Register for Free Membership to

solutions@syngress.com

Over the last few years, Syngress has published many best-selling and critically acclaimed books, including Tom Shinder's *Configuring ISA Server 2000*, Brian Caswell and Jay Beale's *Snort 2.0 Intrusion Detection*, and Angela Orebaugh and Gilbert Ramirez's *Ethereal Packet Sniffing*. One of the reasons for the success of these books has been our unique **solutions@syngress.com** program. Through this site, we've been able to provide readers a real time extension to the printed book.

As a registered owner of this book, you will qualify for free access to our members-only solutions@syngress.com program. Once you have registered, you will enjoy several benefits, including:

- Four downloadable e-booklets on topics related to the book. Each booklet is approximately 20-30 pages in Adobe PDF format. They have been selected by our editors from other best-selling Syngress books as providing topic coverage that is directly related to the coverage in this book.

- A comprehensive FAQ page that consolidates all of the key points of this book into an easy to search web page, providing you with the concise, easy to access data you need to perform your job.

- A "From the Author" Forum that allows the authors of this book to post timely updates links to related sites, or additional topic coverage that may have been requested by readers.

Just visit us at **www.syngress.com/solutions** and follow the simple registration process. You will need to have this book with you when you register.

Thank you for giving us the opportunity to serve your needs. And be sure to let us know if there is anything else we can do to make your job easier.

SYNGRESS®

BEST DAMN Windows
Server 2003
PERIOD
BOOK

Susan Snedaker

KEY	SERIAL NUMBER
001	HJ642HLPMN
002	PO823H7N4C
003	8NJH24589
004	VBP965T5T5
005	CV23GHSES4
006	VB5429IJN6
007	HJJ3EFG6GB
008	29MKFG6932
009	629TGHCXDE
010	IMTGHXWQ39

PUBLISHED BY
Syngress Publishing, Inc.
800 Hingham Street
Rockland, MA 02370

The Best Damn Windows Server 2003 Book Period

Printed in the United States of America
2 3 4 5 6 7 8 9 0

ISBN: 1-931836-12-4

Acquisitions Editor: Jaime Quigley
Page Layout and Art: Patricia Lupien
Cover Designer: Michael Kavish
Indexer: Rich Carlson

Distributed by O'Reilly & Associates in the United States and Canada.

Acknowledgments

We would like to acknowledge the following people for their kindness and support in making this book possible.

Syngress books are now distributed in the United States and Canada by O'Reilly & Associates, Inc. The enthusiasm and work ethic at ORA is incredible and we would like to thank everyone there for their time and efforts to bring Syngress books to market: Tim O'Reilly, Laura Baldwin, Mark Brokering, Mike Leonard, Donna Selenko, Bonnie Sheehan, Cindy Davis, Grant Kikkert, Opol Matsutaro, Lynn Schwartz, Steve Hazelwood, Mark Wilson, Rick Brown, Leslie Becker, Jill Lothrop, Tim Hinton, Kyle Hart, Sara Winge, C. J. Rayhill, Peter Pardo, Leslie Crandell, Valerie Dow, Regina Aggio, Pascal Honscher, Preston Paull, Susan Thompson, Bruce Stewart, Laura Schmier, Sue Willing, Mark Jacobsen, Betsy Waliszewski, Dawn Mann, Kathryn Barrett, John Chodacki, and Rob Bullington.

The incredibly hard working team at Elsevier Science, including Jonathan Bunkell, Ian Seager, Duncan Enright, David Burton, Rosanna Ramacciotti, Robert Fairbrother, Miguel Sanchez, Klaus Beran, Emma Wyatt, Rosie Moss, Chris Hossack, and Krista Leppiko, for making certain that our vision remains worldwide in scope.

David Buckland, Daniel Loh, Marie Chieng, Lucy Chong, Leslie Lim, Audrey Gan, Pang Ai Hua, and Joseph Chan of STP Distributors for the enthusiasm with which they receive our books.

Kwon Sung June at Acorn Publishing for his support.

David Scott, Tricia Wilden, Marilla Burgess, Annette Scott, Geoff Ebbs, Hedley Partis, Bec Lowe, and Mark Langley of Woodslane for distributing our books throughout Australia, New Zealand, Papua New Guinea, Fiji Tonga, Solomon Islands, and the Cook Islands.

Winston Lim of Global Publishing for his help and support with distribution of Syngress books in the Philippines.

Author

Susan Snedaker (MBA, BA, MCSE, MCT, PM) is Principal Consultant and founder of Virtual Team Consulting, LLC, a consulting firm specializing in start-ups and companies in transition, particularly technology companies. Virtual Team Consulting works with technology start-ups to develop viable business plans in preparation for debt/equity funding or due diligence with venture capital firms. Virtual Team Consulting also provides IT consulting, design and implementation services to businesses of all sizes. The firm assists companies with strategic planning, operations improvement and project management. Through its team of subject matter experts, Virtual Team Consulting also offers financial and change management services to targeted companies.

Prior to founding Virtual Team Consulting in May 2000, Susan held various executive and technical positions with companies including Microsoft, Honeywell, Keane, and Apta Software. As Director of Service Delivery for Keane, she managed 1200+ technical support staff delivering phone and email support for various Microsoft products such as Windows Server operating systems. She has contributed technical chapters to six Syngress Publishing books on Windows and security technologies, and has written and edited technical content for a variety of publications. Susan has also developed and delivered technical content from security to telephony, TCP/IP to wi-fi and just about everything in between (she admits a particular fondness for anything related to TCP/IP).

Susan holds a master's degree in business administration and a bachelor's degree in management from the University of Phoenix; she also holds a certificate in project management from Stanford University. She is a member of the Information Technology Association of Southern Arizona (ITASA).

Special Contributors

Thomas W. Shinder M.D. (MVP, MCSE) is a computing industry veteran who has worked as a trainer, writer, and a consultant for Fortune 500 companies including FINA Oil, Lucent Technologies, and Sealand Container Corporation. Tom was a Series Editor of the Syngress/Osborne Series of Windows 2000 Certification Study Guides and is author of the best selling books *Configuring ISA Server 2000: Building Firewalls with Windows 2000* (Syngress Publishing, ISBN: 1-928994-29-6) and *Dr. Tom Shinder's ISA Server and Beyond* (ISBN: 1-931836-66-3). Tom is the editor of the Brainbuzz.com *Win2k News* newsletter and is a regular contributor to TechProGuild. He is also content editor, contributor and moderator for the World's leading site on ISA Server 2000, www.isaserver.org. Microsoft recognized Tom's leadership in the ISA Server community and awarded him their Most Valued Professional (MVP) award.

Debra Littlejohn Shinder (MCSE) is a technology consultant, trainer, and writer who has authored a number of books on networking, including *Scene of the Cybercrime: Computer Forensics Handbook,* published by Syngress Publishing (ISBN: 1-931836-65-5), and *Computer Networking Essentials,* published by Cisco Press. She is co-author, with her husband, Dr. Thomas Shinder, of *Troubleshooting Windows 2000 TCP/IP* (ISBN: 1-928994-11-3), the best-selling *Configuring ISA Server 2000* (ISBN: 1-928994-29-6), and *ISA Server and Beyond* (ISBN: 1-931836-66-3). Deb is also a technical editor and contributor to books on subjects such as the Windows 2000 MCSE exams, the CompTIA Security+ exam, and TruSecure's ICSA certification. She edits the Brainbuzz A+ Hardware News and Sunbelt Software's WinXP News and is regularly published in TechRepublic's TechProGuild and Windowsecurity.com. Deb currently specializes in security issues and Microsoft products. She lives and works in the Dallas-Fort Worth area.

Laura E. Hunter (CISSP, MCSE, MCT, MCDBA, MCP, MCP+I, CCNA, A+, Network+, iNet+, CNE-4, CNE-5) is a Senior IT Specialist with the University of Pennsylvania, where she provides network planning, implementation, and troubleshooting services for various business units and schools within the University. Her specialties include Microsoft Windows NT and 2000 design and implementation, troubleshooting and security topics. As an "MCSE Early Achiever" on Windows 2000, Laura was one of the first in the country to renew her Microsoft credentials under the Windows 2000 certification structure. Laura's previous experience includes a position as the Director of Computer Services for the Salvation Army and as the LAN administrator for a medical supply firm. She also operates as an independent consultant for small businesses in the Philadelphia metropolitan area and is a regular contributor to the TechTarget family of websites.

Laura has previously contributed to the Syngress Publishing's *Configuring Symantec Antivirus, Corporate Edition* (ISBN 1-931836-81-7). She has also contributed to several other exam guides in the Syngress Windows Server 2003 MCSE/MCSA DVD Guide and Training System series as a DVD presenter, contributing author, and technical reviewer. Laura holds a bachelor's degree from the University of Pennsylvania and is a member of the Network of Women in Computer Technology, the Information Systems Security Association, and InfraGard, a cooperative undertaking between the U.S. Government other participants dedicated to increasing the security of United States critical infrastructures.

Chad Todd (MCSE: Security, MCSE, MCSA: Security, MCSA, MCP+I, MCT, CNE, A+, Network+, i-Net+) author of *Hack Proofing Windows 2000 Server* (Syngress, ISBN: 1-931836-49-3) co-owns a training and integration company (Training Concepts, LLC) in Columbia, SC. Chad first certified on Windows NT 4.0 and has been training on Windows operating systems ever since. His specialties include Exchange messaging and Windows security. Chad was awarded MCSE 2000 Charter Member for being one of the first two thousand Windows 2000 MCSEs and MCSA 2002 Charter Member for being one of the first five thousand MCSAs. Chad is a regular contributing author for *Microsoft Certified Professional Magazine*. Chad has worked for companies such as Fleet Mortgage Group, Ikon Office Solutions, and Netbank.

Jeffery A. Martin (MCSE, MCDBA, MCT, MCP+I, MCP, MCNE, CNE, CNA, CNI, CCNA, CCNP, CCI, CCA, CTT, A+, Network+, I-Net+, Project+, Linux+, CIW, ADPM) has been working with computers and computer networks for over 15 years. Jeffery spends most of his time managing several companies that he owns and consulting for large multinational media companies. He also enjoys working as a technical instructor and training others in the use of technology.

Chris Peiris (MVP, MIT) works as an independent consultant for .NET and EAI implementations. He is currently working with the Commonwealth Bank of Australia. He also lectures on distributed component architectures (.NET, J2EE, and CORBA) at Monash University, Caulfield, Victoria, Australia. Chris was awarded the Microsoft Most Valuable Professional for his contributions to .NET technologies by Microsoft, Redmond. Chris is designing and developing Microsoft solutions since 1995. His expertise lies in developing scalable, high-performance solutions for financial institutions, G2G, B2B, and media groups. Chris has written many articles, reviews, and columns for various online publications including 15Seconds, Developer Exchange (www.devx.com), and Wrox Press. He is co-author of *C# Web Service with .NET Remoting and ASP.NET* and *C# for Java Programmers* (Syngress Publishing, ISBN: 1-931836-54-X), and study guides on MCSA/MCSE Exams 70-290 and Exam 70-298, also from Syngress. Chris frequently presents at professional developer conferences on Microsoft technologies.

His core skills are C++, Java, .NET, C#, VB.NET, Service Oriented Architecture, DNA, MTS, Data Warehousing, WAP, and SQL Server. Chris has a bachelor's in computing, a bachelor of business (accounting), and a masters in information technology. He is currently under taking a PhD on web service management framework. He lives with his family in ACT, Australia.

Martin Grasdal (MCSE+I, MCSE/W2K MCT, CISSP, CTT+, A+) is an independent consultant with over 10 years experience in the computer industry. Martin has a wide range of networking and IT managerial experience. He has been an MCT since 1995 and an MCSE since 1996. His training and networking experience covers a number of products, including NetWare, Lotus Notes, Windows NT, Windows 2000, Windows 2003, Exchange Server, IIS, and ISA Server. As a manager, he served as Director of Web Sites and CTO for BrainBuzz.com, where he was also responsible for all study guide and technical content on the CramSession.com Web sit. Martin currently works actively as a consultant, author, and editor. His recent consulting experience includes contract work for Microsoft as a Technical Contributor to the MCP Program on projects related to server technologies. Martin lives in

Edmonton, Alberta, Canada with his wife Cathy and their two sons. Martin's past authoring and editing work with Syngress has included the following titles: *Configuring and Troubleshooting Windows XP Professional* (ISBN: 1-928994-80-6), *Configuring ISA Server 2000: Building Firewalls for Windows 2000* (ISBN: 1-928994-29-6), and *Dr. Tom Shinder's ISA Server & Beyond: Real World Security Solutions for Microsoft Enterprise Networks* (ISBN: 1-931836-66-3).

Contents

Foreword

Any IT professional who's been in the business more than 15 minutes knows that the only constant is change. Staying up-to-date on computing technologies is an unrelenting process. Those that thrive in this industry are those that enjoy continuous learning and new challenges. That said, it's still a daunting task to keep on top of fast-changing technology. From worms and viruses to storage area networks to Wi-Fi, today's IT professional has to constantly take in vast amounts of data, sort through it for relevant pieces, and figure out how to apply it to his or her own network.

Windows Server 2003 is based on the technologies introduced or enhanced in Windows 2000. This updated operating system contains all the technological updates you'd expect, as well as a determined effort by Microsoft to improve security. Out of the box, Windows Server 2003 is more secure than any previous Microsoft operating system. It's locked down, it doesn't install unnecessary components, and it requires activation or enabling of some key features that are installed by default. Overall, this operating system is the most stable, secure operating system Microsoft has built. The focus on security is evident and anyone running a Windows-based network should take a serious look at upgrading to this new version — not only to take advantage of the new features such as support for the latest protocols, but to improve overall security.

This book is designed to give you the best of the best. Each chapter was specifically selected to provide both the depth and breadth needed to work effectively with Windows Server 2003 without extraneous or irrelevant information. Of course, it would be easy to fill volumes on Windows Server 2003 and the technologies that go into this operating system. What we've done instead is focus on what you really need to know to plan, install, manage and secure a Windows Server 2003 network. You won't find arcane references to the technical specifications of RFC 2460 (IPv6 for those of you who were about to jump to the IETF website or geekier still, those who have the RFC index file on their desktop). What you will find is accurate, focused technical information you can use today to manage your Windows Server 2003 systems and networks. You'll find a practical blend of technical information and step-by-step instructions on common Windows Server 2003 tasks. You can read this book from cover to cover and become highly knowl-edgeable about Windows Server 2003, or you can flip to specific chapters as references for particular tasks. Either way, you'll find this is the best damn Windows Server 2003 book . . . period.

— Susan Snedaker

Many thanks for the good-natured guidance from my editor, Jaime Quigley, at Syngress. Thanks also to my fine friend and mentor, Nick Mammana, who long ago taught me it's both what you say and how you say it that matter. And last, but certainly not least, thanks to Lisa Mainz for being such a techno-geek. I've learned a lot watching you break the rules.

Chapter 1

Overview of Windows Server 2003

In this chapter:

- **What's New in Windows Server 2003?**
- **The Windows Server 2003 Family**
- **Licensing Issues**
- **Installation and Upgrade Issues**
- **Planning Tools and Documentation**

Introduction

The latest incarnation of Microsoft's server product, Windows Server 2003, brings many new features and improvements that make the network administrator's job easier. This chapter will briefly summarize what's new in 2003 and introduce you to the four members of the Windows Server 2003 family: the Web Edition, the Standard Edition, the Enterprise Edition, and the Datacenter Edition. We'll also discuss how licensing works with Windows Server 2003, and provide a heads up on some of the issues you might encounter when installing the new OS or upgrading from Windows 2000. We'll look at the tools and documentation that come with Windows Server 2003 to familiarize you with new features in this version of the Microsoft operation system.

Windows XP/Server 2003

Windows XP and Windows Server 2003 are based on the same code and are the client and server editions of the same OS, with the same relationship to one another as Windows 2000 Professional and Windows 2000 Server.

Windows XP is available in four 32-bit editions:

- Windows XP Home Edition
- Windows XP Professional
- Windows XP Media Center Edition
- Windows XP Tablet PC Edition

There is also a 64-bit version of XP, designed to run on the Itanium processor. Windows Server 2003 comes in four editions (discussed later in this chapter):

- Windows Server 2003 Web Edition
- Standard Edition
- Enterprise Edition
- Datacenter Server

Server 2003 comes in both 32-bit and 64-bit versions.

Windows XP introduced a new variation to the 9*x* style GUI. The new interface is called LUNA and is also used by Windows Server 2003. The idea behind LUNA is to clean up the desktop and access everything needed from the Start menu. If you don't care for LUNA, both XP and Server 2003 also support the classic Windows 9x/NT 4.0 style GUI.

What's New in Windows Server 2003?

Windows Server 2003 improves upon previous versions of Windows in the areas of availability, reliability, security, and scalability. Windows 2003 is designed to allow customers to do more with less. According to Microsoft, companies that have deployed Windows 2003 have been able to operate with up to 30 percent greater efficiency in the areas of application development and administrative overhead.

New Features

Microsoft has enhanced most of the features carried over from Windows 2000 Server and has added some new features for Windows Server 2003. For example:

- Active Directory has been updated to improve replication, management, and migrations.
- File and Print services have been updated to make them more dependable and quicker.
- The number of nodes supported in clustering has been increased and new tools have been added to aid in cluster management.
- Terminal Server better supports using local resources when using the Remote Desktop Protocol.
- IIS 6.0, Media Services 9.0, and XML services have been added to Windows Server 2003.

- New networking technologies and protocols are supported, including Simple Object Access Protocol (SOAP), Web Distributed Authoring and Versioning (WebDAV), IPv6, wireless networking, fiber channel, and automatic configuration for multiple networks.

- New command-line tools have been added for easier administration.

- Software Restriction Policies allow administrators to control which applications can be run.

- All features of Windows have been updated to reflect Microsoft's security initiative.

New Active Directory Features

Active Directory was first introduced in Windows 2000 and Microsoft has made improvements to AD in Windows Server 2003. Windows 2003 enhances the management of Active Directory. There are more AD management tools now and the tools are easier than ever to use. Microsoft has made it painless to deploy Active Directory in Windows 2003. The migration tools have been greatly improved to make way for seamless migrations.

In the corporate world where mergers and acquisitions are common, things change all the time. With Windows Server 2003, you can rename your domains, a feature missing from Windows 2000. You can also change the NetBIOS name, the DNS name, or both.

Another problem with changes in the business environment is the need to configure trust relationships. With Windows 2000, if two companies merge and each has a separate Active Directory, they have to either set up manual nontransitive trusts between all of their domains or collapse one forest into the other. Neither of these is an ideal choice and is prone to error. The trusts are easy enough to set up, but then you lose the benefits of being in a single forest. Collapsing forests can require a lot of work, depending on the environment.

Windows Server 2003 Active Directory now supports forest-level trusts. By setting the trusts at the forest roots, you enable cross-forest authentication and cross-forest authorization. Cross-forest authentication provides a single sign-on experience by allowing users in one forest to access machines in another forest via NTLM or Kerberos (Kerberos is the preferred method, if all systems support it). Cross-forest authorization allows assigning permissions for users in one forest to resources in another forest. Permissions can be assigned to the user ID or through groups.

Not all improvements have to do with mergers and multiple forests. In the past, it was common practice for companies with many offices spread out geographically to build their domain controllers locally and ship them to the remote offices. This was because of replication issues. When a new domain controller is created, it must pull a full copy of the Active Directory database from another domain controller. This full replication can easily oversaturate a slow network link. However, with Server 2003, you can create a new domain controller and pull the Active Directory information from your backup media. The newly created domain controller now only has to replicate the changes that have occurred since the backup was made. This usually results in much less traffic than replicating the entire database.

The Active Directory Users and Computers tool (ADUC) has been improved to include a new query feature that allows you to write filters for the type of objects you want to view. These queries can be saved and used multiple times. For example, you might want to create a query to show you all of the users with mailboxes on a specified Exchange server. By creating a query, you can easily pull up a current list with one click of the mouse. ADUC also now supports the following:

- Multi-object selection
- Drag-and-drop capabilities
- The ability to restore permissions back to the defaults
- The ability to view the effective permissions of an object

Group policy management has also been enhanced in Server 2003. The Microsoft Group Policy Management Console (GPMC) makes it easy to troubleshoot and manage group policy. It supports drag-and-drop capabilities, backing up and restoring your group policy objects (GPOs), and copying and importing GPOs. Where the GPMC really shines is in its reporting function. You now have a graphical, easy-to-use interface that, within a few clicks, will show you all of the settings configured in a GPO. You can also determine what a user's effective settings would be if he or she logged on to a certain machine. The only way you could do this in Windows 2000 was to actually log the user on to the machine and run *gpresult* (a command-line tool for viewing effective GPO settings).

In Windows Server 2003, the schema can now be redefined. This allows you to make changes if you incorrectly enter something into the schema. In Windows 2000, you can deactivate schema attributes and classes, but you cannot redefine them. You still need schema admin rights to modify the schema, but now it is more forgiving of mistakes.

The way objects are added to and replicated throughout the directory has been improved as well. The Inter-Site Topology Generator (ISTG) has been improved to support a larger number of sites. Group membership replication is no longer "all or nothing" as it was in Windows 2000. In Windows Server 2003, as members are added to groups, only those members are replicated to your domain controllers and global catalog (GC) servers, rather than the entire group membership list. No more worrying about the universal group replication to your GC servers.

Every domain controller caches credentials provided by GC servers. This allows users to continue to log on if the GC server goes down. It also speeds up logons for sites that do not have a local GC server. No longer is the GC server a single point of failure. In fact, you no longer are required to have one at each site.

Active Directory now supports a new directory partition called the application partition. You can add data to this partition and choose which domain controllers will replicate it. This is useful if you have information you want to replicate to all domain controllers in a certain area, but you do not want to make the information available to all domain controllers in the domain.

Improved File and Print Services

Practically every organization uses file and print services, as sharing files and printers was the original reason for networking computers together. Microsoft has improved the tools used to manage your file system by making the tools run faster than before; this allows users to get their jobs done in less time and requires less downtime from your servers. The Distributed File System (Dfs) and the File Replication Service (FRS) have also been enhanced for Windows Server 2003, and Microsoft has made printing faster and easier to manage.

Enhanced File System Features

Windows 2003 supports WebDAV, which was first introduced in Exchange 2000. It allows remote document sharing. Through standard file system calls, clients can access files stored on Web repositories. In other words, clients think they are making requests to their local file systems, but the requests are actually being fulfilled via Web resources.

Microsoft made it easier to manage disks in Windows Server 2003 by including a command-line interface. From the command line, you can do tasks that were only supported from the GUI in Windows 2000, such as managing partitions and volumes, configuring RAID, and defragmenting your disks. There are also command-line tools for extending basic disk, file system tuning, and shadow copy management.

Disk fragmentation is a problem that commonly plagues file servers. This occurs when data is constantly written to and removed from a drive. Fragmented drives do not perform as well as defragmented drives. Although Windows 2000 (unlike NT) included a disk defragmentation tool, it was notoriously slow. To address this, Microsoft beefed up the defragmenter tool in Windows Server 2003 so that it is much faster than before. In addition, the new tool is not limited to only specific cluster sizes that it can defrag, and it can perform an online defragmentation of the Master Fat Table.

The venerable CHKDSK (pronounced "check disk") tool, which is used to find errors on Windows volumes, has been revamped as well. Microsoft studies show that Windows Server 2003 runs CHKDSK 20 to 35 percent faster than Windows 2000. However, since Windows 2003 (like Window 2000) uses NTFS—which is less prone to errors than FAT file systems—you shouldn't have to run CHKDSK often.

Both the Dfs and the FRS have been improved. Dfs allows you to create a single logical tree view for multiple servers, so that all directories appear to be on the same server. However, they are actually on separate servers. Dfs works hand in hand with Active Directory to determine site locations for clients requesting data, thereby allowing clients to be directed to a server closest to them in physical proximity. FRS is used to replicate Dfs file share data. FRS now allows administrators to configure its replication topology and compress replication traffic.

One of the best file system improvements in Windows 2003 is shadow copies. After you enable shadow copies on the server and install the shadow copy client software on the desktop computer, end users can right-click on a file and view previous versions that were backed up via shadow copies. They can then keep the current version of the file or roll back to an early version. This will remove the burden (to some extent) of simple file restores from your IT staff and allow the users to handle it themselves.

Improved Printing Features

Even though we rely more on electronic communications than ever before, printing is still an important requirement for most companies. One of the more common reasons for small companies to put in a network is for the purpose of sharing printers (a shared Internet connection and e-mail are two other reasons). Microsoft has taken many steps to improve the printing experience in Windows Server 2003. Users who print long documents should notice a performance boost over Windows 2000, because 2003 does a better job of file spooling, print jobs should get to the printer faster.

Microsoft has also made printing easier to manage. Windows Server 2003 has command-line utilities for managing printer configuration, including print queues, print jobs, and driver management. System Monitor has counters for managing print performance.

Installing printers is easy in Windows 2003 because of plug-and-play (PnP) functionality. This allows you to physically connect the printer to the machine and have Windows set it up for you automatically (as long as the printer itself supports PnP). Windows 2003 supports over 3800 new print drivers.

Revised IIS Architecture

Internet Information Services (IIS) is Microsoft's Web server product. IIS 6.0 is included with all versions of Windows Server 2003. With this new version, Microsoft has made great leaps in the area of IIS reliability, availability, management, and security.

IIS 6.0 was designed so a problem with one application won't cause the server or other applications running on the server to crash. It provides health monitoring and disables Web sites and applications that fail too frequently within a defined period of time. IIS 6.0 can stop and restart Web sites and applications based on customized criteria (such as disk, CPU, or memory utilization). IIS 6.0 allows changing the configuration of your Web server without having to restart it. It is the most scalable version of IIS to date, supporting more Web sites on a single server than IIS 5.0. The actual IIS services stop and start much faster than before, helping to decrease Web site downtime.

Management of your Web server is easier in Server 2003, thanks to command-line scripting. The metabase is now stored in a plain-text XML configuration file. This improves backing up, restoring, recovering, troubleshooting, and directly editing the metabase. IIS 6.0 supports ASP .NET, .NET Framework, and a wide variety of languages. Since the .NET Framework doesn't depend on a specific language, almost any programming language will do.

One common complaint about Windows 2000 was that IIS installed by default; thereby creating an instant vulnerability on servers that were never intended to be Web servers. Microsoft recommends that you only install IIS when needed and lock it down so it only offers the services that your organization requires. In Windows Server 2003, IIS is not installed by default and is locked down by default when you do install it. This means that it will only deliver static content, unless you specifically configure it for dynamic content. IIS 6.0 requires an administrator to add necessary dynamic extensions to the Web services extensions list. Until they are added to this list, IIS will not support them; this will stop attackers from calling unsecured dynamic pages.

Enhanced Clustering Technology

A cluster is a group of servers that work together like one computer. Clusters can be used for performance reasons (to balance the load across two or more computers) or for fault tolerant reasons (to provide failover if one computer fails).

Microsoft added clustering support to its OS line in 1997 with Windows NT 4.0 Enterprise Edition. At that time, clustering was not commonly used. Only the really big IT shops could afford to put in clustered solutions because of the cost of the extra servers. Now that hardware has dropped in price, more and more customers are choosing to cluster their mission-critical systems. As Storage Area Networking (SAN) technology becomes more widespread, clusters are becoming fairly easy to set up. Like Windows 2000, Windows 2003 supports two types of clustering: Microsoft Cluster Service (MSCS) and Network Load Balancing (NLB).

Microsoft Cluster Service

MSCS uses two or more physically connected servers, called *nodes,* that communicate with each other constantly. If a node detects that another node is offline, it will take over the services provided by the offline node. However, this happens behind the scenes, and end users are unaware of the process (other than experiencing a small initial delay).

MSCS is traditionally used with mail servers, database servers, and file and print servers. MSCS is supported in Windows Server 2003 Enterprise Edition and Windows Server 2003 Datacenter Edition. Some of the new features of Windows Server 2003 clustering include:

- The support of more nodes in a cluster. Enterprise Edition and Datacenter Edition both support eight nodes.

- Clustering now integrates with Active Directory and creates a computer account for the virtual cluster name.

- Clustered applications can now use Kerberos authentication.

Network Load Balancing

NLB is available in all versions of Windows Server 2003. Unlike MSCS, where only one server offers the services at a time, NLB nodes all offer services at the same time. The NLB cluster is accessed via a virtual name (a name that represents the group of servers as an entity), and whichever server is least busy answers the request (there is a little more to it, but this is good enough for now).

If one server goes offline, there is no transferring of services because all servers offer the services already. When a server goes offline, it is removed from the rotation of servicing requests until it comes back online. NLB is generally used with Web servers, application servers, terminal servers, and streaming media servers. NLB Manager is a new tool in Windows Server 2003 that provides a central point for managing and configuring NLB clusters.

There are many new features for NLB in Server 2003. NLB now supports multiple network interface cards (NICs), allowing a single server to host multiple NLB clusters. You can use virtual clusters to set up different port rules for each cluster IP address, so that each IP address represents a different resource (Web page, application, and so forth). The Internet Group Management Protocol (IGMP) is now supported when NLB is configured in multicast mode. Using IGMP limits cluster traffic on the switch to the ports that have NLB server connected to them. This helps prevent switch flooding. (Switch flooding occurs when every server in an NLB cluster sees every packet addressed to the cluster.) NLB now supports IPSec traffic.

New Networking and Communications Features

Windows Server 2003 adds a number of new networking technologies that enable it to grow with the needs of your business. For example:

- It supports IPv6, which was created to overcome the limited number of addresses in IPv4 (previous versions of NT use IPv4). Windows Server 2003 supports IPv4/IPv6 coexistence through technologies such as Intra-site Automatic Tunnel Addressing Protocol (ISATAP) and 6to4. Internet and remote access functionality have been enhanced in Windows Server 2003.

■ Point-to-Point Protocol over Ethernet (PPPoE) allows making broadband connections to an Internet Service Provider (ISP) without having to load any software.

■ Windows can now use IPSec over NAT.

■ Remote Authentication Dial-In User Service (RADIUS) has been improved to provide better control over network access and easier troubleshooting of authentication problems.

■ Microsoft's implementation of RADIUS, Internet Authentication Service (IAS), can send its logs to a Microsoft SQL Server and it now supports 802.1X authentication and cross-forest authentication.

In Windows 2000, IPSec was not supported through a NAT server. This was a serious drawback for some companies, as it meant they could not VPN through the NAT server using IPSec or the Layer Two Tunneling Protocol (L2TP), which uses IPSec for encryption. This restriction has been removed in Windows Server 2003. Both IPSec connections and L2TP connections using IPSec are supported over NAT when you have a Server 2003 VPN server. This is done using a technology called NAT traversal, or NAT-T. On the client end, the Microsoft L2TP/IPSec VPN client supports NAT-T. It can be downloaded at www.microsoft.com/windows2000/server/evaluation/news/bulletins/l2tpclient.asp and can be installed on Windows 98, ME, and NT 4.0 Workstation.

The Internet Connection Firewall (ICF) functions as a personal software-based firewall and provides protection for computers connected to the Internet or unsecured networks. ICF protects LAN, VPN, dial-up, and PPPoE connections by making it easier to secure your server against attacks. With ICF, only the services that you need to offer are exposed. For example, you can use ICF to filter the network connection of your DNS server so that only DNS requests are passed through. ICF is included with the 32-bit versions of the Standard and Enterprise Editions of Windows Server 2003. It is not included with the Web and Datacenter Editions, or with any of the 64-bit versions.

Improved Security

You might have noticed that Microsoft is paying more attention to concerns about security. Many of the new features discussed thus far relate in one way or another to security. One of the key components of Windows Server 2003 security is the Common Language Runtime (CLR) software engine. It reduces the number of security vulnerabilities due to programming mistakes, and makes sure that applications have appropriate permissions to run and that they can run without any errors.

EFS encrypts files that are stored on NTFS-formatted partitions so that it can only be decrypted by the person who encrypted the file, those with whom he or she shares the file, or a designated recovery agent. The sharing of encrypted files is new to Windows XP/Server 2003. In Windows 2000, this was not possible because only the person who encrypted the file had the correct keys to decrypt it. Now, the person who encrypts the file can choose to give other people the ability to decrypt the file as well, and the file encryption key (FEK) is protected by the public key of each additional person who is given authorization. Encrypted files appear just like normal files in Windows Explorer. However, only authorized users can access them. Anyone else will be denied access. EFS now supports encrypting offline files and storing encrypted files in Web folders.

Microsoft provides a single sign-on environment for users via Credential Manager. Credential Manager provides a secure place for users to store their passwords and X.509 certificates. When a resource is accessed, the correct credentials will be pulled from Credential Manager without prompting the user for action. In large complex environments in which you can have three or four user accounts, this is a great benefit. No longer do you have to key in your domain, username, and password each time; you set it up once and then Credential Manager does all of the work.

You can now control which software can run on a machine via software restriction policies. These policies can be applied at the domain, site, OU, or locally. You define a default security level that either allows or disallows software to run via the Group Policy Object Editor Snap-in. Among other things, software restriction policies can be used to prevent viruses and other harmful programs from running on your PC, and can also be used to limit end users to only running the programs needed for their job.

Windows Server 2003 supports the IEEE 802.1X protocols. This standard allows authorization and authentication of users connecting to Ethernet and wireless local area networks (WLANs). Windows Server 2003 supports authentication via Extensible Authentication Protocol (EAP) methods, such as smart cards.

Auto-enrollment and auto-renewal of certificates makes it easier to quickly deploy smart cards. Certificate Services now supports incremental (a.k.a. delta) Certificate Revocation Lists (CRLs), which means that the server can just push down the changes to the client and not have to push the entire CRL every time.

Another new security feature of Windows Server 2003 is Passport Integration. Passport is integrated with Active Directory and supports mapping AD user accounts to Passport accounts. Users can use Passport for a single sign-on to all of the supported systems.

Better Storage Management

In an effort to keep up with the changing times, Microsoft has greatly increased the level of built-in SAN support in Windows Server 2003. The Virtual Disk Service (VDS) provides a unified interface for multivendor storage devices. VDS discovers the storage devices in your network and gives you a single place to manage them.

You can now create and mount a SAN volume from within Windows. In previous versions of Windows, you had to do this from within your SAN application. Also included in Windows 2003, via the driver development kit, is multipathing input/output (MPIO). MPIO allows up to 32 different paths to external storage (for example, SAN).

Microsoft has also put a lot of work into the backup features of Windows Server 2003. The Volume Shadow Copy Services allows you to create a snapshot (or an exact copy) of volumes on your SAN. Clients can then perform shadow copy restores on their own. In other words, clients can look at a list of shadow copies performed on their data and choose to restore their own data from a given snapshot. *NTBackup* also uses shadow copies to make sure that all open files are backed up.

Improved Terminal Services

Terminal Server allows client workstations to function as terminal emulators. Terminal Services client software is installed on the local workstation, allowing it to connect to the terminal server and receive its own desktop session. Multiple clients can run sessions simultaneously. All processing takes place on the server. The client machine is only responsible for managing the keystrokes and mouse clicks, which are passed over the network to the terminal server via the Remote Desktop Protocol (RDP).

Although RDP is the native protocol for Microsoft Terminal Server and is used with clients running the Windows 2000 Terminal Services client or the XP/2003 Remote Desktop Connection (RDC) client, the Server 2003 terminal server can also be configured to accept connections from Citrix clients using the ICA protocol.

In Windows Server 2003, Remote Administration mode has been renamed to Remote Desktop for Administration and it is installed by default. This works like the Remote Desktop feature in Windows XP. As in Windows 2000, you are still limited to two simultaneous remote desktops at a time. However, there is one improvement: you can now take over the local console session. Terminal Services in Application Server mode is now simply called Terminal Server.

The Windows Server 2003 Terminal Server and Remote Desktop for Administration support more local client devices than in Windows 2000. Now the local client file system, audio output, printers, serial ports, smart cards, and clipboard are supported making it easier for clients to use their local resources while connected to the terminal server. RDP 5.1 is a much more robust client than RDP 5.0 (Windows 2000). It supports display configurations up to 24-bit color at up to 1600x1200 resolution. It also allows customizing the client experience based on available bandwidth. In other words, unnecessary features can be turned off when connecting over a slow link to optimize performance.

Terminal Server is one of the most used features of Windows 2000. It allows users to connect from their local machines and run desktop sessions off of the server. The local workstation at this point is functioning as a "thin client" because all processing is taking place on the server. One common complaint about Terminal Server in Windows 2000 is a lack of support for local resources.

This has been improved in Windows Server 2003. You can now share information easily between your local disk and the server. You no longer must map a drive back to your local workstation. You can print to locally attached printers and use locally attached serial devices. You can redirect the sound from the terminal server to come out of your local speakers. All of these things make using Terminal Server an even more transparent process to the end user.

New Media Services

Microsoft has redesigned Media Services. The version of Media Services in Windows Server 2003 is version 9.0. It is managed via the Windows Media Services Microsoft Management Console (MMC). Media Services provides audio and video content to clients via the Web (Internet or intranet). According to Microsoft, Media Services has been improved in four areas:

- Fast streaming
- Dynamic content
- Extensibility
- Industrial strength

Fast Streaming

Media Services supports fast streaming to ensure the highest quality streaming experience possible even over unreliable networks (for example, wireless networks). Streaming refers to sending video and/or audio in compressed form over the network and playing the data as it arrives. There are four parts that make up fast streaming:

- **Fast start** Supplies instant-on playback without a buffering delay.

- **Fast cache** Supplies always-on playback by streaming to cache as quickly as the network will support and by playing back the stream to the client from cache.

- **Fast recovery** Sends redundant packets to wireless clients to ensure that no data is lost due to connectivity problems.

- **Fast reconnect** Supplies undisturbed playback by restoring connections if the client is disconnected during a broadcast.

Dynamic Content

Media Services supports advertisements and server-side playlists. Advertising support is very flexible, in that ads can be placed anywhere and used as often as wanted in the playlist. You can even use data gathering tools such as cookies to personalize your ads, and all ad data can be logged for further analysis. Server-side playlists are great for clients that don't support client-side playlists. Server-side playlists can contain live data or preexisting content. They allow you to customize the way your content is presented to clients and to make changes quickly and easily without any delay in service.

Extensibility

Microsoft has exposed over 60 Media Services interfaces and their properties, making Media Services a very open platform. Customization can be achieved by using the Microsoft supplied plug-ins or by using the SDK to create your own plug-ins. You can use scripting languages you already know (such as Perl, Visual Basic, Visual Basic Scripting Edition, C, Visual C++, and Microsoft JScript) to customize Media Services.

Industrial Strength

Microsoft boasts that Media Services is the most scalable, reliable, and secure solution on the market today. Media Services in Windows 2003 supports twice as many users per server as Windows 2000. It supports HTTP 1.0/1.1, RTP, RPSP, HTML v3.2, FEC, IPv4/6, IGMPv3, SNMP, WEBM/WMI, SMIL 2.0, SML, SML-DOM, and COM/DCOM. All Media Services plug-ins run in protected memory to guarantee reliability. Many common authorization and authentication methods are supported, such as digital rights management and HTTP Digest. Microsoft provides a Web-based interface, an MMC snap-in interface, and command-line support for administering your media servers.

XML Web Services

XML Web Services are building-block applications that connect together via the Internet. These services provide reusable components that call functions from other applications. It doesn't matter how these applications were built, the types of devices used, or the OS on the devices used as long as they support XML, because XML is an industry standard. XML Web Services are made available in Windows Server 2003 because of the .NET framework. XML Web Services help provide effective business-to-business (b2b) and business-to-consumer (b2c) solutions.

The Windows Server 2003 Family

The Windows Server 2003 family comes in four different editions: Web Edition, Standard Edition, Enterprise Edition, and Datacenter Edition. It also comes in both 32-bit and 64-bit versions.

Why Four Different Editions?

Although all organizations are different, most would fall into one of three categories: small, medium, and large. The networking needs of organizations in each of these categories are different.

Typically, small organizations are concerned with performance versus cost. They want good performance, but it can't cost a fortune. Large companies want the best performance possible. They aren't as concerned with cost, as long as the product performs as expected. Medium-sized companies fall somewhere in the middle. They sometimes need a little more out of an OS than what a small company will settle for, but they don't need the high-end equipment and features used by very large companies.

Microsoft has tried to create a different edition of Windows for each type of organization, so that all companies can use Windows Server 2003 without overpaying or sacrificing performance. Companies should buy the minimum version of Windows that provides all of the needed features.

Members of the Family

As noted, there are four editions of Windows Server 2003: Web Edition, Standard Edition, Enterprise Edition, and Datacenter Edition. Each edition has its own benefits:

- Web Edition is the least expensive and least functional version. However, if your server is only used for hosting Web pages, then it is a perfect choice.

- Standard Edition is the next step up from Web Edition. Most of the features in Windows Server 2003 are supported in Standard Edition.

- If you need features not provided by Standard Edition or hardware not supported on Standard Edition, then Enterprise Edition would be the next logical choice. Almost every feature in Windows Server 2003 is supported in Enterprise Edition.

- If you need to use Windows System Resource Manager or you need super powerful hardware, then Datacenter Edition is your only choice.

Be sure to pick the version that most closely matches your needs. There are huge differences in price as your work your way up the chain. There is no reason to pay for more than what you need, but you don't want your organization hobbled by limited functionality.

Web Edition

Prior to the release of Windows 2003, if you wanted to have a Windows server function only as a Web server, you would have to buy a copy of Windows 2000 Server and use IIS. This was a waste of money and functionality, because most of the features of Server would never be used. Now there is a version of Windows designed to function exclusively as a Web server, Windows Server 2003 Web Edition. This will save companies a great deal of money and possibly give Microsoft a larger share of the Web server market. There is a difference in price (list price) of around $700 to $800 between Web Edition and Standard Edition Server.

Web Edition is meant to host Web pages, Web applications, and XML services. It supports IIS 6.0, ASP.NET, and .NET Framework. Web Edition supports up to two processors and 2GB of RAM. Client access licenses (discussed later in the chapter) are not required when connecting to Web Edition. However, you are only allowed 10 inbound simultaneous SMB connections, to be used for content publishing (this limit does not apply to Web connections). Web Edition allows you to install third-party Web server software such as Apache, Web availability management software such as Microsoft Application Center, and database engine software such as Microsoft SQL Server 2000 Desktop Engine (MSDE).

Web Edition does *not* support the following functions:

- Internet Authentication Services (IAS)
- Microsoft Metadirectory Services
- Domain controller functionality
- Universal Description, Discovery, and Integration Services (UDDI)
- Remote Installation Services

Standard Edition

Windows Server 2003 Standard Edition is the replacement for Windows 2000 Server. It is meant for small to medium-sized businesses and contains most of the features discussed thus far in the book. It is not limited in functionality like Web Edition and it supports up to four CPUs and 4GB of RAM. Standard Edition is a great choice for file and print servers, Web servers, and application servers that don't need to be clustered. It can also function as a domain controller. Microsoft expects Standard Edition to be the most widely used version of Windows Server 2003.

Enterprise Edition

Windows Server 2003 Enterprise Edition is the replacement for Windows 2000 Advanced Server. Enterprise Edition is meant for any sized business, but includes features most often desired by enterprise-level organizations. It provides high performance and reliability. All of the features supported in Standard Edition are supported in Enterprise Edition, as well as support for clustering up to eight nodes. It supports more powerful hardware than Standard Edition, and can use up to eight processors and up to 32GB of memory. There is a 64-bit version of Enterprise Edition for Intel Itanium machines. The 64-bit version supports up to eight processors and up to 64GB of RAM. Enterprise Edition is good for companies that need features or hardware not supported in Standard Edition.

Datacenter Edition

Datacenter Edition is Microsoft's high-end OS. It is meant for companies that need the most reliable and scalable platform available. You cannot buy the Datacenter Edition software and install it yourself; only approved equipment vendors can buy it and they must install it onto approved hardware. Datacenter Edition contains all of the features found in both Standard Edition and Enterprise Edition; in addition, it adds the Windows System Resource Manager to aid in system management. Datacenter Edition supports up to 32 processors and 64GB of memory in the 32-bit version. The 64-bit version supports up to 64 processors and 512GB of memory. If performance and reliability are at the top of your list (and cost is near the bottom), then Datacenter Edition is an excellent choice.

Licensing Issues

Microsoft based the Windows Server 2003 licensing structure on Windows 2000's structure. However, they have changed some things. This section is not the final word when it comes to Microsoft licensing. This section is meant to serve as a guide on the basics of Windows 2003 licensing. To order licenses, contact your Microsoft Software Advisor. In the United States, call (800) 426-9400, or visit the Microsoft Licensing Program Reseller Web page (http://shop.microsoft. com/helpdesk/mvlref.asp). In Canada, call the Microsoft Resource Centre at (877) 568-2495. Outside of the United States and Canada, please review the Worldwide Microsoft Licensing Web site (www.microsoft.com/worldwide).

There are a few rules that you need to know about Microsoft's licensing schemes:

- You have to purchase a product license for every copy of the OS you are going to install.

- Every network connection that is authenticated requires a Windows Client Access License (CAL). Anonymous connections do not require a CAL (for example, anonymous access to a Web page). Windows CALs are not required for Windows 2003 Web Edition, as it is meant to serve Web content only.

- Every Terminal Server session made by a user or device requires a Terminal Server Client Access License (TS CAL). TS CALs are not required for Windows Server 2003 Web Edition, as it is meant to serve Web content only.

The product license allows you to install the OS onto a machine. The CAL allows devices or users to connect to that machine. Microsoft's reasoning behind this is that everyone pays the same price for the base OS, but companies with more connections pay more than companies with fewer connections. This allows them to price according to usage.

There are two licensing modes supported in Windows 2003:

- **Per Server mode** Requires a Windows CAL for each connection. These are assigned to each server and cannot be shared between servers. You are allowed one connection for each CAL assigned to the server. Once the maximum number has been reached, no more connections are allowed.

- **Per Device or Per User mode (formerly called "Per Seat" mode)** Requires that each device or user have its own Windows CAL. These allow the device or user to connect to an unlimited number of servers. With Per Device or Per User mode, the server will not limit the number of connections made as it does in Per Server mode.

Generally, Per Server mode will be most cost effective if you have only one or two servers, and clients that don't always connect at the same time. Per Device or Per User mode will be most cost effective if you have many servers to which your clients need to connect.

Microsoft has two types of CALs, User CALs and Device CALs. User CALs are purchased for every user that makes a connection to a Windows 2003 server. Device CALs are purchased for every machine that makes a connection to a Windows 2003 server. Microsoft recommends that you use either User CALs or Device CALs, but not both at the same time. User CALs are best when you have more machines than users and your users log on to multiple machines to access the servers. Device CALs are better when you have more employees than machines and your users share machines. User CALs and Device CALs are available for both Windows and Terminal Server. Device CALs and User CALs cost the same.

Windows 2000 supported the System Equivalency license for Terminal Server. The System Equivalency license stated that if your client was running the same OS version as the terminal server, then you did not have to buy a Terminal Server CAL (thus, a Windows 2000 Pro machine connecting to a Windows 2000 terminal server did not need a TS CAL). Windows 2003 no longer supports System Equivalency licenses. However, Microsoft does have a Terminal Server licensing transition plan. You can receive a free TS CAL for every copy of Windows XP that you own at the time of the Windows 2003 launch (April 24, 2003). Check out the Microsoft licensing page for more information (www.microsoft.com/licensing).

New to Windows 2003 is the External Connector (EC) license. ECs enable external users to access your server without requiring that you buy CALs for them. External users are people who are not employed by your company. Terminal Server also has an EC license called the Terminal Server External Connector (TS-EC). The EC license is replacing the Internet Connector and TS Internet Connector licenses.

Product Activation

Starting with Windows XP, Microsoft requires OSs to be authorized before a specified number of days pass, after which you won't be able to log on to the OS. Failure to activate only prevents logging on. Services and remote administration are not affected. Windows Server 2003 allows a 30-day grace period for product activation (for retail and OEM products). Companies that use volume licensing do not have to activate their software.

Windows includes an activation wizard. You can activate over the Internet or by phone. One important thing to remember about product activation is that the activation process keeps track of the hardware in your machine. If the hardware changes dramatically, you will have to reactivate your software within three days in order to continue logging on to the server. Microsoft does this to prevent people from purchasing one copy of the OS, activating it, making an image of it, and deploying that image to many more machines.

Installation and Upgrade Issues

Unless your company is buying its first Windows server, you are going to have to decide between upgrading and performing a clean install. Each method has advantages and disadvantages:

- Upgrading preserves many of your existing settings, such as users and groups, permissions and rights, and applications.

- Performing a clean installation can improve the performance of your hard drive, as it will be reformatted during installation. This also gives you a chance to change the partition and volume sizes used on your drives. Clean installs ensure that you don't carry over any existing problems that you might have with your current OS. Some administrators (the authors of this book included) prefer clean installs because they have seen many problems related to OS upgrades in the past. There is something comforting about starting from scratch.

Common Installation Issues

The biggest problems with installing a new OS are hardware and software incompatibilities. It is important to adhere to the recommended hardware specifications for Windows Server 2003. At a minimum, you need the following hardware configuration:

- 133 MHz processor
- 128MB of RAM
- 1.5GB hard drive

Remember that these are the bare minimums on which Windows Server 2003 will run. Obviously, on such old hardware, performance will suffer. Microsoft recommends at least a 550 MHz processor and 256MB of RAM. The more RAM the better.

You should always verify hardware compatibility before you start your installation. There is a system compatibility check you can run from the Windows Server 2003 CD that will check out your hardware for you automatically via the System Compatibility wizard. Even if all of your hardware is supported, you should always update your machine's BIOS to the most recent version.

Common Upgrade Issues

As stated earlier, you should always verify hardware compatibility and BIOS versions. You should always back up your existing system before you start your upgrade. If you have applications on your server, you should read the release notes on application compatibility. These are found in the docs folder on the setup CD (relnotes.htm).

When upgrading servers from NT 4.0 to Windows Server 2003, you must have Service Pack 5 or higher installed. You can perform upgrades from all server versions of NT 4.0 (Server, Enterprise Edition, and Terminal Server Edition). Upgrading Windows 2000 machines to Windows Server 2003 doesn't require any service packs to be installed first. Windows 2000 Server can be upgraded to Windows Server 2003 Standard Edition or Enterprise Edition. However, Windows 2000 Advanced Server can only be upgraded to Windows Server 2003 Enterprise Edition, and Windows 2000

Datacenter Server can only be upgraded to Windows Server 2003 Datacenter Edition. You must have at least 2GB of free hard drive space for all upgrades.

When upgrading Windows NT 4.0 domains to Windows Server 2003 domains, you must first make sure that DNS is installed and properly configured. You don't have to use a Microsoft DNS server, but your implementation of DNS must support service (SRV) records. Optionally, you might want it to support dynamic updates as well. If DNS does not support dynamic updates, you will have to manually create all of the needed SRV records. Before starting the upgrade, you should take one of your BDCs offline. This will allow you to roll back to your existing NT 4.0 environment if you should have problems with the upgrade. Always start your upgrades with the PDC, followed by the BDCs. After upgrading the PDC, you should set your forest functional level to Windows 2003 interim mode.

When upgrading Windows 2000 domains, you must first prepare the forest and the domain for Windows Server 2003 by using the ADPrep tool. You can prepare the forest by running *adprep.exe /forestprep* on the Schema Master, and you can prepare the domain by running *adprep.exe /domainprep* on the Infrastructure Master. ADPrep can only be run from the command line; there isn't an equivalent graphical tool. Unlike when you upgrade from NT 4.0 domains, you do not have to upgrade the PDC (technically the PDC Emulator) first. You can install a new Window 2003 domain controller into an existing Windows 2000 domain. When upgrading your domain controllers, you need to budget a little growing room for the Active Directory database. The database file (ntds.dit) might grow by up to 10 percent.

Windows Server 2003 Planning Tools and Documentation

Planning is the first step in building a reliable, secure, high-performance and highly available Windows Server 2003-based network. In this section, we'll begin with an overview of network infrastructure planning, introducing you to planning strategies and how to use planning tools.

This section also looks at legal and regulatory considerations, how to calculate total cost of ownership (TCO), and how to plan for future growth. We discuss how to develop a test network environment and how to document the planning and network design process.

Overview of Network Infrastructure Planning

Proper planning of a network infrastructure is essential to ensuring high performance, availability, and overall satisfaction with your network operations. In order to create a viable network design, you'll need an understanding of both the business requirements of your organization and current and emerging networking technologies. Accurate network planning will allow your organization to maximize the efficiency of its computer operations, lower costs, and enhance your overall business processes.

When planning for a new infrastructure or upgrading an existing network, you should take some or all of the following steps:

- Document the business requirements of your client or organization.

- Create a baseline of the performance of any existing hardware and network utilization.

- Determine the necessary capacity for the physical network installation, including client and server hardware, as well as allocating network and Internet bandwidth for network services and applications.

- Select an appropriate network protocol and create an addressing scheme that will provide for the existing size of the network and will allocate room for any foreseeable expansions, mergers, or acquisitions.

- Specify and implement the technologies that will meet the existing needs of your network while allowing room for future growth.

- Plan to upgrade and/or migrate any existing technologies, including server operating systems and routing protocols.

Planning Strategies

When designing a new network or significantly upgrading an existing one, you should first use the business requirements of your organization as the primary source of planning information. You'll need to create a network infrastructure that addresses the needs of your management structure, such as fault tolerance, security, scalability, performance, and cost. You'll need to balance these requirements with the types of services that your users and clients will expect from a modern network, including e-mail, calendaring, project collaboration, Internet access, file, print, and application services.

After you've determined the business requirements of your network, you should then analyze the technical requirements of your organization. These requirements may apply to any applications that are already in use or that you plan to implement, as well as to the associated hardware and operating system. You should carefully note all of these requirements so that you won't create any difficulties later on during the implementation process. Be sure to analyze and document the existing network, including any hardware, software, and network services that are already in place. This will make it easier to take the existing configuration into account when planning the new or upgraded network.

Finally, any well-formed network plan should make allowances for future changes to the organization, including support for new technologies and operating systems, as well as additional hardware and users. Your organization's business requirements can change—through a merger, an acquisition, or simple growth and expansion. Although it is impossible to foresee all possible changes of this nature, a good network design will be flexible enough to accommodate as many adjustments as possible.

Using Planning Tools

There are a number of tools available to assist you in developing a plan for your network infrastructure. The first and best of these, however, might be the simplest: pencil and paper. As we discussed in the previous section, you should begin your planning by determining the requirements of the business that will be using the network.

After you have a high-level understanding of your company's organizational structure and computing needs, you should inventory the hardware and software that is already in place. This is especially important to ensure existing hardware and software are supported in Windows Server 2003. In a small office environment, you can accomplish this by simply taking a walk to determine the physical layout of network cables, routers, and the like. In a medium- to large-sized enterprise network, you will probably want to rely on automated inventory tools such as Microsoft's Systems Management Server (SMS) or a third-party equivalent. Take as detailed of an inventory as possible, including the hardware configuration of server and workstation machines, as well as vendor names and the version numbers of the operating system and business applications the systems are running.

You can use a network analyzer, such as the Network Monitor utility built into the Windows Server 2003 operating system or the more full-featured version of Network Monitor included in SMS, to create a baseline of the current utilization of your network bandwidth. If this utilization is already near capacity, you can use this baseline to justify and plan upgrades to your network infrastructure (moving from 10MB Ethernet to 100MB Ethernet, for example).

Windows Server 2003 has introduced new management features that will assist you in planning your network configuration, especially in the areas of user and computer management. The Resultant Set of Policy (RSoP) Microsoft Management Console (MMC) snap-in contains a Group Policy modeling function that will allow you to simulate changes to Group Policy Objects (GPOs) in an Active Directory (AD) environment before actually applying them to a production network. For example, if you want to apply a new GPO to a departmental Organizational Unit (OU), the modeling report will indicate how the new GPO will affect the objects within the OU to which it's being applied. The Group Policy Management Console (GPMC) can also provide detailed configuration reports on existing GPO settings in place on a Windows 2000 or Windows Server 2003 AD installation.

Reviewing Legal and Regulatory Considerations

Depending on the business in which you are involved, your network design plan should address the legal issues associated with your industry, geographic location, and so on. Backup schedules and off-site data availability have become federally regulated matters, especially in the financial arena. Consult your Legal department during the design process, because like everything else in this venture, it's certainly best to get it right the first time.

Don't forget to include your client workstations when making allowances for legal and regulatory matters. For example, if your corporate data-retention policy calls for maintaining e-mail data for twelve months, but some users have copies of every item they've sent or received in the last five years, that fact could come back to haunt you in a legal proceeding.

Some fields of business are subject to very detailed governmental regulations regarding data security. For example, healthcare providers now fall under strict laws regarding electronic patient information since the Health Insurance Portability and Accountability Act (HIPAA) went into effect in 2003. Regardless of your field, if you work on government projects, your network might be required to meet specified security criteria.

Network communications can also subject your company to legal liability when employees misuse the network. For example, pornographic material on the company network can subject the company to charges of the "hostile workplace" definition of sexual harassment under Title VII of the federal Civil Rights Act of 1964 and various state laws. You should also consider intellectual property (copyright, trademark, and patent) laws in establishing your network policies.

Common factors that also need to be reviewed for legal compliance are any Service Level Agreements (SLAs) in place on your network. An SLA attempts to define the scope of a service provider's responsibilities in maintaining applications or services on a network. This provider can be an external vendor to whom you've outsourced a critical service (your ISP, for example), or the SLA can be an internal document detailing the IT department's duties in maintaining network availability. The following are the major components of an external SLA, using an ISP as a real-world example:

- **Scope of services** This spells out exactly which service or application that an SLA is referring to and the level of responsibility that the internal IT department will have in maintaining this service versus the external vendor. This includes outlining the hardware, software, and resources that comprise the particular service, such as the modems, network connectivity equipment, ISP help desk, and engineering personnel in the case of an ISP.

- **Roles and responsibilities** Your ISP should establish a coverage schedule so that at least one primary and one backup support avenue is available to report any service outages. You'll also need to establish a system to escalate support calls if the scheduled support person is unavailable or cannot correct the problem. You can use this information to inform your users of the turnaround time they can anticipate in responding to and resolving any problems.

These are only a few of the legal considerations that are important in a corporate network environment. You should always include a legal advisor as a member of your network planning team.

Calculating TCO

"These upgrade proposals look interesting, but how will they impact our company's TCO?" Total Cost of Ownership (TCO) is a calculation that was designed to assist consumers and corporate managers in assessing the direct and indirect costs and benefits associated with the implementation of new or upgraded computer technology. The purpose of TCO is to quantify the financial bottom line associated with a computer or technology purchase decision.

TCO calculations do not rely on a single formula. For example, a high-end computer will have a higher initial purchase price, but will probably incur fewer repair bills during its active life cycle. TCO is balanced against the benefits created by the technology purchase, such as improved user efficiency or perceived happiness with improved performance, in attempting to make a final purchase decision.

The first part of calculating TCO is relatively simple: What is the initial purchase price of the new technology? Include the cost of hardware, software licensing, networking equipment, installation charges, and so on. Don't forget to factor in the necessary time to train your end users and IT staff in the use and administration of the new technology. Next, determine the ongoing costs for maintenance and support. These costs can include charges for vendor support, as well as in-house labor expended on interoperability issues with third-party and legacy software support. Try to estimate the total costs for the full anticipated life cycle of the proposed technology.

Determining the soft costs associated with a new technology is a bit more complicated. How much money will your company save by reducing the number of times your users are forced to reboot their computers each day? Conversely, how much money is lost when an account manager cannot access the order-entry application for 20 minutes, for an hour, and for a day? These costs are fairly difficult to quantify, but they can be critical when determining the total benefits afforded by a network upgrade. You can start investigating soft costs by talking to your users and reviewing TCO models from network analysts.

Your users can certainly tell you how much it aggravates them when their e-mail or order database is "running too slowly," even if they can't tell you what "too slowly" means in terms of actual response time. This can also point out performance bottlenecks that you may not have known about before. For example, a real estate lending office for a well-known bank shared a T1 line with the bank branch in the lobby of the office building. The real estate lenders encountered severe network performance degradation every day at around 4:30 P.M. Further investigation revealed that this time frame coincided with the bank tellers transmitting their daily totals to the bank's main headquarters when the branch closed each day.

Preconfigured TCO models from organizations like the Gartner Group, IDC, or other independent network analysts can walk you step-by-step through plugging in various budget figures to arrive at the TCO of a specific technology, hardware, or software package. However, remember that these models are not set in stone, and they should be modified as needed to meet the specific needs of your organization. These models will rely more on actual calculations, such as dividing a help desk analyst's salary by the number of support calls he or she is able to process in a day, or determining the "cost per e-mail message" of an e-mail server upgrade that increases the number of messages it can transmit in a day, week, or hour. You can then take these numbers and factor in the soft costs already mentioned. Using a combination of calculations and judgment calls will typically lead you to the most accurate assessment of TCO within your organization.

Developing a Windows Server 2003 Test Network Environment

When implementing a new network or computer solution, you should perform a thorough battery of testing before deploying it into production. Although not specific to Windows Server 2003, you should follow a systematic approach to designing a new or upgraded network. This typically includes developing a test environment in which you can test compatibility, usability, connectivity, security settings and more.

You'll begin the test process in an isolated lab where new technologies will have no chance of adversely affecting the existing computing environment. After you are satisfied with the new technology's performance in the test lab, you can expand testing into a pilot deployment involving a few actual users, analyzing their input and reactions to make any necessary adjustments to your design. Only after you are satisfied with the pilot deployment should you perform a full-scale deployment in your production environment.

Depending on the total number of users you have, you might want to split your full-scale deployment schedule into stages. After each stage, you can verify that your system is accommodating the increased processing load from the additional users as expected, before you begin deploying the next group of users.

The success of any network deployment depends heavily on your ability to develop an effective test environment. This test lab can consist of a single lab or several labs, each of which can test various pieces of the overall design without risking the integrity of your production environment. Working in the test lab will allow you to verify the effectiveness of your design, discover any potential deployment problems, and increase your staff's familiarity with the new technology before it "goes live." In short, a well-developed test environment will reduce the risk of errors during the deployment of a new technology, thus minimizing any potential downtime for your clients and users.

Planning the Test Network

Before you begin testing your Windows Server 2003 network design, you need to plan the test network itself. The first step is to determine the hardware resources required to set up the lab. This involves identifying the standard configurations of your existing or new client computers. (If you support diverse workstations, do your best to include a representative workstation from each supported configuration.) Be sure to include all components and peripherals, including the following:

- BIOS versions
- USB adapters
- CD and DVD drives
- Sound cards
- Video cards
- Network adapters
- Smart card readers
- Removable storage devices, such as Zip drives or external hard drives
- Small Computer System Interface (SCSI) adapters
- Removable storage devices
- Mouse or trackball devices
- Keyboards

Although using separate hardware devices for your test lab is the ideal, many small and medium-sized businesses simply cannot afford to buy dozens of computers for the test lab. Using a third-party product such as VMware (www.vmware.com) will allow you to simulate a multiple server/domain environment, as well as multiple desktop operations systems, fairly closely without the expense of multiple individual machines. VMware can run multiple operating systems—such as Microsoft Windows, Linux, and Novell NetWare—simultaneously on a single PC, including all networking and connectivity that you would need to perform your testing.

In addition to purchasing hardware or virtual PC environments for the test lab, you need to secure appropriate licensing for all necessary software, including operating systems, service packs, management utilities, and business applications. Make sure that you can obtain or duplicate the following configuration and information when creating a test lab for Windows Server 2003:

- **Network services** Install the same services on a test server that will be used in the actual deployment. This can include Domain Name System (DNS), Dynamic Host Configuration Protocol (DHCP), Windows Internet Name Service (WINS), or any other Windows service.

- **User accounts** Create a domain controller in your test environment to effectively simulate any upgrade procedures.

- **Domain structure** Simulate the domain hierarchy of your proposed environment, including forests, trees, parent and child domains, and all necessary trust relationships. Configure sites as necessary to simulate any WAN testing considerations.

- **Network protocols and topology** Re-create the network technologies that will be used in your production environment as completely as possible. For example, if your production environment will be using 100MB cabling, using Gigabit Ethernet will provide erroneous results when doing performance testing. You should also include routers to test for performance latency as well as replication across WAN links.

- **Domain authentication** Use the appropriate authentication to mimic the desired production environment, including mixed mode versus native mode, and NTLM versus Kerberos client authentication. Selecting the appropriate authentication model will allow you to compare apples to apples during testing and avoid any unexpected behavior later. Remember that Windows NT 4 workstations or servers cannot use Kerberos authentication. You will need to rely on either NTLM authentication or its stronger successor, NTLM version 2.

- **Group Policy Object (GPO) settings** Create GPOs with the settings that you wish to deploy in your production environment. You can use the GPMC (discussed earlier) to test the potential behavior of any policy objects on user and group objects.

Although you usually want your test lab to mimic your production environment as closely as possible, there are exceptions to every rule. Some tests that you might wish to perform will affect an entire domain or forest, rather than a single machine. If you are testing this type of functionality, you might wish to create a separate domain within the test lab so that the remainder of the lab environment will not be adversely affected.

Some of the tests for which you might wish to create a separate, isolated domain or forest are as follows:

Switching from mixed mode to native mode Changing from mixed mode to native mode will allow for much tighter security in a Windows 2000 or Windows Server 2003 environment, but it assumes that you have no Windows NT 4 backup domain controllers (BDCs) remaining in your domain. (After the switch to native mode, Windows NT 4 BDCs will no longer be able to replicate with Windows 2000 or 2003 domain controllers.) This change will affect an entire domain and cannot be reversed.

Upgrading the domain or forest functional level This feature was introduced in Windows 2000, where you had the ability to run a domain in mixed mode for backward compatibility or native mode for increased security and functionality. Windows Server 2003 expands on this by creating several levels of both forest *and* domain functionality that can expose different features of the operating system for your use. For example, raising the functional level of a domain to Windows Server 2003 native will prevent any existing Windows NT 4 or Windows 2000 Server domain controllers from participating in domain replication. Like the switch from mixed to native mode, this will affect the entire domain and/or forest in question and cannot be undone.

DNS settings Changes to a DNS server will affect all clients who use that server for name resolution. Although this does not involve the kinds of one-way changes described above, you should still proceed with caution before making changes that can affect other tests that might be running simultaneously in the lab environment.

One important (but often overlooked) step in the planning process is that of carefully selecting a location for your test lab. Too often, the test lab is relegated to a corner of a server room or whatever room is available in a file or storage area. However, if you will be performing tests for an extended period of time, you should consider allocating a permanent or semipermanent location for the lab. Be sure to locate the test lab in an area with enough space for all necessary equipment and personnel. If you will be testing network equipment that will be deployed to multiple locations, you should consider deploying a test lab at each site to test WAN links, replication, and site configurations. Also, identify the personnel you'll need to perform testing, as well as whatever training they will need.

Finally, be sure to provide both physical and technological security measures for the equipment and resources of the test lab. This includes isolating the test lab topology from your corporate network using routers, switches, or firewalls, as appropriate. If you need to provide a connection from the test lab to the corporate network, decide in advance how you will control, secure and monitor that connection, and be sure to devise a way to quickly terminate the connection if something unexpected or adverse occurs.

Exploring the Group Policy Management Console (GMPC)

A prominent new feature of Windows Server 2003 that is helpful in planning and assessing network changes is the GPMC, which allows administrators to monitor, troubleshoot, and plan Group Policy settings across an entire enterprise from a single management console. Along with a console window that provides a graphical representation of GPO settings, the GPMC also includes a collection of scripts that you can run from the command line to streamline administration and planning tasks. You can download and install the GPMC from Microsoft's Web site. Once it's installed, you'll have a shortcut to it in the Administrative Tools folder, and it will be available as an MMC snap-in.

The scripts that are included with GPMC can greatly simplify your life when you attempt to take stock of an existing network environment (for example, when you begin to plan for an upgrade). Using GPMC, you can quickly perform the following tasks using its automated scripting function:

- List all GPOs that are present in a given domain
- List any disabled GPOs
- List GPOs at a backup location
- List GPOs by policy extension or security group
- List any orphaned GPOs (GPOs that are no longer linked to any AD object) that are still present in the SYSVOL directory

- List GPOs with duplicate names
- List GPOs without security filtering
- List unlinked GPOs in a domain

GPMC's reporting functions will also generate HTML-formatted reports in an easy-to-read format, which is always a hit when you're presenting the upgrade proposal to management or a budget committee. Additionally, the GPMC includes the Resultant Set of Policy Planning function to allow you to simulate changes to GPO settings for a user, computer, or container object. Both of these functions will greatly assist you with the administrative and technical aspects of a network design project.

Documenting the Planning and Network Design Process

The importance of documenting your computing environment after you have deployed a new network design such as Windows Server 2003 cannot be overemphasized. As you move through the network design and testing processes, you should also keep detailed documentation of each design, product, or vendor decision that you make, including your reasons for choosing one alternative over another. Personnel changes can occur without warning, and a well-maintained design document will quickly answer the question of "Why did we choose Vendor X over Vendor Y?" when it is posed by the new Vice President of IT, who just started last week. Knowing that Vendor Y's product proved incompatible after several hours of troubleshooting will save you from needing to waste time by repeating portions of the design process.

Because of the effects that ongoing changes can have in a production environment, many organizations use test equipment to test every patch and service pack that is released by their product vendors, so that any potential problems or bugs can be intercepted before the patch is applied globally. Whatever method you use to roll out ongoing updates and changes, you should include detailed documentation, not only of *what* update was rolled out on a given date, but also of *how* the change was applied to client machines or other devices on your network.

Creating the Planning and Design Document

When documenting both your test lab and your overall network design, there are a number of items that need to be discussed. Although maintaining network documentation is often relegated to a backseat behind the numerous fires that we must put out on a daily basis as network administrators, comprehensive records in this area will actually help you in whatever troubleshooting issues come up after the new network is placed into production. Include configuration information about the following components of your final network design (although a complete list is limited only by the amount of time you have in the day!):

- Windows Server 2003 domain structure information, including DNS hierarchy and replication information, AD hierarchy information (site configuration, forest, domains, and OUs), and GPO settings and where they are applied within the AD hierarchy. Be sure to include information about **Enforce** and **Block Inheritance** flags in Group Policy implementation. These affect how GPOs are inherited throughout the AD infrastructure.

- Trust relationships, both transitive and explicitly defined
- Network connectivity hardware (switches, routers, firewalls, and other LAN and WAN connectivity devices)
- Client computer configuration, both hardware and software
- Line-of-business application inventory and configuration
- Backup, restore, and disaster recovery procedures

Windows Server 2003, built upon the same technology as Windows 2000, has been upgraded and improved to address a variety of needs in today's networked environment. We've reviewed the new features in Windows Server 2003 and taken a quick look at some of the tools available to make installing, maintaining and repairing Windows Server 2003 a bit easier. We've also reviewed the basics of network design, planning and testing and we're now ready to jump into the specifics of Windows Server 2003.

Chapter 2

Using Server Management Tools

In this chapter:

- **Recognizing Types of Management Tools**

- **Managing Your Server Remotely**

- **Using Emergency Management Services**

- **Managing Printers and Print Queues**

- **Managing and Troubleshooting Services**

- **Using Wizards to Configure and Manage Your Server**

Introduction

The network administrator's daily tasks can be made easier (or more difficult) by the number and quality of administrative tools available to perform those tasks. In the previous chapter, we quickly reviewed some of the tools. In this chapter, we'll take a more in-depth look at specific server management tools.

In Windows Server 2003, Microsoft has provided administrators with a wealth of graphical and command-line utilities for carrying out their job duties. The Administrative Tools menu is the place to start, and there you'll find predefined management consoles for configuring and managing most of Server 2003's services and components, including Active Directory tools, distributed file system (Dfs), DNS, Security policies, Licensing, Routing and Remote Access, Terminal Services, Media Services, and more.

But that's only the beginning. Administrators can create customized Microsoft Management Consoles as well, just as with Windows 2000. This makes it easier to perform tasks yourself, and easier to delegate administrative tasks to others, because you can create consoles for specific purposes and enable only limited user access to them for specified users or groups.

For those who prefer the power and flexibility of the command line, many of these same administrative tasks can be performed there, as well as other tasks that have no GUI interface. Windows Server 2003 includes a huge number of command-line utilities, including dozens of new ones that were not included in Windows 2000 Server.

Many of the more complex configuration tasks performed by administrators can be done via Wizards that walk you through the steps. This makes it easier to set up services and server components for those who are unfamiliar with the process.

In this chapter, we introduce you to many of the graphical management consoles and command-line administrative utilities that are included in Windows Server 2003, and show you how to use them to manage your server and your network.

Recognizing Types of Management Tools

So many administrative tools are available, located in so many different places, that it can be daunting for a new administrator of a Windows computer to know where to look. Of course, in the fullness of time, experience brings familiarity - but even experienced administrators occasionally discover a tool that they haven't seen before. In this section we will review where most of the common administrative tools are located.

Administrative Tools Menu

The Administrative Tools menu is where many important tools are located. Click **Start | Programs | Administrative Tools** to see what is available. You can change what appears in this folder by editing the **All Users** profile in the **Documents and Settings** folder as shown in Figure 2.1.

Figure 2.1 Location of the Administrative Tools Folder

Another way to access the same folder is by clicking **Start | Settings | Control Panel**, and then double-clicking the **Administrative Tools** icon.

Note that the items in the Administrative Tools menu folder are shortcuts, rather than the programs or console files themselves. Many of the actual management console files (.msc files) are located in the **<systemroot>\system32** folder. You can find the location of the .msc file by right-clicking the shortcut in the right pane as shown in the figure, selecting **Properties**, and then checking the **Target** field on the **Shortcut** menu.

Custom MMC Snap-Ins

The Microsoft Management Console (normally referred to as an MMC) is the framework for nearly all Windows graphical administrative tools. It provides a blank sheet to which you can add your favorite administration tools. The idea is that all administrative tools have a common look and feel and that the management tool for an administrative task, such as adding users and groups, is written as a snap-in for an MMC. The administrator can then choose which snap-ins to have in a console or use one of the many pre-configured ones found in the **Administrative Tools** folder. Some of the MMC snap-ins can be used to manage remote computers as well as the local computer (assuming you have the appropriate rights). Many vendors of third-party management tools provide snap-ins for their products, which you can add to your MMC consoles.

Note that some of the tools in the **Administrative Tools** folder, such as **Licensing,** are stand-alone programs that don't work with an MMC. When you look at the properties of those shortcuts, you'll find that the target files are executables (.exe) instead of MMCs (.msc).

After you've created an MMC, it can be saved as a stand-alone file and even e-mailed to another administrator to use. Possession of an MMC file does not in itself give a user any additional rights. So if you e-mail an MMC file with, for example, the Disk Management snap-in to a non-administrative user, that user won't be able to complete any disk management tasks even though he or she can see the snap-in.

MMC Console Modes

MMC consoles can be configured to prevent anyone from changing them. A console can be saved in one of four modes, each of which has varying restrictions. Table 2.1 shows the four modes and the functionality of each.

Table 2.1 MMC Console Modes

Console Mode	Functionality
Author mode	Full access to the MMC and change all aspects.
User mode –full access	Full access to the windowing commands but can't add or remove snap-ins.
User mode – limited access, multiple window	Access only to the areas of the console as it was when saved. Can create new windows but not close existing windows.
User mode – limited access, single windows	Access to the console as it was when saved. Can't open new windows.

To give you an idea of how you can use the MMC, use the following steps to create a custom MMC. You may choose to use this MMC or you may simply follow the steps to get a better idea of how to create a custom MMC.

1. To create a new console, click **Start | Run** and type **mmc** in the dialog box.

2. Select **Add/Remove Snap-in** from the **File** pull-down menu.

3. In the **Add/Remove Snap-in** dialog-box, click the **Add** button.

4. In the **Add Standalone Snap-in** dialog box, scroll through the list and click **Event Viewer**, and then click the **Add** button.

5. In the **Select Computer** dialog box, click **Finish**.

6. Click **Close** in the **Add Standalone Snap-in** dialog box, and then click **OK** in the **Add/Remove Snap-in** dialog box.

7. Repeat steps 2 to 6, but for step 5 select **Another Computer** and enter the name of or browse to another computer on your network.

8. Repeat steps 2 to 6, but for step 4 select **Services** and in step 5 select **Local Computer**.

9. In the left-hand pane, click the plus signs next to the two Event Viewer folders to expand them.

10. Click **Application** under the Event Viewer (Local) folder.

11. You should now have a console similar to the one shown in Figure 2.2.

Figure 2.2 Viewing the Application Log for the Local Computer

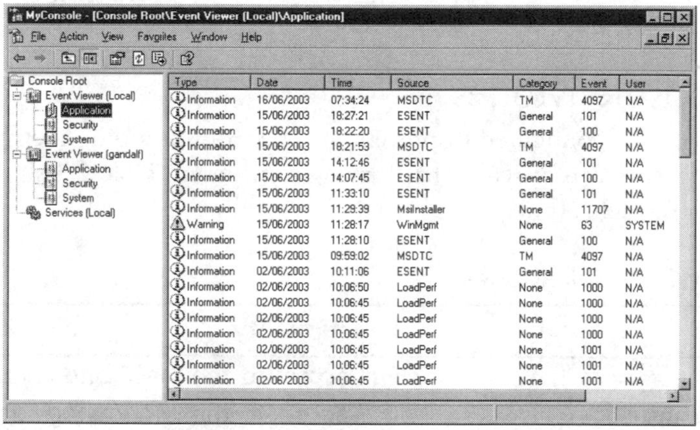

12. To save this console for future use, select **Save** from the **File** pull-down menu. Type **MyConsole** in the **File name** box and click **Save**.

13. The console is saved and can be started again via **Start | Programs | Administrative Tools | MyConsole.msc**.

14. We will now look at opening multiple windows. Highlight **Event Viewer (Local)**, and then right-click and select **New Window from Here**. You now have two windows open, which can be managed using the **Window** pull-down option.

15. Click **Window** and explore the various options for how the two windows are laid out.

16. Switch to the **Event Viewer (Local)** window and close this window by typing **Ctrl-F4**. You should now have only one window called **Console Root**.

17. Click **File** and select **Options**.

18. In the **Options** dialog box that appears, click the pull-down menu for the **Console mode** box and select **User mode – limited access, single window**, and then click **OK**.

19. Click **File** and select **Save**.

20. Click **File** and select **Exit**.

21. Re-open the console by selecting **Start | Programs | Administrative Tools | MyConsole.msc**.

22. Note that the **Window** pull-down option is no longer present, that you cannot add new snap-ins via the **File** pull-down menu, and that you cannot close any of the snap-ins that are in the MMC.

Command-Line Utilities

As the name suggests, command-line utilities are designed to be run in a command window (start by selecting **Start | Run**, and then type **cmd** in the **Open** box and press **Enter**) or as part of batch files or scripts. Administrators are forever looking for ways to simplify administration and using command lines in batch files is a very good way of handling routine, repetitive tasks. You can perform some administrative tasks using only a graphical interface, some using only a command-line utility, and others can be done using either. Later in the chapter, we will examine printer administration, which is a good example of something that can be managed using graphical or command-line tools.

Command-line utilities are written using a language that has to be run using a scripting host such as Windows **cscript** and others run as compiled programs or executables.

Command-line utilities are harder to find because they are not in any of the Start menus (although you can add them). A good place to look for information is in Windows **Help and Support**. Search on **Command-line Reference** and you get an A-Z of Windows command-line tools.

Wizards

Wizards guide you through potentially complex tasks by taking you through a series of dialog boxes where you answer questions or make choices; they are essentially wrappers around the underlying graphical or command-line based tool. Each version of Windows increases the number of wizards in an attempt to make administration easier for the inexperienced administrator. However, in some cases it can be quicker for the experienced administrator to perform a task directly using the appropriate administrative tools rather than using a wizard.

Many wizards can be accessed through the Manage Your Server tool and the Configure Your Server Wizard in Administrative Tools.

Windows Resource Kit

The Windows Resource Kit, available for download from Microsoft's Web site, provides even more tools for administrators to use to manage Windows servers in a large network. If you are responsible for many servers, you should download this kit and spend some time reviewing its contents.

The Run As command

It is good practice for administrators not to log on using an account that has administrative rights. This prevents accidental changes to the file server, viruses having more access than otherwise, and so on. As an administrator, you should log on using an ordinary user account and when you need to perform an administrative task you can use the **Run as** option to choose an administrator account. **Run as** is available by right-clicking an item in the start menu.

The **Run as** option won't appear in the right context menu for every Start menu item, just for executables, management consoles, and other programs that can be run.

You can also use the *runas* command in a command prompt for command-line utilities. Start a command prompt and then type **runas /user:administrator cmd**. This will start a new command prompt with administrator privileges.

Managing Your Server Remotely

How often have you had to walk to the other end of a building to perform a server task or − even worse − had to drive or fly to another office? One of the main aims for any administrator is to be able to manage all the servers without leaving his or her desk! Windows Server 2003 provides you with a variety of methods to remotely manage your servers depending on your scenario.

Remote Assistance

Remote Assistance is designed for users to request help on their PCs (which must be running Windows XP or later) from another user. The user requesting help sends an invitation to assist, using Windows Messenger or e-mail via the **Help and Support Center**. The request includes an attachment (which contains details of how to connect to the user's PC) that the recipient double-clicks to start a Remote Assistance session with the requesting user's PC. Once connected, the helper can view the desktop of the requesting user and chat online with him. The helper can also, with the user's permission, take control of his desktop.

The request can optionally include an "expiry" (expiration) date, after which the Remote Assistance request is no longer valid. This is used to reduce the risk of unauthorized access to the user's computer. The user requesting help can also require the helper to use a password to connect to his computer. The user must communicate this password to the helper.

The user can review his invitations in the **Help and Support Center**. Figure 2.3 shows a summary of invitations that have been sent out.

Although the usual method is for the user requesting help to initiate the Remote Assistance session, it is also possible within a domain for a helper to offer assistance. An administrator can set group policy to prevent users from requesting remote assistance, or to restrict whether users will be able to enable a helper to remotely control their computers or only view them.

Both users need to be connected to the Internet in order to use Remote Assistance and if firewalls are in use, port 3398 must be open. You can disable Remote Assistance completely to prevent any Remote Assistance invitations being sent.

To configure Remote Assistance, right-click **My Computer** and select **Properties**, and then click the **Remote** tab.

Figure 2.3 Summary of Remote Assistance Invitations

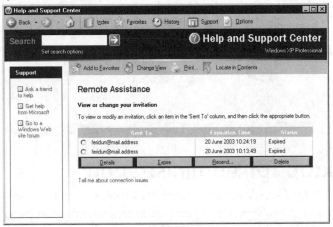

Using Web Interface for Remote Administration

If you need to manage your servers from home or perhaps from another office, one option is to use a standard Web browser to administer your servers using the remote administration component of Windows Server 2003. You must configure your server first, but after you have done this, you can simply point the browser to your server's IP address and you can administer it from anywhere in the world. To access the server over the Internet, the following conditions must be met:

- The Remote Administration (HTML) component must be installed on the server. It is not installed by default (with the exception of Windows Server 2003 Web Edition).

- Port 8098 on the server must be accessible through your Internet connection.

- Your server must have a valid external IP address.

If you want to access your servers only over your company network, an external IP address is not necessary, but you must still be able to communicate with port 8098 on the server. Microsoft recommends that the browser you use for remote administration be Internet Explorer version 6.0 or later.

To access your server over the Web, browse to **https://servername:8098**. You must use a secure connection. The **:8098** in the URL directs the browser to connect to port 8098 on the server instead of the default port 80. You can change your server to work on a different port in Internet Information Services (IIS) Manager. After you've connected to the server, you'll see the Welcome page, as shown in Figure 2.4.

Through this Web site, you can carry out the more common administration tasks, such as configuring Web sites, managing network settings, and administering local user accounts.

Figure 2.4 Welcome Page for Server Web Administration

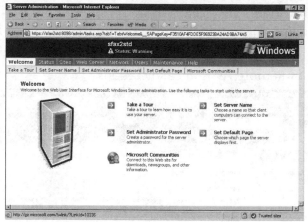

Remote Desktop for Administration

The Remote Desktop (RD) for Administration facility enables users to connect to a Windows Server 2003 or a Windows 2000 Server computer desktop from any computer that has the Remote Desktop client software. In Windows 2000, this facility was called Terminal Services Administration mode. Remote Desktop for Administration is effectively Terminal Server installed in a special mode that enables up to two remote users and one local user (at the console) to connect to a server for administration purposes and does not require any additional licensing. Terminal Server can also be used in application mode to enable many users to connect to your server using Remote Desktop from their computers and run applications in a "thin client" computing model. Application mode requires Terminal Server licensing to be set up.

You can connect to the server from any client computer running the RDC client or the Windows terminal services client. Microsoft provides an RDC client for Windows 95, 98/98SE, ME, NT 4.0 and 2000. You can also download an RDC client for Macintosh OS X.

The Remote Desktop snap-in is a very useful tool for adding Remote Desktop functionality to an MMC. With this tool, you can connect to the server's console session.

Administration Tools Pack (adminpak.msi)

The Windows Server 2003 Administration Tools Pack is used on client computers running Windows XP Professional to provide management tools for Windows Server 2003 computers. The client computers must have Windows XP Service Pack 1 applied.

You can install the Administration Tools from the **adminpak.msi** file, which you can find on the Windows Server 2003 CD or in the system32 folder of a computer running Windows Server 2003. Double-click the adminpak.msi file to install the tools.

After the tools are installed, you'll have all the administrative tools that we looked at earlier in this section available on your Windows XP computer and you'll be able to perform server and network administrative tasks from the XP client. In particular, this includes tools for server-based services such as DNS, DHCP, and Active Directory.

Windows Management Instrumentation (WMI)

Windows Management Instrumentation (WMI) provides an object-based method for accessing management information in a network. It is based on the Web-Based Enterprise Management (WBEM) standard specified by the Distributed Management Task Force (DTMF) organization and is designed to enable the management of a wide range of network devices. WMI is Microsoft's implementation of WBEM for Windows operating systems.

WMI is used with programs or scripts to retrieve management information or change configurations of Windows computers, but using WMI is not trivial and requires programming skills. WMI can be used at the command line using **WMIC**, but you need knowledge of the WMI database of objects. For more information on this topic, refer to Microsoft's WMI Software Development Kit.

Some enterprise Microsoft tools, such as Systems Management Server (SMS) and Health Monitor in the Back Office products use WMI to manage computers. For more information on WMI, have a look at Microsoft's Web site at www.microsoft.com/windows2000/techinfo/howit-works/management/wmiscripts.asp.

Using Computer Management to Manage a Remote Computer

Computer management is available on client and server computers to perform management tasks and is actually a pre-configured MMC console. To start computer management, select **Start | Settings | Control Panel**, double-click **Administrative Tools**, and then double-click **Computer Management**. Alternatively, right-click the **My Computer** icon and select **Manage**.

You can also use computer management to connect to another computer (providing you have the appropriate rights). Select **Connect to another computer…** from the **Action** pull-down menu, and then enter the name of the remote computer in the **Another computer:** box or browse for it by clicking the **Browse** button.

Figure 2.5 shows Computer Management on a server with the Disk Management snap-in expanded. On a server computer, Computer Management has additional snap-ins for server-based services, so you won't see exactly the same snap-ins in Computer Management on a computer running Windows 2000 Professional or Windows XP Professional.

Computer Management has three nodes that group the management tasks, as shown in Table 2.2. Expanding each node reveals the snap-ins. System Tools contains snap-ins for local management tasks, the Storage node contains snap-ins for tasks related to local disks and storage devices (such as tape drives), and the Services and Applications node contains snap-ins for other server-based applications. The contents of this node vary depending on whether the computer is running a client or server operating system and the server components that have been installed. Table 2.2 shows only some of the possible snap-ins under Services and Applications.

Table 2.2 Management Snap-Ins in Computer Management

Computer Management Node	Management Snap-In	Use
System Tools	Event Viewer	Display event logs
	Shared Folders	View shared folders, open files, and active sessions
	Local Users and Groups	Manage local user and group accounts
	Performance Logs and Alerts	Configure performance data logs
	Device Manager	Manage computer hardware
Storage	Removable Storage	Manage devices with removable media
	Disk Defragmenter	Defragment local disks
	Disk Management	Configure disk partitions and volumes
Services and Applications	DHCP (if installed)	Configure the DHCP service for allocating IP addresses
	Services	Manage services
	WMI Control	Configure Windows Management Instrumentation
	Indexing Service	Configure the Indexing Service to provide fast searches
	Routing and Remote Access (if installed)	Manage routing and remote access
	DNS (if installed)	Configure the DNS service

Figure 2.5 Computer Management MMC

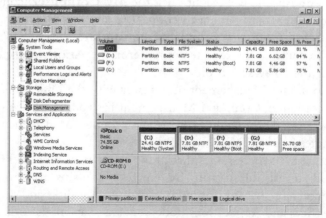

Which Tool To Use?

In this section we've seen a variety of tools for remotely managing servers. How do you decide which one to use in a given situation? It really depends on what you are trying to do and in cases where you can accomplish the same thing with different tools, you might have your favorite tools for administering a server.

- Remote Assistance is really a tool for end users and you are unlikely to use it for remote server management. You should, however, be aware that Remote Assistance invitations can be sent from a Windows Server 2003 computer, and you should know how to turn off Remote Assistance.

- The Remote Desktop tool is useful when you need to have full control of a single server. Because you are effectively at the server, you can administer any function. With the Remote Desktop snap-in, or using RD from the command line, you can even connect to the server console session remotely.

- The Web Interface for Remote Administration is useful in situations where you need to carry out basic tasks when you are away from the corporate network, but still have access to the Internet. It is limited, however, as to which administrative tasks you can carry out.

- The administration tools pack and computer management in conjunction with custom MMCs are likely to be among the tools you use the most, especially if you have to administer a large number of servers. You can put together customized MMCs that contain the snap-ins for tools that you use the most often and for the servers that you have to regularly manage.

Using Emergency Management Services

Emergency Management Services is a new feature in Windows Server 2003 that enables you to remotely manage a server when normal network connectivity has failed. Under normal conditions, you use the tools described in this and other chapters to manage your server either by being physically present at the server or over the network. However, what happens if the network crashes or the server doesn't boot properly?

Providing the server has the appropriate hardware and firmware, you can remotely manage it without the presence of a local keyboard, mouse, or display. This is called out-of-band or "headless" operation. A key aim of out-of-band management is to get a server that is not working properly back to a normal operating state.

A number of situations might require you to resort to out-of-band management:

- The server has stopped responding to normal network management commands.

- The network card in the server has failed.

- The server hasn't booted properly.

- The server has been shut down and you need to bring it up again.

The extent to which you can use out-of-band management depends on the hardware of your server. At the very least, on a server with Windows Server 2003, a serial port and Emergency Management Services enabled, you can connect a VT100-type terminal or a computer with a terminal emulator to the serial port and perform certain tasks using the Special Administration Console (SAC). However, the server must be up and running to be able to manage it in this way.

If you need to be able to manage the server remotely when it has crashed or even switched off, you need special hardware and firmware on the motherboard that provide features such as firmware console redirection. This means that you can monitor the server via the serial port right from the moment it starts up and even check out BIOS settings.

Emergency Management Services is not enabled by default, but can be enabled during an installation, an upgrade, or after setup has been completed.

Managing Printers and Print Queues

Managing printing, which involves many tasks, is a routine part of almost every administrator's job and in this section we will examine the tools that you can use to manage your printers.

Windows Server 2003 offers a variety of methods for managing printers; these include the Control Panel, the Manage Your Server tool, and command-line tools.

Printer management tasks include the following:

- Creating a printer
- Sharing a printer
- Adding printer drivers for earlier operating systems
- Setting permissions
- Managing print queues
- Creating printer pools
- Scheduling printers
- Setting printing priorities

You can carry out all these tasks using graphical or command-line tools. First, we'll cover how to carry out these tasks using the graphical interface.

Using the Graphical Interface

The Graphical Interface for managing printers and print queues includes a number of tools:

- Control Panel | Printers and Faxes folder
- Add Printer Wizard
- Add Printer Driver Wizard
- Manage Your Server

The **Printers and Faxes** folder is where printers defined on the computer are stored. Configuring the properties of printers in this folder carries out nearly all printer tasks.

The **Manage Your Server** tool enables you to configure various server roles, including the print server role, by using the **Configure Your Server** Wizard. We cover roles later in this chapter.

Here, we'll examine the key printer management tasks using the graphical interfaces.

Creating a Printer

Use the **Add Printer Wizard** to create a printer by selecting **Start | Settings | Printers and Faxes** and clicking the **Add Printer** icon.

The wizard asks you a series of questions about which port to use, the driver to use, what name to give the printer, whether it should be shared, optional location and comment information, and whether to print a test page.

The port to choose depends on how the printer is physically connected to the computer. It might be connected to a serial port, parallel port, or USB port. If the printer is connected directly to the network, you need to use a TCP/IP port and specify the IP address of the printer. Usually, if you connect a printer to a USB port, Windows uses Plug and Play to automatically install the printer for you.

Printer drivers are used to convert a print job to the specific commands that a print device understands. Print devices vary in the command languages that they use; for example, most HP printers use PCL. It is therefore very important that you select the correct driver for your printer. Often a new printer comes with an installation CD or disk that contains the driver.

After you've created a printer, it appears in the **Printers and Faxes** folder and you can double-click the printer to change its properties.

Sharing a Printer

If you do not share a printer, only the computer on which you create the printer can use it. Sharing a printer makes it available over the network to other computers.

To share a printer: highlight it, right-click, and then click **Sharing**. In the **Properties** dialog box, select **Share this printer** and choose a share name. This is the name by which the printer will be known over the network.

You need to consider the operating system that the computers using the printer share will be running. When you share a printer on a Windows Server 2003 computer, the installed driver is also suitable for Windows XP and Windows 2000 clients. When a computer running Windows 2000 or Windows XP connects to the share, it automatically downloads the driver. If you have client computers running Windows NT 4.0 or Windows 95/98 or Windows Millennium Edition (ME), install additional drivers.

Adding Printer Drivers for Earlier Operating Systems

To make a shared printer available to users of computers with earlier operating systems, install the appropriate driver on the server computer. To do this, select the **Sharing** tab for the printer and click the **Additional Drivers** button to load the drivers for earlier operating systems. The benefit of doing this is that when a computer running, for example, Windows 98 connects to the shared printer, it downloads the appropriate driver automatically rather than asking the user for the location of the printer driver.

Setting Permissions

Printer permissions control who can print to a printer and whether a user can manage the printer. There are three permissions for printers (refer to Table 2.3) and these can be applied to users and groups. As with file and folder permissions, printer permissions are cumulative, so if a user has permissions to a printer and is also a member of a group that has permissions, the user will have the cumulative effect of the user and group permissions. The exception to this is that if any of the printer permissions have been denied, the user can never have that permission regardless of any groups that he belongs to. Figure 2.6 shows the default permissions on a Windows Server 2003 computer.

Figure 2.6 Default Printer Permissions

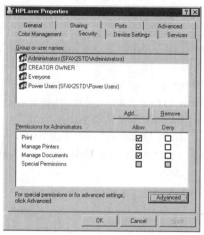

The **Special Permissions** permission enables you to fine-tune the security by specifying who is allowed to read what the permissions are, who can change the permissions. and who can take ownership. The person that created it owns a printer and that person can always change permissions on the printer. To make someone else the owner of a printer, give that user the **Take Ownership** permission and then get the other user to exercise the **Take Ownership** option. The user will then own the printer and can change permissions.

Table 2.3 Printer Permissions

Permission	Use
Print	Users can print and delete their own jobs.
Manage Documents	Users can pause, resume, restart, delete, and change the print order of documents submitted by other users. However, this permission does not, by itself, enable a user to print to the printer.
Manage Printers	Users have complete control over the printer and can change any of its characteristics.

Figure 2.7 The Windows Server 2003 Add Printer Wizard

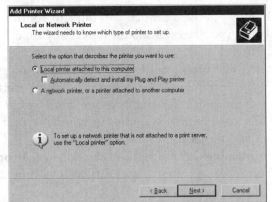

Managing Print Queues

You will often need to see what jobs are waiting to print and perhaps to delete some. You accomplish this via the print queue for a printer. To look at the queue, double-click the printer of interest. In the dialog box that appears you will see a list of jobs waiting to be printed. You can delete or cancel a job by highlighting it and then pressing delete or by highlighting it and then right-clicking and selecting **Cancel**.

To cancel all jobs in a queue, highlight the printer, right-click, and select **Cancel All Documents**. If you have the dialog box for the printer queue open, you can also select **Cancel All Documents** from the **Printer** pull-down menu.

Pausing a print job prevents it from printing but won't delete it from the queue. You might do this if someone has submitted a very large print job and you want to hold it back until all the other jobs have printed. To pause a print job, highlight the job, right-click, and then select **Pause**. To release the job for printing, highlight the job, right-click, and then select **Resume**.

You can also pause the entire queue, perhaps because the printer has failed or jammed and you want to stop a flood of error messages. To pause a printer, highlight it, right-click, and then select **Pause Printing**. To restart printing, highlight the printer, right-click, and then select **Resume Printing**.

Managing Printer Pools

Imagine your printer has become very busy and long queues develop. In this situation, rather than replacing the printer with a much more powerful one, you could purchase another identical printer (perhaps saving money). Connect the printer and, instead of creating a new printer queue on the server, modify the properties of the existing queue on the **Ports** tab, select **Enable Printer Pooling**, and choose the new port that you used to connect the printer (this could be a TCP/IP port).

Whenever a user prints to this queue, the print job is sent to the first printer that is not busy, thus pooling the jobs. You must ensure that the printers you connect are identical, because users cannot control which printer will service their jobs. Differences in capabilities between the printers might mean that a job fails to print properly. You should also locate the printers physically close to each other, because users will not know which printer has printed their job.

Scheduling Printers

As well as controlling which users can use a printer, you can also control when they print by using scheduling. By setting a schedule, users can still submit jobs at any time, but the jobs will only be printed during the scheduled hours.

Consider a scenario where some users print large reports to a printer that is shared by other users. With a single printer queue, printing the large report holds up printing for other users. To resolve this, create a second printer queue that points to the same port as the first queue, change the availability time to out-of-office hours and advise users to use the second printer for the large reports and the first queue for shorter jobs.

To set a schedule for a printer, highlight it, right-click and select **Properties**, and then select the **Advanced** tab. The default is for a printer to be available at all times. Figure 2.8 shows an example of a printer with restricted availability.

Figure 2.8 Example of Restricted Printing Hours

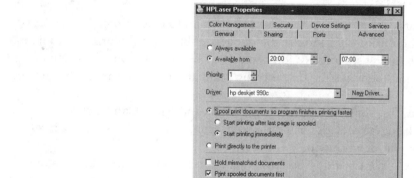

Setting Printing Priorities

You can use priorities to control the order in which print jobs are processed. Normally, jobs are printed in the order in which they are received. All printers and print jobs have a priority setting that can be changed. The default priority is 1 but can range from 1 to 99, with 99 being the highest. When a print job arrives, its priority setting is the same as the priority of the printer. Once in the queue, the priority setting can be changed by anyone with the **Manage Documents** permission. Typically, the priority of a print job will be increased to make it print next despite its position in the queue. Note that by changing the default priority of the printer to 50, for example, it is possible to reduce the priority of a job.

You can also use priorities to give certain users preferential access to a printer. For example, you have a group of managers whose print jobs need to be dealt with before other users. To achieve this, create two print queues pointing to the same printer. Let's say they are called A4 and A4Mgrs. Remove the **Print** permission for the Everyone group from A4Mgrs and add the **Print** permission to the Managers group. This means that only the managers can use this queue. The final step is to increase the priority on the A4Mgrs print queue, so that the managers' print jobs get serviced first.

Using New Command-Line Tools

Windows Server 2003 introduces a number of command-line-based scripts to manage printers. If you have large numbers of printers on your network with many servers, using these new command-line scripts in batch files can save you a lot of time, compared with using the graphical interface.

The scripts are written in Visual Basic and have to be run in a command window using *cscript*, as in this example: ***cscript prncnfg.vbs***.

It isn't necessary to include the .vbs extension. But using *cscript* is necessary because the default scripting host is *wscript* (which is for graphical windows-based scripts) and the printer management scripts have been written for the command line. You can change the default scripting host to *cscript* by using the command ***cscript //h:cscript***.

If you change the default scripting host, you can run the command-line tools without having to type *cscript* each time (however, you will then have to type *wscript* before any windows-based scripts you run). You might also like to set the option that suppresses the *cscript* logo. This prevents a couple of extra lines appearing in the output. Figure 2.9 shows the output of the *prnjobs* script with and without the logo and using the *cscript* command to suppress the appearance of the logo lines.

Figure 2.9 Using the //nologo Option with *cscript*

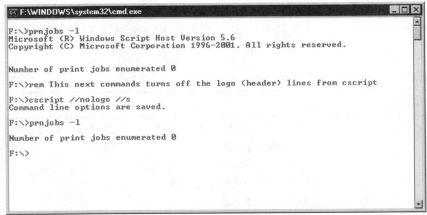

Most of the scripts can also be used to manage printers on a remote computer by using the ***−s computername*** option. If you want to use a script to connect to a remote computer, you might also need to use the ***−u username*** and ***−w password*** options to connect as a user who has administrative privileges on the remote computer.

Each script has many options, so use Windows Help or run the script with the ***/?*** option to display additional help on each option.

Note that with all these scripts you must leave a space between the option and the argument. For example, you should enter ***prnport −l −s computername*** instead of ***prnport −l −scomputerrname***.

The following list describes each of the new scripts:

- **Prncnfg.vbs** Use *prncnfg* to display or change configuration information about a printer or rename a printer on a local or remote computer.

- **Prndrvr.vbs** Use *prndrvr* to delete, add, or list the printer drivers installed on a local or remote computer.

- **Prnjobs.vbs** Use *prnjobs* to manage print jobs. You can pause, resume, or cancel (delete) individual print jobs or list all the jobs in a print queue on a local or remote computer. Note that *prnjobs* is used to manage individual print jobs, not the whole queue. To manage a queue, use *prnqctl*.

- **Prnmngr.vbs** Use *prnmngr* to add and delete printers, list printers, and to display or change the default printer. Some of the options for *prnmngr* work only on the local computer.

- **Prnport.vbs** Use *prnport* to manage TCP/IP ports. You can display or change configuration information, create, delete, or list TCP/IP ports on a local or remote computer.

- **Prnqctl.vbs** Use *prnqctl* to manage a printer queue. You can pause or resume printing of jobs in the queue, cancel all print jobs in the queue, or print a test page.

Table 2.4 shows the main options for each script. Note that you will need to include additional options over and above what is shown in Table 2.4 to specify the particular printer, driver, port, and so on that is to be affected. Table 2.5 shows the command to use for each of the common printer management tasks.

Table 2.4 Options for Printer Management Scripts

Script and Options	Use
Prncnfg -g	Display configuration information for a printer.
Prncnfg -t	Configure a printer.
Prncnfg -x	Rename a printer.
Prndrvr -l	List installed printer drivers.
Prndrvr -a	Install a printer driver.
Prndrvr -d	Delete a printer driver.
Prnjobs -l	List print jobs.
Prnjobs -z	Pause a print job.
Prnjobs -m	Resume a print job.
Prnjobs -x	Cancel a print job.
Prnmngr -a	Add a printer.
Prnmngr -d	Delete a printer.
Prnmngr -l	List all the printers on a computer.
Prnport -l	List TCP/IP ports.
Prnport -g	Display configuration information for a TCP/IP port.

Continued

Table 2.4 Options for Printer Management Scripts

Script and Options	Use
Prnport -t	Change configuration information for a TCP/IP port.
Prnport -a	Create a TCP/IP port.
Prnport -d	Delete a TCP/IP port.
Prnqctl -z	Pause the queue.
Prnqctl -m	Resume printing of the queue.
Prnqctl -x	Cancel all print jobs in the queue.
Prnqctl -e	Print a test page.

Table 2.5 Example of Commands for Printer Management Tasks

Task	Example of Command To Use
Create a printer	prnmngr –a –p printername –m drivername –r portname
Share a printer	prncnfg –t –p printername –h sharename +shared
Add a printer driver	prndrvr -a -m drivername -v versionnumber –e environment
Set permissions	Not available
Manage print queues	prnjobs or prnqctl
Create printer pools	Not available
Schedule printers	prncnfg –t –p printername –st starttime –ut endtime
Set printer priorities	prncnfg –i prioritynumber

The Printer Spooler Service

All printing is managed by the spooler service. If this service is not running, users cannot print. The spooler has a number of configuration options. To change these, open the **Printers and Faxes** folder and select **Server Properties** from the **File** pull-down menu. This opens the **Print Server Properties** dialog box containing four tabs: **Forms**, **Ports**, **Drivers**, and **Advanced**, which are used as follows:

- Use the **Forms** tab to define custom paper sizes.
- Use the **Ports** tab to define new ports (especially TCP/IP ports) and to configure properties of existing ports.
- Use the **Drivers** tab to add new drivers or configure existing drivers.
- Use the **Advanced** tab to modify the behavior of the spooler service.

In particular, note the **Spool Folder** under the **Advanced** tab. This location is where print jobs are stored until they are printed. On larger networks with many printers the spool folder can get quite large.

The Internet Printing Protocol

Windows Server 2003 enables users to print to printers over the Internet or an intranet. Users have to know the URL for the printer so that they can connect to it via their Web browsers. For servers running Windows 2000 Server or Windows Server 2003, the URL http://server/printers shows the printers available on the server. At this URL, users can connect to a printer, review the queue, and manage printers and jobs for which they have permissions. Figure 2.10 shows an example of viewing a queue using a Web page. Internet Printing requires Internet Information Services (IIS) to be running on the server. Internet Printing is installed by default on Windows 2000, but on Windows Server 2003 it has to be specifically installed, as does IIS (which is also not installed by default).

Figure 2.10 Viewing a Printer Queue using a Web Page

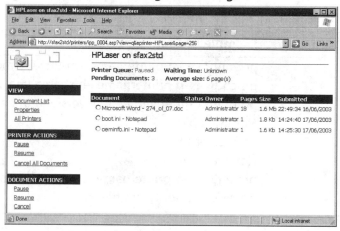

Using the Graphical Interface

Most of the time, you will use the graphical interface for managing services. You can start it in a number of ways:

- Select **Start | Programs | Administrative Tools | Computer Management**. In the Computer Management window, expand **Services and Applications**, and then click **Services**.

- Create a custom Microsoft Management Console that contains the Services snap-in.

- Select **Start | Programs | Administrative Tools | Services**.

Using New Command-Line Utilities

In addition to the graphical interface, Windows Server 2003 has a number of command-line-based programs to manage and troubleshoot services and perform a few other server tasks. These are executable programs rather than scripts, so they do not need to be run with the *cscript* command. In the following sections, we examine each program.

Sc.exe

The *sc.exe* program communicates with the Service controller and has twenty-four different options. We won't examine them all here, but you can refer to the online help for more information. In general, *sc* is used to configure services and manage their status, name, and permissions. For example, *sc stop <servicename>* is used to stop a service but *<servicename>* must be the name as stored in the registry and not the display name. Use *sc getkeyname* to determine the registry name of the service. Figure 2.11 shows how to find the registry name for the Telnet service, how to check the service's current status, and how to stop the Telnet service.

Figure 2.11 Stopping the Telnet Service Using sc

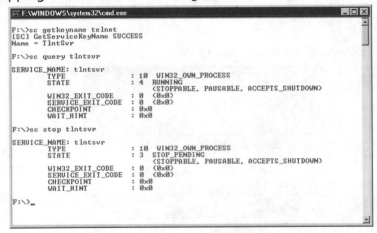

Schtasks.exe

You use *schtasks* to set programs to run at scheduled intervals, delete or change existing scheduled tasks, and stop or run a scheduled task immediately. Table 2.6 lists the six options for *schtasks*. *Schtasks* doesn't provide as much control over scheduled tasks as using the graphical interface.

Table 2.6 Options for the schtasks Command

Schtasks option	Use
schtasks create	Create a new scheduled task.
schtasks change	Change the properties of a scheduled task but not the actual schedule.
schtasks run	Run a scheduled task immediately.
schtasks end	Stop a scheduled task that is currently running.
schtasks delete	Delete a scheduled task.
schtasks query	List all the scheduled tasks on the local or a remote computer.

Setx.exe

You use *setx* to configure environment variables for either the user (the variables apply only to a specific user) or the system environment (variables apply to all users). You can set variables explicitly by specifying their value or using the value of a registry key or the contents of a file. *Setx* is the only way to permanently (i.e., remembered between reboots) set a variable name via the command line.

Shutdown.exe

Use the *shutdown* command to shut down or restart local or remote computers. You can also use it for shutting down several computers at once using the */i* option. With this option, a new window appears where you add the names of the computers that you want to shut down or restart. Figure 2.12 shows the dialog box for the */i* option.

Figure 2.12 The Remote Shutdown Dialog Box

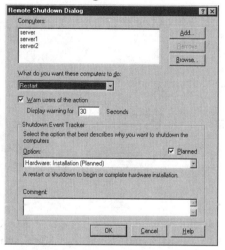

Tasklist.exe

Tasklist shows all the tasks that are running on the local or remote computer. *Tasklist* is a really useful command given its many options as shown in Table 2.7.

- The */S* option connects to a remote computer. You might also have to specify the */U* option to connect as a particular user and the */P* option to specify the password for that user.

- The */M* option lists all the dll modules that a process has loaded. However, you can also use this option to list all the processes that have loaded a particular module by specifying */M module name*. For example, to list all processes that have loaded the *user32.dll* module, use *tasklist /M user32.dll*.

- The */FI* option is particularly useful for restricting the output to list only the tasks that are of interest. This option is used with a variety of filters, which can, for example, be used to display tasks with a particular name, process number, or processes that have used more than a certain amount of CPU time. As an example, to list all processes that start with **H**, use the command *tasklist /FI "IMAGENAME eq H*"*.

■ The */FO* option controls how the output is displayed. There are three formats: Table, List, or CSV.

■ The */V* option adds information to the output.

Table 2.7 Some of the Options for the tasklist Command

Tasklist Option	Use
Tasklist /S	Connect to a remote computer (system).
Tasklist /M	List modules loaded by processes.
Tasklist /FI filter	Display only processes that match the filter.
Tasklist /FO format	Specify how the output is displayed.
Tasklist /V	Display verbose information.

Taskkill.exe

Use *taskkill* to terminate processes on the local or a remote computer. You need to use *tasklist* first to identify the process that needs to be terminated. *Taskkill* has many options and if used without care you could end up ending more processes than you expected.

■ The */S* option connects to a remote computer. You might also have to specify the */U* option to connect as a particular user and the */P* option to specify the password for that user.

■ The */F* option forcefully terminates a process. Without the */F* option a process might not actually terminate, particularly if it raises a dialog box asking whether changes should be saved. The */F* option overrides this but there is a risk of losing the user's work.

■ Use the */FI* option with extreme care, because it can terminate all processes that match a given filter. For example *taskkill /FI "IMAGENAME eq H*"* terminates all processes that start with **H**.

■ The */PID* option terminates a process with a specific process number.

■ The */T* option terminates a process and all child processes that it started.

■ The */IM* option is functionally the same as */FI* with **IMAGENAME** in that it terminates processes with a specific name or names. You can use wildcards to specify the process names.

Table 2.8 Some of the Options for the taskkill Command

Taskkill Option	Use
Tasklist /S	Connect to a remote computer (system).
Tasklist /F	Forcefully terminate a process.
Tasklist /FI filter	Terminate processes that match the filter. **Use with care!**
Tasklist /PID process id	Terminate the process with this ID.
Tasklist /T	Terminate a process and all its child processes.
Tasklist /IM process name	Terminate all processes that match the given image name.

Using Wizards to Configure and Manage Your Server

A lot of effort has been made in Windows Server 2003 to make administrative tasks easy for the administrator through the use of wizards. A key wizard is the **Configure Your Server Wizard**, which, in conjunction with the **Manage Your Server** tool, guides an administrator through the most common administrative tasks.

Using the Configure Your Server Wizard and Manage Your Server

Windows Server 2003 introduces the concept of server roles, which brings related administrative tasks together for management purposes. We'll examine each of these roles in the next chapter. Figure 2.20 shows the server role page of the **Configure Your Server Wizard**. This page shows whether a role has been configured.

You must install server roles using the **Configure Your Server Wizard** before you can manage them using **Manage Your Server**. In the rest of this section we'll look at each of the roles in more detail. The **Configure Your Server Wizard** and **Manage Your Server** can be found in **Start | Programs | Administrative Tools**.

Note that the use of server roles is completely optional and there is no reason you can't perform server administrative tasks without setting up server roles.

Chapter 3

Planning Server
Roles and Server Security

In this chapter:

- **Understanding server roles**

- **Planning a server security strategy**

- **Planning baseline security**

- **Customizing server security**

Introduction

Planning an effective security strategy for Windows Server 2003 requires an understanding of the roles that different servers play on the network and the security needs of different types of servers based on the security requirements of your organization. Securing the servers is an important part of any network administrator's job.

In this chapter, we will first review server roles and ensure that you have an understanding of the many roles Windows Server 2003 can play on the network. We will discuss domain controllers; file and print servers; DHCP, DNS, and WINS servers; Web servers; database servers; mail servers; certification authorities; and terminal servers. Then we will delve into how to plan a server security strategy. We will examine how to choose the right operating system according to security needs, how to identify minimum security requirements for your organization, and how to identify the correct configurations to satisfy those security requirements.

Next, we'll review how to plan baseline security on both client and server machines. We will cover planning the secure baseline installation parameters and enforcing default security settings on new computers. We will look at how to customize server security, securing your servers according to their roles. Then we will walk through the process of creating custom security templates and how to deploy security configurations.

Understanding Server Roles

When Windows Server 2003 is installed on a computer, it provides a wide variety of tools and functionality. However, additional features may still need to be installed on the server to bring clients the services they need. The server may need to supply file and print services, authenticate users, or support a local intranet Web site. Until Windows Server 2003 is configured to supply these services, clients will be unable to use the server in a manner that is required by the organization.

Server roles are profiles that are used to configure Windows Server 2003 to provide specific functionality to the network. When you set up a server to use a specific role, various services and tools are enabled or installed, and the server is configured to provide additional services and resources to network clients. Roles are applied to machines using the Configure Your Server Wizard and managed using the Manage Your Server tool.

As shown in Figure 3.1, Manage Your Server provides information about the roles that are currently configured for a server, and it provides the ability to add and remove roles from a server. Depending on your server's settings, this tool will start automatically upon logon. If you've checked the **Don't display this page at logon** check box at the bottom of this window, Manage Your Server will not start automatically. You can start it manually by selecting **Start | Administrative Tools | Manage Your Server**.

As shown in Figure 3.1, there are a variety of items in Manage Your Server's main window. The left side of the window lists the roles currently configured for the server. Beside each entry, there are buttons that relate to the corresponding role. These buttons differ from role to role, and they are used to invoke other tools for managing the role or to view information on additional steps that can be taken to configure, administer, and maintain the role.

Figure 3.1 The Main Manage Your Server Window

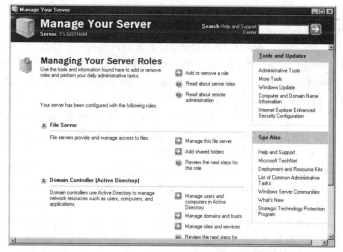

Near the top of the Manage Your Server window are three buttons. Two of these are used to obtain additional information about roles and remote administration. The other button, labeled **Add or remove a role**, is used to invoke the Configure Your Server Wizard. You can also start the Wizard by selecting **Start | Administrative Tools | Configure Your Server**.

When the Configure Your Server Wizard starts, it informs you of possible preliminary steps that need to be taken before a new role is added. As shown in Figure 3.2, these steps include ensuring that network and Internet connections are set up and active for the server, peripherals are turned on, and your Windows Server 2003 installation CD is available. When you finish reading this information, click the **Next** button to have the Wizard test network connections and continue to the next step.

Figure 3.2 Preliminary Steps of the Configure Your Server Wizard

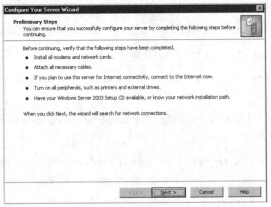

In the next window, shown in Figure 3.3, roles that are available to add and remove through the Wizard are listed in the **Server Role** column; the **Configured** column indicates whether the role has been previously installed. If you want to install a role that isn't listed here, click the **Add or Remove Programs** link to open the Add or Remove Programs applet (in the Windows Control Panel), where you can configure additional services.

Figure 3.3 Configuring Server Roles

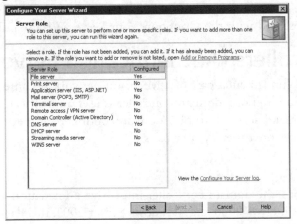

In Figure 3.3, you can see that there are 11 different roles that can be applied to Windows Server 2003 through the Configure Your Server Wizard. These roles are as follows:

- **Domain controller** This role is used for authentication and installs Active Directory on the server.

- **File server** This role is used to provide access to files stored on the server.

- **Print server** This role is used to provide network printing functionality.

- **DHCP server** This role allocates IP addresses and provides configuration information to clients.

- **DNS server** This role resolves IP addresses to domain names (and vice versa).

- **WINS server** This role resolves IP addresses to NetBIOS names (and vice versa).

- **Mail server** This role provides e-mail services.

- **Application server** This role makes distributed applications and Web applications available to clients.

- **Terminal server** This role provides Terminal Services for clients to access applications running on the server.

- **Remote access/VPN server** This role provides remote access to machines through dial-up connections and virtual private networks (VPNs).

- **Streaming media server** This role provides Windows Media Services so that clients can access streaming audio and video.

After you select the role to add to the server, click **Next** to step through the process of setting up that role. Each set of configuration windows is different for each server role. Also, although multiple roles can be installed on Windows Server 2003, only one role at a time can be configured using the Configure Your Server Wizard. To install additional roles, you need to run the Wizard again.

Before setting up a server role, it is important to understand each of the roles that can be applied to Windows Server 2003 so you select the roles most appropriate for the server's use and for your organization. In the sections that follow, we will discuss these roles in greater detail and examine how they are installed with the Configure Your Server Wizard and other tools.

Domain Controllers (Authentication Servers)

Domain controllers are a fundamental part of a Microsoft network because they are used to manage domains. An important function of a domain controller is user authentication and access control. By combining authentication and access control, a domain controller can permit or deny access to network services and resources on a user by user basis.

Active Directory

To perform these functions, the domain controller must have information about users and other objects in a domain. In Windows 2000 and Windows Server 2003, this data is stored in *Active Directory* (AD), which is a directory service that runs on domain controllers.

When AD is installed, the server becomes a domain controller. Until this time, it is a member server that cannot be used for domain authentication and management of domain users or other domain-based objects. This does not mean, however, that AD can be installed on every version of

Windows Server 2003. It can be installed on Standard Edition, Enterprise Edition, and Datacenter Edition, but servers running the Web Edition of Windows Server 2003 cannot be domain controllers. Web Edition servers can be only stand-alone or member servers that provide resources and services to the network.

A Windows Server 2003 computer can be changed into a domain controller by using the Configure Your Server Wizard or by using the Active Directory Installation Wizard (DCPROMO). DCPROMO is a tool that promotes a member server to domain controller status. During the installation, a writable copy of the AD database is placed on the server's hard disk. The file used to store directory information is called NTDS.dit and, by default, is located in *%systemroot%*\NTDS. When changes are made to the directory, they are saved to this file.

Each domain controller retains its own copy of the directory, containing information about the domain in which it is located. If one domain controller becomes unavailable, users and computers can still access the AD data store on another domain controller in that domain. This allows users to continue logging on to the network, even though the domain controller that is normally used is unavailable. It also allows computers and applications that require directory information to continue functioning while one of these servers is down. When a change is made on one domain controller, the changes are replicated, so every domain controller continues to have an accurate copy of AD. This type of replication is called *multi-master*, because each domain controller contains a full read/write copy of the AD database.

Operations Master Roles

In Windows Server 2003, all domain controllers are relatively equal by default. However, there are still some operations that need to be performed by a single domain controller in the domain or forest. To address these, Microsoft created the concept of *operations masters*. Operations masters serve many purposes. Some control where components of AD can be modified; others store specific information that is key to the healthy function of AD at the domain level. Because only one domain controller in a domain or forest fulfills a given role, these roles are also referred to as *Flexible Single Master of Operations* (FSMO) roles. Some FSMO roles are unique to each domain; others are unique to the forest.

There are five different types of master roles, each serving a specific purpose. Two of these master roles are applied at the forest level (forest-wide roles), and the others are applied at the domain level (domain-wide roles). The following are the forest-wide operations master roles:

- **Schema master** A domain controller that is in charge of all changes to the AD schema. The schema determines which object classes and attributes are used within the forest. If additional object classes or attributes need to be added, the schema is modified to accommodate these changes. The schema master is used to write to the directory's schema, which is then replicated to other domain controllers in the forest. Updates to the schema can be performed only on the domain controller acting in this role.

- **Domain naming master** A domain controller that is in charge of adding new domains and removing unneeded ones from the forest. It is responsible for any changes to the domain namespace. This role prevents naming conflicts, because such changes can be performed only if the domain naming master is online.

In addition to the two forest-wide master roles, there are three domain-wide master roles: relative ID (RID) master, primary domain controller (PDC) emulator, and infrastructure master. These roles are described in the following sections.

Relative ID Master

The *relative ID master* is responsible for allocating sequences of numbers (called relative IDs, or RIDs) that are used in creating new security principles in the domain. Security principles are user, group, and computer accounts. These numbers are issued to all domain controllers in the domain. When an object is created, a number that uniquely identifies the object is assigned to it. This number consists of two parts: a domain security ID (or computer SID if a local user or group account is being created) and an RID. Together, the domain SID and RID combine to form the object's unique SID. The domain security ID is the same for all objects in that domain. The RID is unique to each object. Instead of using the name of a user, computer, or group, Windows uses the SID to identify and reference security principles. To avoid potential conflicts of domain controllers issuing the same number to an object, only one RID master exists in a domain. This controls the allocation of RID numbers to each domain controller. The domain controller can then assign the RIDs to objects when they are created.

PDC Emulator

The *primary domain controller (PDC) emulator* is designed to act like a Windows NT PDC when the domain is in Windows 2000 mixed mode. This is necessary if Windows NT backup domain controllers (BDCs) still exist on the network. Clients earlier than Windows 2000 also use the PDC emulator for processing password changes, though installation of the AD client software on these systems enables them to change their password on any domain controller in the domain to which they authenticate. The PDC emulator also synchronizes the time on all domain controllers the domain. For replication accuracy, it is critical for all domain controllers to have synchronized time.

Even if you do not have any servers running as BDCs on the network, the PDC emulator still serves a critical purpose in each domain. The PDC emulator receives preferred replication of all password changes performed on other domain controllers within the domain. When a password is changed on a domain controller, it is sent to the PDC emulator. If a user changes his or her password on one domain controller, and then attempts to log on to another, the second domain controller may still have old password information. Because this domain controller considers it a bad password, it forwards the authentication request to the PDC emulator to determine whether the password is actually valid. In addition, the PDC emulator initiates urgent replication so that the password change can propagate as soon as possible. Urgent replication is also used for other security-sensitive replication traffic, such as account lockouts.

This operations master is by far the most critical at the domain level. Because of this, you should ensure that it is carefully placed on your network and housed on a high-availability, high-capacity server.

Infrastructure Master

The *infrastructure master* is in charge of updating changes that are made to group memberships. When a user moves to a different domain and his or her group membership changes, it may take time for these changes to be reflected in the group. To remedy this, the infrastructure master is used to update such changes in its domain. The domain controller in the infrastructure master role compares its data to the Global Catalog, which is a subset of directory information for all domains in the forest and contains information on groups. The Global Catalog stores information on universal group memberships, in which users from any domain can be added and allowed access to any domain, and maps the memberships users have to specific groups. When changes occur to group membership, the infrastructure master updates its group-to-user references and replicates these changes to other domain controllers in the domain.

File and Print Servers

Two of the basic functions in a network are saving files in a central location on the network and printing the contents of files to shared printers. When file server or print server roles are configured in Windows Server 2003, additional functions become available that make using and managing the server more effective.

Print Servers

Print servers are used provide access to printers across the network. Print servers allow you to control when print devices can be used by allowing you to schedule the availability of printers, set priority for print jobs, and configure printer properties. Using a browser, an administrator can also view, pause, resume, and/or delete print jobs.

By configuring Windows Server 2003 in the role of a print server, you can manage printers remotely through the GUI and by using Windows Management Instrumentation (WMI). WMI is a management application program interface (API) that allows you to monitor and control printing. Using WMI, an administrator can manage components like print servers and print devices from a command line.

Print servers also provide alternative methods of printing to specific print devices. Users working at machines running Windows XP can print to specific printers by using a Uniform Resource Locator (URL).

File Servers

Administrators benefit from *file servers* by being able to manage disk space, control access, and limit the amount of space that is made available to individual users. If NTFS volumes are used, disk quotas can be set to limit the amount of space available to each user. This prevents users from filling the hard disk with superfluous data or older information that may no longer be needed.

In addition to these features, a file server also provides other functionality that offers security and availability of data. File servers with NTFS volumes have the *Encrypted File System* (EFS) enabled, so that any data can be encrypted using a public key system. To make it easier for users to access shared files, the *Distributed File Service* (DFS) can be used, which allows data that is located on servers throughout the enterprise to be accessible from a single shared folder. When DFS is used, files stored on different volumes, shares, or servers appear as if they reside in the same location.

DHCP, DNS, and WINS Servers

The roles of DHCP, DNS, and WINS servers are used for uniquely identifying computers and finding them on the network. A DHCP server issues a unique IP address to computer on the network. DNS and WINS servers resolve the IP address to and from user-friendly names that are easier for users to deal with. With Windows Server 2003 acting as a DHCP, DNS, and/or WINS server, clients can be automatically issued an IP address and find other machines and devices more easily.

DHCP Servers

DHCP is the *Dynamic Host Configuration Protocol*, and it is used to dynamically issue IP addresses to clients on networks using the Transmission Control Protocol/Internet Protocol (TCP/IP). Many enterprises use static IP addresses only for their servers and network infrastructure equipment (switches, routers, and so on). Dynamic addresses are typically used for all clients.

DNS Servers

The *Domain Name System* (DNS) is a popular method of name resolution used on the Internet and other TCP/IP networks. AD is integrated with DNS, and it uses DNS servers to allow users, computers, applications, and other elements of the network to easily find domain controllers and other resources on the network. DNS servers are often the targets of attacks. We'll talk about securing a DNS server later in this chapter.

WINS Servers

The *Windows Internet Name Service* (WINS) is another method of name resolution that resolves IP addresses to NetBIOS names, and vice versa. *NetBIOS* names are used by pre-Windows 2000 servers and clients, and they allow users of those operating systems to log on to Windows Server 2003 domains. They are supported in Windows Server 2003 for backward-compatibility with these older systems. By implementing a WINS server, you allow clients to search for computers and other resources by computer name, rather than by IP address.

Web Servers

Web servers allow organizations to host their own Web sites on the Internet or a local intranet. Implementing a Web server in an organization allows users to benefit by accessing information, downloading files, and using Web-based applications. Web servers are another popular hacker target. We'll discuss steps to secure a web server later in this chapter.

Web Server Protocols

Microsoft's Windows Server 2003 Web server product is *Internet Information Services* (IIS) 6.0, which is included with Windows Server 2003. IIS allows users to access information using a number of protocols that are part of the TCP/IP suite, including the following:

- **Hypertext Transfer Protocol (HTTP)** Used by the World Wide Web Publishing service in IIS. By connecting to sites created on your Web server, users can view and work with Web pages written in the Hypertext Markup Language (HTML), Active Server Pages (ASP), and Extensible Markup Language (XML).

■ **File Transfer Protocol (FTP)** Used for transferring files between clients and servers. Using this service, clients can copy files to and from FTP sites using a Web browser like Internet Explorer or other FTP client software. By using such software, clients can browse through any folders they have access to on the FTP site, and they can access any files they have permissions to use.

■ **Network News Transfer Protocol (NNTP)** Used for newsgroups, which are also called discussion groups. The NNTP service in IIS allows users to post news messages. Other users can browse through messages stored on the server, respond to existing messages, and post new ones using a newsreader program.

■ **Simple Mail Transfer Protocol (SMTP)** Used to provides e-mail capabilities. The SMTP service that is installed with IIS isn't a full e-mail service, but provides limited services for transferring e-mail messages. Using this service, Web developers can collect information from users of a Web site, such as having them fill out a form online. Rather than storing the results of the form locally in a file, the information can be e-mailed using this service.

Web Server Configuration

Although a Web server can facilitate a company's ability to disseminate information, it isn't an actual role that is configured using the Configure Your Server Wizard. It is installed as part of the application server role, which we'll discuss later in this chapter. The Configure Your Server Wizard provides an easy, step-by-step method of configuring Web servers through the application server role; however, it isn't the only way to install IIS. You can also install IIS through the Add or Remove Programs applet in the Windows Control Panel.

Using Add or Remove Programs to install IIS takes a few extra steps, but it allows you to perform the installation without installing other services and features available through the application server role. To use Add or Remove Programs to install IIS, follow these steps:

1. Select **Start | Control Panel | Add or Remove Programs**.

2. Click the **Add/Remove Windows Components** icon to display the **Windows Components Wizard**, which provides a listing of available components to install.

3. In the list, select **Application Server** and click the **Details** button to view the **Application Server** dialog box, shown in Figure 3.4.

Figure 3.4 Installing IIS through the Application Server Dialog Box in the Windows Components Wizard

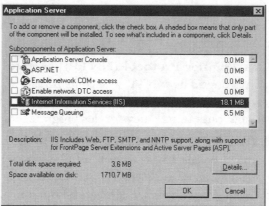

4. The **Application Server** dialog box contains a number of subcomponents. To install IIS, select the check box for **Internet Information Services (IIS),** and either click **OK** to install the default components or click **Details** to view even more subcomponents that can be installed within IIS.

5. When you've made your selections, click **OK** to return to the **Windows Components Wizard**.

6. Click **Next** to have Windows make the configuration changes you requested from your selection.

7. Once the Wizard has finished copying the necessary files and changing system settings, click **Finish** to complete the installation process and exit the Wizard.

Database Servers

Database servers are used to store and manage databases (Microsoft SQL or Oracle, for example) that are stored on the server and to provide data access for authorized users. The Configure Your Server Wizard does not include a configurable role for database servers. Because SQL Server provides additional measures of security that would not otherwise be available (as discussed in the "Securing Database Servers" section later in this chapter) and processing occurs on the server, transactions can occur securely and rapidly.

Mail Servers

Mail servers enable users to send and receive e-mail messages. When a server is configured to be a mail server, two protocols are enabled: SMTP and Post Office Protocol (POP3). SMTP is used by clients and mail servers to send e-mail. POP3 is used by clients when retrieving e-mail from their mail server. Each of these protocols is part of the TCP/IP protocol suite and installed when TCP/IP is installed on a computer. However, even if TCP/IP is installed on Windows Server 2003, the services provided by mail servers still need to be enabled by configuring the machine to take the role of a mail server.

Certificate Authorities

Certificate authorities (CAs) are servers that issue and manage certificates. Certificates are used for a variety of purposes, including encryption, integrity, and verifying the identity of an entity, such as a user, machine, or application. Certificates are typically part of a larger security process, *Public Key Infrastructure* (PKI), discussed in detail later in this book.

Certificate Services

Certificate Services is used to create a Certificate Authority (CA) on Windows Server 2003 servers in your organization. With Certificate Services, you can create a CA, format and modify the contents of certificates, verify information provided by those requesting certificates, issue and revoke certificates, and publish a Certificate Revocation List (CRL). The CRL is a list of certificates that are expired or invalid, and it is made available so that network users can identify whether certificates they receive are valid.

Certificate Services supports implementing a hierarchy of CAs, so that a single CA isn't responsible for providing certificates to the entire network or authenticating the entire intranet or Internet. This isn't to say that multiple CAs must be used in an organization, but it is one possibility. Using a hierarchy of CAs is called *chaining*, where one CA certifies others. In this hierarchy, there is a single root authority and any number of subordinate CAs.

A *root authority* (or root CA) resides at the top of the hierarchy. The root CA is the most trusted CA in the hierarchy—any clients that trust the root CA will also trust certificates issued by any CA below it. This makes securing a CA vital (as discussed in the "Securing CAs section later in this chapter).

Subordinate CAs are child CAs in the hierarchy. They are certified by the root authority and bind its public key to its identity. Just as the root CA can issue and manage certificates and certify child CAs, a subordinate CA can also perform these actions and certify CAs that are subordinate to it in the hierarchy.

In addition to having different levels of CAs in an organization, there are also different types of root and subordinate CAs that can be used. *Enterprise CAs* use AD to verify information that is provided when requesting a certificate and to store certificates within AD. When the certificate is needed, it is retrieved from directory services. *Stand-alone CAs* can be used in environments that do not use AD (CAs do not require AD).

As with IIS, Certificate Services isn't an actual role that can be set up with the Configure Your Server Wizard. Instead, you must follow these steps:

1. Select **Start | Control Panel | Add or Remove Programs**.

2. Click **Add/Remove Windows Components** to display the **Windows Components Wizard**, which provides a listing of available components to install.

3. In the list of available components, click the check box beside the **Certificate Services** item so it is checked. A warning message will appear, stating that after Certificate Services is installed, the name of the machine cannot be changed. This is because the server's name is bound to the CA information stored in AD, and any changes to the name or domain membership would invalidate certificates issued by this CA.

4. Click **Yes** to continue with the installation. (Clicking **No** will cancel it.)

5. You are presented with the window shown in Figure 3.5, which allows you to specify the type of CA that will be set up. As mentioned earlier, you have the option of creating an enterprise root CA, an enterprise subordinate CA, a stand-alone root CA, or a stand-alone subordinate CA.

Figure 3.5 Choosing a CA Type in the Windows Components Wizard

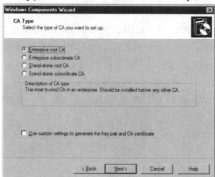

6. For this example, we will assume that this is the first CA being created and AD is used. Select **Enterprise root CA** and click **Next.**

7. You are then presented with a window shown in Figure 3.6, which allows you to provide information to identify the CA you're creating. Enter a common name and distinguished name suffix for the CA. Distinguished names are used to provide each object in AD with a unique name. A distinguished name represents the exact location of an object within the directory. This is comparable to a file being represented by the full path, showing where it is located on the hard disk. With an object in the directory, several components are used to create this name:

- CN, which is the common name of the object, and includes such things as user accounts, printers, and other network elements represented in the directory.

- OU, which is the Organizational Unit. OUs are containers in the directory, which are used to hold objects. To continue with our example of files on a hard disk, this would be comparable to a folder within the directory structure.

- DC, which is a domain component. This is used to identify the name of the domain or server, and the DNS suffix (for example .com, .net, .edu, .gov, and so forth).

When combined, these components of a distinguished name are used to show the location of an object. In the case of the CA being created here, the common name is CertServer, and the distinguished name suffix is the domain components. This makes the distinguished name CN=CertServer,DC=knightware,DC=ca, which you can see in the preview in Figure 3.6.

Figure 3.6 Entering CA Identifying Information in the Windows Components Wizard

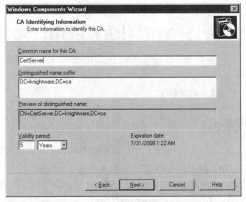

8. Optionally, you can change the **Validity period** of certificates issued by the CA. As shown in Figure 3.6, the default validity period is five years. You can modify this by specifying a different number and whether the period is in **Years**, **Months**, **Weeks**, or **Days**.

9. Click **Next** when you are finished entering CA identifying information.

10. This will bring you to the **Certificate Database Settings** window, shown in Figure 3.7, where you can specify the location of the certificate database and log file. By default, the database and log are named after the common name you specified for the CA, and each is stored in the **System32** folder of the *%systemroot%* (for example, C:\Windows\System32). Click **Next** to continue.

Figure 3.7 Choosing Certificate Database Settings in the Windows Components Wizard

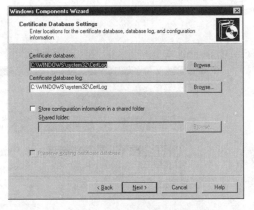

11. A message box will appear informing you that IIS must be stopped before installation can continue. Clicking **No** will return you to the previous window. Clicking **Yes** will stop the service and cause Windows to make the configuration changes you requested from your selection. If ASP is not enabled on the machine, a message box will interrupt the process, asking if you want to enable ASP. Clicking **Yes** will enable ASP and continue the installation.

12. After the Wizard has finished copying the necessary files and changing system settings, click **Finish** to complete the installation process.

Application Servers and Terminal Servers

Application servers and terminal servers provide the ability for users to access applications over the network. These roles are two of the most commonly used server roles and are ones you're likely to implement or manage in your network.

Application Servers

Application servers allow users to run Web applications and distributed programs from the server. Because Web applications require Internet technologies, when Windows Server 2003 is set up as an application server, IIS subcomponents such as ASP can be installed. As explained earlier, IIS is the Web server that comes with Windows Server 2003 and can be used to make Web applications available to users on the network. If IIS has been installed, the application server role will appear as a configured role in the Manage Your Server tool. This is despite the fact that only some components for the application server role have been installed. To modify the installed components, you can either use the Windows Components Wizard or the Configure Your Server Wizard.

Use the following steps to set up an application server in Windows Server 2003.

1. Select **Start | Administrative Tools | Manage Your Server**.

2. When Manage Your Server starts, click the **Add or remove a role** button.

3. When the Configure Your Server Wizard starts, read through the information on the Preliminary Steps window, and then click **Next**.

4. After the Wizard checks your network settings and operating system version, the Server Role window will appear. From the list, select **Application server** (IIS, ASP.NET), as shown in Figure 3.8. Then **click** Next to continue.

Figure 3.8 Choose the Application Server Role

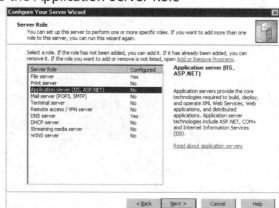

5. The **Application Server Options** window appears, as shown in Figure 3.9. Here, you can add components that are used with IIS. Note that IIS will be installed regardless of what you select on this page. Select the **FrontPage Server Extensions** check box to add Web server extensions that allow content created with FrontPage, Visual Studio, and Web Folders to be published to the IIS Web site. Select **Enable ASP.NET** to allow Web-based applications created using ASP.NET to be used on the site. After selecting the options you wish to add, click **Next** to continue.

Figure 3.9 Select Application Server Options

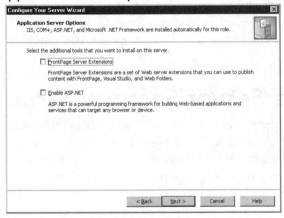

6. The **Summary of Selections** window, shown in Figure 3.10, provides a list of components that will be installed as part of the application server configuration. Review these settings, and then click **Next** to begin installing these components.

Figure 3.10 Review the Summary of Selections

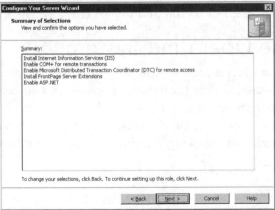

7. After copying files, the **Windows Components Wizard** will open and continue the installation. Once it has completed, you will be returned to the **Configure Your Server Wizard**. Click **Finish** to complete the installation.

Terminal Servers

Terminal servers allow remote access to applications using thin-client technology. A benefit of Terminal Services is that users can run programs that they might otherwise be unable to use. For example, a user running an older version of Windows might need to use Office XP, but she doesn't have the minimal requirements install it. Through Terminal Services, she can connect to and be presented with a Windows Server 2003 desktop. If Office XP is installed on the terminal server, the user can open and use the application. Because all processing occurs on the server, the user can run applications that are impossible to install on her local system.

There are a wide variety of clients that can use Terminal Services. Client software is available for Windows 3.11 and later, as well as Macintosh and UNIX. Internet Explorer can also be used to access a terminal server, using the Web client software. Terminal Services can also interact with Citrix clients.

Planning a Server Security Strategy

The only truly secure network is one that is totally inaccessible. Security is always a trade-off between usability and protection. When planning security, you need to find an acceptable balance between the need to secure your network and the need for users to be able to perform their jobs.

In creating a security plan, it is important to realize that the network environment will never be completely secure. The goal is to make it difficult for intruders to obtain unauthorized access, so it isn't worth their time to try or continue attempting to gain access. It is also critical to protect servers from potential disasters and to have methods to restore systems if they become compromised.

A good security plan considers the needs of a company and tries to balance it with their capabilities and current technology. As you'll see in the sections that follow, this means identifying the minimum security requirements for an organization, choosing an operating system, and identifying the configurations necessary to meet these needs. To develop a security plan, you must identify the risks that potentially threaten a network, determine what countermeasures are available to deal with them, figure out what you can afford financially, and implement the countermeasures that are feasible.

Choosing the Operating System

In planning a strategy for server security, you will need to determine which operating systems will be used in the organization. Different network operating systems provide diverse features that can be used as part of your security strategy.

Of course, there are non-Microsoft network operating systems available to use on your server, but we will consider only the following Windows server systems here:

- Windows NT Server 4
- Windows 2000 Server
- Windows 2000 Advanced Server
- Windows 2000 Datacenter
- Windows Server 2003 Standard Edition

- Windows Server 2003 Enterprise Edition
- Windows Server 2003 Datacenter Edition
- Windows Server 2003 Web Edition

One of the first considerations for the operating system you choose will be the minimum system requirements for installing the operating system. Obviously, if your existing server cannot handle a particular version of Windows, you will not be able to install it. If this is the case, you will need to upgrade the hardware, purchase a new server to support the operating system you want, or choose an operating system that does match the current server's hardware. The minimum system requirements for Windows server operating systems are shown in Table 3.1.

Table 3.1 Minimum System Requirements for Windows Server Operating Systems

Server	Computer/ Processor	Memory (RAM)	Hard Disk	CPU Support
Windows NT Server 4	486/33 MHz or higher/Pentium, or Pentium Pro processor	16MB; 32MB recommended	Intel and compatible systems: 125MB available hard disk space minimum. RISC-based systems: 1 60MB available hard disk space	Up to 4 CPUs (retail version); Up to 32 CPUs available from hardware vendors
Windows 2000 Server	133 MHz or higher Pentium-compatible CPU	At least 128MB: 256MB recommended; 4GB maximum	2GB with 1GB free space; additional free space required for installing over a network	Up to 4 CPUs
Windows 2000 Advanced Server	133 MHz or higher Pentium-compatible CPU	At least 128MB; 256MB recommended; 8GB maximum	2GB with 1GB free space; additional free space required for installing over a network	Up to 8 CPUs
Windows 2000 Datacenter	Pentium III Xeon processors or higher	256MB	2GB with 1GB free space; additional free space required for installing over a network	8-way capable or higher server (supports up to 32-way)
Windows Server 2003 Standard Edition	133 MHz	128MB	1.5GB	Up to 4 CPUs
Windows Server 2003 Enterprise Edition	133 MHz for x86-based computers; 733 MHz for Itanium-based computers	128MB	1.5GB for x86-based computers; 2GB for Itanium-based computers	Up to 8 CPUs

Continued

Table 3.1 Minimum System Requirements for Windows Server Operating Systems

Server	Computer/ Processor	Memory (RAM)	Hard Disk	CPU Support
Windows Server 2003 Datacenter Edition	400 MHz for x86-based computers; 733 MHz for Itanium-based computers	512MB	1.5GB for x86-based computers; 2GB for Itanium-based computers	Minimum 8-way capable machine required; maximum 64
Windows Server 2003 Web Edition	133 MHz	128MB	1.5GB	Up to 2 CPUs

Beyond the minimum requirements, you will need to look at the features available in different versions and editions of Windows, and how they can be used to enhance network security. The progression from one version to another has offered improvements and additions to security, with Windows Server 2003 offering the most security features. By identifying which features are necessary for your organization, you can create a network that provides the necessary functionality and security.

Security Features

Windows 2000 offers a number of new security features that were not previously available in Windows NT. Many of the features we'll discuss next were implemented in Windows 2000 and have been updated in Windows Server 2003. In addition, new features have been added that make Windows Server 2003 the most secure Windows server product to date. The enhanced security features were introduced in Chapter 1 and are discussed in greater detail throughout this book.

Identifying Minimum Security Requirements for Your Organization

Before you can begin implementing security measures, you need to know what needs protecting. For this reason, the security planning process involves considerable analysis. You need to determine which risks could threaten a company, what impact these threats would have on the company, the assets that the company needs to function, and what can be done to minimize or remove a potential threat.

The following are the main types of threats:

■ Environmental threats, such as natural and man–made disasters

■ Deliberate threats, where a threat was intentionally caused

■ Accidental threats, where a threat was unintentionally caused

Environmental threats can be natural disasters, such as storms, floods, fires, earthquakes, tornadoes, and other acts of nature. When dealing with this type of disaster, it is important to analyze the entire company's risks, considering any branch offices located in different areas that may be prone to different natural disasters.

Human intervention can create problems as devastating as any natural disaster. Man-made disasters can also occur when someone creates an event that has an adverse impact on the company's environment. For example, faulty wiring can cause a fire or power outage. In the same way, a company could be impacted by equipment failures, such as the air conditioning breaking down in the server room, a critical system failing, or any number of other problems.

The deliberate threat type is one that results from malicious persons or programs, and they can include potential risks such as hackers, viruses, Trojan horses, and various other attacks that can damage data and equipment or disrupt services. This type of threat can also include disgruntled employees who have authorized access to such assets and have the ability to harm the company from within.

Many times, internal risks are not malicious in nature, but accidental. Employees can accidentally delete a file, modify information with erroneous data, or make other mistakes that cause some form of loss. Because people are fallible by nature, this type of risk is one of the most common.

Each business must identify the risks it may be in danger of confronting and determine what assets will be affected by a potential problem, including:

- **Hardware** Servers, workstations, hubs, printers, and other equipment.
- **Software** Commercial software (off the shelf) and in-house software.
- **Data** Documents, databases, and other files needed by the business.
- **Personnel** Employees who perform necessary tasks in the company.
- **Sundry equipment** Office supplies, furniture, tools, and other assets needed for the business to function properly.
- **Facilities** The physical building and its components.

When identifying minimum security requirements, it is important to determine the value and importance of assets, so you know which are vital to the company's ability to function. You can then prioritize risk, so that you can protect the most important assets of the company and implement security measures to prevent or minimize potential threats.

Determining the value and importance of assets can be achieved in a number of ways. Keeping an inventory of assets owned by the company will allow you to identify the equipment, software, and other property owned by the company.

To determine the importance of data and other assets, and thereby determine what is vital to secure, you can meet with department heads. Doing so will help you to identify the data and resources that are necessary for people in each department to perform their jobs.

In addition to interviewing different members of an organization, review the corporate policies for specifications of minimum security requirements. For example, a company may have a security policy stating that all data is to be stored in specific folders on the server, and that the IT staff is required to back up this data nightly. Such policies may not only provide insight on what is to be protected, but also what procedures must be followed to provide this protection.

Companies may also be required to protect specific assets by law or to adhere to certain certification standards. For example, hospitals are required to provide a reasonable level of security to protect patient records. If such requirements are not met, an organization can be subject to legal action.

Identifying Configurations to Satisfy Security Requirements

To protect assets from risks that were identified as possible threats to a business, countermeasures must be implemented. Servers will need certain configurations to provide security, and plans must be put into practice. Compare the risks faced by an organization with an operating system's features to find support that will address certain threats. Configuring the server to use these services or tools can assist in dealing with potential problems. For example, installing AD and using domain controllers on a network can heighten security and provide the ability to control user access and security across the network. In the same way, configuring a file server to use EFS so that data on the server's hard disk is encrypted can augment file security. Using security features in an operating system allows you to minimize many potential threats.

The same technique should be used when determining which roles will be configured on servers. As described earlier, different server roles provide different services to a network. By comparing the functionality of a server role to the needs of a company, you can identify which roles are required. Although it may be tempting to configure a server with every possible role, this can cause problems. When a server is configured to play a certain role in an organization, a number of different services, tools, and technologies may be installed and enabled. Never instal more roles than are needed to provide required functionality. Always disable any unneeded services on the server.

Although roles are helpful, running a Wizard to configure servers in a particular role isn't enough to create a secure environment. Additional steps should be followed to protect these servers and the data, applications, and other resources they provide. By customizing servers in this manner, you can ensure that the company will be able to benefit from Windows Server 2003 without compromising security. We'll discuss these steps in the "Customizing Server Security" section later in this chapter.

Planning Baseline Security

Security templates allow you to apply security settings to machines. These templates provide a baseline for analyzing security. Templates are .inf files that can be applied to computers manually or by using Group Policy Objects (GPOs). Security templates are discussed in detail in Chapter 4"Security Templates and Software Updates."

Customizing Server Security

Security templates contain predefined configurations, which are a great starting point, but usually, they do not fulfill the needs of many organizations. You may need to make some changes to match the organizational policies of your company. Similarly, configuring roles for servers requires additional steps to make the servers secure from attacks, accidents, and other possible problems. By customizing server security, you can implement security measures that will fulfill the unique needs of your organization.

Securing Servers According to Server Roles

You can use the Configure Your Server Wizard to configure the server for a particular server role. Though this procedure may install and enable a number of different services, tools, and technologies, additional steps usually are required to ensure the server's security. Some tasks are unique to the server's role, but others should be applied to all servers on your network.

Security Issues Related to All Server Roles

Any server used by members of an organization might be at risk of attacks by hackers and malicious programs, as well as accidents or other disasters. You will want to consider taking a number of countermeasures to ensure that any server is well protected.

Physical Security

A large part of physical security involves protecting systems from unauthorized physical access. Even if you've implemented strong security that prevents or limits access across a network, it will do little good if a person can sit at the server and make changes or (even worse) pick up the server and walk away with it.. If people do not have physical access to systems, the chances of unauthorized data access are reduced.

Physical security also involves protecting servers and other assets from environmental disasters. Uninterruptible Power Supplies (UPSs) should be installed to provide electricity during power outages, and fire suppression systems to extinguish fires need to be in place (keep in mind that some fire suppression systems are not suitable for server rooms because they can destroy the servers in the process of extinguishing a fire). By considering natural risk sources within an area, you can determine which measures need to be taken to reduce or remove risks.

Physical security not only includes natural disasters, but also those caused by the workplace environment. Servers need to be stored in stable areas that adhere to the environmental requirements of the equipment, which can include temperature and humidity specifications.

Service Packs and Hotfixes

At times, software vendors may release applications or operating systems with known vulnerabilities or bugs, or these problems may be discovered after the software has been released. Service packs contain updates that may improve the reliability, security, and software compatibility of a program or operating system. Patches and bug fixes are used to repair errors in code or security issues. Failing to install these may cause certain features to behave improperly, make improvements or new features unavailable, or leave your system open to attacks from hackers or viruses. In most cases, the service packs, patches, or bug fixes can be acquired from the manufacturer's Web site.

Updates for Windows operating systems are made available on the Windows Update Web site, which can be accessed through an Internet browser by visiting http://windowsupdate.microsoft.com. The Windows Update Web site determines what software is recommended to secure your system, and then allows you to download and install it from the site.

Windows Update provides updates for only Windows operating systems, certain other Microsoft software (such as Internet Explorer), and some additional third-party software, such as drivers. To update most third-party programs installed on the computer, you will need to visit the manufacturer's Web site, download the update, and then install it.

Windows 2000, Windows XP, and Windows Server 2003 also provide an automated update and notification tool that allows critical updates to be downloaded and installed without user intervention. When enabled, this tool regularly checks Microsoft's Web site for updates, and if one or more are found, automatically downloads and installs the update. You can also just have it notify you that updates that are available. Because this tool requires connecting to Microsoft over the Internet, it can be used only if the servers or workstations have Internet access.

In some situations, administrators may not want Windows Server 2003 to automatically download and install software without their approval, or they may not want computers to connect to the Microsoft Web site in this manner. In these cases, the Automatic Updates service should be disabled or configured so that it is used for notification only. These settings can be accessed by selecting **Start | Control Panel | System** and clicking the **Automatic Updates** tab in the **System Properties** dialog box. As shown in Figure 3.11 the **Automatic Updates** tab provides a number of settings that allow you to configure whether updates are automatically acquired and installed on the computer, when updates occur, and whether intervention is required. These settings include the following:

- **Keep my computer up to date** Enables Automatic Updates on the machine. When this selected, the other settings in this list may be configured.

- **Notify me before downloading any updates and notify me again before installing them on my computer** Informs users that an update is available and asks them if they would like to download it. If the user chooses to have the update downloaded, Automatic Updates will prompt the user when the download is complete, asking if the update should be installed.

- **Download the updates automatically and notify me when they are ready to be installed** Causes any updates to be downloaded from the Microsoft Web site without any notification. Once the update has completed downloading, the user is asked if the update should be installed.

- **Automatically download the updates, and install them on the schedule that I specify** Causes any updates to be downloaded from the Microsoft Web site without any notification. When this option is chosen, you can specify the time when the update can be installed without user intervention.

Figure 3.11 Choosing Automatic Updates Options

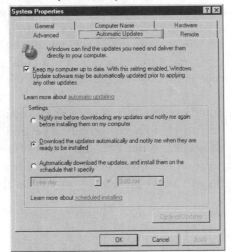

Antivirus Software

To prevent these malicious programs from causing problems, antivirus software should be installed on servers and workstations throughout the network. Signature files are used to identify viruses and let the software know how to remove them. Because new viruses appear every month, signature files need to be updated regularly by downloading them from the vendor's Web site.

Unnecessary Accounts and Services

Hackers and malicious programs can use insecure elements of a system to acquire greater access and cause more damage. To keep these entities from exploiting elements of your system, you should disable any services that are not needed. If a service has a weakness for which a security patch has not been developed, it could be exploited. By disabling unneeded services, you are cutting off possible avenues of attack. In doing so, you will not affect any functionality used by computers and users, and you can avoid any security issues that may be related to them.

Certain accounts in Windows Server 2003 should also be disabled or deleted. If an account is no longer being used, it should be removed to avoid a person or program using it to obtain unauthorized access. Even if an account will not be used temporarily (for example, during an employee's leave or vacation), the account should be disabled during the user's absence. If an employee has left permanently or a computer has been removed from the network, these accounts should be deleted. Properly managing users and groups greatly simplifies this task and methods for doing so are discussed in detail in "Working with User, Group and Computer Accounts" later in this book.

There are other accounts that you should consider disabling due to their access level. Windows Server 2003 and previous versions of Windows all have an account named Administrator that has full rights on a server. Because hackers already know the username of this account, they only need to obtain password to achieve this level of access. Although the Administrator account cannot be deleted, it can be disabled and renamed. If you create new user accounts and add them to the Administrators group, and disable the Administrator account, attackers will find it more difficult to determine which account to target.

Another account that is disabled by default, and should remain so, is the Guest account. This account is used to provide anonymous access to users who do not have their own account. Like the Administrator account, the Guest account is created when Windows Server 2003 is installed. Because there is the possibility that this account could accidentally be given improper levels of access and could be exploited to gain even greater access, it is a good idea to leave this account disabled. By giving users their own accounts, you can provide the access they need and audit their actions when necessary.

For any user, group, or computer account, it is important to grant only the minimum level of access needed. You want users to be unable to access anything beyond the scope of their role within the organization. This will assist in keeping other data and systems on the network protected. Determining what level of security a user needs to perform his or her job usually requires some investigation. By understanding the job a user performs, you will be able to determine which resources the user needs to access.

Strong Passwords

Strong passwords are more difficult to crack than simple ones. These types of passwords use a combination of keyboard characters from each of the following categories:

- Lowercase letters (*a–z*)

- Uppercase letters (*A–Z*)

- Numbers (0–9)

- Special characters (` ~ ! @ # $ % ^ & * ( ) _ + - = { } | [ ] \ : " ; ' < > ? , . /)

The length of a password also affects how easy it is to crack. You can use security templates and group policies to control how long a password is valid, the length of a password, and other aspects of password management. Another requirement that is important to having secure passwords is making sure that each time users change their passwords, they use passwords that are different from previous passwords.

To ensure domain controllers are secure, there are a number of password requirements that are enforced by default on Windows 2003 domain controllers:

- The password cannot contain any part of the user's account name.

- It must be a minimum of six characters in length.

- It must contain characters from three of the four categories: lowercase letters, uppercase letters, numbers, and special characters.

NTFS

Windows Server 2003 supports the FAT, FAT32, and NTFS file systems. Of these, NTFS provides the highest level of security. Disk partitions can be formatted with NTFS when a server is initially installed. If a volume is formatted as FAT or FAT32, you can convert it to NTFS. You can convert partitions to NTFS by using the command-line tool *convert.exe*.

Regular Backups

It is also important to perform regular data backups. Windows Server 2003 also provides Automated System Recovery and the Recovery Console for restoring systems that have failed.

Recovery Console is a text-mode command interpreter that can be used without starting Windows Server 2003. It allows you to access the hard disk and use commands to troubleshoot and manage problems that prevent the operating system from starting properly.

Automated System Recovery (ASR) allows you to back up and restore the Registry, boot files, and other system state data, as well as other data used by the operating system. An ASR set consists of files that are needed to restore Windows Server 2003 if the system cannot be started. In addition, ASR creates a floppy disk that contains system settings. Because an ASR set focuses on the files needed to restore the system, data files are not included in the backup. You should create an ASR set each time a major hardware change or a change to the operating system is made on the computer running Windows Server 2003. ASR should not be used as the first step in recovering an operating system. In fact, Microsoft recommends that it be the last possible option for system recovery and be used only after you've attempted other methods. In many cases, you'll be able to get back into the system using Safe Mode, the Last Known Good Configuration or other options.

To create an ASR set, use the Windows Server 2003 Backup utility. On the **Welcome** tab of the Backup utility, click the **Automated System Recovery Wizard** button. This starts the **Automated System Recovery Preparation Wizard**, which takes you through the steps of backing up the system files needed to recover Windows Server 2003 and creating a floppy disk containing the information needed to restore the system.

Securing Domain Controllers

The methods described in the previous sections can improve the security of a server in any role, but they are particularly important for domain controllers. The effects of an unsecured domain controller can be far-reaching. Information in AD is replicated to other domain controllers, so changes on one domain controller can affect all of them. This means that if an unauthorized entity accessed the directory and made changes, every domain controller would be updated with these changes. This includes disabled or deleted accounts, modifications to groups, and changes to other objects in the directory. Because all Windows 2000 Server domain controllers store a writable copy of AD (unlike Windows Server 2003), additional steps must be taken to secure the directory in a mixed environment.

It is important that group membership is controlled, so that the likelihood of accidental or malicious changes being made to AD is minimized. This especially applies to the Enterprise Admins, Domain Admins, Account Operators, Server Operators, and Administrators groups.

Because anyone who has physical access to the domain controller can make changes to the domain controller and AD, it is important that these servers have heightened security. Consider using smart cards to control authentication at the server console.

Encryption should also be used to protect data and authenticate users. As mentioned, NTFS partitions allow file encryption, and Kerberos provides strong authentication security. In Windows Server 2003, Kerberos is the default authentication protocol for domain members running Windows 2000 or later.

Securing File and Print Servers

File and print servers also need additional security. In addition to setting permissions on files and folders, regularly performing backups, and using antivirus software, organizations may also need to implement greater levels of protection such as encryption. Similarly, print servers need to be protected from improper use and must be configured to prevent unauthorized users from wasting print resources.

File Servers

It is especially important that volumes on a file server are formatted as NTFS and appropriate permissions are set on files and folders. As an added measure of security, these disks should also use EFS.

EFS is used to encrypt data on NTFS volumes. When EFS is used, unauthorized users and malicious programs are prevented from accessing the content of files, regardless of their permissions. EFS file encryption is completely transparent to the user.

Although EFS is an important part of securing a file server, this does not mean that every file on the network is a candidate for being encrypted with EFS. As mentioned, only files on NTFS volumes can be encrypted with EFS. If a volume is formatted as NTFS, files that have the System attribute or are located in *%systemroot%* (for example, C:\Windows) cannot be encrypted. Also, if the file or folder you want to encrypt is compressed, you cannot use encryption. The opposite is also true: if a file or folder is encrypted with EFS, it cannot be compressed.

Another important limitation of EFS is that it encrypts data only on NTFS volumes. When a file is accessed remotely on a file server, Windows Server 2003 decrypts it and sends it across the network in unencrypted form. For data to be encrypted during transmission, other technologies like IPSec must be used.

IPSec ensures that data is sent securely over the network by encrypting packets and authenticating the identity of the sender and receiver. When using IPSec, a policy is applied to both the sender's and receiver's computer, so the systems agree on how data will be encrypted. Other computers that intercept traffic between the machines will be unable to decipher the information contained in the packets.

Print Servers

Files that are being printed may also require protection. IPSec can be implemented to protect the transmission of data being sent to printers. After all, if a document can be captured while being sent to a printer, a hacker can view its information just as if it were being accessed directly from a server.

Physical security issues can be very important for printers. Anyone with access to a printer can remove printed documents from it. This is especially critical for printers that are routinely used to print sensitive documents or financial instruments like checks. A sensitive document may reside on a highly secure file server, but once it is printed, anyone standing by the printer could simply pick it up and walk away. To prevent this from happening, such printers should be located in secure areas that are not accessible to the public and other unauthorized users.

Just as files can have permissions assigned to them, so can printers. Printer permissions are used to control who can print and manage network printing. They are set on the **Security** tab of a printer's properties. Using printer permissions, you can allow or deny the following permissions for users:

- **Print** Allows users to print documents.

- **Manage Printers** Allows users to perform administrative tasks on a printer, including starting, pausing, and stopping the printer; changing spooler settings; sharing the printer; modifying permissions; and changing property settings.

- **Manage Documents** Allows users to perform administrative tasks relating to documents being printed. It allows users to start, pause, resume, reorder, and cancel documents.

Although different permissions exist for printing, only the Print permission gives the ability to print a document. For example, when only the Manage Documents permission is given, the user has the ability to manage other people's documents but cannot send documents to the printer for printing. Because those who manage printers may need to print test pages to determine if the printer is working properly, the Manage Printers permission can be set only if the Print permission is given.

Because the Print permission is assigned to the Everyone group, all users have access to print to a printer once it is shared on the network. For most printers, it's usually a good idea to remove this permission and add the specific groups within your organization that should have access to the printer.

Securing DHCP, DNS, and WINS Servers

DHCP, DNS, and WINS servers provide the ability to connect to the network and find other computers. DHCP is used to provide IP address and configuration information to clients. If you do not secure these servers, malicious persons and programs may be able to prohibit users from connecting to the network, redirect traffic to other locations, and impact the ability to use network resources.

DHCP servers do not require authentication when providing a lease. To avoid unauthorized access, it is important you restrict physical and wireless access to your network. In addition, auditing should be enabled on the DHCP server so that you can review requests for leased addresses. By reviewing the logs, you may be able to identify possible problems.

Just as DHCP is an unauthenticated protocol, so is the NetBIOS naming protocol used by WINS. WINS was designed to work with NetBIOS over TCP/IP (NetBT), which does not require any authentication. Because a user does not need to provide credentials to use WINS, it should be regarded as available to unauthorized persons or programs.

Rogue servers can also be a problem on the network. When a client requests a DHCP lease, it does so by broadcast. If an unauthorized person puts a DHCP server on the network, the incorrect IP address and configuration information could be provided to clients. This isn't the case if the rogue DHCP server is running Windows 2000 or Windows Server 2003, because these must be authorized in AD. If the server determines that it is not authorized, the DHCP service will not start. However, pre-Windows 2000 and non-Windows DHCP servers require no authorization and can be effectively used as rogue DHCP servers in a Windows Server 2003 environment. Handing out bogus DHCP leases that do not expire can be a very effective DoS technique. Because of this, it is important to monitor network traffic for DHCP server traffic that does not come from your network's authorized DHCP servers.

Restricting access to DHCP tools and limiting membership in groups that can modify DHCP settings are other important steps in securing a DHCP server. To administer DHCP servers remotely using the DHCP console or Netsh utility, you need to be a member of the Administrators group or the DHCP Administrators group. By restricting membership in these groups, you limit the number of people who can authorize a DHCP server to service client requests.

Securing Web Servers

Because IIS provides a variety of services that allow users to access information from the Web server service, it provides potential avenues of attack for unauthorized users, malicious programs, and other sources. IIS is not installed by default in Windows Server 2003, though in earlier versions of the OS it was installed by default.. If you do not need a Web server on your network, IIS should remain uninstalled. If it has been installed on servers that do not need it, make sure to uninstall it.

Once IIS is installed on Windows Server 2003, it is locked down to prevent any unneeded services from being exploited. By default, IIS will provide only static content to users. If dynamic content is used on the server, you will need to enable the necessary features. For example, if you your site is going to use ASP, ASP.NET, Common Gateway Interface (CGI), Internet Server Application Programming Interface (ISAPI) or Web Distributed Authoring and Versioning (WebDAV), each of these will need to be enabled before they can be used. As with Windows Server 2003 itself, any components that are not needed should be disabled.

Another default setting of IIS is that it will not compile, execute, or serve files with dynamic extensions. For example, if you have Web pages written as ASPs with the extension .asp, IIS, using default settings, won't provide users with this content. These are not allowed by default because of Microsoft's new security initiatives. Dynamic content can contain malicious code or have weaknesses that can be exploited. If files that provide dynamic content need to be used on the Web server, you must add the file extensions to the Web service extensions list. Any file types that are not needed should not be added.

An important part of protecting Web servers is using firewalls. Rules can be set up on the firewall controlling what kinds of traffic may pass and who can perform certain actions. Recent attacks suggest that firewall software may be a new target for attack, so it's vital to configure your firewall properly and monitor it regularly.

Securing Database Servers

When securing databases, you should take advantage of security features offered by the database software. Microsoft SQL Server, for example, provides two methods of authenticating clients to access data: Windows Authentication Mode and Mixed Mode. When Windows Authentication Mode is used, the SQL Server administrator has the ability to grant logon access to Windows user accounts and groups. If Mixed Mode is used, users can be authenticated through either Windows authentication or separate accounts created within SQL Server.

Regardless of the authentication mode used, like many database applications, SQL Server allows you to control access to data at a granular level. Permissions can be set to determine the operations that a user can perform on the data contained in the database. In many database applications, you can set permissions at the server, database, or table level. While one account might have the ability to create tables and delete data in all databases, another may only be able to view data in a single database. These permissions are different from those that can be set through AD and NTFS, and they apply only within the database program.

Database servers may also need to be secured through other roles that are used to access the database. For example, IIS is set up through the application role, and Web pages on the server can be used to access data stored in a database. Similarly, applications that are developed and made accessible from a terminal server may be used to view and manipulate database information.

To control access to the database server, you can use settings configured through a *data source name* (DSN). A DSN is commonly used by compiled and Web-based programs to gain access to data that is stored in data management systems and data files. A DSN contains information on the database name, the server it resides on, and the directory in which it's stored (if a data file is used). It also holds the username, password, and driver to use when making the connection. Programs use information in the DSN to connect to the data source, make queries, and manipulate data. To create or modify a DSN, use the Data Sources (ODBC) applet (select **Start | Administrative Tools | Data Sources (ODBC))**.

Because a DSN provides the username and password to use when connecting to the data source, a number of security-related issues arise from its use. Any passwords that are used should follow the recommendations for strong passwords that were discussed earlier in this chapter. In cases where a DSN is being used to connect to a SQL Server database, you also have the option of using Windows authentication or SQL Server authentication. If SQL Server authentication is used, you can enter the username and password of an account created in SQL Server. However, you should avoid entering the name of any accounts with access higher than the user will need. For example, entering the system administrator account (**sa**) would provide a DSN with full access to SQL Server and could maliciously or accidentally cause problems. To avoid possible damage to data or access violations, you should provide the username and password of a SQL Server account that has restricted access.

Securing Mail Servers

When Windows Server 2003 is configured with the mail server role, it should be set up to require secure authentication from e-mail clients. As mentioned earlier, clients retrieve their e-mail from mail servers using the POP3 protocol. Client software and the mail server's POP3 service can be configured to accept only passwords that are encrypted in order to prevent them from being intercepted by unauthorized parties.

In Windows Server 2003, the Microsoft POP3 Service uses Secure Password Authentication (SPA) to ensure that authentication between the mail server and clients is encrypted. SPA is integrated with AD, which is used to authenticate users as they log on to retrieve their e-mail. In cases where domain controllers are not used, SPA can authenticate to local accounts on the mail server. When the POP3 service is configured to accept only authentication using SPA, clients must also be configured to use encrypted authentication. If they are not, clients will attempt to authenticate using cleartext (which is plaintext, or unencrypted data) and will be rejected by the mail server.

To prevent mail servers from filling up with undeleted or unchecked e-mail, disk quotas should also be implemented. Disk quotas can be used only on NTFS partitions. When NTFS is used, permissions can also be set on the directories that store e-mail, preventing unauthorized parties from accessing it on the server.

Securing Certificate Authorities

In addition to the basic server hardening techniques mentioned, a CA needs additional levels of security applied it. Recall that a root CA resides at the top of the hierarchy, with subordinate CAs existing below it. Because the root CA is the most trusted one in a hierarchy, any CAs below it automatically trust it. These subordinate CAs use the root CA's public key and bind it to its own identity. In doing so, the subordinate can also issue certificates to users and computers.

Because of the trust between root and subordinate CAs, if the root CA is compromised, subordinate CAs continue trusting it. This compromises all certificates issued by the CAs in the hierarchy. As a security measure, you should disable the root CA's ability to issue certificates online and allow only child CAs to perform this function. An offline root CA is more difficult to compromise, since physical access to it is required.

When certificates are found to be invalid, they should immediately be revoked. After a certificate is revoked, the CRL should be immediately updated and published. The CRL is used to inform the world of certificates that are no longer valid. If the certificate is invalid, the software used to check it often allows the user to decide whether or not to trust the certificate holder.

Securing Application and Terminal Servers

Application and terminal servers are also configurable server roles that need additional steps to ensure that they are secure. Users are able to access applications across the network and execute them on servers using each of these roles. Because of the importance of many network-accessed applications, and the damage that can be done if they are exploited, it is essential that these roles are protected.

Application Servers

Application servers provide access to a wide variety of data on the network, and they need to be hardened using the methods discussed earlier. Using NTFS and enabling EFS where appropriate will help secure data. Configuring IPSec for transmission of highly sensitive files may also be appropriate for some application servers.

Servers configured in the application server role also have IIS 6.0 installed by default. IIS lets the application server provide Web-based applications to users of the network. Because the application server may have a Web server installed on it, steps need to be taken to ensure the Web server is also secure.

Terminal Servers

Because terminal servers provide access to applications and data, setting permissions on connections is important so you can control who can access a server and perform specific tasks. This is in addition to the permissions that can be set on files accessed by users in a terminal server session. By limiting access in these ways, you can control who is able to use files and applications and what actions they are able to perform. Terminal Server is discussed in more detail later in this book.

Custom Security Templates

Windows Server 2003 provides several pre-defined security templates you can modify and customize for your organization's particular needs. You can create custom security templates in a number of ways. As described earlier, modifying the results of an analysis using Security Configuration and Analysis, and then exporting the changes to a new template file, is one way to create a custom security template. In addition, you can create custom security templates using the Security Templates snap-in. The Security Templates snap-in allows you to modify existing templates and create new ones from scratch. Security templates are discussed in detail in "Security Templates and Software Updates" later in this book.

Chapter 4

Security Templates and Software Updates

In this chapter:

- **Security Templates**
- **Software Updates**

Introduction

In the last chapter, we looked at planning server roles and associated security measures. In this chapter we will examine two of Microsoft's key security tools for Windows Server 2003, the Security Configuration and Analysis management console and the Software Update Service.

The Security Configuration and Analysis management console provides a utility for testing baseline security settings and a method for applying a consistent security configuration to machines throughout the enterprise. The Software Update Service provides a mechanism to consistently apply hot fixes and updates to all Microsoft systems in your enterprise. When used together, the Security Configuration and Analysis tool and the Software Update Service are intended to reduce administrative overhead while providing consistent application of current security settings to all Microsoft-based machines in your network.

With the release of Service Pack 4 (SP 4) for Windows NT 4.0, Microsoft introduced a new security configuration tool to ease administration of your Windows NT network. The release of the NT 4.0 Service Pack 4 CD introduced the Security Configuration Manager (SCM). The Security Configuration Manager is a product originally designed for Windows NT 5.0 (now known as Windows 2000). Now, with the release of Windows Server 2003, Microsoft continues to expand on the functionality of the Security Configuration Manager with the Security and Configuration Analysis management console. The Security Configuration and Analysis utility provides a tool for configuring, comparing, and applying security templates.

Security Templates

A security template is a Windows initialization (.ini) file that lists configuration parameters for various operating system settings for different server types. Using the Security Configuration and Analysis utility, you can analyze the current configuration of your server. This analysis creates a template for the existing system configuration while comparing the system configuration against a preconfigured template. The security template is divided into the following seven areas:

- Account Policies
- Local Policies
- Event Log
- Restricted Groups
- System Services
- Registry
- File System

Account Policies determine password policy, account lockout policy, and Kerberos policy. Through this portion of the security template you can configure password complexity, password history, and other password characteristics. Also, through the account policy settings, you can configure account lockout threshold and duration.

Local Policies determine auditing policy, user rights assignment, and security options. Through Local Policy subcategories, you can configure system access settings, recovery options, system control permissions, account and system manipulation, and event auditing.

Event Log configurations modify application, system, and security Event Log settings. Through this category, you can configure event log storage capabilities and features.

The Restricted Groups category controls membership of security-sensitive groups. Through this category, group membership settings can be enforced and forced to override administrative changes to account settings that conflict with Restricted Groups membership settings.

The System Services category controls startup and permissions for system services. This configuration option helps to regulate system services available on the particular system. This carries an elevated level of importance for publicly connected servers, such as Web servers and VPN gateways, for example. Publicly connected servers are exposed to malicious attacks from anywhere in the world. It is considered best practice to enable only services that are needed by the server. Maintaining unneeded services increases the potential vulnerabilities on the server. Different services are known to have certain vulnerabilities. For example, IIS has had a long list of buffer overflow vulnerabilities discovered and subsequently patched. If the machine is not being used as a Web server, there is no need to support IIS and maintain its series of patches and updates.

The Registry category offers configuration options for permissions for registry keys. This helps to control unwanted modification of registry values by users or programs operating under the context of particular users.

The File System category provides options to control permissions for folders and files. Figure 4.1 illustrates the Security Configuration and Analysis management console with a domain controller *DC* security template compared against the existing system configuration.

Figure 4.1 Security Configuration and Analysis Management Console

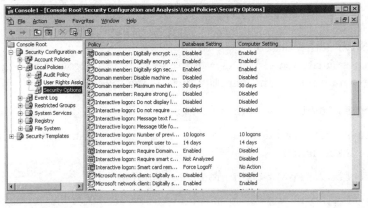

In the next section, we will look at the different types of security templates and explore the uses of and differences between each.

Types of Security Templates

Microsoft offers several preconfigured security templates through the Security Configuration and Analysis utility as well as online. You can apply a preconfigured security template to your system or use it to compare your existing configuration settings to predetermined settings provided by the security template. Templates are available for several configuration scenarios. Microsoft provides templates for the following:

- Default security (Setup security.inf)

- Compatible (Compatws.inf)

- Secure (Secure*.inf)

- Highly Secure (hisec*.inf)

- System root security (Rootsec.inf)

- No Terminal Server user SID (Notssid.inf)

The *Default* security template represents the default settings that are applied during installation of the operating system. This template also applies the default file permissions for the root of the system drive with the post-installation settings. This template was primarily designed for disaster recovery scenarios.

The *Compatible* security template modifies the permissions on files and registry settings to loosen the restrictive standard security settings for user accounts. This template provides limited capabilities for user accounts when compared to Power Users but provides greater freedom and capabilities than a standard user account.

The *Secure* security template increases security by modifying the password, lockout, and audit settings. This template increases security without adversely affecting application compatibility. Also, the Secure security template permits network authentication only through NT LAN Manager version 2 (NTLMv2). Microsoft network clients typically rely on LAN Manager and NTLM for network authentication. Windows for Workgroups, Windows 95, and Windows 98 clients that do not have the Directory Service client pack installed do not have NTLMv2 capabilities. Windows 95 and Windows 98 clients with the Directory Service client pack installed and Windows ME clients have provisions for NTLMv2 authentication.

The *Highly Secure* security template increases the security level provided by the Secure security template. The features modified by this template include the following:

- LAN Manager and NTLM authentication are refused

- Domain-to-member and domain-to-domain trust relationships require strong encryption and SMB packet signing

- All members of the Power Users group are removed

- Only Domain Admins and the local Administrator account remain members of the local Administrators group

The *System root security* template provides the same level of permissions as the default Windows XP file and folder permissions for the root system drive. This template can be used to reapply the default permissions to the root system drive if those permissions have been inadvertently modified or it can be used to apply the default permissions levels to other drives or volumes.

The *No Terminal Server user SID* security template removes the Terminal Server user SIDs that are used by Terminal Servers running in Application Mode. Terminal Server user SIDs provide access control for users logged in to Terminal Servers running in application mode. The Terminal Server user SIDs control access to the file system and default registry locations. Microsoft recommends running the Terminal Server in Full Security mode instead of removing the Terminal Server user SIDs to secure Terminal Servers. This template is generally used on a system that will not be used as a terminal server.

Network Security Settings

It was noted in the previous section that the use of *Secure* and *Highly Secure* security templates affects the authentication mechanisms used in network communication. Several of the security options under Local Policy affect network security for clients and servers. The Security Options listed under Local Policies provides several network security configuration options:

- Network security: Do not store LAN Manager hash value on next password change

- Network security: Force logoff when logon hours expire

- Network security: LAN Manager authentication level

- Network security: LDAP client signing requirements

- Network security: Minimum session security for NTLM SSP-based (including secure RPC) clients

- Network security: Minimum session security for NTLM SSP-based (including secure RPC) servers

The *Network security: Do not store LAN Manager hash value on next password change* security setting controls whether the weak LAN Manager (LM) hash value for the password will be stored in the local database next time the password is changed. The LM value is stored on the local computer in the security database. If the local computer's security database becomes compromised, the LM value might be used to extract the user's password. This setting is disabled by default.

The *Network security: Force logoff when logon hours expire* security setting affects users connected to the local computer through a network connection by manipulating the Server Message Block (SMB) communication between the systems. This setting, enabled by default, will disable network connectivity between the user's PC and the server configured with this security setting.

The *Network security: LAN Manager authentication level* security setting affects the authentication protocols used by clients and servers in a Microsoft network. Table 4.1 illustrates the relationship between security settings, client authentication protocol selection, and server authentication protocol selection.

Table 4.1 Relationships between Client and Server Authentication Settings

Settings	Clients LM	Domain Controllers NTLM	NTLMv2	LM	NTLM	NTLMv2
Send LM & NTLM responses	Yes	Yes	No	Accepted	Accepted	Accepted
Send LM & NTLM—use NTLMv2 session security if negotiated	Yes	Yes	Yes*	Accepted	Accepted	Accepted
Send NTLM response only	No	Yes	Yes*	Accepted	Accepted	Accepted
Send NTLMv2 response only	No	No	Yes	Accepted	Accepted	Accepted
Send NTLMv2 response only\ refuse LM	No	No	Yes	Refused	Accepted	Accepted
Send NTLMv2 response only\ refuse LM & NTLM	No	No	Yes	Refused	Refused	Accepted
*If supported by the server						

Normally, LAN Manager and NTLM authentication are used by Microsoft systems for network authentication. Implementing *Secure* and *Highly Secure* security templates affects network security by altering the typical LAN Manager and NTLM authentication request protocols.

A system configured with the Default security template or not configured with any security modifications will send LAN Manager and NTLM responses. Workstations do not have a defined configuration, meaning they will follow the server requests. Implementing security templates affects the use of LAN Manager and NTLM authentication used by the systems. Security settings determine which authentication protocol is used for network logons. The security settings determine the authentication protocol used by clients, the level of security negotiated, and the level of authentication accepted by servers. Figure 4.2 shows the options available through the *Network security: LAN Manager authentication level* security configuration setting.

Figure 4.2 Setting the Network Security: LAN Manager Authentication Level Options

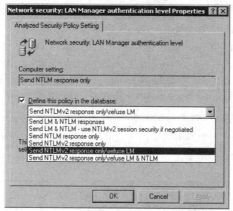

The *Network security: LDAP client signing requirements* security setting establishes the degree of data signing used in LDAP BIND requests. Digital signing is a method used to validate data integrity. This method uses keys to generate a hash of the actual data. This method of hashing, or encrypting the data, provides a mechanism to verify data integrity. If the data is modified in any way, the hash will not match. This ensures that data received by a client is the actual data sent by the server. The default setting is *Negotiate signing*. The three levels of LDAP client signing are:

- **None** Options are specified by the caller.

- **Negotiate signing** If Transport Layer Security/Secure Sockets Layer (TLS\SSL) is not being used, LDAP BIND requests occur with the LDAP data signing option set along with the options specified by the caller. If TLS\SSL is used, the LDAP BIND requests occur with the options that are specified by the caller. This is the default.

- **Require signature** If the client and server configurations do not match in this case, the client will receive an LDAP BIND request failed and the client will be unable to connect to the server.

The *Network security: Minimum session security for NTLM SSP-based (including secure RPC) clients* security setting provides message confidentiality, message integrity, 128-bit encryption, and NTLMv2 security connection requirements for client connections. In the default configuration, no options are set. The following options are available:

- **Require message integrity** Message integrity must be negotiated to continue the connection. Message integrity is verified through message signing. The signature ensures that the message has not been tampered with.

- **Require message confidentiality** Encryption must be negotiated to continue the connection. Encryption converts data into an unreadable format until decrypted.

- **Require NTLMv2 session security** NTLMv2 protocol must be negotiated or the connection will fail.

- **Require 128-bit encryption** Without negotiating strong encryption (128-bit) the connection will fail.

Figure 4.3 demonstrates the available options for Network security: Minimum session security for NTLM SSP-based (including secure RPC) clients configuration.

Figure 4.3 Setting Minimum Session Security for NTLM SSP-based (Including Secure RPC) Clients

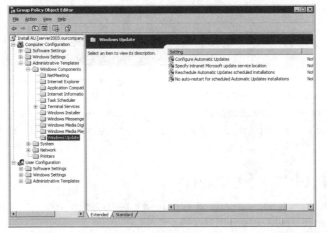

The *Network security: Minimum session security for NTLM SSP-based (including secure RPC) servers* security setting provides message confidentiality, message integrity, 128-bit encryption, and NTLMv2 security connection requirements for server connections. By default, no requirements are set. The following options (the same as those available for clients) are available:

- **Require message integrity** Message integrity must be negotiated to continue the connection. Message integrity is verified through message signing. The signature ensures the message has not been tampered with.

- **Require message confidentiality** Encryption must be negotiated to continue the connection. Encryption converts data into an unreadable format until decrypted.

- **Require NTLMv2 session security** NTLMv2 protocol must be negotiated or the connection will fail.

- **Require 128-bit encryption** Without negotiating strong encryption (128-bit) the connection will fail.

Figure 4.4 illustrates the available options for Network security: Minimum session security for NTLM SSP-based (including secure RPC) servers configuration.

Figure 4.4 Setting Minimum Session Security for NTLM SSP-based (Including Secure RPC) Servers

As mentioned previously, Microsoft provides several security templates to simplify basic security configurations to match common scenarios. In the next section, you will see how a predefined security template can be used to compare existing system security settings with the settings provided by the template.

Analyzing Baseline Security

In most types of analysis, the first step is to determine a baseline. If you want to measure network performance and determine how much difference certain modifications make, you have to start from a baseline or existing performance level. This approach also applies to security. If we want to tighten security on our network or on an individual system, we should first determine the baseline.

Using the Microsoft Security Configuration and Analysis management console, you can compare existing security settings to one of the predefined templates or to a custom template. The baseline analysis is conducted through the following steps:

1. A baseline storage location is determined by creating a database file where the configuration information and comparison information will be saved.

2. A template is selected to compare the current configuration against.

3. To finish the analysis, you run an analysis between the selected template and the current configuration.

4. The analysis will display different icons depending on the comparison results.

Table 4.2 displays the possible results from a security analysis.

Table 4.2 Possible Security Analysis Results

Visual flag	Meaning
Red X	The entry is defined in the analysis database and on the system, but the security setting values do not match.
Green check	The entry is defined in the analysis database and on the system and the setting values match.
Question mark	The entry is not defined in the analysis database and, therefore, was not analyzed.
(No flag)	If an entry is not analyzed, it may be that it was not defined in the analysis database or that the user who is running the analysis may not have sufficient permission to perform analysis on a specific object or area.
Exclamation point	This item is defined in the analysis database, but does not exist on the actual system.

A comparison between the securedc.inf template file and a standard domain controller is displayed in Figure 4.5.

Figure 4.5 Comparing the securedc.inf Template to a Standard Domain Controller

As an example, use the following steps to import and compare the hisecdc.inf security template to a standard installation Windows Server 2003 domain controller.

1. We will customize a Microsoft Management Console (MMC) with the Security Configuration and Analysis snap-in. Open the Microsoft Management Console (MMC) click **Start | Run | MMC.exe |** and click **OK**.

2. To add the Security Configuration and Analysis snap-in, click **File | Add Remove Snap-in...** to open the **Add/Remove Snap-in** pop-up window as shown in Figure 4.6.

Figure 4.6 Adding Snap-ins to the MMC

3. Click **Add...** and scroll down and select the **Security Configuration and Analysis** snap-in as shown in Figure 4.7.

Figure 4.7 Adding the Security Configuration and Analysis Snap-in

4. Click **Add** then click **Close** to return to the **Add/Remove Snap-in** dialog box as shown in Figure 4.8.

Figure 4.8 The Security Configuration and Analysis Snap-in Is Added

5. Click **OK** to move on to the analysis stage.

6. Click **Security Configuration and Analysis** in the left pane of the MMC to view instructions for importing and analyzing the templates as seen in Figure 4.9.

Figure 4.9 The MMC before Importing Templates

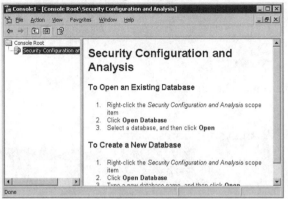

7. Right-click the **Security and Configuration Analysis** folder in the left pane of the MMC and select **Open database…**.

8. Type **Exercise1** in the filename dialog box and click **OK**.

9. Select the hisecdc.inf security template as shown in Figure 4.10 and click **Open**.

Figure 4.10 Selecting the hisecdc.inf Template

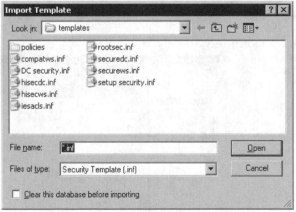

10. You will be returned to the blank Security Configuration and Analysis snap-in. Right-click the **Security Configuration and Analysis** folder in the left pane of the MMC and select **Analyze Computer Now**. A **Perform Analysis** dialog box will be displayed requesting the location for the **Error log file path:** as shown in Figure 4.11.

Figure 4.11 Specifying the Error Log File Path

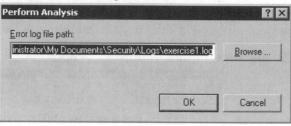

11.   Click **OK** to begin the analysis. A progress screen like the one in Figure 4.12 will be displayed.

Figure 4.12 Analysis Progress Screen

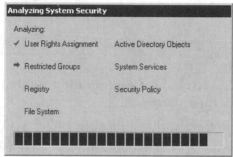

12.   When the analysis is complete, you will see several new items listed below **Security Configuration and Analysis** in your MMC as shown in Figure 4.13.

Figure 4.13 Completed Analysis

13.   Browse through each category to see how the template will affect the configuration of your computer. Each item marked with a red X represents a discrepancy in the policy. Figure 4.14 illustrates an example of several discrepancies between the computer configuration and the template configuration. Each red X represents an increase in security, in this particular situation.

Figure 4.14 Discrepancies in the Analysis between the Current Configuration and the Template

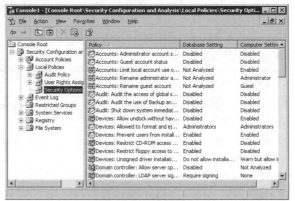

Applying Security Templates

There are multiple methods available for applying security templates in Windows Server 2003. The following tools provide mechanisms for applying security templates:

- Secedit.exe
- Group policy
- Security Configuration and Analysis

Secedit.exe

The **secedit.exe** command line tool provides a command line interface to analyze, modify, and apply security templates. The **secedit.exe** command works with the following switches:

- secedit /analyze
- secedit /configure
- secedit /export
- secedit /validate
- secedit /import
- secedit /GenerateRollback

The syntax used to apply a security template using the secedit.exe command is secedit /configure /db FileName [/cfg FileName] [/overwrite][/areas area1 area2...] [/log FileName] [/quiet].

The FileName attribute used with the /db switch specifies the filename of the database containing the security template to be applied. The FileName attribute used with the /cfg switch is an optional parameter specifying the security template to be imported into the database. This option is valid only when used in conjunction with the /db switch. The /overwrite switch specifies to overwrite any information stored in the database instead of appending to the database. The /areas switch specifies which areas of the template should be applied to the system. If no area is specified, all areas will be applied. The areas are the same categories discussed earlier in this chapter where we dissected the security template. Table 4.3 lists each area with a description of the configuration parameters provided.

Table 4.3 /areas Switch Options

Area Name	Description
SECURITYPOLICY	Local policy and domain policy for the system, including account policies, audit policies, and so on
GROUP_MGMT	Restricted group settings for any groups specified in the security template
USER_RIGHTS	User logon rights and granting of privileges
REGKEYS	Security on local registry keys
FILESTORE	Security on local file storage
SERVICES	Security for all defined services

The **FileName** parameter used with the **/log** switch sets the filename and path for the log file. If this switch is not specified, the log file is stored in the default location. The **/quiet** switch suppresses output to the screen.

Group Policy

Group policy provides several configuration options for systems within your enterprise environment. You can install software packages, configure desktop options, configure Internet Explorer settings, and configure security settings just to name a few. Group policy settings are applied through Active Directory Users and Computers for Domains and Organizational Units and through Active Directory Sites and Services for sites within your enterprise. Group policy is discussed in more detail in "Working with Group Policy in an Active Directory Environment" as well as in "Deploying Software via Group Policy."

The security settings within Group Policy are identical to the configuration options in the Security Configuration and Analysis management console. When Group Policy is used, each area application of policy is applied in a cumulative fashion. The order of application is:

- local
- site
- domain
- organizational unit.

First, locally configured security policies are applied to the system. Next, if a site-based security policy is configured, it will be applied on top of the local policy. This policy will overwrite the settings in the local policy. The domain policy is applied next, again overwriting previously applied policies. Finally, the organizational unit policy is applied. This policy also overwrites any previously written policies. If multiple (nested) organizational units hold the user or computer account, the nearest organizational unit to the user or computer account is applied last. This means that the nearest organizational unit-based policy will be the final policy applied and consequently, the settings from that policy will be the last ones written to the cumulative security settings.

Security Configuration and Analysis

The Security Configuration and Analysis management console provides local security policy application to your system. As discussed in the previous section, the security settings applied by this type of policy are overwritten by site, domain, and organizational unit-based policies used in Group Policy application. The advantage of the Security Configuration and Analysis tool is that it provides analysis capabilities to determine cumulative affects from new policies. You can run the analysis portion of the Security Configuration and Analysis utility to determine what portion of your settings will change by applying a new template or to see where a template might not provide additional benefits to your configuration.

Software Updates

Information technology is a dynamic industry with constant change. Currently, security and cost of ownership are two of the hottest topics in IT. To maintain a secure, consistent environment requires keeping up-to-date on security patches and hot fixes. As new vulnerabilities are discovered, as new services are implemented, the onus is on the IT department to keep systems up-to-date and secure. Most people are now familiar with Windows Update. Using Windows Update, your computer polls Microsoft servers to determine whether your system is up-to-date with hot fixes and security patches. This process simplifies administration but creates a couple of other dilemmas.

Running Windows Update in a large network environment poses a number of questions:

- How do you provide consistency?

- How do you ensure that all systems are being updated?

- How do you make sure that the update will not cause problems with a software package installed on your client systems?

- What about the bandwidth consumed by all of your clients connecting over your expensive WAN links to retrieve the same information over and over again?

There must be a better way to keep clients consistently updated. Enter the Software Update Service.

The Software Update Service (SUS) provides a centralized, LAN-based solution for the Windows Update service. Using SUS, clients connect to a server within your network infrastructure to receive updates. This allows you to centrally control which updates are deployed and which updates are not deployed. In this manner, you are able to test updates before deploying them to clients. This process provides greater control over software updates for your clients while also cutting down on WAN traffic. Your SUS server connects to Microsoft's servers to keep up-to-date with current security patches and hot fixes. Now, instead of having multiple clients connecting through the WAN link to Microsoft's servers to each retrieve the same updates, your server connects once and the clients connect internally to your server. This system reduces WAN bandwidth requirements while also increasing security by minimizing the number of clients connecting outside of your network. Also, this centralized control allows you to test updates before deploying them.

There are basically two components to this system. SUS is the server component responsible for downloading the updates from Microsoft's servers. Also, the SUS component provides centralized control of updates. The second component to the system is the Automatic Updates client software. This software offers a mechanism for clients to connect to either Microsoft's update servers or to your centralized update server. Let's see how this system is configured.

Install and Configure Software Update Infrastructure

The software update infrastructure (SUS) provides centralized administration and distribution of software updates within your organization's network. In this section, we will focus on the server components of the SUS infrastructure. The system is not a single piece of software but actually a combination of components that make up the infrastructure. To provide a centralized in-house SUS infrastructure, SUS uses the following three components:

- A new synchronization service called Windows Update Synchronization Service. This service downloads content to your SUS server.

- A server running an Internet Information Services (IIS) Web site. This server services the update requests from Automatic Updates clients.

- An SUS administration Web page.

SUS has the following software and minimum hardware requirements:

- Windows 2000 Server or Windows Server 2003

- Pentium III 700 MHz or higher processor

- A network card

- 512 megabytes of RAM

- 6 gigabytes (GB) of free hard disk space on an NTFS partition for storage of update packages

- A minimum of 100MB of free space on an NTFS partition for installation of SUS itself

- Microsoft Internet Explorer v5.5 or above

According to Microsoft, this configuration should support up to 15,000 clients using one SUS server. To build the SUS server:

1. Download the Sus10sp1.EXE file from the www.microsoft.com SUS page. The file is approximately 33 megabytes in size.

2. Copy the file to the server where you will install SUS.

3. Double-click the **Sus10sp1.exe file**.

4. In the Welcome screen, click **Next**.

5. Accept the End User License Agreement, and click **Next**.

6. Select the **Typical** check box. At this point, a typical install has been completed for the SUS server. The next screen will display the URL used by client machines to connect to the SUS server being installed. Document the URL and click **Install**.

7. The IIS lockdown tool may run at this point, depending on current server configuration. The **Finish** page will be displayed next. Document the administration URL displayed on the **Finish** page.

8. Click **Finish** to launch the SUS administration Web site in your default Web browser.

At this point, your SUS server has been installed with default configurations. In the next section, we will customize the server configuration. An SUS server provides two basic functions: synchronizing content and approving content. Before the SUS server can download content, it has to be configured.

1. Configuration settings are adjusted from the **Set Options** link, as shown in Figure 4.15.

Figure 4.15 Set Options Configuration Screen

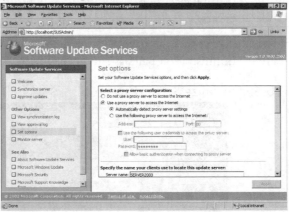

2. From the **Set Options** page, configure your network proxy settings if your network uses a proxy. The default setting is **Automatically detect proxy server settings**. This configuration will detect and automatically configure the proxy connection if your network supports this option. Otherwise, configure the proxy settings for your particular proxy.

3. Depending on whether your network uses DNS or NetBIOS for name resolution, you should configure the SUS server to support the proper name service for your network. This will determine the name used by clients to connect to the SUS server.

4. Configure the SUS server used to provide synchronized content. The options are to use Microsoft servers or to use a server on your internal network.

5. Specify how your server will handle new versions of previously approved updates.

6. Select a storage location for updates. The options are to maintain the updates on a Microsoft Windows Update server or to save the updates to a local folder. Also, locales may

be selected from this portion of the configuration. Note that each locale that is selected will increase the amount of storage space necessary to maintain updates on your server.

There are two types of data associated with the SUS synchronization:

- The metadata stored in a file named Aucatalog.cab. This file stores details about the packages and package availability.
- The actual package file that updates your systems.

No matter how the SUS server is configured, the Aucatalog.cab file will always be downloaded. As previously mentioned, you have the option to store packages in a local folder or to use Maintain the updates on the Microsoft Windows Update servers. The benefit to the second option takes advantage of the global availability of the Microsoft Windows Update servers while still providing control over which updates your clients will receive. This does not provide bandwidth-saving advantages the way that keeping an internal SUS server does. It does, however, reduce the amount of free disk that you need on the SUS server.

Now that we have installed the Windows Update Synchronization Service to our SUS server and configured the update and storage settings, it is time to synchronize the server with the Microsoft Windows Update servers.

1. Click **Synchronize server** in the navigation panel on the left side of the **Software Update Services** administration page as shown in Figure 4.16.

   Figure 4.16 Synchronize Server Page

2. From this page, you should configure a synchronization schedule for your SUS server. The synchronization schedule setting allows for synchronization at a particular time of day on a weekly or daily basis. Determine a time when network traffic is low and your server is not in the process of being backed up or processing other service requests, if possible. Scheduling settings are shown in Figure 4.17.

Figure 4.17 Setting SUS Scheduling

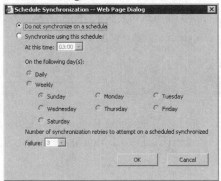

3. After specifying a schedule and completing the SUS server configuration, it is a good idea to manually synchronize the server the first time. Select **Synchronize Now** from the **Synchronize Server** page.

4. After synchronization is complete, depending on your server configuration, your server will either automatically approve the updates or you will have a list of updates to review for your approval. To review the updates, select **Approve updates** from the navigation menu as shown in Figure 4.18.

Figure 4.18 Update Review for Approval

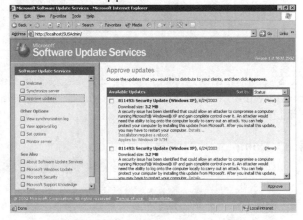

5. Review the updates available and select the updates that you want applied to your client systems, then click the **Approve** button to complete the SUS synchronization and update process. A pop-up message will appear to warn you that your update list will be modified as shown in Figure 4.19. Select **Yes** to continue.

Figure 4.19 Synchronization List Warning

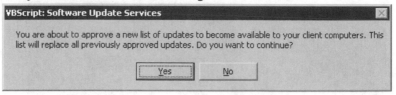

6. Depending on the update or updates selected, you may be prompted to accept an End User License Agreement (EULA) to continue as shown in Figure 4.20. Select **Accept** to continue.

Figure 4.20 EULA Prompt

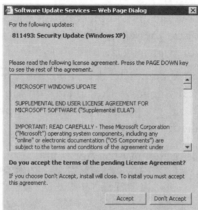

7. After the SUS server finishes downloading the selected updates, you are prompted with another pop-up window informing you that the updates have been successfully approved and are available for clients as shown in Figure 4.21.

Figure 4.21 Completed Approval pop-up

8. The SUS server is now configured, and synchronization and approval have been completed.

9. Your server may display one of the following messages next to each update in the approval list:

- **New** This indicates that the update was recently downloaded. The update has not been approved and will not be offered to any client computers that query the server.

- **Approved** This means that the update has been approved by an administrator and will be made available to client computers that query the server.

- **Not Approved** This indicates that the update has not been approved and will not be made available to client computers that query the server.

- **Updated** This indicates that the update has been changed during a recent synchronization.

- **Temporarily Unavailable** This message is displayed only when updates are stored locally on the server. An update is in the Temporarily Unavailable state if one of the following is true: The associated update package file required to install the update is not available or a dependency required by the update is not available.

10. Depending on your server configuration, the server may need periodic administration to approve new updates for your clients. It is best practice to test updates on non-production machines before approving them for your production environment. This ensures that the updates do not conflict with other software used by your client systems.

A **Monitor server** page is available for a high-level overview of updates available. Also, as synchronizations are performed, log entries are added to the **Event Log** to document the synchronization process and to provide information in the event of a synchronization failure.

In the next section, we will discuss the process used to install and configure SUS clients with the Automatic Client Update software on Windows 2003, Windows XP, and Windows 2000 client systems.

Install and Configure Automatic Client Update Settings

You now have a working SUS server on your corporate LAN so it is time to configure the clients. The updated Automatic Update client is available for Windows 2000 Professional, Windows 2000 Server, and Windows 2000 Advanced Server (all with Service Pack 2 or higher), Windows XP Professional, Windows XP Home Edition, and Windows Server 2003 family. Windows 2000 Data Center Server uses a special service for system update capabilities separate from the standard SUS service. Three options are available for client installation:

- Install Automatic Updates client using the MSI install package.

- Self-update from the STPP version Critical Update Notification (CUN).

- Install Windows 2000 Service Pack 3 (SP3).

- Install Windows XP SP1.

- Install Windows Server 2003.

Microsoft recommends using the MSI install package (filename WUAU22.msi) to update Windows 2000 and Windows XP client systems. The client software may be installed using the MSI package through Microsoft IntelliMirror, Microsoft Systems Management Server (SMS), or through a simple logon script.

Once the client software is installed, there are two basic configuration categories to complete:

- Automatic Updates functionality
- Automatic Updates server to use—from Microsoft Windows Updates servers or from a server running SUS on your local network

SUS clients use the Microsoft Windows Updates servers by default. Clients must be redirected to use the local SUS server or servers. The recommended approach for SUS client redirection to a local SUS server is through Group Policy settings.

To configure Group Policy SUS server redirection in an Active Directory environment:

1. The WUAU.adm file that describes the new policy settings for the Automatic Updates client is automatically installed into the %windir%\inf folder when you install Automatic Updates. This file describes the new policy settings used for the Automatic Update configuration.

2. Load WUAU.adm as an administrative template in the **Group Policy Object Editor**.

3. From an Active Directory domain controller, click **Start | Programs | Administrative Tools | Active Directory Users and Computers**.

4. Right-click the Organizational Unit (OU) or domain where you want to create the policy, and then click **Properties**.

5. Click the **Group Policy** tab, and click **New**.

6. Type a name for the policy, and then click **Edit** to open the **Group Policy Object Editor**.

7. Under either Computer Settings or User Settings, right-click **Administrative Templates**.

8. Click **Add/Remove Templates** and **Add**.

9. Enter the name of the Automatic Updates ADM file: **%windir%\inf\WUAU.adm**.

10. Click Open.

11. From within the **Group Policy Editor**, **Computer Configuration | Administrative Templates | Windows Components | Windows Update** in the right pane of the management console, the two configuration options are listed as seen in Figure 4.22.

Figure 4.22 Configuring Windows Automatic Update Using Group Policy

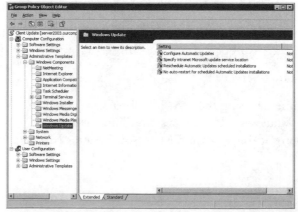

12. Configure the SUS server location information by double-clicking on **Specify intranet Microsoft update service location** and clicking **Enable** as shown in Figure 4.23.

Figure 4.23 Enabling SUS Client Redirection

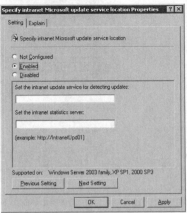

13. In the **Set the intranet update service for detecting updates:** box, enter the URL for the SUS server.

14. In the **Set the intranet statistics server:** box, enter the URL for the statistics server. Click **OK** to continue. This server can be the same server as the SUS server. The server has to have IIS installed and configured to be the statistics server.

15. Configure the **Automatic Update Properties** by double-clicking **Configure Automatic Updates** in the right pane of the management console.

16. Click **Enable** and select one of the three **Configure Automatic Updating:** options as shown in Figure 4.24. The **Notify for download and notify for install** option notifies a logged-on administrative user prior to the download and prior to the installation of the updates. The **Auto download and notify for install** option automatically begins downloading updates and then notifies a logged-on administrative user prior to installing the updates. The **Auto download and schedule the install** option is configured to perform a scheduled installation. The recurring scheduled installation day and time must also be set using the **Scheduled install day:** and **Scheduled install time:** drop-down boxes. Click **OK** to continue.

Figure 4.24 Configuring Automatic Update Properties

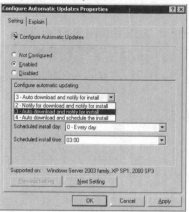

17. If the computer is not running when the scheduled install time arrives, the **Reschedule Automatic Updates scheduled installations** policy setting will provide a means to install the updates after the computer has been started. Double-click **Reschedule Automatic Updates scheduled installations**, click **Enable**, and specify a time in the **Wait after system startup(minutes):** box (a value between 1 and 60). Click **OK** to complete this configuration setting.

Twenty-four hours after the client first establishes a connection with the update service, a local administrator will be presented with a wizard-based configuration for the client update settings if no configuration settings have been specified through other methods. A local administrator can use the Automatic Updates applet in the Control Panel to configure Automatic Update or to modify the settings. If Group Policy has been configured for Automatic Updates, it will override the local settings. The order for policy application is the same as discussed earlier: Local, Site, Domain, Organizational Unit. Each policy overwrites the previous policy if conflicting parameters are encountered.

Supporting Legacy Clients

Legacy clients (running operating systems that predate Windows 2000) do not work with Group Policy. To take advantage of software update capabilities for Windows 98 and Windows 98SE systems, you will have to modify the registry. In a non-Active Directory environment (workgroup or NT 4.0 Domain), there are several ways to configure registry keys for the SUS client settings. The most common ways to set the registry keys in a non-Active Directory environment are:

- Manually editing the registry using Regedit.exe
- Centrally deploying these registry key changes using Windows NT 4 System Policy

First, update the Critical Update Notification system to accommodate the new Automatic Update system. The option to update using self-update from the STPP version Critical Update Notification (CUN) involves editing the registry in the following manner:

1. Open Registry Editor. Click **Start | Run** and type **regedit.exe**. Press **OK**.

2. Navigate to **HKEY_LOCAL_MACHINE\SOFTWARE\Microsoft\Windows\ CurrentVersion\WindowsUpdate\Critical Update**.

3. Create **SelfUpdServer** value under this key as **REG_SZ.."SelfUpdServer"="http:// <YourServer>/SelfUpdate/CUN5_4"**.

4. Navigate to **HKEY_LOCAL_MACHINE\SOFTWARE\Microsoft\Windows\ CurrentVersion\WindowsUpdate\Critical Update\Critical Update SelfUpdate**.

Create the **SelfUpdServer** value under this key as **REG_SZ. "SelfUpdServer"=** where <YourServer> is the name of the SUS server on your network.

After the Critical Update software has been upgraded, it is time to configure the software. Let's take a look at one of the methods used to update the registry on older client systems. To modify the registry with regedit.exe, add the following settings to the registry at this location:

HKEY_LOCAL_MACHINE\Software\Policies\Microsoft\Windows\ WindowsUpdate\AU

- **RescheduleWaitTime**
    - Range: n; where n = time in minutes (1 through 60)
    - Registry value type: REG_DWORD

- **NoAutoRebootWithLoggedOnUsers**
    - Set this to 1 if you want the logged on users to choose whether or not to reboot their systems
    - Registry value type: REG_DWORD

- **NoAutoUpdate**
    - Range = 0|1. 0 = Automatic Updates is enabled (default), 1 = Automatic Updates is disabled
    - Registry Value Type: Reg_DWORD

- **AUOptions**
    - Range = 2|3|4. 2 = notify of download and installation, 3 = automatically download and notify of installation, and 4 = automatic download and scheduled installation. All options notify the local administrator.
    - Registry Value Type: Reg_DWORD

- **ScheduledInstallDay**
    - Range = 0|1|2|3|4|5|6|7. 0 = Every day; 1 through 7 = the days of the week from Sunday (1) to Saturday (7)
    - Registry Value Type: Reg_DWORD

- **ScheduledInstallTime**
    - Range = n; where n = the time of day in 24-hour format (0 through 23)
    - Registry Value Type: Reg_DWORD

- **UseWUServer**
  - Set this to 1 to enable Automatic Updates to use the server running Software Update Services as specified in WUServer
  - Registry Value Type: Reg_DWORD

Now, in **HKEY_LOCAL_MACHINE\Software\Policies\Microsoft\Windows\WindowsUpdate** add the following registry entries:

- **WUServer**
  - Sets the SUS server by HTTP name
  - Registry Value Type: Reg_SZ

- **WUStatusServer**

  - Sets the SUS statistics server by HTTP name
  - Registry Value Type: Reg_SZ

Testing Software Updates

Software updates were designed to fix security problems or to improve the performance or functionality of your network systems. With the enormous amount of software available for current Windows operating systems and with the massive amount of different types of hardware available, it is impossible from a practical standpoint to test every scenario in which a software update might be applied. Some software updates can have adverse affects on your client system performance or operating capabilities. It is considered best practice to try to simulate your network environment as accurately as possible in a test lab environment in an effort to pre-test software updates before deploying them to your production environment.

Testing should occur in a lab environment that models your production network. If possible, you should have at least two instances of each type of hardware used in your environment. This hardware should be configured with the same software and settings that typical clients with this type of system would have. You should have a server configured as a test SUS server for the network and you should have a sufficient number of servers set up in the lab to model the production network. As new updates become available, using the SUS test server, you should approve updates individually and test them against your lab systems to verify proper operation. Try to put the software through its paces, making sure that the update that was applied has not adversely affected the system. Maintain a list of tested updates, documenting any changes that you have observed as a result of the update. Now, once the client test systems seem to be functioning properly, you should approve the tested software updates on your production SUS server.

If, for some reason, an update does have adverse affects on certain systems in the test environment, do not deploy the update until a workaround has been determined. You should look on Microsoft's TechNet site to attempt to find solutions to the problems that the update is causing. Microsoft's TechNet site is located at http://www.microsoft.com/technet. This site maintains the Microsoft Knowledgebase, a database of known problems with Microsoft products and possible solutions. You might have to contact the hardware or software vendor to resolve the problem. It is possible that you may have to go through Microsoft's technical support to resolve the issues as well.

Chapter 5

Managing Physical and Logical Disks

In this chapter:

- **Using Disk Management Tools**

- **Managing Physical and Logical Disks**

- **Optimizing Disk Performance**

- **Understanding and Using Remote Storage**

- **Troubleshooting Disks and Volumes**

Introduction

Disk management is an important aspect of optimizing and maintaining any server and Windows Server 2003 includes a variety of tools that the administrator can use to format, partition, organize, and optimize disks. In this chapter, we take a look at how the operating system enables you to interface with the physical and logical disks in your machine, and how you can optimize disk performance to increase the overall performance of your server.

Like Windows 2000, Server 2003 supports two disk types: basic and dynamic. Upgrading your disks to dynamic status enables you to take advantage of the operating system's software RAID support, so that you can create fault-tolerant volumes. A regular schedule of defragmentation is another way you can enhance disk performance, and in this chapter, we will show you how to use both the graphical interface and the command-line tool to defragment your disks and perform other disk management tasks. You will also learn to configure disk quotas for better management of disk space on the file server, and we show you how to use the Remote Storage feature to manage volumes.

Finally, we will discuss basic troubleshooting techniques for tracking down problems with disks and volumes.

Working with Microsoft Disk Technologies

It is important for you to know the correct terminology relating to the various disk components in Windows Server 2003. There are two primary components to understand: *physical disks* and *logical disks*. Physical disks can be either basic or dynamic. Logically, they can be separated into either partitions or volumes. This section explains when and how each of these is used.

Physical vs Logical Disks

You must be able to distinguish between a physical disk and a logical disk. *Physical* refers to the actual, tangible hard disk itself. A physical disk is a piece of hardware, which can be organized into logical disks. A physical disk by itself is of no use to Windows. It is not until you format the physical disk and create a logical disk that it becomes a resource that is accessible from within Windows.

Logical disks enable you to customize your physical disks to best fit your needs. Depending on the disk type used (basic or dynamic), logical disks consist of either partitions or volumes. These are units made up of all or part of one or more disks. Partitions are divisions of a single disk. Volumes can span multiple physical disks. Conversely, a single physical disk can contain multiple logical disks. The following illustrate a couple of real-world examples:

- You have three physical disks installed in your server, each of which contains 30GB of disk space. However, you don't want to use them as three separate disks. In other words, you do not want the operating system to "see" these disks as a C drive, a D drive, and an E drive. Instead, you want to access all the space contained in the three disks as if it belonged to one 90GB physical disk. To accomplish this, you can create a spanned volume (covered later in this chapter) and combine all three physical disks into one logical disk. You can now access all the storage via one drive letter (e.g., D:).

- Maybe you have the opposite scenario. You have one large 100 GB physical disk, but you don't want one large C: drive. You can create two or more partitions or logical drives to divide up the space. You can assign a separate drive letter for each logical disk and access the single physical disk as if it were multiple smaller physical disks.

Basic vs Dynamic Disks

Windows Server 2003 supports two types of physical disk configurations:

- Basic disks
- Dynamic disks

By default, disks are initially configured as basic. Basic disks use the same disk structure used in Windows NT 4.0 and previous operating systems, all the way back to MS-DOS. That is, they are divided into primary and extended partitions, and logical drives can be created within extended partitions.

Dynamic disks use a new disk structure that was introduced in Windows 2000. The basic unit of a dynamic disk is the volume (rather than the partition). Dynamic disks support features that you don't get with basic disks and give you much more flexibility in structuring your storage space.

With dynamic disks, you can extend simple volumes (make them bigger without reformatting and losing data) to any empty space on any dynamic disk, create spanned volumes across multiple physical disks and create fault tolerant (RAID 1 and 5) volumes.

A single computer can contain both basic and dynamic disks. Each physical disk installed in the computer is separately identified as either basic or dynamic. Basic disks and dynamic disks both support the same file systems (FAT16, FAT32, and NTFS).

Basic disks can be upgraded to dynamic status at any time without losing data. Later in the chapter, you will learn how to upgrade your disks. You do not even have to reboot after upgrading to dynamic unless you are upgrading the system disk or the disk being upgraded is currently in use. As mentioned, basic disks are made up of partitions and logical drives. Basic disks do not support creating volume sets or fault-tolerant volumes. MS-DOS and all versions of Windows can use basic disks.

Although dynamic disks (unlike basic disks) support creating volumes that span multiple disks and creating fault-tolerant volumes, dynamic disks are not always the best solution. The following are some limitations of using dynamic disks:

- Dynamic disks are currently not supported on laptop computers.

- Removable media and disks attached via FireWire (IEEE 1394), Universal Serial Bus (USB), or shared SCSI buses cannot be converted to dynamic.

- You can install Windows Server 2003 only onto a dynamic volume that was converted from a basic boot or system partition. You cannot install onto a dynamic volume that was created from free space. This is because there must be an entry in the partition table for the setup program to recognize the volume, and such an entry does not exist on a newly created dynamic volume.

- Even though Windows 2000, XP Pro, and Server 2003 all use dynamic disks, you cannot convert a basic disk that holds multiple instances of these operating systems to dynamic. The operating systems installed on the disk will not start if you do this.

- Dynamic disks are not supported by Windows Cluster Service. If you need the features of dynamic disks on a clustered shared disk, you can use a third-party program called Veritas Volume Manager 4.0 to accomplish this.

Booting Your Disk

Two disk sectors are vital to starting your computer, the master boot record (MBR) and the boot sector. The MBR is created when a disk is initially partitioned. The boot sector is created when a partition (or volume) is formatted.

The MBR is located in the first sector on the physical hard disk. It contains the master boot code, the partition table, and the disk signature for the physical disk. The master boot code is responsible for booting the machine. The partition table identifies the type and location of partitions on the physical disk. The disk signature identifies the physical disk to the operating system.

The MBR performs the following operations when a disk boots:

1. It scans the partition table (or disk configuration database) for an active partition.

2. It finds the starting sector for the active partition.

3. It loads a copy of the boot sector of the active partition into memory.

4. It passes control to the boot sector.

There is a boot sector for each partition on your physical disk. The boot sector (like the MBR) contains code that is required to boot. Among other things, it also contains information required by the file system to access the partition or volume. The boot sector loads NTLDR (the Windows startup file) into memory and gives it control of the boot process.

Unlike basic disks, dynamic disks do not use a partition table to store their configuration information. Instead, they use a private database that is stored at the end of the disk, called the Logical Disk Manager or LDM database. This database is exactly 1MB in size and is replicated to all the dynamic disks within a machine. This addresses the problem of the partition table as a single point of failure. The LDM database includes such information as volume types, offsets, memberships, and drive letters for each volume on the disk. The LDM replicates and synchronizes the databases across the disks, so that all dynamic disks on the system are aware of one another. There is a unique DiskID in the LDM header of each dynamic disk that enables LDM to identify each disk and distinguish it from the others.

Partitions vs Volumes

Both partitions and volumes enable us to divide one physical disk into sections so that each section appears as a separate disk. Each section is individually formatted (different sections can be formatted in different file systems) and can have its own drive letter. Basic disks contain partitions. Partitions cannot be configured to span disks and therefore cannot provide any fault tolerance. Dynamic disks contain volumes. Volumes can span disks and can provide fault tolerance.

Partition Types and Logical Drives

There are two types of partitions:

- Primary parititons
- Extended partitions

Primary partitions are assigned drive letters and formatted as a whole; they cannot be subdivided. Extended partitions simply group free space so that it can be subdivided into logical drives, which can be individually formatted and used for storage.

Primary Partitions

After a primary partition is formatted and assigned a drive letter, it appears as a separate disk to the OS. Depending on the disk-partitioning method used, basic disks can have between four and 128 primary partitions. When using the 32-bit editions of Windows Server 2003, basic disks use the Master Boot Record (MBR) for partitioning and can have up to four primary partitions. The 64-bit editions of Windows Server 2003 can use the GUID partition table (GPT) for partitioning. The GPT utilizes primary and backup partitions for redundancy and allows for up to 128 partitions.

Extended Partitions

Extended partitions can be created only on an MBR-partitioned disk. Extended partitions enable you to have more than four drives on a basic disk. You can only have one extended partition per basic disk, but it can be divided into multiple logical drives. You do not format the extended partition itself. Creating an extended partition simply pools free space that can then be divided into logical drives. In other words, until you create a logical drive for your extended partition, you cannot access the space on that partition.

Logical Drives

Logical drives are created when you divide up the space contained within an extended partition. Logical drives are formatted and assigned a drive letter just like primary partitions. An extended partition can contain an unlimited number of logical drives. The Windows system partition cannot be stored on a logical drive.

Volume Types

Dynamic disks are made up of volumes. A single dynamic disk can hold up to 2,000 volumes, but Microsoft recommends that you limit the volumes per disk to 32. As with partitions, you can have multiple volumes per disk, but unlike partitions, volumes can span multiple disks. Some volume types are designed to increase performance and some types are designed to provide fault tolerance. Windows Server 2003 supports the following five volume types:

- Simple
- Spanned
- Striped
- Mirrored
- RAID-5

Simple Volumes

Simple volumes are made up of free space on a single dynamic disk. They function much like primary partitions on a basic disk. If you have only one physical disk, all the volumes you create on it will be simple volumes.

Simple volumes are not fault tolerant. However, you can mirror them (discussed below) to make them fault tolerant, in which case they become *mirrored volumes*. Simple volumes can be extended on a single disk as long as the disk is not the boot or system disk. Extending a simple volume involves taking free space on a disk and adding it to the existing volume. You can also extend a simple volume across multiple disks, but then it becomes a *spanned volume*. Note that you can't combine these operations (that is, you can't mirror a spanned volume).

Simple volumes provide almost 100 percent utilization of disk space. In other words, if you purchase two 100 GB disks and format them as simple volumes, you have a total of 200 GB total storage, minus the 1MB per disk overhead for the LDM database. You are able to use more of the purchased disks' space than is true with other types of volumes.

Spanned Volumes

Spanned volumes support two to 32 disks. Each disk can be a different size (as shown in Figure 5.1). Creating a spanned volume is like extending a simple volume except that it spans multiple disks (hence the name, spanned volume). In fact, if you extend a simple volume across multiple disks, by definition it becomes a spanned volume. Spanned volumes are not fault tolerant and cannot be mirrored. Spanned volumes do not provide any performance improvements over simple volumes. They are used merely to increase the amount of space that can be accessed as a single unit. Like simple volumes, spanned volumes provide 100 percent drive utilization (minus the 1MB used for the LDM database). As data is written to the spanned volume, it is first written to the first disk in the set. When the first disk is full, the data is then written to the second disk, and so on.

Figure 5.1 Understanding Spanning Volumes

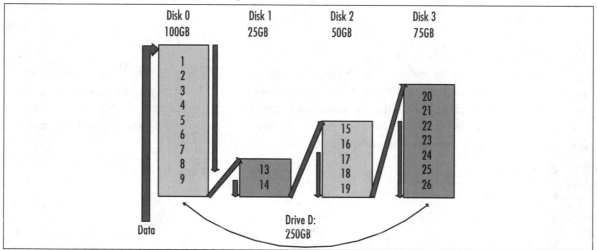

You can extend a spanned volume to make it larger (if it is formatted with NTFS). This consists of adding unallocated space to the volume, like extending a simple volume, except that the unallocated space does not have to be contiguous and can be on any dynamic disk attached to the computer. No data is lost; the new space is formatted without any impact on the existing data.

Striped Volumes

Striped volumes are made up of two to 32 disks. Each disk should be the same size to efficiently use all space. It is possible to use different-sized disks, but the stripe size on every disk will be limited to the amount of free space on the smallest disk, so there will be space wasted on the larger disk(s). In other words, if you created a striped volume with one 5 GB drive and two 10 GB drives, you would only be able to use 5 GB of each drive because that is the maximum amount that is available on all disks. This would create a 15 GB striped volume, wasting 10 GB of disk space (5 GB on each of the 10GB disks). If you use equal-sized disks, striped volumes provide 100 percent drive utilization (minus 1MB overhead for the LDM database).

Striped volumes cannot be mirrored or extended and they are not fault tolerant. However, striped volumes do provide performance advantage. Striping increases read and write access to the volume, because all the disks are working at the same time. In fact, striped volumes offer the best performance of all Windows Server 2003 volume types. This is because of the way data is stored (as shown in Figure 5.2). Data is written evenly across all disks in 64 KB chunks.

Figure 5.2 Understanding Striped Volumes

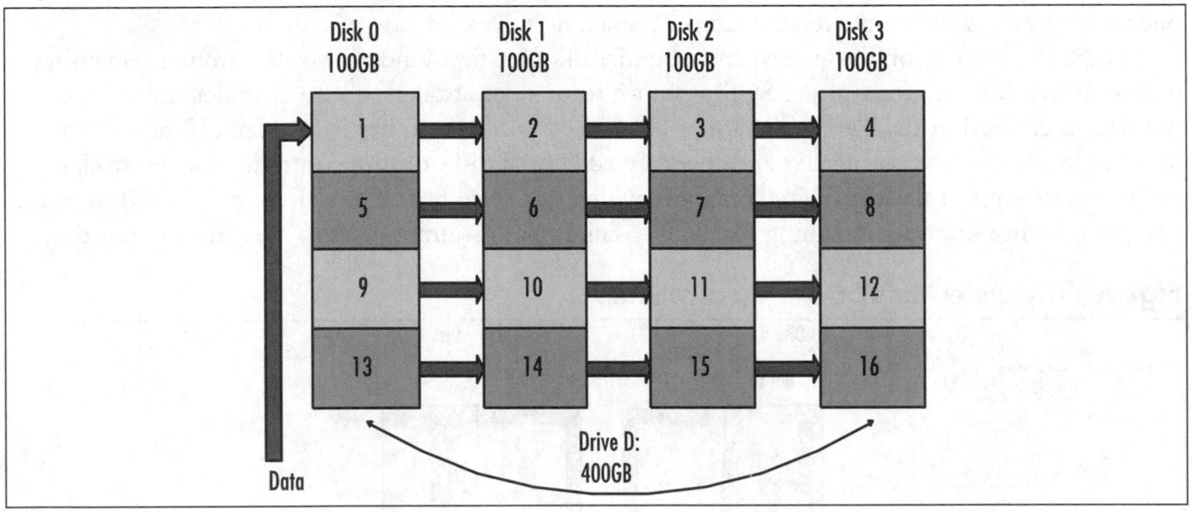

Mirrored Volumes

Mirrored volumes require exactly two disks and these two disks should be identical. Not only should they be the same size, but Microsoft recommends that both disks be the same model, from the same vendor. Mirrored volumes provide fault tolerance by making a duplicate copy of everything that is written to the volume (see Figure 5.3), with one copy on each physical disk. If one disk in the mirrored volume fails, the other disk will take its place. However, when this happens, you no longer have fault tolerance. You need to break the mirror so you can then create a new, mirrored volume with another disk, to restore fault tolerance.

Mirrored volumes cannot be extended, and they provide only 50 percent disk utilization. In other words, every 1 GB of storage space that you buy gets you 500MB of actual storage. The benefit of a mirror is that you have an exact duplicate of everything. With a mirror, you can lose one disk and still have all your data intact. Only if you lost both disks at the same time would you lose your data. Because all the data is there on the duplicate disk, you can get back up and running after a failure much faster than with a RAID-5 volume, where the data must be regenerated from the parity information following a failure before it can be accessed.

Mirroring can have a negative impact on system performance, because of the overhead of writing to two disks at the same time.

An even more fault-tolerant form of disk mirroring is called *disk duplexing*. Disk duplexing is the same as disk mirroring, except that each disk in the mirror is connected to a different disk controller. This eliminates the disk controller as a single point of failure. Duplexed disks appear to the operating system the same as mirrored disks; if you have duplexed disks, they will be shown as mirrored disks in the Disk Management console.

You can mirror any simple volume, including the boot and system volumes. Microsoft recommends that you use separate controllers (duplexing) if you mirror the system or boot volumes. The controllers should be identical (same model and vendor) to prevent problems with starting from the mirror if the primary disk fails. Always test a mirrored system or boot volume to ensure that the operating system will be able to start from a remaining mirror in case of failure.

There are several conditions that must be met in order for Windows to start from a remaining mirror. If the disks in a mirror are SCSI disks on separate controllers, both controllers must have translation enabled or disabled (one cannot be enabled while the other is disabled). If the disks are SCSI disks on the same controller and there are additional disks on the controller, the controller's BIOS has to support the capability to choose which device to boot from. If the disks are IDE disks, you must ensure that the remaining disk after a failure has its jumpers set to the "master" position.

Figure 5.3 Understanding Mirrored Volumes

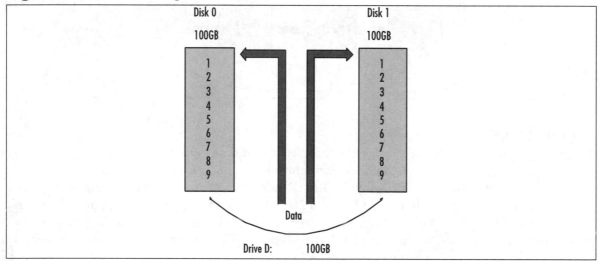

RAID-5 Volumes

RAID-5 volumes consist of three to 32 disks. RAID-5 volumes provide increased performance for read operations, as well as fault tolerance. The performance boost is due to the way RAID-5 volumes stripe data across all the disks and the fault tolerance is provided by parity information. As with a striped volume, data is written evenly across all disks in 64 KB chunks (see Figure 5.4). Unlike with disk striping, the available space (the stripe) on one disk is used for parity information. To increase performance, the parity information is split across all the disks in the volume, written in stripes like the data. Write performance is lower, because the parity must be calculated during the write operation. If most operations are read-oriented (for instance, users accessing files on a file server), RAID-5 provides significant performance advantages.

Windows Server 2003's RAID-5 volumes cannot be extended or mirrored, and the boot and system partitions cannot be part of a RAID-5 volume.

Disk utilization depends on how many disks are part of the RAID array. The equivalent of one disk is used for writing the parity information. If you have three disks, one-third of the total disk space is used for parity information, so you are able to utilize two-thirds of the space you purchase for data. If you have 10 disks in the array, only one-tenth of the total space is used for parity. Thus, the more disks you have in the set, the more efficient disk usage becomes.

Figure 5.4 Understanding RAID-5 Volumes

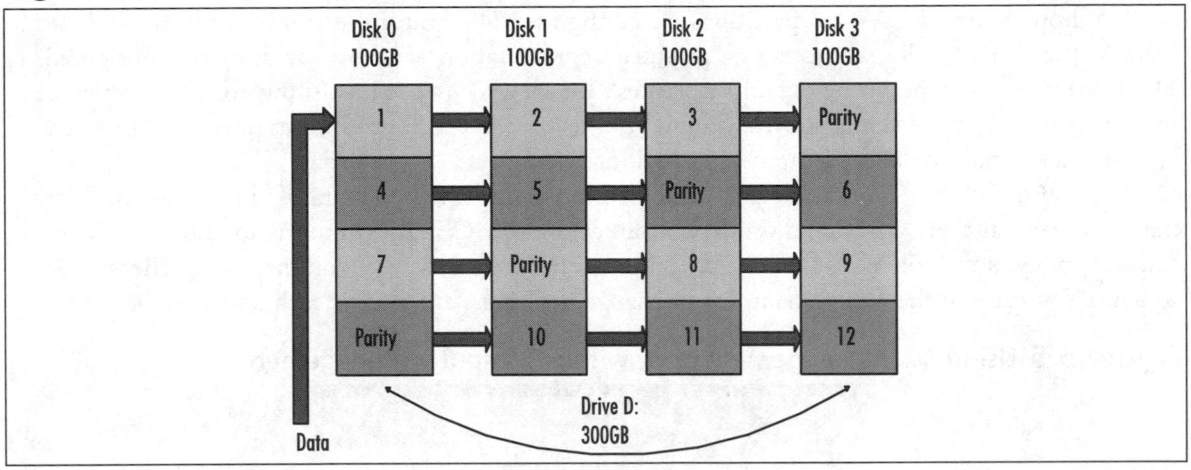

Using Disk Management Tools

Microsoft provides a variety of disk management tools in Windows Server 2003. These include command-line utilities such as **diskpart.exe**, **fsutil.exe**, and **rss.exe**. These tools support scripting, which enables you to automate many of your disk management responsibilities. You can also manage your disks through the graphical interface via the disk management MMC. This section will show you how to manage disks both from the GUI and from the command prompt.

Using the Disk Management MMC

You can access the disk management MMC, shown in Figure 5.5, in a couple of different ways:

- You can get there via Computer Management, by clicking **Start | Programs | Administrative Tools | Computer Management**.
- You can right-click the **My Computer** icon on the desktop or in the **Start** menu and select **Manage** from the context menu.
- You can create a custom MMC console to use the Disk Management snap-in.

Figure 5.5 shows the default view for the Disk Management MMC. Notice that the details pane is divided into two sections, a top section and a bottom section. There are three different views that you can use for either section:

- Disk list
- Volume list
- Graphical view

By default, the top section displays the volume list view and the bottom section displays the graphical view. You can change the view by clicking the **View** menu bar, choosing **Top** or **Bottom**, and selecting the view that you want.

In Figure 5.5, the top section is using the default volume list view. This view uses text in a table to show how your volumes and partitions are configured. The bottom section is using the graphical view. As the name implies, it provides a graphical representation of how your disks are configured. The third view (not shown by default) is the disk list view. It uses text to show you how your disks are configured. It looks similar to the volume list view, except it displays information on a per-disk basis instead of volume and partition information.

Most administrators find the default combination volume list and graphical view to be most efficient. Notice that there is a legend on the bottom of the MMC, as shown in Figure 5.6. The color codes enable you to look at each disk and easily determine what type of volume(s) or partition(s) it contains. You can use the **View** menu bar to change the colors assigned to each disk region.

Figure 5.5 Using Disk Management from within Computer Management

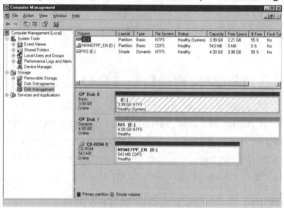

Figure 5.6 Using the Legend in the Disk Management MMC

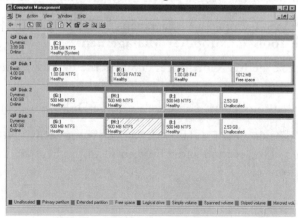

Using the Command-Line Utilities

Microsoft has increased the number of functions that administrators can perform from the command prompt in Windows Server 2003. This gives you more flexibility in accomplishing administrative tasks. Windows Server 2003 includes the following command-line tools for performing disk-related tasks:

- **Diskpart.exe:** for managing disks
- **Fsutil.exe**: for managing the file system
- **Rss.exe:** for managing remote storage

In the following sections, we will discuss each of these utilities in detail.

Using Diskpart.exe

Diskpart.exe enables you to manage disks, partitions, or volumes from the command prompt. You can type the commands directly at the command prompt via interactive mode or you can configure diskpart.exe to use a script for its input.

Diskpart.exe scripting is beneficial if you are automating the deployment of Windows Server 2003 by using unattended setup files. Microsoft recommends that you put all your diskpart.exe commands into a single script to avoid conflicts between multiple scripts. If you must use separate scripts, you must allow at least 15 seconds after each script finishes before the next one starts to execute. Put the command *timeout /t 15* at the beginning of each script to force a 15-second delay.

The syntax for using diskpart.exe with scripts is:

```
diskpart [/s <script>]
```

If you want to use diskpart.exe in interactive mode, type **diskpart.exe** at the command prompt. This will take you to the **DISKPART>** prompt, shown in Figure 5.7. Whenever you see **DISKPART>**, you are in interactive mode and diskpart.exe is awaiting your input. Typing **help** in interactive mode will display all the utility's available commands, as shown in Table 5.1.

Table 5.1 Using Diskpart.exe Commands

Command	Description
ADD	Adds a mirror to a simple volume.
ACTIVE	Marks the current basic partition as active.
ASSIGN	Assigns a drive letter or mount point to the selected volume.
AUTOMOUNT	Enables and disables automatic mounting of basic volumes.
BREAK	Breaks a mirror set.
CLEAN	Clears the configuration information, or all information, off the disk.
CONVERT	Converts between different disk formats.
CREATE	Creates a volume or partition.
DELETE	Deletes an object.

Continued

Table 5.1 Using Diskpart.exe Commands

Command	Description
DETAIL	Provides details about an object.
EXIT	Exits Diskpart.exe.
EXTEND	Extends a volume.
GPT	Assigns attributes to the selected GPT partition.
HELP	Prints a list of commands.
IMPORT	Imports a disk group.
INACTIVE	Marks the current basic partition as inactive.
LIST	Prints out a list of objects.
ONLINE	Onlines a disk that is currently marked as offline.
REM	Does nothing. Used to comment scripts.
REMOVE	Removes a drive letter or mount point assignment.
REPAIR	Repairs a RAID
RESCAN	Rescans the computer looking for disks and volumes.
RETAIN	Places a retained partition under a simple volume.
SELECT	Moves the focus to an object.

Figure 5.7 Using Diskpart.exe in Interactive Mode

Before you can use any of these commands, you must list all disk objects and then choose one on which diskpart.exe will carry out the command(s). After you place the focus on a particular object, all commands entered will target that object until you change the focus to a different object. Use the following steps to walk through the process of focusing diskpart.exe on a disk. Figure 5.8 shows these commands as entered in the command console.

1. Use the appropriate list command from the table to list the disk, volumes, or partitions on your system. For this example, we are going to list the disks. Type **list disk** and press **Enter**. The output is shown in Figure 5.8.

2. Now that you know which disks are available, select one for the focus of your commands. For this example, we select the first disk (disk 0). Type **select disk 0** and press **Enter**.

3. You can now type **list disk** again and press **Enter** to verify that the correct disk was selected. The disk on which diskpart.exe is focused has an asterisk (*) to the left of it.

Figure 5.8 Focusing Diskpart.exe on Disk 0

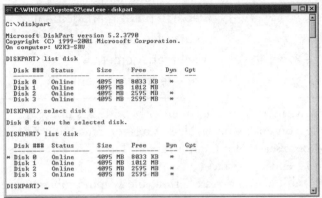

Now you can use the desired command to perform an operation on the selected disk. For example, to change a basic disk to dynamic, you use the **convert** command with the following syntax:

```
DISKPART> convert dynamic
```

Using Fsutil.exe

You can use *fsutil.exe* to manage FAT and NTFS file systems from the command prompt. Some of the actions you can perform with this utility include the following:

- Managing sparse files
- Managing reparse points
- Mounting and dismounting volumes
- Viewing the amount of free space on a volume

Fsutil.exe supports the commands shown in Table 5.2.

Table 5.2 Using Fsutil.exe Commands

Command	Description
behavior	File system behavior control
dirty	Volume dirty bit management
file	File-specific commands
fsinfo	File system information

Continued

Table 5.2 Using Fsutil.exe Commands

Command	Description
hardlink	Hardlink management
objectid	Object ID management
quota	Quota management
reparsepoint	Reparse point management
sparse	Sparse file control
usn	USN management
volume	Volume management

You can perform many different management tasks with this utility that do not have a GUI counterpart. For example, you enable or disable settings for generating 8.3 file names, set the amount of disk space to be reserved for the Master File Table Zone, set a file's valid data length, and create hard links (directory entries for files).

Experimenting with fsutil.exe can create serious file system problems or even make your system unbootable, so Microsoft recommends that only advanced users run this utility.

Using Rss.exe

Rss.exe manages Remote Storage from the command prompt. You can use Remote Storage to extend your server's disk space by moving data off your hard disks and onto magnetic tapes or magneto-optical (MO) disks, with file data cached locally for quick access. We discuss Remote Storage in much more detail in the section "Understanding and Using Remote Storage."

The rss.exe utility enables you to run scripts that enable applications to directly access Remote Storage. You can use rss.exe only after you have set up Remote Storage using the Remote Storage MMC (covered later in this chapter). The basic syntax for rss.exe is as follows:

```
RSS [ADMIN | VOLUME | MEDIA | FILE] [SET | SHOW | JOB | MANAGE | UNMANAGE
    | DELETE | SYNCHRONIZE | RECREATEMASTER | RECALL] <args> <switches>
```

Managing Physical and Logical Disks

We've discussed physical and logical disks and how they're implemented in Windows Server 2003. In this section, we'll look at how you can effectively manage basic and dynamic disks.

Managing Basic Disks

It is important to understand the circumstances that make it desirable to use basic disks. You should not upgrade your disks to dynamic status without knowing all the consequences of that action. If you choose to stick with basic disks, you need to know how to create and delete partitions and logical drives. Basic disks can be managed via the Disk Management MMC or the diskpart.exe utility, and you can use scripts to automate many management tasks as discussed previously.

In the following sections, we discuss the most important aspects of managing basic disks, including:

- When to use basic disks instead of dynamic disks
- How to create partitions and logical drives
- How to assign a new drive letter
- How to format a basic volume
- How to extend a basic volume

When to Use Basic Disks

Basic disks are the default for Windows Server 2003. You should always use basic disk if you are going to dual-boot your machine with another operating system. MS-DOS, Windows 9x, Windows NT 4.0, and Windows XP Home Edition do not support dynamic disks. Windows 2000, Windows XP Professional, and Windows Server 2003 do support dynamic disks, but not when dual booting.

Use basic disk if you will be moving your disks between machines. If you use dynamic disks, you have to go into Disk Management and import dynamic disk every time you move them from one PC to another. With basic disks, you just install them and Windows automatically sees them. Laptop hard disks must be configured as basic disks as most removable storage media.

Creating Partitions and Logical Drives

When you install Windows Server 2003, setup will prompt you to create a primary partition to use as the boot partition for Windows. If you want to create more partitions afterwards, you will need to use the disk management MMC. This section will walk you through creating a primary partition, creating an extended partition, creating a logical drive, and assigning a new drive letter.

Creating a primary partition

1. Right-click the unallocated space on the disk on which you want to create a primary partition.

2. Click **New partition** on the pop-up menu. This will start the **New Partition Wizard**, as shown in Figure 5.9.

3. Click **Next** to continue.

Figure 5.9 Creating a Primary Partition Using the New Partition Wizard

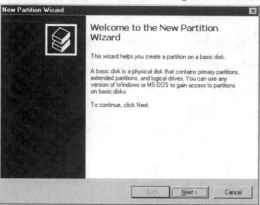

4. On the **Select Partition Type** window (Figure 5.10), select **Primary partition**.

5. Click **Next** to continue. You will now be prompted to specify the partition size as shown in Figure 5.11.

6. Specify the **Partition size in MB** and click **Next** to continue.

Figure 5.10 Selecting to Create a Primary Partition

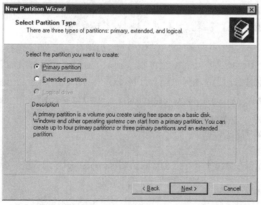

Figure 5.11 Specifying the Partition Size

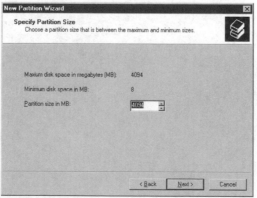

7. Now you need to identify your new partition. Select a drive letter or choose to mount the new volume to an NTFS folder. For this example we are assigning our partition the drive letter **F**, as shown in Figure 5.12.

8. Click **Next** to continue.

Figure 5.12 Assigning a Drive Letter or Path

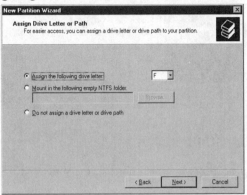

9. You must now format your new partition. You can format partitions as FAT, FAT32, or NTFS. For this example, choose **NTFS**, as shown in Figure 5.13, and then click **Next** to continue.

10. You will now see the **Completing the New Partition Wizard** window, as shown in Figure 5.14. Read over the summary to verify that you made the correct selections and click **Finish** to complete the process.

Figure 5.13 Formatting the Partition

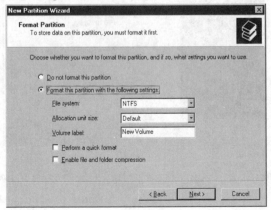

Figure 5.14 Completing the New Partition Wizard

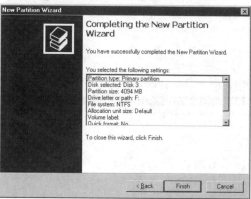

Creating an extended partition

1. Right-click the unallocated space on the disk on which you want to create an extended partition.

2. Click **New partition** on the pop-up menu. This will start the **New Partition Wizard** as shown in Figure 5.15.

3. Click **Next** to continue.

Figure 5.15 Creating an Extended Partition with the New Partition Wizard

4. On the **Select Partition Type** window (Figure 5.16), select **Extended partition**.

5. Click **Next** to continue. You will now be prompted to specify the partition size as shown in Figure 5.17.

6. Specify the **Partition size in MB** and click **Finish** to create the extended partition.

Figure 5.16 Selecting to Create an Extended Partition

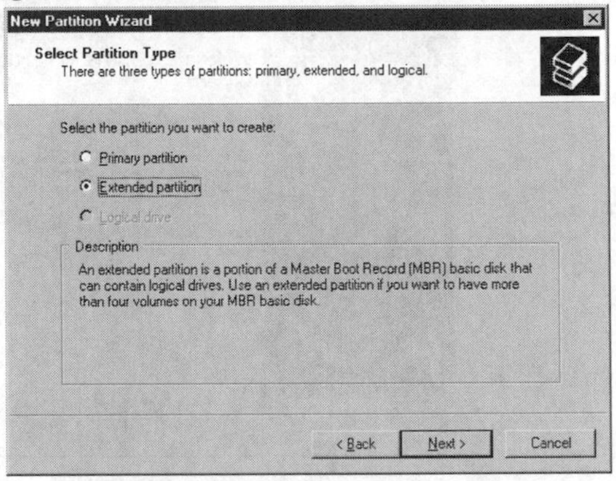

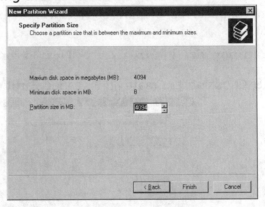

Figure 5.17 Specifying the Partition Size

Creating a logical drive

1. Right-click the Extended partition on the disk on which you want to create a logical drive.

2. Click **New Logical Drive** on the pop-up menu. This will start the **New Partition Wizard**, as shown in Figure 5.18.

3. Click **Next** to continue.

Figure 5.18 Using the New Partition Wizard to Create a Logical Partition

4. On the **Select Partition Type** window (Figure 5.19), select **Logical drive**.

5. Click **Next** to continue. You will now be prompted to specify the partition size as shown in Figure 5.20.

6. Specify the **Partition size in MB** and click **Next** to continue.

Figure 5.19 Choosing to Create an Extended Partition

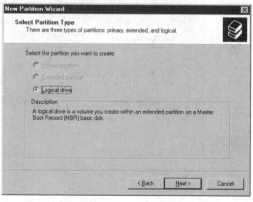

Figure 5.20 Specifying a Partition Size

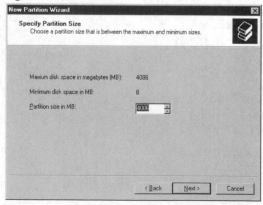

7. Now you need to identify your new partition. Select a drive letter or choose to mount the new volume to an NTFS folder. For this example, we are assigning our partition the drive letter **G**, as shown in Figure 5.21.

8. Click **Next** to continue.

Figure 5.21 Assigning a Drive Letter or Path

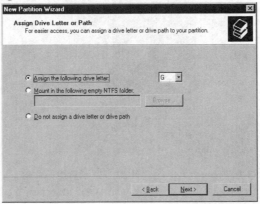

9. You must now format your new partition. You can format partitions as FAT, FAT32, or NTFS. For this example, choose **NTFS**, as shown in Figure 5.22, and then click **Next** to continue.

10. You will now see the **Completing the New Partition Wizard** window, as shown in Figure 5.23. Read over the summary to verify that you made the correct selections and click **Finish** to complete the process.

Figure 5.22 Formatting the New Partition

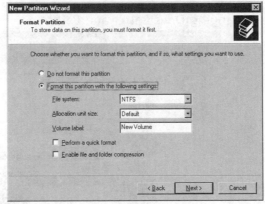

Figure 5.23 Finishing the New Partition Wizard

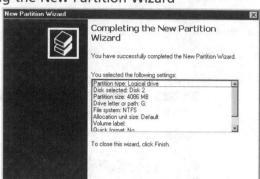

Assign a New Drive Letter

You are given the option to assign a drive letter when you create a primary partition or a logical drive. If you chose not to assign one then or you wish to change the letter, you can use Disk Management or diskpart.exe to assign a new drive letter.

1. Open **Computer Management** by right-clicking **My Computer** and choosing **Manage**.

2. Expand **Storage** and click **Disk Management**. This will give you the window shown in Figure 5.24.

3. Right-click the partition you want to assign a drive letter.

4. Select **Change Drive Letter and Paths** from the pop-up menu as shown in Figure 5.24. You will now see the window displayed in Figure 5.25.

Figure 5.24 Changing Drive Letter and Paths

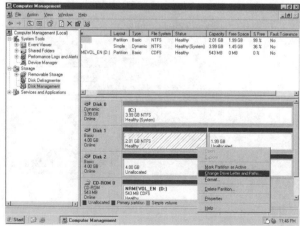

Figure 5.25 Adding a Drive Letter

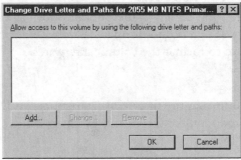

5. Click the **Add** button to add a drive letter. This will give you the window shown in Figure 5.26.

6. Use the drop-down arrow to select the drive letter you want to assign. For this example we are going to use **E**.

7. After you select the drive letter, click **OK** to accept your choice. This will apply your changes. Figure 5.27 shows that our partition now has the drive letter E.

Figure 5.26 Selecting the Letter to Assign

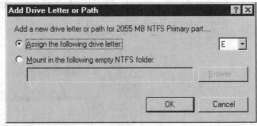

Figure 5.27 Seeing the New Drive Letter

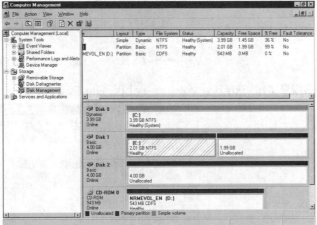

Formatting a Basic Volume

Like assigning a drive letter, you are given the option to format a drive when you create a primary partition or a logical drive. If you do not format the volume during creation, you can use Disk Management or format.exe to format the volume afterwards.

Format a volume

Use the following steps to format the first primary partition on Disk 2. Look at Figure 5.28 and you can see that this partition, unlike the C: and E: drives, has not been formatted. Here are the steps to format it with NTFS:

1. Open **Computer Management** by right-clicking **My Computer** and choosing **Manage**.

2. Expand **Storage** and click **Disk Management**. This will give you the window shown in Figure 5.28.

3. Right-click the partition you want to format.

4. Select **Format** from the pop-up menu, as shown in Figure 5.28. You will now see the window displayed in Figure 5.29.

Figure 5.28 Formatting a Volume

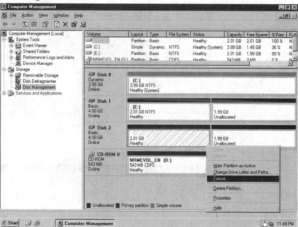

Figure 5.29 Choosing a Volume Label, File System, and Cluster Size

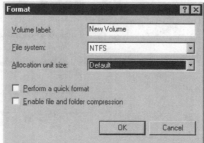

5. Enter the **Volume label** for the volume. For this example we are using **New Volume**.

6. Select the **File system** to use. In this example we are using **NTFS**.

7. Select the **Allocation unit size** (file system cluster). For this example we are using **Default**, which is 4 KB.

8. Optionally, you can choose to perform a quick format and to enable file and folder compression. After you make your choices, click **OK** to continue. You will now be warned that you are going to lose all data, as shown in Figure 5.30.

9. Click **OK** to start the format process. Figure 5.31 shows the volume being formatted and Figure 5.32 shows the volume after the format has completed.

Figure 5.30 Acknowledging Formatting Warning

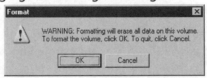

Figure 5.31 Watching the Drive Format

Figure 5.32 Seeing the Formatted Drive

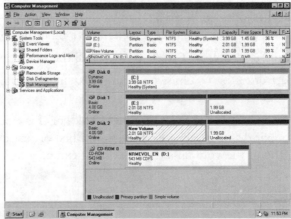

Extending a Basic Volume

Extending a basic volume enables you to add more space to an existing volume without losing data. This is a new feature that was not available in Windows 2000. You can extend a basic volume only onto the same disk and only if it is followed by contiguous unallocated space. You cannot use Disk Management to extend a basic volume. The only way to do it is to use diskpart.exe from the command prompt.

Extending a basic volume

Even though you cannot use Disk Management to extend a basic volume, let's open it anyway so that we can see our volume as it gets extended. We will use diskpart.exe to actually do the extending of the primary partition (F:) on Disk 2.

1. Open Computer Management by right-clicking My Computer and choosing Manage.

2. Expand **Storage** and click **Disk Management**. This will give you the window shown in Figure 5.33. Use this window to see the before and after of extending your volume.

Figure 5.33 Extending a Basic Volume

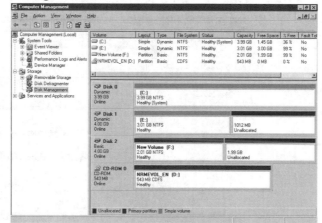

3. Open the command prompt by selecting **Start | Run | CMD | OK**.

4. From within the command prompt, launch diskpart by typing **diskpart** and pressing **Enter**. This will put you into diskpart interactive mode, as shown in Figure 5.34.

5. Type **list volume** and press **Enter** to display all the available volumes on your system.

6. Focus diskpart onto the volume you wish to extend by typing **select volume 3**. For this example we choose to extended volume 3.

7. To extend the volume, type **extend size=1024**. For this example we extended the volume by 1 MB. To exit disk part, type **exit** when finished or just close the command prompt. Figure 5.35 shows the volume after it has been extended.

Figure 5.34 Using Diskpart

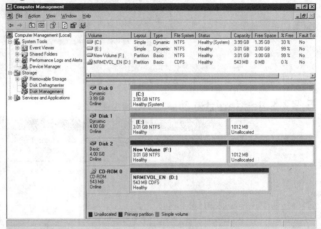

```
C:\WINDOWS\system32\cmd.exe - diskpart

C:\>diskpart

Microsoft DiskPart version 5.2.3790
Copyright (C) 1999-2001 Microsoft Corporation.
On computer: W2K3_DC

DISKPART> list volume

  Volume ###  Ltr  Label       Fs     Type        Size     Status     Info
  ----------  ---  ----------- -----  ----------  -------  ---------  --------
  Volume 0    C                NTFS   Simple      4087 MB  Healthy    System
  Volume 1    E    New Volume  NTFS   Simple      3072 MB  Healthy
  Volume 2    D    NRMEVOL_EN  CDFS   CD-ROM        543 MB  Healthy
  Volume 3    F    New Volume  NTFS   Partition   2055 MB  Healthy

DISKPART> select volume 3

Volume 3 is the selected volume.

DISKPART> extend size=1024

DiskPart successfully extended the volume.

DISKPART>
```

Figure 5.35 Seeing the Extended Volume

Managing Dynamic Disks

Dynamic disks are the required disk structure in Windows Server 2003 if you want to create fault-tolerant volumes or increase read and write performance by spanning disks. Dynamic disks, like basic disks, can be managed via the Disk Management MMC or with the diskpart.exe utility. Managing dynamic disks is a little more complicated than managing basic disks, as you have more options from which to choose. This section discusses converting your disks from basic to dynamic and creating the various types of volumes supported in Windows Server 2003.

Converting to Dynamic Disk Status

By default, all disks are configured as basic disks. It is up to you to convert them to dynamic if you choose to do so. Remember to carefully assess your situation and determine whether you need the features of dynamic disks (and make sure your system is one of those that can use dynamic disks) before performing the conversion. If you convert a disk that is currently being accessed (such as the boot or system disks) then you must reboot in order to convert. Otherwise, you can convert without rebooting. Converting to dynamic does not erase any data.

Converting your system disk to a dynamic disk

1. Right-click the disk that you want to upgrade to dynamic.

2. Select **Convert to Dynamic Disk** from the pop-up menu, as shown in Figure 5.36. This will give you the **Convert to Dynamic Disk** selection window, as shown in Figure 5.37.

Figure 5.36 Converting to Dynamic Disk

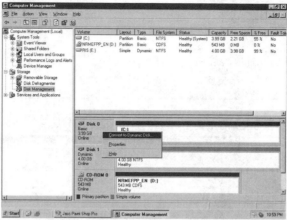

Figure 5.37 Selecting the Disk to Convert

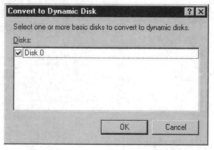

3. The disk you want to upgrade should be checked by default. If not, check its check box and click **OK** to continue.

4. You are next shown a summary screen (Figure 5.38) that indicates which disk(s) will be converted. Click **Convert** to continue.

Figure 5.38 Reviewing Disks to be Converted

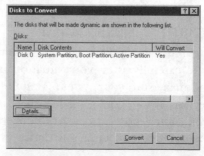

5. Windows will warn you that you are about to convert to dynamic. Click **Yes** on the warning screen (shown in Figure 5.39) to continue.

6. You are next warned that file systems currently in use on the disk will be dismounted during the upgrade (Figure 5.40). This is your last chance to cancel the conversion operation. If you are sure that you want to convert to dynamic, click **Yes** to dismount the file system.

7. Click **OK** on the confirmation window (shown in Figure 5.41) to reboot your PC. The disk(s) you selected will be upgraded when the computer is rebooted.

Figure 5.39 Confirming the Conversion

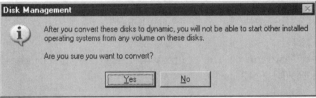

Figure 5.40 Dismounting Disk to be Converted

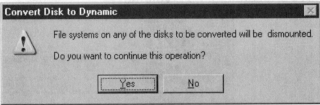

Figure 5.41 Completing the ConversionCreating and Using Dynamic Volumes

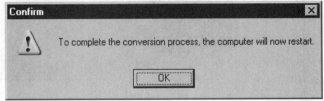

After you have converted your disk to dynamic, you can create volumes. Creating volumes is similar to creating partitions, except that there are some additional steps because, unlike partitions, volumes can span multiple disks. The type of volume you create depends on a variety of factors, such as the following:

- How many disks do you have in your machine?
- Do you want fault tolerance?
- Do you want to increase read or write performance?
- What is being stored (or will be stored) on the volume (e.g., database, system partition, print spooler, etc.)?

Creating and Using Simple Volumes

Simple volumes are the default volume type on a dynamic disk. Use simple volumes in the following situations:

- You only have one disk in a machine.
- You are not concerned with fault tolerance.
- You want the ability to dynamically extend the space used on a volume.

Use the following steps to create a simple volume

1. Right-click the unallocated space on the disk on which you want to create a simple volume.

2. Click **New Volume** on the context menu. This will start the **New Volume Wizard**, shown in Figure 5.42.

3. Click **Next** to continue.

Figure 5.42 Creating Simple Volumes

4. On the **Select Volume Type** window (Figure 5.43), select **Simple**.

5. Click **Next** to continue.

Figure 5.43 Selecting Volume Type

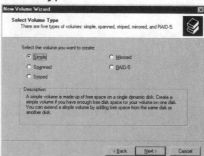

6. You will next be prompted to select the disk to use for the simple volume, as shown in Figure 5.44. The correct disk should already be selected. If not, select it.

7. Select the amount of space to be used for the simple volume and click **Next** to continue.

Figure 5.44 Selecting Disks to be Used in a Simple Volume

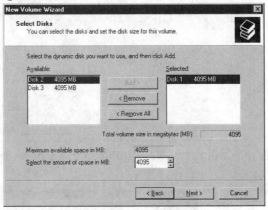

8. Next you need to identify your new volume. Select a drive letter or choose to mount the new volume to an NTFS folder. For this example, we assign the new volume the drive letter **D**, as shown in Figure 5.45

Figure 5.45 Assigning a Drive Letter or Path

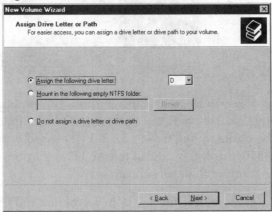

9. Next, you can format your new volume. You can format the volume as FAT, FAT32, or NTFS, or you can choose not to format the volume now. For this example, choose **NTFS,** as shown in Figure 5.46, and click **Next** to continue.

10. You will now see the **Completing the New Volume Wizard** window, as shown in Figure 5.47. Read over the summary to verify that you made the correct selections and click **Finish** to complete the process.

Figure 5.46 Formatting Your New Volume

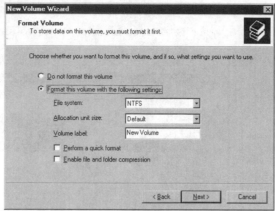

Figure 5.47 Finishing the New Volume WizardCreating and Using Spanned Volumes

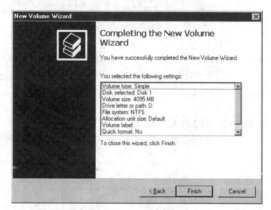

Spanned volumes enable you to group different disks of the same or different sizes and access them as if they were one disk. However, only one disk in the volume is written to at a time. Spanned volumes can be created using two to 32 disks. Spanned volumes provide 100 percent drive utilization (minus the 1MB per disk overhead for the LDM partition).

Use spanned volumes in the following situations:

- You want to access multiple disks as a single volume and you are not concerned about fault tolerance or increased read/write performance.

- Your disks are different sizes and you want to achieve 100 percent drive utilization with a single volume.

- You have a simple volume that is almost full and you need to expand it across multiple disks.

Create a spanned volume

1. Right-click the unallocated space on the disk on which you want to create a spanned volume.

2. Click **New Volume** on the context menu. This will start the **New Volume Wizard**, as shown in Figure 5.48.

3. Click **Next** to continue.

Figure 5.48 Creating a Spanned Volume

4. In the **Select Volume Type** window (Figure 5.49), select **Spanned**.

5. Click **Next** to continue.

Figure 5.49 Selecting the Volume Type to be Created

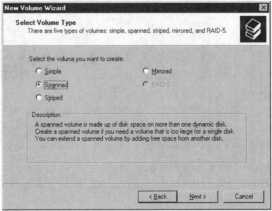

6. You will next be prompted to select the disks to use for the spanned volume, as shown in Figure 5.50. Select the disks you want to use.

7. Select the amount of space to be used for simple volume and click **Next** to continue.

Figure 5.50 Selecting Disks to be Used in Spanned Volume

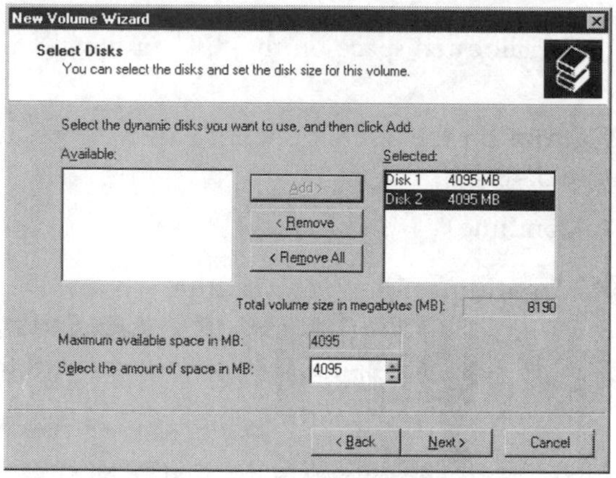

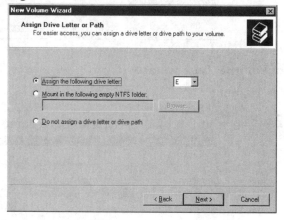

8. Next you need to identify your new spanned volume. Select a drive letter or choose to mount the new volume to an NTFS folder. For this example, we assign the new volume the drive letter **D**, as shown in Figure 5.51.

Figure 5.51 Assigning a Drive Letter or Path

9. Next you can format your new spanned volume. You can format the volume as FAT, FAT32, or NTFS, or you can choose not to format the volume at this time. For this example, choose **NTFS,** as shown in Figure 5.52, and then click **Next** to continue.

10. You will next see the **Completing the New Volume Wizard** window, as shown in Figure 5.53. Read over the summary to verify that you made the correct selections and click **Finish** to complete the process.

Figure 5.52 Formatting the New Spanned Volume

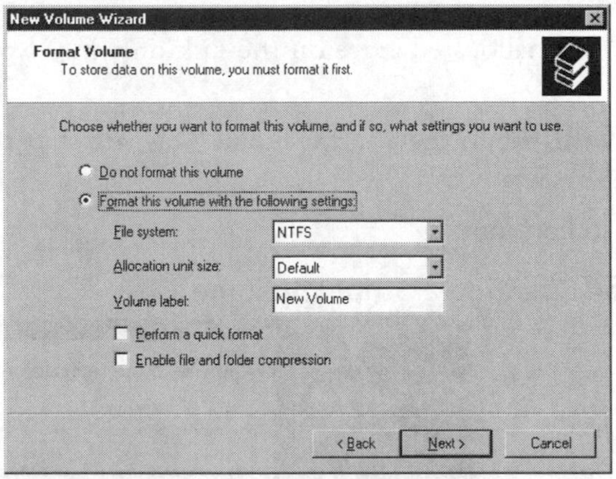

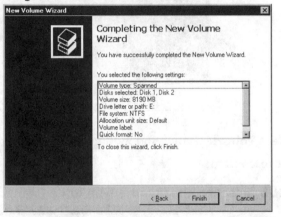

Figure 5.53 Completing the New Volume Wizard

Creating and Using Striped Volumes

Striped volumes require that you use an equal amount of unallocated space on each of the disks that is part of the volume. Ideally, your disks will all be the same size and all space on each will be unallocated. If not, some of the space will be wasted when you create the volume.

Striped volumes increase both read and write performance when accessing the volume by utilizing all the disks at one time. Unlike spanned volumes, striped volumes cannot be extended. Striped volumes can be created using two to 32 disks.

Use stripped volumes in the following situations:

- The primary disk operation will be reading information from a large database such as SQL or Exchange.

- The volume will be used to spool large print jobs.

- You are not concerned with fault tolerance.

- You plan to collect external data on the disk at very fast transfer rates.

Creating a striped volume

1. Right-click the unallocated space on the disk on which you want to create a striped volume.

2. Click **New Volume** on the context menu. This will start the **New Volume Wizard**, as shown in Figure 5.54.

3. Click **Next** to continue.

Figure 5.54 Creating a Striped Volume

4. On the **Select Volume Type** window (Figure 5.55), select **Striped**.

5. Click **Next** to continue.

Figure 5.55 Selecting the Volume Type to be Created

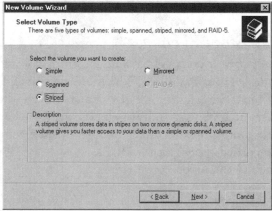

6. You will next be prompted to select the disk to use for the striped volume, as shown in Figure 5.56. Select the disks you want to use.

7. Select the amount of space to be used for the striped volume and click **Next** to continue.

Figure 5.56 Selecting Disks to be Used in Striped Volume

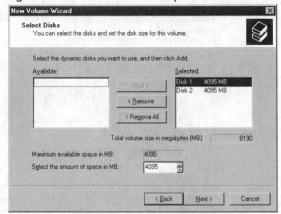

8. Next you need to identify your new striped volume. Select a drive letter or choose to mount the new volume to an NTFS folder. For this example, we assign the new volume the drive letter **E**, as shown in Figure 5.57.

Figure 5.57 Assigning a Drive Letter or Path

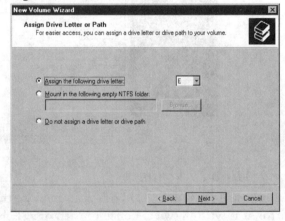

9. Next, you can format your new striped volume. You can format a striped volume as FAT, FAT32, or NTFS, or you can choose not to format the volume at this time. For this example, choose **NTFS**, as shown in Figure 5.58, and click **Next** to continue.

10. You will next see the **Completing the New Volume Wizard** window, as shown in Figure 5.59. Read the summary to verify that you made the correct selections and click **Finish** to complete the process.

Figure 5.58 Formatting the New Striped Volume

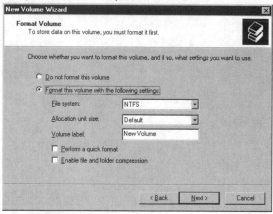

Figure 5.59 Ending the New Volume Wizard

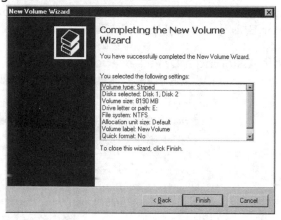

Creating and Using Mirrored Volumes

Mirrored volumes require exactly two disks and both disks must be the same size. When you write information to the mirror, it is written twice – once to each disk. This provides complete redundancy for your data. Should one disk fail, you can use the mirrored copy. Mirrored volumes provide only 50 percent disk utilization (the least cost efficient of all volume types) and cannot be extended. However, they provide excellent fault tolerance.

Use mirrored volumes in the following situations:

- You want to provide fault tolerance for the boot and/or system partition.

- You want an easy way to roll back failed operating system upgrades (break the mirror before the upgrade).

- You need fault tolerance, but you only have two disks.

- You want to be able to get the system up and running quickly after a disk failure.

Creating a mirrored volume

1. Right-click the simple volume you wish to mirror, as shown in Figure 5.60.

2. Choose **Add Mirror** from the context menu.

Figure 5.60 Creating a Mirrored Volume

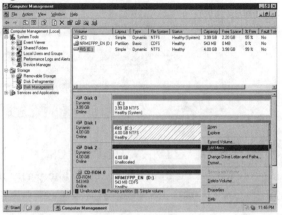

3. You are next prompted, as shown in Figure 5.61, to select a location to hold a mirror of the selected drive. Select the disk on which you want to create the mirror copy.

4. Click **Add Mirror** to continue. You will see your mirror being created, as shown in Figure 5.62.

After the mirror is created, both volumes that make up the two parts of the mirror will appear in the **Disk Management** console with the same drive letter.

Figure 5.61 Selecting a Location for the Mirror

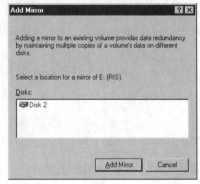

Figure 5.62 Synchronizing a Mirrored Volume

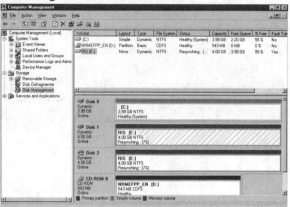

Creating and Using RAID-5 Volumes

RAID-5 volumes can be created using three to 32 disks. The parity information can be used to regenerate the missing data should one disk fail. If you lose more than one disk, however, all your data will be lost.

As with mirrored volumes, RAID-5 volumes cannot be extended. However, RAID-5 volumes offer more efficient disk utilization than mirrored volumes. You lose the storage space equivalent to one disk in the RAID-5 volume because it is used for parity information. For example, if you have five disks and you lose the storage space of one disk, you operate at 80 percent disk utilization. If you increase the number of disks in your RAID-5 volume, you will get even better disk utilization. For example, if you use 10 disks instead of five, you will operate at 90 percent utilization instead of 80 percent utilization. On the other hand, it takes longer to get your system back up and running after a disk failure with RAID-5, as opposed to mirrors, because you must go through the process of regenerating the data from parity.

Use RAID-5 volumes in the following situations:

- You need the boosted read performance of a striped volume, but you must have fault tolerance.

- You want fault tolerance with the most efficient level of disk utilization possible.

- You need fault tolerance, but you have too many disks to use a mirror.

Creating a RAID-5 volume

1. Right-click the unallocated space on the disk on which you want to create a RAID-5 volume.

2. Click **New Volume** on the context menu. This will start the **New Volume Wizard**, as shown in Figure 5.63.

3. Click **Next** to continue.

Figure 5.63 Using the New Volume Wizard to Create a RAID-5 Volume

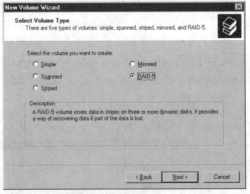

4. In the **Select Volume Type window** (Figure 5.64), select **RAID-5**.

5. Click **Next** to continue.

Figure 5.64 Selecting to Create a RAID-5 Volume

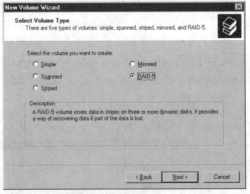

6. You will next be prompted to select the disks to use for the RAID-5 volume, as shown in Figure 5.65. Select the disks you want to use.

7. Select the amount of space to be used for the striped volume and click **Next** to continue.

Figure 5.65 Adding Disks to the RAID-5 Volume

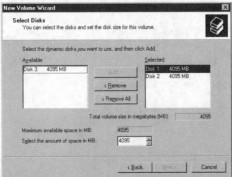

8. Next you need to identify your new RAID-5 volume. Select a drive letter or choose to mount the new volume to an NTFS folder. For this example, we assign the new volume the drive letter **D**, as shown in Figure 5.66.

Figure 5.66 Assigning a Drive Letter or Path

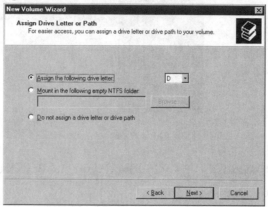

9. Next, you can format your new RAID-5 volume. You can format a RAID-5 volume as FAT, FAT32, or NTFS, or you can choose not to format the volume at this time. For this example, choose **NTFS**, as shown in Figure 5.67, and click **Next** to continue.

10. You will next see the **Completing the New Volume Wizard** window, as shown in Figure 5.68. Read the summary to verify that you made the correct selections and click **Finish** to complete the process.

Figure 5.67 Formatting the RAID-5 Volume

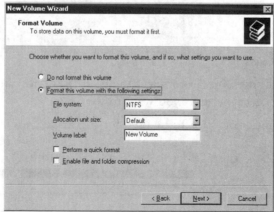

Figure 5.68 Finishing the New Volume Wizard

Optimizing Disk Performance

Optimizing disk performance is an important part of managing a server. Consider the disk-oriented tasks that take place on a typical day on the typical server. Users save data to their home directories. They send e-mail back and forth (which is saved in a database on the server). They print documents. They access shared files. All these tasks require good disk performance.

Two issues you will always run into when managing disks are disk fragmentation and insufficient disk space. Fragmentation problems are not as obvious as disk space problems; when you run out of disk space, you usually find out immediately. However, you may not notice that a disk is fragmented unless you take the time to check or you notice that performance has degraded. With Windows Server 2003, Microsoft provides ways to manage both of these concerns. The disk defragmentation utilities can ensure that your disk is performing at its peak and the disk quotas feature can ensure that you do not run out of disk space. In the following sections, we will discuss how to use these tools to keep your disks at optimum performance levels.

Defragmenting Volumes and Partitions

Defragmenting the disks on all your servers (especially file servers) can ensure optimal performance and enable you to get more use out of your disks. It is not something that you should do every day, but you definitely need to make it part of your server maintenance routine. Microsoft provides two tools for performing defragmentation. Both tools work with basic and dynamic disks that are formatted with the FAT, FAT32, or NTFS file systems. These tools are:

- Disk Defragmenter (graphical utility)
- Defrag.exe (command-line tool)

You will learn how to use each of these tools to defragment your disks.

Using the Graphical Defragmenter

You can access the graphical defragmenter in several different ways:

- Click **Start | All Programs | Accessories | System Tools | Disk Defragmenter**.

- Right-click **My Computer**, select **Manage**, and click **Disk Defragmenter** in the left console pane.

- Click **Start | All Programs | Administrative Tools | Computer Management** and click the **Disk Defragmenter** in the left console pane.

For our examples, we will access the Disk Defragmenter via Computer Management. Note that anyone can open the Disk Defragmenter tool, but only an administrator, or someone with an account that has been delegated the authority, can analyze or defragment a volume.

Using the Disk Defragmenter

1. Open **Computer Management** (click **Start | All Programs | Administrative Tools | Computer Management**).

2. Click **Disk Defragmenter** as shown in Figure 5.69.

3. Click the **Analyze** button. This will analyze your disks and give you a report of how defragmented they are, as shown in Figure 5.70.

Figure 5.69 Using Disk Defragmenter from the GUI

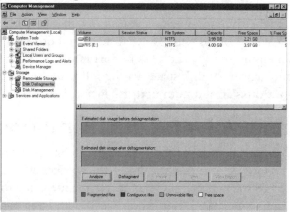

Figure 5.70 Analyzing Your Hard Disk for Defragmentation

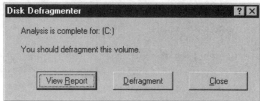

4. Click the **View Report** button to see the status of your disk. This will give you a report similar to the one shown in Figure 5.71.

Figure 5.71 Viewing the Analysis Report

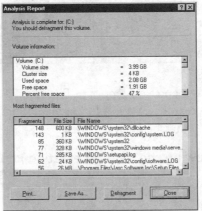

5. At this point, you can click **Close** if you do not want to defragment your disk. If you do want to defragment, click the **Defragment** button to start the process.

6. You will next see the screen shown in Figure 5.72. You can pause or stop the defragmentation process by clicking **Pause** or **Stop** on the **Action** menu. When the defragmentation process is complete, you will be given the option to view a defragmentation report, as shown in Figure 5.73. Click **View Report**.

Figure 5.72 Defragmenting Your Hard Disk

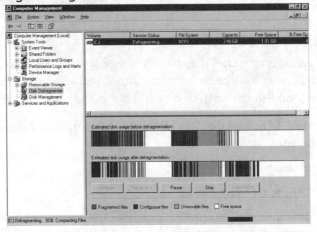

Figure 5.73 Completing Defragmentation

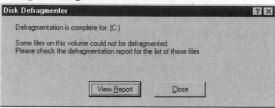

7. Compare the defragmentation report in Figure 5.74 with the analysis report in Figure 5.71. You should see a decrease in file fragmentation. You can print or save your report for later viewing. When finished, click **Close**.

Figure 5.74 Viewing the Defragmentation Report

Viewing the Analysis Report

You don't have to really understand the analysis report in order to defragment your disks. The software is smart enough to let you know whether or not you need to defrag. However, a lot of good information can be found in the analysis report. This includes the following:

- **Fragmented files and folders** Displays the paths and names of the most fragmented files on the volume.

- **Volume size**

- **Amount of free space available**

- **Average number of fragments per file** You can use the average number of fragments per file to gauge how fragmented the volume is. Table 5.3 explains the possible averages.

Table 5.3 Describing the Average Number of Fragments per File

Average Number of Fragments per File	Description
1.00	Most or all files are contiguous.
1.10	Around ten percent of the files are fragmented into two or more sections.
1.20	Around twenty percent of the files are fragmented into two or more sections.
1.30	Around thirty percent of the files are fragmented into two or more sections.
2.00	Most or all of the files are fragmented into two or more sections.

Understanding the Disk Defragmenter Interface

The Disk Defragmenter provides you with analysis reports and defragmentation reports to alert you to the fragmentation status of your disks. However, the graphical interface of the defragmenter tool also provides much of the same information if you know what to look for. The screenshot in Figure 5.75 was taken immediately after running the defragmentation utility. Let's analyze the display to determine the information that is available.

Notice that Disk Defragmenter runs in a standard MMC, which gives it a familiar feel, with the console tree in the left pane and the details pane on the right. On the right side, the pane is split into a top and a bottom section. The top section shows the volumes and partitions on the machine. The bottom section shows a graphical view of the fragmentation status of the selected volume. There are two bars in the bottom pane, which indicate the following:

- Estimated disk usage before defragmentation
- Estimated disk usage after defragmentation

By examining these bars, you can see the status of the disk before the defragmentation and the changes that have occurred afterward. These bars are obviously too small to list every cluster on the disk, but they do provide an accurate representation of how fragmented the volume is.

Table 5.4 explains the color codes used in these two bars. After running Disk Defragmenter, the goal is to see most of the red in the top bar replaced with blue.

Table 5.4 Understanding the Estimated Disk Usage Bars in Disk Defragmenter

Color	Description
Red	Most of the clusters are fragmented files.
Blue	Most of the clusters are contiguous files.
Green	Most of the clusters are files that cannot be moved from their current location. This could include paging files, or files used by the file system.
White	Most of the clusters are free space.

Figure 5.75 Viewing Your Disk After Defragmentation

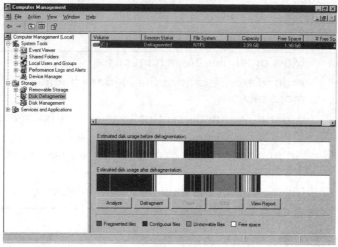

Using Defrag.exe

If you are comfortable with the Disk Defragmenter tool but prefer a character-based utility, you will feel right at home with *defrag.exe*, the command prompt equivalent of Disk Defragmenter. Defrag.exe does everything that Disk Defragmenter does and in addition, it supports scripting. You can use defrag.exe in a script to schedule analysis and defragmentation of your servers. Scripting is the primary reason to use defrag.exe instead of Disk Defragmenter. Table 5.5 explains the parameters for defrag.exe. Defrag.exe uses the following syntax:

```
defrag <volume> [-a] [-f] [-v] [-?]
   volume  drive letter or mount point (d: or d:\vol\mountpoint)
```

Table 5.5 Understanding Defrag.exe Parameters

Parameters	Description
Volume	The drive letter or mount point to be defragmented.
A	Analyzes the volume and displays an analysis summary indicating whether you should defragment the volume.
F	Forces defragmentation of the volume when low on free space.
V	Displays the complete analysis and defragmentation reports (not just a summary). When used with the /a switch, it displays only the analysis report. When used alone, it displays both the analysis and defragmentation reports.
?	Displays help.

Defragmentation Best Practices

As discussed, defragmenting your disks is a good thing. It speeds up access to your files and can make more free space available. However, for best results, here is a summary of the guidelines to follow when defragmenting your servers:

- Make sure that you have at least 15 percent of your volume's total space free. Disk Defragmenter needs to have an area to sort fragments while it is rearranging your volume. If you can't meet this requirement due to low disk space, you will only get a partial defragmentation.

- Always try to schedule your defragmentations during non-production hours. You don't want your users accessing files while the volume is being defragmented. This can cause two problems: users' performance will suffer because of the resources being consumed by Disk Defragmenter and your defragmentation will take longer.

- Always analyze before you defragment to make sure that you actually need to. You should analyze any time a large number of files are added to your server or after installing software on your server. Both of these actions tend to cause high levels of fragmentation.

Configuring and Monitoring Disk Quotas

The capability to set disk quotas is a feature that was on the "wish list" of Windows NT administrators for a long time. Users tend to find a way of consuming every bit (and byte) of space that you offer them. Third-party products provided for setting quotas with NT, and built-in support for disk quotas was first introduced in Windows 2000. Disk quota support has been carried over to Windows XP and Windows Server 2003. In the following sections, we discuss how to enable, configure, and monitor disk quotas.

Brief Overview of Disk Quotas

Disk quotas enable you to track and limit disk space usage on NTFS volumes. You can use disk quotas for two purposes:

- To audit how much space your users are using (enabling quotas without limiting disk space)
- To limit your users to a set amount of space (enabling quotas and setting limits on disk space)

Users are warned when they approach the specified limit. The administrator can set the level at which the warning occurs. After the limit is reached, a user can no longer save data to the volume without first deleting some files to create new space. You can also set the system to log an event to the event log when a user reaches either the warning level or the disk space limit.

Disk quota amounts are calculated based on file ownership. The size of the file is charged against its owner's limit. The only time this poses a problem is when users share single files. For example, if you have the correct permissions, you can write to a file that someone else owns and it would count against the other user's limit.

Disk quotas are set at the volume level only. You cannot create different quotas for individual folders within a volume. If you need to set different quotas for the same users on different folders, you can put those folders on separate volumes or purchase third-party software that allows for more granular setting of quotas. Likewise, you cannot set quotas at the physical disk level. If a disk has three volumes on it, each volume is managed separately. You must have administrative rights to assign quotas.

Use disk quotas in the following situations:

- You have limited shared storage available on public servers and need to ensure that the disks don't become full.

- You want to keep a log of how much disk space is being consumed by each user.

Enabling and Configuring Disk Quotas

You can enable disk quotas by accessing the **Properties** sheet for a volume and using the **Quota** tab. If you do not see a Quota tab on the Properties sheet, either you do not have administrative rights on the machine or the volume is formatted with FAT or FAT32. Remember that disk quotas can only be configured on NTFS volumes.

The Quota tab (Figure 5.76) contains valuable information and you should be familiar with all the options on this tab. The first thing you see on the Quota tab is the "stop light." It indicates the status of disk quotas on the volume:

- When the light is red, disk quotas are disabled.

- When the light is yellow, the system is rebuilding disk quota information.

- When the light is green, disk quotas are enabled and active.

When you select the check box next to **Enable quota management**, the light goes from red to yellow to green. However, the light may appear to go straight to green. This just means that the quota information was built very quickly and didn't register on the light.

After you enable disk quotas, you must configure how they will be used. By default, users are not denied disk space or warned about the amount of disk space they are using. This is the proper setting if you are only using disk quotas to track how much space each user is using, but if you want to limit the amount of space available to users, you must further configure the quotas feature. This is where the **Deny disk space to users exceeding quota limit** check box comes into play. When you check this checkbox, Windows will deny additional disk space to anyone who exceeds his or her limit.

You can either set limits for users individually by using the **Quota Entries** button or you can configure a default limit that will apply to everyone. You can also import quota settings from another volume. This is useful if you want to set the quotas identically on a number of different volumes.

There are two settings to configure for each user (or for all users as the default): a limit level and a warning level:

- Next to **Limit disk space to,** there are two boxes. The first box is a text field into which you can type a number. The second box is a drop-down box that contains a disk measurement unit (KB, MB, GB, TB, PB, EB). By entering a number in the first box and choosing a measurement from the second box, you can restrict each user to a disk space limit ranging from 1KB to 6 EB. The default limit is 1KB.

■ Directly under the limits boxes are identical **Set warning level to** boxes. Quota warnings are configured in the same ways as quota limits. You should set the warning level to a smaller number than the disk limit so that users will know they are approaching their limits before reaching them.

Table 5.6 explains the different disk measurement options available for setting limits and warnings.

Table 5.6 Understanding Disk Measurements

Measurement	Description
KB	KB stands for kilobyte. One kilobyte equals one thousand bytes (1,024 bytes in decimal).
MB	MB stands for megabyte. One megabyte equals one million bytes (1,048,576 bytes in decimal).
GB	GB stands for gigabit. One gigabit equals one billion bytes (1,073,741,824 bytes in decimal).
TB	TB stands for terabyte. One terabyte equals one thousand billion bytes (1,099,511,627,776 bytes in decimal—that is a thousand gigabytes).
PB	PB stands for petabyte. One petabyte equals one thousand terabytes (1,125,899,906,842,624 bytes in decimal).
EB	EB stands for exabyte. One exabyte equals one quintillion bytes (a billion gigabytes—1,152,921,504,606,846,976 bytes in decimal).

Finally, you can configure the logging options. Under **Select the quota logging options for this volume** you have two options:

■ Log event when a user exceeds their quota limit
■ Log event when a user exceeds their warning level

Both options are disabled by default and either or both can be enabled by checking the corresponding check box(es). Both settings log events to the system log of the event viewer. Logging options are set only on a per-volume basis; there is no setting for logging on an individual user's Quota Settings page.

Enabling disk quotas and setting quota limits

1. In Windows Explorer or **My Computer**, right-click the volume on which you want to set quotas and select **Properties** from the context menu. In this example, we enable quotas on the C drive. Note that to manage quotas on a remote computer, you'll need to first map a network drive for the remote volume on which you want to set or manage quotas.

2. Click the **Quota** tab, as shown in Figure 5.76.

3. Check the check box next to "**Enable quota management**" to enable disk quotas for the C drive.

4. Check the check box next to "**Deny disk space to users exceeding quota limit**" to enforce limits.

5. Click the **Quota Entries** button to open the **Quota Entries** console, as shown in Figure 5.77.

Figure 5.76 Enabling Disk Quotas

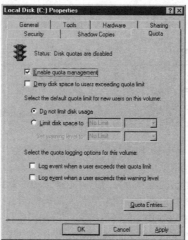

Figure 5.77 Viewing Quota Entries

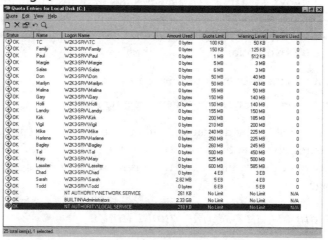

6. Click the **Quota** menu bar.

7. Select **New Quota Entry** from the menu.

8. You are prompted to choose the users for which you want to add quotas, as shown in Figure 5.78. Type the user's name in the box and click **Check Name** to verify that the user exists in the account database.

9. If the name is verified, click **OK** to continue. You next have to customize the quota entry for the user, as shown in Figure 5.79.

Figure 5.78 Choosing Users to Restrict

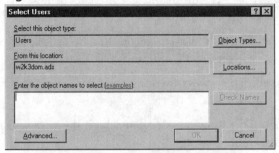

Figure 5.79 Configuring Limits and Warnings

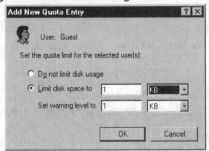

10. Select "**Limit disk space to**" and enter the amount of space you wish to allow the user to use on the volume. Select a unit of measurement.

11. Set the warning level for your user in the same way.

12. Click **OK** to save the settings and add the user to the Quota Entries list.

Monitoring Disk Quotas

Now that you know how to enable disk quotas, we will discuss how to analyze the quota settings and monitor disk usage. Disk quota settings are accessed and disk usage is monitored via the Quota Entries console, as previously shown in Figure 5.77.

The Quota Entries console displays seven items in regard to each user. You can sort by the columns by clicking the corresponding section of the column title bar or by using the View menu (**View | Arrange Items | by…**). For example, if you want to sort by the amount of disk spaced used, click on the **Amount Used** bar. This will arrange the user accounts in order of least to greatest space used. Clicking the same column header again will rearrange the accounts in the opposite order (greatest to least).

- **Status** This indicates how well the user is complying with the quota limit. There are three possible settings: **OK**, **Warning**, or **Above Limit**. A status of **OK** indicates that the user hasn't reached the warning or limit level yet. **Warning** indicates that the user has reached the warning level, but not the limit level. **Above Limit** indicates that the user has passed both the warning and limit levels. Sorting by status makes it easy to find all users that have exceeded their limits.

- **Name** This is the user's full name as it appears in Local Users and Groups or Active Directory Users and Computers.

- **Logon Name** This is the user's account name as it appears in Local Users and Groups or Active Directory Users and Computers.

- **Amount Used** This shows the total amount of disk space currently being used by the user.

- **Quota Limit** This shows the level at which the user will no longer be allowed to save data to this volume.

- **Warning Level** This shows the level at which the user will be warned when saving data to this volume.

- **Percent Used** This displays the percentage of allocated space that has been used by the user. Sorting by **Percent Used** is a good way to discover which users may run out of space soon.

Figure 5.80 Resolving SIDs to Logon Names

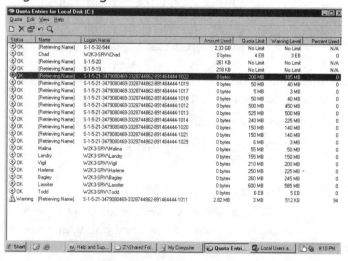

Exporting and Importing Quota Settings

If you have multiple volumes that contain users' data then you will probably want to apply the same quota settings to all volumes. Also, if you migrate your users' data from one volume to another, then you need an easy way to reapply all the disk quotas.

There are a few different ways to copy disk quotas from one volume to another. If you open the Quota Entries window (as shown in Figure 5.81) for both volumes, you can drag and drop quota limits between the two windows. You can also export all quota settings to a file and import them to another volume. You can use the following steps to export quota settings and import quota settings.

Export quota settings

1. Open **My Computer**.
2. Right-click the **volume** you want to manage and choose **Properties** from the pop-up menu.
3. Click the **Quota** tab.
4. Click the **Quota Entries** button. This will give you a window similar to Figure 5.81.
5. Click the **Quota menu bar** and choose **Export** from the drop-down list. You will now be asked where to save the quota settings, as shown in Figure 5.82.
6. Type in a **name** and click the **Save** button to finish the export.

Figure 5.81 Choosing to Export Quota Settings

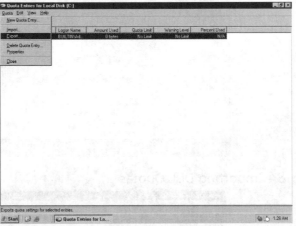

Figure 5.82 Exporting Quota Settings

Import quota settings

The steps for importing quota settings are very similar to the steps for exporting quota settings.

1. Open **My Computer**.

2. Right-click the **volume** you want to manage and choose **Properties** from the pop-up menu.

3. Click the **Quota** tab.

4. Click the **Quota Entries** button. This will give you a window similar to Figure 5.83.

5. Click the **Quota menu bar** and choose **Import** from the drop-down list. You will now be asked which quota settings file to import, as shown in Figure 5.84.

6. Navigate to the quota settings file and click **Open** to import the settings.

Figure 5.83 Choosing to Import Disk Quotas

Figure 5.84 Importing Disk Quotas

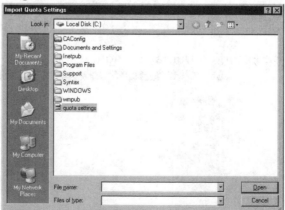

Disk Quota Best Practices

Disk quotas are a powerful feature that give Windows Server 2003 administrators flexible control over disk usage. However, using them incorrectly can be disastrous. Don't let this keep you from using disk quotas – just learn to use them intelligently. Here are few guidelines that will ensure that enabling disk quotas makes your job as an administrator easier, not more difficult:

- Set default limits so that all users are restricted in the amount of space they can use by default. Always make your default settings as restrictive as possible, while still providing users with enough space to do their work. It is easier to give users more space if needed than to take space away. Remember that this is only a default setting. It is not a mandatory setting for all your users; it only applies to those user accounts that do not have specific individual settings configured.

- Use reasonable quota limits. Don't just take the amount of space available and divide it equally among your users. Sit down and calculate a fair limit, based on user needs. Not everyone needs the same amount of disk space. Power users may need more than standard users. Those who work with and save large graphic or video files need more space than those who work primarily with plain text files.

- Be realistic in setting the quotas and stick to them unless/until there is a real need to change them. If you set the default limit at 50MB when you know most users are using 200MB, you are setting yourself up for trouble. Try not to get into the habit of setting quotas excessively low and then increasing them when users complain. It is better to give users the right amount of space up front, and be less flexible about increasing the amount. If users know they can easily get their allocations increased by complaining, they will be less motivated to properly manage their files.

- Delete quota entries for users who no longer need to store files on the volume. Delete or move their files to another volume, to free space for those who need to store data on the volume.

- When calculating the amount of disk space available for allocating quotas, remember to take into account NTFS overhead. Files can contain up to 64KB of metadata (information about the file) that is not counted against a user's quota, but does take up space on the disk.

Using Fsutil to Manage Disk Quotas

If you prefer using a command-line tool instead of the graphical interface, you can perform many of the tasks involved in managing disk quotas with the command-line utility **fsutil.exe**. Use the command **fsutil quota** with one of the following parameters to perform quota-related tasks:

- Fsutil quota disable <volumepathname> To disable quotas on the volume.

- **Fsutil quota enforce <volumepathname >** To enable quota enforcement on the volume.

- **Fsutil quota modify <volumepathname>** To create a new quota or change an existing one.

- **Fsutil quota query <volumepathname>** To list existing quota entries.

- **Fsutil quota track <volumepathname>** To track disk usage on the volume.

- **Fsutil quota violations** To display detected quota violations.

The **fsutil** commands can be used in a script to automate quota tasks (for example, to set a specified quota limit each time you add a new user).

Implementing RAID Solutions

There are several options for setting up a RAID environment. You can use either software-based RAID or hardware-based RAID. Software-based RAID is more cost effective because you don't have to purchase anything extra, but it works only in certain situations and performance is not as good. You cannot easily change from one RAID type to another. If you want to change you must do the following:

1. Back up your data.

2. Erase your existing RAID configuration.

3. Create a new RAID configuration.

4. Restore your data from backup.

This section covers the differences between hardware and software RAID and when it is best to use for a given environment.

Understanding Windows Server 2003 RAID

Windows Server 2003 RAID is software-based RAID. With software-based RAID, all the physical disks are presented to the operating system as they are and the operating system manages them in a RAID configuration. The benefit is that software-based RAID is built into the operating system. The drawback is that the operating system incurs the entire overhead for maintaining the RAID volume. Additionally, there are limitations that apply to software-based RAID that do not apply to hardware-based RAID. You do not have as many RAID options with software-based RAID. Windows Server 2003 supports only three levels of RAID: RAID 0, RAID 1, and RAID 5. In the next sections, we discuss each in more detail.

RAID Level 0

RAID level 0 utilizes disk striping. A RAID level 0 volume in Windows Server 2003 is called a striped volume. This version of RAID does not provide any fault tolerance. Level 0 can be implemented as either a software or hardware solution and is supported by all controllers. Because the operating system must be loaded before the striped volume is initialized and made available, a level 0 array cannot be used for the boot or system partitions. RAID level 0 should be used when you are trying to get maximum performance from your drives. Level 0 is best for data that is not mission-critical or that is backed up regularly. It is good for audio/video streaming, gaming and other applications where performance is important. Windows Server 2003's RAID level 0 works with a minimum of two disks and up to a maximum of 32 disks.

RAID Level 1

RAID level 1 utilizes disk mirroring. A RAID level 1 volume in Windows Server 2003 is called a mirrored volume, and consists of two identical disks. This version of RAID does provide fault tolerance and is the only one of Windows Server 2003's software-based RAID levels that can be used for the boot and system partitions. Level 1 can be implemented as either a software or hardware RAID solution. RAID level 1 should be used when you want to provide fault tolerance for the boot and/or system partitions or if you need fault tolerance and have only two disks available. Level 1 is the most expensive form of Windows Server 2003 RAID because only 50% of the disk space that must be purchased is used for data.

RAID Level 5

RAID level 5 utilizes disk striping with parity. A RAID level 5 volume in Windows Server 2003 is called a RAID-5 volume. As with disk striping, a RAID-5 volume cannot be used for the boot or system partition because the operating system must be loaded first to initialize the volume and make it available. RAID-5 volumes require a minimum of three disks and work with up to 32 disks. You should use RAID level 5 when you need fault tolerance with better performance and drive utilization than RAID level 1 can provide. RAID 5 is one of the most popular RAID implementations. However, software RAID 5 is considerably slower than its hardware counterpart, because of the overhead involved in calculating the parity information. It is better for read-intensive applications as opposed to write-intensive ones.

Hardware RAID

As the name implies, hardware-based RAID uses special hardware to create RAID volumes. A RAID controller is added to your server. The controller handles the overhead of managing the RAID volumes, and this improves performance by removing the processing burden from the operating system. This also removes many of the restrictions imposed by software-based RAID. Because the RAID controller presents the RAID volume to the OS as one disk, you can use hardware-based RAID 0 and RAID 5 volumes for the boot and system partitions. Hardware-based RAID provides you with many more RAID levels to choose from. You should refer to the hardware manufacturer's specification to determine the type of RAID supported and its compatibility with Windows Server 2003. The only real drawback to hardware-based RAID is the price. Server-grade RAID controllers typically cost $750 and up. This can add up quickly when you have a large number of servers.

RAID Best Practices

After you have made the decision to use a RAID volume, you need to determine which solution best fits your needs. Will it be hardware RAID or software RAID? Disk striping or disk mirroring? How should you set it up? There are no hard, fast rules, only recommendations, but the following provide some general guidelines to follow when setting up your RAID volumes:

- Using Hardware RAID

    - Use hardware RAID whenever possible because it offers the best performance.

    - Try to use identical hardware for all your servers. This makes it easier to recover if you have a disaster.

    - Always keep spare disks on hand. When you lose one drive (with most RAID levels), you no longer have any fault tolerance. You need to be able to replace failed hardware as quickly as possible. (This also applies to software RAID).

    - Keep RAID controllers updated with the current firmware revision.

    - Always back up your data before updating the firmware on RAID controllers.

- Using Software RAID

    - Use mirrored volumes for the boot and system partitions.

    - Use RAID-5 volumes for database disks (e.g., Exchange and SQL servers).

    - Use striped volumes on database servers' disks that contain transaction logs (e.g., Exchange and SQL servers).

    - Use striped volumes for disks that are used for printer spooling.

Understanding and Using Remote Storage

Windows Server 2003's Remote Storage provides fast access to data stored on disks and archival capabilities for data that isn't frequently used, and best of all, it handles switching between the two. It automates the archival process and makes accessing archived data easy for the end user. With Remote Storage the server backs up seldom-used files for you automatically, and then automatically restores them when you attempt to access them.

What is Remote Storage?

Remote Storage provides a means of extending the disk space on your servers without having to buy more hard disks. Instead, you use a tape or a magneto-optical (MO) disk library to archive less-frequently used files. It costs significantly less per megabyte to buy a library full of tapes compared to equivalent storage space on hard disks.

After it is set up, Remote Storage runs on autopilot. You tell Remote Storage which volume(s) to manage and you specify how much free space you want to remain available on your managed volume; when the amount of free space drops below that level, Remote Storage kicks in and moves enough files to the media library to bring the disk back within your predefined parameters. A *managed volume* refers to a disk volume in Windows whose files are monitored and managed by Remote Storage.

One big advantage of Remote Storage is that all the files on the server look the same to the end user. When a user needs to open a file, he simply double-clicks it. If the file has not yet been moved to tape, it is opened immediately. If the file has been moved to tape, Remote Storage retrieves it from storage and puts a copy on the local disk (a cached copy). Users might notice a delay while this takes place, but they do not have to take any extra steps to retrieve the file. After the file is cached, it will be automatically opened for the user.

Storage Levels

Remote storage has two defined storage levels. The levels exist in a hierarchical structure:

- Local storage is the top level. It contains the NTFS disks of the computer that is running Remote Storage.

- Remote storage is the bottom level. This is the library that is connected to the server running Remote Storage.

Remote Storage keeps as much information as possible in the top level for faster access. Only when this level is reaching its storage limit is the data moved to the bottom level.

Relationship of Remote Storage and Removable Storage

Removable Storage is a feature of Windows Server 2003 that enables multiple programs to share the same storage media. It organizes all your available media into separate *media pools*. Microsoft defines a media pool as a logical collection of removable media that share the same management policies. Applications use media pools to control access to specific media within the library. Removable Storage requires that all data-management programs run on the computer connected to the library.

In other words, Removable Storage provides a standard way for applications to access a media library. By having all applications access the library through Remote Storage, Microsoft has provided a level of compatibility between applications, including Remote Storage. Remote Storage uses Removable Storage to access the media stored in the library.

Media Pools

Media pools contain either media or other media pools. Using the capability to nest media pools inside each other enables you to create a hierarchical media pool structure for Removable Storage. You can group media pools together and manage them as a single unit. Media pools can span multiple libraries. There are two main types of media pools: system media pools and application media pools.

System media pools hold media not currently being used by an application. Removable Storage creates one of each of the following system media pools (as shown in Figure 5.85) for each media type in your system:

- **Free media pools** These pools hold media not currently in use by applications. This media is readily available for use.

- **Unrecognized media pools** Blank media and media not recognized by Removable Storage go into the unrecognized media pool and are unusable until they are moved into a free media pool.

- **Import media pools** These pools are recognized by Removable Storage, but they have not been used by Remote Storage before. After they have been catalogued they can be used.

Application media pools contain media created and controlled by applications. For example, Backup and Remote Storage use application media pools for storage. Application media pools dictate which media can be accessed by any given application. An application can use more multiple media pools, and more than one application can use a single media pool.

Figure 5.85 Understanding How Media Pools Work Together

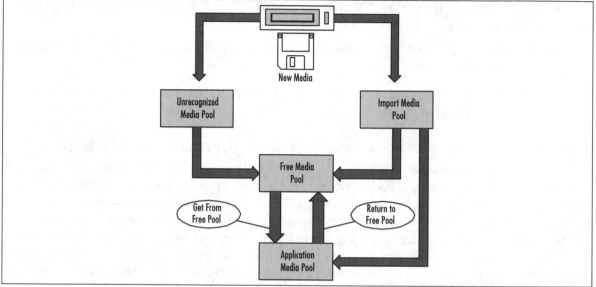

Setting Up Remote Storage

Remote Storage is not installed by default. You add it via the **Add or Remove Programs** applet in Control Panel. Before starting the installation, you must verify that enough tapes or disks have been moved to a free media pool in Removable Storage to hold all the files you wish to move to Remote Storage and that the local disks being managed are running Windows 2000's or Windows Server 2003's versions of NTFS (NTFS version 5). If you want compression and indexing on local disks, enable these before starting setup. You must be logged on with administrative rights to install Remote Storage. You cannot install Remote Storage into a clustered environment. Remote Storage will not fail over. Also, Remote Storage will not work with shared cluster disks but it will work with local disks that are not shared.

Use the following steps to install and configure Remote Storage.

Installing Remote Storage

1. Open Control Panel by clicking **Start | Control Panel**. This will display a screen similar to that shown in Figure 5.86.

2. Double-click **Add or Remove Programs**. This will display the screen shown in Figure 5.87.

Figure 5.86 Opening Control Panel

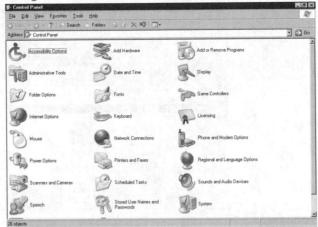

Figure 5.87 Using Add or Remove Programs

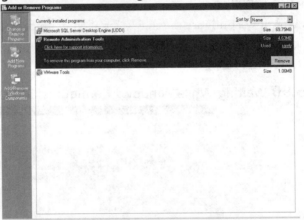

3. From the **Add or Remove Programs** window, click **Add/Remove Windows Components.** You should see a "Please wait…" message, as shown in Figure 5.88

4. You will next be presented with the **Windows Components Wizard,** as shown in Figure 5.89.

Figure 5.88 Waiting on Windows Setup

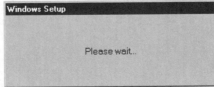

Figure 5.89 Adding Windows Components

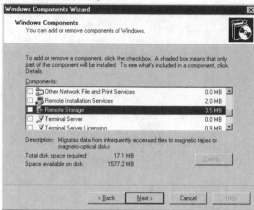

5. Scroll down and click the check box next to **Remote Storage**.

6. Click **Next** to continue.

7. Windows will now configure the newly installed components, as shown in Figure 5.90.

8. Next you will see the **Completing the Windows Components Wizard**, as shown in Figure 5.91. Click **Finish** to close the wizard.

Figure 5.90 Waiting While Windows Configures Components

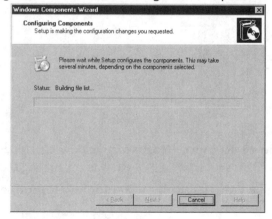

Figure 5.91 Completing the Components Wizard

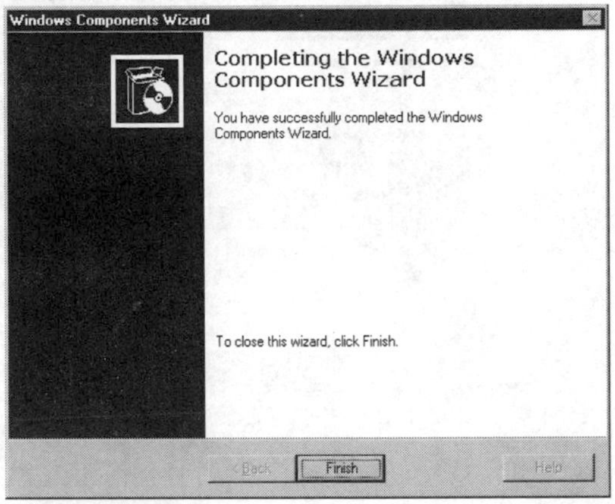

![Windows Components Wizard showing Completing the Windows Components Wizard]

Configuring Remote Storage

1. Open the Remote Storage MMC by clicking **Start | All Programs | Administrative Tools | Remote Storage**.

2. Because this is the first time you have opened the Remote Storage MMC, the Remote Storage Setup Wizard will automatically start, as shown in Figure 5.92. Click **Next** to continue.

Figure 5.92 Running the Remote Storage Setup Wizard

3. You will next be asked which volumes you want Remote Storage to manage, as shown in Figure 5.93. For this example, we select the **C** drive. Select the disk(s) that you want to manage and click **Next** to continue.

Figure 5.93 Selecting the Volumes to be Managed

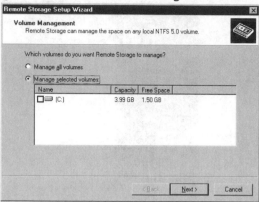

4. Set the criteria for managing free space on the volume with the **Volume Settings** dialog box shown in Figure 5.94. Click **Next** to continue.

5. You will next be asked to choose which media type to use, as shown in Figure 5.95. For this example, select **Removable media** and click **Next** to continue.

Figure 5.94 Managing Free Space on Your Volumes

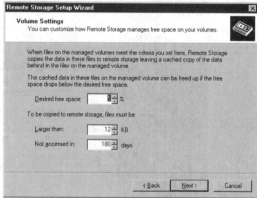

Figure 5.95 Selecting a Media Type

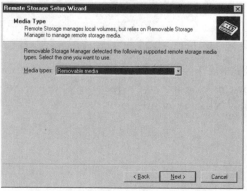

6. The last item to configure is the schedule for copying files, as shown in Figure 5.96. To accept the defaults, click **Next** and skip to step 9. To customize the schedule, click the **Change Schedule** button. This will display the **Schedule** window shown in Figure 5.97.

7. Set the schedule to copy files at a time that is least busy in your environment and click **OK**.

8. You will be returned to the screen shown in Figure 5.96. Click **Next** to continue.

9. On the **Completing the Remote Storage Setup Wizard** screen (5.98), review the settings to make sure they are correct, and then click **Finish** to complete the configuration of Remote Storage.

Figure 5.96 Verifying the Schedule for Copying Files

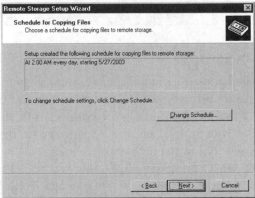

Figure 5.97 Customizing the Schedule for Copying Files

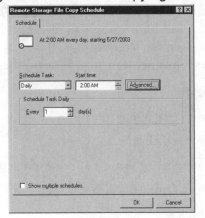

Figure 5.98 Completing the Remote Storage Setup Wizard

Using Remote Storage

Now that you have installed and configured Remote Storage, you need to know how to administer it. Like Microsoft's other administrative tools, Remote Storage is managed through an MMC snap-in. The Remote Storage MMC has two panes: the console pane on the left is used to navigate the various components of Remote Storage and the details pane on the right displays specifics of whichever component is selected in the left console pane.

The Remote Storage MMC (see Figure 5.99) that is accessed from the **Administrative Tools** menu also contains the snap-ins for Removable Storage and Event Viewer. However, Remote Storage itself has only two containers to manage: the **Managed Volumes** container and the **Media** container. We previously discussed storage levels within Remote Storage. We said the top level was for local storage and the bottom level was for remote storage. The **Managed Volumes** container is the top level of storage and is used for managing local storage. The **Media** container is the bottom level and is used for managing remote storage.

The **Managed Volumes** container is used to perform the following tasks:

- Set the desired free space.
- Specify file-selection criteria and rules.
- Change the file-copy schedule.
- Set the maximum number of drives to access simultaneously.
- Set the runaway recall limit.
- Validate files.
- Discontinue volume management.
- Modify files on managed volumes.

The **Media** container is used to perform the following tasks:

- Create media copies.
- Synchronize media copies.
- Recreate the media master.

Figure 5.99 Using the Remote Storage MMC

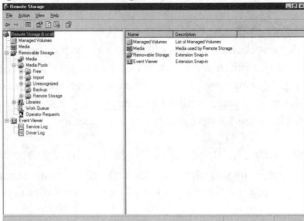

Setting the Desired Free Space

You can configure how much free space you want available on your managed volume. If the volume falls below your specified threshold, then Remote Storage deletes cached files until the volume is back within acceptable limits. You can also tell Remote Storage to delete all cached files from the volume to create a large amount of available free space.

Specifying File-Selection Criteria and Rules

You tell Remote Storage which files to manage on your volume. You set criteria that must be met in order for the file to be copied to remote storage. After the criteria have been met, the files are copied. Minimum files size and elapsed time since last use are the common criteria used by Remote Storage.

In addition to using criteria to control which files get copied to Remote Storage, you can also create rules. There are two types of rules, inclusion and exclusion. Inclusion rules control which files are copied to Remote Storage and exclusion rules control which files are not copied to Remote Storage. Rules are processed in order and the first rule that matches is applied. Change the order of your rules to set their priority.

Remote Storage has a predefined list of rules available for use. You cannot modify these rules or change their order. You can create your own rules and order them however you see fit. By default, all system, hidden, encrypted, extended attribute, and sparse files are excluded from the file rule list as these files cannot be copied to remote storage.

Both types of rules are built on the same options:

- A specified folder, including subfolders
- A specified folder, excluding subfolders
- File name extension
- File name

Changing the File-Copy Schedule

The file copy schedule tells Remote Storage when to copy files from the managed volume to the library. This is set during the initial setup, but it can be changed after the fact. You should always try to copy files into storage during low periods of activity (preferably during non-business hours). You can manually copy files into storage without waiting until the scheduled time by right-clicking the managed volume and choosing Copy Files to Remote Storage.

Setting the Maximum Number of Drives to Access Simultaneously

If you have a multiple-drive device, then you need to tell Remote Storage how many drives to utilize at once. If you have multiple users trying at once to access files on different media, then you may want to increase the number of drives that can be accessed simultaneously to increase your performance. Conversely, if you have an application that accesses Removable Storage, you may want to decrease the amount of disk utilized at once by Remote Storage so that Remote Storage doesn't access all the disks at once and prevent your application from working.

Setting the Runaway Recall Limit

The Runaway call limit defines the number of file recalls a user can make on a file within a single session. It stops Remote Storage from copying the same file from the library to the managed volume over and over. If a user recalls a file within 10 seconds of the original file recall, the runaway recall count is increased by one. After the runaway recall limit is reached, the file is still accessible, it just will be accessed from storage and not cached on the managed volume.

Validating Files

Validation is the process of verifying that the data in Remote Storage points to the correct file on the managed volume. Validation can determine if a file has been moved between volumes. You can manually perform file validation by right-clicking the managed volume, selecting **All Tasks**, and choosing **Validate Files**. Two hours after a backup program restores a file, Remote Storage automatically forces a file validation.

Discontinuing Volume Management

You can easily tell Remote Storage to stop managing a volume by right-clicking a managed volume and choosing **Remove**. If you do so, you have to decide if you want to leave the files on the library or if you want to copy them back to the original volume. If you leave the files in Remote Storage, it will recall them as normal. However, no new files created on the volume will be copied to Remote Storage.

Modifying Files on Managed Volumes

There are special considerations to be aware of when deleting files on managed volumes and moving files between managed volumes. If files on a managed volume are deleted, you must restore the file from backup. Do not think that because the file is stored in the library that it can be restored from there. When you delete a file from the managed volume it is also deleted from the library. If you move or copy files between managed volumes, the files are recalled. If you want to move files back and forth without causing a recall, then you must back up and restore the data to the new location and then run a volume validation.

Creating and Synchronizing Media Copies

You can create copies of your media to provide fault tolerance. These copies are called *media copy sets* and they provide redundancy for your data. If there is a problem with the master media set, the media copy set will be used. In order for Remote Storage to create media copy sets, there must be two or more drives in the library. When using media copy sets, you must make sure that the master set and the copies are in sync. To synchronize the media copies, right-click **Media** and select **Synchronize Copies Now**.

Recreating the Media Master

The *media master* is the tape that holds all the files required for Remote Storage. If the media master were to fail, you could create another one from a media copy set. However, you may lose any data that was created since the last time you synchronized the media copy set with the media master. Recreate the media master only if you get errors when recalling files. Follow the steps below to recreate the media master:

1. Select **Media**.
2. Right-click the **media** you would like to recreate.
3. Select **Properties**.
4. Click the **Recovery** tab.
5. Click **Recreate Master**.

Remote Storage Best Practices

Microsoft provides some guidelines for you to follow when using Remote Storage. You should try to adhere to these best practices whenever possible:

- Make multiple copies of your remote storage tapes and always keep a copy offsite.
- Always configure Remote Storage through the GUI before using rss.exe to manage it.
- Do not create File Replication service (FRS) replicas on a Remote Storage volume.
- Regularly validate your managed volumes.
- Stop managing all volumes before you uninstall Remote Storage.

- Do not manage full volumes.

- Do not format a managed volume.

- Schedule your task to run during periods of low activity.

- Do not change the drive letter of a managed volume.

- Run a system state backup as an administrator to back up the Remote Storage database files.

- Do not install Remote Storage on shared cluster disks.

Troubleshooting Disks and Volumes

Thus far in this chapter, we have focused on how to enable and configure various disk-related features of Windows Server 2003. However, a large part of any administrator's job is dealing with problems and knowing what to do when things go wrong. In this section, we address some of the most common disk-related troubleshooting scenarios you're likely to encounter.

Troubleshooting Basic Disks

Many basic disk-troubleshooting scenarios involve a disk not being recognized by the operating system (and thus not showing up in the Disk Management console) or showing up in a problematic state. Remember the basic rules of troubleshooting any computer/network problem: begin at the physical level. This means you should always check the hardware first to make sure that it is functional.

In the following sections, we will cover these common situations:

- New disks don't show up in the volume list view.

- Disk status is not initialized.

- Disk status is unknown.

- Disk status is unreadable.

- Disk status is failed.

New Disks Are Not Showing Up in the Volume List View

New disks that fail to show up in the volume list view are a common concern. This is usually because there are no designators (drive letters) associated with the disk.

If the disk is not mounted, you will need to use the **diskpart** and **mountvol** commands or use the Disk Management console to mount the volume and assign drive letters. The **mountvol** command enables you to mount a volume without a drive letter. This is useful if you have run out of drive letters.

You have to manually assign drive letters to each volume or partition on the disk before you can format them and use them for storage. Notice in Figure 5.100 that there are three disks shown online in the graphical view (bottom pane), but they do not have drive letters associated with them. Until they do, they will not show up in the volume list view (top pane).

Figure 5.100 Understanding the Default State of Drives

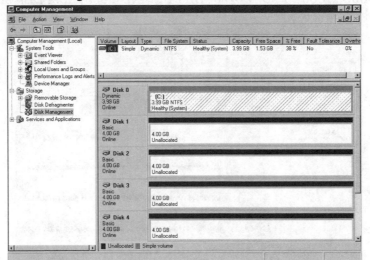

Disk Status is Not Initialized or Unknown

If your disks are showing up as unknown and not initialized, as shown in Figure 5.101, this is generally because no signature has been written to the disk by which Windows can identify it. You need to write a signature to a new disk when you install it, before you can use it. When Windows writes a signature to the disk, it also creates the master boot record (MBR) or GUID partition table. When you add a new disk and start Disk Management, the system automatically starts a wizard that prompts you to write a signature to the new disk. If you cancel the wizard, however, the disk will not have a signature and will be left in an uninitialized state.

To initialize a disk after the wizard has been cancelled, follow these steps:

1. Right-click the disk that needs to be initialized in the bottom graphical pane of the Disk Management console, and then select **Initialize Disk** from the context menu.

2. You will be prompted to select one or more disks to initialize. Ensure that the check box(es) of the appropriate disk(s) is checked and click **OK.**

3. The disk status in the graphical view will change from **Unknown** to **Basic**.

After the disk is initialized, you can create partitions.

Figure 5.101 Troubleshooting Disks That Do Not Have a Signature Disk Status is Unreadable

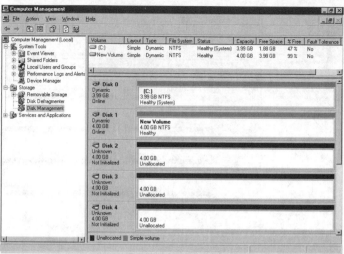

An unreadable disk indicates that you may have a hardware failure or corruption of the disk's copy of the disk configuration database. Unfortunately, there is generally no way to fix failed hardware other than to replace it. Sometimes you will get the "unreadable" message if the disks are still spinning up while you are viewing the Disk Management console. If this is the case, rescanning the computer for disks usually solves the problem. To rescan, click **Action | Rescan Disks**. If rescanning doesn't solve the problem, try rebooting the machine.

Disk Status is Failed

A failed disk indicates that the file system is corrupt, the disk is damaged, or for some other reason the volume could not start. Remember another rule of troubleshooting: always try the easy solutions first. Make sure that the disk has power and is plugged into the server. If your hardware is faulty, you will have to replace it and restore your data from backup. One of the most common causes of disk problems is a loose or bad IDE or SCSI cable. Try tightening or swapping out cables if you suspect this is the problem.

If the hardware is not faulty, we move on to troubleshooting the software. One possibility is that the file system is corrupt. If you can still access the volume, run **chkdsk.exe** against it. Chkdsk.exe may not be able to recover any lost data, but it can usually bring the file system back to a consistent state. Chkdsk.exe uses the following syntax.

```
CHKDSK [volume[[path]filename]]] [/F] [/V] [/R] [/X] [/I] [/C]
    [/L[:size]]
```

Table 5.7 explains chkdsk.exe parameters.

Table 5.7 Understanding Chkdsk.exe Parameters

Parameter	Desription
volume	Specifies the drive letter (followed by a colon), mount point, or volume name.
filename	Specifies the files to check for fragmentation. Used on FAT and FAT32 volumes only.
/F	Fixes errors on the disk.
/V	Displays the full path and name of every file on the disk. Used on FAT and FAT32 volumes only.
/R	Locates bad sectors and recovers readable information (implies /F).
/L:size	Changes the log file size to the specified number of kilobytes. If size is not specified, displays current size. Used on NTFS volumes only.
/X	All opened handles to the volume would then be invalid (implies /F).
/I	Performs a less vigorous check of index entries. Used on NTFS volumes only.
/C	Skips checking of cycles within the folder structure. Used on NTFS volumes only.

Troubleshooting Dynamic Volumes

Dynamic disks can have the same problems as basic disk (discussed above). When troubleshooting dynamic disks, you should always run through the scenarios given for basic disks, as well. In addition to these problems that are common to both disk types, dynamic disks can have additional problems that do not apply to basic disks. In the following section, we will discuss these troubleshooting scenarios that are unique to dynamic disks:

- Disk status is foreign.

- Disk status is online (errors).

- Disk status is offline or missing.

- Disk status is data incomplete.

- Disk status is Stale Data.

- Disk status is Failed or Failed Redundancy.

Disk Status is Foreign

A disk status of **Foreign**, as shown in Figure 5.102, occurs when you move a dynamic disk from one machine to another. This happens because Windows stores all dynamic disk configurations in a private database in the last 1MB of disk space. This database is associated with the machine in which the disk is installed and is replicated to all the dynamic disks installed in that machine. If you connect the disk to a different machine, the second machine will detect that the database doesn't match anything in its database and the disk will be marked as foreign.

To make the new computer recognize the dynamic disk, you must import it. To do so, right-click the foreign disk and select **Import Foreign Disks** from the pop-up menu. This will make the volume visible and incorporate it into the new machine's dynamic disk database.

Figure 5.102 Importing a Foreign Disk

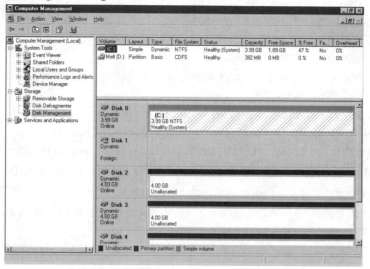

Disk Status is Online (Errors)

A disk status of **Online (Errors)** indicates that the disk is working, but is having problems. I/O errors are being detected somewhere on the disk. If this problem persists, you should replace the hardware. If the problem is temporary, you might be able to reactivate your volume to bring it back online. To do so, right-click the volume and choose **Reactivate Disk** from the pop-up menu. If the reactivation works, the disk will be marked as **Online**.

You can also use the **diskpart** command with the **online** parameter to reactivate a disk (remember to first select the disk so that it is the focus).

Disk Status is Offline

A disk status of **Offline**, where the disk name field indicates **Missing** (as shown in Figure 5.103) usually means that the disk is no longer physically connected to the server. Check to make sure that the disk is powered on and correctly connected to the server. After fixing a physical connectivity problem, right-click the volume and choose **Reactivate Disk**. This will bring the disk back online and make it usable by Windows again.

If this does not fix the problem, it is possible that your disk is corrupt beyond repair. If so, you must remove it from the server. Right-click the volume(s) contained on the disk and choose **Remove Volume** from the context menu. After all volumes have been removed, right-click the disk and choose **Remove Disk**. At this point, all data is lost and the disk has been removed from your system. Do not do this unless you are sure that the disk is irreparably damaged.

Figure 5.103 Troubleshooting Missing Disks

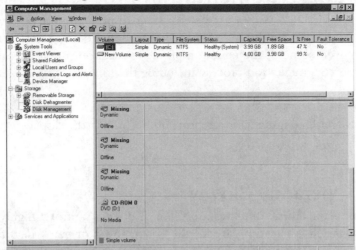

If the disk status shows **Offline**, but the disk name still shows as Disk 0, Disk 1, etc. (instead of "Missing"), you should be able to simply right-click and select **Reactivate** to bring the disk back online. Volumes should be returned to **Healthy** status after the disk comes back online.

Disk Status is Data Incomplete

As discussed earlier, when you move dynamic volumes between servers they are marked as foreign. You must import them in order for Windows to use them. If you have a volume that spans multiple disks (e.g., a spanned volume, striped volume, or RAID 5 volume) and you only import some of the disks, you will see the error message **Data Incomplete**, as shown in Figure 5.104. If this happens, cancel the import process until you can move all the disks in the volume at the same time. When all the disks have been physically installed in the new machine, import them together and Windows will recognize them as being part of the same volume.

Figure 5.104 Importing Part of a Spanned Volume

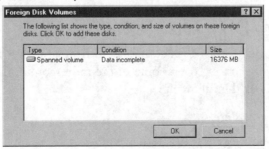

Troubleshooting Fragmentation Problems

Disk fragmentation is inevitable if you ever delete files, install programs, or otherwise use the computer for normal tasks. To optimize disk performance, you should defragment your disks as often as needed. This section covers some of the common problems that you might encounter related to disk fragmentation and the defragmentation process, including the following:

- Computer is operating slowly.

- The Analysis and Defragmentation reports do not match the display.

- Volumes contain unmovable files.

Computer is Operating Slowly

This is a common complaint from computer users. This is often a sign of a highly fragmented disk and commonly occurs when applications are installed or removed or many new files are created. The solution is simple: use **defrag.exe** or Disk Defragmenter to defragment your disks.

The Analysis and Defragmentation Reports Do Not Match the Display

The graphical display is designed to provide a quick look at the level of fragmentation of the volumes on your hard disk. The graphical representation is too small in scale to give a 100-percent accurate representation. The reports created by the defragmentation tools are much more detailed and are very accurate. When there are discrepancies between the display and reports, the information in the reports should be considered more reliable.

My Volumes Contain Unmovable Files

This is normal. Certain files cannot be moved during the defragmentation process. The page file is one of these files. Every volume containing a page file will appear as having files that cannot be moved. Also, on NTFS-formatted volumes, the NTFS Change journal and the NTFS log file cannot be moved.

Troubleshooting Disk Quotas

Disk quotas are a great feature. However, they can lead to trouble if they are improperly configured or not managed properly. This section covers some of the more common issues that appear when using disk quotas. Issues such as the following:

- The Quota tab is not there.

- Deleting a Quota entry gives you another window.

- A user gets an "Insufficient Disk Space" message when adding files to a volume.

The Quota Tab is Not There

Disk quotas are set via the quotas tab on the properties of a volume. If the tab does not appear (Figure 5.105), then one of three things is the cause. Either you do not have administrative rights on the machine, the volume is formatted as FAT or FAT32 and not as NTFS, or the volume is not shared from the volume's root directory.

Figure 5.105 Missing the Quota Tab

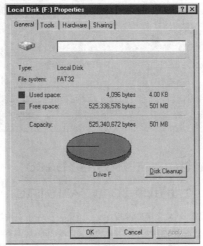

Deleting a Quota Entry Gives you Another Window

Whenever you try to delete a quota entry for a user that still retains ownership of files, you are presented with the Disk Quota window shown in Figure 5.106. This is because you cannot delete a quota entry if the user still owns files. This keeps you from having files on your server that are not being managed by disk quotas because the owner is no longer around. You have three choices:

- Permanently delete all the files.

- Take ownership of the files.

- Move the files to another volume.

After doing so, you will be able to delete the quota entry for your user.

Figure 5.106 Cleaning Up Disk Quotas

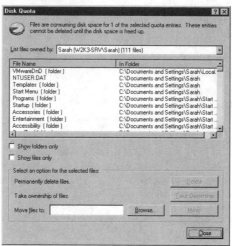

A User Gets an "Insufficient Disk Space" Message When Adding Files to a Volume

The insufficient disk space message (see Figure 5.107) to be expected for any of your users that are over their quota limit. Usually this is a good thing because it means that disk quotas are working. The only way around it is to increase your users' quota limit or to stop denying users who exceed their disk space. If this is happening unexpectedly, verify that your users' limits are set correctly. A common error is to forget to change the quota measurement from KB to MB. You may think that your users have 150MB of available space when they only have 150KB of space.

Figure 5.107 Exceeding Your Quota Limit

Troubleshooting Remote Storage

Remember when you are troubleshooting Remote Storage that you are writing data to backup media. This is going to be slower than writing to disks. This is not to say that your performance should be terrible. Just be realistic with your expectations. Here are some common Remote Storage troubleshooting issues:

- Remote Storage will not install.
- Remote Storage is not finding a valid media type.
- Files can no longer be recalled from Remote Storage.

Remote Storage Will Not Install

Remote Storage is not installed by default. You must add it through **Control Panel | Add or Remove Programs**. You must have administrative rights on the machine on which you are installing Remote Storage. Without administrative rights, setup will not continue.

Remote Storage Is Not Finding a Valid Media Type

During initial setup, Remote Storage searches for an available media type. If Remote Storage is not finding one on your machine, you either have not waited long enough for Remote Storage to finish searching or you do not have a compatible library.

Files Can No Longer Be Recalled from Remote Storage

Remote Storage has a runaway recall limit to deny recalling files from storage more than a specified number of times in a row. It is possible that you have an application that is making too many recalls. Once this threshold is crossed, future recalls are denied. If the recalls are legitimate, you can increase the threshold for the runaway recall limit. If they are not valid, then you need to terminate the application making the request.

Troubleshooting RAID

When troubleshooting RAID volumes, you must first troubleshoot the disk itself. So always start with the basic disk and dynamic disk checklist. However, there are times when the problem is with the RAID volume itself and not the underlying disk. This section covers the following:

- Mirrored or RAID-5 volume's status is Data Not Redundant.
- Mirrored or RAID-5 volume's status is Failed Redundancy.
- Mirrored or RAID-5 volume's status is Stale Data.

Mirrored or RAID-5 Volume's Status is Data Not Redundant

A Data Not Redundant status indicates that your volume is not intact. This is due to moving disks from one machine to another without moving all the disks in the volume. Wait to import your disk until you have all the disks in the volume physically connected to the server. Then when you import them, Windows will see them as a complete volume and retain their configuration.

Mirrored or RAID-5 Volume's Status is Failed Redundancy

Failed Redundancy, as shown in Figures 5.108 and 5.109, occurs when one of the disks in a fault-tolerant volume fails. Your volume will continue to work, but it is no longer fault tolerant. If another disk fails, you will lose all your data on that volume. You should repair the failed disk as quickly as possible.

Your mirrored volume will need to be recreated after replacing the disk. Right-click the defective disk and select **Remove Mirror**. Then right-click the working disk and select **Add Mirror**, selecting the new disk as the mirror. To repair the RAID-5 volume, put in the disk and right-click the volume and choose **Repair RAID-5 Volume**.

Figure 5.108 Recovering a Failed Mirrored Volume

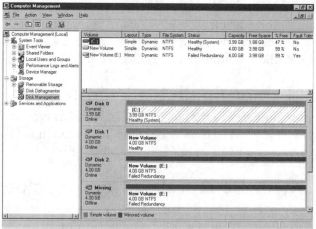

Figure 5.109 Recovering a Failed RAID-5 Volume

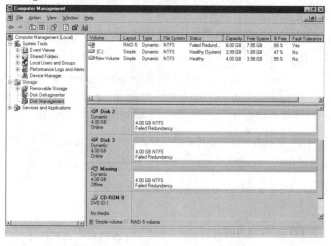

Mirrored or RAID-5 Volume's Status is Stale Data

Stale data occurs when a volume's fault-tolerant information is not completely up to date. This happens in a mirrored volume if something has been written to the primary disk, but for whatever reason it hasn't made it to the mirror disk yet. This occurs in a RAID-5 volume when the parity information isn't up to date.

If you try to move a volume while it contains stale information, you will get a status of **Stale Data** when you try to import the disk. Move the disk back to the machine it was originally in and rescan the machine for new disk. After all the disks are discovered, wait until they say online and healthy before you try to move them again.

Chapter 6

Implementing Windows Cluster Services and Network Load Balancing

In this chapter:

- **Making Server Clustering Part of Your High-Availability Plan**

- **Making Network Load Balancing Part of Your High-Availability Plan**

Introduction

Fault tolerance generally involves redundancy; for example, in the case of disk fault tolerance, multiple disks are used. The ultimate in fault tolerance is the use of multiple servers, configured to take over for one another in case of failure or to share the processing load. Windows Server 2003 provides network administrators with two powerful tools to enhance fault tolerance and high availability: server clustering (only in the Enterprise and Datacenter Editions) and Network Load Balancing (included in all editions).

This chapter looks first at server clustering and shows you how to make clustering services part of your enterprise-level organization's high-availability plan. We'll start by introducing you to the terminology and concepts involved in understanding clustering. You'll learn about cluster nodes, cluster groups, failover and failback, name resolution as it pertains to cluster services, and how server clustering works. We'll discuss three cluster models: single-node, single quorum device, and majority node set. Then we'll talk about cluster deployment options, including N-node failover pairs, hot standby server/N+1, failover ring, and random. You'll learn about cluster administration, and we'll show you how to use the Cluster Administrator tool as well as command-line tools.

Next, we'll discuss best practices for deploying server clusters. You'll learn about hardware issues, especially those related to network interface controllers, storage devices, power-saving features, and general compatibility issues. We'll discuss cluster network configuration and you'll learn about multiple interconnections and node-to-node communications. We'll talk about the importance of binding order, adapter settings, and TCP/IP settings. We'll also discuss the default cluster group. Next, we'll move onto the subject of security for server clusters. This includes physical security, public/mixed networks, private networks, secure remote administration of cluster nodes, security issues involving the cluster service account, and how to limit client access. We'll also talk about how to secure data in a cluster, how to secure disk resources, and how to secure cluster configuration log files.

The next section addresses how to make Network Load Balancing (NLB) part of your high-availability plan. We'll introduce you to NLB concepts such as hosts/default host, load weight, traffic distribution, convergence, and heartbeats. You'll learn about how NLB works and the relationship of NLB to clustering. We'll show you how to manage NLB clusters using the NLB Manager tool, remote-management tools, and command-line tools. We'll also discuss NLB error detection and handling. Next, we'll move onto monitoring NLB using the NLB Monitor Microsoft Management Console (MMC) snap-in or the Windows Load Balancing Service (WLBS) cluster control utility. We discuss best practices for implementing and managing NLB, including issues such as multiple network adapters, protocols and IP addressing, and NLB Manager logging. Finally, we'll address NLB security.

Making Server Clustering Part of Your High-Availability Plan

Certain circumstances require an application to be operational more than standard hardware would allow. Databases and mail servers often have this need. Using *server clustering*, it is possible to have more than one server ready to run critical applications. Server clustering also provides the capability to automatically manage the operation of the application so that if one server experienced a failure another server would automatically take over and keep the application running. Server clustering is a critical component in a high-availability plan. We'll discuss high-availability strategies in the next chapter.

The basic idea of server clustering has been around for many years on other computing platforms. Microsoft initially released its server cluster technology as part of Windows NT 4.0 Enterprise Edition. It supported two nodes and a limited number of applications. Server clustering was further refined with the release of Windows 2000 Advanced and Datacenter Server Editions. Server clusters were simpler to create, and more applications were available. In addition, some publishers began to make their applications "cluster-aware," so that their applications installed and operated more easily on a server cluster. Now, with the release of Windows Server 2003, we see another level of improvement on the server clustering technology. Server clusters now support much larger clusters and more robust configurations. Server clusters are easier to create and manage. Features that were available only in the Datacenter Edition of Windows 2000 have now been made available in the Enterprise Edition of Windows Server 2003.

Terminology and Concepts

Although it has been used previously, a more formal definition of a server cluster is needed. For our purposes, a *server cluster* is a group of independent servers that work together to increase application availability to client systems and appear to clients under one common name. The independent servers that make up a server cluster are individually called *nodes*. Nodes in a server cluster monitor each other's status through a communication mechanism called a *heartbeat*. The heartbeat is a series of messages that allow the server cluster nodes to detect communication failures and, if necessary, perform a *failover* operation. A failover is the process by which resources are stopped on one node and started on another.

Cluster Nodes

A server cluster node is an independent server. This server must be running Windows 2000 Advanced Server, Windows 2000 Datacenter Server, Windows Server 2003 Enterprise Edition, or Windows Server 2003 Datacenter Edition. The two editions of Windows Server 2003 cannot be used in the same server cluster, but either can exist in a server cluster with a Windows 2000 Advanced Server node. Since Windows Server 2003 Datacenter Edition is available only through original equipment manufacturers (OEMs), this chapter deals with server clusters constructed with the Advanced Server Edition of Windows Server 2003 unless specifically stated otherwise.

A server cluster node should be a robust system. When designing your server cluster, do not overlook applying fault-tolerant concepts to the individual nodes. Using individual fault-tolerant components to build fault-tolerant nodes to build fault-tolerant server clusters can be described as "fault tolerance in depth." This approach will increase overall reliability and make your life easier.

A server cluster consists of anywhere between one and eight nodes. These nodes do not necessarily need to have identical configurations, although that is a frequent design element. Each node in a server cluster can be configured to have a primary role that is different from the other nodes in the server cluster. This allows you to have overall better utilization of the server cluster if each node is actively providing services. A node is connected to one or more storage devices, which contain disks that house information about the server cluster. Each node also contains one or more separate network interfaces that provide client communications and support heartbeat communications.

Cluster Groups

The smallest unit of service that a server cluster can provide is a *resource*. A resource is a physical or logical component that can be managed on an individual basis and can be independently activated or deactivated (called bringing the resource *online* or *offline*). A resource can be owned by only one node at a time.

There are several predefined (called "standard") types of resources known to Windows Server 2003. Each type is used for a specific purpose. The following are some of the most common standard resource types:

- **Physical Disk** Represents and manages disks present on a shared cluster storage device. Can be partitioned like a regular disk. Can be assigned a drive letter or used as an NTFS mounted drive.

- **IP Address** Manages an IP address.

- **Network Name** Manages a unique NetBIOS name on the network, separate from the NetBIOS name of the node on which the resource is running.

- **Generic Service** Manages a Windows operating system service as a cluster resource. Helps ensure that the service operates in one place at one time.

- **Generic Script** Manages a script as a cluster resource (new to Windows Server 2003).

- **File Share** Creates and manages a Windows file share as a cluster resource.

Other standard resource types allow you to manage clustered print servers, Dynamic Host Configuration Protocol (DHCP) servers, Windows Internet Name Service (WINS) servers, and generic noncluster-aware applications. (It is also possible to create new resource types through the use of dynamic link library files.)

Individual resources are combined to form *cluster groups*. A cluster group is a collection of server resources that defines the relationships of resource within the group to each other and defines the unit of failover, so that if one resource moves between nodes, all resources in the group also move. As with individual resources, a cluster group can be owned by only one node at a time. To use an analogy from chemistry, resources are atoms and groups are compounds. The cluster group is the primary unit of administration in a server cluster. Similar or interdependent resources are combined into the same group. A resource cannot be dependent on another resource that is not in the same cluster group. Most cluster groups are designed around either an application or a storage unit. It is in this way that individual applications or disks in a server cluster are controlled independently of other applications or disks.

Failover and Failback

If a resource on a node fails, the cluster service will first attempt to reactivate the resource on the same node. If unable to do so, the cluster service will move the cluster group to another node in the server cluster. This process is called a *failover*. A failover can be triggered manually by the administrator or automatically by a node failure. A failover can involve multiple nodes, if the server cluster is configured this way, and each group can have different failover policies defined.

A *failback* is the corollary of a failover. When the original node that hosted the failed-over resource(s) comes back online, the cluster service can return the cluster group to operation on the original node. This failback policy can be defined individually for a cluster group or disabled entirely. Failback is usually performed at times of low utilization to avoid impacting clients, and it can be set to follow specific schedules.

Cluster Services and Name Resolution

A server cluster appears to clients as one common name, regardless of the number of nodes in the server cluster. It is for this reason that the server cluster name must be unique on your network. Ensure that the server cluster name is different from the names of other server clusters, domain names, servers, and workstations on your network. The server cluster will register its name with the WINS and DNS servers configured on the node running the default cluster group.

Individual applications that run on a server cluster can (and should) be configured to run in separate cluster groups. The applications must also have unique names on the network and will also automatically register with WINS and DNS. Do not use static WINS entries for your resources. Doing so will prevent an update to the WINS registered address in the event of a failover.

How Clustering Works

Each node in a server cluster is connected to one or more storage devices. These storage devices contain one or more disks. If the server cluster contains two nodes, you can use either a SCSI interface to the storage devices or a Fibre Channel interface. For three or more node server clusters,

Fibre Channel is recommended. If you are using a 64-bit edition of Windows Server 2003, Fibre Channel is the required interface, regardless of the number of nodes.

Fibre Channel has many benefits over SCSI. Fibre Channel is faster and easily expands beyond two nodes. Fibre Channel cabling is simpler, and Fibre Channel automatically configures itself. However, Fibre Channel is also more expensive than SCSI, requires more components, and can be more complicated to design and manage.

On any server cluster, there is something called the *quorum resource.* The quorum resource is used to determine the state of the server cluster. The node that controls the quorum resource controls the server cluster, and only one node at a time can own the quorum resource. This prevents a situation called *split-brain,* which occurs when more than one node believes it controls the server cluster and behaves accordingly. Split-brain was a problem that occurred in the early development of server cluster technologies. The introduction of the quorum resource solved this problem.

Cluster Models

There are three basic server cluster design models available to choose from: single node, single quorum, and majority node set. Each is designed to fit a specific set of circumstances. Before you begin designing your server cluster, make sure you have a thorough understanding of these models.

Single Node

A single-node server cluster model is primarily used for development and testing purposes. As its name implies, it consists of one node. An external disk resource may or may not be present. If an external disk resource is not present, the local disk is configured as the cluster storage device, and the server cluster configuration is kept there.

Failover is not possible with this server cluster model, because there is only one node. However, as with any server cluster model, it is possible to create multiple *virtual servers.* (A virtual server is a cluster group that contains its own dedicated IP address, network name, and services and is indistinguishable from other servers from a client's perspective.) Figure 6.1 illustrates the structure of a single-node server cluster.

Figure 6.1 Single Node Server Cluster

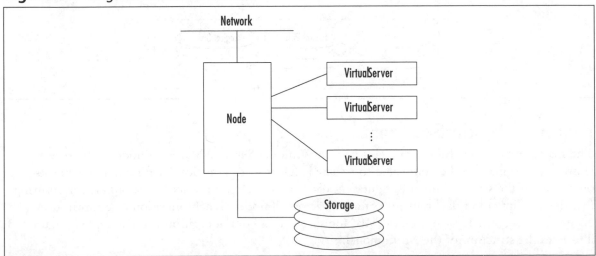

If a resource fails, the cluster service will attempt to automatically restart any applications and dependent resources. This can be useful when applied to applications that do not have built-in restart capabilities but would benefit from that capability.

Some applications that are designed for use on server clusters will not work on a single-node cluster model. Microsoft SQL Server and Microsoft Exchange Server are two examples. Applications like these require the use of one of the other two server cluster models.

Single Quorum Device

The single quorum device server cluster model is the most common and will likely continue to be the most heavily used. It has been around since Microsoft first introduced its server clustering technology.

This type of server cluster contains two or more nodes, and each node is connected to the cluster storage devices. There is a single quorum device (a physical disk) that resides on the cluster storage device. There is a single copy of the cluster configuration and operational state, which is stored on the quorum resource.

Each node in the server cluster can be configured to run different applications or to act simply as a hot-standby device waiting for a failover to occur. Figure 6.2 illustrates the structure of a single quorum device server cluster with two nodes.

Figure 6.2 Single Quorum Device Server Cluster

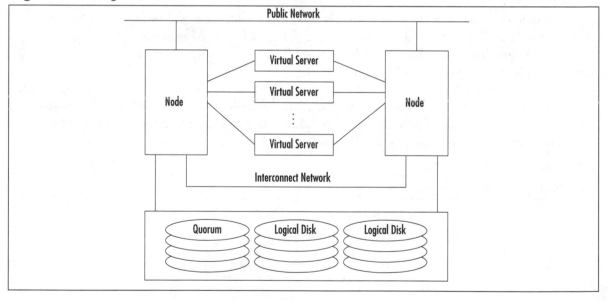

Majority Node Set

The majority node set (MNS) model is new in Windows Server 2003. Each node in the server cluster may or may not be connected to a shared cluster storage device. Each node maintains its own copy of the server cluster configuration data, and the cluster service is responsible for ensuring that this configuration data remains consistent across all nodes. Synchronization of quorum data occurs over Server Message Block (SMB) file shares. This communication is unencrypted. Figure 6.3 illustrates the structure of the MNS model.

Figure 6.3 A Majority Node Set Server Cluster

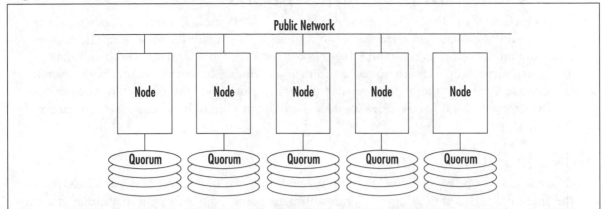

This model is normally used as part of an OEM pre-designed or pre-configured configuration. It has the ability to support geographically distributed server clusters. When used in geographically dispersed configurations, network latency becomes an issue. You must ensure that the round-trip network latency is a *maximum* of 500 milliseconds (ms), or you will experience availability problems.

The behavior of an MNS server cluster differs from that of a single quorum device server cluster. In a single quorum device server cluster, one node can fail and the server cluster can still function. This is not necessarily the case in an MNS cluster. To avoid split-brain, a majority of the nodes must be active and available for the server cluster to function. In essence, this means that 50 percent plus 1 of the nodes must be operational at all times for the server cluster to remain operational. Table 6.1 illustrates this relationship.

Table 6.1 Majority Node Set Server Cluster Failure Tolerance

Number of Nodes in MNS Server Cluster	Maximum Node Failures before Complete Cluster Failure	Nodes Required to Continue Cluster Operations
1	0	1
2	0	2
3	1	2
4	1	3
5	2	3
6	2	4
7	3	4
8	3	5

Server Cluster Deployment Options

When you use either the single quorum device model or MNS model, there are a variety of ways that you can configure your clustered applications to act during a failover operation. The choices vary with the number of nodes in your server cluster, and each has advantages and disadvantages.

These deployment options are not always mutually exclusive. In a server cluster with several nodes and multiple cluster groups, it is possible that some groups will use one deployment option while other groups use a different one. Consider these options carefully when you design larger server clusters.

N-Node Failover Pairs

The N-node failover pairs deployment option specifies that two nodes, and only two nodes, may run the application. This is the simplest option and is, in essence, the only option available in a two-node server cluster. If configured in a larger server cluster with three or more nodes, the application will not be able to function if both nodes are not operational. In larger server clusters made up of nodes with different processing capabilities or capacities, you can use this option to limit an application to running on only the nodes capable of adequately servicing the application.

An N-node failover pair is configured by specifying the two nodes in the Possible Owners property for the cluster resource, as shown in Figure 6.4. You can set the Possible Owners property using the server cluster administrative tools described in the "Server Cluster Administration" section later in this chapter. Every cluster resource has a Possible Owners property that can be configured or left blank.

Figure 6.4 Setting the Possible Owners Property

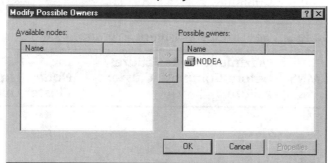

Figure 6.5 illustrates an N-node failover configuration in a server cluster with four nodes—A, B, C and D—in its normal operational state. Nodes A and B are configured as a failover pair, and nodes C and D are also a failover pair. Assorted virtual servers are active and are spread among the nodes.

Figure 6.5 N-Node Failover, Initial State

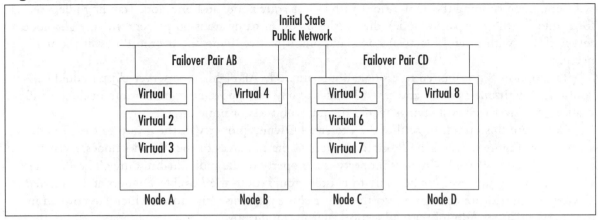

Figure 6.6 shows the same server cluster as Figure 6.5, but after two of the nodes failed. As you can see, node B has taken ownership of the virtual servers that were operating on its failover partner (node A). Node C has also taken ownership of node D's virtual servers.

Figure 6.6 N-Node Failover, Failed State

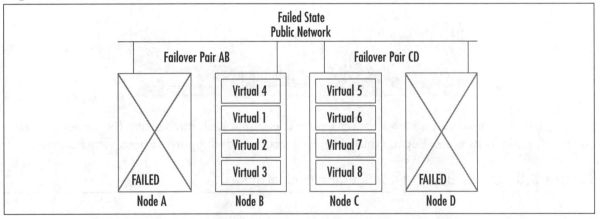

Note that Figures 6.5 and 6.6 depict a single quorum device server cluster. An MNS server cluster with four nodes could not operate with failed two nodes. The storage devices and Interconnects have been removed from the images for clarity.

Hot-Standby Server/N+I

The hot-standby server/N+1 deployment option is possible on server clusters with two or more nodes and is sometimes referred to as an *active/passive* design. In this design, you specify one node in the server cluster as a *hot spare*. This hot-spare node is normally idle or lightly loaded. It acts as the failover destination for other nodes in the cluster.

The main advantage of this option is cost savings. If a two-node server cluster is configured with one node running the application(s) (the *N* or *active* node) and one node standing idle, waiting for a failover (the *I* or *passive* node), the overhead cost in hardware is 50 percent. In an eight-node server cluster with seven N (active) nodes and one I (passive) node, the overhead cost is about 15 percent.

This option is not limited to a single hot-spare node. An eight-node server cluster could be configured with one N node and seven I nodes or any other possible combination. In these config-urations, the overhead cost savings would be quite a bit less or nonexistent.

Configure this option by setting the Preferred Owners property of the group to the N node(s), as shown in Figure 6.7, and the Possible Owners of the resources to the N and I nodes. As mentioned earlier, the Possible Owners property is a property of the individual resource. The Preferred Owner property, however, applies only to cluster groups. Both the Possible Owners and Preferred Owners properties are configured via the server cluster administrative tools, which are covered in the "Server Cluster Administration" section later in this chapter.

Figure 6.7 Setting the Preferred Owners Property

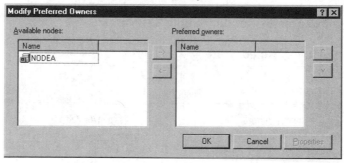

Figure 6.8 illustrates a four-node server cluster configured with three active (N) nodes and one passive (I) node in its normal operational state. Each active node supports various virtual servers.

Figure 6.8 Hot-Standby/N+I Configuration, Initial State

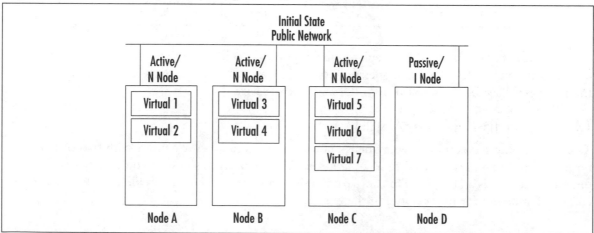

Figure 6.9 shows the same server cluster as Figure 6.8, but after the failure of two of the nodes. The virtual servers that were operating on the failed nodes have failed over to the I node. Again, if this were an MNS server cluster, there would not be enough nodes operating to support the server cluster. The MNS cluster would have failed when the second node failed, but the virtual servers from the first node would have been successfully failed over to the I node. Again, note that the storage devices and Interconnects have been removed from both images.

Figure 6.9 Hot Standby/N+I Configuration, Failed State

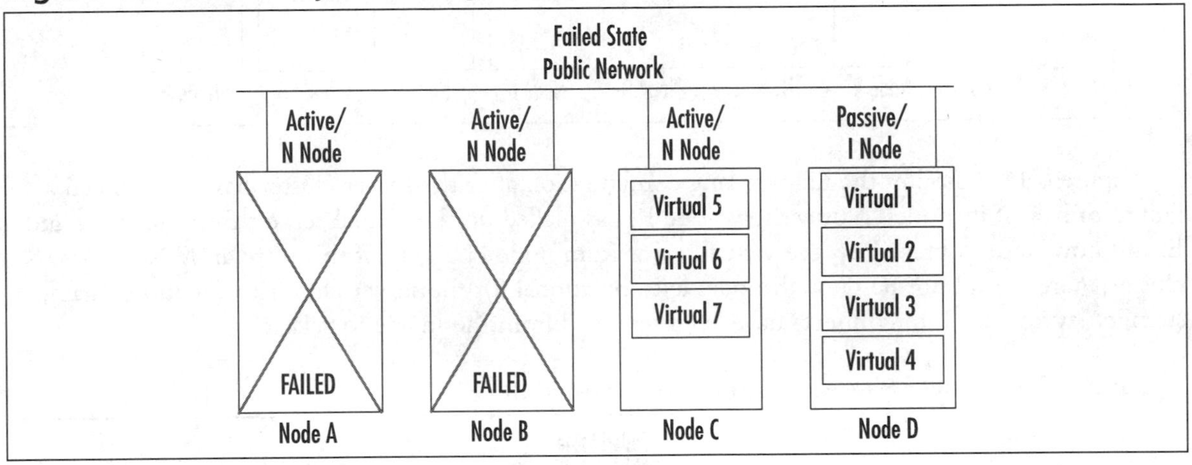

Failover Ring

A *failover ring* is mainly used when all nodes in a server cluster are active. When a failover occurs, applications are moved to the next node in line. This mode is possible if all nodes in the server cluster have enough excess capacity to support additional applications beyond what they normally run. If a node is operating at peak utilization, a failover to that node may reduce performance for all applications running on that node after the failover.

The order of failover is defined by the order the nodes appear in the Preferred Owner list (see Figure 6.7). The default node for the application is listed first. A failover will attempt to move the cluster group to each node on the list, in order, until the group successfully starts.

It is possible to limit the size of the failover ring by not specifying all the cluster nodes on the Preferred Owner list. In effect, this combines the N+I and failover ring options to produce a hybrid option. This hybrid option reduces the N+I overhead cost to zero, but you need to make sure that enough capacity is present to support your applications.

Figure 6.10 illustrates an eight-node server cluster in a failover ring configuration in its initial state. This server cluster is operating with eight nodes. To simplify the diagram, each node is running one virtual server. (The configuration of the failover ring in this scenario is very simple: each node fails over to the next node, with the last node set to fail over to the first, and so on.) Storage devices and Interconnects have been removed for clarity.

Figure 6.10 Failover Ring Configuration, Initial State

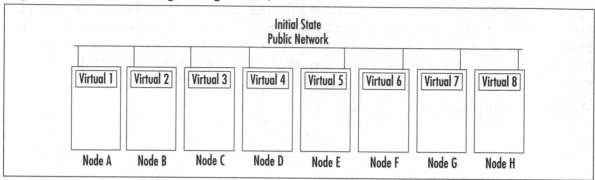

Figure 6.11 illustrates the failover ring configuration after the server cluster has experienced a failure of half of its nodes. Notice how node F has picked up the virtual servers from nodes D and E, and how node A picked up the virtual server from node H. Again, if this were an MNS server cluster, there would not be enough nodes left operational for the server cluster to function. Again, storage devices and Interconnects have been removed from the image for clarity.

Figure 6.11 Failover Ring Configuration, Failed State

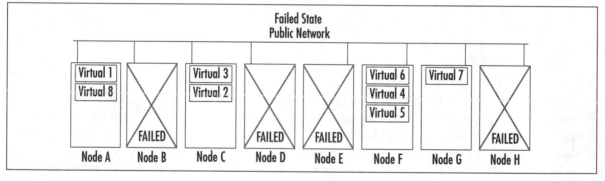

Random

The random deployment option makes the cluster service determine the destination for a failover. This option is used in large server clusters where each node is active and it is difficult to specify an order of failover because of the needs and complexity of the environment. When adopting this option, it is important to make sure that each node has sufficient excess capacity to handle additional load. Otherwise, a failover may reduce performance for applications running on a node that is at or near peak capacity.

This mode is configured by not defining a Preferred Owner for the resource group. The cluster service will attempt to determine a suitable node for the application in the event of a failover. Figure 6.12 illustrates a random failover configuration in the initial state. It shows a server cluster of eight nodes supporting two virtual servers, each in its normal operating mode.

Figure 6.12 Random Configuration, Initial State

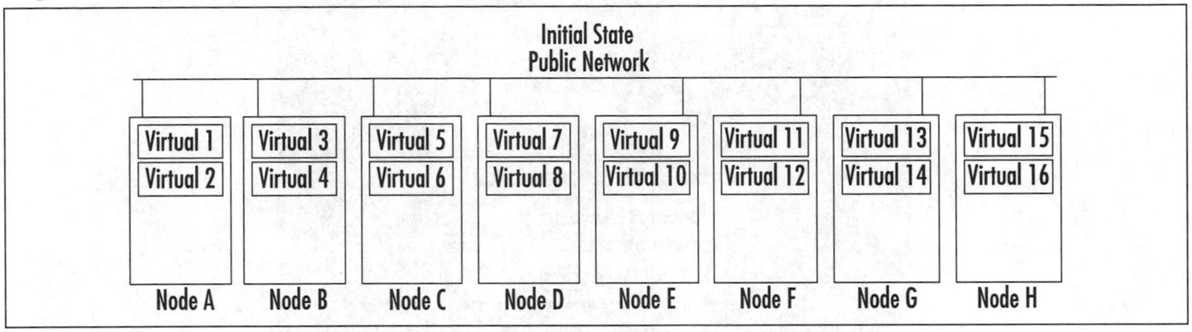

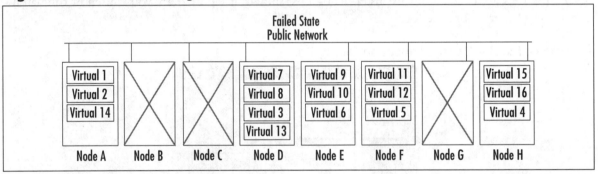

Figure 6.13 shows the same configuration after this server cluster has experienced a failure of three of its nodes. Notice how the virtual servers have been distributed seemingly at random to the surviving nodes. If this were an MNS server cluster, it would still be functioning.

Figure 6.13 Random Configuration, Failed State

Server Cluster Administration

After a server cluster is operational, it must be administered. There are two tools provided to you to accomplish this: Cluster Administrator, an interactive graphical utility, and *Cluster.exe*, provided for use at the command line and in scripts or batch files.

Using the Cluster Administrator Tool

To access the Cluster Administrator utility, select **Start | Administrative Tools | Cluster Administrator**. The Cluster Administrator utility, shown in Figure 6.14, allows you to create a new server cluster, add nodes to an existing server cluster, and perform administrative tasks on a server cluster.

Figure 6.14 The Cluster Administrator Window

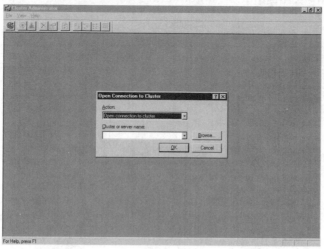

At the Open Connection to Cluster dialog box, shown in Figure 6.15, you can enter the name of a server cluster or browse for it.

Figure 6.15 The Open Connection Dialog Box

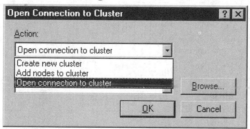

If you wish to create a new server cluster, select **Create new cluster** in the **Action** drop-down list box and click **OK**. This will start the New Server Cluster Wizard, which will step you through the process of creating a new server cluster. Selecting **Add nodes to cluster** in the Action drop-down list will start the Add Nodes Wizard. This Wizard lets you add nodes to an existing server cluster.

Using Command-Line Tools

Cluster.exe is the command-line utility you can use to create or administer a server cluster. It has all of the capabilities of the Cluster Administrator graphical utility and more. Cluster.exe has numerous options. Figure 6.16 shows the syntax of the **cluster.exe** command and the options you can use with it.

Figure 6.16 Cluster.exe Command Options

```
CLUSTER /LIST[:domain-name]


CLUSTER /CHANGEPASS[WORD] /?
CLUSTER /CHANGEPASS[WORD] /HELP
CLUSTER /CLUSTER:clustername1[,clustername2[,...]]
        /CHANGEPASS[WORD][:newpassword[,oldpassword]] <options>


<options> =
  [/FORCE] [/QUIET] [/SKIPDC] [/TEST] [/VERB[OSE]] [/UNATTEND[ED]] [/?] [/HELP]


CLUSTER [/CLUSTER:]cluster-name <options>


<options> =
  /CREATE [/NODE:node-name] [/VERB[OSE]] [/UNATTEND[ED]] [/MIN[IMUM]]
    /USER:domain\username | username@domain [/PASS[WORD]:password]
    /IPADDR[ESS]:xxx.xxx.xxx.xxx[,xxx.xxx.xxx.xxx,network-connection-
        name]
  /ADD[NODES][:node-name[,node-name ...]] [/VERB[OSE]] [/UNATTEND[ED]]
    [/MIN[IMUM]] [/PASSWORD:service-account-password]


CLUSTER [[/CLUSTER:]cluster-name] <options>


<options> =
  /CREATE [/NODE:node-name] /WIZ[ARD] [/MIN[IMUM]]
    [/USER:domain\username | username@domain] [/PASS[WORD]:password]
    [/IPADDR[ESS]:xxx.xxx.xxx.xxx]
  /ADD[NODES][:node-name[,node-name ...]] /WIZ[ARD] [/MIN[IMUM]]
    [/PASSWORD:service-account-password]
  /PROP[ERTIES] [<prop-list>]
  /PRIV[PROPERTIES] [<prop-list>]
  /PROP[ERTIES][:propname[,propname ...] /USEDEFAULT]
  /PRIV[PROPERTIES][:propname[,propname ...] /USEDEFAULT]
  /REN[AME]:cluster-name
  /QUORUM[RESOURCE][:resource-name] [/PATH:path] [/MAXLOGSIZE:max-size-
      kbytes]
  /SETFAIL[UREACTIONS][:node-name[,node-name ...]]
```

Continued

Figure 6.16 Cluster.exe Command Options

```
/LISTNETPRI[ORITY]

/SETNETPRI[ORITY]:net[,net ...]

/REG[ADMIN]EXT:admin-extension-dll[,admin-extension-dll ...]

/UNREG[ADMIN]EXT:admin-extension-dll[,admin-extension-dll ...]

/VER[SION]

NODE [node-name] node-command

GROUP [group-name] group-command

RES[OURCE] [resource-name] resource-command

{RESOURCETYPE|RESTYPE} [resourcetype-name] resourcetype-command

NET[WORK] [network-name] network-command

NETINT[ERFACE] [interface-name] interface-command


<prop-list> =

    name=value[,value ...][:<format>] [name=value[,value ...][:<format>
        ] ...]


<format> =

    BINARY|DWORD|STR[ING]|EXPANDSTR[ING]|MULTISTR[ING]|SECURITY|ULARGE


CLUSTER /?

CLUSTER /HELP


Note: With the /CREATE, /ADDNODES, and /CHANGEPASSWORD options, you
      will be prompted for passwords not provided on the command line
      unless you also specify the /UNATTENDED option.
```

The following are some of the tasks that are impossible to do with Cluster Administrator or are easier to perform with Cluster.exe:

- Changing the password on the cluster service account

- Creating a server cluster or adding a node to a server cluster from a script

- Creating a server cluster as part of an unattended setup of Windows Server 2003

- Performing operations on multiple server clusters at the same time

Recovering from Cluster Node Failure

It is reasonable to assume that on any server cluster, you will have a component failure or need to take part of the server cluster offline for service. A properly designed and maintained server cluster should have no problems. But what if something causes the node to fail? For example, if a local hard disk in the node crashes, how do you recover?

Many of the same basic administrative tasks performed on nonclustered servers apply to clustered ones. Following the same practices will help prevent unplanned downtime and assist in restoring service when service is lost:

- **Have good documentation** Proper and complete documentation is the greatest asset you can have when trying to restore service. Configuration and contact information should also be included in your documentation.

- **Perform regular backups and periodically test restores** Clusters need to be backed up just like any other computer system. Periodically testing a restore will help keep the process fresh and help protect against hardware, media, and some software failures.

- **Perform Automated System Recovery (ASR) backups** When performing an ASR backup on your server cluster, make sure that one node owns the quorum resource during the ASR backup. If you need an ASR restore, this will be a critical component.

- **Develop performance baselines** A performance baseline should be developed for each node and the server cluster as a whole. This will help you determine if your server cluster is not performing properly or is being outgrown.

If a node experiences a failure, any groups that were on the failed node should be moved to another node (unless you are using the single-node model). You should then repair the failed components in the node in the same way as you would repair any computer system.

If repairing the node involves the replacement of the boot and/or system drives, you may need to do an ASR restore. As a precaution, you should physically disconnect the node from the cluster's shared storage devices first. Once the ASR restore is complete, shut down the node, reconnect it to the shared storage devices, and boot the node.

Server Clustering Best Practices

There are many ways to accomplish the setup and operation of a server cluster, but some methods are more reliable than others. Microsoft has published a number of "Best Practices" documents relating to its products and technologies, and server clusters are no exception.

Hardware Issues

The foundation of your server cluster is the hardware. It is critical to build reliable nodes at the hardware level. You cannot build high availability from unreliable or unknown components.

Compatibility List

Microsoft's position since it first began publishing cluster technology is that the hardware components used in a server cluster *and* the entire server cluster configuration itself must be listed on the Hardware Compatibility List (HCL) in order to receive support. With the introduction of Windows XP, Microsoft changed from the HCL to the Windows Catalog. Windows Server 2003-compatible hardware is listed in the Windows Server Catalog, but the concept and support requirements remain the same as they were with the HCL.

In order to receive technical support from Microsoft, ensure that your entire hardware configuration is listed as compatible in the Windows Server Catalog. Using unlisted hardware does not mean you cannot make the hardware work; it simply means that you cannot call Microsoft for help if the need arises.

Network Interface Controllers

A server cluster requires at least two network interfaces to function: one for the public network (where client requests come from) and one for the private interconnect network (for the heartbeat). Since a single private interconnect would present a single point of failure, it is good practice to have at least two interconnects. Do not use a *teamed configuration* with interconnects. A teamed configuration binds two or more physical interfaces together into one logical interface. Using teamed controllers preserves the single point of failure.

Network controllers should be identical. This includes not only the manufacturer and model, but also the firmware and drivers. Using identical controllers will also simplify the design of your server cluster and make troubleshooting easier.

Change the default name of each network interface to a descriptive name. Use Heartbeat, Interconnect, or Private for the interconnect interface. Similarly, use Public, Primary, or some similar name for the public interfaces. You should configure these names identically on each node. Following this procedure will make identifying and troubleshooting network issues much easier.

Storage Devices

No single resource in a server cluster requires more planning and preparation than shared storage. Poor planning can make management tasks quite difficult. Planning cluster disk resources requires attention to numerous details.

First, thorough planning must be done for the acquisition of the shared disk hardware. Develop capacity requirements and design disk layouts. Dynamic disks, volume sets, remote storage, removable storage, and software-based RAID cannot be used for shared cluster disks. Plan on using hardware RAID, and purchase extra hard disks for use as RAID hot spares.

If a single RAID controller is part of the design (likely in a single-node cluster), make sure that you keep an identical spare RAID controller on hand. The spare should be the exact brand and model and have the same firmware version as your production RAID controller.

If you are using Fibre Channel-based controllers, consider using multiple Fibre Channel host bus adapters (HBAs) configured in either a load-balanced or failover configuration. This will increase the cost of the cluster, but fault-tolerance will also increase. Before purchasing redundant HBAs, make sure that they are of the same brand, model, and firmware version. Also, ensure that the hardware vendor includes any necessary drivers or software to support the redundant HBA configuration.

If you are using SCSI–based controllers, ensure that each SCSI adapter on the shared storage bus is configured with a different SCSI ID. Also ensure that the shared SCSI bus is properly terminated. If either of these tasks is not done properly, data could be lost, hardware could be damaged, or the second cluster node may not properly join the cluster.

Use caution with write caching of shared disks. If power fails or a failover occurs before data is completely written to disk, data can be corrupted or lost. Disable write caching in **Device Manager** by clearing the **Enable write caching on the disk** check box on the **Policies** tab in the **Properties** of the drive, shown in Figures 6.17 and 6.18. If the RAID controller supports write caching, either disable the feature or ensure that battery backup for the cache or an alternate power supply for the controller is available.

Figure 6.17 Accessing Disk Drive Properties in Device Manager

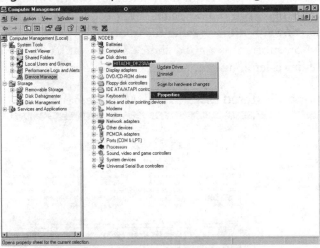

Figure 6.18 Disabling Write Caching on a Drive through Device Manager

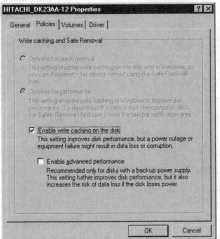

When starting the installation of the first node, ensure that the first node is the *only* node on the shared storage bus. This must be done to properly partition and format the drives in the shared storage. Until the cluster service is installed, other nodes can access the shared disks and cause data corruption.

If you are using a sophisticated disk system for shared cluster storage, use the features of the system to create logical drives that your nodes will access. This step is necessary because the *disk* is the smallest unit of storage that is recognized as a cluster resource. All of the partitions on a disk move with the disk between cluster nodes.

Once the first node is booted, format your shared drives. Only the NTFS file system is supported on clustered disks. The quorum drive should be created first. A minimum of 500MB should be assigned to the quorum drive, and no applications should reside on it. Partition and format the rest of your clustered drives as planned. Assign drive letters as you normally would, as shown in Figure 6.19, and document them. You can assign any drive letters that are not already in use, but it is a good idea to adopt the convention of assigning the quorum drive the same drive letter each time you create a cluster—Q (for quorum) is a good choice. Once you have assigned drive letters, you will need to match these drive-letter assignments on each node in the cluster.

Figure 6.19 Configuring Clustered Disks in Disk Management

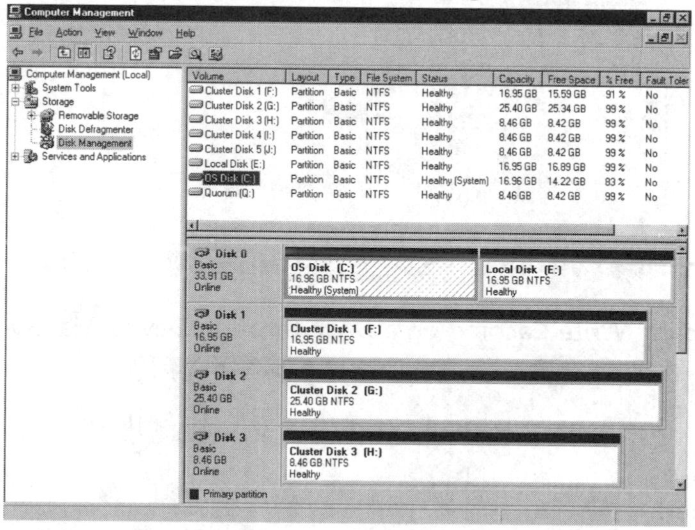

In addition to drive-letter assignments, you also have the option of using NTFS mounted drives. A mounted drive does not use a drive letter, but appears as a folder on an existing drive. Mounted drives on clustered storage must be mounted to a drive residing on shared storage in the same cluster group and are dependent on this "root" disk.

Planning sufficient allocation of disk space for your applications is critical. Since you cannot use dynamic disks on shared storage without using third-party tools, it is difficult to increase the size of clustered disks. Be sure to allow for data growth when initially sizing your partitions. This is a situation where it is better to allocate a few megabytes too many than a few kilobytes too few.

If you plan on using the *generic script* resource type, make sure the script file resides on a local disk, not a shared disk. It is possible for errant scripts to be the cause of a failover, and if a script resides on a clustered disk, the script "disappears" from under the node executing it. By keeping the scripts on a local disk, they remain available to the node at all times, and the appropriate error-checking logic can be used when errors are encountered.

Power-Saving Features

Windows Server 2003 includes power-management features that allow you to reduce the power consumed by your servers. This is very useful on laptop computers and some small servers, but can cause serious problems if used on clustered servers. If more than one node were to enter a standby or hibernation state, the server cluster could fail.

The power-saving options in Windows Server 2003 must be disabled for server clusters. Nodes should be configured to use the **Always On** power scheme, as shown in Figure 6.20. To access this option, select **Start | Control Panel | Power Options**. Using this power scheme will prevent the system from shutting down its hard drives and attempting to enter a standby or hibernation state.

Figure 6.20 Enabling the Always On Power Scheme

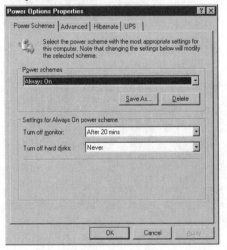

Cluster Network Configuration

Communications are a critical part of server cluster operations. Nodes must communicate with each other directly over the interconnects in order to determine each other's health and, if necessary, initiate a failover. Nodes must also communicate with client systems over the public network to provide services. Both of these networks require proper planning.

When referring to server clusters, there are four types of networks:

- **Internal cluster communications only (private network)** Used by nodes to handle their communication requirements only. No clients are present on this network. This network should be physically separated from other networks and must have good response times (less than 500 ms) in order to avoid availability problems.

- **Client access only (public network)** Used to service client requests only. No internal cluster communication occurs over this network.

- **All communications (mixed network)** Can handle both categories of communications traffic. Normally, this network acts as a backup to a private network, but that is not required.

- **Nonclustered network (disabled)** Unavailable for use by the cluster for either servicing clients or for internal communications.

When you create the server cluster through the New Server Cluster Wizard, it will detect the different networks configured in the server. You will be asked to select the role each network will have in the server cluster. Select **Internal cluster communications only (private network)** for the interconnect(s), as shown in Figure 6.21, instead of accepting the default value (which will mix the server cluster heartbeat traffic with client communication traffic).

Figure 6.21 Configuring Interconnect Networks

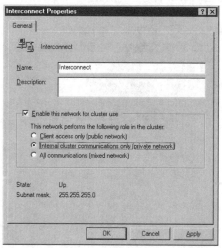

If you are using only a single interconnect, you should configure at least one public network interface with the **All communications (mixed network)** setting, as shown in Figure 6.22. This allows the server cluster to have a backup path for internal server cluster communications, if one is needed. If you have multiple interconnects configured, you should set the public interfaces to the **Client access only (private network)** setting.

Figure 6.22 Configuring Public Networks

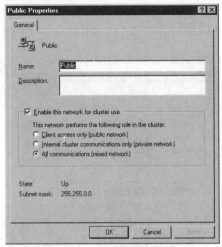

Multiple Interconnections

At least one interconnect between nodes is required. Node status messages are passed over this communication path. If this path becomes unavailable, a failover may be initiated. Because of this, multiple interconnects are recommended.

If your server cluster is configured with multiple interconnects, the reliability of the interconnects goes up. If a heartbeat message on one interconnect path goes unanswered, the node will attempt to use the other interconnect paths before initiating a failover. As with most components in a high-availability system, redundancy is good.

When using multiple interconnects, follow the same rules previously stated for configuration, but try to avoid using multiple ports on the same multiport network interface card (NIC). If the card fails, you will lose the interconnect. If you are using two dual-port cards, try to configure the system to use one port on each card for interconnects and the other port for your public network.

Node-to-Node Communication

The interconnects are used by the nodes to determine each other's status. This communication is unencrypted and frequent. Normal client activity does not occur on this network, so you should not have client-type services assigned to the network interface used for interconnects. Windows Server 2003 normally attaches the following services to each network interface:

- Client for Microsoft Networks
- Network Load Balancing
- File and Printer Sharing for Microsoft Networks
- Internet Protocol (TCP/IP)

You should uncheck the first three services from each interconnect interface (the properties of a network interface are accessible via **Start | Control Panel | Network Connections**). Only TCP/IP should be assigned. Figure 6.23 shows a properly configured interconnect interface.

Figure 6.23 Configuring an Interconnect Interface

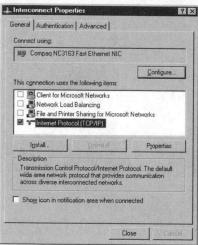

You should also make sure that the Network Priority property of the server cluster is configured with the interconnect(s) given highest priority, as shown in Figure 6.24. This ensures that internal cluster communication attempts are made on the interconnects first. To access this property, in Cluster Administrator, right-click the server cluster name and select **Properties**.

Figure 6.24 Setting the Network Priority Property of the Cluster

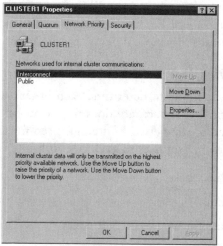

Binding Order

Binding is the process of linking the various communications components together, in the proper order, to establish the communications path. To configure the binding order of communication protocols and services to the network interface, select **Start | Control Panel | Network Connections**. Click the **Advanced** menu and select **Advanced Settings….** When establishing the order of network connections, you should ensure that the public interfaces appear highest on the list, followed by interconnects, and then any other interfaces. Figure 6.25 shows this binding order.

Figure 6.25 Setting the Proper Binding Order of Interfaces

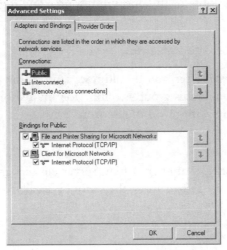

Adapter Settings

All network interfaces in a server cluster should be manually set for speed and duplex mode. Do not allow the network adapters to attempt to auto-negotiate these settings. If the controllers negotiate differently, your communications can be disrupted. Also, in many cases, a crossover cable is used on the interconnects. In these cases, an auto-negotiation may fail entirely, and the interconnect may never be established, affecting cluster operation.

As mentioned earlier, teamed network adapters must not be used for interconnects. However, they are perfectly acceptable for the public network interfaces. A failover or load-balanced configuration increases redundancy and reliability.

TCP/IP Settings

Static IP addresses (along with the relevant DNS and WINS information) should be used on public network interfaces. For the interconnects, you *must* use static IP addresses.

It is also a good practice to assign private IP addresses on interconnects from a different address class than your public class. For example, if you are using class A addresses (10.*x.x.x*) on your public interface, you could use class C addresses (192.168.*x.x*) on your interconnects. Following this practice helps easily identify the type of network you may be troubleshooting just by looking at the address class. Using addresses this way is not required, but it does prove useful.

Finally, you should not configure IP gateway, DNS, or WINS addresses on your interconnect interfaces. Name resolution is usually not required on interconnects and, if configured, could cause conflicts with name resolution on your public interfaces. All public interfaces must reside on the same IP subnet. Likewise, all interconnect interfaces must reside on the same IP subnet.

The Default Cluster Group

Every server cluster has at least one cluster group: the default. This group contains the following resources:

- Quorum disk (which contains the quorum resource and logs)
- Cluster IP address
- Cluster name (which creates the virtual server)

When designing your server cluster, you should not plan on using these resources for anything other than system administration. If this group is offline for any reason, cluster operation can be compromised. Do not install applications on the quorum drive or in the default cluster group.

Security

Security is a consideration for any computer system. Server clusters are no exception. In fact, because they often contain critical information, they should usually be more closely guarded than a standard server.

Physical Security

Nodes should be kept in controlled environments and behind locked doors. More downtime is caused by accident than by intent. It is obvious that you would not want an unhappy or ex-employee to have access to your computer systems, but what about the curious user? Both can lead to the same end.

When setting up physical security, do not forget to include the power systems, network switches and routers, keyboards, mice, and monitors. Unauthorized access to any of these can lead to an unexpected outage.

Public/Mixed Networks

It is a good idea to isolate critical server clusters behind firewalls if possible. A properly configured firewall will also allow you to control the network traffic your server cluster encounters.

If there are infrastructure servers (DNS, WINS, and so on) that are relied on to access the server cluster, make sure that those servers are secured as well. If, for example, name resolution fails, it is possible that clients will not be able to access the server cluster, even though it is fully operational.

Private Networks

The traffic on the private interconnect networks is meant to be used and accessed by nodes only. If high traffic levels disrupt or delay heartbeat messages, the server cluster may interpret this as a node failure and initiate a failover. For this reason, it is a good idea to place the interconnects on their own switch or virtual LAN (VLAN) and to not mix heartbeats with other traffic.

Do not place infrastructure servers (DNS, WINS, DHCP, and so on) on the same subnet as the interconnects. These services are not used by the interconnects and may cause the conflicts you desire to avoid.

Remote Administration of Cluster Nodes

Administration of your server cluster should be limited to a few controlled and trusted nodes. The administrative tools are quite powerful and could be used intentionally or accidentally to cause failovers, service stoppages, resource stoppages, or node evictions.

Use of Terminal Services on nodes is debatable. Terminal Services works just fine on nodes and actually includes some benefits. Evaluate your administrative, security, and operational needs to determine if installing Terminal Services on your nodes is appropriate for your situation.

The Cluster Service Account

The account that the cluster service uses must be a domain-level account and configured to be a member of the local Administrators group on each node. This account should not be a member of the Domain Admins group. Using an account that has elevated domain-level privileges would present a strong security risk if the cluster service account were to become compromised.

Do not use the cluster service account for administration, and be sure to configure it so that it can log on to only cluster nodes. Use different cluster service accounts for each cluster in your environment. This limits the scope of a security breach in the event that one occurs. If any of the applications running on your server cluster require accounts for operation, create and assign accounts specifically for the applications. Do not use the cluster service account for running applications. Doing so would make your cluster vulnerable to a malfunctioning application.

If you are required to permanently *evict* (forcibly remove) a node from a server cluster, you should manually remove the cluster service account from the appropriate local security groups on the evicted node. The cluster administrative tools will not automatically remove this account. Leaving this account with elevated permissions on an evicted node can expose you to security risks for both the evicted node and your domain.

Another possible method of securing a server cluster is to create a *domainlet*. A domainlet is a domain created just to host a server cluster. Each node in the server cluster is a domain controller of the domain. A domainlet allows you to better define and control the security boundary for the cluster. There are advantages and disadvantages to this approach. (For more information about domainlets, visit Microsoft's Web site.)

Client Access

Use the security features built into Windows Server 2003 and Active Directory (AD) to secure the applications and data on your server cluster. Turn on and use the auditing features of the operating system to see what activity is occurring on your server cluster.

Administrative Access

In larger organizations, it may be possible to have a different group of personnel responsible for administering clusters than those that perform other administrative tasks. Evaluate this possibility in your organization. If this strategy is adopted, assign these cluster administrators to a domain group and make that group a member of the appropriate local groups on the nodes. Also, assign NTFS permissions in a similar manner.

Cluster Data Security

As with any server, data should be accessed in a controlled manner. You do not want users accessing, deleting, or corrupting data. Assign appropriate NTFS file system permissions on a server cluster, just as you would assign them on a stand-alone server.

Disk Resource Security

Use NTFS permissions to ensure that only members of the Administrators group and the cluster service account can access the quorum disk. If you use scripts and the generic script resource type, you should assign appropriate NTFS Execute permissions to the scripts. A buggy script, or one run in an unplanned or uncontrolled manner, may cause data loss or a service outage.

Cluster Configuration Log File Security

When a cluster is created or a node is added to a cluster using the Wizard, a file containing critical information about the cluster is placed the *%systemroot%*\System32\LogFiles\Cluster\ directory, unless you do not have administrative permissions on the node; in that case, the file is placed in the *%temp%* directory. The log file, ClCfgSrv.log, should have NTFS permissions that allow access to only the Administrators group and the cluster service account.

Creating a New Cluster

Use the following steps to create a server cluster. Only the creation of the first node is covered. Each server cluster and network configuration is unique. You will need to substitute your TCP/IP addresses and account names, and adjust this process to fit your hardware.

1. Properly assemble your hardware. Ensure that only this first node is connected to and can access the shared storage unit(s).

2. Assign friendly names to your network interfaces and configure them with static IP addresses.

3. Log on to your domain with an account capable of creating user accounts. Open **Active Directory Users and Computers**. In the **Users** container, create an account called **ClusterAdmin** matching the settings shown in Figures 6.26 and 6.27. Close **Active Directory Users and Computers**.

Figure 6.26 Create a New Cluster Service User Account

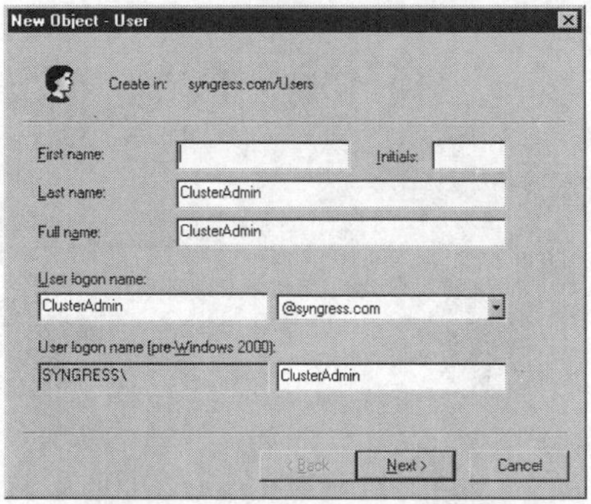

Figure 6.27 Assign a Password and Properties to New Cluster Service User Account

4. Log on to your first cluster node and start Cluster Administrator by selecting **Start | Administrative Tools | Cluster Administrator**.

5. When the **Open Connection to Cluster** dialog box is presented (Figure 6.28), select **Create new cluster** from the **Action** drop-down box and click **OK**.

Figure 6.28 Open Connection to Cluster

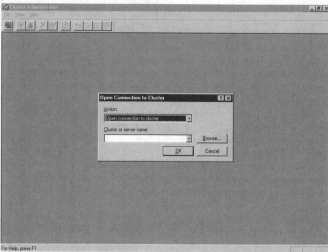

6. The **New Server Cluster Wizard** will start, as shown in Figure 6.29. Click **Next**.

Figure 6.29 The New Server Cluster Wizard's Welcome Window

7. Select your domain in the **Domain** drop-down list and enter **cluster1** in the **Cluster name** text box, as shown in Figure 6.30. Click **Next**.

Figure 6.30 Specify the Cluster Name and Domain

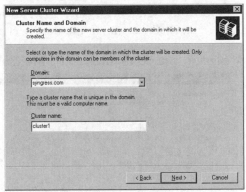

8. Enter the name of the computer that will become your first node in the **Computer name** text box, as shown in Figure 6.31, and click **Next**.

Figure 6.31 Select the Computer Name

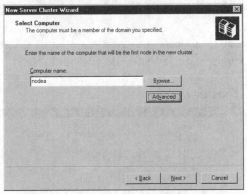

9. The **Analyzing Configuration** window will appear, as shown in Figure 6.32, while the configuration of the node is verified. You can click the **View Log...** button to see the history of actions the Wizard has performed, or click the **Details...** button to see the most recent task.

Figure 6.32 Analyzing the Configuration of the Cluster Node

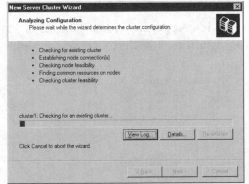

10. When the analysis is completed, the **Analyzing Configuration** window will show the tasks completed, as shown in Figure 6.33. Click the plus signs (+) to see the details behind each step. When you're finished examining the details, click **Next**.

Figure 6.33 Finished Analyzing the Configuration of the Cluster Node

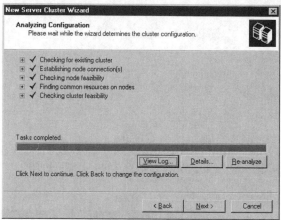

11. You are asked what IP address you want assigned to the server cluster, as shown in Figure 6.34. Enter the appropriate **IP Address** and click **Next**.

Figure 6.34 Enter the Cluster IP Address

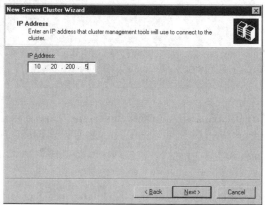

12. In the **Cluster Service Account** window, shown in Figure 6.35, enter the **User name**, **Password**, and **Domain** for the cluster service account you created in step 3. Then click **Next**.

Figure 6.35 Enter the Cluster Service Account Information

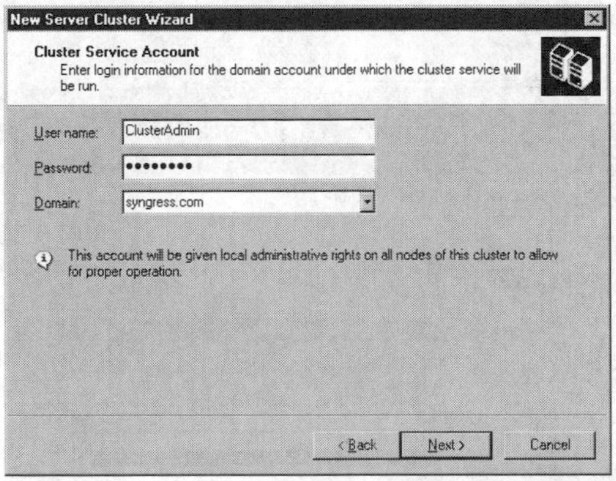

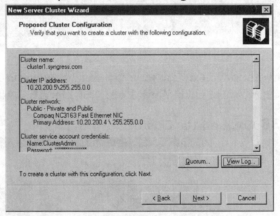

13. The Wizard will display the proposed server cluster configuration, as shown in Figure 6.36. Review the information.

Figure 6.36 Review the Proposed Cluster Configuration

14. Click the **Quorum…** button. Select the correct quorum disk for your configuration from the drop-down list, as shown in Figure 6.37, and select **OK**.

Figure 6.37 Select the Quorum Disk

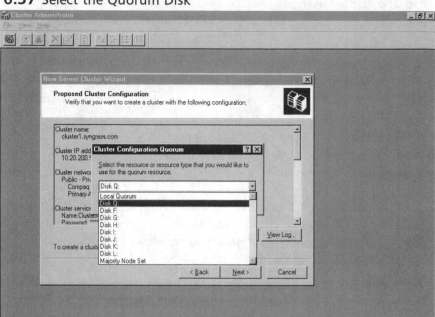

15.   The Wizard will now create the server cluster, as shown in Figure 6.38. As the configuration progresses, you can click **View Log...** or **Details...** to see what the Wizard is doing.

Figure 6.38 Creating the Cluster

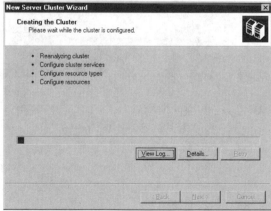

16.   When the Wizard finishes creating the server cluster, the **Creating the Cluster** window will show the tasks completed, as shown in Figure 6.39. Click the plus signs (+) to see details about each step performed. Click **Next**.

Figure 6.39 Completed Cluster Creation

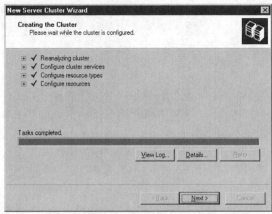

17. The Wizard informs you that the server cluster is created, as shown in Figure 6.40. You can click **View Log…** to examine all of the activity involved in the creation. Click **Finish** to exit the Wizard.

Figure 6.40 The Wizard's Final Window

18. The Cluster Administrator utility appears. As shown in Figure 6.41, it displays the server cluster you just created.

Figure 6.41 The Newly Created Cluster

19. Right-click the server cluster name (CLUSTER1) and select **Properties**. Click the Network Priority tab and move Interconnect to the top of the list, as shown in Figure 6.42. Click Apply.

Figure 6.42 Change Network Priorities

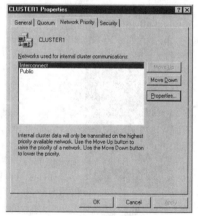

20. Examine the Quorum and Security tabs to become familiar with the default settings on these tabs. When you have finished reviewing the configuration of these tabs, click **OK**. Then close Cluster Administrator.

Making Network Load Balancing Part of Your High-Availability Plan

The other high-availability tool included in Windows Server 2003 is Network Load Balancing (NLB). A primary use for NLB is increasing the scalability and availability of Internet applications (Web, FTP, VPN, firewall, proxy servers, and so on) by having multiple machines simultaneously answering and serving client requests. NLB is included in all versions of Windows Server 2003 and is installed automatically, although it must be configured and activated before it is usable.

Microsoft also considers NLB a clustering technology. The two clustering technologies are very different and serve different purposes. A server cluster requires specialized hardware, and there is typically one installed copy of each application, which moves between server cluster nodes. Only the node actively hosting the application responds to client requests. An NLB cluster does not require any specialized or additional hardware. *Every* host runs a *separate and independent copy* of the application and actively responds to client requests. Server clusters are used mainly for database-type applications. NLB clusters are used for traffic or communication type applications.

NLB has been available since Windows NT 4, when it was an add-in component called Windows Load Balancing Service (WLBS). You will still see NLB called this in some utilities and documentation. Unless specifically referred to in a historical context, the terms *WLBS* and *NLB* should be considered interchangeable.

Terminology and Concepts

NLB introduces some new terms for dealing with this form of clustering. Some terms are similar to those used with server clusters, but they have different meanings.

Hosts/Default Host

When referring to NLB, a *host* is a server running any edition of Windows Server 2003 that has been configured to respond to client requests via the NLB driver. Since NLB is automatically installed, any Windows Server 2003 server has the potential to be an NLB host.

The default host in an NLB cluster is the host with the highest currently active *priority*. The priority is a unique identifying number assigned to each host in an NLB cluster. An NLB cluster can have up to 32 hosts, so the priorities range from 1 to 32. Hosts cannot be configured to have the same priority.

Load Weight

As previously mentioned, an NLB cluster can consist of up to 32 hosts. The hosts do not need to be identical in hardware or configuration. The *load weight* is a mechanism for distributing the traffic load within an NLB cluster to the hosts that are most suited to handle the load. Lighter loads can be configured for hosts with less capacity and heavier loads for more robust hosts.

The load weight is applicable only if specifically configured; otherwise, all hosts are configured with equal load weights. When used, each host is assigned a load weight from 0 (lowest weight) to 100 (highest weight). The weights from all active hosts in the cluster are averaged, and traffic is distributed accordingly. In this way, the load weight is a relative value within the NLB cluster.

Traffic Distribution

The way requests from clients are spread out among the hosts in an NLB cluster is referred to as *traffic distribution*. Each host in an NLB cluster is configured with at least two IP addresses. One address is reserved for the nonclustered traffic directed to the host, and the second IP address is shared among all nodes in the cluster and is called the *cluster IP address*. It is to this second IP address that clients direct their requests.

When a request is sent to the cluster IP address, all hosts in the cluster receive the request. The NLB driver passes the incoming traffic through the defined *port rules*. The host that the port rules specify to receive the request services the request, while all other hosts discard the request. Port rules are the mechanism used to direct incoming traffic on specific TCP/IP ports to specific hosts or groups of hosts. All hosts in an NLB cluster must have the same number and specific port rules. Port rules can apply to a specific cluster IP address, all port numbers, or a specific range of port numbers, and to the TCP, UDP, or both protocols.

In addition, each port rule contains a *filtering mode* for that rule. The filtering mode defines how the hosts in a cluster handle inbound traffic. The options for the filtering mode are as follows:

- **Disabled** All traffic matching the associated cluster IP address, port range, and protocol will be blocked. Applications on the NLB cluster will never see this traffic.

- **Single Host** All traffic matching the associated cluster IP address, port range, and protocol will be handled by one specific host in an NLB cluster. For example, this filtering mode could be used to direct all FTP traffic inbound to an NLB cluster to host 2 of that cluster, while Web traffic is served from all nodes.

- **Multiple Host** All traffic matching the associated cluster IP address, port range, and protocol will be distributed to multiple hosts in the NLB cluster. When using the multiple host filtering mode, you must also select an *affinity*. Affinity describes how multiple requests from the same client are directed among the multiple hosts. There are three affinity options:

  - **None** Any NLB host matching the port rule can service requests from clients. This is the most efficient affinity setting in terms of evenly distributing the workload, but it should not be used with the UDP or Both protocol settings to properly handle fragmented packets.

  - **Single** This is the default setting. Single affinity ensures that only one NLB host will handle traffic requests for the same client session. This setting is necessary if session state preservation is needed. (for example, for Web servers using server-side cookies). This setting reliably supports the UDP or Both protocol setting.

  - **Class C** This affinity setting specifies that all client requests originating from the same class C IP subnet will be directed to the same NLB host. This setting is useful in large NLB clusters handling traffic inbound from the Internet. This setting also reliably supports the UDP or Both protocol setting.

Convergence and Heartbeats

An NLB cluster can be a fluid environment. By design, a host can be added or removed from the operational cluster without affecting the services provided by the NLB cluster. However, each time a host is added to or removed from the NLB cluster, the cluster must reconfigure itself to allow for the new increased or decreased capacity, and calculate for traffic distribution accordingly. This process is called *convergence*. During convergence, the new stable state of the cluster and default host (the host with the highest priority) is determined.

Convergence normally occurs within 10 seconds, and client requests to operational hosts are unaffected. Requests to hosts that have failed or exited the cluster are redistributed to working hosts after convergence is completed.

NLB cluster hosts determine the status of each other by exchanging *heartbeat* messages. Heartbeats in an NLB cluster differ from those used in a server cluster but serve a similar purpose. In essence, the heartbeat messages generated by an NLB host are a way for the host to tell the other members of the cluster "I'm alive." By default, if a host does not send a heartbeat message to the other NLB cluster hosts within five seconds, it will be considered failed and a convergence will be initiated.

How NLB Works

NLB requires between 2 and 32 host systems to be effective. Each host has its own copy of the applications being supported by the cluster. The hosts share one or more IP addresses. When the cluster is started, the hosts perform a convergence. Once convergence is complete, the hosts will begin responding to client requests. Client systems then issue requests directed to one of the cluster IP addresses. All of the cluster hosts receive the request. The host that is next in line to service the request does so, while the other hosts ignore it.

Once per second, a host issues heartbeat messages to the other hosts in the NLB cluster. If another host is added or if a host leaves, the cluster will perform another convergence.

Relationship of NLB to Clustering

Server clustering and NLB clustering differ greatly. You cannot combine NLB and server clustering on the same hosts, but the two technologies can sometimes be used together to increase overall reliability and performance.

Server clustering is used primarily for database-type applications (such as SQL Server, Exchange Server, and Oracle) that run as a single instance of the application, and parallel or concurrent execution is impossible or impractical. Server-clustered databases often operate behind an NLB cluster. For this reason, a server cluster is sometimes referred to as the *back-end*.

NLB is used for applications whose primary resource is TCP/IP communication-related—such as Internet Information Server (IIS), ISA Server, virtual private network (VPN) servers, and terminal servers—that can run in multiple instances or in a parallel fashion. By adding hosts to an NLB cluster, more requests can be serviced simultaneously, increasing responsiveness and performance. The applications on the NLB hosts would then issue requests to the back-end on the client's behalf, process the returned request, and then fulfill the original client request. Since the NLB cluster logically resides between the client and the server cluster, or in "front" of the server cluster, the NLB cluster is usually referred to as the *front-end*.

The combination of these two high-availability technologies can be very powerful and reliable. Figure 6.43 illustrates this front-end/back-end structure.

Figure 6.43 Combining Network Load Balancing and Server Clustering into a Front-end/Back-end Architecture

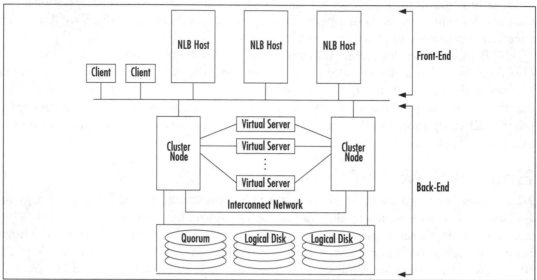

Managing NLB Clusters

Windows Server 2003 includes some useful tools for creating and managing NLB clusters. The NLB Manager (new to Windows Server 2003) is provided to centrally create and manage NLB clusters from a graphical interface. For performing administrative tasks from the command-line interface, the NLB.exe utility is provided.

Using the NLB Manager Tool

Microsoft made many improvements and added many tools to Windows Server 2003, but NLB Manager should earn Microsoft a special thanks. This tool is extremely powerful. It takes what used to be a difficult manual process and simplifies it with a point-and-click interface.

With NLB Manager, you can perform the following tasks:

- Create a new NLB cluster.
- Add and automatically configure a new host.
- Remove a host from an NLB cluster, automatically disabling NLB on the removed host.
- Configure all NLB-related properties on the cluster.
- Configure all hosts in the cluster.
- Replicate the NLB cluster configuration (but not applications) to other NLB hosts.
- Troubleshoot NLB clusters.

To run NLB Manager, you must be a member of the local Administrators group on the host you are adding, configuring, or removing from the cluster. You do not need to have elevated privileges for the system on which you are running NLB Manager.

The NLB Manager utility is a part of the Windows Server 2003 Administration Tools Pack, which can be found in *%systemroot%*\System32\Adminpak.msi. The Administration Tools Pack can be installed on a Windows XP workstation to allow remote administration.

To access NLB Manager, select **Start | Administrative Tools | Network Load Balancing Manager**. When the utility starts for the first time, you are presented with an empty session, as shown in Figure 6.44. From here, you can begin the process of creating or managing an NLB cluster.

Figure 6.44 Starting NLB Manager for the First Time

Remote Management

You must take a series of steps in order to remotely manage an NLB cluster or host with NLB Manager. NLB Manager uses Windows Management Instrumentation (WMI) interfaces. WMI requires Remote Procedure Call (RPC) and Distributed Component Object Model (DCOM) availability. You can verify that these services are available for NLB Manager's use by selecting **Start | Administrative Tools | Services** and viewing the list of services.

If you are attempting to manage an NLB cluster that is on the other side of a firewall from your location, you will need to make sure that your firewall is configured to allow DCOM to pass. Microsoft has a white paper available that describes how to do this at www.microsoft.com/com/wpaper/dcomfw.asp.

Command-Line Tools

Before Windows Server 2003, the only way to manage a load-balanced cluster was with command-line tools. In some situations, this approach still makes sense, because command-line tools can be scripted and scheduled.

Microsoft includes the NLB.exe utility for this purpose. NLB.exe can perform many of the same functions as NLB Manager, but it uses a different mechanism that is disabled by default. NLB.exe uses the remote-control feature of NLB instead of RPC and DCOM. This may be advantageous in certain circumstances, but enabling the remote-control feature exposes the cluster to possible security risks. Microsoft recommends that remote control be disabled and suggests that you perform all NLB administration through NLB Manager.

If you need to use NLB.exe, make sure that you enforce strong passwords on the NLB cluster and keep your NLB cluster behind a firewall. The default UDP ports used by NLM.exe are 1717 and 2504.

Figure 6.45 shows the command-line parameters that can be used with NLB.exe.

Figure 6.45 Output of the NLB.exe /? Command

```
Usage: NLB <command> [/PASSW [<password>]] [/PORT <port>]
<command>

  help                              - displays this help
  ip2mac    <cluster>               - displays the MAC address for the
                                        specified cluster
  reload    [<cluster> | ALL]       - reloads the driver's parameters
                                        from the registry for the
                                        specified cluster (local only).
                                        Same as ALL if parameter is not
                                        specified.
  display   [<cluster> | ALL]       - displays configuration parameters,
                                        current status, and last several
                                        event log messages for the
                                        specified cluster (local only).
                                        Same as ALL if parameter is not
                                        specified.
  query     [<cluster_spec>]        - displays the current cluster state
                                        for the current members of the
                                        specified cluster. If not
                                        specified a local query is
                                        performed for all instances.
  suspend   [<cluster_spec>]        - suspends cluster operations
                                        (start, stop, etc.) for the
                                        specified cluster until the resume
                                        command is issued. If cluster is
                                        not specified, applies to all
                                        instances on local host.
```

Continued

Figure 6.45 Output of the NLB.exe /? Command

```
resume    [<cluster_spec>]           - resumes cluster operations after a
                                       previous suspend command for the
                                       specified cluster. If cluster is
                                       not specified, applies to all
                                       instances on local host.
start     [<cluster_spec>]           - starts cluster operations on the
                                       specified hosts. Applies to local
                                       host if cluster is not specified.
stop      [<cluster_spec>]           - stops cluster operations on the
                                       specified hosts. Applies to local
                                       host if cluster is not specified.
drainstop [<cluster_spec>]           - disables all new traffic handling
                                       on the specified hosts and stops
                                       cluster operations. Applies to
                                       local host if cluster is not
                                       specified.
enable <port_spec> <cluster_spec>    - enables traffic handling on the
                                       specified cluster for the rule
                                       whose port range contains the
                                       specified port
disable <port_spec> <cluster_spec>   - disables ALL traffic handling on
                                       the specified cluster for the rule
                                       whose port range contains the
                                       specified port
drain <port_spec> <cluster_spec>     - disables NEW traffic handling on
                                       the specified cluster for the rule
                                       whose port range contains the
                                       specified port
queryport [<vip>:]<port>             - retrieve the current state of the
          [<cluster_spec>]             port rule. If the rule is handling
                                       traffic, packet handling
                                       statistics are also returned.
params [<cluster> | ALL]             - retrieve the current parameters
                                       from the NLB driver for the
                                       specified cluster on the local
                                       host.
```

Continued

Figure 6.45 Output of the NLB.exe /? Command

```
<port_spec>
  [<vip>: | ALL:](<port> | ALL)    - every virtual ip address (neither
                                     <vip> nor ALL) or specific <vip>
                                     or the "All" vip, on a specific
                                     <port> rule or ALL ports
<cluster_spec>
  <cluster>:<host> | ((<cluster> | ALL) - specific <cluster> on a
      specific
  (LOCAL | GLOBAL))                   <host>, OR specific <cluster> or
                                     ALL clusters, on the LOCAL machine
                                     or all (GLOBAL) machines that are
                                     a part of the cluster
      <cluster>                    - cluster name | cluster primary IP
                                     address
      <host>                       - host within the cluster (default -
                                     ALL hosts): dedicated name |
                                     IP address | host priority ID
                                     (1..32) | 0 for current DEFAULT
                                     host
      <vip>                        - virtual ip address in the port
                                     rule
      <port>                       - TCP/UDP port number

Remote options:
  /PASSW <password>                - remote control password (default -
                                     NONE)
                                     blank <password> for console prompt
  /PORT <port>                     - cluster's remote control UDP port
```

NLB Error Detection and Handling

The objective of NLB is increased availability. Consequently, Microsoft has included mechanisms in NLB to handle and manage error situations without affecting the reliability of the NLB cluster. If an error is encountered, details about the error are recorded in the Windows event log, and NLB isolates the host having the problem by preventing it from joining the cluster and servicing requests.

As previously stated, an NLB cluster performs a convergence when a host joins or leaves the cluster. When a host attempts to join, it notifies the other cluster hosts of its configuration. Likewise, the other hosts notify the joining host of their configurations. A check for consistency in operating parameters (host priority, port rules, and so on) is performed. If the host that is attempting to join does not have a configuration consistent with the hosts already in the cluster, the new host will not be allowed to join, and convergence will not occur. This process ensures that a misconfigured host does not compromise cluster operations.

Monitoring NLB

Events encountered by NLB (convergence, communication errors, and so on) are recorded by NLB in the System event log. You can use Event Viewer to examine these events.

NLB Manager does not use the Windows event logs. Instead, it includes its own logging function that records actions performed by the utility. This log file allows you to see what administrative activity has occurred on your NLB cluster.

The log function must be activated before it can be used. To activate the log, start NLB Manager and select **Options | Log Settings...**, as shown in Figure 6.46.

Figure 6.46 Starting an NLB Manager Log

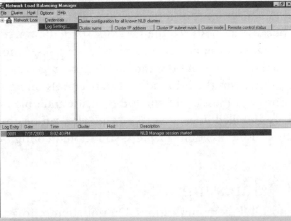

When the **Log Settings** dialog box appears, as shown in Figure 6.47, check **Enable logging** and enter a path and filename for the log. If no path is given, the log file is stored in the profile of the logged-on user account.

Figure 6.47 Enabling the NLB Manager Log

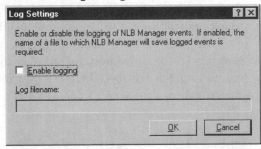

This log file contains sensitive information about your NLB cluster. You should secure it by restricting access to it with NTFS permissions. Be aware, however, that the account under which NLB Manager runs will require Full Control permissions to the log file.

Using the WLBS Cluster Control Utility

If you have enabled the remote-control feature of NLB, you can use the NLB.exe command-line utility to get status information from an NLB cluster. You can use the **NLB query** command to display the current configuration, status, and any recent event log messages for the NLB cluster. The **NLB display** command displays the current state of the NLB cluster and hosts.

NLB Best Practices

As with all technologies, there are certain ways to implement and operate NLB that are better than others. Microsoft publishes a number of items that fall into the best practices category for NLB.

Multiple Network Adapters

NLB can be implemented with a single network interface adapter in each host, but multiple adapters are recommended. A single network interface generates additional communications overhead for the NLB cluster, because all hosts see the network traffic destined for a specific host.

You are also limited in how you can perform administrative tasks. A host with a single network interface (operating in the default unicast mode) cannot perform regular (non-NLB) communications. This means that you cannot run the NLB administrative tools on an NLB host in this configuration. To avoid this situation, you must enable multicast or use multiple network adapters. When multiple network adapters are installed in each host, one adapter can be configured for NLB and the other for regular traffic. When using multiple adapters, you should configure only one adapter for use by NLB.

Protocols and IP Addressing

NLB supports only TCP and UDP communications. Do not attempt to attach any other protocols (IPX/SPX, AppleTalk, ATM, and so on) to the adapter. Only static IP addresses are allowed on an NLB cluster node. DHCP is not supported. This is true for the cluster IP address and the dedicated host IP address.

Each node in an NLB cluster must be on the same TCP/IP subnet. NLB does not support hosts residing on multiple subnets.

When configuring the IP addresses for your hosts, keep in mind that multiple IP addresses can be assigned to an adapter, and *all* of those IP addresses will be load-balanced, *except* for the address configured as the host's dedicated address (the one that handles non-NLB traffic). The host's dedicated IP address must be first on the list of IP addresses assigned to a network interface, so that any outbound traffic from the host is sent from this IP address. Figure 6.48 shows a network adapter with multiple IP addresses configured in the **Advanced TCP/IP Settings** dialog box (to open this dialog box, click **Advanced** in the **Internet Protocol (TCP/IP) Properties** dialog box for the network interface properties).

Figure 6.48 Configuring a Network Adapter with Multiple IP Addresses

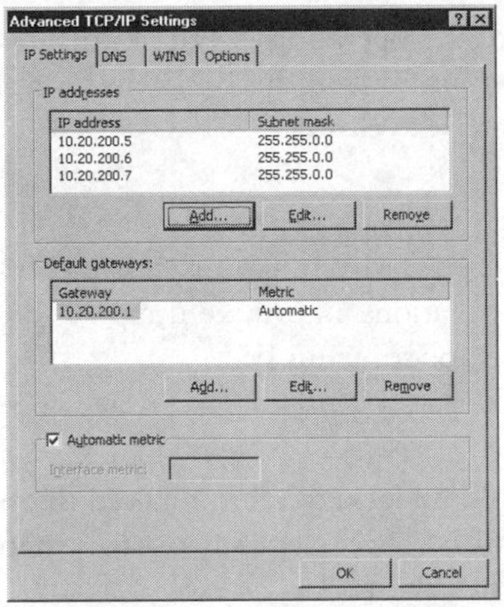

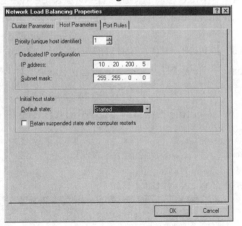

You will notice from the example in Figure 6.48 that the IP address **10.20.200.5** is listed first and is therefore the node's dedicated IP address. This configuration is not complete, however, until the properties of the NLB driver are also configured with this IP address, as shown in Figure 6.49 (check **Network Load Balancing** in the property pages of the network interface, and then click the **Properties** button to open this dialog box).

Figure 6.49 NLB Dedicated IP Address Configuration

Security

Security is of greater concern in an NLB cluster than it is with a stand-alone server. NLB has no inherent security features, and it cannot be used as a firewall or in any other intrusion-prevention role. When improperly configured, NLB can open security holes into your environment. It is critical that you take proper security precautions when using NLB.

Host Security

Consider tightening the security of the operating system. Limit the number of users permitted to access the hosts. Place a secured PC in front of the NLB cluster and behind a firewall. Use this PC to run NLB Manager and administer the cluster.

Application Security

Because NLB provides no additional security functions, it is imperative to use any security features available in your load-balanced applications. If you are using IIS on an NLB cluster, follow the documented procedures and guidelines for securing IIS.

Physical Security

Like any server, an NLB host should be locked behind closed doors for protection, and so should the network equipment that the NLB cluster depends on. It is theoretically possible to cause a service disruption by forging cluster heartbeats.

Host List

If you are using the host list feature of NLB Manager, you should secure the host list file on your administrative system. Restrict access to appropriate users.

Remote Control Option

The remote-control feature of NLB is a known security risk. You should avoid using this feature. If you must enable remote control, ensure that strong passwords are used. It is also advisable to place the cluster behind a firewall and filter the port traffic going to the remote-control ports.

Create A Network Load Balancing Cluster

Use the following steps to create a new NLB cluster using the NLB Manager administrative tool. Where appropriate, use your own TCP/IP addresses.

1. Start NLB Manager by selecting **Start | Administrative Tools | Network Load Balancing Manager**.

2. Select **Cluster | New**, as shown in Figure 6.50.

Figure 6.50 Create a New NLB Cluster

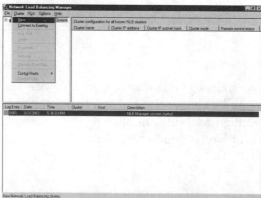

3. You will be presented with the Cluster Parameters window. Enter the IP address, Subnet mask, and Full Internet name (this is the fully qualified domain name) of the cluster in the Cluster IP configuration section, as shown in Figure 6.51.

Figure 6.51 Configure Cluster Parameters

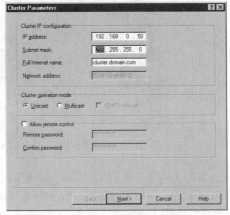

4. Click the Multicast option in the Cluster operation mode section, and notice how the Network address entry changes, as shown in Figure 6.52. The network (media access control, or MAC) changes to fit the correct mode based on the communication mechanism you select. (We will leave Multicast selected for the example.)

Figure 6.52 Select Multicast Cluster Operation Mode

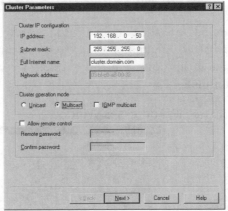

5. Select the check box next to IGMP multicast, as shown in Figure 6.53.

Figure 6.53 Select IGMP Multicast with the Cluster Operation Mode

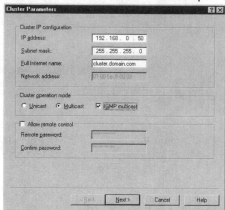

6. You will be presented with the warning message shown in Figure 6.54. This message is intended to remind you that additional configuration of your switches and NIC may be required if you select IGMP support. Click OK to close the Warning dialog box.

Figure 6.54 IGMP Warning Message

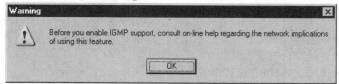

7. You will be presented with the Cluster IP Addresses window, as shown in Figure 6.55. If you want to load-balance multiple IP addresses, you can click the Add... button and add them to the cluster at this point. For this example, we will work with only one address. Click Next to continue.

Figure 6.55 Cluster IP Addresses Window

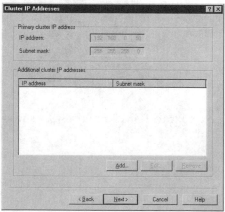

8. In the Port Rules window, you see the default port rule, as shown in Figure 6.56. This rule evenly distributes arriving traffic among all cluster hosts. Select the default port rule and click **Edit**....

Figure 6.56 The Port Rules Window

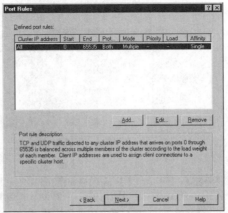

9. The Add/Edit Port Rule dialog box appears, as shown in Figure 6.57. As you can see, the default port rule applies to all cluster IP addresses on all ports and protocols. It also directs all client requests to the same cluster host (Multiple host/Single Affinity). Click **Cancel** to avoid modifying the default port rule.

Figure 6.57 The Add/Edit Port Rule Dialog Box

10. Click **Next** in the Port Rules window to advance to the Connect window.

11. Enter the name of a host in the Host field and click the **Connect** button. When the host is identified, select the network interface to load-balance, as shown in Figure 6.58. Then click **Next**.

Figure 6.58 Connect to an NLB Node

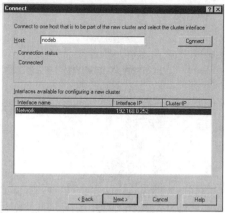

At this point, you may receive the warning message, as shown in Figure 6.59. If you receive this message, you are using DHCP to assign an IP address to your network interface. You must use static IP addresses on your network interfaces when using NLB. You must cancel the configuration, change from DHCP to static IP addresses, and begin this process again.

Figure 6.59 DHCP Warning Message

12. You are now presented with the Host Parameters window, as shown in Figure 6.60. Enter the Priority, Dedicated IP address, and Subnet mask for the cluster host. Set the Default state of the host to Started. (This setting will make the host automatically attempt to join the NLB cluster on startup). Click **Finish**.

Figure 6.60 Configure Host Parameters

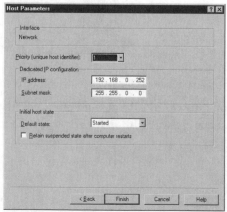

13. You are now taken back to the main window of the NLB Manager utility, which will look similar to Figure 6.61.

Figure 6.61 The Configured NLB Cluster

14. The bottom pane of the window is the log of activities performed by the NLB Manager. Double-click an entry. Figure 6.62 shows an example of the details that appear when Log Entry 0004 was double-clicked. When you are finished viewing the log entry's details, click **OK**.

Figure 6.62 View NLB Manager Log Entry Details

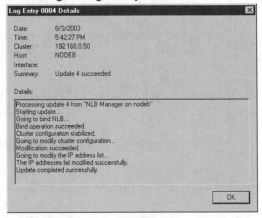

15. Click the NLB cluster you just created. You will see current details about your cluster, similar to those shown in Figure 6.63.

Figure 6.63 Configured NLB Cluster Details

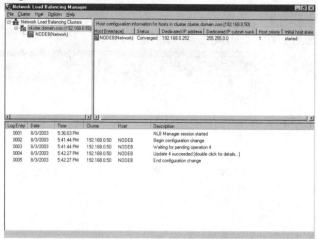

16. Click the host you just configured. You will see the port rules, as shown in Figure 6.64.

Figure 6.64 Configured Port Rules on Cluster Node

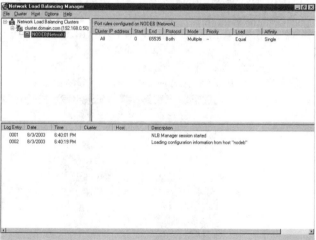

Chapter 7

Planning, Implementing, and Maintaining a High-Availability Strategy

In this chapter:

- **Understanding Performance Bottlenecks**

- **Planning a Backup and Recovery Strategy**

- **Planning System Recovery with ASR**

- **Planning for Fault Tolerance**

Introduction

High availability is a buzzword in today's networking world, and for good reason. Ensuring that the network's resources are available to users when they need them is an important part of the network administrator's job. Downtime—whether caused by a disk failure, a performance slowdown, data loss due to an attack, or the loss of an entire server due to a natural disaster such as fire or flood—cuts into worker productivity and impacts the business's bottom line or the organization's ability to accomplish its goals.

In the previous chapter, we looked at server clustering and network load balancing as part of a high-availability network. In this chapter, we will look at the concept of high availability and how it can be attained. We'll provide an overview of performance bottlenecks and what causes them, and show you how to identify such common system bottlenecks as memory, processor, disk, and network components. We'll walk you through the steps of using the System Monitor utility to track server performance and show you how to use Event Viewer and service logs to monitor server issues, as well.

Next, we show you how to plan a backup and recovery strategy. We'll review the Windows Backup Utility and the differences between full, incremental, and differential backups. We'll also discuss the use of the Volume Shadow Copy feature as a backup option. We'll review how to decide what information should be backed up. We'll also show you how to back up user data, system state data, the Dynamic Host Configuration

Protocol (DHCP) database, Windows Internet Name Service (WINS) database, Domain Name System (DNS) database, cluster disk signatures, and partition layouts. We'll walk you through the process of using the Windows Backup administrative tool, including the Backup and Restore Wizard feature and the Advanced Mode feature. We'll also discuss the use of command-line tools. Then we'll talk about how to select your backup media, and you'll learn about scheduling backups and how to restore data from backup when necessary.

We'll address how to plan for system recovery using the Automated System Recovery (ASR) feature. You'll learn about system services, how to make an ASR backup, and how to do an ASR restore. We'll explain how ASR works and discuss alternatives to ASR such as the Safe Mode and Last Known Good boot options. Finally, we'll discuss the importance of planning for fault tolerance, including solutions aimed at providing fault tolerance for local network connectivity, Internet connectivity, data on disk, and mission-critical servers.

Understanding Performance Bottlenecks

All system administrators want the systems they install to run perfectly out of the box, all the time. We have all wanted to be able to safely turn off our pagers and cell phones. Our servers should run reliably, quickly, and without interruption, right? Well, if that were the case, we would all be terminally bored or changing careers.

Identifying System Bottlenecks

For the most part, a Windows Server 2003 system does run well in its default configuration, and, if designed and maintained properly, operates with a minimum of administrative overhead. However, as a general-purpose operating system, it can often be tuned to perform better when used for certain tasks.

The main hardware resources of any computer system are used by different applications and circumstances in different combinations, often taxing one resource more than another. If multiple applications are run on a system, it is often possible to reach the limit of a resource and suffer slow response time, unreliable services, or missed transactions. We will take a look at each of these resources, discuss some of the common issues related to them, and consider some of the management options available.

Memory

RAM is most often the single resource that becomes a bottleneck. A common cause of slow performance is insufficient physical memory. The minimum recommended amount of memory for running Windows Server 2003 is 128MB (512MB for Datacenter Edition). These are *very* conservative numbers. Even Microsoft recommends at least 256MB. If you have the ability, double (or more) these amounts, and you will be happy you did. The short rule with memory is this: more is better.

The Windows operating system controls the access to and allocation of memory and performs "housekeeping tasks" when needed. Applications request memory from the operating system, which allocates memory to the application. When an application no longer needs memory, the application is supposed to release the memory back to the operating system. An application that does not properly release memory can slowly drain a system of available free memory, and overall performance will suffer. This is referred to as a *memory leak*.

Another performance factor related to memory is the use of *virtual memory* (VM) or *paging*. Virtual memory is a method of increasing the amount of memory in a system by using a *page file* on the hard drive. Access to hard drives, even on the fastest disk subsystems, is dozens or hundreds of times slower than access to RAM. When the operating system needs more RAM than is available, it copies the least recently used pages of memory to the page file, and then reassigns those pages of RAM to the application that requested it. The next time a memory request occurs, the operating system may need to reallocate more pages in RAM or retrieve pages from the page file. This paging process can slow even the fastest system.

Tuning memory is often as simple as adding more memory, reducing the number of applications running (including applications that run in the System Tray), or stopping unnecessary services. However, there is an advanced memory-tuning technique that can be applied if the application supports it. Part of the Enterprise Memory Architecture feature of the Enterprise and Datacenter editions of Windows Server 2003 is *4GB tuning* (4GT), also called *application memory tuning*. Using this feature, you can change the amount of RAM addressable by applications from 2GB to 3GB. Your system must have at least 2GB of physical RAM installed, and the application must be written to support the increased memory range. Consult the application documentation or contact your vendor to make this determination.

Processor

CPUs are commonly described by their type, brand, or model (for example, Pentium 4), and their *clock speed* (for example, 2.0 GHz). In simplest terms, the clock speed is how many times per second the CPU executes an instruction. Generally, the faster the CPU is, the better the computer performs.

The CPU *bus architecture* is another factor when examining performance. A 32-bit CPU (which includes all of Intel's CPUs from the 80386 through the Pentium 4 and AMD's CPUs from the Am486 through the Athlon-XP) can use integers 32 bits wide and access 2^{32} bytes of memory, or 4GB. A 64-bit CPU (Intel's Itanium series and AMD's Opteron series) can use integers 64 bits wide and access (in theory) 2^{64} bytes of memory or 16 exabytes (16 billion gigabytes). No current hardware can support this amount of RAM. Windows Server 2003 supports a maximum of 512GB on Itanium-based hardware with the Datacenter Edition. The point is that 64-bit CPUs can support significantly more memory and run applications that use more of it than 32-bit CPUs, all at a faster speed. Extremely large databases can get a large performance boost on 64-bit systems.

Using multiple CPUs in a computer (called *multiprocessing*) allows a computer system to run more applications at the same time than a single-CPU system, because the workload can be spread among the processors. In effect, this reduces the competition among applications for CPU time. A related programming technology called *multithreading* allows the operating system to run different parts of an application (*threads*) on multiple CPUs at the same time, spreading out the workload. Windows Server 2003 can support up to 64 CPUs, depending on the edition of the operating system in use.

A recent development by Intel is a technology called *hyperthreading*. This feature, introduced in the Xeon and Pentium 4 series of processors, makes a single CPU appear to be two CPUs. Hyperthreading is implemented at the BIOS level and is therefore transparent to the operating system. It typically yields a performance increase of 20 to 30 percent, meaning it is not as efficient as multiple physical CPUs. However, it is included free on hardware that supports the technology.

One of the downsides of multiple processors is the management of *interrupts*. The first CPU in a multiprocessor system (processor 0) controls I/O. If an application running on another CPU requires a lot of I/O, CPU 0 can spend much of its time managing interrupts instead of running an application. Windows Server 2003 manages multiple processors and interrupts quite well, but there is a way to tune the *affinity* of a thread to a specific processor.

Processor affinity is a method of associating an application with a specific CPU. Processor affinity can be used to reduce some of the overhead associated with multiple CPUs and is controlled primarily via the Task Manager utility.

Priority is a mechanism used to prioritize some applications (or threads) over others. Priority can be set when an application is started or can be changed later using the Task Manager utility.

Disk

The disk is the permanent storage location of the operating system, applications, and data. A *disk* is made up of one or more physical *drives*. Often, a computer system will contain multiple disks configured in *arrays*, which can be useful for increasing performance and/or availability.

Several factors contribute to the performance and reliability of disk:

- The disk controller technology
- The life-expectancy (MTBF) of the drive(s)
- The way data is arranged on the drive(s)
- The way data is accessed on the drive(s)
- The ratio of drive controllers to the number of drives

Network Components

The primary (and default) communications protocol used by Windows Server 2003 is TCP/IP. The operating system also supports the next generation of the TCP/IP protocol, IP version 6 (IPv6), as well as the AppleTalk, Reliable Multicast, and NWLink protocols. Multiple protocols installed on a system consume additional memory and CPU resources. Reducing the number of protocols in use will improve performance.

On systems that do have multiple protocols loaded, change the binding order of the protocols to the NIC so that the most frequently used protocol is bound first. This will reduce the amount of processing needed for each network packet and improve performance.

When a packet is received by the NIC, it is placed in a memory buffer. The NIC then either generates an interrupt to have the CPU transfer the packet to the main memory of the computer or performs a direct memory access (DMA) transfer and moves the data itself. The method used depends on the hardware involved. The DMA transfer method is much faster and has less impact on the overall system.

The number and/or size of the memory buffers allocated to the NIC can affect performance as well. Some NICs allow you to adjust the number of memory buffers assigned to the card. A larger buffer space allows the NIC to store more packets, reducing the number of interrupts the card must generate by allowing larger, less frequent data transfers. Conversely, reducing the number of buffers can increase the amount of interrupts generated by the NIC, impacting system performance. Some NICs allow you to adjust the buffers for transmitting and receiving packets independently, giving you more flexibility in your configuration. The trade-off of increasing communication buffers may be a reduction in the amount of memory available to applications in the system.

One feature of Windows 2000 and Windows Server 2003 is support for IP Security (IPSec). This feature allows the securing of data transmitted over IP networks through the use of cryptography. IPSec is computer-intensive, meaning that significant amounts of CPU overhead are incurred with its use. Some NICs made in recent years support the offloading of the IPSec calculations to a highly optimized processor on the NIC. This can greatly reduce the amount of CPU time needed, as well as improve communications performance. NICs that support the offloading of IPSec are not much more expensive than regular NICs and should be strongly considered if you are using IPSec.

Another consideration for network performance is the network topology. Although it is not specific to the Windows operating system, network topology can greatly affect communications performance. If the traffic to your server must travel through routers that convert large incoming packets into multiple smaller packets, your server must do more work to reassemble the original packets before your applications can use the data. For example, if a client system is connected to a Token Ring network (which commonly uses a packet size of 4192 bytes or larger) and your server is connected via Ethernet (with a packet size of 1514 bytes), an intermediary router will "chop" the original packet into three or more packets for transmission on the Ethernet network segment. Your server must then reassemble these packets before passing them to applications. Reducing the number of topologies and/or routers on your network can improve performance by reducing packet conversions and reassembly.

Also, when using Ethernet, consider using switches instead of hubs. Switches are more expensive but allow higher communication rates and also permit more than one device to communicate at the same time. Hubs are cheaper but allow only one computer to be communicating at any given time. Switches are also not susceptible to Ethernet collisions, whereas hubs are at the mercy of collisions.

Another topology-related configuration is the duplex setting of the NICs. Primarily an issue with Ethernet, *duplex* describes how data is transmitted. A full-duplex communication link allows the simultaneous transmission and reception of data. Full duplex is the desired setting for servers, because servers normally need to transmit and receive at the same time. Full duplex typically requires switches. Half-duplex communication is the bi-directional communication of data but not at the same time. When transmitting data, receiving data is not possible and vice versa. Half duplex is often acceptable for workstations but should be avoided on servers.

Using the System Monitor Tool to Monitor Servers

Windows Server 2003 includes tools for monitoring the performance of your server. System Monitor is one such tool. System Monitor is an ActiveX control snap-in that is available as part of the Performance administrative tool. You can start it from the Start menu, as shown in Figure 7.1.

Figure 7.1 Starting the Performance Administrative Tool

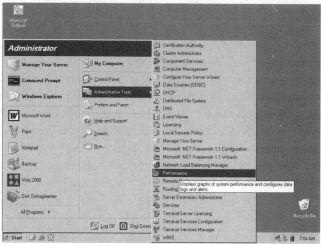

System Monitor works by collecting information from *counters* built in to the operating system. Counters are features of the operating system (as well as some utilities and applications) that count specific events occurring in the system (like the number of disk writes each second or the percentage of disk space in use by files). The graphical view, shown in Figure 7.2, graphs the counter statistics.

Figure 7.2 System Monitor, Graphical View with Default Counters

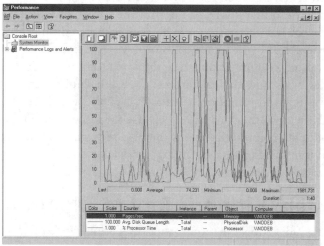

You can also see the counter statistics in System Monitor's report view, as shown in Figure 7.3.

Figure 7.3 System Monitor, Report View with Default Counters

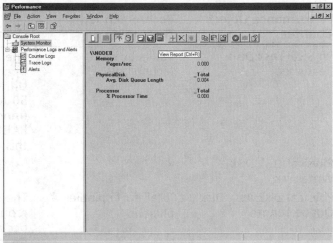

You can access the data collected by counters via System Monitor, other utilities, or third-party applications. This data provides you with an understanding of what is occurring on your system at the moment or over time. Using this information, you can tune your system's operation to best suit your needs, determine if components are being overutilized, plan for expanding or replacing your system, or perform troubleshooting. Some of the most frequently used counters are shown in Table 7.1.

Table 7.1 Commonly Referenced Performance Counters

Resource	Performance Object: Counter	Recommended Threshold	Comments
Disk	Logical Disk:%Free Space	15%	Percentage of unused disk space. This value may be reduced on larger disks, depending on your preferences.
	Physical Disk:%Disk Time	90%	If you're using a hardware controller, try increasing the controller cache size to improve read/write performance. The Physical Disk counter is not always available or may be unreliable on clustered disks.
	Logical Disk:%Disk Time		

Continued

Table 7.1 Commonly Referenced Performance Counters

Resource	Performance Object: Counter	Recommended Threshold	Comments
	Physical Disk:Disk Reads/sec	Varies by disk technology	The rate of read or write operations per second. Ultra SCSI should handle 50 to 70. I/O type (random/sequential) and RAID structure will affect this greatly.
	Physical Disk:Disk Writes/sec		
	Physical Disk:Avg. Disk Queue Length	Total # of spindles plus 2	The number of disk requests waiting to occur. It is used to determine if your disk system can keep up with I/O requests.
Memory	Memory:Available Bytes	Varies	The amount of free physical RAM available for allocation to a process or the system.
	Memory:Pages/sec	Varies	Number of pages read from or written to disk per second. Includes cache requests and swapped executable code requests.
Paging File	Paging File:%Usage	Greater than 70%	The percentage of the page file currently in use. This counter and the two Memory counters are linked. Low Available Bytes and high Pages/sec indicate a need for more physical memory.
Processor	Processor:%Processor Time	85%	Indicates what percentage of time the processor was not idle. If high, determine if a single process is consuming the CPU. Consider upgrading the CPU speed or adding processors.

Continued

Table 7.1 Commonly Referenced Performance Counters

Resource	Performance Object: Counter	Recommended Threshold	Comments
	Processor:Interrupts/sec	Start at 1000 on single CPU; 5000 multiple CPUs	Indicates the number of hardware interrupts generated by the components of the system (network cards, disk controllers, and so on) per second. A sudden increase can indicate conflicts in hardware. Multiprocessor systems normally experience higher interrupt rates.
Server Work Queues	Server Work Queues: Queue Length	4	Indicates the number of requests waiting for service by the processor. A number higher than the threshold may indicate a processor bottleneck. Observe this value over time.
System	System:Processor Queue Length	Less than 10 per processor	The number of process threads awaiting execution. This counter is mainly relevant on multiprocessor systems. A high value may indicate a processor bottleneck. Observe this value over time.

Before you attempt to troubleshoot performance issues, you should to create a *baseline*. Develop a baseline by collecting data on your system in its initial state and at regular intervals over time. Save this collected data and store it in a database. You can then compare this historical data to current performance statistics to determine if your system's behavior is changing slowly over time. Momentary spikes on the charts are normal, and you should not be overly concerned about them. Sustained highs can also be normal, depending on the activity occurring in a system, or they can signal a problem. Proper baselining will allow you to know when a sustained high is detrimental.

The Heisenberg Principal of physics (greatly paraphrased) states that you cannot observe the activity of something without altering its behavior. The same is true with performance monitoring. The collection of statistics requires computer resources. Collect only the counters you specifically need. If the system you wish to examine is extremely busy, consider using the noninteractive Performance Logs and Alerts function, shown in Figure 7.4, rather than System Monitor. Collecting the counters will still incur overhead, but not as much.

Figure 7.4 Performance Logs and Alerts, Accessed from Computer Management

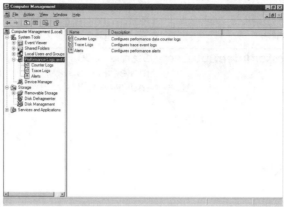

You might also consider lowering the update interval or collecting data from the system on an hourly or daily basis, rather than continuously. If you're monitoring disk counters, store the logs on a different disk (and, if possible, on a different controller channel) than the one you are monitoring. This will help avoid skewing the data. You can also save the collected statistics into a file or database, and then load and review them later (configured on the **Source** tab of the **System Monitors Properties** dialog box, shown later in Figure 7.11).

A counter log called System Overview, shown in Figure 7.5, is provided by Microsoft as an example. This log is configured to collect the same default counters as System Monitor at 15-second intervals.

Figure 7.5 The Sample System Overview Counter Log

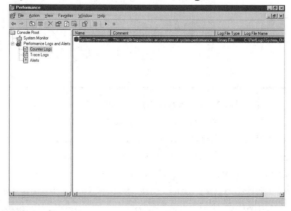

You can view the properties of the System Overview log by right-clicking it and selecting **Properties** from the context menu. Figure 7.6 shows the dialog box that appears.

Figure 7.6 Properties of the System Overview Sample Log

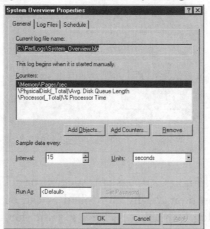

The **Log Files** tab, shown in Figure 7.7, specifies the type (format) of the log file, its location, and the comment assigned to the log. The drop-down menu for the **Log File Type** option (shown in Figure 7.7) lists the formats available for log files. The binary format is compact and efficient. The text formats require more space to store the log, but they can be read by other applications like Microsoft Word and Excel. The binary circular file format overwrites itself when it reaches its maximum size, potentially saving disk space.

Figure 7.7 Properties of the System Overview Sample Log, Log Files Tab

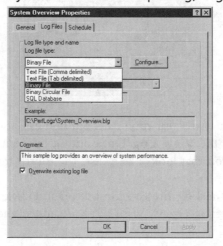

If you click **Configure...** in the **Log Files** tab of the **System Overview Properties** dialog box, you will be presented with the **Configure Log Files** dialog box, as shown in Figure 7.8. Here, you can specify the location, name, and size limit of the log file.

Figure 7.8 Configuring Log Files

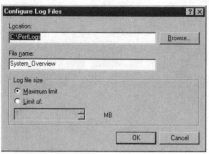

The **Schedule** tab, shown in Figure 7.9, lets you specify the schedule for collecting data from the selected counters. The log can be manually controlled or can be scheduled to start at a specific date and time. You can stop the log manually or after a specific duration, a certain date and time, or when the log reaches its maximum size.

Figure 7.9 Properties of the System Overview Sample Log, Schedule Tab

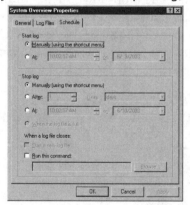

By default, System Monitor tracks real-time data, but you can also have it display data from log files. To view log file data, click the **View Log Data** button in the main System Monitor window, as shown in Figure 7.10 (the icon that looks like a disk, the fourth from the left; circled for clarity in the figure).

On the **Source** tab, select the **Log files** option button and click **Add**. Browse to the log file you wish to view, select it, and click **Open.** With a log file added, the **Source** tab should look similar to Figure 7.11.

Click **OK**, and you will be viewing the data collected in the log file. Figure 7.12 shows an example of viewing log file data.

Figure 7.10 Selecting the View Log Data Button

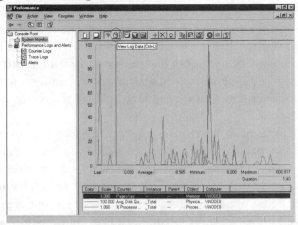

Figure 7.11 System Monitor Properties, Source Tab

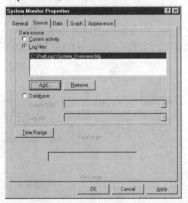

Figure 7.12 System Monitor, Viewing Log File Data

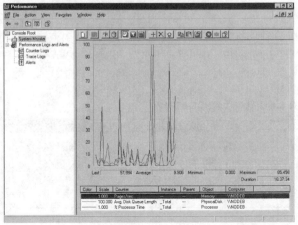

Determining if performance is acceptable can be highly subjective. It varies depending on the system, role, and environment. There are several general counters and specific thresholds for these counters that you can use to monitor performance. You should examine these counters as ratios over a period of regular intervals, rather than as the average of specific instances. This will provide a more realistic picture of the actual activity occurring on your system. In addition, watch for consistent occurrences of the threshold values being exceeded. It is not uncommon for momentary activity in a system to cause one or more counters to exceed threshold values, which may or may not be acceptable in your environment.

You can use System Monitor and Performance Logs and Alerts to monitor the local system or another computer on the network, as shown in Figure 7.13. It can be useful to compare the performance of the same resource on multiple systems. Be cautious when you do this, though. Ensure that you are comparing appropriately similar objects. Watch out for the "apples and oranges" mismatch. Also, consider that a server being monitored locally may have less monitoring overhead than one that is monitored remotely. This is particularly true regarding the network- and server-related counters, which can be skewed by the transmission of the performance data to your monitoring system. Be sure to account for this difference when developing your statistics.

Figure 7.13 Selecting Counters from Another Computer

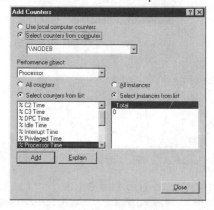

If the **Explain** button in the **Add Counters** dialog box is not grayed out, a supporting explanation of the counter is available. The explanation for the Memory:Pages/sec counter is shown in Figure 7.14.

Figure 7.14 Viewing a Counter Explanation

Once you have become comfortable and proficient with reading counters, developing baselines, unobtrusively monitoring system activity, and comparing performance, you are ready for the final performance task: determining when your system will no longer be capable of performing the tasks that you want it to perform. Eventually, every computer will be outdated or outgrown. If you have developed the skills for monitoring your system, you should be able to determine in advance when your system will be outgrown. This will allow you to plan for the eventual expansion, enhancement, or replacement of the system. By taking this proactive approach, you can further reduce unplanned downtime by being prepared.

Use the following steps to create a system monitor console. Refer to Table 7.1, earlier in the chapter, for information about common counters.

Creating a System Monitor Console

1. Select **Start | All Programs | Administrative Tools | Performance**. Click **System Monitor**. If any counters are already present, click the **Delete (X)** button on the toolbar, circled in Figure 7.16, until the System Monitor window is empty.

Figure 7.15 Empty System Monitor

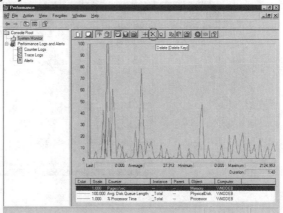

2. Click the Add (+) button on the toolbar. The Add Counters dialog box appears, as shown in Figure 7.16.

Figure 7.16 Add Counters

3. In the Performance object drop-down list, select the Logical Disk object.

4. In the Select counters from list box, select the %Free Space counter.

5. In the Select instances from list box, select _Total, and then click Add.

6. Repeat steps 3, 4 and 5, but select the following performance objects and counters (listed in the form performance object:counter):

   - Physical Disk:%Disk Time
   - Logical Disk:%Disk Time
   - Paging File:%Usage
   - Processor:%Processor Time

7. Click Close.

8. You should now see a System Monitor window similar to Figure 7.17. Observe the graph as it progresses. Compare the scale of the counters to each other.

Figure 7.17 Percentage-based Counters in System Monitor

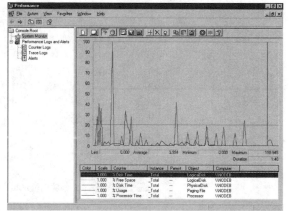

9. Click the Add (+) button.

10. In the Performance object drop-down list, select Physical Disk:Disk Reads/sec.

11. In the Select instances from list box, select _Total, and then click Add.

12. Repeat steps 9, 10, and 11 to add the following counters:

   - Physical Disk:Disk Writes/sec
   - Physical Disk:Avg. Disk Queue Length
   - Memory:Available Bytes
   - Memory:Pages/sec
   - Processor:Interrupts/sec
   - Server Work Queues:Queue Length
   - System:Processor Queue Length

13. Click **Close**.

14. Your System Monitor window should look similar to Figure 7.18. Notice how busy the chart is beginning to look. Again, compare the scale of the counters to each other. Notice how several counters seem to stay at the bottom of the chart even though they are active. This illustrates that you should consider scale and try not to mix percentage-based counters with nonpercentage-based counters on the same graph.

Figure 7.18 All Common Counters in System Monitor

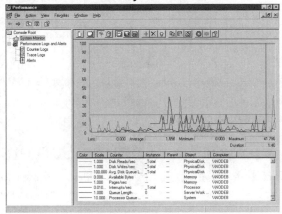

15. Click Logical Disk:%Free Space.

16. Click the Delete (X) button.

17. Repeat steps 9, 10, and 11 to add the following counters:

   - Physical Disk:%Disk Time
   - Logical Disk:%Disk Time
   - Paging File:%Usage
   - Processor:%Processor Time

18. You have removed all of the percentage-based counters from the graph. Your System Monitor window should appear similar to Figure 7.19. Compare the scale of the nonpercentage counters.

Figure 7.19 Common Nonpercentage Counters

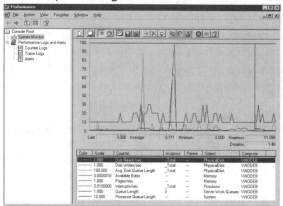

19. Close the Performance console.

Using Event Viewer to Monitor Servers

Windows Server 2003 includes several log files that collect information on events that occur in the system. Using these log files, you can view your system's history of events. A standard Windows Server 2003 system has three event logs that record specific categories of events:

- **Application** Contains events generated by server-based applications, such as Microsoft Exchange and WINS. The specific events logged by each application are determined by the application itself and may be configurable by an administrator within the application.

- **Security** Contains events relating to system security, including successful and failed logon attempts, file creation or deletion, and user and group account activity. The contents of this file will vary depending on the auditing settings selected by the system administrator.

- **System** Contains events relating to the activity of the operating system. Startups and shutdowns, device driver events, and system service events are recorded in the System log. The configuration and installed options of the operating system determine the events recorded in this log. Because of the nature of its entries, this log is the most important for maintaining system health.

In addition to these three basic logs, a Windows Server 2003 system configured as a domain controller will also have the following two logs:

- **Directory Service** Contains events related to the operation of Active Directory (AD). AD database health, replication events, and Global Catalog activities are recorded in this log.

- **File Replication Service** Contains events related the File Replication Service (FRS), which is responsible for the replication of the file system-based portion of Group Policy Objects (GPOs) between domain controllers.

Finally, a server configured to run the DNS Server service will have the DNS Server log, which contains events related to the operations of that service. Client DNS messages are recorded in the System log.

Events entered into these log files occur as one of five different event types. The type of an event defines it level of severity. The five types of events are as follows:

- **Error** Indicates the most severe or dangerous type of event. The failure of a device driver or service to start or a failed procedure call to a dynamic link library (DLL) can generate this type of event. These events indicate problems that could lead to downtime and need to be resolved. The icon of an error event appears as a red circle with a white *X* in the middle.

- **Warning** Indicates a problem that is not necessarily an immediate issue but has the potential to become one. Low disk space is an example of a Warning event. This event type icon is a yellow triangle with a white exclamation point (!) in it.

- **Information** Usually indicates success. Proper loading of a driver or startup of a service will generate an Information event. This icon is a white message balloon with a blue, low-ercase letter *i* in it.

- **Success Audit** In the Security log, indicates the successful completion of an event configured for security auditing. A successful logon will generate this event. This icon is a gold key.

- **Failure Audit** In the Security log, indicates the unsuccessful completion of an event configured for security auditing. An attempted logon with an incorrect password or an attempt to access a file without sufficient permissions will generate this type of event. The event's icon is a locked padlock.

The event logs are very helpful for collecting data, but we need a tool to present, filter, search, and help us interpret the data. That tool is Event Viewer, shown in Figure 7.20, which can be accessed by selecting **Start | All Programs | Administrative Tools | Event Viewer**.

Event Viewer can also be accessed as a component of the **System Tools** snap-in within the **Computer Management** utility, as shown in Figure 7.21.

When viewing an event log, the events appear in the order they occurred. Double-clicking an event will bring up the properties of that event, as shown in Figure 7.22. Click the arrows to navigate to either the next or previous event.

Figure 7.20 The Event Viewer Window

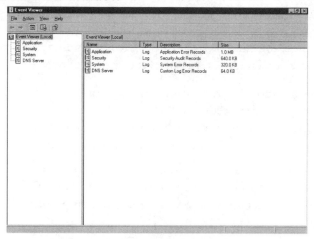

Figure 7.21 Event Viewer, as Viewed from Computer Management

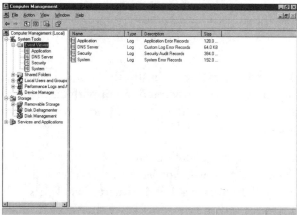

Figure 7.22 Viewing Event Properties

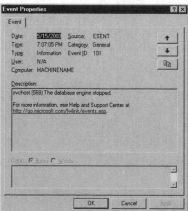

Each event captured follows the same format and contains the same set of data points. Those data points form the *event header* and are as follows:

- **Date** The date the event occurred.

- **Time** The time the event occurred.

- **Type** The applicable type of event (Error, Warning, and so on).

- **User** The user or account context that generated the event.

- **Computer** The name of the computer where the event occurred.

- **Source** The application or system component that generated the event.

- **Category** The classification of the event from the event source's perspective.

- **Event ID** A number identifying the specific event from the source's perspective.

- **Description** A textual description of the event. This may be in any readable structure.

- **Data** A hexadecimal representation of any data recorded for the event by the source.

An event log can contain thousands or even millions of events. Because the event header follows the same structure regardless of the event source, you can use the filter function to focus in on specific patterns of events. The filter function is available from the log's Properties dialog box. Right-click a log in the left tree view and select **Properties** from the context menu, as shown in Figure 7.23, to view its properties.

Click the **Filter** tab to display the filter options, as shown in Figure 7.24. (You can also access the filter function by clicking **View | Filter**.)

By changing the selections on the **Filter** tab, you can exclude from view those events that do not fit the filter selections. Put another way, events that do not match the filter selections are filtered out. The events are still in the log; they are just not displayed as long as the filter is active.

In addition to using the filter function, you can search event logs for specific events. From the Event Viewer main window, select **View | Find…**, as shown in Figure 7.25.

Figure 7.23 Accessing the Properties of an Event Log

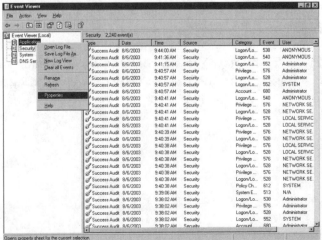

Figure 7.24 Filtering Event Log Data

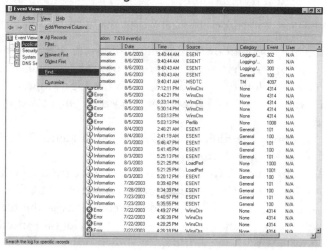

Figure 7.25 Using Find in an Event Log

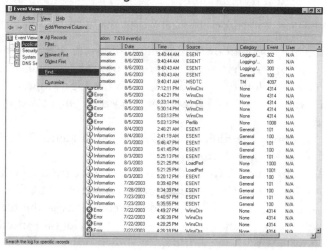

In the **Find** dialog box, enter your criteria for the search and click the **Find Next** button. The next event that matches your criteria will be highlighted in the Event Viewer main window, as shown in the example in Figure 7.26.

The event log files themselves are stored in a compact binary format in the *%systemroot%*\System32\Config directory. You can configure the maximum size of these files and what action is taken when this size is reached on the **General** tab of the log **Properties** dialog box, as shown in Figure 7.27.

Figure 7.26 Finding Event Log Data

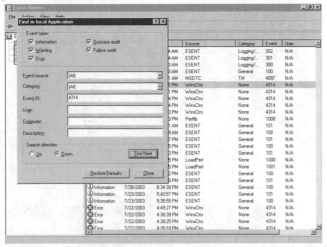

Figure 7.27 Event Log General Properties

Accessing the Properties dialog box of an event log gives you access to information about the log itself and allows you to change certain characteristics of the log. Referring to Figure 7.27, you can see the log's name, location, and size. The **Maximum log size** option allows you to limit the amount of space the log consumes. The three radio buttons below this option allow you to specify what will happen when this maximum size is reached.

Event logs can be archived on the computer on which they occur for long-term storage and analysis. This can be accomplished in two ways. The first is through the use of the **Clear Log** button on the event log Properties dialog box. You can click this button to delete all entries from a log file, but this process will also prompt you to save the events prior to deletion. The second method is through the use of the **Save Log File As…** option on the context menu for a log file, as shown in Figure 7.28.

Figure 7.28 Saving a Log File, Selection Menu

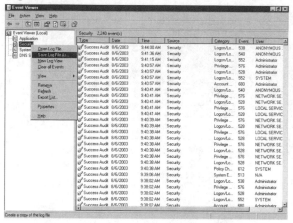

The **Save Log File As…** selection brings up a **Save AS** dialog box, as shown in Figure 7.29, which allows you to choose the name, location, and format of the archive.

Figure 7.29 Saving a Log File

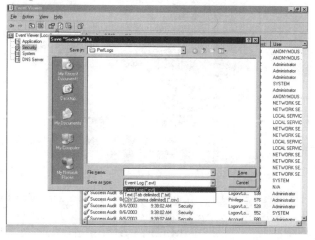

You can save events in a binary .evt, comma-delimited, or tab-delimited text file. You can use the .evt format to retain the log file in a compact format, which you can reopen in Event Viewer by selecting **Action | Open Log File…**, as shown in Figure 7.30. The delimited archive file formats consume more disk space than the .evt format, but they can be imported into a database or an application like Microsoft Excel for further analysis.

Choosing to open a log file brings up an Open dialog box, shown in Figure 7.31. In this dialog box, you can locate and choose the archived file.

Figure 7.30 Opening an Archived Log File

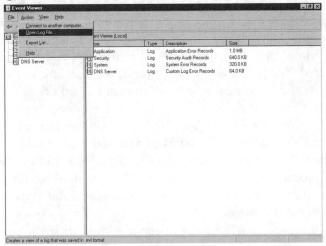

Figure 7.31 Selecting an Archived Event Log

Using Service Logs to Monitor Servers

As mentioned previously, there are additional event logs for servers in certain roles. A server running the DNS server will have a DNS Server log. A server acting as a domain controller will have logs for the Directory Service and File Replication Service. It is also possible that other services or applications may create their own log files, but most do not.

These server log files follow the same format as the other event logs. They can be filtered, searched, and archived using the methods described in the previous sections.

These logs exist mainly to collect the events from these services in one place other than the System log. These services generate a greater number of events than do other services.

Planning a Backup and Recovery Strategy

Backups and documentation are usually of critical importance to the continuing operation of an organization. Organizations often account for the value of their computer and communications equipment, but they overlook their data, which can be difficult to valuate. Equipment can be replaced. Staff can be hired. But if data cannot be restored, it is lost forever.

You should consider good backups as a form of insurance. Hard drives fail. Cooling fan bearings wear out, and systems overheat. Lightning strikes buildings. Viruses contaminate or destroy data. Buildings get flooded. The important point is the ability to recover from any loss that occurs.

When considering the factors that make backups necessary, you should also consider the human side of the situation. The software won't operate itself, and someone must change tapes. Do not forget to develop good procedures for the people (or person) responsible for your backups. It is important to ensure that there is more than one person who is capable of restoring data, which makes good written procedures essential.

When developing your backup and restore procedures, consider the following guidelines:

- **Develop a log** This gives you a hardcopy record of your backup activities.

- **Test your procedures, devices, and media frequently** A failure in any one of these areas can make data impossible to restore.

- **Keep multiple copies** Media can and does go bad. Shelf life, manufacturing defects, and environmental or physical damage can render media impossible to read.

- **Rotate copies offsite** Keep the backups in a different location. That way, a local disaster won't destroy all of your backups.

- **Back up the system** The operating system and your applications are a form of data, too, and should be protected accordingly.

- **Use the new Automated System Recovery (ASR) feature** This feature saves time in the event of a disaster and can also act as a "last-ditch" effort before a complete rebuild. Perform an ASR backup after each major system change and also on a regular basis.

- **Secure your backups** Secure your backup media in the same way that you would secure any other valuable item. Keep your media locked up, if possible, in a safe.

- **Know your data** Data that changes frequently may need more frequent backups. Databases require different strategies than documents and spreadsheets. Encrypted File System (EFS) files and folders should have the recovery agent's EFS private key backed up as well; otherwise, recovering EFS files and folders may not be possible. The DHCP, WINS, DNS, and AD services have specific backup or restore requirements. It is important to understand these requirements when you plan your backup strategy.

Understanding Windows Backup

Windows Server 2003 includes the Backup Utility for performing backups, restores, and running the ASR Wizard. The utility can back up data to and restore data from almost any removable media device identified by the operating systems—tape drives, hard drives, and even file shares on the network. You cannot, however, back up to recordable CD or DVD drives.

In order to perform a backup or restore operation, you must have the appropriate user rights. The Administrators and Backup Operators groups are assigned the necessary rights to perform both functions, so using an account that is a member of either of these groups will suffice.

The specific user rights required to perform a backup or restore can be individually assigned by using the Local Security Policy utility, shown in Figure 7.32, or a GPO if the user is a member of an AD domain. The following are the user rights required to perform backup and restore operations:

- **Back up files and directories** Allows a user to bypass (if necessary) established permissions on files, directories, and Registry keys and values. Be cautious when assigning this right, because this can be a security risk. A user with this right could easily back up all of your company's most sensitive information and carry it out the door.

- **Bypass traverse checking** Gives a user the ability to cross directories, whether or not that user has permissions to those directories.

- **Restore files and directories** The corollary user right to Back up files and directories. Allows a user to bypass (if necessary) the established permissions on files, directories, and Registry keys and values. This effectively gives a user the ability to restore objects, regardless of the objects' assigned permissions. You should be cautious with this right due to the potential security risk and possibility of destroying or corrupting data.

Figure 7.32 Detailed User Rights, Accessed from Local Security Policy

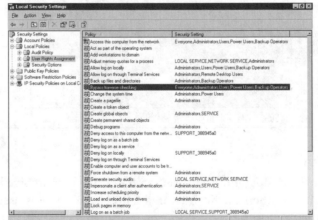

Types of Backups

Most good backup strategies adopt a method of backing up different amounts of data at different times and for different purposes. The length of time required to back up data on a server increases as the amount of data on a server grows. On many systems, a large amount of data is static or changes infrequently. Finally, the costs associated with consumable media (such as tape cartridges) mean that economics force the issue of using the media in cycles. The basic backup cycle includes a complete or *full backup* and several *incremental* or *differential backups*. Each type of backup serves a specific need.

Full Backups

The Windows Backup Utility calls a full backup a *normal* backup. The full backup, as its name implies, backs up everything specified by the user performing the backup operation. A full backup can include the operating system, system state data, applications, and any other data. With a full backup, everything that is backed up has the file system archive bit reset (cleared). This allows the incremental and differential backup types to determine if the file needs to be backed up. If the bit is still clear, the other backup types know that the data has not changed. If the bit is set, the data has changed, and the file needs to be backed up.

The full backup is usually the first backup performed on a server. It takes the longest of all the backup types to complete, because it backs up all specified files, regardless of the state of the archive attribute. A full backup consumes the largest amount of backup media of any backup type. Depending on the amount of information chosen to back up and the underlying backup technology involved, it may require multiple backup media to complete.

The main advantage of the full backup type is the ability to rapidly restore the data. All of the information is contained in a single backup set when this type of backup is used. The disadvantages of full backups are high media consumption and long backup times.

Figure 7.33 illustrates a series of full backups. The values listed are relative.

Figure 7.33 Full (Normal) Backup Pattern

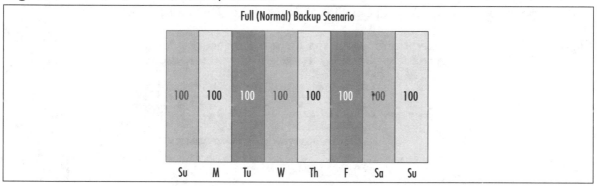

Incremental Backups

During an incremental backup operation, all specified files have their archive bit examined. If the bit is set, the file is backed up, and then the bit is cleared. This backup type is used to back up data that has changed or been created since the last full (normal) or incremental backup. It can also be used after a copy or differential backup, but because these do not reset the archive attribute, there is no way for the incremental backup to tell which files have changed since one of those backups last ran. As a result, every file with the archive attribute set is backed up.

The incremental backup type is used between full backups. It is quick to perform, collects the least amount of data, and consumes the smallest amount of media. A complete restore, however, requires the last full backup and every incremental backup (in sequence) since the full backup was performed.

The primary benefits of using the full/incremental backup combination, as illustrated in Figure 7.34, are time and media savings. The main drawback of this combination is longer and more complex restore operations if there are long periods between full backups.

Figure 7.34 Full (Normal) Backup/Incremental Backup Pattern

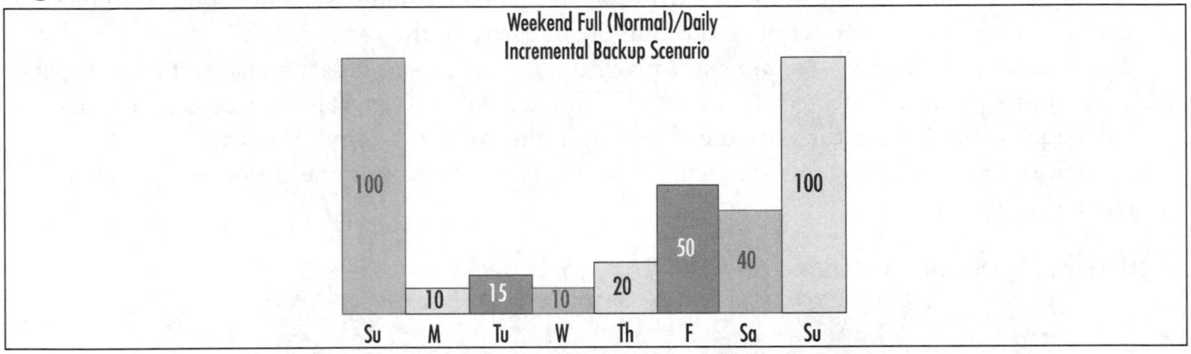

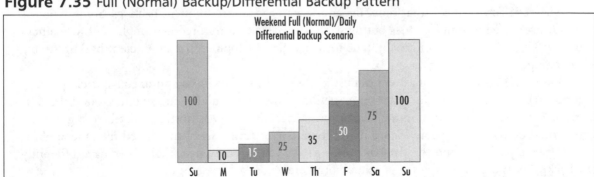

Differential Backups

The differential backup type is sometimes used as a substitute for the incremental type. A differential backup collects data that has changed or been created since the last full (normal) or incremental backup, but it does not clear the archive bit on the file. It can also be used after a copy or differential backup, but as with an incremental backup, every file with the archive attribute set is backed up.

The differential backup is advantageous when you want to minimize the restoration time. A complete system restore with a full/differential backup combination, as illustrated in Figure 7.35, requires only the most recent full backup and the most recent differential backup. Differential backups start with small volumes of data after a recent full or incremental backup, but often grow in size each time, because the volume of changed data grows. This means that the time to perform a differential backup starts small but increases over time as well. In theory, if full or incremental backups are infrequent, a differential backup could end up taking as long and reaching the same volume as a full backup.

Figure 7.35 Full (Normal) Backup/Differential Backup Pattern

Volume Shadow Copy

More of a new feature than a backup type, Volume Shadow Copy allows you to back up all files on the system, including files that are open by applications or processes. In previous versions of Windows, the applications would need to be stopped or users logged out to allow these files to be closed and backed up using the Windows Backup Utility. With Volume Shadow Copy, these files can continue to remain in use without affecting the integrity of the backup.

This feature is enabled by default, but it may need to be disabled if data managed by some critical applications would be affected by the use of Volume Shadow Copy. The feature can be temporarily disabled by clicking the **Advanced** button in the Backup Utility's **Backup Job Information** dialog box, as shown in Figure 7.36. Unless specified by vendor documentation, leave this feature turned on.

Figure 7.36 Disabling Volume Shadow Copy for a Backup

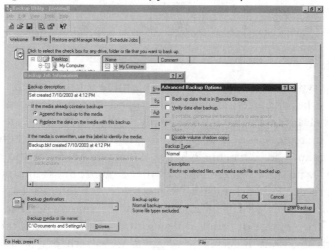

Determining What to Back Up

Because the data on your servers may be largely static, frequent backups of such data may be redundant. The corollary of this is that more dynamic data needs more frequent backups. Some types of data are structured as multiple files but must be backed up and restored as a single unit to maintain integrity. These factors and more combine to make the development of an efficient backup strategy challenging.

One of the basic techniques you can use to assist you in developing an effective backup and restore strategy is to place your data into basic categories and structure the system around them. For example, on a server that is used for file and print sharing as well as hosting a database, a good structure would be to have separate logical drives for the operating system, the shared files, the application software packages, and the databases. This allows you to easily treat each set of data differently for backup purposes, meeting the specific requirements of each type of data.

Data Backup

If you separate your data into categories, the time required to perform backups can be greatly reduced. For example, once a month, the static parts of the system (operating system and software volumes) could be backed up to tape. For the rest of the month, you can perform either incremental or differential backups. The shared file volume can follow a different schedule, depending on the rate and volume of change in the data. The volume that contains the database files may need full backups nightly in order to expedite restore procedures and also due to the nature of the database application. It, too, can be easily backed up on a separate schedule from the rest of the system. Tailoring the behavior of backups to each type of data will speed backup and restore operations and minimize the ongoing costs associated with consumable media.

System State Data

The system state data is a special collection of key system and service information. The system state data is present on all Windows Server 2003 systems and includes the following:

- The Registry
- The COM+ Registration database
- Critical boot and system files
- Files protected by Windows File Protection
- The AD database and logs, and the SYSVOL directory (on domain controllers)
- The Certificate Services database (on Certificate Services servers)
- The Cluster Services data (on cluster member servers)
- The Internet Information Server (IIS) Metadirectory (when IIS is installed)

The system state components are designed to allow a system's full identity to be restored, and therefore they are backed up as an entire unit. You can back up system state only locally (unless you're using a third-party application) and restore it only to the system from which it originated.

The Restore to Alternate Location feature is available with a system state restoration, but only the Registry, SYSVOL, cluster data, and boot files will be restored. The other components of system state cannot be put in an alternate location and will not be restored. The normal (and arguably best) practice is to back up the system state, boot, and system volumes together. Also, use the ASR feature, which is covered in the "Planning System Recovery with ASR" section later in this chapter.

DHCP, WINS, and DNS Databases

DHCP, WINS, and DNS are services that can be hosted by Windows Server 2003. However, each requires some amount of special treatment.

DHCP allows the automatic assignment of IP addresses to systems on the network. When installed, DHCP operates continuously and creates an automatic backup of the DHCP database in *%systemroot%*\System32\Dhcp\Backup. To manually back up the DHCP database, use the **Action | Backup** command in the DHCP utility. You should then use the Windows Backup Utility to copy this file to your backup media. To restore a DHCP database, first restore the database backup from your backup media, and then use the **Action | Restore** command in the DHCP utility. The DHCP service will be temporarily stopped during the restore operation.

WINS is a service that provides a method of mapping NetBIOS names to IP addresses. WINS is commonly (but not exclusively) used with older versions of Windows. WINS has a built-in backup function, but the function is not activated until you first specify a backup path for the database in the WINS administrative tool by selecting the WINS server and selecting **Action | Properties**, as shown in Figure 7.37.

Figure 7.37 Configuring the WINS Backup Path

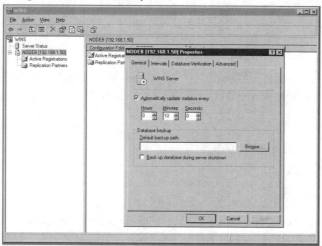

Once you have specified a backup directory path, WINS automatically performs a back up of the local WINS database every 24 hours. You should use the Windows Backup Utility to back up this directory to your backup media.

To restore the WINS database, you must first restore the WINS backup directory path from your backup media. Then stop the WINS service, remove all files from the WINS database path, start the WINS utility, select **Action | Restore Database,** and select the file from which to restore the database.

DNS is the name resolution protocol and service used to convert host names to IP addresses. AD is designed to use DNS, and Windows Server 2003 can be used as a DNS server. How DNS data is backed up and restored depends on how DNS is configured. If DNS is configured as an Active Directory-integrated zone, the DNS information is stored in the AD database. This means it is backed up and restored as part of the system state data.

If DNS is not configured as an Active Directory-integrated zone, the individual zone files are automatically backed up by the DNS service, and these files should be used for backup and restore operations. These files are stored in *%systemroot%*\DNS\Backup.

Cluster Disk Signatures and Partition Layouts

Some special care must be taken when backing up and restoring clustered computers. If a clustered server needs to be restored, the original disk signatures and partition structure must also be restored.

This is best accomplished by using the ASR feature (covered in the "Planning System Recovery with ASR" section later in this chapter). All cluster nodes should have an ASR backup performed on them, making sure that one node has ownership of the cluster's quorum resource when the ASR Wizard is running. In the event that clustered disks need recovery, you can use the ASR backup to restore the clustered disk partitions and disk signatures.

Using Backup Tools

The Windows Backup Utility is included in Windows Server 2003 for backing up and restoring your servers. The Backup Utility uses all of the new backup- and restore-related features of Windows Server 2003, including ASR and Volume Shadow Copy. If you are currently using a third-party backup and restore application, you may be surprised by all of the features that the Backup Utility offers in Windows Server 2003.

Using the Windows Backup Utility

The Windows Backup Utility supports three modes of operation: the Backup or Restore Wizard, Advanced Mode, and command-line operation. Each mode is meant to fit different circumstances. The Backup Utility is accessed from **Start | All Programs | Accessories | System Tools | Backup**. It can also be started from a command-line by typing **NTBackup.exe**.

Backup or Restore Wizard

The first time you start the Backup Utility, you are presented with the Backup or Restore Wizard, as shown in Figure 7.38. The purpose of the Wizard is to simplify the backup or restore process by stepping you through the process, making the most common options available. The Wizard is best used for initial or manual backups on standardized hardware configurations.

Figure 7.38 The Backup or Restore Wizard

The Wizard does allow you to take advantage of some of the more advanced options, like scheduling, but these options are best configured and controlled by using Advanced Mode.

Advanced Mode

Advanced Mode is accessed by clicking the **Advanced Mode** link in the opening Backup or Restore Wizard window (see Figure 7.38). Advanced Mode gives you direct access to the ASR Wizard, customization options, and reporting and media management functions. If you click Advanced Mode, you are presented with the window shown in Figure 7.39.

Figure 7.39 The Windows Backup Utility, Advanced Mode

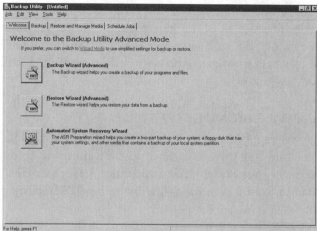

Using Advanced Mode, you can predefine different backup jobs and save their settings. You can then set up schedules for these backup jobs to accommodate the needs of your organization and your data. You can also access the **Report** option (available from **Tools | Report**) to get detailed information on the backup and restore activity that has occurred on your system.

Using the Command-Line Tools

You can also run the Windows Backup Utility as part of a batch file or directly from a command prompt. Using this capability, you can integrate the Windows Backup Utility into sophisticated batch files or scripts. Most of the options available in Advanced Mode are available when using the command-line mode. However, you cannot do a restore from the command-line. Restores must be performed with the Wizard or Advanced Mode.

Selecting Backup Media

An important part of your backup and restore strategy is your choice of backup media. Many different types of media are usable by Windows Backup, and each has advantages and disadvantages. You must consider factors such as backup and restore speed, media capacity, media cost, device cost, media shelf life, and the reliability of the technology.

When analyzing these factors, take a long-term view. Technology changes rapidly, but data stays around for a long time. Examine the necessary life of your data. Accounting data usually needs to be recoverable for seven years. Data relating to legal proceedings may need to be retained for decades. Medical research data may need to be retained for *centuries*. No single media or technology will meet all of these requirements, but with proper planning, you can ensure that you and your successors can manage the retention of data.

Tape technology has been around for a long time. Tape lends itself very well to high-volume, long-term storage of data. Tape is the most common type of backup media used and is almost always the eventual endpoint of saved data.

The Windows Backup Utility can use any type of tape drive and tape technology supported by Windows Server 2003. When purchasing a tape drive, make sure that the operating system supports it. Choosing the type of tape drive and media can be difficult, since tape technology is widely varied and available in several different formats, capacities, and speeds. Extensive research may be required to choose a technology that matches your requirements for data volume, backup speed, and restore speed.

Scheduling Backups

You can use the **Schedule Jobs** tab in the Windows Backup Utility, shown in Figure 7.40, to create an automated schedule of backup jobs. You can define different types of jobs and different schedules. For example, you can define and schedule normal (full) backups every Friday starting at 6:00 P.M. and differential backups every weeknight starting at 10:00 P.M. The jobs will automatically execute when their scheduled times occur.

Figure 7.40 Scheduling Backups with the Backup Utility

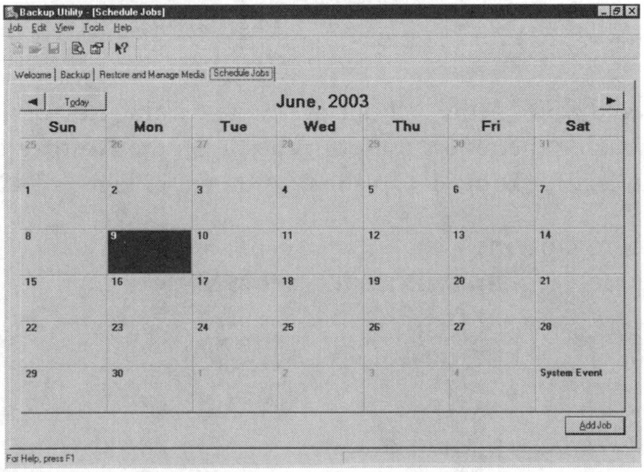

Restoring from Backup

Backing up data is important, but the objective of any backup and restore application is the successful restoration of data after it is lost or corrupted. A backup process without a restore process is useless.

As with backups, knowing your data is important when attempting a restore operation. Some types of data must be restored as a unit (system state), some data may require additional preparation or utilities for a successful restore (AD), and some data may require noting more than a place to put it (normal shared files).

As mentioned previously, you can restore files using either the Backup Utility's Backup or Restore Wizard or Advanced Mode. The first step is to select the backup media to restore from. When using Advanced Mode, you can click the **Restore and Manage Media** tab to select the media, as shown in Figure 7.41. You can expand the media listing on this tab until you find the items you wish to restore, and then select those items by clicking the check box next to each item.

Figure 7.41 Choosing the Restore Source Media

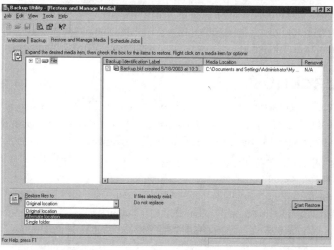

By default, files restored from media will not overwrite existing files of the same name. You can alter this behavior by changing the restore options available on the **Restore** tab of the **Options** dialog box (accessed by selecting **Tools | Options**), as shown in Figure 7.42.

Figure 7.42 The Restore Options

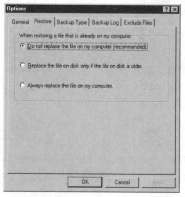

When you have selected the items you wish to restore, you must determine if you want to restore them to their original locations or to an alternate location. This is determined by the setting you select in the **Restore files to** drop-down list on the **Restore and Manage Media** tab (see Figure 7.41). Once you have selected the restore options desired, click the **Start Restore** button to begin the restore process.

Use the following steps to create a backup schedule on your Windows Server 2003 computer.

Create a Backup Schedule

1. Select Start | All Programs | Accessories | System Tools | Backup. In the Backup or Restore Wizard, click Next. Select Back up files and settings, as shown in Figure 7.43, and click Next.

   Figure 7.43 Select Backup Files and Settings

   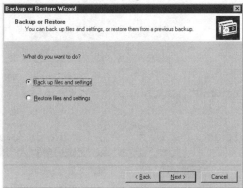

2. Select Let me choose what to back up, as shown in Figure 7.44, and click Next.

   Figure 7.44 Select to Choose What to Back Up

   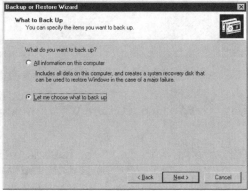

3. For this example, select My Documents in the Items to Back Up window, shown in Figure 7.45, and click Next.

Figure 7.45 Choose Items to Back Up

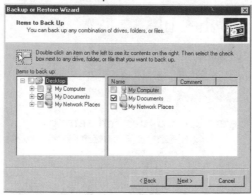

4. Select the destination, location, and name for your backup, and then click Next. Note that for this example, a file has been chosen for the destination, as shown in Figure 7.46.

Figure 7.46 Selecting a Destination for the Backup

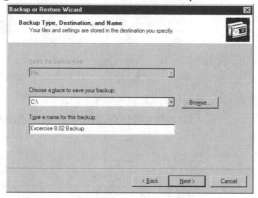

5. In the Completing the Backup or Restore Wizard window, shown in Figure 7.47, click Advanced.

Figure 7.47 Choose Advanced to Specify Backup Options

6. Select Normal as the backup type, as shown in Figure 7.48, and click Next.

Figure 7.48 Select the Backup Type

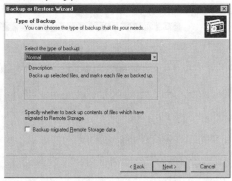

7. Make no changes in the How to Back Up window, shown in Figure 7.49, and click Next.

Figure 7.49 How to Back Up Options

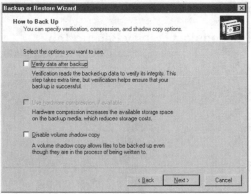

8. In the Backup Options window, select Replace the existing backups, as shown in Figure 7.50, and click Next.

Figure 7.50 Select Backup Options

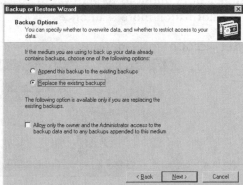

9. In the When to Back Up window, select Later and enter Friday in to the Job name text box, as shown in Figure 7.51. Then click the Set Schedule button.

Figure 7.51 Specify When to Back Up

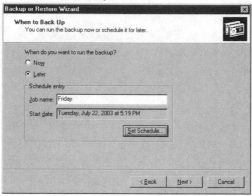

10. In the Schedule Job dialog box, change the backup to run Weekly on Friday at 8:00PM, as shown in Figure 7.52, and click OK.

Figure 7.52 Schedule a Weekly Backup Job

11. In the Set Account Information dialog box, shown in Figure 7.53, enter an account and password with sufficient permissions to perform the backup and click OK. You may be prompted for this information more than once.

Figure 7.53 Set Account Information.

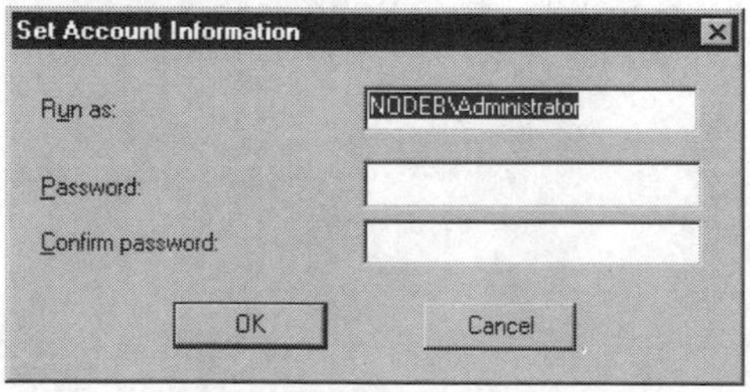

12. Scheduling of the backup is now complete. Close and reopen the Backup Utility.

13. Click Advanced Mode and select the Schedule Jobs tab. You will see your scheduled backups ready to go, as shown in Figure 7.54.

Figure 7.54 View Scheduled Backups in Advanced Mode

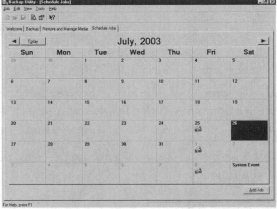

Planning System Recovery with ASR

The *Automated System Recovery* (ASR) feature of Windows Server 2003 is new and replaces the older emergency repair disk (ERD) concept. You might have heard the saying, "Outages take seconds; recoveries take days." ASR was designed to specifically address this issue.

In the past 10 years, the state-of-the art operating system has gone from DOS to Windows Server 2003. The operating system's complexity has increased, along with the difficulty in troubleshooting and repair. If an operating system component of a DOS system became corrupted, often a single command (SYS) could be used to re-create the operating system on the affected disk within minutes. Starting with Windows NT, however, repair was not that simple. The operating system no longer consisted of a few basic files, but hundreds of files that were linked together by the Registry. Troubleshooting became extremely difficult. A complete reinstallation and recovery was often necessary, followed by hours of tweaking and reconfiguration in an attempt to return to the previous operational state.

Now, with ASR, you can re-create *and* restore the entire operating system *exactly as it was* in one simple and quick process. It's important to note that ASR is not meant as a substitute for regular backups. ASR protects only the operating system and any other data that is on the same partitions or volumes as the operating system files. Typically, applications and data must continue to be backed up on a regular basis outside your adopted ASR procedures. However, a proper ASR routine can mean the difference between spending a weekend or a couple of hours on recovery.

What Is ASR?

ASR is a two-part, last-resort, system recovery feature for all components of the operating system, including the system state, system services, disk signatures, and partition layouts. It is similar to some third-party disaster-recovery tools, but it is more specific in purpose.

Unlike an operating system reinstallation, an ASR restore will re-create the *exact state* of the operating system at the time the ASR backup was performed. This means that for ASR to be effective, you should make sure that an ASR backup is performed after each change in the operating system.

How ASR Works

ASR involves two main processes:

- **ASR backup**   The process of creating an *ASR set*, which consists of a 1.44MB floppy diskette and a linked backup media containing ASR-created backup data. These two components are necessary for performing an ASR restore and must be kept together.

- **ASR restore**   The process of re-creating the operating system and system-related disk partitions/volumes from an ASR set. In addition to the ASR set, you will need to have the original media used to install Windows Server 2003 on your server.

An ASR backup creates a set of all of the information necessary to re-create the operating system at the time the ASR backup is performed. When an ASR restore is performed, the operating system is reinstalled using the original Windows Server 2003 media. However, instead of generating new disk signatures, security identifiers, and Registry content, these items are restored from the ASR set.

Alternatives to ASR

Before resorting to an ASR restore, there are a few alternatives that you should attempt for expediency and simplicity. Sometimes, these alternatives resolve the issue, so an ASR restore is unnecessary.

Safe Mode Boot

A Safe Mode startup starts the system with the minimum number of drivers enabled. Only keyboard, mouse, base video, monitor, disk, and default services are loaded. No network is available. This startup option can sometimes be used to get around a failed software application, service, or device driver that is causing system problems. If the system boots successfully, you can then disable or uninstall the problem driver, service, or application.

Last Known Good Boot Mode

The Last Known Good option starts the system normally but uses the Registry settings from the last successful logon to the system. This is useful to get past misconfiguration issues, especially regarding drivers that can cause system instability. A successful boot with this option will wipe out any setting or configuration changes that have occurred since the last successful logon. Once a logon occurs, these settings will then become the new Last Known Good configuration.

ASR As a Last Resort

If none of the above alternatives work, then an ASR restore may be necessary. Remember that ASR restores and re-creates the system as it was when the ASR set was created. Because of this, it is important to keep your ASR set up-to-date. At a minimum, an ASR backup should be performed after each operating system or system change.

Using the ASR Wizard

The ASR Wizard is accessed from the Windows Backup Utility in Advanced Mode. To start the Wizard, click its icon on the **Welcome** tab or select if from the **Tools** menu, as shown in Figure 7.55.

Figure 7.55 Starting the ASR Wizard

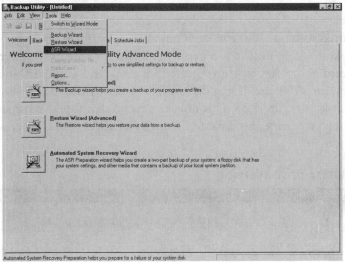

The ASR Wizard will start, prompt you for a destination for the backup, as shown in Figure 7.56, and proceed to create the backup.

Figure 7.56 The ASR Preparation Wizard, Choose a Destination

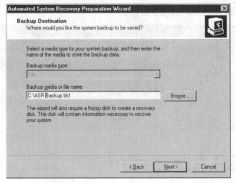

When the partitions or volumes that contain operating system components have been backed up, you will be prompted to insert a blank 1.44MB diskette, as shown in Figure 7.57. Insert the diskette into the floppy drive and click **OK**.

Figure 7.57 Creating the ASR Diskette

You are not required to have a diskette drive installed to perform an ASR backup, but you *are* required to have a diskette drive installed to perform an ASR restore. You can create the ASR diskette after the Wizard completes by copying the files asr.sif and asrpnp.sif (located in the *%systemroot%*\Repair directory) to a diskette. If you do not have a floppy disk drive installed in your system, you will see the warning in Figure 7.58. This does not mean that the ASR process will fail; it just means that you will need to create the diskette manually later. Click **OK** to close the warning dialog box.

Figure 7.58 No Floppy Drive Warning

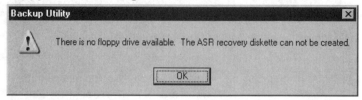

If you are performing an ASR backup without using a diskette, next, you will see the warning shown in Figure 7.59. Click **OK** to close the dialog box.

Figure 7.59 ASR Diskette Warning Message

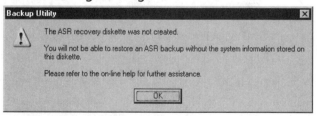

Performing an ASR Restore

An ASR restore is a fairly straightforward process. Boot from your original Windows Server 2003 CD-ROM. If a third-party storage driver needs to be loaded, press **F6** when prompted to load the driver. To begin the ASR recovery process, press **F2** when prompted, as shown in Figure 7.60.

Next, you will be prompted to insert the ASR diskette into the floppy drive, as shown in Figure 7.61.

Figure 7.60 Text-Mode ASR Prompt

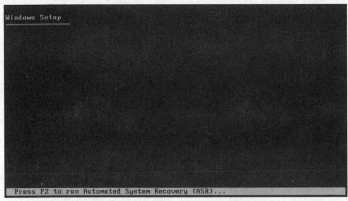

Figure 7.61 Insert the ASR Diskette Prompt

The ASR process will begin partitioning and formatting your server's boot and system partitions/volumes, as well as any other partitions or volumes that contained operating system files. This process will automatically re-create the operating system as it existed at the time the ASR set was created. If the backup media that is part of the ASR set cannot be located, you will be prompted for its location. Once the ASR restore is complete, the system will reboot.

Planning for Fault Tolerance

Fault tolerance is the ability to encounter failures and continue to function. Fault tolerance is created by using a combination of *redundancy* (the duplication of components or resources), efficient distribution of workload, proper planning, proper procedures, and training. When all of these are done correctly and in the right proportions, high availability is the result.

To properly plan for fault tolerance, examine all of the possible areas a failure could occur that would affect continuous operation. The following are the most common areas of failure:

- Hardware (disk, RAM, CPU, power supply, cooling fans, and network)

- Infrastructure (power feeds, environmental, and wide-area communications)

- Operational (documentation, change of media, and procedures)

- Functional (placing too many critical processes into a failure-susceptible area).

One fault-tolerant-related phrase you may have heard before is *five nines*, which is a reference to the larger *scale of nines* measure of computer system availability first developed by Jim Gray. The scale of nines refers to the percentage of downtime allowed per year, described by the number of nines in the availability statistic. Five nines refers to an achievable level of reliability in the middle scale. Table 7.2 illustrates the amount of downtime each level of "nines" means per year.

Table 7.2 The Scale of Nines and What Five-Nines Means

Name	Percentage of Uptime per Year	Effective Downtime per Year
One nine	90%	36 days, 12 hours
Two nines	99%	3 days, 15 hours, 36 minutes
Three nines	99.9%	8 hours, 45 minutes, 36 seconds
Four nines	99.99%	52 minutes, 34 seconds
Five nines	99.999%	5 minutes, 15 seconds
Six nines	99.9999%	31.5 seconds
Seven nines	99.99999%	3.2 seconds
Eight nines	99.999999%	0.32 second
Nine nines	99.9999999%	0.03 second

Five nines reliability is commonly discussed because it is possible to achieve given current technology. The primary factor with the scale of nines is cost. Higher levels of availability are becoming possible to achieve, but they usually come at a steep price.

Network Fault-Tolerance Solutions

One area of component failure is the network interface. If a system has one interface to a network, and a component of that interface fails (the switch, the cable, or the NIC), the whole interface fails. As a result, it is a good idea to build redundancy into your network interfaces.

Several manufacturers sell NICs that have two or more ports. Using the appropriate drivers, these cards usually support either a failover configuration or a load-balanced configuration, which work as follows:

- **Failover** Keeps one port idle and waiting, while the other port(s) handle communications. If a component of that interface fails, the idle port comes online and takes over for the failed port. A failover configuration can be used with switches or nonswitched network hubs.

- **Load-balanced configuration** Uses multiple ports simultaneously and spreads the communication load among the ports. In the event of an interface failure, the communications load is reassigned to the remaining active ports. A load-balanced configuration yields higher availability and performance but can be used only in conjunction with higher-end intelligent switches.

Some network topology issues can affect network availability as well. When designing a network, keep in mind all of the potential failure points, including routers, switches, bridges, and wide area network (WAN) components.

In all but the smallest networks, it is a good idea to have redundant functionality for critical services. If you are using AD, make sure that you have more than one domain controller and DNS server. If you are using WINS, create a secondary WINS server and have it replicate with the primary WINS server. If you are using DHCP, create a secondary DHCP server on each subnet and configure each with the appropriate scopes. Following these guidelines will ensure continued operation of these services in the event of failures.

Internet Fault-Tolerance Solutions

Many of the Internet fault-tolerance solutions are the same as general network fault-tolerance solutions, but there are a few extra considerations.

Network Load Balancing (NLB), discussed in the previous chapter, is a set of features included with all versions of Windows Server 2003 that can increase the redundancy, performance, and availability of Web sites.

Most medium and large networks access the Internet through a *proxy server*. If your environment includes a proxy server, consider building redundancy into it. A secondary proxy server may be in order.

The actual communication circuits and Internet Service Providers (ISPs) are other potential points of failure. It is common for large companies and organizations to have multiple WAN circuits and even multiple circuits to more than one ISP. This increases cost but also reduces the likelihood of a communications failure in an area usually outside your control.

Disk Fault-Tolerance Solutions

The most common hardware component that fails is the hard drive. Even though modern disk drives commonly operate for months or years without incident, failure is a given. As a result, disk fault-tolerance solutions are some of the most well-developed and reliable technologies, and they employ some of the oldest and most simple techniques. These solutions were discussed earlier in Chapter 5.

Server Fault-Tolerance Solutions

The server is our final point of consideration for fault-tolerance. There are two basic methods for introducing fault-tolerance on a server: hardware redundancy and virtualization (called *clustering*). Clustering was covered earlier in Chapter 6.

Modern server hardware is designed around increasing performance and reliability. Higher-end (more complicated and expensive) servers often include many built-in redundancy features. It is possible to find servers that support spare RAM and CPUs, redundant power supplies and cooling fans, built-in hardware RAID support, and many other features integrated into the basic system. In addition, many components in modern higher-end servers are *hot-swappable,* meaning the power does not need to be turned off in order to remove or change the component.

Another hardware component that is often overlooked but is easily acquired and implemented is a redundant power source. Ideally, you want duplicate power sources all the way back to duplicate utility companies, but that is usually not possible. What is possible is the installation of an Uninterruptible Power Supply (UPS) and the software to communicate with it. Size a UPS by the amount of power it must provide and the length of time needed to run when on battery. The more equipment on a UPS or the longer the required runtime, the "larger" the UPS must be. In very large environments, consider multiple UPSs operating in parallel (never "daisy-chain" UPSs) and possibly a backup generator.

Chapter 8

Monitoring and Troubleshooting Network Activity

In this chapter:

- **Using Network Monitor**

- **Monitoring and Troubleshooting Internet Connectivity**

- **Monitoring IPSec Connections**

Introduction

Managing a network involves a great deal of planning, design, and implementation. Even the most efficient networks require analysis and monitoring to validate your network design. Once your network is implemented, you will need to identify baselines for network activity, and be prepared to recognize abnormal behavior, and diagnose unexpected changes and troubleshoot problems with your network. Understanding your network will also provide you with the information necessary to plan for growth by examining trends and identifying the effects of adding hosts.

As challenging as it is to manage a regular local area network (LAN), we are expanding our scope of responsibility by allowing access to the Internet, and allowing our employees to access our networks from their homes, other businesses, and even hotels and coffee houses. With that perspective in mind, you spent all that time and effort to create a secure and reliable environment, and now you have clients transmitting company data from a network about which you know nothing. That fact alone makes it imperative that you implement strong security policies to protect loss of corporate data, and understand how to support and monitor the traffic in and out of your LAN from the Internet. It also places a burden on you to provide highly available and fast Internet access to support the telecommuters and any other remote clients that use the Internet to access the corporate LAN.

Due to the ever growing complexity with network design, and the large quantity of data flow on today's networks, we must understand the traffic and the tools that we use to capture and analyze that traffic. One of the most valuable tools we have at our disposal is Network Monitor. In this chapter, you will become familiar with network monitor and how to use Network Monitor to view your network traffic and identify information about the network traffic. Network Monitor is a great tool to help understand and troubleshoot connectivity problems.

We will discuss the identification and resolution for Internet connectivity problems. We will focus on Network Address Translation (NAT), name resolution, and IP addressing issues. In addition to troubleshooting and monitoring regular network traffic, we will also focus on monitoring network traffic that is encrypted. IP Security (IPSec) is based on open standards that are used to provide reliable transmission of encrypted data and authentication of data over IP. We will discuss how to use IPSec Security Monitor console to monitor and troubleshoot IPSec connections on your network.

Using Network Monitor

As a network administrator, you are tasked with understanding your network. One of the primary functions of the network is the reliable delivery of data. In addition to reliability, you must provide security and ensure that the data is accessible by those who are intended to receive it. Network Monitor provides network administrators with a window to the information being delivered over the network.

Network Monitor captures the frames of data as they are delivered over the wire, time stamps them, and provides statistical data about those frames. After you have captured the frames of data, Network Monitor will decode the headers and provide an easy-to-read summary of the type of packet, the source, the destination, and if the data is not encrypted, the data in the packet as well. In this section we will install Network Monitor. After we install Network Monitor, we explain the general layout of the main console, and then look at some captured frames. We look at how to filter captured data by setting capture filters and capture triggers, and then view more concise data using display filters.

Installing Network Monitor

There are two versions of Network Monitor. The full featured version ships with both Microsoft Systems Management Server (SMS) and the limited version. The limited version is included with the operating system, but is not installed in Windows Server 2003 by default. Installing Network Monitor is actually a simple task—it is installed as a Windows Component via **Add/Remove Programs**.

Use the following steps to install Network Monitor. During the installation, the driver for Network Monitor is automatically installed.

Install Network Monitor

You will need the Windows Server 2003 product disc during the installation. It will be helpful to have other machines available to you after the example is complete to see network traffic and perform the captures.

1. Navigate to **Control Panel | Add or Remove Programs**. The Add or Remove programs dialog is displayed.

2. Select **Add/Remove Windows Components** from the shortcut bar.

3. The **Windows Components Wizard** is displayed (see Figure 8.1).

Figure 8.1 Windows Components Wizard

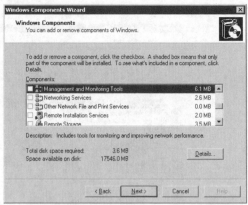

4. Select the item Management and Monitoring Tools as shown in Figure 8.1, and click the Details button.

5. The Management and Monitoring Tools dialog is shown as in Figure 8.2. Click the check box next to Network Monitor Tools and click OK.

Figure 8.2 Management and Monitoring Tools

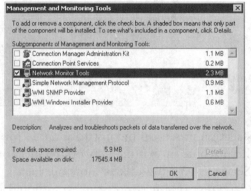

6. The Windows Components Wizard is displayed again (see Figure 8.3), this time with the check box next to Management and Monitoring Tools checked and gray.

7. Click Next to apply the changes and install the necessary software components. You will see what appears to be several components that you did not choose appear in the Status messages seen above the progress bar in Figure 8.4. This is part of a routine and there is no need for alarm. Only the necessary components for Network Monitor will be installed.

Figure 8.3 Windows Components Wizard after Selecting the Network Monitoring Subcomponent

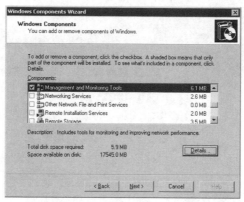

Figure 8.4 Configuring Components

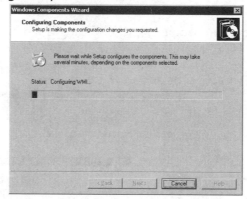

8. During the installation process, if the installation files for Windows Server 2003 are not accessible on the machine or existing network connections, then you will be prompted for the Windows Server 2003 setup disk as shown in Figure 8.5. If the installation files are located on the hard disk or a network share, you should still click OK and then you'll be able to enter the path on the next screen.

Figure 8.5 Insert Disk

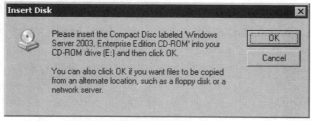

9. When the installation is complete, you will see the Completing the Windows Components Wizard message (see Figure 8.6). Click Finish.

Figure 8.6 Windows Components Wizard—Completing the Windows Components Wizard

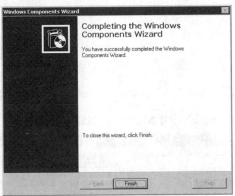

In this example, we installed the operating system component version of Network Monitor. Now it is possible to capture and view frames of data from your network. We can now become more familiar with using Network Monitor and understand how to use it effectively.Let's take a look at how to capture frames. Click **Start | Administrative Tools | Network Monitor**. The first time you launch Network Monitor, you will see a message informing you that you must select a network to monitor, or Network Monitor will select one for you, as shown in Figure 8.7.

Figure 8.7 Microsoft Network Monitor Console

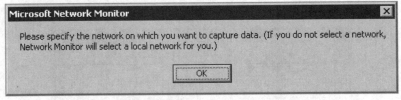

Figures 8.8 and 8.9 show the dialog that you will use to select the network on which you will monitor traffic using this instance of Network Monitor. If you are capturing data from multiple LANS simultaneously, you must install and configure one adapter for each network and start a unique instance of Network Monitor for each adapter. You must select the network for each instance of Network Monitor by selecting **Capture | Networks** and selecting the appropriate network. The network for newly installed adapters will not be available until you restart Network Monitor.

Figure 8.8 Select a Network

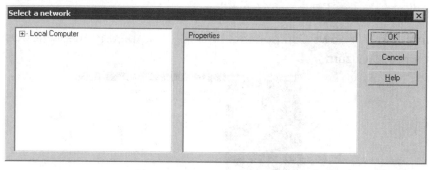

Figure 8.9 Select a Network with Multiple Adapters

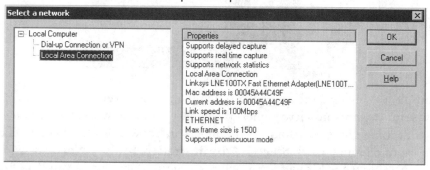

After you have selected a network, you will see the **Network Monitor Capture window** that is shown in Figure 8.10.

Figure 8.10 Network Monitor Console

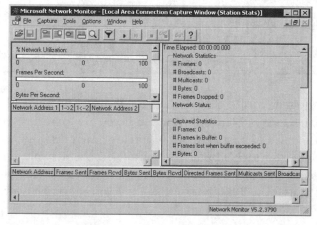

There are four panes in the Capture window:

- **Graph pane** is in the upper left corner and displays a graphical representation of the current total capture statistics from the collected capture data. See the Network Monitor help file for an explanation of each counter in this pane.

- **Session Statistic pane** is located in the left center of the console and displays the current session statistics that constitute data sent to or from your computer. It displays the session's participants and the amount of data exchanged in either direction. See the Network Monitor help file for an explanation of each counter in this pane.

- **Station Statistics pane** is the bottom-most pane that shows your computer's network activity. See the Network Monitor help file for an explanation of each counter in this pane.

- **Total Statistics pane** is located in the upper right corner of the console. The Total Statistics pane shows the network traffic summaries for the inbound and outbound traffic on your computer.

Begin your first capture by selecting **Capture | Start** or clicking **Play** on the tool bar. You will begin to see data transmissions immediately, as shown in Figure 8.11.

Figure 8.11 Network Monitor Console Capturing Data

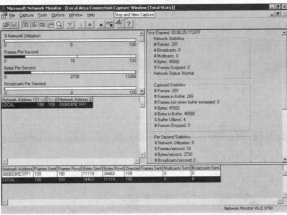

Click the **Stop and View Capture** icon (with the glasses and the square) shown in Figure 8.11, or **Capture | Stop** and **View** or **Shift+F11** to view the captured frames.

Figure 8.12 Network Monitor Frame Viewer Window Summary Data

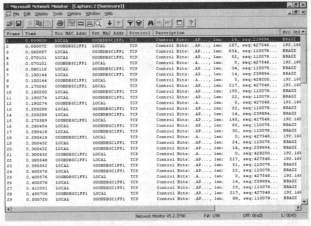

The window shown in Figure 8.12 is called the **Frame Viewer** window. Currently it is displaying a full window that contains the **Summary Pane**, which contains frames and their statistics to analyze. Three panes are part of the Frame Viewer window (see Figure 8.13):

- **Summary Pane** shows the list of captured frames. You can filter this list to isolate the frames that you want to analyze. If you double-click an item in the list, the other two panes are visible.

- **Detail Pane** shows the detail of the frame that is currently selected in the Summary Pane, which now occupies only a third of the Frame Viewer window. This hierarchical representation is very informative, and can provide a valuable insight as to how you approach design and implementation for your network.

- **Hexadecimal Pane** is broken down into two views. The first view is the actual data in hexadecimal form that makes up the frame, and the second section is the alphanumeric ASCII representation of that frame.

Figure 8.13 Network Monitor Frame Viewer Window with All Panes Visible

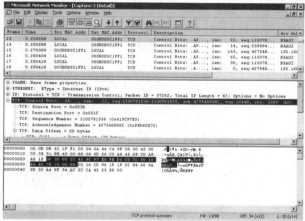

Basic Configuration

As discussed previously, there are certain settings that are required to monitor your network. For example, you must select a local network. If you don't set one, then Network Monitor will select your default adapter, which is the first in the network binding order. This may suit your current needs, but you might need to install additional adapters later to monitor multiple networks at the same time.

If you want to monitor more than one network, then you must have the additional adapter installed and configured prior to launching Network Monitor. If you install an adapter while Network Monitor is running, then you will need to restart Network Monitor after you install the adapter in order to select that network. Note, however, that if you want to monitor a specific protocol on the network, it is possible to capture that traffic without installing that protocol.

Network Monitor captures data by frames, which means that each packet contains the source and destination address, the header information, and the data itself. All the frames transmitted on the segment are processed by all the machines on that network. If the destination is not addressed to that adapter, then the frame is dropped. Broadcast frames are captured as well since technically they are destined for the local computer as part of the segment. If the adapter has initiated multicast traffic, then it will also be shown.

Network Monitor Default Settings

There are several settings that are accessible from the Capture menu. Two of the most important are:

- The **Capture | Addresses** menu item, which allows you to define addresses and the metadata about the addresses and stores them in a database. By default, the information about your local adapters is part of this database.

- The **Capture | Buffer settings** item, which allows you to set the Buffer Size in megabytes (MB), and Frame size in bytes. The buffer size determines how much data you can capture at one time before ceasing to gather data. The default setting for buffer size is 1MB. The maximum value for buffer size is 1024 MB. Frame size is the setting that allows you to configure the number of bytes to capture from each frame. This is useful when on token ring networks that are particular about frame size. The default frame size is set to Full, which is the maximum size or 65,535 bytes. The list of frame sizes is a list of numbers that are incremented 64 bytes at a time, and the highest number listed is 65472, even though 65535 (Full) is the largest frame size. You have the option to type your own custom value in the range of 32 bytes to the maximum value, or you can select the values provided in the list.

The other menu items on the Capture menu are **Filter**, **Networks**, and **Trigger**. **Networks** has been discussed earlier in the chapter; **Filter** and **Trigger** will be discussed in later sections. By default there are no filters or triggers, and the network is the primary adapter on your machine.

Configuring Monitoring Filters

Capture filters allow you to isolate different types of data transmitted to and from your machine on the specified network. You can use an address database to add addresses to your filter and restrict data to capture to those addresses. You can save the filter to a file so that you can use it again, and create standard address filters for your network. Using filters will reduce the buffer usage and save time fishing through an excessive number of frames captured. You can further restrict frames of data by designing a capture filter.

When you select **Capture | Filters** you will be presented with a **Capture Filter** dialog box (see Figure 8.14). You can use this dialog to create a logic base filter using a graphical representation of the Boolean logic you are using to define the filter.

Figure 8.14  Capture Filter Dialog

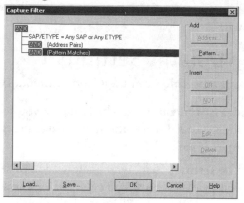

You can filter on a specific protocol by clicking the **SAP/ETYPE=** line of the Capture Filter dialog and clicking **Edit**. For example, if you want to capture only IPv6 frames on your network, open the **Capture Filter** dialog and edit the **SAP/ETYPE** line, then select and disable all protocols except **IP ETYPE 0x86DD**.

You can add additional filters on addresses for up to four address pairs at the same time. This will capture packets only from that computer in Network Monitor, or you can define the filter to *exclude* that computer and its frames from the capture.

You can also specify a pattern to match in the frames you capture. It is possible to use pattern filters to limit the frames to only the ones that contain ASCII or hexadecimal data that you define in the pattern filter. If you have an idea where the data is located in the frame, you can improve the filter performance by defining bytes offsets from the **Start of the Frame**. The filter will ignore the offset number of hex bytes and then start searching for the filter criteria from that point in the frame. You can also specify **From End of Topology Header**. Topology Header is the definition of the network medium, such as Ethernet or Token Ring. If you are using Ethernet or Token Ring, you should specify the **From End of Topology Header** option, since Ethernet and token ring have variable size frames in the media access control (MAC) protocol. Pattern filters require the offset to be defined, and it defaults to 0 bytes from the start of the frame.

Configuring Display Filters

Once you have captured data, you can filter the data further by using a display filter. Display filters allow you to focus on the types of frames that you really care about. Display filters apply only to data that you have already captured and have no effect on the actual traffic. You can filter data that you want to analyze in the Frame Viewer window, or if you need only a subset of the information for later, you can apply a filter to restrict the data as you save it to a capture file.

Display filters can include criteria based on source or destination address, and protocol information in the frame. It is possible to use the properties of the protocol and the values the protocol contains in the header to filter data. Protocol properties are the definition of the protocol and its function. If you are inundated with unwanted traffic that is specific to a protocol or a machine address you can simply add a filter to exclude it by modifying the **Protocol==** line in the Display

Filter dialog. By applying display filters, you reduce the data in the Capture window to a more manageable size. So if you want to limit the amount of frames that you want to allow Network Monitor to capture, use a capture filter to drop the frames you don't care about instead of adding the frames to the trace. After you have captured the data, use a display filter to hide the unwanted frames that are already captured.

Interpreting a Trace

Network Monitor can be used to capture frames of data transmitted to and from you machine. The captured frames are referred to a **network trace**. As previously discussed, you can identify capture filters that can be used to focus the trace on the types of frames that contain the information you need. For example, you can define capture filters that would enable you to trace IPSec traffic to your machine from a specific client, and view the data to ensure that it is encrypted. Use the following steps to perform a network trace.

Perform a Network Trace

In this example, you will begin a trace, identify a specific type of frame, and look at its contents. (Before you begin, you must have installed Network Monitor.)

1. Open Network Monitor. Click Start | Administrative Tools | Network Monitor.

2. Click Capture | Start Capture or press F10 to begin capturing frames.

3. From another computer, ping the interface that Network Monitor is capturing frames on for one series.

4. Once the ping is complete, click Capture | Stop or press F11 to stop capturing frames.

5. Examine each of the panes in the Capture window and note the various values.

6. When you are satisfied that you did capture frames on that interface, click Capture | Display Captured Data or press F12. The Capture Summary (see Figure 8.15) appears.

Figure 8.15 Capture Summary

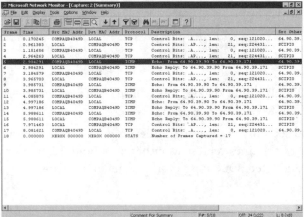

7. Use Display | Filter to open the filter dialog (see Figure 8.16).

Figure 8.16 Filter Dialog

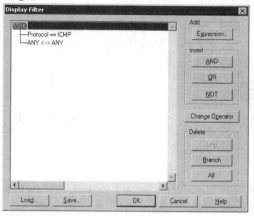

8. Click Protocol ==ANY and then click Edit Expression.

9. The Expression dialog is displayed. Make sure you are on the Protocol tab, and click Disable All.

10. Locate ICMP in the Disabled protocols list and click Enable or double-click ICMP. The expression dialog should look like Figure 8.17.

Figure 8.17 Expression Dialog with ICMP Enabled

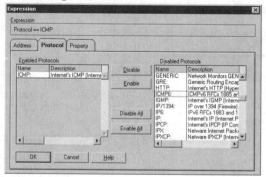

11. Click OK.

12. From the Display filter dialog, you will see that Protocol==ANY is now Protocol==ICMP. Click OK.

13. You should see only eight lines in the Capture Summary window as shown in Figure 8.18. Each of the lines represents either an inbound frame or an outbound frame for the ping we conducted. One ping cycle is four round trips.

Figure 8.18 Capture Summary with ICMP Display Filter Enabled

14. Double-click one of the entries where the description begins "Echo: From…". You should see the Capture Detail (middle) pane in Figure 8.19.

Figure 8.19 Capture Detail of ICMP Ping Traffic

15. Expand the ICMP tree in the Detail pane and click the last item that begins ICMP: Data: ….

16. Look in the Hexadecimal (bottom) pane at the highlighted text. Note the contents.

17. In the Capture Summary pane (top), click the next frame in the list. The Description should begin "Echo Reply: To…".

18. Expand the ICMP tree in the Detail pane and click the last item that begins ICMP: Data: ….

19. Look at the highlighted text in the bottom pane. Note the contents. They should be identical to the Data contents in the ICMP Echo. This is how ping is validated.

Now that you have analyzed a basic capture, locate a good TCP/IP reference and monitor traffic on your network for short periods of time and practice identifying details about the frames of data on your network. Don't forget to use capture and display filters to minimize the data gathered and then impact on network traffic.

Monitoring and Troubleshooting Internet Connectivity

Accessing the Internet has become commonplace over the last few years. The accessibility of information resources on the Internet alone makes it a necessity for day-to-day access. The ability to conduct business transactions using e-commerce applications has developed an online marketplace for business-to-business and business-to-consumer sales. It is also possible to provide remote technical support, connectivity between different company locations and voice communication over the Internet, and reduce the cost of travel and support.

With the onset of these new possibilities, you are now tasked with ensuring the high availability of Internet access. In addition to reliable access, you must ensure that the data transmitted over the Internet is protected from prying eyes, and that your network is not blatantly exposed to security threats from inside and outside your network. This section covers some of the various issues associated with Internet access and some of the tools used to monitor and troubleshoot Internet access.

NAT Logging

If you have a small, nonrouted network, you may have implemented the Network Address Translation protocol (NAT) to allow your private network users to access the Internet. There will be a need to monitor and possibly identify problems with applications that use the Internet over the interface that uses the NAT protocol. NAT requires Routing and Remote Access Services (RRAS) on a multi-homed computer. One of the network interfaces must be configured with a public IP address or you may configure it to use demand dial routing, and obtain the public address from your Internet Service Provider (ISP). Take a look at this excellent overview at www.microsoft.com/WINDOWSXP/pro/techinfo/planning/networking/nattraversal.asp for more details on how NAT works.

The first step in troubleshooting NAT is to verify your configuration. There are a few basic settings to verify. Let's look at the RRAS server settings and identify some of the key details. Both the public interface to the Internet and the private LAN interfaces must be added to the NAT routing protocol and configured to use the correct settings. Figure 8.20 shows the **NAT/Basic Firewall** tab of the private interface. It must have the **Private interface connected to private network** option selected. Another common area for trouble is the **Static packet filters** options shown in the bottom of the dialog in Figure 8.21. The Static Packet Filters dialog is accessed by clicking the **Inbound Filters** button shown on the dialog in Figure 8.20. You can configure filters on the traffic Inbound (destined for the private network in this case) and Outbound (destined for the Internet in this case).

Figure 8.20 NAT/Basic Firewall Tab of the Private Interface

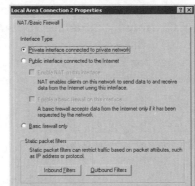

Filters are defined by two criteria. The first criterion is the action. The two actions are:

- Receive all packets except those that meet the criteria defined in the Filters list.
- Drop all except those that meet the criteria defined in the Filters list.

The second criterion is the filters that are listed in the Filters list. The filters contain settings for the following:

- The **Source network** IP address and subnet mask define where the packet is coming from.
- The **Destination network** IP address and subnet mask define where the packet is going.
- **Protocol to filter** defines the protocol such as TCP, UDP, ICMP, and so on, and the source and destination ports used by the filter. You may also use **Any**, which includes all possible ports and protocols.

If you have defined filters that permit only specified traffic or deny all traffic except that which is defined in the filter list, you may use NAT logging to identify blocked traffic. We will discuss logging a little later in the chapter. Now you should examine the external interface.

Figure 8.21 Inbound Static Packet Filters Dialog

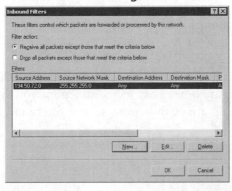

Shown in Figure 8.22 is the **NAT/Basic Firewall** tab of the public interface, which is configured as **Public interface connected to the Internet.** This properties dialog can be accessed from the **Routing and Remote Access Console** by expanding the **NAT/Basic Firewall** node, then right-clicking the LAN connection that is the external (public) interface adapter and selecting **Properties.** Also note that the check box for **Enable NAT on this interface** is checked. This turns the NAT protocol on, and is required for NAT protocol to map internal address and port requests to the public IP interface.

Figure 8.22 NAT/Basic Firewall Tab of the Public Interface

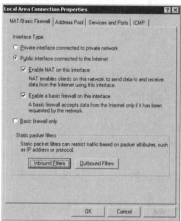

You can have the **Enable a basic firewall on this interface** option checked, which will block all public Internet access to the local private network. This is equivalent in concept to enabling filters on an interface. There are several methods you can use to define filters:

- **The TCP/IP filtering option**, which is located in the LAN properties, contains filter settings that are defined on the **Internet Protocol (TCP/IP) Properties**, **Advanced TCP/IP Settings**, **Options** tab.

- **In the RRAS snap-in, in the NAT/Basic Firewall node**, the Internal and each LAN Connection Interface properties there are the filters discussed previously.

- **In the RRAS snap-in, in the General node**, the Internal and each LAN Connection Interface properties there are the filters discussed previously.

You should check each location for filter settings to make sure that you are allowing or disallowing the appropriate traffic.

You can enable common services to access your network by simply checking the box next to the service name in the **Services and Ports** tab shown in Figure 8.23. You can also manage the behavior of ICMP by checking the boxes next to the functions you wish to allow on the ICMP tab seen in Figure 8.24. These settings are equivalent to setting filters and are disabled by default.

Figure 8.23 Services and Ports Tab

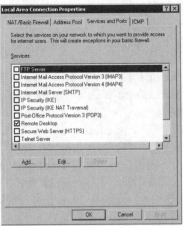

Figure 8.24 ICMP Tab

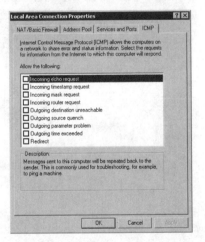

The client machines that use the NAT server will need their TCP/IP configuration set to obtain their IP addresses automatically. When the clients receive the IP configuration from the NAT server, they will be assigned:

- IP address from the defined pool (Defaults to 192.168.0.0/24)

- Subnet mask (Defaults to 255.255.255.0)

- Default gateway (NAT computer internal IP address)

- DNS server (NAT computer internal IP address)

Clients that obtain their address from the NAT server will use the NAT server to resolve DNS queries. The DNS server that is defined on the NAT server actually handles the request that is forwarded from the NAT server for the NAT client. This will limit your capabilities to resolve hostnames on your internal network if you have a DNS server providing the name resolution for internal hosts.

If the client machine is configured to use DHCP, or any of the TCP/IP settings were manually configured incorrectly, then it may not be able to access the Internet. If you are running DHCP service on another server on your network, and the client computer gets its IP address from the DHCP server, then it may not be able to access the Internet or resolve host names on the Internet. We will discuss name resolution in a later section. A nice feature of NAT is that you can disable NAT address assignment and allow your DHCP clients to use a DHCP server. This will simplify your network administration and provide you with the means to provide additional configuration information to DHCP clients in the scope options, such as WINS servers, which type of name resolution to use, and many others. With ICS you cannot disable address assignment.

To disable NAT addressing, using the **RRAS Console**, right-click on **NAT/Basic Firewall** and select **Properties**. You will be presented with the **Properties** dialog. Click the **Address Assignment** tab as shown in Figure 8.25. Simply uncheck the **Automatically assign IP addresses by using the DHCP allocator** check box, then click **OK**. Clients on your internal network will no longer obtain IP addresses from the NAT server.

Figure 8.25 NAT/Basic Firewall Properties—Disable NAT Address Assignment

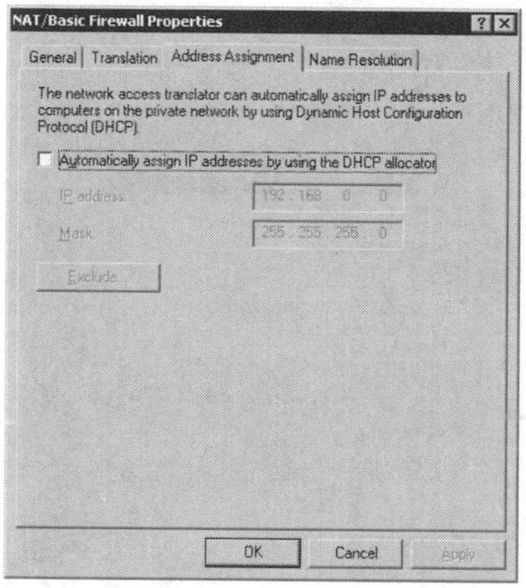

Monitoring NAT Activity

Now that your LAN clients are using NAT, you will need to be able to monitor use, and to identify and resolve issues associated with NAT. There are several tools to provide you with the necessary information for identifying which clients are connected and to which address and port they are connected with what protocol. You may also need to identify causes of unreliable Internet access. All clients that use NAT to access the Internet will have their internal IP address mapped to an external IP address and the private address will need to map the appropriate port for the desired protocol to an external port for the same protocol.

You can view the mappings of NAT clients in the **Network Address Translation Mappings Table** shown in Figure 8.26, by right-clicking the interface listed in the NAT/Basic Firewall pane of RRAS console. The route table (see Figure 8.27) and other TCP, UDP, and IP information is also accessible from RRAS by right-clicking the interface listed in the **General** pane.

Figure 8.26 Network Address Translation Mappings Table

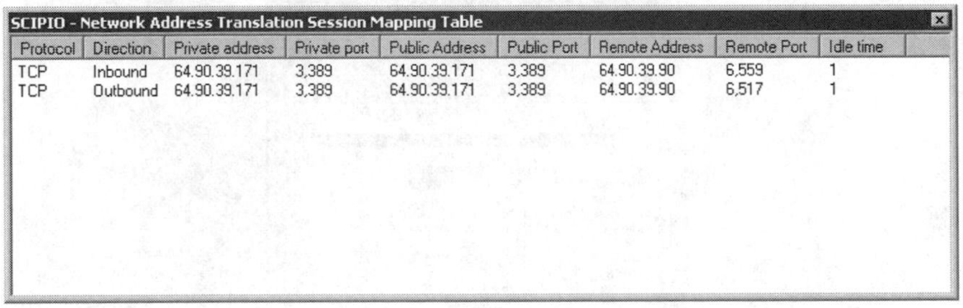

SCIPIO - Network Address Translation Session Mapping Table

Protocol	Direction	Private address	Private port	Public Address	Public Port	Remote Address	Remote Port	Idle time
TCP	Inbound	64.90.39.171	3,389	64.90.39.171	3,389	64.90.39.90	6,559	1
TCP	Outbound	64.90.39.171	3,389	64.90.39.171	3,389	64.90.39.90	6,517	1

Figure 8.27 Routes Table

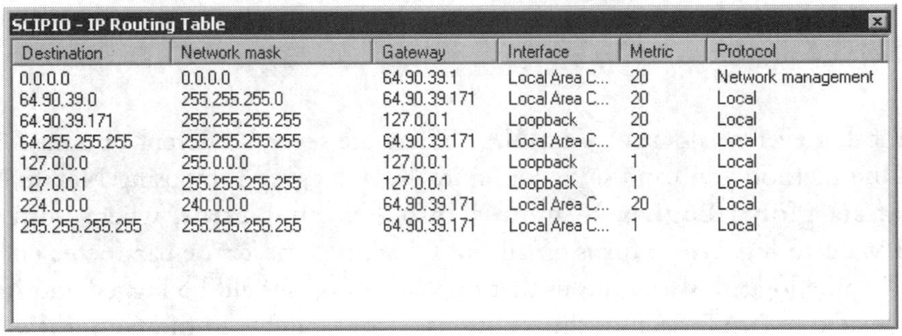

SCIPIO - IP Routing Table

Destination	Network mask	Gateway	Interface	Metric	Protocol
0.0.0.0	0.0.0.0	64.90.39.1	Local Area C...	20	Network management
64.90.39.0	255.255.255.0	64.90.39.171	Local Area C...	20	Local
64.90.39.171	255.255.255.255	127.0.0.1	Loopback	20	Local
64.255.255.255	255.255.255.255	64.90.39.171	Local Area C...	20	Local
127.0.0.0	255.0.0.0	127.0.0.1	Loopback	1	Local
127.0.0.1	255.255.255.255	127.0.0.1	Loopback	1	Local
224.0.0.0	240.0.0.0	64.90.39.171	Local Area C...	20	Local
255.255.255.255	255.255.255.255	64.90.39.171	Local Area C...	1	Local

There are other options to monitor the client Internet connections over NAT. In addition to providing an overview of mappings, the Netstat utility has a new option that allows you to find out what process is the owner of the connection. This is helpful when you have many connections through a routing server and need to identify what application is using which connection. The command is **Netstat –o** and adds the Process column as you can see in Figure 8.28. The process can then be cross-referenced by id using Task Manager (see Figure 8.29). Another helpful utility to get details about a process is Process Explorer, a free utility from www.sysinternals.com. You can also enable logging.

Figure 8.28 Netstat Command with –o Option

```
C:\WINDOWS\system32\cmd.exe
Microsoft Windows [Version 5.2.3790]
(C) Copyright 1985-2003 Microsoft Corp.

C:\Documents and Settings\Administrator.SCIPIO>netstat -o

Active Connections

  Proto  Local Address          Foreign Address        State           PID
  TCP    SCIPIO:epmap           SCIPIO:3046            ESTABLISHED     716
  TCP    SCIPIO:epmap           SCIPIO:3057            ESTABLISHED     716
  TCP    SCIPIO:3046            SCIPIO:epmap           ESTABLISHED     1624
  TCP    SCIPIO:3057            SCIPIO:epmap           ESTABLISHED     3636
  TCP    SCIPIO:3389            xzozx90.august.net:6517  ESTABLISHED     792
  TCP    SCIPIO:3389            xzozx90.august.net:6559  ESTABLISHED     792

C:\Documents and Settings\Administrator.SCIPIO>_
```

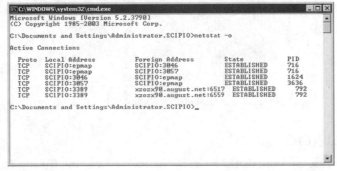

Figure 8.29 Task Manager Listing at the Same Time of the Netstat –o Command

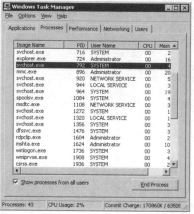

You can also log events associated with NAT. There are several different options for logging NAT events. One method you can use to configure NAT logging is by using **Netsh**: **Netsh routing ip nat set global LogLevel= none | info | warn | error**, where **LogLevel** specifies the events you want to log. **None** turns off all NAT logging. The **error** parameter enables errors related to NAT to be logged, **warn** means that only warnings should be logged and **info** parameter logs all events related to NAT. Each of these options is configurable in the **General** tab of the **NAT/Basic Firewall Global** properties, as shown in Figure 8.30. The events that are logged are written to the Application Event log.

Figure 8.30 NAT/Basic Firewall Global Properties

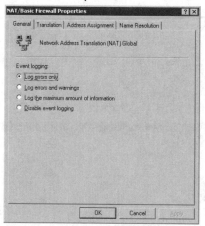

Name Resolution

The resources you provide on your LAN must be accessible by some means. In order to facilitate the use of friendly names, we must provide readily available services or mechanisms to resolve names to IP addresses. There are two basic types of name resolution, Host Name Resolution and NetBIOS Name Resolution.

Host Name Resolution Troubleshooting Tools

You can use **nslookup** to troubleshoot host name resolution. **Nslookup** is an interactive command line utility that can be used to perform domain name queries against a specific DNS server, examine zone files, and validate the entries in the zone records in the DNS database. If the forward look up zone is not available, when you run **nslookup** to query that zone, it will timeout. **Netdiag**, **Dnscmd**, and **dcdiag** are all enhanced command line utilities that can also be used to resolve more Active Directory/DNS related issues. **Netdiag** is used to check distributed and network services such as IPSec, and to verify WINS and DNS name resolution and consistency. You can install the **netdiag** utility from the **suptools.msi** file located in the **Support\Tools** folder on the Windows Server 2003 product disc.

Dnscmd is the command line version of the DNS configuration utility. This tool can be used to add, delete, or verify records in a DNS database, configure DNS servers, and manage zones. **Dcdiag** can be used with **netdiag** and **dnscmd** to check the domain controllers in your enterprise and verify that the domain controllers are running properly.

NetBIOS Name Resolution

A NetBIOS name is a 16-byte address that maps to a network node that is defined as a NetBIOS resource on your network. NetBIOS name resolution entails resolving the NetBIOS name to the NetBIOS resource. NetBIOS names are unique names used by a host exclusively or a group name that can be resolved to more than one computer or process. If you request a single resource, then you use a unique name, otherwise you will use a group name to request resolution of more than one process on more than one computer.

NetBIOS Node Types

There are different methods for resolving NetBIOS names to IP addresses. The order in which each of the methods is used to resolve NetBIOS names depends on the NetBIOS node type defined for the client host. You can configure DHCP scope to define the node type setting for each host that gets an address from that scope. See Table 8.1 for a description of each of the node types that can be defined.

Table 8.1 Definition of NetBIOS Node Types

Type of Node	Definition
B-node (broadcast)	B-node broadcasts NetBIOS name queries for resolution of NetBIOS names and registering NetBIOS resources. Since B-node is broadcast-based, it is confined to local segments and contributes a good deal to overall net-work traffic on a segment.
P-node (peer-peer)	P-node resolves NetBIOS names with a direct request to a NetBIOS name server (NBNS).

Continued

Table 8.1 Definition of NetBIOS Node Types

Type of Node	Definition
M-node (mixed)	M-node basically is made up of B-node and P-node resolution combined. M-Node hosts attempt to resolve hosts by using B-node broadcasts, and if that fails, then it will query a NetBIOS Name Server using a direct request using P-node.
H-node (hybrid)	H-node is a Hybrid made up of P-node and B-node resolution combined. H-Node requests are the opposite of M-node requests. The first attempt to resolve hosts is by a direct query to NetBIOS Name Server using P-node, and then it will use B-node broadcasts.

If a Windows Server 2003 machine is configured to use NetBIOS over TCP/IP, then it will use B-node broadcast to resolve NetBIOS names, unless a WINS server is defined, which will cause it to use H–Node resolution. You can also define the node type setting in DCHP for those hosts on your network that are set to dynamically configure the IP address.

LMHOSTS File

The LMHosts file is also located in the WINDIR\System32\Drivers\etc folder. There are differences in the file format of LMHosts. Instructions in the LMHosts.sam file located in the WINDIR\System32\Drivers\etc folder can be used to create a file without the full name LMHosts (no .sam extension). You can configure the clients with the option to use LMHosts files for resolution if you like. NBTStat can be used to purge the NetBIOS name cache and load the LMHosts file to the cache using **NBTStat –RR**, as well as troubleshooting NetBIOS name resolution. It is strongly recommended that if you are using a Windows operating systems other than Windows 2000/XP or Windows Server 2003, that you implement a WINS server to reduce broadcast traffic and aid in the resolution of the other Windows resources.

Using IPConfig to Troubleshoot Name Resolution

The front line in host name resolution problem solving is Ipconfig. You can use ipconfig to give you the details of your IP address settings for all your adapters. This allows you to verify the subnet mask, default gateway, and other settings for every adapter on the machine. The **ipconfig** utility with no command line options will provide the simple view as shown in Figure 8.31. For more detail you can use **ipconfig /all** for the results shown in Figure 8.32. In addition, you can now use **ipconfig** with the option **/displaydns** to give you the list of host name resolutions cached on the client machine as shown in Figure 8.33.

Figure 8.31 Results of ipconfig

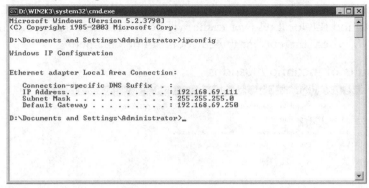

Figure 8.32 Results of ipconfig /all

Figure 8.33 Results of ipconfig /displaydns

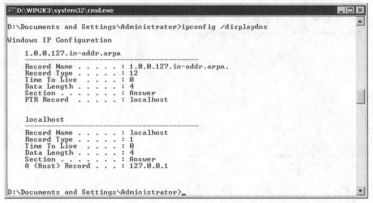

If you are having trouble resolving hosts, you can try clearing the resolver cache using **ipconfig /flushdns** as in Figure 8.34. On occasion, IP addresses change on the network. A common scenario is one in which a machine has a host name registered in DNS, you remove the computer account from Active Directory, and remove the entry from DNS. Then you add the machine with the same name as it had before, only now, it gets assigned a new IP address. When other machines attempt to resolve the machine by using the host name, if they have the old address for the same host name in cache, then the client machine will not be able to connect to the rebuilt machine. Simply use **ipconfig /flushdns** and the local resolver cache will be cleared, thus requiring the client to request resolution from DNS, where the current information can be obtained.

Figure 8.34 Results of ipconfig /flushdns

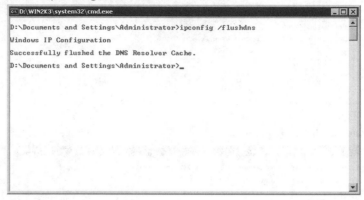

If required, you can use **ipconfig /registerdns** (see Figure 8.35) to add the client to the Dynamic DNS server if you are using Active Directory integrated DNS and your host name is not registered in DNS. Your machine name may not be registered in DNS if you have assigned a static IP address.

Figure 8.35 Results of ipconfig /registerdns

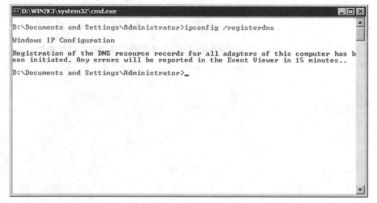

IP Addressing

The flexibility of TCP/IP contributes to the complexity of troubleshooting addresses and connections. There are several tools that can help isolate and identify issues with addressing, but it is also imperative that you understand IP addressing rules and subnetting. **Ipconfig**, **ping**, and **tracert** are the most useful tools in identifying addressing problems with the client configurations and connections to other hosts on the Internet.

Client Configuration Issues

Some of the issues that occur with manual configuration of IP addresses include duplicate addresses, invalid subnet masks, invalid default gateways, and invalid or missing host name resolution settings (such as DNS and WINS). To help identify the problem, start by typing **ipconfig /all** at a command prompt. Verify the information that is output by the command is correct, and then continue by using **ping** to help isolate the problem.

1. Ping the loopback address (127.0.0.1) to verify that the TCP/IP protocol stack is configured correctly on the local computer.

2. Ping the external IP address of the local computer to ensure the host is on the network and using a valid IP address; that is, no address conflicts.

3. Ping the IP address of the default gateway to verify that the default gateway is accessible and your local network configuration contains the correct subnet mask.

4. Ping the IP address of a remote host to verify that you can transmit data over the default gateway.

If you are not able to get traffic through to a site, but you are making it through the default gateway, then you should use **tracert** to identify the break in the route to the destination. An example of using **tracert** is shown in Figure 8.36, using the command line **tracert www.syngress.com.** To prevent the resolution of the hostnames that are shown in the results of Figure 8.36, specify the command with the **–d** option: **tracert -d www.syngress.com.**

Figure 8.36 Results of tracert

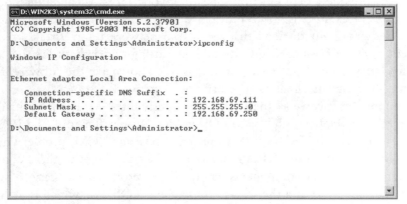

Another utility that is more useful than **tracert** and **ping** combined is **pathping**. **Pathping** is basically **tracert** and **ping** combined. The **pathping** command line utility provides an overview of latency and loss of data over a network at each hop from a source to a destination. The **pathping** utility will continue to ping over a specified period of time in seconds, but it will default to a value related to the total number of hops from the source to the destination. **Pathping** computes the latency and packet loss from each router. This allows you to identify firewalls that block **icmp** but still provide information about latency on the hops past the firewall. You can also use **pathping** to zero in on problem routers, or slow connections on a route. An example of the command **pathping** *destination address* is shown in Figure 8.37. It is also possible to use **pathping** to trace the latency from a different source to the same destination. This provides a means for you to troubleshoot a connection on another machine, from a different client on the network. The command for specifying a different source address is **pathping –i<***IP address of source***> *destination address***. It can also provide means for you to monitor a specific set of links in the route that may reduce the overall time to perform the trace. **Pathping** command line options are case sensitive.

Figure 8.37 Results of pathping

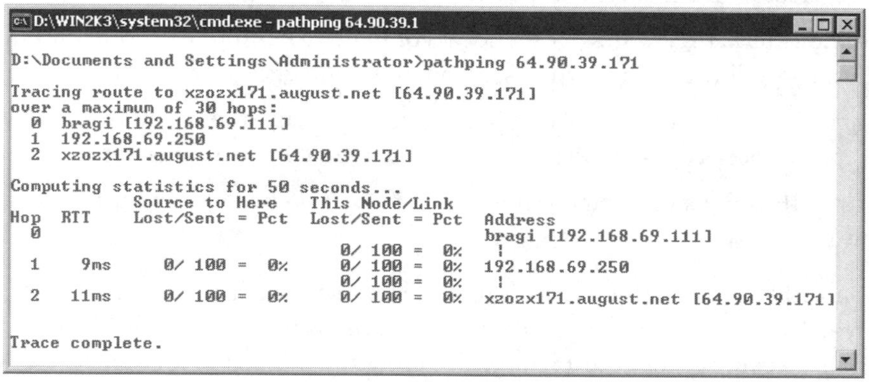

```
D:\WIN2K3\system32\cmd.exe - pathping 64.90.39.1                    _ □ ×

D:\Documents and Settings\Administrator>pathping 64.90.39.171

Tracing route to xzozx171.august.net [64.90.39.171]
over a maximum of 30 hops:
  0  bragi [192.168.69.111]
  1  192.168.69.250
  2  xzozx171.august.net [64.90.39.171]

Computing statistics for 50 seconds...
             Source to Here   This Node/Link
Hop  RTT     Lost/Sent = Pct  Lost/Sent = Pct   Address
  0                                              bragi [192.168.69.111]
                                0/ 100 =  0%       |
  1   9ms    0/ 100 =  0%      0/ 100 =  0%     192.168.69.250
                                0/ 100 =  0%       |
  2  11ms    0/ 100 =  0%      0/ 100 =  0%     xzozx171.august.net [64.90.39.171]

Trace complete.
```

Network Access Quarantine Control

Internet Authentication Service (IAS), combined with Remote Authentication Dial-In User Service protocol and RRAS, provide a new function called Network Access Quarantine Control (NAQC). The primary function of NAQC is not to provide additional security, but to help protect your network from improperly configured clients that access your network using Virtual Private Networking (VPN). A perfect example of using NAQC would be ensuring that a client has the correct version of virus scan software, with the latest virus definitions, and also enable the software if it is currently disabled, all before allowing the client to access any other network resources.

The basic components involve all the services previously listed—RRAS, with MS Quarantine IPFilter and remote access policies such as MS Quarantine Session Timeout, and RADIUS with IAS. The client components to NAQC are a Connection Manager (CM) profile, which can be distributed with a CM policy from the RRAS servers, and a script using the client component **RQC.exe**. The remaining server components consist of the resources necessary to provide name resolution, script and file access, and the service component **RQS.exe**, which is installed on the RRAS server.

Generally, NAQC would function basically by a client using a CM profile that has the quarantine policy to connect to a RRAS server with quarantine capabilities and configured with the MS Quarantine IPFilter and MS Quarantine Session Timeout policies. The RRAS server forwards the RADIUS access request to the IAS server that will validate the user credentials and match the quarantine policy. The IAS server will provide a quarantine restricted access acceptance via RADIUS that will allow the client limited access to network resources such as obtaining an IP address, DNS access for name resolution, and the attributes that are part of the quarantine policies. Once the client has an IP address and policies, the client is restricted to accessing resources that match the quarantine filters, and only for the time allotted in the MS Quarantine Session Timeout policy.

The script is executed on the client by the CM profile, and is used to verify that the client configuration meets the requirements of the network policies. Once the verification is complete, the script executes **rqc.exe** with the necessary command line settings, which will send an unencrypted, unauthenticated notification to the RRAS server **rqs.exe** service. The rqs traffic is allowed to pass through the RRAS filters, since it is defined in the RRAS IPFilter settings with the MS Quarantine IPFilter attributes. Rqs then verifies the information and parameters passed from rqc, one of which is the script version passed in the rqc command line. If the client meets the requirements, then RRAS will get a notification from rqs that the client is valid, and subsequently RRAS will lift the MS Quarantine IPFilter and MS Quarantine Session Timeout policy restrictions and allow the client normal access to the LAN. Once this process is complete, the rqc component will write a message to the System event log.

Unfortunately, due to the fact that NAQC requires RRAS and the post connect script in the CM profile, it cannot be used on the LAN for regular clients. You can, however, implement similar functionality in logon scripts and domain policies since the LAN clients are very likely to be using domain accounts to access the network.

DHCP Issues

DHCP is an easy way to manage IP addressing schemes for larger networks. Some of the items to consider when you implement and use DHCP include:

- Lease time
- Number of hosts in a scope
- Network traffic
- Scope options
- Topology

When a machine acquires an IP address from a DHCP server, it acquires a *lease*. The request for the lease is a message called a DHCPREQUEST, which is broadcast by the DHCP client looking for DHCPOFFERs of a lease from a DHCP server. The *lease duration* for a DCHP address is specified in the scope set on the server and defaults to eight days. At 50 percent of the lease duration, the DCHP client sends a directed request to the DHCP server that issued the lease and requests a renewal of the lease. If no DHCPACK (acknowledgement) is received from the server, the DHCP Client waits until 87.5 percent of the lease time and makes a final request to renew the IP address. If no DHCPACK is received at this point, then the client waits until the lease is expired and starts the process over. If a DHCP Client is unable to receive an IP address lease, then it will use an alternate configuration if one is specified. If there is no alternate configuration, the client will use APIPA to start the TCP/IP services and assign itself an address from the APIPA pool (169.254.0.0/16).

To determine the appropriate lease time for your network, consider the following:

- **Number of hosts** If the number of hosts is close to the number of total IP addresses in your DHCP server's scope, then the lease should be shorter—about three days. If there are a great deal more IP addresses than hosts, then a longer lease can be assigned.

- **Mobile Users** If you have a small number of mobile users and the client machines do not frequently move from one network to the other, then a longer lease duration is recommended; conversely, if you have more mobile users, then a shorter lease will be preferred so that the IP addresses will be released sooner and return to the available pool of addresses.

- **Unlimited** It is possible to set the lease duration to unlimited, but it presents a challenge if you wish to change the DHCP settings, since this setting requires the client to initiate the DHCPREQUEST.

Because they are broadcast, the DHCPREQUEST messages do not cross router boundaries, unless the router is capable of forwarding DHCP broadcast messages, in compliance with RFC 2131. You can also configure a DHCP Relay Agent to forward the requests to a DHCP server.

Using DHCP can reduce IP address conflicts, by preventing the need for static IP addresses. It also can eliminate invalid subnet masks, since they are assigned by the DHCP server as well. Another advantage is the scope properties. By assigning scope properties, you can define default gateways, DNS servers, WINS servers, and the type of name resolution that is preferred. By managing name resolution settings, you can help eliminate broadcast traffic.

Monitoring IPSec Connections

The connections established using the IPSec protocol are end-to-end connections, and are sometimes difficult to troubleshoot. Often the problems are related to connectivity of the networks over which the IPSec connection is established. There are also many different policies that we can apply that could have different effects depending on whether they are applied by the domain the machines are members of, or the ones that exist on the local computer. The network traffic is also a challenge, since it is responsible for delivering the data between the destinations. In this section, we are going to discuss the different methods to obtain useful information about IPSec connections and their settings.

IPSec Monitor Console

Information about IPSec traffic can be obtained using several different methods. One of the simplest methods is using the IPSec Monitor Console. IPSec monitor gives you information about domain and computer polices that are applied to the machine you are monitoring. In addition, it gives you information about main mode and quick mode statistics and filters. Most often, we may use IPSec monitor on the machine we are troubleshooting; however, it is possible to connect to a remote computer and view IPSec polices and settings using the IPSec Monitor snap-in.

IPSec Security Monitor allows us to watch for developing trends of security and authentication failures. This will help you to identify policy conflicts for specific IPSec tunnels. You can also determine the volume of traffic, the policies and associations, and how they are distributed. You can also evaluate the ESP packets with the total packets to identify potential holes in the security of the transmitted data and correct the security polices on the affected machines.

Network Monitor

The Network Monitor software that is part of Windows Server 2003 includes all the necessary protocol parsers for Internet Key Exchange (IKE) Internet Security Association and Key Management Protocol (ISAKMP), IP Authentication Header (AH), and IP Encapsulating Security Payload (ESP) protocols. The ESP parsers only function if null-encryption is being used and the entire ESP packet is captured. Network Monitor cannot parse the encrypted portions of ESP traffic that is encapsulated by IPSec unless encryption is being performed by an IPSec hardware offload network adapter. This implies that the packets are decrypted by the hardware and as a result, the ESP packets are decrypted when Network Monitor captures them. This allows Network Monitor parsers to parse and interpret the data for the upper-layer protocols.

Netsh

IPSec packet event logging can be enabled using netsh command line utility. The command is **netsh ipsec dynamic set config ipsecdiagnostics** *Level,* where *level* is a whole value between 1 and 7. The option values are listed in Table 8.2. To see dropped packet events, you must set the logging level to 7. The change will be written to the registry and will not take effect until the next reboot, when the IPSec driver reads the registry on start up. The registry key that contains the logging level value is **HKEY_LOCAL_MACHINE\System\CurrentControlSet\Services\IPSec\ EnableDiagnostics**, and the value is a valid whole number in the DWORD registry setting between 1 and 7. All the events that are defined for the specified log level are written to the System event log once every hour or when the event buffer is full and must be written to the log.

Table 8.2 Log Level Options for IPSec Driver Using Netsh

Log level	Effective logging
1	Total number of incorrect Security Parameters Index (SPI) packets
2	Inbound only per-packet drop events
3	Combined effect of level 1 and 2 logging is enabled, as well as any unexpected plaintext packets (clear-text events) inbound or outbound
4	Outbound only per-packet drop events
5	Combined effect of level 1 and 4 logging is enabled
6	Combined effect of level 2 and 4 logging is enabled
7	All logging levels are enabled

The logging occurs at regular intervals based on the **LogInterval** setting in the registry, located in **HKEY_LOCAL_MACHINE\System\CurrentControlSet\Services\IPSec**. You can set this value by using the registry, or by the preferred method of using **netsh ipsec dynamic set config ipsecloginterval** *Interval*, where *Interval* is the number of seconds between event log writes. The recommended value of the Interval parameter for troubleshooting is 60 seconds, which is also the minimum value. You can set the interval as high as 86400 seconds, which is equal to 1440 minutes or 24 hours. You can view information about IPSec policies using either the **netsh ipsec static show** command or the **netsh ipsec dynamic show** command.

Ipseccmd

The command line tool **Ipseccmd** is used to script the creation of IPSec policy, and display active SAs and policy assignments. **Ipseccmd** is no longer supported on Windows Server 2003 and its functionality is replaced by **netsh**. All IPSec-specific functionality is present in the **netsh** utility. You can view information about IPSec policies using either the **netsh ipsec static show** command or the **netsh ipsec dynamic show** command.

Netdiag

Although **Netdiag.exe** can still be used to obtain information about networking, Windows Server 2003 no longer uses the **netdiag /test:ipsec** option; it has been removed and replaced with the **netsh** commands for IPSec. All IPSec-specific functionality is present in the **netsh** utility. You can view information about IPSec policies using either the **netsh ipsec static show** command or the **netsh ipsec dynamic show** command.

Event Viewer

To view Internet Key Exchange (IKE) events in the security log, you must enable success or failure auditing for the Audit logon events policy for your domain or workgroup, although these events are not exclusive to IPSec services. Enabling success or failure auditing will cause IPSec to record the success or failure of the negotiation, establishment, and termination of each main mode and quick mode connection as events.

You should be very cautious when enabling IKE events, especially if the server is exposed to the Internet, or provides IPSec services to lots of clients. Hack attempts on the IKE protocol could cause the security log to fill very quickly. IKE events can also fill the security log for servers that use IPSec to secure traffic to many clients. To avoid this, you can disable auditing for IKE events in the security log by modifying the registry.

To view IPSec policy change events in the Security log, enable success or failure auditing on the Audit policy node Audit Policy Change policy for your domain or local computer.

Active Directory Infrastructure Overview

In this chapter:

- **Introducing Directory Services**

- **Understanding How Active Directory Works**

- **Using Active Directory Administrative Tools**

- **Implementing Active Directory Security and Access Control**

- **What's New in Windows Server 2003 Active Directory?**

Introduction

The Active Directory is the foundation of an enterprise-level Windows network, and Windows Server 2003 includes a number of improvements and enhancements to its directory services that will make a network administrator's job easier. Windows Server 2003 administrators must understand the basics of how directory services work and the role they play in the network, and specifically how the directory services concept is implemented in Microsoft's Active Directory.

In this chapter, we start with the basics by defining directory services and providing a brief background of the directory services standards and protocols. You'll learn how the Active Directory works, and be introduced to the terminology and concepts required to understand the Active Directory infrastructure.

We discuss how the directory is structured into sites, forests, domains, domain trees, and organizational units (OUs), and you'll learn about the components that make up the Active Directory, including both logical and physical components. These include the schema, the Global Catalog (GC), domain controllers (DCs), and the replication service. You'll learn to use the Active Directory administrative tools, and we discuss directory security and access control. Finally, we provide an overview of what's new for Active Directory in Windows Server 2003.

This chapter lays the groundwork for the specific Active Directory-related administrative tasks that you will learn to perform throughout the rest of the book. Even if you're very familiar with AD concepts, this chapter may still serve as a good refresher.

Introducing Directory Services

As anyone familiar with networking knows, a network can be comprised of a vast number of elements, including user accounts, file servers, volumes, fax servers, printers, applications, databases, and other shared resources. Because the number of objects making up a network increases as an organization grows, finding and managing these accounts and resources becomes harder as the network gets bigger. To make a monolithic enterprise network more manageable, directory services are used to store a collection of information about users and resources, so they are organized and accessible across the network.

A directory allows accounts and resources to be organized in a logical, hierarchical fashion so that information can be found easily. By searching the directory, users can find the resources they need, and administrators are able to control and configure accounts and resources easily and effectively. Keeping this information in a centralized location ensures that users and administrators don't have to waste time looking at what's available on each server, they only have to refer to the directory.

Any directory is a structured source of information, consisting of objects and their attributes. Those who have access to the directory can look up an object, and then view its attributes. If they have sufficient rights (as in the case of an administrator), the object can be modified. These attributes can be used to provide information that's accessible to users, or control security at a granular level.

Because a user can access account information from anywhere on the network, directory services allow a user to log on to multiple servers using a single logon. A single logon is an important feature to directory services, because without it, a user must log on to each server that provides needed resources. This is common on Windows NT networks, where the administrator must create a different account on each server the user needs to access. The user then needs to log on to each server individually. This is significantly different from the way Windows 2000/2003's directory services work, where a user logs on to the network once and can use any of the resources to which he or she has been given access.

Sophisticated directory services give administrators the ability to organize information, control security, and manage users and resources anywhere on the network. Information resides in a central repository that's replicated to different servers on the network. It allows the data to be accessed when needed and saves the administrator from having to visit each server to manage accounts. This lowers the amount of work needed to manage the network, while providing granular control over rights and permissions. The administrator only needs to modify a user account or other object once, and these security changes are replicated throughout the network.

Directory services have been used on different network operating systems for years, and have proven to be a useful and powerful technology. Following suit, Microsoft created its own implementation of directory services on Windows NT called NTDS, and then followed with Active Directory on newer versions of servers. NTDS used a flat namespace, which provided limited functionality in comparison with Active Directory's hierarchical structure and feature set. Active Directory was first introduced in Windows 2000, and continues to provide directory services to the Windows Server 2003 family of servers. It can be installed on the Standard, Enterprise, and Datacenter Editions of Windows Server 2003, and provides a necessary foundation for any network using these servers.

NOTE

Installation of Active Directory on a Windows 2000 or Windows Server 2003 server makes that computer a DC. Windows Server 2003 Web Edition cannot function as a DC, and thus cannot have Active Directory installed.

Terminology and Concepts

Before delving too far into the specifics of Active Directory, it is important to discuss a number of concepts and terms to appreciate the features and functionality of a directory service. As with anything dealing with technology, certain words and phrases associated with Active Directory and Windows Server 2003 are useful in identifying and defining specific components of the network. Whether you're new to Active Directory or experienced from using previous versions, the information provided here will help you to understand other topics that follow in this book.

In reading this section, it is important to realize that this is an overview of topics that we discuss later in greater detail. We define some of the terms used throughout this book, and look at concepts that we'll build on in later sections.

Some of the terms and concepts we discuss in the following subsections include:

- Directory data store
- Directory partitions
- Policy-based administration
- DAP and LDAP
- Naming schemes used in Active Directory

Directory Data Store

Active Directory isn't just a service that provides access to directory services; it's also a method of storing data about network elements. If you didn't have a place where configurations and directory data are saved, you'd lose this information every time you shut down your server. The data store contains a vast amount of information, including data dealing with users, groups, computers, the resources they can access, and other components of the network. Because the Active Directory data store is a database of all directory information, it is also referred to as the directory.

When you install the directory on a Windows Server 2003 server, the Active Directory data source is placed on the server's hard disk. The file used to store directory information is called NTDS.DIT, and is located in the NTDS folder in the systemroot (for example, C:\WINDOWS). Any changes made to the directory are saved to this file.

The presence of Active Directory's data store on a Windows Server 2003 server has a major impact on that server's role in the network. As shown in Figure 9.1, the directory is stored on DCs, which are servers with writable copies of the data store. A DC is used to manage domains, which are groups of computers, users, and other objects that share (or are included in) the same directory.

Domains that use different Active Directory data sources can still communicate with one another, but (as we'll see later in this chapter) secure relationships between them must be configured.

Figure 9.1 Relationship Between Active Directory, Domain Controllers, Member Servers, and Clients

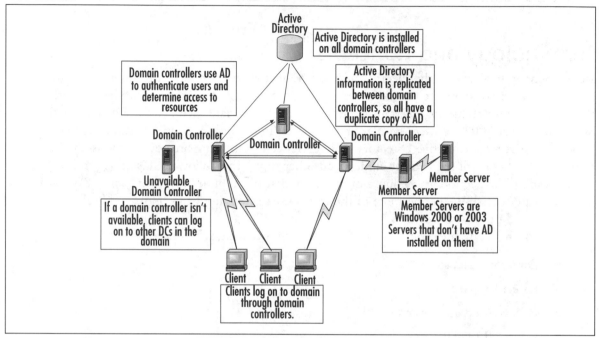

Each DC retains its own copy of the directory, containing information on the domain in which it is located. If one DC becomes unavailable, users and computers can still access the Active Directory data store on another DC in that domain. This allows users to continue logging on to the network even though the DC that's normally used is unavailable. It also allows computers and applications that require directory information to continue functioning while one of these servers is down.

Because a domain can have more than one DC, changes made to the directory on one DC must be updated on others. The process of copying these updates is called *replication*, and is used to synchronize information in the directory. Without replication, features in Active Directory would fail to function properly. For example, if you added a user on one DC, the new account would be added to the directory store on that server. This would allow the user to log on to that domain controller, but he or she still couldn't log on to other DCs until these changes to the directory were replicated. When a change is made on one DC, the changes need to be replicated quickly so that each DC continues to have an accurate duplicate copy of Active Directory.

Because replication is so important to making the directory consistent across the network, the data source is organized in a way to make replication more efficient. Not every piece of data is saved in the same location of the data source. As shown in Figure 9.2, information resides in different areas of the directory, called directory *partitions*. Because Active Directory is a logical, hierarchical structure, it has a treelike structure similar to that of the Windows Registry or folders on a hard disk.

Data is stored within subtrees of the directory, much like data on your hard disk is stored within folders that are nested within one another. Each contiguous subtree in the directory is a partition. Any data that changes within a directory partition is replicated as a single unit to other DCs.

Figure 9.2 Active Directory Is a Hierarchical Structure

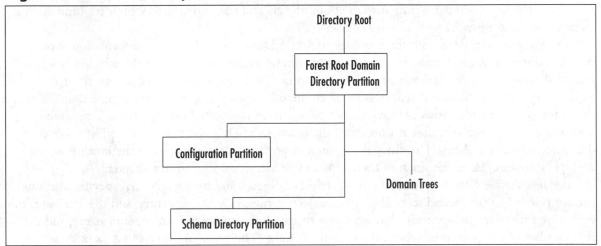

In Active Directory, three partitions exist on any DC and must be replicated, as these contain data that the Microsoft network needs to function properly:

- Domain partition
- Configuration partition
- Schema partition

The domain partition contains information about the domain. This includes information about users, computers, resources, and attributes associated with each. Without this data being replicated, any changes would be limited to the server on which the changes were made, and other servers would use older settings. For example, if the domain data wasn't replicated and you disabled a user's account on one DC, the user would still be able to log on to other DCs. The domain partition is important because it contains information about objects and their attributes, which are fundamental elements of your network.

Configuration data deals with the topology of Active Directory, and includes information about how the domains, domain trees, and forests within a network are configured. A domain tree is a structure of domains. If more than one domain is in a domain tree, trusts are set up between those domains so that they can share data and resources between them. A forest also consists of multiple domains that share directory data. It consists of one or more trees that are connected through trusts. The configuration partition also includes information about the locations of DCs and the GC, which is a subset of the data contained in Active Directory that is used to provide search and logon functionality across multiple domains. We discuss each of these topics in greater detail later in this chapter.

Because Active Directory is made up of different objects, and each object has specific attributes, certain rules must be created to control what objects can exist in the directory, and the attributes of each. For example, a user account has attributes that include a password, an account name, and the first and last of the person to whom the account belongs. The types of objects that exist in Active Directory, and which attributes each type has, is determined by the schema. The *schema partition* contains information that defines object classes and attributes used within the domain. It determines what objects can exist within Active Directory, and what attributes each can have.

Windows Server 2003 servers can also create one or more application partitions, which are used to store data that is specific to different applications running on the network. Programs can use this partition to store settings that are needed while the programs are running on a server. We discuss this in greater detail later in the chapter.

Protecting Your Active Directory Data

In addition to Windows 2000 servers, Active Directory can only be installed on Microsoft Windows Server 2003, Standard Edition; Windows Server 2003, Enterprise Edition; and Windows Server 2003, Datacenter Edition. When a server is configured to be a DC on any of these editions, a writable copy of the directory is stored on the server's hard disk. Because any file can be damaged, destroyed, or compromised (such as in the case of a hacking attempt or virus), you should take steps to ensure that the directory is safe on your server(s).

If only one DC is used, then only one NTDS.DIT file will exist, meaning there is only one copy of the directory for that domain. Failure of this server or damage to the NTDS.DIT file will disable the network. Users will be unable to log on, computers will be unable to access needed information from the directory, and any configurations on your network could be lost. Rather than hoping that nothing ever happens to your one DC, it is wise to use multiple DCs on your network.

If more than one DC exists in a domain, any updates to the NTDS.DIT will be replicated to other DCs. This will allow multiple copies of the directory to exist on the network, providing a level of fault tolerance if one server fails. If one fails, another can continue authenticating users, supplying services, and providing access to resources.

Because of the importance of the NTDS.DIT file, the drive on which it is stored should be formatted in NTFS format. NTFS is a file format that allows the best possible level of protection, allowing you to set permissions on who can access the directory and NTDS.DIT file locally and across the network. Such permissions cannot be set on hard disks that are formatted as FAT16 or FAT32. Limiting the access to this file lessens the chance that someone might accidentally or maliciously damage or delete the data source.

It is also important to remember that any measures you take to protect Active Directory from harm do not negate the need to perform regular backups. When backups are performed, the data on a computer is copied to other media (such as a tape, CD, or DVD), which can then be stored in another location. Should any problem occur, you can restore any files that were damaged or lost.

Policy-Based Administration

There can be hundreds or thousands of users and computers in a large network. Having to go through each account and configure settings can be an arduous task. For example, imagine having to go to each computer to change the desktop so that it displays a company logo as the background image. Rather than visiting each computer, it would be far easier to make such changes in one location, and have these settings apply to everyone. This is why policy-based administration is such a benefit to Active Directory: it makes managing accounts easier.

Group policies allow you to apply default settings to groups of users and groups. Policies can be used to:

- Control desktop settings that determine the display properties of a computer.

- Assign scripts that run at logon, logoff, startup, and shutdown.

- Enforce password security, such as by setting minimum password lengths, maximum length of time before a password must be changed, and so on.

- Redirect folders from the local computer to a folder on a networked computer, such as when the My Documents folder is redirected to use specific folders on a server.

- Deploy applications, so that certain members have programs available to them to install or have them automatically installed.

As we'll see in the chapters that follow, these are just a few of the options available to administrators in managing users and computers on a network.

When policies are created, they are stored as Group Policy Objects (GPOs) in Active Directory. The settings in a GPO can be applied to a site, domain, or OU. An OU is a container in Active Directory that can contain users, groups, computers, or other OUs. We'll discuss OUs in greater detail later in this chapter. Because GPOs can be applied at different levels, you can set different policies for different areas of your company. For example, you could create a group policy for users in Finance and another for the Sales department (by placing Finance users in one OU and Sales users in another). If you have different domains for different branch offices, you could have different settings for the Sales divisions in each domain. Using GPOs in this manner, you can configure which settings will be used for specific groups of users and computers.

Directory Access Protocol

For clients to search for objects, update information, and communicate with DCs when logging on to the network, a directory access protocol must be used. A protocol is a set of rules that dictate how data is sent over a network. A directory access protocol is used for the specific purpose of exchanging information with the directory service.

Active Directory uses LDAP for communications between clients and directory servers. LDAP is a version of the X.500 Directory Access Protocol (DAP), and is considered lightweight because it uses less code than DAP does.

The Internet Engineering Task Force (IETF) established industry standards for LDAP, enabling LDAP to be used over local networks and the Internet by a variety of directory services. Many network operating systems that use directory services (including Novell NetWare, Windows 2000, and Windows Server 2003) implement LDAP for accessing the directory, while other products (such as Internet browsers) support it as a method for finding resources or managing the directory. Since its inception in 1994, there have been several versions of LDAP, with features being added to accommodate changing needs. Active Directory supports versions 2 and 3.

Naming Scheme

Active Directory supports several common formats for naming objects. By using different methods of naming objects, it allows objects to be accessed in a variety of ways. Providing different naming schemes also provides backward compatibility to older systems that might not support one or more of these formats. The naming schemes supported by Active Directory include:

- Domain Name System (DNS)

- User principal name (UPN)

- Universal Naming Convention (UNC)

- Uniform Resource Locator (URL)

- Lightweight Directory Access Protocol Uniform Resource Locator (LDAP URL)

In Active Directory, domains are usually given DNS names (such as syngress.com). Because Windows domains didn't use this naming scheme prior to Windows 2000, each domain is also given a name that's compatible with those used in Windows NT networks. These pre-Windows 2000 names are NetBIOS names, and are one-word names that users of older operating systems can use to log on to Active Directory. This allows clients to log on to domains by entering the domain name and username using the format: *domain name\username.*

UPNs are based on the IETF's RFC 822. Each user account in Active Directory has a logon name and UPN suffix. The logon name is the account name, and the UPN suffix is the domain that the user will log on to. The two are connected by the @ symbol, making the logon appear like an Internet e-mail address (username@domain). After entering a username, the user will generally be required to enter a password to prove that he or she is authorized to use this account.

When the UPN is created for a user account, it also suggests a pre-Windows 2000 logon name that is used by the Security Account Manager (SAM) to log on to a server. The SAM is a service that stores information about user accounts and groups to which they belong. Local computer accounts use the SAM to store accounts that are used to access the local computer, and Windows NT servers use it for allowing network users access to resources on the server. Although you can create your own logon name, Active Directory will suggest a pre-Windows 2000 user logon name that's based on the first 20 bytes of the Active Directory logon name.

Every computer account that is created in Active Directory also has multiple names, so that the account can be identified and accessed in a variety of ways. When a computer account is created in Active Directory, you need to enter a name for the computer, which will uniquely identify it in the domain. This is the host name for the machine, which can be used by DNS to indicate its place in the domain, and can be used to help find the computer when clients search for it and its resources on the network.

In DNS, the host name is combined with the domain name to create the computer's fully qualified domain name (FQDN). This combines the host name with the domain name, and separates the two with a period. For example, if you have a computer named COMP100 in the domain called knightware.ca, the FQDN for this computer would be comp100.knightware.ca. No two computers in a domain can have the same name, as this would create conflicts.

When the computer account is created, it will also require the computer be given a pre-Windows 2000 name, so older clients and servers can identify and access it. As with user accounts, Windows Server 2003 will suggest a name, which is based on the first 15 bytes of the name used to create the account. If you don't want to use this default name, you can enter a new one at any time.

The UNC path is a tried-and-true method of accessing shared resources over a network. It uses the format of two backslashes, followed by the domain name or server name, the name of the share, and (where applicable) the name of the resource. The shared resource is often the name of a shared directory, and might be followed by the name of a file, application, or other resource on the server. In other words, the format would be \\domain name\share\filename or \\servername\share\filename. For example, if you were accessing a file named SPREADSHEET.XLS in a shared directory called XLS on a server named FS-GOTHAM, the UNC to access it would be \\fs-gotham\xls\spreadsheet.xls. You can use UNC names in the address bar of browsers, from the Run command of the Windows Start menu, or any other place where UNC names are allowed.

Another common method of accessing resources through a browser is by using URLs. A URL generally begins with http (for HyperText Transfer Protocol), a colon, and two forward slashes, followed by a server name such as www, a domain name such as syngress.com, and a filename path (which can contain a directory name such as files, or just a filename such as file.htm or file.html for an HTTP document, file.asp for an Active Server Pages document, or file.jpg for a graphic in .JPG format).

The final naming scheme we'll discuss is LDAP URL. This method is similar to using URLs, but uses the X.500 naming structure to locate a resource. An LDAP URL uses the format LDAP://domain name/CN=common name/OU=organizational unit/DC=domain component. In this format, the common name is the name of an object in Active Directory, OU is the organizational unit, and DC is the DNS domain name in which the object exists. This allows you to specify an object that is uniquely identified in the directory. As we'll see in the sections that follow, this information is built on X.500/LDAP standards.

X.500/LDAP standards

Both the X.500 DAP and LDAP work by interacting with the directory. The directory is designed as a hierarchy, and has a tree-like structure called the *directory information tree*. Information in subtrees branch off the trunk, much as folders on the hard disk branch off a root directory. These subtrees contain objects that represent elements of the network, and are called *directory service entries*. Just as there can't be two files with the same name in a folder on your hard disk, each object must have a unique name in the directory structure.

Distinguished Name

To accommodate the need for each object being identified with a unique name in the directory, objects have a distinguished name (DN). A DN represents the exact location of an object within the directory. This is comparable to a file being represented by the full path, showing where it is located on the hard disk. With an object in the directory, several components are used to create this name:

- **CN** The common name of the object, and includes such things as user accounts, printers, and other network elements represented in the directory.

- **OU** The organizational unit. These are containers in the directory that are used to hold objects. To continue with our example of files on a hard disk, this would be comparable to a folder within the directory structure.

- **DC** A domain component. This is used to identify the name of the domain or server, and the DNS suffix (for example, .com, .net, .edu, and .gov).

When combined, these components of the DN are used to show the location of an object. Each DN can be used more than once to fully identify the object's place within the directory. For example, let's say a user account named BobSmith was stored in the Accounting OU in the syngress.com domain. In this case, the DN of this object would be:

```
CN=BobSmith, OU=Accounting, DC=syngress, DC=com
```

Relative Distinguished Name

An RDN is a portion of the DN, and is used to uniquely identify an object with a parent container. As each object must have a unique name with the directory structure, the RDN identifies an object within a particular OU. This is comparable to a file in a folder, where you specify the name of the file and not the full path to it. Just as a file in one folder might have the same name as a file in another folder, an object in one OU might have the same name as another object in another OU. While the RDN would be the same, the DN would indicate that each is in a different OU.

To illustrate this, let's look at the previous example, which used the DN /CN=BobSmith, /OU=Accounting, /DC=syngress, /DC=com. In this case, CN=BobSmith is the RDN of the object. It is a subset of the DN, and the only one by that name in the Accounting OU. However, you could have a user account named BobSmith in the Sales OU. Even though the RDNs are identical, the full DNs are unique.

DNS and RDNs apply to user accounts and any other objects within the directory. When a computer account is created, the name used for the computer is used by LDAP as the RDN. For example, if a computer were named COMP100, this would be its RDN.

Canonical Name

A canonical name is another way of showing the DN of an object. It contains the same information, but shows it in a way that is easier to read. Using the example of the BobSmith object, if we convert its DN to a canonical name, it would read:

```
syngress.com/Accounting/BobSmith
```

In the preceding example, the CN, OU, and DC components of the DN have been removed and replaced with slashes (similar to the way in which a pathname to a file on a DOS/Windows machine is notated with backslashes). The canonical format also reverses the information. Rather than beginning with the lowest level component of the DN (in other words, the object) and moving up through higher levels, it starts at the highest level of the directory structure and works its way down to the object's name. While it relates the DN of an object, it removes the extraneous notations in the name and makes it easier to read.

Installing Active Directory to Create a Domain Controller

When Windows Server 2003 is installed on a computer, it doesn't mean that the directory is also installed. Active Directory is installed when you create a DC. It can be installed as part of the Windows Server 2003 installation, and can also be installed on member servers, which are computers running Windows Server 2003 that don't have Active Directory installed. A server without Active Directory installed on it can still deliver a variety of services, file storage, and access to other resources, but until Active Directory is installed, it can't authenticate users or provide the other functions of a DC. Once Active Directory is installed, the member server ceases to be a member server and becomes a DC.

To install Active Directory on a member server, the Active Directory Installation Wizard (DCPROMO) is used. DCPROMO is a tool that promotes a member server to DC status. Because a DC is a server with a writable copy of Active Directory installed on it, this tool will install a copy of the directory database on the server, and configure the structure of Active Directory based on your input. After Active Directory is installed, you can then perform other tasks that will allow users of your network to access resources on the domain.

Use the following steps to install Active Directory on a Windows Server 2003 computer.

Install Active Directory

As with many of the example in this book, this example should *not* be performed on a production server. Moreover, while readers who have previous knowledge of Active Directory can perform these steps, those who are new to Active Directory might want to read the next section to understand how Active Directory works before attempting to install it.

1. From the Run command on the Windows Start menu, type **DCPROMO** and then click **OK**.

2. A welcome screen will appear that identifies the program as the Active Directory Installation Wizard. Click **Next** to continue.

3. An information screen will appear, warning that clients running Windows 95 or Windows NT 4.0 SP3 and earlier won't be able to log on to Windows Server 2003 DCs or access domain resources. Click **Next** to continue.

4. The Domain Controller Type screen appears after this, allowing you to specify whether you want the server to be a DC for a new or existing domain (see Figure 9.3). Selecting the **Domain controller for a new domain** will allow you to create a new domain, while selecting **Additional domain controller for an existing domain** will add this server to a domain that already exists. Select the first of these options to create a new domain. Click **Next** to continue.

Figure 9.3 Domain Controller Type Screen of Active Directory Installation Wizard

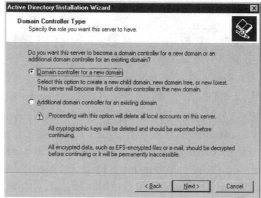

5. The next screen allows you to configure or install DNS on the server. If DNS is already running, then select Yes, I will configure the DNS client. If not, select No, just install and configure DNS on this computer. If you select Yes and DNS is not running, a warning screen will appear informing you of this. If DNS isn't running, select the second option (No), and click **Next** to continue.

6. Enter the DNS name for the new domain (for example, syngress.com). Click **Next** to continue.

7. As shown in Figure 9.4, the screen that appears next asks you to enter the NetBIOS name for this domain, which older versions of Windows will use to access the domain. Windows Server 2003 suggests a name based on your previously entered DNS name. Accept the default value, and click **Next** to continue.

Figure 9.4 NetBIOS Domain Name Screen of the Active Directory Installation Wizard

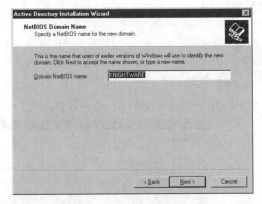

8. The next screen, shown in Figure 9.5, allows you to specify where the Active Directory database and log files will be stored. By default, this will be a directory called NTDS in the systemroot folder. Accept the default values and click **Next** to continue.

Figure 9.5 Database and Log Folders Screen of the Active Directory Installation Wizard

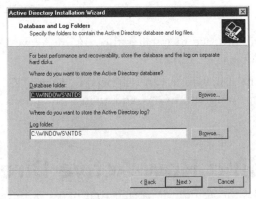

9. The next screen asks for the location of where public files that will be copied to other DCs will be stored. By default, this is stored in the SYSVOL directory in the systemroot folder. Accept the default value and click **Next** to continue.

10. The next screen is used to set proper permissions based on whether you will be running server programs that were designed for pre-Windows 2000 domains. If this were the case, you would select the first option Permissions compatible with pre-Windows 2000 Server operating systems. Selecting this will allow anonymous users to read information on the domain, so it is best to select Permissions compatible only with Windows 2000 or Windows Server 2003 operating systems whenever possible. Assuming you will not be running such software, select the second option, and click **Next**.

11. The following screen asks that you enter a password used when the server is started in Directory Services Restore mode. This mode is used to restore Active Directory after it has become damaged. Enter a password in the first field, and then enter it in the field below to confirm your password. Click **Next** to continue.

12. The screen that appears next displays all the settings you chose for your installation of Active Directory (see Figure 9.6). Review the summary information that's shown on this screen, and then click **Next** to continue.

Figure 9.6 Summary Screen of the Active Directory Installation Wizard

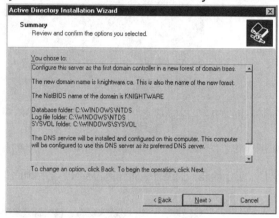

13. The wizard will proceed to install and configure Active Directory based on your choices. Once this is done, click **Finish**.

14. To complete the installation, you will need to restart Windows Server 2003. A message box will appear informing you of this, and giving the options of restarting now or not. Click **Restart Now**.

Understanding How Active Directory Works

Active Directory provides the ability to manage your network through a single source of information. Using tools in Windows Server 2003, you can administer users, computers, printers, and a variety of other resources. Changes made to objects in the directory are replicated to other DCs. This ensures that each DC has an up-to-date copy of all directory objects and their attributes.

Directory Structure Overview

When you compare the directory structure of different organizations, you will find that they are different. Active Directory is organized in a hierarchical structure that is built from a variety of different components that represent elements of your network. For example, there are user objects, computer objects, and various containers to organize them. The way you organize these elements will make the hierarchical structure of Active Directory in your company different from other companies. The components that are part of this hierarchy (which we discuss in the sections that follow) include:

- Sites
- Domains
- Trees
- Forests
- Objects
- DCs

In addition to these, we will also look at the components of Active Directory that are used to organize and manage this hierarchy. These components are:

- GC
- Schema

Active Directory allows you to administrate your network by dealing with the physical and logical structure. The physical structure of your network consists of tangible elements that make up your network, while the logical structure is used to organize components into a hierarchy that matches the structure of your company. As we'll see in the sections that follow, sites represent the physical structure of a network, while domains, trees, and forests represent the logical structure.

Sites

A *site* is one or more IP subnets connected by a fast and reliable link. The term *subnet* is short for "subnetwork," and refers to a group of neighboring computers that have been subdivided within the network. Computers in the subnet use a different network ID from those in other subnets, essentially becoming a smaller network within the network. Sites are used to store information about the topology of your network in Active Directory, so that the directory has information about the physical structure of the network.

Active Directory uses information about the physical elements of a network in a number of ways. It allows Active Directory to determine the fastest connections between sites, so that updates in the directory can be replicated to other DCs. Sites contain computer and connection objects, which are used to configure replication between sites, allowing this information to be copied in the fastest, most effective way to DCs in other sites. It is also useful to users, as it will allow each user to be authenticated by the DC that's closest to that user.

Although not required, it is a good idea to have a DC in each site. When a client logs on to a domain, a DC must be contacted. The client will search the local site for a DC and then, if one is not found, attempt to connect to DCs in other sites. If the client has to connect to a DC in a different site, it might take a long time for the user to be authenticated. Creating different sites will group computers together, so they will authenticate to the DC that's closest to them.

An important feature of a site is that subnets are *well connected*. This means that the links between sites are reliable and fast. While determining what is fast can be subjective, Microsoft has traditionally defined a fast link as being at least 512 Kbps, while acknowledging that 128 Kbps or higher is sufficient. Because the bandwidth needed by an organization depends on the amount of data being transferred between sites, some companies will require a greater bandwidth to meet their needs.

As shown in Figure 9.7, there can be multiple domains in a site, or multiple sites in a domain. Because sites represent the physical structure, they are different from domains, trees, and forests (which we'll discuss next) that represent the logical structure. Sites are separate from these entities, and unfettered by issues that determine the logical structure of a Windows Server 2003 network.

Figure 9.7 Sites Can Contain Multiple Domains, and Domains Can Contain Multiple Sites

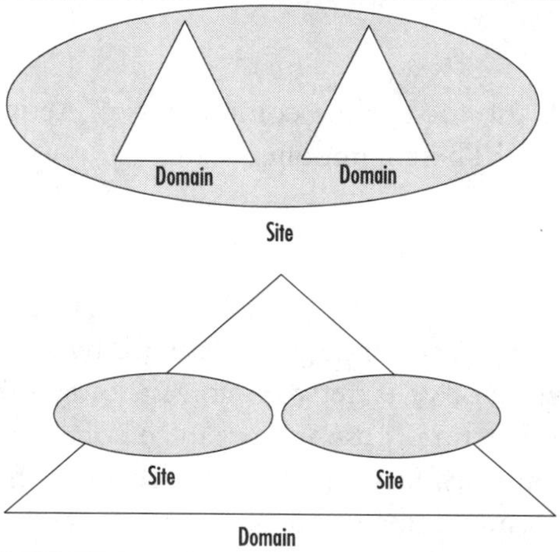

Domains

Domains have been a cornerstone of a Microsoft network since the days of Windows NT. A domain is a logical grouping of network elements, consisting of computers, users, printers, and other components that make up the network and allow people to perform their jobs. Because domains group these objects in a single unit, the domain acts as an administrative boundary, in which you can control security on users and computers. In Windows Server 2003, a domain also shares a common directory database, security policies, and (when other domains exist in the network) relationships with other domains. They are important logical components of a network, because everything is built upon or resides within the domain structure.

Sites and domains are different structures, and aren't bound by one another. Just as a site can include users and computers from multiple domains, domains can include multiple sites. This allows you to have objects from different areas of your network in the same domain, even if they're in different subnets or geographical locations.

In serving as an administrative boundary, each domain uses its own security policies. Group policies can be applied at a domain level, so that any users and computers within that domain are affected by it. This allows you to control access to resources, password policies, and other configurations to everyone within the domain. These security settings and policies only affect the domain, and won't be applied to other domains in the network. If large groups of users need different policies, you can either create multiple domains or apply settings in other ways (for example, using OUs, which we'll discuss later).

When a domain is created, a DNS domain name is assigned to identify it. DNS is used on the Internet and other TCP/IP networks for resolving IP addresses to user-friendly names. Because an

Active Directory domain is integrated with DNS, this allows users, computers, applications, and other elements of the network to easily find DCs and other resources on the network.

As you can imagine, a significant number of objects can potentially exist within a domain. To allow for significant growth in a network, Microsoft designed Active Directory to support up to 10 million objects per domain. While Microsoft concedes this to be a theoretical estimate, the company provides a more practical estimate that each domain can support at least 1 million objects. In either case, chances are your domain will never reach either of these limits. If it does, you'll need to create additional domains, and split users, computers, groups, and other objects between them.

Earlier in this chapter, we mentioned that updates to the directory are replicated to other DCs, so that each has an identical copy of the directory database. We'll explain replication in greater detail later in this chapter, but for now it is important to realize that Active Directory information is replicated to every DC within a domain. Each domain uses its own directory database. Because the information isn't replicated to other domains, this makes the domain a boundary for replication as well as for administration and security.

Domain Trees

Although domains serve as boundaries for administration and replication, this does not mean that you should only use one domain until you reach the limit on the number of objects supported per domain. That depends on your organizational structure. You might want to use multiple domains for any of the following reasons:

- To decentralize administration

- To improve performance

- To control replication

- To use different security settings and policies for each domain

- If you have an large number of objects in the directory

For example, your company might have branch offices in several countries. If there is only one domain, directory information will have to be replicated between DCs in each country, or (if no DCs resides in those locations) users will need to log on to a DC in another country. Rather than replicating directory information across a WAN, and having to manage disparate parts of the network, you could break the network into several domains. For example, you might create one domain for each country.

Creating separate domains does not mean there will be no relationship between these different parts of your network. Active Directory allows multiple domains to be connected together in a hierarchy. As shown in Figure 9.8, a domain can be created beneath an existing domain in the hierarchy. The pre-existing domain is referred to as a "parent domain," and the new domain created under it is referred to as a "child domain." When this is done, the domains share a common namespace. They also share a schema, configuration, and GC, as do all domains in the same forest, whether or not they have a parent-child relationship (we'll discuss these elements in greater detail later in this chapter).

As seen in Figure 9.8, domains created in this parent-child structure and sharing a namespace belong to a *domain tree*. Trees follow a DNS naming scheme, so that the relationship between the parent and child domains is obvious and easy to follow. To conform to this naming scheme, a child domain appends its name to the parent's name. For example, if a parent domain used the domain name sygress.com, a child domain located in the United Kingdom might have the name uk.syngress.com. Names can also indicate the function of a domain, rather than its geographical location. For example, the child domain used by developers might use the name dev.syngress.com. Because domain trees use a contiguous namespace, it is easy to see which domains are child domains of a particular parent domain.

Figure 9.8 A Domain Tree Consists of Parent and Child Domains in a Contiguous Namespace

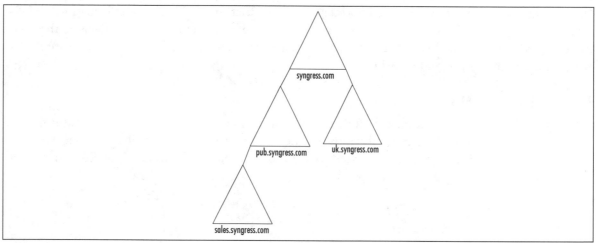

When a child domain is created, a two-way transitive trust relationship between the parent and child domains is automatically created. A trust relationship allows pass-through authentication, so users who are authenticated in a trusted domain can use resources in a trusting domain. Because the trust between a parent and child domain is bidirectional, both domains trust one another, so users in either domain can access resources in the other (assuming, of course, that the users have the proper permissions for those resources).

The other feature of the trust relationship between parent and child domains is that they are transitive. A transitive relationship means that pass-through authentication is transferred across all domains that trust one another. For example, in Figure 9.9, Domain A has a two-way transitive trust with Domain B, so both trust one another. Domain B has a two-way transitive trust with Domain C, so they also trust one another, but there is no trust relationship between Domain A and Domain C. With the two-way transitive trust, Domain C will trust Domain A (and vice versa) because both trust Domain B. This will allow users in each of the domains to access resources from the other domains. Trusts can also be manually set up between domains so that they are one-way and nontransitive, but by default, transitive bidirectional trusts are used in domain trees and forests. These trusts are also *implicit,* meaning that they exist automatically by default when you create the domains, unlike *explicit* trusts that must be created manually.

Figure 9.9 Adjoining Domains in a Domain Tree Use Two-Way Transitive Trusts

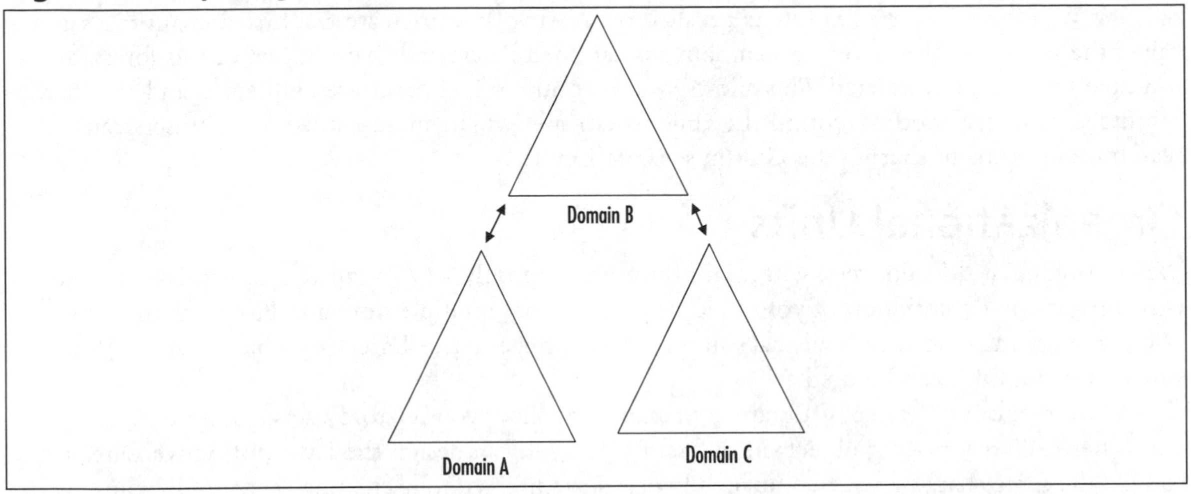

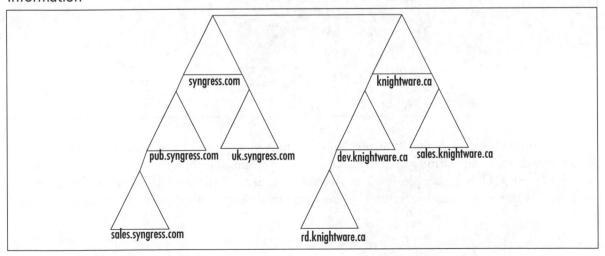

Forests

Just as domains can be interconnected into trees, trees can be interconnected into forests. A forest is one or more domain trees that share the same schema, GC, and configuration information. As is the case with domain trees, domains in the same forests use two-way transitive trusts between the roots of all domain trees in the forest (that is, the top level domain in each tree) to allow pass-through authentication, so users can access resources in domains throughout the forest. As shown in Figure 9.10, although trees require a contiguous namespace, a forest can be made up of multiple trees that use different naming schemes. This allows your domains to share resources across the network, even though they don't share a contiguous namespace.

Figure 9.10 A Forest Allows Multiple Domain Trees to Be Connected and Share Information

Every Active Directory structure has a forest, even if it only consists of a single domain. When the first Windows Server 2003 DC is installed on a network, you create the first domain that's also called the *forest root domain*. Additional domains can then be created that are part of this forest, or multiple forests can be created. This allows you to control which trees are connected and can share resources with one another (within the same forest), and which are separated so that users can't search other domains sharing the GC (in separate forests).

Organizational Units

When looking at domain trees, you might think that the only way to create a directory structure that mirrors the organization of your company is to create multiple domains. However, in many companies, a single domain is all that's needed. To organize Active Directory objects within this single domain, OUs can be used.

As we mentioned earlier, OUs are containers that allow you to store users, computers, groups, and other OUs. By placing objects in different OUs, you can design the layout of Active Directory to take the same shape as your company's logical structure, without creating separate domains. As shown in Figure 9.11, you can create OUs for different areas of your business, such as departments, functions, or locations. The users, computers, and groups relating to each area can then be stored inside the OU, so that you can find and manage them as a single unit.

Figure 9.11 Organizational Units Can Contain Other Active Directory Objects

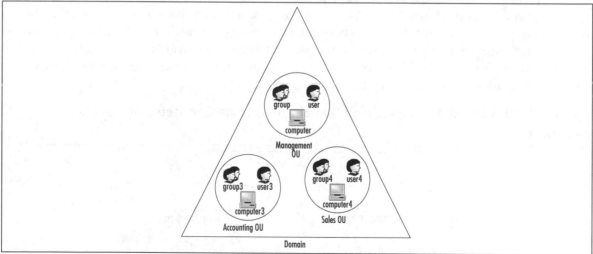

OUs are the smallest Active Directory unit to which you can delegate administrative authority. When you delegate authority, you give specific users or groups the ability to manage the users and resources in an OU. For example, you can give the manager of a department the ability to administer users within that department, thereby alleviating the need for you (the network administrator) to do it.

Active Directory Components

When looking at the functions of domains, trees, forests, and OUs, it becomes apparent that each serves as a container. These container objects provide a way to store other components of Active Directory, so that they can be managed as a unit and organized in a way that makes administration easier. OUs also provide the added feature of allowing nesting, so that you can have one OU inside another.

The bulk of components in Active Directory, however, are objects that represent individual elements of the network (in Novell's NDS structure, these are called *leaf objects,* in keeping with the tree analogy, because they are at the end of the hierarchical "branch" and don't contain any other objects). Objects are divided into *classes*, and each object class includes a set of *attributes*, which are properties that hold data on characteristics and configurations. Just as people are defined by their characteristics (for example, eye and hair color, height, weight), attributes define an object. A printer object might have attributes that include the make, model, and configuration information related to that device, whereas a user object would include attributes such as username, password, and other data that defines the user.

Logical vs. Physical Components

The components making up Active Directory can be broken down into logical and physical structures. Logical components in Active Directory allow you to organize resources so that their layout in the directory reflects the logical structure of your company. Physical components in Active Directory are similarly used, but are used to reflect the physical structure of the network. By separating the logical and physical components of a network, users are better able to find resources, and administrators can more effectively manage them.

Many directories are designed to follow the logical structure of an organization. You're probably familiar with organizational charts; maps that show the various departments in a company, and illustrate which departments are accountable to others. In such a map, a Payroll department might appear below the Finance department, even though they are physically in the same office. Just as the chart allows you to find where a department falls in the command structure of a company, the logical structure of a directory allows you to find resources based on a similar logical layout. As we saw earlier, you can organize your network into forests, trees, and domains, and then further organize users and computers into OUs named after areas of your business. A map of the directory structure can be organized to appear identical to the logical structure of the company.

Physical components are used to design a directory structure that reflects the physical layout, or *topology,* of the network. For example, as we saw earlier, a site is a combination of subnets, and a DC is a server that has a copy of the directory on it. DCs are physically located at specific locations in an organization, while subnets consist of computers using the same grouping of IP addresses. In both cases, you could visit a room or building and find these components. Thus, physical components can be used to mirror the physical structure of an organization in the directory. As illustrated in Figure 9.12, this makes the physical structure considerably different from the logical structure of a network.

Figure 9.12 Logical Structure vs. Physical Structure

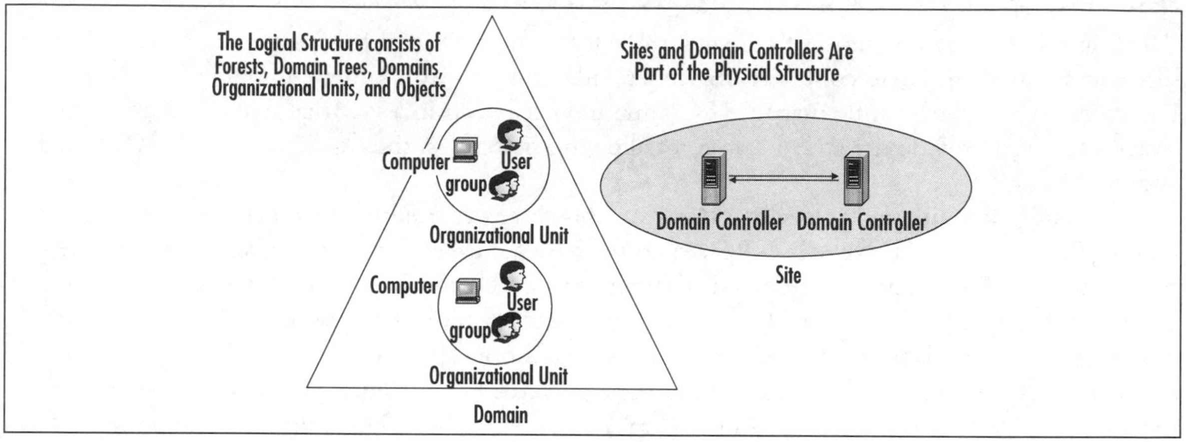

Domain Controllers

DCs are used to manage domains. As mentioned, the directory on a DC can be modified, allowing network administrators to make changes to user and computer accounts, domain structure, site topology, and control access. When changes are made to these components of the directory, they are then copied to other DCs on the network.

Because a DC is a server that stores a writable copy of Active Directory, not every computer on your network can act as a DC. Windows Server 2003 Active Directory can only be installed on Microsoft Windows Server 2003, Standard Edition; Windows Server 2003, Enterprise Edition; and Windows Server 2003, Datacenter Edition. Servers running other the Web Edition of Windows Server 2003 cannot be DCs, although they can be member servers that provide resources and services to the network.

When a DC is installed on the network, the first domain, forest, and site are created automatically. Additional domains, forests, and sites can be created as needed, just as additional DCs can be added. This allows you to design your network in a way that reflects the structure and needs of your organization.

While only one DC is required to create a domain, multiple DCs can (and usually should) be implemented for fault tolerance and high availability. If more than one DC is used and one fails, users will be able to log on to another DC that is available. This will allow users to continue working while the DC is down. In larger companies, a number of DCs can be added to accommodate significant numbers of users who might log on and log off at the same time of day or need to access resources from these servers.

Master Roles

Certain changes in Active Directory are only replicated to specific DCs on the network. Operations Masters are DCs that have special roles, keeping a master copy of certain data in Active Directory and copying data to other DCs for backup purposes. Because only one machine in a domain or forest can contain the master copy of this data, they are also referred to as Flexible Single Master Operations (FSMO) roles.

Five different types of master roles are used in an Active Directory forest, each providing a specific purpose. Two of these master roles are applied to a single DC in a forest (forestwide roles), while three others must be applied to a DC in each domain (domainwide roles). In the paragraphs that follow, we will look at each of these roles, and discuss how they are significant to Active Directory's functionality.

Forestwide master roles are unique to one DC in every forest. There are two master roles of this type:

- Schema Master
- Domain Naming Master

The *Schema Master* is a DC that is in charge of all changes to the Active Directory schema. As we'll see in the next section, the schema is used to define what object classes and attributes are used within the forest. The Schema Master is used to write to the directory's schema, which is then replicated to other DCs in the forest. Updates to the schema can be performed only on the DC acting in this role.

The *Domain Naming Master* is a DC that is in charge of adding new domains and removing unneeded ones from the forest. It is responsible for any changes to the domain namespace. Such changes can only be performed on the Domain Naming Master, thus preventing conflicts that could occur if changes were performed on multiple machines.

In addition to forestwide master roles, there are also domainwide master roles. There are three master roles of this type:

- Relative ID (RID) Master
- Primary domain controller (PDC) Emulator
- Infrastructure Master

The *RID Master* is responsible for creating a unique identifying number for every object in a domain. These numbers are issued to other DCs in the domain. When an object is created, a sequence of numbers that uniquely identifies the object is applied to it. This number consists of two parts: a domain security ID (SID) and a RID. The domain SID is the same for all objects in that domain, while the RID is unique to each object. Instead of using the name of a user, computer, or group, this SID is used by Windows to identify and reference the objects. To avoid potential conflicts of DCs issuing the same number to an object, only one RID Master exists in a domain, to control the allocation of ID numbers to each DC, which the DC can then hand out to objects when they are created.

The *PDC Emulator* is designed to act like a Windows NT primary DC. This is needed if there are computers running pre-Windows 2000 and XP operating systems, or if Windows NT backup domain controllers (BDCs) still exist on the network. The PDC Emulator is responsible for processing password changes, and replicating these changes to BDCs on the network. It also synchronizes the time on all DCs in a domain so servers don't have time discrepancies between them. Because there can only be one Windows NT PDC in a domain, there can be only one PDC Emulator.

Even if there aren't any servers running as BDCs on the network, the PDC Emulator still has a purpose in each domain. The PDC Emulator receives preferred replication of all password changes performed by other DCs within the domain. When a password is changed on a DC, it is sent to the PDC Emulator. The PDC Emulator is responsible for this because it can take time to replicate password changes to all DCs in a domain. If a user changes his or her password on one DC and then attempts to log on to another, the second DC he or she is logging on to might still have old password information. Because this DC considers it a bad password, it forwards the authentication request to the PDC Emulator to determine whether the password is actually valid. Whenever a logon authentication fails, a DC will always forward it to the PDC Emulator before rejecting it.

The *Infrastructure Master* is in charge of updating changes made to group memberships. When a user moves to a different domain and his or her group membership changes, it can take time for these changes to be reflected in the group. To remedy this, the infrastructure manager is used to update such changes in its domain. The DC in the Infrastructure Master role compares its data to the GC, which is a subset of directory information for all domains in the forest. When changes occur to group membership, it then updates its group-to-user references and replicates these changes to other DCs in the domain.

Schema

The *schema* is a database that is used to define objects and their attributes. Information in the schema is used to control the types of objects (classes) that can be created in Active Directory, and the additional properties (attributes) associated with each. In other words, the schema determines what you can create in Active Directory, and the data that can be used to configure these objects.

The schema is made up of classes and attributes. Object classes define the type of object, and include a collection of attributes, which are used to describe the object. For example, the User class of object contains attributes made up of information about the user's home directory, first name, last name, address, and so on. While the object class determines the type of object that can be created in Active Directory, the attributes are used to provide information about it. An object's attributes are also known as its *properties,* and in most cases, you can configure its attributes by editing its properties sheet (usually accessed by right clicking the object and selecting **Properties**).

Active Directory comes with a wide variety of object classes, but additional ones can be created if needed. Because the schema is so important to Active Directory's structure, *extensions* (additions and modifications) to the schema can only be made on one DC in the forest. Modifications to the schema can only be made on the DC that's acting in the *Schema Master* role. Schema information is stored in a directory partition of Active Directory, and is replicated to all DCs in a forest.

Attributes are created using the Active Directory Schema snap-in for the Microsoft Management Console (MMC) (which we'll discuss later in this chapter). When a new class or attribute is added to the schema, it cannot be deleted. If a class or attribute is no longer needed, it can only be deactivated, so it cannot be used anymore. Should the class or attribute be needed later, you can then reactivate it.

Global Catalog

As anyone who's tried to search a large database can attest, the more data that's stored in a database, the longer it will take to search. To improve the performance of searching for objects in a domain or forest, the GC is used. The GC server is a DC that stores a copy of all objects in its host domain, and a partial copy of objects in other domains throughout the forest. The partial copy contains objects that are most commonly searched for. Because the GC contains a subset of information in Active Directory, less information needs to be replicated, and increases performance when users search for specific attributes of an object.

In addition to being used for searches, the GC is also used to resolve UPNs that are used in authentication. As discussed earlier, the UPN has a format like an e-mail address. If a user logs on to a DC in a domain that doesn't contain the account, the DC will use the GC to resolve the name and complete the logon process. For example, if a user logged on with the UPN myname@us.syngress.com from a computer located in ca.syngress.com, the DC in ca.syngress.com would be unable to find the account in that domain. It would then use the GC to find and authenticate the user's account.

The GC is also used to store information on Universal Group memberships, in which users from any domain can be added and allowed access to any domain. When a user who is a member of such a group logs on to a domain, the DC will retrieve his or her Universal Group membership from the GC. This is only done if there is more than one domain in a forest.

The GC is available on DCs that are configured to be GC servers. Creating a GC server is done by using the Active Directory Sites and Services snap-in for the MMC (which we'll discuss later in this chapter). After a GC server is configured, other DCs can query the GC on this server.

Replication Service

The Windows Server 2003 replication service is used to replicate Active Directory between DCs, so that each DC has an up-to-date copy of the directory database. Because each DC has an identical copy of the directory, they can operate independently, allowing users to be authenticated and use network resources if one of the DCs fails. This allows Windows Server 2003 DCs to be highly reliable and fault tolerant.

Multimaster replication is used to copy changes in the directory to other DCs. With multimaster replication, DCs work as peers to one another, so that any DC accepts and replicates these updates (with the exception of the special types of data for which an Operations Master is assigned). Rather than having to make changes on a primary DC, changes can be made to the directory from any DC.

Replication occurs automatically between DCs, and generally, no additional configuration is required. However, because there are times when network traffic will be higher, such as when employees log on to DCs at the beginning of the workday, replication can be configured to occur at specific times. This will enable you to control replication traffic so it doesn't occur during peak hours.

To replicate the directory effectively, Windows Server 2003 uses the Knowledge Consistency Checker (KCC) to generate a replication topology of the forest. A *replication topology* refers to the physical connections used by DCs to replicate the directory to other DCs within the site and to DCs in other sites. After initially creating a replication topology, the KCC will review and modify the topology at regular intervals. This allows it to see if certain connections or DCs are unavailable, and if changes need to be made as to how replicated data will be transferred to other DCs.

Replication is handled differently within a site as opposed to when the directory is replicated to other sites. *Intra-site replication* (in which Active Directory is replicated within a site) is handled by using a ring structure. The KCC builds a bidirectional ring, in which replication data is passed between DCs in two directions. Because the data is only being transferred within the site, the replicated data isn't compressed.

The KCC creates at least two connections to each DC, so if one connection fails, the other can be used. For example, in Figure 9.13, connections that are functional are shown with a straight line, while broken connections are shown with dotted lines. Because one of the four servers in Figure 9.13 has failed, replication data cannot be passed through it, so another connection between the servers is used. Using multiple connections provides fault tolerance.

Figure 9.13 Replication Topology

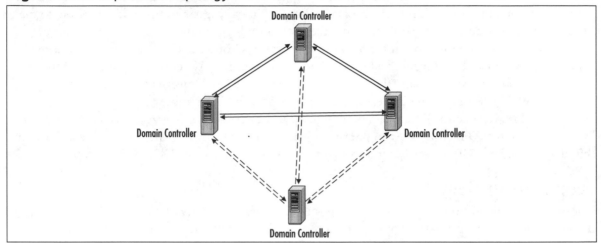

Intra-site replication is automated to occur at regular intervals, and only occurs when DCs are notified of a change. By default, when a change is made on a DC, it will wait 15 seconds and then send notification to its closest replication partner. If it has more than one replication partner, it will send out notifications in three-second intervals to each additional partner. When a partner receives this notification, it will send out a request for updated directory information to the original DC, which then responds by sending the updated data. The exception to this process is when an account is locked out, the DC account is changed, or there are changes in account lockout policy or domain password policy. In these circumstances, there is no 15-second waiting period, and replication occurs immediately.

Replication between sites is called *inter-site replication*. Because the bandwidth between sites might be slower than that within a site, inter-site replication occurs less frequently and is handled differently. Rather than informing other DCs shortly after a change occurs, replication occurs at scheduled times. Information about *site link objects* is used to determine the best link to use for passing this data between sites.

Site links are used to define how sites replicate Active Directory information between one another. These objects store data controlling which sites are to replicate traffic between one another, and which should be used over others. For example, you might have an ISDN connection between your offices and one located overseas. If the overseas link were slower and more costly to use than others, you could configure the link so it is only used as a last resort. Through the site link object, the fastest and least expensive connection between sites is used for replication.

A DC acts in the role of an inter-site topology generator in each site, and serves the purpose of building this topology. It considers the cost of different connections, whether DCs are available, and whether DCs have been added to sites. By gathering this information, the KCC can then update the topology as needed, and provide the method of passing data between the sites.

How often replication occurs is configurable, so that it occurs as frequently or infrequently as your needs dictate. By default, inter-site replication occurs every 180 minutes (three hours), and will use the site link to meet this schedule 24 hours a day, 7 days a week. The frequency of replications can be modified as needed to occur at certain times and days of the week.

Using Active Directory Administrative Tools

Just as organizations have the tendency to grow and change, so do the networks they use. In a Windows Server 2003 network, the number of domains, sites, OUs, users, computers, and other objects populating Active Directory can grow exponentially with a business. Every new employee needs a new account, and every new computer added to the network means another object added to the directory. Even when growth is limited, there can be a considerable amount of maintenance to these objects, such as when users change jobs, addresses, or other issues that involve changes to information and access. To aid administrators with these tasks, Active Directory provides a number of tools that make management easier.

Two types of administrative tools can be used to manage Active Directory. Windows Server 2003 provides a variety of new command-line tools that individually administer different aspects of the directory and its objects. By clicking on the Windows **Start** menu and clicking **Programs | Accessories | Command Prompt** (or simply clicking **Start | Run** and typing **cmd**), a prompt will appear allowing you to enter these commands and control objects and elements of Active Directory. The other method of managing Active Directory is with tools using a graphical user interface (GUI). These tools allow you to point and click through objects, and modify them using a graphical display. Most of the graphical tools are available through the **Start | Programs | Administrative Tools** menu.

Graphical Administrative Tools/MMCs

A primary administrative tool for managing Windows Server 2003 and Active Directory is the Microsoft Management Console (MMC). The MMC isn't a management tool in itself, but an interface that's used to load snap-ins that provide administrative functionality. Snap-ins provide a specific functionality, or a related set of functions. Because of the design of the MMC interface, you can load several snap-ins into one console, and create custom tools to deal with specific tasks. In addition, because these snap-ins run in the same environment, it becomes easier to learn how to use these tools because you don't have to learn a different interface for each.

MMCs can be started by opening pre-made consoles that are available under the **Administrative Tools** folder in the Windows **Start** menu. An empty MMC can be started by using the **Run** command in the Windows **Start** menu. By typing **MMC** in the **Run** command in the Windows **Start** menu, an empty MMC will start as shown in Figure 9.14.

Figure 9.14 Microsoft Management Console

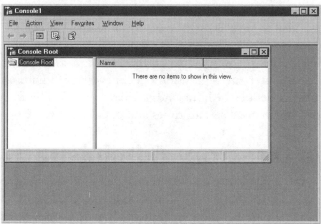

The windows appearing in the MMC are interfaces with individual snap-ins or custom console files. Each child window in the MMC has two panes. The left pane displays the console tree, which is a hierarchical display of tools available through the console. These can be multiple snap-ins that have been loaded into the MMC and saved as a custom console. The right pane is called the detail pane, and provides commands and information relating to what is selected in the console tree.

You can add snap-ins for specific tasks by clicking on the **File** menu and selecting **Add/Remove Snap-in**. When this is done, a new dialog box will appear with two tabs: Standalone and Extensions.

The Standalone tab is used for standalone snap-ins, which are designed to run without any additional requirements. The Extensions tab is used to load a special type of snap-in, called an extension snap-in. These are used to add additional functions to a standalone snap-in that's already been installed.

The Standalone tab is used to add or remove snap-ins from the console. As shown in Figure 9.15, clicking the **Add** button on this tab will display a list of available standalone snap-ins. After selecting the one you want to add, click the **Add** button on this dialog. Clicking **Close** will exit this screen, and return you to the previous one, which will now include your selected snap-ins in a list of ones to install in this console. Clicking **OK** confirms the selection, and installs them.

Figure 9.15 Add/Remove Snap-in Dialog Box

As you can see by in Figure 9.15, there are three snap-ins available for Active Directory:

- Active Directory Users and Computers
- Active Directory Domains and Trusts
- Active Directory Sites and Services

While we'll discuss each of these in the sections that follow, it is important to realize that these aren't the only snap-ins that you can use with Windows Server 2003. The MMC supplies these three snap-ins for use with Active Directory, but others are also available for specific purposes and management tasks. Each has an individual functionality or set of related functions for administering Windows Server 2003 and Active Directory. Note that although the three Active Directory-related snap-ins are available to be added to a custom MMC, each is already installed in a separate pre-configured MMC available through the Administrative Tools menu.

Because multiple snap-ins can be added and configured in the MMC, you can create custom consoles to perform specific tasks. After setting up a console, you can save it to a file that has the .msc extension. The console can be saved in one of two modes: Authoring and User.

Authoring mode is used to provide full access to the functions of an MMC console. When saved in this mode, users who open the console can add and remove snap-ins, create new Windows, create Favorites and taskpads, view everything in the console tree, and save consoles.

User mode is used to limit another user's ability to use certain functions of the console. If you were creating a console for users to perform a specific task, but didn't want them to access other functions, then User mode would be ideal. There are three access levels for User mode:

- **Full Access** The same as Author mode, except that snap-ins can't be added or removed, console settings can't be changed, and users can't create Favorites and taskpads.

- **Limited Access, Multiple Windows** Allows users to view parts of the console tree that were visible when the console was saved, and prohibits users from closing existing windows. Users can, however, create new windows.

- **Limited Access, Single Window** Also allows users to access parts of the console tree that were visible when the console was saved, but prohibits users from creating new windows.

Active Directory Users and Computers

The Active Directory Users and Computers console is one of the MMC snap-ins for use with Active Directory. It allows you to administer user and computer accounts, groups, printers, OUs, contacts, and other objects stored in Active Directory. Using this tool, you can create, delete, modify, move, organize, and set permissions on these objects.

As shown in Figure 9.16, when this tool is loaded, a node will appear in the console tree (left pane) showing the domain. Expanding this node will show a number of containers that are created by default. While additional containers can be created, the ones that appear here after creating a DC are:

- Builtin
- Computers

- Domain Controllers
- Users

These containers store objects that can be managed with this tool, and allow you to view and modify information related to these different objects.

Figure 9.16 Active Directory Users and Computers

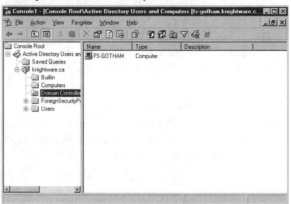

The *Builtin* container holds groups that were created by Windows Server 2003, and can be used to control access. You can add users to these Builtin groups to give them the ability to perform certain tasks. For example, rather than allowing everyone in the IT department to use the same Administrator account, users can be added to the built-in Administrators group. This gives them the ability to administer Windows Server 2003, but allows you to track which person with this level of security performed certain tasks.

The *Computers* container is used to store computer objects. These are (as the name implies) computers running on the network that have joined the domain and have accounts created in Active Directory. The Computers container can also include accounts used by applications to access Active Directory.

The *Domain Controllers* container contains objects representing DCs that reside in the domain. The ones shown in this container are ones running Windows 2000 Server and Windows Server 2003. Earlier versions are not displayed.

The *Users* container is used to store user accounts and groups. Users and Groups that appear in this container are ones that were created using application programming interfaces (APIs) that can use Active Directory, and ones that were created in Windows NT prior to upgrading.

Additional containers can be displayed when Active Directory Users and Computers is running with Advanced Features activated. You can enable Advanced Features by clicking on the menu item with this name, found in the View menu. When Advanced Features have been activated, LostAndFound and System containers are displayed in the left console tree.

The *LostAndFound* container is used to store stray objects whose containers no longer exist. If an object is created at the same time its container is deleted, or if it is moved to a location that's missing after replication, the object is placed in this container. This allows you to manage the lost object, and move it to a container that does exist.

The *System* container is used for system settings. These are built-in settings for containers and objects used by Active Directory and Windows Server 2003.

Active Directory Domains and Trusts

The Active Directory Domains and Trusts console is used to manage domains and the trust relationships between them. As shown in Figure 9.17, the console tree of this tool includes a node for domains making up the network. By selecting the **Active Directory Domains and Trusts** node, a listing of domains will appear in the right pane. Using this tool, you can create, modify, and delete trust relationships between domains, set the suffix for UPNs, and raise domain and forest functional levels. This enables administrators to control how domains function, and how they interoperate.

Figure 9.17 Active Directory Domains and Trusts

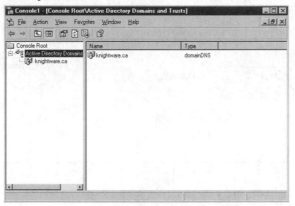

Using the Active Directory Domains and Trusts console, you can create a variety of different types of trusts between domains and forests. Earlier, we discussed how parent and child domains and domain trees use a two-way transitive trust to share resources between domains. The two-way transitive trust means that both domains trust one another, as well as any other domains with which they have similar trust relationships. In addition to this type of trust, additional trusts can be created:

- Shortcut trust
- Forest trust
- Realm trust
- External trust

A *shortcut trust* is transitive, and can be either one-way or two-way. This means that either one domain can trust another but not vice versa, or both domains can trust each other. This type of trust is used to connect two domains in a forest, and is particularly useful when the domains are in different trees. By creating a shortcut, one domain can connect with another quickly, improving logon times between domains. Connection is quicker because, when two domains in different trees connect via the implicit trusts that exist by default, the trust path must go all the way up the tree to the root domain, across to the other tree's root domain, and back down the second tree. A shortcut trust, as its name indicates, creates a direct trust between the two domains in different trees.

To illustrate this, let's look at the situation in Figure 9.18. If a user in DomainD wanted to use resources in Domain2, he or she would be authenticating to a domain that is located in a different tree. Without a shortcut trust, the connection would go through DomainA, across the trust between the two trees to Domain1, and then to Domain2. With a shortcut trust, DomainD and Domain2 would have a direct trust between them that could be used for authentication. As we can also see in Figure 9.18, multiple shortcut trusts can exist, allowing users to be authenticated to other domains that they commonly need to access.

Figure 9.18 Shortcut Trusts

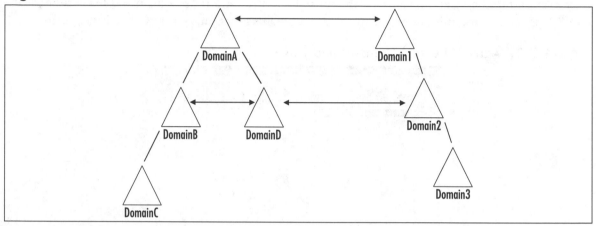

A *forest trust* is also transitive, and can be one-way or two-way. As shown in Figure 9.19, this type of trust is used to connect two different forests, so that users in each forest can use resources in the other. Using this type of trust, a user in a domain in one forest could be authenticated and access resources located in a domain that's in another forest. This allows different areas of the network to be interconnected, even though they are separated by administrative boundaries.

Figure 9.19 Forest Trust

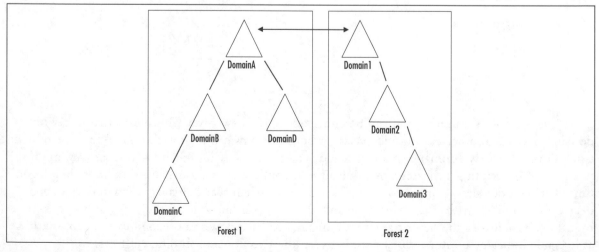

A *realm trust* can be one-way or two-way, and can also be either transitive or nontransitive. *Nontransitive* means that the trust relationship doesn't extend beyond the two parties. For example, let's say DomainA trusts DomainB, and DomainB trusts DomainC. Because the trust is nontransitive, DomainA and DomainC don't trust one another because there isn't a trust relationship between them. As shown in Figure 9.20, the realm trust is used when a relationship needs to be created between a Windows Server 2003 domain and a non-Windows realm that uses Kerberos version 5 (such as one running UNIX).

Figure 9.20 Realm Trust

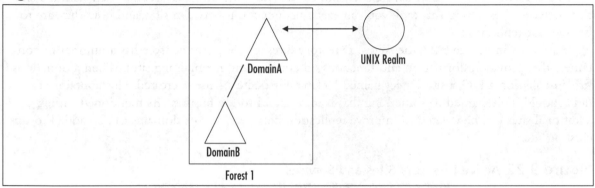

The final type of trust that can be created is an *external trust*. An external trust is always nontransitive, and can be either one-way or two-way. As shown in Figure 9.21, this type of trust is used to create a relationship between a Windows Server 2003 domain and one running Windows NT 4.0. It can also be used to connect two domains that are in different forests, and don't have a forest trust connecting them.

Figure 9.21 External Trust

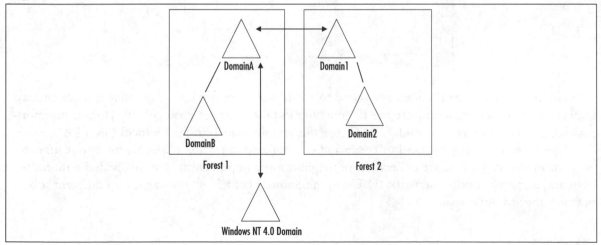

The Active Directory Domains and Trusts console is also used for raising domain and forest levels, which enables additional features in Active Directory. Raising domain and forest functional levels depends on what operating systems are running on servers, and is something we discuss in greater detail later in this chapter.

Active Directory Sites and Services

Earlier in this chapter, we discussed how sites represent the physical structure of your network, and are important to replicating information in Active Directory. The Active Directory Sites and Services console is used to create and manage sites, and control how the directory is replicated within a site and between sites. Using this tool, you can specify connections between sites, and how they are to be used for replication.

As shown in Figure 9.22, the Active Directory Sites and Services console has a number of containers that provide information and functions on creating and maintaining sites. When a domain is first installed on a DC, a site object named Default-First-Site-Name is created. This container can (and should) be renamed to something that is meaningful to the business. As mentioned earlier, additional sites can be created to improve replication between sites, or domains can be added to this existing site.

Figure 9.22 Active Directory Sites and Services

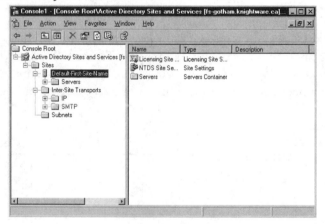

The *Inter-Site Transports* container is used to create and store site links. A *site link* is a connection between sites. Links created under the IP container use the Internet Protocol (IP) as their transport protocol, while those created under SMTP use the Simple Mail Transfer Protocol (SMTP).

The *Subnets* container is used to create and store objects containing information about subnets on your network. Subnets are collections of neighboring computers that are subdivided within the network, using a common network ID. Using the Subnets container, you can group different subnets together to build a site.

Command-Line Tools

Windows Server 2003 provides a number of command-line tools that you can use for managing Active Directory. These tools use commands typed in at the prompt, and can provide a number of services that are useful in administering the directory. The command-line tools for Active Directory include:

- **Cacls** Used to view and modify discretionary access control lists (DACLs) on files.
- **Cmdkey** Used to create, list, and delete usernames, passwords, and credentials.
- **Csvde** Used to import and export data from the directory.
- **Dcgpofix** Restores Group Policy Objects (GPOs) to the state they where in when initially installed.
- **Dsadd** Used to add users, groups, computers, contacts, and OUs.
- **Dsget** Displays the properties of an object in Active Directory.
- **Dsmod** Used to modify users, groups, computers, servers, contacts, and OUs.
- **Dsmove** Renames an object without moving it, or moves an object to a new location.
- **Ldifde** Used to create, modify, and delete objects from Active Directory.
- **Ntdsutil** Used for general management of Active Directory.
- **Whoami** Provides information on the user who's currently logged on.

In the sections that follow, we will briefly discuss each of these tools, and show you how they can assist you in performing certain tasks when administering Active Directory.

Cacls

Cacls is used to view and modify the permissions a user or group has to a particular resource. Cacls provides this ability by allowing you to view and change DACLs on files. A DACL is a listing of access control entries (ACEs) for users and groups, and includes permissions the user has to a file. The syntax for using this tool is:

```
Cacls filename
```

Cacls also has a number of switches, which are parameters you can enter on the command line to use a specific functionality. Table 9.1 lists the switches for Cacls.

Table 9.1 Switches for the Cacls Tool

Parameter	Description
/t	Change the DACLs of files in the current directory and all subdirectories.
/e	Edit the DACL.
/r *username*	Revokes the users' rights.

Continued

Table 9.1 Switches for the Cacls Tool

Parameter	Description
/c	Ignore any errors that might occur when changing the DACL.
/g username:permission	Grants rights to a specified user. Rights that can be granted are: n (None), r (Read), w (Write), c (Change), and f (Full Control).
/p username:permission	Replaces the rights of a specified user. The rights that can be replaced are: n (None), r (Read), w (Write), c (Change), and f (Full Control).
/d username	Denies access to a specified user.

Cmdkey

Cmdkey is used to create, view, edit, and delete the stored usernames, passwords, and credentials. This allows you to log on using one account, and view and modify the credentials of another user. As with other command-line tools we'll discuss, cmdkey has a number of switches that provided needed parameters for the tool to function. Table 9.2 lists these parameters.

Table 9.2 Switches for the Cmdkey Tool

Parameter	Description
/add:targetname	Adds a username and password to the list, and specifies the computer or domain (using the targetname parameter) with which the entry will be associated.
/generic	Adds generic credentials to the list.
/smartcard	Instructs cmdkey to retrieve credentials from a smart card.
/user: username	Provides the username with which this entry is to be associated. If the username parameter isn't provided, you will be prompted for it.
/pass:password	Provides the password to store with this entry. If the password parameter isn't provided, you will be prompted for it.
/delete: {targetname | /ras}	Deletes the username and password from the list. If the targetname parameter is provided, the specified entry will be deleted. If /ras is included, the stored remote access entry is deleted.
/list: targetname	Lists the stored usernames and credentials. If the targetname parameter isn't provided, all of the stored usernames and credentials will be listed.

Csvde

Csvde is used to import and export data from Active Directory. This data is comma delimitated, so that a comma separates each value. Exporting data in this way allows you to then import it into other applications (for example, Microsoft Office tools such as Access and Excel). Table 9.3 lists the parameters for this command.

Table 9.3 Switches for the Csvde Tool

Parameter	Description
-i	Used to specify the import mode.
-f *filename*	Specifies the filename to import or export data to.
-s *servername*	Sets the DC that will be used to import or export data.
-c *string1 string2*	Replaces the value of string1 with string2. This is often used when importing data between domains, and the DN of the domain data is being exported from (string1) needs to be replaced with the name of the import domain (string2).
-v	Verbose mode.
-j *path*	Specifies the location for log files.
-t *portnumber*	The portnumber parameter is used to specify the LDAP port number. By default, the LDAP port is 389 and the GC port is 3268.
-d *BaseDN*	The BaseDN parameter is used to specify the DN of a search base for data export.
-p *scope*	Used to set the search scope. The value of the scope parameter can be Base, OneLevel, or SubTree.
-l *LDAPAttributeList*	Specifies a list of attributes to return in an export query. If this parameter isn't used, then all attributes are returned in the query.
-o *LDAPAttributeList*	Specifies a list of attributes to omit in an export query.
-g	Used to omit paged searches.
-m Active Directory.	Used to omit attributes that apply to certain objects in
-n	Specifies that binary values are to be omitted from an export.
-k	If errors occur during an import, this parameter specifies that csvde should continue processing.
-a *username password*	Specifies the username and password to be used when running this command. By default, the credentials of the user currently logged on are used.

Continued

Table 9.3 Switches for the Csvde Tool

Parameter	Description
-b username domain password	Specifies the username, domain, and password to use when running this command. By default, the credentials of the user currently logged on are used.

Dcgpofix

Dcgpofix is used to restore the default domain policy and default DC's policy to they way they were when initially created. By restoring these GPOs to their original states, any changes that were made to them are lost. This tool has only two switches associated with it:

- **/ignoreschema** Ignores the version number of the schema.
- **/target: {domain | dc | both}** Specifies the target domain, DC, or both.

When the /ignoreschema switch is used, dcgpofix will ignore the version number of Active Directory's schema when it runs. This will allow it to work on other versions of Active Directory, as opposed to the one on the computer on which dcgpofix was initially installed. You should use the version of dcgpofix that was installed with your installation of Windows Server 2003, as GPOs might not be restored if versions from other operating systems are used.

Dsadd

Dsadd is used to add objects to Active Directory. The objects you can add with this command-line tool are users, computers, groups, OUs, contacts, and quota specifications. To add any of these objects, you would enter the following commands at the command prompt:

- *dsadd user* Adds a user to the directory
- *dsadd computer* Adds a computer to the directory
- *dsadd group* Adds a group to the directory
- *dsadd ou* Adds an OU to the directory
- *dsadd contact* Adds a contact to the directory
- *dsadd quota* Adds a quota specification to the directory

While the commands for this tool are straightforward, there is a variety of arguments associated with each. For full details on these arguments, type the command at the command prompt followed by /?. This will display a list of parameters for each command.

Dsget

Dsget is used to view the properties of objects in Active Directory. The objects you can view with dsget are users, groups, computers, servers, sites, subnets, OUs, contacts, partitions, and quota specifications. To view the properties of these objects, enter the following commands:

- ■ *dsget user* Displays the properties of a user

- ■ *dsget group* Displays the properties of a group and its membership

- ■ *dsget computer* Displays the properties of a computer

- ■ *dsget server* Displays the properties of a DC

- ■ *dsget site* Displays the properties of a site

- ■ *dsget subnet* Displays the properties of a subnet

- ■ *dsget ou* Displays the properties of an OU

- ■ *dsget contact* Displays the properties of a contact

- ■ *dsget partition* Displays the properties of a directory partition

- ■ *dsget quota* Displays the properties of a quota specification

While the commands for this tool are straightforward, there is a variety of arguments associated with each. For full details on these arguments, type the command at the command prompt followed by /?. This will display a list of parameters for each command.

Dsmod

Dsmod is used to modify existing objects in Active Directory. The objects you can modify using dsmod are users, groups, computers, servers, OUs, contacts, partitions, and quota specifications. To edit these objects, enter the following commands:

- ■ *dsmod user* Modifies the attributes of a user in the directory

- ■ *dsmod group* Modifies the attributes of a group in the directory

- ■ *dsmod computer* Modifies a computer in the directory

- ■ *dsmod server* Modifies the properties of a DC

- ■ *dsmod ou* Modifies the attributes of an OU in the directory

- ■ *dsmod contact* Modifies the attributes of a contact in the directory

- ■ *dsmod partition* Modifies a directory partition

- ■ *dsmod quota* Displays the properties of a quota specification

While the commands for this tool are straightforward, there is a variety of arguments associated with each. For full details on these arguments, type the command at the command prompt followed by /?. This will display a list of parameters for each command.

Dsmove

Dsmove is used to either rename or move an object within a domain. Using this tool, you can rename an object without moving it in the directory, or move it to a new location within the directory tree. The dsmove tool can't be used to move objects to other domains.

Renaming or moving an object requires that you use the DN, which identifies the object's location in the tree. For example, if you have an object called JaneD in an OU called Accounting, located in a domain called syngress.com, the DN is:

```
CN=JaneD, OU=Accounting, DC=syngress, DC=com
```

The *–newname* switch is used to rename objects using the DN. For example, let's say you wanted to change a user account's name from JaneD to JaneM. To do so, you would use the following command:

```
Dsmove CN=JaneD, OU=Accounting, DC=syngress, DC=com –newname JaneM
```

The *–newparent* switch is used to move objects within a domain. For example, let's say the user whose name you just changed was transferred from Accounting to Sales, which you've organized in a different OU container. To move the user object, you would use the following command:

```
Dsmove CN=JaneM, OU=Accounting, DC=syngress, DC=com –newparent OU=Sales,
  DC=syngress, DC=com
```

In addition to the *–newname* and *–newparent* switches, you can also use the parameters listed in Table 9.4 to control how this tool is used.

Table 9.4 Switches for Dsmove

Parameter	Description
{-s Server –d Domain}	Specifies a remote server or domain to connect to. By default, dsmove will connect to the DC in the domain you logged on to.
-u Username	Specifies the username to use when logging on to a remote server.
-p {Password | *}	Specifies the password to use when logging on to a remote server. If you type the * symbol instead of a password, you are then prompted to enter the password.
-q	Sets dsmove to suppress output.
{-uc | -uco | -uci}	Specifies dsmove to format input and output in Unicode.

Ldifde

Ldifde is used to create, modify, and delete objects from the directory, and can also be used to extend the schema. An additional use for this tool is to import and export user and group information. This allows you to view exported data in other applications, or populate Active Directory with imported data. To perform such tasks, ldifde relies on a number of switches that enable it to perform specific tasks, listed in Table 9.5.

Table 9.5 Switches for Ldifde

Parameter	Description
-I	Sets ldifde to import data. If this isn't specified, then the tool will work in Export mode.
-f *Filename*	Specifies the name of the file to import or export.
-s *Servername*	Specifies the DC that will be used to perform the import or export.
-c *string1 string2*	Replaces the value of string1 with string2. This is often used when importing data between domains, and the DN of the domain data is being exported from (string1) needs to be replaced with the name of the import domain (string2).
-v	Verbose mode.
-j *path*	Specifies the location for log files.
-t *portnumber*	The *portnumber* parameter is used to specify the LDAP port number. By default, the LDAP port is 389 and the GC port is 3268.
-d *BaseDN*	The *BaseDN* parameter is used to specify the DN of a search base for data export.
-p *scope*	Used to set the search scope. The value of the scope parameter can be Base, OneLevel, or SubTree.
-r *LDAPfilter*	Specifies a search filter for exporting data.
-l *LDAPAttributeList*	Specifies a list of attributes to return in an export query. If this parameter isn't used, then all attributes are returned in the query.
-o *LDAPAttributeList*	Specifies a list of attributes to omit in an export query.
-g	Used to omit paged searches.
-m Active Directory.	Used to omit attributes that apply to certain objects in
-n export.	Specifies that binary values are to be omitted from an
-k	If errors occur during an import, this parameter specifies that ldifde should continue processing.
-a *username password*	Specifies the username and password to be used when running this command. By default, the credentials of the user who's currently logged on are used.
-b username domain password	Specifies the username, domain, and password to use when running this command. By default, the credentials of the user who's currently logged on are used.

Ntdsutil

Ntdsutil is a general-purpose command-line tool that can perform a variety of functions for managing Active Directory. Using Ntdsutil, you can:

- Perform maintenance of Active Directory
- Perform an authoritative restore of Active Directory
- Modify the Time To Live (TTL) of dynamic data
- Manage domains
- Manage data in the directory and log files
- Block certain IP addresses from querying the directory, and set LDAP policies
- Remove metadata from DCs that were retired or improperly uninstalled
- Manage Security Identifiers (SIDs)
- Manage master operation roles (Domain Naming Master, Schema Master, Iinfrastructure Master, PDC Emulator, and RID Master)

Typing **ntdsutil** at the command prompt will load the tool and the prompt will change to **ntd-sutil:**. As shown in Figure 9.23, by typing **help** at the command line, you can view different commands for the tasks being performed. After entering a command, typing **help** again will provide other commands that can be used. For example, typing **metadata cleanup** after first starting **ntd-sutil**, and then typing **help** will display a list of commands relating to metadata cleanup. This allows you to use the command as if you were navigating through menus containing other commands. You can return to a previous menu at any time, or exit the program by typing **Quit**.

Figure 9.23 NTDSUTIL

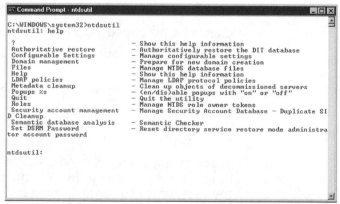

Whoami

Whoami is a tool for displaying information about the user who is currently logged on. Using this tool, you can view your domain name, computer name, username, group names, logon identifier, and privileges. The amount of information displayed depends on the parameters that are entered with this command. Table 9.6 lists the available parameters.

Table 9.6 Switches for Whoami

Parameter	Description
/upn	Displays the UPN of the user currently logged on.
/fqdn	Displays the FQDN of the user currently logged on.
/logonid	Displays the Logon ID.
/user	Displays the username of the user currently logged on.
/groups	Displays group names.
/priv	Displays privileges associated with the currently logged-on user.
/fo *format*	Controls the format of how information is displayed. The *format* parameter can have the value of: table (to show output in a table format), list (to list output), or csv to display in a comma-delimited format.
/all	Displays username, groups, SIDs, and privileges for the user currently logged on.

Figure 9.24 Results of Using the *WHOAMI /ALL* Command

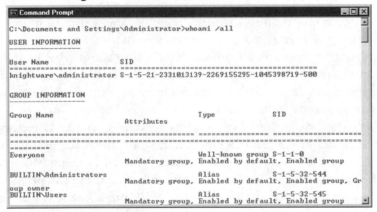

Implementing Active Directory Security and Access Control

Security is an important part of Windows Server 2003 and Active Directory. Two primary methods of implementing security are user authentication and access control. *Authentication* is used to verify the identity of a user or other objects, such as applications or computers. After it's been determined they are who or what they say they are, the process continues by giving them the level of access they deserve. *Access control* manages what users (or other objects) can use, and how they can use them. By combining authentication and access control, a user is permitted or denied access to objects in the directory.

Access Control in Active Directory

In Active Directory, permissions can be applied to objects to control how these objects are used. Permissions regulate access by enforcing whether a user can read or write to an object, has full control, or no access. Active Directory permissions are separate from share permissions and NTFS permissions, and work in conjunction with both. Three elements determine a user's access, and define the permissions they have to an object:

- Security descriptors
- Object Inheritance
- Authentication

Objects in Active Directory use security descriptors to store information about permissions, and control who has access to an object. The security descriptor contains information that's stored in access control lists (ACLs), which define who can access the object and what they can do with it. There are two different types of ACLs in the security descriptor:

- Security access control list (SACL)
- Discretionary access control list (DACL)

The SACL is used to track an object's security based on how a user or group accesses the object. For example, you can audit whether a user was able to access the object using a particular permission (such as Read, Write, or Full Control). Information about what to audit is kept in ACEs, which are stored within the SACL. These entries control what is audited, and contain information about the events to be logged. In doing this, records can be kept on the security of objects, and whether specific users or groups are able to successfully access them.

As we saw earlier, when we discussed command-line tools for Active Directory, a DACL is a listing of ACEs for users and groups, and includes information about the permissions that a user or group has to a file. The DACL controls whether a user is granted or denied access to an object. ACEs in the DACL explicitly identify individual users and groups, and the permissions granted to each. Because only users and groups identified in the DACL can access an object in Active Directory, any user or group that isn't specified is denied access.

Active Directory places the permissions you can apply to objects into two categories: standard permissions and special permissions. *Standard permissions* are those that are commonly applied to objects, whereas *special permissions* provide additional access control. For most objects in Active Directory, five permissions are available as standard permissions:

- **Full Control** Allows the user to change permissions, take ownership, and have the abilities associated with all other standard permissions.
- **Read** Allows the user to view objects, attributes, ownership, and permissions on an object.
- **Write** Allows the user to change attributes on an object.

- **Create All Child Objects** Allows the user to add objects to an OU.
- **Delete All Child Objects** Allows the user to delete objects from an OU.

Permissions can be set on objects by using the **Active Directory Users and Computers** snap-in for the MMC. As shown in Figure 9.25, you can set permissions by using the **Security** tab of an object's **Properties** dialog box. The **Security** tab is hidden in the **Properties** dialog box, unless the **Advanced Features** menu item is toggled on the **View** menu first. After this is done, you can then bring up the **Properties** dialog box by selecting an object and clicking **Properties** on the **Action** menu, or right-clicking on the object and selecting **Properties**.

Figure 9.25 Permissions Are Set on the Security Tab of the Object's Properties

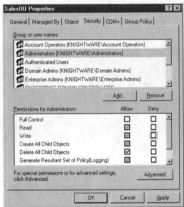

The top pane of the Security tab lists users and groups, and the lower pane lists the various permissions that can be applied to these users and groups. You can set permissions by selecting one of these users and groups, and checking the applicable permissions. Special permissions can be set for objects by clicking the **Advanced** button, which displays a dialog box where additional permissions can be applied.

Because it would take a while to assign permissions to every object in Active Directory, object inheritance can be used to minimize how often and where permissions are assigned. *Object inheritance* refers to how the permissions of a parent object are inherited by child objects. When permissions are applied to a container, they are propagated to objects within that container. For example, if a group had Full Control permissions on an OU, the group would also have Full Control of any of the printer objects within that OU. The permissions of one object flow down to any objects within the hierarchy, so child objects have the same permissions as their parents.

Since there might be times when you don't want the permissions from a parent to propagate to child objects, inheritance can be blocked. By clearing the **Allow Inheritable Permissions From Parent To Propagate To This Object** check box, the permissions from containers higher in the hierarchy are blocked. When this is done, any permissions that are modified on parent objects don't apply to the child. Permissions for the child object must be explicitly assigned. Use the following steps to set permissions on AD objects.

Set Permissions on AD Objects

1. Open Active Directory Users and Computers by clicking selecting **Administrative Tools** in the Windows Start menu, and then clicking on the **Active Directory Users and Computers** menu item.

2. When the MMC opens with this snap-in installed, expand the console tree so that your domain and the containers within it are visible.

3. Select your domain from the console tree. From the **Action** menu, select **New** and then click the **Organizational Unit** menu item. As shown in Figure 9.26, when the dialog box appears, name the new OU TestOU, and then click **OK**. A new OU with this name should now appear in the console tree beneath your domain.

Figure 9.26 New Object Dialog Box

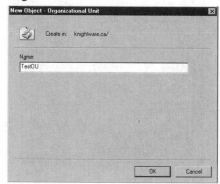

4. In the **View** menu, click **Advanced Features**.

5. Select the TestOU OU. From the **Action** menu, click **Properties**.

6. When the Properties dialog box appears, click the **Security** tab. In the list of usernames, select the name of the account you're currently logged on with.

7. In the pane below the list of usernames and groups, click the **Full Control** check box under **Allow**, so that a check mark appears in it. You now have full control of the OU.

8. Click the **Advanced** button to display the **Advanced Security Settings** dialog box. When the dialog box appears, click the Permissions tab. As shown in the Figure 9.27. Ensure that the Allow inheritable permissions from the parent to propagate to this object and all child objects check box is checked. This will allow inheritable permissions to be applied to this OU, and any within the container. Click **OK** to return to the previous screen.

Figure 9.27 Advanced Settings Dialog Box

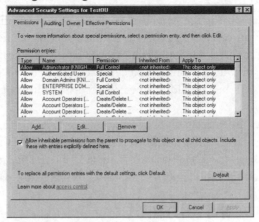

9.   Click **OK** to exit the Properties dialog box.

Role-Based Access Control

Access control can be managed based on the *role* an Active Directory object plays in an organization. Since objects represent users, computers, and other tangible elements of an organization, and these people and things serve different purposes in a company, it makes sense to configure these objects so that they reflect the tasks they perform. *Role-based administration* is used to configure object settings, so that computers and users have the necessary permissions needed to do their jobs based on the roles they fill.

The roles that users and computers are assigned correspond to the functions they serve in a company. Two categories of roles can be used for role based access control: authorization and computer configuration.

Authorization roles are based on the tasks a person performs as part of his or her job. For example, Help Desk personnel would need the ability to change passwords, while accountants would need to be able to access financial information and audit transactions. Using role-based access control, you can give each person the access he or she needs to perform these tasks.

Authorization roles are similar to security groups, to which users can become members and acquire a level of security that gives them the ability to perform certain tasks. However, authorization roles differ in that they are used for applications. Role-based access can be applied to a single application, set of applications, or a scope within the application. Another important difference is that role-based authorization can be dynamic, so that users become part of a group membership as an application runs. This is different from security groups that require membership to be set beforehand.

In the same way that users have different purposes in a company, so do computers. A business might have DCs, mail servers, file servers, Web servers, and any number of other machines providing services to users and applications in an organization. *Computer configuration roles* are used to control which features, services, and options should be installed and configured on a machine, based on the function it serves in the company.

Authorization Manager

Authorization Manager is a snap-in for the MMC that allows you to configure role-based access for applications. By using roles, you ensure that users only have access to the functions and resources they need to perform their jobs, and are prohibited from using other features and resources they're not authorized to use. For example, personnel in Payroll would need to view information on employees (so they can be paid), but wouldn't need to access administrative features that allow them to modify passwords.

In Authorization Manager, roles are designed based on the tasks that are supported by the application. After the role is developed, users and groups can then be assigned to the role so they have the access necessary to perform these tasks. The tasks that are available for users to use depend on the application, as the ability to support roles and the functions available are part of the software design.

Active Directory Authentication

When you log on to a Windows Server 2003 domain, a single logon gives access to any resources you're permitted to use, regardless of their location on the network. A user doesn't need to re-enter a password every time the user accesses a server or other resources, because any authentication after initially logging on is transparent. Because only one logon is needed, the system needs to verify a person is who he or she claims to be, before any access is given.

Operating systems such as Windows NT, 2000, and Server 2003 store account information in the SAM database. The SAM stores credentials that are used to access the local machine. When a user logs on to a computer with a local user account that's stored in the SAM, the user is authenticated to the local machine. The user's access is limited to just that computer when logging on to the machine.

When users log on to the Windows Server 2003 domain, an account in Active Directory is used to access network resources located within the domain, or in other trusted domains. When a user logs on, the Local Security Authority (LSA) is used to log users on to the local computer. It is also used to authenticate to Active Directory. After validating the user's identity in Active Directory, the LSA on the DC that authenticates the user creates an access token and associates a SID with the user.

The access token is made up of data that contains information about the user. It holds information about the user's name, group affiliation, SID, and SIDs for the groups of which he or she is a member. The access token is created each time the user logs on. Because the access token is created at logon, any changes to the user's group membership or other security settings won't appear until after the user logs off and back on again. For example, if the user became a backup operator, he or she would have to log off and log back on before these changes affected the user's access.

Standards and Protocols

Authentication relies on standards and protocols that are used to confirm the identity of a user or object. Windows Server 2003 supports several types of network authentication:

- Kerberos
- X.509 certificates

- Lightweight Directory Access Protocol/Secure Sockets Layer (LDAP/SSL)
- Public Key Infrastructure (PKI)

As we'll see in the paragraphs that follow, some of these standards and protocols not only provide a method of authenticating users, but also the ability to encrypt data.

Kerberos

Kerberos version 5 is an industry standard security protocol that Windows Server 2003 uses as the default authentication service. It is used to handle authentication in Windows Server 2003 trust relationships, and is the primary security protocol for authentication within domains.

Kerberos uses mutual authentication to verify the identity of a user or computer, and the network service being accessed. Each side proves to the other that they are who they claim to be. Kerberos does this through the use of *tickets*.

X.509 Certificates

X.509 is a popular standard for digital certificates, published by the International Organization for Standardization (ISO). X.509 certificates are used to verify that the user is who he or she claims to be. Digital certificates work as a method of identifying the user, much as your birth certificate is used to identify you as a person. They can also be used to establish the identity of applications, network services, computers, and other devices.

LDAP/SSL

LDAP is used by Active Directory for communication between clients and directory servers. LDAP allows you to read and write data in Active Directory, but isn't secure by default. To extend security to LDAP communications, LDAP can be used over Secure Sockets Layer/Transport Layer Security. Secure Sockets Layer (SSL) and Transport Layer Security (TLS) provide data encryption and authentication. TLS is the successor to SSL, and is more secure. It can be used by clients to authenticate servers, and by servers to authenticate clients. Communication using TLS allows messages between the client and server to be encrypted, so data being passed between the two isn't accessible by third parties.

PKI

PKI is a method of authentication that uses unique identifiers called "keys," which are mathematical algorithms used for cryptography and authentication. PKI uses two different types of keys: public keys and private keys. PKI is discussed at length in "Planning, Implementing, Maintaining Public Key Infrastructure" later in this book.

What's New in Windows Server 2003 Active Directory?

A number of enhancements and new features in the Windows Server 2003 Active Directory weren't available in Windows 2000 Server. These improvements allow various tasks and network operations to be performed more efficiently. However, although there are many new features, the availability of a number of them depends on the environment in which DCs are running.

When a Windows Server 2003 DC is created on a network, Active Directory is installed with a basic set of features. Additional features can be enabled, but this is dependent on the operating systems running as DCs and the functional level (formerly called the mode) that's configured for the domain or forest. There are four different levels of functionality for Active Directory:

- Windows 2000 mixed

- Windows 2000 native

- Windows 2003 interim

- Windows 2003

If you're upgrading from Windows 2000 Server on your network, you're probably familiar with the first two levels. Each of these appeared in Windows 2000, and provided backward compatibility to older operating systems such as Windows NT 4.0, and allowed control of what features were available in Active Directory. Windows Server 2003 interim and Windows Server 2003 functionality are new to Active Directory, and weren't available in previous versions.

Windows 2000 mixed allows domains to contain Windows NT BDCs that can interact with Windows 2000 and Windows Server 2003 servers. In this level, the basic features of Active Directory are available to use. However, you aren't able to nest groups within one another, use Universal Groups that allow access to resources in any domain, or use Security ID Histories (SIDHistory). Because it accommodates the widest variety of servers running on your network, this is the default level of functionality when a Windows Server 2003 DC is installed.

Windows 2000 native is the highest mode available for Windows 2000 and the next highest level for Windows Server 2003 DCs. Windows 2000 native removes support for replication to Windows NT BDCs, so these older servers are unable to function as DCs. In this level, only Windows 2000 and Windows Server 2003 DCs can be used in the domain, and support for Universal Groups, SIDHistory, and group nesting becomes available.

Windows 2003 interim is a new level that's available in Windows Server 2003. This level is used when your domain consists of Windows NT and Windows Server 2003 DCs. It provides the same functionality as Windows 2000 mixed mode, but is used when you are upgrading Windows NT domains directly to Windows Server 2003. If a forest has never had Windows 2000 DCs, then this is the level used for performing an upgrade.

The highest functionality level for Active Directory is *Windows 2003*. The Windows 2003 level is used when there are only Windows Server 2003 DCs in the domain. When this level is set for the domain, a considerable number of features are enabled. We discuss these features later in this chapter, when we discuss new features that are available with domain and forest functionality.

The number of features available for Active Directory is also dependent on whether the functionality level has been raised for the domain or the entire forest. With domain-level functionality, all servers in the domain are running Windows Server 2003. With this level, different domains in a forest can be set to use different functionality levels. With forest-level functionality, all domains in the forest are running Windows Server 2003 and have their domain functionality raised to Windows Server 2003. As stated previously, there are four different levels for Windows Server 2003 domain functionality.

Forest functionality can also be raised to enable features that apply to all domains in the forest. With forest functionality, there are three different levels available:

- Windows 2000
- Windows 2003 interim
- Windows 2003

Windows 2000 level allows Windows NT, Windows 2000, and Windows Server 2003 DCs on the network, and is the default level for a forest. The other two levels are the same as the domain levels, in that Windows 2003 interim supports Windows Server 2003 DCs and NT BDCs, while Windows 2003 level supports only Windows Server 2003 DCs on the network. When the default level is raised to either of these other levels, additional features in Active Directory become available.

To raise the forest functionality, you must first raise the functionality of domains within the forest. Each domain in the forest must be raised to either Windows 2000 native or Windows 2003 before the forest functionality can be raised to Windows 2003. When the forest functional level is then raised to Windows 2003, any DCs in the forest's domains will have their domain functional level automatically raised to Windows 2003.

The tool used to raise domain and forest functional levels is *Active Directory Domains and Trusts*. Raising domain levels is done by right-clicking the domain in the left console pane and then clicking **Raise Domain Functional Level** from the menu that appears. As shown in Figure 9.28, you then select the level to which you want to raise the domain, and then click the **Raise** button. Raising forest functional levels is done similarly. To raise the forest level, right-click the **Active Directory Domains and Trusts** node, and then click **Raise Forest Functional Level** from the menu that appears (see Figure 9.28). Select the level to which you want to raise the forest, and click **Raise** to complete the task.

Figure 9.28 Raise Domain Functional Level Dialog Box

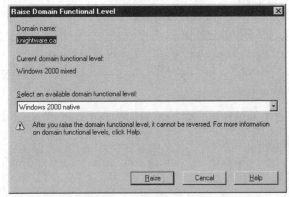

When raising the forest or domain functional levels, it is important to remember that it is a one-way change. After raising the level, you cannot lower it again later. For example, if you raise the domain from Windows 2000 mixed to Windows 2003, you cannot return the level to Windows 2000 mixed again. This means that you can't add Windows NT BDCs or Windows 2000 DCs to your domain after the upgrade, and any existing DCs need to be upgraded or permanently removed from service. If you attempt to change the domain or forest level after raising it to Windows 2003, a screen similar to Figure 9.29 will appear.

Figure 9.29 Raise Domain Functional Level Dialog Box After Raising the Domain Functional Level

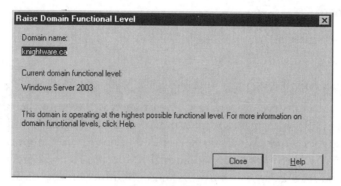

New Features Available Only with Windows Server 2003 Domain/Forest Functionality

In Chapter 1, we discussed the new features of Windows Server 2003 that apply to all computers running this latest OS. However, there are new features discussed in this section that are available only with Windows Server 2003 domain and forest functionality.

When the domain or forest functional levels have been raised so that all DCs are running Windows Server 2003, a number of new features become enabled. These features allow you to modify elements of both your domain and forest, and provide advanced functions that aren't available until functionality levels are raised. In the paragraphs that follow, we will look at the new features available in Active Directory when all DCs have been upgraded to Windows Server 2003, and the functionality has been raised to Windows 2003.

Domain Controller Renaming Tool

The DC renaming tool allows you to rename a DC without having to demote it first. This can be useful when you need to restructure the network, or simply want to use a more meaningful name for a particular DC. When this tool is used, the DC name changes, and any Active Directory and DNS entries are automatically updated.

Domain Rename Utility

Domains can also be renamed. Using the domain rename utility (rendom.exe), you can change the NetBIOS and DNS names of a domain, including any child, parent, domain-tree, or forest root domains (from which all others branch off in the hierarchy). By renaming domains in this manner, you can thereby move them in the hierarchy. For example, you can change the name of dev.web.syngress.com to dev.syngress.com, making the web.syngress.com and dev.syngress.com domains on the same level of the hierarchy. You could even rename the domain so that it becomes part of a completely different domain tree. The only domain that you can't reposition in this manner is the forest root domain.

Forest Trusts

As we saw earlier, forest trusts can also be created, so that a two-way transitive trust relationship exists between two different forests. In creating such a trust, the users and computers in each forest are able to access what's in both forests. This expands the network, so users are able to use services and resources in both forests.

Dynamically Links Auxiliary Classes

Additional features have also been added to the schema. Windows Server 2003 supports *dynamically linked auxiliary classes,* which allow additional attributes to be added to individual objects. For example, you can have an auxiliary class that has attributes that are used for the Accounting department, and others that are useful for the Sales department. By applying the auxiliary classes to the objects, only those objects are affected. Rather than adding attributes to an entire class of objects, dynamically linking auxiliary classes allows you to apply additional attributes to a selection of objects.

Disabling Classes

Because certain objects in Active Directory might no longer be needed after a specific point, you can disable classes and attributes that are no longer needed in the schema. Classes and attributes can be disabled, but cannot be deleted. If schema objects are not longer required, you can deactivate them, and reactivate them later if the situation changes.

Replication

Improvements have also been made in how Active Directory replicates directory data. Rather than having the entire group membership replicated as a single unit, individual members of groups can now be replicated to other DCs. In addition, changes have been made to GC replication. When there is an extension of a partial attribute set, only the attributes that have been added are replicated. These improvements decrease the amount of network traffic caused by replication because less data is transmitted across the network. You can use the following steps to raise domain and forest functionality.

Raise Domain and Forest Functionality

This should not be performed on a production network. It assumes that all DCs in the domain are running Windows Server 2003. After raising the functional levels, you will **NOT** be able to roll back to a previous level.

1. From the Windows **Start** menu, select **Administrative Tools**, and then click the **Active Directory Domains and Trusts** menu item.

2. When Active Directory Domains and Trusts opens, expand the **Active Directory Domains and Trusts** node, and select your domain.

3. From the **Action** menu, click **Raise Domain Functional Level**.

4. When the **Raise Domain Functional Level** dialog box appears, select **Windows Server 2003** from the drop-down list. Click the **Raise** button.

5. A warning message will appear, informing you that this action will affect the entire domain, and after you raise the domain functional level, it cannot be reversed. Click **OK**.

6. After you raise the level, a message box will inform you that the action was successful. Click **OK** to continue.

7. In the context pane of Active Directory Domains and Trusts, select the **Active Directory Domains and Trusts** node.

8. From the **Action** menu, click **Raise Forest Functional Level**.

9. When the **Raise Forest Functional Level** dialog box appears, select **Windows Server 2003** from the drop-down list. Click the **Raise** button.

10. A warning message will appear, informing you that this action will affect the entire forest, and after you raise the forest functional level, it cannot be reversed. Click **OK**.

11. After you raise the level, a message box will inform you that the action was successful. Click **OK** to continue.

Chapter 10

Working with User, Group, and Computer Accounts

In this chapter:

- ☑ **Understanding Active Directory Security Principal Accounts**

- ☑ **Working with Active Directory User Accounts**

- ☑ **Working with Active Directory Group Accounts**

- ☑ **Working with Active Directory Computer Accounts**

- ☑ **Managing Multiple Accounts**

Introduction

An important part of the network administrator's job involves management of the network's users and computers. Windows Server 2003 assigns accounts to both users and computers for security and management purposes. User accounts can be further managed by placing them in groups so that tasks—such as assigning permissions—can be applied to an entire group of users simultaneously rather than having to do so for each individual user account.

We show you how to work with Active Directory user accounts, including the built-in accounts and those you create. You'll also learn to work with group accounts, and you'll learn about group types and scopes. You'll learn to work with computer accounts, and how to manage multiple accounts. We'll show you how to implement *User Principal Name* (UPN) suffixes, and we'll discuss how to move objects within Active Directory.

You'll learn to use the built in tools—both graphical and command line—to perform the common administrative tasks associated with the users, groups, and computers including creating and managing all three types of accounts.

Understanding Active Directory Security Principal Accounts

Active Directory is made up of a wide variety of different directory service objects. Among these objects are security principal accounts, which consist of the following:

- User accounts
- Computer accounts
- Groups

Security principal accounts are used in authentication and access control, and provide a means to manage what can be accessed on the network. Based on the security settings associated with a security principal account, you can control whether a user, group, or computer has access to Active Directory, printer, and file system objects, as well as domain controllers (DCs), member servers, client computers, applications, and other elements of the network. They are a major factor in keeping your network protected and controlling what users and computers are authorized to access.

Security Principals and Security Identifiers

Security principals get their name because they are Active Directory objects that are assigned *Security Identifiers* (SIDs) when they are created. The SID is used to control access to resources and by internal processes to identify security principals. Because each SID is unique, unless security is breached, there is no way for accounts to mistakenly gain access to restricted resources when the system is properly configured by an administrator.

SIDs are able to remain unique because of the way they are issued. In each domain, there is a DC that acts as a Relative ID (RID) Master. The RID Master is responsible for generating relative identifiers, which are used in creating SIDs. The SID is a number that contains a domain security identifier and relative identifier. The domain ID is the same for all objects in the domain, but the relative identifier is unique. A pool of these numbers is issued to each DC within the domain, so they can be assigned to security principals that are created on the DC. When 80 percent of the numbers in the pool have been assigned to objects, DCs will then request a new pool from the RID Master.

SIDs are used because unlike the names associated with objects, SIDs don't change. When the object is created, a unique alphanumeric value is associated with it, and this stays with the object until it is deleted. Such things as changing the object's name or other attributes don't affect the SID. Because the SID is used to determine access, the user's identity remains constant, and any access the user has will be unaffected.

As shown in Figure 10.1, the SID is used as part of the authentication process. When a user logs on to a domain, the Local Security Authority (LSA) is used to authenticate to Active Directory, and create an access token. The access token is used for controlling a user's access to resources, and contains the user's logon name and SID, the names and SIDs for any groups the user is a member of, and privileges assigned to the user. The token is created each time the user logs on, and holds all of the information needed for access control.

Figure 10.1 How Security Identifiers Are Used in Access Control

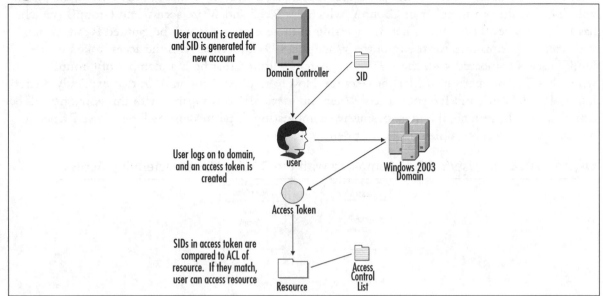

When a user attempts to access a resource, Windows Server 2003 compares the SID with the resource's security descriptor. A security descriptor contains two components, the discretionary access control list (DACL) and the system access control list (SACL). An ACL contains access control entries (ACEs), which are used to control or monitor access to a resource. An ACE determines whether a user associated with a particular SID is to be allowed or denied access, or whether the user is to be audited.

The SACL is used for auditing access to a resource. An ACE in a SACL contains information on whether logging should be generated on attempts to access a resource. This logging can be generated when a specified user or group attempts to access a resource and is successful, fails, or both.

The DACL is used for a different purpose. DACLs determine whether a security principal is granted or denied access to a resource. The DACL catalogs who has access to the resource and what level of access they have. When a user tries to access an object, the user's SID is compared to entries in the DACL. If the user's SID or the SID of a group he or she belongs to matches an entry in the DACL, that user can be either explicitly permitted or denied access to use the resource.

When a security principal attempts to access a resource that is protected by a DACL, each ACE in the DACL is analyzed in sequence to determine if access should be allowed or denied. As shown in Figure 10.2, the SID of the user and any groups he or she belongs to is compared to the ACEs in the DACL. Windows Server 2003 will look at each ACE until one of the following occurs:

- An entry is found that explicitly denies access to the resource.

- One or more entries are found that explicitly grants access to the resource.

- The entire DACL is searched but no ACE is found that explicitly grants or denies access. Since no entry is found, the security principal is implicitly denied access.

In Figure 10.2, one user is granted access while the other is denied access. When the SIDs associated with the access token of the JaneS user is compared with the entries in the DACL, the system will find that she is a member of GroupA (which has Read and Write access) and GroupB (which has Execute access). Because of her membership in these groups, she will be granted Read, Write, and Execute permissions for the resource. When the SIDs associated with the access token of the JohnD user is compared with the DACL, the system will find that he is a member of GroupB, which has Execute permission for the resource. However, there is also an ACE that explicitly denies JohnD Read, Write, and Execute access. When the user's SID is compared with this entry, he will be denied access. In general, the most permissive combination of permissions will be allowed when a user accesses a resource, unless an explicit deny is assigned.

Figure 10.2 The User's SID Is Compared with the DACL's ACE to Determine Access

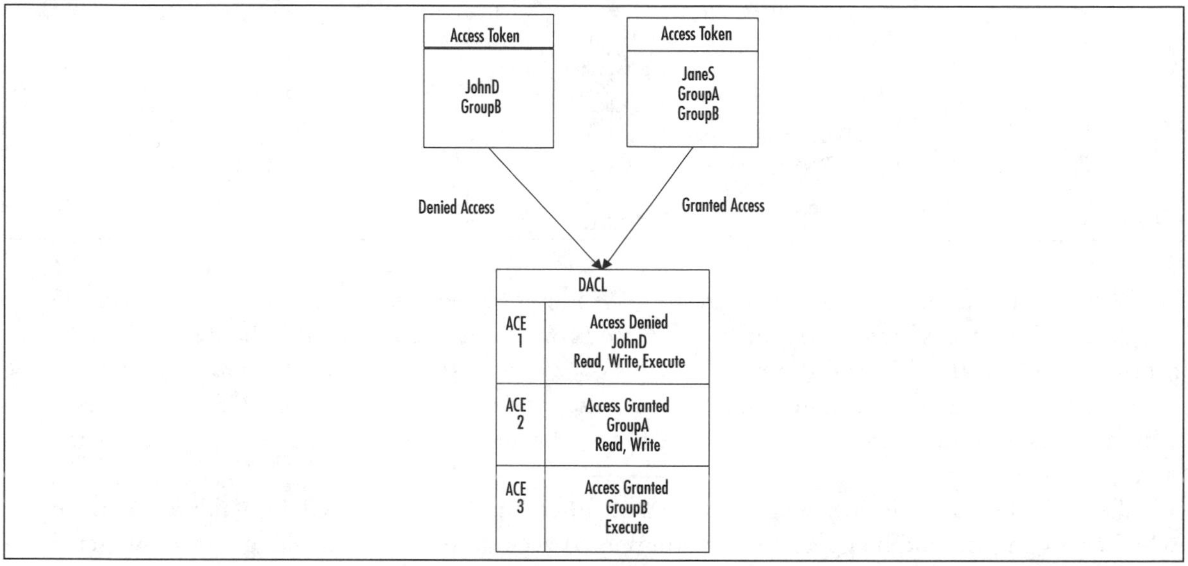

In addition to containing the user's SID and the SIDs of any groups the user is a member of, the access token might also contain additional SIDs that result from group membership the operating system assigns dynamically or other special logon scenarios. These SIDs are common to installations of Windows Server 2003 in a stand-alone and/or Active Directory environment, and for this reason are referred to as *well-known security identifiers*. Table 10.1 lists the different types of well-known SIDs.

Table 10.1 Well-Known Security Identifiers

Type of SID	SID	Description
Anonymous Logon	S-1-5-7	Used when a user logs on without supplying a username and password.
Authenticated Users	S-1-5-11	Used when users or computers have been authenticated with individual accounts. The exception is when someone logs on with the Guest account, as this isn't considered an authenticated user.
Batch	S-1-5-3	Used when users log on through a batch queue facility, such as when scheduled tasks are run under a specific account.
Creator Owner	S-1-3-0	Used as a placeholder in inheritable ACEs. When an ACE is inherited, this SID is replaced with the SID of the current owner of the object.
Creator Group	S-1-3-1	Used as a placeholder in inheritable ACEs. When an ACE is inherited, this SID is replaced with the SID of the primary group to which the object's current owner belongs.
Dialup	S-1-5-1	Used when the user logs on to the system using a dial-up connection.
Everyone	S-1-1-0	Used to specify the Everyone group. In Windows Server 2003, this includes authenticated users and the Guest account. Earlier versions of Windows include these accounts and anonymous logons.
Interactive	S-1-5-4	Used for users who are logged on to the local machine (as opposed to connecting via the network) or connected through Terminal Services.
Local System	S-1-5-18	Used for a service account that's run by Windows.
Network	S-1-5-2	Used when a user logs on through a network connection. Because of the methods in which interactive users log on to the system, this type of SID isn't used for their access tokens.
Other Organization	S-1-5-1000	Used to determine whether users from other domains or forests are permitted to authenticate to services.
Self/Principal Self	S-1-5-10	Used as a placeholder in ACEs. When permissions are granted to Principal Self, they are given access to the security principal represented by the object. The SID acting as a placeholder is replaced during access checks with the SID for the user, group, or computer represented by the object.
Service	S-1-5-6	Used for security principals that log on as a service.

Continued

Table 10.1 Well-Known Security Identifiers

Type of SID	SID	Description
Terminal Server Users	S-1-5-13	Used for users that log on to a Terminal Services server running in Terminal Services version 4.0 application compatibility mode.
This Organization	S-1-5-15	Used to add data to the authentication information of the user who's logged on by the authentication server. This is used if the Other Organization SID isn't used.

Tools to View and Manage Security Identifiers

Windows Server 2003 provides command-line utilities that can be used to view and manage SIDs. Because of the way in which SIDs are handled in a domain, it is rare to ever need this capability. However, should the need arise, it is useful to know these tools exist.

As we saw in Chapter 9, "Active Directory Infrastructure Overview," the WHOAMI tool allows you to display information about the user who is currently logged on. By using the */ALL* parameter, you can display all of the user's access token information, including information on the username, groups, associated SIDs, and privileges, for the user who is currently logged on. The syntax for viewing this information is:

```
WHOAMI /ALL
```

The NTDSUTIL tool is another tool that can be used to manage SIDs in rare instances where duplicate SIDs exist. To avoid potential conflicts of DCs issuing the same SID to an object, only one RID Master exists in a domain. While this will generally ensure that SIDs are unique within a domain, there is the remote possibility that duplicate SIDs can be still be issued. Duplicate SIDs can be found and dealt with by using the Security Account Management menu of NTDSUTIL. By typing **security account management** from the NTDSUTIL prompt, commands shown in Table 10.2 can be accessed. Using these commands, you can check the domain for any objects with duplicate SIDs and delete them to resolve the issue.

Table 10.2 Commands Available in NTDSUTIL from the Security Account Management Menu

Command	Description
Check duplicate SID	Checks the local SAM or domain database for objects with duplicate SIDs.
Cleanup duplicate SID	Checks the local SAM or domain database for objects with duplicate SIDs and deletes them.
Connect to server %s	Specifies the server or DC to connect to. %s is a variable denoting the server or DC to connect to.

Continued

Table 10.2 Commands Available in NTDSUTIL from the Security Account Management Menu

Command	Description
Log file %s	Specifies where to create a log file. %s is a variable denoting a location. If this parameter isn't used, events will be logged to a file named dupsid.log that will be placed in the root folder of the profile for the user who executes the command.
Quit	Returns to previous menu. When the main menu is displayed again, this command will exit you from NTDSUTIL.
? or help	Displays help.

Naming Conventions and Limitations

In looking at the relationship between security principals and SIDs, it becomes apparent that it would be difficult to use SIDs as the sole method of identifying an account. While SIDs uniquely identify users, computers, and groups, trying to remember the SID of users and computers you commonly access through the directory would be almost impossible. For this reason, various naming conventions are used to distinguish objects in Active Directory.

In Windows Server 2003, a number of different boundaries exist to logically group objects and manage them. For example, domains provide a boundary that allows two computers with the same name to exist in different domains. Similarly, the *User Principal Name* (UPN) in Windows Server 2003 must be unique in each forest, and Pre-Windows 2000 logon names must be unique in each domain. Even if you're new to Windows Server 2003 networks, you're probably familiar with how domains are named on the Internet, which is the largest DNS namespace in the world. Active Directory domains follow the same naming conventions as DNS.

As shown in Figure 10.3, an Active Directory namespace is arranged in a hierarchy. This contiguous namespace provides a way of conveying how the hierarchical structure of the domains is designed in a network.

Figure 10.3 Hierarchical Structure of an Active Directory Namespace

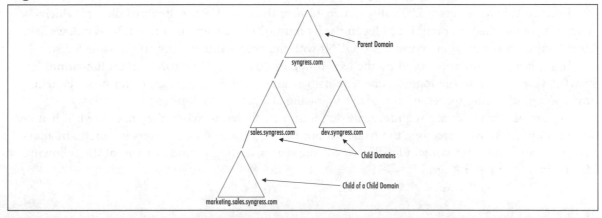

In looking at Figure 10.3, you can see that syngress.com is the parent domain, and that it has two child domains (sales.syngress.com and dev.syngress.com). Because a child domain can also have child domains beneath it, we also see that sales.syngress.com has its own child domain called marketing.sales.syngress.com.

In addition to providing a method to uniquely identify domains within a namespace, individual computers are also provided with unique names that relate to the hierarchy. To show the place of these computers in a DNS domain structure, *Fully Qualified Domain Names* (FQDNs) are used, which combine the host name with the domain name. In Active Directory, the computer name is also appended to the name of the domain of which it is a member. This combination can be up to 255 characters in length. When creating computer accounts in Active Directory, the name of the computer can only consist of letters (a to z, A to Z), numbers (0 to 9), and hyphens (-). The name cannot consist of all numbers.

Because pre-Windows 2000 computers didn't use a DNS-like naming scheme, Active Directory also allows NetBIOS names to be used for backward compatibility. By providing support for NetBIOS names and pre-Windows 2000 domain naming schemes, older clients can access Windows Server 2003 computers and domains.

In addition to names used by computers and domains, user accounts also have distinct methods of being named. User accounts have a UPN that can be used to log on from Windows 2000, XP Professional, and Server 2003 machines. They also have a backward-compatible login name known as the pre-Windows 2000 name. During the process of creating a new user account, Active Directory will suggest a pre-Windows 2000 name that is based on the first 20 characters of the UPN that you type in. Either name can be changed at any time. The pre-Windows 2000 logon name is limited to 20 characters. Although the pre-Windows 2000 name can still be used to log on to domains on newer operating systems, the UPN logon name is preferred when logging on from Windows 2000 or later. UPNs consist of a logon account name and a UPN suffix, which is the domain name that contains the user account by default. The logon name and UPN suffix is connected together using the at (@) sign. This makes it appear like an Internet e-mail address (username@domain).

While the default UPN suffix for a user account is the domain containing the account, other UPN suffixes can also be used. To make it simpler to log on to the network, Active Directory allows you to implement a single UPN suffix for all users. In such a case, you could have all users have the forest root domain name as their UPN suffix, or even create alternate UPN suffixes. In using alternate UPN suffixes, you aren't limited to using valid DNS or Active Directory domain names. You can use any UPN suffix you choose.

Because Windows Server 2003 allows users to have the same UPN suffix regardless of which domain contains their account, UPN logon names must be unique within a forest. In Windows Server 2003, Active Directory won't permit two UPNs with the same name to exist in the same forest.

In creating a name that's used by the user to log on to Active Directory, certain limitations exist in what you can use in the logon name. The name cannot contain all spaces, or must not contain any leading or trailing spaces, or any of the following characters: " / \ [ ] : ; | = , + * ? < >

Groups also have certain requirements that must be adhered to when they're created. When creating groups in Active Directory, the name cannot be longer than 64 characters in length. In addition, the name must not contain leading or trailing spaces, trailing periods, or any of the following characters: / [ ] : | = ? * , + " \ < > ;

Security principals also make use of three other types of naming conventions, which are common to all objects in Active Directory:

- Relative Distinguished Name (RDN)
- Distinguished name (DN)
- Canonical name

Through these naming conventions, security principals can be located in the directory using the *Lightweight Directory Access Protocol* (LDAP). Each of these is used to identify objects in Active Directory, and provide methods of locating objects within the directory, regardless of how many layers of organizational units (OUs) it is stored under.

Relative Distinguished Names (RDNs) refer to the name of the object in relation to where it is located in the directory. In other words, it doesn't show the path to where you can find the object in the directory structure. For example, a user object named John Smith would be a valid RDN. In looking at this name, however, you wouldn't know whether it was stored in the Users container or another location.

Because the RDN identifies the object within a container, this name must be unique within the container in which it is stored. In other words, you can't have two users named John Smith in the same OU. If two objects did exist with the same name, confusion could occur as to which object you really wanted to access.

To provide more specific information concerning the exact location of an object within the directory's hierarchy, a *Distinguished Name* (DN) is used. The DN is used to show the *path* to an object. It says that the object is located in a particular domain, and possibly even within a specific OU. This path identifies the name of the object, and the hierarchy to the container in which it is stored. To provide this information, the DN uses the following notations:

- **CN** The common name of the object.
- **OU** An organizational unit that contains the object, or contains another OU in the hierarchical path to the OU that contains the object.
- **DC** A domain component that specifies a DNS name in the hierarchy to the object. Just as with OU objects, there may be multiple domain components in the hierarchical path to the object.

As shown in Figure 10.4, the DN uses these notations to provide a map to how you can find a single object within the structure of Active Directory. In Figure 10.4, we see that there are a number of users located in the Accounts Receivable OU, which resides in the Accounting OU of knightware.ca. If you wanted to find a user object named John Doe within this structure, you would use the following DN:

```
CN=John Doe,OU=Accounts Receivable,OU=Accounting,DC=knightware,DC=ca
```

In comparing the DN to Figure 10.4, you can see that it starts with the object, and works its way up to the highest level of the structure.

Figure 10.4 Distinguished Names Are Used to Show Location of Objects

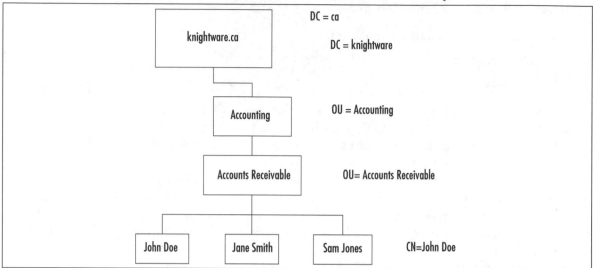

As mentioned earlier, the CN within the DN is also the RDN of the object. The RDN uniquely identifies an object within a parent container, and in the case of our previous example, refers to the John Smith object. In this case, we could refer to the RDN as follows:

```
CN=John Smith
```

Another way of looking at this same information is with the canonical name. *Canonical names* provide the same information as the DN, but in reverse. Rather than beginning with the object and working its way up the highest level, the canonical name starts at the highest level and works its way down. In looking at the previous example, the DN "CN=John Doe, OU=Accounts Receivable, OU=Accounting, DC=knightware, DC=ca" would be translated to the following canonical name:

```
knightware.ca/Accounting/Accounts Receivable/John Doe
```

By providing different options for identifying objects and their location in the directory, there is greater versatility in the methods tools that you can use to access these objects. Before using DNs, RDNs, and canonical names, you need to give the object a unique name. As we'll see in the sections that follow, the names for users, computers, and groups are specified when the security principal itself is created.

Working with Active Directory User Accounts

In Windows Server 2003, two different types of user accounts can be created: local and domain-based user accounts. Local user accounts are used to control access to the computer on which you are working. They are created on Windows Server 2003 by using the Local Users and Groups snap-in, or the Users node under the Local Users and Groups node in the Computer Management utility. Once created, the account information is stored in a local database called the *Security Accounts Manager* (SAM). The account information only applies to the local computer, and isn't replicated to other machines within the domain. When a user logs on to the computer, Windows Server 2003 authenticates the user with this information, and either permits or denies access to the machine.

Domain accounts are created in Active Directory and are considerably different from local user accounts. Rather than storing information on the local machine, account information is stored in the directory and replicated to other DCs. As we discussed earlier in this chapter, when the user logs on to a DC, the account information is used to build an access token. This access token is used for the duration of time that the user is logged on to the network, and determines what the user is allowed to access on the network, and actions he or she can perform.

Active Directory user accounts are created and managed using the Active Directory Users and Computers snap-in. As shown in the Figure 10.5, this snap-in provides a graphical user interface (GUI) that allows you to point-and-click through the various tasks related to administering user objects. The left pane of this tool is the console tree, which contains nodes representing your domain and the container objects within your domain such as OUs. Expanding the node of a domain displays the containers, which can be selected to view objects stored within them. These objects within the container are displayed in the right pane of the console.

Figure 10.5 Active Directory Users and Computers

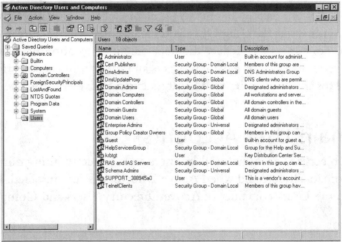

As mentioned in Chapter 9, a number of containers are automatically created when Active Directory is first installed. Each stores different types of objects, some of which are used in managing users and computers on the network. These containers are:

- **Builtin** The default location for most domain local groups that are created during the installation of Windows Server 2003 and Active Directory. A few service-specific domain local groups, such as the DnsAdmins group, are created in the Users container.

- **Computers** The default location that is used to store computer objects for members of the domain. This container does not contain objects for Active Directory DCs.

- **Domain Controllers** The default location that is used to store Active Directory DC objects.

- **ForeignSecurityPrincipals** The Active Directory location used to store foreign SIDs for user accounts in external trusted domains.

- **Users** The default location for user accounts, global groups, and universal groups that are created during the installation of Active Directory. This container often contains additional domain local groups that are used by services such as RRAS and DNS.

In addition to these containers, others also exist that are hidden. You must enable Advanced Features to display these additional containers. To do this, select **View | Advanced Features**. Once enabled, the following containers can then be seen:

- **LostAndFound** Used to store objects whose parent containers no longer exist. If an object is created on one DC close to the time that its parent container is deleted on another DC (or if it is moved to a location that's missing after replication), the object is considered orphaned and is placed in this container.

- **System** Contains information about the domain, objects used by Active Directory, and the underlying Windows Server 2003 operating system. Unlike most of the other containers, the objects in this container generally cannot be modified by the administrator.

While these containers are created by Active Directory, objects can also be stored in OUs that are created by the administrator. By using OUs, you can arrange user accounts, computer accounts, and other objects into containers that reflect the department or location of these objects. For example, you could create an OU for a branch office, and then store accounts for users at that location within the OU. This makes it easier to delegate administrative control, and manage users using Group Policy.

Built-In Domain User Accounts

You can create user objects for accounts used by users and services within your organization in addition to those automatically created when Active Directory is first installed. These built-in accounts are stored in the Users container of Active Directory Users and Computers, and are:

- Administrator
- Guest
- HelpAssistant
- SUPPORT_388945a0
- InetOrgPerson

While we'll discuss each of these accounts in the sections that follow, it is important to realize that each of the accounts created by Active Directory is assigned group memberships and user rights that provide different levels of access.

Administrator

The Administrator account is the first account that's created when Active Directory is installed. As we saw in the previous chapter, when you use the Active Directory Installation Wizard and set up a new domain, this account is created to give you the access to perform domain configuration. Once created, it can be used to create and manage security principals and other objects, administer policies, assign permissions, and other tasks needed in the design and administration of Active Directory.

The Administrator account has the highest level of access of any default account created in Active Directory. It is a member of the Administrators, Domain Admins, Domain Users, Enterprise Admins, Group Policy Creator Owners, and Schema Admins groups. Due to the importance of the Administrator account, it cannot be deleted from Active Directory, or removed from the Administrators group. It can, however, be disabled or renamed to make it more difficult for unauthorized or malicious users to use this account by guessing its password.

Guest

The Guest account is another built-in account, but provides the lowest level of access. It is designed to be used by occasional users who need minimal access and don't want to log on with their own account, or users who don't have an account of their own in the domain.

When Active Directory creates this account, it makes the Guest account a member of the Guests group and Domain Guests global group. Membership in these groups allows a person using this account to log on to the domain. Just as with other accounts, you can control what rights and permissions this account has, and add or remove this account from group memberships.

Because it is better for users to have their own accounts when logging on to the domain, the Guest account is disabled by default. Having this account disabled prevents unauthorized persons from using this account to access the domain, and potentially use it to obtain additional levels of access. As we saw with the Administrator account, the Guest account can't be deleted, but can be renamed.

HelpAssistant

The HelpAssistant account is automatically created in Active Directory when a Remote Assistance session is established. Remote Assistance allows a user to connect to a machine and assist them, such as by taking control of the computer remotely. For example, a person working Help Desk could take over a user's computer remotely, and show the user how to perform a particular task.

To prevent others from indiscriminately taking over a computer and performing tasks while a person is logged on, this connection is established with the permission of the person using the computer. This account is managed by the Remote Desktop Help Session Manager service, and is deleted automatically when there are no pending Remote Assistance requests. Because it is removed when no longer needed, it doesn't always appear in the Users container of Active Directory Users and Computers.

SUPPORT_388945a0

The Support_388945a0 account is used by the Help and Support Service to provide interoperability with and allow access to signed scripts that are made available within Help and Support Services. An administrator can delegate the ability for a normal user to run these scripts from links in Help and Support Services. The scripts can be programmed to use the Support_388945a0 account instead of the logged-on user's credentials to perform administrative tasks on the local system that the user would not typically be allowed to perform without administrative-level access.

InetOrgPerson

InetOrgPerson accounts are used to represent users in non-Microsoft directory services. While Active Directory is the only directory service used by Windows 2000 and Windows Server 2003, it isn't the only directory service in existence. Other network operating systems, such as Novell NetWare, use their own implementations of a directory service, which aren't always compatible with Active Directory. The InetOrgPerson is used to assist applications written for other directories, or when migrating from these directory services to Active Directory.

Unlike the previous accounts we've discussed, InetOrgPerson accounts don't actually refer to an account named InetOrgPerson, but an object class used to create accounts. Because it exists as a type of user class, accounts created with this class are security principals. InetOrgPerson accounts are created in the same way that user accounts are created.

Creating User Accounts

Windows Server 2003 provides multiple ways of creating user accounts in Active Directory. As mentioned, Active Directory Users and Computers provides a GUI that allows you to create new accounts quickly and efficiently. As a new method of adding user accounts to Active Directory, you can also use the *DSADD* command. In the paragraphs that follow, we will look at each of these tools.

Creating Accounts Using Active Directory Users and Computers

Active Directory Users and Computers is a tool that is installed on DCs, and is used by those with the appropriate access to create domain accounts. Only members of the Administrators group, Account Operators group, Domain Admins group, Enterprise Admins group, or someone who's been delegated authority can create a user account. Responsibility can be delegated through the Delegation of Control Wizard, Group Policy, or security groups (which we'll discuss later in this chapter).

Active Directory Users and Computers is started in a number of ways. The Active **Directory Users and Computers** snap-in can be loaded into **Microsoft Management Console** (MMC). Using the Windows **Start** menu can also start this tool by clicking on **Start | Administrative Tools | Active Directory Users and Computers**. The final method of starting it is through the Control Panel. In **Control Panel**, open **Performance and Maintenance | Administrative Tools | Active Directory Users and Computers**. Use the following steps to create a user object in Active Directory.

Create a User Object in Active Directory

1. Open **Active Directory Users and Computers from Start | Administrative Tools Active Directory Users and Computers**.

2. When the utility opens, expand the console tree so that your domain and the containers within it are visible.

3. Select the **TestOU** OU that you created in Chapter 9 from the console tree. If you did not create a TestOU earlier, create one now. From the **Action** menu, select **New | User**.

4. When the **New Object – User** dialog box appears, enter the following information in the corresponding fields:

Field	Data to Enter
First name	John
Initials	Q
Last name	Public
Full name	John Public
User logon name	Jpublic
User logon name (pre-Windows 2000)	Jpublic

5. After entering this information, click the **Next** button to continue.

6. Enter a password of your choosing in the **Password** field, and then reenter it in the **Confirm password** field.

7. Clear the **User must change password at next logon** check box.

8. Click **Next** to continue. When the summary screen appears, review the settings you have entered and click **Finish** to create the account.

9. From the **Action** menu, select **New | User**.

10. When the **New Object – User** dialog box appears, enter the following information in the corresponding fields:

Field	Data to Enter
First name	Jane
Last name	Doe
Full name	Jane Doe
User logon name	Jdoe
User logon name (pre-Windows 2000)	Jdoe

11. After entering this information, click the **Next** button to continue.

12. Enter a password of your choosing in the **Password** field, and then reenter it in the **Confirm password** field.

13. Click **Next** to continue. When the summary screen appears, review the settings you have entered and click **Finish** to create the account.

14. Log off and then log back on as the jdoe user. Notice that you are required to change the password.

15. Log off and then log back on as the jpublic user. Notice that you aren't required to change the password.

Creating Accounts Using the DSADD Command

Windows Server 2003 includes a number of command-line tools that allow you to perform common administrative tasks from a command prompt. Using the **DSADD** command, you can create new objects in Active Directory, including user objects. As is the case when using Active Directory Users and Computers, only members of the Administrators group, Account Operators group, Domain Admins group, Enterprise Admins group, or someone who's been delegated authority can create a user account. This means that the DSADD command can't be used as a workaround to creating an account without authorization.

Create a new user with DSADD by entering the following syntax:

```
DSADD USER UserDN [-samid SAMName] -pwd {Password|*}
```

In entering this command, the following parameters must be entered:

- *UserDN* This is the DN of the user object you are adding. This provides information on where the account will be created.

- *SAMName* This is a NetBIOS name, which is used when logging on from pre-Windows 2000 computers. If this parameter isn't added, DSADD will create one, based on the first 20 characters of the common name you entered for the UserDN parameter.

- *Password* This is the password that will be used for this account. If an asterisk (*) is entered for this parameter, you will be prompted to enter a password.

In addition to these parameters, additional settings can be applied when creating a user account by using the following syntax. Note that this is all one long line.

```
dsadd user UserDN [-samid SAMName] [-upn UPN] [-fn FirstName] [-mi
Initial] [-ln LastName] [-display DisplayName] [-empid EmployeeID]
[-pwd {Password | *}] [-desc Description] [-memberof Group;...]
[-office Office] [-tel PhoneNumber] [-email Email] [-hometel
HomePhoneNumber] [-pager PagerNumber] [-mobile CellPhoneNumber]
[-fax FaxNumber] [-iptel IPPhoneNumber] [-webpg WebPage] [-title Title]
[-dept Department] [-company Company] [-mgr ManagerDN] [-hmdir
HomeDirectory] [-hmdrv DriveLetter:] [-profile ProfilePath] [-loscr
ScriptPath] [-mustchpwd {yes | no}] [-canchpwd {yes | no}]
[-reversiblepwd {yes | no}] [-pwdneverexpires {yes | no}] [-acctexpires
```

NumberOfDays] [**-disabled** {**yes** | **no**}] [{**-s** *Server* | **-d** *Domain*}]

[**-u** *UserName*] [**-p** {*Password* | ***}] [**-q**] [{**-uc** | **-uco** | **-uci**}]

As you can see, a considerable number of options can be set in using the DSADD command, which are not available when initially creating an account with Active Directory Users and Computers. We'll explain how such information can be added to an account with Active Directory Users and Computers in the next section. First, let's examine the various parameters that can be used in association with the DSADD command. The parameters in this syntax are explained in Table 10.3.

Table 10.3 DSADD Parameters for Creating Users

Parameter	Description
-upn *UPN*	Specifies the UPN for the account.
-fn *FirstName*	Specifies the first name of the user.
-mi *Initial*	Specifies the initial(s) of the user.
-ln *LastName*	Specifies the last name of the user.
-display *DisplayName*	Specifies the display name of the account.
-empid *EmployeeID*	Specifies the user's employee ID.
-desc *Description*	Information that describes the account.
-memberof *Group*	Specifies the DNs of groups of which this account will be a member.
-office *Office*	Specifies the office location of the user.
-tel *PhoneNumber*	Specifies the telephone number of the user.
-email *Email*	Specifies the user's e-mail address.
-hometel *HomePhoneNumber*	Specifies the user's home telephone number.
-pager *PagerNumber*	Specifies the pager number of the user.
-mobile *CellPhoneNumber*	Specifies the cellular telephone number of the user.
-fax *FaxNumber*	Specifies the user's fax number.
-iptel *IPPhoneNumber*	Specifies the user's IP phone number.
-webpg *WebPage*	Specifies the URL of the user's Web page.
-title *Title*	Specifies the title of the user.
-dept *Department*	Specifies the user's department.
-company *Company*	Specifies company information.
-mgr *ManagerDN*	Specifies the DN of the user's manager.
-hmdir *HomeDirectory*	Specifies the home directory of the user.
-hmdrv *DriveLetter*:	Specifies the drive letter used by the user to access his or her home directory. This parameter is used if the *HomeDirectory* is specified using the universal naming convention.
-profile *ProfilePath*	Specifies the profile path for the account.

Continued

Table 10.3 DSADD Parameters for Creating Users

Parameter	Description
-loscr *ScriptPath*	Specifies the logon script path for the account.
-mustchpwd {yes | no}	Specifies whether the user needs to change his or her password the next time he or she logs on. By default, the user doesn't need to change the password, so this would be the same as specifying no for this parameter.
-canchpwd {yes | no}	Specifies whether the user is allowed to change his or her password. By default, the user can change his or her password, so this would be the same as specifying yes for this parameter.
-reversiblepwd {yes | no}	Specifies whether the password is stored using reversible encryption, which is used by Macintosh computers and some forms of Windows-based authentication. By default, reversible encryption isn't used, so this is the same as this parameter being set to no.
-pwdneverexpires {yes | no}	Specifies whether the password expires. By default, a password will expire, so this is the same as this parameter being set to no.
-acctexpires *NumberOfDays*	Specifies the number of days before the account expires. If the value of *NumberOfDays* is set to 0, the account will expire at the end of the day. If the value of *NumberOfDays* is set to a negative value, it will set that the account has already expired that many days ago. If set to a positive value, it will expire that many days in the future. If the value of *NumberOfDays* is set to Never, the account will never expire.
-disabled {yes | no}	Specifies whether the account has been disabled. By default, the account is enabled, so this is the same as this parameter being set to no.
{-s *Server* | -d *Domain*}	Specifies to connect to a remote server or domain. By default, the computer is connected to the DC in the logon domain.
-u *UserName*	Specifies the username to log on to a remote server. By default, the username that the user is logged on to the local system with is used. The following formats can be used for the *UserName* variable: Username Domain\username User principal name
-p {*Password* | *}	Specifies the password to log on to a remote server. If an asterisk (*) is used, you will be prompted for a password.
-q	Specifies quiet mode, and suppresses output.

Continued

Table 10.3 DSADD Parameters for Creating Users

Parameter	Description
{-uc | -uco | -uci}	Specifies Unicode to be used for input or output. If –uc is used, then input or output is to a pipe (|). If –uco is used, then output is to a pipe or file. If –uci is used, then input is from a pipe or file.

Managing User Accounts

Managing user accounts is done through the properties of the object, which is accessible by using Active Directory Users and Computers. You can access the properties of a user object by selecting the object, and then clicking on **Action | Properties**. You can also right-click on the object and select **Properties** from the context menu.

Upon opening the Properties of the user, you will see a number of tabs that allow you to set various options and provide information dealing with the account including general information, settings for Terminal Services, certificate information and group membership, among others. Individually, each of the tabs allows you to manage different settings related to the user account. However, a number of these tabs are related, in that they deal with particular aspects of user account management. As we'll see in the sections that follow, by using them together, you can configure how the account can be used.

Personal Information Tabs

In looking at what properties can be set with these tabs, you will see that there are four tabs that contain personal information about the user: General, Address, Telephones, and Organization. As shown in Figure 10.6, the General tab contains a number of fields that contain information provided when the account was initially created.

In looking at this tab, notice that Telephone and Web page fields have a button beside them named Other. When this button is clicked, a dialog box will open that allows you to enter additional entries. As you might guess, this is because many users might have more than one Web page or telephone number associated with them. If additional entries exist, you can also click the **Other** button to view these entries in the dialog box that appears.

Figure 10.6 General Tab of User's Properties

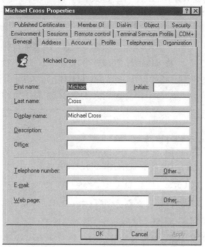

The Address tab is used to store contact information dealing with a user's physical or mailing address, as shown in Figure 10.7.

Figure 10.7 Address Tab of a User's Properties

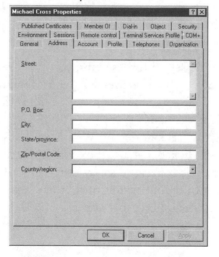

The Telephones tab is another tab that contains personal properties related to the user. As shown in Figure 10.8, this tab provides contact information relating to various methods of verbal or digital communication. Because users might have multiple telephone numbers, pagers, and other methods of communication, each of these fields (except for Notes) also includes an Other button.

Figure 10.8 Telephones Tab of User's Properties

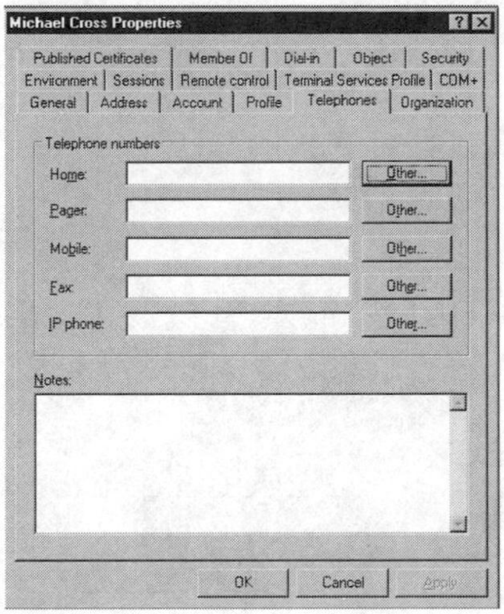

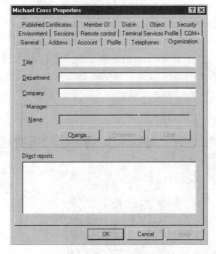

The Organization tab is the final tab that contains personal properties for the user. This tab allows you to enter information relating to the organization in which the user works, as seen in Figure 10.9.

Figure 10.9 Organization Tab of User's Properties

Account Settings

Not all of the tabs in the user's Properties deal with personal information. As seen in Figure 10.10, the Account tab is used to store information relating to the domain user account, including password options. The fields on this tab include:

Figure 10.10 Account Tab of User's Properties

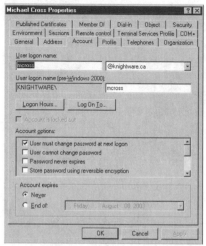

In addition to the fields shown, the Account tab also includes a Logon Hours button, which opens a dialog box that allows you to control when this user can log on or remain logged on to the network. By default, users are able to log on and remain logged on to the network 24 hours a day, 7 days a week. However, in secure environments, you might want to control when a user is able to log on. To provide a maintenance window, you might want to limit users' ability to log on or remain logged on after regular hours of work, or during weekends.

As shown in Figure 10.11, the Logon Hours dialog box contains a series of boxes that determine the times and days when a user can log on. After selecting the boxes representing the times and dates to log on, click the **Logon Permitted** or **Logon Denied** option buttons to respectively permit or deny access during those times. If all of the boxes are selected and **Logon Permitted** is selected, then there are no restrictions set for the user.

Figure 10.11 Logon Hours Dialog Box

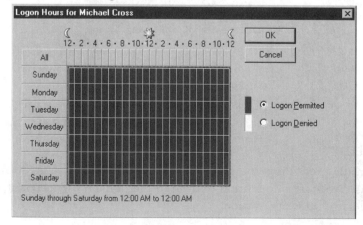

The other button that appears on the Account tab is the Log On To button. When this button is clicked, the Logon Workstations dialog box shown in Figure 10.12 appears. On this dialog box, you can control what computers the user can use when logging on to the domain. By default, users can log on from any computer. However, by using the fields on this tab you can heighten security by limiting users to working on the machine at their desk, or a group of computers within their department. For example, you might want to prevent users from logging on to the domain from a specific machine so that they cannot access another user's data that is stored on that computer.

Figure 10.12 Logon Workstations Dialog Box

The Profile tab is also used to configure elements of the user's account, relating to profiles, logon scripts, and home folders. Roaming profiles can be used to provide consistency across the network, by ensuring that a user has the same desktop environment, application settings, drive mappings, and personal data regardless of which computer he or she uses on the network. The **Profile path** field on this tab is used to specify the path to the user's profile. Similarly, logon scripts are also used to apply settings to a user's account, by running a script when the user logs on to the network. The **Logon script** field is used to set where this script is located, so it will automatically run each time the user logs on to this account. Through these, the user's environment is configured each time he or she logs on to a DC.

Finally, as shown in Figure 10.13, the **Home folder** section of this tab is used to specify the location of a home directory that will contain the user's personal files. The **Local path** text box is used to specify a path to the directory on the local system. Alternatively, you can specify a network location by using the **Connect** drop-down box to specify a drive letter that the path will be mapped to, and then enter a UNC path to the directory in the **To** text box.

Figure 10.13 Profile Tab of User's Properties

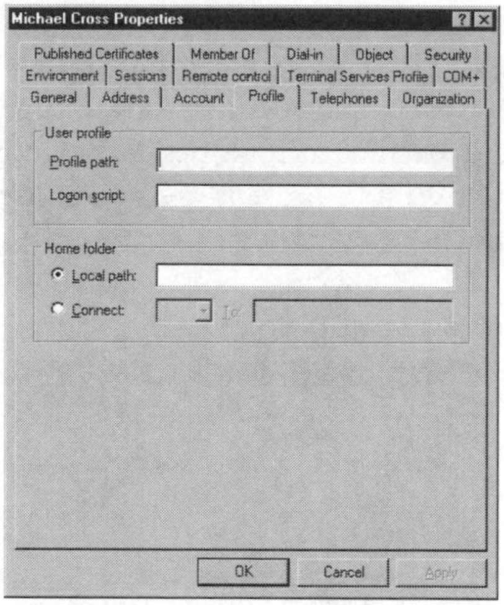

Terminal Services Tabs

Terminal Services allows users to access applications that are run on the server. Terminal Services is discussed in detail at the end of this book.

The Properties dialog box of a user provides four tabs that specifically deal with Terminal Services: Environment, Sessions, Remote Control, and Terminal Services Profile. As seen in Figure 10.14, the **Environment** tab is used to configure settings for Terminal Service's startup environment. By default, users receive a Windows Server 2003 desktop when connecting using Terminal Services. The **Starting program** section contains fields for specifying a particular program to run when logging on to Terminal Services. If this option is enabled, users will receive the program instead of a desktop. When the **Start the following program at logon** check box is selected, you can enter the path and executable name for the program.

Figure 10.14 Environment Tab of User's Properties

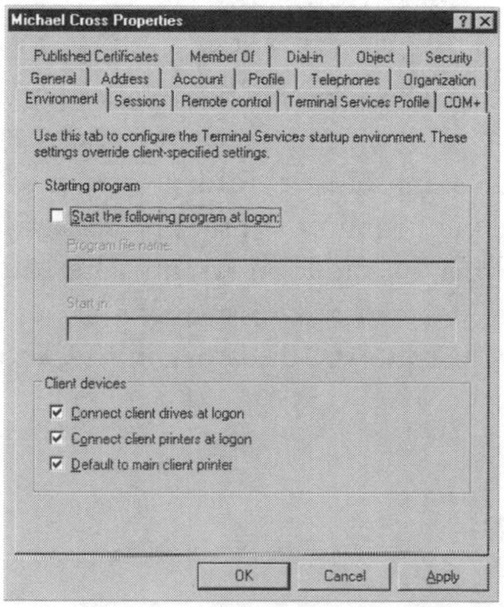

The **Client devices** section also allows you to configure how devices on the computer you're working on will be dealt with. In addition to the settings on the Environment tab, the Sessions tab is also used for configuring Terminal Services. As seen in Figure 10.15, this tab includes numerous settings for configuring timeout and reconnection settings for Terminal Services sessions.

Figure 10.15 Sessions Tab of User's Properties

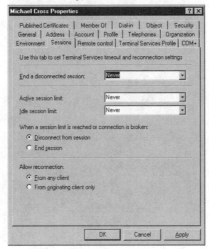

The Remote Control tab allows you to configure remote control settings for the user, which enables others to take over a session. By taking over the computer, the other person can then perform actions on the remote computer, enabling that person to perform various actions and show the user how to do certain tasks. As shown in Figure 10.16, the fields available to configure these settings are:

Figure 10.16 Remote Control Tab of User's Properties

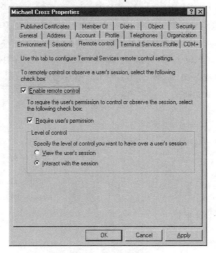

The Terminal Services Profile tab is similar to the Profile tab discussed earlier, except that settings on this tab exclusively relate to a user's Terminal Services session, as shown in Figure 10.17.

Figure 10.17 Terminal Services Profile

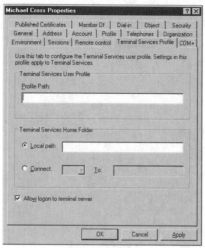

Security-Related Tabs

Several tabs are available through the user object's properties that control security settings associated with the account. These tabs are Published Certificates, Dial-in, Security, and Member Of. Together, they allow you to manage issues related to access control and authentication.

The Published Certificates tab provides a listing of certificates that are used by the account, and allows you to add others. As shown in Figure 10.18, this tab allows you to view any X.509 certificates that have been published for the user account, and includes fields that explain who it was issued by, who it was issued to, the intended purpose of the certificate, and its expiration date. The **Add from Store** button can be used to add additional certificates to the listing from the computer's local certificate store. The **Add from File** button can also be used to add a certificate from a file. If a certificate is no longer needed, you can select the one you no longer want to be applied to the account and click the **Remove** button. Finally, the **Copy to File** button will export the certificate that is selected in the list to a file.

Figure 10.18 Published Certificates

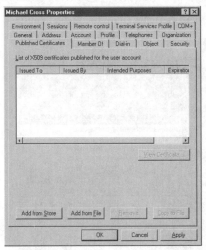

The Dial-in tab allows you to configure settings that are used when the user attempts to connect to the network remotely using a dial-up or VPN connection. Remote access is discussed in detail later in this book. This section describes the user account settings related to remote access. These settings are applied when the user dials in to a Windows Server 2003 remote access server or attempts to use a VPN connection, as shown in Figure 10.19.

Figure 10.19 Dial-In Tab

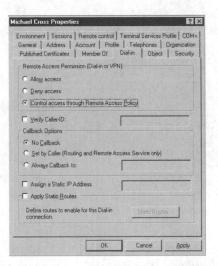

The Security tab (Figure 10.20) is used to configure what permissions other users and groups have to an object. This tab consists of two panes. The top pane lists users and groups that have been added to the DACL for the account. It also allows you to add or remove users and groups from the DACL. In the lower pane, you can enable or disable specific permissions by checking a check box in the Allow or Deny column. Special permissions can also be set for objects by clicking the

Advanced button, which displays a dialog box (seen in Figure 10.21) where additional permissions can be applied.

Figure 10.20 Security Tab

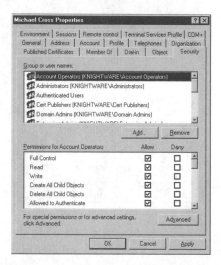

Figure 10.21 Special Permissions Dialog Box

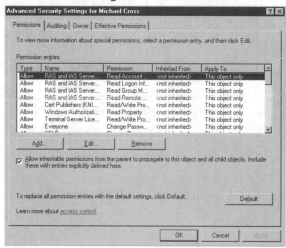

As seen in Figure 10.21, the Special Permissions dialog box that's access through the **Advanced** button of the Security tab allows you to configure advanced settings and apply additional permissions to an account. As seen in this dialog, the Permissions tab also provides an option labeled **Allow inheritable permissions from the parent to propagate to this object and all child objects**. When this check box is checked, any permissions applied to the parent object (which in this case would be an OU) are also applied to this account. If this check box is unchecked, then any permissions applied at the higher level will not be applied, and the object will only have the permissions that have been explicitly set for it.

The final tab we'll discuss is the Member Of tab. As seen in Figure 10.22, this tab provides a listing of the user's group membership(s). By clicking the **Add** button, a dialog box will appear with a list of available groups of which the user can become a member. Selecting a group from the list on the **Member Of** tab and clicking the **Remove** button will remove that user from the group's membership.

Figure 10.22 Member Of Tab

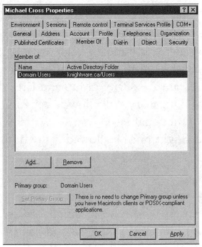

At the bottom of this tab is a button called **Set Primary Group**, which only applies to a limited number of users. A primary group is needed by users who use Macintosh computers, and log on to the network through File or Print Services for Macintosh. The other users who require a primary group are users who are running POSIX-compliant applications.

To fully understand how the **Member Of** tab affects a user's level of security, we must look at how groups impact a user's access. In the section that follows, we will look at the various groups that users can become members of, and see what each group offers.

Working with Active Directory Group Accounts

Using groups, you can perform a variety of tasks that will affect the accounts and groups that are members. These include:

- Assigning rights to a group account to authorize them to perform a certain task

- Assigning permissions on shared resources to a group, so that all members can access the resource in the same manner

- Distributing bulk e-mail to all members of the group

As we'll see in the sections that follow, group accounts are a powerful tool for managing large numbers of users as if they used a single account. In associating accounts with groups, you will find that some groups will have a much larger membership than others, and some will be used for purposes other than dealing with security issues.

Group Types

The first step in working with group accounts is deciding on the type of group you want to create and work with. In Active Directory, there are two different types, which are used for two different purposes:

- Security groups
- Distribution groups

The difference between these groups resides in how they are used. Security groups are designed to be used for security purposes, while distribution groups are designed to be used for sending bulk e-mail to collections of users. Once you create a particular type of group account, it is possible to switch its type at any time. If you create a security group and later decide to convert it into a distribution group (or vice versa), Active Directory will allow it depending on the domain functional level that's been set. If the domain functional level is set to Windows 2000 native or higher, the conversion can take place. However, it might not be allowed if the domain is running at the Windows 2000 mixed level.

Security Groups

A security group is a collection of users who have specific rights and permissions to resources. Although both can be applied to a group account, *rights* and *permissions* are different from one another. *Rights* are assigned to users and groups, and control the actions a user or member of a group can take. In Windows Server 2003, rights are also sometimes called *privileges*. You might have noticed this earlier when viewing the output of the command *WHOAMI /ALL*. *Permissions* are used to control access to resources. When permissions are assigned to a group, it determines what the members of the group can do with a particular resource.

Security groups are able to obtain such access because they are given a SID when the group account is first created. Because it has a SID, it can be part of a DACL, which lists the permissions users and groups have to a resource. When the user logs on, an access token is created that includes their SID and those of any groups of which they're a part. When they try to access a resource, this access token is compared to the DACL to see what permissions should be given to the user. It is through this process and the use of groups that the user obtains more (and in some cases, less) access than has been explicitly given to his or her account.

Another benefit of a security group is that you can send e-mail to it. When e-mail is sent to a group, every member of the group receives the e-mail. In doing so, this saves having to send an e-mail message to each individual user.

Distribution Groups

While security groups are used for access control, distribution groups are used for sharing information. This type of group has nothing to do with security. It is used for distributing e-mail messages to groups of users. Rather than sending the same message to one user after another, distribution groups allow applications such as Microsoft Exchange to send e-mails to collections of users.

The reason why distribution groups can't be used for security purposes is because they can't be listed in DACLs. When a new distribution group is created, it isn't given a SID, preventing it from being listed in the DACL. Although users who are members of different security groups can be added to a distribution group, it has no effect on the permissions and rights associated with their accounts.

Group Scopes in Active Directory

Scope is the range that a group will extend over a domain, tree, and forest. The scope is used to determine the level of security that will apply to a group, which users can be added to its membership, and the resources that they will have permission to access. As we'll discuss in the sections that follow, Active Directory provides three different scopes for groups:

- Universal
- Global
- Domain Local

Universal

Universal groups have the widest scope of any of the different group scopes. Members of this group are able to contain accounts and groups from any domain in the forest, and can be assigned permissions to resources in any domain in the forest. In other words, it is all encompassing within any part of the forest.

Whether a universal security group can be used depends on the functional level that the domain has been set to. Domains that have the functional level set to Windows 2000 mixed won't allow universal security groups to be created. However, if the domain functional level is Windows 2000 native or Windows Server 2003, then universal security groups can be created. In this situation, the group can contain user accounts, global groups, and universal groups from any domain in the forest, and be assigned permissions to resources in any domain. Universal distribution groups can be used at any functional level, including Windows 2000 mixed.

Universal groups can be converted to groups with a lesser scope. Providing the group doesn't contain any universal groups as members, a universal group can be converted to a global group or a domain local group. If universal groups are members of the universal group that's being converted, you won't be able to perform the conversion until these members are removed.

Global

Global groups have a narrower scope than universal groups. A global group can contain accounts and groups from the domain in which it is created, and be assigned permissions to resources in any domain in a tree or forest. Because it only applies to the domain in which it's created, this type of group is commonly used to organize accounts that have similar access requirements.

As we saw with universal groups, however, the members that can be part of a global group depend on the domain functional level. If the functional level of the domain is set to Windows 2000 mixed, then the membership of a global group can only consist of user accounts from the same domain. If the functional level of the domain is set to Windows 2000 native or Windows Server

2003, then the global group can have user accounts and other global groups from the same domain as members. User accounts and global groups from other domains cannot become members of a global group.

Global groups can also be converted into a universal group, provided that the global group isn't a member of any other global groups. If other global groups are members of the global group, then these must be removed before the conversion can take place. The domain functional level must be Windows 2000 native or Windows Server 2003 to convert to a universal security group.

Domain Local

Domain local groups also have a scope that extends to the local domain, and are used to assign permissions to local resources. The difference between domain local and global groups is that user accounts, global groups, and universal groups from any domain can be added to a domain local group. Because of its limited scope, however, members can only be assigned permissions within the domain in which this group is created.

As you might expect from the two previous scopes, the abilities of a domain local group depends on the domain functional level. If the functional level is set to Windows 2000 mixed, then the domain local group can only contain user accounts and global groups from any domain. It cannot contain universal groups when Windows Server 2003 is using this level of functionality. If the functional level is set to Windows 2000 native or Windows Server 2003, then the domain local group can contain user accounts and global groups from any domain, as well as universal groups. In addition, it can contain other domain local groups from the same domain. These abilities, however, have no impact on permissions. In all cases, permissions can only be assigned to resources in the local domain.

Domain local groups can be converted to a universal group, provided that there are no other domain local groups in its membership. If the domain local group does have other domain local groups as members, then these must be removed from the membership before a conversion is made.

Built-In Group Accounts

As we saw when we discussed user objects, a number of built-in accounts are automatically created when you install Active Directory. This not only applies to user accounts, but group accounts as well. Many of these groups have preconfigured rights, which allow members to perform specific tasks. When users are added to these groups, they are given these rights in addition to any assigned permissions to access resources.

The groups that are created when Active Directory is installed can be accessed through Active Directory Users and Computers, and are located in two containers: *Builtin* and *Users*. Although they are stored in these containers, they can be moved to other OUs within the domain. Those in the Built-in container have a domain local scope, while those in the Users container have either a domain local, global, or universal scope. In the paragraphs that follow, we will look at the individual groups located in each of these containers, and see what rights they have to perform network-related tasks.

Default Groups in Builtin Container

Up to 14 different built-in groups that might be located by default in the Builtin container, including:

- **Account Operators**, which allows members to manage accounts
- **Administrators**, which gives members full control
- **Backup Operators**, which allows members to back up and restore files
- **Guests**, which gives members minimal access
- **Incoming Forest Trust Builders**, which is only available in forest root domains, and gives members permission to Create Inbound Forest Trusts
- **Network Configuration Operators**, which allows members to manage network settings
- **Performance Monitor Users**, which allows users to manage performance counters and use System Monitor
- **Performance Log Users**, which allows users to manage performance counters and use Performance Logs and Alerts
- **Pre-Windows 2000 Compatible Access**, which is used for backward compatibility
- **Print Operators**, which allows members to manage printers
- **Remote Desktop Users**, which allows members to connect to servers using Remote Desktop
- **Replicator**, which is used for replication purposes
- **Server Operators**, which allows members to manage servers
- **Users**, which contains every user account created in the domain

Default Groups in Users Container

In addition to the groups we've discussed, up to 13 built-in groups can be located by default in the Users container, including:

- **Cert Publishers**, which gives members the ability to publish certificates
- **DnsAdmins**, which provides administrative access to the DNS Server service
- **DnsUpdateProxy**, which provides members with the ability to perform dynamic updates for other clients
- **Domain Admins**, which gives members full control of the domain
- **Domain Computers**, which includes computers that are part of the domain
- **Domain Controllers**, which includes DCs
- **Domain Guests**, which includes guests of the domain
- **Domain Users**, which includes users of the domain

- **Enterprise Admins**, which gives full control over every domain in the forest

- **Group Policy Creator Owners**, which allows members to manage group policies in the domain

- **IIS_WPG**, which is used by Internet Information Service (IIS)

- **RAS and IAS Servers**, which allows members to manage remote access

- **Schema Admins**, which allows members to modify the schema

- **Telnet Clients**, which is used for clients to connect using Telnet

Creating Group Accounts

In addition to the built-in groups that are created when Active Directory and other services are installed on DCs, you can also create group accounts to suit the needs of your organization. To create group accounts, you can use either Active Directory Users and Computers or the DSADD command-line tool. Regardless of the method you use, only members of the Administrators group, Account Operators group, Domain Admins group, Enterprise Admins group, or another user or group that's been delegated authority can create a new group.

Creating Groups Using Active Directory Users and Computers

Creating new groups in Active Directory Users and Computers begins by selecting the container or OU in which you want the group to be stored. Once this is done, click **Action | New | Group**. Alternatively, you can right-click on the container, and select **New | Group**. In either case, this will open the **New Object – Group** dialog box.

The **New Object – Group** dialog box requires a minimal amount of information to create the new group. As shown in Figure 10.23, the **Group name** text box is where you enter the Active Directory name of the group. As you enter information into this field, it will also fill out the **Group name (pre-Windows 2000)** text box. This is the name that older operating systems will use to refer to the group. By default, it is the same as the **Group name**, but can be modified to any name you want within the naming rules covered previously in the chapter.

Figure 10.23 New Object Dialog Box for Creating New Groups

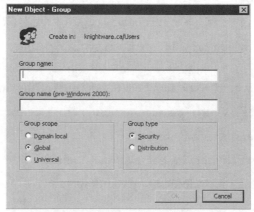

Below the fields designating the group's name is a section that allows you to control the scope. As discussed previously in this chapter, there are three different scopes for groups: *Domain local*, *Global*, and *Universal*. A Security group type can only be given a universal scope if the functionality level has been raised to Windows 2000 native or higher. If the functionality level is Windows 2000 mixed, then the Universal option on this dialog box will be disabled when creating a Security type group, and the only available options will be Domain local and Global.

To the right of this section is another one that allows you to specify the type of group you are creating. Two different types of groups can be created: *Security* and *Distribution*. As mentioned earlier in this chapter, security groups are used to control access, while distribution groups are used by applications for sending bulk e-mail to collections of users.

Once you have provided the information about the new group, click the **OK** button to create the group. After clicking this button, this new object will appear in the container that you initially selected to store the group. As we'll see later in this chapter, you can then modify the properties of this object to provide additional information, such as membership, descriptions, and other factors.

Creating Groups Using the DSADD Command

As we saw earlier in this chapter, the DSADD command is a useful tool for creating accounts from the command line. In addition to creating user accounts, you can also use it to create groups. Creating a new group with DSADD is done by entering the following syntax:

DSADD GROUP *GroupDN* **-samid** *SAMName* **-secgrp** *yes | no* **-scope** *l | g | u*

When using this command, the following parameters must be entered:

- **GroupDN** This parameter is used to specify the DN of the object being added to Active Directory and where the object will be created.

- **SAMName** This parameter is the NetBIOS name that will be used by pre-Windows 2000 computers.

- **yes | no** This *parameter* is used to specify whether the account will be created as a security or distribution group. If a security group is being created, then you would enter **yes**. If you were going to create a distribution group, then you would enter **no**.

- **l | g | u** This parameter is used to specify the scope of the group. If you were creating a domain local group, you would enter **l**. If you were creating a global group, you would enter **g**. If you were creating a universal group, you would enter **u**.

In addition to these parameters, you can also specify others by using the following syntax:

DSADD GROUP *GroupDN* **[-secgrp {yes | no}] [-scope {l | g | u}] [-samid**
SAMName] **[-desc** *Description*] **[-memberof** *Group* ...] **[-members**
Member ...] **[{-s** *Server* | **-d** *Domain*}] **[-u** *UserName*] **[-p {**Password
| *}] [-q] [{-uc | -uco | -uci}]

These options provide a variety of settings that can be applied to the group when creating it. In addition to the ones already mentioned, the meanings of these different parameters are explained in Table 10.4.

Table 10.4 DSADD Parameters for Creating Groups

Parameter	Description
-desc *Description*	Specifies the description you want to add for the group.
-memberof *Group ...*	Specifies the groups to which this new group should be added.
-members *Member ...*	Specifies the members that should be made a part of this group.
{**-s** *Server* | **-d** *Domain*}	Specifies to connect to a remote server or domain. By default, the computer is connected to the DC in the logon domain.
-u *UserName*	Specifies the username to use when logging on to a remote server. By default, the username that the user is logged on to their local system is used. The following formats can be used for the *UserName* variable: Username Domain\username User principal name
-p {*Password* | ***}	Specifies the password to use when logging on to a remote server. If an asterisk (*) is used, you will be prompted for a password.
-q	Specifies quiet mode, and suppresses output.
{-uc | -uco | -uci}	Specifies Unicode to be used for input or output. If –uc is used, then input or output is to a pipe (|). If –uco is used, then output is to a pipe or file. If –uci is used, then input is from a pipe or file.

Managing Group Accounts

As we've seen, the DSADD command provides a number of options for configuring new groups, while there are only a minimal number of options available when creating them through Active Directory Users and Computers. However, most of these options can be configured and reconfigured at any time by using the object's properties. By modifying the group's properties, you can perform a variety of administrative tasks related to managing group accounts.

Accessing the properties of a group account is done through **Active Directory Users and Computers**. Select the object and click **Action | Properties**. You can also right-click on the object, and select **Properties** in the context menu. Regardless of the method used to display the properties, a dialog box similar to that shown in Figure 10.24 will appear.

The dialog box contains a great deal of information about the group, and a number of options that can be configured. As seen in this figure, the title bar states the group's name followed by the word "Properties." In the case of this figure, the properties being viewed are those of a group called "Accounting Users." The dialog also provides six different tabs, which can be used for managing different facets of the account.

The **General** tab, shown in Figure 10.24, allows you to modify much of the information you provided when creating the account in Active Directory Users and Computers. On this tab, the **Group name (pre-Windows 2000)** field contains the NetBIOS name that older operating systems use to access the group. As you'll notice, this name can be modified, so it is different from the Active Directory group name. A group can have the name "Accounting Users," but have the name "Accounting" for its pre-Windows 2000 name.

Figure 10.24 General Tab in the Properties of a Group

The **Members** tab is used to view current group members and add new ones. As shown in Figure 10.25, this tab provides a field that shows all current members of the group. To add new members, you click the **Add** button, which opens a dialog box that allows you to enter the names of accounts to add. Clicking **OK** in this dialog adds the name of the user, computer, or group to the list on the **Members** tab. Removing accounts from membership is also simple. Just select the account to remove from the list, and then click the **Remove** button.

Figure 10.25 Members Tab in the Properties of a Group

By clicking the **Add** button, the dialog box shown in Figure 10.26 appears. In this dialog, you can search for the objects you want to add to the Members list. By clicking the **Object Types** button, a dialog will appear allowing to you specify the object types you want to find. In this dialog, you can click check boxes to specify whether to search for Contacts, Computers, Groups, Users, or Other objects. To limit the search to only start from a specific point in the directory structure, you can click the **Locations** button to open a dialog box showing the directory tree, where you can select the point to begin the search. Finally, the **Enter the object names to select** is where you would enter the name of the object. Upon clicking **OK**, Active Directory will use these parameters to find the object to add to the Membership list.

Figure 10.26 Select Users, Contacts, Computers, or Groups Dialog Box

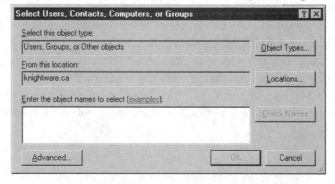

The Member Of tab, shown in Figure 10.27, is used to add this group to other existing groups in Active Directory. This tab provides a field that lists all groups to which this group belongs. To add this group to other groups, click the **Add** button to open a dialog box where you can enter the names of the groups you'd like this one to be a member of. Upon clicking **OK**, the name of the group is added to the listing on the **Member Of** tab. Removing this group from membership in another group is done by selecting that group from the list, and then clicking the **Remove** button.

Figure 10.27 Member Of Tab in the Properties of a Group

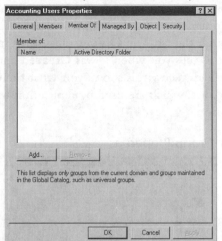

The Managed By tab is used to designate an account that is responsible for managing this group. This makes it easy for users to determine who they have to contact to request membership in the group, and how to establish contact. Checking the **Manager can update membership list** check box also allows the account listed on this tab to add and remove members from the group. To designate a manager, click the **Change** button and specify the account. Once added, it will be displayed in the **Name** field on this tab. The properties of this account can then be viewed by clicking the **Properties** button; however, many of the commonly viewed elements of this account will automatically appear on the tab. As shown in Figure 10.28, information such as the **Office**, **Street**, **City**, **State/province**, **Country/region**, **Telephone number**, and **Fax number** will appear. To remove this account from a managerial role, click the **Clear** button.

Figure 10.28 Managed By Tab in the Properties of a Group

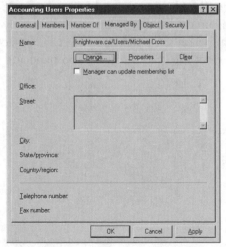

To view information about the group, you can use the **Object** tab. As shown in Figure 10.29, this tab allows you to view information about this Active Directory object. The **Canonical name of object** field displays the canonical name of the group, while the fields below this provide other data that can't be modified through the tab. The **Object class** field informs you that this is a Group, and information below this tells you when it was **Created** and last **Modified**. The **Update Sequence Numbers (USNs)** fields below this shows you what the original and current update sequence numbers for this object are, which are used by replication to ensure that all DCs have an updated copy of object information.

Figure 10.29 Object Tab of Group Properties

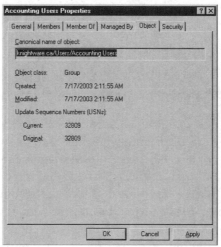

The Security tab is used to configure the permissions that other accounts have over the group. As shown in Figure 10.30, the top pane of this tab lists users and groups with permissions over the account, while the lower pane shows the permissions of an account that's selected in the top pane. New accounts can be given access by clicking the **Add** button. Once an account is added and selected in the top pane, you enable or disable specific permissions by selecting the check box in the **Allow** or **Deny** column. Special permissions can also be set for objects by clicking the **Advanced** button. To remove an account, select the account in the top pane and click the **Remove** button.

Figure 10.30 Security Tab of Group Properties

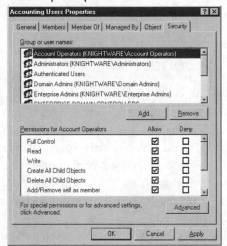

Working with Active Directory Computer Accounts

Computer accounts are objects that are stored in Active Directory and used to uniquely identify computers in a domain. With computer accounts, data on the computer is stored within Active Directory, allowing you to view information about the machine and use the account to set privileges on resources, install applications, and perform other actions related to its usability on the network.

Creating Computer Accounts

Computer accounts can be created in the Computers container or OUs that have been created in Active Directory. To create a new computer account, you need the same privileges as when creating user and group accounts. Only members of the Administrators group, Account Operators group, Domain Admins group, Enterprise Admins group, or a user or group that has been delegated authority can create a new account. If a user has been issued the **Add workstations to a domain** right, then he or she can create up to 10 computer accounts in a domain.

There are three different methods in which a new computer account can be created:

- Joining a workstation to a domain using a user account that has the right to create a new computer account in the domain

- Creating a computer account in Active Directory Users and Computers and then joining the workstation to the domain

- Creating the computer account using DSADD and then joining the workstation to the domain

While accounts can be created before a workstation is added to the domain, only minimal information about the computer will be included in the account. Once the workstation is added to the domain, data is retrieved from the computer that is added to the account. This includes such facts as the operating system installed on the machine, the version of the operating systems, and other relevant information.

Creating Computer Accounts by Adding a Computer to a Domain

Computer accounts can be created when adding a computer to a domain. Computers can be added to a domain by using the same dialog box you use to change the computer's name. On a Windows 2000 Professional machine, this is done on the Network Identification tab of the System Properties dialog. To access this dialog, you can right-click the **My Computer** icon located on the desktop, and select **Properties** on the context menu. You can also access this dialog by double-clicking the **System** icon in **Control Panel**. Once the System Properties dialog appears, click the **Properties** button on the **Network Identification** tab.

As shown in Figure 10.31, the dialog box that appears after clicking the **Properties** button allows you to modify the name of the computer, and choose whether the computer is part of a workgroup or domain. The **Member Of** section provides two options. The **Domain** option enables a text box that allows you to provide the name of a domain this computer will join. The **Workgroup** option enables a text box that allows you to provide the name of a workgroup this computer will join. At any time, the computer can be switched from being a member of a workgroup or domain. If the computer is joining a domain where a computer account doesn't exist for this machine, then the **Computer name** field is used to specify the new Active Directory account's name.

Figure 10.31 Identification Changes Dialog Box

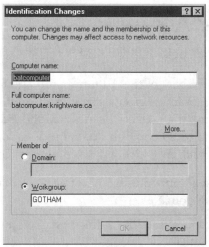

After entering the name of a domain this computer will join, click the **OK** button. The computer then proceeds to connect to a DC for the domain you are attempting to join, and if it finds one, a dialog box will be displayed asking you for the username and password of an account permitted to add workstations to the domain. Once this information is provided and you click **OK**, the username and password you provided will be authenticated and (if the user account has the necessary privileges) the workstation will be joined to the domain. If a computer account already exists for the computer, then data is retrieved and the account is updated. If no account exists, the account is created.

Creating Computer Accounts
Using Active Directory Users and Computers

Computers can also be created using Active Directory Users and Computers. Right-click on the container or OU that you want to create the object in, and select **New | Computer**. Alternatively, you can select the container or OU in which you want to create the computer account, and then click **Action | New | Computer**. A dialog box similar to the one shown in Figure 10.32 will appear.

Figure 10.32 New Object – Computer Dialog Box

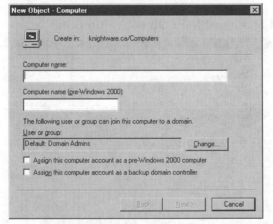

The first field on this screen is used to identify the computer. The **Computer name** text box is used to specify the name that you want this computer account to be called in Active Directory. This will be the RDN of the computer. The **Computer name (pre-Windows 2000)** text box is where you would enter the NetBIOS name of this computer, which older operating systems will use when connecting to this computer. As mentioned before, the NetBIOS name of a computer can be up to 15 characters in length. When you enter a value in the **Computer name** text box, a NetBIOS name will be suggested based on the first 15 characters of the **Computer name** field. However, this can be changed to another name.

Below this is a field that states which user or group can join the computer to the domain. As we saw in the previous section, when the computer is added to a domain, a username and password of a user account with the necessary rights is required. By default, the Domain Admins group has this ability, but this can be changed. To specify another user or group, click the **Change** button and enter the name of the user or group that should be given this privilege. The selected user or group will appear in the **User or group** field of this screen. The final options on this screen deal with older machines in a domain. The **Assign this computer account as a pre-Windows 2000 computer** designates that this machine is running an older operating system, such as Windows NT. The **Assign this computer account as a backup domain controller** specifies that this is a Windows NT BDC. Only Windows NT and newer operating systems can have accounts in Active Directory.

The remaining screens require little input. Click the **Next** button to continue to the screen that allows you to specify whether the computer is managed. A managed computer is a Remote Installation Services (RIS) client. If the **This is a managed computer** check box is checked, you must then enter the client computer's globally unique identifier (GUID). After providing this information and clicking **Next**, a screen will appear that offers the following options:

- **Any available Remote Installation Services (RIS) server**, which specifies that any RIS server can provide remote installation services to this computer.

- **The following RIS server**, which specifies that only designated RIS servers can service this computer.

Figure 10.33 Managed Screen of New Object – Computer

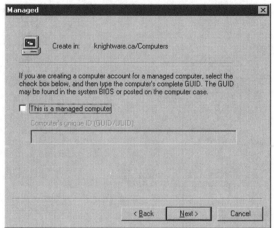

While the screen with these RIS options will appear if the computer is managed, this will not occur if the **This is a managed computer** check box isn't checked. Upon clicking **Next**, you proceed to the final summary screen, which you can review before creating the computer account. As shown in Figure 10.34, this screen informs you of what the computer will be called in Active Directory, and other information on options you chose during setup. Click the **Finish** button on this screen to close the wizard and create the account.

Figure 10.34 Final Screen of New Object – Computer

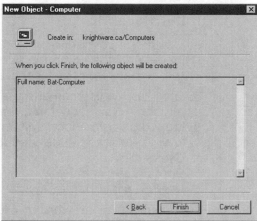

Creating Computer Accounts Using the DSADD Command

As was the case with users and groups, computer accounts can also be created using the DSADD command. The command-line method can be used in scripts to automate the addition computer objects to Active Directory. You can use the DSADD command to create computer objects using the following syntax:

DSADD COMPUTER *ComputerDN*

In using this command, *ComputerDN* specifies the DN of the computer that's being added. This provides information on where in the directory structure this account will be created. However, this isn't the only parameter that's available for DSADD. As shown in Table 10.5, each of these parameters provides different information that is used to set up the account. To use additional options, the following syntax can be used:

```
dsadd computer ComputerDN [-samid SAMName] [-desc Description] [-loc
     Location] [-memberof GroupDN ...] [{-s Server | -d Domain}] [-u
          UserName] [-p {Password | *}] [-q] [{-uc | -uco | -uci}]
```

Table 10.5 DSADD Parameters for Creating Computers

Parameter	Description
-samid *SAMName*	Specifies the NetBIOS name used by pre-Windows 2000 computers.
-desc *Description*	Specifies a description to be used for the account.
-loc *Location*	Specifies the location of the computer.
-memberof *GroupDN*	Specifies the groups that this new computer account will be a member of.

Continued

Table 10.5 DSADD Parameters for Creating Computers

Parameter	Description
{-s *Server* | -d *Domain*}	Specifies a connection to a remote server or domain. By default, the computer is connected to the DC in the domain that the local user is logged on to.
-u *UserName*	Specifies the username to use when logging on to a remote server. By default, the username that the user logged on to the local system with is used. The following formats can be used for the *UserName* variable: Username Domain\username User principal name
-p {*Password* | *}	Specifies the password to use when logging on to a remote server. If an asterisk (*) is used, you will be prompted for a password.
-q	Specifies quiet mode, and suppresses output
{-uc | -uco | -uci}	Specifies Unicode to be used for input or output. If –uc is used, then input or output is to a pipe (|). If –uco is used, then output is to a pipe or file. If –uci is used, then input is from a pipe or file.

Managing Computer Accounts

As seen previously, accounts can be administered through the properties of the object, which can be accessed using Active Directory Users and Computers. To view the properties, select the object and click **Action | Properties**. You can also right–click on the object, and select **Properties** from the context menu. Using either method, a dialog box with nine tabs will be displayed.

The **General** tab of a computer account's properties allows you to view common information about the computer, as seen in Figure 10.35.

Figure 10.35 General Tab in the Properties of a Computer Account

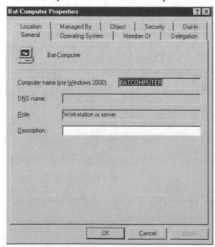

As shown in Figure 10.36, the **Operating System** tab provides information about the operating system running on the computer that has joined the domain. The **Name** field provides the name of the operating system, **Version** provides the version of the operating system, and **Service pack** displays the service pack level that has been applied to the operating system. These values are retrieved from the computer and can't be modified.

Figure 10.36 Operating System Tab in the Properties of a Computer Account

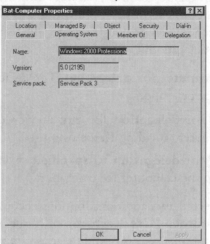

The Member Of tab shown in Figure 10.37 displays existing group memberships for this computer and allows you to add the computer to groups in Active Directory. By default, it will be a member of the Domain Computers or Domain Controllers group depending on its network role. The computer account can be made a member of other groups by clicking the **Add** button. To remove the computer from a group, select the group in the list and click the **Remove** button.

Figure 10.37 Member Of Tab in the Properties of a Computer Account

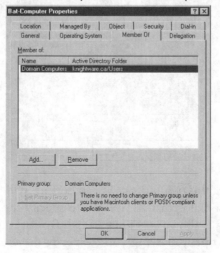

At the bottom of this tab is a section that allows you to set the primary group to which the computer belongs. By default, computers are made a member of the Domain Computers group, which is displayed in the **Primary group** field on this tab. To change the primary group, you could use the **Set Primary Group** button, but this generally isn't required. Primary groups are used by Macintosh computers and POSIX-compliant applications, and aren't required by other operating systems or applications.

The Delegation tab shown in Figure 10.38 is used to control whether services can act on behalf of another user from this computer. Using this tab, you can specify that the account can be used by specific services. By using the account's credentials, they are able to impersonate the account. This tab has three options relating to delegation:

- **Do not trust this computer for delegation** The default value, and doesn't allow the computer to be used for delegation.

- **Trust this computer for delegation for any service (Kerberos only)** Allows any service to use the computer providing Kerberos is used.

- **Trust this computer for delegation to specified services only** Only allows the services you specify to use the computer for delegation.

When the final option is selected, two additional options become available: **Use Kerberos only** and **Use any authentication protocol**. **Use Kerberos only** specifies that delegation can only be performed if Kerberos is used for authentication, while **Use any authentication protocol** allows any protocol to be used.

Figure 10.38 Delegation Tab in the Properties of a Computer Account

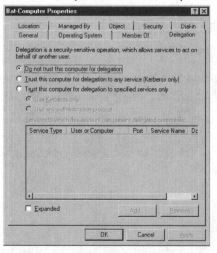

In addition to these options, the two buttons at the bottom will also be enabled. The **Add** button can be clicked to open a dialog that allows you to specify the services that can use the computer for delegation. This dialog is shown in Figure 10.38. By clicking the **Users or Computers** button, another dialog box will open, allowing you to specify the user or server that has these services associated with them. This will populate the **Available Services** field on this screen. By selecting services in this listing or alternatively clicking **Select All**, the selected services are delegated for the user or computer accounts selected. By selecting a service from this list and clicking the **Remove** button, a selected service is removed from being able to use this computer.

Figure 10.39 Add Services Dialog

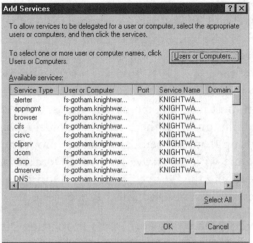

The **Location** tab of Computer Properties allows you to provide information on the location of the computer within the organization. This tab has a single text box that allows you to enter a location name, and a button labeled **Browse**. If no locations are available to select using browse, the **Browse** button will be grayed out.

The **Managed By** tab is similar to the tab we saw earlier in Figure 10.28 when we discussed group accounts.

The **Object** tab provides information about the object, and is similar to the tab we saw in Figure 10.29 when discussing groups.

The **Security** tab is similar to the one in Figure 10.30 that we saw when discussing group accounts. This tab is used to configure the permissions that other accounts have in Active Directory for this computer object.

The final tab in a computer's properties is the **Dial-in** tab. This tab is similar to the one we saw in Figure 10.19 when we discussed user accounts. It allows you to configure settings that are used when the computer attempts to connect to the network remotely using a dial-up or VPN connection.

Managing Multiple Accounts

So far, we've discussed how you can use tools for Active Directory to create and manage individual objects. In addition to creating and modifying user accounts, computer accounts, and group accounts, you can also perform actions that affect large numbers of accounts at once. Next, we'll look at how you can manage UPNs, move objects, and how to troubleshoot problems that might result when working with accounts in Active Directory.

Implementing User Principal Name Suffixes

As discussed earlier in this chapter, *User Principal Names* (UPNs) consist of a logon account name and UPN suffix, which is connected together with an @ symbol. When combined they often look just like an e-mail address, and can in fact be used by programs to send messages to Active Directory accounts. The UPN is used when logging on to Windows 2000 and Windows Server 2003 domains from Window 2000 or later clients.

In Active Directory, alternative UPN suffixes can be created, so the user can log on using a UPN suffix that is different from the name of the domain in which their user account resides. For example, if a user had to log on to a domain with an exceptionally long name, you could provide an alternate UPN suffix as part of the user's UPN. In doing so, the UPN is simplified, making it easier for users to enter it when logging on.

To add a UPN suffix, you must have the appropriate rights. UPN suffixes can only be added by a member of the Domains Admins group in the forest root domain, a member of the Enterprise Admins group, or a user or group that has been delegated the proper authority.

Adding UPN suffixes is done with the Active Directory Domains and Trusts console. It can also be started through MMC, by adding the **Active Directory Domains and Trusts** snap-in. Figure 10.40 shows the Active Directory Domains and Trusts Properties dialog box.

Figure 10.40 Active Directory Domains and Trusts Properties Dialog Box

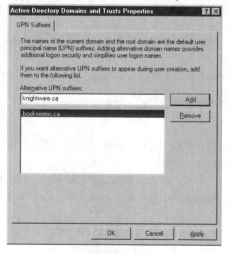

Use the following steps to add and use alternative UPN suffixes.

Add and Use Alternative UPN Suffixes

1. From the Windows Start menu, select **Administrative Tools | Active Directory Domains and Trusts**.

2. When the Active Directory Domains and Trusts console appears, select **Active Directory Domains and Trusts** from the console tree.

3. From the Action menu, select the **Properties** menu item.

4. When the Active Directory Domains and Trusts Properties dialog box appears, click in the **Alternative UPN suffixes** text box, and, enter the alternative UPN suffix you want to use (for example, eu.syngress.com).

5. Click the **Add** button. The listing should now appear in the lower pane.

6. Click **OK** to finish and close the Active Directory Domains and Trusts utility.

7. From the Windows Start menu, select **Administrative Tools | Active Directory Users and Computers**.

8. When Active Directory Users and Computers opens, expand the console tree and then expand your domain. Once this is done, select the **TestOU** container.

9. In the right pane, select the Jane Doe user that you created previously.

10. From the **Action** menu, select the **Properties** menu item.

11. When the Properties dialog box for the Jane Doe user account opens, select the Account tab.

12. In the User logon name field, use the drop-down list to select the new UPN suffix for this user.

13. Click **OK** to save the change and exit.

Moving Account Objects in Active Directory

Windows Server 2003 provides a number of tools that allow you to move objects within domains and between them. The tools that can be used for moving objects include **Active Directory Users and Computers**, and two command-line utilities. As we've seen, Active Directory Users and Computers is an MMC snap-in that allows you to interact with Active Directory through a graphical interface. The **DSMOVE** and **MOVETREE** are command-line tools that allow you to move objects by entering textual commands at the command prompt. In the sections that follow, we will look at these tools, and see how they can be used to move objects within and between domains.

Moving Objects with Active Directory Users and Computers

Active Directory Users and Computers can be used to move user, computer, and group accounts to other locations of the directory. With this tool, objects can be moved within a domain. It can't, however, be used to move objects to other domains.

Active Directory Users and Computers is the only tool that allows you to move accounts using a GUI. Because it's a graphical tool, you can move Active Directory objects using your mouse. Select an object by holding down your left mouse button, drag the object to a different container or OU, and release the left mouse button to drop it into the new location.

In addition, you can also move objects within the directory by right-clicking on the object, and selecting **Move** from the context menu. A dialog box will appear asking you to choose the container or OU the object should be moved to. As seen in Figure 10.41, the Move dialog box displays a tree that represents the directory tree. By browsing the folders in this tree, you can select the container you want the object moved to, and then click **OK** to being the move.

Figure 10.41 Move Dialog Box

When using Active Directory Users and Computers, multiple objects can be selected and moved to other locations. You can select these objects as you would files in Windows Explorer, by dragging your mouse over the objects to be moved. You can also select a series of objects by holding down the **Shift** key as you click on objects, or select a number of individual objects by holding down the **Ctrl** key as you click on them. After selecting the objects to be moved, perform the actions we just discussed to move them to another container or OU.

Moving Objects with the DSMOVE Command

DSMOVE is used to move objects within a domain, and can be used to rename objects. DSMOVE is a command-line utility that is used from the command prompt. Providing you don't need to move an object to another domain, you can use this tool to move an object to other locations in the directory tree. The syntax for using this tool is as follows:

DSMOVE *UserDN* [**-newparent** *ParentDN*] **-pwd** {*Password*|***}

In using this syntax, several different parameters must be entered for moving the object. The *UserDN* parameter specifies the DN of the object being moved. The *–newparent* switch indicates that you are using DSMOVE to move an object, and is used with the *ParentDN* variable to specify the DN of the new location.

To illustrate how this command is used, let's say you wanted to move an object called **BuddyJ** from the **Sales** OU in knightware.ca to the **Finance** OU in the same domain. To move this object, you would use the following command:

Dsmove CN=BuddyJ,OU=Sales,DC=knightware,DC=ca **-newparent**

    OU=Finance,DC=knightware,DC=ca

DSMOVE also provides additional parameters to perform actions such as renaming an object, or controlling the type of input and output for this command. To review these parameters, refer to the section on DSMOVE in Chapter 9.

Moving Objects with the MOVETREE Command

MOVETREE is the Active Directory Object Manager tool. In addition to other capabilities, it is a command-line tool that allows you to move objects to other domains in a forest. By using this tool, you have the freedom to move a user account, computer account, group, or OU to any location within the directory, regardless of the domain.

When an object is moved using this tool, it is first copied to the Lost and Found container before being moved to the destination domain. Objects that can't be moved remain in this container, so you can manage them as needed. Because orphaned data might reside in this domain after using MOVETREE, you should check this container after performing a move.

A variety of information isn't moved with this tool. This includes data such as profiles, logon scripts, and personal information when moving user accounts. Local groups and global groups also aren't moved, but membership in these groups remains unaffected so that security involving the moved objects remains the same.

In addition to the limitations on data associated with accounts, there are also limitations when **MOVETREE** is used to move OUs between domains. When an OU is moved, group policies aren't affected, as clients will continue to receive these settings from a link to the policy in the original domain. In other words, although the OU is now in another domain, clients will connect to the Group Policy Object (GPO) that is located in the original domain. Because this can cause performance issues, it is wise to recreate these policies in the domain where the OU has been moved, and then delete the GPO in the original domain (which is no longer needed).

As a command-line tool, **MOVETREE** requires that certain parameters be used to effectively complete operations. The syntax for **MOVETREE** is as follows, and the parameters are explained in Table 10.6.

```
MoveTree [/start | /continue | /check] [/s SrcDSA] [/d DstDSA]
    [/sdn SrcDN] [/ddn DstDN] [/u Domain\Username] [/p Password]
        [/quiet]
```

Table 10.6 Parameters for MOVETREE

Parameter	Description
/start	Specifies whether to start a move with a /check option, or with the /startnocheck option, which starts the operation without a check.
/continue	Specifies to continue the move after a failure.
/check	Specifies to check the entire tree before moving an object.
/s SrcDSA	The SrcDSA variable is used to specify the FQDN of the source server.

Continued

Table 10.6 Parameters for MOVETREE

Parameter	Description
/d *DstDSA*	The *DstDSA* variable is used to specify the FQDN of the destination server.
/sdn *SrcDN*	The *SrcDN* variable is used to specify the source subtree's root DN.
/ddn *DstDN*	The *DstDN* variable is used to specify the destination subtree's root DN.
/u *Domain\Username*	Specifies the domain and user account to use for the operation.
/p *Password*	Specifies the password of the account to use for the operation.
/quiet	Specifies that quiet mode should be used, suppressing output.

The Active Directory Object Manager tool isn't installed with Active Directory, and thereby isn't initially available for use. **MOVETREE** is available as part of the Active Directory Support Tools on the installation CD, and can be installed through Windows Explorer. By accessing the **Support\Tools** folder on the installation CD, right-clicking on **SUPTOOLS.MSI**, and then choosing **Install** from the menu that appears, the **Windows Support Tools Setup Wizard** will start. By following the instructions in this wizard, **MOVETREE** and the other support tools will be installed.

You can use the following steps to install **MOVETREE** with AD support tools.

Install MOVETREE with AD Support Tools

1. Insert the Windows Server 2003 Server installation CD into your CD-ROM drive.

2. From the Windows **Start** menu, select **Windows Explorer**.

3. When Windows Explorer opens, expand the node representing your CD-ROM drive, and then expand the **Support | Tools** folder.

4. When the contents of the **Tools** folder is displayed in the right pane, right-click on the **SUPTOOLS.MSI** file and click **Install** in the context menu.

5. When the **Windows Support Tools Setup Wizard** appears, click **Next** to continue.

6. On the **End User License Agreement** screen, click **I Agree** to install these tools, and then click **Next** to continue.

7. On the **User Information** screen, enter your name in the **Name** field, and the company you work for in the **Organization** field. By default, these fields will already be completed from information acquired from Windows Server 2003 Server. Click **Next** to continue.

8. On the **Destination Directory** screen, accept the default settings, and click **Install Now** to install the tools.

9. A dialog box will appear showing that files are being copied to the folder specified in the **Destination Directory** screen, and being installed on Windows Server 2003. Once completed, the final screen of the wizard will appear, informing you that the tools were successfully installed. Click **Finish** to exit the wizard and complete the installation process.

Troubleshooting Problems with Accounts

Troubleshooting problems with accounts relies on the same methodologies and practices involved in troubleshooting other problems in Windows Server 2003. It requires an understanding of functions, configurations, and limitations. It also requires starting at the simplest possible solution for a problem and working up to the most complex. For example, if a user's account wasn't working, you wouldn't start by restoring Active Directory from a previous backup from when the user was able to log on. You might, however, check to see if the account was disabled or locked out.

It is important that you determine whether the problem exists with the user who's logging on from a computer, or with the machine itself. You'll remember that Active Directory uses both computer and user accounts. If a problem is resulting from the computer account, no user will be able to perform a certain action from the machine, regardless of what user account is used.

At times, the problems that exist in a computer account might require resetting it. If you want to reset a computer account, in **Active Directory Users and Computers**, you can right-click on the account you want to reset, and then click **Reset** from the menu that appears. After a moment, a message box will appear stating that the account was reset.

Another important part of troubleshooting is determining the scope of a problem. Is only one person experiencing a problem, or are a number of people experiencing the same difficulties?   In doing so, you can determine whether the problem is with a user or computer account, or with a group of which these members are a part.

The problem might not exist in the user's account settings, but with DCs in the domain. For example, if you couldn't create security principals in Active Directory, the problem could stem from the fact that the RID Master is unavailable. The DC that has the RID operations master role allocates RIDs used for SIDs. Because SIDs can't be issued to new user accounts, computer accounts, and groups, these security principals can't be created.

You could use the command *netdom query fsmo* to identify which computers are holding single operation master roles. Once you've identified the DC serving in a particular master role, you could either repair the machine, or assign the operations master role to another machine. Before going through all this work, however, you should remember that the reason why others can't perform such actions might be because they don't have the proper rights, privileges, or permissions. In all cases, remember to start by looking at the simplest possible solution first.

Chapter 11

Creating User and Group Strategies

In this chapter:

- ☑ **Create a password policy for domain users.**
- ☑ **Plan a security group strategy.**
- ☑ **Plan a user authentication strategy.**

Introduction

Knowing how to create users and groups and the procedures for moving and managing them is only half the battle when it comes to effectively using these security objects on the network. The network administrator must also be able to develop strategies for authenticating the identity of anyone who uses network resources, and plan how to use groups most effectively to provide the security and access needed.

In today's connected world, proof of your identity is often required to ensure that someone else is not trying to use your identity. It used to be that a username and password were sufficient to authenticate someone to a network. However, password authentication is only the first step in true authentication of a user's identity in today's environment. You must have a well-defined password policy, which includes account lockout, password rotation, and other options to ensure limited access to your network. In this chapter, we develop a password policy for your Windows Server 2003 network. However, sometimes passwords and password policies are not enough, and we have to take authentication to the next plateau.

Tools such as biometric devices, token devices, voice identification, and smart cards are becoming much more mainstream for user authentication as the price continues to drop and acceptance continues to rise. Smart cards are discussed in a later chapter "Planning, Implementing, Maintaining Public Key Infrastructure."

An effective authentication strategy works hand in hand with a security group strategy. A well-designed group strategy will ensure that users receive only the appropriate

431

level of access to resources on the network. It will also reduce the workload of the administrator and make it easier to manage large numbers of users.

Creating a Password Policy for Domain Users

Since they are largely created and managed by end users, passwords have the potential to be the weakest link in any network security implementation. Since passwords are the "keys to the kingdom" of any computer system, the database that Windows Server 2003 uses to store password information will be a common attack vector for anyone attempting to hack your network. Windows Server 2003 offers several means to secure passwords on your network. A combination of technical measures, along with a healthy dose of user training and awareness, will go a long way toward protecting the security of your network systems.

Creating an Extensive Defense Model

In modern computer security, a system administrator needs to create a security plan that uses many different mechanisms to protect a network from unauthorized access. Rather than relying solely on a hardware firewall and nothing else, *defense in depth* would also use strong passwords as well as other mechanisms on local client PCs, in the event that the firewall is compromised. The idea is to create a series of security mechanisms so that if one is circumvented, other systems and procedures are in place to help impede an attacker. Microsoft refers to this practice as an *extensive defense model*. The key points of this model are the following:

- A viable security plan needs to begin and end with user awareness, since a technical mechanism is only as effective as the extent to which the users on your network adhere to it. As an administrator, you need to educate your users about how to best protect their accounts from unauthorized attacks.

- Use the system key utility (*syskey*) on all critical machines on your network. This utility, discussed later in this chapter, provides additional encryption for password information that is stored in the Security Accounts Manager (SAM) and Active Directory databases.

- Educate your users about the potential hazards of selecting the Save My Password feature or any similar feature on mission-critical applications, such as remote access or VPN clients.

- If you need to create one or more service accounts for applications to use, make sure that these accounts have different passwords. Otherwise, compromise of one account might leave multiple network applications open to attack.

- If you suspect that a user account has been compromised, change the password immediately. If possible, consider renaming the account entirely, since it is now a known attack vector.

- Create a password policy and/or account lockout policy that is appropriate to your organization's needs. It's important to strike a balance between security and usability in designing these types of account policies.

Strong Passwords

In discussing security awareness with your user community, one of the most critical issues to consider is that of password strength. A weak password will provide potential attackers with easy access to your users' computers, and consequently the rest of your company's network. Well-formed passwords will be significantly more difficult to decipher. Even though password-cracking utilities continue to evolve and improve, educating your users regarding the importance of strong passwords will provide additional security for your network's computing resources.

According to Microsoft, a weak password is one that contains any portion of your name, your company's name, or your network logon ID. For example, if a username was assigned as *JSmith*, and the user's password was *Smith12!@!*, that would be considered a weak password. A password that contains any complete dictionary word—*password, thunder, protocol*—is also considered weak. It should be understood that blank passwords are weak as well.

By comparison, a strong password will not contain any reference to your username, personal information, company name, or any word found in the dictionary. Strong passwords should also be at least seven characters long and contain characters from each of the following groups:

- **Uppercase letters** A, B, C …
- **Lowercase letters** z, y, x …
- **Numeric digits** 0, 1, 2, 3, 4, 5, 6, 7, 8, or 9
- **Non-alphanumeric characters** !, ★, $, }, etc.

Each strong password should be appreciably different from any previous passwords that the user has created. P!234abc, Q!234abc, and R!234abc, although each meeting the described password criteria, would not be considered strong passwords when viewed as a whole.

System Key Utility

Most password-cracking software used in attacking computer networks attempts to target the SAM database or the Active Directory database in order to access passwords for user accounts. To secure your password information, you should use the *system key* utility (the *syskey.exe* file itself is located in the %systemroot%\System32 directory by default) on every critical machine that you administer. This utility provides additional encryption for password information, which provides an extra line of defense against would-be attackers. To run the utility, click **Start | Run** then type **syskey** and click **OK**.

Defining a Password Policy

Using Active Directory, you can create a policy to enforce consistent password standards across your entire organization. The options you can specify include: how often passwords must be changed, the number of unique passwords a user must use before being able to reuse one, and the complexity level of passwords that are acceptable on your network. Additionally, you can specify an account lockout policy that will prevent users from logging on after a specified number of incorrect logon attempts. In this section, we discuss the steps necessary to enforce password and account lockout policies on a Windows Server 2003 network. You can use the following steps to create a domain password policy.

Create a domain password policy

1. From the Windows Server 2003 desktop, open **Start | Administrative Tools | Active Directory Users and Computers**. Right-click the domain that you want to set a password policy for, and select **Properties**.

2. Select the **Group Policy** tab, followed by the **Default Domain Policy**, as shown in Figure 11.1. Click the **Edit** button.

Figure 11.1 The Group Policy Tab

3. Navigate to **Computer Configuration | Windows Settings | Security Settings | Account Policies | Password Policy**. You'll see the screen shown in Figure 11.2.

Figure 11.2 Configuring Password Policy Settings

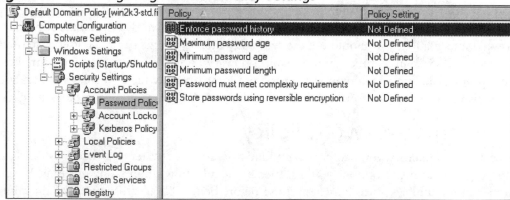

Using password policies, you can configure the following settings:

- **Enforce password history** This option allows you to define the number of unique passwords that Windows will retain.

- **Maximum password age** This setting defines how frequently Windows will prompt your users to change their passwords.

- **Minimum password age** This setting ensures that passwords cannot be changed until they are more than a certain number of days old.

- **Minimum password length** This option dictates the shortest allowable length that a user's password can be. Enabling this setting also prevents users from setting a blank password.

- **Password must meet complexity requirements** This policy setting, when activated, forces any new passwords created on your network to meet the complexity requirements.

- **Store passwords using reversible encryption** This option stores a copy of the user's password within the Active Directory database using reversible (cleartext) encryption. This is required for certain message digest functions and authentication protocols to work properly. This policy is disabled by default and should be enabled only if you are certain that your environment requires it.

4. For each item that you want to configure, right-click the item and select **Properties**. In this case, we're enforcing a password history of three passwords. In the screen shown in Figure 11.3, place a check mark next to **Define this policy setting**, and then enter the appropriate value.

Figure 11.3 Defining the Password History Policy

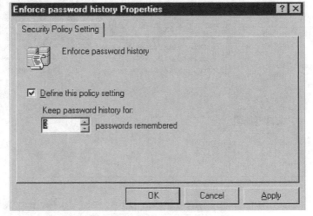

Modifying a Password Policy

You can modify an existing Windows Server 2003 password policy by navigating to the policy section of the appropriate computer or domain and make the changes. New and modified password policies are only enforced when passwords are changed. Therefore, altering password policy does not place an immediate burden on users. Typically, users won't notice the policy change until their passwords expire and they are forced to set new ones. If you need to ensure that all passwords are forced to comply with the new policy, you can set the **User must change password at next logon** option in the properties of the user accounts you administer.

Applying an Account Lockout Policy

In addition to setting password policies, you can configure your network so that user accounts will be locked out after a certain number of incorrect logon attempts. This can be a *soft lockout*, in which the account will be re-enabled after an administrator-specified period of time. Alternatively, it can be a *hard lockout* in which user accounts can only be re-enabled by the manual intervention of an administrator. Before implementing an account lockout policy, you need to understand the potential implications for your network.

Create an account lockout policy

1. From the Windows Server 2003 desktop, click **Start | Administrative Tools | Active Directory Users and Computers**.

2. Right-click the domain you want to administer, and then select **Properties**.

3. Select the **Default Domain Policy**, and click the **Edit** button.

4. Navigate to the account lockout policy by clicking **Computer Configuration | Windows Settings | Security Settings | Account Policies | Account Lockout Policy**. You'll see the screen shown in Figure 11.4.

Figure 11.4 Account Lockout Policy Objects

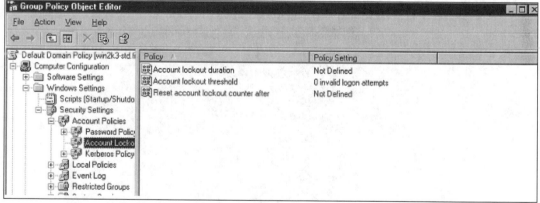

Using Account Lockout Policy, you can configure the following settings:

- **Account lockout duration** This option determines the amount of time that a locked-out account will remain inaccessible. Setting this option to 0 means that the account will remain locked out until an administrator manually unlocks it.

- **Account lockout threshold** This option determines the number of invalid logon attempts that can occur before an account will be locked out. Setting this option to 0 means that accounts on your network will never be locked out.

- **Reset account lockout counter after** This option defines the amount of time in minutes after a bad logon attempt that the "counter" will reset.

5. For each item that you want to configure, right-click the item and select **Properties**. To illustrate, we create an Account lockout threshold of three invalid logon attempts. In the screen shown in Figure 11.5, place a check mark next to **Define this policy setting**, and then enter the appropriate value.

Figure 11.5 Configuring the Account Lockout Threshold

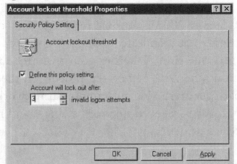

Creating User Authentication Strategies

Any well-formed security model needs to address the following three topics: authentication, authorization, and accounting (or *auditing*). *Authentication* deals with *who* a person is, *authorization* centers around *what* an authenticated user is permitted to do, and *accounting/auditing* is concerned with tracking *who did what* to a file, service, or other resource. Windows Server 2003 addresses all three facets of this security model.

Regardless of which protocol or technical mechanism is used, all authentication schemes need to meet the same basic requirement of verifying that a user or other network object is in fact who or what it claims to be. Windows Server 2003 offers several protocols and mechanisms to perform this verification, including (but not limited to) the following:

- Kerberos
- NT LAN Manager (NTLM)
- Secure Sockets Layer/Transport Security Layer (SSL/TLS)
- Digest authentication
- Smart cards

The following sections cover the details of each authentication mechanism available with Windows Server 2003, and the appropriate use for each. The most common authentication mechanism dates back to mainframe computing, *password authentication*. Concerns regarding password authentication have largely been connected with ensuring that user passwords are not transmitted in an easily intercepted and decipherable form over a network connection. In fact, many modern password authentication schemes, such as NTLM and Kerberos, never transmit the actual user password at all.

Need for Authentication

User authentication is a necessary first step within any network security infrastructure because it establishes the identity of the user. Keep in mind as we go along that a fully functional authentication strategy will almost certainly involve a combination of the methods and protocols. Your goal as a network administrator is to create an authentication strategy that provides the optimum security for your users while allowing you to administer the network as efficiently as possible.

Single Sign-On

A key feature of Windows Server 2003 is support for single sign-on, an authentication mechanism that allows your domain users to authenticate with any computer in the domain, while only providing their logon credentials one time. Whether your network authentication relies on single sign-on or not, any authentication scheme is a two-step process. At the very least, the user must perform an *interactive logon* in order to access the local computer. If network access is required, *network authentication* will allow the user to access needed network services and resources. In this section, we'll review both of these processes briefly.

Interactive Logon

A network user performs an interactive logon when presenting valid network credentials to the operating system of the physical computer the user is attempting to logon to—usually a desktop workstation. The logon name and password can either be a local user account or a domain account. Accounts stored in a SAM database can only be used for access to that specific computer.

When using a domain account, the user's logon information is authenticated against the Active Directory database. This allows the user to gain access to not only the local workstation but also to all resources he or she has been granted permission to use in the domain and any trusting domains.

Network Authentication

Once a user has gained access to a physical workstation, it's almost inevitable that the user will require access to files, applications, or services hosted by other machines on the LAN or WAN. *Network authentication* is the mechanism that confirms the user's identity to whatever network resource the user attempts to access. Windows Server 2003 provides several mechanisms to enable this type of authentication, including Kerberos and NTLM.

The mechanism used depends on the configuration of the network and the operating systems involved. Because this happens in the background, the network authentication process is transparent to users in an Active Directory environment. The network operating system handles everything behind the scenes without the need for user intervention. This feature provides the foundations for single sign-on in a Windows Server 2003 environment by allowing users to access resources in their own domains as well as other trusted domains.

Authentication Types

Windows Server 2003 offers several different authentication types to meet the needs of a diverse user base. The default authentication protocol for a homogeneous Windows 2000 or later environment is Kerberos version 5. This protocol relies on a system of tickets to verify the identity of network users, services, and devices. For Web applications and users, you can rely on the standards-based encryption offered by the SSL/TLS security protocols as well as Microsoft Digest. To provide backward compatibility for earlier versions of Microsoft operating systems, Windows Server 2003 provides support for the NTLM protocol. In this section, we examine the various authentication options available to you as a Windows administrator.

Kerberos

Within a Windows Server 2003 domain, the primary authentication protocol is Kerberos version 5. Kerberos provides thorough authentication by verifying not only the identity of network users but also the validity of the network services themselves. This latter feature was designed to prevent users from attaching to "dummy" services created by malicious network attackers to trick users into revealing their passwords or other sensitive information. The process of verifying both the user *and* the service that the user is attempting to use is referred to as *mutual authentication*. Only network clients and servers that are running the Windows 2000, Windows Server 2003, or Windows XP Professional operating system will be able to use the Kerberos authentication protocol. When these operating systems are members of a domain, Kerberos will be enabled as their default authentication mechanism for domain-based resources. In a Windows 2000 or later Active Directory environment, pre-Windows 2000 computers that attempt to access a "Kerberized" resource will be directed to use NTLM authentication.

The Kerberos authentication mechanism relies on a *Key Distribution Center* (KDC) to issue *tickets* that allow client access to network resources. Each domain controller in a Windows Server 2003 domain functions as a KDC. Network clients use DNS to locate the nearest available KDC so that they can acquire a ticket. Kerberos tickets contain cryptographic information that confirms the user's identity to the requested service.

These tickets remain resident on the client computer system for a specific amount of time, usually 10 hours. This ticket lifetime keeps the Kerberos system from being overwhelmed, and is configurable by an administrator. If you set the threshold lower, you must ensure that your domain controllers can handle the additional load that will be placed on them. It is also important, however, not to set them too high. A ticket is good until it expires, which means that if it becomes compromised it will be valid until expiration.

Understanding the Kerberos Authentication Process

When a user enters his or her network credentials on a Kerberos-enabled system, the following steps take place. These transactions occur entirely behind the scenes. The user is only aware that he or she has entered the password or PIN number (if using a smart card) as part of a normal logon process. The following steps occur in a single domain environment:

1. Using a smart card or a username/password combination, a user authenticates to the KDC. The KDC issues a *ticket-granting ticket (TGT)* to the client system. The client retains this TGT in memory until needed.

2. When the client attempts to access a network resource, it presents its TGT to the *ticket-granting service (TGS)* on the nearest available Windows Server 2003 KDC.

3. If the user is authorized to access the service that it is requesting, the TGS issues a *service ticket* to the client.

4. The client presents the service ticket to the requested network service. Through mutual authentication, the service ticket proves the identity of the user as well as the identity of the service.

The Windows Server 2003 Kerberos authentication system can also interact with non-Microsoft Kerberos implementations such as UNIX-based Kerberos realms. In Kerberos, a realm is similar to the concept of a domain. This "realm trust" feature allows a client in a Kerberos realm to authenticate against Active Directory to access resources, and vice versa. This interoperability allows Windows Server 2003 domain controllers to provide authentication for client systems running other types of Kerberos, including clients that are running operating systems other than Windows. It also allows Windows-based clients to access resources within a non-Windows Kerberos realm.

Secure Sockets Layer/Transport Layer Security

Any time you visit a Web site that uses an https:// prefix instead of http://, you're seeing *Secure Sockets Layer* (SSL) encryption in action. SSL provides encryption for other protocols such as HTTP, LDAP, and IMAP, which operate at higher layers of the protocol stack. SSL provides three major functions in encrypting TCP/IP-based traffic:

- **Server authentication** Allows a user to confirm that an Internet server is really the machine that it is claiming to be. It's difficult to think of anyone who wouldn't like the assurance of knowing that he or she is looking at the genuine Amazon.com site, and not a duplicate created by a hacker, before entering any credit card information.

- **Client authentication** Allows a server to confirm a client's identity during the exchange of data. For example, this might be important for a bank that needs to transmit sensitive financial information to a server belonging to a subsidiary office. Combining server and client authentication provides a means of mutual authentication.

- **Encrypted connections** Allow all data that is sent between a client and server to be encrypted and decrypted, allowing for a high degree of confidentiality. This function also allows both parties to confirm that the data was not altered during transmission.

The *Transport Layer Security* (TLS) protocol is currently under development by the Internet Engineering Task Force (IETF). It will eventually replace SSL as a standard for securing Internet traffic while remaining backward compatible with earlier versions of SSL. RFC 2712 describes the way to add Kerberos functionality to the TLS suite, which will potentially allow Microsoft and other vendors to extend its use beyond LAN/WAN authentication, to use on the Internet as a whole.

SSL and TLS can use a wide range of ciphers (authentication, encryption, and/or integrity mechanisms) to allow connections with a diverse client base. You can edit the Registry in Windows Server 2003 to restrict the ciphers allowed. Within the Registry Editor on the server, browse to the following key: HKEY_LOCAL_MACHINE\SYSTEM\CurrentControlSet\Control\SecurityProviders\SCHANNEL\Ciphers, as shown in Figure 11.6. Each available cipher has two potential values:

- **0xffffffff** (enabled)
- **0x0** (disabled)

Figure 11.6 Editing SSL/TLS Ciphers

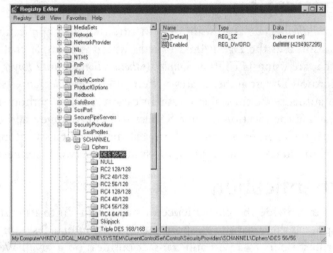

NT LAN Manager

Versions of Windows earlier than Windows 2000 used *NT LAN Manager* (NTLM) to provide network authentication. In a Windows Server 2003 environment, NTLM is used to communicate between two computers when one or both of them is running a pre-Windows 2000 operating system. NTLM will also be used by Windows Server 2003 computers that are not members of a domain. NTLM encrypts user logon information by applying a mathematical function (or *hash*) to the user's password. A user's password isn't stored in the SAM or Active Directory database. Rather, the value of a hash that is generated when the user's account is first created or the user's password is changed, is stored. If the password is less than 15 characters long, two hashes are actually stored: an NT hash and a LM hash. The LM (or LAN Manager) hash is weak and can easily be broken by password crackers. Because of this it is recommended that you configure the **Network security: Do not store LAN Manager hash value on next password change** Group Policy setting.

During logon, the domain controller sends a challenge to the client. This is a simple string of characters that the client mathematically applies to the hash value of the user's password. The result of this mathematical algorithm is a new hash that is then transmitted to the domain controller. In this way, the user's password is never actually transmitted across the network.

The domain controller also has the hash for the user's password. Moreover, it knows the challenge it sent, so it is able to perform the same calculation. It compares the hash that it mathematically calculated with the one received from the client. If they match, logon is permitted.

The NTLM hash function only exists in Windows Server 2003 for backward compatibility with earlier operating systems. Windows Server 2003 domains support both NTLM and NTLM version 2. If your network environment is exclusively running Windows 2000 or later, you might want to consider standardizing on a stronger form of authentication such as Kerberos. Using NTLM is preferable to sending authentication information using no encryption whatsoever, but NTLM has several known vulnerabilities that do not make it the best choice for network authentication if your operating system supports more advanced schemes.

Digest Authentication

Microsoft provides *digest authentication* as a means of authenticating Web applications that are running on IIS. Digest authentication uses the *Digest Access Protocol*, which is a simple challenge-response mechanism for applications that are using HTTP or *Simple Authentication Security Layer* (SASL) based communications. When Microsoft Digest authenticates a client, it creates a *session key* that is stored on the Web server and used to authenticate subsequent authentication requests without needing to contact a domain controller for each authentication request. Similar to NTLM, digest authentication sends user credentials across the network as an encrypted hash so that the actual password information cannot be extracted in case a malicious attacker is attempting to "sniff" the network connection.

Passport Authentication

Any business that wants to provide the convenience of single sign-on to its customers can license and use Microsoft Passport authentication. Passport authentication enables your company to provide a convenient means for customers to access and transact business on a given Web site. Sites that rely on Passport authentication use a centralized Passport server to authenticate users, rather than hosting and maintaining their own authentication systems. From a technical perspective, Passport authentication relies on standards-based Web technologies, including SSL, HTTP redirects, and cookies.

Educating Users

The more highly publicized network security incidents always seem to center on a technical flaw: an overlooked patch that led to a global denial-of-service (DoS) attack, a flaw that led to the worldwide propagation of an e-mail virus, or something similar. However, many network intrusions are caused by a lack of knowledge among corporate employees. For this reason, user education is a critical component of any security plan. Make sure that your users understand the potential dangers of sharing their logon credentials with anyone else or leaving that information in a location where others could take note of it. Your users will be far more likely to cooperate and comply with corporate security standards if they understand the reasons behind the policies and the damage that they can cause by ignoring security measures. By combining user education with technical measures, such as password policies and strong network authentication, you will be well on your way to creating multiple layers of protection for your network and the data it contains.

Smart Card Authentication

Smart cards provide a portable method of providing security on a network for tasks like client authentication and securing user data. Smart cards and smart card authentication are discussed in detail in the chapter "Planning, Implementing, Maintaining Public Key Infrastructure, later in this book.

Using a smart card for network logons provides extremely strong authentication because it requires two factors: something the user *knows* (the PIN), and something the user *has* (the smart card itself). This system provides stronger authentication than a password alone, since a malicious user would need to have access to both the smart card and the PIN in order to impersonate a legitimate user. It's also difficult for an attacker to perform a smart card attack undetected, because the user would notice that his or her smart card was physically missing.

Planning a Security Group Strategy

As discussed in Chapter 10, a set of default groups is created during the installation of Windows Server 2003 on a computer. These groups reside in the local SAM database of the stand-alone or member server, and can only be granted rights and permissions on that computer. Domain controllers also have a set of default groups. These groups reside within the Active Directory database structure and can be used throughout the domain.

You aren't limited to using the default groups. Windows Server 2003 allows you to create your own groups both at the SAM and Active Directory database levels. This book deals with Active Directory, so we will assume that you are working in a Windows Server 2003 Active Directory environment when we discuss planning group strategy.

Security Group Best Practices

Microsoft has a number of different recommended methods for using groups in a domain environment. You should expect to be asked a number of complex questions about the appropriate use of groups. Most of their recommendations fall into one of two models:

- A single domain forest
- A multiple domain forest

Designing a Group Strategy for a Single Domain Forest

AGDLP. This simple acronym sums up everything you need to remember for the use of groups in a single domain forest environment. Each of the letters has a specific meaning:

- **A** Accounts
- **G** Global groups
- **DL** Domain local groups
- **P** Permissions

The acronym can be read as: **A**ccounts (user and computer objects) are placed into **G**lobal groups, which are placed into **D**omain **L**ocal groups, which are added to ACLs and granted **P**ermissions to a resource.

Consider this scenario: You have a new employee who is joining the benefits team within a company. The new user needs to access to both benefits-related resources and all general HR resources. Therefore, you add the user into both the Benefits and HR global groups. These global groups are themselves members of domain local groups, one of which is illustrated in Figure 11.7. The HR global group is a member of the HR_Print domain local group. This group is used to grant access to the general printers that all members of the HR department are allowed to use.

Figure 11.7 AGDLP in a Single Domain Forest

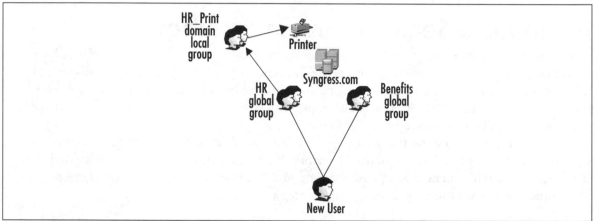

When the domain functional level is elevated to Windows 2000 native or Windows Server 2003, Microsoft specifies a new group model, AGGDLP. The meaning of the letters does not change. Therefore, this model means: **A**ccounts are placed into **G**lobal groups that can be placed into other **G**lobal groups and/or **D**omain **L**ocal groups, which are added to ACLs and granted **P**ermissions to resources. This can make a huge difference, because it allows you to potentially reduce the number of groups that you have to add a new user to.

Consider the example used previously. If you nest the Benefits global group into the HR global group, you gain a tremendous advantage. When a new user joins the benefits team, you only have to add that user's account to a single user group, Benefits. Because this group is also a member of the HR global group, the user will receive all of the permissions and rights assignments associated with both groups. Figure 11. 8 shows the AGGDLP model.

Figure 11.8 AGGDLP in a Single Domain Forest

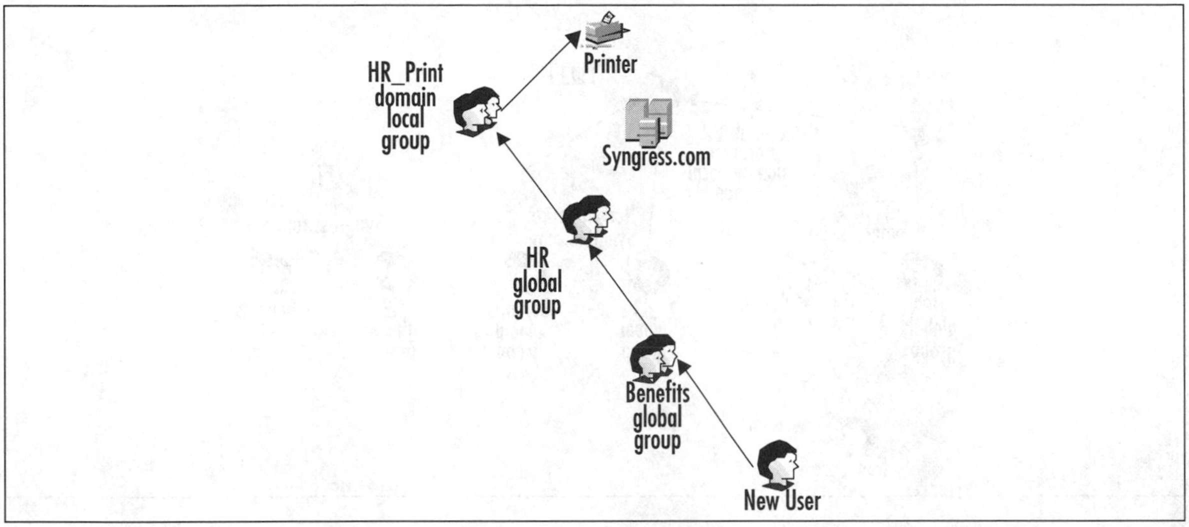

Designing a Group Strategy for a Multiple Domain Forest

These existing models can also be extended to a multiple domain forest. In a Windows 2000 mixed functional level domain, it takes quite a few resource assignments to grant permissions across domains. Extending the previous example, two additional domains will be added. Each domain is for a different region of the world, and each has an HR department. The company needs all HR employees to be able to access files that are located in the North America office. Because the domain is at the Windows 2000 mixed functional level, the AGDLP model is used.

Again, a new user joins the benefits team, this time in the Europe domain. The user is added to the Benefits and HR global groups in the Europe domain. The HR global group in each domain has also been added to the Global_HR_Resources domain local group in the North America Domain. The Global_HR_Resources DLG has been granted the necessary permissions on the ACL for the files. Because all HR employees are (directly or indirectly) members of the HR global group in their domain, and each HR global group is a member of the Global_HR_Resources domain local group, they all have permission to access the required files. These complex relationships are shown in Figure 11.9.

Figure 11.9 AGDLP in a Multiple Domain Forest

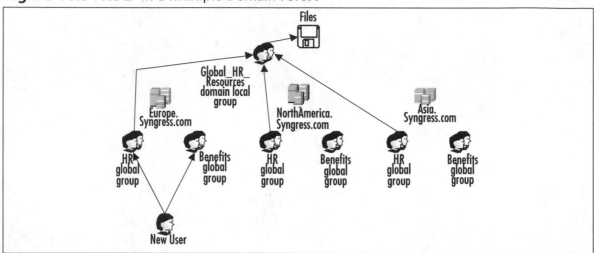

Moving all of the domains in the forest to the Windows 2000 native or Windows Server 2003 functional level greatly reduces the complexity. Just as we saw in the previous section, when a new benefits user joins the company, the only group his or her account needs to be made a member of is the Benefits global group in his or her regional domain. Again, this is because the Benefits global group is nested in the HR global group.

The real power in a multiple domain environment, however, comes in the ability to use universal security groups. You no longer have to add each HR global group into the Global_HR_Resources domain local group. Instead, you can add all of the HR global groups into a universal group called ALL_HR. You then add this group into the Global_HR_Resources DLG. These group memberships are shown in Figure 11.10.

When universal groups enter the design, we are using the AGGUDLP model (sometimes abbreviated AGUDLP), where **U** represents Universal group. This model means: **A**ccounts should be placed into **G**lobal groups that can be placed into other **G**lobal groups and/or **U**niversal groups, and then into **D**omain **L**ocal groups, which are added to ACLs and granted **P**ermissions to resources.

Figure 11.10 AGGUDLP in a Multiple Domain Forest

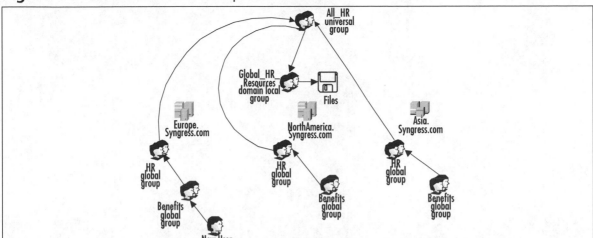

While this might look like a similar amount of work when compared with Figure 11.9, the real power of this design becomes evident when you attempt to grant all HR users access to another resource, such as a printer in Asia. In this case, you simply need to create a new DLG and grant the print permission for the printer in the Asia domain to that group. In Figure 11.11, the group is called HR_Print_Asia. You then simply add the All_HR universal group to the HR_Print_Asia domain local group. Imagine what the diagram would look like if you couldn't use a universal group and how much more work would be involved. You would need to add each HR global group to the HR_Print_Asia domain local group. Now imagine that you have dozens of similar situations in your forest, and you'll no doubt appreciate the simplicity and reduced management requirements that universal groups bring with them.

Figure 11.11 Using AGGUDLP to Grant Access to an Additional Resource

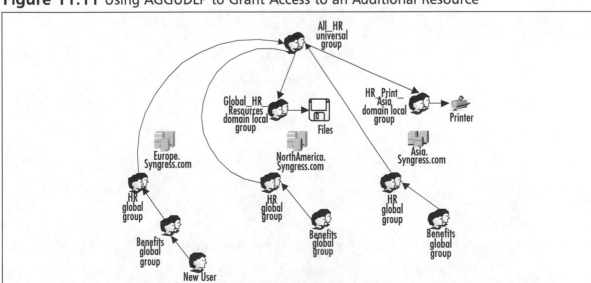

Chapter 12

Working with Forests and Domains

In this chapter:

☑ **Understanding Forest and Domain Functionality**

☑ **Creating the Forest and Domain Structure**

☑ **Implementing DNS in the Active Directory Network Environment**

Introduction

A Microsoft Active Directory network has both a physical and a logical structure. Forests and domains define the logical structure of the network, with domains organized into domain trees in which subdomains (called *child domains*) can be created under parent domains in a branching structure. Forests are collections of domain trees that have trust relationships with one another, but each domain tree has its own separate namespace.

In this chapter, you will learn all about the functions of forests and domains in the Windows Server 2003 Active Directory infrastructure, and we will walk you through the steps of creating a forest and domain structure for a network. You'll learn to install domain controllers (DCs), create the forest root domain and a child domain, find out how to name and rename domains, and how to set the functional level of a forest and domain.

The Domain Name System (DNS) is an integral part of a Windows Server 2003 network, as it is used for providing name resolution within the network. We will discuss the role of DNS in the Active Directory environment, and you'll learn about the relationship of the DNS and Active Directory namespaces, how DNS zones are integrated into Active Directory, and how to configure DNS servers for use with Active Directory.

Understanding Forest and Domain Functionality

Active Directory is composed of a number of components, each associated with a different concept, or layer of functionality. You should understand each of these layers before making any changes to the network. The Active Directory itself is a distributed database, which means it can be spread across multiple computers within the forest. Among the major logical components are:

- Forests
- Trees
- Domains
- The domain namespace

Aspects of the physical structure include the following:

- Sites
- Servers
- Roles
- Links

Administrative boundaries, network and directory performance, security, resource management, and basic functionality are all dependent on the proper interaction of these elements.

Note that the differentiation between forests and trees is most obvious in the namespace. By its nature, a *tree* is one or more domains with a contiguous namespace. Each tree consists of one or more domains, while each *forest* consists of one or more trees. Because a forest can be composed of discrete multiple trees, a forest's namespace can be discontiguous. By *discontiguous*, we mean that the namespaces anchor to different forest-root DNS domains, such as cats.com and dogs.com. Both are top-level domains and are considered two trees in a forest when combined into a single directory.

The Role of the Forest

An Active Directory always begins with a *forest root domain*, which is automatically the first domain you install. This root domain becomes the foundation for additional directory components. Certain forest objects and services are only present at the root (for example, the Enterprise Administrators and Schema Administrators groups, and the Schema Master and Domain Naming Master roles). These cannot be easily recreated, depending on the type of failure.

New Forestwide Features

Many of the new features offered by Windows Server 2003 are only available in a forest where you have raised the forest functional level to Windows Server 2003. For more information on functional levels and a breakdown of when these new features become available, see the section *Forest and Domain Functional Levels* later in the chapter.

Defunct Schema Objects

In Windows 2000 Active Directory, you could deactivate a schema class or attribute. Now, once your forest has been raised to the Windows Server 2003 functional level, you can not only deactivate them, you can even rename and redefine them. This feature protects against the possibility of one application irreversibly claiming another application's schema. It allows for the redefinition of classes and attributes without changing their unique identities. These items are called *reused*. If the class or attribute is left deactivated, it is called *defunct*.

Domain Rename

This is a complex and sweeping modification to the namespace of a domain. DNS names, and NetBIOS names of any child, parent, or forest-root domain can now be changed. As far as Windows Server 2003 Active Directory is concerned, the identity of a domain rests in its domain *Globally Unique Identifier* (GUID), and its domain SID. Creating new DNS or NetBIOS names will leave those attributes unchanged. The domain rename function is not able to promote a domain to the forest root role. Even if you rename the forest root domain, its role will remain unchanged.

The renaming process will temporarily interrupt the functionality of the domain and its interaction with the forest, until the DCs are rebooted. Client workstations will not function properly until they are each rebooted *twice*. Due to the complexity of the operation, the risks of such a sweeping change, and the unavoidable domain and workstation service interruptions, domain renaming should not be considered a routine operation.

Forest Restructuring

Existing domains can now be moved to other locations within the namespace. During this restructuring, you will manually break and reestablish the appropriate trust relationships among the domains. A requirement for namespace changes, or a need to decrease administrative overhead, typically drives forest restructuring. This reduction in overhead is accomplished by reducing replication traffic, reducing the amount of user and group administration required, and simplifying the administration of Group Policy. The smallest possible number of domains will provide the most efficient design. Minimizing the number of domains reduces administrative costs and increases the efficiency of your organization. Reasons to restructure include:

- Decommissioning a domain that is no longer needed
- Changing the internal namespace
- Upgrading your network infrastructure to increase your bandwidth and replication capacity, which enables you to combine domains

Before you begin restructuring Windows Server 2003 domains within your forest, make sure that the forest is operating at the Windows Server 2003 functional level.

Universal Group Caching

Universal Group caching is a new feature of the Windows Server 2003 DC, which caches a user's complete Universal Group membership. The cache is populated at first logon, and subsequent logons use the cache, which is refreshed periodically.

Some of the benefits of Universal Group caching include faster logon times and authenticating DCs no longer have to consult a GC to get Universal Group membership information. In addition, you can save the cost of upgrading a server to handle the extra load for hosting the GC. Finally, network bandwidth is minimized because a DC no longer has to handle replication for all of the objects located in the forest.

Application Partitions

Another DC enhancement allows for the creation of application-specific Active Directory partitions, also known as *naming contexts*. Active Directory stores the information in a hierarchy that can be populated with any type of object except for security principles such as users, groups, and computers. This dynamic body of data can be configured with a replication strategy involving DCs across the entire forest, not just a single domain. With application partitions, you can define as many or as few replicas as you want. Site topologies and replication schedules are observed, and the application objects are not replicated to the GC. Conveniently, application partitions can leverage DNS for location and naming. The Windows Server 2003 Web Edition cannot host application partitions because they do not support the DC role.

Install from Backups

The *Install from backups* feature provides the capability to install a DC using backup media rather than populating the Active Directory through a lengthy replication period. This is especially useful for domains that cross-site boundaries using limited WAN connectivity. To do this, back up your directory store using **Windows Backup**, restore the files at the remote site's candidate DC, and run **dcpromo** using the **source replication from files** option. This also works for GC servers.

Active Directory Quotas

The new Active Directory quotas (not to be confused with disk quotas) are defined as the number of objects that can be owned by a given user in a given directory partition. Fortunately, Domain Admins and Enterprise Administrators are exempt from the quota, and they do not apply at all to the schema partition. Replicated operations do not count toward the quota; only the original operations do. Quota administration is performed through a set of command-line tools, including *dsadd*, *dsmod*, *dsget*, and *dsquery*. No graphical interface exists for quota administration.

Linked Value Replication

Linked value replication provides an answer to Windows 2000's limit of 5000 direct group members. Instead of treating a large group as a single replication unit, linked value replication allows a single member to be added or removed from the group during replication, thereby reducing network traffic. Without it, for example, any changes to a 10,000-member distribution group will trigger a complete replication. With a group that large, this would be likely to occur many times in a typical day.

Improved Knowledge Consistency Checker

The Windows 2000 Knowledge Consistency Checker (KCC) would not operate properly within a forest containing more than 200 sites due to the complexity of the inter-site replication topology generator algorithms. The service had to be turned off in that case, and the replication topology had to be managed manually. The Windows Server 2003 KCC can automatically manage replication among up to 5000 sites due to new, more efficient algorithms. In addition, it uses greatly improved topology generation event logging to assist in troubleshooting.

Reduced NTDS.DIT Size

The Windows Server 2003 directory takes advantage of a new feature called *Single Instance Store* (SIS). This limits the duplication of redundant information. The new directory store is about 60 percent smaller than the one in Windows 2000.

Forest Trusts

In Windows NT 4.0, there were few options for the interoperability of business units; for example, either Calico.cats.com trusted Labs.dogs.com or they didn't. There were no other real options. In addition, if trust existed at all, it tended to be complete. When Windows 2000 introduced the Active Directory, many more options became available so that partnerships and integrated project teams could form on the network just as they did in real life. The problem with that approach was that there always had to be a dominant partner at the root— the playing field could never be completely even.

Understanding the politics of business, Microsoft stepped in with a solution called *multiple-forest trusts* in Windows Server 2003, which, when used, result in a configuration called *federated forests*. Without the forest trust, Kerberos authentication between forests would not work. Remember that having two forests means two Active Directory databases and two completely distinct sets of directory objects, such as user accounts. Accessing resources across the federated forest boundary requires a more complex trust path than the one between domains within a single forest.

Routing Hints for Forest Trusts

Routing hints are a new feature of GCs. The problem with creating trusts between forests is that all traditional authentication channels stop at the forest boundary. DCs and traditional GCs are sometimes not enough. When these fail to produce a *Service Principal Name* (SPN) describing the location of the service being requested, routing hints from the Windows Server 2003 GC help guide the workstation toward the correct forest within the *Federated Forest* boundary. The GC server does this by checking the forest trust's *Trusted Domain Object* (TDO) for trusted name suffixes that match the one found in the destination SPN. The routing hint always goes back to the originating device so that it can resume its search for the SPN location in the other forest. This new functionality has some limitations. If the TDO contains outdated or incorrect information, the *hint* might be incorrect since the GC does not actually check for the existence of the other forests.

Cross-Forest Authentication

Although some types of data access are supported, Windows Server 2003 does not support NetBIOS name resolution or Kerberos delegation across forests. NTLM authentication for down-level clients continues to be fully supported, however. A Universal Group in one forest might contain global groups from one or more additional forests across any available forest trusts.

Federated Forest, or cross-forest, authentication takes two forms. In the default *forest-wide authentication*, an "allow-all deny-some" approach is used. In other words, external users have the same level of access to local resources as the local users do. The other form of access control takes the security conscious approach of "deny-all allow-some." This optional method is called *selective authentication*, and requires more administrative overhead by granting explicit control over the outside use of local resources. You must set a control access right called *allowed to authenticate* on an object for the users and groups that need access from another forest. If selective authentication is enabled, an *Other Organization* SID is associated with the user. This SID is then used to differentiate the external user from local users and determines if an attempt can be made to authenticate with the destination service.

For reliable authentication using Kerberos, system time must be accurate across every workstation and server. Servers are best synchronized with the same time source, while workstations are synchronizing time with the servers. In an upgraded Active Directory domain, this is usually not a problem.

New Domainwide Features

There are many new features in Windows Server 2003 related to domainwide features, the most significant of which we discuss next.

Domain Controller Rename

Not to be confused with domain renaming, *domain controller rename* is the ability to rename a DC without following the Windows 2000 procedure of demoting, renaming, and promoting again. In a large domain, this saves considerable time, especially over a slow WAN link, since the process of re-promoting the DC requires a replication of the Active Directory.

Universal Groups and Group Conversions

Universal Groups are able to contain members from any domain in any forest, and they replicate to the GC. They are particularly useful for administrative groups. One of the best uses for groups with universal scope is to consolidate groups above the domain level. To do this, add domain user accounts to groups with global scope and nest these Global Groups within Universal Groups. Using this strategy, changes to the Global Groups do not directly affect the membership of groups with universal scope. Taking it one step further, a Universal Group in one forest can contain Global Groups from one or more *additional* forests across any available forest trusts.

Here is an example. You have two domains in different forests with NetBIOS names of CATS and DOGS. Each domain contains a Global Group called Birdwatchers. To take advantage of this new capability, you add both of the Global Groups, CATS\Birdwatchers and DOGS\Birdwatchers, to a Universal Group you create called ALLBirdwatchers. The second step is to create an identical Universal Group in the other forest as well. The ALLBirdwatchers group can now be used to authenticate users anywhere in both enterprises. Any changes in the membership of the individual Birdwatchers groups will not cause replication of the ALLBirdwatchers group.

Table 12.1 Summary of Universal Group Capabilities by Domain Functional Level

Functional Level	Universal Group Members	Universal Group Nesting
Windows 2000 mixed	None	None
Windows 2000 native	User and computer accounts, Global Groups, and Universal Groups from any domain	Universal Groups can be added to other groups and assigned permissions in any domain
Windows Server 2003 interim	None	None
Windows Server 2003	User and computer accounts, Global Groups, and Universal Groups from any domain	Universal Groups can be added to other groups and assigned permissions in any domain

Security Group Nesting

Security Groups are used to grant access to resources. Using nesting, you can add a group to a group. This reduces replication traffic by nesting groups to consolidate member accounts. A Security Group can also be used as an e-mail distribution list, but a Distribution Group cannot be used in a discretionary access control list (DACL), which means it cannot be used to grant access to resources. Sending e-mail to a Security Group sends the message to all members of the group.

Distribution Group Nesting

Distribution Groups are collections of users, computers, contacts, and other groups. They are typically used only for e-mail applications. Security Groups, on the other hand, are used to grant access to resources *and* as e-mail distribution lists. Using nesting, you can add a group to a group. *Group nesting* consolidates member accounts and reduces replication traffic. Windows NT did not support Distribution Groups within the OS, but they are supported in all versions of Active Directory. Distribution Groups cannot be listed in DACLs in any version of Windows, which means they cannot be used to define permissions on resources and objects, although they *can* be used in DACLs at the application layer. Microsoft Exchange is a common example. If you do not need a group for security purposes, create a Distribution Group instead.

Number of Domain Objects Supported

In Windows 2000, group membership was stored in Active Directory as a single multivalued attribute. When the membership list changed, the entire group had to be replicated to all DCs. So that the store could be updated in a single transaction during the replication process, group memberships were limited to 5000 members. In Windows Server 2003, *Linked Value Replication* removes this limitation and minimizes network traffic by setting the granularity of group replication to a single principle value, such as a user or group.

Distribution Groups

Distribution Groups, unlike Security Groups, are not primarily used for access control, although they can be used in an ACL at the application layer. Distribution groups are designed to be used with e-mail applications only. You can convert a Distribution Group to a Security Group (or vice versa), if the functional level is Windows 2000 native or higher. You have to be a domain or enterprise admin, or a member of the Account Operators Group (or have the appropriate authority delegated) to convert a group. Changing the group type is as simple as right-clicking the group in **Active Directory Users and Computers**, clicking **Properties**, and clicking the desired group type on the **General** tab.

Domain Trees

A domain tree can be thought of as a DNS namespace composed of one or more domains. If you plan to create a forest with discontiguous namespaces, you must create more than one tree. Referring back to Figure 12.1, you see two trees in that forest, Cats.com and Dogs.com. Each has a *contiguous namespace* because each domain in the hierarchy is directly related to the domains above and below it in each tree. The forest has a *discontiguous namespace* because it contains two unrelated top-level domains.

Forest and Domain Functional Levels

Functional levels are a mechanism that Microsoft uses to remove obsolete backward compatibility within the Active Directory. It is a feature that helps improve performance and security. In Windows 2000, each domain had two functional levels (which were called "modes"), native mode and mixed mode, while the forest only had one functional level. In Windows Server 2003, there are two more levels to consider in both domains and forests. To enable all Windows Server 2003 forest and domainwide features, all DCs must be running Windows Server 2003 and the functional levels must be set to *Windows Server 2003*. Table 12.2 summarizes the levels, DCs supported in each level, and each level's primary purpose.

Table 12.2 Domain and Forest Functional Levels

Type	Functional Level	Supported DCs	Purpose
Domain Default	Windows 2000 mixed	NT, 2000, 2003	Supports mixed environments during upgrade; low security, high compatibility
Domain	Windows 2000 native	2000, 2003	Supports upgrade from 2000 to 2003
Domain	Windows Server 2003 interim	NT, 2003	Supports upgrade from NT to 2003; low security, no new features

Continued

Table 12.2 Domain and Forest Functional Levels

Type	Functional Level	Supported DCs	Purpose
Domain	Windows Server 2003	2003	Ideal level, best security, least compatibility, all new Active Directory features are enabled
Forest Default	Windows 2000	NT, 2000, 2003	Supports mixed environments during upgrade; low security, high compatibility
Forest	Windows Server 2003 interim	NT, 2003	Supports upgrade from NT to 2003; low security, some new features
Forest	Windows Server 2003	2003	Ideal level, best security, least compatibility, all new Active Directory features are enabled

Domain Functionality

When considering raising the domain functionality level, remember that the new features will directly affect only the domain being raised. Once the domain functional level has been raised, no prior version DCs can be added to the domain. In the case of the Windows Server 2003 domain functional level, no Windows 2000 servers can be promoted to DC status after the functionality has been raised. Table 12.2 summarizes the levels, DCs supported in each level, and the level's primary purpose. See Table 12.3 for a summary of the capabilities of the current Windows 2000 and new Windows Server 2003 domain functional levels.

Table 12.3 Domain Functional Level Features

Domain Feature	Windows 2000 Mixed	Windows 2000 Native	Windows Server 2003 Interim	Windows Server 2003 Native
Local and Global Groups	Enabled	Enabled	Enabled	Enabled
Distribution Groups	Enabled	Enabled	Enabled	Enabled
GC support	Enabled	Enabled	Enabled	Enabled
Number of domain objects supported	40,000	1,000,000	40,000	1,000,000
Kerberos KDC key version numbers	Disabled	Disabled	Disabled	Enabled
Security Group nesting	Disabled	Enabled	Disabled	Enabled
Distribution Group nesting	Enabled	Enabled	Enabled	Enabled
Universal Groups	Disabled	Enabled	Disabled	Enabled
SIDHistory	Disabled	Enabled	Disabled	Enabled
Converting groups between Security Groups and Distribution Groups	Disabled	Enabled	Disabled	Enabled
DC rename	Disabled	Disabled	Disabled	Enabled
Logon timestamp attribute updated and replicated	Disabled	Disabled	Disabled	Enabled
User password support on the *InetOrgPerson objectClass*	Disabled	Disabled	Disabled	Enabled
Constrained delegation	Disabled	Disabled	Disabled	Enabled
Users and Computers container redirection	Disabled	Disabled	Disabled	Enabled

Windows 2000 Mixed Domain Functional Level

The Windows 2000 mixed domain functional level is primarily designed to support mixed environments during the course of an upgrade. Typically, this applies to a transition from Windows NT to Windows 2000, although it is also the default mode for a newly created Windows Server 2003 domain. It is characterized by lowered security features and defaults, and the highest compatibility level possible for Active Directory.

In the *Windows 2000 mixed* functional level, which is the default level, Windows 2000 and greater DCs can exist, as well as Windows NT backup domain controllers (BDCs). Newly created Windows Server 2003 domains always start at this level. Windows NT primary domain controllers (PDCs) do not exist in any version of Active Directory.

Windows 2000 Native Domain Functional Level

The Windows 2000 native domain functional level is primarily intended to support an upgrade from Windows 2000 to Server 2003. Typically, this applies to existing Active Directory implementations since mixed and interim modes support the upgrade from Windows NT. It is characterized by better security features and defaults, and an average compatibility level.

In *Windows 2000 native* functional level, DCs have all been upgraded to Windows 2000 or Windows Server 2003. Native mode enables Universal Security Groups, nested groups, group conversion between distribution and security types, and SIDHistory.

Windows Server 2003 Interim Domain Functional Level

The Windows Server 2003 interim domain functional level is the preferred method of supporting Windows NT environments during the course of an upgrade. This level *only* applies to a transition from Windows NT to Windows Server 2003 because it does not allow for the presence of Windows 2000 DCs. It is characterized by lowered security features and defaults, similar to the Windows 2000 mixed domain functional level, and a high compatibility level for Windows NT.

In the *Windows Server 2003* interim domain functional level, no domainwide features are activated, although many forest level features are activated at this level (see the section *Windows Server 2003 Interim Forest Functional Level* later in the chapter). This mode is only used during the upgrade of Windows NT 4.0 DCs to Windows Server 2003 DCs. If a Windows 2000 Active Directory domain already exists, then the Windows Server 2003 interim domain level cannot be achieved.

Remember that any domain joined to an existing forest inherits its domain functional level from the child, top-level, or root-level domain that it connects to during the joining process. The domain level of Windows 2000 is only the default when you create a new forest root.

Windows Server 2003 Domain Functional Level

The Windows Server 2003 domain functional level is the ideal level. This level does not allow for the presence of Windows NT or Windows 2000 DCs. It starts out with the best security defaults and capabilities, and the least compatibility with earlier versions of windows. All new 2003 Active Directory domain features are enabled at this level, providing the most efficient and productive environment. In the Windows Server 2003 domain functional level, only Windows Server 2003 DCs can exist.

Forest Functionality

The Windows Server 2003 *forest functional levels* are named similarly to the domain levels. Windows 2000 originally had only one level, and that level was carried over into Windows 2003. The two other available functional levels are Windows Server 2003 *interim* and Windows Server 2003, sometimes referred to as Windows Server 2003 *native* mode. Table 12.2 summarizes the levels, DCs supported in each level, and the level's primary purpose. See Table 12.4 for a summary of the capabilities of the new Windows Server 2003 forest functional levels.

Table 12.4 New Forest Functional Level Features

Forest Feature	Windows 2000	Windows Server 2003 Interim	Windows Server 2003 Native
Support for more than 5000 members per group	Not available	Enabled	Enabled
Universal Group caching	Enabled	Enabled	Enabled
Application partitions	Enabled	Enabled	Enabled
Install from backups	Enabled	Enabled	Enabled
Quotas	Enabled	Enabled	Enabled
Rapid GC demotion	Enabled	Enabled	Enabled
SIS for system access control lists (SACL) in the Jet Database Engine	Enabled	Enabled	Enabled
Improve topology generation event logging	Enabled	Enabled	Enabled
Windows Server 2003 DC assumes the Intersite Topology Generator (ISTG) role	Enabled	Enabled	Enabled
Efficient group member replication using linked value replication	Disabled	Enabled	Enabled
Improved KCC inter-site replication topology generator algorithms	Disabled	Enabled	Enabled

Continued

Table 12.4 New Forest Functional Level Features

Forest Feature	Windows 2000	Windows Server 2003 Interim	Windows Server 2003 Native
ISTG aliveness no longer replicated	Disabled	Enabled	Enabled
Attributes added to the GC, such as: *ms-DS-Entry-Time-To-Die*, *Message Queuing-Secured-Source*, *Message Queuing-Multicast-Address*, *Print-Memory*, *Print-Rate*, and *Print-Rate-Unit*	Disabled	Enabled	Enabled
Defunct schema objects	Disabled	Disabled	Enabled
Cross-forest trust	Disabled	Disabled	Enabled
Domain rename	Disabled	Disabled	Enabled
Dynamic auxiliary classes	Disabled	Disabled	Enabled
InetOrgPerson objectClass change	Disabled	Disabled	Enabled
Application groups	Disabled	Disabled	Enabled
15-second intrasite replication frequency for Windows Server 2003 DCs upgraded from Windows 2000	Disabled	Disabled	Enabled
Reduced NTDS.DIT size	Disabled	Disabled	Enabled
Unlimited site management	Disabled	Disabled	Enabled

Windows 2000 Forest Functional Level (default)

The Windows 2000 forest functional level is primarily designed to support mixed environments during the course of an upgrade. Typically, this applies to a transition from Windows 2000 to Windows Server 2003. It is also the default mode for a newly created Windows Server 2003 domain. It is characterized by relatively lower security features and reduced efficiency, but maintains the highest compatibility level possible for Active Directory. The Windows 2003 interim forest functional level handles upgrades from Windows NT to Windows Server 2003.

In the *Windows 2000* functional level, which is the default level, Windows 2000 and greater DCs can exist, as well as Windows NT BDCs. Newly created Windows Server 2003 forests always start at this level. Windows NT PDCs do not exist in any version of Active Directory. Features available in the Windows 2000 forest functional level of Windows Server 2003 carry over the old features and add many new ones.

Windows Server 2003 Interim Forest Functional Level

The Windows Server 2003 interim forest functional level is the preferred method of supporting Windows NT environments during the course of an upgrade. This level *only* applies to a transition from Windows NT to Windows Server 2003 because it does not allow for the presence of Windows 2000 DCs anywhere in the forest. It is characterized by lowered security features and defaults, but provides many efficiency improvements over the Windows 2000 forest functional level.

In the *Windows Server 2003* interim forest functional level, unlike the Windows Server 2003 interim domain functional level, many new features are activated while still allowing Windows NT 4.0 BDC replication. This mode is only used during the upgrade of a Windows NT 4.0 domain to a Windows Server 2003 forest. If a Windows 2000 Active Directory forest already exists, then the Windows Server 2003 interim forest level cannot be achieved.

To revert your Windows Server 2003 forest back to the interim level for an upgrade, you must manually configure the forest level with LDAP tools such as Ldp.exe or Adsiedit.msc. Remember that any domain joined to an existing forest inherits its domain functional level from the child, top-level, or root-level domain that it connects to during the joining process. The default forest level of Windows 2000 only applies when you create a new forest.

Windows Server 2003 Forest Functional Level

The Windows Server 2003 forest functional level is the ideal level. This level does not allow for the presence of Windows NT or Windows 2000 DCs anywhere in the forest. It starts out with the best security defaults and capabilities, and the least compatibility with earlier versions of Windows. All new 2003 Active Directory forest features are enabled at this level, providing the most efficient and productive environment. In the Windows Server 2003 forest functional level, only Windows Server 2003 DCs can exist.

Raising the Functional Level of a Domain and Forest

Before increasing a functional level, you should prepare for it by performing the following tasks. First, inventory your entire forest for earlier versions of DCs. The Active Directory Domains and Trusts MMC snap-in can generate a detailed report should you need it. You can also perform a custom LDAP query from the Active Directory Users and Computers MMC snap-in that will discover Windows NT DC objects within the forest. Use the following search string:

```
(&(objectCategory=computer)(operatingSystem Version=4*)
(userAccountControl:1.2.840.113556.1.4.803:=8192))
```

There should be no spaces in the query, and type it in all on one line. The search string is shown on two lines for readability.

Second, you need to *physically* locate all down-level DCs for the new functional level in the domain or forest as needed, and either upgrade or remove them.

Third, verify that end-to-end replication is working in the forest using the Windows Server 2003 versions of Repadmin.exe and Replmon.exe.

Finally, verify the compatibility of your applications and services with the version of Windows that your DCs will be running, and specifically their compatibility with the target functional level. Use a lab environment to test for compatibility issues, and contact the appropriate vendors for compatibility information.

Domain Functional Level

Before raising the functional level of a domain, all DCs must be upgraded to the minimum OS level as shown in Table 12.2. Remember that when you raise the domain functional level to Windows 2000 native or Windows Server 2003, it can never be changed back to Windows 2000 mixed mode. The steps that follow take you systematically through the process of verifying the current domain functional level. Then, we'll step through the process of raising the domain functional level. To raise the level, you must be an enterprise administrator, a domain administrator in the domain you want to raise, or have the appropriate authority.

Verify the domain functional level

1. Log on as a Domain Admin of the domain you are checking.

2. Click on **Start | Control Panel | Performance and Maintenance | Administrative Tools | Active Directory Users and Computers**, or use the Microsoft Management Console (MMC) preconfigured with the Active Directory Users and Computers snap-in.

3. Locate the domain in the console tree that you are going to raise in functional level. Right-click the domain and select **Raise Domain Functional Level**.

4. In the Raise Domain Functional Level dialog box, the current domain functional level appears under **Current domain functional level**.

This check can also be performed using the Active Directory Domains and Trusts MMC snap-in.

Raise the domain fuctional level

1. Log on locally as a Domain Admin to the PDC or the PDC Emulator FSMO of the domain you are raising.

2. Click on **Start | Administrative Tools | Active Directory Domains and Trusts**, or use the MMC preconfigured with the Active Directory Domain and Trusts snap-in.

3. Locate the domain in the console tree that you are going to raise in functional level. Right-click the domain and select **Raise Domain Functional Level**.

4. A dialog box will appear entitled **Select an available domain functional level**. There are only two possible choices, although both might not be available.

- Select **Windows 2000 native**, and then click the **Raise** button to raise the domain functional level to Windows 2000 native.

- Select **Windows Server 2003**, and then click the **Raise** button to raise the domain functional level to Windows Server 2003.

Forest Functional Level

Before raising the functional level of a forest, all DCs in the forest must be upgraded to the minimum OS level as shown in Table 12.2. In practice, since the only forest functional level that will be available to you is Windows Server 2003, all DCs in the forest must be running Windows Server 2003. Locate all down-level DCs and either upgrade them or remove them from the domain. You do not have to upgrade the domain functional level before the forest functional level. The reason for this is that all domains in the forest will automatically raise to the level of Windows Server 2003 to match the forest level after Active Directory replicates the changes. The forest Schema Master performs this operation. The steps below take you through the process of verifying the current forest functional level. You can then step through the process of raising the forest functional level. To raise the forest level, you must be an enterprise administrator, a domain administrator at the forest root, or have the appropriate authority.

Verify the forest functional level

1. Log on as an Enterprise Administrator in the forest you are checking.

2. Click on **Start | Administrative Tools | Active Directory Domains and Trusts**, or use the MMC preconfigured with the Active Directory Domains and Trusts snap-in.

3. In the console tree, right-click the **Active Directory Domains and Trusts** folder and select **Raise Forest Functional Level**.

4. In the Raise Forest Functional Level dialog box, the current forest functional level appears under **Current forest functional level**.

Raise the forest functional level

1. Log on locally as an Enterprise Administrator on the PDC Emulator FSMO of the forest root domain you are raising.

2. Click on **Start | All Programs | Administrative Tools | Active Directory Domains and Trusts**, or use the MMC preconfigured with the Active Directory Domains and Trusts snap-in.

3. In the console tree, right-click the **Active Directory Domains and Trusts** folder and select **Raise Forest Functional Level**.

4. Where it asks you to Select an available forest functional level, click Windows Server 2003, and then click the **Raise** button.

Optimizing Your Strategy for Raising Functional Levels

There are two basic strategies for traveling the path from the Windows 2000 native level and Windows 2000 mixed-mode levels to the goal of Windows Server 2003 functional levels across your forest.

- The Windows 2000 native mode path.
  - Raise the level of all domains to the Windows 2000 native functional level.
  - Raise the forest level to Windows Server 2003.

Benefits of this method include:

- You do not have to perform the domain level-raising procedure on every domain before raising the forest level.

- It automatically does the work of tracking down all down-level domains and DCs for you. The process fails if these exist, but then you have a ready list of preparation work to do. This is helpful if your forest is not well documented. See the sidebar *If Raising the Forest Functional Level Fails* for more information.

- The Windows Server 2003 level path.
  - Raise the level of all domains to the Windows 2000 native functional level.
  - Raise the level of all domains to the Windows Server 2003 functional level.
  - Raise the forest level to Windows Server 2003.

The benefits of this method are:

- All of the new Windows Server 2003 domain-level features are turned on before you make the commitment to raising the level of the forest.

- You can perform integration and interoperability testing on a smaller scale without committing the forest to the functional upgrade.

There are three basic approaches for the use of interim modes when upgrading Windows NT to Windows Server 2003. Interim level should be avoided if you will ever have a need to implement Windows 2000 DCs. Here are the three strategies:

- When upgrading the Windows NT PDC into a *new* Windows Server 2003 forest, select the interim level from the dcpromo utility.

- When upgrading the Windows NT PDC into an *existing* Windows Server 2003 forest, manually set the interim level with Ldp.exe or Adsiedit.msc, and join the forest during the upgrade. The upgraded domain inherits the interim setting from the forest.

- Upgrade or remove all Windows NT BDCs, and then upgrade the Windows NT PDC. Since no Windows NT DCs remain in the domain, the Windows Server 2003 interim functionality level is not needed.

Creating the Forest and Domain Structure

The process of creating the forest and domain structure is centered on the use of the Active Directory Installation Wizard. This utility installs and configures DCs, which in turn provide the Active Directory directory service to networked computers and users. The first step is to install Windows Server 2003 as a member server or a stand-alone server. At this point, you should be familiar with that process, so it will not be covered here.

Next comes the decision process leading to the installation of a DC. Essentially, there are two reasons to install a DC: to create a new domain, or to add an additional DC to an existing domain. Depending on your current forest structure, you will end up with one of four results:

- A new forest
- A new domain tree in an existing forest
- A new child domain in an existing domain
- A new DC in an existing domain

Deciding When to Create a New DC

Since a domain cannot exist without a DC, you must create at least one for each domain. The process of creating the first DC also creates the domain itself. The domain can be either a new child domain or the root of a new tree. The difference is in the namespace. See the section *Domain Trees earlier* in the chapter. Here are the four main reasons to create a new DC:

- Creating the first domain in your network
- Creating a new domain in your forest
- Improving a domain's reliability
- Improving network performance between sites

If you want to create a domain with a name that is not related to any other namespace in your forest, you will create a new tree. If you want to create a domain that will function as an additional subunit within an existing domain, you will create a child domain.

To improve a domain's reliability, you should always create at least a second DC in each domain. That way, if the first one fails, you will still be able to use the second. If your existing DCs are overloaded, simply adding another DC to your domain will help spread the load. If any of your domains are divided by WAN links, then it is a good practice to place a DC in each site. Besides lowering WAN bandwidth utilization and improving logon response times, you also provide a level of fault tolerance. If the WAN link fails, users on both sides of the link will continue to be able to log on if your domain is at the Windows Server 2003 functional level.

Active Directory requires DNS. The Active Directory Installation Wizard will look for an authoritative DNS server that accepts dynamic updates for the domain. If a DNS server that can accept dynamic updates is not available, the Active Directory Installation Wizard will optionally create one for you that is preconfigured for the name of your domain. When you restart the new DC, it will register itself with DNS.

Installing Domain Controllers

You should know what type of domain you want to install before you begin, and the namespace it will use. Read the procedure for the type of domain you want to install and know what your responses will be. For example, if you want the *shared system volume* (SYSVOL) on its own disk volume, you will need to prepare it ahead of time. Before you run the Active Directory Installation Wizard, make sure that the authoritative DNS zone allows dynamic updates and that your DNS server supports SRV records. As always, no matter how small the domain, it should always have two DCs for fault tolerance and availability.

Creating a Forest Root Domain

The initial DC that you install will provide your users with the Active Directory. Consider making this an empty root domain where your Enterprise Administrators have accounts, but no regular users. With the procedure that follows, you will simultaneously create your first domain, called the root domain, and your first forest.

Create a new domain in a new forest

1. Log on as a local Administrator.

2. Click **Start | Run**.

3. Type **dcpromo**.

4. Click **OK** to start the Active Directory Installation Wizard.

5. In the **Welcome to the Active Directory Installation Wizard** window, click **Next.**

6. In the **Operating System Compatibility** window, click **Next.**

7. In the **Domain Controller Type** window, click **Domain controller for a new domain | Next.**

8. In the **Create New Domain** window, click **Domain in a new forest | Next.**

9. In the **New Domain Name** window, type the full DNS domain name for the new domain, and click **Next.**

10. In the **NetBIOS Domain Name** window, verify the NetBIOS name and click **Next.** The default name is generally the best one to use.

11. In the **Database and Log Folders** window, type or browse to the location where you want the database and log folders. Click **Next.**

12. In the **Shared System Volume** window, type or browse to the location where you want the SYSVOL folder. Click **Next.**

13. In the **DNS Registration Diagnostics** window, verify an existing DNS server to be authoritative for this new forest, or click **Install** and configure the DNS server on this computer, and set this computer to use this DNS server as its preferred DNS server. Click **Next.**

14. In the Permissions window, you have two options: **Permissions compatible with pre-Windows 2000 server operating systems** and **Permissions compatible only with Windows 2000 or Windows Server 2003 operating systems**. Select one, and then click **Next**.

15. In the **Directory Services Restore Mode Administrator Password** window, input and confirm the password for the **Directory Services Restore Mode**. Click **Next**.

16. Read the **Summary** window. Click **Next**. The installation will continue for several minutes.

17. Restart your new DC.

18. Verify that the installation was successful. Open a command prompt and enter the *Net Share* command. It should report the existence of the *Netlogon* and *SYSVOL* shares. To verify that the DNS service locator records for the new DC were successfully created, follow these steps:

   1. Click **Start | Administrative Tools | DNS** to start the DNS administrator console.

   2. Expand the server name.

   3. Expand **Forward Lookup Zones**.

   4. Expand the domain.

   5. Verify that the _msdcs, _sites, _tcp, and _udp folders are present and contain records for your new DC. These service location records are crucial to the operation of the DC. See Figure 12.1 for a view of the DNS administrator tool used to view them.

Figure 12.1 The DNS Administrator Tool Used to Verify a Successful Forest-Root

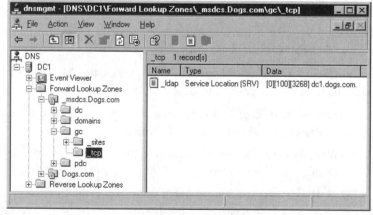

Creating a New Domain Tree in an Existing Forest

This will often be the second domain that you install. This type of arrangement accommodates a forest comprised of two different company divisions, or two companies within a larger corporation. Domains are used as boundaries for security and administration. With the procedure that follows, you will simultaneously create your first nonroot top-level domain, and the second tree in your forest. Note that a new bidirectional, transitive trust is automatically created with the forest root.

Create a new domain tree in an existing forest

1. Log in as a local Administrator.

2. Click **Start | Run**.

3. Type **dcpromo**.

4. Click **OK** to start the Active Directory Installation Wizard.

5. In the **Welcome to the Active Directory Installation Wizard** window, click **Next**.

6. In the **Operating System Compatibility** window, click **Next**.

7. In the **Domain Controller Type** window, click **Domain controller for a new domain | Next**.

8. In the **Create New Domain** window, click **Domain in an existing forest | Next**.

9. In the **Network Credentials** window, type in the username, password, and domain name of an Enterprise Administrator or Domain Admin in the forest-root domain. Click **Next**.

10. In the **New Domain Tree** window, type the full DNS domain name for the new domain, and click **Next**.

11. In the **NetBIOS Domain Name** window, verify the NetBIOS name and click **Next**. The default name is generally the best one to use.

12. In the **Database and Log Folders** window, type or browse to the location where you want the database and log folders. Click **Next**.

13. In the **Shared System Volume** window, type or browse to the location where you want the SYSVOL folder. Click **Next**.

14. In the **DNS Registration Diagnostics** window, configure an existing DNS server to be authoritative for this tree, or click **Install and configure the DNS server on this computer, and set this computer to use this DNS server as its preferred DNS server**. Click **Next**.

15. In the Permissions window you have two options: **Permissions compatible with pre-Windows 2000 server operating systems** and **Permissions compatible only with Windows 2000 or Windows Server 2003 operating systems**. Select one, and then click **Next**.

16. In the **Directory Services Restore Mode Administrator Password** window, input and confirm the password for the **Directory Services Restore Mode**. Click **Next**.

17. Read the **Summary** window. Click **Next**. The installation will continue for several minutes.

18. Restart your new DC.

19. Verify that the installation was successful. Open a command prompt and enter the **Net Share** command. It should report the existence of the Netlogon and SYSVOL shares. To verify that the DNS service locator records for the new DC were successfully created, follow these steps:

    1. Click **Start | Administrative Tools | DNS** to start the DNS administrator console.

    2. Expand the server name.

    3. Expand Forward Lookup Zones.

    4. Expand the domain.

    5. Verify that the _msdcs, _sites, _tcp, and _udp folders are present and contain records for your new DC. These service location records are crucial to the operation of the DC. See Figure 12.1 for a view of the DNS administrator tool used to view them.

Creating a New Child Domain in an Existing Domain

This will often be the third domain that you install. This type of arrangement accommodates a tree comprised of two different company groups, sometimes in physically separate locations. Since domains are used as boundaries for security and administration, there are many reasons for segregating a subgroup. If a group requires higher or lower levels of security, or if a different group of administrators requires complete control, then a child domain is a good idea. Now that you have created a new domain (in the steps outlined earlier), you can easily create a new child domain in an existing domain.

Once complete, you should verify that the installation was successful. Open a command prompt and enter the **Net Share** command. It should report the existence of the *Netlogon* and *SYSVOL* shares. To verify that the DNS service locator records for the new DC were successfully created, follow these steps:

1. Click **Start | Administrative Tools | DNS** to start the DNS administrator console.

2. Expand the server name.

3. Expand **Forward Lookup Zones**.

4. Expand the domain.

5. Verify that the _msdcs, _sites, _tcp, and _udp folders are present and contain records for your new DC. These service location records are crucial to the operation of the DC. See Figure 12.1 for a view of the DNS administrator tool used to view them.

Creating a New DC in an Existing Domain

This is the only situation where you will run the Active Directory Installation Wizard without creating a new domain. We'll step through using the AD Installation Wizard in the procedure that follows. Usually, you will need to perform this procedure when your domain has grown to the point that it needs additional DCs to spread the workload.

Create a new domain controller in an existing domain using the conventional across-the-network method

1. Log in as a local Administrator.

2. Click **Start | Run**.

3. Type **dcpromo /adv**.

4. Click **OK** to start the Active Directory Installation Wizard.

5. In the **Welcome to the Active Directory Installation Wizard** window, click **Next**.

6. In the **Operating System Compatibility** window, click **Next**.

7. In the **Domain Controller Type** window, click **Additional domain controller for an existing domain | Next**.

8. In the **Copying Domain Information** window, click **Over the network | Next**.

9. In the **Network Credentials** window, type in the username, password, and domain name of an Enterprise Administrator in the forest-root domain, or a Domain Admin in the parent domain, and click **Next**.

10. In the **Additional Domain Controller** window, type in or browse to the top-level domain name where you are adding the new DC, and click **Next**.

11. In the **Database and Log Folders** window, type or browse to the location where you want the database and log folders. Click **Next**.

12. In the **Shared System Volume** window, type or browse to the location where you want the SYSVOL folder. Click **Next**.

13. In the **Directory Services Restore Mode Administrator Password** window, input and confirm the password for the **Directory Services Restore Mode**. Click **Next**.

14. Read the **Summary** window. Click **Next**. The installation will continue for several minutes.

15. Restart your new DC.

16. Verify that the installation was successful. Open a command prompt and enter the *Net Share* command. It should report the existence of the Netlogon and SYSVOL shares. To verify that the DNS service locator records for the new DC were successfully created, follow these steps:

    1. Click **Start | Administrative Tools | DNS** to start the DNS administrator console.

    2. Expand the server name.

    3. Expand **Forward Lookup Zones**.

    4. Expand the domain.

5. Verify that the _msdcs, _sites, _tcp, and _udp folders are present and contain records for your new DC. These service location records are crucial to the operation of the DC. See Figure 12.1 for a view of the DNS administrator tool used to view them.

Using the New System State Backup Method

This final DC installation procedure covers the new method of installing the Active Directory database on your new DC from backups, as illustrated in Figure 12.2. You should use a healthy Windows Server 2003 DC as the source of the system state, and DNS should be working before you begin.

The procedure that follows is an advanced procedure, and assumes certain skills such as installing Windows Server 2003 as a member server, the use of Windows Backup, and general Windows administrative abilities. You should also test this procedure in a lab environment before trying it on an operational network. In addition, this procedure will show you how to use an *answer file* to automate the promotion process, making this the optimal procedure for unattended installations. Figure 12.3 shows a sample answer file. The */ADV* switch with **dcpromo** is only necessary for promoting

Figure 12.2 Using the New System State Backup Method

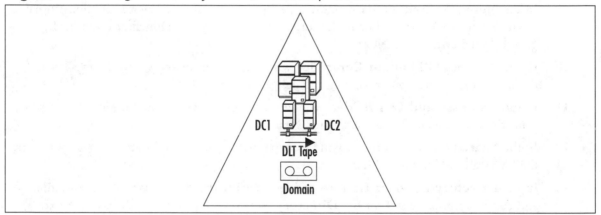

from a backup file.

Create a new domain controller in an existing domain using the new system state backup method

Steps 1 through 3 walk you through taking the snapshot.

1. Log in as a local Administrator on the healthy DC.

2. Create a directory called C:\Backup. If the folder already exists, remove any files that it contains.

3. Using **Windows Backup**, save the *system state*. It is a good practice to name the file after your source DC, giving it a .bkf extension.

You now must transport the file. Use the backup media of your choice, ensuring your ability to perform the restore at the other end. Remember that the backup file can be many GBs in size. If you choose to use the network to transport the file, you can perform the restore and the copy at the same time using the following steps. There are various ways to accomplish this. If you choose to use a third-party backup program to transport the file on physical media such as DLT tape, CD, or DVD, you will still need to use **Windows Backup** at the other end to extract the data from the backup file. Adjust the procedure to your preferences.

4. Log on as a local Administrator on the member server that you want to promote, and create a shared folder called C:\Restore. It might be on your LAN or across a WAN at this point, so you might need a helping hand at the other end.

5. Back at the DC, map a drive to the shared folder created previously if you choose to copy the file over the network.

6. You have two options, depending on your choice of transport. If you are copying the file across the network, use the **Restore Wizard** within **Windows Backup** from the existing DC to restore the domaincontrollername.bkf file to the shared folder in the member server. If you have created *physical* media for transport, use the **Restore Wizard** directly on the member sever using the local physical media.

7. Create a file on the member server containing the following settings. For this example, we call this file DCUnattend.txt. Examine the options in Figure 12.3. They allow for unattended Active Directory installations in other configurations such as directly across the network from an established DC. Remember to rename the member server *before* promoting it, or you will be faced with the opportunity to perform a *domain controller rename* procedure, which is another new feature of Windows Server 2003.

Figure 12.3 Sample DCUnattend.txt File

[Unattended]

Unattendmode=fullunattended

[DCINSTALL]

UserName=(domain or Enterprise admin account)

Password=(password)

UserDomain=(domain of the user account)

DatabasePath=c:\Windows\ntds

LogPath=c:\Windows\ntds

SYSVOLPath=c:\Windows\sysvol

SafeModeAdminPassword

CriticalReplicationOnly

SiteName=

ReplicaOrNewDomain=Replica

ReplicaDomainDNSName=(domain name, not including any server name)

ReplicationSourceDC=

ReplicateFromMedia=yes

ReplicationSourcePath=c:\NTDSrestore

RebootOnSuccess=yes

8. Open a command prompt and type the following command: **Dcpromo /adv /answer:C:\DCUnattend.txt**. After it is complete, the system will reboot. If dcpromo stops and asks for information, then some information was missing from the answer file.

9. Verify that the installation was successful. Open a command prompt and enter the *Net Share* command. It should report the existence of the Netlogon and SYSVOL shares. To verify that the DNS service locator records for the new DC were successfully created, follow these steps:

   1. Click **Start | Administrative Tools | DNS** to start the DNS administrator console.

   2. Expand the server name.

   3. Expand Forward Lookup Zones.

   4. Expand the domain.

   5. Verify that the _msdcs, _sites, _tcp, and _udp folders are present and contain records for your new DC. These service location records are crucial to the operation of the DC.

Assigning and Transferring Master Roles

The advantage of a single-master model is that conflicts cannot be introduced while the Operations Master is offline. The alternative involves resolving conflicts later, with possibly negative results. The disadvantage is that all Operations Masters must be available at all times to support all dependant activities within the domain or forest. The Active Directory supports five operational master roles: the Schema Master, Domain Master, RID Master, PDC Emulator, and the Infrastructure Master. Two of these operate at the forest level only, the Schema Master and the Domain Naming Master. Conversely, the RID Master, PDC Emulator, and Infrastructure Master operate at the domain level.

Table 12.5 Valid Authorization Levels for Viewing, Transferring, and Seizing Operations Master Roles

Role	Task	Domain Administrator on the Local Domain	Domain Administrator on the Forest-Root Domain	Enterprise Administrator
Schema Master	Viewing, transferring, or seizing		X (Plus *Schema Admins* membership)	X
Domain Naming Master	Viewing, transferring, or seizing		X	X
Infrastructure Master	Viewing, trans-ferring, or seizing	X		X
RID Master	Viewing, transferring, or seizing	X		X
PDC Emulator	Viewing, transferring, or seizing	X		X

The forest level, therefore, has five roles—one of each. Each domain added after the forest root domain has three additional masters. With that information, we can determine the number of operations master servers required in a given forest with the following formula:

((*Number of domains* * 3)+2)

Given the formula, we can determine that a forest with three domains, needs a maximum of 11 server platforms to support the 11 FSMO roles (3*3=9, and 9+2=11), unless you assign multiple roles to a single DC. Often, small domains, empty root domains, or best practices will make combining several of these roles onto a single DC desirable.

The first DC that you install in the forest root will automatically host all five roles. The first DC that you install in any additional domains will automatically host the three roles of PDC Emulator, RID Master, and Infrastructure Master.

You can use the ntdsutil.exe command-line utility to transfer FSMO roles, or you can use an MMC snap-in tool. Depending on which role you want to transfer, you can use one of the following three MMC snap-in tools:

- Active Directory Schema snap-in (Schema Master role)

- Active Directory Domains and Trusts snap-in (Domain Naming Master role)

- Active Directory Users and Computers snap-in (RID Master, Infrastructure Master, and PDC Emulator roles)

To seize a role, you must use the *ntdsutil* utility. If a computer cannot be contacted due to a hardware malfunction or long-term network failure, the role must be seized.

Locating, Transferring, and Seizing the Schema Master Role

The DC that hosts the Schema Master role controls each update or modification to the schema. You must have access to the Schema Master to update the schema of a forest.

Refer to the first procedure that follows for instructions on how to identify the DC that is performing the Schema Master operation role for your forest using the command line or the GUI. Refer to the second procedure that follows for instructions on how to transfer the Schema Master operations role for your forest to a different DC. The steps for seizing the role to another DC in case of failure are outlined later in this section (see *Seize the FSMO master roles*) .

Temporary loss of the Schema Master is not noticeable to domain users. Enterprise and domain administrators will not notice the loss either, unless they are trying to install an application that modifies the schema during installation or trying to modify the schema themselves. You should seize the schema FSMO role to the standby operations master only if your old Schema master will be down permanently.

Locate the Schema Operations Master

1. Log on as an Enterprise Administrator in the forest you are checking.

2. Click **Start | Run**.

3. Type **regsvr32 schmmgmt.dll** in the **Open** box, and click **OK**. This registers the *Schmmgmt.dll*.

4. Click **OK** in the dialog box showing that the operation succeeded.

5. Click **Start | Run**, type **mmc**, and then click **OK**.

6. On the menu bar, click **File | Add/Remove Snap-in**, click **Add**, double-click **Active Directory Schema**, click **Close**, and then click **OK**.

7. Expand and then right-click **Active Directory Schema** in the top left pane, and then select **Operations Masters** to view the server holding the Schema Master role as shown in Figure 12.4.

Transfer the Schema Operations Master Role

1. Log on as an Enterprise Administrator in the forest where you want to transfer the Schema Master role.

Figure 12.4 Locating the Schema Operations Master

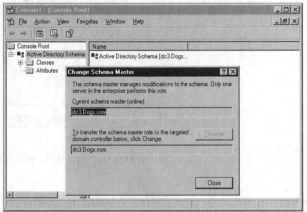

2. Click **Start | Run**.

3. Type **regsvr32 schmmgmt.dll** in the **Open** box, and then click **OK**. This registers the *Schmmgmt.dll*.

4. Click **OK** in the dialog box showing that the operation succeeded.

5. Click **Start | Run**, type **mmc**, and then click **OK**.

6. On the menu bar, click **File | Add/Remove Snap-in**, click **Add**, double-click **Active Directory Schema**, click **Close**, and then click **OK**.

7. Right-click **Active Directory Schema** in the top left pane, and then click **Change Domain Controller**.

8. Click **Specify Name** as shown in Figure 12.5, type the name of the DC that will be the new role holder, and then click **OK**.

9. Right-click **Active Directory Schema** again, and then click **Operations Master**.

10. Click **Change**.

Figure 12.5 Transferring the Schema Operations Master Role

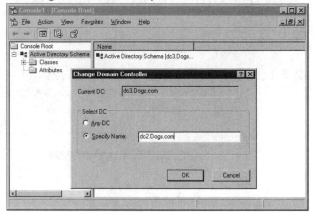

11.   Click **OK** to confirm that you want to transfer the role, and then click **Close**.

Locating, Transferring, and Seizing the Domain Naming Master Role

The Domain Naming Master DC controls the addition or removal of domains in the forest, AND adding and removing any cross-references to domains in external LDAP directories. There can be only one Domain Naming Master in the forest.

Refer to the first procedure that follows for instructions on how to identify the DC that is performing the Domain Naming Master operation role for your forest. Refer to the second procedure that follows for instructions on how to transfer the Domain Naming Master operations role for your forest to a different DC. The steps for seizing a role to another DC in case of failure are described later in this section (see *Seize the FSMO Master Roles*).

Locate the Domain Naming Operations Master

1.   Log on as an Enterprise Administrator in the forest you are checking.

2.   Click **Start | Run**, type: **mmc**, and then click **OK**.

3.   On the menu bar, click **File | Add/Remove Snap-in**, click **Add**, double-click **Active Directory Domains and Trusts**, click **Close**, and then click **OK**.

4.   Right-click **Active Directory Domains and Trusts** in the top left pane, and then click **Operations Masters** to view the server holding the domain naming master role.

Transer the Domain Naming Master Role

1. Click **Start | Administrative Tools | Active Directory Domains and Trusts**.

2. Right-click Active Directory Domains and Trusts, and click **Connect to Domain Controller**, *unless you are already on the DC to which you are transferring to the role*. In the Enter the name of another domain controller window, type the name of the DC that will be the new role holder, and then click **OK**. Optionally, in the Or, select an available domain controller list, click the DC that will be the new role holder, and click **OK**.

3. In the console tree, right-click **Active Directory Domains and Trusts**, and then select **Operations Master**.

4. Click **Change**.

5. Click **OK** for confirmation, and click **Close**.

Locating, Transferring, and Seizing the Infrastructure, RID, and PDC Operations Master Roles

The Infrastructure Master is responsible for updating references from objects in the local domain to objects in other domains. There can be only one Infrastructure Master DC in each domain. The RID Master processes Relative ID (RID) pool requests from all DCs in the local domain. There can be only one RID Master DC in each domain. The PDC Emulator is a DC that advertises itself as the PDC to workstations, member servers, and BDCs running Windows NT. It is also the Domain Master Browser, and handles Active Directory password collisions, or discrepancies. There can be only one PDC Emulator in each domain.

Refer to the first procedure that follows for instructions on how to identify the DCs that are performing the FSMO roles for your forest using the Active Directory Users and Computers GUI interface. Refer to the second procedure that follows for instructions on how to transfer the Infrastructure, RID, and PDC Master operations roles for your forest to different DCs. Again, if you need to seize a role, follow the steps later in this section (see *Seize the FSMO Master Roles*).

Locate the Infrastructure, RID and PDC Operations Masters

1. Log on as an Enterprise Administrator in the forest you are checking.

2. Click **Start | Run**, type **dsa.msc**, and click **OK**. This is an alternate method for opening the **Active Directory Users and Computers** administrative tool.

3. Right-click the selected Domain Object in the top left pane, and then click **Operations Masters**.

4. Click the **Infrastructure** tab to view the server holding the Infrastructure Master role.

5. Click the **RID** tab to view the server holding the RID Master role.

6. Click the **PDC** tab to view the server holding the PDC Master role.

Transfer the Infrastructure, RID and PDC Master Roles

1. Click **Start | Administrative Tools | Active Directory Users and Computers.**

2. Right-click **Active Directory Users and Computers**, and click **Connect to Domain Controller** *unless you are already on the DC you are transferring to.* In the Enter the name of another domain controller window, type the name of the DC that will be the new role holder, and then click **OK**; or in the Or, select an available domain controller list, click the DC that will be the new role holder, and click **OK**.

3. In the console tree, right-click **Active Directory Users and Computers**, and click **All Tasks | Operations Master.**

4. Take the appropriate action below for the role you want to transfer.

5. Click the Infrastructure tab, and click **Change**.

6. Click the RID tab, and click **Change**.

7. Click the PDC tab, and click **Change**.

8. Click **OK** for confirmation, and click **Close**.

Seize the FSMO Master Roles

1. Log on to any working DC.

2. Click **Start | Run**, type **ntdsutil** in the Open box, and then click **OK**.

3. Type **roles**, and press **Enter**.

4. In ntdsutil, type **?** at any prompt to see a list of available commands, and press **Enter**.

5. Type **connections**, and press **Enter**.

6. Type **connect to server** *servername*, where *servername* is the name of the server that will receive the role, and press **Enter**.

7. At the server connections: prompt, type **q**, and press **Enter**.

8. Type the appropriate seizing command as shown next. See the example in Figure 12.6. If the FSMO role is available, *ntdsutil.exe* will perform a transfer instead. Respond to the Role Seizure Confirmation Dialog box.

```
seize Schema master
seize domain naming master
seize Infrastructure master
seize RID master
seize PDC
```

Figure 12.6 Seizing the PDC Master Role

```
D:\WINDOWS\system32\ntdsutil.exe: roles

fsmo maintenance: connections

server connections: connect to server DC4

Binding to DC4 ...

Connected to DC4 using credentials of locally logged on user.

server connections: q

fsmo maintenance: seize PDC

Attempting safe transfer of PDC FSMO before seizure.

FSMO transferred successfully - seizure not required.

Server "DC4" knows about 5 roles

Schema - CN=NTDS Settings,CN=DC3,CN=Servers,CN=Default-First-Site-
    Name,CN=Sites,

CN=Configuration,DC=Dogs,DC=com

Domain - CN=NTDS Settings,CN=DC3,CN=Servers,CN=Default-First-Site-
    Name,CN=Sites,

CN=Configuration,DC=Dogs,DC=com

PDC - CN=NTDS Settings,CN=DC4,CN=Servers,CN=Default-First-Site-
    Name,CN=Sites,CN=

Configuration,DC=Dogs,DC=com

RID - CN=NTDS Settings,CN=DC4,CN=Servers,CN=Default-First-Site-
    Name,CN=Sites,CN=

Configuration,DC=Dogs,DC=com

Infrastructure - CN=NTDS Settings,CN=DC4,CN=Servers,CN=Default-First-Site-
    Name,C

N=Sites,CN=Configuration,DC=Dogs,DC=com

fsmo maintenance:q
```

9. After you seize the role, type **q**, and then press **Enter** repeatedly until you quit the Ntdsutil tool.

Placing the FSMO Roles

It is a good idea to place the RID and PDC Emulator roles on the same DC. Down-level clients and applications target the PDC, making it a large consumer of RIDs. Good communication between these two roles is important. If performance demands it, place the RID and PDC Emulator roles on separate DCs, but make sure they stay in the same site and that they are direct replication partners with each other.

As previously stated, you should place the Infrastructure Master on a non-GC server to maintain proper replication. Additionally, ensure that the Infrastructure Master has a direct connection object to a GC server somewhere in the forest, preferably in the same site. There are two exceptions to this rule:

- **Single domain forest** If your forest contains only one Active Directory domain, then there can be no phantoms. The Infrastructure Master has no functionality in a single domain forest. In that case, you can place the Infrastructure Master on any DC.

- **Multidomain forest where every DC holds the GC** Again, there can be no phantoms if every DC in the domain hosts a GC. There is no work for the Infrastructure Master to perform. In that case, you can place the Infrastructure Master on any DC.

Considering the forest level, the Schema Master and Domain Naming Master roles are rarely used and should be tightly controlled. For that reason, you can place them on the same DC. Another Microsoft-recommended practice is to place the Domain Naming Master FSMO on a GC server. Taking all of these practices together, a Microsoft-recommended best-practice empty root domain design would consist of two DCs with the following FSMO/GC placement:

- **DC 1:**
    - Schema Master
    - Domain Naming Master
    - GC

- **DC 2:**
    - RID Master
    - PDC Emulator
    - Infrastructure Master

This preferred design remains valid until performance degradation forces you to separate the roles. Consider upgrading the hardware instead, or adding additional GCs, since the recommended configuration is the most efficient. For extremely large forests, install additional DCs and separate roles as needed. For these reasons and more, you need to be able to locate and assess your GC placement in relation to your FSMO roles. Here is how you find GCs:

1. Log on to any working DC.

2. Click **Start | Programs | Administrative Tools | Active Directory Sites and Services**.

3. Double-click **Sites** in the left console pane, and browse to the appropriate site, or click Default-first-site-name if no other sites are available.

4. Expand the **Servers** folder, and click the name of the DC that you want to check.

5. In the DC's folder, double-click **NTDS Settings**.

6. Click **Action | Properties**.

7. On the **General** tab, locate the **Global Catalog** check box to see if it is selected as shown in Figure 12.7.

Figure 12.7 Locating the Global Catalog Function

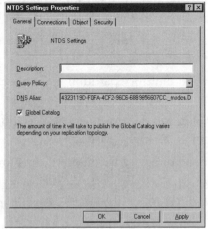

Using Application Directory Partitions

The Active Directory contains several partitions for the storage of object data. These *directory partitions*, also called *naming contexts*, are contiguous Active Directory subtrees that are replicated across DCs. As a minimum, each DC contains a replica of three partitions: the schema partition, the configuration partition, and the domain partition in addition to any application directory partitions that you might choose to create. An instance of an application directory partition on another DC is called a *replica*.

The default security descriptor for objects in the application directory partition is defined by an attribute called the *security descriptor reference domain*. By default, this attribute is the parent domain of the application directory partition. If the partition is a child of another application directory partition, the default security descriptor reference domain is the security descriptor reference domain of its parent. If it has no parent, the forest root domain becomes the default security descriptor reference domain. This attribute can be modified using the following steps.

Administer Application Directory Partitions

1. Log on as an Enterprise Administrator.

2. Click **Start | Run**, type **ntdsutil**, and click **OK**.

3. At the **ntdsutil** command prompt, type **domain management**.

4. At the **domain management** command prompt, type **connection**.

5. At the **connection** command prompt, type **connect to server** *servername,* where *servername* represents the DNS name of the DC where you want to create the application directory partition.

6. At the **connection** command prompt, type **quit**.

7. At the **domain management** command prompt, consult the following list of commands for the function you want to perform:

    ■ Create an application directory partition: use the command **create nc** *application_directory_partition domain_controller*

    ■ Delete an application directory partition: use the command **delete nc** *application_directory_partition*

    ■ Add an application directory partition replica: use the command **add nc replica** *application_directory_partition domain_controller*

    ■ Remove an application directory partition replica: use the command **remove nc replica** *application_directory_partition*

    ■ Display application directory partition information: use the command **list**

    ■ Add an application directory partition replica: use the command **set nc reference domain** *application_directory_partition domain_controller*

In this context, *application_directory_partition* is the DN of the application directory partition that you want to operate on, and *domain_controller* is the DNS name of the DC where you want to perform the operation. If you are operating on the DC that you connected to in step 5, use "NULL" as the *domain_controller* parameter.

8. Enter **q** until ntdsutil exits.

Establishing Trust Relationships

External trusts are a concept left over from Windows NT, but are still necessary for sharing resources with a Windows NT domain or any other Windows domain outside your forest. A *realm* trust allows cross-platform interoperability with non-Windows Kerberos V5 (version 5) realms, such as those commonly used with UNIX systems. As you can see, trusts are varied in properties and purposes. The most important concepts to understand about trusts before you create them are *direction* and *transitivity*. Always be aware of the extent of any internal access that you grant to external users.

Direction and Transitivity

Two primary attributes of trusts are direction and transitivity. The *direction of trust* flows from the trusting domain to the trusted domain as shown by the arrow in Figure 12.8. Cats.com *trusts* Dogs.com. The *direction of access* is always in the opposite direction; Dogs.com *accesses* resources in Cats.com. This is a one-way trust. Likewise, Dogs.com trusts Fish.com, but does not trust Cats.com. Two one-way trusts can combine to simulate a single two-way trust.

Figure 12.8 The Nontransitive Trust

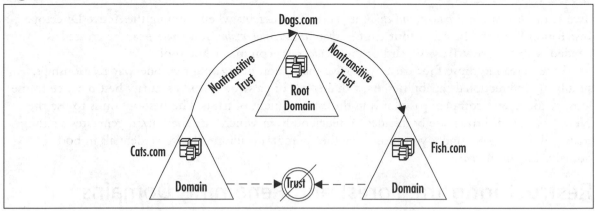

The second attribute of the trust is *transitivity*, or a measure of how far the trust extends. A non-transitive trust has limits. The trusted domain, *and only the trusted domain*, can access resources through the trust to the trusting domain. As shown in Figure 12.8, if the Dogs.com domain has trusts to other domains such as Fish.com, those other domains are barred from access to Cats.com unless they have a nontransitive trust of their own. The absence of the third leg of the trust breaks the circle of access. This is the behavior of all trusts in Windows NT.

Conversely, transitive trusts, like the ones shown in Figure 12.9, are the skeleton keys of access. Anyone on the trusted side of the trust relationship can enter, including anyone trusted by the trusted domain. When a user or process requests access to a resource in another domain, a series of hand-offs occurs within the authentication process down the *trust path* as shown in Figure 12.9. When Cats.com trusts Dogs.com, they must trust all Dogs.com child domains equally at the level of the trust. There are two types of trusts in Figure 12.9, *parent and child* and *tree-root*. All trusts shown are bidirectional and transitive, as they are by default in Windows Server 2003. Calico.cats.com has a trust relationship with Yellow.labs.dogs.com because of the trust path that extends through all three intervening domains. If Calico.cats.com has no reason to trust Yellow.labs.dogs.com, then the cats must apply permissions to limit or block the access.

Figure 12.9 The Transitive Trust

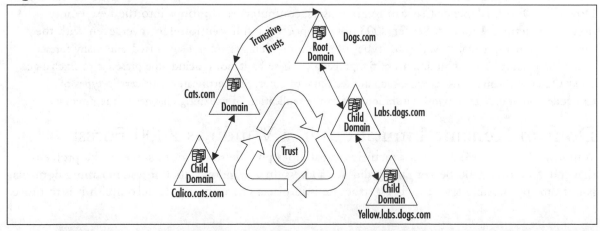

Types of Trusts

Two trusts, *tree-root* and *parent and child*, are created by default when running the Active Directory Installation Wizard. The other four trusts—*shortcut, external, realm,* and *forest*—can be created as needed with the New Trust Wizard or the *Netdom.exe* command-line tool.

When creating those four trusts, you have the option of creating two one-way relationships, simulating bidirectional capabilities. As with any use of passwords, it is a security best practice to use long, random, and complex passwords in the establishment of trusts. The best option is to use the New Trust Wizard to create both sides simultaneously, in which case the wizard generates a strong password for you. Naturally, you must have the appropriate administrative credentials in both domains for this to work.

Restructuring the Forest and Renaming Domains

In Windows Server 2003, you can rename domains in an Active Directory forest after the forest structure is in place. This was not true in the Windows 2000 Server family. You build your Active Directory forest structure one domain at a time, and the resulting relationships are the result of the order in which you create them and the DNS names you assign. Renaming domains allows you to change the forest structure. For example, you can raise a child domain to be a new tree-root domain, or lower a top-level domain to child status in another tree. In each case, you rename an existing domain to create a different forest structure. In cases where restructuring is not your goal, you can rename domains without affecting the trust relationships between domains. For example, you do not create a different domain-tree structure if you rename a root domain, although the names of all child domains below it are also changed.

This is a complex and sweeping modification to the namespace of one or more domains. During the domain rename procedure, you can change DNS and NetBIOS names, but the true identity of a domain lies in its domain GUID and its domain SID. Creating new DNS or NetBIOS names will leave those attributes unchanged.

Domain Rename Limitations

Windows NT had no supported method for domain renaming, other than a complete rebuild of the new domain. The best option that Windows 2000 offers is only the first half of the solution—you still have to create a new domain from scratch. Microsoft released a support tool called the Active Directory Object Manager that can migrate users, computers, and groups into the new empty domain structure. Windows Server 2003 now supports the full solution. However, even with the new restructuring capability, certain types of structural changes are not supported, and many forests cannot be renamed due to limitations of the procedure. These limitations include the presence of Exchange 2000. Other problematic issues arise, such as the failure of enterprise certificates with certain types of embedded pointers, and network saturation due to the replication of sweeping changes to the directory.

Domain Rename Limitations in a Windows 2000 Forest

Windows Server 2003's forest restructuring capabilities provide solutions to some of the problems that the Windows 2000 Server family did not address. In a Windows 2000 forest, renaming domains is not directly possible after the forest structure is in place. The only way to accomplish it is to move or recreate the domain contents. These constraints make domain name changes or forest restructuring prohibitive in Windows 2000.

- You cannot change the DNS name or the NetBIOS name of a domain. You can, however, achieve similar results by moving its contents into a new domain using the Active Directory Object Manager (MoveTree) in the Windows 2000 Support Tools.

- Using the Active Directory Object Manager method, you cannot move a domain within a forest in a single operation.

- Using the Active Directory Object Manager method, you cannot split a domain into two domains in a single operation.

- Using the Active Directory Object Manager method, you cannot merge two domains into a single domain in a single operation.

Domain Rename Limitations in a Windows Server 2003 Forest

Windows Server 2003 Standard, Enterprise, and Datacenter Editions provide tools that you can use to safely rename domains. Since domain renaming is at the core of forest restructuring, you can leverage this capability with very powerful results. When considering restructuring an existing Windows Server 2003 forest, be sure to consider the limitations of domain renaming. Adding, removing, merging, and splitting domains are operations outside the scope of the domain rename process.

- You cannot change which domain is the forest root domain, although you can still give it a new DNS or NetBIOS name.

- You cannot remove or add domains to the forest. The number of domains before and after the restructuring must remain the same (you can, of course, add new domains after the name change).

- You cannot move a domain name from one domain to another in a single operation.

The resulting forest, no matter how sweeping the DNS and NetBIOS changes are, must result in a well-formed forest. A *well-formed forest* has the following characteristics:

- All domains within the forest must form one or more DNS trees.

- The forest-root domain must be the root of one of these trees.

- A domain directory partition must not have an application directory partition as a parent.

Domain Rename Dependencies

Other conditions that must be eliminated, or prerequisites that must be met before you can attempt the domain rename procedure, include the following:

- Domain rename is not supported in a domain where Exchange 2000 is installed.

- All of your DCs must be running Windows Server 2003, and the Active Directory *forest* functional level must be raised to Windows Server 2003.

- The domain rename procedure requires Enterprise Administrator privileges.

- The control station for the domain rename operation must not be a DC. You must use a member server to perform the operation.

- All domain-based DFSroot servers must be running Windows 2000 with Service Pack 3 or higher.

Domain Rename Conditions and Effects

The domain rename procedure is complex, requires a great deal of care in planning and execution, and should always be tested in a lab environment before performing it on an operational forest. The time required to go through a complete domain rename operation varies; the number of domains, DCs, and member computers is directly proportional to the level of effort required.

Before undertaking a domain rename operation, you must fully understand the following conditions and effects. They are inherent in the process and must be dealt with or accommodated.

- Each DC requires individual attention. Some changes are not replicated throughout the Active Directory. This does not mean that every DC requires a physical visit. Headless management can greatly reduce the level of effort required, depending on the size and structure of the domain and the number of sites it contains.

- The entire forest will be out of service for a short period. Close coordination is required with remote sites, especially those in other time zones. During this time, DCs will perform directory database updates and reboot. As with other portions of the procedure, the time involved is proportional to the number of DCs affected.

- Any DC that is unreachable or fails to complete the rename process must be eliminated from the forest for you to declare the procedure complete.

- Each client workstation requires individual attention. After all DCs have updated and rebooted, each client running Windows 2000 or Windows XP must be rebooted two times to fully adapt to the renamed domain. Windows NT workstations must disjoin from the old domain name and rejoin the new domain name, a manual process that requires a reboot of its own.

- The DNS host names of your DCs are not changed automatically by the domain rename process. To make them reflect the new domain name, you must perform the *domain controller rename procedure* on each DC. Having the host name of a DC decoupled from its domain name does not affect forest service, but the discrepancy will be confusing until you change the names.

- The DNS suffix of client workstations and member servers will automatically update through the domain renaming process, but not all computers will match the DNS name of the domain immediately. As with most portions of this process, the period of time required is proportional to the number of hosts in the domain.

Rename a Windows Server 2003 Domain Controller

As you know, renaming a DC is different than renaming a domain. Follow these steps to rename your Windows Server 2003 DC.

1. Log in as a domain administrator and open a command prompt.

2. Execute the rename command:

Netdom Computername *OldComputerNetBIOSname* **/add:** *NewComputerFQDN*

3. Verify the secondary name with the following command:

Netdom Computername *OldComputerNetBIOSname* **/enumerate**

    The command will report old and new DNS names. Allow some time for the computer account to be replicated throughout the domain, and the DNS resource records to be distributed to the authoritative DNS servers.

4. Select the new computername as the primary one:

Netdom Computername *OldComputerNetBIOSname* **/makeprimary:** *NewComputerFQDN*

    The */enumerate* option should have displayed both computer names. Type the new name exactly as shown by the command in step 3. Now that you have changed the primary name, the */enumerate* command will not work again until you reboot.

5. Reboot and log on as a domain admin.

6. Check the names again:

Netdom Computername *NewComputerNetBIOSname* **/enumerate**

7. Delete the old computer name:

Netdom Computername *NewComputerNetBIOSname* **/remove:** *OldComputerFQDN*

    Type the old name exactly as shown by the */enumerate* command in step 6.

8. Confirm the functionality of the new name. Using the DNS administrator, expand the DNS server icon. Click the forward lookup zone and check for an (A) record for the new computer name. Verify that it points to the correct IP address. There should not be a host record for the old name. If you find one, delete it.

Implementing DNS in the Active Directory Network Environment

Whatever implementation of DNS you use with your Active Directory, it must support DNS SRV records. Using the Windows implementation of DNS gives you additional features that make it easier to use. For example, when you install a new domain, the DNS zones are automatically created and configured for you, significantly reducing the time you must spend manually configuring each DNS server. If you do have problems, the Windows Server 2003 DNS service has configuration enhancements that simplify the debugging and logging of incorrect DNS configurations. This helps you solve problems faster by suggesting troubleshooting steps for you to take. Another way in which Active Directory helps you configure DNS is through Group Policy for DNS clients. This greatly simplifies the implementation of DNS changes. Windows 2000, Windows XP, and Windows Server 2003 are similar in their user interfaces for DNS, but Windows NT is significantly different. Table 12.6 shows a comparison of the administrative tools used in NT versus more recent versions.

Table 12.6 Comparison of Administrative Tools in Windows NT vs. Windows Server 2003

DNS Task	Windows NT 4.0 uses	Windows 2000, XP, and Server 2003 use
Installing the DNS server service	**Network** control panel	Windows Components wizard
Starting the DNS Manager	**Start | Administrative Tools | DNS Manager**	**Start | Administrative Tools | DNS**
Starting, stopping, or restarting the DNS service	**Services** control panel	**Start | Administrative Tools | DNS,** then right-click **Computername | All Tasks** and select **Start, Stop, Pause, Resume,** or **Restart**
Adding a remote server to DNS Manager	**Server** menu in DNS Manager	In the DNS tool, right-click **DNS | Connect to DNS Server...,** **The following computer:** type **Computername,** click **OK**

DNS and Active Directory Namespaces

In Windows Server 2003, Active Directory supports multiple discontiguous interforest namespaces through the implementation of GCs, and multiple discontiguous extraforest namespaces through the use of routing hints. This means that multiple namespaces can coexist within the same Active Directory. You should, however, be aware that *name collisions* are possible using cross–forest trusts if namespaces overlap within the federated forest.

DNS Zones and Active Directory Integration

Standard DNS zones are stored in text files in the *%systemroot*/System32/Dns folder. After DNS is integrated into the directory, it exists in a *dnsZone* container object identified by the name of the zone. DNS and Active Directory can use identical names for different namespaces. For this reason, it is important to understand that they are *not* the same namespace. DNS contains zones and records, while Active Directory contains domains and domain objects.

Windows Server 2003 brings in a new feature that blurs the line between DNS and Active Directory, called *application partitions*. With this release of Windows, DNS zones and records can be contained within the Active Directory itself, and are subject to the same replication and authentication parameters. Some advantages of this include a reduction in the number of objects stored in the GC, and a finely tuned replication domain. Regular Active Directory integrated DNS zones are replicated in their entirety to the domain partition of every DC whether it needs it or not and to the GC. By contrast, application partition-integrated DNS zones only replicate to DNS servers, reducing replication traffic and unused replicas. There are two automatically configured application partitions. One has a forestwide scope and resides on DCs running DNS in the forest root. The other application partition has a more limited domain scope, and resides on DCs running DNS in each domain.

Some of the benefits to be gained by integrating DNS with Active Directory include:

- An upgrade from the standard DNS single-master update model to the multi-master model. Updates can take place at any DNS server, not just the one that is authoritative for each zone. The multi-master model eliminates the single point of failure for dynamic updates.

- Access control lists (ACLs) on directory-integrated zones, allowing you to specify who can delete, modify, or even who can read records within the zone.

- Secure updates, which protect the integrity of your DNS zones by protecting against DNS poisoning and other malicious attacks.

- The automatic replication and synchronization of DNS zones whenever you install a new DC.

- A common replication topology for DNS zones and Active Directory domains. The non-integrated DNS requires the design, implementation, testing, and administration of two different replication topologies.

- Added replication efficiency, since Active Directory replication is faster and more efficient than standard DNS replication.

Configuring DNS Servers for Use with Active Directory

It is a good practice to add additional DNS servers to eliminate concerns over a single point of failure. Traditionally, you would install a standard secondary DNS server. With Active Directory integration, all you need to do is convert your standard primary DNS server to an Active Directory integrated primary DNS server. Once that is done, simply configure additional DCs to take on the DNS role for redundancy.

There are a few things to be acquainted with when you integrate your DNS into the directory. For one thing, there are no more secondary DNS servers. Once integrated into Active Directory, all DNS servers are primary. Zone transfers no longer take place; instead, Active Directory replication is used to distribute changes as they occur. With legacy DNS systems, Standard DNS zones are administered using a text editor. DNS zones stored in Active Directory are administered using the DNS console or the *dnscmd* command-line tool only—no more text editing.

The following sections take you through the Windows Server 2003 versions of common DNS administrative procedures related to Active Directory and application partition integration. By default, the DNS Server service will attempt to discover and build the standard DNS application directory partitions in Active Directory. Depending on how DNS was originally implemented, these default partitions might already exist. If necessary, you can manually create them as shown in the following steps. Some DNS procedures require the Windows support tool's *dnscmd* utility, which you can install by double-clicking **suptools.msi** on the Windows Server 2003 CD in the \Support\Tools folder.

Integrating an Existing Primary DNS Server with Active Directory

To integrate an existing primary DNS server with Active Directory, follow these steps:

1. On the current DNS server, click **Start | Programs | Administrative Tools | DNS** to start the DNS Administrator console.

2. Expand the server name.

3. Right-click your primary DNS zone, click **Properties**, click the **General** tab, and note the *Type* value. This will be *Primary zone*, *Secondary zone*, or *Stub zone*.

4. Click **Change**.

5. In the **Change Zone Type** box, click the check box for **Store the zone in Active Directory**.

6. Click **Yes** to verify, and then click **OK**.

7. In the Domain properties, the type should now read **Active Directory-Integrated**. You can add as many additional DNS servers as you want.

To force replication to occur immediately instead of waiting for the regular replication cycle, follow these steps:

1. Click **Start | Administrative Tools | Active Directory Sites and Services**.

2. Expand the sites. If no additional sites are configured, you will use the one called *default-first-site-name*.

3. Expand the following folders: *your site, Servers, your Computer, NTDS Settings*. One or more DC objects are listed in the right pane. Right-click each entry to see its "friendly" name. Right-click an entry, and select Replicate Now to begin replication immediately. The time it takes to update the target controller depends on network performance and the amount of data replicated.

Creating the Default DNS Application Directory Partitions

To create the default DNS application directory partitions, follow these steps:

1. Log on to your DNS server as an Enterprise Administrator.

2. To open DNS, click **Start | Administrative Tools**, and double-click **DNS**.

3. In the console tree, expand and right-click the DNS server and select **Create Default Application Directory Partitions**. Follow the instructions to create the DNS application directory partitions. The options are:

   - **Would you like to create a single partition that stores DNS zone data and replicates that data to all DNS servers in the Active Directory domain *DnsDomainName*. Yes, or No.** This option creates one DNS application directory partition for each domain in the forest. DNS zones stored in this partition are replicated to all Active Directory-integrated DNS servers in the domain. Depending on your domain structure and the context of the command, you might get this question multiple times for different domains.

   - **Would you like to create a single partition that stores DNS zone data and replicates that data to all DNS servers in the Active Directory forest *DnsForestName*? Yes, or No.** This option creates one DNS partition named for your forest. It contains all the DNS servers running on the DCs in the forest, and replicates the DNS data to all DNS servers. DNS zones stored in this application directory partition are replicated to all Active Directory-integrated DNS servers in the forest.

Using dnscmd to Administer Application Directory Partitions

There are some differences between standard DNS and the Active Directory-integrated version of DNS. For example, when you uninstall a DNS server hosting Active Directory-integrated zones, these zones will either be saved or deleted. Since the zone data is stored on other DNS servers, it will not be deleted unless the DNS server that you uninstall is the last one hosting that zone. Windows gives you a warning if this is the case.

Only Enterprise Admins can create a DNS application directory partition. Most other DNS tasks can be handled by the DnsAdmins or Domain Admins group.

1. Log on to your DNS server with the credentials needed for the given task.

2. Open a command prompt. Click **Start | All Programs | Accessories | Command Prompt**, or click **Start | Run** and type **cmd**.

3. Use the following dnscmd.exe options. See the example following for assistance:

   - Type the following command as an Enterprise Administrator to create a DNS application directory partition: **dnscmd *ServerName* /CreateDirectoryPartition *FQDN***.

   - Type the following command as a member of the DnsAdmins or DomainAdmins group to enlist a DNS server in a DNS application directory partition: **dnscmd *ServerName* /EnlistDirectoryPartition *FQDN***.

- Type the following command as a member of the DnsAdmins or DomainAdmins group to n-enlist a DNS server in a DNS application directory partition: **dnscmd** *ServerName* **/UnenlistDirectoryPartition** *FQDN*.

In this case, *ServerName* specifies the DNS host name or IP address of the DNS server, and *FQDN* specifies the name of the target DNS application directory partition.

Here is an example. Note the "." at the end of the FQDN:

```
D:\SupportTools>dnscmd DC4.Fish.com /CreateDirectoryPartition Fish.com.
DNS Server DC4.Fish.com created directory partition: Fish.com.
Command completed successfully.
```

Securing Your DNS Deployment

DNS is full of information. It helps users find services, and services find resources. Unfortunately, it sometimes provides malicious users with that same wealth of information about your network. To help keep this from happening, use the following guidelines as a minimum approach to your DNS security architecture.

- Use a split DNS design with internal DNS servers protected by your firewall and external DNS servers on the outside. Your internal namespace can be a child domain of your external namespace, or be completely different.

- Use your internal DNS servers to host your internal namespace and your external DNS servers to host your external namespace. The external servers should not be able to forward name lookups from the Internet to your internal network, but internal servers can forward queries to the outside.

- Use a packet-filtering firewall to lock down DNS port 53 so that only external DNS servers under your control can communicate with your internal DNS servers.

- Configure secure dynamic updates. With this setting, only computers joined to the Active Directory can authenticate with DNS; hence, register their service locator records. Computers that are unable to authenticate cannot make changes to DNS data.

- Carefully monitor and contril who has the ability to control DNS zones through the DACL in Active Directory

Chapter 13

Working with Trusts and Organizational Units

In this chapter:

- ☑ **Working with Active Directory Trusts**

- ☑ **Working with Organizational Units**

- ☑ **Planning an OU Structure and Strategy for your Organization**

Introduction

Trust relationships define the ways in which users can access network resources across domains and forests. Without a trust between the domain to which a user belongs and the domain in which a resource resides, the user won't be able to access that file, folder, printer, or other resource. Hence, it is important for network administrators to understand how the built-in (implicit) trusts in the Active Directory network function, and how to create explicit trusts to provide access (or faster access) between domains.

Organizational units (OUs) are container objects within the directory structure that can be used, as the name implies, to organize resources, including (but not limited to) users, groups, and computers. Group policies can be applied to OUs, and administration of an OU can be delegated, making it easy to perform tasks that need to apply to only select objects.

This chapter addresses these two important components of Active Directory: trust relationships and OUs. You'll learn about the different types of trusts that exist in the Active Directory environment, both implicit and explicit, and you'll learn to create shortcut, external, realm, and cross-forest trusts. You'll also learn to verify and remove trusts, and how to secure trusts using SID filtering.

Next, we discuss the creation and management of OUs and you learn to apply group policy to OUs and how to delegate control of an OU. We show you how to plan an OU structure and strategy for your organization, considering delegation requirements and the security group hierarchy.

Working with Active Directory Trusts

One of the many issues that need to be dealt with in any computer organization is how to protect resources. The main difficulty that administrators face is the dilemma of how to ensure that the resources of the company are not accessible by those who do not need access. The other side of that coin, equally important, is how to ensure that people who do need access are granted access with the least amount of hassle. In small companies, the issues are simpler, because multiple domains rarely exist. In today's larger corporations and conglomerates, the issues of security are compounded. What administrators need is an easy tool to manage access across multiple domains and, often, across forests.

The tool is **Active Directory Domains and Trusts**. With Active Directory Domains and Trusts, an administrator can establish relationships between domains that will allow users in one domain to access the resources in another. This way, the administrator can ensure that all users who need access can have it without the hassles involved in having user accounts in multiple domains.

Types of Trust Relationships

Two or more Active Directory domains are implicitly or explicitly connected using trust relationships. The authentication requests made from one domain to the other domains use these relationships. The trusts provide a seamless coexistence of resources within the forest structure. Users are granted access to the resources in the other domain(s) after being authenticated in their own domain first. Once authenticated in their own domain, they can traverse the other domains to gain access to their resources.

The primary advantage of these relationships is that administrators no longer need to create multiple user accounts for each user who needs access to resources within each domain. Administrators can now add the users of the other domains to their access control lists (ACLs) to control access to a resource. To take full advantage of these relationships, the administrator must know about the various types of trust that exist, and when to use them.

Default Trusts

When the Active Directory Installation Wizard is used to create a new domain within an existing forest, two default trusts are created: a parent and child trust, and the tree-root trust. Four additional types of trusts can be created using the **New Trust Wizard** or the command-line utility **netdom**. The default trust relationships inside a Windows 2000 and Windows Server 2003 forest are transitive, two-way trusts.

A parent and child trust is a transitive, two-way trust relationship. It allows authentication requests made in the child domain to be validated in the parent domain. Because the trusts are transitive, these requests pass upwards from child to parent until they reach the root of the domain namespace. This relationship will allow any user in the domain to have access to any resource in the domain if the user has the proper permissions granted.

An additional transitive, two-way trust is created to simplify the navigation, the tree-root trust. This is especially needed in large organizations that might have multiple levels of child domains. The tree-root trust is a trust that is created between any child domain and the root domain. This provides a shortcut to the root. This trust relationship is also automatically created when a new domain is created.

Shortcut Trust

Shortcut trusts are transitive in nature and can either be one-way or two-way. These are explicit trusts that you create when the need exists to optimize ("shortcut") the authentication process. Without shortcut trusts in place, authentication travels up and down the domain tree using the default parent and child trusts, or by using the tree-root trusts. In large complex organizations that use multiple trees, this path can become a bottleneck when authenticating users. To optimize access, the network administrator can create an explicit shortcut trust directly to the target domain (see Figure 13.1).

Figure 13.1 Shortcut Trust

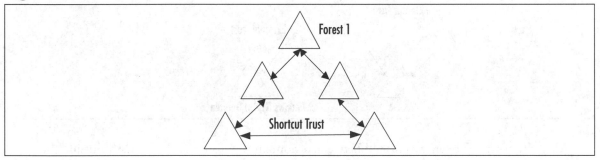

These trusts are used when user accounts in one domain need regular access to the resources in another domain. Shortcut trusts can be either one- or two-way.

One way shortcut trusts should be established when the users in one domain need access to resources in the other domain, but those in the second domain do not need access to resources in the first domain.

Two-way trusts should be created when the users in both domains need access to the resources in the other domain. The shortcut trust will effectively shorten the authentication path, especially if the domains belong to two separate trees in the forest.

Realm Trust

Realm trusts are explicit trusts that are created to join a Windows Server 2003 domain to a non-Windows Kerberos v5 realm. This allows you the flexibility of creating a trust for your non-Windows networks to interoperate with the security services based on other Kerberos v5 implementations, such as with UNIX. This extension of security can be switched from one-way or two-way trusts and from transitive to non-transitive.

External Trust

An external trust is used when you need to create a trust between domains outside of your forest. These trusts can be one- or two-way trusts. They are always non-transitive in nature. This means that you have created an explicit trust between the two domains, and domains outside this trust are not affected. You can create an external trust to access resources in a domain in a different forest that is not already covered by a forest trust (see Figure 13.2).

Figure 13.2 External Trust

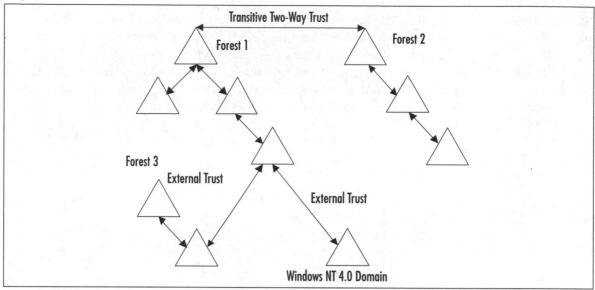

After the trust has been established between a domain in a forest and a domain outside the forest, the security principals from the domain outside the forests will be able to access the resources in the domain inside the forest. Security principals can be the users, groups, computers, or services from the external domain. They are account holders that are each assigned a security identifier (SID) automatically to control access to the resources in the domain.

The Active Directory in the domain inside the forest will then create foreign security principal objects representing each security principal from the trusted external domain. You can use these foreign security principals in the domain local groups. This means that the domain local groups can have members from the trusted external domain. You use these groups to control access to the resources of the domain.

The foreign security principals are seen in Active Directory Users and Computers. Since the Active Directory automatically creates them, you should not attempt to modify them.

Forest Trust

A forest trust can only be created between the root domains in two forests. Both forests must be Windows Server 2003 forests. These trusts can be one- or two-way trusts. They are considered transitive trusts because the child domains inside the forest can authenticate themselves across the forest to access resources in the other forest.

Forest trusts help manage the Active Directory infrastructure. They do this by simplifying the management of resources between two forests by reducing the required number of external trusts. Instead of needing multiple external trusts, a two-way forest trust between the two root domains will allow full access between all the affected domains. Additionally, the administrator can take advantage of both the Kerberos and NTLM authentication protocols to transfer authorization data between forests.

Forest trusts can provide complete two-way trusts with every domain within the two forests. This is useful if you have created multiple forests to secure data within the forest or to help isolate directory replication within each forest.

Creating, Verifying, and Removing Trusts

Trust relationships are created and managed using the **Active Directory Domains and Trusts** utility in the **Administrative Tools** menu. To create or manage trusts, you must be a member of the Domain Admins group or the Enterprise Admins group in the Active Directory, or have the appropriate authority delegated to you.

Most administrators will use the **RunAs** command to manage trusts. This is generally accepted as a security best practice. Use the following steps to create a transitive, one-way incoming realm trust.

Create a transitive, one-way incoming realm trust

1. Open Active Directory Domains and Trusts by clicking **Start | Programs | Administrative Tools**, and then selecting **Active Directory Domains and Trusts**.

2. In the console tree, right-click the domain node. Select **Properties** in the context menu.

3. On the Trusts tab, click the **New Trust** button.

4. When the **New Trust Wizard** opens, click **Next**.

5. On the **Trust Name** page, enter the target realm's name and click **Next**.

6. On the **Trust Type** page, select **Realm Trust** and click **Next**.

7. On the **Transitivity of the Trust** page, click **Transitive**, and then click **Next**.

8. On the **Direction of Trust** page, click **One-way: incoming**, and then click **Next**.

9. On the **Summary** page, review the information, and then click **Finish**.

This wizard will allow you to also create non-transitive trusts and two-way and one-way outgoing realm trusts. Alternatively, you can use the **netdom** command to create a realm trust.

Securing Trusts Using SID Filtering

One security concern when using trusts is a malicious user who has administrative credentials in the trusted domain sniffing the trusting domain to obtain the credentials of an administrator account. With the credentials of the trusting domain administrator, the malicious user could add his SID to allow full access to the trusting domain's resources. This type of threat is called an *elevation of privilege attack*.

The security mechanism used by Windows Server 2003 to counter an elevation of privilege attack is *SID filtering*. SID filtering is used to verify that an authentication request coming in from the trusted domain only contains the domain SIDs of the trusted domain. It does this by using the SIDHistory attribute on a security principal.

SID filtering uses the domain SID to verify each security principal. If a security principal includes a domain SID other than one from trusted domains, the SID filtering process removes the SID in question. This is done to protect the integrity of the trusting domain. This will prevent the malicious user from being able to elevate his or her own privileges or those of other users.

There are some potential problems associated with SID filtering. It is possible for a user whose SID contains SID information from a domain that is not trusted to be denied access to the resources in the trusting domain. This is can be a problem when universal groups are used. Universal groups should be verified to contain only users that belong to the trusted domain.

SID filtering can be disabled if there is a high level of trust for all administrators in the affected domains, there are strict requirements to verify all universal group memberships, and any migrated users have their SIDHistories preserved. To disable SID filtering, use the **netdom** command. Working with Organizational Units

Creating OUs inside a domain allows for two different types of hierarchies. One hierarchy is the structure of the domain and child domains; the other hierarchy is the structure of the OU and its child OUs. The two hierarchies give you flexibility in how to manage the organization. The concept of placing one OU inside another is called *nesting*. Although there are no limits to the number of nested OUs, Microsoft recommends that you not exceed 10 levels of nesting.

Understanding the Role of Container Objects

OUs are not security principals. Security principals are user accounts, group accounts, and computer accounts. OUs are containers that are used to organize the Active Directory.

The purpose of creating OUs is to allow the administrator to create a container that can be used to implement security policies, run scripts, deploy applications, and delegate authority for granular administrative control.

Creating and Managing Organizational Units

OUs are created and managed in the **Active Directory Users and Computers** tool in the **Administrative Tools**. This tool allows you to add OUs to the domain. After adding an OU, you have the ability to delegate control, add members, and move the OU. All of these activities can be accomplished by right-clicking on the OU that you want to manage and selecting the appropriate action from the context menu. The context menu will give you options to delete, rename, and enter the properties of the OU as well.

The Properties window of an OU has three tabs:

- General
- Managed By
- Group Policy

The **General** tab allows you to enter a description of the OU, street, city, state/providence, zip/postal code, and country/region information.

The **Managed By** tab allows you to change the user account that manages the OU. When a user account has been selected, the tab will display information about the account, such as office, address, and telephone numbers. This is read for the corresponding section of the user information stored about that user account. The **Managed By** tab has three buttons to manage this section of the OU Properties: **Change, View**, and **Clear**. The **Change** button opens a user window so you can select the account that will be used to manage the OU. The **View** button lets you see the user's account Properties window. You have the opportunity of making any necessary changes to the user's account. The **Clear** button removes the user account from the Managed By tab.

The **Group Policy** tab is discussed in the next section.

Create an Organizational Unit

1. Open **Active Directory Users and Groups** by clicking **Start | Control Panel | Performance and Maintenance | Administrative Tools**, and then double-click **Active Directory Users and Groups**.

2. In the console tree, right-click on the domain node. Select **New** in the context menu, and then select **Organizational Unit.**

3. In the **New Organizational Unit** window, type the name of the OU.

4. Click **OK** to create the OU.

5. Right-click on the new OU and select **Properties** from the menu.

6. On the **General** tab, enter a description to explain the purpose of the OU

7. Click on the **Managed By** tab. Click the **Change** button. Select a user account to manage the OU from the **Users and Groups** window.

8. Click the **Group Policy** tab. Click the **New** button to create a new GPO.

9. Rename the GPO by typing the new name.

10. Right-click on the GPO, and select **No Override** from the menu. Notice the check mark by the GPO in the **No Override** column (see Figure 13.3).

Figure 13.3 No Override Option

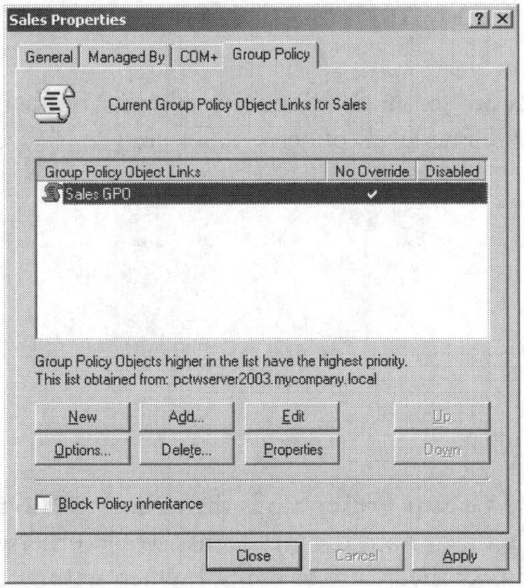

11. Click the **Edit** button. From the GPO window, double-click **User Configuration | Administrative Templates | Start Menu & Taskbar**. Double-click **Remove Favorites menu from Start Menu**. In the window that opens, click **Enable** to remove favorites from the Start menu.

12. Click the **Explain** tab. This defines what the impact of your actions will be.

13. Click **OK** to close the **Remove Favorites menu from Start Menu** window.

14. Close the GPO window.

15. Check the **Block Inheritance** option.

16. Right-click on the GPO and select **Disable** from the menu.

17. Close all windows.

Applying Group Policy to OUs

One of the fundamental reasons for creating an OU is to apply a GPO to it. After creating the OU, you can then create a new GPO or apply an existing GPO. The **Group Policy** tab found in the **OU Properties** window is the most important tab of the OU properties. This is where you create, associate, and edit the GPOs that will affect the OU. This tab has the following buttons:

- New
- Add
- Edit
- Options
- Delete
- Properties

The permissions that are set via the **Security** tab control the level of access that a user or group of users has over the GPO. The levels of permissions are:

- Full Control
- Read
- Write
- Create Child Objects
- Delete Child Objects
- Apply Group Policy

At the bottom of the **Group Policy** tab is the option to **Block Inheritance**. **Block Inheritance** will block settings from the GPOs that would otherwise be inherited from a parent OU. This gives the child OU the ability to control which settings to accept from the parent OUs. However, if the parent has set the **No Override** and the child sets **Block Inheritance**, the **No Override** setting takes precedence.

Delegating Control of OUs

Delegation of control over an OU is done to alleviate the tasks of the network administrators from performing the routine functions of an OU. Often, a manager or supervisor whose account is in the OU will have a better understanding of the daily tasks associated with the users and computers that belong to the OU, and is thus well positioned to take care of the OU. Delegation is a simple process. A wizard will walk you through the process. The Delegation of Control Wizard is discussed later in the chapter.

After you have decided to whom you want to delegate control, decide on which tasks to delegate. You have the ability to delegate management control over users and groups as well as the Group Policy Links. You can pass control of different activities to different people in the organization.

Specifically, the levels of delegations are:

- Create, delete, and manage user accounts
- Reset passwords on user accounts
- Read all user information
- Create, delete, and manage groups
- Modify the membership of a group
- Manage Group Policy Links

As you can see, delegation can reduce the amount of daily management tasks required by the network administrator.

Planning an OU Structure and Strategy for Your Organization

The OU structure can make your life easier—or it can do the opposite. If you spent time planning the structure and the implementation, the chances improve that your life will become easier and that you will be able to focus on the many facets of network administration without having to perform daily maintenance on the OUs and user issues such as resetting passwords. Your strategy should include the following:

- What OUs to create
- What policies need to be applied to cover the security requirements of the OU
- Who needs to be in charge of the OU (so you can delegate control to that user)

As with any structure, you will be faced with many decisions that need to be addressed; for example, whether a domain or OU is more appropriate for a given scenario. When making these decisions, remember to factor in the ease with which growth and changes can be accommodated.

Delegation Requirements

Delegation of control over an OU is frequently a necessity for many organizations. The delegation allows a local manager or IT staff member to control the OU. To delegate the control, you must be a member of the Enterprise Admins or Domain Admins global groups, or you must have been granted the privilege of delegating control.

From a security standpoint, when you delegate control, you should first determine the level of control that you want to grant. Just because you delegate basic administrative control over the OU does not mean that you fully relinquish control of the OU. The following procedure steps through how to delegate authority for an OU.

Delegate authority for an OU

1. Click **Start | Programs | Administrative Tools | Active Directory Users and Computers**.

2. In the console tree, right-click the OU to be delegated. Select **Delegate Control** in the context menu. This invokes the **Delegation of Control Wizard**.

3. In the **Delegation of Control Wizard**, click **Next** to continue.

4. In the **User or Groups** window, click **Add** and then select the user who will receive the delegated control. Click **Add** and then click **OK**. Click **Next** to continue.

5. In the **Tasks to Delegate** window, select the tasks that you want to delegate. Click **Next** to continue.

6. In the **Completing Delegation of Control** window, review the information and click **Finish**.

Security Group Hierarchy

One of the issues that will need to be evaluated as you deploy Active Directory is the answer to this question: What is the *effective policy* that will be applied to a specific user? Because it is possible for a user to have several layers of GPOs applied, it is very possible to have conflicting policies. This section discusses how to evaluate which policy will ultimately apply.

The first concept that needs to be covered is the order in which policies are applied. The first rule to remember is that a policy always overrides a profile setting. This becomes a factor as users might be moved from one OU where they use roaming profiles that allow the user a lot of liberty to configure their own settings. As these users are moved to another OU where the users' privileges are more controlled, they might notice that the user profile settings are overwritten by the OU policies.

The next concept is the order of the application of polices. Group policy is applied in this order:

- Local computer policy
- Site policy
- Domain policy
- OU policies, starting with the parent OU and working inward toward the security object through the child OUs

As an administrator, you still have further control over the application of policies. Windows Server 2003 Active Directory has two settings that help you with this control: **No Override** and **Block Inheritance**. The **No Override** setting is set to prevent a child OU policy setting from overwriting the policy setting of the parent. It does not apply if the policy setting is not set in the parent GPO.

The **Block Inheritance** setting allows you to control the inheritance of a policy setting in the parent by blocking it from being applied to the child. Even though you can set **Block Inheritance**, if the **No Override** option is set, **No Override** will be the setting that takes effect.

Chapter 14

Working with Active Directory Sites

In this chapter:

- ☑ **Understanding the Role of Sites**

- ☑ **Relationship of Sites to Other Active Directory Components**

- ☑ **Creating Sites and Site Links**

- ☑ **Understanding Site Replication**

Introduction

In the previous chapter, we saw the logical structure of the network as defined by forests and domains. Sites and the subnets, of which sites are comprised, define the physical structure of an Active Directory network. Sites are important in an enterprise-level multiple location network, for creating a *topology* that optimizes the process of replicating Active Directory information between domain controllers (DCs). Sites are used for replication and for optimizing the authentication process by reducing authentication traffic across slow, high-cost WAN links. Site and subnet information is also used by Active Directory-enabled services to help clients find the nearest service providers.

In this chapter, we discuss the role of sites in the Active Directory infrastructure, and how replication, authentication, and distribution of services information work within and across sites. We explain the relationship of sites with *domains* and *subnets*, and how to create sites and site links.

You'll also learn about site *replication* and how to plan, create, and manage a replication topology. We'll walk you through the steps of configuring replication between sites, and discuss how to troubleshoot replication failures.

Understanding the Role of Sites

In today's distributed network environment, the communication must always be rapid and reliable. Geographical and other restrictions resulted in the need to create smaller networks, known as *subnets*. These subnets provide rapid and reliable communication between locations, which can also be attained in larger networks by using Microsoft Windows Server 2003 Active Directory Sites. They ensure rapid and reliable communication by using the methods offered by Microsoft Windows Server 2003 Active Directory Sites to regulate inter-subnet traffic.

A *site* defines the network structure of a Windows Server 2003 Active Directory. A site consists of multiple *Internet Protocol* (IP) subnets linked together by rapid and reliable connections. The primary role of sites is to increase the performance of a network by economic and rapid transmission of data. The other roles of sites are replication and authentication. The Active Directory physical structure manages when and how the authentication and replication must take place. The Active Directory physical structure allows the management of Active Directory replication scheduling between sites. The performance of a network is also based on the location of objects and *logon authentication* as users log on to the network.

Replication

Replication is defined as the practice of transferring data from a data store present on a source computer to an identical data store present on a destination computer to synchronize the data. In a network, the directory data must live in one or more places on the network to be equally available to all users. The Active Directory directory service manages a replica of directory data on one or more DCs, ensuring the availability of directory data to all users. The Active Directory works on the concept of sites to perform replication efficiently, and uses the *Knowledge Consistency Checker* (KCC) to choose the best replication topology for the network automatically.

Authentication

The authentication process includes the confirmation of the source and integrity of information, such as verifying the identity of a user or computer. An important characteristic of authentication in the Windows Server 2003 family is its support for *single sign-on*. The single sign-on feature allows a user to log on to the network once, using a single password, and authenticate to any computer in a network. Interactive logon authentication verifies the user's logon information to either a domain account or to a local computer. Network authentication verifies the user's identification to a network service to which the user tries to gain access. Windows Server 2003 supports Kerberos V5 and Secure Socket Layer/Transport Layer Security (SSL/TLS) authentication mechanisms.

Distribution of Services Information

Active Directory distributes a wide range of service information. The DCs are also used to distribute directory information and generate responses for each service request. The Active Directory distributes service-centric information such as configurations and bindings. The distribution of this type of information enables the services to be more accessible by clients and is easily manageable for administrators. Figure 14.1 shows how the services information is accessed between the client, server, and a DC in a network.

Figure 14.1 Services Information Shared between a Client, Server, and a Domain

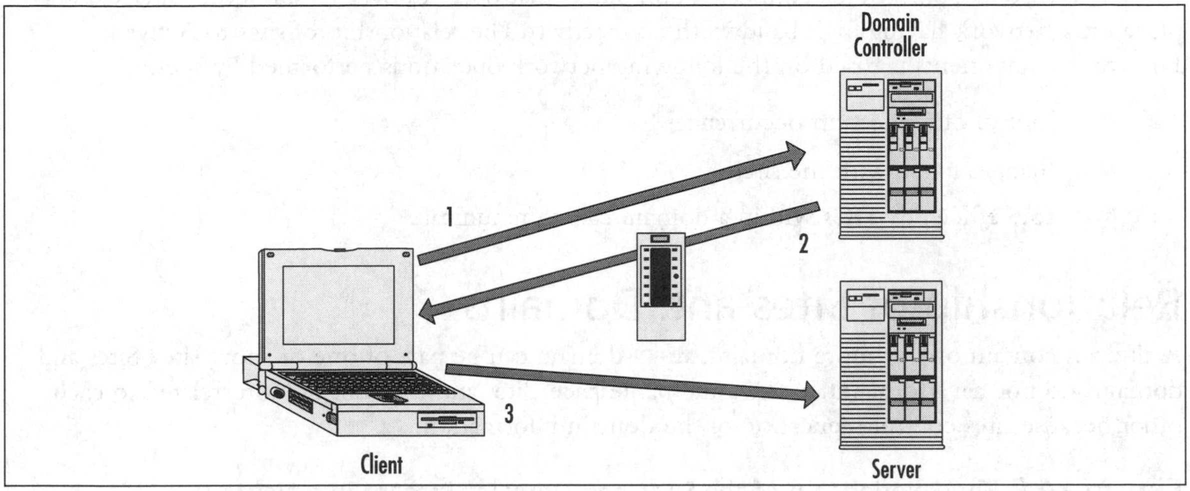

In Figure 14.1, the client shares the services information between a client, server, and a DC in three steps:

1. The client makes a request.
2. The client receives the services information from a DC as a response.
3. The clients available on the network server then use the services information.

Certain sets of services are distributed by the directories by default, including file and print services, storage management, Active Directory, and management services. These sets of services can be modified in the directories to meet the needs of your network environment. The distribution of services to the directory provides the following benefits:

- **Resource availability** This Active Directory model is a service-centric model that enables the client to provide access to the distributed network services. Since the services information is distributed to the directory, clients needn't store the resource's location.

- **Administration** Distributing services in Active Directory enables the administrator to resolve configuration-related problems in a network centrally, instead of having to visit individual computers. This feature ensures that all the services employ the latest configuration information.

- **Publishing services** This process enables the data or operations available to the network users. Publishing a service in Active Directory enables users and administrators to move from a machine-centric view of the network to a service-centric view.

Relationship of Sites to Other Active Directory Components

A *site* is as a collection of inter-connected computers that operates over IP subnets. A site is also a place on a network having high bandwidth connectivity. The relationship of sites to Active Directory components is based on the following network operations performed by sites:

- Control of replication occurrences
- Changes made with the sites
- How efficiently DCs within a domain can communicate

Relationship of Sites and Domains

A site can contain one or more domains, and a domain can be part of one or more sites. Sites and domains do not have to maintain the same namespace. Sites and domains are interrelated to each other because sites control replication of the domain information.

Figure 14.2 The Relationship of the Sites and Domains Present in a Network

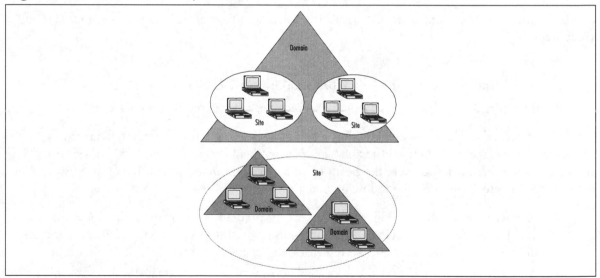

For more information on the working of domains, see Chapter 12, "Working with Forests and Domains" and Chapter 15, "Working with Domain Controllers."

Physical vs. Logical Structure of the Network

The sites present in an Active Directory denote the *physical structure* of a network, domains represent the *logical* or *administrative structure* of the organization. The physical structure information is available as site and site link objects in the directory. This information is used to build the most efficient replication topology. Generally, Active Directory Sites and Services are used to define sites and site links.

This partitioning of physical (sites) and logical (domains) structure offers the following advantages:

- You can develop and manage the logical and physical structures of your network independently.

- You do not have to base domain namespaces on your physical network.

- You can deploy DCs for multiple domains within the same site.

- You can deploy DCs for the same domain in multiple sites.

The Relationship of Sites and Subnets

In Active Directory, a site consists of a set of computers that are inter-connected in a local area network (LAN). Computers within the same site typically exist in the same building, or on the same campus network. A single site consists of one or more IP subnets. Sites and subnets are represented in Active Directory by site and subnet objects, which we create through the Active Directory Sites and Services administrative tool. Each site object is associated with one or more subnet objects.

Creating Sites and Site Links

In this section, we'll look at creating sites and site links, as well as planning for your site. As with most other administrative tasks in Windows Server 2003, planning is a key component that improves the end result and reduces error and downtime.

Site Planning

You should plan thoroughly before creating and deploying an Active Directory. Site planning enables you to optimize the efficiency of the network and reduce administrative overhead. High-performance sites are developed based on the proper planning of the physical design of your network. Site planning enables you to determine exactly which sites you should create and how they can be linked using *site links* and *site link bridges*. Site information is stored in the *configuration partition*, which enables you to create sites and related information at any point in your deployment of Active Directory.

Site planning enables you to publish site information in the directory for use by applications and services. Generally, the Active Directory consumes the site information. You'll see how replication impacts site planning later in the chapter.

Criteria for Establishing Separate Sites

When you initially create a domain, a single default Active Directory site called *Default-Site-First-Name* is created. This site represents your entire network. A domain or forest consisting of a separate site can be highly efficient for a LAN connected by high-speed bandwidth.

If a single LAN consists of a separate subnet or if a network consists of multiple subnets connected by a high-speed connection, establishing a separate site topology offers the following advantages:

- Simplified replication management
- Regular directory updates between all DCs

Establishing separate site topology enables all replication to occur as *intra-site* replication, which requires no manual replication configuration. A separate site design enables DCs to receive updates with respect to directory changes.

Creating a Site

Sites are created using the Active Directory Sites and Services tool of Windows Server 2003. This tool can also be used to create new sites, site links, subnets, and so forth. Use the following steps to create a new site.

Create a new site

1. To open the **Active Directory Sites and Services** tool, click **Start | Control Panel | Administrative Tools | Active Directory Sites and Services**. The Active Directory Sites and Services console opens.

2. Highlight the **Sites** folder in the left-hand tree pane of the **Active Directory Sites and Services** console. Right-click and select **Sites** folder **New | Site** option from the context menu.

3. Selecting the **New Site** option opens a **New Object – Site** dialog box.

4. Type the name of the site in the **Name** box present in the **New Object – Site** dialog box.

5. Select an initial site link object for the site from the **New Object – Site** dialog box.

6. Click **OK**. This completes the process of creating a site using the **Active Directory Sites and Services** tool. Figure 14.3 shows the initial site link object of the site.

Figure 14.3 The Initial Site Link Object for the Site

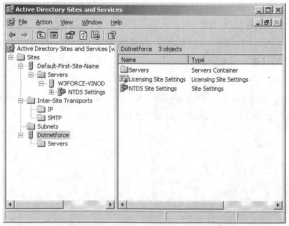

Renaming a Site

Renaming a site is one of the first tasks you should perform when administering a site structure. When you create a site initially, it is created with the default name *Default-First-Site-Name*. This name can be changed based on the purpose of the site, such as the name of the physical location.

A site is also renamed when a network of an organization is expanded by one or more sites. Even if an organization is located in a single location, it makes sense to rename the Default-First-Site-Name, because you never know when the network will expand. Renaming a site enables administrators to differentiate sites present in a network easily and perform administration tasks efficiently.

When a DC becomes aware that its site has been renamed, it will update its DNS records appropriately. Because of issues with cached DNS lookups and client caching of site names that will lead to temporary delays in connectivity directly after a rename, it's best to name and rename sites as early as possible in the deployment. After renaming a site, it's advisable to manually force replication with other DCs in the same site.

Sites are renamed using the Active Directory Sites and Services tool of Windows Server 2003. Use the following procedure to rename a site.

Rename a new site

1. To open the **Active Directory Sites and Services** tool, click **Start | Control Panel | Administrative Tools**. Double-click **Active Directory Sites and Services**. The Active Directory Sites and Services dialog box opens.

2. Highlight the **Sites** folder in the left-hand tree pane of the **Active Directory Sites and Services** console. Expand the **Sites** folder, and you'll see the sites shown with icons of small, yellow office buildings.

3. Right-click the site you want to rename and select the **Rename** option from the context menu.

4. Type the new name of the site in the **Name** box in the left console pane.

5. Click **OK**. This completes the process of renaming a site using the Active Directory Sites and Services tool.

Creating Subnets

Subnets are associated with the Active Directory sites to match client computers. As you know, the subnets are denoted by a range of IP addresses. The Active Directory Sites and Services user interface prevents you from having to provide the subnet names manually; instead, you are prompted for a network address. Subnets are created using the Active Directory Sites and Services tool of Windows Server 2003. You can use the following steps to create subnets.

Create subnets

1. To open the **Active Directory Sites and Services** tool, click **Start | Control Panel | Administrative Tools**, and then double-click **Active Directory Sites and Services**. The Active Directory Sites and Services console opens.

2. Highlight the **Sites** folder in the left tree pane of the **Active Directory Sites and Services** console. Expand the **Sites** folder.

3. Right-click **Subnets** and select **New Subnet** from the context menu.

4. Selecting the New Subnet option opens a **New Object – Subnet** dialog box.

5. Type the network address and subnet mask in the form of dotted decimal notation in the text boxes present in the **New Object – Subnet** dialog box.

6. Select a site object for this subnet from the list provided in the **New Object – Subnet** dialog box.

7. Click **OK**. This completes the process of creating a subnet using the Active Directory Sites and Services tool.

Associating Subnets with Sites

After creating sites and subnets, the next step is to associate your subnets with sites. You specify the subnets associated with each site on your network by creating subnet objects in the Active Directory Sites and Services console. The association of subnets with sites enables the computers on the Active Directory network to use the subnet information to find a DC in the same site, so that authentication traffic will not cross over WAN links. Active Directory also uses subnets during the replication process to determine the best routes between DCs.

Subnets are associated with sites using the Active Directory Sites and Services tool of Windows Server 2003. Once you've created sites and subnets, you need to associate them. The following steps walk you through that process.

Associate subnets with sites

1. To open the **Active Directory Sites and Services** tool, click **Start | Control Panel | Administrative Tools,** and then double-click **Active Directory Sites and Services**.

2. Highlight the **Subnet** folder present in the left tree pane of the Active Directory Sites and Services console.

3. Right-click the newly created subnet and select the **Properties** option; this will open a Properties dialog box.

4. Associate any site with this subnet by selecting the available site from the site drop-down menu, and click **OK**, as shown in Figure 14.4.

Figure 14.4 Subnet Dialog Box for Associating/Changing the Site

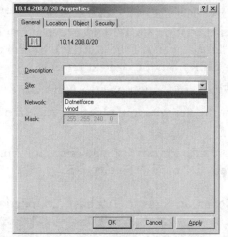

5. Click **OK**. This completes the process of associating a subnet with a site using the Active Directory Sites and Services tool.

Creating Site Links

After creating and defining the scope of each site, the next step in the site configuration process is establishing connections between the sites. The physical connectivity between the sites is established between the Active Directory databases by site link objects. A *site link object* is an Active Directory object that embodies a set of sites that can communicate at uniform cost. A *site link* that connects only two sites using the IP transport typically corresponds to a WAN link. A site link that connects more than two sites typically corresponds to Asynchronous Transfer Mode (ATM) and metropolitan area network (MAN) through leased lines and IP routers. Each site link is based on the following four components:

- **Transport** The networking technology to move the replication traffic.
- **Sites** The sites that the site link connects.
- **Cost** The value to calculate the site links by comparing to others, in terms of speed and reliability charges.
- **Schedule** The times and frequency at which the replication will occur.

Site links are created using the Active Directory Sites and Services tool of Windows Server 2003. Use the following steps to create site links.

Create site links

1. To open the **Active Directory Sites and Services** tool, click **Start | Control Panel | Administrative Tools**, and then double-click **Active Directory Sites and Services**.

2. Highlight the **Inter-Site Transports** folder in the left tree pane of the Active Directory Sites and Services console. Expand the **Inter-Site Transports** folder.

3. Right-click either the **IP** or **SMTP** folder (depending on what protocol the network is based on) in the left tree pane of the **Active Directory Sites and Services** console. Select **New Site Link** from the context menu.

4. Selecting **New Site Link** option opens a **New Object – Site Link** dialog box.

5. Type the name of the new site link object in the **Name** box in the **New Object – Site Link** dialog box.

6. Select two or more sites for establishing connection from the **Sites not in this site link** box, and click **Add** as shown in Figure 14.5.

Figure 14.5 Selecting Sites to Establish Connection

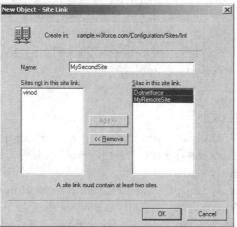

7. Click **OK**. This completes the process of creating a new site link object using the Active Directory Sites and Services tool. Figure 14.6 shows the final screen shot of the process.

Figure 14.6 ADSS Tool After Creating the New Site Link

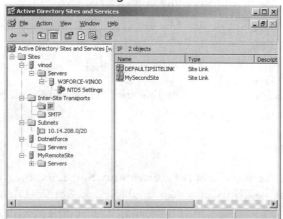

Configuring Site Link Cost

Site link costs are calculated to determine how expensive an organization considers the network connection between two sites that the site link is connecting.

Higher costs represent more expensive connections. If there are two site links available between two sites, the lowest cost site link will be chosen. Each site link is assigned an IP or SMTP transport protocol, a cost, a replication frequency, and an availability schedule. All these parameters reflect the characteristics of the physical network connection.

The cost assigned to a site link is a number on an arbitrary scale that should reflect, in some sense, the expense of transmitting traffic using that link. Cost can be in the range of 1 to 32,767, and lower costs are preferred. The cost of a link should be inversely proportional to the effective bandwidth of a network connection between sites. For example, if you assign a cost of 32,000 to a 64 kbps line, then you should assign 16,000 to a 128 kbps line and 1000 to a 2 Mbps line. It makes sense to use a high number for the slowest link in your organization. As technology improves and communication becomes cheaper, it's likely that future WAN lines will be faster than today's, so there's little sense in assigning a cost of two for your current 128 kbps line and a cost of 1 for your 256 kbps line.

Site link costs are configured using the Active Directory Sites and Services tool of Windows Server 2003. The following procedure walks you through assigning and configuring site link costs.

Configure site link costs

1. To open the **Active Directory Sites and Services** tool, click **Start | Control Panel | Administrative Tools**, and then double-click **Active Directory Sites and Services**.

2. Highlight the **Sites** folder in the left tree pane of the Active Directory Sites and Services console and expand the **Sites** folder.

3. Highlight the **Inter-Site Transports** folder in the left tree pane of the Active Directory Sites and Services console and expand the **Inter-Site Transports** folder.

4. Right-click the site link whose cost you want to configure in the left tree pane of the **Active Directory Sites and Services** console, and select **Properties**. Selecting **Properties** opens a dialog box.

5. Type the value for the cost of replication of the site link object in the **Cost** box in the dialog box as shown in Figure 14.7.

Figure 14.7 The Cost of the Site Link Object

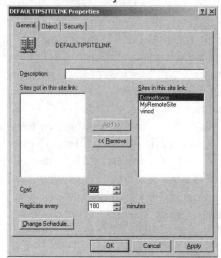

6. Click **OK**. This completes the process of configuring the site link costs using the Active Directory Sites and Services tool.

Site Replication

An essential process for any domain that has multiple DCs is replication. Replication ensures that each copy of the domain data is up to date, and is done by sending information about changes from one DC to another. In Windows Server 2003, every DC is capable of making changes to the database that has domain user and computer accounts.

Types of Replication

Replication in a Windows Server 2003 environment is one of two types:

- **Intra-site replication** Replication that occurs between DCs within a site.
- **Inter-site replication** Replication that occurs between DCs in different sites.

It is important to understand the differences between these methods when planning the site structure and replication.

Intra-site Replication

Intra-site replication occurs between DCs within a site. The system implementing such replication uses high-speed, synchronous Remote Procedure Calls (RPCs).

Within a site, a ring topology is created by the KCC between the DCs for replication (see Figure 14.8). The **KCC** is a built-in process that runs on all DCs and helps in creating replication topology. It runs every 15 minute by default and delegates the replication path between DCs based on the connection available. The KCC automatically creates replication connections between DCs within the site. The ring topology created by the KCC defines the path through which changes flow within the site. All the changes follow the ring until every DC receives them.

Figure 14.8 Ring Topology for Replication

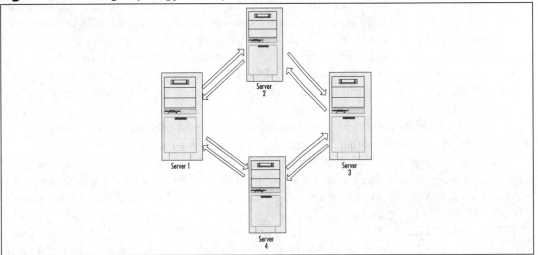

The KCC analyzes the replication topology within a site to ensure efficiency. If a DC is added or removed, it reconfigures the ring for maximum efficiency. It also configures the ring so that there will be not more than three hops between any two DCs within the site, which sometimes results in the creation of multiple rings (see Figure 14.9).

Figure 14.9 The Three-Hop Rule of Intra-site Replication

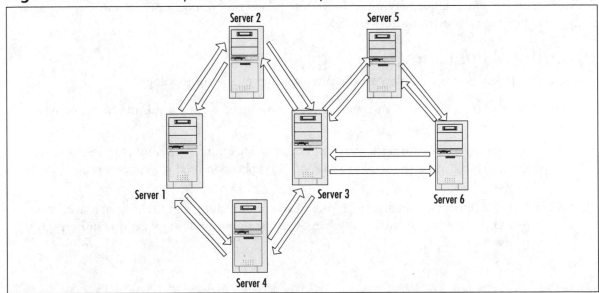

Inter-site Replication

Inter-site replication takes place between DCs in different sites. The drawback of inter-site communication is that it has to be configured manually. Active Directory builds an efficient inter-site replication topology with the information provided by the user. The directory saves this information as site link objects. A DC running a service called the *Inter-site Topology Generator* (ISTG) is used to build the topology. An ISTG is an Active Directory process that runs on one DC in a site and considers the cost of inter-site connections. It ensures that the previous DCs are no longer available, and checks to determine if new DCs have been added. The KCC process updates the inter-site replication topology. A least-cost spanning-tree algorithm is used to eliminate superfluous replication paths between sites.

An inter-site replication topology is updated regularly to respond to any changes that occur in the network. It would be useful if the traffic needs to cross a slower Internet link.

An inter-site replication across site links occurs every 180 minutes; this can be changed if necessary. In addition, you can schedule the availability of the site links for use. By default, a site link is accessible to carry replication 24 hours a day, 7 days a week, and this can also be changed if necessary. A site link can also be configured to use low-speed synchronous RPCs over TCP/IP or asynchronous SMTP transport. That is, replication within a site always uses RPC over IP, while replication between sites can use either RPC over IP or SMTP over IP. Replication between sites over SMTP is supported for only DCs of different domains. DCs of the same domain must replicate by using the RPC over IP transport. Hence, a site link can be configured to point-to-point, low-speed synchronous RPC over IP between sites, and low-speed asynchronous SMTP between sites

Planning, Creating, and Managing the Replication Topology

An important job when implementing replication topology is planning, creating, and managing the replication topology discussed in this section.

Planning Replication Topology

There are three key points to understand before planning replication topology:

- Before starting a replication planning process, we need to first finish the forest, domain, and DNS.

- It is essential to have an understanding of Active Directory replication, the File Replication Service (FRS), and system volume (SYSVOL) replication used to replicate group policy changes.

- For Active Directory replication, a rule of thumb is that a given DC that acts as a bridgehead server should not have more than 50 active simultaneous replication connections at any given time.

Creating Replication Topology

The next step is to create the replication topology.

- Active Directory replication is a one-way *pull* replication whereby the DC that needs updates (target DC) gets in touch with the replication partner (source DC). Then, the source DC selects the updates that the target DC needs, and copies them to the target DC. Because Active Directory uses a multi-master replication model, each DC functions as both source and target for its replication partners. From the view of a DC, it has both inbound and outbound replication traffic, depending on whether it is the source or the destination of a replication sequence.

- Inbound replication is the incoming data transfer from a replication partner to a DC, while outbound replication is the data transfer from a DC to its replication partner.

- System policies and logon scripts that are stored in SYSVOL use FRS to replicate. Each DC keeps a copy of SYSVOL for network clients to access. FRS is also used for the Distributed File System (DFS).

- Components of the replication topology such as the KCC, connection objects, site links, and site link bridges are to be checked by the administrator.

- There are two methods for creating a replication topology:

  - Use the KCC to create connection objects. This method is recommended if there are 100 or fewer sites.

  - Use a scripted or third-party tool for the creation of connection objects. This method is recommended if there are more than 100 sites.

Managing Replication Topology

Data is usually replicated based on a change notification within sites. It's up to the administrator to force immediate replication. To do so for all data on a given connection in a single direction, perform the following steps:

1. Choose **Start | Programs | Administrative Tools | Active Directory Sites and Services**. Expand **Sites** in the left tree pane.

2. Expand the name of the site that has to replicate to.

3. Expand the name of the server for replicating.

4. Select the server's **NTDS Settings** object. The right console pane will be populated with the server's inbound connection objects.

5. In the right pane, right-click the name of the server from which you want to replicate, and select **Replicate Now**.

Replication can also be forced from the command line by using the *repadmin.exe* utility from the Support Tools.

Configuring Replication between Sites

To ensure that users can log on within a given span of time, it is necessary to locate DCs near them, which sometimes involves moving the DCs between sites.

The purpose of a site is to help manage the replication between DCs and across slow network links. In addition to creating the site and adding subnets to that site, we also need to move DCs into the site, as replication happens between DCs. The DC has to be added to a site to which it belongs so that clients within a site can look for the DCs in the site and can log on to it.

To move DCs, follow these steps:

1. Select **Click Active Directory Sites and Services**.

2. Choose the **Sites** folder and then select the site where the server is located.

3. In the site, expand the **Servers** folder.

4. Right-click on the DC you want to move, and choose **Move**.

5. Select the destination subnet from the dialog box and click **OK**.

Configuring Replication Frequency

Replication frequency can be configured by providing an integer value that informs the Active Directory as to how many minutes it should wait before it can use a connection to check replication updates. The interval of time must be not less than 15 minutes and not more than 10,080 minutes. For any replication to happen, a site link is essential. Follow these steps to configure site link replication frequency:

1. Choose **Start | Programs | Administrative Tools | Active Directory Sites and Services**.

2. Expand the **Inter-Site Transports** folder, select either the **IP** or **SMTP** folder, and then right-click the site link for which the site replication frequency is to be set.

3. Click **Properties**, and in the Properties dialog box for the site link, enter in the **Replicate Every** box the number of minutes between replications. The default value is 180.

4. Click **OK**.

Configuring Site Link Availability

After the DCs are moved, a site link has to be created between sites, as it provides a path through which replication takes place. The creation of site links gives the KCC information about which connection object should be created in order to replicate directory data. Site links also imply where the connection object should be created. Follow these steps to configure a site link:

1. Choose **Start | Programs | Administrative Tools | Active Directory Sites and Services**.

2. Open the **Sites** folder and then the **Inter-Site Transports**.

3. Right-click on the **IP** or **SMTP** folder depending on the protocol needed and then choose **New Site Link**.

4. Enter the name for the site link in the **Name** text box. From the **Sites not in this site link** list, choose the site to connect and click **Add**.

5. Click **OK**.

When creating site links, there is the option of using either IP or SMTP as the transport protocol:

■ **SMTP replication** SMTP can be used only for replication over site links. It is asynchronous; that is, the destination DC does not wait for the reply, so the reply is not received in a short amount of time. SMTP replication also neglects Replication Available and Replication Not Available settings on the site link schedule, and uses the replication interval to indicate how often the server requests changes .When choosing SMTP, you must install and configure an enterprise certification authority (CA), as it signs the SMTP messages that are exchanged between DCs.

■ **IP replication** All replication within a site occurs over synchronous RPC over IP transport. The replication within a site is fast and has uncompressed delivery of updates. Replication events occur more frequently within a site than between sites, and the overhead of compression would be inefficient over fast connections.

Configuring Site Link Bridges

Often, there is no need to deal with site link bridges separately, as all the links are automatically bridged by a property known as a *transitive site link*. Sometimes when you need to control through which sites the data can flow, you need to create site link bridges. By default, all the site links created are bridged together.

The bridging enables the sites to communicate with each other. If this is not enabled by the automatic bridging due to the network structure, disable the same and create an appropriate site link bridge. In some cases, it is necessary to control the data flow through the sites using site link bridges. To disable transitive site links (automatic bridging), follow these steps:

1. Choose **Start | Programs | Administrative Tools | Active Directory Sites and Services**.

2. Expand the **Sites** folder and then expand the **Inter-Site Transports** folder.

3. Right-click on the transport for which the automatic bridging should be turned off, and choose **Properties**.

4. On the **General** tab, clear the **Bridge all site links** check box and click **OK**.

To create a site link bridge, follow these steps:

1. Choose **Start | Programs | Administrative Tools | Active Directory Sites and Services**.

2. Expand the **Sites** folder and then the **Inter-Site Transports** folder.

3. Right-click on the transport that needs to be used, and choose **New Site Link Bridge**.

4. In the **Name** box, enter a name for the site link bridge.

5. From the list of **Site links not in this bridge**, select the site link to be added.

6. Remove any extra site links in the **Site links in this bridge** box and click **OK**.

Configuring Bridgehead Servers

A *bridgehead server* is a server that is mainly used for inter-site replication. The bridgehead server can be configured for every site that is created for each of the inter-site replication protocols. This helps to control the server that is used to replicate information to other servers.

To configure a server as a bridgehead server, follow these steps:

1. Choose **Start | Programs | Administrative Tools | Active Directory Sites and Services**.

2. Expand the **Sites** folder.

3. Expand the site in which a bridgehead server has to be created, and then expand the **Servers** folder.

4. Right-click on the server and choose **Properties**.

5. In the **Transports available for inter-site transfer** area, select the protocol for which this server should be a bridgehead and click **Add**.

6. Click **OK** to set the properties, and then close **Active Directory Sites and Services**.

The ability to configure a server as a bridgehead server gives you greater control over the resources used for replication between intersites.

Troubleshooting Replication Failure

DCs usually handle the process involved with replication automatically. Unsuccessful network links and incorrect configurations prevent the synchronization of information between DCs. There are many ways to monitor the behavior of Active Directory replication and correct problems if they occur.

Troubleshooting Replication

A common symptom of replication problems is that the information is not updated on some or all DCs. There are several steps that you can take to troubleshoot Active Directory replication, including:

- **Check the network connectivity** The basic requirement for any type of replication to work properly in a distributed environment is network connectivity. The ideal situation is that all the DCs are connected by high-speed LAN links. In the real world, either a dial-up connection or a slow connection is common. Check to see if the replication topology is set up properly. In addition, confirm if the servers are communicating. Failed dial-up connection attempts can prevent important Active Directory information from being replicated.

- **Examine the replication topology** The Active Directory Sites and Services tool helps to verify whether a replication topology is logically consistent. This is done by right-clicking the **NTDS Settings** within a Server object and selecting **All Tasks | Check Replication Topology**. If there are any errors, a dialog box will alert you to the problem.

- **Validate the event logs** Whenever an error in the replication configuration occurs, events are written to the Directory Service event log. The Event Viewer administrative tool can provide the details associated with any problems in replication.

- **Verify whether the information is synchronized** Many administrators forget to execute manual checks regarding the replication of Active Directory information. One of the reasons for this is that Active Directory DCs have their own read/write copies of the Active Directory database. Therefore, no failures are encountered while creating new objects if connectivity does not exist. It is important to regularly check whether the objects have been synchronized between DCs. The manual check, although tedious, can prevent inconsistencies in the information stored on DCs.

- **Check router and firewall configurations** Firewalls restrict the types of traffic transferred between networks. In some cases, firewalls might block the types of network access that should be available for Active Directory replication to occur.

- **Verify site links** Before any DCs in different sites can communicate, the sites must be connected by site links. If replication between sites doesn't occur properly, verify whether the site links are in proper positions.

Using Replication Monitor

The Replication Monitor tool helps you to determine whether the DCs replicate the Active Directory information correctly. This tool is available as part of the Windows Server 2003 Support Tools, which have to be installed separately. After installing the Support Tools, go to **Startup menu | Windows Support Tools | Command Prompt** and enter **replmon.exe**, which will open the Replication Monitor console (see Figure 14.10).

Figure 14.10 Replication Monitor Console

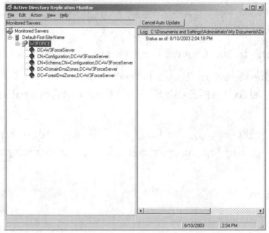

When you open the tool, you see a blank screen that is divided into two panels: *Monitored Server* and *Log*. Follow these steps to perform replication monitoring:

1. Select the **Add Monitored Server** option from the **Edit** menu.

2. Enter the server name (if known) to be monitored, or search for a specific domain for a server to monitor. After this is done, the **Monitored Server** panel displays the Active Directory information, and the log panel shows the information stored in the log file.

3. To save the log information, select the **Save Monitored List As** and **Open Log** options from the **File** menu.

4. The **Active Directory Replication Monitor** tool can also be used for synchronizing the directory partition. DCs listed for a directory partition are treated as source servers, while the direct replication partners are represented by an icon that indicates the network-connected servers. Right-clicking a server and selecting **Properties** can also identify it. The **Properties** box displays the source server as a Direct Replication Partner, a Transitive Replication Partner, or a Bridge Head Connection.

5. Right-click the direct replication partner, and select **Synchronize Replica**. **replmon.exe** initiates replication and reports the success or failure of the request.

6. Apart from these functionalities, the **Replication Monitor** tool has various options under different menus, such as **Action**, **View**, and so forth. Under the **Action** menu you have different options. For example, under the **Domain** option you can select **Search Domain Controller**, which is used for replication errors. There is a **Server** option that is basically used for replication-related work and helps to check the replication topology.

7. Apart from these submenus, there are options such as **Site**, **Naming Context**, and **Replication Partners** that are enabled when the appropriate function for a server is selected.

The Active Directory Replication Monitor is simple and easy to use. It provides a great deal of information and is useful for fixing Active Directory replication problems.

Using Event Viewer

The Event Viewer is used for configuring Active Directory event logging. To configure Active Directory event logging, follow these steps:

1. Select **Start | Run**. In the **Open** box, type **regedit**, and click **OK**.

2. Locate and click the following Registry key:
   HKEY_LOCAL_MACHINE\SYSTEM\CurrentControlSet\Services\NTDS\Diagnostics

3. Each entry in the right pane of the Registry Editor window represents a type of event that Active Directory can log. All entries are set to the default value of 0 (None).

To configure event logging for the appropriate component, follow these steps:

1. In the right pane of the Registry Editor, double-click the entry that represents the type of event that is to be logged; for example, **Security Events**.

2. Type the logging level that's needed in the **Value data** box, and click **OK**.

3. Repeat step 2 for each component that you want to be logged. Then, on the **Registry** menu, click **Exit** to quit the Registry Editor.

Some of the events that can be written to the event log include:

- KCC
- MAPI events
- Security events
- Replication events
- Directory access
- Internal configuration
- Internal processing
- Inter-site messaging
- Service control setup

Each entry is assigned a value of 0 through 5, which determines the level of details of the events that are logged:

- **0** (None): Only critical events and error events are logged at this level. This is the default setting for all entries.

- **1** (Minimal): Very high-level events are recorded in the event log at this setting. Events can include one message for each major task that is performed by the service. This can be used when the location to start an investigation is not known.

- **2** (Basic)

- **3** (Extensive): This level records more detailed information than the lower levels, such as steps that are performed to complete a task.

- **4** (Verbose)

- **5** (Internal): This level logs all events, including debug strings and configuration changes. A complete log of the service is recorded.

Using Support Tools

As mentioned earlier, the Support Tools must be installed separately from the Windows Server 2003 operating system. In addition to the Replication Monitor, there are other support tools that will be useful to you in managing sites, subnets, and your overall network. Table 14.1 lists some of the support tools that are used most frequently.

Table 14.1 Categorizing Support Tools

Tool	Description
Repadmin.exe: Replication Diagnostics Tool	A command-line interface that is used for Active Directory replication. This tool provides a powerful interface into the inner workings of Active Directory replication, and is useful in troubleshooting Active Directory replication problems.
Active Directory Replication Monitor (Replmon.exe)	Used to display replication topology, status, and performance of Active Directory DCs.
ADSI Edit	MMC snap-in that acts as a low-level editor for Active Directory.
Browstat.exe: Browser Status	A network browser diagnostic tool.
Dsacls.exe	Facilitates management of ACLs for directory services.
Dsastat.exe: Active Directory Diagnostic Tool	Compares and detects differences between naming contexts on DCs.

Chapter 15

Working with Domain Controllers

In this chapter:

- ☑ **Planning and Deploying Domain Controllers**
- ☑ **Backing Up Domain Controllers**
- ☑ **Managing Operations Masters**

Introduction

In the preceding chapters, we discussed forests, domains, sites and subnets. The common link? Domain Controllers (DC), the backbone of any Windows Server 2003 network. Server roles were discussed in Chapter 3 and managing domain controllers was covered at length in Chapter 12. In this chapter, we're going to take a quick look at DCs in more detail. Implementing and managing DCs is an important part of the network administrator's job, because the DCs play such a vital role in the operation of the network. The focus of this chapter is the Active Directory DC and how to plan and deploy DCs on your network. You'll learn about server roles, where DCs fit in, and how to create and upgrade DCs. We discuss placement of DCs within sites, and how to back up your DCs.

Planning and Deploying Domain Controllers

Remember that a DC does not equal a domain. A domain is a logical entity containing potentially millions of objects, while a DC, in the context of this chapter, is simply a computer running Windows Server 2003 with a copy of the Active Directory database (of course, an NT Server or Windows 2000 Server computer can also be a DC). This server takes on a management role in granting or denying access to resources throughout the entire domain, not just those resources located on this physical machine.

In order to provide acceptable connectivity performance, it is imperative that all users have adequate access to a DC close to their physical locations.

Understanding Server Roles

You might recall that, before Windows 2000, in order to install a server operating system, you had to decide the server's role during installation. Switching between the roles of primary domain controller (PDC), backup domain controller (BDC) and member or standalone server was difficult and required new installations with each change. Starting with Windows 2000 and continuing with Server 2003, *all* servers begin as standalone or member servers, and then you promote the server to be a DC as needed. In addition, you can now *demote* the DC back to a member server.

As already mentioned, a server that contains a copy of the Active Directory database is a DC. A DC has domain responsibilities and those can interfere with other tasks. Because the Active Directory is the most important part of the domain, your DC will delay your print job or file access until it is finished with its DC duties. Your users, however, don't care about the domain and its needs. Their own needs are more important to them. Therefore, you should separate file and print access, e-mail and Internet access, and other application-based duties from the DC. Plan your servers according to the needs of the users in your area of stewardship, and balance that with the needs of your domain.

Function of Domain Controllers

We have alluded to the responsibilities of DCs, and now we will iterate those responsibilities or functions:

- Track all user and computer accounts
- Authenticate access to resources
- Verify passwords
- Establish secure connections
- Replicate all changes to all other DCs

A DC receives changes to its copy of the Active Directory database. By default, all DCs within a site replicate everything to each other within about 15 minutes. Between sites, the replication is managed, which is the main reason to create separate sites. If replication is immediate over fast WAN connections, then replication will be as well. If the replication is based on time or activity, the change will have to wait in Denver until the site policy decides to talk to Philadelphia and exchange data. What this means is that it could take 12 to 24 hours before Jett can use his Manager-level access. Kim knows that Jett can't wait this long, so to avoid this, she changes her DC connection to go directly to a DC in Philadelphia, over the WAN. Now the change is accomplished within 15 minutes. Of course, Kim's time to make the change is slowed by that WAN connection, but Jett is much happier!

Although the previous list of DC responsibilities is by no means exhaustive, it represents most of the functions you should be concerned about first. Additionally, your DC integrates with other services for ease of administration and security. The following is a short list of some of these services.

- DNS
- DHCP
- Kerberos security
- Remote access
- Virtual private networking

Important to note here is that Active Directory, which is on the DCs, provides these services to give you centralization and control of resources. Making them work efficiently is accomplished by understanding the various services and knowing when to use them and more importantly when *not* to use them. It is easy to turn on the services and let them run, but each service has an effect on the hardware resources involved, which are limited. Enabling unused services also creates a security risk because the unused (and often unmonitored) service could be exploited by a hacker.

Determining the Number of Domain Controllers

Since you just learned about sites in Chapter 14, "Working with Active Directory Sites," you know that each site requires at least one DC. Your site topology is very important, because of the speed factors (actually the lack of speed) involved in the WAN connections between these sites. You must keep firm control of the replications crossing the WAN. Without sites, you break the age-old rule originally established by Novell: *Don't span the WAN.* The information that follows applies to DCs in *each* site.

Table 15.1 lists the factors you must consider in determining the number of DCs to install.

Table 15.1 Domain Controller Functions Affecting Performance

DC Functions	Description of Effect
PDC Emulator	This FSMO is assigned to the first DC installed, and is designed to respond to Windows NT 4 BDCs. Additionally, this FSMO receives all new password and lockout information changes immediately for the entire domain.
Active Directory replication	The process of synchronizing the Active Directory database between DCs.
Workstation logon	Computer accounts authenticating to domain.
Global Catalog (GC) operations	Required in a multidomain Active Directory forest to facilitate logons.
File and print services	A DC can store files and be a print server too.
Network services	A DC can host other important network services such as: DNS DHCP WINS
User logon	User authentication on startup and resource access.

Continued

Table 15.1 Domain Controller Functions Affecting Performance

DC Functions	Description of Effect
LDAP searches	If you use LDAP applications or services, be aware of this need.
Other FSMOs	

Depending on the number of users, computers, and application needs in your domain, you most likely need more than one DC. At the very least, you should have two DCs for fault tolerance in case one goes down. As your network size increases, so will the number of DCs. This facilitates both load balancing and redundancy of the Active Directory. The number of nondomain functions, such as file and print services, will have to go to dedicated member servers. Then, how many DCs do you need?

Microsoft has outlined a way to determine this and even created a Job Aid to help you. The first issue is, how much can your server physically handle? Microsoft has issued *minimum* guidelines in Table 15.2 for processors and memory, based on the number of users in the domain and the number of DCs handling the load.

Table 15.2 Minimum DC, GC, RAM, and CPU per Site

Number of Domain Users in Site	Number of DCs	Global Catalog	RAM	CPU
1 to 499	1	DC is a GC server	512MB	Uniprocessor PIII 500+
500 to 999	1	DC is a GC server	1GB	Dual PIII 500+
1,000 to 10,000	2	Both DCs are GC servers	2GB	Quad PIII Xeon+
10,000+	1 for every 5000 users	Half of all DCs are GC servers with a minimum of two GCs	2GB	Quad PIII Xeon+

When the term "minimum" is used, remember that it means just that: the *bare* minimum! Your servers should have much more than the minimum if you want more than minimal performance. According to the experts, if you have to choose between CPU and RAM, get more RAM. It's always easier to get more RAM up front. Although we always say that we can add more RAM later, we often don't, or when we want to, it is not available for that particular server because it has become obsolete.

Using the Active Directory Installation Wizard

You know what a DC is, what hardware to buy, how many to buy, and where to put them, and now we will show you how to create one. Microsoft's Active Directory Installation Wizard (ADIW) is used to create DCs, domains, trees, and forests, so you need to understand how to start it and which options to choose.

To start the ADIW, click **Start | Run**. Type **dcpromo** and press **Enter**. The initial Welcome window contains a link to Windows' Help files. Use the Help files if you have to—they are very good. Click **Next**.

Operating system compatibility is described in the next window. Click **Next**.

The next window shows the **Additional domain controller for an existing domain** dialog, used to create all other DCs within that same domain. Use this to set up DCs for each site. Selecting this option takes you to a window that requires administrator-level credentials in order to create the DC. The server you are promoting must be able to find another DC via DNS, so make sure you are connected to the network and you have set up your TCP/IP settings to find both the DNS and the DC.

Choosing **Domain controller for a new domain** will make this server a DC, and it will be the first DC in a new domain. Use this for each *new* domain. Following most experts' recommendations, you will only do this once, because a single domain network is the best way to go. Of course, reality dictates that you might have to create additional domains, and this is where you do it.

Three choices are presented to you to create a new:

- **Domain in a new forest** This choice is for the very first DC in your first tree in your first forest.

- **Child domain in an existing domain tree** This choice is used when you already have a domain tree (for example, yourfirm.biz) and you need a second domain or child to this domain (for example, MyPlace.YourFirm.biz).

- **Domain tree in an existing forest** With this option you are sharing the forest and allowing some communication, but you have different tree names. For example, you could have a forest like YourFirm.biz and then add another domain tree that uses a different DNS name, like MyFirm.biz.

The options of **Child domain in an existing forest** and **Domain tree in an existing forest** require an existing entity to which you are adding. The next window requests administrator credentials at the tree and forest levels. Again, the TCP/IP settings must already be in place in order to find the corresponding DCs to authenticate your credentials and allow you to add on to the tree or forest. Refer to Chapter 12 for specific step-by-step instructions for creating and naming new domains.

Creating Additional Domain Controllers

To add more DCs to your new domain, yourfirm.biz, you must install Windows Server 2003 on another machine. Remember the initial server installation is either a standalone or member server and then it can be promoted to a DC. Dcpromo, otherwise known as the ADIW, accomplishes this feat. You just created your first DC, so the steps are still fresh in your mind, right?

Since the domain and DNS servers already exist, when you see the window shown in Figure 15.1, select the second option, **Additional domain controller for an existing domain**. Next, enter the credentials for your parent domain administrator, and the ADIW creates the new DC with replication, dynamic updates, and DNS SRV records all in place. Use the following procedure to promote a Windows Server 2003 member server to an additional domain controller.

Figure 15.1 Domain Controller Type

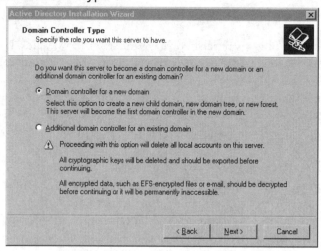

There are a few prerequisites you will need to meet before you begin:

- One DC
- One standalone or member server
- Both of these servers connected on the same network
- Both of these servers set up with TCP/IP pointing to the same DNS server

Once these have been met, follow these steps:

1. On your member or standalone server, make sure you are logged on with administrator permissions and that the prerequisites are met.

2. Begin the promotion process by clicking **Start | Run** and typing **dcpromo**. Click **OK**.

3. The ADIW is launched. Click **Next**.

4. Click **Next** on the next dialog labeled **Operating System Compatibility**.

5. Select **Additional domain controller for an existing domain, and** click **Next**.

6. Type in the Administrator account and password. Type in the domain name if it is not already there.

7. This dialog requires the FQDN that matches the A record in your DNS server. By default, it puts whatever was in the last dialog. Make sure it is correct and click **Next** (see Figure 15.2).

Figure 15.2 Full DNS Name of Existing Domain

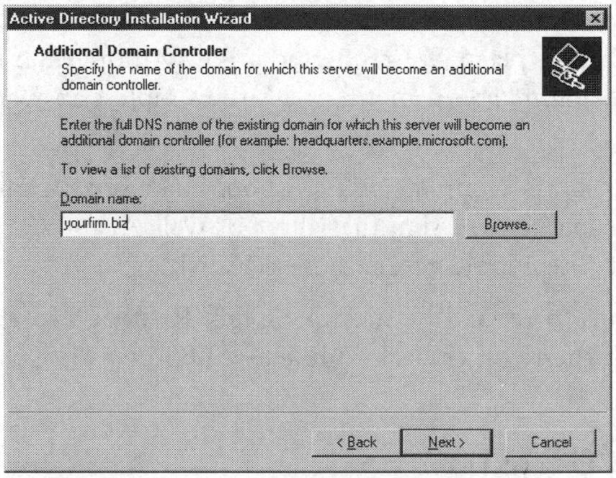

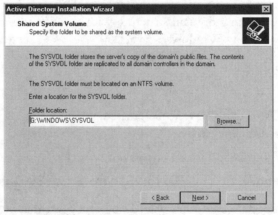

8. The next two dialogs should seem familiar. You must specify the location of the Active Directory database and log. Keep the defaults of \WINDOWS\NTDS. Click **Next**.

9. Specify the location of your system volume (SYSVOL) folder, which *must* be on an NTFS partition. The default is fine as long as you formatted your disk with NTFS. Click **Next** (Figure 15.3).

Figure 15.3 Shared System Volume Location

10. Type in the same password you used for your domain password. This dialog requests a password for the directory services restore administrator which is different from the domain administrator; however, unless there are compelling reasons otherwise, put in the same password. It can be difficult enough dealing with the crash requiring a restore, without adding to the stress of remembering a password not often used. Click **Next**.

11. Think about what dcpromo is about to do and what must be in place for it to work. After clicking Next, you will test the settings outlined in the prerequisites. The ADIW must find a DNS server, ask for the location of a DC in the existing domain, locate and authenticate

to that DC, and transfer a copy of the Active Directory database, making a new DC. If this fails, you have a great opportunity to determine why. Use the hints just mentioned and verify that all is in place. We requested a Retry more than once before noticing the we misspelled *administrato*r—sometimes, it's the simplest answer. Review the **Summary** and click **Next**.

12.   After the transfer is complete, which should take several minutes, you will see the Complete dialog box—a sign that all went well. Again, note the location of the DC in the Default-First-Site-Name site, and click **Finish**.

13.   The last step is to restart the machine.Click **Restart Now**. This obviously reboots the server, which then comes back online as a DC in your existing domain.

Upgrading Domain Controllers to Windows Server 2003

If you administer an existing domain and are looking to upgrade to Windows Server 2003, your best bet is to upgrade the DCs one by one until they are all at the same level. Server 2003 can co-exist with Server 2000 and NT, as long as you are aware of the caveats associated with such an environment. Even if you plan to upgrade all of the DCs, you must still temporarily run the network as a mixed environment.

Upgrading your existing domain can be done in one of two ways: *in-place upgrade* or *migration*. An in-place upgrade means that you take your existing DC and install Windows Server 2003 right over the top of it. Your existing domain structure with all of its user, group, and computer accounts will be migrated into the new Windows Server 2003 Active Directory. The advantages are clear:

- It's simple and quick.
- You don't need a new computer.
- No new SIDs or trusts have to be created, which keeps all your existing member servers and resource domains happy.
- Everyone gets to keep his or her password.
- Migrating from Windows 2000 to Windows Server 2003 in this manner works well.

Why would you upgrade any other way? Experts suggest that you avoid the in-place upgrade in the following situations:

- If you are trying to get an NT 4 PDC to become an Active Directory DC in an existing Active Directory domain, you can't do it this way. Upgrading an NT 4 PDC will always create a new Active Directory domain.
- Upgrading an NT 4 DC allows you to create a new Active Directory domain name, but you are forced to keep the NetBIOS name.
- You cannot merge your NT 4 domain into your Active Directory domain.
- All accounts are upgraded and there is no way to roll this back. We suggest that you take one of your BDCs in NT or one of your Active Directory DCs in 2000 and move it

offline in case there are any problems. You can then bring the DC back online, and your original domain will still exist.

- All the extra "stuff," such as unused groups and users, in the NT SAM is there in your new Active Directory domain.

A migration is accomplished by creating a new pristine Active Directory on a new server. Then, you use a migration tool to copy the domain information from your old domain to your new one. Here are some of the advantages of this method:

- Migration is gradual. You can migrate one department at a time.

- Accounts are copied rather than moved, so you can return to the old domain if necessary.

- You avoid the complexity of taking existing database bugs and moving them into your new Active Directory.

- You can re-evaluate your existing domain structure and consolidate or expand your domains, as you deem necessary.

There are also disadvantages to migration:

- You need new computers to install your new domain.

- Generally, users have to create new passwords.

- A migration tool might have to be purchased. Microsoft has a free migration tool, Active Directory Migration Tool (ADMT), but it is designed for the small to medium domains. You can purchase other tools for enterprise-level migrations. At around $10 per user, this can get expensive.

- You cannot use the same NetBIOS name that exists in your old domain.

- Migration is more work. You might have to go to every member server and re-do all of the groups (some migration tools provide ways to avoid this by using Security ID histories (SIDHistory).

Whether to upgrade or to migrate is an important decision. You must understand the differences and know the pros and cons involved. Either choice will produce issues to consider and plan for.

Placing Domain Controllers within Sites

Sites were discussed earlier in this book, in Chapter 12, "Working with Active Directory Sites." Remember that you don't need more than the default site unless you have a network with subnets that are connected by slower WAN links. If you have multiple sites, you need to put your DCs in the right places; otherwise, you will "span the WAN"; in other words, your DCs will replicate continuously over your WAN, eating up the bandwidth needed by your users.

Here is a brief review of what you need to manage your sites. The tool of choice is the Active Directory Sites and Services console.

- Create a site name
- Create subnets to match your actual IP subnets
- Move the servers listed in ADSS to their respective assigned sites

First, you define the site itself. We suggest at least renaming the Default-First-Site-Name to something befitting your company location, such as CorpHQ. Next, you need to define subnets. Your physical and logical IP subnets should already exist, but you need to define them in the site tool, by specifying the subnet address and assigning it to your site. To place your DC in a site, open the **Servers** folder and move the DC into the appropriate site. Remember that all servers within a site will automatically determine the replication process, but you must configure the replication between sites.

Backing Up Domain Controllers

Every Windows server has a *system state* that includes the Registry of that server (among other things). On a DC, the system state also includes Active Directory. Since replication of Active Directory occurs automatically, you only need to back up the system state of one of your DCs to back up Active Directory. However, your other DCs might run other applications or have files that only exist on that machine, so be sure that those are included in your routine backup. If you have multiple sites, consider backing up the system state of one DC per site to facilitate easier access to the Active Directory backup data should you need to restore it.

To back up the system state of any computer, you must be connected locally. In other words, the computer that you are logged on to, and are running the backup application from, is the only system state you can back up. If you are using a tape drive and you want to back up the Active Directory, you will have to connect the tape drive to a DC directly. The local computer rule applies to a restore as well: you must be directly connected to the computer on which you want to restore the system state. Backup media options have been increased from the limited Windows 2000 Backup to include removable media (CD, DVD) or a shared resource.

Restoring Domain Controllers

To restore a DC from backup, you must determine which part needs to be restored. The first question to ask is, does the Active Directory need to be restored authoritatively or non-authoritatively?

- **Non-authoritative restore** means that you just restore the Active Directory to whatever point it was at when you backed it up, and then let the new changes from the other DCs automatically replicate to this DC to bring it up to the most current state.

- **Authoritative restore** means that the Active Directory that you restore is the master, and even though the data on it is "old" compared to the other DCs, its data is to be taken as the *authority* or final word on the Active Directory.

Use the non-authoritative restore when you have lost the DC but the data on the other DCs is accurate; in other words, there is nothing the "downed" DC knows that no other DC knows. Authoritative restore is used when the "downed" server *does* know something the other DCs don't.

For example, suppose you delete the user account Hannah on Monday. On Friday, you learn that Hannah was not supposed to be deleted. You can't just create a new user called Hannah because the new account takes on a new SID, and all the permissions, rights, and privileges that were associated with the first Hannah are lost. You must restore the original account, which by now is removed from all the DCs. Fortunately, you can perform an authoritative restore from Sunday night's backup to get Hannah's account back. This forces all the other DCs to re-accept Hannah's original account.

That is a simplified version of what the backup and restore capabilities can do. When you restore authoritatively, you can restore the entire Active Directory or select different levels of the domain hierarchy, even down to the single object restore, as was needed in the previous scenario. As long as you know the exact FQDN for the object to be restored, you can recover it.

The steps to restore Active Directory start with a good recent backup. Remember that your restore is only as good as your backup. Spend the time, effort, and money to ensure that you have good valid backups. With the backup in hand, you are ready. On which DC should you run the restore? See Chapter 19, "Ensuring Active Directory Availability," for more information about backing up and restoring the Active Directory. Also remember that you can now use a backup from a DC running Windows Server 2003 to create additional DCs.

Managing Operations Masters

Flexible Single Master Operations (FSMO, pronounced *fizz-moe*) are certain roles assigned to DCs that need only exist on one DC and not all DCs. They are also called *operations masters*. These operations are critical in managing such objects as the schema and determining uniqueness among a forest, tree, and domain. Earlier in the chapter we declared all Windows Server 2003 DCs equal— that was not entirely accurate. FSMOs make some DCs more important than others, at least in regard to certain domain tasks, and it is your job to know which DCs perform these roles and what to do if a role needs to be switched to another DC. You must also know how to *seize* a role should you lose one. Those various roles, as well as how to seize and transfer roles, were discussed in detail in Chapter 12.

Chapter 16

Working with Global Catalog Servers and Schema

In this chapter:

- ☑ **Working with the Global Catalog and GC Servers**
- ☑ **Working with the Active Directory Schema**

Introduction

In previous chapters, we've discussed forests, domains, trusts, sites, and organizational units. In this chapter, we're going to take a closer look at the Global Catalog and Global Catalog servers. We'll also look at the Active Directory schema. Understanding the structure of AD is important in order to be an efficient Windows Server 2003 administrator.

Active Directory uses the Global Catalog (GC), which is a copy of all the Active Directory objects in the forest, to let users search for directory information across all the domains in the forest. The GC is also used to resolve user principal names (UPNs) when the domain controller (DC) that is authenticating logon isn't aware of the account (because that account resides in a different domain). When the DC can't find the user's account in its own domain database, it then looks in the GC. The GC also stores information about membership in Universal Groups.

Because the GC performs all these functions for the multidomain network, it is important for administrators to understand how it works and how to create, manage, and place the GC servers that hold the GC. In this chapter, we look at this special type of domain controller: the Global Catalog Server. You'll learn about the role the GC plays in the network, and how to customize the GC using the Schema Microsoft Management Console (MMC) snap-in. We show you how to create and manage GC servers, and we'll explain how GC replication works. You'll learn about the factors to consider when placing GC servers within sites.

Next, we address the Active Directory schema itself. You'll learn about schema components: classes and attributes, and the naming of schema objects. We show you how to install and use the Schema management console, and you'll learn how to extend the schema and how to deactivate schema objects.

Working with the Global Catalog and GC Servers

The GC is a vital part of Active Directory functionality. Given the size of enterprise-level organizations, on many networks, there will be multiple domains and at times, multiple forests. The GC helps in keeping a list of every object without holding all the details of those objects; this optimizes network traffic while still providing maximum accessibility.

Whenever a user is searching for an object in the directory, the GC server is used in the querying process for multiple reasons. The GC server holds partial replicas of all the domains in a forest, other than its own (for which it holds a full replica). Thus, the GC server stores the following:

- Copies of all the objects in the domain in which it resides
- Partial copies of objects from other domains in the forest

The key point is that the GC is designed to have the details that are most commonly used for searching for information. This allows for efficient response from a GC server. There is no need to try to find one item out of millions of attributes, because the GC has the important search-related items only. This makes for quick turnaround on queries.

Functions of the GC

The GC serves various purposes, which we discuss later in the chapter. GC servers are important for the UPN functionality of Active Directory. Universal Groups are also a responsibility of the GC server.

The scope of Directory Services has changed from the days of Windows NT 4.0 Directory Services. With Active Directory, a user record holds more than just a username for an individual. The person's telephone number, e-mail address, office location, and so forth can be stored in Active Directory. With this type of information available, users will search the directory on a regular basis. This is especially true when Microsoft Exchange is in the environment.

Whether a person is looking for details on another user, looking for a printer, or simply trying to locate another resource, the GC will be involved in the final resolution of the object. As mentioned previously, the GC server holds a copy of every object in its own domain and a partial copy of objects in other domains in the forest. Therefore, users can search outside their own domains as well as within, something that could not be done with the old Windows NT Directory Services model.

UPN Authentication

The UPN is meant to make logon and e-mail usage easier, since the two (your user account and your e-mail address) are the same. An example of a UPN is Brian@syngress.com. The GC provides assistance when a user from a domain logs on and the DC doesn't know about the account. When the DC doesn't know the account, it generally means that the account exists in another domain. The GC will help in finding the user's account in Active Directory. The GC server will help resolve the user account so the authenticating DC can finalize logon for the user.

Directory Information Search

With Active Directory, users have the ability to search for objects such as other users or printers. To help a user who is searching the database for an object, the GC answers requests for the entire forest. Since the complete copy of every object available is listed in the GC, searches can be completed quickly and with little use of network bandwidth.

When you search the entire directory, the request is directed to the default GC port 3268. The GC server is also known to other computers on the network because of SRV records in DNS. That is how a node on the network can query for a GC server. There are SRV records specifically for GC services. These records are created when you create the domain. The DNS entry for a GC server uses the mnemonic *Gc* and the record type *SRV.*

When users search for information in Active Directory, their queries can cross WAN links, depending on the network layout. Each organization is different. Figure 16.1 shows an example layout with GC servers in the corporate office in Chicago and a branch office in Seattle. The other two sites do not have GC servers. When queries are initiated at the Chicago branch office, the queries use the corporate office GC server. With a high-speed fiber connection, bandwidth isn't an issue.

Figure 16.1 Example GC Search Query

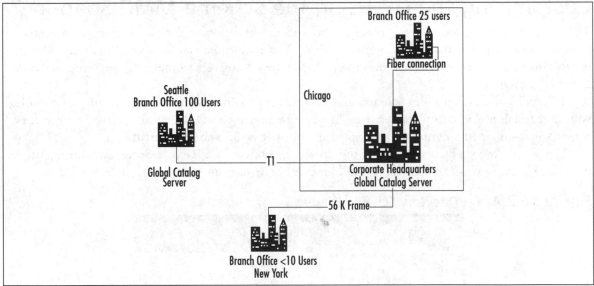

The branch office in New York has a slow link but less than 10 users. These users will use the GC in Chicago as well. Even though the pipe between these locations is only 56K, the minimal amount of users doesn't warrant having a GC server in New York. The Seattle office has a T1, which is decent connectivity, but there are over 100 users in this location. Considering that, searches will be more efficient with a GC server locally. We will look at sites later in the chapter, but Figure 16.1 will help you get a basic understanding of how the query process works.

Universal Group Membership Information

When setting up your network, you will have certain features available based on the Forest Functional Level and Domain Functional Level. Universal Groups is one of these features that will or will not be available depending on your functional level. If your Domain Functional Level is set to at least Windows 2000 Native or later, you will have Universal Groups available on your network. Universal Groups can have members belonging to various domains in the forest. Without a GC server, Universal Groups could not exist. That is because Universal Group membership is stored in the GC only. This means that every DC will not have a copy of Universal Group membership; only the DCs serving as GC servers have this information. When users log on, their Universal Group membership is checked. The GC provides this information to the authenticating DC.

Universal Group membership information is stored in all GC servers, so you need to consider the design of your GC server layout when adding to or changing the GC server configuration. The number of users at a location will help determine when you need a GC server. A large number of queries of the GC information over slow links isn't recommended; placing a GC at each site is a better design. With sites with a small number of users, you can get away with not having a GC server at each site. We discuss this in more detail later in the section *Placing GC Servers within Sites*.

Customizing the GC Using the Schema MMC Snap-In

There might be occasions when you need to make a modification to the GC. You might want to include more attributes than were originally set up. You have to be careful, though, and consider the replication of data. The more attributes there are for the GC servers to replicate, the more network traffic is generated.

To modify the GC, use the Schema snap-in within the MMC. Before you can run the console, you must install it. You complete the installation by registering a .dll. To install the Active Directory Schema snap-in, open a command prompt and type **Regsvr32 schmmgmt.dll**.

You should then see a message that the dll was registered ("DllRegisterServer in schmmgmt.dll succeeded"). Now you can run the Active Directory Schema snap-in as shown in Figure 16.2.

Figure 16.2 Active Directory Schema Snap-In

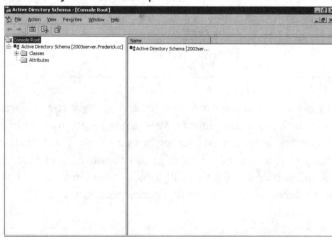

Now that the .dll is registered, you can create a custom MMC. If you click **Start** and select **Run**, you can start a blank console by typing **MMC** in the Run window and clicking **OK**. You have to add the snap-in to the blank MMC. The following procedure walks you through the steps of registering and running the Active Directory Schema snap-in. Remember that you must be a Schema Admin member to make changes to the schema. If you are not, you will be able to run the Schema Admin snap-in and view properties of classes and attributes, but you won't be able to makes changes.

Setup Active Directory Schema MMC Snap-in

You need to be logged on as an Enterprise Administrator in Active Directory.

1. Log on to your server with an Enterprise Administrator account.
2. Open a command prompt by Clicking **Start**, and then select **Run**.
3. In the **Run** box, type **cmd** and press **Enter**.
4. At the command prompt, type **regsvr32 schmmgmt.dll**.
5. You should see a box that shows registration if the dll was successful.
6. Click **OK** in the dialog box confirming that the registration succeeded.
7. Now, click **Start**, type **mmc /a**, and press the **Enter**.
8. In the MMC window, click on **File** and select **Add/Remove Snap-in**.
9. In the **Add/Remove Snap-in** window, click **Add**.
10. Find the **Active Directory Schema** snap-in listed in the **Add Standalone Snap-in** window.
11. Select the snap-in and then click **Add**.
12. Now, click **Close** in the **Add Stand Alone Snap-in** dialog box.
13. Click **OK** in the **Add/Remove Snap-in** dialog box.
14. You should now have a console that you can use for modifying the schema or GC. You can save this as a .msc file to easily click on it next time versus adding a custom snap-in.

Creating and Managing GC Servers

When you initially install Active Directory, the first DC created is also the first GC server. As your network changes, you might require additional GC servers to help manage network traffic. To specify whether a server is a GC server, use the Active Directory Sites and Services console. Open the **Active Directory Sites and Services** console, expand **Sites**, and then expand the site with the DC you want to be a GC server. Next, expand **Servers** and find the *Domain Controller* object. In the details pane you should see NTDS Settings.

If you right-click **NTDS Settings** and select **Properties**, you will have the option to enable or disable the GC on the DC you select, as Figure 16.3 shows.

Figure 16.3 General Tab of NTDS Settings Properties

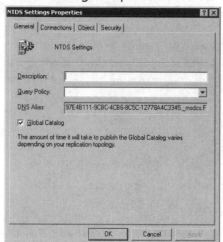

The check box on the **General** tab is used to enable or disable GC functionality. To be able to change the state of the GC check box, you must be a member of the Domain Admins group or the Enterprise Admins group.

As stated previously, the planning of GC server placement is important for a successful network. Each GC server creates additional replication traffic on the network.

Understanding GC Replication

You know now that GC servers hold information for all of the objects in their own domains and a partial copy of the objects from other domains in the forest through replication. The default attributes included in the GC make up the most commonly searched for items. These items are part of normal Active Directory replication.

The Knowledge Consistency Checker (KCC) generates the GC replication topology. The GC is only replicated between DCs that are GC servers; the information is not replicated to other DCs. A few things can affect replication; for example, Universal Group membership, and the number of attributes included in the GC.

Universal Group Membership

The GC holds the sole responsibility of maintaining Universal Group membership. The names of the Global Groups and Domain Local Groups are also in the GC, but their membership lists are not. This helps keep the size of the database small enough to efficiently answer queries.

For replication purposes, it is best to keep Universal Group membership relatively static. Every change made to a Universal Group is replicated to every GC server. Keeping these changes to a minimum will keep the GC replication traffic to a minimum.

Attributes in GC

When you first set up Active Directory, there is a series of default attributes from Active Directory in the GC. Sometimes, the default set of attributes is missing an item you would like to see. For example, perhaps you want to have a coworker's department number as part of his user record; you can accomplish this by adding an attribute. You can use the Active Directory Schema snap-in to include additional attributes in the GC by using the General tab as shown in Figure 16.4. To get to this option, open the **Schema** snap-in, and expand the **Attributes** section. Right-click any attribute, and select **Properties**.

Figure 16.4 Adding Attributes to the GC

Prior to Windows Server 2003, each time the attribute set was extended, a full synchronization of all attributes stored in the GC was completed. In a large network, this can cause a serious amount of network traffic. With Windows Server 2003, only the additional attribute or attributes are replicated to other GC servers. This makes more efficient use of network bandwidth.

Placing GC Servers within Sites

Another consideration when it comes to replication is placement of your GC servers. In a small network with one physical location, GC server placement is easy. Your first DC that is configured will hold the GC role. If you have one site, but more than one DC, you can move the role to another DC if you want to. Most networks today consist of multiple physical locations, whether in the same city or across the country. If you have high-speed links connecting your branch offices you might be okay, but many branch office links use limited bandwidth connections. If the connection between locations is less than a T1, you might have limited bandwidth depending on what traffic is crossing the wire. As a network administrator, you will have to work with your provider to gauge how much utilization there is across your WAN links.

Another factor is reliability. If your WAN links are unreliable, replication traffic and synchronization traffic might not successfully cross the link. The less reliable the link, the more the need for setting up sites and site links between the locations.

Without proper planning, replication traffic can cause problems in a large network. Sites help control replication traffic. Making the most of available bandwidth is an important factor in having a network that allows your users to be productive. Logon and searching Active Directory are both affected by GC server placement. If users cannot find the information they need from Active Directory, they might not be able to log on or find the information or data they need.

Bandwidth and Network Traffic Considerations

Active Directory replication works differently depending on whether it is *intersite* or *intrasite* replication, as we discussed in Chapter 14. DCs that are part of the same site (intrasite) replicate with one another more often than DCs in different sites (intersite). If you have sites that are geographically dispersed, you need to be careful how you handle your GC server placement. The bandwidth between geographically dispersed offices is often minimal. The rule of thumb is to have GC servers in selected sites. In most cases, you do not want to have a GC server in every site because of the vast amount of replication that would occur. The following examples describe situations in which you should have a GC server within a site:

- If you have a slow WAN link between geographic locations. If you have a DC at each location, a good rule is to also have a GC server at each location. If the WAN link supports traffic for normal DC traffic, it should also handle GC traffic.

- If you have an application that relies heavily on GC queries across port 3268, you'll want to have a GC server in the site that the application runs in. An example of this is Exchange 2000, which relies heavily on GC information.

- If the domain functionality level is Windows 2000 native or later, you'll want to have GCs in as many sites as possible because Universal Group membership comes into play. We look at caching of Universal Groups, which can reduce traffic related to this, in the next section.

Data replicated between sites is compressed, which makes better use of available bandwidth. Because the data is compressed, more can be sent over a limited amount of bandwidth. This is how site placement and design can be critical to efficient network operation. For more information in site replication, refer to Chapter 14.

Universal Group Caching

The Windows Server 2003 Active Directory introduces Universal Group caching as a new feature. When a user logs on to the network, his or her membership in Universal Groups is verified. For this to happen, the authenticating DC has to query the GC. If the GC is across a WAN link, the logon process will be slow every time. To alleviate this, the DC that queries the GC can cache this information, which cuts down on the amount of data traveling across the WAN link for Universal Group information.

The cache is loaded at the first user logon. Every eight hours by default, the DC will refresh the cache from the nearest GC server. Caching functionality is administered in Active Directory Sites and Services as shown in Figure 16.5, and can be turned off if desired. You can also designate the GC server from which you want the cache to refresh, giving you more control over traffic distribution on the network.

Figure 16.5 Configuring Universal Group Caching

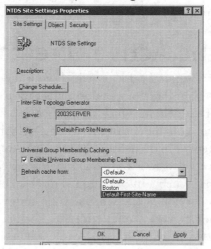

Prior to Windows Server 2003, Active Directory logon failed if a GC could not be located to check Universal Group membership. With Universal Group caching, DCs cache complete group membership information, so even if a GC server cannot be reached, logon will still happen based on cached Universal Group information.

Troubleshooting GC Issues

As with anything on your network, you will spend a certain percentage of your time troubleshooting issues. Common issues with GC include:

- Replication latency between GC servers
- Slow query response
- Overall load too high

Determining the proper course of action depends on the problem you are encountering. The basic answer to any of the preceding issues will result in either moving or adding GC servers.

If you are experiencing replication latency, you need to look at your GC servers and possibly your site configuration. Adding sites might help with replication traffic, as traffic between sites replicates differently than it does within sites. Between sites, the data is compressed and will cut down on bandwidth usage, which could help with the latency problem.

Slow query response can be a result of slow links between locations. Adding a GC server to the location experiencing this problem if one isn't already present will help. In addition, checking your site configuration can help as well. Workstations within a site will query the local GC server versus going across a WAN link.

If the overall load is too high, you need to look at adding more GC servers to balance the traffic. This also results in more replication traffic if you are not careful, so planning and consideration of the impact on your network is important.

There is no one single answer to troubleshooting your GC and the servers involved. Even with proper planning, problems sometimes arise. Working through the problem and testing will take time, and location of GC servers can make all the difference in a successful Active Directory layout.

Working with the Active Directory Schema

To have a directory, you must have a framework on which your directory structure is based. The Active Directory schema defines your directory. For an object to store data such as a username or telephone number, there has to be a field in which this information can be entered. These fields have names and belong to another component of the schema, which we will look at shortly. As with any other type of database, a schema simply defines the structure for the data.

It is important to remember that there is only one schema per forest. Thus, all the domains in the forest share this single schema. Schema information is the backbone of your Active Directory and the data within. If problems develop in the schema, your entire network could be out of commission. This means that you must be very careful with the schema.—which is why only members of the Schema Admins groups have write permission to the schema. The only default member of that group is the Administrator account in the forest root domain. You should be very selective when choosing members of the Schema Admins group.

Understanding Schema Components

Every database is built on a foundation that defines its structure, the database model. The foundation, or model, is based on various components (see Figure 16.6). The first component of the foundation for the schema in Active Directory is the *class*. Objects in the database belong to classes. A little later in the chapter, we look at how the class defines the structure of your data.

Associated with each object are fields, or *attributes*, that you fill in with data. We'll look at how this component relates to the class, and then bring it all together. For now, remember that the important components of the schema are:

- Object classes
- Object attributes

As with any database, there must be a naming standard. Within this section, we will look at schema object naming and how information can be referenced in different ways. If you decide that you need to extend the schema by adding additional classes or attributes, you need to plan exactly how you want it done. It is important to take extreme care in extending the schema. In most circumstances, software installations will extend the schema rather than an administrator manually editing it. Software such as Microsoft Exchange or Microsoft SQL can use the schema and sometimes require that changes be made. This is generally done as part of the software installation process and is the reason why you have to be logged on with a particular user account when installing that type of software.

Figure 16.6 Schema Components Diagram

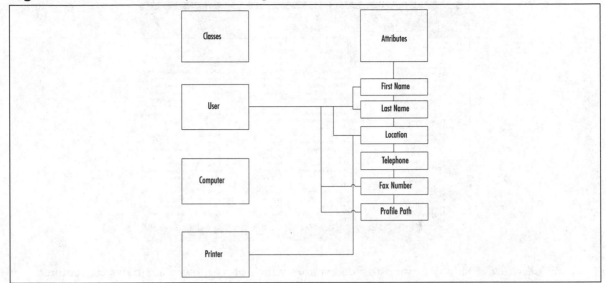

Classes

Object classes define your objects in the directory. Examples of *Object* classes include:

- User
- Printer
- Computer

When you create a new object in Active Directory, such as a new user account, you are creating a new instance of the existing *User* class. The class determines what attributes the object can contain. Classes are defined separately from attributes because there can be attributes that different classes share. A good example would be the location attribute. This attribute can be shared by the *User* class, *Site* class, and *Printer* class. Thus, the attribute is only defined once in Active Directory and is then linked to the respective classes of which it is a part. Figure 16.7 is a screen from the Active Directory Schema snap-in and some of the default *Object* classes.

Figure 16.7 *Object* Classes in Schema

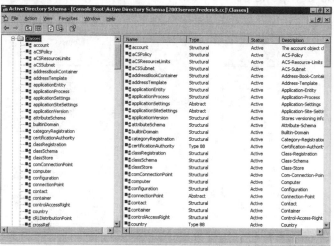

Each *Object* class has a definition that determines which of its allowed attributes are required and which are optional. These are known as *ClassSchema* objects in Active Directory, and define the common name for the object, a list of "must have" attributes, and a list of "might have" attributes, among other things. There are three types of *Object* classes in Windows Server 2003: *structural* objects that give an identity to the physical objects that make up your network (for example, servers or users); *abstract* objects that are used to define the structure objects (these are like a template for creating structural objects); and *auxiliary* objects, which are a predefined list that contains attributes that can be included in structural and abstract objects. The Type 88 in Figure 16.7 is an example of an *auxiliary* object.

Attributes

You need to define various attributes for each object you create. Remember that the *Object* class determines which attributes are required and which are optional. All attributes associated with that class will exist, but some (the optional attributes) can be left blank. You will be required to enter information for the required attributes. An example of an attribute is *First Name* or *Telephone Number*. This attribute is associated with the *User Object* class. These attributes can be filled in when you create the user account and are defined in Active Directory as containing a certain type of data. The *AttributeSchema* object defines the characteristics of a given attribute. Configuration items such as common name, syntax rules, and other things make up the *AttributeSchema* object. For example, a *Telephone Number* attribute is generally in a specified format, such as Access code–Area or Country Code–Prefix–Number (for example, 1-512-555-1234). However, the schema is not this specific; it specifies that the syntax must be a Unicode string of characters, with a minimum of one and a maximum of 64 characters.

In addition to defining the syntax, each attribute's properties will also include an X.500 object identifier (OID) for interoperability with other directories that comply with X.500 specifications, and a statement as to whether the attribute is single or multivalued as shown in Figure 16.8. Recall that X.500 is the directory standard upon which AD is built.

Figure 16.8 Properties of an Attribute

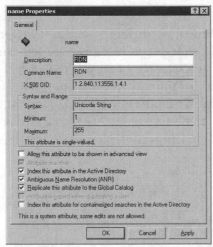

You use the Active Directory Schema snap-in to maintain attributes just as you do with objects. Figure 16.9 shows some of the default attributes within Active Directory.

Figure 16.9 Default Attributes in Active Directory

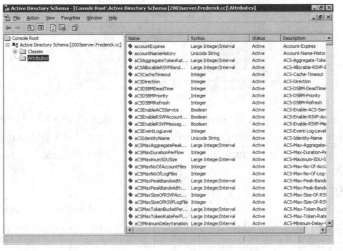

Single-Value Attributes

Most of the attributes you will work with will be single-value attributes. A single-value attribute is just what its name implies; it is an attribute with one piece of data entered. An example would be *First Name*. The *First Name* attribute cannot hold multiple values of data. After the first name is entered, you have to create a completely different object if you want to have another object with a different *First Name* attribute.

Multivalue Attributes

Although most attributes are of the single-value variety, there are also cases where an attribute will hold more than one piece of information. Attributes such as *Telephone Number* can hold multiple values. When you create a user account or edit its properties, you can enter a main number of 555-5555 for a user, and if that user has a secondary line, you can click the Other button to add additional data as shown in Figure 16.10. (You can access the properties for a user account by opening the **Active Directory Users and Computers (ADUC)** administrative tool, clicking the **Users** container in the left console tree, right-clicking the username whose properties you want to edit in the right console pane, and selecting **Properties**.)

Figure 16.10 Multivalue Attributes

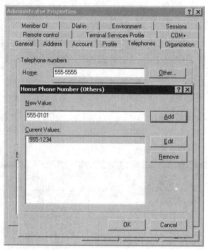

Multivalue attributes do not sort or keep track of the order of the entries if there are multiple entries. They are simply there for convenience in the case of common attributes that can have more than one entry. Each value within a multivalue attribute must be unique.

Indexing Attributes

When you index data in a database, you are organizing the information so you can have efficient responses to queries based on that data. You can set attributes as *indexed* to help users find the information they need. This means that the attribute will be indexed in the Active Directory. With indexing attributes, wildcard searches will function, allowing the user the ability to enter a partial word with an asterisk and return multiple hits.

When deciding which attributes to index, you have to be careful because you can slow your network down with extra replication traffic. When you mark an attribute as indexed, every attribute in that instance is added to the index. For example, if an attribute such as *Location* is part of a *Printer* object and a *User* object, both objects would be added to the index. With multivalued attributes, you could be using more bandwidth because you are replicating a large amount of information. The rule of thumb is to only index common attributes.

To index an attribute, use the Active Directory Schema snap-in. Expand the **Attributes** section and right-click on the attribute you want to index. Select **Properties**, and then check the option to **Index this attribute in the Active Directory** as shown in Figure 16.11.

Figure 16.11 Indexing Attributes

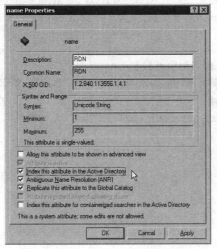

Naming of Schema Objects

If you are going to be working with *Schema* objects a lot, you need to be comfortable with the naming conventions that apply to *Schema* objects. There are different ways to reference objects in Active Directory, the most common of which are:

- **Lightweight Directory Access Protocol (LDAP)** LDAP is the primary access protocol for Active Directory. LDAP is an industry standard protocol for commonality among directories, and is based on the ISO's X.500 directory naming conventions. LDAP names identify an entire path within the directory; for example, CN=JDoe, OU=Sales, DC=Frederick, DC=cc.

- **Common name** The common name is a simplified way to identify an object. Common names are much easier to read than LDAP names. Common names must be unique within the container. An example common name would be JDoe.

- **Object Identifier (OID)** An identification number issued by another authority. The International Organization for Standardization (ISO) and American National Standards Institute (ANSI) have developed standards for OIDs as part of the X.500 directory services specifications. Every OID is unique. An example is the *Department* attribute in Active Directory. The OID for Department is 1.2.840.113556.1.2.141. This same OID will be used for the *Department* attribute in any directory that follows X.500 standards.

You should follow the LDAP or common name naming standards when setting up *Schema* objects. If you write software that modifies the schema, certain standards must be followed for the software to meet the "Certified for Windows" requirements. If you stick with the standards, any changes you make will be less likely to cause problems.

Working with the Schema MMC Snap-In

When working with the Schema snap-in, you need to be aware of some other configuration items. If you right-click **Active Directory Schema**, you are presented with various options as shown in Figure 16.12.

Figure 16.12 Schema Administrative Options

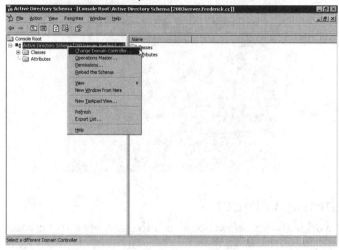

If you select **Change Domain Controller**, you can choose what DC you want to feed the schema information. If you select **Operations Master**, you can see what server is holding the **Schema Master role**, or change the server responsible for that role. You can use the Permissions option to change permissions on the schema. In most cases, network administrators would have no reason to go into the Permissions tab.

The last option in the first section of the list is Reload the Schema. This option will reload the schema from the database to make sure you don't have cached information that could be outdated.

When working with the Schema snap-in in a mixed environment, you might find yourself at a Windows 2000 server. If you are making schema modifications from a Windows 2000 server, you must ensure that Service Pack 3 for Windows 2000 has been installed.

Modifying and Extending the Schema

There will be times when the default schema layout doesn't meet your needs. If this is the case, you can modify the schema by changing existing classes or attributes. You could also extend the schema by adding classes or attributes that do not exist. Again, you must be extremely careful when making changes to the schema; modifying or extending the schema should only be done when absolutely necessary.

To modify or extend the schema, use the Schema snap-in. Begin by making your changes in a test environment and testing thoroughly before making modifications or extensions on your production network. Remember that the user using the snap-in must be a member of the Schema Admins group. Before you modify the schema by changing or adding classes or attributes, keep the following guidelines in mind:

- Double-check to be certain that the existing schema configuration does not meet your needs. It is possible that there is an existing class or attribute that will work for your requirements.

- When you add a class or attribute, that class or attribute *cannot* be removed. You can, however, deactivate a class or attribute. We will look at that in the next section.

- Make sure you have a valid OID; do not just pick one out of thin air.

- Default system classes cannot be modified. Windows uses these classes for basic functionality.

- Review documentation on the schema. In particular, review the Active Directory Programmer's Guide, which can be downloaded at www.microsoft.com, if you intend to make extensive modifications or extensions.

- Remember that schema changes affect the entire forest, because only one schema exists in a Windows Server 2003 forest and is shared by all domains in that forest.

When creating a new class, various attributes need to be filled out as shown in Figure 16.13. The first section is the Identification section. You will have to complete both Common Name and LDAP Display Name. You also have to enter the object ID, so you need to know how they are assigned. There is also an optional *Description* attribute that you use if you want to.

The other section is Inheritance and Type. The *Parent* class will have permissions assigned. Being a *Child* class, we would inherit the permissions from the *Parent* class objects.

Figure 16.13 Create a New Object Class

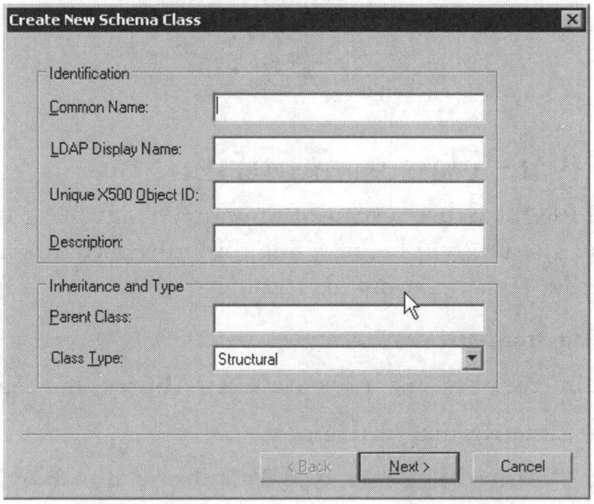

Deactivating Schema Classes and Attributes

If changes or additions are made to the schema, they cannot be deleted. Windows Server 2003 does not allow for deletion of classes or attributes after they are defined in the schema. However, you can deactivate a class or attribute if you don't want to use it anymore. This is essentially the same as deletion, because the class or attribute is no longer available for use. However, the class or attribute still exists within the schema. The deactivated class or attribute is called *defunct*. Default classes and attributes cannot be deactivated. If you decide that you need to have the attribute available, you can reactivate it later.

When you deactivate a class or attribute, you can redefine it if your forest is at the Windows Server 2003 functional level. For example, if you have an attribute that has the wrong syntax, you can deactivate the existing attribute and then create a new attribute with the proper syntax. You can reuse the LDAP display name and the OID. Note that you have to rename the original attribute after you deactivate it and before you create the new attribute to prevent conflicts.

You use the Schema snap-in to deactivate or reactivate an attribute or class. Figure 16.14 shows where you can activate or deactivate an attribute.

Figure 16.14 Activating or Deactivating

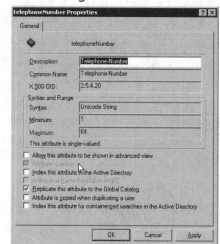

Create and deactivate classes or attributes

In this procedure, you will use the Schema snap-in to create an attribute, and then you will deactivate it. You should work on a test system before using this procedure on a live schema since additions to the schema cannot be removed (only deactivated).

1. Open the **Schema snap-in**.
2. Expand Active Directory Schema, right-click **Attributes**, and select **Create Attribute**.
3. Click **Continue** at the warning dialog box.
4. In the **Common Name** dialog box, type **Telephone number 2**.

5. In the **LDAP Name** dialog box, type **Telephone number 2**.

6. For the **OID**, type **2.5.4.20.2**.

7. Change the syntax drop-down to **Integer**, and then click **OK**.

8. Now, find the new attribute, right-click, and choose **Properties**.

9. On the **General** tab, you should see a check box for Attribute is Active.

10. Click the check box to remove the check. Click **Yes** to the question about the making the object defunct.

11. Click **OK** and the status window in the details pane should show **Defunct** under the **Status** column.

Troubleshooting Schema Issues

You might run into issues when working with the schema. They could be as simple as not finding the Schema snap-in to not being able to extend the schema. The most common problem is running or finding the snap-in. Make sure you register the .dll for the snap-in, and then create a customized MMC to run the snap-in.

There might be times where you simply cannot extend the schema; for example, if you are trying to add a class and are unable to complete the operation. A few things could cause this; the most common being that the user trying to make the changes is not a member of the Schema Admins group. In addition, the Schema Operations Master role has to be up and available on the network. If the Schema Operations Master role is across a WAN link, you might be experiencing too much latency. You can move this role if needed to solve network connectivity problems. You might also experience an issue where you cannot associate an attribute with a class. This is because the schema cache is not up to date. If this happens, you need to make sure the Schema cache is updated by reloading the schema. This could also be caused by trying to make changes on a server other than the Schema Operations Master. When modifying the schema, it is recommended that you make changes on the server running the Schema Operations Master role.

Chapter 17

Working with Group Policy in an Active Directory Environment

In this chapter:

- ☑ **Understanding Group Policy**

- ☑ **Planning a Group Policy Strategy**

- ☑ **Implementing Group Policy**

- ☑ **Performing Group Policy Administrative Tasks**

- ☑ **Applying Group Policy Best Practices**

- ☑ **Troubleshooting Group Policy**

Introduction

We briefly touched on Group Policy in earlier chapters. In this chapter, we'll take an in-depth look at Group Policy in Windows Server 2003. Group Policy is used to manage and control various features and components of the Windows Server 2003 network. Group Policy settings can be used to define users' desktop environments, to specify security settings, and to configure and control application behavior. Group Policy can be used to automatically deploy software to users and computers. You can also use group policies to assign scripts and redirect folders. Policies can be applied to a site, a domain, an organizational unit (OU) or a local computer.

Because Group Policy is used for so many important management functions, it is important for network administrators to be intimately familiar with how Group Policy works, and how they can use it for more flexibility and control of network components.

This chapter starts with a brief review of the basics of Group Policy terminology and concepts, including user and computer policies and Group Policy Objects (GPOs). We discuss the scope and application order of policies, and you'll learn about Group Policy integration in Active Directory. We show you how to plan a Group Policy strategy, and then walk you through the steps of implementing Group Policy. We show you how to perform common Group Policy tasks, and discuss Group Policy propagation and replication. You'll also learn best practices for working with Group Policy, and we'll show you how to troubleshoot problems with Group Policy.

Understanding Group Policy

Group Policy is derived from the System Policies of the Windows NT days, and has been significantly enhanced, first in Windows 2000 and now again in Windows Server 2003. Implementing Group Policy in the Active Directory allows system administrators to control aspects of the user or service environment within the network from a global perspective.

You can use Group Policy to accomplish the following tasks, among others:

- **Assign scripts** You can specify scripts that will run at login, logoff, startup, shutdown, and other times.

- **Manage applications** You can designate applications that will be installed on, updated on, or removed from computers.

- **Redirect folders** You can specify alternate locations for system folders, such as My Documents, My Pictures, and others.

- **Change Registry settings** You can designate a set of Registry settings that will be applied to the local computer when a user logs on.

Gaining a full understanding of how Group Policy can impact the network requires a full understanding of the terminology and concepts.

Terminology and Concepts

You will encounter a number of terms, acronyms, and jargon when designing and implementing a group policy in your organization. When we refer to Group Policy, we are actually talking about the superset of all the individual components that make up the larger whole. You will find policy elements that affect only users or computers, policies that are set at the workstation level or applied to an OU in Active Directory, and ways to apply basic security to policies. Let's review the basic terms used as the foundation of building Group Policy.

Local and Non-Local Policies

Group Policy allows you to set policies that will impact resources connecting to a specific computer or interacting with the entire directory. The terms *local policy* and *non-local policy* identify where the group policy settings originate. A local policy is stored on a specific computer (a workstation or a member server) and applies only to activities on that computer. For example, a local policy only affects a user object when the user logs on interactively on the server, either at the console or via terminal services. Local policies can also affect the way a user object accesses data from the specific server across the network. Generally, local policies should only be used on workstations; however, there are a few situations where local policies on a server would make sense.

Non-local policies are applied primarily to group objects. These policies affect objects in the directory and are enacted when the object is active in the network. If a non-local policy affects a user object, its effect is applied every time that user object logs on, no matter what PC is used as the logon console. Group policies can apply to any of the following:

- A local computer
- An entire site
- A domain
- A specific OU

Group policies can be filtered through security settings, much like NTFS file and folder permissions control access to data on a server volume. As you will see shortly, there is a specific order in which policies are applied if local and group policies differ in a specific area, but the best practice for policies in general is to apply the policies at the group level, not at the local level.

User and Computer Policies

As you might have guessed, some policies apply to user accounts, and other policies apply to computer accounts. You can only apply policies to user and computer objects, not security groups or other objects (however, policies can be filtered by security groups by setting the security group Access Control Entry on the GPO). These two types of policy application work as follows:

- User policies affect how user accounts interact with the network and are applied when a user logs on to the network.
- Computer policies affect how computer objects interact with the network and only apply to those computers that participate in the Active Directory.

You configure each of these types of policies in separate areas in the GPO Editor.

User and computer policies are divided into three groups: Software Settings, Windows Settings, and Administrative Templates.

Software Settings

The primary use of this setting is to install, update, or remove software on computers on the network. The Software Installation node is located in this group, and other policy groups can be added in this area by other applications.

Software policies set in this area under Computer Configuration apply to all users who log on to the computer where the policy applies. This policy setting could be used to designate a specific computer on the network where a particular application should be installed, no matter who logs on to the computer. Software policies set in this area under User Configuration apply to all computers that a particular user logs on to. This setting is useful if a particular user has a specific application that he or she needs to use, no matter where that user uses a computer in the organization. The policies can be set so that if an application is installed on a computer this way, only the user to whom the policy is applied is able to see or run the application.

Windows Settings

Policies applying to scripts, security, folder redirection, and Remote Installation Services, among others, are located in this area. There are significant differences between these policy settings depending on whether they are applied in the Computer Configuration or User Configuration node. Table 17.1 details some of the policy groups and whether they are applied to user or computer settings.

Table 17.1 Group Policies for Windows Settings

Policy	Location	Description
Scripts	Computer Configuration	Specifies startup and shutdown scripts to be run on the computer.
Scripts	User Configuration	Specifies logon and logoff scripts to be run by users.
Account policies	Computer Configuration\ Security Settings	Contains policies related to password and account lockout settings.
Folder redirection	User Configuration\Security Settings	Contains policies to redirect certain user folders, such as Application Data, My Documents, and Start Menu, to alternate locations.
Internet Explorer maintenance	User Configuration\Security Settings	Contains settings to modify defaults for Internet Explorer, such as user interface settings, favorites, connection settings, and security zone settings.
Public Key policies	Computer Configuration\ Security Settings	Contains policies related to system-level public key activities, such as Encrypted File System, Enterprise Trust, Autoenrollment settings, and Automatic Certificate Request settings.
Public Key policies	User Configuration\Security Settings	Contains policies related to user-level public key activities, such as Enterprise Trust and Autoenrollment settings.

Administrative Templates

Policy settings that appear in the Administrative Templates node of the GPO Editor contain Registry settings to achieve each of the settings contained in the hierarchy. Policies for user configuration are placed in the HKEY_CURRENT_USER (HKCU) area of the Registry, while those for computer configurations are placed in the HKEY_LOCAL_MACHINE (HKLM) area.

Administrative templates contain settings for Windows components such as NetMeeting, Internet Explorer, Terminal Services, Windows Media Player, and Windows update, to name a few. Other components common to both user and computer configurations include settings for user profiles, script execution, and group policy.

While the different policy settings between user and computer configurations are too numerous to list here, there are some key components available for the user configuration. These include the Start Menu, Taskbar, Desktop, Control Panel, and Shared folder settings.

Group Policy Objects

All group policy information is stored in Active Directory in GPOs. You can apply these objects at the site, domain, or OU level within the directory. Since the GPO is an object in the directory, you can set security permissions on the objects to determine who will access the policy settings stored in the GPO.

Because GPOs can impact a large portion of the directory, you should update GPOs infrequently. Each GPO update must propagate across the entire directory to take effect, and this could be a time-consuming process if the directory structure is very large. You should also restrict the number of individuals who make changes to GPOs that can impact the entire organization. Otherwise, you can run into the situation where two administrators make contradictory changes to a GPO in different locations of the tree, and the changes propagate differently around the tree, potentially causing problems until the directory has completely updated the GPO changes.

Scope and Application Order of Policies

A single object in the network can be subject to multiple policy settings, depending on how Group Policy is configured on the local machine and in the directory. Active Directory processes policy settings in a specific manner when an object connects to the network. Knowing this process will help you troubleshoot problems with policy settings as they arise.

Local, Site, Domain, OU

Group Policy settings are applied in the following order:

1. **Local settings** Each computer has its own local GPO, and these settings are applied before any others. There is only one local GPO per computer.

2. **Site settings** Group policies associated with the site in Active Directory are processed next. The system administrator can set a specific order in which the site policies are to be applied, if more than one policy is defined.

3. **Domain settings** Group policies associated with a domain object follow the completion of the site settings. If multiple domains are involved, the administrator can set the order of preference in which those settings will be applied.

4. **OU settings** Group policies associated with an OU are applied last in the processing order, but the processing starts with the OU highest in the directory structure. The remaining OU GPOs will be processed in descending order until the OU that contains the directory object is reached. If multiple policy settings are applied for a particular OU, the administrator can set the order in which the settings are applied.

Figure 17.1 details the order in which multiple policies are applied when a user object logs on to the domain. In the diagram, the user object exists in the OU 4 OU, which is in the OU 3 OU of Domain 1 of Site. When the user logs on, the local policy of the computer is applied, followed by any GPOs attached to Site, then Domain 1, then OU 3, and finally OU 4.

Figure 17.1 Processing Policy Settings at User Logon

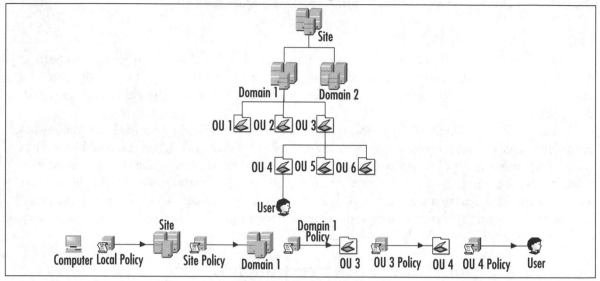

Understanding Policy Inheritance

We saw in Figure 17.1 that when the user logged on, policies from the Site, Domain, and OUs were applied to the user object. The example indicated that any policies associated with OU 3 would be applied before the policies in OU 4. Through policy inheritance, the policies in OU 3 will apply to all objects in OU 3, OU 4, OU 5, and OU 6, even if no specific policies are assigned to OU4, OU5, or OU6.

Objects in child containers generally inherit policies from the parent containers within a domain. If a policy setting is enabled in OU 3 and that same policy setting is not configured in OU 4, then objects in OU 4 inherit the policy setting from OU 3. If a policy setting is disabled in OU 3 but that same policy setting is enabled in OU 4, then the policy setting is enabled in OU 4, as the GPO for OU 4 overrides policy settings from OU 3. This is the way it works by default.

However, administrators can block inheritance on group policy settings at the OU level. If you want to start with a clean slate at a particular OU, you can use the Block Policy Inheritance setting at that OU, and only the settings in the GPO for that OU will apply to objects in the OU. Blocking policy inheritance does not impact local computer policy settings, only Active Directory group policy settings.

In addition, policies set at a higher container can be marked as No Override, which prevents any lower container settings from changing the policy settings of the higher container. Going back to Figure 17.1, if the GPO for OU 3 is marked for No Override, and a policy setting in the GPO for OU 4 conflicts with a setting from OU 3, the setting in OU 4 will not take effect. You cannot block a policy that is set to No Override.

You should use great care in using the Block Policy Inheritance and No Override settings when configuring Group Policy. Changing the default way in which policy is applied can complicate troubleshooting of policy settings if problems are encountered.

Filtering Scope by Security Group Membership

As mentioned, you can further control which policies are applied to which objects by filtering policy application by security group membership. Similar to setting permissions on files and folders with NTFS security settings, you can set security on a GPO so that only certain groups can see the GPO, which means that only those groups will have the policies applied.

Looking back at Figure 17.1, the diagram assumes that there is no security filter on the GPOs at any level. Now let's suppose that the user object is a member of the Accounting group, and that the GPO in OU 4 has security permissions set. If the security permissions on the GPO in OU 4 do not give members of the Accounting group access to read the GPO, then the user will not have the GPO settings for OU 4 applied when he or she logs on.

If you find yourself needing to filter GPO settings based on group membership, you might need to set multiple GPOs on a container and adjust the security settings accordingly. Again, adding a number of GPOs to a container increases the complexity of the policy setting process, which can cause complications for troubleshooting.

Group Policy Integration in Active Directory

As mentioned earlier, non-local group policy settings are stored in objects in the Active Directory. These objects are linked to specific containers: sites, domains, and OUs. Since GPOs are objects in the directory, they are subject to all the settings and rules of other objects.

Group Policy Propagation and Replication

Active Directory replication has an impact on group policy application in a large directory structure. Because GPOs are objects in the directory, they must be replicated to all copies of the directory partition on all domain controllers (DCs) before the settings can take effect in all circumstances. Replication is a concern for GPOs linked to a site or domain with multiple controllers.

When group policy is set for a domain, by default the actual object is tied to the server that has the primary domain controller (PDC) Emulator operations master token. The other DCs will receive the updated policy information as the token is passed around through replication. Users who authenticate to DCs other than the PDC might not receive the updated policies upon logon if the directory has not had ample time to replicate the settings.

You can specify a particular DC to be used for editing group policy by using the **DC Options** command in the **View** menu of the GPO Editor. As mentioned, the default is the DC with the PDC Emulator operations master token, but you can change this setting.

Sites that have multiple servers connected over slow WAN links have several issues related to policy propagation and replication. Obviously, a DC with an updated group policy is impacted by a slow WAN link when attempting to replicate the data across the link. Depending on how the directory is configured, DCs across the slow link can be set up to replicate much less frequently than those on a faster link.

Also of concern are users who authenticate to a DC across a slow WAN link. While the normal authentication process might not be all that network-intensive, more GPOs that have to be processed by the user significantly increases the time needed for full authentication.

Planning a Group Policy Strategy

You must consider a number of factors when planning the group policy strategy for your organization. Some of these factors include size of the organization, geography of the organization, structure of the organization, and so on. More importantly, you must determine the effective policy settings you want to have for each object in the directory.

One way to test your policy plan is to create the policies and then log on with user accounts from different locations of the directory and see how the policies impact the user experience. This is time consuming, cumbersome, and has a definite impact on the production network. Fortunately, Microsoft provides a way for evaluating the proposed policy environment without impacting the production system.

Using RSoP Planning Mode

The **Resultant Set of Policy** (RSoP) tool, included with Windows Server 2003, has a special planning mode that system administrators can use to evaluate the design of the group policy within the directory. The planning mode of RSoP can simulate a number of situations where group policy settings can be affected by a number of factors, including slow network links.

Opening RSoP in Planning Mode

To use RSoP in planning mode, you will need to run the **Resultant Set of Policy Wizard** from inside the Microsoft Management Console (MMC). You can follow these steps to open RSoP in planning mode to collect information for an RSoP report.

1. Open **Microsoft Management Console (MMC)** and add the **RSoP snap-in**.

   - Select **File | Add/Remove Snap-in**.

   - Click **Add**.

   - Select **Resultant Set of Policy** from the list.

   - Click **Add**, and then click **Close**.

   - Click **OK**.

2. Right-click on **Resultant Set of Policy** and select **Generate RSoP Data**.

3. Click **Next** in the Resultant Set of Policy Wizard window.

4. Click the **Planning Mode** option button, and click **Next**.

The RSoP wizard will walk you through the steps of gathering the data that can be collected and included in the RSoP report. On each page, there is a **Skip to the final page of this wizard without collecting additional data** check box. If you select the check box, only the data specified up to that point in the wizard will be included in the RSoP query. All other settings will take their default values.

The first page of the wizard collects user and computer information on which the query will run. This is the only data that is required in the wizard, as all subsequent pages can be skipped by clicking the **Skip to the final page of this wizard without collecting additional data** check box. On this page, you must select a specific user or user container, and a specific computer or computer container. You can use the **Browse** buttons to search for a user or computer or the parent container, or you can enter the information directly into the fields. After the information for the user and computer selections is complete, the **Next** button will enable and you can move to the next page of the wizard.

The next page of the wizard allows you to specify any advanced simulation options. On this page, you can specify the report to simulate a slow network connection and loopback processing options, if any. You can also specify which site's policies to test, if there are multiple sites available.

If you specified a specific user or computer in the initial page of the wizard, the next page of the wizard will allow you to specify an alternate location for the object or objects specified. Changing the location of the object will let you test what changes would occur if you moved the object to a different location in the directory. If you only select containers in the initial page, this page will not display.

The next page of the wizard identifies the security groups for the user object selected. If a specific user is selected in the first page of the wizard, the security groups for that user are displayed. If a user container is specified, the Authenticated Users and Everyone groups are listed as defaults. You can add user groups to the list or remove groups from the list to see what changes will occur as a result.

The next page of the wizard identifies the security groups for the computer object selected. As with the user selection in the previous page, you can specify which security groups to use when running the query.

The next options page of the wizard allows you to select the Windows Management Instrumentation (WMI) filters to use on the user object or container in the query. The default selection is for all linked WMI filters, or you can select only specific WMI filters.

The last options page of the wizard selects the WMI filters for the computer object or container. As on the previous page, you can accept the default selection of all WMI filters, or you can specify which filters to use.

After you complete all the pages of the wizard, or if you select the option to skip the remaining information pages, a summary page will display the options that will be used when running the query. Figure 17.2 shows the summary page and the information specified for a sample query. In this window, you can choose to gather extended error information or select a different DC to process the simulation. Clicking **Next** will start the query based on the information listed in this page.

Figure 17.2 Reviewing the Settings of the RSoP Query Prior to Execution

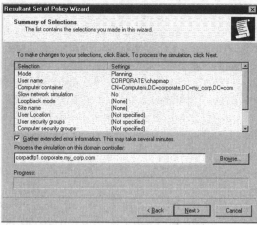

When the query has completed (which might take several minutes depending on the size and configuration of your environment), the wizard's finish page will display. Clicking **Finish** will close the wizard and return you to the MMC to review the RSoP report.

Reviewing RSoP Results

The results of the RSoP query displayed in the MMC will look similar to the Group Policy Object Editor window, with a few important differences. Figure 17.3 shows the RSoP results window in the MMC. This particular query was run on the user *chapmap* and the *Computers* container. When looking at the policy settings in the window, you only see the policies that will be in effect for the user when logged on to a computer in that particular container. You will also only be able to view the policy settings in this interface. You will not be able to change any policy.

Figure 17.3 Reviewing the RSoP Planning Results

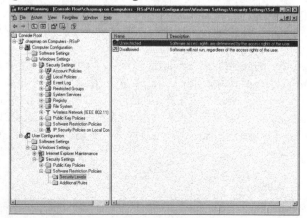

When you right-click either the **Computer Configuration** or **User Configuration** node in the tree and select **Properties**, you will find information about the policies that were processed to

generate the results found in the report. You can select to view all GPOs and their filtering status to see which GPOs were processed and which were not, and why not if they were not. You can display revision information to see how many times a particular GPO has been modified, and you can display scope information that tells where the GPO resides. If you click the **Security** button, you can see the security permissions set for the GPO.

If you open a policy setting, you can view the properties of that policy setting. Figure 17.4 shows the properties of the setting selected in Figure 17.3. As shown in the figure, the option to set this particular setting as default is grayed out, because no changes can be made in this interface. If you click on the **Precedence** tab, you will see a list of GPOs where this particular policy is set, including the order in which this policy was processed.

Figure 17.4 Viewing the Properties of a Policy Setting in the RSoP Report

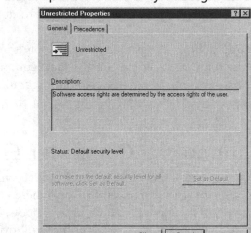

You can run an additional query on a different set of user and computer objects from this interface by right-clicking on the RSoP result object in the left pane, **chapmap on Computers – RSoP** in this instance, and selecting **Change Query**. If you go in and make group policy changes that would impact the results of the query and want to see how those changes actually affect the system, you can right-click the RSoP result object and select **Refresh Query**. This second option will re-run the query with the same options

Strategy for Configuring the User Environment

When setting group policy at the user level, you are creating an environment that will follow the user around the network. No matter what computer the user logs on to, the group policy settings inherited by that user will apply. This section covers some of the "shoulds" and "should nots" related to the user environment.

One policy setting that will follow the user around no matter where he or she logs on is *roaming profiles*. Enabling roaming profiles for a user community will store all the user settings on a server rather than on the local computers. When a user logs on, all of his or her profile settings (Desktop items, My Documents, Registry settings, etc.) will be pulled off the server, ensuring that the user has the same environment on each computer he or she uses. This approach has many advantages, but it has disadvantages as well. Some profile settings are hardware-dependent, and if the computers used by the user do not have the same hardware, the user could encounter difficulty upon logon (video cards can be especially problematic in this regard).

Software Installation is another policy that can be of great benefit to the organization. If a certain group of users has a particular application that is critical to performing their work tasks, you can set up software installation policies that will download and install the application on any computer the user uses throughout the company. This policy also keeps unauthorized users from being able to run the application even though it is installed on the computer they are using. The same caveat applies to software installation as to roaming profiles. Not all software packages are compatible with other programs that might be installed on a computer. Before implementing this type of policy in the organization, you'll need to make sure that the applications being installed will work well with other programs that already exist on the computer. The last thing you want to do is to break one program on a system by installing another.

The vast majority of other group policy settings that you can apply to users in the directory have little chance of causing conflict with other settings on the local computer. Logon and logoff scripts, application settings, folder redirection, and environment configurations can help to standardize the user's computing experience across multiple machines, which can, in turn, ease the support burden on your IT staff.

Strategy for Configuring the Computer Environment

When setting policy for the computer environment, the settings applied will impact every user who logs on to the computer. Unlike user settings, there are two places where computer policy is applied. The first is the local policy set at the computer each time it boots. These settings are applied first, and any subsequent policy that conflicts with the local settings will override the local settings. However, computer policy can also be set in Active Directory. These settings follow the same rules as user settings in terms of priority order. Any computer policies set at the site level will be overwritten by additional policy settings at the domain or OU level when the settings conflict.

One case where computer policy overrides user policy is when a GPO containing computer settings is configured to operate in *loopback mode*. Loopback mode is a special setting that is only used in cases where a very specific set of policies needs to be applied in a controlled environment. Loopback mode allows administrators to apply group policy based on the computer at which the user is logging on. In other words, this setting is used if a particular user should have different policies applied, depending on where he or she logs on. When loopback processing is enabled, the computer policies set for the system override any user policy settings applied during logon.

Loopback operates in two modes—*replace* and *merge*. When loopback is enabled, one of these two modes must be selected. Replace mode will eradicate any user policy settings applied at logon and only retain the computer policy settings. Merge mode will allow user settings that do not conflict with computer settings to be applied. If there is a conflict between the two, the computer settings override the user settings.

The philosophy of "less is more" applies directly to the approach for setting computer policy in the domain. In general, you should try to have only one set of policies apply to computers. If you do have cases where you need different policy settings to apply to different sets of computers within the organization, set up the separate policy objects, but restrict access to those objects so that only the systems that need to be affected by the object will process the settings.

Run an RSoP Planning Query

This following procedure walks you through the process of generating an RSoP planning report based on changing a user object from one OU to another. For this example, we will use the user object for Robert Smith, which exists in the Marketing OU, and build an RSoP report showing the policy settings that would apply to the object if it were moved into the Accounting OU. As long as you have appropriate permissions to run an RSoP query on a system, you should be able to emulate the steps in this example on a system to which you have access, as you will not be changing any settings on the system in the process.

1. Open an MMC window and load the RSoP snap-in (see the steps outlined earlier in this section if needed).

2. Right-click the **Resultant Set of Policy** object in the console tree, and select **Generate RSoP Data**.

3. In the Resultant Set of Policy Wizard, click **Next**.

4. Select the **Planning Mode** option button, and click **Next**.

5. In the **User and Computer Selection** window, select the **User** option button, and click the **Browse** button in the **User information** frame.

6. In the **Select User** dialog box, choose a user object and click **OK**.

7. In the **User and Computer Selection** window, click the **Computer** option button, and click the **Browse** button in the **Computer information** frame.

8. In the **Select Computer** dialog box, choose a computer object and click **OK**.

9. The **User and Computer Selection** window should now appear as in Figure 17.5. Click **Next**.

Figure 17.5 Specifying the User and Computer Objects in the RSoP Wizard

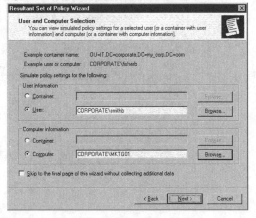

10. In the **Advanced Simulation Options** page, select the appropriate site from the **Site** drop-down list, shown in Figure 17.6, and click **Next**.

Figure 17.6 Specifying a Site in the Simulation Options Page

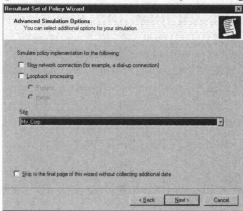

11. In the **Alternate Active Directory Paths** page, change the location for the user and computer objects. When the new locations have been selected, click **Next**.

12. In the **User Security Groups** page, change the security groups to match those of the new location. Select the groups that the user would no longer belong to, and click **Remove**.

13. To add new security groups to the query, click the **Add** button and select the appropriate groups. Click **Next**.

14. In the **Computer Security Groups** page, you can leave the security group setting as it is, or you can change group assignments by using the **Add** and **Remove** buttons. Figure 17.7 shows the settings used for this query. When complete, click **Next**.

Figure 17.7 Selecting Computer Security Group Settings

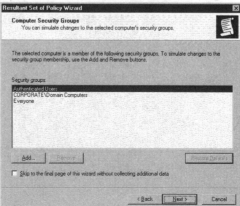

15. In the **WMI Filters for Users** page, select the **All linked filters** option button to include all WMI filters in the query, as shown in Figure 17.8, or select the **Only these filters** option button to specify which filters to use. When finished, click **Next**.

Figure 17.8 Selecting WMI Filters for Users

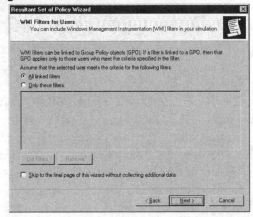

16. In the WMI Filters for Computers page, select the **All linked filters** option button to include all WMI filters in the query, or select the **Only these filters** option button to specify which filters to use. When finished, click **Next**.

17. Review the selections made in the Summary of Selections page, and click **Next** to start the query.

18. When the query has completed, click the **Finish** button to close the wizard and view the RSoP report, shown in Figure 17.9.

Figure 17.9 Viewing the RSoP Report

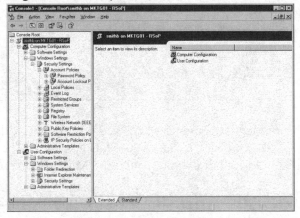

19. Browse through the report looking at the policies that would be enabled for user smithb on computer MKTG01. Close the MMC when done.

Implementing Group Policy

Now that you know how to evaluate the effects of group policy on the directory, it is time to start creating policy objects and applying policy to the environment. In this section, you will learn about the different places where you can create GPOs, and the tools to modify and manage them.

The Group Policy Object Editor MMC

The **Group Policy Object Editor** is a snap-in for the MMC. Because group policy can be applied at several locations, opening the Group Policy Object Editor can differ depending on where you want to apply group policy.

From within an MMC, you can select the **Group Policy Object Editor** snap-in from the **Add/Remove Snap-in** window. When selecting the Group Policy Object Editor from the list of stand-alone snap-ins, the Group Policy Wizard will open, allowing you to select the scope of the group policy to work with. Clicking the **Browse** button in this wizard will open the **Browse for a Group Policy Object** window, shown in Figure 17.10. The first three tabs in the window allow you to search for GPOs of a specific type: Domain/OU, Site, and Computer. The fourth tab, selected in Figure 17.10, displays a list of all policy objects in the domain, regardless of location. Local computer policy objects will not show in this listing, because they are stored on the computer, not in the domain.

Figure 17.10 Viewing all Group Policy Objects in the Domain

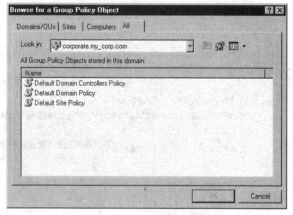

To edit one of the existing GPOs stored in Active Directory, select the GPO from one of the tabs and click **OK**. This will take you back to the Group Policy Wizard. When you click **Finish** in the wizard, the Group Policy Object Editor will open in the MMC, and you can begin editing the GPO.

Creating, Configuring, and Managing GPOs

Loading the Group Policy Object Editor snap-in in an MMC will allow you to edit existing policies in the network. When the domain is first created, there are three default policies created:

- Default Site Policy
- Default Domain Policy
- Default Domain Controllers Policy

You will probably want to create new policies and associate them with specific areas of the directory.

Creating and Configuring GPOs

There are two ways to create new GPOs in the directory. You already know how to load the Group Policy Object Editor snap-in into the MMC, so let's look at how to create a new GPO from the Group Policy Wizard.

In Figure 17.10, you saw the **Browse for a Group Policy Object** window that opens when you click the **Browse** button in the Group Policy Wizard. Next to the **Look in** drop-down menu, you will find the **Create New Group Policy Object** button. When you click this button, a new GPO will be created in the scope you have selected in the **Look in** menu. Creating the GPO in this scope will automatically link the object to the container that was selected in the scope.

Another way to open the GPO Editor and create a new GPO is from within the **Active Directory Sites and Services** or **Active Directory Users and Groups** tools. Right-click the object in the container list where you want the GPO to be created, and select **Properties**. Then, select the **Group Policy** tab in the **Properties** window to see what policies are already linked to the container or to create a new object for the container. Figure 17.11 shows the **Group Policy** tab for the IT Management container. In this example, there is only one object tied to this container. To create and edit a new GPO, click the **New** button, give the policy a name, and then click **Edit** to open the Group Policy Object Editor for the new GPO.

Figure 17.11 Viewing the Group Policy Objects for a Container

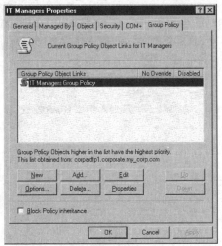

Naming GPOs

All GPOs created in the directory should have unique names. Even though each GPO is associated with a specific container and could have the same name as another object in the tree, there will be much less confusion when troubleshooting if each GPO name is unique. GPO names can contain letters, numbers, and special characters, but the name cannot be longer than 255 characters. Any GPO name longer than 255 characters will be automatically truncated to the 255-character maximum.

There are no other specific rules as to how to name each GPO. In the same way that you should name each object in the directory to match its function or purpose, you can consider the same approach when naming GPOs. If you have a set of policies that will impact a single container in the directory, such as an OU, you could include the name of the OU in the name of the GPO. If the policies contained in a GPO are going to be linked to a number of containers in the directory, you could name the GPO after the function its policies are designed to perform.

Managing GPOs

From the Group Policy tab of the container Properties window, you can perform a number of functions on the GPOs associated with the container. We have already covered creating and editing a new GPO from the interface. Now let's take a look at some of the other ways you can manage the GPOs from this interface.

Figure 17.12 shows the Group Policy tab of the root of the domain of My Corp. There are three GPOs stored within this container in Active Directory: Default Domain Policy, Folder Redirection Policy, and Manager Tools Policy. Based on the information displayed in the figure, the Default Domain Policy and the Folder Redirection Policy objects will be processed by objects logging on within this domain. The Manager Tools Policy will not be processed with the other two GPOs at this level because it has been disabled at this level, as indicated by the check mark under the Disabled column next to the policy object. We can also see that none of the GPOs have been marked as No Override.

Figure 17.12 Managing the Group Policies for the Root Domain

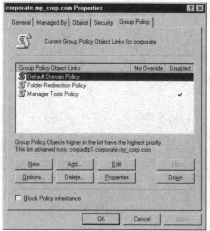

The No Override and Disabled settings can be set in two places. Clicking the **Options** button will open an Options window for the selected GPO. The Options window allows you to set the **No Override** and **Disabled** settings for the object. In addition, you can set both options by right-clicking the GPO in the list and selecting either the No Override or Disabled entries in the pop-up menu.

Clicking the **Properties** button in this interface will bring up the Properties window for the object. Within the GPO properties, you can modify a number of settings that will control who accesses the policy and how it is applied. These properties are covered in detail in the next section.

You can also click the **Delete** button to remove a policy from this container. When clicking Delete, you will be asked if you want to remove the link to the GPO from the container or if you want to permanently remove the GPO from the directory altogether. If the policy is linked to multiple containers and you only want to remove the link from the current container, select the **Remove the link from the list** option button. Otherwise, click the **Remove the link and delete the Group Policy Object permanently** button to completely eliminate the GPO from the directory.

If there are multiple GPOs linked to a container, as there are in Figure 17.12, you can specify the order in which the GPOs are processed within the container. When multiple GPOs are present in the list, use the **Up** and **Down** buttons to arrange the order of the GPOs in the list.

Finally, you can block policy inheritance for the container by enabling the **Block Policy inheritance** check box. If the container is a child object in the directory, turning on this option will prevent the container from inheriting any policy settings from parent containers. The only time that the Block Policy inheritance setting can't prevent settings from inheriting is if a parent container has a policy with the No Override option set. It should also be noted that the Block Policy inheritance setting applies only to the container and not the specific GPOs associated with the container.

Configuring Application of Group Policy

Placing a GPO in a container enables the policy settings within the object on all objects that log on as part of that particular container. There are times when you will not want all objects associated with a container to have the policy settings applied, either for security or performance reasons. This section deals with ways of governing access to the settings within a GPO from within the GPO properties interface.

General

Figure 17.13 shows the **General** tab of the GPO Properties window. This is the view that is opened by default when the Properties window is opened. This view provides system information about the GPO and allows you to exclude certain portions of the policy from application. If the policy object only contains user configuration policies, you can check the **Disable Computer Configuration settings** check box, and the Computer Configuration settings will be ignored when the object is processed. This will help to cut down on processing time at bootup if there are no policies specifically set in the object for computer settings. Alternately, you can check the **Disable User Configuration settings** check box to prevent the user configuration settings in the GPO from processing at logon.

Figure 17.13 Viewing the General Properties of a GPO

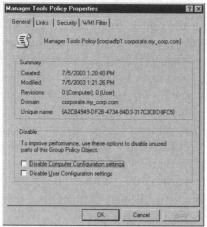

Links

In the **Links** tab of the GPO Properties window, you can search for all the places where the specific GPO has been linked. By default, this window is empty when first opened. Select the appropriate domain from the drop-down list and click **Find Now** to search for all the containers where the GPO is linked. While you cannot change any of the settings for the GPO in this view, you can find all the places where the GPO is enabled when troubleshooting policy problems.

Security

Figure 17.14 shows the Security tab of the GPO Properties window. In this view, you can set all the security permissions necessary to govern how the policy will be applied and managed. In this example, the Authenticated Users group is not listed. When a new GPO is created, the Authenticated Users group is given Read and Apply Group Policy permissions on the GPO. Those two permissions are the minimum needed to be able to have policy settings applied to a group.

Figure 17.14 Viewing the Security Settings on a GPO

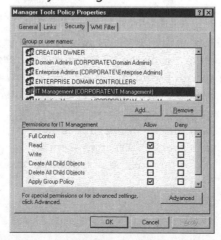

In this case, the IT Management security group has been given the Read and Apply Group Policy permissions to the object, so members of the IT Management security group can see and process the policy settings contained within this object. However, these permissions alone do not allow members of this security group to process the policy object. Members of this group have to log on within the context of a container that was linked to this GPO. Only members of the IT Managers security group who are located in the IT Managers container process the GPO, because in Figure 17.12, we saw that the Manager Tools Policy object was disabled in the root container of the domain.

WMI Filter

Figure 17.15 shows the WMI Filters tab of the GPO Properties window. In this view, you can set WMI filters to further restrict who does and does not have access to the GPO for processing. You can use WMI queries to further filter application of a GPO beyond what you can achieve with security settings. WMI filters are written in the WMI Query language (WQL) and are generally used for exception processing.

Figure 17.15 Viewing the WMI Filter Settings on a GPO

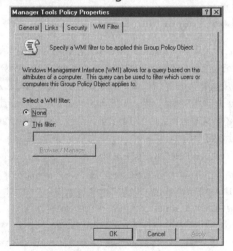

Delegating Administrative Control

You might be in an Active Directory environment where one group or organization only controls a small portion of the directory. Because Active Directory allows you to delegate control of parts of the directory tree, you might find yourself needing to delegate control over Group Policy as well. By default, only the following are allowed to create and manage GPOs in the directory:

- Domain administrators
- Enterprise administrators
- Members of the Group Policy Creator Owners group.

Granting the ability to create and manage GPOs to a non-administrator user takes two steps:

1. The user must become a member of the Group Policy Creator Owners group. Membership in this group will allow users to create GPOs in the area of the directory where they have access. When a member of this group creates a new policy object, he or she will become the owner of the object and will have full control over the object through the Group Policy Creator Owners permissions.

2. The user must be given permissions to a container in the directory where he or she will be managing group policy. This is done through delegation of control. When in Active Directory Users and Computers, right-click the designated container from the console list and select the **Delegate Control** item. Work your way through the Delegate Control Wizard to select the users who should be given control in the container. Add the Manage Group Policy Links item from the Permissions list, and then finish the wizard.

After these two steps have been performed, the user will be able to create new GPOs in the container where control was given. If you want the user to be able to edit the policies in other objects, you can give the user explicit permissions on the GPO in the directory. The user will only be able to create GPO links in containers where he or she has been granted that permission.

Verifying Group Policy

After you have created and linked GPOs in the directory, you should verify the correct operation of the policy settings before allowing the policy to be processed by users. To do this, you can use the Resultant Set of Policy tool in *logging mode* instead of planning mode. Access the RSoP tool just as you did for planning mode, but in the first page of the wizard, select the **Logging mode** option button instead of the **Planning mode** button. The settings for generating an RSoP report in logging mode are different from those in planning mode. The next few paragraphs detail the wizard pages and the settings needed to generate the report.

The first data page of the wizard allows you to select which computer to generate the report for. Your options are the current computer or another computer on the network. You can also select not to include computer configuration settings in the report.

The next page allows you to select the user for which the report will be run. You can select the current user or identify a different user from the directory. If you do not want to include user configuration data in the report, you can select the option to only include computer configuration information.

After completing the wizard, you can browse through the policy settings that will be in effect for the user once he or she logs on. There are fewer options needed for the logging mode of RSoP because the tool is not generating any "what if" information in the report. Instead, this report looks at the existing user and designated computer and reviews the policy settings that will be in effect for the user when he or she logs on.

Delegate Control for Group Policy to a Non-Administrator

In the following procedure, we walk through the process of setting up a non-administrator user to create and manage group policy in a specific container. For this example, one of the managers in the

Marketing department will be given permissions to create GPOs in the Marketing container of the directory. After we have her permissions configured, we will log on as the user and create a simple GPO for the container.

1. Open **Active Directory Users and Computers**.

2. Find the user object in the tree, and open the **Properties** for the user.

3. Click the **Member of** tab, and click **Add**.

4. Enter group policy in the object name field, and click **Check Names**.

5. The Group Policy Creator Owner group will be recognized. Click **OK**.

6. The group should now be listed in the groups list.

7. Click **Apply**, and then click **OK** to close the user Properties window.

8. Right-click the appropriate container in the console tree (in this case, the Marketing container) and select **Delegate Control** from the menu.

9. In the Delegation of Control Wizard, click **Next**.

10. In the Users or Groups window, click **Add**.

11. Select the username from the directory and click **OK**. Repeat the process to add more users if necessary.

12. When the user list is complete, click **Next.**

13. In the **Tasks to Delegate** page, click on the **Manage Group Policy links** check box as shown in Figure 17.16. If you would like the user to be able to work with RSoP, enable the **Generate Resultant Set of Policy (Planning)** and **Generate Resultant Set of Policy (Logging)** items as well. Click **Next**.

Figure 17.16 Enabling the Group Policy Settings

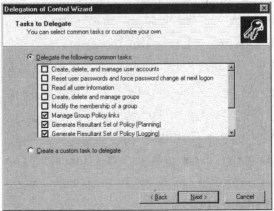

14. Click **Finish** to close the wizard.

15. Log on as the user and run Active Directory Users and Computers, or use **Run As** to run the tool as the user.

16. Active Directory Users and Computers should open to the container to which the user was just added.

17. Right-click the container and select **Properties**.

18. Click the **Group Policy** tab.

19. Click **New**.

20. Type in the name of the policy object.

21. Click **Edit**.

Now you can go through and set the appropriate policy items as needed.

Performing Group Policy Administrative Tasks

A number of tasks can be performed with group policy settings. This section of the chapter covers some of the more typical administrative tasks that you might perform in setting up group policy for your organization.

Automatically Enrolling User and Computer Certificates

If your organization is using Certificate Services to manage user and computer certificates, you might want to enable autoenrollment of the certificates. Your certification authorities (CAs) need to be configured to support autoenrollment, but without enabling this setting in policy, users have to go through a manual process to enroll.

You will set the autoenrollment policy in both the user configuration and the computer configuration of the GPO. Since you will probably want the settings to apply to all systems in the organization, enable the settings in the Default Domain Policy object at the root of each domain in the organization. Follow these steps to enable this security setting:

1. Open **Active Directory Users and Computers**.

2. Right-click the domain container in the console tree and select **Properties**.

3. Click the **Group Policy** tab and select the **Default Domain Policy**.

4. Click **Edit** to open the Group Policy Object Editor.

5. Expand the **Computer Configuration** object, and then the **Windows Settings** object.

6. Expand the **Security Settings** object, and then select the **Public Key Policies** object.

7. Double-click the **Autoenrollment Settings** object in the right-hand pane.

8. Click the **Enroll certificates automatically** option button.

9. Enable the **Renew expired certificates, update pending certificates, and remove revoked certificates** check box.

10. Enable the **Update certificates that use certificate templates** check box. Your settings should now appear as shown in Figure 17.17.

Figure 17.17 Configuring Autoenrollment Settings

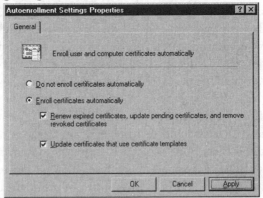

11. Click **Apply**, and then click **OK**.

12. Expand the **User Configuration** object in the console tree, and then the **Windows Settings** object.

13. Expand the **Security Settings** object, and then select the **Public Key Policies** object.

14. Double-click the **Autoenrollment Settings** object in the right-hand pane.

15. Click the **Enroll certificates automatically** option button.

16. Enable the **Renew expired certificates, update pending certificates, and remove revoked certificates** check box.

17. Enable the **Update certificates that use certificate templates** check box.

18. Click **Apply**, and then click **OK**.

If your organization has multiple domains, repeat this process for each domain in the environment. Remember that only systems running Windows 2000 or later will be able to participate in autoenrollment of certificates.

Redirecting Folders

Another feature that is becoming increasingly popular is folder redirection, especially since group policy makes this an easy task to perform. Through group policy, you can specify folder redirection for the following four system folders on the user system:

- Application Data
- Desktop
- My Documents
- Start Menu

Folder redirection can be seen as a subset of roaming profiles. By specifying an alternate location for these folders on a network share, the user has access to these folders no matter which computer he or she uses to log on.

Of the four folders that can be redirected, setting the My Documents folder for redirection is probably the most advantageous. Not only will the user have his or her data available at any computer, but storing this data on the server allows the data to be easily backed up to tape or other offline storage media. As an administrator, you can also set quotas on server storage, helping to keep the size of the My Documents folder in check. You can also take advantage of the offline folders feature of Windows 2000 and Windows XP to keep the data available to users when they are not on the network.

When setting up folder redirection, you should allow the system to create the folders in the location where the data will be directed. A number of permissions must be set correctly to maintain security on the redirected folders. Your best bet is to let the system handle this part of the process.

Folder redirection settings are located in the User Configuration area of the GPO under Windows Settings. To enable redirection of one of the four folders, follow these steps:

1. Right-click the folder name and select **Properties**.

2. In the **Target** tab of the window, you can select the setting to use for redirection, as shown in Figure 17.18. You can select between two options for the location of the redirected folder. The basic option redirects the folder to the same folder path for all users. For the Application Data and Desktop folders, there are three options for the folder location:

   - Creating a directory for each user in the path specified

   - Redirecting all users to the same location

   - Pointing the folder to the local user profile location

Figure 17.18 Selecting Options for Redirecting My Documents

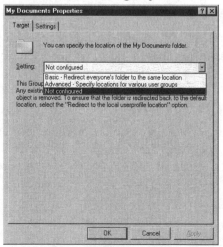

If you choose to point the folder to the path in the user profile, the folder will point to the default location as if no redirection had been applied. Redirecting the folder to a specific location will create that location either on the network or on a local path, and all users who have this policy applied will point to the same folder. For the Start Menu and Desktop folders, this might be a beneficial setting, as you can centrally control the appearance and contents of those folders in one location, but you need to be aware of the security settings on the folder.

The primary choice for this setting will probably be to create a folder for each user in a location specified, as shown in Figure 17.19. As you can see, when the root path is specified, the dialog box gives you an example of what the folder path will be.

Figure 17.19 Setting the Folder Location for Redirection

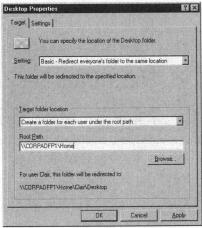

The Start Menu and My Documents folders have slightly different options for redirection. When redirecting the Start Menu, you do not have the option of specifying a unique path for each individual user. Whether setting up basic or advanced redirection of the Start Menu, you can only specify one common location for all users or redirect the folder back to the local user profile.

The Start Menu options are simpler than the Application Data and Desktop folder settings, but the My Documents options are more complex. When redirecting the My Documents folder, there are four location options for storing the folder. As with the Application Data and Desktop folders, you can store the My Documents folder in the local user profile, a common directory for all users, or have the system create a folder for each user in a common location. There is a fourth option, however, for My Documents. That option allows you to redirect the My Documents folder to the user's home folder on the network. This option will not create a My Documents folder *in* the user's home folder. It will simply point the My Documents folder to the user's home directory on the network.

There are a few items you should pay attention to if you consider implementing this option. First, you must have implemented the home folder settings for all users, and you must have created those folders prior to implementing this option. Second, the security settings on the home folder are not changed by the folder redirection policy, so you need to be aware of the settings applied to the user home folder on the network. Finally, you have the choice of including the My Pictures folder with the redirected My Documents folder, or having the My Pictures folder stored in a different location. This might be advisable if server disk storage is a concern. If you choose this option, the My Pictures item in the My Documents folder will be a shortcut pointing to the correct location for the actual folder.

The advanced option allows you to select the folder location based on security group. This is one way to specify a different target location for the folder for different groups of users. You can set multiple security groups to have different target locations within a single GPO in the domain. Another way to accomplish this, especially if you only have a small set of users whose folders should be redirected, is to set folder redirection GPOs at other locations within the directory and filter access to those GPOs based on security.

When selecting the advanced redirection option, you can add the individual security groups for redirection, and have the same choices for folder location as with the basic option. Setting advanced folder redirection is functionally equivalent to setting up multiple GPOs with basic redirection settings and security filtering. The difference is that there is only one GPO to manage instead of several.

Configuring User and Computer Security Settings

When browsing through the Group Policy Object Editor, you might have noticed that there are security settings for both the user configuration and computer configuration. Some of these settings are the same for both configurations, such as the Autoenrollment Settings for certificates discussed earlier. There are many differences between the two options, however, and we cover some of those differences in this section.

Computer Configuration

With these security settings, you can provide additional control and management over objects in the directory. The settings contained in this area can govern how users authenticate to computers and other resources on the network, can provide additional permissions or restrictions for resources in the directory, can control audit settings, and can alter group membership. The settings in this area of group policy are primarily used to specify alternate settings for specific computers on the network.

Table 17.2 lists the main option groups under Security Settings in the Computer Configuration in the Group Policy Object Editor, along with a description of the security setting.

Table 17.2 Security Settings for Computer Configuration

Security Setting Collection	Description
Account Policies	Contains setting groups for password policy settings, account lockout settings, and Kerberos policy settings.
Local Policies	Contains setting groups for auditing policy settings, user rights assignment settings, and security options settings.
Event Log	Contains settings for application, system, and security event logs.
Restricted Groups	Contains groups for specific security restrictions.

Continued

Table 17.2 Security Settings for Computer Configuration

Security Setting Collection	Description
System Services	Contains settings for controlling startup and permissions for system services.
Registry Keys	Contains Registry keys and permissions to add.
File System	Contains files or folders and permissions to add.
Wireless Network Policies	Contains policies governing specific wireless network connections.
Public Key Policies	Contains setting groups for Encrypted File System policy settings, Automatic Certificate Request settings, Trusted Root Certification Authorities settings, and Enterprise Trust settings.
Software Restriction Policies	Contains settings, when enabled, for restricting access to certain software, such as 16-bit applications.

User Configuration

There are fewer options for configuring security settings in the User Configuration area of group policy. The two groups of policies in this area are listed in Table 17.3.

Table 17.3 Security Settings for User Configuration

Security Setting Collection	Description
Public Key Policies	Contains settings for certificate autoenrollment and Enterprise Trust.
Software Restriction Policies	Contains settings that identify, through various means, applications that are authorized to run on a system.

Redirect the My Documents Folder

In this example, we walk through the process of redirecting the My Documents folder for a specific group of users in the directory. We will take the Information Technology group and redirect their folders to a shared location on the network, and use advanced redirection to limit folder redirection only to members of that group. We will point the My Documents directory to a common location and use the network's home directory path as the root folder for the redirected folder.

1. Open **Active Directory Users and Computers**.

2. Right-click the domain container and select **Properties**.

3. Click the **Group Policy** tab and click **New**.

4. Name the policy *Folder Redirection Policy* and click **Edit**.

5. Under **User Configuration**, expand **Windows** Settings.

6. Expand **Folder Redirection**.

7. Right-click **My Documents** and select **Properties**.

8. In the Setting drop-down menu, select **Advanced** – Specify locations for various user groups.

9. In the **Security Group Membership** pane, click **Add**.

10. In the **Security Group Membership** pane, enter the name of the security group, or click **Browse** and find the group in the directory. This example uses the Information Technology group.

11. In the **Target Folder Location** pane, select **Create** a folder for each user under the root path from the drop-down menu.

12. Enter the UNC path to the desired folder in the Root Path field, or click **Browse** to find the desired path. This example uses the path \\CORPADFP1\Home for the root path.

13. Click **OK**.

14. The **My Documents Properties** window should now appear as shown in Figure 17.20. Click the **Settings** tab.

Figure 17.20 Viewing the Redirection Settings for My Documents

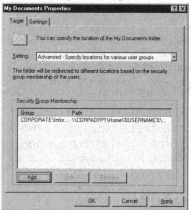

15. Make sure the check boxes for **Grant the user exclusive rights to My Documents** and **Move the contents of My Documents to the new location** are enabled.

16. Click the **Redirect the folder back to the local user profile location when policy is removed** option button.

17. The **Settings** tab should appear as shown in Figure 17.21. Click **OK**.

Figure 17.21 Configuring the Settings for My Documents Folder Redirection

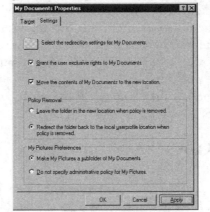

Now when members of the Information Technology group log on, their My Documents folders will be created in the network share, and the data from their existing folders will be moved into the new folders.

Using Software Restriction Policies

One of the relatively new challenges facing system administrators today is the significant increase of malicious code. Not only are more and more individuals writing malicious code, such as viruses, but with the ever-increasing use of e-mail and the Internet, these programs are being spread faster and faster. Some organizations are struggling with the proliferation of other programs, not specifically malicious in nature, but productivity killers nonetheless. Or users might download and install programs that cause conflicts with existing programs, generating additional support calls to your help desk.

Making use of software restriction policies will allow you to place controls on "untrusted" code within your organization. Through a combination of rules, you can identify specific applications or types of applications that are either allowed to run or prevented from running. These rules are powerful and complex, but by themselves cannot provide full protection against malicious code. Use of software restriction policies will augment the protections you might already have in place, but you should not plan to rely solely on these policies to completely protect your environment.

Setting Up Software Restriction Policies

The settings for Software Restriction are located in the Security Settings area of Group Policy. You might have to enable software restriction policies before you can make changes, as most systems do not have these policies enabled by default. When software restriction policies are enabled, you will find a number of settings in the area. The *Enforcement* policy determines if the software policies will apply to all files or exclude library (.dll) files. This policy also identifies whether the policies apply to all users of the system or just to non-administrators. If you want to exclude administrators from software restriction policies, this is where you would set that option.

Another policy you will find here is the *Designated file types* policy. You can specify which file types, based on file extension, to which software restriction policies should apply. You can add additional file types by adding the file extension to the list in this policy window.

The third policy you will find here is the *Trusted Publishers* policy. In this policy setting, you can specify what user level is allowed to enable trust for software publishers, and how to check for expired certificates for those publishers.

The other area located here is the *Additional Rules* folder, where the specific rules you will create for your system will be located.

Software Policy Rules

There are four types of rules that you can use to identify applications to which policy should apply: the hash rule, certificate rule, path rule, and Internet zone rule. Each rule identifies a different way to identify files that should have rules applied. Within the rule, you can set the security setting for the resulting file or files to either Disallowed or Unrestricted. A Disallowed setting in a rule will prevent the user from accessing the file or files. An Unrestricted setting will allow the user to access the file or files.

Hash Rule

When you create a hash rule, you identify a specific file to which you want the rule to apply, and the system generates a hash on the file, including attributes such as date and time of creation and file size. After the policy is in place, the system performs a hash on each file accessed, and if the hash matches the hash in the rule, the rule is applied.

Certificate Rule

When you create a certificate rule, you identify a set of files that are signed by a specific certificate. In creating the rule, you select the specific certificate for the rule. When the system processes a file request, it will check the certificate settings on the file to check for a match against the certificate in the rule, and will process the rule if there is a match. Certificate rules to not apply to .exe and .dll files, but will apply to all other file types listed in the Designated File Types policy.

Path Rule

When you create a path rule, you identify a file or set of files based on their location on disk. The path can identify the path to a folder, a specific file, or a set of files based on a wildcard. When the system processes a file request when path rules are in place, it will compare the file requested to the path rules, and process the rule if there is a match.

Internet Zone Rule

When you create an Internet zone rule, you specify settings based on the Internet zones identified in Internet Explorer: Internet, Local Computer, Local Intranet, Restricted Sites, and Trusted Sites. Internet zone rules only apply to Windows installer packages. If a user downloads an installer package from a site in one of the zones, the zone settings will determine if the user will be able to execute the installer.

Precedence of Policies

Since several rules can be applied to the same program, there is an established order of precedence that is applied. A rule based on a higher precedence will override a conflicting rule applied with a lower precedence.

1. Hash rule

2. Certificate rule

3. Path rule

4. Internet zone rule

Based on this order, if a program is unrestricted based on a hash rule but disallowed based on a path rule, the program will run, as the hash rule has precedence over the path rule. For path rules, there is an additional order of precedence based on the path specified. If there are conflicting path rules, the more restrictive path rule will apply. The following list identifies the precedence of paths from most restrictive to least restrictive.

1. Drive:\Folder1\Folder2\filename.extension

2. Drive:\Folder1\Folder2*.extension

3. *.extension

4. Drive:\Folder1\Folder2\

5. Drive:\Folder1\

When similar rules are applied, such as multiple path rules, the more restrictive rule applies. For example, if a program is set to Disallow in one path rule and set to Unrestricted in another, access to the program will be denied, as Disallow is the more restrictive setting.

Best Practices

The following items include some of the recommendations for implementing software restriction policies.

- **Test, test, test** Never implement software restrictions without testing, especially when applying a Disallow setting. Placing restrictions on certain types of files can negatively impact the operation of your computer and/or the network environment.

- **Couple software restriction policies with access control restrictions** Using access control in conjunction with software restriction makes a more complete restriction solution.

- **Use anti-virus software** Software restriction policies are not a sufficient substitute for a solid anti-virus package. The tools used in conjunction can increase the security of the system, but do not plan on using software restriction in place of anti-virus tools.

- **Use Disallow as default with great caution** If you take the approach of using Disallow as the default and identifying specific applications to allow, be sure you test the system thoroughly. Some applications can launch other applications in normal course of operation. As stated in the first item, test your implementation thoroughly before unleashing it on an unsuspecting audience.

Applying Group Policy Best Practices

If you have been reading straight through this chapter, you've seen that there are a vast number of ways that group policy can be implemented in an Active Directory environment. How should you approach a group policy implementation in your environment? This section covers some of the best practices related to implementing group policy.

- **The fewer, the better** Keep the number of policies defined as small as possible. Since each user policy the user encounters must be processed at logon, you can keep user logon delays to a minimum by reducing the number of user policies. In addition, a smaller number of policy objects means fewer places for you to look for problems or conflicts when troubleshooting group policy issues. Computer policies are processed at boot time, so reducing the number of these will speed the boot process of the computer.

- **Avoid conflicting policies whenever possible** Although you can set up a lower-level policy to override a higher-level one, you should avoid doing this unless necessary. Again, simplicity should be the rule.

- **Filter out unnecessary settings** If you set up a policy object that only contains user policy settings, set the properties on the object so that only the user configuration portion is processed. This will help cut down on unnecessary processing time.

- **Avoid nonstandard group policy processing whenever possible** Even though you can use Block Policy Inheritance, No Override, and loopback processing options, you should only do so for special cases. Because each of these options alters the standard way in which policy is applied, they can cause confusion when attempting to troubleshoot policy problems.

- **Keep policy objects contained within the domain** It is possible to link a container to a GPO that resides in another domain, but it is unwise to do so. Pulling a GPO from a different domain slows the processing of policy settings at logon time.

- **Use WMI filters sparingly** This suggestion relates to processing time. The more WMI filters there are to process, the longer it takes to apply policy at logon.

- **Keep policy object names unique** If you name each policy object to describe its function, this should not be a difficult practice to adopt. Even though the directory can support multiple GPOs with the same name, it could get very, very confusing for you when trying to troubleshoot a policy problem.

- **Link policies to a container only once** You can link the same GPO to a container more than once, but you shouldn't. The system will attempt to process each policy linked to a container, and even if there are different options set on each instance of the policy link, it can still yield unexpected results.

Troubleshooting Group Policy

Even the most experienced system administrator is going to encounter times when he or she has misapplied policy or inadvertently created a policy conflict where it was not expected. Fear not, however, because our good friend Resultant Set of Policy and its sidekick, *gpresult.exe*, can help us out of these jams. Along with a few guidelines, these tools can help you resolve even the stickiest policy problems.

The first step in troubleshooting policy problems is *mapping*. Ideally, when you first start developing a plan for group policy, you will map out policy settings as they apply to your Active Directory environment. Not only will a policy map help you to understand how policy settings will impact the network during planning, but an up-to-date map can help you know where to go looking for problems when they occur. If you do not have a policy map, you should draw one up before you get too far into your troubleshooting process. It might take some extra time up front, but it can save you time and headaches later.

Figure 17.22 shows a sample policy map drawn up based on information used in the examples in this chapter. The diagram was created in Visio, but you can use any diagramming tool (including a pencil and paper) that will help you understand the layout of your policy settings. In the diagram, solid lines indicate a logical connection of Active Directory containers, specifically a domain and its associated OUs. The dashed lines indicate links between containers and GPOs. The policy object is located on the level where it is defined. In Figure 17.22, the Manager Tools policy was created at the domain level, but because the policy was disabled at that level, it is not linked in the diagram.

Figure 17.22 Viewing a Sample Policy Map

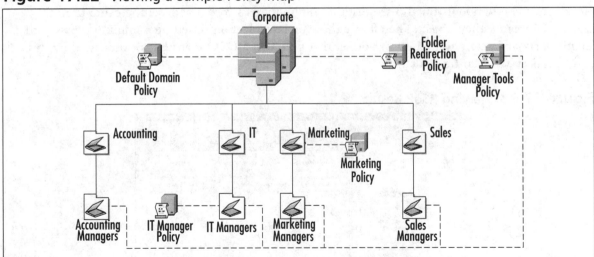

Let's walk through a couple of quick scenarios. A user whose user object is in the Marketing container will have group policy applied in the following order upon logon: Local Computer policy, Default Domain policy, Folder Redirection policy, and Marketing policy.

A user whose user object is in the IT Managers container will have group policy applied in this order: Local Computer policy, Default Domain policy, Folder Redirection policy, IT Manager policy, and Manager Tools policy.

A user whose user object is in the Accounting container will have group policy applied in this order: Local Computer policy, Default Domain policy, and Folder Redirection policy. Therefore, if the user in the Accounting container is supposed to have folders redirected by the Folder Redirection policy, but the folders are not being redirected, You should look at the Folder Redirection Policy object and see what options or permissions are on the object that would prevent the user from having the policy applied, and so on.

Using RSoP

Just having a policy map will not help you identify the location of policy conflicts in all cases. That's where RSoP comes in. Previously, we've used RSoP to plan our policy environment and test the environment prior to implementation. You can also use RSoP to discover what policy is applied to a user object and where the policy setting came from. To do this, add the RSoP snap-in into the MMC and generate a report based on the user and computer in question as described earlier in the chapter.

Let's say that a user is attempting to change his password, but he continually gets an error saying that his password is too short. You seem to recall that you had set a policy that allowed six character passwords as a minimum, but the user continually gets a message that his password must be at least seven characters. You run an RSoP report on the user and get the result shown in Figure 17.23. Remembering that password settings are a part of computer configuration, you open to that portion of the report and find the minimum password length policy. Sure enough, it's set to seven characters. However, in the window you also see that the minimum password length setting came from the Default Domain Policy object. Therefore, either your recollection of setting a minimum password length of six characters was faulty, or you set that policy in a GPO that was not processed by this user, and now you can find out why.

Figure 17.23 Viewing RSoP Results

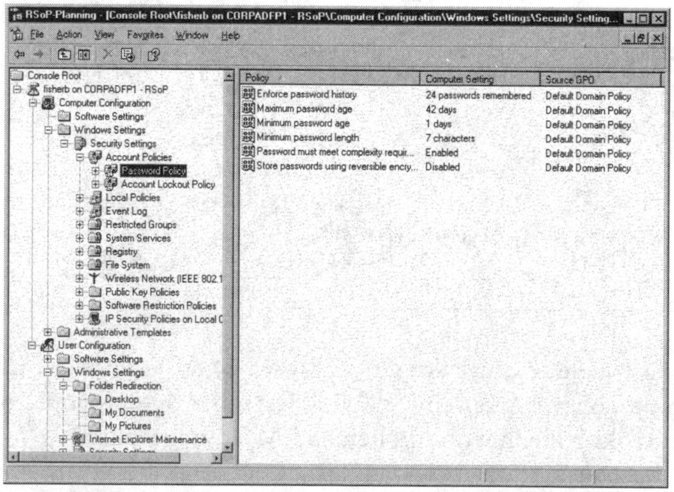

Other settings do not display as clearly in the MMC window. Let's take a quick look at a folder redirection setting that was applied to this same user. When you click the **My Documents** folder under **User Configuration | Windows Settings | Folder Redirection**, the MMC will display information about the Redirection policy. However, the default format of the display does not show all the information at one time, so you can double-click the entry to bring up the **Properties** window shown in Figure 17.24. You can see in the Properties window the location where the My Documents folder has been directed and the settings of the policy that caused this user's folder to be redirected. In this case, the GPO that triggered the redirection is the Folder Redirection Policy object, and it was created in advanced mode, with the user matching the Information Technology group membership. In addition, you can see the settings enabled for this particular redirection policy in the grayed-out check boxes and option buttons.

Figure 17.24 Viewing the Folder Redirection Policy Properties

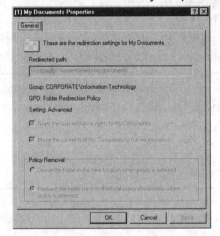

Using gpresult.exe

Sorting through the information provided by RSoP can be a little daunting, especially if there is a lot of customization occurring through group policy settings. Some types of information can be easier to track down using a different tool—gpresult.exe. gpresult is a command-line tool that produces a text report of the resultant set of policy. Table 17.4 lists some of the command-line parameters that can be used with gpresult.exe. By default, running gpresult.exe with no parameters will generate an RSoP report for the current user on the local computer. Different options can be used to specify alternate users and different computers, as well as limiting the scope of the query.

Table 17.4 Command-Line Parameters for gpresult.exe

Parameter	Description
/s *Computer*	Identifies the location of a remote computer for the query. *Computer* can be the name or IP address of the remote system. Do not use backslashes in the computer name.
/u *Domain\User*	Identifies the user to run the program as, in case the current user does not have permission to generate RSoP data.
/p *Password*	Identifies the password to use for the user object identified with the /u parameter.
/user *TargetUserName*	Identifies the user for which RSoP data is to be generated.
/scope {user | computer}	Identifies the specific scope, user or computer, for which the RSoP report should be run.
/v	Generates verbose policy information.
/z	Displays all available information about the policy settings. This setting generates much more output than the /v parameter.

The output of gpresult.exe is grouped into several different sections. The first section of the output gives basic information about the user and computer analyzed in the query. This output is shown in Figure 17.25. One of the items of interest in this section is the indication of a slow link connection, listed in the last line of the figure.

Figure 17.25 Viewing the Results of gpresult.exe

```
RSOP data for CORPORATE\fisherb on CORPADFP1 : Logging Mode



_____



OS Type:                 Microsoft(R) Windows(R) Server 2003, Standard Edition
OS Configuration:        Primary Domain Controller
OS Version:              5.2.3790
Site Name:               My_Corp
Roaming Profile:
Local Profile:           C:\Documents and Settings\fisherb
Connected over a slow link?: No
```

The next section of output contains information about the computer settings of the resultant policy. The output lists the directory path to the computer objects, the last time policy was applied to the computer, and the object from which the policy was applied. The output also lists the specific

GPOs that were applied to generate the resultant policy. Following that list is a section containing security group information for the computer.

The next information contained in the output is a breakdown of the user configuration settings. You will find the directory container for the user object, the GPOs that were applied, and a listing of the security groups to which the user belongs.

Running gpresult.exe in verbose mode (/v) or really verbose mode (/z) will give you additional information about the specific policy settings that apply to the user/computer combination. One such entry is listed in Figure 17.26.

Figure 17.26 Viewing a Sample Policy Listing from a gpresult.exe Verbose Output

```
Folder Redirection


        GPO: Folder Redirection Policy
            KeyName:
            InstallationType:  basic
            Grant Type:        Exclusive Rights
            Move Type:         Contents of Local Directory moved
            Policy Removal:    Redirect the folder back to user profile location
            Redirecting Group: Everyone
            Redirected Path:   \\corpadfp1\home\fisherb\desktop
```

Run an RSoP Query in Logging Mode

In the following procedure, we walk through the steps required to generate an RSoP query in logging mode to produce a report on actual policy settings for a user in the directory. The steps in the example will use the sample user and computer information, but you can run this report for any user and computer in your environment, provided you have access to the tools. Running this query will not impact a production system.

1. Open the Microsoft Management Console.

2. Select **File | Add/Remove Snap-in.**

3. In the **Standalone** tab, click **Add**.

4. Scroll through the list until you find the **Resultant Set of Policy** item, and then click **Add** and **Close**.

5. Click **OK** to return to the MMC window.

6. Right-click the **Resultant Set of Policy** object in the tree and select **Generate RSoP Data**.

7. In the RSoP Wizard, click **Next**.

8. Make sure the *Logging mode* option button is selected, and then click **Next**.

9. Click the *Another Computer* option button, and then click **Browse**.

10. Find a computer in the directory and select it.

11. In the **Computer Selection** window, after selecting the computer, click **Next**.

12. In the **User Selection** window, click the *Select a specific user* option button.

13. Select one of the users listed, and then click **Next**.

14. In the **Summary of Selections** window, click **Next**.

15. Click **Finish** to close the wizard.

16. Browse through the policy settings in the MMC window.

Chapter 18

Deploying Software via Group Policy

In this chapter:

- ☑ **Understanding Group Policy Software Installation Terminology and Concepts**

- ☑ **Using Group Policy Software Installation to Deploy Applications**

- ☑ **Troubleshooting Software Deployment**

Introduction

In the preceding chapter, you learned what Group Policy is and how to work with Group Policy Objects (GPOs). One of the most important functions of Group Policy in an enterprise-level network is the ability to automate software deployment throughout the organization, saving network administrators and users a great deal of time and trouble.

In this chapter, you will learn about Group Policy's software installation feature. We'll provide an understanding of the terminology and concepts behind software installation, and we'll show you how to use the components of software installation: Windows installer packages, transforms, patches, and application assignment scripts. You'll find out how to deploy software to users and to computers by assigning or publishing applications.

After covering the concepts, we walk you through the steps of preparing for Group Policy software installation, working with the GPO Editor and setting installation options. You'll find out how to upgrade applications, configure automatic updates, and remove managed applications. We'll also cover how to troubleshoot problems that can occur with Group Policy software deployment.

Understanding Group Policy Software Installation Terminology and Concepts

Maintaining the correct applications, service packs, and so forth on users' workstations can be a daunting task, but with Group Policy, software can be distributed, configured, and maintained in a centralized fashion. From the applications users need to complete their work, to patches and updates that fix bugs or enhance security, software deployment via Group Policy is a very powerful feature.

Some of the terms associated with Group Policy software deployment may be unfamiliar if you haven't used this feature before. For example, we'll be talking about two types of deployed applications: *published* and *assigned*. A published application is made available to users through the Add/Remove Programs applet in Control Panel. Each user has the option to install the application, or not, when it is published. An assigned application is "pulled" down to the user's computer or the computer itself. During startup or logon, Group Policy assignments are checked. If software is part of a group policy linked to the organizational unit (OU), domain, or site, then the software is "*advertised*" to the user or to the computer. *Advertising* refers to making the application ready for installation when a triggering action occurs (the user clicks the application shortcut, the user attempts to open a document associated with the application, or the computer starts up).

Another term with which you'll need to be familiar is *software package* or *Windows Installer package*. A package is a file with the .msi extension that contains a database with all the instructions and information necessary to install the application. We'll talk about *transforms,* which are files with the .mst extension that make modifications to the database contained in the .msi file.

If you don't know the basic concepts, you can easily misconfigure software installation policies, and that can create problems on your network. Before implementing a new feature such as software installation, you should first ensure that you understand both the concepts and the procedures involved. Then, you can start to develop a software deployment plan. When you have a viable plan in place, you can begin to put the software installation feature to work for you on your network. In the next section, we will provide more detailed information about Group Policy software installation concepts.

Group Policy Software Installation Concepts

You can use Group Policy to deploy software within a domain environment by editing an existing GPO or creating a new one. The GPO must be applied to a domain, OU, or site in Active Directory. When you open a GPO that is applied to one of these units, you'll see two nodes labeled **Software Installation** in the left pane of the Group Policy Editor console: one that is under the **Computer Configuration** node and one that is under the **User Configuration** node.

As mentioned earlier, Group Policy software installation deals with two basic types of software deployment: assigning and publishing. Which of these you choose determines when the software will actually be installed on the user's workstation.

In the following sections, we will look at exactly how each of these options works, and help you determine which is most appropriate for a given situation.

Assigning Applications

The first option is to assign an application. You should assign applications if you want selected users to have the applications available regardless of which computer they are logged on to. An assigned application will "follow" the user from computer to computer within the domain environment.

Applications can be assigned to a user or to a computer by using the appropriate Software Installation node in Group Policy. Using the **Software Installation node** under **Computer Configuration | Software Settings** in the left pane of the Group Policy Editor console will allow you to assign the application to a computer. Using the **Software Installation node** under **User Configuration | Software Settings** in the same console tree will allow you to assign the application to a user.

After determining that you want to assign applications (rather than publish them), next you must decide whether to assign applications to users or to computers. Assigned applications are configured based on use. If a particular user will require a word processing or spreadsheet application, you can assign the application to that user. If you will be installing a particular application on every computer in the organization, or to specific computers (for example, all the computers in the Financial department), you can assign the application to the computer objects in Active Directory.

When an application is assigned to a user, the application will show up as a shortcut, on which the user can click. This shortcut does not mean that the application is installed, however. The shortcut can be configured to show up in the Start menu or on the desktop. There are also file association changes made to the workstation. This shortcut will "follow" the user, so that it appears on whichever computer the user uses to log on to the network. When the user clicks the shortcut, the application is then deployed to the workstation where the user is logged on. This ensures that users will have the appropriate software, regardless of which workstation they are logged on to.

When an application is assigned to a computer, the software is deployed when it is safe to do so (that is, when the operating system files are closed). This generally means that the software will be installed when the computer starts up, which ensures that the applications are deployed prior to any user logging on. Large application deployments can be done this way so users won't have to click and wait. Applications that are assigned to computers are available to any user who logs on to that computer. Often, administrators will do large deployments to computers during off hours so when users arrive the next day, they have the updated and installed software ready for use.

Publishing Applications

When an application is published, it is advertised to users through the **Add/Remove Programs** applet in **Control Panel**. This allows users to control when (and whether) the applications will be deployed. Applications that are not required, but which you want to make available as an option for users, are generally deployed this way. If an application isn't used by everybody but might be useful for some to complete a project or task, it can be published for the users to install when and if they need it.

Publishing an application also allows users to uninstall the application from their workstations. This gives users more control over their workstations, whereas assigned applications maintain themselves as installed applications even if the user manually deletes the files.

Figure 18.1 shows the matrix between assigning and publishing software to users and computers.

Figure 18.1 Assigning and Publishing Software Matrix

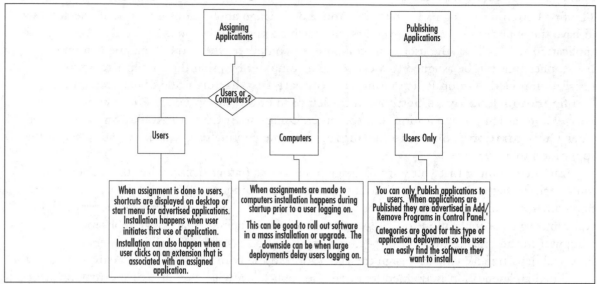

Document Invocation

Whether you assign or publish an application, file association changes can be made in the Registry on the workstation where the new application is installed. *Document invocation* refers to the ability of the system to install an application in response to the user's attempt to open a document that is associated with that application. This is also referred to as *file extension activation*. You can control whether applications will be automatically installed by file extension activation. This selection is made by checking a check box on the **Deployment** tab of the **Properties** sheet of the application. You will learn more about editing the Properties options later in the chapter.

For example, if Microsoft Word has been assigned to a computer or user but has not yet been installed, and a user receives a Word document and attempts to open it by double-clicking it, the Installer will immediately install the application and then open the document with it. It is not necessary for the user to install it via the desktop or Start menu icon, or (in the case of an application assigned to the computer) reboot the computer. The same thing happens if the application has been published, but the user has not chosen to install it via **Add/Remove Programs**. When the user attempts to open the documents, it will be installed automatically. This is also called *on-demand installation*.

What happens if more than one application is associated with the same file extension? Normally, the associated application that was most recently installed on the computer is the one that is used to open the file. You can configure the GPO to set priorities on file extensions, so that you can ensure that the published application that installs when users try to open a file with a specific extension is the right one. This is done by editing the Software Installation Properties of the **User Configuration** or **Computer Configuration** node in the GPO Editor. You will learn more about editing these options later in the chapter.

Application Categories

To make it easier for users to find applications, you can put software into categories. With a large number of applications, users must scroll through the entire list of programs in **Add/Remove Programs** to find the applications they want. To simplify the process, you can categorize the applications you assign or publish.

Categories are not predefined and thus need to be set up by the administrator. Grouping common applications together will assist your users in finding the software they need. You can group applications by department, by job function, or in other ways that are logical and meet the needs of your organization's structure. For example, all members of a particular department might need to use the same application, or all secretaries—regardless of department—might need a particular software application. It is not necessary to define categories for each individual GPO; instead, you create categories that will apply to the entire domain.

Group Policy Software Deployment vs. SMS Software Deployment

Software deployment via Group Policy differs from software deployment via Systems Management Server (SMS). The one simple difference is that SMS is a more controlled software distribution environment. With Group Policy, you set up the deployment as either assigned or published and that is it. With SMS, you can control configuration of items such as bandwidth usage, load balancing, scheduling, and so forth. To accomplish load balancing with Group Policy, you would have to introduce a Distributed File System configuration. Scheduling and bandwidth throttling are available through SMS only, not through Group Policy.

Another key difference between using SMS and using Group Policy is that one is a *pull* model and the other is a *push* model. Software deployment through Group Policy is a *pull* configuration, meaning that the client pulls the software down to a workstation. SMS uses a *push* model where the SMS servers take the responsibility along with the agents to determine what software is needed and the best time to copy the package.

Group Policy Software Installation Components

Now that we have discussed the concepts of when and how software should be deployed, let's look at the components involved in using Group Policy to deploy software. In Windows 2003 as in Windows 2000, the Windows Installer technology is the driving force behind this feature.

You will become familiar with four file types as you work with software installation:

- The *application package* is the first and basic file type you will encounter.

- The *transform* gives you the ability to make changes to a package, or transform the package.

- *Patches* are available for many software programs, and you can deploy these with Group Policy.

- The *application assignment script* stores the information regarding assignment or publishing of the application.

In the following sections, we will discuss each of these in more detail.

Windows Installer Packages (.msi)

In the early days of Windows computing, you could use a third-party installation and packaging tool to simplify software deployment (including Microsoft's SMS). Beginning with Windows 2000, the new Windows Installer technology became available, this provides a native packaging and distribution tool for Windows operating systems, and Group Policy provides a way to distribute software without buying a distribution product.

The Installer technology is made up of the following components:

- The Installer service, which is an operating system service that uses Windows Installer packages to perform software installation, modification, and uninstallation.

- The .msi file, which is a group of files compressed together along with the appropriate scripting to install and configure the software. It is essentially a relational database containing a number of tables that holds information about the application. The package can be configured to handle upgrades as well as new installations.

- The application programming interface (API) by which applications interface with the Installer service.

A big advantage of Windows Installer is its ability to "roll back" to the former state if problems occur during an installation. The Installer service can also monitor the state of installed "self-repairing" applications, and detect missing or corrupt program files. The service can then automatically restore the damaged or missing components so that the application will work properly again.

The database design of the Installer package makes it fast to query and provides for smaller file sizes. The information in the tables includes data that will allow for different installation scenarios, so that there is a set of information about how to install the application clean for the first time, how to install it over a previous version, and so forth. Because the Installer service tracks the installation of the application's features and components, it makes it easier to remove the application completely, without leaving remnants that can cause problems later.

Transforms (.mst)

Packages provided by vendors with their applications are configured and ready to install. This means there isn't much room for flexibility if, for example, you want different installation options for computers in different departments. This is where *transforms* come into play. Transforms are also called *modifications*. That's because a transform is a record of changes to the original package file that allows you to customize the installation by including or excluding particular features. A transform is applicable to a specific Windows Installer package.

Transforms are especially important when you are doing silent or unattended installations. The ability to add or remove certain features or make Registry changes in applying your package makes configuration easier for the administrator. Installing and configuring applications via Group Policy cuts down on the time spent by the administrator in setting up, configuring, and troubleshooting applications for users.

Transforms customize the installation features at the time you assign or publish the application. You can create transforms using the authoring and repackaging utilities we discussed earlier, or the utilities included with applications themselves. Office 2000 included a Custom Installation Wizard to create transforms for making modifications to the application's package when deploying it in your organization. It is often easier to apply a transform rather than repackage an application to make changes.

You associate your transforms with the application when you configure software installation for the application. In the new package that you add via the GPO Editor, you need to select **Advanced published or assigned** in the **Deploy software** dialog box that begins the software deployment process.

Patches and Updates (.msp)

There are times when an application has to be updated because of fixes or new features that are available through a service pack, patch, or other update software. An .msp file is a special type of modification that is used to update an existing Windows Installer package with new information. This allows for easy updates of users' workstations and application of important security patches and other fixes.

With an .msp file, only the updated information needs to be distributed to users. This cuts back on the time and effort required to deploy updates and patches, and cuts down on the amount of network traffic generated by application updates.

To deploy an .msp update, you generally should advertise the package again to those to whom the original application was assigned or published. Sometimes, the software vendor will provide an entire new .msi package if changes are extensive. In this case, you should just replace the old .msi file with the new one. Otherwise, use the .msp file to make the changes to the original .msi file, and then redeploy the application. This will automatically install the new version for those users and computers where the original was installed, and make it available instead of the old version for those users to whom the original was published, who haven't yet installed the application.

Note that .msp files are not able to make certain changes. For example, they cannot be used to remove Registry keys, or remove or change the names of shortcuts and files. They cannot be used to change product codes, and you can't use them to remove features. These tasks require the use of an .mst transform or a new .msi package.

Application Assignment Scripts (.aas)

When you set up Group Policy Software Installation and publish or assign applications, an Application Assignment Script (with the file extension .aas) is generated automatically. The Application Assignment Script is stored in the GPO in Active Directory. The script contains information regarding the configuration of the Software Installation. Advertisement information is also stored within the assignment script.

Deploying Software to Users

GPOs can be linked to a site, domain, or OU (or to a local computer). With that in mind, we will now discuss deployment of software to user objects in Active Directory. Because software installation cannot be done through local group policies, we will be concerned with deploying software at the site, domain, or OU level. The easiest way to deploy software to a specific group of users is to use the OU that contains the user objects. A link can be made to an existing GPO, or you can create a new GPO for this purpose.

Remember that when you deploy software to users, it might be installed soon after they log on. This is determined by whether you assign the software or publish it. If the software is assigned, the software will be installed when the user attempts to run the application from the shortcut or clicks on an associated file. Large installations might make users think that the workstation is locked or froze up, so you have to be careful about whether you assign, publish, or deploy to the workstation instead.

If the application is published, the user can install the application from **Add/Remove Programs** in **Control Panel**. This makes it more likely that the user will know what's going on, since he or she will have chosen to install the application. However, the published application will be installed via document invocation if file associations were set up within the package, which can result in the same problem of a user not realizing an installation is taking place and thinking there is a problem with the computer.

Deploying Software to Computers

Most of the same rules discussed in regard to deploying software to users also apply to deploying software to computer objects in Active Directory. However, you need to remember that you can only assign software to computers; there is no publishing to computer objects. Software installation policies can be applied like any group policy to sites, domains, or OUs. In Active Directory, by default each computer object is added to the **Computers** container in the root domain. You will most likely want to set up software deployment to computers by creating an OU, but this depends on your Active Directory design.

When software is deployed to computer objects, the installation generally takes place when the computer boots, prior to the appearance of the **Ctrl + Alt + Del** screen. This means the user cannot log on until all of the software has been installed. This must be considered prior to designing or assigning software installation packages. Assigning too many applications at the same time can cause the workstation to take a long time to start up.

Using Group Policy Software Installation to Deploy Applications

Now that you know the basics of software installation, let's look at the details and step-by-step procedures involved in completing the process. We will look at the interface used to add software installation packages: the GPO Editor MMC snap-in.

In this section, we will review the Microsoft Windows Installer technology and packages, in the context of how they are used in the process of software deployment. We will also look at how to create your own Windows Installer packages using Veritas WinINSTALL LE. Because the configuration of legacy applications is often an issue in real-world deployment scenarios, we will show you how to deploy software when you don't have a Windows Installer package and do not want to create one. Finally, we will discuss how to set up distribution points.

Preparing for Group Policy Software Installation

Determining which applications you plan to distribute with Group Policy Software Installation is an important first step in the deployment process. Because the GPOs used to deploy software can be linked to a site, domain, or OU, some planning is required. You must take into consideration your Active Directory design and the application needs of your organization.

Some departments will require a particular application, whereas there is no need for that application in other departments. For example, the Financial department may need accounting software that is not used elsewhere. In other cases, an application is required for all those in a particular job function. For example, all project managers may need a particular project management application, regardless of department. There are also times when an application must be distributed throughout the entire enterprise. For example, the software that is used to open and read personnel policies or security policies that apply to all employees will be needed by everyone, regardless of department or job function. Your Active Directory design and organizational needs will ultimately determine your plans for where you will configure Software Installation within Group Policy.

Creating Windows Installer Packages

Although Microsoft provides Installer packages with most of their software programs, the situation is not quite as simple when you have third-party software to install. Then, you may not have the convenience of having a Windows Installer package available, but when this happens, you can use a utility to create an Installer package. One such tool that has been available since Windows 2000 is WinINSTALL. The original version of WinINSTALL LE (Limited Edition) was included on the Windows 2000 Server installation CD-ROM. The software is no longer included on the Windows Server 2003 CD-ROM, but a free MSI repackager, WinINSTALL LE 2003, can be downloaded at no cost at the OnDemand Software Web site at www.ondemandsoftware.com/FREELE2003/. Alternatively, you can download a trial version of the full WinINSTALL product. The full product can be used in environments where deployment needs are more complex, and provides features such as hardware and software inventory, conflict assessment, MSI validation, and multicast replication—many of the same features offered by Microsoft's SMS.

Figure 18.2 shows the WinINSTALL LE interface.

Figure 18.2 WinINSTALL LE 2003 Console

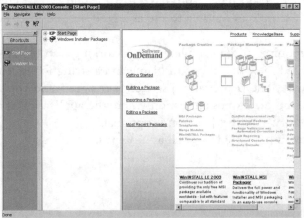

Before you begin to create your own packages, you should configure a freshly installed workstation to use for this purpose. This will ensure that you have a clean Registry and standard configuration of the operating system. Using a workstation that has had software installed and removed and other changes made to it can cause problems with package deployment.

If you cannot dedicate a workstation for creating .msi packages, you must use a computer that is as close as possible to the configuration of the workstations that will receive the package. The workstation on which you create the packages should be running the same version of the operating system as the computers on which the packages will be deployed. As simple as package creation seems, if configuration steps are not followed closely, you might spend more time troubleshooting problems than successfully deploying software.

Using .zap Setup Files

It is possible to publish applications that don't have .msi packages by using the application's Setup program. If you want to deploy software via Group Policy, do not have an .msi file, and do not want to create one, you can instead create a .zap file for the program. The key point to remember in using .zap files is that they can only be published to users; you cannot assign software to users or to computers by this method. This type of software deployment also has some additional limitations when compared to Windows Installer packages, including the following:

- These installations cannot take advantage of elevated user privileges. This means that if the application requires an account with administrative privileges to be used to install it, users who don't have administrative privileges won't be able to install it even though it is published to them.

- The programs cannot be installed on first use by double-clicking a shortcut, as with Windows Installer packages.

- The system does not automatically repair or remove an application, and you cannot roll back a failed deployment.

- You cannot install features upon first use of the feature, as you can with .msi packages.

If these limitations don't present a problem with the application you want to deploy, the first step is to create a .zap file for the application being deployed. To create a .zap file, you must follow the format prescribed by Microsoft. The .zap file is a text file and can be created in any text editor (for example, Notepad). A sample is available to use as a guide in the Microsoft Knowledge Base article Q231747.

Only two items are required to be completed for a working .zap file. As long as *FriendlyName* and *SetupCommand* are filled in with a Program Name and a string for executing the Setup program, the .zap file will work. The [Application] section is required, and you can also include an [Ext] section; the latter is the file extension section where the application is associated with a file extension in Active Directory. The [Ext] section is optional.

The .zap file is created in a text editor such as Notepad.

After you create the .zap file, you have to add it to your Software Installation configuration within Group Policy. The following example walks you through the steps of publishing an application with a .zap file.

Publish Software Using a .ZAP File

When publishing software with a .zap file, you first need to determine which GPO you want to edit. After you determine whether to use a GPO that is applicable to a site, a domain, or an OU, open the appropriate GPO (see the section titled *Working with the GPO Editor* later in this chapter) and make the appropriate addition by following these steps:

1. In the GPO Editor's left console pane, expand **User Configuration**, and then expand **Software Settings**.

2. Right-click **Software Installation**, select **New**, and then select **Package**.

3. Change the **Files of type** field to **ZAW Down-level applications package (*.zap)**.

4. In the **Open** dialog box, navigate to the location of your .zap file or type the path in the **File Name** field.

5. Click the .zap file you created and click the **Open** button.

6. Click **Published** as the deployment method in the **Deploy Software** dialog box, and click **OK**.

Creating Distribution Points

To distribute software, you must ensure that the users are able to access the needed files from the network. As a network administrator, you must create shared folders on the network known as *distribution points*, to hold the necessary files for installing the deployed applications. A distribution point can be part of a Distributed File System (Dfs) hierarchy or any share point that is available to all users who will need to install the software.

Each share point needs to be configured with the appropriate NTFS permissions to allow access to those who will install the software. This will allow you to control the software that can be installed. If a user doesn't have permissions to access the folder where a package is stored, the software cannot be deployed to that user.

In most cases, it is preferable to control who is able to receive the software through their association and permissions to the GPO itself, but the NTFS permissions must be at least Read and Execute for the distribution point and its subfolders.

Working with the GPO Editor

For those who have worked with the Window NT 4.0 System Policy Editor, learning to use the Active Directory GPO Editor should be relatively easy. However, deploying applications via Group Policy can be a bit complex. There are many different options to configure when you are setting up a package for deployment. You can deploy software for fresh installations, manage the upgrade of previously installed packages, and remove software from workstations by forcibly uninstalling the software. Every tool is available for managing software within your organization.

In the following sections, we will show you how to use the GPO Editor to set installation options, assign and publish applications, upgrade applications, and remove managed applications.

Opening or Creating a GPO for Software Deployment

The first step in deploying software via Group Policy is to create a new GPO or open an existing GPO that applies to the site, domain, or OU to which you want to deploy the software. You can open an existing domain policy by following these steps:

1. Click **Start | All Programs | Administrative Tools | Active Directory Users and Computers**.

2. In the left console pane of the ADUC tool, right-click the name of the domain and select **Properties**.

3. Click the **Group Policy** tab.

4. Select the policy you want to edit under **Group Policy Object Links**. Click the **Edit** button. This will open the policy in the GPO Editor.

To deploy software at the OU level, follow the same steps except, in step 2, expand the node for the domain, right-click the name of the OU to which you want to deploy the software, and then click **Properties**.

If you want to deploy software at the site level, follow these steps:

1. Click **Start | All Programs | Administrative Tools | Active Directory Sites and Services**.

2. In the left console pane, expand the **Sites** node.

3. In the right details pane, right-click the site to which you want to deploy the software, and click **Properties**.

4. Click the **Group Policy** tab.

5. Select the policy you want to edit under **Group Policy Object Links**. Click the **Edit** button. This will open the policy in the GPO Editor.

Assigning and Publishing Applications

Earlier we discussed the concepts of assigning versus publishing applications. Now we will look at the GPO Editor console's interface to become more familiar with the step-by-step process. After you open the GPO Editor, right-click on **Software Installation** under either **Computer Configuration** or **User Configuration** (depending on whether you want to assign the software to computers or assign or publish it to users) and choose **New Package** from the right context menu as shown in Figure 18.3.

Figure 18.3 Configuring a New Package

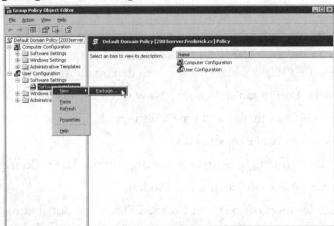

A dialog box will open asking you for the package you want to use. Navigate to a network location where the .msi file for the software you want to deploy is located. Package files should be stored in a central location. This central location is your distribution point for your software packages. Software packages can generally be downloaded from the manufacturer. Some organizations choose to create their own with other third-party software products.

When you choose a new package, it should be located on a network share. Otherwise, you will receive a message informing you that clients will not be able to install the package, as shown in Figure 18.4.

Figure 18.4 Error Message When Selecting Drive Letter

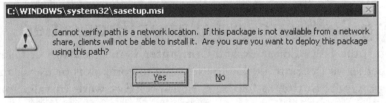

Next, a prompt will ask you if you want to assign or publish the application, or use the Advanced method. If you choose **Advanced**, you will be presented with the Properties window for your new package. We discuss the options that you can configure in this Properties box in the section titled *Configuring Software Installation Properties* later in this chapter.

Assign Software to a Group

This procedure will walk you through the steps of assigning software to an Active Directory group at the OU level. This gives more granularity to the configuration, and this example will give you some good hands-on practice in using the interface.

1. Ensure that you have a distribution point (a shared folder containing the .msi package) set up with the appropriate NTFS permissions assigned.

2. Log on as a Domain Administrator.

3. Open **Active Directory Users and Computers** from the **Administrative Tools** menu and right-click the OU to which you want to deploy the software. Select **Properties**.

4. Click the **Group Policy** tab and choose **New** to create a new GPO.

5. Select the new GPO in the list and type a distinguishing name for it.

6. Click **Edit** to make changes to the GPO.

7. In the GPO Editor, highlight **Software Settings** under **User Configuration**.

8. Right-click, select **New**, and then select **Package**.

9. Navigate to the location of your .msi package. This is the distribution point that you shared earlier. Enter the UNC path so the workstations can find the software.

10. Next, you are prompted to select whether to publish or assign the application or choose the **Advanced** option. Select **Assigned**.

11. Click **OK**. The software package name should show up in the right details pane of the GPO Editor.

12. Close the GPO Editor window. In the OU's **Properties** dialog box, select the GPO under **Group Policy Object Links** and click the **Properties** button.

13. In the GPO's **Properties** dialog box, click the **Security** tab.

14. Remove **Authenticated Users** on the **Security** tab and add the appropriate group that contains the users to whom you want to assign this application.

15. Click **OK** and the application should be ready for deployment.

Configuring Software Installation Properties

When you first open the GPO Editor, expand **Computer Configuration** or **User Configuration** (depending on whether you want to deploy the software to computers or users), and then expand **Software Settings**. Under **Software Settings,** right-click **Software Installation** and choose **Properties**.

There are four tabs within the Properties of Software Installation. In the following sections, we will discuss the configuration options that can be made with each of these tabs.

The General Tab

On the General tab, you can specify the default location of all packages. Under the New Packages section on that same tab, you can specify the default value for publishing or assigning. The default is to prompt the user to decide at the time of object creation. The last item to be configured on this tab is the User Interface options. This setting determines how much of the installation the user sees. The *Basic* option only shows minimal screen display during software deployment. The *Maximum* option shows all the installation screens as the installation happens.

The Advanced Tab

The Advanced tab has options to be configured such as how to handle 64-bit machines as well as OLE information being published in Active Directory. Figure 18.5 shows the Advanced tab.

Figure 18.5 Advanced Tab of Software Installation

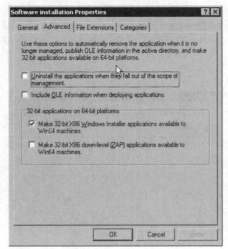

The first option in this window is **Uninstall applications when they fall out of the scope of management**. This means that if a software program was installed with Group Policy and later the account was moved to a different OU, the software could be uninstalled automatically.

You can also choose to have Object Linking and Embedding (OLE) information stored in Active Directory. OLE can be a key part of user interaction and collaboration.

The File Extensions Tab

The File Extensions tab is where you can associate documents and other file types to a specific application that is configured for deployment as shown in Figure 18.6.

Figure 18.6 File Extensions Tab

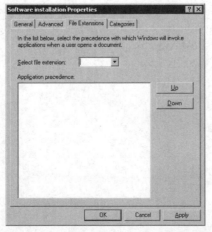

When you select an extension, you also have to consider some type of order since there are applications that have the same extension for the main file. The Up and Down buttons determine application preference.

The Categories Tab

The Categories tab has the option to create categories so that published applications will be easier to find in the **Add/Remove Programs** applet from **Control Panel**. Figure 18.7 shows the Categories tab.

Figure 18.7 Categories Tab

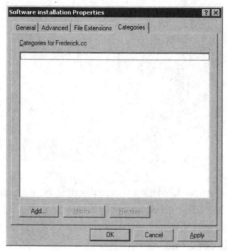

The Add button allows you to specify new categories. Categories help in finding software installations for users. This is especially helpful when software is published so that users do not have to scroll through the entire list of available software.

Upgrading Applications

For most applications, there will occasionally be upgrades released to address issues with the existing version. The software deployment tools available with Group Policy allow you to maintain control over upgrades by linking the upgrade package together with the original application package. Figure 18.8 shows the Upgrades tab in the Properties of an application.

Figure 18.8 Software Upgrades Tab

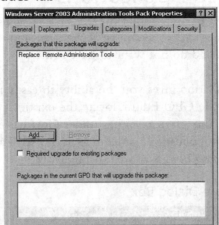

The Upgrades tab shows you packages that this package will upgrade, while the bottom pane shows other packages that will be affected by this package. Use the **Add** button to associate this package with the package it is replacing. A good rule of thumb is to use version numbers or exact names with application upgrades to keep things easy to administer. Generally, when software is deployed as an upgrade, the user is prompted to install the upgrade or the user can select to wait until later if he or she is busy and wants to delay the installation.

As we saw earlier, most software installation packages will come from the software manufacturer. These are known as natively authored packages. With natively authored packages, there can be a *declared upgrade relationship* between a package that is an upgrade and other packages. This is part of the database information that makes up a package. The package will know what previous versions it can upgrade and how to handle issues such as files that need to be deleted or kept.

The one catch is that a declared upgrade relationship only works with natively authored packages. With repackaged applications, you have to manually create the upgrade relationship using the Upgrades tab. This is done be clicking the **Add** button on the **Upgrades** tab and selecting the previous versions of those repackaged applications. Active Directory and Group Policy can use this information to upgrade the appropriate users or workstations.

Configuring Required Updates

You can use the Upgrades tab to specify whether an upgrade is required or optional. If you want to force users to use the most recent version of an application, you can put a check in the **Required upgrade for existing packages** box. This will automatically upgrade the users' workstations the next time they run the application, or when the computer next reboots if the application is assigned to the computer. A required upgrade is performed whether or not the user wants to upgrade. This is good for applications such as service packs, virus updates, patches, and so forth, and is desirable for productivity applications such as Office if you want to ensure that all users have the same version to make it easier to support and troubleshoot the application.

Removing Managed Applications

In some situations, you may want to discontinue the use of a particular software application in your organization. This might occur because you want to replace the application with a comparable product from a different vendor, and do not want to have some users working with one vendor's product and some with the other's.

Group Policy Software Installation gives you the ability to easily remove software that was deployed with Group Policy. In the GPO Editor, locate the existing package in the right pane and select **Software Installation** in the left pane either under **Computer Configuration** or **User Configuration.** Right-click the application name and choose **All Tasks | Remove**. This will invoke the Remove Software dialog box, as shown in Figure 18.9.

Figure 18.9 Remove Software Dialog Box

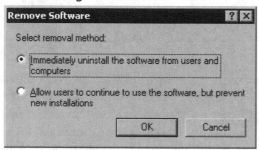

There are two removal methods available:

- If you choose **Immediately uninstall the software from users and computers**, the software will be removed the next time the computer reboots (if the application is assigned to the computer) or the next time the user logs on (if the application is assigned to the user). This is called *forced removal*, and automatically removes the software regardless of users' wishes.

- If you want to leave the software on users' workstations but prevent new installations of it, select the **Allow users to continue to use the software, but prevent new installations** option. Users who have it installed will still be able to use it, but no one will be able to install it.

You can select to have the application automatically removed if the GPO no longer applies to a user. To do this, you need to edit the **Deployment** tab of the application's **Properties** dialog box. Check the check box labeled **Uninstall this application when it falls out of the scope of management**.

There is one other thing to remember about software removal. If you have a legacy application that requires the use of a .zap file, you will not be able to take advantage of the removal feature described previously. For the removal feature to work, you must use Windows Installer (.msi) packages to deploy the software.

Managing Application Properties

After packages are configured, you generally will not have to do much with them. However, there might be occasions when you need to edit an application's properties. To do this, double-click the package in the right details pane of the GPO Editor, with **Software Installation** selected in the left pane, and select **Properties**. Figure 18.10 shows the resulting dialog box.

Figure 18.10 Application Properties

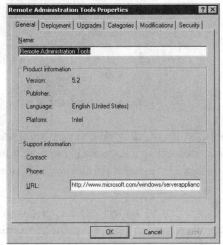

You are presented with six tabs that are used to configure various features, as follows:

- **General** Allows you to rename the package display name and add a URL for support information if desired. Programmers can put contact and telephone information into the package, which will be displayed in those fields. This tab also provides information about the software, including a version number, the publisher's name, language, and the platform on which the software is designed to run.

- **Deployment** As discussed earlier, this tab indicates whether the software is assigned or published as shown in Figure 18.11. This is also where you can select whether the application is to be installed by file extension activation (document invocation); this option is selected by default. Other deployment options include the ability to have the system automatically uninstall the application when it falls out of the scope of management, and the ability to prevent the package from being displayed in the Add/Remove Programs applet in Control Panel. You can also select to have the package installed at logon. This tab also allows you to choose the interface that the user will see during installation (basic or maximum). The Advanced button allows you to ignore language when deploying the package, and you can also select to make a 32-bit x86 application available to 64-bit Windows machines. Some advanced diagnostic information, including the product code, deployment count, and script name/path, are also provided in the Advanced Deployment Options dialog box.

Figure 18.11 Deployment Tab

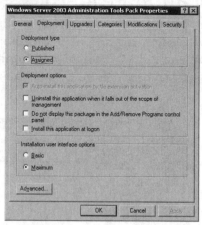

- **Upgrades** As discussed previously, this tab contains upgrade information, including the name(s) of the package(s) that this package will upgrade, whether the package is to be a required upgrade that will be deployed regardless of the user's wishes, and packages in the GPO that will upgrade this package.

- **Categories** This tab allows you to associate the application with a category that is already configured as shown in Figure 18.12. This is especially useful when you publish applications, as they make it easier for users to find the applications within the list in the Add/Remove Programs applet. However, both published and assigned applications can be categorized.

Figure 18.12 Categories Tab

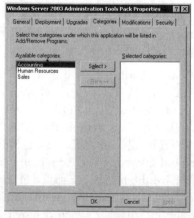

- **Modifications** This tab is used to associate transforms with the package, and control the order in which the transforms are applied to the package, as described in the section titled *Adding and Removing Modifications for Application Packages* later in the chapter.

- **Security** This tab is used to control which users and groups are able to see and use the object in Active Directory, and define the level of access each has. Figure 18.13 shows the Security tab.

Figure 18.13 Security Tab

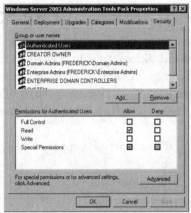

By default, the permissions shown in Table 18.1 will apply.

Table 18.1 Default Active Directory Permissions When Adding Packages

User or Group	Default Permissions
Authenticated Users	Read
Creator/Owner	Read/Write
Domain Admins	Full Control
Enterprise Admins	Read/Write
Enterprise Domain Controllers	Read
SYSTEM	Full Control

Categorizing Applications

We mentioned that you can set up categories for your applications to make it easier for users to find the software they need. Categories are set up first. This is done within the Properties of Software Installation. If you right-click on **Software Installation** and go to **Properties**, there is a **Categories** tab.

Administering categories is simple. The Add button allows you to create new category. You can name it however you want. Many organizations use department names or division names as part of their naming plan.

The Modify button allows you to select an existing category and make modifications. The Remove button will remove a category.

Once the categories are created, the Properties of a package that is already set up will have a Categories tab also. This was shown in Figure 18.11 earlier. There is a list on the left of available categories, and the list on the right tells you what categories this application is setup for.

Adding and Removing Modifications for Application Packages

Often you will need more than one version of an application in use on the network, or even on a single machine. You may also need different features enabled for different users. Instead of creating a different package for each unique configuration of an application, you can use modifications, or transforms, to customize the package. To make a transform or modification, you must have the appropriate software. The packaging programs discussed earlier also can be used to create transforms based on a package.

To add and remove modifications, open the application's **Properties** dialog box and click the **Modifications** tab.

You can assign multiple modifications to a package. Use the **Add** and **Remove** buttons to add the appropriate .mst file to the list or to remove it, and use the **Up** and **Down** buttons to organize the various transforms within the package and control the order in which they will be applied.

Apply a Transform to a Software Package

When working with packages, you might have to apply a transform or modification to the original installation in order to customize the package. This can be because of .ini file changes, Registry changes, or other customization required by your organization. To complete this example, you need an existing .msi file and an .mst file. In this example, we will apply a transform to a package that is deployed to users at the domain level.

1. Open **Active Directory Users and Computers** and right-click the domain name. Click **Properties**.

2. Select the **Group Policy** tab, select the **Default Domain Policy**, and click **Edit**.

3. In the **GPO Editor**, navigate to the **Software Installation** node under **User Configuration** in the left console pane.

4. Right-click **Software Installation,** select **New**, and then select **Package**.

5. In the **Open** dialog box, navigate to the package (.msi file) you chose for this lab and select it. Click the **Open** button.

6. Select **Advanced** when asked about published or assigned. Click **OK**.

7. Click the **Modifications** tab.

8. On the **Modifications** tab, click the **Add** button and browse to the .mst file you chose earlier.

9. Click **OK** to apply the transform to the package.

The tricky part about working with modifications is that you must use the Modifications tab when you are initially setting up the package within the group policy. When you select **Advanced** when setting up a package, you are presented with the Properties dialog box for your application. If you select the **Modifications** tab, you will have the opportunity to click the **Add** button.

However, if you select **Assigned** or **Published** and are not immediately presented with a configuration dialog box, you will not be able to add modifications. The Apply button will be grayed out.

Troubleshooting Software Deployment

An important part of any administrator's job is troubleshooting. With software deployment, as with any other aspect of networking, sometimes things go wrong, and when they do, you need to know how to track down the source of the problem and correct it. The Application log in Event Viewer can be a helpful first step in diagnosing some common problems. Various types of Event Log Error messages might be observed here:

- If you see a series of *MsiInstaller* messages in Event Viewer, you are experiencing a problem with the Windows Installer service. These errors can range from a permissions issue on the distribution point to a problem with the version of Windows Installer you have running on the workstation.

- Watch for *Application Management* messages. These sometimes can indicate the reason why an application didn't deploy properly.

- *Userenv* is another source to look for that may give clues to why software installation failed.

Some common problems encountered with Group Policy software installation and possible methods of resolutions include:

- **Published application doesn't show up in Add/Remove Programs**
    - Check the Group Policy Object link. If there are filters configured or permissions have been changed, the policy may not be getting applied to the user resulting in the software not showing up in **Add/Remove Programs**.

    - Use tools such as gpresult.exe and GPOTool.exe to further troubleshoot the group policy settings and their application to the workstation or user.

    - Check to see what categories are displaying. All Categories will show all available software for installation.

    - There is an option to mark that does not allow the application to display in Add/Remove Programs control panel.

    - Directory replication not being synchronized can cause software not to show up until all domain controllers are up to date.

- **Software installation not completed when assigned**
    - Check the Group Policy Object link. Make sure there aren't any conflicting Group Policy settings. When planning software installation via Group Policy you need to be careful when you have other policies at higher levels like Domain or OU. This

can be especially true if you have the same package configured within multiple GPOs.

- Check permissions on the GPO. Users or Computers must have Read and Apply Group Policy permissions on the GPO. To check permissions, you must right-click on the site, domain, or OU, select **Properties**, go to the **Group Policy** tab, and click **Edit**. On the **Properties** window of the group policy, the **Security** tab has the permission entries.

- Check permissions on the distribution point (the shared folder where the .msi package is located). Users need Read and Execute permissions to the distribution point hierarchy.

- Make sure the software is on a Windows 2003 Share. If you are in a mixed environment, putting shares on Windows NT 4.0 servers is not supported.

- Double check that if the group policy is set for Computers that it is associated with the appropriate OU. The same thing applies to the group policy set for Users; if software installation is assigned to a user and linked to an OU with only Computer objects, then of course the result would not be successful.

- **Name resolution problems**

  - Name resolution is necessary for users to access the shares where packages are located, whether they are stored on a regular share or within a Dfs hierarchy. Ensure that your DNS servers are running properly. One possibility you should always check when it comes to Active Directory is whether the DNS server is overloaded. Ensure that it is responding to client name resolution requests properly. If name resolution ceases to function, many components of Active Directory will not work properly.

Verbose Logging

When you are experiencing serious application deployment problems, you can turn on verbose logging. This will create a special log file that records information about software installation and group policy application. To turn these features on, you must make a Registry change. For software installation, make sure the following entry exists in the Registry:

```
HKLM\Software\Microsoft\Windows NT\CurrentVersion\Diagnostics
DWORD  Appmgmtdebuglevel = 0000009b
```

Turning this feature on will created an appmgmt.log located in the %windir%\debug\usermode\ folder. Only turn this feature on as needed, as it can create a large amount of overhead on the network.

You can also turn on logging for Windows Installer services. You also make a change in the Registry to turn this feature on:

```
HKLM\Software\Policies\Microsoft\Windows\Installer
DWORD  Debug = 00000003
```

Setting this value will cause logging to happen for Windows Installer actions. The log created depends on the action itself. Two types of log files can created: deployment-related or user-related.

With a deployment-related action you will see a log created in %windir%\temp%\msi*.log. This is because deployment-related actions run in the system context so the system temp folder is used. User action would include using add/remove programs to install software. These log files end up in the user's temp folder. The path would be %temp^\msi*.log.

Software Installation Diagnostics Tool

Another tool that you can use comes from the Resource Kit. This tool is Software Installation Diagnostics and can be used to gain additional insight into problems you may be experiencing. This tool is also a command-line tool; you have to open a command prompt to run it.

The file is called addiag.exe. You can type **addiag.exe /?** and receive a list of commands to become familiar with the tool. You can use this tool to print out information possibly related to problem deployments. It will also generate Event Log entries related to software installation.

Chapter 19

Ensuring Active Directory Availability

In this chapter:

- ☑ **Understanding Active Directory Availability Issues**

- ☑ **Performing Active Directory Maintenance Tasks**

- ☑ **Backing Up and Restoring Active Directory**

- ☑ **Troubleshooting Active Directory Availability**

Introduction

In earlier chapters, we looked at the Active Directory (AD) infrastructure, as well as various interacting elements, such as forest, sites, domains, and trusts. We also examined the Global Catalog, Schema, and Group Policy in order to fully understand AD in a Windows Server 2003 environment. Now that we've thoroughly reviewed this information, we can discuss how to ensure AD availability.

This chapter deals with how to maintain high availability of your Active Directory services. You'll learn about the Active Directory database, and the importance of system state data to Active Directory availability. We'll discuss fault tolerance plans as well as Active Directory performance issues. You'll find out how to perform necessary maintenance tasks, such as defragging the database, and you'll learn how to monitor or move the database.

Next, we'll address backup and restoration of the Active Directory, and show you the different restoration methods that you can use and when each is appropriate. We'll walk you through the steps of performing both an authoritative and a normal restore. Finally, you'll learn how to troubleshoot Active Directory availability problems.

Understanding Active Directory Availability Issues

In this section, we look at the core components of the Windows Server 2003 Active Directory service. First, we discuss the structure and type of database, including its files and related components. You'll also learn how updates are written to the Active Directory database, and how it recovers in the event of a failure during the update process. We will review the key system configuration components that comprise the system state data, and look at fault tolerance and performance issues involving Active Directory.

The Active Directory Database

The Active Directory service is based on a transactional database system. The word *transactional* refers to the transaction logs that enable the system to have robust recovery and data tracking in the event of unscheduled hardware outages, data corruption, and other problems that can arise in a complex network operating system environment. The heart of the Active Directory service is the database and its related transactional log files, which include the following:

- **Ntds.dit** This file is the primary Active Directory database file (sometimes referred to as the *data store*) that resides on each domain controller (DC). It stores all of the objects, attributes, and properties for the local domain, as well as the configuration and schema portions of the database. By default, this file is installed into the %SYSTEMROOT%\NTDS folder. Although not required, it is recommended that you store this file on an NTFS partition for security purposes.

- **Edb*.log** This file format identifies transaction logs. Transaction log names can take one of several forms, including edb.log, edb00001.log, edb00002.log, and so forth. Each log file is a fixed 10MB in size, regardless of the amount of actual data stored in it. The current log file that is receiving updates to Active Directory is named edb.log. When this file is full, it is renamed to edb00001.log (or whatever the next number is in the sequence, if 00001 is taken), and a new empty edb.log is created. However, these logs don't keep piling up forever; they are regularly purged through a process called garbage collection, discussed later in the chapter.

- **Res1.log** and **Res2.log** These files are known as the reserved (Res) log files. Their primary purpose is to ensure that Active Directory does not run out of disk space to use when logging transactions. If there is not enough free space to create a new transaction log, the reserved log is used. Because of this role, these log files are often referred to as *placeholders*. Like the edb.log files mentioned previously , these files are 10MB each.

- **Edb.chk** The "checkpoint" file is used to track the updates that have been written to the Active Directory database. You can think of this file as a list that is checked off as updates are flushed to disk from the Active Directory log files. If you shut down the system before all transactions have been written to the database, the checkpoint file will be consulted when you reboot the system so that any remaining transactions can be written to Active Directory.

Microsoft recommends that you place the database and the log files on different physical disks, for performance purposes. Now, let's take a deeper look at how Active Directory works, and the roles these files play in the process of updating and storing data.

Data Modification to the Active Directory Database

The Extensible Storage Engine (ESE) lies at the heart of the Active Directory database system. Changes to the Active Directory database on a DC occur through two primary means:

- An administrator creates, deletes, or updates objects in the database.

- Replication information, which contains new objects, deletion requests, or changes to existing objects is received from other DCs.

When changes to the database occur, the ESE captures each change as a single unit known as a *transaction*. A transaction contains the changed data and a set of metadata. This metadata can include the Globally Unique Identifier (GUID) assigned to the object, a timestamp, version, and other information. It's important to note that this update procedure applies to all changes in Active Directory, including objects, properties, and attributes.

A write request occurs when a change is made to the Active Directory. This initiates a transaction that consists of the changes, as well as the metadata described previously. ESE writes the transaction to the transaction buffer in memory, and then writes the transaction to the Edb.log file. After it has been successfully written in the log file, it is written to the Active Directory database file.

If a failure occurs, when Active Directory recovers, it examines the Edb.chk file to determine which transactions have not been written to the database. Transactions are not marked as written in this file until they have been fully committed to the database. This ensures that a failure that occurs partially through the process of writing data will not be marked as completed and leave inconsistent data in the Active Directory database. When a transaction has been committed, Active Directory compares the information written to the database with the information contained in the log file(s). When the two have been verified as identical, the Edb.chk file is updated and the transaction is marked as committed to the database.

Windows Server 2003 uses *circular* transaction logging. This means that, with the exception of the Edb.log, Res1.log, and Res2.log files, the log files are deleted after all of the transactions they contain have been committed to the database. Another important note about logging is that when you back up Active Directory by backing up the system state data (a process we discuss in the next section of this chapter), all events currently waiting to be written in your transaction logs are committed. The logs are fully committed when you shut down or reboot your server. Figure 19.1 illustrates this process.

Figure 19.1 The Active Directory Data Commitment Process

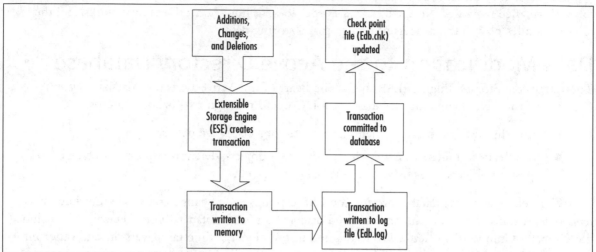

The Tombstone and Garbage Collection Processes

The use of transaction logs is designed to ensure the integrity of data that changes on a single DC. Other mechanisms assure the integrity of changed information in relation to the Active Directory replication process. One of these is the *tombstone* process, which is used to replicate deletions from one DC to another.

When an object is deleted within Active Directory, the ESE engine creates a transaction for it (as described in the previous section) and it is moved to the deleted object's container within the database. It is important to note that the object is not immediately purged from the database. There is a delay between when the item is deleted and when it is finally removed from the database altogether. This delay is known as the *tombstone interval* and is set at 60 days by default. The tombstone process exists to support the multimaster replication strategy of Windows Server 2003's Active Directory service. Each DC holds the object in its deleted items container for the length of the tombstone interval. The default of 60 days allows for plenty of time to pass and ensures that all DCs on the network have sufficient time to receive the delete request. When this interval is reached, the object is marked as *expired*.

You should ensure that backups are performed during the tombstone interval. Restores of directory service data older than the tombstone interval should not be performed to prevent the reintroduction of objects that were deleted during this period but have since been purged from the database.

The garbage collection process works in conjunction with the tombstone process. It runs every 12 hours on DCs by default, and one of its primary functions is to purge expired objects from the database. After the expired objects are purged, any remaining unnecessary log files are deleted and an online defragmentation of the database occurs. This consolidates the free space that was generated by the deletions and increases the performance of the database.

System State Data

System state data is a term Microsoft uses to refer to a set of core configuration information in Windows 2000, XP, and 2003. The actual information included in the system state depends on the underlying configuration of the operating system, and which components are installed.

System state data is most commonly associated with backup and restore operations. The backup tool released with Windows 2000 (and all subsequent versions) included the option to back up all of these critical open resources by selecting the system state backup option.

Fault Tolerance and Performance

You can take several key actions to ensure fault tolerance and maximize performance for the Active Directory database. Maintaining proper backups is, by far, the most important action you can take to provide fault tolerance. We discuss this in more detail later in the chapter. Defragmentation of the Active Directory database is also is a key performance component, and we cover this later in the chapter as well.

For performance reasons, Microsoft recommends that the Active Directory database and log files be on separate physical disk drives attached to separate hard drive controllers or channels. In other words, they recommend that each disk be in its own data path so that there is no contention between these components in the file system. This means that both drives can be read from and/or written to at the same time. This provides both fault tolerance and improved performance.

Performing Active Directory Maintenance Tasks

In this section, we'll look at some of the day-to-day and less routine tasks that you can expect to perform in the process of managing your Active Directory environment including offline and online AD defragmentation, moving the database files and backing up and restoring AD.

Defragmenting the Database

As mentioned previously, by default, Windows Server 2003 begins a maintenance cycle every 12 hours, known as the garbage collection process. The final portion of the Garbage Collection process is the performance of an online defragmentation and re-index of the Active Directory database. This is done to improve the performance of the database.

The Offline Defragmentation Process

Although Windows Server 2003 runs an online defragmentation twice per day by default, there might be times when you need to actually recover available free space from the Active Directory database file. This can only be done by performing an *offline defragmentation*. This type of defragmentation process is much more invasive than its online counterpart, and should be done only when absolutely necessary. For example, when the GC role is removed from a server, this information is deleted from its Active Directory database file, leaving a large amount of free space that can be recovered.

As with many invasive Active Directory database operations, you must be booted into a special mode known as the *Directory Services Restore Mode* to perform an offline defragmentation. The local administrator account is used when performing database maintenance operations in Directory Services Restore Mode.

You can access the Directory Services Restore Mode by booting or rebooting the computer, pressing the **F8** key when prompted, and selecting **Directory Services Restore Mode** from the Windows Advanced Options menu. You will be prompted to log on, and you must use the administrator account. Note that this account is not the domain administrator account; it is a special local account. The password for this local account is set during the installation of directory services on the local computer.

After you are authenticated by the local SAM, you can perform advanced directory services maintenance functions. Many of these are performed with the Ntdsutil utility.

To perform an offline defragmentation of the Active Directory database, use the following steps.

Perform an Offline Defragmentation of the Active Directory Database

1. Back up the system state data for fault tolerance purposes. See the *Backing Up Active Directory* section later in this chapter for more information.

2. Boot or reboot the computer.

3. When prompted, press **F8** during Windows Server 2003 startup.

4. Select **Directory Services Restore Mode (Windows DCs only)** on the Windows Advanced Options menu that appears, and press the **Enter** key.

5. Select your operating system (for example, **Windows Server 2003, Enterprise**), and press the **Enter** key.

6. You will see a number of checks performed while the system is booting, and you eventually will receive the Safe Mode logon prompt.

7. Log on by providing the password for the local administrator account and clicking the **OK** button.

8. Click the **OK** button in the dialog box that notifies you that Windows is running in safe mode.

9. Open a command prompt.

10. Type **ntdsutil** to enter the Ntdsutil utility. Note that this is a command-line utility, so the command prompt will change to ntdsutil:.

11. Type **files**. The command prompt should change to display file maintenance.

12. Type **compact to <*drive*>:\<*directory*>** to create a defragmented and compacted copy of the Active Directory database in the specified new location. For example, **compact to C:\ADTemp** creates a defragmented, re-indexed, and re-sized database file in the C:\ADTemp directory, as shown in Figure 19.2. The location specified can be on a local disk or on a mapped network drive. If there are spaces in the path where the file needs to be placed, it must be surrounded in quotes; for example, **"compact to c:\ad\july defrag"**.

Figure 19.2 The Ntdsutil Compact To Command

13. Type **quit** to return to the ntdsutil: prompt.

14. Type **quit** again to exit the utility.

15. Open Windows Explorer and rename the previously used **ntds.dit** file to **ntds.old.dit**.

<table>
<tr><td>

> **NOTE**
>
> Step 15 is not specified in Microsoft's instructions, but we recommend it for fault tolerance purposes. As mentioned, an offline defragmentation is very invasive. It is possible that the compacted file will be corrupt and that Active Directory will not start after the procedure. If you don't take this step, you will be forced to do a system state restore to recover the previous database file. By simply renaming the file, you can boot back into Directory Services Restore Mode, delete the corrupt file, and rename ntds.old.dit back to ntds.dit to recover the system.

</td></tr>
</table>

16. In Windows Explorer, copy the new **ntds.dit** file from the location you specified, using the **compact to** command to specify the location of the primary **ntds.dit** file location.

17. In Windows Explorer, delete all files that end with the .LOG extension in your Active Directory log files folder.

18. Close the command prompt window and reboot the server normally.

Moving the Database or Log Files

At some point, it might become necessary to move the Active Directory database or log files. Most often, this occurs because you need to move the files to a new hard drive or array of hard drives. Performance might dictate this decision. New faster drives and controllers can be used to replace slower ones as usage increases. The decision might also be dictated by a lack of free space as the Active Directory database and components grow.

Moving the database or log files is relatively simple. It is done from the command line using the Ntdsutil utility. Because the database and log files cannot be open when they are moved, the operation must be carried out while in Directory Services Restore Mode. The following steps outline how to move the Active Directory database and log files.

1. Back up the system state data for fault tolerance purposes. See the *Backing Up Active Directory* section later in this chapter for more information.

2. Boot or reboot the computer.

3. When prompted, press **F8** during Windows Server 2003 startup.

4. Select **Directory Services Restore Mode (Windows DCs only)** on the Windows Advanced Options menu that appears, and press the **Enter** key.

5. Select your operating system (for example, **Windows Server 2003, Enterprise**), and press the **Enter** key.

6. You will see a number of checks performed while the system is booting, and eventually you will receive the Safe Mode logon prompt.

7. Log on by providing the password for the local administrator account and clicking the **OK** button.

8. Click the **OK** button in the dialog box that notifies you that Windows is running in safe mode.

9. Open a command prompt.

10. Type **ntdsutil** to enter the Ntdsutil utility. This is a command-line utility so the command prompt will change to ntdsutil:.

11. Type **files**. The command prompt should change to display file maintenance:.

12. Use one of the following commands to move the Active Directory database or log files, or update their paths.

    ■ Type **move DB to <*drive*>:\<*directory*>** to move the ntds.dit database file to the new location specified. For example, **move DB to C:\AD** moves the database file to the C:\AD directory and updates the Registry to point to this new location, as shown in Figures 19.3 and 19.4.

    ■ Type **move logs to <*drive*>:\<*directory*>** to move the Active Directory log files to the new location specified. For example, **move logs to C:\AD** moves the log files to the C:\AD directory and updates the Registry to point to this new location.

Figure 19.3 Moving the Active Directory Database with Ntdsutil, First Screen Portion

Figure 19.4 Moving the Active Directory Database with Ntdsutil, Second Portion of the Screen

13. Ensure that the database (or log files) is now referenced in the proper location by typing **info**.

14. Type **quit** to return to the ntdsutil: prompt.

15. Type **quit** again to exit the utility.

16. Close the command prompt window and reboot the server normally.

Monitoring the Database

It's important to implement a consistent Active Directory monitoring strategy to ensure database integrity, reliability, and performance within your forest. Regular monitoring can also improve your knowledge of Active Directory and assist you in determining when a problem is in the early stages of unfolding. This will lead to performance and service issues being resolved in a much more timely manner.

It is important to remember that Active Directory does not exist in a vacuum. Performance and service issues that seem to relate to Active Directory can be caused by other key infrastructure components, such as name resolution services. In the following sections, we look at some of the primary tools that you can use to monitor Active Directory.

Using Event Viewer to Monitor Active Directory

You can use the Windows Server 2003 Event Viewer tool is accessed via **Start | Programs | Administrative Tools | Event Viewer**, to view a variety of event logs on the DC. For monitoring the directory service, the following event logs are of particular interest:

- **DNS Server** This event log displays information relating to the DNS server service if it is installed on the DC. It is common in small environments and remote offices to have a single server acting as both DC and DNS server (along with other roles). Because clients running Windows 2000 and later operating systems use DNS to locate DCs and GC servers, problems with this service can severely impact Active Directory availability on the network.

- **System** This event log displays critical information concerning the state of the operating system as a whole. Examining the System log should be part of the review procedure because underlying system stability is critical to optimum functionality of a DC. The System event log is also used to display messages that notify you when the DC's DNS record was not registered or updated properly.

- **Application** This event log displays extensive information from Group Policy and other related Active Directory components.

- **Directory Service** This is the primary event log for Active Directory. It includes information related to when the directory service starts and stops, the Garbage Collection process, online defragmentation, and much more.

- **File Replication Service** This service controls the replication of SYSVOL, which contains critical data such as Group Policy and replication topology connection information.

In a large domain, event logs can grow quite rapidly, which makes it difficult to search through them for key events. Microsoft recommends using the filter or search functionality to specifically seek out events matching the following criteria:

- All records with an Error severity level in the Directory Service or FRS event logs.

- All LSASS records in the System event log with a severity level of Error. The Local Security Authority subsystem (LSASS) is the primary security subsystem for Active Directory.

- All Kerberos V5 Key Distribution Center (KDC) records in the System event log with a severity level of Error. The KDC is the primary logon service for Windows 2000 and later clients in Active Directory.

- All USERENV records in the Application event log with a severity level of Error. This setting can indicate problems with the application of Group Policy.

Using the Performance Console to Monitor Active Directory

The Performance console is another tool that comes preinstalled in Windows Server 2003 and can be very helpful in monitoring Active Directory. The Performance console is accessed via **Start | Programs | Administrative Tools | Performance**, is capable of monitoring the server on which it is installed, and other remote servers. Data from any number of Windows Server 2003 computers can be combined for tracking or display purposes. Windows contains a variety of performance metrics that can be monitored with this utility. The Performance utility consists of the three following components:

- **System Monitor** This portion of the utility is used to graphically display performance metrics.

- **Counter and Trace logs** These options allow for detailed levels of logging over time. In most cases, you won't have time to sit around all day watching the System Monitor, which charts real-time information. Instead, you'll need data that you can review and work with when it is convenient.

- **Alerts** The Alerts option allows you to specify critical thresholds that, when exceeded, cause some type of action to take place. The default action is to have the alert generate a message in Event Viewer. You can also have it send a network message, start logging to a preconfigured counter log, or execute a script, batch file, or program.

The metrics that are monitored using the Performance console are called *counters*. These counters are grouped according to the *objects* to which they pertain. Figure 19.5 some of the counters available for the NTDS (directory services) object.

Figure 19.5 The Add Counters Dialog Box

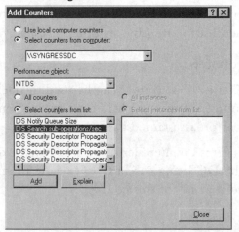

Microsoft recommends that you use the following performance counters for monitoring Active Directory:

- **NTDS performance object counters**:

  - **DRA inbound and outbound counters** These counters are used to track the amount of replication information that flows into and out of a site. Significant changes can indicate a major increase in the amount of replication traffic or a shift in the site replication topology.

  - **DS Search sub-operations/sec** Significant changes in this counter can indicate an application that is incorrectly targeting a DC, or performance problems involving the DC.

  - **LDAP Searches/sec** This counter corresponds to the overall number of LDAP searches per second on the DC. It should be relatively consistent across all of your DCs in a well-planned and balanced environment. If it isn't, this counter can indicate that an application is incorrectly targeting a DC (rather than spreading its use out across several DCs). It can also indicate uneven client loads. This counter is also useful for tracking trends over time for capacity planning.

  - **LDAP Client Sessions** This counter displays the number of clients that are connected to the LDAP services. It can also be used to track uneven client loads, which might be indicative of connection failures to other DCs in a well-planned and balanced environment. Like the LDAP Searches/sec counter, this counter is useful for tracking trends over time for capacity planning.

  - **NTLM Authentications** This counter indicates the number of domain authentications taking place using the NTLM protocol. Windows 2000 and later clients should use Kerberos for authentication, but will fail back to NTLM when they are unable to authenticate using Kerberos. This counter can be used to indicate Kerberos authentication issues in these types of environments.

  - **Kerberos Authentications** This counter indicates the number of domain authentications that take place using the Kerberos protocol. This counter is helpful in tracking authentication trends over time for capacity planning.

- **Processor object counters**:

  - **% Processor Time** This counter can be used to track the overall consumption of processor resources in the DC. Microsoft recommends that this counter not exceed 85 percent on a sustained basis.

  - **% DPC Time** This counter alerts you to delayed execution of processes resulting from the DC being too busy to execute them. Microsoft recommends a sustained threshold of 10 for this counter.

- **System object counters**:

  - **Processor Queue Length** This counter indicates that the system cannot keep up with processing requests. When you see the word *queue* in any counter, the counter tracks the number of things "waiting in line" to use the resource. Microsoft recommends that this counter not exceed a value of 6 on a sustained basis.

  - **Context Switches/sec** Most modern processors can only execute one thread at a time. Although it appears that the computer is running many programs at once, each program is actually sharing the processor with all others. Each *thread* (the smallest unit of executable code in a program) uses the processor for a short period of time and then passes it on to the next. This concept is referred to as *time slicing*. A context switch occurs when the processor switches between waiting processes. This counter can indicate too many applications (including operating system applications) for the processor to service, or applications that are too busy for the processor to keep up with. Microsoft recommends that this counter not exceed 70,000 on a sustained basis.

- **Memory object counters**:

  - **Page Faults/sec** This counter indicates when needed program code is not resident in memory and must be loaded from disk (from the page file). This is often an indication of a system in need of more physical RAM. Microsoft recommends a sustained threshold of 700 for this counter.

  - **Available MBytes** This counter indicates the amount of available system memory. Microsoft recommends using this counter to configure an alert that will notify you when the DC is running low on memory resources.

- **PhysicalDisk:Current Disk Queue Length counter** This counter can be used to track the number of disk reads and writes that are waiting to be filled. This can be the result of a busy processor that is not able to keep up with IRQ requests, or a slow disk drive or subsystem. Microsoft recommends that this counter not exceed a value of 2 on a sustained base.

Use the following steps to configure System Monitor to display the key NTDS object counters.

Use System Monitor to Monitor Active Directory

1. Open the Windows Server 2003 Performance console from **Start | Programs | Administrative Tools | Performance**.

2. Select the **System Monitor** node in the left pane.

3. In the right pane, right-click on the graph and select **Add Counters...** in the context menu that appears. Note that you can also click the **+** button on the toolbar above the graph to add a new counter.

4. In the **Add Counters** dialog box, select **NTDS** from the **Performance object:** drop-down box.

5. In the **Select counters from list:** box, select the **DS Search sub-operations/sec** counter.

6. Click the **Add** button.

7. Repeating steps 5 and 6 after each addition, add the following counters: **LDAP Searches/sec**, **LDAP Client Sessions**, **NTLM Authentications**, and **Kerberos Authentications**.

8. Click the **Close** button in the Add Counters dialog box.

9. Your new counters should appear in the list in the right pane under the graph, as shown in Figure 19.6. Select one of these counters by clicking on it in this list.

Figure 19.6 The Performance Console without Highlighting Enabled

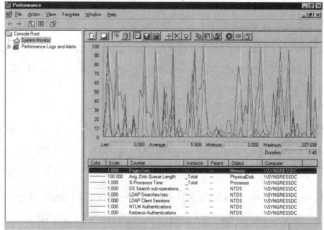

10. Press **Ctrl + H** to highlight the counter in the graph. This tool is often used to display a large number of counters, making it very difficult to tell them apart in the graph. Using the highlight feature makes this much easier.

11. Close the Performance console.

Backing Up and Restoring Active Directory

Although it's technically just a collection of files, Active Directory has its own unique backup and restore methods. In this section, we'll discuss backing up and restoring the Active Directory database.

Backing Up Active Directory

Several different methods can be used to back up Active Directory:

- As part of a full system backup
- As part of a partial system backup
- Back up the system state data only

In the past, the Active Directory database had to be backed up as system state data. Microsoft Backup and some other third-party backup programs are now able to use a new Windows Server 2003 feature known as the Volume Shadow Copy service to work around this open file issue.

Volume Shadow Copy makes a read-only copy of the information in these open files, which can be used for backup purposes. The original files continue to be accessed without any interference from the backup operation. When the backup is complete, the Volume Shadow Copy is deleted. The amount of disk space required by the Volume Shadow Copy will vary, based on the amount of data that changes on the disk during the backup procedure. If the underlying disk does not have enough free space to support Volume Shadow Copy, open files are not backed up.

When preparing a backup job, rather than specifying the individual files for Active Directory to be backed up, it is best to always use the *system state data* selection in the utility. System state will be backed up automatically when a full system backup is selected, and can be specified manually when a partial backup is selected. Using the system state backup feature ensures that all necessary files are backed up. When using the Windows Server 2003 backup utility, if you select system state data, Volume Shadow Copy is enabled by default and cannot be disabled. If you do not select system state data, you can choose to use Volume Shadow Copy (still selected by default) or not within the Backup Wizard.

Backing Up at the Command Line

Instead of using the graphical Backup utility, you can back up the system state data by using the command-line version of the Backup utility. This might be desirable for use with administrative scripts. The command-line utility is a full-featured backup program that can specify many of the same options covered in the previous section. To back up the system state data, open a command prompt (**Start | Run** and type **cmd)** and use the following command and options: **ntbackup backup systemstate /J "Syngress Backup Job" /F "C:\backupfile.bkf"**.

- **Ntbackup** is the name of the command-line backup utility.
- **Backup** is the option to specify a backup operation.
- **Systemstate** is the option used to specify that the system state data should be backed up.
- **/J** specifies the backup job name, which should be surrounded in quotes if it contains spaces.
- **/F** specifies the name of the backup file.

Note that when you run this command, the graphical utility appears to show you the progress of the job.

There are many more switches that you can use with the Ntbackup command-line utility; those described here are the ones you will most commonly use to back up the system state data.

Restoring Active Directory

Windows Server 2003 includes three types of directory services restore methods:

- Primary
- Normal
- Authoritative

The Active Directory restore options have seen some significant changes since Windows 2000. In Windows 2000, there were only two methods of restoration: Authoritative and Non-Authoritative. With Windows Server 2003, Authoritative restores remain unchanged; however, Non-Authoritative restores are now referred to as Normal restores. Despite the name change, they function exactly as they always have.

A new type of restore is added, the Primary restore. This is designed to be used when all DCs for a given domain have been wiped out and need to be restored. Under Windows 2000, this could be an exhaustive Authoritative restore process involving many hours of labor and double-checking. With the new Primary restore type, it is as simple as selecting a check box.

Directory Services Restore Mode

Before we discuss the three different restore methods that can be used, it is important to discuss the Directory Services Restore Mode. Remember that the special feature of this mode is that it allows a DC to boot without initializing its copy of the Active Directory database. Because you must always log on to a Windows Server 2003 computer before you can use the operating system, a small version of a local directory service database (called a SAM database) remains on the computer after it has been promoted to a DC. This database has a single account, the local administrator account.

When you have booted to the Directory Services Restore Mode using the directions given earlier in the chapter, you must log on with this account. After you are authenticated, you can perform certain limited maintenance functions, such as running the Ntdsutil utility mentioned earlier. You can also run the Backup utility to perform restores of the Active Directory database. It is necessary to perform all restores while running in this mode, because the Active Directory database must be offline to be restored. In this mode, you are logged on to a local account and the Active Directory database is not in use.

Normal Restore

The simplest of all restore methods is the normal restore. This method can be used in the following circumstances:

- When a domain only has one DC, and the DC needs to be restored. You can also opt to use the primary restore method (covered later) for this scenario.

■ If there are multiple DCs on the network for the domain, and at least one remains functional, a normal restore can be used to bring the downed DCs back to life.

Like all Active Directory restores, a normal restore is performed by running the Backup utility while logged on to Directory Services Restore Mode. When the restore has completed, the DC is rebooted. When it comes back up, it begins normal replication with its replication partners. Because it was restored from a backup, some of its objects will have older version numbers than ones currently on the network. This will cause updates and deletions to be replicated to the DC and will bring its Active Directory database up to date. To perform a normal restore, follow these steps:

1. Boot or reboot the computer.

2. When prompted, press **F8** during Windows Server 2003 startup.

3. Select **Directory Services Restore Mode (Windows DCs only)** in the **Windows Advanced Options** menu that appears, and press the **Enter** key.

4. Select your operating system (for example, **Windows Server 2003, Enterprise)**, and press the **Enter** key.

5. You will see a number of checks performed while the system is booting, and eventually you will receive the Safe Mode logon prompt.

6. Log on by providing the password for the local administrator account and clicking the **OK** button.

7. Click the **OK** button in the dialog box that notifies you that Windows is running in safe mode.

8. Open the Windows Server 2003 Backup utility from **Start | All Programs | Accessories | System Tools | Backup**.

9. On the initial page of the wizard, click the **Next** button.

10. Select the option button next to **Restore files and settings** and click the **Next** button.

11. The **What to Restore** page contains an Explorer style interface similar to the one you encountered while configuring your backup job. Click the plus sign next to **File** in the left pane. This should reveal the file to which you backed up the system state data earlier. If it doesn't, you can click the **Browse...** button and select the file from the **Open Backup File** dialog box. Click the plus sign next to the file to which you backed up and select the check box next to the backup you want to restore that appears beneath it. Click the **Next** button after making your selection.

12. At this point in the wizard, you can click the **Finish** button and allow the restore to proceed with the default advanced settings. However, we want you to see more of the settings that are available within the wizard, so click the **Advanced...** button.

13. The **Where to Restore** page appears with three options that can be selected from the **Restore files to:** drop-down box.

    ■ **Original location** This option restores all files to their original locations and is the default. When you select this option and click the **Next** button, a dialog box appears, informing you that restoring system state will always overwrite the current system state information unless you restore to an alternate location. Click the **OK** button to proceed to the next screen.

- **Alternate location** Selecting this option reveals the **Alternate location:** text box and a **Browse...** button that opens the **Restore Path** dialog box. You can use this option to restore the files to a different location. This can be helpful for verification and file comparison purposes.

- **Single folder** This option reveals the **Alternate location:** text box and **Browse...** button, which opens the **Restore Path** dialog box. As with the **Alternate location** setting, you can use this option to restore the files to an alternate location. When this option is selected, all restored files are placed in a single directory, rather than having their directory structures restored.

14. Click the **Next** button after making your selection.

15. Depending on your selection, a **Warning** dialog box (shown in Figure 19.7) might appear to inform you that a restore of system state data will always overwrite the current system state data unless you choose to restore it to an alternate location. Click the **OK** button if you receive this dialog box.

Figure 19.7 The System State Restore Warning Dialog Box

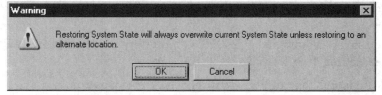

16. The **How to Restore** page contains the following three options:

- **Leave existing files (Recommended)** This option ensures that the restore process does not overwrite any files that currently exist on the DC.

- **Replace existing files if they are older than the backup files** This option permits the files on the disk to be overwritten, but only if the backup file is newer than the one currently on the DC.

- **Replace existing files** Always copies the files from the backup media to the DC and replaces all files existing on the DC, regardless of whether they are newer.

17. After making your selection, click the **Next** button to proceed.

18. The **Advanced Restore Options** page contains the following five check boxes:

- **Restore security settings** This option is selected by default, and should remain selected. It shows the power that a user with restore rights has, because any such user can, by deselecting this check box, restore the files without their associated permissions. In some circumstances, difficulties can arise when restoring data that was on a disk formatted in the NTFS file system, which supports file level permissions, to one using the FAT file system, which does not support file level permissions. In circumstances like these, clearing this check box has been known to resolve some of the issues. This is because selecting this box restores a wide range of extended data (permissions, auditing information, and ownership information) that is not supported by the FAT file system.

- **Restore junction points, but not the folders and file data they reference** Among other things, junction points are used to reference mounted drives. In Windows Server 2003, volumes can be mounted in folders of another volume, instead of being accessed through a drive letter. If you do not restore junction points, you will not be able to restore the information on mounted drives unless you recreate the junction points manually.

- **Preserve existing volume mount points** This option relates to the preceding point. When using mounted drives, it is necessary to create mount points, which are the empty folders to which the volume is mounted (thus creating the mounted drive). When selected, this box protects existing mount points on the volume being restored. This is helpful if you have already formatted the disk to which you are restoring and added these mount points prior to beginning the restore. However, if you have formatted the disk to which you are restoring and have not added these mount points back manually, clearing this check box will restore your old mount points from tape. This option is selected by default.

- **Restore the Cluster Registry to the quorum disk and all other nodes** This option restores the cluster quorum database and replicates it to all of the nodes in the server cluster. This option will be grayed out if the DC is not part of a server cluster.

- **When restoring replicated data sets, mark the restored data as the primary data for all replicas** This option is used to perform a primary restore and is covered in detail later in the chapter.

19. Click the **Next** button after making your selections.

20. Click the **Finish** button to begin the restore.

21. The restore will take at least a few minutes and display its progress as shown in Figure 19.8. When it is finished, click the **Close** button (shown in Figure 19.9) to close the **Restore Progress** dialog box, or click the **Report...** button to view the backup log associated with the job. Clicking the **Report...** button will display the Notepad application with the log file displayed, as shown in Figure 19.10. You should review the log for any error messages, such as those pertaining to files that had to be skipped. When you have finished reviewing the log, close the Notepad application.

Figure 19.8 The Restore Progress Dialog Box During a Restore

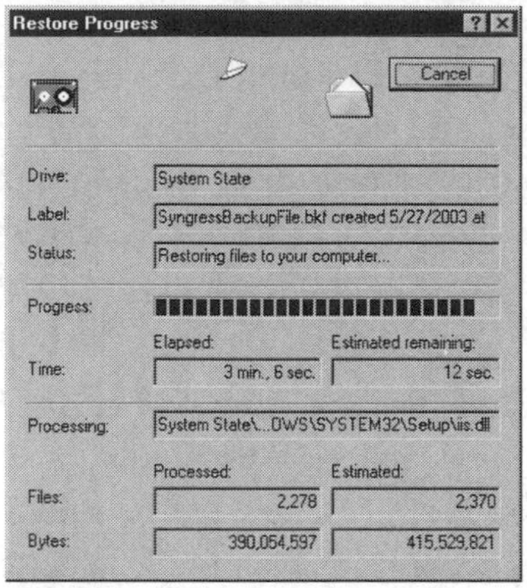

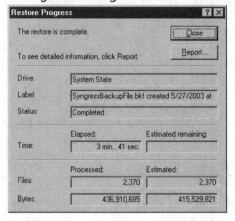

Figure 19.9 The Restore Progress Dialog Box After the Restore Has Completed

Figure 19.10 The Restore Log

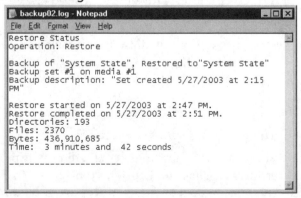

22.   Click the **Yes** button in the **Backup Utility** dialog box when prompted to restart and reboot the server normally.

Authoritative Restore

There are times when a normal restore of Active Directory isn't sufficient; for example, when you accidentally delete an OU. Within a few minutes, the deletion will have replicated to the other DCs in the domain. If you perform a normal restore in an effort to repopulate the OU back into Active Directory, it will not work. When the DC reboots after the restore and replicates with its replication partners, they will have a higher version number for the deleted OU, and the restored DC will be told to delete the object all over again. To restore the object, you must use an authoritative restore.

An authoritative restore is like a normal restore, up to a point. Once the system state data has been restored, rather than rebooting the server, the Ntdsutil command-line utility is used to mark one or more objects as *authoritative*. This gives them a very high version number so that when the server is rebooted and the replication process takes place, the other servers in the domain will see the high version number and replicate the object to their own Active Directory databases. To restore a database authoritatively, follow the steps from the preceding section up to number 18, and then proceed to these steps:

1. Click the **No** button in the **Backup Utility** dialog box when asked to restart.

2. Close the Backup utility, if it does not close by itself.

3. Open a command prompt (click **Start | Run** and type **cmd**).

4. Type **ntdsutil** to enter the Ntdsutil utility. Note that this is a command-line utility so the command prompt will change to ntdsutil:.

5. Type **authoritative restore**. The command prompt should change to display authoritative restore:.

6. Use one of the following commands to mark Active Directory or a portion of it as authoritative.

   - Type **restore database** to mark the domain and configuration containers of the database as authoritative. The schema container cannot be marked as authoritative; consequently, an authoritative restore can not be performed for the schema. Because you cannot delete objects from the schema, this is not an issue.

   - Type **restore subtree** followed by the distinguished name of the object in Active Directory that you want to restore; for example, **restore subtree OU=student,DC=syngress,DC=com** to restore the OU named "student" in the syngress.com domain.

   - The **verinc** option can be used with either the **restore database** or **restore subtree** command. Remember, when an object or the database is restored authoritatively, a large version number is applied to it. The **verinc** option is designed to be used when you need to perform another authoritative restore, on top of an existing authoritative restore. It allows you to choose your own version number, thus ensuring that it will be higher than the one used previously by the utility. The proper syntax is **restore database verinc %d** or **restore subtree**

\<distinguished name of object to mark authoritative\> verinc %d, with **%d** being the desired increment for the version number.

7. Click **Yes** in the **Authoritative Restore Confirmation** dialog box, as shown in Figure 19.11.

Figure 19.11 The Authoritative Restore Confirmation Dialog Box

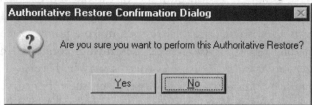

8. Review the screen output while the command completes. Figure 19.12 shows the completed operation.

Figure 19.12 The Completed Authoritative Restore Process

9. Type **quit** to return to the ntdsutil: prompt.
10. Type **quit** again to exit the utility.
11. Close the command prompt and reboot the server normally.

Primary Restore

The primary restore method is new in Windows Server 2003., and is designed for situations where all DCs for a given domain have gone down and you need to rebuild the domain from backup. The first server that is restored in this situation should be restored using this method. Additional DCs can be restored using the normal restore method. A primary restore is also the new preferred method to use when restoring what Microsoft refers to as a *standalone DC*, which means the DC in a domain with only one DC. If you have a domain with only one DC and that server goes down, use this method to restore it.

Performing a primary restore is similar to performing a normal restore. The only difference is that you select the check box next to **When restoring replicated data sets, mark the restored data as the primary data for all replicas** in the Advanced portion of the Restore wizard.

Troubleshooting Active Directory Availability

Microsoft recommends checking the Event Viewer logs and careful monitoring of performance counters as initial steps when troubleshooting Active Directory availability. Another important factor to consider when troubleshooting Active Directory is name resolution. Windows 2000 and later computers use the DNS service to locate Active Directory components, including GC servers and DCs.

Setting Logging Levels for Additional Detail

The default level of logging for all aspects of Active Directory is 0. This is the lowest level of logging, and while it guarantees that fatal and critical errors will be logged, it omits substantial amounts of information that can be beneficial when troubleshooting. The possible range is from 0 (which logs the least amount of information) to 5 (which logs the most). Most of the information is logged to the application log in Event Viewer.

Setting the logging value above 3 for any aspect of Active Directory can fill the application log very quickly and substantially degrade system performance. In general, the level should be elevated temporarily only in instances when you need more information for troubleshooting purposes.

There is a wide range of individual aspects of Active Directory for which you can specify individual logging levels by editing the Registry. All of the pertinent values are located in the HKEY_LOCAL_MACHINE\SYSTEM\CurrentControlSet\Services\NTDS\Diagnostics Registry subkey.

In addition to the additional detail that can be specified for logging to the Event Viewer, Active Directory provides log sources for tracking and troubleshooting purposes. These are located in the %SYSTEMROOT%\Debug folder. Included are logs that were created during the installation of AD that provide significant information about the configuration of Active Directory and its related services. When the maximum number of 5 log files is reached, the oldest is deleted and a new one is created in its place, and all existing log file names will be decremented by 1. New logs will also be created when existing logs get full. By default, these logs generally hold between 1.5 to 2.5MB of information before Active Directory considers them full.

Using Ntdsutil Command Options

A number of repair options within the Ntdsutil command-line utility provide assistance in ensuring the consistency of the database. In the following subsections, we'll examine the use of these options in troubleshooting and maintaining Active Directory health and availability.

Using the Integrity Command

The *integrity* command is used to detect low-level corruption of the database. It performs its work at the binary level, which means that it reads every byte of the ESE database structure looking for corruption. Note that although the ESE structure forms the basis of Active Directory, this command might not parse all Active Directory database information. Some critical Active Directory information is additional to and outside the knowledge of the *esentutl* command that this option uses. Because of the detailed checking it performs, this tool often takes a while to complete its operations.

In addition to the byte-level corruption check mentioned previously, the *Ntdsutil integrity* command also performs a full check on the integrity of the directory service files. After successfully running the command, Microsoft suggests that you perform a semantic database analysis (covered in a later section). The *Ntdsutil integrity* command must be performed when the database is offline, so you have to run it from Directory Services Restore Mode. To use the command, follow these steps:

1. Boot or reboot the computer.

2. When prompted, press **F8** during Windows Server 2003 startup.

3. Select **Directory Services Restore Mode (Windows DCs only)** in the **Windows Advanced Options** menu that appears, and press the **Enter** key.

4. Select your operating system (for example, **Windows Server 2003, Enterprise**), and press the **Enter** key.

5. You will see a number of checks performed while the system is booting, and eventually you will receive the Safe Mode logon prompt.

6. Log on by providing the password for the local administrator account and clicking the **OK** button.

7. Click the **OK** button in the dialog box that notifies you that Windows is running in safe mode.

8. Open a command prompt.

9. Type **ntdsutil** to enter the Ntdsutil utility. This is a command-line utility so the command prompt will change to **ntdsutil:**.

10. Type **files**. The command prompt should change to display **file maintenance:**.

11. Type **integrity**.

12. View and evaluate the information displayed on the screen as the process runs. Figure 19.13 shows an error-free display, and Figure 19.14 shows a display showing errors.

Figure 19.13 A Successful Integrity Check Showing No Errors

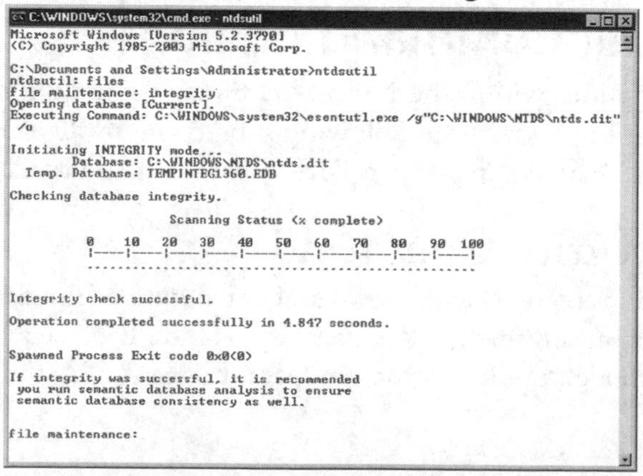

Figure 19.14 An Integrity Check Showing Errors

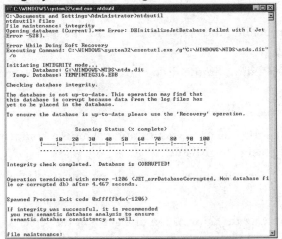

13. Type **quit** to return to the ntdsutil: prompt.

14. Type **quit** again to exit the utility.

15. Close the command prompt window and reboot the server normally.

Using the *recover* Command

Remember that transactions are written to log files before being committed to the Active Directory database file. In the event of power failure or other system problems, not all transactions will be written to the database. When the system is booted, ESE should use the checkpoint, log, and database files to determine what was committed properly to the database and what still needs to be written. Although this process works in most cases, occasionally inconsistencies result and it is necessary to run the process again manually. The *recover* command performs a "soft" recovery of the database log files, which means that it writes transactions from the log files to the directory service database. This process is sometimes also referred to as "re-running" the log files manually.

Like the other commands used in conjunction with the *Ntdsutil* command, the *recover* command must be run from Directory Services Restore Mode. As with the other maintenance commands covered in this section, Microsoft recommends running a semantic database analysis after the *recover* command has completed successfully. To run the *recover* command, follow these steps:

1. Boot or reboot the computer.

2. When prompted, press **F8** during Windows Server 2003 startup.

3. Select **Directory Services Restore Mode (Windows DCs only)** in the Windows Advanced Options menu that appears, and press the **Enter** key.

4. Select your operating system (for example, **Windows Server 2003, Enterprise**), and press the **Enter** key.

5. You will see a number of checks performed while the system is booting, and eventually you will receive the Safe Mode logon prompt.

6. Log on by providing the password for the local administrator account and clicking the **OK** button.

7. Click the **OK** button in the dialog box that notifies you that Windows is running in safe mode.

8. Open a command prompt.

9. Type **ntdsutil** to enter the Ntdsutil utility. This is a command-line utility, so the command prompt will change to **ntdsutil:**.

10. Type **files**. The command prompt should change to display **file maintenance:**.

11. Type **recover**.

12. View and evaluate the information displayed on the screen as the process runs. Figure 19.15 shows a successful recover operation, and Figure 19.16 shows a failed recover operation.

Figure 19.15 A Successful Recover Operation

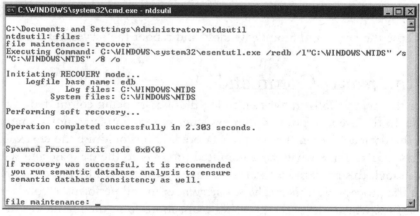

Figure 19.16 A Failed Recover Operation

13. Type **quit** to return to the **ntdsutil:** prompt.

14. Type **quit** again to exit the utility.

15. Close the command prompt window.

Using the Semantic Database Analysis Command

The *semantic database analysis* command is the primary command that is used to verify the full integrity of the Active Directory database. You might be wondering what the difference is between this command and the *integrity* command from the **files:** prompt. Recall that the *integrity* command works by calling the **Esentutl** utility, which has full knowledge of the ESE database system but not necessarily all portions of the Active Directory database. The *semantic database analysis* command is specific to Active Directory and does not use the *Esentutl* command. As its name implies, it analyzes the Active Directory database, based on Active Directory semantics (whereas the *integrity* command bases its check on ESENT database semantics). Running *semantic database analysis* includes checks for the following:

- **Reference counts**
    - Counts references from the data table and the link table to ensure that they match the listed counts for the record.
    - Ensures that each object has a full distinguished name, GUID, and nonzero reference count.
    - For each deleted object, the utility verifies that it does not have a distinguished name or GUID and makes sure that it has a deleted time and date.

- **Deleted objects**
    - Verifies that the object has a deleted time and date.
    - Ensures that the object has a special relative distinguished name.

- **Ancestor checks** Determines if the Distinguished Name Tag is equal to:
    - The ancestor list of the parent
    - The current Distinguished Name Tag

- **Security descriptor checks**
    - Verifies a valid descriptor.
    - Ensures that it has a control field.
    - Verifies that the discretionary access control list is not empty.
    - A warning is generated if deleted objects without a discretionary control access list are located.

- **Replication checks**

  - Checks the up-to-dateness vector in the directory partition head to ensure that the correct number of cursors exist.

  - Checks to ensure that every object has a property metadata vector.

Errors generated by the *semantic database analysis* command are written to dsdit.dmp.xx log files, which are located in the profile directory of the user running the utility (for example, C:\Documents and Settings\Administrator). As with most low-level database tools, this command must be run when the database is not initialized (in other words, in Directory Services Restore Mode). Microsoft recommends that you perform a full backup of the system state data prior to running this command. Follow these steps to perform a semantic database check:

1. Boot or reboot the computer.

2. When prompted, press **F8** during Windows Server 2003 startup.

3. Select **Directory Services Restore Mode (Windows DCs only)** in the **Windows Advanced Options** menu that appears, and press the **Enter** key.

4. Select your operating system (for example, **Windows Server 2003, Enterprise**), and press the **Enter** key.

5. You will see a number of checks performed while the system is booting, and eventually you will receive the Safe Mode logon prompt.

6. Log on by providing the password for the local administrator account and clicking the **OK** button.

7. Click the **OK** button in the dialog box that notifies you that Windows is running in safe mode.

8. Open a command prompt.

9. Type **ntdsutil** to enter the Ntdsutil utility. This is a command-line utility, so the command prompt will change to **ntdsutil:**.

10. Type **Semantic database analysis**, and press the **Enter** key.

11. At the **semantic checker:** prompt, type **Verbose on**, and press **Enter**. This option displays the Semantic Checker.

12. Choose one of the following options:

    - To start the Semantic Checker and not have it repair any of the errors it encounters, type **Go**, and press the **Enter** key.

    - To start the Semantic Checker and have it repair the errors it encounters, type **Go Fixup**, and press the **Enter** key.

13. View and evaluate the information displayed on the screen as the process runs. There is very little difference visually between the two modes. Figure 19.17 shows the **go** mode.

Figure 19.17 Semantic Database Analysis Using Go Mode

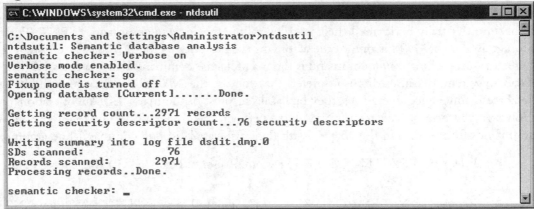

```
C:\WINDOWS\system32\cmd.exe - ntdsutil

C:\Documents and Settings\Administrator>ntdsutil
ntdsutil: Semantic database analysis
semantic checker: Verbose on
Verbose mode enabled.
semantic checker: go
Fixup mode is turned off
Opening database [Current].......Done.

Getting record count...2971 records
Getting security descriptor count...76 security descriptors

Writing summary into log file dsdit.dmp.0
SDs scanned:            76
Records scanned:       2971
Processing records..Done.

semantic checker: _
```

14. Type **quit** or **q** to return to the ntdsutil: prompt.

15. Type **quit** or **q** again to exit the utility.

16. Close the command prompt window.

17. Navigate to your profile directory and use Notepad to open the log file (shown in Figure 19.18) that you saw in step 15 (for example, dsdit.dmp.0).

Figure 19.18 The Log File Produced by Semantic Database Analysis Go Mode

```
dsdit.dmp.0 - Notepad
File Edit Format View Help
Property Metadata vector missing for 2($ROOT_OBJECT$)
INFO: UpToDate vector found for NC head 1458(syngress)
INFO: UpToDate vector found for NC head 1459(Configuration)
WARNING: Deleted object 1471 has timestamp[12/29/9999] later than now
WARNING: Deleted object 1477 has timestamp[12/29/9999] later than now
INFO: UpToDate vector found for NC head 1480(Schema)
Warning SE_DACL_PROTECTED for 1687(VolumeTable)
Warning SE_DACL_PROTECTED for 1693({31B2F340-016D-11D2-945F-00C04FB984F9})
Warning SE_DACL_PROTECTED for 1696({6AC1786C-016F-11D2-945F-00C04FB984F9})
Warning SE_DACL_PROTECTED for 1743(AdminSDHolder)
Warning SE_DACL_PROTECTED for 1746(WMIPolicy)
Warning SE_DACL_PROTECTED for 1748(SOM)
Warning SE_DACL_PROTECTED for 1814(Administrator)
Warning SE_DACL_PROTECTED for 1820(Administrators)
Warning SE_DACL_PROTECTED for 1825(Print operators)
Warning SE_DACL_PROTECTED for 1826(Backup Operators)
Warning SE_DACL_PROTECTED for 1827(Replicator)
Warning SE_DACL_PROTECTED for 1859(krbtgt)
Warning SE_DACL_PROTECTED for 1861(Domain Controllers)
Warning SE_DACL_PROTECTED for 1862(Schema Admins)
Warning SE_DACL_PROTECTED for 1863(Enterprise Admins)
Warning SE_DACL_PROTECTED for 1865(Domain Admins)
Warning SE_DACL_PROTECTED for 1870(Server Operators)
Warning SE_DACL_PROTECTED for 1871(Account operators)
INFO: UpToDate vector found for NC head 1885(DomainDnsZones)
WARNING: Deleted object 1888 has timestamp[12/29/9999] later than now
INFO: UpToDate vector found for NC head 1895(ForestDnsZones)
WARNING: Deleted object 1898 has timestamp[12/29/9999] later than now
2971 total records walked.
Summary:
Active Objects     2960
Phantoms              1
Deleted              10
Security descriptor summary:
SD count:            76
Total SD size before single-instancing:          815 Kb
Total SD size after single-instancing:            69 Kb
```

18. View the contents of the log, paying careful attention to any warning messages, and then close Notepad.

19. Reboot the server normally.

Using the *esentutl* Command

Although all of the operations covered previously in this section used the Ntdsutil command-line utility, most actually performed their work by calling the *Esentutl* command. ESENT (Extensible Storage Engine for NT) is one of the acronyms used to refer to the ESE database system that Active Directory uses. The *Esentutl* command is the maintenance command that is associated with this database system. Because Microsoft prefers that you use the *Ntdsutil* command for all low-level database maintenance operations, they built calls to most of the major *Esentutl* operations into it. However, you do not have to use Ntdsutil to perform these operations. The following are two of the commands from earlier in the chapter with their associated *Esentutl* command-line arguments:

- **Integrity** %SYSTEMROOT% \System32\esentutl.exe /g "C:\Windows\NTDS\ntds.dit" /o

- **Recover** %SYSTEMROOT%\System32\esentutl.exe /redb /l"C:\Windows\NTDS" /s "C:\WINNT\NTDS" /8 /o

The *esentutl.exe* command used in conjunction with the /p switch, shown in Figure 19.19, is considered the most dangerous of all the low-level database commands. In Windows 2000, this command was available as the *repair* option in Ntdsutil, and has been removed in the version of Ntdsutil that ships with Windows Server 2003. This option performs a very low-level and highly invasive binary database repair operation. It is very likely that you will lose some data when using this option, and it is highly possible that it will be data essential to your Active Directory database.

You should use this command with the /p switch only when you have been advised to do so by Microsoft support personnel, or when you feel that you have tried everything else to get Active Directory to initialize. *Always make a backup of your database file before you run this utility.* In most cases, you will be resorting to this option when Active Directory can no longer initialize, and you will be booted to Directory Services Restore Mode. The simplest way to back up the database and related components in this scenario is to copy them to a second location in the file system, using Windows Explorer.

If Active Directory can initialize and you still feel you should (or Microsoft tech support asks you to) run this command, you must boot into Directory Services Restore Mode first. The database must be offline for low-level operations such as this. Microsoft recommends running a semantic database analysis after this command has completed successfully. To use the *repair* command, enter the following at a command prompt: **%SYSTEMROOT%\system32\esentutl.exe /p "C:\Windows\NTDS\ntds.dit" /!10240 /8 /o**

Figure 19.19 The *esentutl* Repair Process

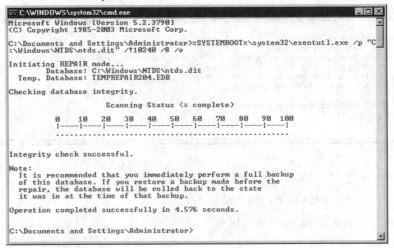

Changing the Directory Services Restore Mode Password

Because the Directory Services Restore Mode password is set during the installation of Active Directory, administrators often have difficulty remembering the password that was used when it is needed later. Fortunately, there is a way to change this password without having to remember what it was originally: by using the Ntdsutil command-line utility. To use this feature, the server on which you want to change the password cannot be running in Directory Services Restore Mode. Ntdsutil can be used to change the password on the DC locally, or another DC within the forest. To change the Directory Services Restore Mode password, follow these steps:

1. Open a command prompt.

2. Type **ntdsutil** to enter the **Ntdsutil** utility. This is a command-line utility, so the command prompt will change to **ntdsutil:**.

3. Type **Set DSRM Password**.

4. At the **Reset DSRM Administrator Password:** prompt, type **Reset Password on server *<SERVER NAME>*.**

5. At the **Please type password for DS Restore Mode Administrator Account:** prompt, type the new password that you want to use.

6. At the **Please confirm new password:** prompt, re-type the new password that you want to use.

7. Review the feedback on the screen to ensure that the operation was successful. Figure 19.20 shows the full procedure.

Figure 19.20 Using *Ntdsutil* to Reset the DSRM Password on a Server

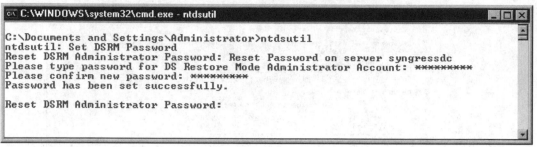

8. Type **quit** or **q** to return to the ntdsutil: prompt.

9. Type **quit** or **q** again to exit the utility.

10. Close the command prompt window.

Chapter 20

Planning, Implementing, and Maintaining a Name Resolution Strategy

In this chapter:

- ☑ **Planning for Host Name Resolution**

- ☑ **Planning for NetBIOS Name Resolution**

- ☑ **Troubleshooting Name Resolution Issues**

Introduction

In this chapter, you'll learn how to plan for the best way of resolving host and NetBIOS names on your network. We'll discuss issues involved in designing a DNS namespace, such as choosing the parent domain name, the conventions and limitations that govern host names, the relationship of DNS and Active Directory (AD), and how to support multiple namespaces.

Then we move onto planning DNS server deployment. You'll find out how to consider factors such as the number of servers, server roles, server capacity, and server placement. We'll also show you how to plan for zone replication between your DNS servers, and we'll address planning for forwarding and how DNS interacts with the Dynamic Host Configuration Protocol (DHCP) on a Windows Server 2003 network. We'll discuss Windows Server 2003 DNS server interoperability with Berkeley Internet Name Domain (BIND) and other non-Windows DNS implementations. You'll learn about zone transfers between Windows Server 2003 DNS servers and BIND servers, and we'll discuss supporting AD with BIND. You'll learn about split DNS configurations and how interoperability relates to other services such as Windows Internet Name Service (WINS) and DHCP. Next, we'll address DNS security issues, including common DNS threats such as footprinting, redirection, and DNS denial-of-service (DoS) attacks. You'll learn how to best secure your DNS deployment by using a split namespace and packet filtering. We'll discuss how to determine the best DNS security level for your network. Next, we'll look at DNS performance issues. We'll show you how to monitor DNS server performance and how to analyze DNS server tests.

In the next section, you'll find out what's new for WINS in Windows Server 2003, and we'll show you how to plan WINS server deployment and WINS replication. We'll walk you through the process of configuring WINS replication partnerships, including push-only, pull-only, and push/pull configurations. We'll also discuss common WINS issues, including configuration, performance, and security issues. We'll show you how to plan for WINS database backup and how to troubleshoot name resolution problems related to both host names and NetBIOS names.

Planning for Host Name Resolution

One of the most common sources of trouble on any Windows network—whether it's a Windows NT, Windows 2000, or Windows Server 2003 network—is faulty name resolution. When name resolution (the process of finding the IP addresses associated with computer names and services running on those computers) is not working perfectly, a multitude of problems can arise, including (but not limited to) the following:

- Users might not be able to log on to the network.

- Users might not be able to connect to applications and services residing on remoter computers.

- Domain controllers might not be able to communicate with each other.

In fact, problems with name resolution are so common that a typical first step in troubleshooting problems on a Windows network is to ensure that name resolution is working flawlessly. A common mantra that reflects this situation is the following: "The problem is irrelevant. The answer is DNS." Although this is a gross oversimplification of the problems that can arise on a Windows network, it does contain a germ of truth.

Planning for host name resolution on a Windows Server 2003 network means developing and implementing a fault-tolerant and secure strategy, whereby host computers on the network are always able to resolve computer names to IP addresses and locate services running on the network in a timely manner. On a Windows Server 2003 network, the primary mechanism for locating the domain controllers is host name resolution through DNS.

DNS Name Resolution Process

Distributing DNS Resource Records (RRs) among many different zones and domains has an effect on the name resolution process that needs to occur for a DNS client to find a host name-to-IP address mapping. Let's take the example of a client trying to connect to www.research.microsoft.com. The DNS client is configured to use another DNS server to perform *recursion* on its behalf. (Performing recursion simply means that the DNS server will issue *iterative queries* to other DNS servers and accept referrals from these servers, until it receives a positive or a negative response, and then forward that response to the DNS client.) The DNS client issues a *recursive query* to the DNS server; the DNS server subsequently issues a series of iterative queries to resolve the name. Figure 20.1 shows the process that occurs in order to resolve www.research.microsoft.com to the IP address.

Figure 20.1 DNS Server Issuing Iterative Queries to Resolve an IP Address on Behalf of a DNS Client

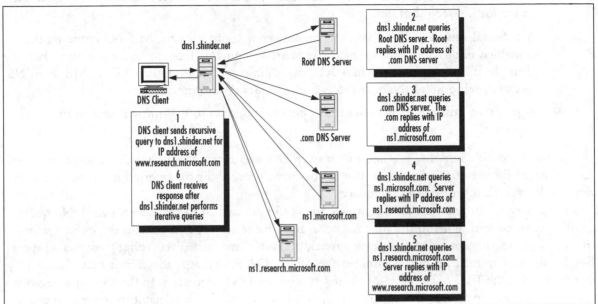

The process of recursion begins with the contacting of the root DNS servers, which are authoritative for the top-level domain on the Internet. To find these authoritative servers, the DNS server will consult its *root hints file*, which is a list of RRs that provides information about the name servers that are authoritative for the top-level domain on the Internet. Windows 2000 and Windows Server 2003 servers will automatically install this file when you install the DNS service on your server, in most circumstances. You can also get the most current version of this file from ftp://rs.internic.net/domain/named.root.

Note that the root hints file is present on the DNS server *only* if the DNS server has *not* itself been configured with a root, or **.**, zone. If this zone is present on your DNS server, it means that this server is the highest level of authority for the root domain, and the server will not be able to perform DNS queries on the Internet. If you use the Dcpromo utility to install and configure the DNS server as a prerequisite for installing a domain controller, that utility will automatically configure the DNS server with the **.** zone. If you wish to use the root hints file on this server to perform recursion on the Internet, you will need to first delete the **.** zone from the DNS server.

This recursion process assumes that no information about the FQDN for www.research.microsoft.com is cached on either the DNS client or dns1. However, over a period of time, dns1 would cache information about the domain namespace and would learn the IP addresses of authoritative name servers for domains and hosts on the Internet, thereby eliminating steps and speeding up the process of name resolution. But even without cached information, DNS host name resolution is very efficient, because it will normally use small UDP packets (512 bytes), unless the response is too large to be contained in a single UDP packet; in which case, TCP will be used.

In our example, three kinds of common responses to DNS queries are used:

- **An authoritative answer** This means that a response is sent from a server that is authoritative for the record of domain.

- **A referral answer** This means that an answer was sent back to the DNS requester that contained information not originally requested to provide hints to find the answer. For example, if the request is for an A RR, the DNS server might return a CNAME or an NS record in response to the query to help the requester find the answer.

- **A positive answer** This means that a positive response to the query is sent to the requester.

A fourth possible response is a negative answer. This means that the authoritative server does not have a record for the queried name or that it does have a record for the queried name, but for a different RR type than specified in the query.

Regardless of the answer that is returned, the results are cached so that subsequent DNS queries can be answered with nonauthoritative responses from name servers that contain the cached information. With the exception of a negative answer, the results are cached according to the value specified for the minimum TTL in the authoritative zone's SOA RR; that is, the authoritative name server controls the TTL of the RR for cached records on DNS requesters. In the case of a negative response, this information is also cached for a period of five minutes by default to prevent unnecessary consumption of resources if the name is queried again. The period for caching negative responses is relatively short, to allow the query to be resolved if the RR becomes available in the future. Negative caching is a DNS standard that is documented in RFC 2308.

It is possible to set up *caching-only* DNS servers. These are DNS servers that contain no zone information and function only to provide support for the recursion process for DNS clients. We will discuss the various DNS server roles later in this chapter.

Forward versus Reverse Lookup Zones

In most of the preceding discussion, we have focused on *forward lookup zones*. These are DNS data files that provide answers to *forward* queries that ask for the IP address of a particular FQDN. However, *reverse lookup zones* are also widely used to provide answers to *reverse* queries that ask for the FQDN of a particular IP address. For example, if you wanted to find the FQDN associated with a particular IP address, you would perform a reverse lookup against a reverse lookup zone.

To handle reverse lookups, a special root domain called in-addr.arpa was created. Subdomains within the in-addr.arpa domain are created using the reverse ordering of the octets that form an IP address. In order for reverse lookup zones to work properly, they use a special RR called a PTR record, which provides the mapping of the IP address in the zone to the FQDN.

Reverse lookup zones are used by certain applications, such as NSLookup (an important diagnostic tool that should be part of every DNS administrator's arsenal). If a reverse lookup zone is not configured on the server to which NSLookup is pointing, you will get an error message when you invoke the nslookup command.

Install Windows Server 2003 DNS Service and Configure Forward and Reverse Lookup Zones

This procedure assumes that a single Windows Server 2003 server is installed as a stand-alone server and is not a member of any domain.

Before you install the DNS service, you might wish to ensure that the domain name in the FQDN for the computer name matches the domain name of the DNS forward lookup zone you plan to install. It is not a requirement that the domain name of the FQDN and the DNS forward lookup zone match. However, if they do match, you will find that Windows Server 2003 adds the appropriate records to the forward lookup zone for the DNS server. To change the FQDN for the computer, follow these steps:

1. On the Windows Server 2003 desktop, right-click the **My Computer** icon and select **Properties** from the context menu.

2. Select the **Computer Name** tab, and then click the **Change** button.

3. In the **Computer Name Changes** property pages, click the **More** button.

4. In the **DNS Suffix and NetBIOS Computer Name** property page, change the primary DNS suffix to **tacteam.local** (or a name of your own choosing) and click **OK.** Reboot the computer when prompted.

Another prerequisite for installing DNS is that your TCP/IP properties should be configured with a static IP address and the primary DNS settings should be configured to point to the address of the computer on which you are installing DNS. To configure TCP/IP properties, follow these steps:

1. On the Windows Server 2003 desktop, right-click the **My Network Places** icon and select **Properties** from the context menu.

2. In the **Network Connections** folder, right-click the **Local Area Connection** icon and select **Properties** from the context menu.

3. Highlight TCP/IP, and then select Properties.

4. In the **TCP/IP** properties page, configure a static IP address, and then configure the primary DNS server settings to point to the IP address of the server. (For the examples in this chapter, we are using addresses on the **192.168.100.0/24** network.)

After you have configured your computer with the appropriate FQDN and IP address, you can install the DNS service. There are a couple of ways you can do this. You can install the DNS service through the **Manage Your Server** page that appears when you first log on to your Windows Server 2003 computer, or you can install the service through **Control Panel | Add/Remove Programs | Windows Components**. In this example, we will install the service through **Control Panel**. To install the DNS service, follow these steps:

1. Select **Start | Control Panel | Add or Remove Programs**.

2. Select **Add/Remove Windows Components**.

3. In the Windows Component Wizard dialog box, scroll down the list of Windows components, highlight **Networking Services**, and then click **Details**.

4. In the Networking Services dialog box, click **Domain Name System** (DNS) to place a check mark in its box, and then click **OK**.

5. If prompted, insert the Windows Server 2003 source CD to provide the installation files for the DNS service, or enter the name of a network path to the installation files.

The DNS service is now installed on your Windows Server 2003 computer. By default, the DNS server is installed with the root hints file and will resolve queries to the Internet. If you have an Internet connection, you can verify this by using the browser on the Windows Server 2003 server and connecting to a Web site. (Alternatively, you can verify this by performing the test labeled **Perform a recursive query to other DNS servers**, which you can find in the DNS console on the **Monitoring** tab of the properties of the DNS server.)

Next, we cover the steps to add a forward lookup zone. We begin by creating a standard primary forward lookup zone:

1. Navigate to the DNS console by selecting **Start | Programs | Administrative Tools | DNS**. (You can also invoke the DNS console through the **Manage Your Server** page that is displayed when logging on to the Windows Server 2003 computer.)

2. In the DNS console, right-click **Forward Lookup Zones** and click **New Zone** in the context menu.

3. The **New Zone Wizard** appears. Click **Next**. Ensure **Primary Zone** is selected as the zone type and click **Next**.

4. Type in **tacteam.local** as the zone name, and then click **Next**. (You can also type in a domain name of your own choosing. For ease of configuration later, it should match the domain name portion of the FQDN of the computer name.)

5. Select the option to **Create a new file with this name.** (A filename has already been created based on the domain name.) Click **Next**.

6. On the subsequent page, click **Next** again to accept the default setting not to allow dynamic updates, and then click **Finish**.

We now need to verify the records in the new zone. To do this, perform these steps:

1. In the DNS console, expand **Forward Lookup Zones,** and then click the zone you just created.

2. Examine the contents of the zone on the right side of the window. You should see three records: an SOA, an NS, and a Host (A) record. If you are missing any of these records, the reason is that the domain you chose to create did not match the domain in the FQDN for the computer name, or the TCP/IP configuration was not pointing to the configured IP address for the primary DNS.

We now can create a reverse lookup zone. The reverse lookup zone is used to resolve IP addresses to names. In addition, if we want to use NSLookup to query the DNS server, we need a reverse lookup zone containing a PTR RR that points to the authoritative DNS server in the zone.

The domain name will be based on the IP subnet and the suffix, in-addr.arpa. In these examples, we are using the subnet 192.168.100.0/24, so the reverse lookup domain will be 100.168.192.in-addr.arpa.

1. In the DNS console, right-click **Reverse Lookup Zones** and click **New Zone** in the context menu.

2. Follow the previous steps for creating a forward lookup zone. However, you will need to type the network ID of your network when prompted. (The **New Zone Wizard** will create the appropriate domain name based on your network ID, so do not change the order of the octets in your address. If you are following the setup for these examples, you should type **192.168.100** as the network ID in the Wizard.)

After you have created the reverse lookup zone, examine the records that are created in it. You should see only two records: an SOA record and an NS record. Open a command prompt and invoke the **nslookup** command. You should see an error message, such as the following:

```
*** Can't find server name for address 192.168.100.21: Non-existent
    domain
Default Server:  UnKnown
Address:  192.168.100.21
```

To correct this situation, we need to add a PTR RR for the DNS server. To do so, follow these steps:

1. Right-click the reverse lookup zone you just created and select **New Pointer (PTR)** from the context menu.

2. In the **New Resource Record** dialog box, enter the host ID for the DNS server (the last number in the IP address), click **Browse,** and navigate to the A record for your DNS server in the forward lookup zone you created previously.

3. Finish creating the record. You should now have a PTR record in addition to the NS and SOA records. To verify the record is correct, invoke the **nslookup** command from a command prompt. You should see the name of the DNS server (instead of "Unknown") in the output.

Now that you have installed a DNS server and have created forward and reverse lookup zones, you will be able to explore and examine DNS server settings. You should use the **New Delegation Wizard** to create a delegation of authority to a subdomain of the domain you just created. To create a delegation of authority from a parent domain, right-click the forward lookup zone for the parent domain and select **New Delegation**. Follow the steps presented by the Wizard.

It's obviously better if a DNS server that is authoritative for the subdomain actually exists, but if this is not the case, you can still create the records used to delegate authority. If you are able, you should install a second Windows Server 2003 server to further explore the features of DNS, such zone transfers, stub domains, and so on. This server can be installed on a virtual machine using VMware; you can run multiple virtual machines, all of which can communicate with one another on the network.

Designing a DNS Namespace

Designing a DNS namespace is a critically important function for any business that relies on both the public and the private identities provided by the DNS namespace(s) for interaction with its customers and for the smooth and secure operation of its network. You should take some of the following considerations into account:

- **Uniqueness** Domain names on the Internet must be unique. Although it is not a requirement that your internal domain namespace be unique, it is prudent to ensure its uniqueness.

- **Integration and interaction of public and private DNS namespaces** It is possible to use the same or different DNS namespace(s) for the public and private networks. Each of these alternatives provides different challenges. To separate the public and private zones requires both planning and administrative effort.

- **Security** Designing a DNS namespace should take into account the security requirements and configuration of your network. For example, it is extremely inadvisable to allow any RRs that are specific to your internal network to be publicly available through DNS queries. You should set up separate name servers to respond to queries for the IP addresses of the organization's Internet hosts, such as Web and mail servers. Deploying a private root zone can also help to enhance the security of your DNS infrastructure. Additionally, you need to consider firewall placement and access rules when designing the DNS namespace.

- **Administration** The design of the DNS namespace will affect administration. For example, using the same domain namespace for both the private and the public networks will require, at a minimum, a split DNS configuration, where two name servers (one that is authoritative for the public RRs and one that is authoritative for the private RRs) will need to be implemented and maintained. In this scenario, special configurations might need to be implemented to allow users on the corporate network to connect to the organization's public Web servers.

Host Naming Conventions and Limitations

Regardless of the choice you make for the domain namespace of your internal and external networks, you should abide by host naming conventions and limitations. According to RFC 1123, "Requirements for Internet Hosts—Application and Support," which defines naming standards for host names, the following US-ASCII–based characters are allowed:

- Uppercase letters (A through Z)

- Lowercase letters (a through z)

- Numbers (0 through 9)

- The hyphen (-)

Note that, according to RFC 1053, DNS resolution is supposed to be case-insensitive. For this reason, the Microsoft DNS service will "downcase" any uppercase characters that it encounters to lowercase (it is an *optional* requirement that case be preserved for use with DNS; to ensure maximum compatibility Microsoft does not implement the optional requirement for case preservation). In other words, all uppercase characters will be treated as lowercase characters.

To allow for the use of more characters than are available with US-ASCII, Windows 2000 and Windows Server 2003 DNS servers provide support by default for UTF-8, which is a *Unicode Transformation Format*. Furthermore, Windows 2000 and higher client operating systems, such as Windows XP, are UTF-8 aware.

UTF-8 is a superset of extended ASCII and additionally provides support for UCS-2, which is a Unicode character set that allows for the use of the majority of the world's writing systems. UTF-8 is backward-compatible with US-ASCII in that the binary representations of characters are identical between the two formats. It is important to remember that not all DNS servers are UTF-8–aware. It is also possible to turn off UTF-8 support on individual Microsoft DNS servers by configuring the name-checking format in the DNS server property pages. Therefore, care must be taken in environments where not all name servers support UTF-8. In particular, when zone information is being transferred between UTF-8 and non–UTF-8 name servers, the zone can fail to reload on servers that do not support UTF-8 if the zone contains UTF-8 information.

The Underscore Character

While it is legitimate to use the underscore character in NetBIOS names, the inclusion of this character in a host name is problematic in environments that use older DNS standards in which its use is prohibited. (The underscore character is allowed in domain names, however, so its use is legitimate in SRV records.) Support for UTF-8 guarantees that the underscore character can be used safely in Microsoft environments. In fact, the underscore is a reserved character that is used extensively in Microsoft DNS to identify SRV records, as per RFC 2782. However, third-party standard DNS servers, such as older UNIX BIND DNS servers, might not recognize host records that use the underscore. Consequently, host names, especially those used by Internet-facing servers, should not use the underscore character as a best practice. If you are upgrading a Windows NT 4 environment to Windows Server 2003, you might wish to consider changing the NetBIOS and host names of computers whose names include the underscore character before performing the upgrade.

DNS and Active Directory (AD)

As a prerequisite to installing AD, you must first have a DNS infrastructure in place on your network and your TCP/IP stack must be configured to use an appropriate DNS server. The DNS server must be authoritative for the domain name of your AD and must be able to support a special kind of RR known as an SRV record, which provides information about well-known network services and replaces the legacy WKS record. By default, Windows 2000 and Windows Server 2003 DNS servers provide support for these records. Other DNS servers, such as those that implement the most recent version of BIND (BIND 9 as of this writing), might support these records as well, but this needs to be confirmed beforehand if you are using something other than Microsoft DNS.

The DNS server should also be capable of supporting the following:

- **Dynamic DNS (DDNS) updates** DDNS is a protocol that allows servers and DNS clients to update DNS records in the master zone file. Although it is not a requirement that the DNS server support DDNS, it is highly recommended that it do so. Support for

DDNS eliminates a considerable amount of administrative work that must be performed in the form of manually adding DNS records to support AD and the network infrastructure in general. Windows 2000 and Windows Server 2003 DNS servers support DDNS, as does BIND 9.

■ **Incremental zone transfers (IXFR)** When a zone file on a master DNS server is updated on a secondary DNS server, the entire file is transferred over TCP port 53 using the AFXR protocol. To eliminate unnecessary traffic associated with zone transfers, the IXFR protocol allows for the transfer of specific updated records, rather than the entire file, between master and secondary servers. The Microsoft DNS service supports IXFR, as do BIND versions 8 and 9.

If an appropriate DNS server is not available when you install your first Windows Server 2003 domain controller, the Dcpromo.exe application will prompt you to install and configure the DNS service on the computer you are promoting to a domain controller.

AD is capable of storing DNS zone information in the form of Active Directory-integrated zones. We will discuss this feature in more detail later in this chapter.

Supporting Multiple Namespaces

When you plan to use DNS for name resolution on your intranet and also plan to have a presence on the Internet, you need to consider how to support one or multiple namespaces. Assuming that you have a publicly registered Internet domain name and wish to base the internal domain name on this one, you have three choices for the selection of your internal domain name:

■ **Same domain name for external and internal use** This configuration requires that you manage separate DNS servers for your internal network and the external network that are both authoritative for the same domain name. This configuration is sometime referred to as a *split DNS*. However, the internal DNS servers will contain RRs that are specific to your internal network and possibly contain RRs for your publicly available Web and mail servers. The DNS servers that are authoritative for the internal network should not be available to external clients. Depending on your security requirements and network configuration, you might find it necessary to maintain a copy of your Internet-facing servers, such as your Web server, on your intranet for use by your internal clients. The external DNS server that is authoritative for the domain will contain RRs for your publicly available Internet-facing servers only (such as the Web and mail servers) and will not contain RRs for your internal network. This model increases the administrative effort for managing DNS records and security, so it is not a recommended solution. However, a key advantage is that your organization's users do not need to remember different domain names for your organization's externally available servers.

■ **Different namespace for internal use** In this scenario, you would use either a completely different name for the internal name of the intranet or use a domain namespace based on the registered domain name but with a different top-level domain suffix, for example, mydomain.local. Microsoft recommends using a namespace based on a registered domain name in the (unlikely but possible) event that two organizations that are using the same AD name merge. If the domain name is registered, it must be unique by definition. A key advantage of this approach is that it provides you with a unique and separate namespace for use on your internal network. With this configuration, the administrative effort required to manage the domain namespace is minimized, compared to using the same domain name for internal and external use. Also, security is enhanced and easier to manage.

A disadvantage of this option is that it requires that you manage two separate DNS namespaces, increasing administrative complexity. For example, using an unrelated internal domain name might require you to register this name with ICANN. Furthermore, using an unrelated internal domain name might cause confusion among users in your company.

- **Delegated subdomain for internal use** In this scenario, your internal domain namespace begins at a subdomain of the publicly registered domain namespace. For example, if your domain name is mydomain.com, you would use something like internal.mydomain.com for your internal namespace on your intranet. To support this configuration, you need internal DNS servers that are authoritative for the subdomain and are available only to your internal network (that is, the child domain namespace is not accessible to external users). Your internal clients, however, would be able to gain access to both the internal and external DNS servers. This approach has a number of advantages:

    - Administrative effort to maintain the DNS namespace is minimized.

    - Both your internal and Internet-facing servers share the same contiguous namespace, making it easier for users to connect to these resources.

    - Any DNS records used for AD are isolated in the child domain and its subdomains. The delegated child domain becomes the forest root domain for AD.

Disjointed Namespaces

Many companies have needed to deploy a disjointed namespace; that is, they design their DNS infrastructure to support two or more noncontiguous namespaces.

In Windows Server 2003, it is now possible to create to create one-way or two-way, cross-forest transitive Kerberos trusts. A two-way transitive trust simplifies resource management because it automatically enables trusts between all domains in the separate forests. This feature, along with complex business needs to deploy disjointed namespaces for separate business units, will make disjointed namespaces more common. Implementing a stable DNS infrastructure to support DNS resolution for a disjointed namespace creates challenges for the DNS administrator. For example, the DNS administrators in the separate forests might need to host secondary zones for the primary zones in the remote forests. The Windows Server 2003 DNS service includes two new features that make it easier to support disjointed namespaces:

- **Conditional forwarding** Makes it possible to configure a DNS server to automatically contact predefined DNS servers based on the domain name in the query request. Thus, when a DNS server encounters a query request for name resolution for resources in a separate namespace, it can forward this query to a particular, predefined set of DNS servers.

■ **Stub zone** A concept borrowed from implementations of BIND. The stub zone is a special kind of secondary zone and consists of only a subset of records from the primary zone of the child domain: the SOA, NS, and A records that identify the DNS servers that are authoritative for the child domain. The NS and A records (sometimes known as *glue records)* are updated on the DNS server hosting the stub zone based on the refresh interval specified in the SOA record. A DNS server hosting a stub zone can respond to recursive queries and contact the DNS servers that are authoritative for the child domain, or it can respond to iterative queries and provide referrals to the DNS servers that are authoritative for the child domain.

When a DNS server hosts a stub zone for another domain, the server can contact the authoritative servers for the domain directly when it receives a request to resolve a name query, helping to reduce DNS name query traffic and the load on the primary DNS server.

Stub zones are useful in situations where authority is delegated to DNS servers in a child domain from a parent domain, such as when you are deploying your own internal root (discussed in the next section) and need to support a disjointed namespace. Stub zones remove the need to manually maintain glue records for the child domain in the parent domain. If a DNS administrator changes the NS or glue records in the child domain, this information will be updated in the stub zone, making it unnecessary for the DNS administrator in the parent domain to manually update records used to delegate authority.

These automatic updates serve to prevent a specific and common problem in a DNS infrastructure, which is known as *lame delegation.* A lame delegation occurs when the NS and glue address records used to delegate authority from a parent to a child domain are incorrect and prevent DNS servers from contacting DNS servers that are authoritative for a child domain.

Deploying an Internal DNS Root Zone

In considering your DNS infrastructure, you should determine whether it is necessary or desirable to deploy an internal DNS root zone (the **.** zone). When you deploy a private root zone, you create a configuration whereby your DNS servers are authoritative for the entire DNS namespace. The private root zone contains only delegations to your internal top-level domains. Consequently, these DNS servers will not perform DNS name resolution on the Internet. If you wish your DNS servers to perform name resolution outside your organization (for example, to servers belonging to a partner or merged organization), you can add delegations from your root zone and top-level domains in the form of NS and glue A records to external DNS servers that are authoritative for other domains. In this situation, it might be advantageous to deploy a stub zone on dns1.syngress.local so that the NS and glue A records for DNS servers in the tacteam.net domain are automatically updated.

A primary advantage of this approach is enhanced security. Your DNS clients and servers that are authoritative for your DNS zones never send DNS information on the Internet. Furthermore, for large and complex networks that span WAN links, deploying a private root zone helps to simplify your DNS infrastructure.

If Internet name resolution is a requirement on your network, you might not be able to deploy a root zone. However, if your client computers are capable of using proxy servers, such as ISA Server 2000, client computers can access Internet resources through the proxy server, which will perform name resolution on their behalf. The proxy server and computers that cannot use the proxy client software need to be configured to use separate, internal DNS forwarders or other DNS servers for Internet name resolution.

Figure 20.2 shows a possible deployment of an internal private root zone in combination with a proxy server to allow connectivity to external Web sites for client PCs. The figure also shows a delegation to a disjointed namespace (tacteam.net) to allow an internal DNS server to resolve host names on the tacteam.net network. Note that dns1.syngress.local does not perform Internet name resolution for client PCs. The ISA Server contacts a DNS server capable of performing name resolution on the Internet. However, dns1.syngress.local, by virtue of a name server delegation, performs recursive DNS resolution for hosts in the tacteam.net network.

Figure 20.2 Deployment of a Private Root Zone

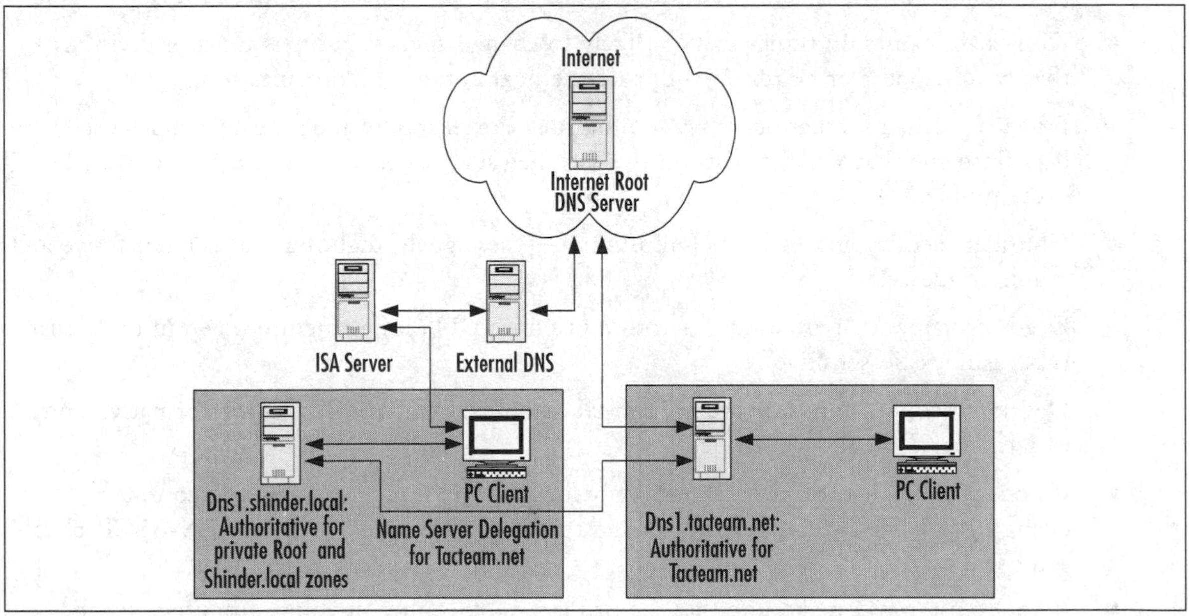

In the example in Figure 20.2, a considerable amount of DNS name resolution traffic can cross a WAN link between the syngress.local and the tacteam.net networks. To reduce this traffic, you can host a secondary zone for tacteam.net on dns1.syngress.local and host a secondary zone for syngress.local on dns1.tacteam.net. In fact, in order for dns1.tacteam.net to perform name resolution for hosts on the syngress.local network, you must either host a secondary zone for syngress.local or use some other configuration, such as conditional forwarding, to make it possible for this name resolution to occur.

General Guidelines for Internal Domain Namespaces

In deciding which approach is best for your organization, take into account a number of complex factors, such as the presence of firewalls and proxy servers, client software, and the number and location of DNS servers under your control. Regardless of the approach you take, you should follow some common-sense guidelines:

- Keep it simple. Don't create a DNS infrastructure with too many subdomains (limit the number to five or fewer subdomains). As a corollary to this, try to limit the number of authoritative zones to a minimum number; don't create separate zones of authority for individual subdomains, unless it is necessary.

- Use your own company or product names, not those of another company.

- Register the domain names used by your company and base internal names on registered names.

- Avoid acronyms and geographical names that might not be easily understood.

- Don't base names on things that are likely to change, such as business units or divisions that can disappear or be renamed during the next company reorganization.

- Don't repeat names that occur on the Internet. For example, don't create a top-level domain name that already exists on the Internet, such as .ca, .biz, and so on. This will cause problems for external name resolution.

- Consider security and ease of administration—these goals might be mutually exclusive and require trade-offs.

- Use host names that are unique across your entire DNS infrastructure (keep in mind that DNS is not case-sensitive).

- Develop a convention for naming internal computers that is consistent, informative, and easily understood and remembered.

- If possible, use US-ASCII characters only for host and domain names and consider changing any NetBIOS computer names to ensure conformity with the US-ASCII character set.

- If you're using AD, make sure that the primary DNS suffix on your computers matches the AD domain name.

Planning DNS Server Deployment

Once you have determined your requirements for your DNS namespace and host names and have determined the number of subdomains, you must plan for the deployment of the DNS infrastructure on DNS servers. The goal of this planning is to ensure maximum availability, fault tolerance, currency of updated DNS records, and security, while at the same time minimizing the amount of traffic associated with DNS query and zone transfer traffic. The size and placement of zone files in your DNS topology will have a direct bearing on these considerations. Your network topology also has a direct bearing on these considerations. For example, the presence of WAN links connecting remote subnets and the available bandwidth on those links will affect the deployment of your DNS infrastructure.

Planning the Number of DNS Servers

To reduce administrative complexity and to ensure fast query response times and fault tolerance, you can configure servers in a variety of roles. For example, you can configure *conditional forwarders* and other types of *caching-only* servers and use these in combination with DNS servers that are authoritative for particular domains. We will discuss forwarders and other DNS server roles later in this chapter.

To determine the number of DNS servers you need, you should keep the following guidelines in mind:

- A Windows Server 2003 DNS server on a 700 MHz Pentium III or higher computer with at least 256MB RAM can handle a large number of queries, more than 10,000 per second. If you experience slow response times, you can add additional DNS servers in the form of secondary servers or Active Directory-integrated zones.

- A DNS server can host many different zones—as many as 20,000 small zones that contain only a few RR in addition to the SOA, NS, and glue address records. If there is excessive traffic related to recursive queries on the network as a result of delegation to other zones, DNS servers can be configured as secondary servers to remote primary servers.

- If you have high-speed, reliable WAN links, you can use centrally located DNS servers to resolve queries for clients located in remote subnets.

- If WAN links are not reliable, you can set up a secondary DNS server on the remote network to ensure availability of zone information.

- Because DHCP servers and clients can automatically update DNS zone records using DDNS, zone replication traffic can become an issue on large networks, even though Windows Server 2003 DNS supports incremental zone updates. If zone replication traffic across WAN links is a consideration, you can set up caching-only forwarders on the remote subnets to eliminate this traffic.

- DNS servers can have multiple roles. For example, a DNS server hosting a primary zone for a particular domain can be configured as a conditional forwarder for other domains. Configuring a server as a conditional forwarder allows it to build up a cache of frequent queries for host name resolution, helping to reduce DNS-related traffic for particular domains.

Planning for DNS Server Capacity

On startup, an authoritative DNS server loads its zone files into RAM. A typical RR consumes approximately 100 bytes of RAM, although the precise value is determined by the kind of RR; for example, an SRV RR consumes more RAM than an A RR. The DNS service itself uses 4MB of RAM without loading any zones. You can use these figures to determine the amount of RAM you need to support your zone files.

You should also keep in mind that a DNS server caches query results in RAM and can return *nonauthoritative* responses to query requests from its cache. (When a DNS server performs a recursive query on behalf of a DNS client, it stores the result in cache. The next time a DNS client makes a query request for the same record, the DNS server responds with a nonauthoritative answer from its cache.) The more RAM available for caching responses, the better the performance for returning nonauthoritative answers to DNS clients on the network.

The performance of the DNS server is also influenced by the number and types of DNS queries to which it must respond. Also, a multihomed DNS server (a DNS server with more than one network interface) that is listening on more than one IP address for DNS queries consumes additional resources. If the DNS server is also a primary server, the number of secondary servers that are polling for updates of the primary zone also have an effect on performance.

Another factor that has an effect on performance is whether the DNS server is processing dynamic updates to zone files and whether the computer is also configured as a domain controller and processing secure updates to the zone files.

To gain a more precise understanding of the resources required for your DNS server, you can gather information from the DNS-related Performance Monitor counters that are installed with the DNS service. We will discuss the topic of monitoring DNS performance in more detail later in the chapter.

Planning DNS Server Placement

In considering where to place DNS servers, you should try to eliminate single points of failure to ensure the availability of DNS and AD services. This means that for every zone in your control, you should have at least two authoritative servers for fault tolerance. All DNS clients should be configured with the IP addresses of primary and at least one alternate DNS server to contact for name resolution. The following guidelines might assist in determining placement of your DNS servers:

- On segmented LAN environments, you should have at least two authoritative servers. These servers should be installed on different subnets.

- On a WAN, you should try to ensure that an authoritative DNS server is installed at each geographic location.

- If you are hosting an authoritative DNS for your Internet-facing hosts, such as your Web and mail servers, consider hosting an offsite secondary DNS server at your ISP or on your domain name registrar's network.

- Consider what services will be unavailable if the router fails on your network segment. For example, if you have a small branch office that lacks a domain controller, users will not be able to use the services provided by AD if the router fails. In this case, there might not be any advantage to deploying a secondary server that is authoritative for your AD zones.

- Consider zone replication traffic across slow WAN links. If zone replication traffic consumes too much bandwidth, consider using forwarding servers in the remote location.

Planning DNS Server Roles

In order to properly plan, implement, and maintain a DNS infrastructure for your network, you should have an understanding of the various DNS server roles that you can install and configure.

- **Authoritative name servers** These are servers that contain the complete zone information for a domain and possibly its subdomains. Any domain will be served by one or more authoritative name servers. For purposes of fault tolerance and load balancing, there should be at least two authoritative name servers for each zone. In a Windows 2000 and Windows Server 2003 environment, it is possible to configure three types of authoritative name servers:

  - A *primary master server* is the authoritative name server that holds the updatable RRs. Any changes made to the zone file information must be made on this server. Unless you are using Active Directory-integrated zones, there is only one primary master DNS server for each zone of authority. A stand-alone server, member server, or Windows 2000 or Windows Server 2003 domain controller can be configured as a primary server.

  - *Secondary servers,* sometimes known as *slave servers*, hold a read-only copy of zone information that is transferred from the primary master server during a process known as *zone transfer* to ensure that RRs are synchronized between the secondary servers and the primary server. A zone transfer occurs in one of two ways. One way is for the secondary servers to poll the primary master server according to the refresh interval in the SOA RR and compare the version number in the SOA RR in the primary's zone file with its own. If the number is larger, it will initiate the zone transfer process. Alternatively, the primary master server can notify the secondary servers on its list whenever updates are made to the zone file. A secondary server can also be configured to do zone transfers to other secondary servers. This configuration is used primarily in situations where the polling of the primary DNS server by a large number of secondary servers puts an unacceptable load on it. The trade-off is currency of records, since updates from the primary DNS server must travel through more than one secondary server before all the records are synchronized among DNS servers.

  - The *Active-Directory-integrated* configuration is specific to Windows 2000 and Windows Server 2003. Instead of zone information being stored in flat text files, as is the case with the primary and secondary DNS servers, zone information is stored in AD. Rather than relying on the mechanism of zone transfers, AD replication is responsible for ensuring that zone information is synchronized among all the participating DNS servers. Another key advantage of using Active Directory-integrated zones is that any DNS server that stores the zone information can update RRs; that is, more than one DNS server can update the zone information.

Secondary zones cannot be stored in AD. Active Directory-integrated zones provide enhanced security for DNS updates and zone replication traffic in several ways: all DNS servers hosting Active Directory-integrated zones must be registered in AD, AD replication traffic is encrypted, and you can use access control lists (ACLs) to restrict the hosts that are allowed to update RRs using DDNS (*secure dynamic updates*).

- **Stealth servers** When you register the name servers that are authoritative for your Internet domain namespace, you must supply at least one or two name servers that are authoritative for the zone, so that authority can be delegated from the parent domain (.com, .net, and so on) to your servers. It is possible, however, for these servers to be secondary, or slave, servers to a primary master server that is not listed in the registered NS records for the zone listed by the registrar as being authoritative for your domain. Usually, the primary master server is located behind a firewall, and access to the primary server itself and zone transfers to the secondary servers are tightly controlled by access rules on the firewall.

- **Caching name servers** A caching name server performs queries on behalf of DNS, but the server itself is not authoritative for any zones. When you first set up a Windows DNS server with the root hints file, it is a caching name server that can resolve queries for Internet hosts using information it possesses about the name servers that are authoritative for the root zone. After time, the caching name server builds up a list of commonly queried names in its cache, which is subsequently used to answer queries on behalf of clients.

- **Forwarding servers** A forwarding server is a kind of caching name server that sends queries to a predetermined list of name servers, known as *forwarders*, which can perform recursive queries on its behalf. The forwarding server will send its query to each forwarder in its list until it receives a positive or negative response. After it exhausts the name servers in its list, it can be configured to send requests to servers on the Internet using its root hints file. Alternatively, a forwarder can be configured to stop at this point, by disabling recursion, and send a negative response back to the original DNS requester if the forwarder cannot resolve the query. If recursion is disabled on the forwarding server, it is referred to as a *forward-only server*. There are a number of uses for forwarding servers and forwarders. They are often used when you want to tightly control which DNS servers (the forwarders) are able to send and receive DNS traffic through your firewall. Another common use of forwarders is to handle DNS queries performed across relatively slow WAN links on a corporate network. In the remote network, a name server is configured to forward queries to a more powerful caching name server that has a larger cache and is better able to resolve DNS queries as result of having access to more bandwidth, rather than send its queries directly to the Internet. A new feature of Windows Server 2003 DNS allows the configuration of *conditional forwarding*. Conditional forwarding allows the DNS administrator to configure the forwarding server to contact specific name servers based on the domain name specified in the query. To configure a conditional forwarder, you specify the domain name and the IP addresses of the servers that are responsible for resolving host names in these domains. Conditional forwarders provide intelligent name resolution and are typically used to reduce the amount of traffic related to recursion on your network.

■ **Nonrecursive servers** A nonrecursive server is one on which you have disabled recursion so that it is not able to perform recursive queries on behalf of DNS requesters. Disabling recursion on a name server also prevents it from using forwarders to resolve queries. Usually, recursion is disabled on authoritative name servers that provide name resolution for DNS requesters on the Internet, performing queries to locate your Internet hosts, such as your Web and mail servers. By disabling recursion on these name servers, you ensure that the servers will respond positively only to queries for RRs in zones for which they are authoritative, and hence tighten the security of these servers. DNS clients on the Internet will not be able to configure their TCP/IP settings to point to your DNS servers for name resolution.

These name server roles are only logically separate from one another. It is possible to combine roles on a single name server. For example, a DNS server can be configured to be a primary master for one domain zone file and as a secondary for other domain zone files. However, it is often advantageous to separate these roles and place them on separate servers. By doing so, you are better able to design your DNS infrastructure to take into account the contingencies of your network infrastructure, such as the speed of your WAN links, the presence of firewalls, the need for security, and so on.

Domain Controller versus Member Server

In an AD environment, you have the choice to install and configure DNS on your domain controllers or on member servers. If you install DNS on your domain controllers, you can configure Active Directory-integrated zones.

Active Directory-integrated zones provide the following advantages over standard DNS zones:

■ There is not a single point of failure for the primary zone. In a standard DNS environment, if the primary master DNS server fails and is not brought online within a particular amount of time (specified in the SOA record), the secondary servers will remove the RRs from their zone, and name resolution will fail for the entire domain.

■ In large environments where DHCP servers and clients are updating RRs, this load can be distributed among domain controllers that store zone information in AD.

■ Active Directory-integrated zones provide enhanced security for zone replication in that DNS servers must be registered in AD and AD replication traffic is encrypted.

■ You can use secure dynamic updates with Active Directory-integrated zones to tighten security further.

■ Synchronization of zone information occurs automatically through AD replication. No further configuration is necessary to facilitate transfer of zone information among participating servers.

■ AD replication is more efficient than the standard zone transfer mechanisms. For example, AD replication propagates only the last changes. Even though an incremental zone transfer copies only the changes to the RRs, it propagates all the incremental changes to the RRs that have occurred since the last update. If you are not using IXFR, the entire zone file is copied whenever an update is made.

■   AD replication will compress replication traffic in certain circumstances, further reducing the bandwidth needed for DNS-related traffic.

Active Directory-integrated zones can be used in combination with secondary servers. For example, you can use secondary zones on servers that are not configured as domain controllers. This is advantageous in situations where you do not want AD traffic replicated across a WAN link, but you do want to have an authoritative DNS server available at a remote location. You cannot simultaneously load a standard text-based primary zone file and an Active Directory-integrated zone for the same domain on the same domain controller. However, you can combine primary, secondary, and Active Directory-integrated zones on the same domain controller. On a stand-alone or member server, primary and secondary zones can be combined on the same server. Furthermore, if you have multiple IP addresses bound to the server, you can emulate a secondary server on the same computer where the primary is located. This configuration is useful in very small environments where you have only one server.

Planning for Zone Replication

In planning your DNS infrastructure, you need to decide on the number and placement of your DNS servers. In particular, you must decide which servers will host zone files for your domains. Distributing zone files across your network has a number of advantages. For example, distributed zone files reduce the network traffic caused by DNS queries, increase availability and fault tolerance, provide load balancing, and result in shorter query response times. However, distributing zone files requires that you replicate zone information among your DNS servers, increasing traffic associated with zone transfers or AD replication (if you have enabled Active Directory-integrated zones). Zone files also increase the storage space requirements on DNS servers. Furthermore, replicating zone information increases the administrative effort required to maintain the DNS infrastructure.

In planning for zone replication, you must decide which mechanism you will use for zone replication: either standard DNS zone transfers or AD replication. This decision will depend on a number of factors, including the storage location (file-based or AD), the type of zone information (primary, secondary, or stub), and whether you need enhanced security.

If you are using stand-alone, member servers, or other implementations of DNS, such as BIND, you must use standard DNS mechanisms for zone transfers. Depending on the version of DNS or BIND you are using, you can use either full (AXFR) or incremental (IXFR) zone transfers to propagate zone information. Incremental zone transfers reduce traffic by propagating only the incremental changes since the last update.

Microsoft and other DNS servers optimize traffic associated with standard zone transfers by compressing the zone transfer information and including multiple RRs in individual TCP packets. This mechanism is referred to as *fast zone transfers* (it should not be confused with IXFR). Versions of BIND earlier than 4.9.4 do not support fast zone transfers. Support for fast zone transfers to BIND secondaries is enabled by default on Microsoft DNS servers, but it can be disabled.

A zone transfer is initiated when the secondary servers determine that the version number in their SOA RR is lower than the version number in the primary's SOA RR, indicating an update to the primary zone. The secondary servers will compare the SOA version number in the following situations:

- When they are notified of a change by the primary server.
- When the refresh interval specified in the SOA has elapsed.
- When the DNS service on the secondary server is started.
- When a zone transfer is manually initiated by the administrator.

When the secondary server determines it needs to update its zone file, it will make a request for an incremental zone transfer (IXFR) or a full zone transfer (AXFR).

The notify list should contain only the IP addresses of secondary servers. It is not necessary to use this list to notify other domain controllers that have a copy of the Active Directory-integrated zone. Active Directory-integrated zones poll approximately every 15 minutes for updates. In fact, adding domain controllers to the notify list can actually degrade performance. Figure 20.3 shows the property pages for configuring a secondary zone transfer notify list.

Figure 20.3 Configuring a Notify List for Zone Transfers

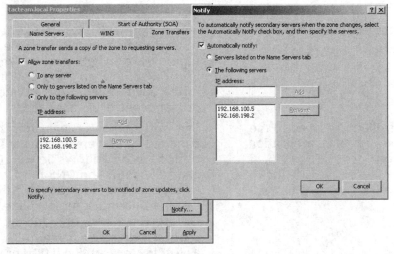

Active Directory-integrated Zone Replication Scope

In a Windows Server 2003 environment, you must specify an Active Directory-integrated scope. The choices for the replication scope are described in Table 20.1.

Table 20.1 Active Directory-integrated Zone Replication Scope Options

DNS Zone Replication Scope	Description and Usage
All DNS servers in the AD forest	This is the broadest scope for DNS zone replication and produces the most replication traffic. Zone data is replicated to all Windows Server 2003 domain controllers on which the DNS service is installed in the entire forest. You can use this option only when all your domain controllers are running Windows Server 2003.
All DNS servers in a specified AD domain	This is the default zone replication setting for DNS installed on Windows Server 2003 domain controllers. Zone information is replicated to all the Windows Server 2003 domain controllers on which the DNS service is installed in the domain. This option is desirable when you want to limit or restrict replication of zone information to only the domain controllers in your AD domain. Zone information is *not* replicated to Windows 2000 domain controllers.
All domain controllers in the AD domain	This option replicates DNS zone information to all domain controllers in the AD domain, regardless of whether or not the DNS service is installed on them. This option is desirable in mixed environment where Windows 2000 domain controllers are used.
All domain controllers specified in the replication scope of a DNS application directory partition	This option allows the customization of your zone replication environment. To use this option, your Windows Server 2003 domain controllers running DNS must be enlisted in the application directory partition. You can use the Dnscmd command-line utility to enlist DNS servers. The syntax for the command is **dnscmd [DNS_server_name] /EnlistDirectoryPartition [FQDN of partition]**. All fields are required.

A significant advantage of using the application directory partition to store zone data is that the data is not replicated throughout the AD forest in the Global Catalog. This would be the case if AD zone data were stored in the domain partition, as it is in Windows 2000. When using intersite replication (replication between different sites), the application directory partition is replicated according to the same schedule as the domain partition.

To change the replication scope, you can use the DNS console, which presents the choices indicated in Figure 20.4. There are four choices, corresponding to the descriptions in Table 20.1. The choices are to replicate zone data to all DNS server in the AD forest, to all DNS servers in the AD domain, to all domain controllers in the AD domain, and to all domain controllers specified in the scope of [a specified] application directory partition. The last choice to customize the zone replication environment is grayed out and unavailable because the server has not been enlisted in other partitions.

Figure 20.4 Changing Replication Scope for Windows Server 2003 Active Directory-integrated Zones

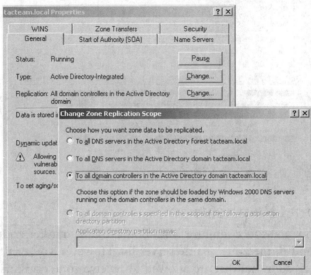

By default, when you first create an Active Directory-integrated zone and an application directory partition has not been created, you have the option of creating the partition using the DNS console utility. You can also use the Ntds utility to create or delete application directory partitions and the Dnscmd utility to create the default application directory partitions. If the default partitions have already been created, you will get an error message indicating that the partition already exists. When you use the DNS console utility to create the application directory partition, you are presented with two exclusive choices:

- To create a single application directory partition that stores DNS zone data and replicates that data to all DNS servers in the domain. If you respond **No** to this choice, you will be presented with the second choice.

- To create a single application directory partition that stores DNS zone data and replicates that data to all DNS servers in the forest. This creates the broadest scope for replication of DNS zone data.

Figure 20.5 shows the choices for creating an application directory partition using the DNS console. The two dialog boxes below the DNS console window appear when you use the DNS console to create the default application directory partitions.

Figure 20.5 Creating the application directory partition using the DNS console

Security for Zone Replication

To secure zone replication, you can configure Microsoft DNS to transfer zone information to only those servers that are found in the zone's name server list. However, you can further tighten security by specifying individual IP addresses that are allowed to receive zone transfers.

In situations where you are transferring zone transfer information over the Internet or you are concerned that this traffic can be intercepted, you should also consider using virtual private network (VPN) tunnels or Internet Protocol Security (IPSec) to encrypt this traffic.

Using Active Directory-integrated zones also increases the security of your replication data by ensuring that all DNS servers are registered in AD and by using the security mechanisms inherent in AD replication. The security for zone transfers arises from the security of AD when you use Active Directory-integrated zones. Where possible, you should use Active Directory-integrated zones exclusively to improve performance and security of zone replication traffic.

General Guidelines for Planning for Zone Replication

You should keep the following guidelines in mind when planning for the distribution of zone files in your infrastructure:

- Limiting the number of zones of authority in your DNS infrastructure simplifies adminis-tration. For each subdomain that has a separate zone of authority, you must ensure that the delegation of authority is correct for the subdomain and plan for the appropriate zone replication for each of these subdomains.

- Distributing zone files increases the traffic associated with zone transfers or AD replication.

- Distributing zone files reduces the amount of traffic associated with name resolution queries.

- Distributing zone files provides a means for supporting a disjointed namespace.

- Distributing zone files increases availability and fault tolerance. It also reduces query response times.

- If you are using Active Directory-integrated zones and all your DNS servers are installed on Windows Server 2003 domain controllers, you can use an application directory partition to reduce the replication traffic associated with the transfer of zone information.

- You can minimize the bandwidth consumed by standard zone transfers by modifying the schedule for transfers to secondary zones.

- You should configure a primary server to notify only secondary servers. However, you should note that configuring the notify list to transfer zone information with the IP addresses of servers hosting the Active Directory-integrated zone can actually degrade performance.

- If you are using standard DNS zone transfers, you should try to implement incremental zone transfers and fast zone transfers where possible.

- A DNS server that is hosting an Active Directory-integrated zone or a standard primary zone can also host a standard secondary zone for another domain.

- A stub zone is a synchronized copy of a subset of an authoritative zone's RRs: the SOA, NS, and glue address records that identify authoritative name servers for a particular domain.

- A stub zone can reduce cross-domain referral and other DNS traffic.

- Security of zone data should be a consideration in your design and implementation. Active Directory-integrated zones provide more security than standard zone types. If you are using standard zone types, security can be enhanced by restricting the hosts that are allowed to receive zone transfers and by encrypting zone transfer traffic using VPN tunnels or IPSec, using the strongest level of encryption possible.

Planning for Forwarding

Distributing zone files throughout your infrastructure provides one means of ensuring efficient DNS name resolution. However, it is not always desirable or possible to distribute zone files to facilitate efficient DNS name resolution.

A forwarder is simply a DNS server that receives queries that are *forwarded* to it by other DNS servers that are not capable of resolving the DNS query. Whenever a DNS server receives a query, it will try to answer the query from the data stored in its zone files or cache. Unless it has been configured otherwise (that is, as a nonrecursive server or a root-level server), if the DNS server cannot answer the query from its data, it will either contact authoritative root servers or forward the query to a forwarder.

Servers that are configured to not use recursion are called *forward-only servers*. You configure a forward-only server by checking the box labeled **Do not use recursion for this domain** in the **Forwarders** property page (see Figure 20.7 in the next section).

Using forwarders can help reduce the amount of DNS traffic related to recursion, in addition to reducing the traffic related to zone replication. Their use can also help to enhance security by minimizing the number of DNS servers that need to communicate with one another across firewalls. Other advantages can be realized by using conditional forwarding, a new feature of Windows Server 2003 DNS.

Conditional Forwarding

Conditional forwarding adds intelligence to the forwarding of DNS queries. In previous versions of Microsoft DNS, you could configure a forwarding server to forward queries for all domains it could not resolve to only a single set of forwarders. In this setup, the list of forwarders was responsible for resolving names for the entire domain namespace on behalf of the forwarding server. With conditional forwarding, it is possible for the DNS administrator to configure a forwarding server to contact different sets of forwarders based on the domain name in the query. Figure 20.6 shows a possible design configuration for conditional forwarding.

Figure 20.6 Conditional Forwarding Configured to Send Queries Directly to an Authoritative Server

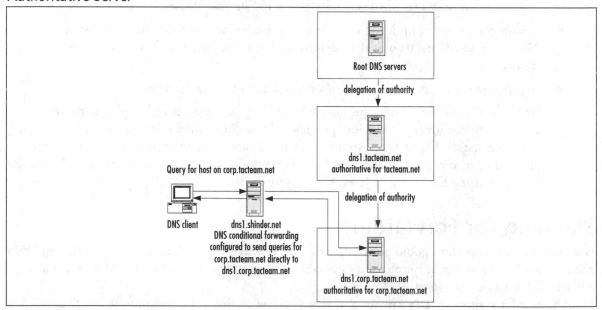

In Figure 20.6, dns1.syngress.net has been configured to send any query requests for hosts in the corp.tacteam.net domain directly to a dns1.corp.tacteam.net, which is authoritative for the zone. If conditional forwarding had not been configured, dns1.syngress.net would need to send a set of iterative queries to the root servers and dns1.tacteam.net in order to find the server that is authoritative for corp.tacteam.net. This configuration helps to eliminate network traffic related to DNS name resolution and reduces DNS query response time. Also, since dns1.syngress.net is a direct point of contact with dns1.corp.tacteam.net, over time, it would acquire a significant number of cached RRs for hosts in the corp.tacteam.net domain.

Figure 20.7 shows conditional forwarding configured for the corp.tacteam.net domain. Note that you can disable recursion on a per-domain basis.

Figure 20.7 Conditional Forwarding for the corp.tacteam.net Domain

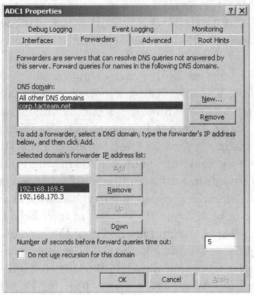

General Guidelines for Using Forwarders

The following guidelines might assist you in planning to use forwarders as part of a DNS infrastructure:

- Forwarders can eliminate the need to host secondary zone files across slow WAN links that might otherwise saturate bandwidth during zone replication.

- Conditional forwarders can directly query authoritative name servers based on the domain name in the query.

- Conditional forwarders can assist in providing support for a disjointed namespace and are a preferred solution over using stub zones for the same purpose.

- Fault tolerance can be enhanced by specifying multiple forwarders and by enabling recursion if queries to forwarders fail.

- Using forwarders can enhance security by minimizing the number of DNS servers that need to communicate with each other across firewalls.

DNS/DHCP Interaction

As is the case with Windows 2000, Windows Server 2003 supports the DDNS standard (RFC 2136) to dynamically update both forward and reverse lookup zones with A and PTR RRs, respectively. (A forward lookup zone resolves host names to IP addresses; a reverse lookup zone resolves IP addresses to host names.) DDNS reduces much of the administrative burden in managing a zone files in a DNS infrastructure. In particular, DDNS makes it possible for AD domain controllers to create and update the SRV RRs that are fundamental to the proper operation of AD. DDNS is also used in combination with DHCP to ensure that DHCP clients will have the appropriate records registered for them in DNS and the DNS records are updated whenever IP addresses change or DHCP leases expire.

Both clients and DHCP servers are capable of updating the zone records. However, only clients that are running Windows 2000, Windows XP, or Windows Server 2003 operating systems are capable of directly updating DNS zones. This is the default configuration for these clients and can be disabled on the **DNS** tab of the **Advanced** property page for TCP/IP. Usually, DHCP clients will update their own A records in the forward lookup zone, but the DHCP servers will update the PTR record in the reverse lookup zone (the computer "owns" the host name, but the DHCP server "owns" the IP address). Clients with manually configured IP addresses will always try to register both an A and a PTR record. Other level clients, such as Windows 9x and Windows NT 4, must rely on DHCP servers to update both A and PTR RRs on their behalf.

DHCP clients that are capable of dynamically updating DNS records use the DHCP client option 81 to provide the FQDN, as specified by the full computer name in the properties of the **My Computer** object, and instructions for the DHCP server to handle DDNS registration. (This is configured on the **DNS** tab of the **Advanced** property page for TCP/IP of the client computer.) The client's FQDN is used to register the name with the appropriate DNS server that is authoritative for the zone. Other level clients will be registered with DNS servers that are authoritative for the domain name configured for the DHCP scope.

A DHCP server will do the following, depending on its configuration:

- Update the A and PTR records, if requested by the client.
- Always update the A and PTR records, regardless of the client request.

A DHCP server will, by default, attempt to update A and PTR records if requested by the client. Figure 20.8 shows the default configuration for the DHCP server on the properties page for the DHCP server in the DHCP console. A similar property page exists for the DHCP scope.

Figure 20.8 Default DHCP Configuration for Dynamic DNS Updates

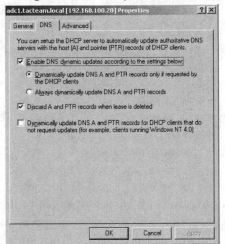

To configure the DHCP server to update DNS records, regardless of the client request, you can select the radio button labeled **Always dynamically update DNS A and PTR records**. If you wish to configure DHCP to perform DNS updates on behalf of legacy clients, you can select the check box labeled **Dynamically update DNS A and PTR records for DHCP clients that do not request updates (for example, clients running Windows NT 4.0)**. By default, the DHCP server is configured to remove both the A and the PTR records from the DNS zone. You can change this behavior by clearing the box labeled **Discard A and PTR records when lease is deleted**. When you clear this box, the DHCP will attempt to remove the PTR record when the lease expires.

Security Considerations for DDNS and DHCP

Implementing DDNS creates some security risks in that unauthorized computers and users might be able to update DNS records. In the case of public Web servers, the consequences of the unauthorized registration of a rogue Web server IP address to replace a valid one can be very significant indeed. For this reason, it is not a good idea to enable DDNS on any zones that are used to resolve names for your Internet-facing servers.

To mitigate the risk of unauthorized updates, you can require the use of *secure dynamic updates*. However, the option to use secure dynamic updates is available only if you are using Active Directory-integrated zones. When you enable this option, you are able to control which computers, users, or groups are able to modify RRs in the zone. For this reason alone, you should consider the using DDNS only if you are using Active Directory-integrated zones.

If you have enabled secure updates, there is a potential for problems caused by the ownership of records. When a DNS client or a DHCP server updates a zone file with an RR, it becomes the owner of that record. Normally, this does not create a problem. However, in some circumstances, the ownership of an RR can prevent a valid update to it. Consider the case of a client that is upgraded to Windows XP. After the upgrade, it attempts to update the RR in the zone. The attempt will fail, because the record is owned by the DHCP server that originally created the record on the client's behalf. Or, consider the case where a different DHCP server, other than the original one, tries to register an update on the client's behalf. Again, the attempt will fail. To resolve this problem, you can use a special security group called DnsUpdateProxy.

DnsUpdateProxy Group

Any objects that are created by members of the DnsUpdateProxy group have no security and are ownerless. Consequently, the first authenticated computer that updates the record is able to take ownership of the object. Therefore, if you enable secure dynamic updates only, you should place all DHCP servers in this group before they start registering names.

The DnsUpdateProxy group can create a security risk, however, if the DHCP server is installed on a domain controller. If the DHCP server that is a member of the DnsUpdateProxy group is installed on a domain controller, all the SRV, the A records for domain controller on which DHCP is installed, and other critical records created by the domain controller for AD functionality will be ownerless, allowing the first authenticated user who tries to update them to become the owner. For this reason, you should not install a DHCP server on a domain controller if you are using the DnsUpdateProxy group.

If, for whatever reason, you do need to install DHCP on a domain controller, or if DHCP is updating A records for clients in forward lookup zones, you should configure your DHCP server(s) to use DNS dynamic update credentials. To do this, you configure a security principal (a user account in this case) for use by all your DHCP servers when they update a DNS zone. You then configure your DHCP servers to use this account for dynamic updates. (This is a new feature of Windows Server 2003 and is not available on Windows 2000.) This obviates the problems arising from ownerless records created by DHCP servers in the DnsUpdateProxy group. In particular, enabling this configuration prevents a DHCP server from using the elevated permissions it inherits by virtue of its being installed on a domain controller. Figure 20.9 shows the **Advanced** tab on the DHCP server property page where you configure credentials for dynamic updates.

Figure 20.9 Configuring Credentials for DHCP Updates to Dynamic Zones

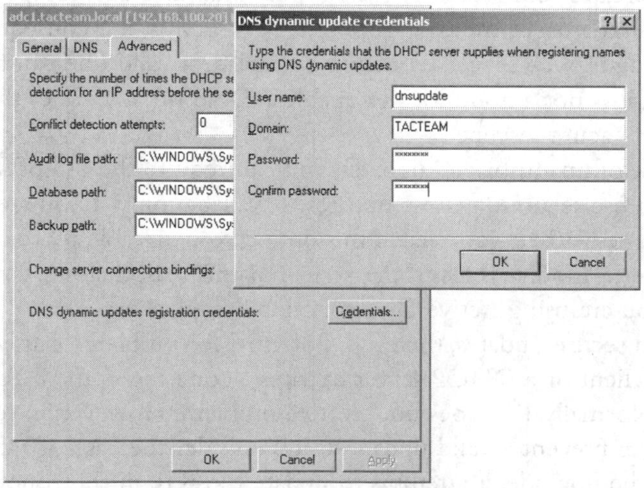

Aging and Scavenging of DNS Records

When you enable zones for dynamic updates, it is possible that the zone data files will acquire, over time, a large number of superfluous and outdated records that might have a negative effect on DNS performance. For example, if you retire a user's workstation and disconnect it from the network, the RRs for that computer might remain in the DNS data. To help ensure the integrity and currency of DNS data, you can enable aging and scavenging of outdated DNS records. (By default, the aging and scavenging option is not enabled.)

Aging and scavenging can be set on a per-zone or per-DNS server basis. Per-zone settings override per-DNS server settings. Figure 20.10 shows the server-wide aging and scavenging property page.

Figure 20.10 Aging and Scavenging Settings for a DNS Server

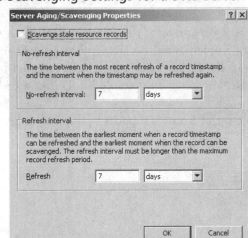

The **No-refresh interval** setting is the amount of time that must elapse before a DNS client or DHCP server can refresh a timestamp for a record. When a DNS client creates a record, it is assigned a timestamp. The DNS client attempts to refresh this record every 24 hours. Unless the record is changed (for example, the client receives a new IP address), the timestamp cannot be refreshed for a default period of seven days. After the seven days have elapsed, the DNS client can refresh the timestamp, which starts the timer on the no-refresh interval for the record. If the record is not refreshed in the seven-day period, it can be scavenged. When the record is scavenged, however, depends on another setting, the **Scavenging period**. This setting is enabled and configured on the **Advanced** tab of the property pages for the DNS server. To enable scavenging, you must enable this setting, as well as the settings for **No-refresh interval** and **Refresh interval**.

Windows Server 2003 DNS Interoperability

In addition to it interoperability with DHCP, the Windows Server 2003 DNS is designed to interoperate with other implementations of DNS, such as BIND, and with other Windows Server 2003 services, such as WINS. In this section, we examine the interoperability of Windows Server 2003 with other DNS servers and Windows Server 2003 services.

BIND and Other DNS Server Implementations

One of the design goals of Windows 2000 and Windows Server 2003 is to ensure that they conform as much as possible with TCP/IP and other standards, as defined by various organizations and governing bodies. This, in turn, helps to ensure that Windows can interoperate with a wide variety of heterogeneous systems.

With some exceptions, such as the addition of functionality required for the interoperability of DNS and WINS, Windows Server 2003 DNS is a completely standards-based implementation of DNS. As such, it will interoperate with other standards-based implementations of DNS, such as BIND. In fact, in many cases, it is not necessary to forsake a current implementation of DNS for Windows Server 2003 DNS, as long as the implementation of DNS supports current DNS standards. That said, management of your DNS infrastructure is easier if all your DNS servers are Windows Server 2003 servers.

BIND 9.2. is the most current version as of this writing. BIND 8 is still widely used. The latest version is 8.4.1, and it should be implemented because it fixes a number of security holes and bugs with earlier versions. Version 4 of BIND has been officially deprecated by ISC, and its use is not recommended. However, if BIND 4 cannot be upgraded to BIND 8 or 9, you should upgrade to BIND 4.9.11.

Table 20.2 shows a comparison of features support by various implementations of DNS.

Table 20.2 Windows DNS and BIND Compatibility Comparison

Feature	Windows Server 2003	Windows 2000	Windows NT 4	BIND 9.2	BIND 8.4.1	BIND 4.9.3
RFC 2782–SRV RRs	Yes	Yes	Yes, with Service Pack 4 or higher installed	Yes	Yes (minimum version is BIND 8.1.2)	No
Fast zone transfer	Yes	Yes	Yes	Yes	Yes	No (but is supported in versions of BIND later than 4.9.4)
Incremental zone transfer	Yes	Yes	No	Yes	Yes (but not supported in versions of BIND earlier than 8.1.2)	No
Dynamic updates	Yes	Yes	Yes	Yes	Yes	No
Stub zones	Yes	No	No	Yes	Yes	Experimental
Conditional forwarding	Yes	No	No	Yes	No	No
DNSSec	Limited support to allow loading of DNSSec RRs in secondary zones	No	No	Yes	Yes	No
ACLs on RRs	Yes, if using AD-integrated zones with secure updates only	Yes, if using AD-integrated zones with secure updates only	No	No	No	No
GSS-TSIG for secure dynamic updates	Yes	Yes	No	No (support for only simple secure updates, as per RFC 3007)	No (support for only simple secure updates, as per RFC 3007)	No

Continued

Table 20.2 Windows DNS and BIND Compatibility Comparison

Feature	Windows Server 2003	Windows 2000	Windows NT 4	BIND 9.2	BIND 8.4.1	BIND 4.9.3
TSIG for securing zone transfers and notify messages	No	No	No	Yes	Yes	No
Kerberos for secure zone transfers	Yes, when using AD-integrated zones	Yes, when using AD-integrated zones	No	No	No	No
WINS and WINS-R records	Yes	Yes	Yes	No	No	No
UTF-8 character encoding	Yes	Yes	No	No	No	No
Aging and scavenging of RRs	Yes	Yes	No	No	No	No

Zone Transfers with BIND

BIND supports standard primary and secondary DNS zones. Thus, BIND servers can be used as both primary DNS servers that transfer zone files to Microsoft DNS secondary servers and vice versa. A BIND server can also be configured as a secondary server to an Active Directory-integrated zone. However, an Active Directory-integrated cannot be a secondary zone, so it is not possible for a BIND server to host a primary zone that transfers zone information to a secondary zone configured in AD. Also note that if you want to secure zone transfers between BIND and Microsoft DNS servers, you will not be able to use the TSIG mechanisms available to recent implementations of BIND. Versions of BIND earlier than BIND 4.9.4 do not support the fast transfer method for zone replication. Disabling fast zone transfers does not affect zone replication between Windows DNS servers. Figure 20.11 shows the default configuration that enables fast zone transfers. To disable fast zone transfers for BIND secondary servers, navigate to the **Advanced** tab of the property pages for the DNS server and clear the check box for **BIND secondaries**.

Figure 20.11 Enabling Fast Zone Transfers for BIND Secondaries

Windows DNS zone files can contain RRs that can cause problems for BIND secondaries. These records include those that use an underscore in the host or domain name and the WINS and WINS-R records. On some versions of BIND, notably BIND 8.0, the presence of these records can cause the zone to fail to load.

Although the underscore is a valid character in a NetBIOS name, it is not a valid character for DNS host names, according to RFCs 851, 952, and 1123. BIND version 8, in particular, will have problems if it encounters underscores in the host or domain names when it loads the data for the secondary zone. If underscores are present in host names, you have two choices: rename the computers so that their names do not have underscores, or disable name checking on the BIND 8 server by changing the default **check-name** setting on the BIND 8 server from **Fail** to **Warn** or **Ignore**.

If a BIND 8 server is hosting a primary or secondary zone for AD SRV records, the only choice is to disable name checking, because these records contain underscores in the domain names, and these cannot be changed. (BIND 9 does not restrict the character set for domain names, so this is not an issue if you are running BIND 9.)

The proprietary WINS forward and reverse lookup records also create problems for BIND secondaries. In this case, the issue is caused by the fact WINS record is not part of the DNS standard and not recognized by other DNS servers. Non-Microsoft DNS servers will see the WINS forward and reverse lookup records as bad records, causing either data errors or the failure of the zone to load. If you are using BIND secondaries for a zone hosting WINS records, you have two choices: configure the WINS records to not replicate or configure a separate referral zone for WINS records. It is preferable to configure a separate referral zone for WINS records, because clients who contact secondary DNS servers might get different answers from those clients who contact the primary DNS server. We will discuss WINS and DNS interaction in more detail later in this chapter.

Supporting AD with BIND

As we mentioned earlier, you can support AD using BIND servers, rather than Windows Server 2003 DNS. The minimum requirement for a DNS server to support AD is that it be able to host SRV records in its data. DDNS is only an optional requirement for a DNS server. Thus, a Windows NT 4 DNS with Service Pack 4 or later could be used to support AD records.

To host AD records, the minimum version of BIND that must be used is version 8.2.2 patch 7. If you use BIND 8, you must configure the **check-name** setting to **Ignore** so that it will load a zone containing underscores in domain names. This setting is not necessary on BIND 9 servers, because they do not restrict character sets used for domain names.

Both BIND 9 and BIND 8.2.2 are capable of supporting dynamic updates. To allow domain controllers to dynamically register their DNS data, you can configure the **allow-update** setting in the named.conf configuration file on the BIND servers. However, it is not possible to configure ACLs on individual RRs (as it is when you are using Active Directory-integrated zones configured for secure updates only).

BIND administrators might be uncomfortable, for security and other reasons, with allowing dynamic updates in the master zone file that hosts the DNS records currently in use. The **allow-update** setting allows you to specify the IP addresses of the servers that can dynamically update records in the zone. However, IP addresses can be spoofed, so this isn't a very strong level of security.

One way to mitigate the risk of using BIND servers for dynamic updates is to create subdomains to host the AD DNS data. For example, if the domain name is mycompany.com, you can create a separate zone called ad.mycompany.com. To create this zone, you must issue a zone statement specifying the zone name and the location of the files in the named.conf file on the BIND server. However, Microsoft Active Directory-integrated zones still provide a much higher level of security. For this reason, it is preferable to use Active Directory-integrated zones. BIND administrators can delegate authority to a subdomain hosted in Active Directory-integrated zones and configure BIND servers as secondaries to this zone to enhance fault tolerance and availability.

Split DNS Configuration

Many organizations want to use the same name on their internal network as they do on their publicly available external network. This situation creates a number of challenges. Foremost among these is security of internal DNS records. It is not desirable to expose internal host names and IP addresses to external clients, even if these hosts cannot be reached by external clients because of restrictions on the firewall. Also, it is not a recommended DNS best practice to include any record in a zone file for a host that is unreachable.

At a minimum, a properly secured DNS configuration requires that the DNS records for the internal namespace be accessible to internal clients only and not accessible to external clients. Furthermore, internal clients should be able to resolve queries for external hosts on the Internet so that e-mail servers are able to send mail to external hosts and users are able to connect to the Internet. Finally, the bastion hosts (computers that can communicate with both the Internet and the intranet) that are responsible for delivering e-mail to the internal network should be able to successfully locate and communicate with the appropriate internal servers through the firewall.

This situation implies the use of a *split DNS* configuration. A split DNS configuration requires two sets of name servers for the same namespace. Depending on the configuration of the infrastructure, this can create some challenges. For example, if the company is using ISA Server as its firewall and making a Web server in its DMZ available to external clients via Web server publishing rules, internal clients might not be able to connect to the internal Web server if the internal DNS uses an A record for the Web server that points to an external address. Supporting this kind of configuration requires that the internal DNS servers use A records that point to the internal IP address of the Web server and not the external IP address that is used to publish the Web server for external clients. In other words, the A records for the Web server will differ in the internal and external DNS servers that are authoritative for the zone. Figure 20.12 shows a possible configuration for a split DNS to allow internal clients to connect to the publicly available Web server.

Figure 20.12 Split DNS Configuration to Allow Internal Clients to Connect to the Web Server in the DMZ

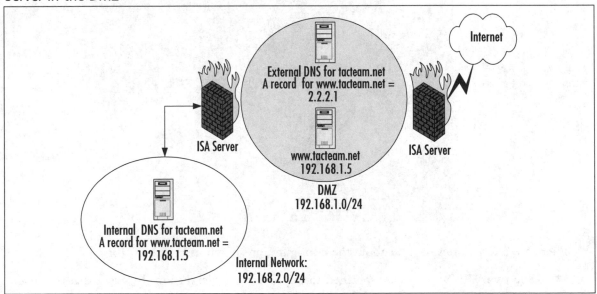

Interoperability with WINS

In a mixed environment that includes downlevel clients, such as Windows NT 4 and Windows 95, you must continue to support NetBIOS name resolution. The primary mechanism for supporting NetBIOS name resolution in a segmented network is through WINS, which allows clients on different subnets to register and resolve NetBIOS computer names on WINS servers. In some situations, it might be necessary for UNIX clients, which do not support NetBIOS, to connect to Windows NT 4 computers. In order to resolve the Windows NT 4 computer names, the UNIX hosts must use DNS. However, if the Windows NT 4 server is configured with a static IP address, it will not be able to dynamically register its host name and IP address in DNS.

One way to support DNS resolution for NetBIOS computer names is to integrate WINS with DNS through WINS forward and reverse lookup records. When a DNS zone is configured with WINS forward or reverse lookup records, it will consult a WINS server to resolve host names for records that are not present in its zone data.

As a result of this integration with WINS and DNS, it is not necessary for the DNS administrator to manually update the DNS zones with A records for NetBIOS computers that are incapable of updating DNS data on their own. The configuration of WINS forward and reverse lookup records is performed on a per-zone basis. To configure WINS lookup records, go to the forward or reverse lookup zone for which you wish to configure WINS integration, go to the property pages for the zone, and click the **WINS** tab. Figure 20.13 shows the **WINS** tab property pages.

Figure 20.13 WINS tab for a DNS Forward Zone Showing Advanced Configuration Options

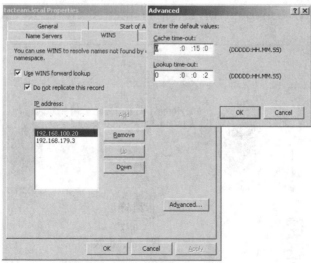

There are a few things to note about the configuration shown in Figure 20.13:

- The two WINS servers are specified to improve fault tolerance in the event that the first WINS server does not have the record or is unreachable.

- The check box for **Do not replicate this record** is selected. The purpose of this configuration is to prevent the replication of WINS records to BIND secondaries that might encounter data errors or fail to load the zone if they encounter the proprietary WINS record in the replicated data.

- **Cache time-out** and **Lookup time-out** values are configured in the **Advanced** properties of the WINS tab. The **Cache time-out** value indicates the length of time the DNS server will cache WINS records. The **Lookup time-out** value indicates the length of time the DNS server will wait for a response from a WINS server.

The WINS forward record has the following format in the zone file:

```
@        WINS     LOCAL   L2 C900 (192.168.100.20 192.168.179.3)
```

The @ is a kind of shorthand used in DNS files to indicate the domain name, also known as the *origin* for the domain, in this case tacteam.local. The LOCAL label indicates that the record should not be sent to secondary servers as part of zone replication. The L2 label refers to the lookup timeout value of two seconds. The C900 label indicates the cache timeout value of 900 seconds, or 15 minutes. Both of these represent the default values. If you have a relatively static environment, it can be advantageous to configure a longer cache timeout value of perhaps an hour or more.

WINS Reverse Lookup Records

Reverse lookup zones are used to resolve IP addresses to host names, rather than host names to IP addresses, as is the case with forward lookup zones. WINS records are not indexed by IP address. Therefore, the WINS server cannot do a reverse lookup. Consequently, in a reverse lookup zone, A WINS-R RR will cause the DNS server to issue a remote adapter node status query using the nbtstat command to determine the NetBIOS name associated with an IP address.

Configuring a WINS-R record in a reverse lookup zone is similar to configuring a WINS record. Figure 20.14 shows the property pages of the **WINS-R** tab for a reverse lookup zone.

Figure 20.14 The WINS-R Tab for a DNS Reverse Lookup Zone Showing Advanced Configuration Options

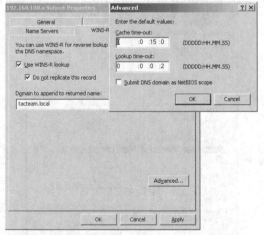

As with WINS forward lookup records, you have the option of preventing the WINS-R record from replicating to secondary servers. This will prevent problems with BIND secondaries encountering this record in the zone data.

Note that the values in the WINS-R record are different. Instead of specifying the IP address of a WINS server, you specify the domain name that should be appended to the reverse lookup query response. Also, in the **Advanced** property page, you can check a box to **Submit DNS domain as NetBIOS scope**. This option should be used *only* if you are using NetBIOS scopes on a subnet. When this option is selected, DNS uses the host name as a NetBIOS computer name to query the remote adapter node status, but submits the domain name as a NetBIOS scope identifier.

A WINS-R RR has a similar format to a WINS forward record in the zone data file:

```
@                        WINSR    LOCAL  L2 C900 (tacteam.local. )
```

The @ indicates the origin of the domain, in this case the 100.168.192.in-addr.arpa reverse lookup domain. The tacteam.local. value is the domain name that will be appended to the host name.

WINS Referral Zones

In a mixed DNS infrastructure where you are not replicating WINS RRs to secondaries, clients will get varying answers to queries if they query a secondary zone for a WINS record. To get around this problem and to provide a means of organizing and distinguishing between WINS and DNS records, you should configure a WINS referral zone. A WINS referral zone is a delegated child subdomain of the parent domain. The WINS child domain contains only the SOA for the child domain and the WINS RRs. For example, if the parent domain is tacteam.local, you would configure a child domain named something like wins.tacteam.local. If you have a large network with multiple WINS servers for different locations, you could use multiple child domains, such as dallas.tacteam.local and edmonton.tacteam.local. However, in order for this configuration to work in your environment, you need to populate the DNS suffix search list on your DNS clients so that they will append the domain name of the WINS referral zone to unqualified queries (queries that do not use the FQDN). Figure 20.15 shows a possible configuration of a DNS client to support WINS referral zones.

Figure 20.15 DNS Client Suffix Search List Configured to Support WINS Referral Zones

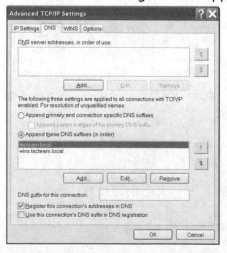

You should note that this configuration overrides the default configuration, which is to **Append primary and connection specific suffixes** and **Append parent suffixes of the primary DNS suffix**. The default configuration allows a client to send a query for an unqualified host name based on the suffix configured for it in the properties of **My Computer** and to *devolve* the domain name to the suffix of the parent domain. For example, if the client FQDN is host1.dev.research.tacteam.local, and it issues a recursive query to resolve the name PServer1 to an IP address, it will first append dev.teacteam.local to the name query. If the query fails, it will subsequently devolve the suffix to the parent domain and append tacteam.local to the name query.

Overriding the default settings for the DNS suffix search list increases administrative effort. However, you can reduce the administration of DNS client settings by using Group Policy settings to supply the clients with a DNS suffix search list. You cannot use DHCP options to specify a custom DNS suffix search list because Option 015 (DNS Domain name), which is used to specify the DNS domain name to append to unqualified queries, allows only one value. If you are implementing a custom DNS suffix search list, you should keep this list as small as possible to reduce DNS traffic on your network.

DNS Security Issues

Security measures that you can take to mitigate risk to your DNS infrastructure include those available to standard DNS implementations, such as disabling recursion on Internet-facing servers, as well as those available to Windows Server 2003 DNS only, such as using Active Directory-integrated zones for zone transfers and secure dynamic updates.

As with developing any security policy, it is important to understand the nature and likelihood of the threats involved to determine the cost to the organization if a particular threat is realized, and then compare this cost with that of implementing countermeasures to mitigate the risk to the organization. Certain trade-offs need to be considered. For example, to completely secure your DNS infrastructure from attacks launched from the Internet, the only completely reliable countermeasure is to not have an Internet connection. Obviously, many organizations could not survive without Internet access, so this particular countermeasure is not appropriate.

In the next section, we will take a look at common threats to a DNS infrastructure. Then we will review the standard and Windows-specific countermeasures you can take to mitigate the risk from these threats.

Common DNS Threats

An unsecured DNS infrastructure is vulnerable to a number of common threats. These include footprinting, redirection, and DoS attacks. These threats are described in the following sections.

Footprinting

Footprinting is the process whereby attackers gain information about your internal DNS RRs and are subsequently able to use this information to infer the identity and purpose of servers on your internal network.

Footprinting often occurs when zone transfers are not secured and the attacker is able to perform a name dump from authoritative servers using the **nslookup** command with the **ls** option or the **dig** command with the **afxr** option—both of these commands initiate a zone transfer from the target domain.

To mitigate the risk from footprinting, it is important to ensure that zone transfers are secured. At the very least, zone transfers should be allowed to only a predetermined list of IP addresses that can be configured in the properties of the primary zone on the DNS server, as shown in Figure 20.16. You should also remember to secure your secondary name servers from unauthorized zone transfers, not just your primary server. Keep in mind that a secondary name server can also transfer zone information. However, even this configuration is vulnerable. For maximum security of zone transfers, you should ensure that zone transfers occur only within Active Directory-integrated zones. If you must transfer zone information over the Internet, you should also consider the use of VPN tunnels or IPSec to secure this traffic.

Figure 20.16 Configuring a Primary Zone with a List of Secondaries Authorized to Do Zone Transfers

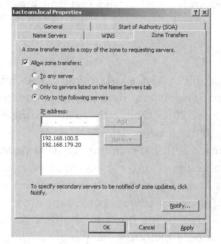

Redirection

A *redirection attack* occurs when an attacker is able to modify DNS records to redirect Web server or other traffic to servers under the attacker's control. This attack occurs when an attacker is able to write information to the zone file. For example, this might happen if dynamic updates are enabled on a zone that is located on an Internet-facing DNS server. For this reason, it is always prudent to disable dynamic updates on zone files that are accessible to clients on the Internet.

Another common cause of redirection attacks is *cache pollution* (also called *cache poisoning*). Cache pollution can occur when a DNS server queries another DNS server and receives a reply from the queried DNS server that is outside the domain namespace in the original query. Unless counter-measures are taken, the DNS server will store this referral information in its cache, even though it did not originally request the information. DNS servers are vulnerable to cache pollution if an answer to a DNS query can be falsified. The consequences of cache pollution can be severe. Imagine what might happen if the poisoned cache of a DNS server redirected users to bogus Web site that contained malicious code designed to install Trojan viruses on client computers.

When cache pollution protection is enabled, the DNS server will discard from its cache the records it receives in response to queries if those responses contain information unrelated to the domain subtree of the requested resource. In our example, if protection against cache pollution is enabled, the DNS server will cache the MX record for the mail server in sampledomain.com, but will not cache the record for the a.root-servers.net, since it is not part of the queried domain subtree. Cache pollution protection is a DNS server-wide setting (**Secure cache against pollution**) and is enabled by default on Windows Server 2003 DNS servers (see Figure 20.11 earlier in this chapter).

Another way to mitigate the risk of cache pollution is to disable recursion on the DNS server. An attacker can use recursion to query the DNS server for resources in the attacker's domain. The recursive name server is then forced to query DNS servers in the attacker's domain that might attempt to pollute the cache of the recursive server.

Denial of Service Attacks

A *Denial of Service* (DoS) attack occurs when a DNS server is deliberately flooded with traffic to the extent that it cannot respond to legitimate requests. DoS attacks on a DNS can be *in-band* on UDP and TCP port 53 (the ports used for DNS queries and zone transfers), or they can be *out-of-band*. In the case of an in-band attack, DNS servers are flooded with recursive queries to the extent that they become unable to handle legitimate queries, or the DNS service is subjected to a buffer overflow attack specific to the DNS service. In an out-of-band DoS attack, the DNS server is the victim of an attack that is not specific to the DNS service, such as buffer overflow, SYN, and Smurf attacks. When a DoS attack occurs on a DNS server, mail servers and Web servers become unavailable as well, because the host names for these servers cannot be resolved to IP addresses.

One approach to mitigate the risk of DoS attacks against your DNS server is to eliminate single points of failure by having multiple DNS servers that are located on separate subnets served by separate routers. Also, you can arrange to have secondary servers hosted offsite by a third party, such as your ISP.

To provide further protection against in-band DoS attacks, you can disable recursion on Internet-facing DNS servers. Recursive queries take a relatively long time to process, making a DNS server that performs recursion vulnerable to a DoS attack that involves sending a large number of recursive queries to the DNS server. When you disable recursion on a DNS server, it will not respond to recursive queries issued by DNS clients. DNS clients will not be able to use this server to resolve names on the Internet. However, the DNS server will still respond to iterative queries issued by other DNS servers. This means that it will respond to queries for resources in zones for which it authoritative.

Recursion is a server-wide DNS setting and is enabled by default. (You can also disable recursion for forwarding servers on a per-domain basis.) If you disable recursion for the entire DNS server, you will not be able to use that DNS server as a forwarder. You can see the **Disable recursion (also disables forwarders)** option in Figure 20.11, shown earlier in the chapter. On internal DNS servers, it is often not desirable to disable recursion. In this case, these DNS servers need to be protected by firewall access rules that prevent their use by DNS clients on the Internet.

To provide further protection against both in-band and out-of-band DoS attacks, it is important to ensure that you apply the latest service packs and harden the servers as much as possible. In addition, your firewall access rules and packet filtering should be configured to prevent any external traffic that is not related to the DNS service from reaching the DNS server. For example, a firewall that is in front of a DNS server in a DMZ should allow traffic to reach the DNS server only on TCP and UDP port 53.

Securing DNS Deployment

In the preceding section, we identified some of the common threats to the DNS infrastructure and provided a number of countermeasures, such as securing zone transfers, disabling recursion, and enabling protection against cache pollution. However, securing a DNS infrastructure requires more than just fine-tuning settings of the individual DNS servers.

Securing the DNS infrastructure starts with the design and implementation of your DNS namespace, and continues with the implementation and configuration of the DNS servers themselves, along with the implementation and configuration of firewalls, routers, and other network devices that can serve to protect individual servers and the network itself. It is possible, for example, to use a private root zone on your intranet and tightly control DNS query access to the Internet. Using a private root in combination with a DNS security policy that restricts DNS queries to the Internet can result in enhanced security for your organization.

DNS Security Levels

To assist in the secure deployment of a DNS infrastructure, Microsoft has published guidelines on its Web site and within the Windows Server 2003 help files that categorize three basic levels of DNS security: low level, medium level, and high level. In the following sections, we will discuss each level in more detail. In considering these models, you should assume that they represent a set of ideal guidelines for the purposes of conceptualization and example. Many organizations do not want to slavishly abide by the models in their purest form.

Low-level DNS Security

The low level of DNS security is precisely that: *low*. In fact, some of the default security configurations of DNS are removed entirely. The effective security is none at all. As the Windows Server 2003 help files state, this kind of configuration should be used only when there is no concern for the integrity of your DNS data or there is no threat that the DNS data on a private network is accessible from the Internet. The characteristics of low-level security are as follows:

- The DNS infrastructure is fully exposed to the Internet.

- All the DNS servers in your network use standard DNS resolution.

- All DNS servers are capable of performing queries to the Internet using root hints that point to the root servers for the Internet.

- Zone transfers are allowed to any server, which represents a removal of the default setting to allow zone transfers only to servers listed in the Name Servers tab.

- The default setting to prevent cache pollution is disabled on the DNS server.

- Multihomed DNS servers (servers with multiple IP addresses) are configured to listen for DNS queries on all configured interfaces.

- All zones are configured to accept dynamic updates from DNS clients.
- UDP and TCP port 53 are open on the firewall for both the source and destination address (that is, the firewall allows any DNS traffic to traverse your firewall, regardless of whether it is initiated by an external or an internal host).

Some organizations may have such a deployment; however, it would be extremely unwise to deploy something like this yourself. Turning off cache pollution protection, in particular, exposes your DNS infrastructure to an unacceptable level of risk, relative to the cost of leaving the default configuration enabled.

Medium-level DNS Security

The medium level of DNS security takes advantage of the countermeasures that are available in a DNS infrastructure where zone data is stored in standard primary or secondary zone files. The security features available through Active Directory-integrated zones are not employed here. The characteristics of medium-level security are as follows:

- Exposure of your DNS infrastructure to the Internet is minimized.
- Internal DNS servers are configured to use a limited list of forwarders when they cannot resolve names locally.
- The default configuration to limit zone transfers to DNS servers listed on the Name Servers tab is left in place.
- In the case of multihomed DNS servers, the DNS servers are configured to listen on only specified IP addresses.
- The default setting to prevent cache pollution is left in place.
- No dynamic updates are allowed on any zones.
- The firewall is configured to limit the traffic traversing the firewall to a limited set of source and destination addresses. Only the external DNS servers under your control are allowed to communicate with internal DNS servers.
- Only the external DNS servers in front of your firewall are configured with root hints to perform recursion.
- All name resolution required by a host on your internal network is performed by proxy servers or gateways.

This represents a more reasonable and prudent approach to mitigating risk to the DNS infrastructure than is offered by the low level, with a low cost of implementation relative to the advantages gained.

High-level DNS Security

A high-level security policy starts with the medium-level security policy and furthers enhances security by leveraging the security available with Active Directory-integrated zones. Furthermore, the high-level security policy assumes that there is no DNS communication with the Internet. This is an unlikely configuration, but something like it might be implemented by organizations that have strict security requirements, and the risk of connectivity to the Internet is deemed to be too great. The characteristics of a high-level security policy are as follows:

- No DNS communication is allowed between the Internet and internal DNS servers.

- The internal DNS infrastructure deploys a private, internal root namespace and is authoritative for all zones.

- The root hints file on all DNS servers points to only the IP addresses of the internal DNS servers that are authoritative for the private root zone.

- Zone transfers are limited to specific IP addresses, rather than just servers listed on the Name Server tab.

- DNS servers are configured to listen on specific IP addresses.

- All DNS servers run on domain controllers, with discretionary access control lists (DACLs) configured to allow only specific authorized individuals to perform administrative tasks on the DNS servers.

- All DNS zones are configured as Active Directory-integrated zones, with DACLs configured to allow only specific authorized individuals to create, modify, or delete DNS zones.

- All RRs stored in Active Directory-integrated zones have DACLs to allow only specific individuals to create, delete, or modify zone data.

- *No* dynamic updates are allowed on the root and top-level domains.

- Only secure dynamic updates are allowed on the child domains.

For many organizations, none of these models will be adequate. The cost, for example, of not allowing DNS communication with the Internet, and hence connectivity, might be too great. The reality is that many organizations will want to develop and deploy a DNS security model that is hybrid of the medium-level and high-level security models.

General DNS Security Guidelines

In planning for the security of your DNS infrastructure, you will want to take into account the design of your DNS namespace, the number and type of DNS servers and zones you plan to deploy, and whether the DNS servers will be serving internal or external clients. You will also want to take into account the security already present or needed in your current infrastructure, such as the location, type, and configuration of firewalls that protect your network.

Security Guidelines for an External DNS Infrastructure

Integrity and availability of DNS data are primary considerations for an external DNS infrastructure, and your design should be informed by these considerations:

- Place all DNS servers in a DMZ or a perimeter network to ensure that access rules and packet filtering on firewalls and routers tightly control source and destination addresses and ports. If possible, configure single-purpose DNS servers and allow traffic on only UDP and TCP port 53 to reach these servers from the Internet.

- Uninstall all unnecessary services from these servers, install current service packs, and harden the servers as much as possible.

- Eliminate single points of failure by hosting DNS servers on different subnets served by different routers. Consider hosting a secondary server at your ISP, for example. This will help mitigate the risk of DoS attacks.

- Consider using a stealth primary server to update read-only secondary servers that are registered with ICANN.

- Allow zone transfers to only a specific set of IP addresses and consider using IPSec or VPN tunnels to enhance the security of zone transfer traffic.

- Do not enable dynamic updates on Internet-facing DNS servers.

- Enable protection against cache pollution on Internet-facing DNS servers.

- Disable recursion on Internet-facing servers.

- Regularly monitor DNS logs and Event Viewer.

Security Guidelines for an Internal DNS Infrastructure

Confidentiality, integrity, and availability of DNS data are primary considerations for an internal DNS infrastructure. The following are security guidelines to consider:

- Consider using a separate, internal namespace to enhance security.

- Do not allow external access from the Internet to your internal DNS servers.

- Consider using a proxy server or a gateway to manage Internet DNS requests for internal clients.

- Use Active Directory-integrated zones and allow only secure updates to these zones.

- Specify and limit the servers that are able to receive zone transfers.

- Eliminate single points of failure and consider how internal DNS clients will resolve names in the event that the primary DNS server in their TCP/IP configuration fails.

- Consider that delegating authority of child domains can involve a security trade-off if different administrators are responsible for the authoritative DNS servers.

Monitoring DNS Servers

An important task in maintaining a DNS environment is monitoring the DNS servers to ensure that they are resolving names and IP addresses properly, and to ensure that they have sufficient resources to handle their workload. Windows Server 2003 and the Windows Server 2003 DNS service provide a number of tools for monitoring DNS servers. These tools include the Monitoring tab on the

DNS console, DNS debug logging, DNS event logging, and DNS Performance Monitor counters, as well as command-line tools such as NSLookup.exe, Dnscmd.exe, and DNSLint.exe. In this section, we will briefly cover the use of these tools to monitor a DNS server environment.

Testing DNS Server Configuration with the DNS Console Monitoring Tab

The DNS console provides a simple but effective tool for ensuring that the DNS service is working properly. To use this tool, click the **Monitoring** tab of the properties for the DNS server, as shown in Figure 20.17.

Figure 20.17 Performing Simple and Recursive Queries Using the Monitoring Tab of the DNS Server Properties

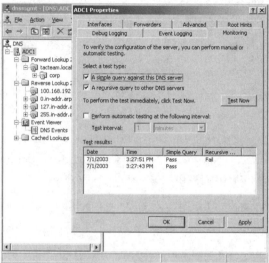

The Monitoring tab allows you to perform a simple and a recursive query test to ensure proper operation. A simple query test uses the DNS client installed on the DNS server to send a local query to the DNS server. A recursive query test uses the local DNS client as well. However, in this case, the DNS client requests that the DNS service use recursion to resolve an NS-type query for the root zone. Failure of this test usually indicates a problem with network connectivity or incorrectly configured root hints. (In the example in Figure 20.17, the recursive query test failed because the network adapter was unplugged before the test was run, and the DNS server could not connect to the servers listed in the root hints file.) When a DNS server fails one of these tests, a warning symbol is displayed on the DNS server in the DNS console. Note that you can set up automatic simple and recursive query testing in the Monitoring tab.

It is a good practice to use these tests after you have set up a DNS server or have made a configuration change on a current DNS server.

Debug Logging

If you need to analyze and monitor the DNS server performance in greater detail, you can use the optional debug tool that you can enable in the **Debug Logging** tab of the DNS server property pages. Because debug logging consumes significant resources, it is not enabled by default and should be enabled only on a temporary basis, such as when you're trying to troubleshoot a problem with DNS. Figure 20.18 shows the configurable properties for DNS debug logging.

Figure 20.18 Debug Logging Properties

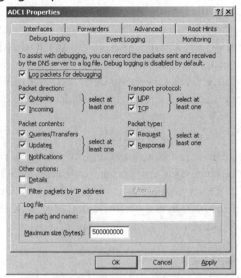

As you can see in Figure 20.18, you have a lot of flexibility and control with regard to the filtering of DNS traffic you wish to include in the debug logs. You can choose to log packets based on the following:

- Their direction, either outbound or inbound
- The transport protocol, either TCP or UDP
- Their contents: queries/transfers, updates, or notifications
- Their type, either requests or responses
- Their IP address

Finally, you can choose to include detailed information.

Let's assume you were trying to troubleshoot a problem with dynamic updates. You could configure the debug utility to log any update packets, but exclude queries/transfers and notifications. This configuration would exclude information that isn't relevant to the problem. You could further refine the information contained in the logs by monitoring for either requests or responses or for incoming or outgoing packets.

Depending on the amount of DNS traffic the server processes and the logging options you select, the log files can grow quite large. You should, therefore, configure logging to occur on a separate hard drive. When the log file reaches the maximum size or the hard drive runs out of room, newer events will overwrite older events.

Event Logging

By default, the DNS service will log all DNS events to the *DNS Event log*. In Windows Server 2003, DNS events are kept in a separate system event log that can be accessed from either the DNS console or Event Viewer. The **Event Logging** tab on the properties of the DNS server allows you to configure the events you would like to log in the DNS Event log. There are four options on the **Event Logging** tab: **No events, Errors only, Errors and warnings**, and **All events**. The default is to log **All events**, which include informational messages that indicate service startup, a new version number for a zone file, and so on. On a busy DNS server, the default size of the event log might not be large enough. You should consider increasing the size of the DNS Event log in this case.

Monitoring DNS Server Using the Performance Console

The Windows Server 2003 Performance console provides a means of monitoring DNS performance, either in real time through the System Monitor or as events logged over a period time by Performance Logs. When the DNS service is installed on Windows Server 2003, more than 60 performance counters are installed for measuring performance of the DNS service. Figure 20.19 shows some of the DNS performance counters that you can select in System Monitor.

Figure 20.19 DNS Performance Counters

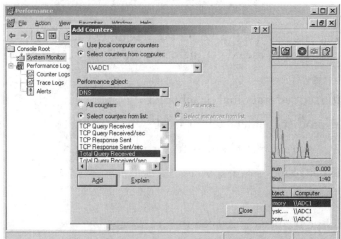

Because the DNS is a critical service, you should log its performance over a period of time using Performance Logs to establish a baseline for normal operating conditions. Once you've established a baseline, you can then use this information to predict effects of planned changes to the infrastructure, such as adding or removing other DNS servers or adding more DNS clients.

Performance baselines also help you to optimize services on your network by providing real-world data about the performance of your servers and your network.

Having a baseline also allows you to detect and troubleshoot problems with your DNS and network infrastructure. For example, if the number of **Secure Update Failures** suddenly increased, you might be prompted to investigate further to determine the cause of the problem.

In choosing DNS counters to monitor, you should consider the role(s) of the DNS server:

- If the DNS server is installed on a domain controller and configured for secure only updates in Active Directory-integrated zones, you should monitor counters that are relevant to dynamic updater performance and security, such as **Secure Update Failure, Dynamic Update Written to Database/sec, Dynamic Update Received/sec,** and so on.

- If the DNS server is used to perform recursion on behalf of clients, you should monitor counters that are relevant to the performance of recursive queries, such as **Recursive Queries/sec** or **Recursive Query Failures/sec**. If you have disabled recursion on your server, a spike in the number of recursive queries the DNS server receives could warrant further investigation.

- If the DNS server replicates zone data with other servers, either as a primary or secondary server, you should monitor counters relevant to zone transfers, such as **AFXR Requests Received**, which would indicate that a number of secondary DNS servers are requesting a full, rather than incremental, zone transfer. A sudden increase in the number of zone transfer requests could indicate the presence of an attacker trying to footprint your DNS records.

Command-line Tools for Maintaining and Monitoring DNS Servers

Windows Server 2003 provides three command-line utilities for maintaining and monitoring DNS servers:

- **NSLookup** This is a standard tool used for monitoring and troubleshooting DNS servers. It provides a means to obtain detailed results for queries performed against a DNS server. NSLookup has two modes: interactive and noninteractive. Interactive mode allows you enter more than one command at an NSLookup prompt. Noninteractive mode is invoked as a single command with options from a command prompt. For NSLookup to work properly, the DNS server that NSLookup is pointing to must have a PTR record for it in a reverse lookup zone.

- **Dnscmd** This utility is found in the \Support\Tools folder on the Windows Server 2003 installation CD. The Dnscmd tool can be used as an alternative to the DNS MMC. With DNScmd, you can create and delete zones, view records, update zone records, and perform other administrative tasks that you would normally perform using the DNS console. Dnscmd can be used to script batch operations and perform remote administration, providing an efficient way to manage multiple, remote DNS servers.

- **DNSLint**   This utility is found in the \Support\Tools folder on the Windows Server 2003 installation CD. DNSLint is new to Windows Server 2003. Its primary purpose is to assist in troubleshooting problems arising from lame (incorrect) delegations and common AD DNS problems, such as verifying records for AD replication. A key advantage of the tool is that it can examine multiple servers in a single operation and display the output as an HTML file. For example, if you were trying to troubleshoot a problem with delegation, you would need to traverse the DNS namespace in multiple steps. With DNSLint, you can diagnose the problem in a single operation. You can also use DNSLint with the **/c** switch to test well-known e-mail ports on all e-mail servers that it finds in the zone records of the DNS servers it checks in the domain.

These tools can be used for a variety of purposes, such as verifying the presence of RRs, checking for lame delegations, checking for missing AD replication records, configuring DNS server settings on multiple servers, and so on.

Planning for NetBIOS Name Resolution

In a Windows 2000 or Windows Server 2003 environment, DNS is the primary method for name resolution. However, even in these environments, NetBIOS name resolution might still be extensively used. For example, if the network consists of older clients, such as Windows NT 4 and Windows 9x clients, you must still support NetBIOS name resolution. Also, certain applications, such as Microsoft Exchange Server, still rely on NetBIOS for their functionality. So, even if the domain is upgraded to AD and all of the clients on the network are upgraded to Windows 2000 or Windows XP, it might still be necessary to support NetBIOS name resolution.

The primary means for ensuring fault-tolerant and timely NetBIOS name resolution is through the implementation of WINS. Through its ability to replicate information with other WINS servers, WINS provides a distributed database that allows NetBIOS clients to register their NetBIOS names to ensure uniqueness and to resolve NetBIOS-to-IP address mappings consistently throughout the network infrastructure. Because WINS servers are capable of replicating database information to one another, this means that multiple WINS servers can provide both fault tolerance and availability of records for NetBIOS resolution to even very large networks that involve many different sites.

Understanding NETBIOS Naming

NetBIOS names have been used in all past versions of Windows and you are no doubt quite familiar with NetBIOS names. Recall that a NetBIOS name is a 16-character string that is used to identify computers, groups, or services on the network. The first 15 characters of the name are configured on the computer by the user or the administrator. The sixteenth and last character of a NetBIOS name identifies a resource type associated with the NetBIOS-related services that are running on the computer.

There are two kinds of NetBIOS names:

- **Unique names**   These names are used to uniquely identify computers and the NetBIOS-related services running on them.

- **Group names** These names are used primarily to support browsing and browser elections.

Collectively, NetBIOS names comprise a *flat* namespace. This differs from a DNS namespace, which provides a hierarchical namespace. And, while it is possible to group NetBIOS names according to a workgroup or domain name for display by the browser service, NetBIOS names must be unique within the NetBIOS namespace.

NetBIOS Name Resolution Process

In a NetBIOS environment that does not employ LMHOSTS files or WINS servers, NetBIOS is completely dependent on broadcasts to register names and to resolve NetBIOS names to addresses. Without the presence of WINS or LMHOSTS files to assist in name resolution, NetBIOS name resolution would generate considerable broadcast traffic for name resolution, adding to the traffic generated to support NetBIOS registration and the browser service. Furthermore, since NetBIOS broadcast traffic normally does not cross routers, it would not be possible to resolve computer names on remote subnets.

To support NetBIOS name resolution on a segmented network, you can use two methods. The first relies on the deployment of LMHOSTS. The second relies on the deployment of WINS servers. A third method, opening routers to forward NetBIOS broadcast traffic, is neither a sensible nor a viable solution in most instances, with the exception of small networks that must use separate networks because they are in different physical locations. That said, it is generally recommended that routers not be configured to forward NetBIOS broadcast traffic and that LMHOSTS files or WINS servers be used to support NetBIOS name resolution across subnets.

Understanding the LMHOSTS File

LMHOSTS files are a good solution in small environments that have a segmented network. In addition, they can be useful in situations where you want some computers to communicate with others across a WAN link, but you do not want to combine the NetBIOS namespace of the offices on either side of the link. However, in large environments, LMHOSTS files are difficult to maintain. An LMHOSTS file must be present on each computer that needs it for name resolution. You can create centralized LMHOSTS files, but the client computers must first have an LMHOSTS file to gain access to the centralized LMHOSTS files. Also, you must manually enter NetBIOS name-to-IP address mappings, increasing the possibility for error. Finally, the use of LMHOSTS files is not possible in an environment that uses DHCP to assigned TCP/IP address configurations to client computers.

To support NetBIOS name resolution in a segmented network or one that uses multiple broadcast domains, a better approach than LMHOSTS files is to use WINS. If a network has been using LMHOSTS files extensively, it is relatively easy to migrate to WINS by importing LMHOSTS files to the database to create static mappings. However, you need to exercise care to ensure that these mappings can be overwritten by WINS clients that use dynamic mappings.

Understanding WINS

In segmented network environments that use DHCP, the best solution to allow for proper NetBIOS name resolution is to use WINS servers. A WINS server provides a database that NetBIOS clients can use to register their NetBIOS names and resolve NetBIOS-to-IP address mappings.

Furthermore, WINS traffic is unicast-based. This means that, instead of relying on broadcasts to register and resolve names, WINS clients will send unicast messages directly to the WINS server, whether on the same or different subnet. The use of unicast helps to reduce the amount of broadcast traffic on the network that is the result of NetBIOS name resolution.

The ability for different WINS servers to replicate database information with each other is another significant advantage in that the replication of this information ensures that clients can resolve NetBIOS names regardless of their location or the WINS server they contact.

When a NetBIOS registration is successful, the WINS server stores the name mapping with the following information:

- **Record Name** The NetBIOS name of the computer, group, or service registered in the database.

- **Type** The resource type associated with the name. Common resource types are [00h] for the workstation service, [03h] for the messenger service, [020h] for the server service, and [1Ch] for the domain name.

- **IP Address** The IP address for the registered name.

- **State** The state of the registration, such as Active, Released, or Tombstoned.

- **Static** Indicates if record is a static mapping (column entry marked with an *x*).

- **Owner** Indicates the owner (specific WINS server where the record was registered) of the record.

- **Version** Indicates the version ID of the record.

- **Expiration** Indicates the date and time the record will expire, if it is not refreshed.

NetBIOS clients that do not use a WINS server must constantly register and defend their NetBIOS names. However, the registration occurs by means of a broadcast and, thus, the registrations are local to the subnet. Whenever a computer attempts to register a duplicate name, it will receive a negative response from the computer that actively possesses the name. Whenever NetBIOS name registration fails, the computer receives an error message, and NetBT won't initialize on the computer until the problem is resolved.

Whenever a WINS client is gracefully shut down, it sends a name release request to the WINS server. The WINS server marks the entry as *released* and gives it a timestamp of the current time plus the *extinction interval*. This interval indicates the time that must elapse before the record is marked as extinct (or *tombstoned*) and can be scavenged from the database. However, if the WINS server that receives the release request is not the original owner of the name registration, it will immediately mark the record as *extinct*. The reason for this is to prevent inconsistencies between primary and secondary servers configured as replication partners.

What's New for WINS in Windows Server 2003

The WINS service was significantly improved in Window 2000, which introduced a number of significant enhancements, such as enhanced filtering and searching for records display and burst handling of WINS registrations. The WINS service in Windows Server 2003 maintains these improvements and adds two more improvements:

- **Filtering records** It is now possible to combine filters used to query the WINS database. The available filters include record owner, record type, NetBIOS name, and IP address with or without subnet mask. You can also cache the results of queries in the RAM of the local computer from which the query is performed, improving performance for subsequent queries and reducing network traffic.

- **Accepting replication partners** For pull replication, you can configure the WINS server to either accept or reject only the name records that are owned by a list of prede-termined WINS servers. (Figure 20.20 later in this chapter shows the Advanced replication property page where accepting replication partners are configured.) In Windows 2000, it was possible to create only a list of replication partners to block.

Planning WINS Server Deployment

Clients can be configured to use multiple WINS servers (up to 12) to register and resolve computer names in the event that the primary WINS server is unavailable. WINS servers can be configured to replicate with one another to ensure both fault tolerance and the availability of records for name resolution in a distributed environment where WINS clients are registering with different WINS servers. The number of WINS servers that should be deployed depends on several complex factors, such as the number of WINS clients that will be registering and resolving names and the network topology (in particular, the presence, number, and capacity of WAN links). If you require WINS replication to meet the goals of fault tolerance and availability, the WINS replication topology needs to be designed to ensure optimal performance in the replication of WINS records and the currency of those records, as well as to ensure optimal query response times, given the constraints of the network topology.

Server Number and Placement

The number of WINS servers you deploy will be determined by the number of WINS clients and the network topology. In general, you should try to design the WINS infrastructure to minimize the number of WINS servers. Having too many WINS servers can complicate network problems, so Microsoft recommends a conservative approach in determining the number of WINS servers and further recommends one primary and one backup WINS server set up as replication partners to each other for every 10,000 clients.

The WINS traffic between clients and servers is relatively small, about 40 bytes, which is the average size of a WINS registration for a client. So, 10,000 WINS records would be approximately 400KB. Through a 56 Kbps WAN link, this amount of data would take a minute to transfer, assuming you could transfer at this rate. It is more likely, though, that the effective bandwidth is somewhat lower than 56 Kbps, and the transfer of 400KB of information would take longer. This delay might or might not be acceptable. However, it is unlikely that 10,000 WINS registrations or 10,000 updated WINS records would need to be transferred simultaneously across the WAN.

To determine the actual number of WINS servers to deploy, you will need to take into account server hardware, WAN links, the number of clients, and the need for redundancy and availability. You should also take into account peak-load conditions that could occur, for example, if the power to client computers were suddenly terminated and then resumed, resulting in a large number of simultaneous registration requests.

Planning for WINS Replication

Even in simple environments, it is a good idea to have two WINS servers configured as replication partners to provide greater fault tolerance and availability. This kind of replication is relatively easy to set up, for example by specifying automatic partner configuration, and requires little planning.

In larger and more complex networks, however, the replication topology will need to be carefully designed to ensure an optimal *convergence time* for the replication of WINS records, given the size, topology, and available bandwidth of the network. Convergence time refers to the maximum amount of time it takes for an updated record to be replicated to all WINS servers in the infrastructure. Generally, convergence time is a function of replication pull schedules and the number of hops in a given replication path that a changed object must travel.

In reality, the amount of time it will take for a record to be synchronized depends on a number of factors. For example, a WINS server configured to send push notifications immediately upon receiving an update will replicate the record faster than the time determined by the replication schedule of the WINS servers that have configured it as a pull partner. Factors that can affect convergence time include the following:

- The kind of replication partnership that is configured. A push/pull replication partnership is more efficient for replicating records than a limited partnership (push or pull only).

- The settings for pull and push partnerships that determine the frequency of replication between servers.

- The ability to use persistent connections for push and pull replication partners (this setting is the default and found in the Replication properties pages of the WINS server console.) The ability to use this setting depends on the presence of stable, high-speed links.

- The particular replication model. The longer the replication path that a replicated object must travel, the longer the convergence time. In a complex replication environment involving multiple WINS servers, a hub-and-spoke replication topology provides the shortest replication paths.

- The particular kind of update that occurs in the WINS database. For example, a name release update will not propagate as quickly as a name registration update, because it is more common for a name-to-IP address mapping to be reused by the same computer, even in an environment that uses DHCP. Since this kind of update is not as urgent as a new name registration, the WINS server provides it with a greater *latency* period for replication.

Along with these factors, you will need to take into account the network topology in planning for WINS replication. Your WINS replication design should, if possible, mirror your network topology. For example, if the organization has a centrally located head office that is connected by high-speed, persistent WAN links to satellite branch offices, you should consider a hub-and-spoke replication model with full push/pull partnerships. In this model, the WINS server in the head office receives replicated records through the push/pull partnership, and then propagates updates it receives from its own WINS clients and those changes it receives from the individual branch offices to the other branch offices.

To plan for WINS replication, it is important to first understand partnership agreements and the settings that can be configured on them.

Replication Partnership Configuration

In order for WINS servers to replicate WINS records with each other, a replication partnership must be configured between them. There are three possible kinds of replication partnerships that can be configured between WINS servers: *push/pull* (also known as *full*), *push-only*, and *pull-only* (also known as *limited*). You can set up a replication partnership manually or implement it automatically.

Automatic Partner Configuration

Automatic partner configuration is an option that can be implemented on small networks to eliminate the administrative effort for configuring replication partnerships between WINS servers. When the automatic partner configuration is enabled, the WINS server will send announcements using the multicast Internet Group Messaging Protocol (IGMP) address at 224.0.1.24, which is the well-known multicast address for WINS servers. When the WINS server discovers other WINS servers that are announcing themselves, the WINS server will automatically configure a partnership agreement between itself and the discovered WINS server. (Both must be enabled for automatic partner configuration.) When the WINS server discovers another WINS server, it will add the server to its list of replication partners, configure push/pull replication between the servers, and set the pull replication interval for every two hours.

Figure 20.20 shows the **Advanced** tab of the **Replication Partners Properties** dialog box, which contains the **Enable automatic partner configuration** option. To view this page, you need to view the properties of the **Replication Partners** node in the **WINS** console.

Figure 20.20 Enabling Automatic Partner Configuration

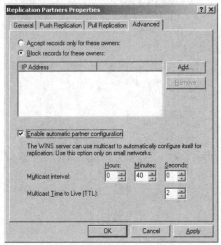

Normally, routers do not forward IGMP traffic, so this configuration is best used on small, unsegmented LANs. However, it is possible to configure routers to forward this traffic, allowing automatic partner configuration to be used in a routed environment. If there are only a few routers in the environment, the amount of multicast broadcast traffic should be minimal.

Push Partnerships

As the name implies, when a push partnership is configured, changes in the WINS database are *pushed* to the remote WINS server. More accurately, a WINS server with records to replicate sends a push notification to target servers (those configured to use it as a pull partner), alerting them that it has records to update on the target WINS servers. The push notification includes an owner table that lists the owner IDs and the highest version ID for each owner. The target servers compare this information with their own owner tables to determine which records to replicate. The target servers reply to the push notification with a pull request, and the transfer of records takes place. Accordingly, since a transfer of records will not take place until a pull request has been received by the server that sent the push notification, pull replication is the single mechanism for replication. The process for push replication occurs as follows:

1. The source WINS server receives updates to its database and, based on a configurable threshold, sends a push notification to the destination WINS server (its push partner), indicating that it has updates to replicate.

2. The destination WINS server for the notification (the push partner) responds by initiating a pull request to its pull partner (the WINS server that sent the notification), and the replication is initiated between the replication partners.

Push replication is not schedulable according to an interval of time. Rather, the WINS administrator configures an update threshold that will trigger a push notification. For example, the WINS server could be configured to send a notification to its push partner after it has received 100 updates. Figure 20.21 shows the **Push Replication** tab of the **Replication Partners Properties** dialog box with the default settings for push replication.

Figure 20.21 Push Replication Settings

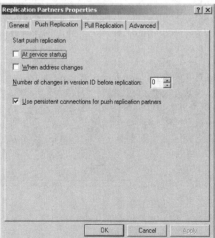

The settings that you enter here will determine the threshold trigger for the push notification. In the configuration shown in Figure 20.21, a push notification is sent to the replication partner as soon as an update occurs in the WINS database. This is the result of setting the value for **Number of changes in version ID before replication** to **0**. However, the value could be set to a higher number, such as 100. It is also possible to configure a push notification to occur when the service starts up or when there is an address change in a WINS registration.

The setting to **Use persistent connections for push replication partners** allows the connections between WINS servers to remain open. This is a useful feature when the WINS servers are connected by a high-speed LAN. Earlier versions of WINS would close the connection after each replication cycle. Opening the connection to initiate a new replication cycle could cause delays, however modest, that are not acceptable in an environment where records need to be synchronized as soon as possible.

It is also possible to manually initiate the push notification, as shown in Figure 20.22. When you manually initiate the push notification, you can choose to push the notification to the replication partner or to trigger the replication to send a notification to all of its partners as well. As an example, consider a replication topology where three WINS servers are configured as push replication partners. WINS-A replicates to WINS-B, which replicates to WINS-C. So, if you manually sent a push notification from WINS-A to its replication partner, WINS-B, you could force WINS-B to also send a push notification to its other replication partner, WINS-C.

Figure 20.22 Manually Starting Push Notification

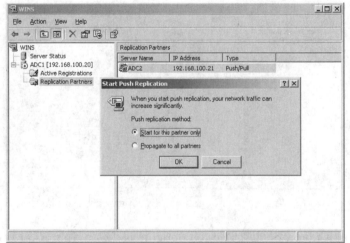

In certain rare situations, it might be desirable to use a *push-only* replication partnership for one-way replication, for example, from a head office to a branch office. For example, suppose that WINS-A in the head office configures WINS-B in the branch office as its push-only partner. (WINS-B should also configure WINS-A as its pull-only partner.) When WINS-A receives updates to its records, it notifies WINS-B, which sends an update (pull) request to WINS-A for the changed records since the last replication cycle. In this scenario, WINS-B never sends its updated records to WINS-A.

Push partnerships are generally configured in LAN environments where bandwidth is not an issue, and it is not necessary to schedule replication to occur during off-peak hours. In general, you should use push replication partnerships in the following situations:

- There is ample bandwidth over LAN or WAN connections.
- There is a need to ensure that updates are replicated as soon as possible and the frequency of replication traffic is not a consideration.

Pull Partnerships

Pull replication differs from push replication in that the replication frequency is defined as an interval of time. At regularly scheduled intervals, a pull partner requests updates from other WINS servers (those configured to use it as a push partner) for updated records that have a higher version ID than the ones it currently has in its database.

Pull replication is configured similarly to push replication. The primary difference is that the WINS administrator schedules the times that the pull replication will take place. Figure 20.23 shows the settings for pull replication that an administrator can configure for individual replication partners.

Figure 20.23 Choosing Replication Partnership Type and Push/Pull Settings

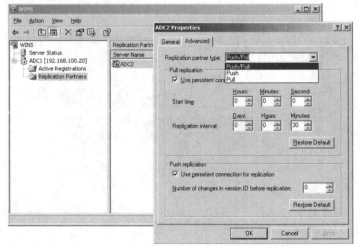

In some situations, it might be desirable to configure *pull-only* replication between replication partners. Usually, this configuration is implemented where WAN links are operating close to capacity and there is a need to schedule WINS replication during off-peak hours. Pull-only replication has an advantage over push-only replication in that the replication schedule can be known in advance. With push-only replication, replication is triggered by reaching a configured threshold of updates, and you can only estimate when this would occur based on experience with the network. However, a disadvantage of pull-only replication is that the WINS server could potentially have acquired a large number of updates to replicate between cycles.

In general, you should use pull replication partnerships in the following situations:

- There is limited bandwidth between WINS servers that requires replication to be scheduled during off hours.

- There is a need to consolidate updates and reduce frequency and amount of replication traffic.

- There is a need to exercise finer control over the timing and frequency of replication traffic.

Push/Pull Partnerships

A push/pull partnership is the default when you configure replication between WINS servers. In fact, Microsoft recommends a push/pull partnership as a best practice and it further recommends that all WINS partnerships be set up this way, unless there is an overriding need to implement a limited partnership. The only need that Microsoft cites for a limited partnership is the presence of a large network connected by relatively slow WAN links. Microsoft often stresses the need for simplicity in a WINS environment.

With a push/pull partnership, a WINS server will be configured both to send push notifications and to make pull requests to its replication partner. The replication partner will also be configured in a similar way. Such a configuration helps to ensure that synchronization among WINS server is optimal, depending on the pull schedule and the configured threshold for push notifications, among other factors. For example, suppose that a WINS server that suddenly experiences a large number of updates immediately sends a push notification to its push partner. The push partner would immediately request these updates, without waiting for the request to be triggered by its pull schedule. Conversely, a WINS server always pulls up-to-date records from its pull partner according to the replication schedule, regardless of how few records have been updated on the pull partner WIN server.

You should always try to deploy a push/pull partnership, unless there is an overriding concern that requires the implementation of a limited partnership.

Replication Models

As we mentioned earlier, the replication model you design will have an effect on the convergence time for replicated WINS records and fault tolerance for replicated records. A replication model that is appropriate for your network topology will ensure the shortest convergence time for replicated WINS records. Where possible, it is recommended that your replication model mirror your network topology and that you keep this model as simple as possible.

In WINS environments where there are three or more WINS servers, you can employ either a *ring* replication model or a *hub-and-spoke* replication model. In more complex environments, these models can be combined to ensure optimal convergence time and fault tolerance for a given network topology. In the following sections, we will discuss each of these models in more detail.

Ring Model

In a ring model, three or more WINS servers are configured to replicate with one another in a circular fashion. The ring model provides for good convergence times for all replication partners when there are no more than four WINS servers. Figure 20.24 shows a ring replication model.

Figure 20.24 Ring Replication Model for WINS Servers

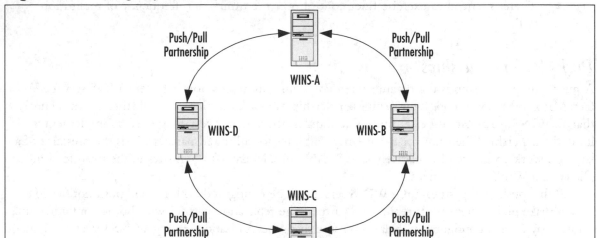

In this model, fault tolerance for replication of WINS records is given priority. Imagine that a record is updated on WINS-A. The record must travel through either WINS-B or WINS-B before it is replicated to WINS-C. However, suppose that the WAN link connecting WINS-A and WINS-D fails. The updated record can still arrive at WINS-C and WINS-D (via WINS-C). Conversely, a record created on WINS-D can still be replicated to WINS-A via WINS-C and WINS-B.

Hub-and-Spoke Model

In the hub-and-spoke model, all WINS servers replicate with a centrally located hub WIN server. The hub-and-spoke model provides for the shortest convergence time in a replication environment that comprises five or more WINS servers, because it provides for the shortest replication paths between any two WINS servers. Furthermore, by implementing a hub-and-spoke model, you reduce the number of replication partnership agreements that you need to maintain. Figure 20.25 shows a typical hub-and-spoke implementation.

Figure 20.25 Hub-and-Spoke Replication Model for WINS Servers

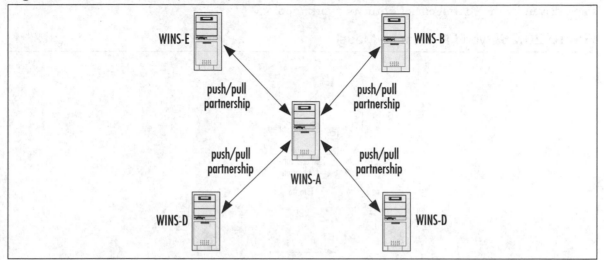

Even though there are five WINS servers that replicate information, there are only four replication agreements to maintain. Furthermore, no server is more than two hops from any other server, regardless of the number of servers added to the topology.

A disadvantage of this model is that it is not as fault tolerant as the ring model. If WINS-A fails, no WINS server will be able to replicate its records to other WINS servers. Furthermore, depending on the average number of records the spoke WINS servers need to replicate and the settings for the push and pull triggers, WINS-A can be continuously replicating with other servers and processing updates. It should be well connected to the other WINS servers and have the capacity to handle the load.

A Windows cluster gives you the ability to set up separate WINS servers, known as *cluster nodes*, that use the same database located in a shared SCSI or Fibre Channel device. When the WINS server that is the active node in the cluster fails, the services will *failover* to another node. Failover is the process of taking resources offline in one node and bringing them online on a new node. The primary advantage of using a Windows cluster is that in the event of a failure of a WINS server, no subsequent replication needs to occur to synchronize records when the failed server is brought online, since only a single database is used. Windows Server 2003 Standard, Enterprise, and Datacenter editions support clustering. For more information about clustering, see the Windows Server 2003 help files.

Hybrid Replication Model

In many situations, it is desirable to combine replication models. As an example, consider a large organization that has three divisions in different geographic locations. Each of these divisions has a number of branch offices that are connected to their respective divisional offices. It might be advantageous to use a ring model of WINS replication among the divisional offices and use hub-and-spoke replication for replication between the divisional offices and their respective branch offices. Figure 20.26 shows a conceptual representation of a hybrid model. Many other variations are possible. A hybrid replication model can employ any mixture of full and limited replication partnerships, driven by the contingencies of the network topology.

Figure 20.26 Hybrid Replication Model

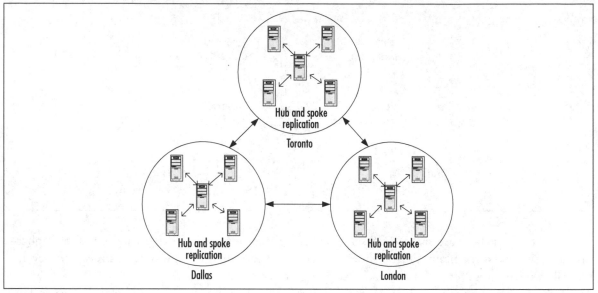

WINS Issues

After establishing the need for WINS planning for the replication topology of the WINS infrastructure, the WINS servers need to be installed and configured. In this section, we will look at the various configuration issues that a WINS administrator needs to be familiar with to ensure an efficient and secure WINS infrastructure, such as handing static WINS entries, client configurations, database maintenance, and WINS infrastructure security.

Static WINS Entries

One of the advantages of using WINS is that it provides a way to dynamically register NetBIOS names, eliminating the need for static entries in LMHOSTS files. However, there are situations that require the use of static mappings in the WINS server database. For example, if you have non-WINS clients that are running NetBIOS applications, you might find it desirable to have entries for these clients in the WINS database, so that you can allow WINS clients to resolve the NetBIOS names of those clients. Static mappings are superior to entries in an LMHOSTS file because they can be replicated throughout the WINS infrastructure.

The use of static mappings can create problems on your network. Unlike dynamic mappings, static mappings stay in the WINS database until they are manually removed. (The expiration date for the static mapping entry in the WINS database is labeled as *infinite*.) Furthermore, unless the migrate on setting is enabled, static mappings are not overwritten by dynamic mappings. For example, a client computer might be given a static mapping in the WINS database, or an LMHOSTS file might be imported to the WINS database, creating a number of static WINS entries. If the clients that are associated with the static mappings were later configured as WINS clients, they would not be able to perform dynamic registration of their NetBIOS names, unless the migrate on setting was enabled. Figure 20.27 shows the **Replication Partners Properties** dialog box, where the **Overwrite unique static mappings at this server (migrate on)** setting is enabled.

Figure 20.27 Configuring Static Entries to Be Overwritten

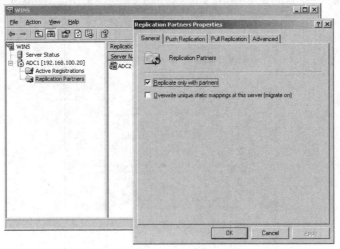

In general, static entries should never be created for WINS-capable client computers. However, it is sometimes desirable for security purposes to use static entries for mission-critical servers to prevent redirection.

Using Static Entries to Prevent Redirection

Unlike with Active Directory-integrated DNS zones, you cannot restrict clients from dynamically registering names according to Windows group memberships. The only mechanism by which WINS prevents clients from registering duplicate names is to send a challenge to the IP address of the active record. If the client responds to the challenge, the duplicate name registration is denied. However, during periods when WINS clients are offline for maintenance or are being rebooted, a rogue computer could register the same name as the original computer, with the malicious intent of redirecting traffic to the rogue computer. In high-security environments, it might be desirable to enter static mappings for critical computers and to ensure that the **Overwrite unique static mappings at this server (migrate on)** setting is disabled.

Multihomed WINS Servers

A multihomed WINS server is one that has more than one active network connection. You should avoid this configuration of a WINS server. Name resolution and replication problems are often the result of using a multihomed computer as a WINS server.

Client Configuration

WINS client configuration is accomplished either through a DHCP server or manually by configuring the settings in the **WINS** tab of the **Advanced TCP/IP Settings** property pages of the TCP/IP properties. Figure 20.28 shows these settings for a Windows XP client.

Figure 20.28 Advanced TCP/IP Settings for WINS Client Configuration

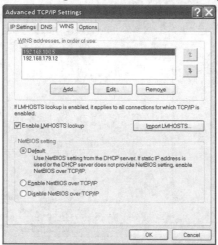

With the configuration shown in Figure 20.28, the client will use an LMHOSTS file if WINS name resolution fails. This is the default configuration. Also, the client is configured to get information about whether NetBT should be enabled from the DHCP server. (This information is provided by a special Microsoft-specific DHCP option.) If the client does not get this information from the DHCP server, it will default to enabling NetBT. You would disable NetBT only when you need to, such as on the Internet-facing interface of a multihomed server or if you have determined that the interface does not need to be able to provide access to NetBIOS applications.

If you are using a DHCP server, you do not need to specify static addresses for WINS servers in this dialog box. If you do configure WINS addresses here, these settings will override those that are supplied by the DHCP server. If you are using DHCP to supply the client settings, you will need to configure two DHCP options:

- **Option 044 WINS/NBNS Servers** You use this option to provide DHCP clients with the IP addresses of WINS servers to contact.

- **Option 046 WINS/NBT Node Type** This option governs the order of NetBIOS name resolution mechanisms that will be used. The hybrid setting option (0x08) is the one most commonly used. With the hybrid node option specified, the WINS client will contact a WINS server before using broadcasts and other methods to resolve names. The mixed node setting option (0x04) forces WINS clients to use broadcasts before contacting the WINS server. This setting is useful in situations where there is a single subnet in a small branch office connected by a slow WAN link. In this case, you might want broadcasts to resolve local NetBIOS names before contacting the remote WINS server. (NetBIOS node types and name resolution were discussed earlier in this chapter.)

Figure 20.29 shows the configuration of DHCP server options to support WINS client configurations.

Figure 20.29 DHCP Options for WINS Client Configurations

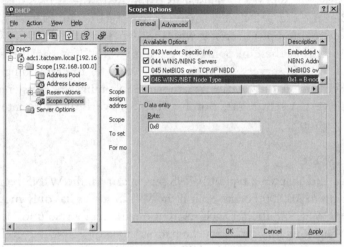

Multiple WINS Server Addresses

If you specify multiple WINS server addresses in the client configuration, the client will try to use the first WINS server in the list for registration and name resolution requests. If the primary server fails to respond, the client will then attempt to contact the alternate WINS servers in the order listed. Up to 12 WINS servers can be specified for Windows XP and Windows 2000 clients.

WINS Proxy Agent

For the rare case where you have a NetBIOS client that is not capable of querying a WINS server for NetBIOS name resolution, you can set up a WINS proxy agent. The WINS proxy agent is a WINS client that is set up on a subnet to provide limited WINS support for b-node and non-WINS NetBIOS clients. A WINS proxy agent listens for name registration and name query broadcasts, and it forwards these to its configured WINS server. This process ensures that the b-node client does not initialize with a duplicate name that is already registered in the WINS database and provides name resolution on behalf of the b-node client.

A common misconception is that a WINS proxy client will register the name on behalf of the non-WINS client. This is not the case. The WINS proxy merely contacts the WINS server to verify that the non-WINS client name does not exist. If there is a duplicate name in the WINS database, the WINS proxy client will send a negative response to the b-node client.

The proxy agent will use its NetBIOS name cache to temporarily store the results of responses to its queries to the WINS server. Performance of the WINS proxy agent could, therefore, be potentially improved by lengthening the amount of time an entry would persist in cache beyond the default 10 minutes.

Preventing Split WINS Registrations

A WINS server is also a WINS client to itself. A common configuration error is to specify a different WINS server to use as an alternate WINS server. The problem with doing this is that during startup of the WINS server, it will try to register its names with the WINS servers configured in the TCP/IP properties. Because the WINS server service won't start until NetBT has initialized, this causes the WINS server to attempt to register with the alternate or secondary WINS. However, it will continue to try to register these mappings in the local WINS database. Once the local WINS database is available, the WINS server will switch to it to register the remaining mappings. This results in what is known as a *split registration*, where name mappings are registered in and owned by two different WINS servers. A split registration for WINS servers can cause intermittent problems with WINS name resolution.

Performance Issues

As mentioned earlier in the chapter, a typical WINS server can handle WINS registrations and name resolution requests for up to 10,000 clients, even if the WINS server has only modest amounts of CPU power and RAM. WINS traffic for each registration and name resolution request is relatively small. However, a number of factors can affect the performance of WINS server. These factors include the presence of other services running on the WINS server, the performance of database maintenance on the WINS server, various WINS server settings, and the flooding of the network with NetBIOS name registration requests. In this section, we'll look at WINS server performance issues.

Hardware Considerations

Even a modestly powered computer can handle a large number of registrations and name resolution requests. However, WINS can generate intensive CPU and disk activity. WINS server performance is, therefore, significantly improved by using fast disks and multiple CPUs. For mission-critical WINS servers that handle large amounts of data, it is a good idea to use RAID arrays to enhance fault tolerance and performance. If you don't use a RAID array, you should consider placing the WINS database on a separate hard disk from the operating system. You can specify the location of the database on the **Advanced** tab of the property pages for the WINS server (see Figure 20.30 in the next section).

If the organization requires a very high degree of fault tolerance and availability, you should consider using a Windows Server 2003 server cluster for the WINS service. This will require at least two WINS servers configured as cluster nodes to use a shared SCSI or Fibre Channel storage device. On large networks, adding more WINS servers to distribute the load will improve response times for WINS queries, but will add more replication traffic and require more administration.

Burst Handling

Since Windows NT 4.0 Service Pack 3, WINS servers have been capable of *burst handling*. Burst handling, which is enabled by default, allows the WINS server to handle a large volume of simultaneous registration requests. This situation can occur, for example, when power is suddenly returned to many computers after a power outage. With burst handling configured, the WINS server will respond positively to name registration and refresh requests before it writes them to the database. However, it will supply the WINS clients with varied and short TTLs for the name registrations to stagger the load for subsequent WINS client refresh attempts.

By default, burst handling occurs when the server has more than 500 requests in its queue. However, you can adjust this setting in the WINS console. As shown in Figure 20.30, the **Advanced** tab for the properties of the WINS server allows you to select a **Low** (300 requests), **Medium** (500), **High** (1000), or **Custom** (where you specify the number of requests). If the WINS server has more than 25,000 requests in its queue, it will start dropping queries.

Figure 20.30 Configuring Burst Handling

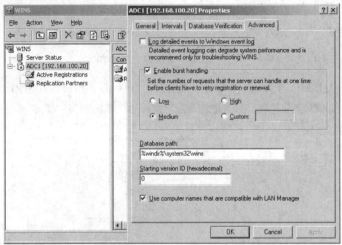

It's a good idea to ensure that burst handling is enabled for reasons other than improving the performance of the WINS server under peak-load conditions. When burst handling is enabled, it writes events to the event log. The presence of burst handling events can provide an indication that the WINS server hardware is not adequate. Furthermore, the presence of burst handling events can indicate a possible DoS attack on the WINS server. You can use Network Monitor or some other tool for analyzing network traffic to capture packets and track down the possible causes of the presence of burst handling events.

Scavenging of WINS Records

Performance of a WINS server will be affected by the settings that are used to determine how frequently clients refresh their registrations, how long it takes for a released or deleted registration to be removed from the database, and how frequently the database verifies its records to ensure the integrity of data. *Scavenging* is the process by which WINS records are removed from the database. More specifically, scavenging is a preset process that periodically runs on the WINS server and either deletes or changes the status of WINS records based on their timestamps and current state. The settings that control these intervals are found in the **Intervals** tab in the property pages of the WINS server. It might be useful to change these settings to improve the performance of the WINS server:

- **Renewal interval** Governs the TTL of the client registration. WINS clients will attempt to renew registrations after half the renewal interval has elapsed. Increasing this interval will reduce the frequency of client renewal attempts and reduce the load on the WINS server. However, increasing the interval also makes the database less consistent with the network over time when computer names are changed. The renewal interval should be the same for all WINS servers when they are replicating with one another.

- **Extinction interval** Governs the period that must elapse from when a name is marked as released and when it is marked as tombstoned.

- **Extinction timeout** Governs the period that must elapse from when a name marked as tombstoned and is subsequently scavenged (removed) from the database.

- **Verification interval** Dependent on the previous values and governs when a WINS server must validate active records it does not own; that is, records learned of via replication with other WINS servers.

Figure 20.31 shows the Intervals tab with the default settings.

Figure 20.31 Interval Settings for Registration Renewal, Removal, and Verification

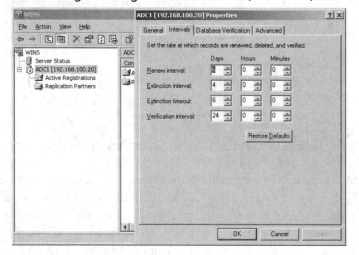

Database Compaction

When records are deleted from the WINS database, the space formerly occupied by them should be recovered to ensure optimal performance of the database. The process of recovering this space is referred to as *compaction*. The WINS service automatically and periodically performs online compaction of the WINS database. However, online compaction of the WINS database is not as efficient as offline compaction. It is, therefore, sometimes desirable for the WINS administrator to stop the WINS service (take the database offline) and perform a manual compaction of the database.

The WINS administrator can use Jetpack.exe, found in the System32 folder, for manual database compaction. The Jetpack utility works by creating a temporary database in which to compact the records, and then replacing the original database with the compacted one. To manually compact the database, the WINS administrator must first stop the WINS service and then issue the **jetpack** command, using the following syntax:

```
jetpack %systemroot%\system32\Wins\Wins.mdb [name_of_temp_database.mdb]
```

After running the jetpack command, the WINS administrator can start the WINS service again.

Using the **net stop** and **net start** commands, the WINS administrator can automate offline compaction in a batch file. For example, you can create a simple batch file that contains the following three lines:

```
net stop wins
jetpack %systemroot%\system32\Wins\Wins.mdb [name_of_temp_database.mdb]
net start wins
```

Once you have created the batch file, you can configure it to run at preconfigured intervals using the Task Scheduler or the AT command-line utility. For example, you could configure the batch file to run once a month during off hours to ensure that the database uses space optimally.

Scheduling Consistency Checking

In order to maintain database integrity in environments that employ replication, it is recommended that automatic periodic consistency checking be enabled. Consistency checking is the process whereby a local WINS server compares local entries that it has acquired by replication with the entries in WINS servers that own the record. If a WINS server detects that the records are identical between its locally stored copy and the remote database, it will update the record with a new timestamp. However, if the record has a lower version ID in the local database, it will pull the updated record from its replication partner and mark the original one for deletion.

Because consistency checking puts a significant load on the resources of a WINS server, it should be scheduled to run during off-peak hours. Figure 20.32 shows the **Database Verification** tab of the property pages of the WINS server, where you can set the schedule for consistency checking.

Figure 20.32 Enabling and Scheduling Consistency Checking

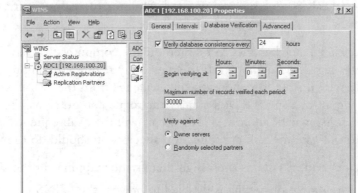

In Figure 20.32, consistency checking is enabled and scheduled to run every 24 hours at 2:00 A.M. Additional settings allow the WINS administrator to specify the maximum number of records to verify and to select randomly selected replication partners. Consistency checking can also be manually initiated from the context menu of the WINS server in the WINS server console.

Security Issues

As with any service that you implement on your servers and your network, it is important for you to understand the service and take measures that mitigate the risk to the service and the network as a whole. These measures include setting up restricted ACLs, logging, auditing, and monitoring, as well as using VPNs or IPSec to secure WINS replication traffic. In the next section, we briefly examine issues related to the security of the WINS service.

NetBIOS Security Issues

With regard to NetBIOS in general and the WINS service in particular, administrators need to be aware that NetBIOS is an unauthenticated protocol. That is, users are not required to submit credentials before using the services provided by a WINS server, such as name registration, renewal, release, and queries. This makes WINS susceptible to a number of different kinds of attacks, primarily DoS attacks and redirection attacks.

In a DoS attack, an attacker attempts to tie up the WINS service with a large number of requests that compromise the WINS server's ability to process legitimate requests. To mitigate the risk of DoS attacks, you should do the following:

- Secure the physical network from unauthorized access.

- Enable burst handling. When burst handling is enabled, burst handling events are recorded in Event Viewer, providing an alert to a possible DoS attack. (This is set in the Advanced tab for the properties of the WINS server, shown in Figure 20.30 earlier in this chapter.)

- Enable detailed WINS logging to provide more complete and specific logging of WINS events in the System log. (Also set in the Advanced tab for the properties of the WINS server, shown in Figure 20.30).

- Use a protocol-analysis tool, such as Network Monitor, to analyze traffic in the case of a suspected attack.

In a redirection attack, an attacker tries to register a rogue computer that has the same name mappings as a previously registered computer. If the previously registered computer is down for maintenance or is otherwise unable to respond to the challenge from the WINS server (for example, if it is also a victim of a specific DoS attack), the rogue computer will be able to register the name mappings with its own IP address. WINS clients will then subsequently be redirected to the rogue computer. To mitigate the risk of redirection attacks, you should do the following:

- Identify mission-critical systems and assign them static mappings in the WINS database.

- Ensure that the migrate on setting is disabled to prevent the WINS server from overwriting the static mappings with dynamic mappings. (This is controlled by the **Overwrite**

unique static mappings at this server (migrate on) setting in the **Replication Partners Properties** dialog box, shown in Figure 20.27 earlier in this chapter.)

Protecting the WINS Database and Log Files

The WINS databases and log files contain important information about your network. The information in these files could be used by attackers to glean confidential information about your company. For example, by an analysis of the number of computers, the attacker could learn the names of those computers, the NetBIOS applications running on the computers, and so on. Furthermore, the integrity and availability of the WINS database and the log files are critical to the operation of the network.

It is particularly important to note that, if you change the default location of the WINS database files, they will inherit the ACLs of the new destination folder, removing the effective security they inherited by virtue of being located in a subfolder of the System32 folder. Also, the WINS backup files inherit the ACL of the folder used to store the backup files. To mitigate the risks to the confidentiality, integrity, and availability of WINS databases, you should consider doing the following:

- Do not store WINS database files on anything except an NTFS formatted partition.
- Ensure that the ACLs for the WINS database, backup, and log files are restricted to allow access to only the Local System Account and the Administrators group.
- Enable file auditing on the WINS files to track attempts of objects that try to access these files.
- Ensure that the WINS server is physically secured from remote access.
- Do not transfer WINS database files over the network using FTP or other unsecured protocols.

WINS Users Group

Only members of the Administrators group can modify the settings for WINS servers. However, it is desirable, in some situations, to provide read-only access to the configuration and database information of WINS servers. To provide users with read-only access to the WINS server, you can use the special WINS Users group. Users who are members of this group are able to query the WINS server database to find records and to view configuration information.

Planning for WINS Database Backup and Restoration

Although it is possible to rely on replicated copies of WINS records to restore a corrupted database, you should only do so as a method of last resort. It is far better to back up the WINS database, either manually or automatically, and restore WINS records from the backup, if necessary.

By default, the WINS database is not backed up automatically. To back up a WINS database automatically, you need to do the following:

1. Specify a backup directory in the **General** tab of the WINS server properties. (WINS will create a folder called **Wins_bak** under this folder to store the backups).

2. Perform a manual backup of the WINS database to the specified location. You can do this by choosing the **Backup Up Database** option from context menu of the WINS server object in the WINS console tree.

After you have performed these steps, backups will occur every 24 hours or upon service shutdown (if so configured). In the event that the WINS service detects a corrupt WINS database upon startup, it will automatically restore the backed up version from the location that you specified for the WINS backups. You cannot use a network drive for this location. Figure 20.33 shows the settings for configuring automatic backups.

Figure 20.33 WINS Backup Configuration

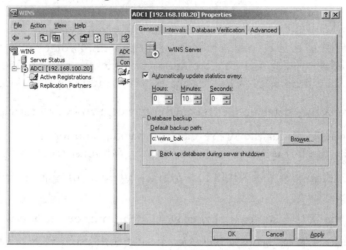

To restore the WINS database, you can stop the WINS service, delete the original database, and restore the backup. If you do not stop the WINS service, the option to restore the WINS database will be grayed out.

Troubleshooting Name Resolution Issues

Proper name resolution is critical to the smooth operation of the network. When name resolution fails, for whatever reason, users might be inconvenienced, and connectivity to critical systems might be compromised. Usually, a name resolution failure requires immediate action on the part of the administrator, even if the failure is not widespread.

Often, problems that appear to be related to name resolution are, in fact, the result of problems that occur further down in the OSI or DoD networking models for TCP/IP. For example, if a router fails, and the DNS or WINS servers are on the other side of the router from the client, clients will not be able to resolve names. The failure of a router occurs at Layer 3 (Network layer) of the ISO model.

As part of a prudent and successful troubleshooting strategy, it is important to troubleshoot from the bottom of the OSI model up, ensuring the following:

- The hardware is functioning properly.

- The computer is configured properly.

- The computer is able to communicate with hosts on the local subnet.

- The computer is able to communicate with the router configured as the default gateway.

- The computer can communicate with remote networks on the far side of the router.

Usually, this troubleshooting will rely on tools such as Ipconfig to verify configuration and PING (using IP addresses) to test communication.

Name resolution occurs further up in the OSI or DoD model. You need to discover if is the failure specific to NetBIOS or DNS (host name resolution). To make this determination, you can test name resolution using applications that are specific to these interfaces. For example, to test NetBIOS name resolution, try to connect to shares using a UNC path or the net commands, invoked from the command line. As long as the name you are trying to resolve does not include dots or is less than 15 characters long, Windows clients will default to using NetBIOS resolution first. If name resolution is successful, but you encounter a delay, chances are that NetBIOS resolution failed but that the fallback host name resolution was successful. To test host name resolution, you can use WinSock applications, such as NSLookup, Telnet, FTP, HTTP, and so on.

You should also consider whether NetBT is enabled, either by means of a DHCP server option or as a configuration on the client computer. Some applications, such as Microsoft Exchange Server, still require that NetBT be enabled to work properly. In troubleshooting name resolution problems, you should therefore take into account the applications that may be involved and their dependence on either the WinSock or NetBT interfaces to work properly.

It is sometimes obvious that the problem is specific to either host name or NetBIOS name resolution. In any event, after you have made the determination, you can proceed to troubleshoot according to the interface (WinSock or NetBT) that is involved.

Troubleshooting Host Name Resolution

Assuming you have eliminated any antecedent causes that have to do with connectivity and communication on the network, troubleshooting host name resolution is easier if you can isolate whether the problem is caused by problems with client configuration or by problems with the DNS server. Problems with DNS clients include improperly entered addresses for the primary and secondary DNS server, in addition to improperly configured DNS suffix search list settings. Problems with DNS servers include improperly configured delegations; improperly configured restrictions on zone transfers; missing, incorrect, or stale resource records; and so on.

Effective troubleshooting of Microsoft DNS issues requires a familiarity with the process of DNS name resolution (for example, recursive versus iterative queries and authoritative versus nonauthoritative responses), dynamic updates, zone transfers, stub zones, forwarding, and so on.

A familiarity with DNS-related troubleshooting tools, such as NSLookup, Ipconfig, Dnscmd, and DNSLint, will help to ensure that you can trace the source of the problem effectively. Using NSLookup, you can request either an authoritative or nonauthoritative response from the DNS server, which can help you to narrow down the problem further; for example, to determine whether a stale record is coming from the DNS cache or not. Furthermore, with NSLookup, you can use debug mode to provide a great amount of detail in the output of the command. You can use DNSLint to check all your delegations and verify the correct configuration of well-known services, such as SMTP. Issues with dynamic registration can sometimes be resolved by using the command **ipconfig /registerdns**. Incorrect entries in the client DNS cache can be resolved with the **ipconfig /displaydns** and **ipconfig /flushdns** commands. Some tools that are not specific to DNS, such as Nltest, can help to troubleshoot DNS-related issues with domain controllers.

Issues Related to Client Computer Configuration

Many problems with DNS resolution have their origins in the client configuration, so verifying the correct client configuration is a good place to begin. To troubleshoot problems with client configuration, use the **ipconfig /all** command to verify the DNS configuration, and then use PING and NSLookup to verify communication with the DNS server. If you can ping the DNS servers, but an NSLookup query against them fails, the issue is most likely related to a problem with the DNS servers. (This is the kind of situation where troubleshooting from the bottom to the top of the OSI model really pays off in helping to narrow down the problem.)

One of the more common and serious problems with client configuration is an improperly configured FQDN, which is set up in the properties of My Computer on Windows 2000 and Windows XP clients. If the FQDN is not present or is incorrectly configured on the client computer, name resolution can fail for domains that would otherwise be searched according to a domain suffix search list. For example, if the computer is a member of the corp.tacteam.net domain, and the user enters and uses an unqualified name (for example, PServer1) in a DNS query for a host in the tacteam.net domain, the query will fail unless the FQDN of the computer is properly configured. (An unqualified name is one that doesn't have a trailing dot.) By default, the DNS client uses a domain suffix search list based on the FQDN. So, if the host name cannot be resolved in the corp.tacteam.net domain, the suffix will be devolved to tacteam.net to find the host. To troubleshoot problems with domain suffix search lists, try to resolve the name at the client using the FQDN (that is, include the trailing dot). If this query succeeds, but an unqualified query does not, the problem is related to the domain suffix search list.

Clients that have improperly configured FQDNs might also have problems with dynamic registration in the DNS zone. The client registration of a host record in a DNS requires that the primary suffix be properly configured. If the domain suffix is improperly configured, the client may be trying to register in a nonexistent or an unintended domain. To troubleshoot and resolve this problem, verify that the client computer is correctly configured with a primary domain suffix and that it can reach a name server that is authoritative for the domain name (you can simulate this by using NSLookup to perform an SOA RR query type for the authoritative zone). If the client receives its TCP/IP configuration from a DHCP server, verify that the DHCP server option for the domain suffix and other settings are configured correctly. Also, the client needs to be configured with the IP address of a DNS that contains the primary zone in order for the updates to occur. Meeting these conditions and then using the **ipconfig /registerdns** command to register the host in the domain might solve the problem. However, if the problem is still not resolved, chances are the source of the problem is the DNS server; for example, an ACL on the RR may be preventing the update. Using Event Viewer on the client computer can help you determine the nature of the problem.

If the DNS clients are getting incorrect responses to DNS queries, the problem might be related to their DNS cache. To clear the cache and force a new query to a DNS server for the host name, use the command **ipconfig /flushdns**. (Alternatively, you can use NSLookup to request an authoritative response.) If you have cleared the cache and are still getting incorrect responses to queries, it is likely the source of the problem has to do with the DNS server; for example, there might be an incorrect entry in the cache of the DNS server, a problem with zone transfers, or a delay in AD replication.

Issues Related to DNS Services

If you have determined that the problem you are experiencing is unrelated to DNS client settings or the client's ability to communicate with the network, the problem is most likely related to DNS server configuration. To troubleshoot DNS server problems, you need to let the symptoms of the problem guide you to a likely cause and solution. Again, using a tool like NSLookup will help you get a clearer picture of the problem, since it can provide more detailed information and be used to get either authoritative or nonauthoritative responses from DNS servers. The following is a brief list of guidelines to help troubleshoot problems with DNS servers:

- If clients cannot resolve names on the Internet or in domains for which their DNS servers are not authoritative using recursive queries, the problem might be related to the ability of the DNS server to perform recursion or to forward the query to a server that will perform recursion for it. In this case, check to make sure that the root hints file is present and the records are correct. If these settings are correct, your DNS server might be experiencing cache pollution. In this case, you should enable protection against cache pollution and restart the DNS service.

- If clients do not get correct records or are getting stale records, the cause could be the cache on the DNS client or DNS server. Examining and clearing the cache will eliminate the problem. However, if the problem is unrelated to cache, the cause could be failed or slow zone transfers to the secondary zones. If you are using Active Directory-integrated zones, the cause could be related to problems with AD replication. Comparing the RRs in the various zone files and looking at events in Event Viewer will help to confirm zone transfers as being the cause or the problem.

- If some clients cannot get responses to DNS queries from a multihomed DNS server but others can, the problem might be related to the listener settings on the DNS server. These settings can restrict which interfaces the DNS service will use to respond to queries.

- If you are implementing a round-robin configuration to provide load balancing and are not getting the desired results, check the settings for subnet prioritization. Round robin is a kind of load balancing that can be configured using multiple host records that have the same name but different IP addresses. When round robin is enabled, the DNS server will rotate responses among all the records. However, if subnet prioritization is also enabled, the DNS server will try to respond with a record that is on the same subnet as the DNS client.

- If zone transfers are failing between DNS servers, the cause could be improper restrictions on DNS servers that are authorized to pull zone information from the primary server. By default, the DNS server will allow zone transfers to only those DNS servers listed as name servers for the zone. However, you might need to reconfigure these restrictions so that you specify the IP addresses of computers that are authorized to pull zone information.

- Another cause of failed zone transfers is the use of nonstandard characters in DNS names. By default, Microsoft DNS servers are configured to load the zone even if they encounter bad data. However, BIND servers are not as forgiving. In addition, WINS forward and reverse lookup records can cause problems if replicated to BIND servers. You can prevent WINS records from replicating to BIND servers. If you are replicating to BIND servers, you should use only standard DNS characters.

- Another common cause of zone transfer problems is an incorrect version number in the SOA of the primary or secondary zone. To determine whether to request a zone transfer from the primary server, the secondary server will compare the version number of the primary's SOA with its own. If the primary's number is higher, the secondary will request either a full or an incremental zone transfer. If the version number is reset on the primary so that it is lower than the version number in the secondary's SOA, the zone transfer will fail.

- If queries to subdomains are failing, the cause is most likely a lame delegation of authority. A lame delegation occurs when the name server and glue address records do not point correctly to the servers that are authoritative for the subdomain. NSLookup and DNSLint are useful tools in helping to troubleshoot problems with delegations.

- If dynamic updates are failing, the cause of the problem might be related to the security settings and ownership of RRs in their ACLs. For example, if a DHCP server is the original owner of a record and a client subsequently gets its IP address from another DHCP server, the dynamic update will fail. Another cause of failed dynamic updates is that the primary zone is, for whatever reason, unavailable. Dynamic updates can occur in only primary or Active Directory-integrated zones.

Troubleshooting NetBIOS Name Resolution

To avoid problems with NetBIOS name resolution in the first place, you should take very seriously the best practices that Microsoft recommends for the deployment of WINS servers and clients. In general, these best practices require the following:

- Be conservative in your estimates of the number of WINS servers you need.

- Use full replication partnership agreements.

- Use a hub-and-spoke replication topology to reduce convergence time in large environments.

- Do not install WINS on a multihomed server.

To troubleshoot problems with NetBIOS name resolution, you should first analyze the problem to determine whether it is a client configuration problem or a problem related to WINS server records or WINS server configuration, such as failed replication.

Issues Related to Client Computer Configuration

First, you should determine whether a problem that appears to be related to client configuration affects a single computer or a group of computers that all get their TCP/IP configuration from the same DHCP server or the same DHCP server scope. You should also verify the WINS server configuration by using the **ipconfig /all** command. The output of this command will list any WINS servers that are either manually configured or dynamically configured through DHCP. You should ping the IP addresses of the WINS servers listed in the client configuration to verify that communication is possible with these computers.

Another command you can use to troubleshoot problems related to client configuration is the **nbtstat** command. With the nbtstat command, you can cause a release and refresh of the NetBIOS registration for the client computer, view the remote name cache, view statistics on recent NetBIOS name resolution activity, and so on. Sometimes, a recently cached but incorrect entry in the remote name cache is causing a specific problem. You can also use the nbtstat command to clear the contents of the cache, except for those entries that are preloaded with the #PRE tag in an LMHOSTS file (these entries are obvious when you view the remote name cache using the nbtstat command).

In addition to verifying the correct configuration of the WINS server entries, you might want to consider whether the client is configured as an h-node, an m-node, a b-node, or a p-node client. For example, if the client is configured as an m-node client, it will use name query broadcasts before reverting to unicast name queries to the WINS server. If there is a duplicate NetBIOS name on the subnet, resolution to this name will occur first in the case of an m-node client.

Furthermore, you should consider the presence of an LMHOSTS file on the client computer and the order in which LMHOSTS will be used in name resolution queries. If the clients are using an LMHOSTS file and it appears that an LMHOSTS file is involved in the problem, you need to verify that the entries in the file are correct.

Issues Related to WINS Servers

In troubleshooting problems with name resolution that involve the WINS server, it is useful to first determine the scope of the problem. For example, does the problem involve dynamic or static name mappings, deleted records, replication, or a corrupted database? You should also consider any error messages that the NetBIOS client receives, such as "Network path not found" or "Duplicate name." In addition, you should look at any events that are recorded in the System event log for the WINS service that might provide an indication of a corrupted database or problems with replication. Finally, you should confirm whether the problem affects one or multiple WINS servers. If the problem affects only one WINS server, you should first verify that the WINS service has started properly and that the database is not corrupted.

Problems Related to Static Mappings

You should avoid the use of static mappings except in situations where you need WINS to provide resolution to NetBIOS applications running on non-WINS clients or you want to provide static, permanent name mappings to mission-critical servers to mitigate the risk of redirection attacks. However, if you are using static mappings and the problem is related to these entries, you should do the following:

- Verify that the entries are correct and that they have replicated properly.

- If you have deleted the static mapping, you need to verify that the tombstoned record, in the case of a tombstone rather than simple deletion, has replicated properly.

- If the client error message refers to a "duplicate name" and there is a static mapping for the name, you need to ensure that the migrate on setting is enabled to allow the dynamic name registration to overwrite the manual registration.

Problems Related to Multihomed WINS Servers

Multihomed WINS servers are not a recommended configuration and are the cause of many WINS-related problems. Some of the problems you might experience with multihomed WINS servers can be hard to track down. If you are experiencing intermittent problems with name resolution or if you are having problems with replication, chances are that these can be traced to the configuration of the multihomed WINS server.

However, if you must use a multihomed WINS server and if you are experiencing problems, you should do the following:

- Verify that all network devices on the multihomed WINS servers are configured as routable interfaces with correct TCP/IP information. (You should never colocate the WINS service with the RAS service—that is just asking for trouble.)

- Verify that all TCP/IP configurations use the IP address of the WINS server for both their primary and alternate WINS servers. (You can leave this configuration blank if you like, because the WINS server will register itself without this configuration.)

- Verify that all the replication partners of the multihomed WINS servers are configured to replicate with *all* the configured IP addresses of the WINS server, and not the NetBIOS name.

Problems Related to Replication

Problems related to replication almost always are the result of not following Microsoft's recommended practices, such as installing too many WINS servers, installing WINS on a multihomed computer, or using limited replication partnerships. For example, installing too many WINS servers (more than 20, according to Microsoft) can cause intermittent and hard-to-locate problems with replication.

In troubleshooting replication problems, you should first consider whether the problem is related to network communication and name resolution to the replication partners themselves. Consider the following questions:

- Can you ping the IP address of the replication partner?

- If the replication partner is a multihomed computer, have you configured the replication partner settings with the IP addresses of the multihomed computer, rather than the NetBIOS name?

- Does the NetBIOS name of the WINS server resolve to the correct IP address?

If you are using limited replication partnerships (push-only and pull-only) replication partners, you should ensure that these partnerships are set up correctly. Also, you might achieve best results by setting up reciprocal partnerships on the push and pull partners. For example, a computer that is configured as a pull-only partner to another WINS server should also configure that WINS server as its push partner. To illustrate, WINS-A has configured WINS-B as its pull partner; WINS-B in turn should configure WINS-A as its push partner. (To ensure that records are never pushed and replicated strictly according to the pull replication schedule, you can set the push trigger threshold to a very high number that will never be reached between pull replication cycles.)

If replication partnerships are configured correctly and there is good connectivity, but you are still experiencing intermittent problems, the version IDs on some replicated records may not be correctly incremented. You can resolve this problem by entering a new starting version ID for the WINS database in the WINS console or using the netsh command.

Chapter 21

Planning, Implementing, and Maintaining the TCP/IP Infrastructure

In this chapter:

- ☑ **Understanding Windows 2003 Server Network Protocols**

- ☑ **Planning an IP Addressing Strategy**

- ☑ **Planning the Network Topology**

- ☑ **Planning Network Traffic Management**

Introduction

Transmission Control Protocol/Internet Protocol (TCP/IP) is the default network/transport protocol stack for a Windows Server 2003 network, and it is important for all network administrators to be intimately familiar with the TCP/IP protocols, IP addressing, and how to plan an IP infrastructure.

This chapter deals with the TCP/IP infrastructure. We'll discuss Internet Group Management Protocol version 3 (IGMPv3), IP version 6 (IPv6) support, the alternate configuration feature, and automatic determination of interface metrics.

You'll find out how to plan an IP addressing strategy, including how to analyze your addressing requirements and how to create an effective subnetting scheme. You'll learn about transitioning to the next generation of IP, IPv6, and we'll introduce IPv6 utilities such as Netsh, Ipsec, PING, and Tracert. We'll discuss 6to4 tunneling, the IPv6 Helper service, and connecting to the 6bone.

Next, we'll discuss the planning of the network topology. This includes analyzing hardware requirements and planning for the placement of physical resources. You'll learn how to plan network traffic management, as well as how to monitor network traffic and devices using Network Monitor and System Monitor. We'll show you how to determine bandwidth requirements and how to optimize your network's performance.

Understanding Windows 2003 Server Network Protocols

The networking architecture of Windows Server 2003 uses the *Network Driver Interface Specification* (NDIS). NDIS provides a kind of wrapper in the I/O Manager layer of Windows that allows the hardware driver to be independent of the protocols used to communicate on your network. Additionally, this allows for multiple network adapters with virtually any device driver, without having any effect on the transport protocols used. Let's take a look at some of the details involved with networking.

The Multiprotocol Network Environment

Microsoft Windows Server 2003, like its predecessors, uses a layered network architecture. Since it is layered, it is possible to extend the functionality of networking Windows Server 2003 with third-party software components. The layered structure also provides the Windows Server 2003 platform with the ability to allow different protocols to communicate using the same structure and methods, so users can access data in the same fashion, regardless of what networking protocol is used.

Windows Server 2003 products use the TCP/IP protocol stack by default. The following network protocols are supported on Windows Server 2003:

- **TCP/IP version 4** The default protocol for Windows Server 2003.
- **TCP/IP version 6** The next generation of TCP/IP.
- **IPX/SPX** Used by many networks running Novell NetWare.
- **AppleTalk** Provides the basis for Services for Macintosh and AppleTalk routing and seed routing support.

The Windows Server 2003 architecture that supports multiple protocols also allows multiple network adapters. Each adapter can use any combination of protocols or networking components, known as *binding*. It is also possible for you to change the order in which protocols are bound to the adapter. You can choose to move the most commonly used protocols on the client up to the top of the binding order to provide faster performance.

When configuring protocols on your computer, it is always desirable to make the fewest possible changes on the client in order to simplify the administration of the network. On a TCP/IP network with more than 25 hosts, it is a good idea to implement a DHCP server. By default, all Windows XP and Windows Server 2003 machines are configured to use DHCP. Occasionally, you might need to manually configure the IP address of your machine. If you do configure the address manually, pay close attention to the information you provide in the dialog box. Errors in the configuration will hinder network communication for that machine, and in some cases, cause problems that could prevent other machines from functioning properly.

What's New in TCP/IP for Windows Server 2003

There are many enhancements to the networking and communications components of Windows Server 2003. The TCP/IP protocol suite has been enhanced with some of the latest technologies, as well as improvements on existing functionality. For more information about other networking and communication feature enhancements, see the white paper titled "Microsoft Windows Server 2003-Technical Overview of Networking and Communication" (www.microsoft.com/windowsserver2003/techinfo/overview/netcomm.mspx).

IGMPv3

Typical communications over an IP-based network are directed unicast communications. Unicast is basically a single, direct request sent from one host to another, and only the two hosts interact over the established route. For example, when you click a hyperlink in a Web browser, you are requesting HTTP data from the host defined in the link, which, in turn, delivers the data to your browser. This is useful in the Web-browsing environments we have grown accustomed to, where there is a demand for a personal, user-controlled experience.

Unicast is not useful for delivering streams of audio or video to large audiences, since a single stream of audio/video data is very costly for only one user. This is where multicast communications are effective. Multicast provides a single stream for multiple hosts. The hosts select the data by requesting the local routers to forward those packets of data from the host providing the multicast data to the subnet of the listening host. When the host decides to stop listening to the multicast traffic, IGMP is responsible for notifying the router that the host is no longer participating.

A set of listening hosts is called a *multicast group*. IGMP is responsible for providing the functionality necessary for hosts to join and leave those groups that receive IP multicast traffic. Each of the versions of IGMP—versions 1, 2, and 3—is automatically supported by Windows Server 2003. IGMPv3 adds functionality to distribute multiple multicast sources regionally and allow the host to select the multicast source that is located closest to the host.

An example of this would be a situation in which you send a video stream broadcasting a speech from the president of your company and have several machines scattered across the United States providing the feed. Then IGMPv3 allows the hosts to provide an *include* list or an *exclude* list of those servers. The multicast routers would be responsible for forwarding the multicast traffic from the include list of servers and for preventing the forwarding of traffic from the excluded sources. As you can see, this feature can be very useful to help reduce network bandwidth utilization.

IPv6

The next generation of TCP/IP is here! Previously, it was possible to experiment with IPv6, but under the covers, the protocol stack was still dependent on IPv4 calls for WinSock functions. With the release of Windows Server 2003, the IPv6 protocol stack is designed for production use.

IPv4 has a limited number of host addresses available (2^{32}, or about 4 billion hosts). That might sound like a lot, but over the past 30 years, the pool of available addresses has been exhausted due to the popularity and growth of the Internet. With IPv6, the host address is 128 bits instead of 32, which means that we will have 2^{128} (about 340,000,000,000,000,000,000,000,000,000,000,000,000) host addresses available. That means we could have about 2^{96} (about 75 trillion trillion, or 75,000,000,000,000,000,000,000,000,000) addresses of our very own. That should last for at least a couple of years. We will discuss transitioning to IPv6 and its features in more detail in the "Transitioning to IPv6" section later in this chapter.

Alternate Configuration

Automatic alternate configuration is an enhancement to TCP/IP that allows for a valid static IP address configuration on a DHCP-configured machine. Without an alternate configuration defined, a computer that is unable to obtain an IP address lease from a DHCP server will automatically receive an Automatic Private IP Addressing (APIPA) address from the 169.254.0.0/16 pool.

Automatic Determination of Interface Metric

The automatic metric feature is enabled by default. The purpose of the automatic metric feature is to determine the speed of the interface for each default gateway and to assign the *metric*, which is the cost of using a particular route.

The metric is weighted by the number of hops to the destination. The number of hops to any host on the local subnet is one. Every router that must be used to reach the destination is another hop. When it is determined that there are multiple routes to the same destination, the metric is evaluated to determine which is the lowest metric and subsequently the fastest route to the destination.

The metric for the loopback adapter and the limited broadcast is always 1. The other addresses have a metric based on the cost of using that route for that network adapter. With multiple network adapters, a multihomed computer, the route table would indicate a different metric for each default route, but only one would be used. Table 21.1 shows a configuration with identical network adapters: one adapter on the 192.168.69.0/24 network and the other on the 192.168.70.0/24 network.

Table 21.1 Description of Routes with a Multihomed Computer

Description	Network Destination	Netmask	Gateway	Interface	Metric
Default route	0.0.0.0	0.0.0.0	192.168.69.111	192.168.69.111	20
Default route	0.0.0.0	0.0.0.0	192.168.70.100	192.168.70.100	30
Loopback network	127.0.0.1	255.0.0.0	127.0.0.1	127.0.0.1	1
Local network	192.168.69.0	255.255.255.0	192.168.69.111	192.168.69.111	20
Local IP address	192.168.69.111	255.255.255.255	127.0.0.1	127.0.0.1	20
Local network	192.168.70.0	255.255.255.0	192.168.70.100	192.168.70.100	30
Local IP address	192.168.70.111	255.255.255.255	127.0.0.1	127.0.0.1	30
Subnet broadcast	192.168.69.255	255.255.255.255	192.168.69.111	192.168.69.111	20
Multicast address	224.0.0.0	240.0.0.0	192.168.69.111	192.168.69.111	20
Multicast address	224.0.0.0	240.0.0.0	192.168.70.100	192.168.70.100	20

Table 21.1 Description of Routes with a Multihomed Computer

Description	Network Destination	Netmask	Gateway	Interface	Metric
Limited broadcast	255.255.255. 255	255.255.255. 255	192.168.69.111	192.168.69.111	1
Limited broadcast	255.255.255. 255	255.255.255. 255	192.168.70.100	192.168.70.100	1

Note that the metric for the default route for the second network, on the adapter for the 192.168.70.100 interface, is higher than the metric for the default route on the 192.168.69.111 interface. This indicates that the 192.168.69.111 network adapter is first in the binding order. Since the metric for the default gateway for the second adapter is higher than the first network adapter, the second gateway is never used and is not necessary.

You can use the **route** command to add routes and change metrics. The command is **route add –p** *Destination Mask Gateway IF Metric,* where:

- *Destination* is the network destination address.

- *Mask* is the appropriate subnet mask defined for the destination network.

- *Gateway* is the address of the router interface used to interface with the network.

- *IF* is the interface you want to associate this route to.

- *Metric* is the metric for this gateway.

The –p parameter specifies that you want to persist this route, so that it will be there if you reset the adapter or restart the machine. If you do not specify –p, the route is temporary and will not be saved.

If you want to delete a route, use the **route delete** *Destination* command to remove the destination route from the route table.

You can disable the automatic metric feature by accessing the properties for the desired connection, as follows:

1. Select **Internet Protocol (TCP/IP)** and click **Properties**.

2. In the **Internet Protocol (TCP/IP) Properties** dialog box, click the **Advanced** button.

3. Uncheck **Automatic metric.**

4. Provide an **Interface metric.** The minimum value is 1.

5. Click **OK.**

6. Run the **route print** command. What changed? You will notice that all of the metric values are now 1.

You can change the values manually, which can allow you to redirect traffic over a slower interface that would normally have a higher metric.

Planning an IP Addressing Strategy

Before you can implement an IP network infrastructure, there are many details that you must consider. Here, we will take a look at how to plan your network by identifying the appropriate addressing requirements and limitations that will shape the network. Understanding subnetting is a requirement to implement your addressing scheme. You will need to identify hardware requirements, decide what class of address you will need, and determine if access to the Internet is necessary for all or just some of your hosts.

Subnetting will allow you to create logical segments on your network that will overlay the physical topology. By using a well-planned subnetting scheme, you can handle your current needs and plan for expansion for future needs. You can also make use of these segments to isolate and distribute heavy traffic, without having a major impact on other segments of your network.

Analyzing Addressing Requirements

Since the host IP address must be unique, the simple rule to calculate the number of hosts for our network is *one IP address per host,* plus one IP address for each additional network adapter in a host machine. We have a concept of one network in the corporate sense, but when determining address requirements, there are a few more details we must consider.

You can define IP addresses using one of the three classes available for standard IP communications: classes A, B, and C. Before we decide which class to use, we need to determine the type of network we are implementing and how many hosts there are per segment. This material provides only a brief review of the topic, and assumes you are familiar with IP addressing concepts and practices.

Creating a Subnetting Scheme

As mentioned, host addresses can belong to one of three classes of IP address, and each has a range of addresses. The range is defined by the value of the first octet. Table 21.2 shows the classes and their ranges, as well as the binary representations of the ranges. Classes D and E are also classes of IP addresses, but Class D is restricted to multicasting and Class E addresses are reserved for future use. 127.0.0.0 is reserved for connectivity testing. 127.0.0.1 is a special address that represents the local loopback adapter that resolves as *localhost*. We can ping the local host to troubleshoot the protocol stack. We will discuss this in more detail in the "Troubleshooting IP Addressing" section later in this chapter. Each class also has a default subnet mask.

Table 21.2 IP Address Classes and Their Ranges

Class	Range of Values	Default Mask	Networks	Hosts	Binary
A	0 to 126	255.0.0.0	126	16,777,214	00000001 to 01111110
B	128 to 191	255.255.0.0	16,384	65,534	10000000 to 10111111
C	192 to 223	255.255.255.0	2,097,152	254	11000000 to 11011111
D	224 to 239	Not applicable			Not applicable

As you know, the default mask for each class defines the number of networks and the number of hosts for each network. An IP address contains information about the network on which the host resides and the address of the host. The network ID is the reference to the logical subnet, and it refers to the octets that are predefined as the network ID and implemented with the default mask. The remaining octets are for the hosts.

The first address in each network refers to "this network" (itself), such as 24.0.0.0/8 or 204.79.26.0/24. The last address in each network or subnetwork is the broadcast address for that segment, such as 179.54.255.255 or 204.79.26.255. We can derive the formula for determining the number of hosts per network as $2^n - 2$, where n is the number of bits available for host IDs.

Class A addresses are used for networks that have a large number of hosts. Based on the default mask, we have the first octet for networks and the last three for hosts. So, we have 126 networks and $2^{24} - 2$ hosts, or 16,777,214. Likewise, with class B, the default mask is 255.255.0.0, so the first two octets are for the network IDs, for a total of 16,384, and the last two are for the hosts. So, class B networks have $2^{16} - 2$ hosts, or 65,534. Class C networks have more networks but are smaller, with $2^8 - 2$ hosts, or 254.

We could implement our network now very simply. Determine the number of hosts and the number of networks, and pick the class that fits. If you do not wish to assign a public IP address to all your machines, there is a solution. There are three banks of IP addresses that are called *private IP address* ranges. They are listed in Table 21.3. Typically, a network will need only one or two public addresses for the Internet interfaces, and everything internal to the company can use the private IP addresses internally.

Table 21.3 Private IP Addresses

Network ID	Subnet Mask	Range
10.0.0.0	255.0.0.0	10.0.0.1 to 10.255.255.254
172.16.0.0	255.240.0.0	172.16.0.1 to 172.31.255.254
192.168.0.0	255.255.0.0	192.168.0.1 to 192.168.255.254

Troubleshooting IP Addressing

The flexibility of TCP/IP also contributes to the complexity of troubleshooting addresses and connections. There are several tools that can help isolate and identify issues with addressing, but it is also imperative that you understand IP addressing rules and subnetting. The ipconfig, ping, and tracert commands are the most useful tools for identifying addressing problems with client configurations and connections to other hosts on the Internet.

Client Configuration Issues

Some of the issues that occur with manual configuration of IP addresses include duplicate addresses, invalid subnet masks, invalid default gateways, and invalid or missing host name resolution settings (such as DNS and WINS). To help identify the problem, start by typing **ipconfig /all** at a command prompt. Verify the information that is output by the command is correct, and then continue by using **ping** to help isolate the problem.

1. Ping the loopback address (127.0.0.1) to verify that the TCP/IP protocol stack is configured correctly on the local computer.

2. Ping the external IP address of the local computer to ensure the host is on the network and using a valid IP address; that is, there are no address conflicts.

3. Ping the IP address of the default gateway to verify that the default gateway is accessible and your local network configuration contains the correct subnet mask.

4. Ping the IP address of a remote host to verify that you can transmit data over the default gateway.

If you are not able to get traffic through to a site, but you are making it through the default gateway, you should use **tracert** to identify the break in the route to the destination.

DHCP Issues

DHCP is an easy way to manage IP addressing schemes for larger networks. DHCP makes it possible to boot a machine and access the network without configuring any protocol information. This eliminates many of the manual configuration issues, such as using the wrong subnet mask, duplicate IP addresses, and limited or no host name resolution. Some of the items to consider when you implement and use DHCP are lease time, number of hosts in a scope, network traffic, scope options, and topology.

When a machine acquires an IP address from a DHCP server, it acquires a *lease*. The request for the lease is a message called a DHCPREQUEST, which is broadcast by the DHCP client looking for DHCPOFFERs of a lease from a DHCP server. The *lease duration* for a DCHP address is specified in the scope set on the server and defaults to eight days. At 50 percent of the lease duration, the DCHP client sends a directed request to the DHCP server that issued the lease and requests a renewal of the lease. If no DHCPACK (acknowledgment) is received from the server, the DHCP client waits until 87.5 percent of the lease time, and then makes a final request to renew the IP address. If no DHCPACK is received at this point, the client waits until the lease is expired and starts the process over. If a DHCP client is unable to receive an IP address lease, it will use an alternate configuration, if one is specified. If there is no alternate configuration, the client will use APIPA to start the TCP/IP services and assign itself an address from the APIPA pool (169.254.0.0/16).

To determine the appropriate lease time for your network, you should consider the following:

- **Number of hosts** If the number of hosts is close to the number of total IP addresses in your DHCP server's scope, the lease should be shorter—about three days. If there are a great deal more IP addresses than hosts, a longer lease can be assigned.

- **Mobile users** If you have a small number of mobile users and the client machines do not frequently move from one network to the other, a longer lease duration is recommended. Conversely, if you have more mobile users, a shorter lease will be preferred, so that the IP addresses will be released sooner and returned to the available pool of addresses.

- **Unlimited** It is possible to set the lease duration to unlimited, but it presents a challenge if you wish to change the DHCP settings, since this setting requires the client to initiate the DHCPREQUEST.

Because they are broadcast, the DHCPREQUEST messages do not cross router boundaries, unless the router is capable of forwarding DHCP broadcast messages, in compliance with RFC 2131. You can also configure a DHCP relay to forward the requests to a DHCP server.

Using DHCP can reduce IP address conflicts by preventing the need for static IP address. It also can eliminate invalid subnet masks, since they are also assigned by the DHCP server. Another advantage is the scope properties. By assigning scope properties, you can define default gateways, DNS servers, WINS servers, and the type of name resolution that is preferred. By managing name resolution settings, you can help eliminate broadcast traffic.

Transitioning to IPv6

IPv6, defined in RFC 2460, is now production ready to use on most operating system platforms. At this point, it is still early in the transition from IPv4. The change to IPv6 will take some time, but with each day, it becomes more necessary due to the growing shortage of IPv4 addresses. Although the larger address space is the most immediate need, IPv6 offers other advantages over IPv4, including the following:

- Better security (built in support for IPSec)

- Support for both stateful and stateless address configuration

- An efficient hierarchical routing infrastructure

- A new header format that provides lower overhead

- Neighbor Discovery (ND) for managing nodes on the same link, replacing ARP, ICMPv4 router discovery, and ICMPv4 redirect messages

- Virtually unlimited extension headers (in comparison to IPv4's limit of 40 bytes)

- Quality of service (QoS) related header fields

The utilities and concepts associated with IPv6 are similar to IPv4, but not identical. In the following sections, we'll take a look at how to install IPv6 and start to familiarize ourselves with the new utilities used to manage it.

IPv6 on Windows Server 2003 provides a new header format that is streamlined to minimize overhead and provide more efficient processing while crossing intermediate routers. All the option fields and any other fields in the header that are not required for routing are placed after the IPv6 header. The IPv6 header also added more QoS support by adding Flow Label fields that provide special handling for a series of packets that travel between a source and destination.

ND is a set of process and messages that are used in an IPv6 environment to identify relationships between neighboring nodes. This allows hosts to discover routers on the same segment, addresses, and address prefixes. With ND, hosts can also resolve neighboring nodes and determine when the MAC address of a neighbor changes (similar to ARP in IPv4). ND also provides the process for address autoconfiguration, also referred to as *stateless address configuration*. In the absence of a stateful address configuration server, such as a DHCP version 6 (DHCPv6) protocol server, ND provides a complex process that allows each interface to use router advertisement messages to define an IPv6 address, and then subsequently ensure the uniqueness of the selected address. Currently, the standards for DHCPv6 and IPv6 stateful addressing are still under development, so neither feature is supported on Windows XP/2003 products at this time.

The new routing structure provides a hierarchical addressing and routing structure that includes a global addressing scheme. Global addresses are the equivalent of public IPv4 addresses and are accessible over the Internet. The global addressing scheme defines new ways to summarize global addresses to facilitate smaller routing tables on the Internet backbone, and thus improve the efficiency and performance on the Internet.

IPv6 Utilities

The traditional IPv4 utilities are still very useful for IPv4, but new utilities and features have been added to accommodate IPv6 functionality. To gain access to the new tools or functionality, you need to install the TCP/IP version 6 protocol.

Install TCP/IP Version 6

1. Open **Network Connections** and double-click the **Local Area Network** icon. You will see the **Local Area Connection Status** dialog box.

2. Click **Properties.**

3. In the **Local Area Network Connection Properties** dialog box, click **Install**.

4. In the **Select Network Component Type** dialog box, select **Protocol** and click **Add**.

5. In the **Select Network Protocol** dialog box, select **Microsoft TCP/IP version 6** and click **OK**.

6. You should return to the **Local Area Connection Properties** dialog box and see that Microsoft TCP/IP version 6 is installed.

7. Click **Close**.

8. Test the TCP/IP version 6 installation by opening **Internet Explorer** and navigating to **www.ipv6.org**. You should see a line under the line "Welcome to the IPv6 Information Page!" that states, "You are using IPv6 from <*your IPv6 address*>," as shown in Figure 21.1. If you are behind a firewall or using 6to4 tunneling, you may not see the message that indicates you have an IPv6 address. If you are able to access the site described in step 9, then you are successfully using IPv6.

Figure 21.1 Test the IPv6 Configuration

9. You can also navigate to an IPv6-only site from Microsoft Research on the Internet by going to **http://ipv6.research.microsoft.com**.

Another way to test whether your IPv6 installation was successful is to run the **ipconfig** command. If IPv6 is installed, your IP address will be shown in IPv6 format, as shown in Figure 21.2.

Figure 21.2 Ipconfig Results after Installing IPv6

```
C:\WINDOWS\system32\cmd.exe                                          _ □ X
Ok.

netsh interface ipv6>exit

C:\Documents and Settings\Administrator>ipconfig

Windows IP Configuration

Ethernet adapter WAN:

        Connection-specific DNS Suffix  . :
        IP Address. . . . . . . . . . . . : 192.168.1.97
        Subnet Mask . . . . . . . . . . . : 255.255.255.0
        IP Address. . . . . . . . . . . . : fe80::20c:29ff:feee:4176%4
        Default Gateway . . . . . . . . . : 192.168.1.7

Tunnel adapter Automatic Tunneling Pseudo-Interface:

        Connection-specific DNS Suffix  . :
        IP Address. . . . . . . . . . . . : fe80::5efe:192.168.1.97%2
        Default Gateway . . . . . . . . . :

C:\Documents and Settings\Administrator>
```

Now that TCP/IP version 6 is installed, additional utilities are available with the IPv6 functionality. Other than the utilities to manage, monitor, and troubleshoot IPv6, only Telnet, FTP, and Internet Explorer actually use the IPv6 protocol stack.

Netsh Commands

Netsh is an interactive command-line utility that allows you to manage local or remote network configurations of active machines. Netsh also supports scripting, so you can create batch configurations that run against the local machine or a specified host on the network. You can also use the Netsh utility to generate a configuration script to use as a backup configuration or as an aid to configure new machines in an identical fashion.

Netsh works with the existing components installed with the operating system by using helper dynamic link libraries (DLLs). Each helper DLL contains the information necessary to execute the commands for the component to which it applies. The set of commands and features supported by the DLLs is called a *context,* and each context is unique to the networking component.

The IPv6 interface has its own context with commands to manage and display information pertaining to the routes, interfaces, addresses, and caches specific to IPv6. There are currently no graphical user interface (GUI) applications to configure IPv6, so Netsh is necessary for configuring IPv6 and its associated components. The component called 6to4 has a subcontext within the IPv6 context, for configuring and managing 6to4 routers and hosts. For more information about Netsh, see the Windows Help and Support Center topic titled "Netsh Overview."

To put the netsh command into IPv6 context, type **netsh** at the command prompt, then at the **netsh>** prompt, type **interface ipv6.** Then you can use the IPv6 context commands, which include the following:

- **6to4** Changes to 6to4 context.
- **Add** Adds a configuration entry.
- **Delete** Deletes a configuration entry.
- **Dump** Shows a configuration script.
- **Install** Installs IPv6.
- **Isatap** Changes to isatap subcontext within IPv6 context.
- **Renew** Restarts IPv6 interfaces.
- **Reset** Resets IPv6 configuration.
- **Set** Sets configuration information.
- **Show** Displays information.
- **Uninstall** Uninstalls IPv6.

Ipsec6.exe

Ipsec6.exe is used to configure and implement IPSec security policies (SPs) and security associations (SAs) for IPv6. Using this utility, you can save and load security policies and security associations to a file that can be edited in a text editor. This can be a real timesaver when you implement IPSec for IPv6 on multiple machines. The command to save a configuration is **ipsec6 s** *FilenameWithNoExtension.* The filename specified from the command line will be appended with the extension automatically. The extension .spd is added to security policy files, and the extension .sad is added to security association files. If you are executing this command for the first time, and there are no current policies and no current security associations, the files created can act as templates to help you get started.

Other ipsec6 commands are available to works with security policies and security associations:

- To load the configuration from these files, type **ipsec6 l** *FilenameWithNoExtension.* The security policies will be loaded from *Filename*.spd and the security associations from *Filename*.sad.

- To delete security policies and security associations, type **ipsec6 d [{sp | sa}]** *[Index]* from a command line. Use the **sp** parameter with the *Index* of the policy you wish to delete, or the **sa** parameter to delete all of the security associations.

- To determine what the current security policies are, type **ipsec6 sp** *[Interface]* from the command line, where *Interface* is optional and applies to the security policies for the specified network interface.

- To view the current security associations, type **ipsec6 sa** from the command line. Note that the output from the commands to view the security policies and security associations is not formatted well for a command line, so you might prefer to save the configuration and view the files in Notepad.

IPv6 PING and Tracert Parameters

Use the following steps to use IPv6 PING to verify connectivity:

1. From a command prompt, type **netsh interface ipv6 show interface**.

2. Find the **Idx** value for **Local Area Connection.**

3. Type **netsh interface ipv6 show interface** *Idx,* where *Idx* is the number from the previous step. The Local Area Connection index number is usually **4**.

4. Right-click in the command window and select **Mark**. Then highlight the address. Once it is highlighted, right-click in the command prompt window. When you release the mouse button, the address will be copied to the Clipboard. Take note of your **Zone ID** for **Link**, which should match the **Idx** number in step 3.

5. Exit the **netsh** command. At a regular command prompt, type **ping,** and then right-click in the command prompt window and select **Paste.**

6. Without adding any spaces, add **%<ZoneID>,** where *ZoneID* is the number noted in step 4, so the command looks like this:

```
Ping fe80::204:5aff:fe08:fb4b%4
```

7. Press **Enter**. You should see four successful replies.

8. Continue by pinging another address on the same local network.

9. To test external hosts, ping the global address of another node.

10. To test name resolution with DNS or a hosts file, ping a node with **ping –6** *Name*, where *Name* is the site name. The **–6** parameter tells PING to use IPv6 only.

You can use Tracert to trace the path taken by IPv6 data packets from this host to the destination host. From a command prompt, type **tracert *IPv6Address%ZoneID,*** where *IPv6* is a valid IPv6 address and *ZoneID* is the destination address. Alternatively, type **tracert –d -6 *Hostname,*** where *Hostname* is the name of the remote machine.

6to4 Tunneling

6to4 tunneling is used to encapsulate IPv6 data packets in IPv4 headers before they are transmitted to the destination host. 6to4 tunneling uses a 6to4 host and 6to4 routers to deliver the IPv6 data. It is an Internet standard, defined in RFC 3056, and is used for interoperability between IPv4 and IPv6 networks. 6to4 hosts and routers are defined as follows:

- **6to4 host** Any IPv6 host that is configured with at least one 6to4 address. 6to4 can be configured with the **netsh interface ipv6 6to4** commands. As you might have noticed when you ran the **show interface** command, by default, your IPv6-enabled host will have a 6to4 pseudo-interface, as well as an automatic tunneling pseudo-interface.

- **6to4 router** Uses IPv4 and IPv6 to forward 6to4 traffic to the destination 6to4 hosts. It is also possible to implement a 6to4 relay router to forward 6to4 router traffic on the IPv6 Internet.

With 6to4 tunneling, it is not necessary for IPv6 hosts to get an IPv6 global address prefix from their ISPs. The host can create a 6to4 address automatically.

IPv6 Helper Service

The IPv6 Helper service is responsible for automatically configuring itself with the appropriate 6to4 addresses, but it uses a specific 6to4 router on the Internet. You can test functionality with the **ping –6** command.

The 6bone

The 6bone is a dedicated IPv6 network that exists on the Internet. It began as a virtual network using IPv6 over IPv4 encapsulation. It contains links to many sites and includes a great deal of IPv6 data, testing plans, news, current events, and implementation instructions. It will be a valuable resource for managing IPv6 on your network. For more information about the 6bone, see www.6bone.net. For instructions on how to connect to the 6bone, see www.opus1.com/ipv6/whatisthe6bone.html.

Teredo (IPv6 with NAT)

Teredo is the name for IPv4 network address translator (NAT) traversal for IPv6. It provides an IPv6/IPv4 translation over NAT and address assignment. Teredo also provides the mechanism for host-to-host automatic tunneling for unicast IPv6 connectivity when IPv6/IPv4 hosts are located behind one or more NAT servers.

Currently, to provide IPv6 connectivity over the Internet, you must have a 6to4 router with a public IPv4 address, which is not always feasible. Teredo provides a mechanism for IPv6 traffic to traverse NATs and access the Internet using IPv6. Basically, IPv6 packets are sent as IPv4-based UDP messages, and this allows the IPv6 packets to pass through the IPv4 NAT server. For more information about Teredo, see the Teredo Overview document located at www.microsoft.com/windowsxp/pro/techinfo/administration/p2p/overview.asp.

Planning the Network Topology

The next phase in planning your TCP/IP infrastructure is planning the IP routing solution to manage the traffic on your network. This will depend on the physical location of your equipment and users, as well as on how you want to distribute the addresses. When your implement your strategy, you will also need to determine how the hosts on your network will resolve host names and implement the necessary services to provide that functionality. You will need to identify where the services such as DHCP, WINS, DNS, and so on must exist in your network to function properly and reduce the network bandwidth utilization.

Analyzing Hardware Requirements

Before you implement your network topology, you should identify the hardware needs. For each physical location, you will need to provide some sort of routing. You might need to implement a WAN solution using a T1 line, which also requires special hardware. You will need DHCP servers at each location or a DHCP relay agent. You will need to provide some form of name resolution, most likely DNS and possibly WINS. Depending on the traffic and if you have a large number of users, you may decide to install switches to help manage network traffic.

For a DHCP server, the two major factors that affect performance are the amount of physical random access memory (RAM) and the speed of the disk input/output (I/O). You should always provide the largest amount of RAM possible and the fastest disk I/O for the best performance on a DHCP server. The same rules apply for WINS and DNS servers, although DNS is more dependent on network bandwidth. In any case, frequent zone updates require more RAM for better performance.

If you are using Active Directory (AD) DNS, there are other considerations related to AD, such as these:

- Increased network utilization due to dynamic DNS updates related to DCHP integration and WINS reverse lookups
- Increased RAM requirements due the increased data volume

Planning the Placement of Physical Resources

The quantity of data and the type of network traffic affect the location of IP resource servers in your enterprise. If the WAN link is slow, you might want to place DNS caching servers at each location to reduce WAN traffic related to DNS resolution. You might also consider providing a DNS server at each location to provide redundancy. In addition, by creating an AD integrated primary zone, you will allow clients to update their resource records locally. Defining which DNS servers can act as forwarders and perform iterative queries will help manage the Internet traffic.

You should also provide a DHCP server at each location. When you have multiple DHCP servers on your network, use the 80/20 rule to balance the load on the subnet: 80 percent of the scope will be on the primary server, with 20 percent on the other server. The DHCP server must have an interface on each network for which it has a scope defined, or you must locate a DHCP relay server on the same subnet as the DHCP clients.

If you implement WINS, you will need to examine the quantity of data replicated between WINS servers and the cost of WINS reverse lookups from DNS servers. You should minimize the number of WINS servers you implement in order to minimize the impact of WINS replication traffic on your network.

Use the Help and Support Center on Windows Server 2003 to see examples of performance statistics in a high traffic environment to help you gauge your enterprise needs.

Planning Network Traffic Management

After you decide where to place your physical equipment, the users will begin accessing the services supplied by DHCP, DNS, and WINS. Other traffic comes from accessing the Internet, file sharing, and the many other network resources that will be used. You can estimate the amount of traffic at peak times by using some of the utilities provided with the operating system. The tools can be used to create baselines, identify the peak network usage areas, and identify the traffic sources.

You will also need to monitor network traffic and analyze the usage. You might be able to identify illicit network access from external sites, find Trojan horse viruses that generate broadcast storms, or just discover who is actually hogging all that Internet bandwidth. You can also determine whether your server-to-server traffic is managed well, or if it is necessary to modify the physical location of equipment.

Monitoring Network Traffic and Network Devices

Every network administrator should be familiar with two key utilities:

- **Network Monitor** Allows you to capture data, identify the source, and analyze the content and format of the message.

- **System Monitor** Allows you to monitor other resources and determine the performance of those resources.

Network Monitor should be run during low-usage times or for short intervals to minimize the impact on performance of capturing all that data on your machine. It is also useful to identify the type of traffic you are concerned with and use the filters to capture only the data you need.

Using System Monitor

System Monitor is a Microsoft Management Console (MMC) snap-in tool that allows you to use counters to monitor the performance of hardware, applications, and operating system components on Windows Server 2003 machines.

System Monitor also allows you to view more than one log file at the same time, so you can compare baseline logs with the current data. The Performance Logs and Alerts service can gather data and store it in a Microsoft SQL Server database that can be viewed by System Monitor. You can also save portions of log files or SQL Server data to a new file. This can help save space, simplify comparisons of data, and reduce analysis time.

Determining Bandwidth Requirements

When you have captured performance statistics and viewed the network traffic during various times of the day, you can identify the different sources of traffic on your network. You will need to analyze how name resolution occurs, where the requests for name resolution initiate, and the server-to-server traffic when replicating the information.

You will need to identify the following:

- The slow connections and the quantity of data transmitted over those connections. This will help you to identify how often servers transmit replicated data to other servers.

- The cost of one client obtaining information from these servers. You can then use that information to calculate the cost of many users.

- Broadcast traffic, so that you can isolate that to certain networks. You will be able to identify areas where clients communicate heavily with other clients, such as file servers, and locate those resources on the same segment as the heavy users.

Optimizing Network Performance

TCP traffic uses a *sliding window* method of transmitting data. As data is successful transmitted to the destination, the window slides over the remaining data and transmits the next packets of data. Window size is basically the maximum number of packets that can be sent without waiting for positive acknowledgment. If you transmit large amounts of TCP data, then larger TCP windows will improve TCP/IP performance. The maximum window size is limited to 64 kilobytes by default and is determined by the windows size setting of the destination host machine. It is possible to increase the size of the TCP window dynamically on Windows Server 2003 to accommodate this by enabling large TCP window support. Client computers can be set to request large windows by editing their Registries. These are then called TCP1323Opts-enabled computers. The window size is negotiated during the TCP three-way handshake process. TCP1323 is a TCP extension defined in RFC 1323.

With Windows Server 2003, it is possible to disable NetBIOS encapsulation over TCP/IP (disable NetBT). This can significantly reduce the overhead of data transfer and eliminate the need for WINS and any other NetBIOS name resolution. It will also reduce the browse master traffic. The drawback to disabling NetBIOS encapsulation is that you can no longer browse network resources. In addition, some applications depend on NetBIOS and will not work without it. If you are using NetBIOS name resolution, you should have WINS servers to allow for directed send requests for name resolution, rather than broadcast for that information. WINS servers share data with each other on a regular interval. You might wish to reduce that traffic by modifying the replication intervals to increase the time between synchronizations. You should minimize the number of WINS servers used on your network. It is not necessary to have a WINS server on every LAN. The more WINS servers you implement, the more network traffic is generated due to WINS database replication.

The placement of other servers that provide network services is also important. DHCP servers must have an interface on the same segment as the clients that will use the DHCP server, or you must provide a means for DHCP requests to cross routers (such as a DHCP relay or using routers that allow DHCP and BOOTP requests). Place DNS servers on each LAN to minimize the amount of traffic generated when performing host name resolution. You can also designate which DNS servers can act as forwarders to control which machines can perform iterative DNS queries over the Internet.

Chapter 22

Planning, Implementing, and Maintaining a Routing Strategy

In this chapter:

- ☑ **Understanding IP Routing**

- ☑ **Security Considerations for Routing**

- ☑ **Troubleshooting IP Routing**

Introduction

In the preceding chapter, you learned about the TCP/IP protocols and how to set up a TCP/IP infrastructure. One of the biggest advantages of TCP/IP as a network/transport protocol stack is its capability to route packets between different networks or subnets. Dealing with routing issues is an important part of the job of a Windows Server 2003 network administrator for a typical medium-to-large size network. In this chapter, we first review the basics of IP routing, including the role of routing tables, static and dynamic routing, and routing protocols such as Routing Information Protocol (RIP) and Open Shortest Path First (OSPF).

You'll learn to use the Netsh commands related to routing, and then we'll show you how to evaluate routing options. This includes selecting the proper connectivity devices, and we'll discuss hubs, bridges, switches (Layer 2, 3, and 4 varieties), and routers. We'll look at how you can use a Windows Server 2003 machine as a router and how to configure the Routing and Remote Access Service (RRAS) to do so.

Next, we look at security considerations related to routing. We'll show you how to analyze requirements for routing components from a security-conscious point of view, and we'll discuss methods of simplifying the network topology to provide fewer attack points. This includes minimizing the number of network interfaces, the number of routes, and the number of routing protocols. We will also discuss router-to-router virtual private networks (VPNs), packet filtering, firewalls, and logging levels.

Finally, we cover how to troubleshoot IP routing issues. We'll identify troubleshooting tools and take a look at some common routing problems, including those related to interface configuration, RRAS configuration, routing protocols, TCP/IP configuration, and routing table configuration.

Understanding IP Routing Basics

Understanding the concepts concerning IP addressing is critical to understanding how IP routing works. A good understanding of IP addressing, and subsequently the art of subnetting, requires that you be comfortable with binary notation and math.

You already know that an IP address is a numeric identifier assigned to every machine on a network. This address tells where the device is located on the specific network.

As a quick review, IP addresses are currently made up of 32 bits of information. These bits are divided into four sections (octets) that each contains 1 byte (6 bits). You will see IP addresses specified in three basic formats:

- Binary such as in 11000000.10101000.00000000.00000001

- Dotted-decimal such as in 192.168.0.1

- Hexadecimal such as in C0 A8 00 01

All three of these examples represent the same IP address. In reality, the computer can use only the binary version. The other two formats are provided because they are easier for people to understand and use.

There are three basic types of IP addresses:

- **Unicast addresses** IP addresses assigned to a single network interface that is attached on the network. Unicast IP addresses are used for one-to-one communications between hosts.

- **Broadcast addresses** IP addresses designed to be received and processed by every IP address located on a given network. They're basically one-to-many communications.

- **Multicast addresses** IP addresses where one or more IP nodes can listen in on the same network segment. Multicast IP addresses are also one-to-many communications.

Next, you should also understand the differences between routed and Network Address Translation (NAT) connections. NAT is the process of switching back and forth between the IP addresses used on an internal network, sometimes referred to as *private addresses*, and Internet IP addresses, sometimes known as *public addresses*.

There are three address blocks set aside and defined as private address space:

- **10.0.0.0 with a subnet mask of 255.0.0.0, or 10.0.0.0/8** This network is a private address space that has 24 host bits that can be used.

- **172.16.0.0 with a subnet mask of 255.240.0.0, or 172.16.0.0/12** This network is a private address space that has 20 host bits that can be used. This provides a range of 16 class B network IDs from 172.0.0.0/16 through 172.31.0.0./16.

- **192.168.0.0 with a subnet mask of 255.255.0.0, 192.168.0.0./16** This network is a private address space that has 16 host bits that can be used. This provides a range of 256 class C network IDs from 192.168.0.0/24 through 192.168.255.0/24.

Remember that private and public spaces do not overlap. Machines on an intranet with a private IP address cannot directly connect to the Internet. Instead, they must be connected indirectly via either a proxy server of NAT. Essentially, all of the computers on your intranet are masquerading behind a single public IP address.

Routed connections require a single public IP address for each connection to the Internet. Using NAT allows you to connect multiple private addresses to a single public IP address. This is done by translating and modifying packets to reflect the changed addressing information.

There are three basic components that make up NAT:

- **Translation** This component maintains the NAT table for inbound and outbound connections.

- **Addressing** This component is handled by a stripped-down version of a Dynamic Host Configuration Protocol (DHCP) server that assigns the IP address, subnet mask, default gateway, and IP address of the Domain Name System (DNS) server.

- **Name resolution** This component forwards all name-resolution requests to the DNS server defined on the Internet-connected adapter, and then returns the reply. It can be thought of as a DNS proxy.

Keep in mind that NAT is not always the solution. It is extremely limited when it comes to security. You cannot encrypt anything carrying or that has been derived from an IP address. Tracking hackers and other problems is also extremely difficult, because the source IP address is stripped away in the NAT process. Another problem arises when you try to use NAT with large networks that have many hosts attempting to communicate with the Internet at the same time. The size of the mapping tables in this kind of environment is overwhelming and can cause performance problems. NAT is discussed in detail later Chapter 25, "Planning, Implementing and Maintaining Routing and Remote Access."

Another basic concept related to IP routing is how the Internet Control Message Protocol (ICMP) works. ICMP is a maintenance protocol used to create and maintain routing tables. It supports router discovery and advertisements to hosts on a network. Very simply, its designed to pass control and status information between TCP/IP devices. When a client computer starts up on your network, it usually has only a few entries in its routing table. When that host sends data out to a specific destination on a network, the host first checks its routing table to see if there is already an entry matching the destination's IP address. If no match is found, the packet is sent to the default gateway. When the default gateway receives the packet, it will check to see if it has a matching entry in its routing table. If it does, it forwards the packet to the destination. At the same time, it sends an ICMP message back to the originating host, telling that host about the better route available. ICMP can also let hosts on a network know if a specific router is still active by sending out periodic messages with this kind of information.

Routing Tables

A routing table is basically a list, a huge list sometimes, that is used to direct traffic on a network. The table includes information about what other networks are reachable from a given network by providing the network address and subnet mask, as well as the metric, or cost, for that specific network route. Another way to think of it is as a database of routes to other locations.

The way this works is simple. When a packet arrives at the routing device (which could be a dedicated router or a Windows Server 2003 computer), the routing table is queried to discover the lowest cost route to the intended destination. Sometimes, when there is no specific information concerning that network in the routing table, the packet will be forwarded to the default gateway, assuming that the default gateway will get the packet where it needs to go.

The level of detail, or the number of routes in the table, depends on whether the IP node is a host or a router. Usually, a host will have fewer entries in this table than a router has in its table. For instance, it would be normal to find an IP host configured with a default gateway. Creating a default route in the table allows for the effective summarization of all destinations. Routing tables on a router, on the other hand, will normally contain an entry for each and every reachable network on the IP network system.

Let's turn our attention back to the table itself. Each of the rows in this list, or entries in this database, is commonly referred to as a *route*. There are three basic types of routes:

- **Host route** A route to a specific IP address in the network. A host is a particular computer, or more specifically, an interface on a computer or device. In these cases, the network mask is always 255.255.255.255 (/32). Host routes are typically used for custom routes to specific hosts. This helps in the optimization and control of a network.

- **Network ID route** A route for classful, classless, subnet, and supernetted destinations. The network mask in these cases will be somewhere between 129.0.0.0 (/1) and 255.255.255.254 (/31).

- **Default route** A route to all other destinations. This route is used when the routing table cannot find a host or network ID route that matches the destination in the packet's header. The default route has a destination of 0.0.0.0 and a network mask of 0.0.0.0 (/0), and it is sometimes expressed as 0/0. All destinations not found in the routing table are simply forwarded to this destination, where the specific destination address will be found.

Each route in the routing table contains the necessary forwarding information for a range of destination IP addresses. This information includes two values for the destination IP address: the next-hop interface and the next-hop IP address. The *next-hop interface* is just a representation of the next physical or logical device over which the IP packet will be forwarded. The *next-hop IP address* is the IP address of the node to which the IP packet is being forwarded. In an indirect delivery, the next-hop IP address is the IP address of a directly reachable intermediate router to which the packet is being forwarded.

The routing table shown in Figure 22.1 (viewed from the Windows Server 2003 **Routing and Remote Access** utility) is for a computer running Windows Server 2003 Enterprise Edition with one 10MB network adapter, an IP address of 192.168.0.13, a subnet mask of 255.255.255.0, and a default gateway of 192.168.0.1.

Figure 22.1 IP Routing Table

Destination	Network mask	Gateway	Interface	Metric	Protocol
ARIES - IP Routing Table					
0.0.0.0	0.0.0.0	192.168.0.1	Local Area Connection	1	Static (non demand-dial)
0.0.0.0	0.0.0.0	192.168.0.1	Local Area Connection	30	Network management
127.0.0.0	255.0.0.0	127.0.0.1	Loopback	1	Local
127.0.0.1	255.255.255.255	127.0.0.1	Loopback	1	Local
192.168.0.0	255.255.255.0	192.168.0.5	Local Area Connection	30	Local
192.168.0.5	255.255.255.255	127.0.0.1	Loopback	30	Local
192.168.0.255	255.255.255.255	192.168.0.5	Local Area Connection	30	Local
224.0.0.0	240.0.0.0	192.168.0.5	Local Area Connection	30	Local
255.255.255.255	255.255.255.255	192.168.0.5	Local Area Connection	1	Local

Let's look at the individual rows more closely:

- The first row in the table, beginning with 0.0.0.0, is the default route.

- The second and third rows, beginning with 127.0.0.0 and 127.0.0.1, are the loopback network.

- The fourth row, beginning with 192.168.0.0, is the local network.

- The fifth row, beginning with 192.168.0.13, is the local IP address.

- The second-to-last row, beginning with 224.0.0.0, is the multicast address.

- The final row, beginning with 255.255.255.255, is the limited broadcast address.

We'll now turn our attention to the upkeep of these tables. You can perform the maintenance of the routing tables manually or automatically. If you do it manually, you'll be using *static routing*. If you do it automatically, you'll be using *dynamic routing*. Let's take a closer look at these two concepts.

Static versus Dynamic Routing

Remember that the basic idea of routing is that each packet you find on your network has a source and a destination. That means that any device that receives the packet inspects the packet's headers to determine where it came from and where it's going. When the device has information about the network, such as how long it would take a packet to go from one point to another, that device can change the routing intelligently to improve the performance of the network.

Static routing uses manually configured routes. Here, there is no attempt to discover other routers or systems on a network. All entries into the routing table are entered by hand, and the routing table is used to get information to other networks. This type of routing works well with classless routing, because each route must be added with a network mask. It works well for small networks, but it doesn't scale well. Static routes are often used to connect to the Internet. Static routing is, however, not fault tolerant.

Dynamic routing doesn't depend on fixed, unchangeable routes to remote networks being added to the routing tables. In other words, you don't need to enter the routes by hand. Dynamic routing uses routing protocols to maintain the routing tables. Dynamic routing allows for the discovery of the networks surrounding the router by finding and communicating with other nearby routers in the network. Routes are discovered using routing protocol traffic and are then added or removed from IP routing tables as required. Dynamic routing can provide fault tolerance. When a route is unreachable, the route is removed from the routing table. Figure 22.2 shows a more complex network using dynamic routing.

Figure 22.2 A More Complex Network Using Dynamic Routing

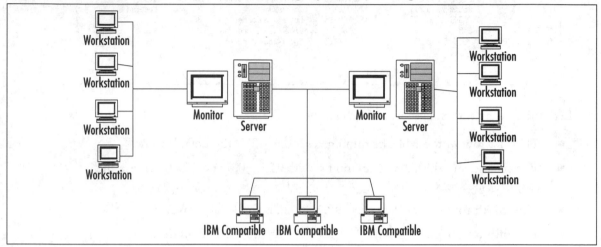

Gateways

As you know, a *gateway* is a device that connects networks using different communication protocols in a way that allows for information to pass from one network to the other. It both transfers and converts the information into a form that can be used by the protocols on the receiving network. In other words, a gateway is somewhat of a router. A router, by definition, is a device or computer that sends packets between two or more network segments as necessary, using logical network addresses, most often IP addresses. The default gateway is a router that connects your host to remote network segments. It's the exit point for all the packets in your network that have destinations outside your network.

Routing Protocols

Router discovery enables new, or rebooted, routers to configure themselves automatically. The two major and most common dynamic-routing protocols are RIP and OSPF. Both of these protocols are supported by the Windows Server 2003 family. Both are interior gateway protocols (IGPs) that use routers to communicate (not to be confused with the proprietary Cisco IGRP). But before we discuss these two protocols, we need to explore how protocols make routing decisions.

In general, routing protocols can use one of two different approaches to making routing decisions:

- **Distance vectors** A distance-vector protocol makes its decision based on a measurement of the distance between the source and the destination addresses.

- **Link states** A link-state protocol bases its decisions on various states of the links that connect the source and the destination addresses.

Distance-vector algorithms, also known as *Bellman-Ford algorithms*, periodically pass copies of their routing tables to their immediate network neighbors. The recipient adds what is called a distance vector, which is little more than a distance value, to the routing table it has just received, and then forwards it on to its immediate neighbors. The process results in each router learning about the other routers and thereby developing a cumulative table of network distances to other routers. This table is then used to update the router's own routing table. Keep in mind that the only thing the router learns about is distance.

The main drawback to distance-vector routing is that it requires time for the changes in a network to propagate across the network. This makes distance-vector routing inappropriate for larger, more complex networks. The advantages of distance-vector routing are its ease of configuration, use, and maintenance. As we will discuss shortly, RIP is the epitome of distance-vector routing.

Link-state routing algorithms are usually known cumulatively as *shortest path first* (SPF) protocols. OSPF, which will be discussed shortly, is an example of this protocol group. These protocols maintain a complex database that describes the network's topology. Link-state protocols develop and maintain extensive information concerning the network's routers and how they interconnect. They do this by exchanging link-state advertisements (LSAs) with each other. Any change in the network will trigger the exchange of LSAs. Each router then constructs an extensive database using these received LSAs, so it can compute different routes and determine how reachable the networked destinations really are. This information is then used to update the routing table. Component failures and growth of the network are easily documented.

The main drawbacks to using link-state protocols involve the heavy use of bandwidth, memory, and processor time. Especially during the initial discovery process, link-state protocols flood the network with messages, thereby lowering the overall network efficiency. Also, overall, link-state protocols require more memory and higher processor speeds than distance-vector protocols need for efficient operation.

The main advantage of link-state protocols comes into play with large and complicated networks. A well-designed network will be more able to withstand the effects of unexpected changes using link-state protocols. Overhead of the frequent, time-driven updates required for distance-vector protocols can be avoided. Networks using a link-state protocol are also more scalable. For most large networks, the advantages of using link-state protocols will outweigh the disadvantages.

RIP

RIP is simple and easy to configure and is used widely in small and medium-sized networks. RIP is an IGP used to route data within autonomous networks. RIP does have performance limitations, however, that restrict its usefulness on medium-sized to large networks. RIP is a distance-vector routing protocol. This means it distributes routing information in the form of a network ID and the number of hops (or the distance) from the destination. RIP has a maximum distance of 15 hops. Anything over that is considered unreachable.

There are two versions of RIP: version 1 described in RFC 1058 and version 2 described in RFC 1723. Windows Server 2003 supports both RIP versions.

RIP version 1 is a class-based routing protocol. Only the network ID is announced here. RIP version 2 is a classless routing protocol. This version includes both a network ID and a subnet mask in its announcement. It also provides more information, allowing for both authentication and a measure of security.

There are several shortcomings to RIP version 1:

- RIP version 1 uses MAC-level broadcasting, requiring all hosts on a network to process all packets.

- RIP version 1 doesn't support sending a subnet address with the route announcement. This can be a problem when there is a shortage of available IP addresses.

- Because RIP version 1 route announcements are being addressed to the IP subnet and MAC-level broadcast, non-RIP hosts may also be receiving the RIP announcements, contributing to the broadcast clutter and possibly lowering the efficiency and performance of your network.

- By default, every 30 seconds, RIP routers broadcast lists of networks they can reach to every other adjacent router. Again, this can contribute to lower network performance.

- RIP version 1 does not handle subnetted addresses well, since it doesn't send the subnet address along with the broadcast.

- RIP version 1 provides no defense from a rogue router. A *rogue router* is an RIP router that advertises false or erroneous route information.

- RIP version 1 is difficult to troubleshoot. In general, most problems in RIP routing stem from incorrect configuration or from the propagation of bad routing information.

So, what does RIP version 2 do to attempt to correct the problems with RIP version 1?

- RIP version 2 advertisements include the subnet mask with the network ID.

- RIP version 2 sends multicast announcements to the multicast IP address 224.0.0.9 with a time to live (TTL) of 1 instead of broadcasting announcements, so it does not require IGMP.

- RIP version 2 allows for authentication to substantiate the source of the incoming routing announcements.

- RIP version 2 is compatible with RIP version 1.

RIP routers begin with a basically empty routing table and start sending out announcements to the networks to which they're connected. These announcements include the appropriate routes listed for all interfaces in the router's routing table. The router also sends out a RIP General Request message asking for information from any router receiving the message. These announcements can be broadcast or multicast. Other routers on other networks hear these announcements and add the original router and its information to their own routing tables. They then respond to the new router's request for information. The new router hears the announcements from these other routers on the network and adds them and their information to its own routing table.

After the initial setup, the RIP router will send out information based on its routing table. The default time period is 30 seconds. Over time, the routers of the network develop a consensus of what the network looks like. The process of developing this consensual perspective of the network's topology is known as *convergence*. Basically, this means that the network's routers individually agree on what the network looks like as a group. It is this very process of convergence, however, that can sometimes lead to problems. A typical network using convergence is shown in Figure 22.3. One of the occasional problems that occurs is called *counting to infinity*. Let's look at how that happens.

Figure 22.3 Typical Network Using Convergence

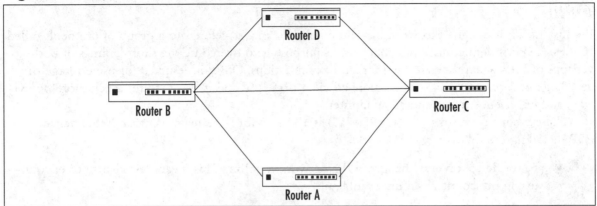

In our example, we will assume that Router A has failed. With its failure, all the hosts on the A network will no longer be accessible from the other three networks. After missing six updates from Router A, Router B will invalidate its B–A route and advertise its unavailability. Routers C and D remain ignorant of the failure of Router A until notified by Router B. At this point, both Router B and Router D still think they can get to Router A through Router C, and they raise the metric of this route accordingly. So, Routers B and D send their next updates to Router C. Router C, having timed out its route to Router A, still thinks it has access through Router B or Router D. Thus, a loop is formed between Routers B, C, and D, based on the mistaken belief that both Routers B and C can still access Router A. With each iteration of updates, the metrics are incremented an extra hop for each route. This count speeds up the process by which the router approaches its definition of infinity—the point where the router says the destination is unreachable.

There are two methods of preventing this counting to infinity loop: split horizon and triggered updates. If the router is implementing split horizon, routes will not be announced back over the interfaces by which they were learned. The limitation of the split-horizon approach is that a route will not timeout until it has been unreachable for six tries, so each router has five opportunities to transmit incorrect information to the neighboring routers. If the router is implementing split horizon with poison reverse, routes learned on interfaces are announced back as unreachable. Split horizon with poison reverse is much more dependable than simple split horizon. However, although split horizon with poison reverse will stop loops in small networks, loops are still possible on larger, multipath networks.

Fault tolerance in RIP networks is based on the timeout of RIP-learned routes. When changes happen in the network, RIP routers send out triggered updates, rather than waiting for a scheduled time for routing announcements. These triggered updates contain the routing update and are sent immediately. Triggered updates are nothing more than a method of speeding up split horizon with poison reverse. However, triggered updates are not foolproof. While the triggered updates are being propagated around the network, routers that have not received the triggered update are still sending out the incorrect information. It's possible that a router could receive the triggered update and then receive an update from another router reintroducing the incorrect information, so the count-to-infinity problem, though not as likely, is still possible.

OSPF

Because OSPF is designed to work inside the network area, it belongs to a group of protocols called IGRPs. OSPF is defined in RFC 2328 and its purpose is to overcome the shortcomings of both versions of RIP when they are used for large organizations. OSPF is designed for use on large or very large networks. OSPF is much more efficient than RIP, and it also requires much more knowledge and experience to set up and administer.

There are many reasons why OSPF is a better choice for large networks than either version of RIP, including the following:

- Faster detection and changes of the network topology. This means less chance of encountering the count-to-infinity problem.

- OSPF routes are loop-free.

- In OSPF, large networks can be broken down into smaller contiguous groups of networks, called *areas*. (RIP does not allow for the subdivision of a network into smaller components.) Routing table entries can then be minimized by using the technique called *summarizing*. Summarizing allows for the creation of default routes for routes outside the area.

- The subnet mask is advertised with OSPF. This provides support for disjointed subnets and supernetting.

- Route exchanges between OSPF routers can be authenticated.

- Because external routes can be advertised internally, OSPF routers can calculate least-cost routes to external destinations.

OSPF is a link-state routing protocol that uses LSAs to send information to other routers in the same area, known as *adjacencies*. Included in the LSA is information about interfaces, gateways, and metrics. OSPF routers collect this information into a link-state database (LSDB) that is shared and synchronized among the various routers. Using this database, the various routers are able to calculate the shortest path to other routers using the SPF algorithm. The cost of each router interface is assigned by the network administrator. This unitless number can include the delay, the bandwidth, and any monetary cost factors. The accumulated cost of any OSPF network can never be more than 65,535. So, the way OSPF works can be divided into three main phases:

- The LSDB is put together from neighboring routers.

- The shortest path to each node is then calculated.

- The router creates the routing table entries containing the information about the routes.

When the router initializes, it sends out an LSA that contains only its own configuration. Each router has its own unique ID that it sends out with the LSA. This ID is not, however, the destination address of that router. Usually, it is the highest IP address assigned to that router, thereby ensuring that each router ID is unique. Over time, the router receives LSAs from other routers. The original router includes these routes in its own LSA and eventually will again send out its LSA, now containing the information it received. This process is called *flooding*. Every router in the area will soon have the information from all other routers in the area.

After the LSDB is compiled, the router determines the lowest cost path to each destination using the Dijkstra algorithm. Now, every other router and network reachable from that router will have a shortest, least-cost path calculated. The resulting data structure is called the *SPF tree*. The SPF tree is different for each router in the network, because the routes are calculated based on each router as the root of the tree. After the SPF tree is calculated, the routing table is created from the information it contains. An entry will be created for each network in the area of the router. The routing table will contain the network ID, the subnet mask, the IP address of the appropriate router for traffic to be directed to for that network, the interface over which the router is reachable, and the OSPF-calculated cost to that network. This cost is the metric unit, not the hop count as it would be in an RIP-routed network.

OSPF router interfaces must be configured for an appropriate network type because the OSPF message address will be set for the network type specified. There are three network types supported by OSPF:

- **Broadcast** This type of network is connected by two or more routers and broadcast traffic is passed between them. Examples of broadcast networks include Ethernet and FDDI.

- **Non-broadcast multiple access (NBMA)** Broadcast traffic doesn't pass on this network, even though it is connected by two or more routers. OSPF must be configured to use IP unicasting instead of multicasting. Examples of this type of network include Asynchronous Transfer Mode (ATM) and Frame Relay.

- **Point-to-Point** Only two routers can be connected using this type of network. Examples of point-to-point networks include WAN links like Digital Subscriber Line (DSL) or Integrated Services Digital Network (ISDN).

Your network is divided into areas by placing routers in specific locations to join or divide the network in the manner you want. What the router does and what designation it is given are determined by its location and role in the network area. The roles that an OSPF router might file include the following:

- **Internal router** All interfaces of the router are connected to the same area. An internal router will have only one LSDB because it is connected to only one area.

- **Area border router (ABR)** When a router's interfaces are connected to different areas, that router is an ABR. An ABR has one LSDB for each area it's connected to, as illustrated in Figure 22.4.

Figure 22.4 An Area Border Router

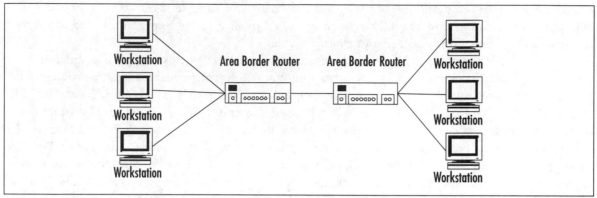

- **Backbone router** If one of a router's interfaces is on the backbone area, that router is considered a backbone router. This applies to both ABRs and internal routers.

- **Autonomous system boundary router (ASBR)** If a router exchanges routes with sources outside the network area, it is known as an ASBR. These special routers announce external routes throughout the area network.

Using Netsh Commands

Administering your routing server through the Routing and Remote Access console is easy. You might wonder why anyone would want to use the command line when a perfectly acceptable and easy-to-use console is available. There are two main reasons:

- You can administer a routing server much more quickly from the command line. This might be especially important over slow network links.

- You can administer multiple routing servers more efficiently and consistently by creating scripts using these commands, which can then be run on many servers.

The Netsh utility is available in the Windows 2000 Resource Kit and is a standard command in Windows XP and Windows Server 2003. This utility displays and allows you to manage the configuration of your network, including both local and remote computers. It is designed to simplify the process of creating command-line scripts such as batch files. The utility itself is little more than a command interpreter that connects and interfaces with a number of services and protocols through the aid of a number of dynamic link libraries (DLLs). Each of these DLLs provides the utility with an extensive set of commands that applies specifically to that DLL's service or protocol. These DLLs are referred to as *helper files*, and sometimes helper files are used to extend other helper files.

You can use the Netsh utility to perform the following tasks:

- Configure interfaces
- Configure routing protocols

- Configure filters

- Configure routes

- Configure remote-access behavior for Windows 2000 and Windows Server 2003-based remote-access routers that are running RRAS

- Display the configuration of a currently running router on any computer

- Use the scripting feature to run a collection of commands in batch mode against a specific router

The syntax for the Netsh utility is as follows:

```
netsh [-r router name] [-a AliasFile] [-c Context] [Command |     -f ScriptFile]
```

Context strings are appended to a command and passed to the associated helper file. The helper file can have one or more entry points that are mapped to contexts. The context can be any of the following: **DHCP**, **ip**, **ipx**, **netbeui**, **ras**, **routing**, **autodhcp**, **dnsproxy**, **igmp**, **mib**, **nat**, **ospf**, **relay**, **rip**, and **wins**. Under Windows XP, the available contexts include **AAAA**, **DHCP**, **DIAG**, **IP**, **RAS**, **ROUTING**, and **WINS**. Appending a specific context to the input string makes a whole different set of commands available that are specific to that context.

The easiest way to learn how the Netsh utility works is by viewing its help information. Open a command prompt window on your Windows Server 2003 computer and enter the **netsh** command at the prompt. The command prompt changes to the **netsh** prompt. Enter a **?** to display a list of available commands. To see the subcontexts and commands that are available to use with the routing context, type **routing ?** at the **netsh** prompt (or simply type **netsh routing ?** at the command prompt), and then press **Enter**. You can get command-line help for each command by typing **netsh,** followed by the command, followed by **?**.

Rather than entering commands through the Netsh utility, it is more efficient to use the DLLs without needing to load the Netsh shell. This reduces the amount of coding time required, and you can use multiple DLLs within a single script. To use Netsh commands this way, follow the **netsh** command with the name of the DLL and the command string. For example, to use the **show helper** command to see a complete list of the available DLLs, type **netsh show helper**, as shown in Figure 22.5.

Figure 22.5 Type netsh show helper at the Command Prompt to View Available DLLs

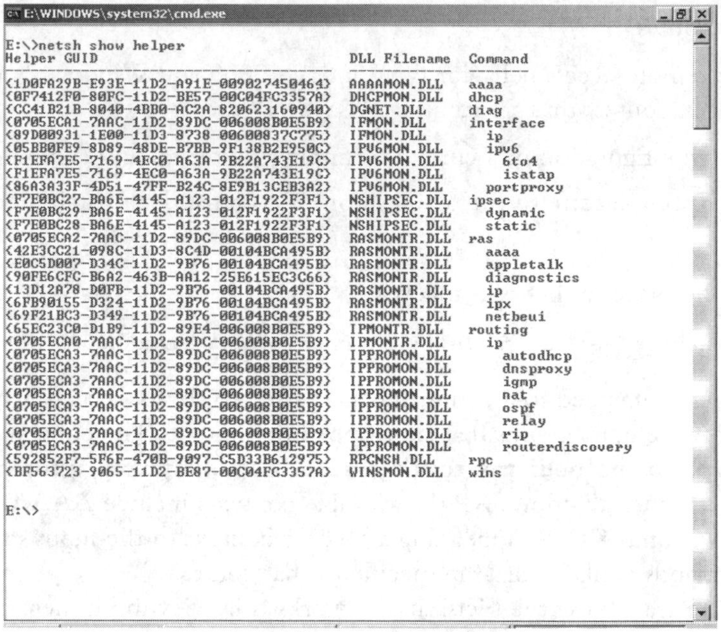

As you can see in Figure 22.5, when the script is processed, you see the results of the script and then are returned to the command prompt, from which you can execute your next script.

Evaluating Routing Options

In order to make good decisions about routing in your network, you need to evaluate potential network traffic, as well as the number and types of hardware devices and applications used in your environment. For the most part, the heavier the routing demand, the higher the need for dedicated hardware routers. Lighter routing demands can be met sufficiently by less expensive software routers. Your routing decisions should be based on your knowledge and understanding of both options.

Selecting Connectivity Devices

For small, segmented networks with relatively light traffic between subnets, a software-based routing solution such as the Windows Server 2003 RRAS might be ideal. On the other hand, a large number of network segments with a wide range of performance requirements would probably necessitate some kind of hardware-based routing solution. Evaluating your routing options includes selecting the proper connectivity devices: hubs, bridges, switches, or routers.

Hubs

Hubs, sometimes referred to as *switches*, are devices used to connect communication lines in a central location and help provide common connections to all other devices on the network. A hub usually has one input and several outputs. These outputs are known as *ports*, but don't confuse them with TCP/IP ports (as in port 80, the one used for HTTP traffic). These ports are just connections and nothing more. They generally accept RJ-45 connectors. Think of a hub as like the center of an old wagon wheel with all the spokes radiating out to the other part of the wheel.

A hub simply takes the data that comes into its ports and sends it out on the other ports of the hub. For this reason, it is sometimes referred to as a *repeater*. It doesn't provide or perform any filtering or redirection of the data from the various sources plugged into it. Hubs are commonly used to connect various network segments of a LAN.

Hubs generally come in three flavors:

- **Passive** Serves simply as a pipeline allowing data to move from one device, or network segment, to another.

- **Intelligent** Sometimes referred to as an *active*, *managed*, or *manageable* hub, it includes additional features that allow you to monitor the traffic passing through the hub and configure each port for specific purposes.

- **Switching** Reads the destination address of each packet and forwards that packet to the correct port. Most hubs of this variety also support load balancing.

Bridges

There are several definitions for a *bridge*, each carrying a specific meaning when used in a particular context. In one context, a bridge can be thought of as a gateway, connecting one network to another using the same communication protocols and allowing the information to be passed from one to the other. In another context, a bridge can be used to connect two networks with dissimilar communication protocols at the Data Link layer (Layer 2), in much the same manner as a router itself. There is also a bridge called a *bridge router*, which supports the functions of both the bridge and the router using Layer 2 addresses for routing.

Here, we'll look at the traditional bridge and the context that is most often associated with this device. Bridges work at both the Physical (Layer 1) and Data Link (Layer 2) layers of the OSI reference model. That means that a bridge knows nothing about protocols but forwards data depending on the destination address found in the data packet. This destination address is not an IP address, but rather a Media Access Control (MAC) address that is unique to each network adapter card. For this reason, bridges are often referred to as *MAC bridges*.

Basically, all bridges work by building and maintaining an address table. This table includes information such as an up-to-date listing of every MAC address on the LAN, as well as the physical bridge port connected to the segment on which that address is located.

There are three basic types of bridges:

- **Transparent bridge** Links together segments of the same type of LAN. A transparent bridge effectively isolates the traffic from one LAN segment from the traffic of another LAN segment, as shown in Figure 22.6.

Figure 22.6 Transparent Bridge

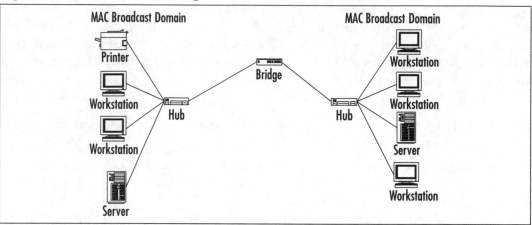

Translating (or translational) bridge Like a transparent bridge, links together segments of the same type of LAN, but also can provide conversion processes needed between different LAN architectures. This allows you to connect a Token Ring LAN to an Ethernet LAN, as shown in Figure 22.7.

Figure 22.7 Translating Bridge

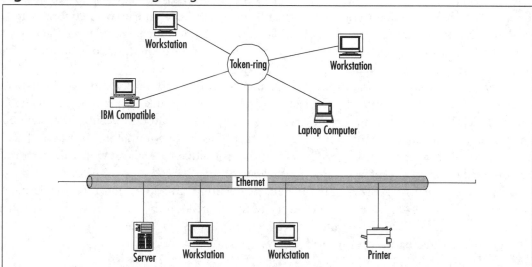

Speed-buffering bridge Used to connect LANs that have similar architectures but different transmission rates. Figure 22.8 shows how you might use a speed-buffering bridge to connect a 10-Mbps Ethernet network to a 100-Mbps Ethernet network.

Figure 22.8 Speed-buffering Bridge

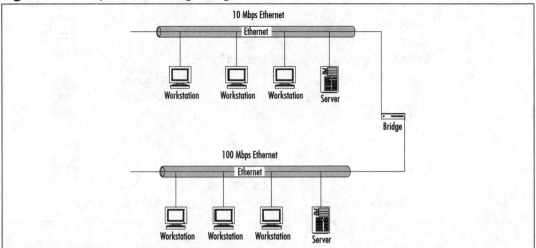

Bridges are self-learning, so the administrative overhead is small. The functionality of bridges has been built into routers, hubs, and switches.

Switches

Switches are like bridges, except that they have multiple ports with the same type of connection (bridges generally have only two ports) and have been described as nothing more than fast bridges. Switches are used on heavily loaded networks to isolate data flow and improve the network performance. In most cases, most users get little, if any, advantage from using a switch rather than a hub.

That's not to oversimplify and suggest that a switch doesn't have many benefits. Switches can be used to connect both hubs and individual devices. These approaches are known as *segment switching* and *port switching*, respectively.

Segment switching implies that each port on the switch functions as its own segment. This process tends to increase the available bandwidth, while decreasing the number of devices sharing each segment's bandwidth, but at the same time maintaining the Layer 2 connectivity. Each shared hub and the devices that are connected to it make up their own media access domain, while all devices in both domains remain part of the same MAC broadcast domain. Figure 22.9 illustrates how a segment-switched LAN can be divided to improve performance.

Figure 22.9 Segment Switching

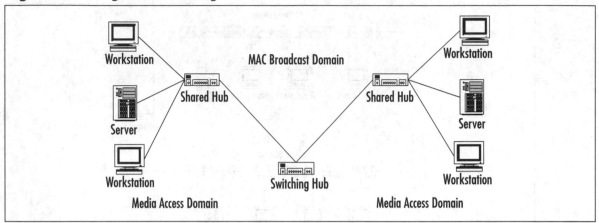

Port switching implies that each port on the switching hub is directly connected to an individual device. This makes the port and the device their own self-contained media access domain. All of the devices in the network still remain part of the same MAC broadcast domain. Figure 22.10 illustrates how the media access and MAC broadcast domains are configured in a port-switched LAN.

Figure 22.10 A Port-switched LAN

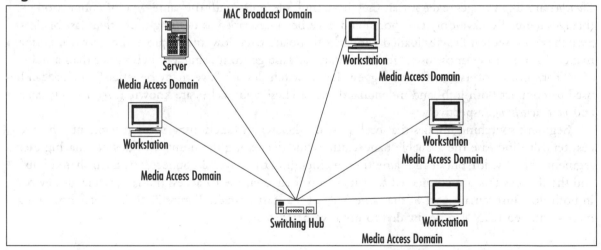

Layer 2 Switches

Layer 2 switches, operating at the Data Link layer, can be programmed to respond automatically to a wide range of circuit conditions. By monitoring control and data events, these switches automatically reroute circuits or switch to backup equipment, as the need requires. These switches operate using physical network, or MAC, addresses. These switches will be fast but not terribly smart. They only look at the data packet to find out where it's headed.

Layer 3 Switches

Layer 3 switches, operating at the Network layer, are designed for disaster recovery service (or, more importantly, for disaster avoidance). These network backup units are usually designed specifically to provide high levels of automation, intelligence, and security. Layer 3 switches use routing protocols such as RIP or OSPF to calculate routes and build their own routing tables.

Layer 3 switches use network or IP addresses to identify locations on the network, identifying the network location as well as the physical device. These switches are smarter than Layer 2 switches. They incorporate routing functions to actively calculate the best way to get a packet to its destination. Unless their algorithms and processor support high speeds, though, these switches are slower.

Layer 4 Switches

Layer 4 switches, operating at the Transport layer, allow network managers to choose the best method of communicating for each switching application. Because Layer 4 coordinates communication between systems, these switches are able to identify which application protocols (HTTP, SMTP, FTP, and so forth) are included in the packets, and they use this information to hand off the packet to the appropriate higher layer software. This means that Layer 4 switches make their packet-forwarding decisions based not just on the MAC and IP addresses, but also on the application to which the packet belongs.

Because these devices allow you to set up priorities for your network traffic based on applications, you can assign a high priority for your vital in-house applications and use different forwarding rules for low-priority packets, such as generic HTTP-based traffic. Layer 4 switches can also provide security, because company protocols can be confined to only authorized switched ports or users. This feature can be reinforced using traffic filtering and forwarding features.

All these devices can be used to segment your network, but segmentation does not create separate LANs. LANs exist at only the first two layers of the OSI reference model. There's another way to segment your network: use a router.

Routers

Routers are Layer 3 devices that forward data depending on the network address, not the MAC address. Since we are dealing with TCP/IP here, this means they use the IP address. Routers read the header information from each packet and determine the most efficient route by which to send that packet on its way. Think of the router as providing the link between the various networks that make up the Internet, or any other network that consists of multiple subnets. Routers isolate each LAN into separate subnets.

Like bridges, routers control bandwidth by keeping data out of subnets where it doesn't belong. Routers, however, need to be set up before they can be used. Once they are set up, they can communicate with other routers and learn the topology of the network.

Windows Server 2003 As a Router

So, can Windows Server 2003 be used to provide routing services within your network? The answer is yes. Any computer running a member of the Windows Server 2003 family can act as a dynamic router supporting RIP, OSPF, or both. To have Windows Server 2003 provide routing services, you install multiple network interface adapters, and then enable and configure RRAS. Each network interface adapter is assigned its own IP address and subnet mask to define the directly attached network ID routes. Because you will probably use dynamic routing, default routes won't be used, so you do not need to configure a default gateway for either network adapter.

Static IP routing will be enabled by default when the RRAS is enabled. Your next step should be to use the Routing and Remote Access administration tool to install RIP for IP or OSPF routing protocols. Next, enable the protocols on your installed network adapters by adding them to the appropriate routing protocol.

But we're getting ahead of ourselves. Let's start by building a check list to follow when setting up Windows Server 2003 as a router:

- Install and configure any necessary network adapters.

- Install RRAS.

- Configure RIP or OSPF.

- Configure the remote-access devices.

- Install and configure the DHCP Relay Agent.

- Install a WINS or DNS name server.

Because you're setting up this Windows Server 2003 machine as a router, you'll need to install two network adapters in it. You'll also need to make sure that the necessary drivers are installed, that the TCP/IP protocol is installed, and that IP addresses have been configured on both of the network adapters. Table 22.1 shows how you might set up the IP addresses for this router.

Table 22.1 Typical Network Adapter Setup

Network Card	Connected to	IP Address
1	Backbone	192.168.0.1
2	Subnet	192.168.1.1

Your next step will be to enable RRAS on your Windows Server 2003 machine. The following steps walk you through this process.

Configure a Windows Server 2003 Computer As a Static Router

1. If this server is a member of an Active Directory (AD) domain and you're not a domain administrator, you'll need to get your domain administrator to add the computer account of this server to the RAS and IAS Servers security group in the domain that this server is a member of. There's two ways this can be accomplished.

   - Add the computer account to the **RAS and IAS Servers** security group using Active Directory Users and Computers.

- Use the netsh ras add registeredserver command.

2. Select **Start | Administrative Tools | Routing and Remote Access**. The Welcome window appears.

3. The default is that the local computer will be listed as a server. If you want to add another server, right-click **Server Status** in the console tree on the left, and then click **Add Server**.

4. Click the appropriate option in the **Add Server** dialog box then click **OK**.

5. In the console tree on the left side of the **Routing and Remote Access** window, right-click the server you want to enable and click **Configure and Enable Routing and Remote Access**.

6. You've now started the Routing and Remote Access Server Setup Wizard. Click **Next**.

7. In the next window, choose the **Custom configuration** option. Click **Next**.

8. In the **Custom Configuration** window, choose **LAN routing** and click **Next**.

9. A summary of your selections will now be presented. Verify that the selections you made are correct, and then click the **Finish** button.

10. A dialog box will appear, telling you that the Routing and Remote Access Service has been installed and asking you if you want to start the service. Click **Yes**.

11. You should still have the **Routing and Remote Access** window open, and it should now look something like Figure 22.11. To add a static default route to the server, right-click **Static Routes** and then click **New Static Route**.

Figure 22.11 Routing and Remote Access Window after RRAS Installation

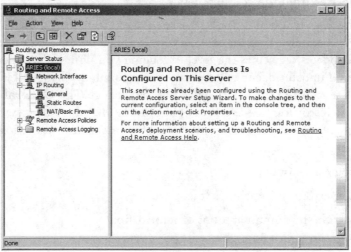

12. Choose the interface you want to use for the default route. In the **Destination** text box, type **0.0.0.0**. Do the same in the **Network mask** text box.

13. If this is a demand-dial interface, the Gateway text box will be unavailable. Select the **Use this route to initiate demand-dial connections** check box. This will initiate a demand-dial connection when any traffic matching this route occurs.

14. If this interface is an Ethernet or Token Ring LAN connection, in the **Gateway** text box, type the IP address of the interface that is on the same network segment as the LAN interface.

15. In the **Metric** box, type **1**. Then click **OK**. You've now added a default static IP route to your router. Follow the same process (steps 11 through 15) for any other route that you want to add to the router.

After you've enabled RRAS, you can also add a static IP route from the command prompt using the **route add** command.

Configure RIP Version 2

After you have enabled RRAS and configured a default static route, you need to enable and configure RIP on your router. This is an easy process using the **Routing and Remote Access** console. Follow these steps:

1. Open the Routing and Remote Access window.

2. In the console tree on the left side of the window, right-click **General**, and then select **New Routing Protocol**.

3. From the **New Routing Protocol** dialog box, choose **RIP Version 2 for Internet Protocol** then click **OK**.

4. **RIP** now appears under your server and IP Routing. Right-click **RIP** and choose **Properties** from the context menu.

5. On the **General** tab of the **RIP Properties** dialog box, shown in Figure 22.12, you can set the maximum amount of time you want this router to wait before it sends out triggered updates, as well as the level of logging you wish to have performed. Remember that triggered updates occur when the network topology changes. Updated routing information is sent out immediately reflecting that change. The **General** tab of the **RIP Properties** dialog box lets you set an interval that these triggered updates will wait before being sent. The default is five seconds. There are four levels of logging you can choose from:

   - Log errors only
   - Log errors and warnings (the default)
   - Log the maximum amount of information
   - Disable event logging

Figure 22.12 The General Tab of the RIP Properties

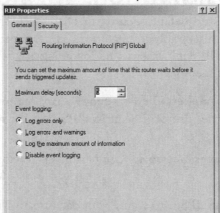

6. Choose the **Security** tab, shown in Figure 22.13. On this tab, you can designate if this router will process announcements from routers. You can accept all announcements from all routers; you can accept announcements from the listed routers only; or you can ignore announcements from those routers listed.

7. After you've made your choice, click **OK**.

Figure 22.13 The Security Tab of the RIP Properties

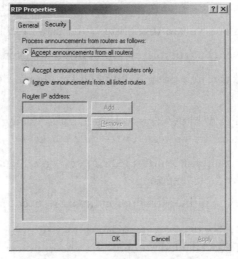

You can also configure your RRAS for OSPF using the same steps you used to add RIP v. 2.

Security Considerations for Routing

Keep in mind that IPv4 has no default security mechanism. Unless you take security into consideration, your network will be susceptible to unauthorized monitoring and access. To prevent this, develop a strategy for your IP deployment. The following are two methods that you can use to help you enhance security when deploying IP:

- **Secure your IP packets** End-to-end security requires that you not use address translation (NAT). Internet Protocol Security (IPSec) is the most efficient method of providing for a secure data stream.

- **Set up a perimeter network** Use perimeter networks to help secure your internal network.

Let's talk first about using IPSec to secure your data stream. The Windows Server 2003 IPSec protocol provides end-to-end security of your data stream using encryption, digital signatures, and hashing algorithms. IPSec resides at the Transport layer of the OSI reference model and protects the individual packets before they reach your network, and then removes the protection on receipt. Even data passed through from applications not having any security features can be protected using IPSec.

Keep in mind that IPSec protects the actual packets of data, not the link. Because of this, IPSec provides security even on insecure networks, and only the computers actually involved in the communication are even aware of it. IPSec provides a number of security features, including the following:

- Authentication by using digital signatures to identify the sender

- Integrity through the use of hash algorithms ensuring that the data has not been altered

- Privacy through encryption that protects the data from being read

- Anti-replay prevents unauthorized access by an attacker who resends packets

- Nonrepudiation through the use of public-key digital signatures that prove the message's origin

- Dynamic rekeying to allow keys to be generated during communication, so that the different transmissions are protected with different keys

- Key generation using the Diffie-Hellman key agreement algorithm, allowing computers to agree on a key without exposing it

- Configurable key lengths, allowing for export restrictions or highly sensitive transmissions

The process of how IPSec works is relatively simple. In order for data to be transmitted and protected between two IPSec-enabled computers, the computers must agree on which keys, mechanisms, and security policies will be used to protect the data. This agreement, or negotiation, produces a security association (SA).

The first SA established between the two computers, called Internet Security Association and Key Management Protocol (ISAKMP), provides the method of key exchange. Using ISAKMP to provide protection, the two computers negotiate the production of a pair of IPSec SAs and keys:

one for inbound transmissions and one for outbound transmissions. These SAs include the agreed-upon algorithm for encryption and integrity and the agreed-upon IPSec protocol to use. Two IPSec protocols can be used:

- **Authentication Header (AH)** Provides data authentication, integrity, and anti-replay to IP packets.

- **Encapsulating Security Payload (ESP)** Provides confidentiality, along with data authentication, integrity, and anti-replay to IP packets.

Using the IPSec SAs and keys, the two computers protect the data during transmissions.

The second method that you can use to enhance security is a perimeter network. These are also sometimes called a *demilitarized zone* (DMZ) or a *screened subnet*. This type of network is generally an additional network between the protected network and the unprotected network. These types of networks are usually small LANs connecting border routers with internal routers. Servers that are required to be exposed to the Internet, like your Web server or mail server, can be placed in the DMZ and be protected by a firewall. Then additional firewalls are placed between the DMZ and your network. Figure 22.14 demonstrates how this type of configuration might look.

Figure 22.14 A Perimeter Network or DMZ

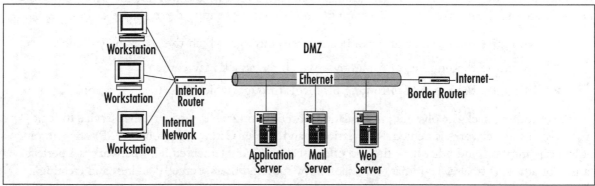

Analyzing Requirements for Routing Components

A router is nothing more than a very specialized computer. It's made up of the following elements:

- A central processing unit (CPU)

- Random access memory (RAM)

- Input/output system (BIOS)

- Operating system (OS)

- A motherboard

- Input/output (I/O) ports

- A power supply

- A case to hold all of this

Most of these parts remain hidden, but that's okay because these components are generally extremely reliable. Most of the time, you won't need to worry about them at all. The components that you will have the most interaction with are the operating system and the I/O ports.

As you know, the operating system is the software that controls the various hardware components and makes the computer usable. The router usually has a configuration file that includes the number, location, and type of each I/O port, as well as details about bandwidth, addressing, and security.

The I/O ports are the one component that you will get to know on a personal basis. These ports function like NICs, in that they define the medium and framing mechanisms and provide the appropriate physical interfaces.

Simplifying Network Topology to Provide Fewer Attack Points

Attacks on your network can come in a variety of ways, in both active and passive forms. An active form of attack is launched with the purpose of damaging or destroying your data and/or your network infrastructure. Passive attacks, on the other hand, can be thought of more in the lines of "fishing expeditions." In these situations, the attackers are mostly snooping—just looking around.

One of the best defensive postures against both forms of attacks is to limit the paths to your network an attack can take. You can accomplish this by implementing three simple tactics:

- Minimize the number of network interfaces through which the attack may come
- Minimize the number of routes over which the attack may come
- Minimize the number of routing protocols through which the attack may come

Most router attacks involve the manipulation of the routing table entries so that service to legitimate systems or networks is denied. RIP version 1 and Border Gateway Protocol (BGP) offer no or little authentication, and what little they do offer usually isn't implemented. This network is a perfect target for attackers to alter legitimate routes, often by spoofing their source IP address and creating a denial-of-service (DoS) condition. The easiest remedy is to use whatever tools you have available. If your routing protocol offers authentication, implement it. If it doesn't, consider changing to one that does.

Minimizing the Number of Network Interfaces and Routes

You want to limit the number of network interfaces through which an attacker could gain entrance. Every NIC you have exposed to the Internet is a potential doorway through which someone could enter. The fewer interfaces exposed, the less work for you in preventing someone coming through an open port and wrecking havoc on your network.

Minimizing the number of routes an attacker might take to your network is similar to minimizing the interfaces. You are restricting the paths through which an attack may come.

Minimizing the Number of Routing Protocols

You also want to limit the options of attackers if they do manage to gain access to your network. By reducing the number of routing protocols, you reduce the options available to the attacker.

Demand-dial routing allows you to use impermanent, dial-up WAN lines to exchange data between two networks. It allows for the effective use of these impermanent connection methods, such as analog modems and ISDN, to mimic dedicated Internet connections. Demand-dial routing brings up the connection only when outbound traffic is addressed to an associated link. With a demand-dial connection, you can use additional leased lines to add needed bandwidth at peak use times. However, you should check all the potential costs before you choose this alternative, to avoid any unexpected and unpleasant surprises when the telephone bill arrives.

Demand-dial routing concepts are relatively simple. A link is created when needed, and the connection is dropped when it's no longer needed. There are three basic phases of demand-dial connection setup:

- Configure the first router to initiate and receive demand-dial connections from the second router.

- Configure the second router to initiate and receive demand-dial connections from the first router.

- Initiate the demand-dial connection from the first router to the second router.

Router-to-Router VPNs

Take two separate networks and put the Internet between them. Now, connect them using a tunnel through the Internet. You create this tunnel using the Point-to-Point Tunneling Protocol (PPTP) or Layer Two Tunneling Protocol (L2TP), so that the data being exchanged between the two networks is encrypted. But what's the difference between a normal client VPN connection and this type of VPN? What can you use to connect the two networks together? You can use routers.

You can use a router-to-router VPN to connect two separate networks together over the Internet and still maintain security. Before we get into the specifics of setting up a router-to-router VPN, let's look briefly at how to set up a client VPN connection first. That way, you will understand the difference between the two and why you might want to use one over the other. The first step is to turn on Windows Server 2003 VPN Server.

Install and Enable Windows Server 2003 VPN Server

Use the following procedure to install and enable the VPN server on a Windows Server 2003 computer.

1. Select **Start | Administrative Tools | Routing and Remote Access.** If you have not set up RRAS, you'll see a red circle in the server icon. If you have set up your server to be a VPN server when you were installing the Windows Server 2003 software, you will see a green arrow.

2. If the service has already been turned on, you may want to reconfigure your server. You can reconfigure it by right-clicking the server icon and choosing **Disable Routing and Remote Access**. Click **Yes** to continue when you are prompted. Your server icon should now have the red circle rather than the green arrow.

3. Right-click your server's icon and choose **Configure and Enable Routing and Remote Access** to start the Setup Wizard. Click **Next** to continue.

4. Select the **Remote Access (dial-up or VPN)** option, as shown in Figure 22.15, and then click the **Next** button.

Figure 22.15 Choose Remote Access

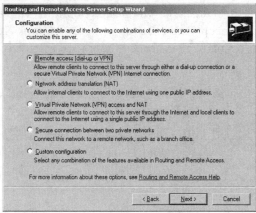

5. Check the **VPN** check box, and then click the **Next** button.

6. In the **VPN Connection** window, shown in Figure 22.16, select the network interface that is connected to the Internet, and then click the **Next** button.

Figure 22.16 Choose the Interface Connected to the Internet

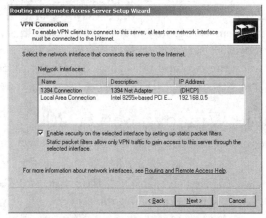

7. In the **IP Address Assignment window**, you have two choices:

   ■ **Automatically** Choose this option if you have a DHCP server you can use to automatically assign IP addresses to the remote clients. This setup will be easier to administer than assigning addresses manually. (However, if you do not have a DHCP server, you must specify a range of static addresses.) Click **Next** to continue.

- **From a specified range of addresses** Choose the option if the remote clients can only be given an address from a specified pool of addresses. Click **Next** to continue. In the **Address Range Assignment** window, click the **New** button. In the **Start IP address** box, type the first IP address in the range of addresses you want to use. Then type in the last IP address in the range you've chosen. Windows Server 2003 will automatically calculate the number of addresses for you. Click the **OK** button to return to the **Address Range Assignment** window, and then click the **Next** button to continue.

8. In the next window, accept the default value of **No, use Routing and Remote Access to authenticate connection requests**, and click the **Next** button to continue.

9. Click **Finish** to turn on RRAS and to configure the server as a remote-access server.

Once you have your server set up to provide VPN service, you can allow client machines to connect to it over the Internet.

Using your new VPN connection is simple: click **Start | Connect To** and choose your new connection. If you don't already have a current connection to the Internet, you'll be offered the opportunity to connect. When the connection is made, the VPN server will prompt you for your name and password. Enter the necessary information and click the **Connect** button. All of the same resources available when you are directly connected to the network are available now. When you're ready to disconnect, simply right-click the connection and choose **Disconnect**.

Now that you know how to create and use a client VPN connection, what are the differences in setting up a router-to-router VPN? There are actually not very many differences. The following steps will walk you through the process of setting up a router-to-router VPN server.

Set Up Windows Server 2003 As Router-to-Router VPN Server

1. Select **Start | Administrative Tools | Routing and Remote Access.**

2. Right-click your server's icon and choose **Configure and Enable Routing and Remote Access** to start the Setup Wizard. Click **Next** to continue.

3. Select the **Secure connection between two private networks** option, as shown in Figure 22.17, and then click the **Next** button.

Figure 22.17 Choose Secure Connection between Two Private Networks

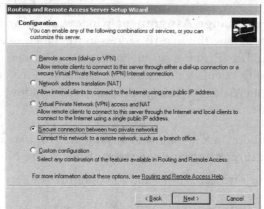

4. Choose the **No** option when you are asked if you want to use demand-dial connections, unless you need to use them, and then click the **Next** button again. If you choose **Yes** to use demand-dial connections, you'll have the opportunity to set up the demand-dial connections when this Wizard is finished. If you are using a full-time connection, you don't need the demand-dial connection.

5. Click **Finish** to turn on RRAS and to configure the server as a router-to-router VPN server.

Make sure you have addresses assigned to all the installed interfaces and that you've installed and set up your routing protocols on each interface. Then you should be able to use this router.

Packet Filtering and Firewalls

One of the best features available in RRAS is the ability to filter TCP/IP packets traveling in either direction. For all practical purposes, enabling packet filtering creates a firewall on your server. You can build filters that can either allow or deny packet traffic into or out of your network. You do this by specifying rules that designate source and destination addresses and ports.

Normally, you set up these filters to block information that the machines in your network should not receive. The filters are set up on a specific interface. This means that the filters on one interface are completely independent of the filters on another. Incoming and outgoing filters are independent of one another also.

Simply put, you have two choices with input filters: accept all traffic over the interface except the traffic you specify, or drop all traffic except the traffic you specify. Output filters are configured in the same manner. Which choice you should make most often depends on the context and purpose of the filter. The second option is the most secure. If you are attempting to keep all but very specific traffic out of your network, this would be the correct choice. The first choice is appropriate if you are just trying to stop specific traffic.

For instance, say you have a Web server and the only traffic you want to allow on this server is traffic traveling to and from the Web server service. All you need to do is configure an input filter for the destination IP address of the Web server and the TCP destination port 80. At the same time, you will want to configure an output filter for the source IP address of the Web server and the TCP source port 80. If these two filters are the only two filters operational on this server, the only traffic that will be allowed across the interface is TCP traffic to and from the Web server service on your Windows Server 2003 machine.

You need to be careful about how you implement these filters, so that you don't make them too restrictive, which would impair the functionality of the other protocols operating on the server. For instance, given our example of a Web server, we can't use PING or any other basic IP troubleshooting tool on that computer now, because we've restricted it to only Web traffic on port 80. We'll talk more about troubleshooting shortly.

It's a good idea to use packet filtering to block unwanted traffic from your VPN servers. There are two basic sets of rules for this process: PPTP packet filters and L2TP packet filters.

For PPTP, there are at least two filters that are required to block non-PPTP traffic. You need to allow Generic Routing Encapsulation (GRE) packets to pass. You also need to allow inbound traffic on TCP port 1723. If the PPTP server is also acting as a PPTP client, you can add a third filter to allow outbound traffic on TCP port 1723 also. After these packets are established, choose the **Drop All Packets Except Those That Meet The Criteria Below** radio button. Then close the dialog box. Repeat the process on the output side.

For L2TP packet filters, you will need four filters: two for input and two for output, as follows:

- A filter with the VPN interface address and a network mask of 255.255.255.255, filtering the User Datagram Protocol (UDP) with a source and destination port of 500

- An input filter with a destination of the VPN address and a network mask of 255.255.255.255, filtering UDP traffic with a source and destination port of 1701

- An output filter with a source of the VPN interface address and a network mask of 255.255.255.255, filtering UDP traffic with a source destination of 500

- An output filter with a source of the VPN interface address and a network mask of 255.255.255.255 filtering UDP with a source and destination port of 1701

Logging Level

Coming up with a good logging strategy is important to the proper maintenance of your network and the devices that are used on it. What to log is probably one of the most important questions you will consider. If you have too much logging, the performance of your server and the network will decline sharply. If you have too little logging, when you have a problem, you won't have the information you need to determine the source and cause. The best choice is to log only those options you really need, and when you don't need a particular type of log data anymore, stop recording it.

In order to set the logging levels, open the RRAS module, right-click the server you wish to administer, choose **Properties,** and then click the **Logging** tab. As shown in Figure 22.18, the **Logging** tab contains several options for the various types of events that you can log. The default is to log all errors and warnings. You can also check the **Log additional Routing and Remote**

Access information (used for debugging) check box, which, as its name implies, will assist you in debugging.

Figure 22.18 Set the Logging Level

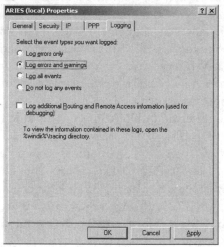

Troubleshooting IP Routing

Here, we will look at the two main tools you might use in troubleshooting IP routing and the common problems that occur with IP routing, which is critical to maintaining a network.

Identifying Troubleshooting Tools

Your best troubleshooting tools are those tools you should be using on a daily basis for network management and monitoring. Windows Server 2003 ships with the Network Monitor tool (NETMON.exe), which is an excellent protocol analyzer you can use to monitor your network. This tool captures and displays information about the IP packets moving in your network and can tell you about the traffic patterns, the broadcast rates, how the network is being used, what kinds of errors you might be experiencing, and many other aspects concerning the behavior of your network.

The Routing and Remote Access console is another excellent troubleshooting tool. Using this tool, you can show your network's TCP/IP information, your IP routing table, the router's RIP neighbors, its OSPF area, the LSDB, the router's OSPF neighbors, and the OSPF virtual interface.

Other familiar tools that you can use for troubleshooting include PING, pathping, Tracert, mrinfo, and Netsh. Let's take a look at how you can these tools to verify and troubleshoot your connections.

Another useful troubleshooting tool is the pathping command. This command combines aspects of PING and Tracert, and adds in some additional features that make it an excellent troubleshooting tool. This tool works by measuring the packet loss across each router between the source machine and the destination. This information can help you determine where your network reliability problems may be coming from. The syntax for the pathping command is as follows:

```
pathping [-n] [-h maximum_hops value] [-g host-list] [-p value]
    [-q value] [-w value] final_destination
```

Where:

- **-n** Tells pathping not to resolve addresses to host names.

- **-h maximum_hops** *value* Sets the maximum number of hops you want the command to search for the target. The default is 30 hops.

- **-g host-list** Provides a loose source route along the host list.

- **-p** *period* Sets the wait period in milliseconds between pings. The default is 250 milliseconds.

- **-q** *num_queries* Sets the number of queries per hop. The default is 100 queries.

- **-w** *timeout* Sets the time length in milliseconds for each reply before the command times out on that hop. The default is 3000 milliseconds.

- **-T** Tests the connectivity to each hop with Layer-2 priority tags.

- **-R** Tests to see if each hop is RSVP-aware.

- *final_destination* The host name or IP address of the network, domain, or machine that you are testing the route to.

The tool will first trace the route to the destination, and then analyze the traffic running through each hop. Keep in mind that one test is not sufficient to give you a good idea about what is going on. There is no specific number of lost packets that signify that a link is causing you problems. If the number is in double digits, though, you should probably examine that route carefully. To get a realistic picture of what is going on in your network, test a router over time and test in both peak and off-peak usage.

If you're using multicast routing, another useful troubleshooting command is mrinfo. This command displays multicast router configuration information. The syntax is as follows:

```
mrinfo [-n] [-?] [-i address] [-t secs] [-r retries] destination
```

Where:

- **-n** Displays the IP addresses in numeric format.

- **-?** Prints usage information.

- **-i** Specifies the IP address of the local interface from which the query was sent.

- **-r** Specifies how many times an SNMP query is to be resent. The default value is 0.

- **-t** Specifies how long to wait for an IGMP neighbor query reply. The default is three seconds.

The mrinfo command displays the interfaces for both the multicast router and its neighbors on each interface. It also provides the names of the neighboring domains, the multicast routing metric, and the TTL.

Also, the Netsh utility, discussed in the "Using Netsh Commands" section earlier in this chapter, can display the configurations of protocols, filters, and routes. It also allows you to reconfigure interfaces. Don't overlook this valuable tool as an option for troubleshooting IP routing.

Common Routing Problems

If you suspect that your RRAS server isn't functioning properly, start by making sure the RRAS server is running. You might be surprised how many times the problem turns out to be the RRAS not being turned on.

Most TCP/IP administrators spend much of their time troubleshooting the hardware. Connectors go bad, NICs die, and cables break or are cut. You need to troubleshoot and repair these elements before you start looking at the software. Consider these potential trouble spots first:

- Check for basic communication between systems first. Broken cables, loose connections, and so on can cause what might look like much more complex problems.

- Make sure that your systems are in compliance with the standards you've chosen. This means you need to verify all devices on your Ethernet are broadcasting Ethernet and not something else. Make sure you have the correct types of cables. An example of this is the common mistake beginners sometimes make using RG59A/U cable instead of RG58A/U. The former cable type is used in broadcasting specifically with video; the latter is used with IEEE 802.3 10Base2 networks.

- Carefully isolate your problem to a single LAN, MAN, or WAN segment by going through each individually. Keep in mind it is extremely rare for two segments to go down at the same time.

Interface Configuration Problems

Make sure that the RRAS server is configured to perform as an IP router. Open the RRAS Microsoft Management Console (MMC) and verify all your settings. Make sure that you have enabled RRAS on the Windows Server 2003 machine you are expecting to perform as a router. It could be that you have the wrong server configured. Also, keep in mind that the system must first make the physical connection to the network. After that, it must make the logical connections.

The router also might not be receiving routed data from other routers. Take a look at the routing table to see that the router is receiving routes from the other routers. If there is anything there other than **Local** in the **Protocol** column, the router is receiving routes via the routing protocols. If not, double-click the rest of the settings in this section and pay particular attention to the appropriate protocol.

RRAS Configuration Problems

Routing for the correct LAN protocol may not be enabled. If you're using IP routing, make sure that IP routing is enabled on the IP tab of the server's property sheet. Also, make sure that you have IP routing protocols attached to each of the interfaces where they are needed.

The wrong protocol could be installed, or the right protocol could have been installed on the wrong interface. The correct protocol must be installed on the appropriate interface for this to work correctly.

Routing Protocol Problems

One of the most common problems you'll face with RIP for IP is incorrect routing table entries. If you're seeing wrong or inconsistent routes in the routing tables, or if routes are totally missing, you should look at the following possibilities:

- The wrong version of RIP could be in use.

- Silent RIP hosts might not be receiving hosts.

- The subnetting scheme on your network could be incompatible with your routing infrastructure.

- A router might be using the wrong password.

- Routing filters might be too restrictive.

- Packet filters might be too restrictive.

- Neighbors might be incorrectly configured.

- Default routes might not be being propagated.

If your router is using OSPF, make sure that the **Enable OSPF on this interface** check box is selected. This option is in the interface's **OSPF Properties** dialog box.

Also make sure that your router is receiving routing information from the other routers on the network. Do this by opening the routing table and looking at the **Protocol** column. One of the following might be the problem with OSPF:

- OSPF might not be enabled on the desired interface.

- The neighboring router might be unreachable.

- The OSPF settings may not match on each of the neighboring routers.

- The stub area configuration or area ID on neighboring routers may not match.

- Interfaces may not be configured with OSPF neighbor IP addresses.

- There may not be a designated router (DR) for the network.

- Packet filtering may be too restrictive.

- Summarized routes may be configured improperly.

- ASBR source or route filtering may be too restrictive.

- Virtual links may be incorrectly configured.

If a routing table entry is marked as being either OSPF or RIP, then information from some of the other routers on your network is getting through. If you do not see any OSPF or RIP entries in the table, you have a problem.

TCP/IP Configuration Problems

Verifying that the router's TCP/IP configuration is correct first may save you a lot of time. You must use the correct IP address and subnet mask.

Routing Table Configuration Problems

You'll need to have a static default route defined and enabled so that your router will forward any packets when there is no specific route designated for them. If the default route is incorrect or missing, you will have problems. If you're using default routing, the default route must be learned through the routing protocols or statically configured on the router over the correct interface.

Chapter 23

Planning, Implementing, and Maintaining Internet Protocol Security

In this chapter:

☑ **Understanding IP Security (IPSec)**

☑ **Deploying IPSec**

☑ **Managing IPSec**

☑ **Addressing IPSec Security Considerations**

☑ **Using RSoP for IPSec Planning**

Introduction

Securing sensitive or mission-critical data is an important part of the network administrator's job. Data is especially vulnerable to interception as it travels across the network. Windows Server 2003 includes Microsoft's implementation of the Internet standard IP Security (IPSec) protocol, for the purpose of protecting data in transit. This chapter deals with how to work with Windows Server 2003's IPSec. We start by introducing IPSec terminology and concepts and explaining how IPSec works "under the hood" to secure data in transit over the network. We discuss the purposes of IPSec encryption: authentication, integrity, and confidentiality. You'll learn about how IPSec operates in either of two modes: tunnel or transport.

Although we refer to IPSec as a protocol, it is actually a framework, or a collection of protocols and standards designed to protect IP data in transit. In this chapter, you'll learn about the protocols used by IPSec. These include the two primary protocols: the Authentication Header (AH) protocol and the Encapsulating Security Payload (ESP) protocol. We'll also discuss the roles of additional protocols used by IPSec, including the Internet Security and Key Management Protocol (ISAKMP), Internet Key Exchange (IKE), and the Oakley key-determination protocol, and the Diffie-Hellman key-agreement protocol. You'll learn about Windows Server 2003's IPSec components—the IPSec driver and the IPSec Policy Agent service. We'll also discuss the relationship of IPSec to Internet Protocol version 6 (IPv6).

Next, we'll show you how to deploy IPSec on your network, taking into consideration organizational needs and security levels, and help you determine the appropriate authentication methods. You'll learn about managing IPSec, and we'll walk you through the process of using the IP Security Policy Management Microsoft Management Console (MMC) snap-in, as well as the command-line tools. We'll discuss the role of IPSec policies, including default and custom policies, and we'll show you how to assign and apply policies. We'll also talk about IPSec security considerations and issues, including the use of a strong encryption algorithm (Triple Data Encryption Standard, or 3DES), authentication methods, firewall packet filtering, unprotected traffic, Diffie-Hellman groups, and the use of pre-shared keys. We'll show you how to use the Resultant Set of Policy (RSoP) and the RSoP MMC snap-in to view policy assignments and to simulate policy assignments for deployment planning.

Understanding IP Security (IPSec)

The Internet Engineering Task Force (IETF) designed the IP Security (IPSec) specifications. The IP Security Working Group of the IETF developed IPSec as an industry standard for encrypting TCP/IP traffic within networking environments. The two main goals of IPSec are to protect IP packets and to give network administrators the ability to use packet filtering as a defense against network attacks. Microsoft's Windows Server 2003 IPSec deployment includes the following features:

- Enhanced IPSec security monitoring with the MMC

- IPSec integration with Active Directory that allows for security policies to be centrally administered

- Use of Kerberos version 5 authentication as the default method by IPSec policies to verify the authenticity of connecting computers

- Backward compatibility with the Windows 2000 Security Framework

- Client and application transparency, because IPSec works at the Network layer of the OSI model

- Automatic security negotiation

IPSec is not required to be supported by any intermediary computer that routes data from the source to destination IP address, unless *network address translation* (NAT) or packet filtering has been implemented on the firewall. IPSec can be deployed with IPSec policy in Windows Server 2003 under any of these circumstances:

- Client-to-client and peer-to-peer support

- Gateway-to-gateway and router-to-router support

- Remote-access client dial-up and Internet access from private networks

The IP Security Policy Management MMC allows network administrators to set security policy settings and options that will allow the systems to negotiate with other systems regarding the traffic that is sent and received from that system.

How IPSec Works

Before secure data can be exchanged, a security agreement between the two communicating computers must be established. This security agreement is called a security association (SA). Both IPSec-enabled computers agree on how to send and receive data, as well as how to protect the information contained in the data packets. Because IPSec SAs are unidirectional, at least two separate SAs are established to protect the data for every communication: one for inbound traffic and one for outbound traffic. There is a unique SA for each direction and for each protocol. Thus, if you are using both AH and ESP, there will be two SAs for AH and two for ESP.

Using the IP Security Policy Management console, you can configure the security policy to block, permit, or negotiate security within your networked environment. Because this security is transparent to users, it is easy to implement and administer.

Securing Data in Transit

An SA is a combination of three things:

- Security protocols
- A negotiated key
- A security parameters index (SPI)

These items together define the security settings that are used to protect the communication from the source IP to the destination IP. The SPI is a unique entry in the IPSec header of each packet and is used to identify which SA is being used to secure data. As mentioned earlier, there will always be separate SAs for inbound and outbound traffic. If a computer is communicating with multiple machines (for example, a database server with multiple clients sending queries), many SAs will exist. The receiving computer uses the SPI to determine which SA should be used to process incoming IP packets.

IPSec Cryptography

IPSec uses cryptography to provide three basic services:

- Authentication
- Data integrity
- Data confidentiality

There are times when only one or two of these services is needed, and other times when all of these services are needed. IPSec can use different methods to authenticate identities, including pre-shared keys, digital certificates, and Kerberos authentication. IPSec can also provide *anti-replay*. This refers to ensuring that an unauthorized person cannot capture the authentication credentials as they're sent across the network and "replay" them to establish a communications session with the server. IPSec uses the *hash functions* to ensure that the contents of the data packet have not changed between the time it was sent and the time it was received. IPSec provides data confidentiality only through the ESP protocol. AH does *not* provide for encryption of the data. ESP uses the 3DES and DES algorithms to ensure data confidentiality.

IPSec Modes

IPSec in Windows Server 2003 has two different modes: *tunnel* mode and *transport* mode. Your choice of which IPSec mode to use depends on your organizational needs. We will take a look at how each of these works and when each is appropriately used.

Tunnel Mode

In tunnel mode, IPSec encrypts the IP header and the payload, thereby securing the entire IP packet. It is used primarily when end systems or gateways do not support the L2TP/IPSec or the Point-to-Point Tunneling protocol (PPTP). In other words, tunnel mode allows you to use IPSec to create a tunnel, in addition to encrypting the data within the tunnel, with servers that cannot use the traditional VPN tunneling protocols (L2TP and PPTP). However, Windows Server 2003 does not support using IPSec as the tunneling protocol for remote access VPNs; it is only supported between gateways, routers, and servers. Remote-access clients must use PPTP or L2TP for VPN connections. The entire packet is encrypted by either AH or ESP.

Transport Mode

Transport mode, the default mode for IPSec, provides for end-to-end security. It can secure communications between a client and a server. When using the transport mode, only the IP payload is encrypted. AH or ESP provides protection for the IP payload. Typical IP payloads are TCP segments (containing a TCP header and TCP segment data), User Datagram Protocol (UDP) messages (containing a UDP header and UDP message data), and ICMP messages (containing an ICMP header and ICMP message data).

IPSec Protocols

As we mentioned earlier, IPSec itself is merely a framework within which a number of components work together. The primary IPSec protocols are ESP and AH. You can configure IPSec to use both of these protocols together to secure the data if you need both data encryption and integrity/authentication for the entire packet. Other IPSec protocols include ISAKMP, IKE, and Oakley, which uses the Diffie-Hellman algorithm.

Determine IPSec Protocol

Use the following steps to determine which IPSec protocol is in use by using the Network Monitor. This procedure assumes the Network Monitor has been installed via **Control Panel | Add/Remove Programs**.

1. Select **Start | Programs | Administrative Tools | Network Monitor**.

2. When the Network Monitor opens, begin the capture by either clicking the **Capture** button and selecting **Start** or by pressing the **F10** key.

3. Allow the capture to run for a few minutes. To stop it, either click the **Capture** button, and then the **Stop and View** button, or press the **F11** key.

4. To view the IPSec protocol traffic on the captured packets, choose the **Display**, and then select the **Captured Data** option.

5. Choose **Display | Filter Data**. Then choose **Edit Expression** option and select the **Protocol** tab.

6. All protocols are enabled by default. You can chose to **Disable All** and then reenable the AH and ESP traffic. Enabled traffic will appear in the left pane, and disabled traffic will appear in the right pane.

7. Click **OK** after the IPSec protocols have been enabled.

8. Select the **OK** option again, and the frames should be displayed in the Network Monitor window. Notice that when you open a packet that is IPSec-secured, you are unable to read the data inside.

ESP

ESP provides confidentiality (in addition to authentication, integrity, and anti-replay protection) for the IP payload. ESP in transport mode does not sign the entire packet. Only the IP payload (not the IP header) is protected. ESP can be used alone or in combination with AH (in order to provide for signing of the entire packet).

Figure 23.1 illustrates how ESP affects the data. You can see that the IPSec AH header has been placed after the IP header and before the TCP header.

Figure 23.1 The Effects of the ESP Header in Tunnel Mode

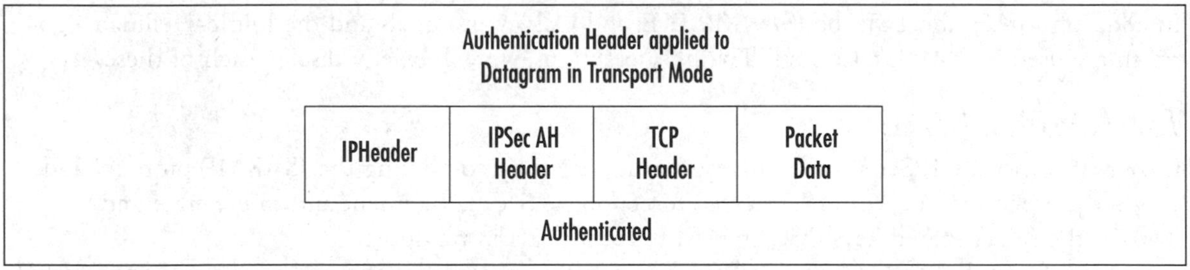

AH

AH does not provide confidentiality, which means that the data is not encrypted. Without data encryption, unauthorized people could use a sniffer-type program on your network to capture and read the packets, but they could not modify the data. AH works by using keyed hash algorithms, which are used to sign the packet for integrity verification. The AH packet signature is shown in Figure 23.2.

Figure 23.2 AH Using Transport Mode

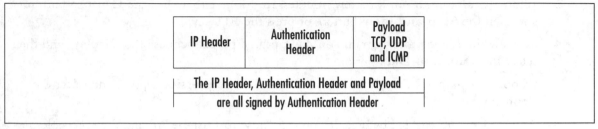

If you need both data integrity and authentication for the IP header, use ESP and AH in combination, as illustrated in Figure 23.3.

Figure 23.3 ESP Used with AH Transport Mode

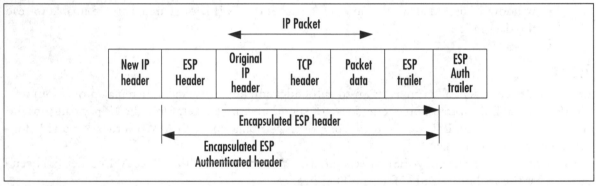

Additional Protocols

In addition to AH and ESP, the ISAKMP, IKE, and Oakley protocols and the Diffie-Hellman algorithm are used with IPSec. In the following subsections, we will briefly discuss each of these.

ISAKMP and IKE

ISAKMP is used by IPSec as a key management system by combining the ISAKMP protocol and another protocol named IKE. IKE is used to centralize SA management and to generate and manage the secret shared keys that are used to secure data in transport.

Often, firewalls, proxy servers, and security gateways must be configured to allow IPSec and IKE traffic to be forwarded. If the packets are not encrypted, the firewall, proxy server, or security gateway can inspect the packet contents or the TCP and UDP ports. If any type of modification has been made to the contents of these packets, the receiving IPSec computer will detect the modification and discard the packets.

In Windows 2000, a major drawback of IPSec was that it could not be used when one of the communicating computers was behind a NAT system. That is because NAT changes the IP headers when it translates multiple internal private IP addresses to a single public external address (which it does so that many computers can access the Internet via one public address). NAT has been an important mechanism for addressing the growing shortage of available public IP addresses, which is a limitation of the IPv4 protocol currently used for most Internet communications. Thus, many networks use NAT to reduce their need for additional public IP addresses.

However, Windows Server 2003's implementation of IPSec provides support for a new Internet specification that allows IPSec packets to be modified by a network address translator (NAT). This is called *NAT traversal*. IPSec's ESP packets can pass through NATs that allow UDP traffic. The IKE protocol automatically detects the presence of a NAT and uses UDP-ESP encapsulation to allow IPSec traffic to pass through the NAT.

Oakley

Oakley is a key-determination protocol. It is used to define how to acquire keying material after it has been authenticated. The Diffie-Hellman algorithm is the basic mechanism for the Oakley protocol.

Diffie-Hellman

The Diffie-Hellman key-exchange algorithm is a secure algorithm that offers high performance, allowing two computers to publicly exchange a shared value without using data encryption. The exchanged keying material that is shared by the two computers can be based on 768, 1024, or 2048 bits of keying material, known as Diffie-Hellman groups 1, 2, and 2048, respectively. Note that Diffie-Hellman does not provide authentication. For protection against man-in-the-middle attacks, identities are authenticated after the Diffie-Hellman exchange occurs. Diffie-Hellman algorithms can be embedded within a protocol that does provide for authentication.

IPSec Components

In addition to the protocols that operate within the IPSec framework, there are a number of operating system components involved in Microsoft's implementation of IPSec. The major IPSec components that are installed with Windows XP and Windows Server 2003 family are the IPSec Policy Agent service and the IPSec driver.

IPSec Policy Agent

The IPSec Policy Agent is a service that resides on each computer running the Windows Server 2003 operating system. It is shown in the Service console as IPSec services. The IPSec Policy Agent begins when the system is started.

For all domain member computers, the IPSec policy will be retrieved by the IPSec Policy Agent when the machine boots up or at the default Winlogon polling interval, unless an IPSec policy is in place that has the interval already set. Active Directory can be manually polled by typing the command **gpupdate** */target:computer* at the command prompt.

If the IPSec Policy Agent is unable to find or connect to the Active Directory domain, it will wait for the policy to be activated or assigned. This is also true if there are no IPSec policies in Active Directory or the Registry.

IPSec Driver

The IPSec driver is used to match all packets against filters in the filter list. Once it finds a packet that matches the filter, it applies the appropriate filter action. If a packet does not match any filter, the packet is not changed and is sent back to the TCP/IP driver. The packet will then be either received or transmitted. After the transmission has been allowed by the filter action, the packet will be sent or received and not modified. If the packet is blocked by the filter action, it will be discarded. If the action requires security negotiation, main mode and quick mode SAs will be negotiated. The IPSec driver uses a database to store all current quick mode SAs. Any outbound packet that matches an IP filter list that is in need of security negotiation will be queued. After the packet has been queued, IKE is notified and will begin the security negotiation. After the negotiation has been successfully completed, the sending computer's IPSec driver will receive the session key from IKE. It will look in its database and locate the outbound SA, and then insert the SPI into the AH or ESP header. The packet will be signed, and if confidentiality is required, it will be encrypted and sent to the IP layer so it can be forwarded to the destination machine.

IPSec and IPv6

IPSec is an important part of the specifications for IPv6, which is supported by Windows Server 2003. As noted earlier, IPv6 is the "next generation" of IP, and its primary design goals were to create a larger address space to alleviate the shortage of IP addresses available under IPv4 and to provide for security of IP communications. IPSec is the means by which IPv6 provides the following:

- Authentication via the mechanism of digitally signing IPSec traffic with the shared encryption key so that the recipient of the data packet can verify that it was sent by the IPSec client transmitter

- Integrity via signing of the packet to ensure that any modifications made in transit will be detected by the recipient

IPSec and IPv6 work together to provide these services by using cryptographic security services. The Windows Server 2003 implementation of IPv6 does not support making data confidential by using data encryption. Keep this in mind when considering deploying IPSec and IPv6 within your network.

Deploying IPSec

With Windows Server 2003, Microsoft has made it relatively easy to deploy security for transmitted data throughout your organization by using the IP Security Policy Management MMC. However, before you begin to deploy IPSec on your network, you need to do your homework and determine the needs of your particular organization.

Determining Organizational Needs

It is very important to find a balance between protecting unauthorized access to data and choosing to make the information available to the largest group of users. The network administrator's dilemma is that security and accessibility are always at opposite ends of the continuum, and increasing one inevitably decreases the other.

After you've identified your organizational needs, you can begin to configure your policy. Only one policy configuration can be assigned at each of the following levels: domain, site, Organizational Unit (OU), and local level. Each IPSec policy consists of one or more IPSec rules. Each IPSec rule consists of the following:

- Selected filter list
- Selected filter action
- Selected authentication method or methods
- Selected connection type
- Selected tunnel setting

To configure IPSec policy, you can create a new policy, and then define the set of rules for the policy by adding filter lists and filter actions. Alternatively, you can create the set of filter lists and filter actions first, and then create the IPSec policies. Finally, you add rules that combine the appropriate filter list with the appropriate filter action. Additionally, you specify authentication methods, connection types, and tunnel settings.

Security Levels

When you begin to consider security levels within your organization, you must take into account the type of data each computer typically will be processing. For example, the configuration you would need for a Web server is different from the one you would need for a domain controller. When planning to deploy IPSec on your network, take into account the following general guidelines for each type of computing environment:

- **Minimal security** No sensitive data is exchanged and IPSec is not active by default.

- **Standard security** This guideline is most appropriate for file servers and similar computers. You can implement the Client (Respond Only) option or Server (Request Security) option for your IPSec policies. These policies enforce security when the client supports it, but they are also efficient because they do not require security if the client is not IPSec-enabled.

- **High security** The computers that need high security are the ones that contain sensitive or valuable data and/or are located in a public network setting. You can implement the Secure Server (Require Security) default policy on these machines. This requires IPSec protection for all traffic being sent to or received from the server (except initial inbound communication) with stronger security methods.

Managing IPSec

Windows Server 2003 comes with two handy tools for managing IPSec. These include the IP Security Policy Management MMC snap-in and the netsh utility (for those who love to use the command-line to execute commands).

Using the IP Security Policy Management MMC Snap-in

You can use the IPSec console to manage IPSec policies and to add and remove filters applied to the IPSec policies. IPSec filtering is used to permit or block certain types of IP traffic. With IPSec filtering, you can secure workstations from outside security hazards.

Install the IP Security Policy Management Console

Use the following steps to install and access the IP Security Policy Management console.

1. Select **Start | Run,** type **mmc,** and click **OK**.

2. In the empty console, select **File | Add/Remove Snap-In**.

3. Click the **Add** button and scroll down to the **IP Security Policy Management** snap-in.

4. Click the **Add** button. The next window asks you to select the appropriate computer or domain that this snap-in will be used to configure. For this example, choose **Local computer**. Then click the **Finish** button.

5. Select **Close,** and then click **OK.** The IP Security Policy Management console will open.

6. Double-click **IP Security Policies on Local Computer.** The three basic policy templates are now displayed in the right pane, as shown in Figure 23.4.

Figure 23.4 The Three Standard IPSec Policies in the IP Security Policy Management Console

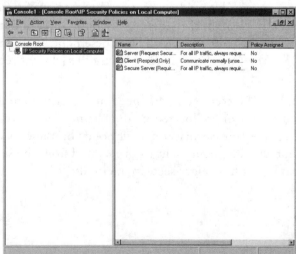

Now you can use the IP Security Policy Management console to define, assign, and manage IPSec policies.

Using the netsh Command-line Utility

Throughout this book, we've look at various uses of the netsh command-line utility. It can also be used to control IPSec in Windows Server 2003.

To use the netsh utility to manage IPSec, you need to change it to the *ipsec* context. Open a command prompt window (select **Start | Run,** type **cmd,** and click **OK**). In the command prompt window, type **netsh ipsec**. The IPSec command syntax you use at the prompt will depend on whether you are using IPSec static or dynamic mode commands. These two command modes have different functions in IPSec, as follows:

- **netsh ipsec static mode commands** Used to perform the same functions as the IP Security Policy Management and IP Security Monitor consoles. These commands allow you to create, modify, and assign IPSec policies, without affecting the current IPSec policy configuration.

- **netsh IPSec dynamic mode commands** Used to display the current state of IPSec; using this configuration will immediately affect the configuration of the IPSec policy.

Some netsh commands and switches are shown in Table 23.1. To view all of the available switches, type **netsh /?** at the prompt. All computers on which you wish to use the netsh utility for IPSec policy configurations must be members of the Windows Server 2003 family.

Table 23.1 netsh Command Switches

Command	Description
netsh ipsec static add policy *name*	Creates an IPSec policy with the specified name
netsh ipsec static delete all	Removes all IPSec policies, filter lists, and filter actions
netsh ipsec dynamic set policy *name*	Immediately sets a policy name
netsh ipsec dynamic delete policy *name*	Immediately removes a policy name
netsh ipsec dynamic export policy *name*	Immediately exports all IPSec policies to a specific file
netsh ipsec dynamic set policy *name*	Immediately sets a policy name

Default IPSec Policies

IPSec has a predefined set of default policies that can be implemented via the IP Security Policy Management console. The set includes Client (Respond Only), Server (Request Security), and Server (Require Security). The following sections explain the usage and settings for each default policy.

Client (Respond Only)

Client (Respond Only) is the least secure default policy. You might wish to implement this policy for intranet computers that need to respond to IPSec requests but do not require secure communications. If you implement this policy, the computer will use secured data communications when requested to do so by another computer.

This policy uses the default response rule, which creates dynamic IPSec filters for inbound/outbound traffic based on the port/protocol requested. The policy settings are as follows:

- IP Filter List: All
- Filter Action: None
- Authentication: Kerberos
- Tunnel Setting: None
- Connection Type: All

Server (Request Security)

The Server (Request Security) policy consists of three rules and can be used when a computer needs to be configured to accept unsecured traffic from other computers that are not IPSec-enabled. However, it will always check for secure communication and use it if the other computer is able to use IPSec. The policy settings for the three rules are shown in Table 23.2.

Table 23.2 Policy Settings for Server (Request Security) Rules

Setting	First Rule	Second Rule	Third Rule (Default Response Rule)
IP Filter List	All IP Traffic	All ICMP Traffic	Dynamic
Filter Action	Request Security (Optional)	Permit	Default Response
Authentication	Kerberos	N/A	Kerberos
Tunnel Setting	None	None	None
Connection Type	All	All	All

Secure Server (Require Security)

The Secure Server (Require Security) policy consists of three rules and can be used for computers that require high security. Filters used in this policy require all outbound communication to be secured. This allows only initial inbound communication requests to be unsecured. The policy settings for the three rules are as shown in Table 23.3.

Table 23.3 Policy Settings for Secure Server (Require Security) Rules

Setting	First Rule	Second Rule	Third Rule (Default Response Rule)
IP Filter List	All IP Traffic	All ICMP Traffic	Dynamic
Filter Action	Require Security	Permit	Default Response
Authentication	N/A	Kerberos	Kerberos
Tunnel Setting	None	None	None
Connection Type	All	All	All

Custom Policies

In addition to the default policies that can be implemented with the IPSec Security Policy MMC, you can also create your own custom policies for implementation by using the New IPSec Policy in the IP Security Policy Management MMC.

To create your own custom policies with the IP Security Policy Management MMC, open the console and select the policy you wish to customize. Use the following steps to customize an IP Security Policy.

Customize IP Security Policy

1. Open the **IP Security Policy Management** console and click **IP Security Policies**.

2. Locate the policy you wish to customize in the right pane and double-click it, or right-click it and select **Properties**.

3. Click on the **Rules** tab, locate the rule you wish to modify and click **Edit.** Switch to the **Filter Action** tab, double-click the filter action that you want to modify.

4. Next, switch to the **Security Methods** tab, and do one of the following:

   ■ To add a new security method, select the **Add** option.

   ■ To modify an existing security method, select the security method that you want to modify and click the **Edit** option.

   ■ To remove a security method, click the security method that you wish to delete and select the **Remove** option.

5. To add or modify a security method, select the **Security Method** tab, choose the **Custom** option button, and then click **Settings**.

6. Set the security method as follows, depending on your policy's need for encryption:

   ■ Select the **Data and address integrity without encryption (AH)** check box if you need to provide data integrity for the packet's IP header and the data. Then for **Integrity algorithm**, select either **MD5** (which uses a 128-bit key) or **SHA1** (which uses a 160-bit key).

- If you need to provide both integrity and encryption for data confidentiality, select the **Data integrity and encryption (ESP)** check box. Then under **Integrity algorithm,** click **None** (for no data integrity; if you have AH enabled and for increased performance, you can choose this), **MD5**, or **SHA1**. Under **Encryption algorithm,** choose **None**, **DES**, or **3DES.**

7. You can also change the default session key lifetime settings, as follows:

- You can set the number of kilobytes of data that is transferred before a new key is generated by choosing the **Generate a new key every** check box and typing in a value in kilobytes.

- You can choose the **Generate a new key every** option to enter the number of seconds to elapse before a new session key is to be generated.

Using the IP Security Policy Wizard

You can open the IP Security Policy Management console by clicking **Start | Run** and typing **mmc**, and then clicking **OK.** Select **File | Add/Remove Snap-in**, and then click **Add,** Click **IP Security Policy Management**, and then click **Add**. For each computer scenario, you need to select a specific option. Table 23.4 shows the scenario and specific snap-in you would need to use.

Table 23.4 IPSec Policy Management Scenarios

Scenario	Snap-In to Choose
Manage IPSec policy for local computer	Select the **Local computer** snap-in
Manage IPSec policies for any domain members	Select **The Active Directory domain of which this computer is a member** snap-in
Manage IPSec policies for a domain that this computer that not a member of	Select the **Another Active Directory domain** snap-in
Manage a remote computer	Select the **Another computer** snap-in

After you've chosen the snap-in, you can close the management console by selecting **Finish**, choosing **Close**, and clicking the **OK** button. To save your console settings select **File | Save**.

You can also access the IP Security Policy Management console from the Group Policy console. To do this, select **Start | Administrative Tools | Active Directory Users and Computers** and right-click the domain or OU for which you need to set Group Policy. (To open Active Directory Users and Computers utility, select **Start | Control Panel | Administrative Tools | Active Directory Users and Computers**.)

Create an IPSec Policy with the IP Security Policy Wizard

To create your own IPSec policy using the IP Security Wizard, follow these steps:

1. Open the IPSec Security Management Snap-in, right-click **IP Security Policies** in the left console pane, and then choose **Create IP Security Policy** from the context menu.

2. The IP Security Policy Wizard Welcome window appears. Click the **Next** button.

3. The IP Security Policy Name window appears, prompting you to give your IPSec policy a name and description. You can choose to accept the default name (not recommended, as it's not very descriptive), or you can enter a new name and description. Then click the **Next** button.

4. The next window allows you to specify how the policy will respond to requests. Accept the default (**Activate the default response rule**) or clear the check box, and then click the **Next** button

5. The Default Rule Authentication Method window appears, as shown in Figure 23.5. Select a different authentication method or accept the default, **Active Directory default (Kerberos V5 protocol)**, and then click **Next**.

Figure 23.5 Select the Default Rule Authentication Method

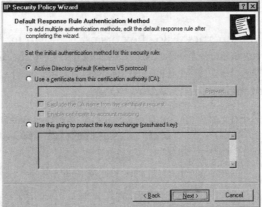

6. The **Completing the IP Security Policy Wizard** window appears. You can choose to edit the properties of the policy (the default) or clear the check box if you do not wish to edit the properties at this time. Click **Finish** to complete the Wizard. For this example, we will leave the **Edit properties** box selected.

7. When you select the option to edit properties, the **New IP Security Policy Properties** dialog box opens, as shown in Figure 23.6. This dialog box allows you to edit the IP security rules and change the general properties of the rule, such as the name and description. Click the **Edit** button in this dialog box.

Figure 23.6 IP Security Policy Properties

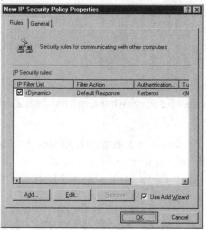

8. The Edit Rule Properties dialog box opens, as shown in Figure 23.7. Here, you can add, edit, or remove security methods; set the security methods that can be used when working with another machine; and select to use session key perfect forward secrecy (PFS). Next, click the **Authentication Methods** tab.

Figure 23.7 Edit the IP Security Policy Security Methods

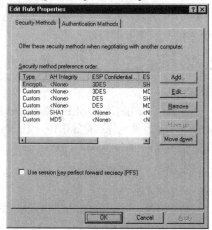

9. The **Authentication Methods** tab allows you to choose a trust method for communicating client computers. Click **Add** to add a method (again, your selections include using a certificate or a pre-shared key). Click **OK** to close the dialog box.

10. After the policy has been edited, you need to assign the policy. Before you assign the policy, make sure that you have the IPSec service started. To assign the policy, right-click the policy name in the right pane and select Assign, as shown in Figure 23.8.

Figure 23.8 Assign the Newly Created IP Security Policy

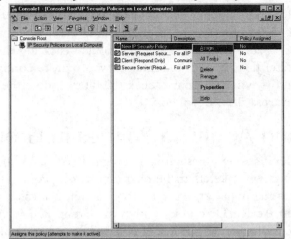

Defining Key Exchange Settings

You can define key exchange settings that apply to IP security policy. Open the MMC containing the security policy, and follow these instructions for modifying the policy:

1. Select the policy you wish to modify by double-clicking that policy.

2. Select the **General** tab and click the **Settings** button.

3. To force reauthentication and the negotiation of new master key keying material each time a new session key is required, click **Master key perfect forward secrecy (PFS)**.

4. To cause the reauthentication and new master key regeneration based on number of minutes, type in a value for **Authenticate and generate a new key after every** *number* **minutes.**

If you require a different setting, you can add a value in the **Authenticate and generate a new key after every** *number* **sessions.** This will set a maximum limit on the number of times a master key or its base keying material can be reused to generate the session key. When this limit is reached it will force a reauthentication with a new master key generation.

If you have enabled **Master key perfect forward secrecy (PFS),** the number of sessions is set to **1** by default and cannot be reconfigured. For special requirements on the master key exchange, select the methods and use master key PFS where it is required for interoperability. By default, this setting is disabled, which should be appropriate in most environments. If you set the session limit to **0,** it will cause rekeys to be determined based only on time. If you work in a performance-based environment, keep in mind that if you enable master key PFS, it could affect performance because each quick mode will require a new main mode negotiation.

Managing Filter Lists and Filter Actions

To manage IP filter lists and filter actions, open the IP Security Policy Management MMC and select the policy you wish to modify by double-clicking that policy. In the **Rules** tab, select the rule you wish to modify that contains the IP filter and double-click it. Select the **IP Filter List** tab and double-click the IP filter that contains the filter list you want to configure. To edit or modify a filter in the IP Filter properties window, double-click the filter, choose the **Addresses** tab, and then select the **Source Address** drop-down box.

Assigning and Applying Policies in Group Policy

Now we will take a look at how to assign or unassign IPSec policy in Group Policy for Active Directory. These settings will take effect the next time Group Policy is refreshed, and if a new policy is assigned over an existing policy, the current policy is automatically unassigned. Use the **IP Security Policies on Active Directory** within the Group Policy console to assign policies to apply to Active Directory objects. To assign or unassign a local computer policy, select **Start | Run,** type **mmc,** and click **OK.** Then choose **File | Add/Remove Snap-in** and click **Add.** Click the **Group Policy Object Editor** and click **Add.** Choose **Finish,** click **Close,** and then click **OK.**

Active Directory Based IPSec Policies

Any IPSec policy that is applied for the domain will take precedence over local IPSec policy that is located on the member computer. After the IPSec policy has been applied to one of the Active Directory Group Policy Objects, it will be broadcast to all of the computer accounts that are affected by that GPO.

Group Policy has backup and restore tools that you can use to save policy information on assigned GPOs. These tools *do not* back up the IPSec policies. To back up and restore IPSec policies, use the **Export Policies and Import Policies** command in the **IP Security Policy Management** console. The Group Policy console will back up and restore only information pertaining to the IPSec policy assignments in relation to GPOs.

The IPSec Policy Agent on client computers running Windows XP Professional or a Windows Server 2003 operating system will poll Active Directory for updates to the assigned IPSec policy. This does not detect domain or OU changes or whether new IPSec policies have been assigned. The Winlogon service polls for these changes every 90 minutes. If a change has been made, the Winlogon service will notify the IPSec Policy Agent, and the IPSec policy changes will be applied.

Cached IPSec Policy

A copy of the currently assigned IPSec policy for a site, a domain, or an OU is cached in the local Registry of each computer to which it applies. If the computer that has the IPSec policy assigned cannot log on to the domain for any reason, the cache copy will be applied. The cache copy of the IPSec policy cannot be changed or managed.

Local Computer IPSec Policy

All Windows Server 2003 servers and Windows XP Professional computers have one local GPO called the local computer policy. With this local policy, Group Policy settings can be stored on individual computers, even when they are not Active Directory domain members. You can manage the local IPSec policy by using the IP Security Policy Management console. Alternatively, you can use the following netsh command at the prompt:

```
netsh ipsec static set store location=local
```

If a computer on which you've applied local IPSec policies later joins an Active Directory domain that has IPSec policies applied, the domain policies will override the local IPSec policy.

IPSec Monitoring

It is important for network administrators to monitor IPSec settings and traffic on a regular basis after deploying IPSec. You can perform monitoring with the netsh command-line utility or with the IP Security Monitor MMC snap-in. In the following sections, we will look at each of these tools.

Using the netsh Utility for Monitoring

Earlier in the chapter, we discussed the use of the netsh command-line utility as equivalent to the IP Security Policy Management console. However, the netsh utility provides some features that are not available with the IP Security Policy Management console. These include the following:

- IPSec diagnostics
- Client computer startup security
- Client computer startup traffic exemptions
- Default traffic exemptions
- Strong certificate revocation list checking Certificate Revocation List
- IKE /Oakley logging

netsh Dynamic Mode Policy

If you want the IPSec rules you have configured to take effect without any wait time, you can use the *netsh ipsec dynamic* commands at the command prompt to add, modify, and assign IPSec policies immediately. Dynamic policies, as their name implies, are not saved; they will be lost if the IPSec service is stopped. However, not all dynamic policies take effect immediately. In some cases, you must restart the computer or the IPSec service first. If you need to make these changes permanent, you need to use the *netsh ipsec dynamic set config* command. This will ensure that the changes are not lost if the computer is restarted.

IPSec Diagnostics

You can use the *netsh diag* command with additional diagnostics at the command prompt. The following are the additional diagnostics switches:

- **netsh diag connect** Used to connect to mail, news, and proxy servers.
- **netsh diag dump** Used to display a script that is used for configuration.

- **netsh diag show** Used to show computer, operating system, network, news, mail, and proxy server information.

- **netsh diag gui** Used to display diagnostics on a Web page. Once this command has been run, you can scan the computer for network diagnostics.

Here are two important things to remember when using the netsh utility:

- If you stop the IPSec service when configuring a dynamic policy, you will lose the settings.

- Use caution because some commands will require you to stop and restart the IPSec service.

Using the IP Security Monitor MMC Snap-in

Microsoft provides the IP Security Monitor MMC snap-in for monitoring IPSec activity. To use the IP Security Monitor, open the MMC and add the IP Security Monitor to the console. We will discuss the use of the IP Security Monitor in more detail in the next section, which covers troubleshooting IPSec.

Troubleshooting IPSec

Troubleshooting is always a big part of any network administrator's job. The following sections will cover how to troubleshoot your IPSec configuration. We include tables that will list specific tools and scenarios you can use to perform the troubleshooting tasks. The IP Security Monitor and the Network Monitor are important tools for troubleshooting IPSec problems, as are the IP Security Policy Management MMC and the netsh utility. An additional tool that is introduced in this section is the Network Diagnostics Tool, netdiag.exe.

Using netdiag for Troubleshooting Windows Server 2003 IPSec

The netdiag tool is provided on the Windows Server 2003 family servers, Windows XP, and Windows 2000 machines. However, it it stored in different locations on each platform, as described below:

- **Windows Server 2003 family** On the Windows Server 2003 installation CD, locate the Support/Tools folder and run the **Suptools.msi** installation package with the **Complete** option to install the tool.

- **Windows XP Professional** On the Windows XP Professional installation CD, locate the Support/Tools folder and run the **Setup.exe file** with the **Complete** setup option to install the tool.

- **Windows 2000** Download the updated version of the tool from the Microsoft Web site.

Viewing Policy Assignment Information

The Policy Assignment option allows you to view policy assignment and precedence. For troubleshooting, it is often important to be able to view IPSec policy assignments and determine the precedence in which policies are applied. Table 23.5 shows a list of the tools to be used with different Microsoft operating systems for viewing the IPSec policy name viewing the Group Policy object to which the IPSec policy is assigned.

Table 23.5 Viewing the IPSec Policy Precedence on Windows Server 2003 Family Machines

Operating System	IPSec Viewing Tools	IPSec Policy Assignment for Group Policies
Windows Server 2003	IP Security Monitor console or the netsh command: *netsh ipsec static show gpoassignedpolicy*	Resultant Set of Policy (RSoP) console or the netsh command *netsh ipsec static show gpoassignedpolicy*
Windows XP	IP Security Policy Management console for local IPSec policy viewing	netdiag.exe *netdiag /test:ipsec* command netdiag.exe command *netdiag /test:ipsec:ipsec*
Windows 2000	netdiag.exe command: *netdiag /test:ipsec* Go to the properties option in the TCP/IP network connections and select **Properties | Advanced | Options | IPSec**. The assigned IPSec policy that is shown is the global policy.	netdiag.exe command: *net diag /test:ipsec* gpresult.exe -Group Policy Results gpotool.exe Group Policy Verification Tool (these can be downloaded from the Windows 2000 Server Resource Kit Web site)

Additionally, you can view all IPSec policies that are available by using the IP Security Policy Management console. Just because an IPSec policy is available, this does not mean that it has been assigned or applied to a computer. In the Windows Server 2003 family, you can determine the assigned (but not applied) policies on IPSec clients by using the RSoP console.

Viewing IPSec Statistics

To view IPSec statistics and items such as filters and security associations, use the tools listed in Table 23.6. These tools work on Windows Server 2003, Windows 2000, and Windows XP Professional machines.

Table 23.6 Viewing IPSec Policy and IP Statistic Details

Operating System	Group Membership Required	Tools
Windows Server 2003 family	Administrators group on that server	IP Security Monitor console or the netsh command *netsh ipsec dynamic show all*
Windows XP Professional	Administrators group on the local computer	IP Security Monitor console or the IPseccmd.exe command *ipseccmd show all* at the command prompt
Windows 2000	Administrators group for the debug command. If you need to view ActiveDirectory-based IPSec policies, you must be a member of the Domain Admins group in Active Directory. IPsecmon.exe displays outbound quick mode security associations.	Netdiag.exe command *netdiag /test:ipsec /v /debug Ipsecmon.exe*

To monitor IPSec policies on a remote computer that is running Windows XP or Windows Server 2003, you can use the Remote Desktop Connection (RDC) to connect to that computer and view its policies as if you were sitting at its desktop. You can do this from any computer that has the RDC client or the Windows 2000 Terminal Services client installed. You can connect remotely in the same way to a Windows 2000 server that is running Terminal Services. However, you cannot connect remotely to the desktop of a computer running Windows 2000 Professional or Windows 9*x*.

Using IP Security Monitor to View IPSec Information

For Windows Server 2003 and Windows XP, the **IP Security Monitor** is implemented as an MMC snap-in. This MMC snap-in allows administrators to view details regarding active IPSec policies that have been applied by the domain or applied locally, the quick mode and main mode statistics, and the active IPSec SAs. You can use the IP Security Monitor to search for specific main mode or quick mode filters and to troubleshoot complex IPSec policy configurations, as well as for filter searches that match a certain traffic type. To view IPSec information on computers running Windows 2000, you need to use the **ipsecmon.exe** command at the **run** prompt.

Using Event Viewer to Troubleshoot IPSec

Event Viewer is a great troubleshooting tool to use to view IPSec information. However, most IPSec-related information will be contained in the Security log, which is not enabled by default. Verify that security auditing is enabled so security events will be entered in the Security log. For domains, use the **Group Policy Editor**. For local computers, use the **Local Security Policy** setting for this procedure. When enabling auditing for Windows Server 2003 machines, you can also turn on the auditing for the security policy database (SPD). Next, you need to edit the audit policy on your domain or local computer. Enable success or failure auditing for **Audit logon events** to allow Event Viewer to record this information.

Your Security log will fill up with IKE events, so you might wish to edit the Registry and disable auditing of IKE events by creating the **DisableIKEAudits** value. Use special care when editing the Registry. Editing errors can make the system unstable and unusable.

To disable auditing of IKE events, perform the following steps:

1. Open the Registry Editor by selecting **Start | Run**, typing **regedit** or **regedt32**, and clicking **OK**.

2. Navigate to **HKEY_LOCAL_MACHINE\System\CurrentControlSet\Control\Lsa\Audit**.

3. Right-click the **Audit** key, select **New**, and then choose **DWORD Value**.

4. In the right pane, change the default name of the new value to **DisableIKEAudits**.

5. Double-click the new value, or right-click and select **Modify**.

6. In the **Edit DWORD Value** dialog box, under **Value data,** type **1**. Then click the **OK** button and close the Registry Editor.

After this modification has been completed, you can stop and restart the IPSec service or restart the system to have the new Registry information read.

Using Packet Event Logging to Troubleshoot IPSec

You can enable packet event logging for the IPSec driver in Windows Server 2003, Windows XP Professional, and Windows 2000 Server by modifying the Registry. This will cause the System log to capture logging information on all dropped inbound and outbound packets. This information can be useful in troubleshooting IPSec problems.

You can also enable IPSec driver logging of dropped inbound and outbound packets by using netsh command-line tool utility. From a command prompt window, issue the following command:

```
netsh IPSec dynamic set config ipsecdiagnostics 7
```

Next, restart the computer so that the settings will take effect.

By default, the IPSec driver will write to the System log on an hourly basis, or after the event threshold value has been met. For troubleshooting purposes, you can change this setting to an interval of 60 seconds. To change this setting, you can modify the Registry by creating the following DWORD value:

1. Open the Registry Editor by selecting **Start | Run,** typing **regedit** or **regedt32**, and clicking **OK**.

2. Navigate to **HKEY_LOCAL_MACHINE\System\CurrentControlSet\Services\IPSec**.

3. Right-click the **IPSec** key and select **New**, and then select **DWORD Value**.

4. In the right pane, change the default name of the new value to **LogInterval.**

5. Double-click the new value, or right-click and select **Modify**.

6. In the **Edit DWORD Value** dialog box, under **Value data**, type **60**.

7. Under **Base**, click the **Decimal option** button.

8. Click the **OK** button.

9. Close the Registry Editor.

After you've made this change, you can restart the system.

Again, you can use a netsh command to change this setting. Open the command prompt window and type the following command:

```
netsh ipsec dynamic set config ipsecloginterval 60
```

Then restart the computer so the changes can take effect.

Packet event logging is disabled by default. After you create the HKEY_LOCAL_MACHINE\System\CurrentControlSet\Services\IPSec\EnableDiagnostics value as described earlier, you can control the logging level by editing the value. Table 23.7 lists the possible values that you can set. To disable logging altogether after the DWORD value has been created without deleting the value (if you will want to enable it again later), set the value to **0**.

Table 23.7 Value Settings and Level of Logging

Value	Logging Performed
1	Bad SPI, IKE negotiation failures, and invalid packet syntax are logged.
2	System log records the inbound per-packet drop events.
3	Unexpected cleartext events and level 1 and level 2 logging are performed.
4	Outbound per-packet drops are recorded.
5	Level 1 and level 4 logging are performed.
6	Level 2 and level 4 logging are performed.
7	All logging is performed.

The value of 7 enables all logging, creating a great deal of information in the logs. Before you enable logging of this magnitude, realize that your system logs will fill up quickly. To prevent problems, do one or more of the following:

- Set your system log size to at least 10MB.

- Clear all events so the log is empty before you start logging.

- Save the current log to a file.

Using IKE Detailed Tracing to Troubleshoot IPSec

Enabling audit logging for IKE events and viewing the events in Event Viewer provide the fastest and simplest way to troubleshoot failed main mode or quick mode negotiations. If you need a more detailed analysis of these negotiations, you can enable tracing for IKE negotiations. This is an extremely detailed log intended for troubleshooting IKE interoperability under controlled circumstances. Before you try to decipher the log, you will need to have expert-level knowledge of RFCs 2408 (defining ISAKMP) and 2409 (defining IKE).

The IKE tracing log is 50,000 lines long and will overwrite if necessary. This log is located in the *systemroot*\Debug\Oakley.log file. Each time the IPSec service is started, the previous version of the file is renamed Oakley.log.sav, and a new Oakley.log file is created. If the Oakley.log file becomes full before the IPSec service is started, the full log will be named Oakley.log.bak, and a new Oakley.log file will be created.

Using the Network Monitor to Troubleshoot IPSec

The Windows Server 2003 Network Monitor is a protocol analyzer (also called a *packet sniffer*) that Microsoft includes with its server operating systems.

The Network Monitor includes parsers for the AH, ESP, and ISAKMP (IKE) IPSec protocols. However, the Network Monitor cannot parse the encrypted portions of IPSec-secured ESP traffic when encryption is software-based. If you are using encryption on a hardware offload network adapter, ESP packets are decrypted when the Network Monitor captures them and therefore can be parsed and interpreted into the upper-layer protocols. The following types of traffic should be exempt from filtering: broadcast, multicast, IKE, Kerberos, and RSVP.

IPSec will exempt all multicast, broadcast, IKE, Kerberos, and RSVP traffic if you are using Windows XP and Windows 2000. The Windows Server 2003 family only exempts IKE traffic from traffic filtering by default. Actions such as block, configure, and permit filter actions can be configured just for broadcast and multicast traffic. SAs will not be negotiated for broadcast and multicast traffic. If you wish to change the filtering behavior on your Windows Server 2003 machines to match the default behavior on Windows 2000/XP machines (that is, to exempt multicast, broadcast, RSVP, and Kerberos traffic, along with IKE), you can use the following netsh command at the prompt on the Windows Server 2003 machine:

```
netsh ipsec dynamic set config ipsecexempt 0
```

After issuing this command, you will need to reboot the computer for the changes to take effect.

By design, Windows 2000 and Windows XP default exemption settings for IPSec are configured for low-risk environments, such as corporate LANs, because the risk of attack is minimal. The Windows 2000 and Windows XP default exemption settings should be used in only low-risk environments and be applied only when necessary for troubleshooting purposes.

To exempt all multicast, broadcast, RSVP, Kerberos, and IKE traffic from IPSec filtering, you need to edit the Registry to create a DWORD value called **NoDefaultExempt** in the **HKEY_LOCAL_MACHINE\System\CurrentControlSet\Services\IPSEC** Registry key and set its value to **0**. Follow the instructions given previously for creating new DWORD values.

Disabling TCP/IP and IPSec Hardware Acceleration to Solve IPSec Problems

IPSec offload is a process by which some network adapters can do the processing for the mathematical calculations involved in encrypting IPSec data and TCP checksums. This speeds up, or *accelerates*, the process because it is being handled by a chip on the network interface card (NIC) instead of by the operating system software. NICs that are capable of offloading IPSec cryptographic functions can also perform a *large-send offload*, which is the processing of very large TCP segments for accelerated transmissions. If a Plug and Play NIC has this capability, its driver can make an advertisement to IPSec and TCP/IP. This results in the protocols passing these tasks to the NIC driver. Although hardware acceleration speeds up processing, it can sometimes cause problems with packet processing. Disabling the hardware offload function can help in troubleshooting IPSEC problems

IPSec offload is a process by which some network adapters can do the processing for the mathematical calculations involved in encrypting IPSec data and TCP checksums. This speeds up, or accelerates, the process because it is being handled by a chip on the network interface card (NIC) instead of by the operating system software. NICs that are capable of offloading IPSec cryptographic functions can also perform a large-send offload, which is the processing of very large TCP segments for accelerated transmissions. If a Plug and Play NIC has this capability, its driver can make an advertisement to IPSec and TCP/IP. This results in the protocols passing these tasks to the NIC driver. Although hardware acceleration speeds up processing, it can sometimes cause problems with packet processing. Disabling the hardware offload function can help in troubleshooting IPSec problems.

Addressing IPSec Security Considerations

As you begin to deploy IPSec throughout your organization, you will need to decide on the encryptions methods you wish to implement and whether to use firewall packet filtering. The following sections provide some guidelines to use when considering IPSec security.

Strong Encryption Algorithm (3DES)

DES and 3DES are *block ciphers*. This refers to an algorithm that takes a block of plaintext of a fixed length and changes it into a block of *ciphertext* (encrypted data) of the same length. The key length for DES is 64 bits total, but because 8 of the bits are used for parity information, the effective length is only 56 bits. With 3DES, the DES process is performed three times with different 56-bit keys, making the effective key length 168 bits. When using 3DES in encrypt-encrypt-encrypt (EEE) mode, 3DES works by processing each block as follows:

1. A block of plaintext is encrypted with key one.

2. The resulting block of ciphertext is encrypted with key two.

3. The result of step 2 is encrypted with key three.

When using 3DES in encrypt-decrypt-encrypt (EDE) mode, step 2 is run in decryption mode. When 3DES is decrypting a packet, the process is done in reverse order. 3DES offers you the best mode for data confidentiality.

Firewall Packet Filtering

To allow for secured packets to be passed through a firewall, you need to configure the firewall or other device, such as a security gateway or router, to allow these packets to pass through the external interface.

The following ports and protocols can be used for firewall filtering:

- IP protocol and port 50, ESP traffic
- IP protocol and port 51, AH traffic
- UDP port 500, IKE negotiation traffic

Diffie-Hellman Groups

As we discussed earlier in the chapter, Diffie-Hellman groups are used to define the length of the base prime numbers that are used during the key-exchange process. There are three types of Diffie-Hellman groups, as follows:

- **Diffie-Hellman group 1** This is the least secure group and it provides only 768 bits of keying strength.
- **Diffie-Hellman group 2** This group is set to a medium level, at 1024 bits of keying strength.
- **Diffie-Hellman group 3** This group is set to the highest level, at 2048 bits of keying strength.

Diffie-Hellman group 3 is available only on Windows Server 2003 family machines. If you wish to use this algorithm on Windows 2000 machines, you must have either Service Pack 2 or the High Encryption Pack installed. If you configure one client machine for a Diffie-Hellman group 1 key exchange and another client machine for the Diffie-Hellman group 3 exchange, negotiation will fail.

For the best security, use the highest Diffie-Hellman group 3 key exchange. When using the quick mode, new keys are created from the Diffie-Hellman main mode master key material. If you have the master key or session key PFS enabled, a new master key will be created by performing a Diffie-Hellman exchange. The master key PFS will require a reauthentication of the main mode SA in addition to the Diffie-Hellman exchange. The session key PFS will not require this reauthentication.

Pre-shared Keys

To authenticate L2TP protocol and IPSec connections, you can select to use a pre-shared key. This is the simplest of three choices of authentication methods that you have with IPSec. The other two authentication methods are Kerberos and digital certificates. Before selecting to use a pre-shared key, you should be aware of all the implications of doing so.

A pre-shared key is a string of Unicode characters. You can use the Routing and Remote Access management console to configure connections to support authenticated VPN connections using the pre-shared key. A server that has the Windows Server 2003 operating system installed may also be configured to use a pre-shared key to authenticate connections from other routers via the Routing and Remote Access console.

Advantages and Disadvantages of Pre-shared Keys

Pre-shared key authentication does not have the overhead costs that a PKI implementation does. This type of authentication is relatively easy to configure using the Routing and Remote Access console (for L2TP/IPSec connections) or the IP Security Policy Management console (for IPSec secured communications).

Pre-shared keys are stored as plaintext. This means the key can be compromised if a hacker is able to access the file on the computer. Thus, the pre-shared key is the weakest of the three IPSec authentication methods.

Another drawback of pre-shared keys in relation to L2TP/IPSec connections is that a remote-access server can use one pre-shared key for all L2TP/IPSec connections that require a pre-shared key for authentication. In this case, you need to issue the same pre-shared key to all L2TP/IPSec VPN clients that connect to the remote-access server using a pre-shared key. Unless you are using the Connection Manager profile to distribute the pre-shared key, each user must manually type the pre-shared key. If you change the pre-shared key on a remote-access server, clients with manually configured pre-shared keys will not be unable to connect to the server until the pre-shared key on the client is changed.

Considerations when Choosing a Pre-shared Key

Remember that a pre-shared key is just a sequence of characters that is configured on both computers that are parties to an IPSec-secured communication. The pre-shared key can be any non-null string of any combination, up to 256 Unicode characters.

When you choose a pre-shared key, consider that users who use the New Connection Wizard to create a VPN client connection must type the pre-shared key manually. A key that is long and complex enough to provide adequate security might be difficult for the majority of your users to remember or type accurately. If the pre-shared key presented by one party to the communication deviates in any way from the pre-shared key configured on the other, IPSec authentication will fail.

Soft Associations

A *soft association* refers to an SA that was created with a computer that hasn't responded to main mode association attempts since the last time the IPSec service was started. If the IPSec policy is so configured, the communications will be allowed, even though there was no response to the main mode negotiation attempt. It's important to understand that a soft association is *not* protected by IPSec.

The soft association is just a communication that is not secured. This occurs when one of the two communicating computers doesn't support IPSec, and the IPSec policy allows unsecured communications in this situation.

Security and RSoP

Administrators can use Resultant Set of Policy (RSoP) features to determine which particular security policies meet their organization's needs. You can use RSoP security templates to create and assign security options for one or many computers. You can apply a template to a local computer, and then import that template into the GPO in the Active Directory. After the template has been imported, Group Policy will process the security template and apply the changes to the all members of that GPO. RSoP will also verify the changes that have been made by polling the system and then showing the resultant policy. RSoP can correct a security breach by taking the invalidly applied or overwritten policy setting or the priority policy setting. Group Policy filtering will report the scope of the GPO, based on the security group membership.

Through individual security settings, administrators can define a security policy in Active Directory that contains specific security settings for nearly all security areas. Security settings in a local GPO can establish a security policy on a local computer. When there are conflicts, security settings that are defined in Active Directory always override any security settings that are defined locally.

The settings of the IPSec policy with the highest precedence apply in their entirety; they are not merged with the settings of IPSec policies that are applied at higher levels of the Active Directory hierarchy.

Planning, Implementing, and Maintaining a Public Key Infrastructure

In this chapter:

- ☑ **Planning a Windows Server 2003 Certificate-Based PKI**

- ☑ **Implementing Certification Authorities**

- ☑ **Planning Enrollment and Distribution of Certificates**

- ☑ **Implementing Smart Card Authentication in the PKI**

Introduction

The Public Key Infrastructure (PKI) is the method of choice for handling authentication issues in large enterprise-level organizations today. Windows Server 2003 includes the tools you need to create a PKI for your company and issue digital certificates to users, computers, and applications. This chapter addresses the complex issues involved in planning a certificate-based PKI. We'll provide an overview of the basic terminology and concepts relating to the public key infrastructure, and you'll learn about public key cryptography and how it is used to authenticate the identity of users, computers, and applications/services. We'll discuss the role of digital certificates and the different types of certificates (user, machine, and application certificates).

You'll learn about certification authorities (CAs), the servers that issue certificates, including both public CAs and private CAs such as the ones you can implement on your own network using Windows Server 2003's certificate services. Next, we'll discuss the CA hierarchy and how root CAs and subordinate CAs act together to provide for your organization's certificate needs. You'll find out how the Microsoft certificate services work, and we'll walk you through the steps involved in implementing one or more certification authorities based on the needs of the organization. You'll learn to determine the appropriate CA type – enterprise or stand-alone CA – for a given situation and how to plan the CA hierarchy and provide for security of your CAs. We'll show you how to plan for enrollment and distribution of certificates, including the use of certificate requests, role-based administration, and auto-enrollment deployment.

Next, we'll discuss how to implement the use of smart cards for authentication within the PKI. You'll learn what smart cards are and how smart card authentication works, and we'll show you how to deploy smart card logon on your network. We'll discuss smart card readers and show you how to set up a smart card enrollment station. Finally, we'll discuss the procedures for using smart cards to log on to Windows, for remote access and VPNs, and to log on to a terminal server.

Planning a Windows Server 2003 Certificate-Based PKI

Computer networks have evolved in recent years to enable an unprecedented sharing of information between individuals, corporations, and even national governments. The need to protect this information has also evolved and network security has consequently become an essential concern of most system administrators. Even in smaller organizations, the basic goal of preventing unauthorized access while still enabling legitimate information to flow smoothly requires the use of more and more advanced technology.

In the mid-1990s, Microsoft began developing what was to become a comprehensive security system of authentication protocols and technology based on already developed cryptography standards known as Public Key Infrastructure (PKI). With the release of Windows 2000 Server, Microsoft used various existing standards to create the first Windows-proprietary PKI – one that could be implemented completely without using third-party companies. Windows Server 2003 expands and improves on that original design in several significant ways, which we'll discuss later in this chapter.

Understanding Public Key Infrastructure

To understand how a PKI works, you first need to understand what it is supposed to do. The goals of your infrastructure should include the following:

- Proper authentication
- Trust
- Confidentiality
- Integrity
- Non-repudiation

By using the core PKI elements of public key cryptography, digital signatures, and certificates, all of these equally important goals can be met successfully. The good news is that the majority of the work involved in implementing these elements under Windows Server 2003 is taken care of automatically by the operating system and is done behind the scenes.

The Function of the PKI

Most of the functionality of a Windows Server 2003-based PKI comes from a few crucial components, which are described below. Although there are several third-party vendors, such as VeriSign (www.verisign.com), that offer similar technologies and components, using Windows Server 2003 can be a less-costly and easier-to-implement option – especially for small- and medium-sized companies.

Components of the PKI

Properly planning for and deploying a PKI requires familiarity with a number of components, including but not limited to the following:

- Digital Certificates
- Certification Authorities
- Certificate Enrollment
- Certificate Revocation
- Encryption/Cryptography Services

In the following sections, we will discuss each of these in more detail.

Understanding Digital Certificates

Think of a certificate as a small and portable combination safe. The primary purpose of the safe is to hold a public key (although quite a bit of other information is also held there). Someone you trust must hold the combination to the safe – that trust is the basis for the entire PKI system. The main purpose of certificates is to facilitate the secure transfer of keys across an insecure network. Figure 24.1 shows the properties of a Windows certificate. Notice that the highlighted public key is only part of the certificate.

Figure 24.1 A Windows Server 2003 Certificate

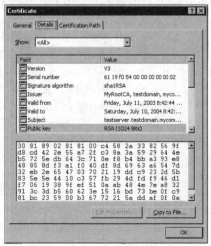

User Certificates

Of the three general types of certificates found in a Windows PKI, the *user certificate* is perhaps the most common. User certificates are certificates that enable the user to do something that would not otherwise be allowed. The Enrollment Agent certificate is one example. Without it, even an administrator is not able to enroll smart cards and configure them properly at an enrollment station. Under Windows Server 2003, required user certificates can be requested automatically by the client and subsequently issued by a certification authority (discussed below) with no user intervention necessary.

Machine Certificates

Also known as computer certificates, *machine certificates* (as the name implies) give the system – instead of the user – the capability to do something out of the ordinary. The main purpose for machine certificates is authentication, both client-side and server-side. As stated earlier, certificates are the main vehicle by which public keys are exchanged in a PKI. Machine certificates are mainly involved with these behind-the-scenes exchanges and are normally overseen by the operating system. Machine certificates have been able to take advantage of Windows' auto-enrollment feature since Windows 2000 Server was introduced. We will discuss auto-enrollment later in this chapter.

Application Certificates

The term *application certificate* refers to any certificate that is used with a specific PKI-enabled application. Examples include IPSec and S/MIME encryption for e-mail. Applications that need certificates are generally configured to automatically request them and are then placed in a waiting status until the required certificate arrives. Depending upon the application, the network administrator or even the user might have the capability to change or even delete certificate requests issued by the application.

Understanding Certification Authorities

Certificates are a way to transfer keys securely across an insecure network. If any arbitrary user were allowed to issue certificates, it would be no different from that user simply signing the data. For a certificate to be of any use, it must be issued by a trusted entity – an entity that both the sender and receiver trust. Such a trusted entity is known as a *certification authority* (CA).

In a third-party, or external, PKI, it is up to the third-party CA to positively verify the identity of anyone requesting a certificate from it. Beginning with Windows 2000, Microsoft has allowed the creation of a trusted *internal* CA – possibly eliminating the need for an external third party. With a Windows Server 2003 CA, the CA verifies the identity of the user requesting a certificate by checking that user's authentication credentials (using Kerberos or NTLM). If the credentials of the requesting user check out, a certificate is issued to the user. When the user needs to transmit his or her public key to another user or application, the certificate is used to prove to the receiver that the public key inside can be used safely.

CA Hierarchy

For a very small organization, it might be possible under Windows Server 2003 for you to use only one CA for all PKI functions. However, for larger groups, Microsoft outlines a three-tier hierarchical structure starting at the top with a root CA, moving downward to a mid-level CA, and finally an issuing-level CA. Both the mid-level CA and issuing-level CA are known as subordinate CAs.

Root CAs

When you first set up an internal PKI, no CA exists. The first CA created is known as the root CA, and it can be used to issue certificates to users or to other CAs. As mentioned above, in a large organization there usually is a hierarchy where the root CA is not the only certification authority. In this case, the sole purpose of the root CA is to issue certificates to other CAs to establish their authority.

The question then becomes: who issues the root CA a certificate? The answer is that a root CA issues its own certificate (this is called a *self-signed* certificate). Security is not compromised for two reasons. First, you will only implement one root CA in your organization and second, configuring a root CA requires administrative rights on the server. The root CA should be kept highly secured because it has so much authority.

Subordinate CAs

Any certification authority that is established after the root CA is a subordinate CA. Subordinate CAs gain their authority by requesting a certificate from either the root CA or a higher-level subordinate CA. After the subordinate CA receives the certificate, it can control CA policies and/or issue certificates itself, depending on your PKI structure and policies.

How Microsoft Certificate Services Works

The Windows Server 2003 PKI does many things behind the scenes. Thanks in part to auto enroll-ment (discussed later in this chapter) and certificate stores (places where certificates are kept after their creation), some PKI-enabled features such as EFS work with no user intervention at all. Others, such as IPSec, require significantly less work than would be required without an advanced operating system.

Even though a majority of the PKI is handled by Windows Server 2003, it is still instructive to have an overview of how certificate services work.

1. First, a system or user generates a public/private key pair and then a certificate request.

2. The certificate request, which contains the public key and other identifying information such as user name, is forwarded to a CA.

3. The CA verifies the validity of the public key. If it is verified, the CA issues the certificate.

4. After it is issued, the certificate is ready for use and is kept in the certificate store, which can reside in Active Directory. Applications that require a certificate use this central reposi-tory when necessary.

In practice, it isn't terribly difficult to implement certificate services. Configuring the CA requires a bit more effort, as does planning the structure and hierarchy of the PKI – especially if you are designing an enterprise-wide solution. We'll cover these topics later in this chapter. You can use the following steps to install Certificate Services in Windows Server 2003.

Install Certificate Services

1. After logging on with administrative privileges, click **Start | Control Panel**, and then click **Add/Remove Programs**.

2. Click **Add/Remove Windows Components**, and then check **Certificate Services**. This selects both sub-components of certificate services, which are Certificate Services CA and Certificate Services Web Enrollment Support.

3. A warning dialog box appear, telling you that after certificate services have been installed, you will not be able to change the machine's domain membership or change its computer name. Click **Yes** to continue.

4. You now must choose the type of CA to establish. You have two decisions to make – that of root vs. subordinate and enterprise vs. standalone (discussed later in this chapter). For this example, click **Enterprise root CA** and click **Next**. If you checked the **Use custom settings to generate the key pair and CA certificate**, you would be prompted to choose a custom cryptographic service provider (CSP), a hash algorithm, and a key length. You could also elect to use an existing key or to use an imported one.

5. The next dialog box presented is the **CA Identifying Information** box. Enter a common name for the CA. For this example, type **My Root CA**. The distinguished name suffix is provided by the operating system and is used along with the common name you just typed in to form the distinguished name. Note that you can also change the default five-year validity period of the CA. You can set the validity period as a number of days, weeks, months, or years. Click **Next** to continue.

6. After the key pair is generated, the Certificate Database Settings dialog box appears. Notice that both the certificate database and certificate database log textboxes are already filled with default values. You may elect to **Store configuration information in a shared folder**, but do not check it for purposes of this example. Click **Next** to complete the installation. After Windows Server 2003 has completed its work (you might be notified during this process that the Internet Information Service (IIS) will stop if you have IIS running on this machine), click **Finish**. During the configuration process, you might be prompted to insert your Windows Server 2003 installation CD or enter the path to the installation files on the hard disk or on a network share. You will also be notified that Active Server Pages (ASP) must be enabled in IIS to provide Web enrollment services. Click **Yes** to enable ASP.

Implementing Certification Authorities

Planning a PKI structure that includes multiple CAs in a hierarchy with proper security can be a test in patience and fortitude. The actual implementation, however, is relatively simple. Before we talk about the differences between enterprise and stand-alone CAs, and the security concerns involved, we'll go over the many options you have control over in the following example.

Configure a Certification Authority

In this example, we'll explore the different properties you have control over when configuring a CA. We won't go over all the options now, but we will cover them all in this chapter.

1. Click **Start | Administrative Tools | Certification Authority** (note that certificate services must be installed before this step – see the example earlier in this chapter; otherwise, this choice will not appear in the **Administrative Tools** menu).

2. In the left pane of the **Certification Authority** snap-in, click **My Root CA** (or whichever CA name you have listed) and expand it. This is where you can view revoked and issued certificates, pending and failed certificates, and certificate templates (discussed later in this chapter).

3. Highlight **My Root CA** and right-click it. Click **Properties**. Figure 24.2 shows the **General** tab. Here, all installed CA certificates are listed as well as the CSP and hash algorithms used. Click **View Certificate** if you want to see the certificate itself.

Figure 24.2 General Tab of the CA Property Sheet

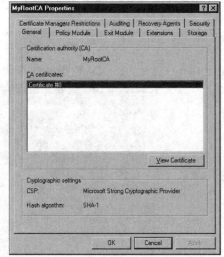

4. Click the **Policy Module** tab. A policy module defines how the CA handles incoming certificate requests. Notice that the Windows default policy is listed. The **Select** button is used to choose a different policy module, usually a customized version. Click the **Properties** button. The default setting tells the CA to follow the settings in the certificate template if applicable and to automatically issue the certificate otherwise. The other setting tags all incoming requests to *pending* status, forcing the administrator to manually approve or deny each certificate request. Keep the default setting and click **OK** to return to the CA property sheet.

5. Click the **Exit Module** tab. Whereas a policy module defines how a CA handles incoming certificate requests, an exit module defines what a CA does with certificates that it issues. The Windows default policy is listed. In addition to the **Add** and **Remove** buttons, there is a **Properties** button. Click the **Properties** button. The only setting is to allow certificates to be published to the file system if a certificate template dictates, which the default policy does not allow. Again, keep the default setting and click **OK** to return to the CA property sheet. Skip the **Extensions** tab for now; we'll discuss it when we talk about certificate revocations later in the chapter.

6. Click the **Storage** tab. Note that the default settings cannot be changed because Active Directory is being used. We'll discuss more about the relationship between Active Directory and enterprise CAs later in this chapter.

7. Click the **Certificate Managers Restrictions** tab. The default setting here tells the CA to not restrict certificate managers. As an administrator, you can designate certificate managers by giving them the **Issue and Manage Certificates** permission. By changing the default, you can specifically restrict the users, groups, and computers over which a certificate manager has control.

8. Click the **Auditing** tab. As seen in Figure 24.3, there are many events that you can monitor – each concerned with a different aspect of security. Especially important are the **Change CA configuration, Change CA security settings,** and **Issue and manage certificate requests** events. Skip the Recovery Agents tab; we'll cover it during our discussion of key archival and recovery.

Figure 24.3 Auditing Tab of the CA Property Sheet

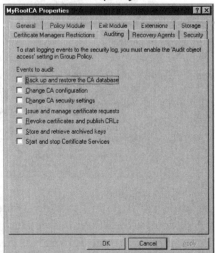

9. Click the **Security** tab. The **Security** tab, shown in Figure 24.4, enables you to grant or deny access to users over several key areas of the CA. Note that the **Issue and Manage Certificates** permission denotes a certificate manager, whereas the **Manage CA** permission gives authoritative access to the entire CA. Click **Cancel** to return to the CA snap-in.

Figure 24.4 Security Tab of the CA Property Sheet

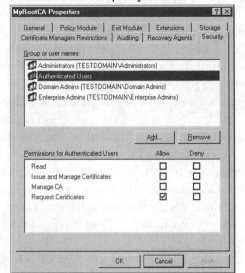

Analyzing Certificate Needs within the Organization

You've just concluded a tour of most of the properties associated with a CA, but knowing what you *can* do does not mean that you know what you *should* do. To find out more about what you should do, you need to analyze the certificate needs of your organization and then move on to create an appropriate CA structure.

When designing a PKI/CA structure, you need to understand the different uses for certificates and whether your organization needs to use certificates for different purposes. Examples include SSL for a secure Web server, EFS for encryption of files, and S/MIME for encryption of e-mail messages. The use of S/MIME might dictate that your CA hierarchy has a trust relationship with external CAs, and the use of SSL might lead you to implement a stand-alone CA instead of an enterprise CA. Thus, analyzing these needs *before* you implement your PKI can save you a lot of time and trouble.

Determining Appropriate CA Type(s)

For most administrators, the most significant factor in designing a CA structure is the amount of PKI-reliant traffic on the network. If you run a small organization without an Internet presence, for example, a single-root CA that issues certificates directly to users will probably fit the bill. However, in a larger organization, a CA hierarchy is likely to be more appropriate.

The first choice when determining appropriate CA types for your PKI is how many subordination levels to use. One level, the root, is of course required. Two, three, and even four subordination levels are relatively common, but the three-tier model is the one most referenced and most-frequently used. So how does the three-tier model work? We've discussed previously the differences between a root CA and a subordinate CA and that a root CA issues certificates to the second-tier subordinates. In the standard three-tier model, the root CA has the job of issuing certificates to the second-tier. That's all it really does. Certainly it has the capability of doing more – it could even issue certificates to users. However in a large company, the amount of traffic generated by even a few PKI-aware applications could easily overwhelm a single CA. Also, if you shift the responsibility of issuing certificates to subordinate CAs, you can take the root CA *offline* – meaning that you detach it from the network entirely. This provides a very high level of security, because attackers have no way of getting to the machine. When a subordinate CA requires a certificate from the root, you can either briefly connect the root CA to the network and then remove it again, or you can literally use a floppy disk.

The intermediate level of CAs, the one just below the root, has the responsibility for controlling certificate policy and issuing certificates to the bottom-level CAs. These bottom-level CAs are the ones that actually issue certificates to users, machines, and applications. The question then becomes: why don't the intermediate CAs just issue the user certificates directly? The answer is that although they can, it just isn't as scalable as the three-tier model. It is easier to add CAs to the hierarchy that are concerned only with issuing certificates and not involved with policies such as key length and CSP choice.

After you have determined the hierarchical structure of your CAs, you will need to determine which CAs are set up as enterprise CAs and which ones are set up as stand-alone CAs before implementing them. You may recall that in the example earlier in this chapter you installed certificate services and chose an enterprise root CA. The choice in your network will depend on several different factors, such as your needed level of security. Both enterprise and stand-alone CAs have advantages and disadvantages. We'll explore some of them in the following sections.

Enterprise CAs

An enterprise CA is tied into Active Directory and is required to use it. In fact, a copy of its own CA certificate is stored in Active Directory. Perhaps the biggest difference between an enterprise CA and a stand-alone CA is that enterprise CAs use Kerberos or NTLM authentication to validate users and computers before certificates are issued. This provides additional security to the PKI because the validation process relies on the strength of the Kerberos protocol and not a human administrator. Enterprise CAs also use templates, which are described later in this chapter, and they can issue every type of certificate.

There are also several downsides to an enterprise CA. In comparison to a stand-alone CA, enterprise CAs are more difficult to maintain and require a much more in-depth knowledge about Active Directory and authentication. Also, because an enterprise CA requires Active Directory, it is nearly impossible to remove it from the network. If you were to do so, the Directory itself would quickly become outdated – making it difficult to resynchronize with the rest of the network when brought back online. This forces an enterprise CA to remain attached to the network, leaving it vulnerable to attackers.

Stand-Alone CAs

Stand-alone CAs do not require Active Directory (although they *can* use AD information if it is available), and are usually used as either secure root CAs or as an issuer to such applications as stand-alone Web servers. Stand-alone CAs are generally not suitable for enterprise-type applications.

Because certificate templates are not used on a stand-alone CA, a standalone is more basic and easier to maintain than an enterprise CA. A stand-alone CA keeps a copy of its CA certificate in a shared folder and if Active Directory is not used, users that need to request certificates need to know the location of the CA. Finally, stand-alone servers can be secured by removing them from the network.

The disadvantages to a stand-alone CA are that an administrator must manually approve or deny every certificate request individually; a stand-alone CA cannot issue log-on certificates; and templates cannot be used with a stand-alone CA, so a key recovery agent cannot be established (we discuss the key recovery agent template below).

Planning the CA Hierarchy

There is more than meets the eye when planning a CA hierarchy. We've already discussed choices you will need to make between root and subordinate and between enterprise and standalone. You will also need to consider possible cross-trust hierarchies and the establishment of the key recovery agent.

Cross-Trust Hierarchies

For a PKI entity to use a certificate provided by a CA, the entity must trust that CA. This trust is established when the entity has a copy of the CA's certificate located in its local certificate store. Using the public key contained in the certificate, the entity can verify the CA's digital signature. How, then, does the certificate get from the CA to the entity's local store? Unfortunately, there is not just one answer. Group policies under Active Directory, preloaded certificates in Windows Server 2003, and downloads from the Windows Update Web site are the most common ways.

The chain of trust from an issuing CA all the way up to the root CA must be verified by an entity requesting a certificate for the certificate to be accepted. In a small, local network operation this is easy to accomplish. However, when your organization must exchange data with external parties, there needs to be a way to recognize and trust a third-party CA as if it were a part of your local chain of trust. There are two ways to do this:

- You can use a certificate trust list, or CTL.

- You can create a cross-trust hierarchy, which enables an external CA to be viewed as a subordinate CA in your local trust chain.

Using a CTL or a cross-trust hierarchy under previous versions of Windows presented a central problem. When an external CA gained trust status, every certificate issued by it and all of its subordinate CAs were automatically trusted. New to Windows Server 2003 is a feature called *qualified subordination*. Qualified subordination enables you to specify how many subordinates can be trusted and it also enables you to specify the purposes of certificates that can be accepted from the external CAs.

Key Recovery Agent

As when a person has locked his or her keys inside the car, lost encryption keys in a PKI can be troublesome. Luckily, Windows Server 2003 provides a locksmith of sorts (called a Registration Authority, or RA) that earlier versions of Windows did not have. A key recovery solution, however, is not easy to implement and requires several steps. The basic method follows:

1. Create an account to be used for key recovery.

2. Create a new template to issue to that account.

3. Request a key recovery certificate from the CA.

4. Have the CA issue the certificate.

5. Configure the CA to archive certificates by using the **Recovery Agents** tab of the CA property sheet (shown in Figure 24.5).

6. Create an archive template for the CA.

Figure 24.5 Recovery Agents Tab of the CA Property Sheet

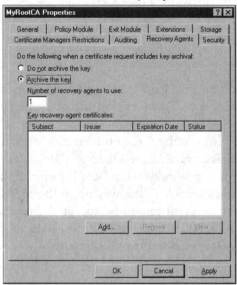

Each of these steps requires many substeps, but can be well worth the time and effort. It is worth noting again that key recovery is not possible on a stand-alone CA, because a standalone cannot use templates. It is also worth noting that only encryption keys can be recovered – private keys used for digital signatures cannot be.

Planning CA Security

As we have already discussed, configuring the root CA as a standalone is probably the most important measure you can take to prevent accidental or intentional tampering. With no network connectivity, attacks become virtually impossible, as a user would have to log on while sitting at the physical location of the server. Other security considerations are really more a function of general server security – things such as requiring complex passwords, implementing file encryption and physically limiting access to the server.

In guarding the hierarchy, you cannot solely concentrate on the root CA. After all, if a subordinate CA is tampered with, every entity below it in the PKI hierarchy becomes compromised. Most subordinate CAs are attached to the network. This obviously increases their vulnerability. Beyond securing the network itself (by using IPSec and group policies, for example), there is another part of a standard PKI that helps maintain CA integrity. That part is *certificate revocation*, which we will go into in greater detail shortly. Certificate revocation enables an administrator to warn PKI clients about certificates that might not be authentic or that might have been issued by a rogue CA.

Disaster recovery applies to every CA in the hierarchy, but especially at the root. That being said, the importance of performing proper backups cannot be overstated.

Certificate Revocation

A CA's primary duty is to issue certificates, either to subordinate CAs or to PKI clients. However, each CA also has the capability to revoke those certificates when necessary. The tool that the CA uses for revocation is the *certificate revocation list*, or CRL. The act of revoking a certificate is simple: from the **Certification Authority** console, simply highlight the **Issued Certificates** container, right-click the certificate and choose **All | Revoke Certificate**. The certificate will then be located in the **Revoked Certificates** container.

When a PKI entity verifies a certificate's validity, that entity checks the CRL before giving approval. The question is: how does a client know where to check for the list? The answer is the CDPs, or CRL Distribution Points. CDPs are locations on the network to which a CA publishes the CRL; in the case of an enterprise CA under Windows Server 2003, Active Directory holds the CRL and for a standalone, the CRL is located in the *certsrv\certenroll* directory. Each certificate has a location listed for the CDP, and when the client views the certificate, it then understands where to go for the latest CRL. Figure 24.6 shows the Extensions tab of the CA property sheet, where you can modify the location of the CDP.

Figure 24.6 Extensions Tab of the CA Property Sheet

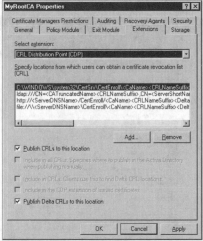

For a CA to publish a CRL, use the **Certification Authority** console to right-click the **Revoked Certificates** container and choose **All Tasks | Publish**. From there, you can choose to publish either a complete CRL or a Delta CRL.

Whether you select a New CRL or a Delta CRL, you are next prompted to enter a publication interval (the most frequent intervals chosen are one week for full CRLs and one day for Delta CRLs). Clients cache the CRL for this period of time and then check the CDP again when the period expires. If an updated CDP does not exist or cannot be located, the client automatically assumes that all certificates are invalid.

Planning Enrollment and Distribution of Certificates

For a PKI client to use a certificate, two basic things must happen. First, a CA has to make the certificate available and second, the client has to request the certificate. Only after these first steps can the CA issue the certificate or deny the request. Making the certificate available is done through the use of certificate templates and is a topic that we discuss in detail below. As for the client, there are three methods of requesting certificates – all three of which are essential to a thorough understanding of PKI: auto-enrollment, the Certificates snap-in, and the Certificates web page. We will discuss each in more detail in the section titled *Certificate Requests*.

Certificate Templates

A *certificate template* defines the policies and rules that a CA uses when a request for a certificate is received. Many built-in templates can be viewed using the **Certificate Templates** snap-in (see Figure 24.7). The snap-in can be run by right-clicking the **Certificate Templates** container located in the **Certification Authority** console and clicking **Manage**. You can use one of the built-in templates or create your own.

Figure 24.7 Certificate Templates Snap-In

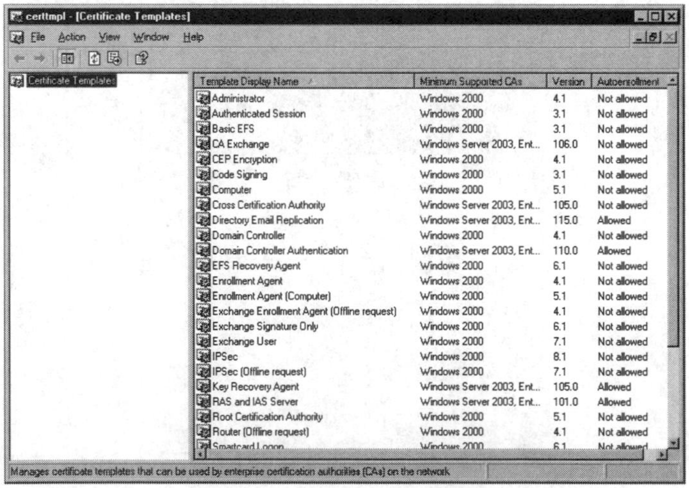

When creating your own template, you have multiple options that will guide the CA in how to handle incoming requests. The first step in the creation process is to duplicate an existing template.

You do this by using the **Certificate Templates** snap-in, then right-clicking the template you wish to copy and selecting *Duplicate Template*. On the **General** tab that appears by default, there are time-sensitive options such as validity period and renewal period. Note the default validity period of one year and the default renewal period of six weeks. There are also general options such as the template display name and a check box for publishing the certificate in Active Directory.

The **Request Handling** tab, shown in Figure 24.8, has options including minimum key size and certificate purpose. The certificate purpose can be encryption, signature, or signature and encryption. There is also an option to allow the export of the private key. Finally, you can instruct the CA how to act when the subject's request is received and which CSPs to use.

Figure 24.8 Request Handling Tab of the New Template Property Sheet

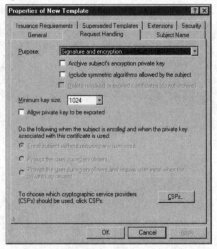

The **Subject Name** tab seen in Figure 24.9 gives you the choice of obtaining subject name information from Active Directory or from the certificate request itself. In the latter case, auto-enrollment (which we'll discuss later in the chapter) is not available.

Figure 24.9 Subject Name Tab of the New Template Property Sheet

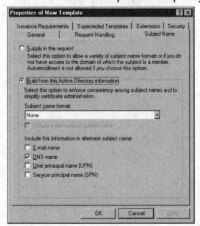

The **Issuance Requirements** tab enables you to suspend automatic certificate issuance by selecting the CA certificate manager approval check box.

The **Superseded Templates** tab is used to define which certificates the current template supersedes. Usually, this tab is used to configure a template that serves several functions; e.g., IPSec and EFS. In this case, a template used *only* for IPSec or a template used *only* for EFS would be placed on the superseded templates list.

The **Extensions** tab, as seen in Figure 24.10, can be used to add such things as the Application Policies extension, which defines the purposes for which a generated certificate can be used. The Issuance Policies extension is also worth mentioning, because it defines when a certificate may be issued.

Figure 24.10 Extensions Tab of the New Template Property Sheet

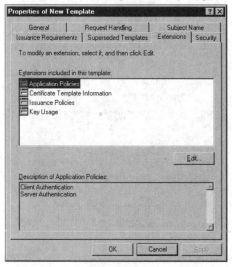

The **Security** tab is similar to the **Security** tab that we saw in an earlier example, except that this tab is used to control who may edit the template and who may request certificates using the template. Figure 24.11 shows the default permission level for the **Authenticated Users** group. For a user to request a certificate, however, the user must have at least the **Enroll** permission assigned to him or her for manual requests and the **Autoenroll** permission for automatic requests.

Figure 24.11 Security Tab of the New Template Property Sheet

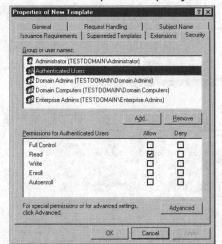

After you have configured a particular template, the CA still cannot use it to issue certificates until it is made *available*. To enable a template, use the **Certification Authority** console and right-click the **Certificate Templates** container. Selecting **New | Certificate Template to Issue** completes the process.

Certificate Requests

A client has three ways to request a certificate from a CA. The most common is auto-enrollment, and we'll discuss its deployment shortly. A client can also request a certificate by use of the **Certificates** snap-in. Clicking **Start | Run** and typing in **certmgr.msc** and pressing **Enter** can launch the snap-in. Note that the **Certificates** snap-in does *not* appear in the **Administrative Tools** folder as the **Certification Authority** snap-in does after installing certificate services.

Next, by expanding the **Personal** container and right-clicking the **Certificates** container beneath it, you can start the **Certificate Request Wizard** by choosing **All Tasks | Request New Certificate**. After the welcome screen, the first screen of the wizard enables you to choose the certificate type. You can only choose a type for which the receiving CA has a template.

If you select the **Advanced** check box, the next screen (Figure 24.12) enables you to choose the Cryptographic Service Provider (CSP) and key length. You can also mark the key as exportable and/or enable strong private key encryption.

Figure 24.12 Cryptographic Service Provider Screen of the Certificate Request Wizard

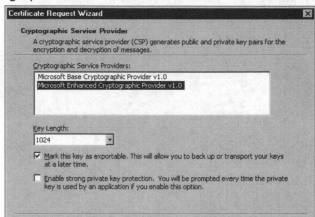

Continuing with the advanced options, you can choose **Browse the domain** to choose a CA to which you want to send the request. Finally, the wizard finishes by prompting you for a friendly name and description for the certificate. The last method for requesting a certificate is to use a Web browser on the client machine. Note that if you use this option, IIS must be installed on the CA.

Auto-Enrollment Deployment

Perhaps the most exciting new feature of the Windows Server 2003 PKI is the capability to use auto-enrollment for user certificates as well as for computer certificates. The request and issuance of these certificates may proceed without user intervention. There are, however, some strict requirements:

- Only Windows Server 2003 clients or Windows XP clients can use auto-enrollment.

- Windows Server 2003 Enterprise Edition or Datacenter Edition is required to configure auto-enrollment for version 2 templates.

Group policies are used in Active Directory to configure auto-enrollment. In **Computer Configuration | Windows Settings | Security Settings | Public Key Policies**, there is a group policy entitled **Automatic Certificate Request Settings**. The property sheet for this policy enables you to choose to either **Enroll certificates automatically** or not. Also, you will need to ensure that **Enroll subject without requiring any user input** option is selected on the **Request Handling** tab of the certificate template property sheet. Finally, be aware that doing either of the following will cause auto-enrollment to fail:

- Setting the **This number of authorized signatures** option on the **Issuance Requirements** tab to higher than one.

- Selecting the **Supply in the request** option on the **Subject Name** tab.

Role-Based Administration

PKI administration, which can be as daunting as general network administration, can be divided among various groups or individuals. Microsoft defines five different roles that can be used within a PKI to facilitate administration:

- CA Administrator
- Certificate Manager
- Backup Operator
- Auditor
- Enrollee

At the top of the hierarchy is the CA administrator. The role is defined by the *Manage CA* permission and has the authority to assign other CA roles and to renew the CA's certificate. Underneath the CA administrator is the certificate manager. The certificate manager role is defined by the *Issue and Manage Certificates* permission and has the authority to approve enrollment and revocation requests.

The Backup Operator and the Auditor roles are actually operating system roles and are not CA specific. The Backup Operator has the authority to back up the CA and the Auditor has the authority to configure and view audit logs of the CA. The final role is that of the Enrollees. All authenticated users are placed in this role and are able to request certificates from the CA.

Implementing Smart Card Authentication in the PKI

If security is a primary concern for your organization, you might want to consider the use of smart cards for both local and remote authentication. This adds a second level of security to the authentication process. Whereas traditional authentication via password requires only "something you know" (the password), smart card authentication also requires "something you have" (the card).

Along with biometric devices such as fingerprint readers and retinal scanners, smart cards represent a more secure way for users to gain access to the network. Smart cards are not as secure as most biometric devices, but they are more widely implemented and have a longer history of use (more than 11 years). In fact, there are many companies that issue smart cards and smart card readers, along with Windows Server 2003-compliant drivers and software. Primarily because of several competing standards, smart card adoption has been slow, but their popularity continues to grow and although they might not replace the standard log-on password anytime soon, smart card technology is full of potential.

How Smart Card Authentication Works

After setting up an enrollment station (described below), any user with the enrollment agent certificate can issue smart cards to users. Enrollment is the process by which a CA grants a certificate to the card. The card itself generates a public/private key pair, and the certificate is used to protect the public key during transport. After enrollment, the user can insert the card at any workstation on the network, including terminal services clients and remote access clients, as long as a smart card reader is present.

If possible, clients logging on to a Windows Server 2003 network will be authenticated with the Kerberos protocol. In traditional authentication, a username and password typed in via the keyboard are used to encrypt communication between the client and the Key Distribution Center (KDC). With smart cards, however, the private key stored in the card digitally automatically signs the timestamp that is sent to the KDC, eliminating the need for a password. In addition to the encrypted timestamp, the card's certificate (including of course the card's public key) is sent as well. When the KDC receives the package, known as a ticket-granting ticket (TGT) request, it verifies the public key and then uses the public key to verify the digital signature on the request. If everything checks out, the server authenticates the client by returning a ticket that is also encrypted with the card's public key. Finally, the ticket is decrypted at the client's workstation by the private key stored in the smart card.

Deploying Smart Card Logon

Even though smart cards have been around for some time, many different standards still exist. This can complicate the deployment of a smart card solution, especially if Windows Server 2003 does not natively support the hardware you've chosen; in that case, several extra steps are required. Windows Server 2003, out of the box, contains drivers for two companies that manufacture smart cards and readers – Schlumberger and Gemplus. For any other vendor's equipment, you'll need to install drivers and the CSP that the vendor uses.

The first step in deployment is to prepare the appropriate certificate templates. These templates include the following:

- Enrollment agent
- Smart card logon
- Smart card user certificates

The templates are not enabled by default and require some configuration.

The second step is to issue the enrollment agent certificate. Finally, the smart cards need to be enrolled at the enrollment station. We'll guide you through the step-by-step deployment process later in this chapter.

Smart Card Readers

Most smart card readers in today's market attach to the computer's USB or serial port. USB equipment is strongly recommended if your clients have USB ports. Readers are available in external or internal models, and many cost less than fifty dollars at retail. Readers that are built into a keyboard are also gaining in popularity. Make certain that the readers you choose will read the kind of smart card you plan on issuing.

Smart Card Enrollment Station

The enrollment station you choose should be a secure system and must be running Windows 2000 or higher. Of course a smart card reader must be installed, and appropriate drivers and CSPs loaded if necessary. Finally, you should install any vendor-supplied utility software.

Using Smart Cards To Log On to Windows

Smart cards can be used for more than secure authentication. In fact, there are two different templates in Windows Server 2003 that are both used for smart card certificates. The first is the smart card log-on certificate, which, as the name implies, is used only for logons. The second is the smart card user certificate, which, in addition to logons, provides secure e-mail services. For the following example, you'll use the more common of the two, which is the smart card logon certificate. You will have to have a PKI implemented with at least one CA already running before beginning. You will also need a smart card reader and a smart card to complete this example.

Implement and Use Smart Cards

1. On the system acting as the CA, log on as an administrator and open the Certification Authority console by clicking **Start | Programs | Administrative Tools | Certification Authority**.

2. Expand the appropriate CA container, right-click **Certificate Templates**, and choose **New | Certificate Template to Issue**.

3. Select **Smartcard Logon** and click **OK**. Repeat step 2 and select **Enrollment Agent** and then click **OK**.

4. Right-click **Certificate Templates** and choose **Manage**. This displays the Certificate Template snap-in.

5. Right-click the **Smartcard Logon** template and choose **Properties**. Click the **Security** tab.

6. For this example, assign the administrator the role of enrollment agent. Add the **Administrator** by clicking the **Add** button. After selecting the **Administrator**, select the **Read** and **Enroll** check boxes. Click **OK** to finish. Close the console.

7. Log on to the enrollment station system as an administrator. Click **Start | Run**, type **certmgr.msc**, and then click **OK**. This launches the **Certificates** snap-in.

8. Expand the **Personal** container, right-click **Certificates**, and choose **All Tasks | Request New Certificate**. Proceed past the **Certificate Request Wizard**'s opening screen by click **Next**.

9. The next screen shows the **Certificate Types** screen. Choose **Enrollment Agent** and click **Next**. On the next screen, do not type anything in for the **Certificate Friendly Name** and **Description** fields. These fields are optional, and you will not use friendly names or their descriptions in this example. Click **Next**, and then click **Finish**. A message appears when the certificate has been issued. Close the console.

10. You will now use a certificate-requesting technique similar to one in a previous example , but with more advanced options. Launch **Internet Explorer** and type **http://*servername*/certsrv** in the **Address** bar, where *servername* is the server name of the CA you used in step 1.

11. Click **Request a certificate** and then click **Advanced certificate request** on the next screen.

12. Figure 24.13 shows the **Advanced Certificate Request** screen. Click **Request a certificate for a smart card on behalf of another user by using the smart card certificate enrollment station**.

Figure 24.13 Advanced Certificate Request Screen

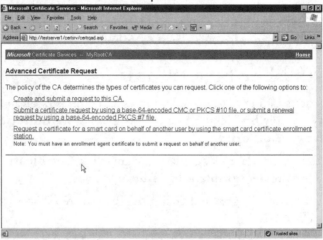

13. Figure 24.14 shows the Smart Card Certificate Enrollment Station screen. Select **Smartcard Logon** from the **Certificate Template** drop-down box.

Figure 24.14 Smart Card Certificate Enrollment Station Screen

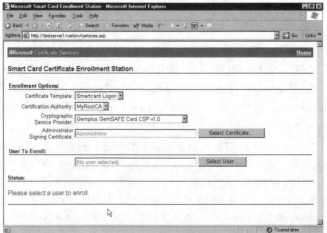

14. Select the CA used in step 1 from the **Certification Authority** drop-down box.

15. Select the appropriate CSP from the **Cryptographic Service Provider** drop-down box.

16. Click the **Select User** button and choose the user you are enrolling.

17. Place the smart card into the attached reader and click **Enroll**.

18. The CSP will now enable you to enter a PIN for the card. Enter the PIN and click **OK**.

19. Distribute the card to the user for testing.

Using Smart Cards for Remote Access VPNs

To use smart cards to log on to a remote access VPN server, the server must first be configured to enable it. This includes selecting a protocol, as discussed below. It also includes obtaining a machine certificate for the VPN server. When the server is able to accept smart card certificates, the client must be configured to send them. This means attaching a smart card reader and establishing a VPN connection. If you view the Properties of the client's VPN connection, you will notice a **Networking** and a **Security** tab. For smart card use, the type of VPN selected under the **Network** tab should be the Level 2 Tunneling Protocol, or L2TP.

The **Security** tab, shown in Figure 24.15, is a bit more complex. There are two options, **Typical** and **Advanced**.

Figure 24.15 Security Tab of the VPN Client's Properties Sheet

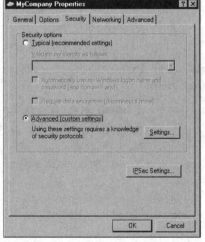

Choose **Advanced** (**custom settings)** and click the **Settings** button. Choose the **Use Extensible Authentication Protocol (EAP)** option and select **Smart Card or other certificate (encryption enabled)** from the drop-down box. Click the **Properties** button and the **Smart Card or Other Certificates** dialog box appears, as shown in Figure 24.16. Choose the **Use my smart card** option. Your configuration of the VPN client is now complete.

Figure 24.16 Smart Card or Other Certificate Properties Sheet

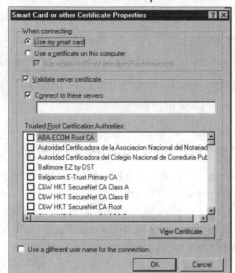

Using Smart Cards To Log On to a Terminal Server

Using smart cards to log on to a terminal server is inherently more secure than using passwords, as we've discussed previously. Similar to using a smart card on a local workstation, using a smart card on a terminal client enables the server to verify your identity and give you appropriate access. Also, if you want the information contained in the card to be available for the entire terminal session, perform the following steps:

1. Click **Start | Programs** or **All Programs | Accessories | Communications | Remote Desktop Connection**.

2. Click **Options** and proceed to the **Local Resources** tab.

3. Under **Local Devices**, click the **Smart Card** option and click **Connect**.

Chapter 25

Planning, Implementing, Maintaining Routing and Remote Access

In this chapter:

☑ **Planning the Remote Access Strategy**

☑ **Addressing Dial-In Access Design Considerations**

☑ **Configuring the Windows Server 2003 Dial-up RAS Server**

☑ **Configuring RRAS Packet Filters**

☑ **Addressing VPN Design Considerations**

☑ **PPP Multilink and Bandwidth Allocaiton Protocol (BAP)**

☑ **Addressing Wireless Remote Access Design Considerations**

☑ **Planning Remote Access Security**

☑ **Configuring Wireless Security Protocols**

☑ **RRAS NAT Services**

☑ **ICMP Routher Discover**

☑ **Creating Remote Access Policies**

☑ **Troubleshooting Remote Access Client Connections**

☑ **Troubleshooting Remote Access Server Connections**

☑ **Configuring Internet Authentication Services**

Introduction

In this chapter, we will explore planning, configuring and maintaining routing and remote access. We will explore the Routing and Remote Access Service (RRAS) for Windows Server 2003 along with the protocols used to support remote access. One of the key protocols used in dial-up and VPN environments is Point-to-Point Protocol (PPP). We will look at PPP and special features available to PPP connections in Windows Server 2003.

We will also look examine some of the features used to implement network security for Windows Server 2003. We'll look at designing and implementing wireless networking and how to secure wireless communications.

We'll conduct an analysis of the Windows Server 2003 RRAS policy configuration and packet filter implementation. Because most internal systems today do not have a sufficient number of public IP addresses, we will discuss RRAS Network Address Translation (NAT) services. Finally, because even the best of intentions do not always go according to plan, we will look at troubleshooting remote access client and server configurations followed by a thorough review of Microsoft's implementation of Remote Access Dial-in User Service (RADIUS), also known as Internet Authentication Service (IAS) in the Microsoft world.

Planning the Remote Access Strategy

Even if your network is small, chances are you have a need for remote access, whether it be for traveling employees, telecommuters, or remote branches. You can choose from several methods of remote access, including dial-in access, VPN access through the Internet, and wireless networking. Which methods you support and how you configure them will depend on the needs of your organization and its individual users.

Analyzing Organizational Needs

Different organizations have different needs in a remote access strategy. The following are some of the organizational needs you might need to address:

- Security of dial-in and VPN connections

- Availability of modems and connections

- Determining which resources or subnets must be reached remotely

- Deermining whether existing network servers can adapt to provide remote access

Analyzing User Needs

You also need to consider the needs of individual users when planning a strategy for remote access. The following are some needs you may have to address:

- The bandwidth requirements of users, and what their modems or connections can support

- How frequently users need to connect to the network and how critical network availability is

- The types of operating systems and computers used by clients
- Whether clients have existing Internet connections that could be used for VPN access

Selecting Remote Access Types To Allow

When planning which types of remote access to allow, you should consider how they meet your organization's needs and the needs of the users, the expense and administrative effort involved in implementing each one, and their relative levels of security. In the next sections, we'll look in more detail at those aspects of each of the remote access types mentioned earlier: dial-in, VPN, and wireless.

Dial-In

The traditional method of remote access uses a pool of modems and a server running the Routing and Remote Access (RRAS) service. Although there are popular alternatives, such as VPN access, modems still have some advantages. Because they do not communicate via the Internet, modem transmissions are often more secure and less prone to interception. If bandwidth is not an issue, modems can provide a consistent, low-cost solution.

Dial-in access typically uses PPP (point-to-point protocol) for communication. This is an Internet-standard protocol for dial-in connections. PPP supports a negotiation process that authenticates and authorizes the user and can also assign an IP address, DNS server addresses, and other critical configuration elements for remote access.

VPN

A VPN (virtual private network) uses encryption to create a virtual connection, or tunnel, between a remote node and your network, using a public network such as the Internet. VPN access has a number of advantages over dial-in remote access including speed, ability to work with large amounts of data and the increasing availability of Internet access.

While VPN access is theoretically less secure than a dial-up connection, because data is transmitted over a public network, Windows Server 2003 supports strong levels of encryption to minimize this risk. You can also mandate a level of encryption so that clients that do not support your minimum encryption level cannot connect to the network.

Wireless Remote Access

Wireless network access is rapidly becoming more popular as a facet of remote access strategies. Wireless networks using the 802.11 standard enable a number of wireless users to connect to your network by connecting to a wireless access point, or WAP. The 802.11 standards do allow for security, but many wireless networks are not configured for maximum security, and allowing wireless access is always a security risk. You should plan for wireless access when your users will be within range of a WAP but without access to a wired connection, and when security is not the highest priority.

Addressing Dial-In Access Design Considerations

When you plan a system for dial-in access, you need to consider a number of factors, including: how IP addresses are assigned, the number and type of incoming ports to configure and security and administration procedures.

Allocating IP Addresses

When clients connect to RRAS, whether through a dial-in or VPN connection, the RRAS server assigns each client an IP address. You can configure the RRAS server to allocate IP addresses from a static address pool, to use DHCP or Automatic Private IP Addressing (APIPA).

Static Address Pools

You can configure the RRAS server to assign IP addresses from a static pool of addresses specified in the RRAS server's configuration. This requires a range of addresses that are dedicated for this purpose. Although this is often the simplest approach, keep these considerations in mind:

- Make sure the static address pool does not overlap the range of addresses assigned by a DHCP server. Two machines with the same address will cause a conflict and a loss of connection for both.

- If you are using multiple RRAS servers with separate modem pools, you will need to define a static address pool for each one and make sure there are no conflicts between the ranges you assign.

- Be sure the address pool includes at least as many addresses as there are modems for incoming connections.

You can also assign a static address for a single user, group, or a particular type of connection using a remote access policy.

Using DHCP for Addressing

Rather than using a static address pool, you can configure the RRAS server to request IP addresses from a DHCP (Dynamic Host Configuration Protocol) server. If you are using DHCP to assign addresses in the network already, this technique allows you to assign remote client addresses from the same address pool and eliminate the possibility of address conflicts. It also makes it easy to manage addressing with multiple RRAS servers, because you can configure them to use the same DHCP server.

Using APIPA

Finally, you can configure the RRAS server to assign addresses using Automatic Private IP Addressing (APIPA). This system uses private addresses in the range of 169.254.0.1 through 169.254.255.254, a range reserved for use by Windows networks, and is usually used when a DHCP server is unavailable. APIPA provides some of the advantages of DHCP without a dedicated server, but is usually only suitable for small networks.

If you enable the DHCP option on the RRAS server but a DHCP server is unavailable on the network, it will automatically use APIPA to issue addresses to remote clients. Clients must be configured to obtain an IP address when they connect, rather than with a specific IP address, to use this feature.

Determining Incoming Port Needs

When you are designing a dial-in remote access solution, one of the most important considerations is the number of incoming ports (modems) you will need. The following are some of the factors you should take into account:

- An estimate of the number of users who will need to concurrently access the network remotely. Keep in mind that a single user who requires access for several hours a day will require an additional modem for reliable access, but several users who use the network for only a few minutes at a time could be easily served by a single modem.

- The bandwidth available on the RAS server's connection to the LAN. If the bandwidth of all the modems combined approaches this limit, dial-in users will experience slow connections.

- The number of IP addresses available. If an address pool or DHCP server is out of addresses, additional modems will not allow additional users.

Multilink and BAP

Another factor that can affect the number of incoming ports you will need is whether you will be supporting multilink connections. This is a Windows Server 2003 feature that enables two or more ports on the RRAS server to be connected to a single client and combined into a higher-bandwidth connection.

For example, if a client connects with two 56K modems and multilink enabled, their bandwidth with a perfect connection would be 112K. In practice, if you've spent time trying to get a single modem to work at 56K, you can imagine how unlikely this best-case scenario is, and few client computers have two modems installed. Nonetheless, multilink is sometimes the cheapest way to get a high-bandwidth connection. Multilink is also often used to combine two 64K ISDN channels into a single 128K connection.

Windows Server 2003 also supports BAP (bandwidth allocation protocol). This is a system that automatically disconnects one or more ports from a multilink connection if it is using only a small percentage of its capacity. This enables you to make the best use of multiple ports without relying on users to reconfigure their connections.

You can configure multilink and BAP settings as part of a dial-in profile. Remote access policies and profiles are described in detail later in this chapter. The **Multilink** settings tab for a dial-in profile enables you to enable or disable multilink and BAP and change their settings, as shown in Figure 25.1.

Figure 25.1 Multilink Options

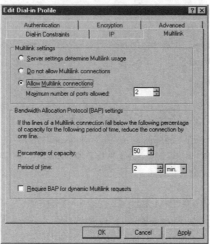

Selecting an Administrative Model

There are two basic ways for you to control remote access to your network. You can configure individual user accounts to allow or disallow remote access, or configure one or more remote access policies to control access based on users, groups, times of day, and many other criteria.

Access by User

You can allow or disallow remote access from the **Dial-in** tab of a user's **Properties** dialog box in the **Active Directory Users and Computers** console.

Access by Policy

You can also configure one or more Remote Access Policies for precise control of which users can reach the network through remote access. Whether a user is affected by policies depends on the setting you choose in the Dial-in tab of the user's Properties dialog box:

- **Allow access:** The user is allowed remote access regardless of policy settings.
- **Deny access:** The user is denied remote access regardless of policy settings.
- **Control access through Remote Access Policy:** Allows a Remote Access Policy to control whether the user has access.

Configuring the Windows 2003 Dial-up RRAS Server

Dial-up connectivity is generally provided through the Point-to-Point Protocol (PPP). PPP will be discussed later in this chapter. First, let's look at how an RRAS Dial-up server fits into a Windows Server 2003 network. The dial-up scenario using analog phone lines is most typically for local phone calls to the corporate office. To configure a RRAS Dial-up server, open **Routing and Remote Access** from **Administrative Tools.** Right-click the server name and select **Configure and Enable Routing and Remote Access.** This will launch the **Routing and Remote Access Server Setup Wizard.** The Setup Wizard will prompt you to enter the configuration information to easily setup a simple RRAS Dial-up server.

Configuring RRAS Packet Filters

Routing and Remote Access packet filters provide network security by controlling certain types of network traffic into or out of your LAN. RRAS packet filters are applied through the Routing and Remote Access Service MMC on a per-interface basis. RRAS packet filters work on an exception basis. This means that the filters can do either of the following:

- Allow all traffic except that specified in the filter
- Deny all traffic except that specified by the filter

Packet filtering rules are a vital part of security in the Windows Server 2003 remote access network environment. You can use the following steps to configure RRAS packet filtering.

Figure 25.2 RRAS Network to Be Filtered

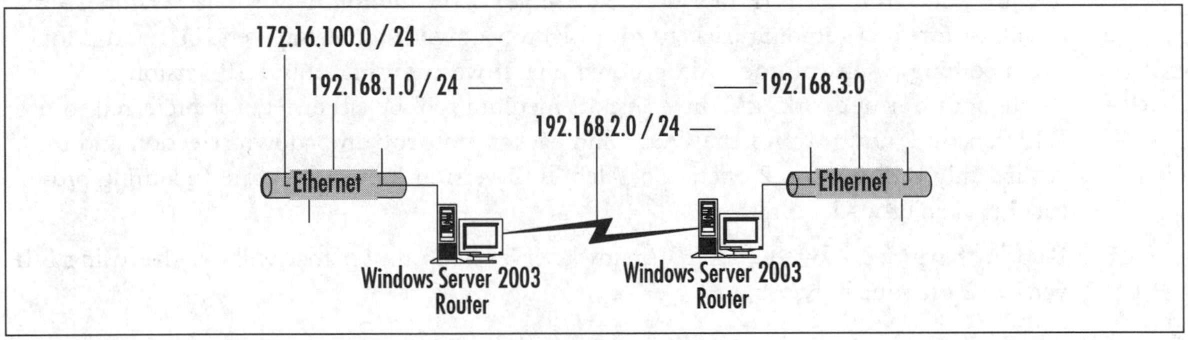

RRAS Packet Filter Configuration

In this example, we will configure inbound and outbound packet filters. We will configure the LAN interface to allow only traffic from the 192.168.0.0/16 series of networks. Figure 25.2 shows the network that we are configuring. To start our configuration, we will configure a basic RIP version 2 network.

1. Start by opening Routing and Remote Access by selecting **Start | Programs | Administrative Tools | Routing and Remote Access.**

2. From the Routing and Remote Access management console, right-click the server name and select **Configure and Enable Routing and Remote Access**. If this option is grayed out, select Disable Routing and Remote Access to start with a fresh configuration.

3. On the first page of the Routing and Remote Access Server Setup Wizard, click **Next**.

4. Select **Custom Configuration** and click **Next**.

5. Select **LAN Routing** followed by **Next**, and then select **Finish**. A message box will display asking if you would like to enable the Routing and Remote Access Service. Select **OK** to enable LAN routing.

6. Now that the Routing and Remote Access Service is enabled, we have to configure RIP v2.

7. In the left pane, select IP Routing. Right-click **General** and select **New Routing Protocol**.

8. On the next screen, select **RIP Version 2** for Internet Protocol and click **OK**.

9. Now an entry for RIP will be displayed in the left pane beneath the IP Routing icon. This means that RIP is enabled on the server but at this point, RIP will not advertise any routes because we have to tell RIP which interfaces to use for route advertisement.

10. In the left pane, right-click **RIP** and select **New Interface….**

11. From the New Interface for RIP Version 2 for Internet Protocol dialog box, select the interface that provides the common link between the routers as shown in Figure 25.2. In this case, the common interface has been named WAN.

12. The default setting for RIP in a Windows Server 2003 environment is Rip version 2 broadcast for the Outgoing packet protocol: drop-down list and Rip version 1 and 2 for the Incoming packet protocol: drop-down box. If we are using only RIP version 2 throughout our network, and the transport medium will be Ethernet, it is preferred to use RIP version 2 multicast for the Outbound packet protocol: drop-down selection and to ensure only RIP version 2 operation, select RIP version 2 only from the Incoming protocol packet: drop-down list.

13. Repeat this process for the other Windows Server 2003 router that will be advertising RIP version 2 on your network.

In our example, we have configured another network at 172.16.100.0/24. This is the network we wish to block using the packet filters. The direct approach would be to specifically block this network. We intend to block all network traffic except for our current network addresses. We will begin with the **Routing and Remote Access** management console to configure the packet filters for inbound and outbound traffic.

1. Before we begin filtering, verify connectivity to the 172.16.100.0/24 network by pinging the 172.16.100.3 interface from your server.

2. We intend to block all traffic except traffic to and from the 192.168.1.0, 192.168.2.0, and 192.168.3.0 networks. To accomplish this, we will apply inbound and outbound packet filters on our WAN interface. Select **General** under the **IP Routing** icon in the left pane of the management console.

3. Right-click the **WAN** interface in the right pane of the management console and select **Properties**.

4. Under the **General** tab of the **WAN Properties** dialog box, select the **Inbound Filters...** button.

5. The inbound filters should allow traffic coming from the 192.168.2.0 and 192.168.3.0 networks only. We will add those networks as source networks for the inbound filter. Select **New** from the **Inbound Filters** dialog box. Then, select the **Source Network** check box and enter **192.168.2.0** for the **IP address:** and **255.255.255.0** for the **Subnet mask:** as shown in Figure 25.3.

Figure 25.3 Adding an Inbound Filter

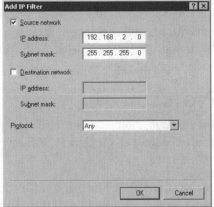

6. Click **OK** to add the first filter to the inbound filter list.

7. Repeat this process for the 192.168.3.0 network. Select **New** from the **Inbound Filters** dialog box. Then, select the **Source Network** check box and enter **192.168.3.0** for the **IP address:** and **255.255.255.0** for the **Subnet mask:**.

8. Change the **Filter Action** to **Drop all packets except those that meet the criteria below** and click **OK**.

9. We will now configure **Outbound Filters** in the same fashion that we just configured the **Inbound Filters**. Select the **Outbound Filters...** button. The outbound filters should allow traffic going to the 192.168.2.0 and 192.168.3.0 networks only. We will add those networks as destination networks for the outbound filter. Select **New** from the **Outbound Filters** dialog box. Then, select the **Destination Network** check box and enter **192.168.2.0** for the **IP address:** and **255.255.255.0** for the **Subnet mask:**.

10. Repeat step number 9 for the 192.168.3.0 network. Select **New** from the **Outbound Filters** dialog box. Then, select the **Destination Network** check box and enter **192.168.3.0** for the **IP address:** and **255.255.255.0** for the **Subnet mask:**.

11. Change the **Filter Action** to **Drop all packets except those that meet the criteria below** and click **OK**.

12. From the **WAN Properties** dialog box, click **OK** to complete the configuration.

13. To verify your configuration, test connectivity to the 172.16.100.0/24 network by pinging the 172.16.100.3 interface from your server.

Addressing VPN Design Considerations

Rather than using individual modem or ISDN ports for remote access, you can configure a VPN (virtual private network) and enable any number of connections through the Internet. A VPN uses an encrypted tunnel to create a secure virtual connection and transmit private data over the public network.

Although using a VPN for remote access does not require any special hardware beyond an Internet connection for clients and the RRAS server, there are still a number of choices you must make when planning a VPN strategy. These include the VPN protocols you will support, the need for machine certificates, IP filtering, and remote access policies.

Selecting VPN Protocols

A VPN connection is created through the use of a tunneling protocol, (sometimes called a VPN protocol), supported by both the client and the server. Windows Server 2003 supports two tunneling protocols:

- **PPTP** (point-to-point tunneling protocol) is an Internet standard for VPN connections based on PPP (point-to-point protocol). PPTP uses the MPPE (Microsoft Point-to-Point Encryption) system to encrypt data.

- **L2TP** (layer 2 tunneling protocol) is a newer standard for a tunneling protocol, developed in cooperation between Microsoft and Cisco. L2TP is used with IPSec (IP Security) to provide encryption.

You can support one or both of these VPN protocols in your remote access strategy. Which protocols you support depends on the needs of clients, the requirements for public-key security, and whether you need the higher-security features of L2TP. These considerations are discussed in the following sections.

Client Support

Of course, a major factor in deciding which tunneling protocols you should support is the protocols supported by the client machines. The following is a summary of the VPN tunneling protocol support of Windows clients:

- **PPTP** is supported by Windows 95, Windows 98, Windows ME, Windows NT 4.0 and later, Windows 2000, Windows XP, and Windows Server 2003.
- **L2TP** is supported by Windows 2000, Windows XP, and Windows Server 2003.

If you are supporting non-Windows clients, you should determine which VPN protocols they support. The easiest way to support a wide variety of clients is to enable both VPN protocols at the server level; clients that support L2TP will use it, and other clients will use PPTP.

Data Integrity and Sender Authentication

The IPSec encryption used with L2TP supports two features that are not available with PPTP and MPPE encryption, along with the data confidentiality that is provided by both encryption protocols. You should make sure your network supports L2TP if you require either of the following:

- **Data integrity** L2TP over IPSec verifies the integrity of data by using hash algorithms (checksums).
- **Sender authentication** IPSec provides mutual authentication for the client computer and VPN server. This authentication is based by PKI (public key infrastructure) certificates and is in addition to the user authentication handled by protocols such as MS-CHAP v2 and EAP-TLS.

PKI Requirements

To support L2TP over IPSec for VPN connections, you need to install computer certificates at both the VPN server and the clients. If you do not have an existing certificate server configured on the network, this might require additional planning and configuration. PPTP does not require a PKI at all and is the only choice if you do not wish to install certificates.

Installing Machine Certificates

To use IPSec with L2TP, you need to install computer certificates at each client for encryption. Windows 2000 and Windows Server 2003 support auto-enrollment, a feature that automatically distributes certificates to computers the first time they connect to the network. If you are not using auto-enrollment, you can manually request a certificate for the computer. You can do this using the Certificates MMC snap-in or by connecting to the certificate server with a Web browser.

If you do not have a certification authority (CA) on the network, you can install Certificate Services on a domain controller.

Configuring Firewall Filters

Because a VPN server is connected to the Internet, it is often used in conjunction with a software or hardware firewall to prevent unauthorized traffic from the Internet from reaching the internal network. You can arrange the firewall and VPN server in one of two ways:

- The VPN server is directly connected to the Internet and the firewall separates it from the internal network.
- The firewall is connected to the Internet and the VPN server is behind the firewall.

Figure 25.4 shows these two configurations.

Figure 25.4 Firewall Configurations

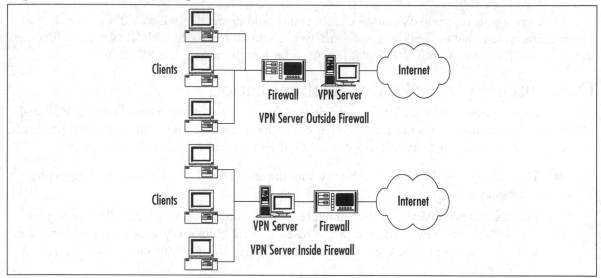

The more common of the two arrangements is to connect the firewall to the Internet and keep the VPN server behind the firewall. In this scenario, you set up packet filters to allow all VPN traffic through the firewall. Since the VPN connection between the client and server handles authentication and security itself, this does not represent a security risk.

PPP Multilink and Bandwidth Allocation Protocol (BAP)

The Point-to-Point Protocol (PPP) provides encapsulation, authentication, and encryption functions for remote access connectivity. Most VPN and remote access technology today is built upon PPP or extensions of this protocol. One of the many features of PPP is Multilink. PPP is generally used for different types of dial-up connections. Sometimes, there is an advantage to providing a single virtual link that encompasses multiple physical links, like the B-channels on an ISDN connection.

Since ISDN has traditionally been billed per usage, and analog long distance phone calls are also typically billed per usage, maintaining the virtual link when the bandwidth requirements are low could prove costly. Multilink itself does not include provisions to monitor the connection requirements. Enter Bandwidth Allocation Protocol (BAP). BAP adds features to PPP and Multilink to monitor the connection requirements and to adjust accordingly. If our ISDN link does not need the bandwidth provided through two B-channels, BAP will drop one of the two connections, based on our configuration settings. If the bandwidth requirements increase and the single B-channel in use cannot provide sufficient bandwidth, BAP will connect the second B-channel to double our bandwidth capabilities. This same configuration could include two analog phone lines at each end of the connection as opposed to the 2B+D ISDN configuration for Multilink. In order to take advantage of the capabilities of BAP, the remote access client and server must support BAP and have it enabled.

PPP Multilink Protocol

The PPP Multilink Protocol must be enabled on both the remote access client and the remote access server. PPP Multilink is enabled on the remote access server via remote access policy, using the Routing and Remote Access Service management console or the Internet Authentication Service (IAS). The nature of multilink requires dialing to multiple devices or endpoints. To enable Multilink on a remote access client, you must enable multiple device dialing on the client system through the **Network and Dial-up Connections** folder. Again, if unlimited connectivity is not available, the nature of Multilink presents cost prohibitive problems due to the lack of provisions to link and unlink extra physical connections on an as-needed basis.

BAP Protocols

To facilitate dynamic allocation of links for Multilink, Microsoft provides dynamic BAP. Dynamic BAP is a series of interrelated protocols. Dynamic BAP consists of the following protocols:

- Bandwidth Allocation Protocol (BAP)
- Bandwidth Allocation Control Protocol (BACP)
- Extensions to the Link Control Protocol (LCP)

BAP provides additional links on an as-needed basis, in response to specific configuration settings. BAP is the control mechanism used in dynamic BAP. BAP automatically will initiate a connection with your second modem to increase your available bandwidth to 112kbps (56kbps+56kbps) when needed. Once the bandwidth requirement drops below a predetermined setting for a predetermined amount of time, the second modem will disconnect.

BACP works in conjunction with BAP, utilizing the same mechanism as PPP's Link Control Protocol to provide connection control in a dynamic BAP environment. The sole purpose of BACP is to provide a negotiated, favored peer whose requests are implemented during a request to add or drop a connection.

PPP provides connections for upper layer protocols through the Link Control Protocol. Extensions to LCP are an integral part of dynamic BAP, just as they are with any other implementation or PPP. To transport TCP/IP traffic over an analog dial-up connection, Internet Protocol Connection Protocol (IPCP), an extension of LCP, carries the IP traffic through the PPP connection. Likewise, to carry IPX/SPX traffic over a PPP connection, Internetwork Packet Exchange Control Protocol (IPXCP) provides the connection between the PPP endpoints and the IPX/SPX client. This encapsulation of upper layer data is commonly known as *tunneling*.

Multilink with BAP support is implemented through the Routing and Remote Access management console and it is enabled by default. BAP is enabled via **Routing and Remote Access** in **Administrative Tools.** Once you select the server, right click and select **Properties**. On the **PPP** tab, select **the Dynamic bandwidth control using BAP and BACP** checkbox. Multilink is enabled within the Routing and Remote Access applet and selecting Remote Access Policies. Select the remote access policy to modify, click **Edit Profile** and configure the specifics of the Multilink policy on the **Multilink** tab.

Addressing Wireless Remote Access Design Considerations

Wireless networks are fast becoming one of the most common network types. Although they are not cost-effective or efficient as a replacement for wired networking, wireless networks are a great choice for temporary networks, networking in areas where networking is normally difficult, or offering wireless access to customers or employees with portable computers.

Windows Server 2003's RRAS server can be used to manage wireless connections to the network. If you will be allowing wireless access, you will need to do the following:

- Configure remote access policies.

- Determine whether to use IAS for authentication.

- Configure the WAPs.

The 802.11 Wireless Standards

Today's wireless networks generally use one of the standards developed by the IEEE under the 802.11 working group and based on the original 802.11 protocol, which supported speeds of 2 Mbps in the 2.4 GHz radio spectrum. The newer standards support higher speeds and are popularly known as *Wi-Fi*. There are three current versions of 802.11 that define different wireless standards:

- 802.11b was the first standard to be widely accepted. It operates at 11 Mbps and has a range of about 50 meters. It uses the 2.4 GHz spectrum.

- 802.11a appeared in products in 2001. This standard uses the 5 GHz spectrum, has a theoretical maximum speed of 54 Mbps, but does not handle distance and obstacles as well as 802.11b.

- 802.11g is the latest standard, ratified in 2003. It uses the 2.4GHz band and is backward compatible with 802.11b equipment, but supports a theoretical throughput of 54 Mbps.

Using IAS for Wireless Connections

Many WAPs support RADIUS authentication. Because the security of normal wireless authentication with the 802.11 protocols is minimal, using RADIUS provides stronger authentication as well as a centralized source for authentication and accounting for all wireless access. IAS can be used for this purpose.

Because WAPs configured for RADIUS authentication rely on the presence of a RADIUS server, you might need to configure a second IAS server and specify it as a backup server in the WAP configuration. This ensures that wireless users can still connect if the primary IAS server is unavailable. The steps to configure an IAS Server are included at the end of this chapter.

Configuring Remote Access Policies for Wireless Connections

To enable wireless connections, you need a basic remote access policy to allow wireless users. This policy can restrict access to a group, require certificate-based authentication, and/or mandate a high level of encryption. You can use the following steps to create a policy for wireless access.

Create a Policy for Wireless Access

1. From the IAS or RRAS console, select **Remote Access Policies** in the left-hand column.

2. Select **Action | New Remote Access Policy** from the menu.

3. A welcome message is displayed. Click **Next** to continue.

4. The **Policy Configuration Method** dialog box is displayed. Select **Use the wizard to set up a typical policy** and enter **Wireless access** in the policy name field. Click **Next** to continue.

5. The **Access Method** dialog box is displayed. Select **Wireless** and click **Next**.

6. The **User or Group Access** dialog box is displayed. Select **Group** and click **Add**. Enter **Domain Admins** and click **OK**, and then click **Next**.

7. You are prompted to choose an EAP type to allow. Select **Smart card or other certificate** and click **Next**.

8. A completion message is displayed. Click **Finish** to exit the wizard.

Multiple Wireless Access Points

You can support multiple WAPs for wireless access using RRAS or IAS for authentication. Because each access point covers only a limited area, it is common to have multiple WAPs. Keep the following considerations in mind when planning to deal with multiple WAPs:

- IAS authentication will enable all WAPs to use a central server for authentication.

- Each WAP will need to be added to the IAS server's list of clients and configured to use RADIUS authentication.

- There are several variations of the 802.11 protocols and not all devices are compatible. Be sure all WAPs and clients support the same protocols.

Placing CA on VLAN for New Wireless Clients

Wireless clients typically use certificate-based authentication, either using the EAP-TLS protocol with a user certificate or using a certificate stored in a smart card. Each client also needs a computer certificate installed in order to use EAP-TLS authentication. You need to configure a certificate server to issue certificates to wireless clients.

For new clients that might not have a certificate already, one strategy is to create a virtual LAN (VLAN) and place a certification authority (CA) on the VLAN to issue certificates. You can use a remote access policy to restrict new wireless clients to this VLAN so they will be unable to access other network resources and to limit their connection time. After a client successfully connects to the VLAN and is issued a certificate, it can reconnect using the standard wireless access policy and gain full access.

Configuring WAPs as RADIUS Clients

For WAPs to use the IAS server for authentication, you must configure both ends:

- In the IAS MMC snap-in, add each WAP as a RADIUS client.
- In the WAP's configuration, enable RADIUS authentication and specify the IAS server (or both servers, if you have a backup server configured.)

How you configure the WAP varies depending on the hardware in use. Consult the documentation provided by the manufacturer to find out how to do this.

Planning Remote Access Security

Windows Server 2003 includes a number of security features for remote access, including some new features that were not available in Windows 2000. When you plan a strategy for remote access security, you need to take several things into account:

- The functional levels of your domains
- The methods you will use for data encryption and authentication
- Whether you will use advanced security features such as callback security and smart cards

These items are discussed in the following sections.

Domain Functional Level

Domains hosted on Windows Server 2003 computers can have one of several different domain functional levels. The functional level of your domain affects which remote access security features you can use. Depending on your needs, you might need to raise the functional level of the domain to take advantage of new security features.

Selecting Authentication Methods

When a user attempts to connect to a remote access server, one or more protocols are used for authentication, verifying the user's identity. After the user is authenticated, the RRAS server can determine what resources the user is authorized to access.

When you configure a remote access server you can select which authentication methods will be allowed. You should choose authentication methods based on their relative levels of security. Additionally, the methods you choose will depend on the client operating systems and the authentication methods they support.

Disallowing Password-Based Connections (PAP, SPAP, CHAP, MS-CHAP v1)

A number of the available authentication methods use simple user names and passwords for authentication. The simplest of these is PAP (Password Authentication Protocol). In PAP, the client transmits the user's password as unencrypted text. To ensure a secure network, you should disable PAP and SPAP, a variation of the same protocol that is used by Shiva clients.

CHAP (Challenge Handshake Authentication Protocol) improves security by creating an encrypted challenge and enabling the client to create a response using the password. This avoids sending the password over the network. However, CHAP stores passwords using reversible encryption, and is therefore also considered insecure. MS-CHAP v1, Microsoft's adaptation of CHAP, improves security but is superceded by the more secure version 2.

To ensure secure remote access, you should disable the less-secure authentication methods. You can use the following steps to disable password-based authentication.

Disable Password-Based Authentication Methods

1. From the **Start** menu, select **Programs | Administrative Tools | Routing and Remote Access**.
2. Highlight the RRAS server name in the left-hand column.
3. Select **Action | Properties** from the menu.
4. The Properties dialog box is displayed. Click the **Security** tab.
5. The Security properties are displayed. Click the **Authentication Methods** button.
6. The Authentication Methods dialog box is displayed. *Uncheck* the box next to Microsoft encrypted authentication (MS-CHAP).
7. *Uncheck* the box for Encrypted authentication (CHAP).
8. *Uncheck* the boxes next to Shiva Password Authentication Protocol (SPAP) and Unencrypted password (PAP).
9. Click **OK** to exit the Authentication Methods dialog box, and then click **OK** to exit the Properties dialog box and save the changes.

Using RADIUS/IAS vs. Windows Authentication

Windows Server 2003 supports RADIUS, an Internet standard for a centralized server to handle a network's authentication and accounting needs. Internet Access Server (IAS) is Microsoft's implementation of a RADIUS server, and is included with Windows Server 2003 but is not installed by default. You can install it through the **Add/Remove Programs** applet in Control Panel as a Windows component. We'll walk through the steps for setting up an IAS Server at the end of this chapter. When you configure an RRAS server, you can choose one of two authentication methods:

- **Windows Authentication:** The traditional method. Each RRAS server handles authentication itself, and you can configure the authentication methods supported in the Remote Access Policy section of the Routing and Remote Access MMC snap-in. Policies you create for one RRAS server apply only to that server.

- **RADIUS Authentication:** The RRAS server acts as a RADIUS client and contacts an IAS (or RADIUS) server to authenticate users. When RADIUS is in use, you configure authentication methods and other remote access security settings from the Remote Access Policy section of the Internet Access Server MMC-snap-in. The policies you create for the IAS server apply to any RRAS server that authenticates using that server.

Selecting the Data Encryption Level

In a VPN, you can control the level of encryption that is allowed for access. By disallowing unencrypted connections or those that use less-secure encryption, you can decrease the risk of network snooping. You can enable or disable the following levels of encryption:

- **No encryption**: Unencrypted connections, unsuitable for VPN use.

- **Basic encryption**: Encryption with a 40-bit key, considered relatively easy to break.

- **Strong encryption**: Encryption with a 56-bit key. In IPSec, this uses the DES standard for encryption. Although more secure, DES-encrypted data has been demonstrated to be breakable.

- **Strongest encryption**: Encryption with a 128-bit key for MPPE connections, or triple DES (3DES), which uses a 168-bit key (56-bit times three) for IPSec connections.

The Strongest Encryption option might not be available in international versions of Windows Server 2003 or US editions without the High Encryption Pack installed. You can enable or disable these encryption levels using remote access policies. This process is described later in this chapter.

Using Callback Security

Callback security is a high-security system used for dial-in connections. When a client connects to a system using callback, the system disconnects and calls the client back at the client's phone number. There are two variations of callback:

- **Allowing the user to specify the callback number**. This does not provide a high level of security, but does ensure that the client's phone number can be logged and can be used to avoid long-distance charges being incurred by the client.

- **Using a callback number specified by the administrator**. This is very secure because it is difficult to impersonate a valid client, but it requires that a client always connect from the same number.

You can configure callback security as part of a remote access profile.

Managed Connections

For a user to connect to a remote access server via dial-in or VPN, the client computer must have the correct settings configured to match the server. Because this can be a daunting process for administrators, Windows Server 2003 supports two components to simplify the process of managing connections:

- **Connection Manager** is the client software Windows clients use to make a connection to a dial-in server or VPN server. Current versions of Windows include Connection Manager.

- **Connection Manager Administration Kit (CMAK)** is an administrator's tool that enables you to create a customized version of Connection Manager to distribute to clients. The customizations are stored in a dial-in profile and can include settings for your server, phone numbers, and even custom graphics, icons, and help files.

Mandating Operating System/File System

Windows Server 2003 supports a new feature called Network Access Quarantine control. This feature enables you to restrict access to particular operating systems, file systems, and other aspects of the client's configuration. You use a script to accomplish this.

When Quarantine control is enabled, clients can connect normally to the RRAS server and are issued IP addresses. However, when a client first connects, it is put into quarantine mode and allowed only limited access to network resources. A script is then run through Connection Manager on the client machine to determine if the client's configuration matches the requirements. If it does, the quarantine is released and the client gains full access to the network.

Using Smart Cards for Remote Access

Smart cards are typically used with the EAP-TLS authentication method. Because IPSec encryption is used with L2TP VPN connections, smart cards can be used to encrypt a VPN connection that uses L2TP over IPSec. Smart cards are discussed in more detail in the "Planning, Implementing, Maintaining Public Key Infrastructure" chapter.

Configuring Wireless Security Protocols

The IEEE 802.1X standard provides for authenticated network access using either wired Ethernet networks or 802.11 WLANs. Extensible Authentication Protocol (EAP) is an extension to the PPP that provides for modular authentication mechanisms to be employed. EAP supports Kerberos, certificates, tokens, smart cards, and one-time passwords. The 802.1X standards use EAP to provide WLAN networking with a few security options:

- EAP-Transport Layer Security (EAP-TLS)
- EAP-Microsoft Challenge Handshake Authentication Protocol version 2 (EAP-MS-CHAP v2)
- Protected EAP (PEAP)

EAP-TLS uses certificates to provide the strongest authentication available using Windows Server 2003. Certificate-based security relies on a special text file or certificate. EAP-MS-CHAP v2 supports password-based authentication of the user, the client computer, and the server. This method of authentication is not as strong as EAP-TLS due to the inherent weakness of password-based security. EAP-MS-CHAP v2 authentication requires proof of knowledge of the user's password to be demonstrated by the client and the server.

PEAP relies on TLS to provide several enhancements to EAP. PEAP authenticates servers to prevent the use of rogue access points. Also, PEAP has provisions for session caching, which allows fast reconnection while wireless users roam between access points. PEAP provides a special encryption conduit to protect other EAP processes running within PEAP.

Windows Server 2003 wireless networking relies on Active Directory-based wireless network policies. To configure the Active Directory-based wireless network policies, open the **Active Directory Users and Computers** management console and navigate to the **Wireless Network (IEEE 802.111) Policies** as follows:

1. Click **Start | Programs | Administrative Tools | Active Directory Users and Computers**.

2. In the left pane, right-click the domain or organizational unit for which you want to set Group Policy.

3. Select **Properties**, and then click the **Group Policy** tab.

4. Select **Edit** and open the Group Policy object that you want to edit. If you will be creating a new policy, click **New** to create a new Group Policy object, and then click **Edit**.

5. In the left pane, click **Computer Configuration | Windows Settings | Security Settings | Wireless Network (IEEE 802.11) Policies**.

Now we need to configure the actual policy settings. Windows Server 2003 provides a wizard to walk us through the configuration settings for the policy.

1. Right-click **Wireless Network (IEEE 802.11) Policies** and select **Create Wireless Network Policy**. Click **Next** on the Welcome page of the Wizard.

2. **The Wireless Network (IEEE 802.11) Policy** wizard requests a policy name and description. Name the policy by typing a unique name in the **Name** field. Provide a description of the wireless network policy by typing a description in the **Description** field. The description should contain something such as the groups or domains the policy affects.

3. Click **Next** and leave the **Edit properties** check box.

4. Click **Finish** to complete the initial wireless network policy configuration and to open the **Domain Wireless Network Policy Properties** dialog box.

5. Specify how often Active Directory is to be polled for updates by typing a value in **Check for policy changes every number minutes**.

6. Specify the type of wireless network that clients can access by clicking a network type in the **Networks to access** list. Choices include any available network (access point pre-

ferred), access point (infrastructure) networks only, or computer to computer (ad hoc) networks only.

7. If you want to allow client systems to dictate wireless network settings, select the **Use Windows to configure wireless network settings for clients** check box. This is the default setting. If, instead, you wish to prevent clients from using Windows to configure their wireless network settings, clear the **Use Windows to configure wireless network settings for clients** check box.

8. If clients will be allowed to connect to available networks that do not appear on the Preferred Networks tab, select the **Automatically connect to non-preferred networks** check box. If, instead, you wish to ensure that clients connect only to networks that appear on the Preferred Networks tab, clear the **Automatically connect to non-preferred networks** check box (cleared by default).

9. Preferred Networks may be configured from the **Preferred Networks** tab.

10. Click **Add** to add a preferred network.

11. In the **Network name (SSID)** box, enter a unique name.

12. In the **Description** box, enter a description of the wireless network.

13. From the **Wireless network key (WEP)** box, specify network encryption and authentication by configuring the following check boxes:

    ■ **Data encryption (WEP enabled)** setting will require a network key to be used for encryption.

    ■ **Network authentication (Shared mode)** setting will require that a network key be used for authentication. Not selecting this option means that a network key is not required for authentication. In this configuration, the network will operate in open system mode.

    ■ **The key is provided automatically** setting determines whether a network key is automatically provided for clients.

14. To configure the network to operate as a computer-to-computer (ad hoc) network, click **This is a computer-to-computer (ad hoc) network; wireless access points are not used check box**. The **Move Up** and **Move Down** buttons provide capabilities to change the preferred network search order.

15. The **IEEE 802.1x** tab provides configuration options for 802.1x—a port-based network access control.

16. Click **OK | OK**. Close the Group Policy Editor by clicking on the **X** in the upper right corner of the **Group Policy Editor** management console. Click **OK** to close the domain properties dialog box. Close **Active Directory Users and Computers** by clicking the **X** in the upper-right corner of the **Active Directory Users and Computers** management console.

Following the steps below, you can configure a client and server to use 802.11 wireless networking. The recommended best-practice for wireless networking in a Microsoft environment is to configure IAS/RADIUS to centralize authentication for the wireless access points used in the network. The instructions for IAS installation and configuration listed here are just specific enough to meet the requirements for wireless networking. EAP-TLS is the recommended authentication protocol for wireless networking. EAP-TLS requires installation of a certificate on the IAS server. Begin by installing a certificate for the IAS server. It is recommended that you use the automatic certificate allocation feature available through Active Directory Group Policy.

Configure Wireless Networking

1. Open Active Directory Users and Computers. **Start | Administrative Tools | Active Directory Users and Computers.**

2. In the left pane, double-click **Active Directory Users and Computers**, then right-click the domain name where your CA exists, and then click **Properties**.

3. On the **Group Policy** tab, click **Default Domain Policy**, and then click **Edit**.

4. In the left pane, click **Computer Configuration | Windows Settings | Security Settings | Public Key Policies.**

5. In the right pane, right-click Automatic Certificate Request Settings, point to **New**, and then click **Automatic Certificate Request.**

6. From the **Automatic Certificate Request** wizard, click **Next**.

7. In **Certificate templates**, click **Computer** as seen in Figure 25.5, and then click **Next**.

Figure 25.5 Specifying Computer Certificates

8. Your enterprise root CA appears on the list.

9. Click the CA, click **Next**, and then click **Finish**.

10. To create a computer certificate for the CA computer, type the following at the command prompt: **gpupdate /target:Computer**.

11. Install the IAS Windows component through **Add or Remove Programs**. **Start | Settings | Control Panel | Add or Remove Programs**. Click the **Windows Components** icon in the left side of the applet.

12. From the **Windows Components Wizard** dialog box, click **Networking Services**, then select **Details**.

13. From the **Networking Services** dialog box, click **Internet Authentication Service | OK | Next**.

14. You may be prompted to insert the Windows Server 2003 compact disc.

15. Once IAS is installed, click **Finish | Close**.

16. Open the **Internet Authentication Service** management console. **Start | Programs | Administrative Tools | Internet Authentication Service**.

17. The default port and event logging setting for IAS are sufficient for this example.

18. The default log file parameters for the IAS are sufficient for this example.

19. From the IAS management console, right-click **RADIUS Clients**, and select **New RADIUS Client**.

20. Using the **New RADIUS Client Wizard,** add basic client information for the wireless access point Also add your wireless clients as RADIUS Clients.

21. Click **Next**. Select **RADIUS Standard** from the **Client-Vendor** drop-down list on the **New RADIUS Client** screen and enter the shared secret password; select **Finish**.

22. Configure a remote access policy for the IAS clients. From the IAS management console (**Start | Administrative Tools | Internet Authentication Service**) double-click **Internet Authentication Service** in the left pane.

23. In the left pane, click **Remote Access Policies**.

24. In the right pane, double-click the policy that you want to configure.

25. Click **Edit Profile**.

26. On the **Authentication** tab, click **EAP Methods**.

27. In **Select EAP providers**, click **Add**. Select the **Protected EAP (PEAP)** and then click **OK**.

28. In **Select EAP providers**, click the **Protected EAP (PEAP)** and then click **Edit**.

29. From the **Protected EAP Properties** dialog box in **Certificate Issued**, select the certificate that the server uses to identify itself to client computers. Enable PEAP fast reconnect for 802.11 wireless client computers by selecting **Enable Fast Reconnect** as shown in Figure 25.6.

Figure 25.6 Configuring PEAP Properties

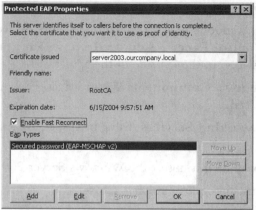

30.   Secure password user authentication with EAP-MSCHAPv2 as the default EAP Type. The
       default settings for EAP-MSCHAPv2 are sufficient for this example.

31.   Select **OK**. Click **OK** again to complete the PEAP configuration. We will use PEAP as
       the only authentication protocol allowed for our wireless clients. Remove the other
       authentication check boxes as shown in Figure 25.7.

Figure 25.7 Using PEAP Exclusively for Authentication

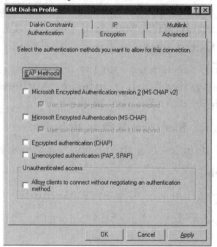

32.   Select **OK** and select **OK** again to complete the configuration.

RRAS NAT Services

Network Address Translation (NAT) was introduced in response to the concern that available public IP version 4 addresses were rapidly being depleted. NAT is defined in RFC 1631. NAT typically provides a translation service for private IP addresses to a public IP address or addresses. *IP masquerading* is another term frequently used (especially in the UNIX community) to describe this process. NAT works in the following manner:

1. A system on the private network attempts to connect to a public address on the outside of the network.

2. The NAT system (the client's default gateway) looks at the source and destination addresses and TCP and/or UDP port numbers.

3. The NAT system enters this information into its NAT table, replaces the client address with the NAT system's public address, and possibly modifies the source port numbers.

4. The remote system responds to the NAT system, sending any return information to the NAT system's public address and advertised port number or numbers.

5. The NAT system checks its NAT table to determine whether or not to forward the request to the internal network.

6. If a match is made in the NAT table, what is now the destination address for this traffic stream (the computer on the private network) replaces the NAT public address and again port numbers are modified if necessary.

7. The client that originated the traffic receives the responses from the public computer.

NAT can provide address mappings for hundreds or even thousands of addresses. NAT also provides a level of security for private networks because NAT typically does not allow inbound TCP/IP traffic without initiation from the internal network. In other words, unless a client on the private network requests to connect to a system on the public network, the system on the public network will not be allowed to connect to the private network.

So, what happens when you want to host a public service that is connected to your private network? Figure 25.8 illustrates an example in which public systems need access to a Web server that is housed on the private network.

Figure 25.8 Private Network Web Server Available to the Public

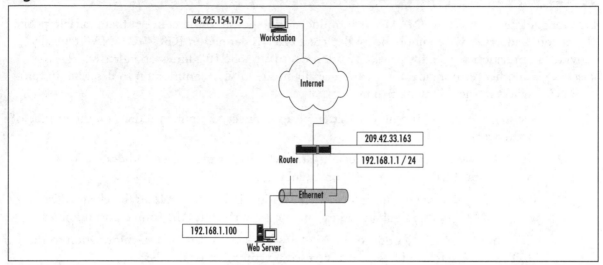

For a public system to reach a system on a private network hidden by NAT, the NAT system needs a static mapping for the service being requested. This static mapping will map the TCP or UDP port request to a private address on the inside of the NAT translated network. Let's look at an example to see how this works.

1. A user on the public network at address 64.225.154.175 attempts to connect to the Web server hidden behind a NAT translator at 209.42.33.163.

2. The public system sends a TCP Synchronize (SYN) segment from 64.225.154.175 on TCP port 2481 to the NAT translator at 209.42.33.163 on TCP port 80.

3. If the NAT translator did not have a static mapping, the connection would fail and the public system attempting to make the connection would display an error message. In our example, the NAT translator finds a mapping for 192.168.1.100, the private address for the Web server on the private LAN segment behind the NAT system.

4. The NAT translator removes the destination address of 209.42.33.163, replaces it with 192.168.1.100, and forwards the traffic out the NAT private interface to the private network Web server.

5. The Web server replies to the NAT system with traffic destined for 64.225.154.175.

6. The NAT system sees the mapping in the NAT table for this transaction and replaces the source address of 192.168.1.100 with the NAT server's public address of 209.42.33.163 and forwards the traffic out of its public interface.

7. The 64.225.154.175 system receives the response from 209.42.33.163 to complete the connectionThere are limitations to NAT. NAT relies on information in the IP header and TCP header of packets. If IP information or port information is not stored in the header, the way it is in most TCP/IP traffic, NAT may not be able to translate the traffic stream.

FTP, PPTP, and other forms of tunneled traffic can cause problems for NAT. A NAT editor is needed to translate FTP traffic through a NAT system, for example.

Typical NAT traffic is translated based on TCP port, UDP port, and IP addresses listed in the TCP header, UDP header, and IP header, respectively. NAT editors are special software components that translate traffic that contains TCP, UDP, or IP information in places other than their respective headers. Microsoft provides built-in NAT editor functions for some common protocols like FTP and PPTP within their recent operating system offerings. Use the steps below to configure NAT and static NAT mapping.

Configure NAT and Static NAT Mapping

1. Open Routing and Remote Access. **Start | Administrative Tools | Routing and Remote Access.**

2. From the Routing and Remote Access management console, right-click the server name and select **Configure and Enable Routing and Remote Access**. If this option is grayed out, select **Disable Routing and Remote Access** to start with a fresh configuration.

3. From the **Routing and Remote Access Server Setup Wizard**, click **Next**.

4. Select **Network address translation (NAT)** and click **Next**.

5. From the **NAT Internet Connection** dialog box, select the WAN interface and remove the Enable security on the selected interface by setting up basic firewall check box as shown in Figure 25.9; click **Next**.

Figure 25.9 Specifying the Public Interface and Removing Firewall Settings

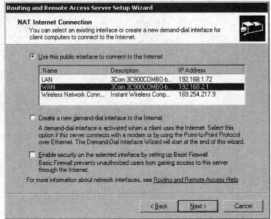

6. Select the **LAN** interface for the private NAT interface as shown in Figure 25.10 and select **Next**.

Figure 25.10 Specifying the LAN Interface as the Private NAT Interface

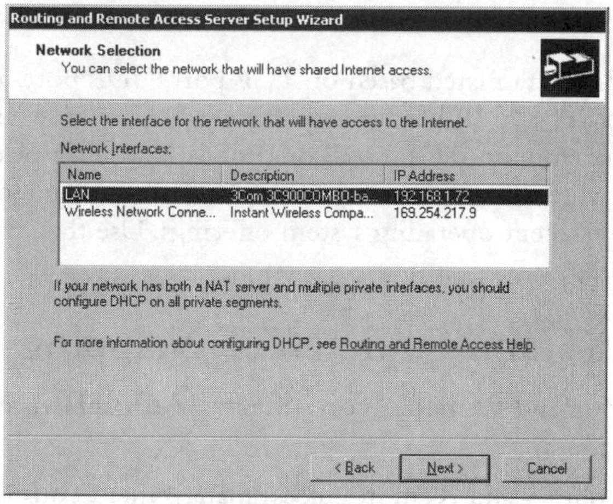

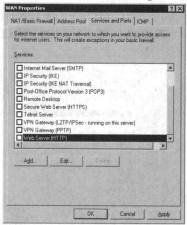

7. Click **Finish** to complete the basic NAT configuration. Now we will modify the configuration to provide public inbound requests for our private Web servers.

8. Click **NAT/Basic Firewall** in the left pane of the management console and right-click the **WAN** interface in the right pane of the management console. Select **Properties**.

9. From the **WAN Properties** dialog box, select the **Service and Ports** tab as shown in Figure 25.11.

Figure 25.11 Specifying Services Available through NAT

10. Select the **Web Server (HTTP)** check box. In the **Private address** box, enter **192.168.1.100** as shown in Figure 25.12 to direct inbound Web traffic to the Web server located at 192.168.1.100.

Figure 25.12 Specifying the Private Network Web Server Address

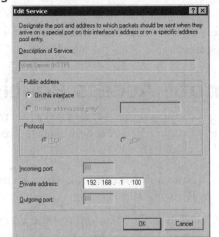

11. Click **OK**. Click **OK** again to complete the configuration.

ICMP Router Discovery

RFC 1256 describes a method for IP hosts to detect a router's availability by using Internet Control Message Protocol (ICMP). ICMP Router Discovery, the name for this process, works in two ways:

- Hosts send router solicitations using ICMP to discover available routers on the network.
- Routers send ICMP advertisements in response to the IP host solicitations as well as periodic ICMP updates to notify the hosts that the router is still available.

Although Windows Server 2003 supports ICMP Router Discovery, it is disabled by default. You can use the following procedure to configure ICMP router discovery.

Configure ICMP Router Discovery

1. Open Routing and Remote Access. **Start | Programs | Administrative Tools | Routing and Remote Access.**

2. In the left pane of the RRAS console, click **General**.

3. In the right pane, right-click the interface on which you want to enable router discovery, and then click **Properties**.

4. On the **General** tab, select the **Enable router discovery advertisements** check box.

5. In **Advertisement lifetime (minutes),** type or select the time after which a router is considered down after hearing its last router advertisement.

6. In **Minimum time (minutes),** type or select the minimum rate at which the router periodically sends ICMP router advertisements.

7. In **Maximum time (minutes),** type or select the maximum rate at which the router periodically sends ICMP router advertisements.

8. In **Level of preference**, type or select the level of preference for this router to be a default gateway for hosts.

Creating Remote Access Policies

You can manage the security of your remote access server by creating one or more remote access policies. Depending on your configuration, you will need to create policies in one of these two places:

- If you are using Windows authentication, use the Remote Access Policies item under each RRAS server in the Routing and Remote Access MMC snap-in.

- If you are using RADIUS authentication, use the Remote Access Policies item under the IAS server in the Internet Authentication Service MMC snap-in.

Regardless of the type of authentication you are using, the policies you create will work the same way, and the dialog boxes for creating and modifying policies are the same.

Policies and Profiles

Remote access security includes two key components:

- **Remote Access Policies** Determine which users can connect remotely and the connection methods they can use. You can have any number of remote access policies.

- **Remote Access Profiles** Provide further restrictions after the connection is established. Each policy contains exactly one profile.

Each remote access policy has an order number, or priority. You can define the order by using the Move Up and Move Down actions in the policy window. The list of policies in a default Windows Server 2003 RRAS installation is shown in Figure 25.13. Each policy can have various criteria against which connection attempts are checked. The policy can be set to either Grant or Deny access for users who match these criteria.

Figure 25.13 Remote Access Policies

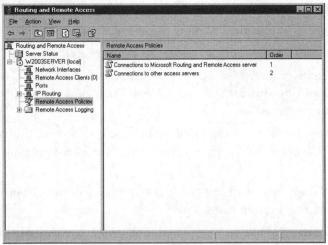

When a user attempts to connect, his or her connection criteria are compared to each policy's conditions in order until a policy matches. The Grant or Deny setting of that policy then determines whether the user is allowed access. If a policy grants access, its associated profile is used to further restrict the connection.

In the following sections, you will learn how to make practical use of remote access policies and profiles to authorize or restrict remote access and to control aspects of the connections using remote access profiles.

Authorizing Remote Access

The simplest use for a remote access policy is to authorize remote access for a particular user or group. Windows Server 2003 includes a wizard that you can use to quickly create these types of policies. After you have created a policy, you can modify the properties of the policy to make more specific settings or restrictions. You can launch the wizard through Start | Administrative Tools | Routing and Remote Access. In the left pane, select Remote Access Policies then from the menu select Action | New Remote Access Policy. The wizard will step you through the process to authorize remote access by user. A similar process is used to authorize remote access by group.

Authorizing Access By Group

Unlike user accounts, security groups do not include dial-in properties. If you wish to enable access for a group, you can use the wizard to create a remote access policy that includes a condition to check the user's group membership. You can use the following steps to authorize remote access by group.

1. Select **Programs | Administrative Tools | Routing and Remote Access** from the Start menu. If you are using RADIUS authentication, select Internet Authentication Service instead.

2. Click **Remote Access Policies** in the left-hand column. A list of the current policies is displayed in the window.

3. From the menu, select **Action | New Remote Access Policy**.

4. The wizard displays a welcome message. Click **Next** to continue.

5. The Policy Configuration Method screen is displayed. Select the **Use the wizard to set up a typical policy option** and enter **Allow Admin Access** in the Policy name field. Click **Next** to continue.

6. The Access Method screen is displayed. You can select whether this policy will apply to Dial-up, VPN, Wireless, or Ethernet access. Select the Dial-up option and click **Next** to continue.

7. The User or Group Access dialog box is displayed. Select the Group option and click the **Add** button to add a group name.

8. The Select Groups dialog box is displayed. Enter **Domain Admins** in the **Enter the object names to select** field and click **OK**.

9. You are returned to the User or Group Access dialog box. Click **Next** to continue.

10. The Authentication Methods dialog box is displayed. Click **Next** to continue.

11. The Policy Encryption Level dialog box is displayed. Click **Next** to continue.

12. The wizard displays the completion dialog box. Click **Finish** to create the policy.

Restricting Remote Access

You can add any number of conditions to a remote access policy to restrict the users, connection types, and other criteria that can match the policy. Each policy can be configured to either allow access or deny access based on those criteria.

To restrict access, you can create a policy that denies access based on a set of criteria. Because each connection will use the first policy that it matches, be sure your policies for denying access are placed early in the list, before any other policy that might match the same users.

The current conditions for a policy are listed in its **Properties** dialog box. You can use the **Add** button to add a condition. There are a variety of attributes you can test to create a condition.

Restricting by User/Group Membership

You already used the wizard to create a simple policy to restrict by group membership earlier in this section. You can also add this condition manually to any policy using its properties. The attribute for group membership is **Windows-Groups**. You can specify one or more group memberships to match and set the policy to either grant or deny access.

Restricting by Type of Connection

You can use the NAS-Port-Type attribute to restrict a remote access policy to a particular type of connection. Connection types include modem, ISDN, wireless, VPN, and other network connections that can be used for remote access. For example, suppose you were discontinuing the use of dial-in remote access and want to add a policy to prevent dial-in access. You would create a policy to deny access when the NAS-Port-Type attribute indicates a modem connection and place it at the top of the list to override other policies.

Restricting by Time

You can use the **Day-and-Time-Restrictions** attribute to control the day of the week and times of day that a policy will be effective. You can use this feature to deny access at a specific time or day or to explicitly grant access at a certain time. To use this feature, use the **Add** button in the **Properties** dialog box to add a condition to a policy, and then select **Day-and-Time-Restrictions**. The **Time of day Constraints** dialog box enables you to allow or deny access for each hour of the day and each day of the week.

Restricting by Client Configuration

You can use the Network Access Quarantine Control (NAQC) feature to restrict connections based on aspects of a client's configuration: the operating system, file system, and even details of which security updates have been installed. You need to create a custom script or program to check the client's configuration to implement this feature.

NAQC is included with the Windows Server 2003 Resource Kit. It includes several components:

- The Remote Access Quarantine Agent service (RQS.EXE) runs on the RRAS servers.

- A custom script to check the configuration. The script can use RQC.EXE, included in the resource kit, to notify the quarantine agent whether the client passed its tests.

- Connection Manager, using a custom profile and a post-connect action to run the script.

- A RADIUS (IAS) server to manage authentication.

- A remote access policy that uses the quarantine attributes, installed with the quarantine agent, to determine whether the connection has been authorized by the script.

NAQC is supported by Windows 98 SE and later clients that support Connection Manager. For details on implementing a quarantine script, consult Microsoft's TechNet site.

Restricting Authentication Methods

You can use the **Authentication-Type** attribute to restrict a policy to certain authentication types. When you add this attribute, you can use the **Authentication-Type** dialog box to add one or more of the possible authentication types, as shown in Figure 25.14.

Figure 25.14 Restricting by Authentication Method

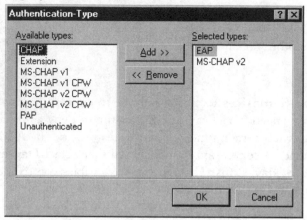

Restricting by Phone Number or MAC Address

You can use the following two attributes to add a phone number condition to a remote access policy:

- **Called-Station-ID**: The phone number the user called.
- **Calling-Station-ID**: The phone number the call originated from (Caller ID).

Controlling Remote Connections

After a connection is established by matching a remote access policy, the profile associated with the policy is used to control what the user can do with the connection. Some of the most useful profile settings include the following:

- The amount of time the user is allowed to remain connected or remain idle
- The encryption methods that will be allowed
- Which traffic will be filtered using packet filters
- The client IP address

Controlling Idle Timeout

The *idle timeout* is the amount of time the RRAS server will keep a session connected when there has not been any traffic to or from the remote access server. You can use this setting to ensure that clients who finish using their remote connection but fail to disconnect are disconnected automatically.

The idle timeout is part of a remote access profile. You can change the timeout on the **Dial-in Constraints** tab of the **Edit Dial-in Profile** dialog box.

Controlling Maximum Session Time

Along with the idle timeout, you can define a maximum amount of time a client can remain connected to the server whether they use the connection or not. When your supply of incoming ports is limited, this is one way to ensure that ports are opened up to enable other users to connect. The maximum session time is also defined in the **Dial-in Constraints** tab of a profile.

Controlling Encryption Strength

You can use the settings in the **Encryption** tab of a remote access profile's **Properties** dialog box to allow or disallow particular types of encryption for a VPN connection. Encryption types include the following:

- Basic encryption (MPPE 40-bit)

- Strong encryption (MPPE 56-bit)

- Strongest encryption (MPPE 128-bit)

Any three of these encryption settings can be used, depending on what the server and the client support, to prevent unauthorized access.

Controlling IP Packet Filters

You can use IP packet filters to filter incoming or outgoing traffic for connections that match a particular remote access profile. You might find this useful for denying access to a VPN from particular locations or only allowing access from a particular address. You can manage outgoing and incoming packet filters from the IP settings tab of the **Profile Properties** dialog box, as shown in Figure 25.15.

Figure 25.15 IP Settings

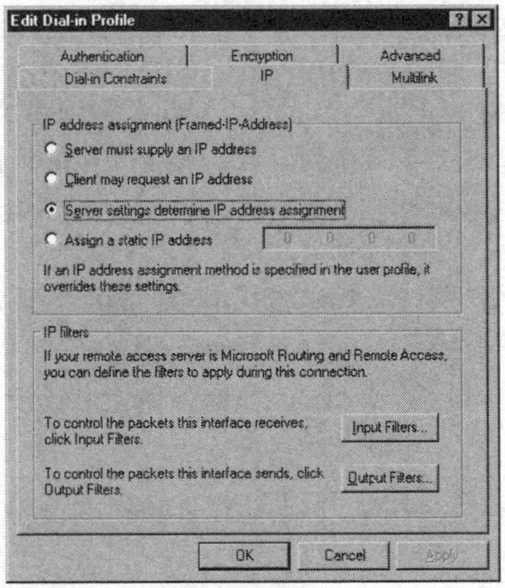

Controlling IP Address for PPP Connections

You can also use the **IP settings** to control IP address assignment for PPP (dial-in) connections. The following options are available:

- Server must supply an IP address

- Client may request an IP address

- Server settings determine IP address assignment

- Assign a static IP address

The last option enables you to specify a single IP address to be a assigned to clients that match this profile. If you use this feature, be sure only one client at a time will match the profile, because the IP address can only be assigned to one client.

Troubleshooting Remote Access Client Connections

Remote access client connections are often the most difficult connection problems to troubleshoot. In many cases, the system you are troubleshooting is not physically in front of you or even remotely accessible via remote control software, which makes it an added challenge. The best practice to follow when troubleshooting any type of connectivity problem is to start with the simpler areas and work your way up. The Open Systems Interconnect (OSI) reference model proves to be a handy guide for troubleshooting. Troubleshoot by starting at the lowest layers first, as seen in Table 25.1.

Table 25.1 The OSI Reference Model

Layer Number	Layer	Description
1	Physical Layer	Cabling, connectors
2	Data Link Layer	Network card, Hardware address (ARP, MAC, LLC)
3	Network Layer	Logical Addressing (IP address, IPX address)
4	Transport Layer	Segment and assemble upper layer information (TCP ports, UDP ports)
5	Session Layer	Connection control (RPC, SQL, NFS)
6	Presentation Layer	Data formatting (ASCII, MPEG, JPEG)
7	Application Layer	Applications (e-mail client, Web browser, word processor)

Most, if not all, networking problems will be solved within the first three or four layers. Begin the troubleshooting process with cabling. Work your way up the OSI reference model to test hardware settings and drivers next. At layer 3, the network layer, verify connectivity based on logical addressing like phone numbers or IP addresses. At the transport layer, verify available port numbers for your applications. Usually, transport layer problems will occur at a firewall or NAT system. This should be one of the first things to check if you have made it to layer 4 in the troubleshooting process. Session layer troubleshooting would entail verifying that services are started and running properly on your systems. Presentation and application layer problems do not generally affect network and/or remote access connectivity. Let's take a closer look at the different types of remote access to see how our methodology applies.

If the client is connecting through a modem, check the phone cable connectors to make sure they are securely connected to the wall and the modem. Ensure the modem is getting power and displays proper diagnostic indicators if you are working with an external modem. You might try shutting off and restarting an external modem. Check the Windows Device Manager to verify operation and driver information. If necessary, update the drivers. Working our way toward the network layer, test full operation of the modem by dialing a phone number with the phone dialer. Test the modem itself to ensure it is dialing a different number using phone dialer. If possible, ensure that the routing and remote access service is operational on the remote access server. Make sure you are using the correct authentication algorithm.

If you are connecting through VPN using an Internet connection, first verify Internet connectivity. If you are using a dial-up Internet connection to provide a transport for the VPN, follow the steps in the previous paragraph to ensure dial-up connectivity to your ISP and the Internet. If you are able to reach Internet servers, verify connectivity to the VPN server by issuing a ping command to the VPN server's FQDN or IP address. Make sure that there are a sufficient number of L2TP or PPTP ports available on the VPN server. Make sure you are using the proper authentication algorithms and the proper encryption strength. Finally, verify remote access policy settings will allow connectivity. If any one of the remote access policy rules matches your client computer or your user account, rule processing ends at that step and the requested action is processed.

If you are able to connect to the remote access server but you are unable to connect to resources within the remote LAN, you have already ruled out the first two layers of the OSI reference model. Typical problems in this scenario include IP connectivity problems, name resolutions problems, and incorrect upper layer protocol selection. An approach here would be to check the IP address assigned to the PPP adaptor. Verify IP connectivity to the inside interface of the remote access server. This is the LAN interface on the RRAS server. Next, in a Windows 2000 or Windows Server 2003 Active Directory environment, issue an nslookup command to test DNS resolution for the client. If IP connectivity fails, name resolution will fail. When testing IP connectivity, verify that the address assigned to the PPP adaptor is a valid address for one of your LANs. If the address is in the range of 169.254.0.1 and 169.254.255.254, this is an Automatic Private IP Address assignment (APIPA). This signifies a problem in the address request process with the DHCP server. This problem could be between the client and the RRAS server or between the RRAS server and the DHCP server.

Some utilities for troubleshooting Windows Server 2003 connectivity include:

- Ipconfig
- Netsh
- Nslookup
- Ping

The **ipconfig** command, when used with the **all** switch (**ipconfig /all**), provides information about existing network interfaces, both real and virtual. Figure 25.16 shows the output from the **ipconfig** command when used with the **all** switch.

Figure 25.16 Ipconfig Command Display

The **netsh** command utility was introduced with Windows 2000. It provides scripting, display, and modification capabilities for virtually every aspect of Windows Server 2003 networking. Figure 25.17 displays a list of available options from the **netsh** command line interface. The **netsh** command has been expanded with additional helper files and so has more functionality in its Windows Server 2003 version (for example, the IPSec context).

Figure 25.17 Netsh Command Line Options

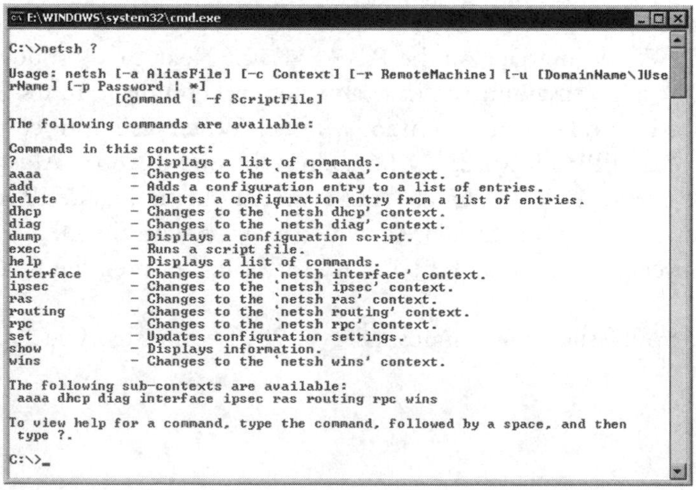

Several of the **netsh** commands typically are used more from the server but **netsh** provides functions for client side interaction as well.

The **nslookup** command is used to troubleshoot and test DNS information for client systems. When used with a computer name or FQDN within an Active Directory environment, **nslookup** can illustrate DNS name resolution mappings, as well as general DNS information. Figure 25.18 illustrates the output from a typical **nslookup** command.

Figure 25.18 Using the Nslookup Command

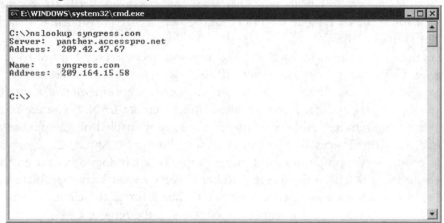

The **ping** command is used to test general network layer connectivity between hosts. Several switches are available for use with the **ping** command. **Ping** sends an ICMP echo request to the host that the **ping** command was issued to. The host, if available, will reply with an ICMP reply to the **ping** issued to the initiating system. From the initiating system, a successful **ping** will list the responses with TTL times displayed next to each request. Figure 25.19 displays one successful **ping** command and one failed **ping** command.

Figure 25.19 Using the Ping Command

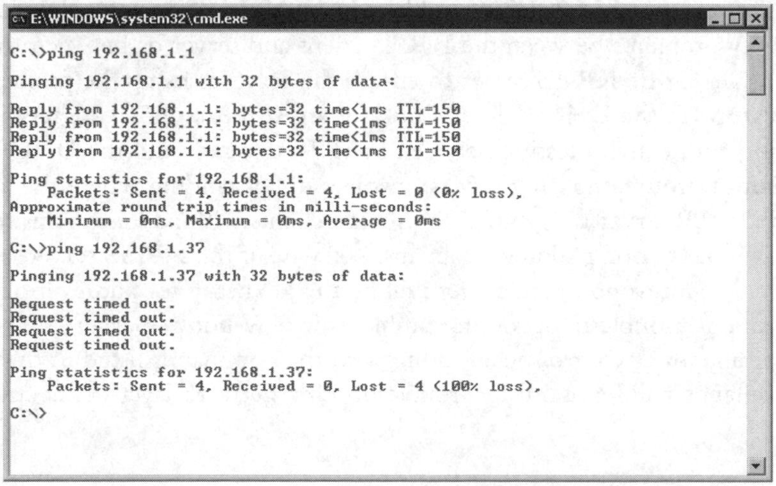

Troubleshooting Remote Access Server Connections

Troubleshooting remote access server connections is not so different from troubleshooting remote access client connections. The best approach is to follow the OSI reference model from the simple lower layers, working your way up through the various upper layers. Again, begin by checking physical layer attributes. Make sure cables are properly connected and secured. Ensure hardware is configured with the right drivers and, if necessary, hardware configurations. Verify the problem is truly a server problem. If some clients are able to connect and others are not, it is possible that the problem is with the client configurations.

It is quite common for clients to have access to a remote access server, but not to systems beyond the server. This could be a problem with IP routing on the remote access server. Verify IP connectivity beyond the remote access server by pinging either the inside network interface on the remote access server or ping another internal address on the remote LAN. If you are unable to reach internal addresses on the remote LAN, verify that IP Routing is enabled on the remote access server. For AppleTalk clients, verify that network access is allowed for AppleTalk clients on the **AppleTalk** tab on the server properties sheet. If the **AppleTalk** tab does not exist on the server, AppleTalk needs to be installed on the server. Another possible network layer problem involves static routing. If the remote LAN does not have a static route entry back to the client system, client traffic will enter the remote LAN only to die within the confines of the remote LAN.

Other network layer problems can occur with dynamic routing enabled (RIP or OSPF). One possible compatibility problem to consider: Windows XP 64-bit and Windows Server 2003 64-bit do not support OSPF routing. RIP v1 is a classful routing protocol. This means that RIP v1 networks must be divided at standard default subnet mask boundaries. If two networks exist within your IP network that do not use standard network masks, this can present routing problems. RIP v1 cannot properly advertise a network that does not use default subnet masks. Also, when using DHCP to allocate addresses, it is possible to run out of addresses or to lose proper connectivity with the DHCP server. As mentioned in the previous section, this will result in APIPA assignment (unless APIPA has been disabled or there is an alternate configuration set). APIPA addresses fall within the range of 169.254.0.1 and 169.254.255.254, and having an APIPA assigned address could be the result of connectivity problems between the RRAS client and server or between the RRAS server and DHCP server. Check the RRAS server to ensure the server is using the proper network interface to communicate with the DHCP server. Look for an APIPA assigned address at the RRAS server. Also, try ping connectivity testing between the RRAS server and the DHCP server. Part of the address distribution troubleshooting process involves understanding where the addresses are coming from. If a DHCP server is supposed to provide clients with addresses, this server should be the next stop for troubleshooting address problems. Likewise, if the RRAS server is distributing addresses from a static address pool, this server will be the next stop for address troubleshooting.

In order to properly troubleshoot routing problems in a Windows Server 2003 environment, you have a few commands at your disposal. Along with the commands listed in the previous section, the following commands will be useful for troubleshooting network layer connectivity and routing problems:

- Pathping
- Tracert
- Route

The **pathping** command was introduced with Windows 2000. This command combines characteristics of the **ping** command, discussed in the previous section, with the **tracert** command. This command enumerates the routing path that IP traffic will take to a given destination, as well as listing statistical information about the path to each router along the route to the destination. This command is useful for testing packet loss along a path. If you suspect a router along the path is dropping packets, this is the command to use. From a command prompt, type **pathping w.x.y.z**, where **w.x.y.z** is the remote system address whose path you are testing. The results from a **pathping** are displayed in Figure 25.20.

Figure 25.20 Pathping Test Results

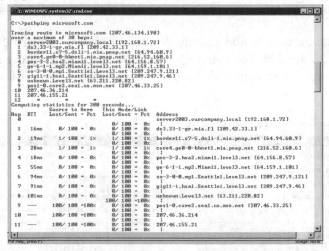

The **tracert** command enumerates the routing path that IP traffic will take to a given destination. Again, some basic statistical information is also listed with the trace. This command is a little less detailed than the **pathping** command. . From a command prompt, type **tracert w.x.y.z**, where **w.x.y.z** is the remote system address whose path you are testing. The results from a **tracert** are displayed in Figure 25.21.

Figure 25.21 Tracert Results

```
E:\WINDOWS\system32\cmd.exe

C:\>tracert microsoft.com

Tracing route to microsoft.com [207.46.134.222]
over a maximum of 30 hops:

  1    16 ms    17 ms    18 ms  ds3.33-1-gr.mia.fl [209.42.33.1]
  2    18 ms    19 ms    23 ms  border11.s7-5.dsli-1.mia.pnap.net [64.94.60.9]
  3    18 ms    19 ms    19 ms  core4.ge0-0-bbnet1.mia.pnap.net [216.52.160.6]
  4    21 ms    20 ms    24 ms  pos-3-2.hsa2.miami1.level3.net [64.156.8.57]
  5    20 ms    27 ms    20 ms  ge-6-2-1.mp2.Miami1.level3.net [64.159.1.177]
  6    91 ms    92 ms    91 ms  so-1-0-0.mp2.Seattle1.Level3.net [209.247.10.133
]
  7    91 ms    91 ms    92 ms  gig10-1.hsa1.Seattle1.level3.net [209.247.9.70]

  8    97 ms    97 ms    96 ms  unknown.Level3.net [63.211.220.82]
  9    96 ms    96 ms    97 ms  207.46.33.229
 10    95 ms    98 ms    97 ms  207.46.36.78
 11    98 ms    98 ms    98 ms  207.46.155.21
 12     *         *         *   Request timed out.
 13     *         *         *   Request timed out.
 14     *         *         *   Request timed out.
 15    ^C
C:\>_
```

The **route** command is used to add, modify, delete, and display routing information for a Windows Server 2003 router. This command is useful in determining existing routes available for IP traffic passing through the server. Figure 25.22 illustrates the **route** command with the **print** switch.

Figure 25.22 Using the Route Command

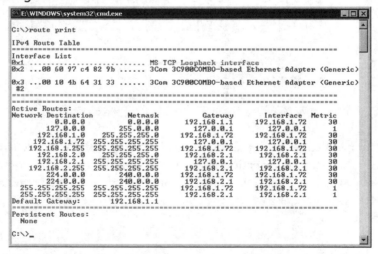

Finally, completing our network layer troubleshooting and working up to the transport layer, make sure the client traffic passes through any packet filters that might be in place. If the client's network settings match any single rule in the packet filter criteria for denied access, the client will be denied access. If this is the case, determine how the rule might be rewritten to allow client access. Another option would be to determine a way to modify the client configuration so the packet filter rule does not prevent client access to the network.

Configuring Internet Authentication Services

The Windows Server 2003 Internet Authentication Services (IAS) provide open standard centralized connection authentication, authorization, and accounting for several types of network access. This open standard is more commonly known as Remote Authentication Dial-In User Service (RADIUS). This Microsoft implementation of RADIUS provides authentication for the following network connection types:

- Authenticating switch
- Dial-up
- Router-to-router connections
- Virtual private network (VPN) remote access
- Wireless

The major advantage of IAS/RADIUS is that it provides an open standard solution. This means that equipment and software from various vendors can be tied together through the RADIUS authentication service, thereby simplifying account administration for remote access users and systems. Windows Server 2003 IAS supports the IETF RADIUS standards specified in RFC 2865 and 2866. One advantage to using the Microsoft implementation of RADIUS in conjunction with Active Directory is the capability for a single sign-on. The centralized authentication capabilities for IAS provide for authentication forwarding to Active Directory for authentication. In this fashion, all users are authenticated from the same source. If a user logs in to the local LAN, his or her username and password will be the same as the one used for remote access through VPN, wireless networking, or any other network connection whose authentication is provided by Microsoft IAS.

IAS must be installed as a separate Windows component. The first step in IAS configuration is installing the IAS component. Next, we must configure the properties for one of the IAS servers. After that, the remote access servers that will act as clients to this IAS server must be added. When IAS is implemented the IAS servers will carry out remote access policies. Remote access policies should be configured at this time on the IAS server. Logging methods must be configured for authentication and accounting. As the configuration of the first server is nearly complete, we can now copy the configuration from this IAS server to additional IAS servers on our network. The IAS servers must be registered in the correct Active Directory domains as a final configuration step. After completing the actual configuration, it is considered best practice to verify all configurations and operational settings. There are three ways to register the IAS servers in the appropriate Active Directory domains. You can use any one of these methods:

- Register the IAS server in the default domain using Active Directory Users and Computers.
- Register the IAS server in the default domain using Internet Authentication Service.
- Register the IAS server in the default domain using the **netsh** command.

We have completed the installation and configuration for the IAS server. Before placing the server into production, we should verify the configuration of RADIUS accounting and authentication on the access servers. Also, depending on the role of the server, we should verify that the access servers are properly configured for operation. For example, for dial-up and VPN connections we should establish a connection through standard dial-up as well as a VPN connection. The following steps walk you through configuring IAS in Windows Server 2003.

Configure IAS

1. Click **Start | Control Panel | Add Remove Programs**.
2. Click **Add/Remove Windows Components**.
3. From the dialog box in the Windows Components Wizard, select **Networking Services | Details**.
4. Select **Internet Authentication Service** followed by **OK | Next**.

Now that IAS is installed, it is time to configure the properties for the IAS server as follows:

1. Click **Start | Programs | Administrative Tools | Internet Authentication Service.**
2. Right-click Internet Authentication Service and select **Properties**.
3. Select the **Ports** tab, and configure the RADIUS authentication and accounting UDP ports if they differ from the defaults of 1812 and 1645 for authentication, and 1813 and 1646 for accounting.
4. Continuing from Properties, on the **General** tab, select each required option for IAS event logging , and then click **OK**.
5. Right-click RADIUS Clients and select **New RADIUS Client**.
6. From the **New RADIUS Client Wizard** add basic client information. Click **Next**.
7. Select **RADIUS Standard** from the **Client-Vendor** drop-down list on the **New RADIUS Client** screen and enter the shared secret password; then select **Finish**.
8. Configure the remote access policies. In our example, we will grant access to a Windows Global Group called Radius-Clients. Configure the remote access policy to grant access to members of the Radius-Clients group.
9. From the left pane of the Microsoft management console, select **Remote access logging**.
10. From the right pane, right-click **Local File** or **SQL Server**, and then select **Properties**.
11. From the **Settings** tab, select one or more check boxes for recording authentication and accounting requests in the IAS log files:

    - For accounting request and response captures, select **Accounting requests**.
    - For authentication requests, Access-Accept messages, and Access-Reject messages captures, select Authentication requests.
    - For periodic status update captures, select **Periodic status**.

Now that we have a configuration nearly completed, we can copy the IAS configuration from the first IAS server to additional IAS servers.

1. Begin from a Command Prompt. Click **Start | Run** and type **cmd**, then click **OK**.

2. From the command prompt, type **netsh aaaa show config > path\file.txt.** This stores all configuration settings in a text file. You can use a relative or absolute path, or a UNC path.

3. Copy this file to the destination computer or computers.

4. From a command prompt on the destination computer, type **netsh exec path\file.txt**.

As a final configuration step, we have to register the IAS servers in the appropriate Active Directory domains. There are three ways to accomplish this task:

- Register the IAS server in the default domain using Active Directory Users and Computers:

  1. Log on to the IAS server with an account that has administrative credentials for the domain.

  2. Open **Active Directory Users and Computers**. Click **Start | Programs | Administrative Tools | Active Directory Users and Computers**.

  3. In the left pane of the ADUC console, click the **Users** folder for your domain.

  4. In the right pane, right-click **RAS and IAS Servers**, and then click **Properties**.

  5. In the **RAS and IAS Servers Properties** dialog box, on the **Members** tab, add each of the IAS servers.

- To register the IAS server in the default domain using Internet Authentication Service:

  1. Log on to the IAS server with an account that has administrative credentials for the domain.

  2. Open **Internet Authentication Service**. Click **Start | Programs | Administrative Tools | Internet Authentication Service**.

  3. Right-click **Internet Authentication Service**, and select **Register Server in Active Directory**.

  4. Select **OK** when the **Register Internet Authentication Service in Active Directory** dialog box appears.

- To register the IAS server in the default domain using the **netsh** command:

  1. Log on to the IAS server with an account that has administrative credentials for the domain.

  2. Open **Command Prompt**. Click **Start | Run** and type **cmd,** then click **OK**.

  3. Type **netsh ras add registeredserver** at the command prompt.

Chapter 26

Managing Web Servers with IIS 6.0

In this chapter:

☑ **Installing and Configuring IIS 6.0**

☑ **What's New in IIS 6.0?**

☑ **Managing IIS 6.0**

☑ **Troubleshooting IIS 6.0**

☑ **Using New IIS Command-Line Utilities**

Introduction

Microsoft's Internet Information Services (IIS) is one of the most popular Web servers in use on the Internet and in intranets throughout the world. Windows Server 2003 includes the latest version, IIS 6.0. There have been changes, additions and improvements to the software in the areas of core functionality and services, administration, security, and performance. IIS 6.0 has been redesigned to provide better reliability and more flexibility in configuring application environments.

A Web server is a common point of vulnerability to hackers. In the past, it has been common for servers to be running "rogue" Web services without the knowledge of administrators. Thus, for security reasons, IIS 6.0 is not installed by default on Windows Server 2003 servers (with the exception of the Web Server Edition), and when you do install it, it is initially configured in a high security ("locked") mode. Because Web servers are common targets of attack due to their exposure to those outside the local network, security is a priority in this new version. Consequently, a number of important Web services features – which worked automatically in previous versions – now have to be explicitly enabled before they will work. This new focus on security means administrators need to familiarize themselves with these changes to provide the Web server services needed on their networks.

In this chapter, we take you through the installation and configuration process for IIS 6.0 and introduce you to its new features, including security features, reliability features, and other new features. We'll show you how to use the Web Server Security Lockdown Wizard and how to manage security issues for your Web servers. We'll also discuss troubleshooting issues, and you'll learn to use the new IIS command-line utilities.

Installing and Configuring IIS 6.0

Before you can use IIS's services, you have to install it (unless you're using the Web Server Edition of Windows 2003 Server), so we will first concentrate on the installation process. IIS is not installed by default in any of the other Windows Server 2003 family members. You will learn about all these new security features as we progress though this chapter. First, let's learn about the prerequisites for installing IIS 6.0 on Windows 2003 Server.

Pre-Installation Checklist

You should take some precautions before installing IIS. These steps will ensure that your new IIS installation will run smoothly. Here is a checklist to go through prior to the installation:

- **Domain Name Registration for an IP address for the IIS server**: If it is to be an Internet Web server (as opposed to an intranet server), the IIS server will be referred by the domain name from outside the enterprise, so you must register a domain name and obtain a public IP address for it. You'll also need to obtain DNS services for your domain, from your ISP or another public DNS server. You also need to assign an IP address or a unique machine name for references inside the enterprise.

- **Access privileges for installation**: Make sure you are logged in with an account (*Administrator* or a member of the *Administrator group* for the machine) that has the correct authentication privileges to access the machines and network components. (i.e., – configuring routers to channel IIS requests).

Internet Connection Firewall

Windows 2003 comes with a very basic internal software firewall called the *Internet Connection Firewall* (ICF). This feature is disabled by default. If you enable it, the firewall can be configured to enable or disable protocol access through IIS. The protocols in question that relate to IIS are HTTP, HTTPS, FTP, and SMTP. IIS 6.0 will *not* function correctly if the ICF is *enabled* and the relevant protocols are *disabled*. For example, the IIS 6.0 Web server will not function if the HTTP and HTTPS protocols are disabled. You basically have two options when it comes to the ICF:

1. Disable the firewall. (Warning: You are at the mercy of the corporate firewall!)

2. Enable the firewall and filter the correct protocols.

The most cost-effective method is to use the second option and maximize Windows 2003's built-in functionality. Follow these steps to configure the protocols:

1. Open **Start | Control Panel | Network Connections | Local Area Connection**.

2. Navigate to the **Advanced** tab and select the **Protect my computer and network by limiting or preventing access to this computer from the internet** checkbox.

3. Click the **Settings** button and navigate to the **Services** tab. This will bring up a window to select or deselect the access protocols to your server. This is the list of protocols the IIS server will understand to process user requests. Select the correct checkbox next to the protocol name to enable requests using the particular protocol. You can disable the protocol access by clearing the checkbox.

4. Select the appropriate protocols for your organization. Most organizations will enable HTTP, HTTPS, SMTP, and FTP access through the firewall. As part of security best practices, avoid enabling protocols your organization will not be using. Each time you select a protocol, a small window will appear, prompting you to enter the machine name or IP address of the server that hosts the service.

5. Click **OK** and repeat the process for all other protocols.

These are some of the prerequisites for your IIS 6.0 installation. Application of IIS security templates and operating system hardening are some of the other prerequisites. The next step is to initiate the installation process. There are several ways to install IIS in Windows 2003 Server. We will discuss each of these in the next section.

Installation Methods

IIS is not installed by default in the Windows 2003 Server setup, except in the Web Server Edition. There are three different ways to install IIS. They are listed below:

- Use the **Configure Your Server** wizard.

- Use the **Add or Remove** option from the **Control Panel**.

- Use the **Unattended Setup**.

Using the Configure Your Server Wizard

In addition to its other possible roles (domain controller, file server, DNS server, and so forth), the Windows 2003 Server can act as an application server. When the computer is configured as an application server, IIS is installed.

Follow these steps to install ISS 6.0 from the **Configure Your Server** Wizard:

1. Click the **Start | Manage Your Server** option. You will see the **Manage Your Server** window. Click the **Add or remove a role** link.

2. The next screen is the **Preliminary Steps** window. This is a warning screen that prompts the user to confirm that all prerequisites are met for the installation. Most of these warnings relate to hardware not being configured correctly. Click **Next**.

3. The next screen is the **Configuration Options** screen. This screen is presented to the user only once. You can select from two options to configure the server. The **Typical**

configuration for a first server option will enable the basic server communication options. It will set up a domain controller by installing Active directory, DNS services, and DHCP services. The second option is **Custom Configuration**. This will enable you to configure your server by selecting specific options from a list. For this walk-through, we will choose this option.

4. The next screen displays a list of server roles that you can assign to your Windows 2003 server. This screen lists all the server services that are available. We will select the **Application Server (IIS, ASP.NET)** option from the list. You can also use this screen to install Print, Terminal, DNS, DHCP services, and more, as shown in Figure 26.1. Click **Next**.

Figure 26.1 Server Role Screen

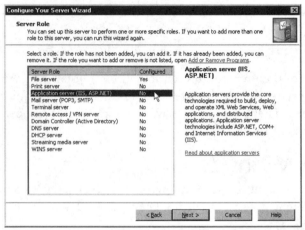

5. The next screen is the **Application Server Options** window. This screen enables you to configure dynamic options for IIS installation. The options you can select here include **ASP.NET** and **FrontPage Extensions**. ASP.NET is a scripting framework that is used to execute IIS applications. The FrontPage extensions will enable your Web application to be ported to another Integrated Development Environment (IDE). That is, the same Web project can be modified using Visual Studio .NET and Web Matrix. The FrontPage extensions also will enable users to develop Web content and manage the Web site remotely. Click **Next**.

6. The next screen is a summary of the items you have selected. Review these, and use the **Back** button if you want to change anything. Note that **Enable COM+ for remote transactions** option is added by the installation process. Click **Next**.

7. The installation process will begin. You will be presented with an **Application Selections** screen and a progress bar will indicate the installation progress. The installation process will automatically bring up the **Configuration Components** window and will start to copy the correct files from the Windows 2003 installation CD, DVD, or network share. A confirmation screen will appear to complete the installation.

Figure 26.2 Configuring Components Window

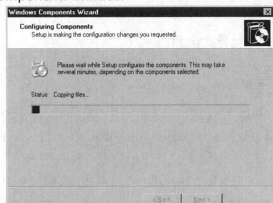

Using the Add or Remove Programs Applet

The previous section explained how to install IIS 6.0 by using the **Configure Your Server Wizard**. The second option is to install IIS through the **Add or Remove Programs** applets in **Control Panel**. Select Application Server and click the Details button to configure the application server options.

Using Unattended Setup

The third option for installing IIS is using the unattended setup feature, which is commonly used by system administrators to install IIS 6.0 on multiple computers. When you use this option, the setup program does not need any manual intervention. The configuration settings (the selections that you would make during an attended setup) are read from a text file and applied automatically by the operating system. You only need to initiate the process and IIS 6.0 will be installed according to the text file settings.

After you create the answer file, you run **winnt32.exe** or the **sysocmgr.exe** command-line utility with the answer script as the parameter. The answer file has a *.inf* file extension. Some of the important options that are included in the answer file are shown in Table 26.1.

Table 26.1 Answer File Parameters for IIS Unattended Setup

Component	Answer File Parameter
ASP.NET	asp.net = on/off
FTP service	iis_ftp = on/off
IIS Manager	iis_inetmgr = on/off
NNTP Service	iis_nntp = on/off
SMTP Service	iis_smtp = on/off
WWW Service	iis_www = on/off
Active Server Pages	iis_asp = on/off
WebDAV Publishing (discussed later)	iis_webdav = on/off

Installing IIS with unattended setup is very straightforward. You can also get the help files available for unattended setup by using the **syscomgr.exe /?** syntax.

Installation Best Practices

Installation best practice will ensure the optimum scalability and performance of IIS 6.0. Here are some of the important steps to ensure maximum value from IIS:

- The file system onto which you install IIS should be NTFS.

- Make sure the **Internet Connection Firewall** (ICF) is enabled and configured properly unless you will be relying on a separate firewall product.

- Use unattended setup to install IIS on multiple machines.

- **Configure Your Server Wizard** will enable you to install multiple application server components (DNS, File server, etc.). Therefore, you can install other components parallel to IIS 6.0 setup.

What's New in IIS 6.0?

There are many new features in IIS 6.0. Many of these features are designed to address technical and architectural issues in IIS 5.0. The new features can be divided into several broad categories. The most important categories are security and reliability. Microsoft has invested a large number of resources on its new **Trustworthy Computing** initiative. IIS 6.0 is one of the first products to be developed under this security-focused strategy. Performance is also enhanced by some key architectural modifications to the IIS 6.0 object model. In the following sections, we investigate these changes in detail.

New Security Features

IIS 5.0 and earlier versions were constantly patched by hot fixes from Microsoft. IIS was once considered one of the main security holes in Windows architecture. This was a major deterrent to using IIS as a commercial Web server. IIS 6.0 comes with an extensive list of new security features.

Advanced Digest Authentication

Advanced Digest Authentication is an extension of **Digest security**. Digest security uses MD5 hashing to encrypt user credentials (user name, password, and user roles).

Advanced Digest Security takes the digest authentication model further by storing the user credentials on a domain controller as an MD5 hash. The Active Directory database on the domain controller is used to store the user credentials. Thus, intruders would need to get access to the Active Directory in order to steal the credentials. This adds another layer of security to protect access to Windows 2003 Web sites.

Server-Gated Cryptography (SGC)

Communication between and IIS Web server and the Web client is done using Hypertext Transfer Protocol (HTTP). These HTTP network transmissions can be easily compromised due to their text-based massaging formats. To improve security, the HTTP calls between the client and the server can be encrypted. Secure Sockets Layer (SSL) and Transport Layer Security (TLS) are the most common encryption mechanisms used on Web sites. SSL/TLS will enable a secure communication by encrypting the communication channel with a cipher algorithm. TLS is the later version of the SSL protocol and is more secure than SSL.

Server-Gated Cryptography (SGC) is an extension of SSL/TLS. It uses strong 128-bit encryption to encode data. SGC does not require an application to run on client's machine. A special SGC certificate is needed to enable SGC support built into IIS 6.0. IIS 6.0 supports both 40-bit and 128-bit encryption sessions. This means older 40-bit SGC certificates are still valid in IIS 6.0. SGC is commonly used for financial sector applications to protect data.

Selectable Cryptographic Service Provider (CSP)

SSL/TLS offer a secure environment in which to exchange data though it places a heavy load on the CPU. IIS 6.0 comes with a new feature called **Selectable Cryptographic Service Provider (CSP)** that enables the user to select from an optimized list of cryptography providers. A cryptographic provider will provide you with an interface encrypt communication between the server and the client. CSP is not specific to IIS and can be used to handle cryptography and certificate management. Microsoft implements two default security providers. Those are Microsoft DH SChannel Cryptographic provider and Microsoft RSA SChannel Cryptographic provider. The Microsoft implementations are optimized to IIS 6.0 for faster communications. The private keys for these to Microsoft implementations are stored in the registry. The Microsoft Cryptographic API (Crypto API) for every provider contains identical interface for all providers. This will enable developers to switch between providers without modifying the code. The CSP can be configured using the **Welcome to the Web Server Certificate Wizard**. Click on **Properties** of a Web site and select the **Directory Security** tab. Then click the **Server Certificate** button.

Configurable Worker Process Identity

One of the most serious problems with previous IIS versions was the instability of the World Wide Web (WWW) Publishing Service. The failure of this service could result in the shutdown of the machine. IIS 6.0 runs each Web site in an isolated process environment. This isolated process environment is called a **Worker Process**. Therefore, a Web site malfunction could be limited to its process environment and therefore avoid a web server shutdown. IIS 6.0 can also run using the IIS 5.0 isolated environment. The IIS system administrator can choose between worker process model or IIS 5.0 isolation model by selecting the correct option from **Services** Tab by right-clicking **Web Sites**. You can click the **Run WWW service in IIS 5.0 isolation mode** option box to run IIS in IIS 5.0 isolation mode. IIS will run on worker process model if you do not check the box. You cannot run worker process model Web sites and IIS 5.0 isolation mode Web sites simultaneously.

The worker process can be run with a lower level of permission than the system account. The worker process will shut down the application if the IIS server is targeted with malicious code. IIS

6.0 (which is by default run by the local system account) is not affected since the worker process can be configured to run under a less-privileged account.

Default Lockdown Status

The default installation of IIS 6.0 will result in a "*light-weight*" Web server. The only default feature available will be the access to static content. This *restricted* functionality is referred as **Default Lockdown** status. You can enable or disable IIS features through the Web Services Extensions node of the IIS Manager.

New Authorization Framework

Authorization refers to the concept of confirming a user's access for a given resource. (Authentication refers to obtaining access to the resource. When a user is authenticated we need to make sure that he or she is authorized to perform any tasks on the resource. This is the basis of authorization.) There are two types of ASP.NET authorization options available for IIS 6.0:

- **File Authorization** *FileAuthorizationModule* class is responsible for file authorization on Windows 2002 systems. The module is activated by enabling **Windows Authentication** on a Web site. This module does access control list (ACL) check on the authorization access on an ASP.NET file for a given user. (It could be either ".asmx" file for ASP.NET application or a ".asmx" file for a Web service.) . The file is available for the user if the ACL confirms the user access to the file.

- **URL Authorization** *URLAuthorizationModule* class is responsible for URL authorization on Windows 2003. This mechanism uses the URL namespace to store user details and access roles. The URL authorization is available to use at any time. The authorization information is stored on text file on a directory. The text file will have <authorization> tag to allow or deny access to the directory. (This will apply to the subdirectories if not specified). Here is a sample authorization file:

```
<authorization>
    <allow users="Chris"/>
    <allow roles="Admins"/>
    <deny users="Kirby"/>
    <deny users="?"/>
</authorization>
```

This file will enable *Chris* to access its content. It will also enable anyone with *Admins* user roles. The user *Kirby* is denied access. Any one else will not be able to gain access to this directory (indicated by the ? wild card).

New Reliability Features

The most significant modification to reliability in IIS 6.0 is the emphasis on the *Worker Process Model*. This concept was initially embedded into IIS 4.0 as "*Running an application in a separate memory space.*"

IIS separates all user code from its WWW service. The user application (different Web sites) functions as a separate *Internet Server Application Programming Interface* (ISAPI) application. The separate ISAPI workspace is referred as a **worker process**. IIS 5.0 ran each Web site within its own **inetinfo.exe** memory space. The IIS 6.0 worker process Web sites do not run within the **inetinfo.exe (WWW services)** memory space. Because the worker process runs in an isolated environment from the WWW service, an error in the Web site application code (or malicious attack) will not cause the Web server to shut down. The worker process model can store application-specific data on its own memory space. IIS 5.0 stored all the application data within the inetinfo.exe memory space. Therefore, we can assign a Web site to run on specific CPU.

Health Detection

Health detection is performed by IIS over all its worker processes. This adds another level of reliability to the Web applications. The **inetinfo.exe** process (IIS) will check the availability of each worker process (different Web sites) periodically. IIS manager can configure this time limit. (It is 240 seconds by default). Therefore IIS will maintain a heartbeat between its worker processes

New Request Processing Architecture: HTTP.SYS Kernel Mode Driver

In Windows 2003 server, the HTTP stack is implemented as a kernel mode device driver called **HTTP.sys.** All incoming HTTP traffic goes through this kernel process. This kernel process is independent of application process. IIS 6.0 is an application process and external to HTTP.sys. Recall that application processes (IIS) run in *user mode* and the operating system functions are run in *kernel mode*. HTTP.sys is responsible for the following:

- Connection management (managing the database connections from the ASP.NET pages to data bases),

- Caching, (reading from a static cache as opposed to recompiling the ASP.NET page),

- Bandwidth throttling (limiting the size of the Web requests to a Web site), and

- Text-based logging. (Writing IIS information into a text log file.)

In IIS 5.0, the HTTP request was consumed by the IIS inetinfo.exe. HTTP.sys in IIS 6.0 relieves IIS of this responsibility. In doing so, it enhances IIS performance in the following ways:

- HTTP.sys enables caching (referred as **flexible caching**) at kernel level so that static data can be cached for faster response time (independent of the user-mode caching). This will be faster than user-mode caching. We need to be careful with flexible caching. Because HTTP.sys is separate from IIS we may still cache old data after an IIS restart.

- HTTP.sys introduces a mapping concept called "**application pool**." Application pooling enables Web sites to run together in one or more processes, as long as they share the same pool designation. Web sites that are assigned different application pools never run in the same process. A central Web site (credit card verification Web site) can be accessed by all the other miscellaneous sites (shopping cart E- Commerce sites) by using this method. By using the correct application pool information HTTP.sys can route the HTTP traffic to the correct Web site.

- HTTP.sys increases the number of Web sites you can host using the application pool concept. This architecture also increases performance and more controlled access to valuable IIS resources.

Other New Features

Lets concentrate on some of the other new features in IIS 6.0. All of these changes are designed to improve IIS scalability. Some of these changes are a byproduct of the Microsoft .NET strategy.

ASP.NET and IIS Integration

IIS is a Web server, and one of its functions is to accept HTTP requests. We need to have scripting language that can communicate with IIS in order to do this. Earlier versions of IIS (2.0 through 5.0) used a scripting language called Active Server Pages (ASP). IIS 6.0 uses ASP.NET scripting languages for the same purpose. There are some significant changes to the ASP.NET architecture (compared to the older ASP). Some of those advantages include the following:

- ASP.NET is based on MS .NET framework. ASP.NET can be coded in multiple languages. (C#, VB.NET, Jscript.NET, etc.)

- You can have multiple language code in the same ASP.NET page. In other words, you can have a VB.NET function in a C# ASP.NET page.

- ASP code is interpreted (the code is complied *line by line*, not as the complete source file at once), while ASP.NET code is compiled. (The complete source file is complied once, not line-by-line compilation.) This makes for a *significant performance increase* in IIS 6.0.

- ASP.NET allows you three levels of caching. You can cache complete pages. The second option is to cache selected parts of the pages. (Referred to as *fragment caching*). The third option is to use *Caching API*. Developers can use this to exert extensive control over caching behavior, and thus increase performance.

Unicode Transformation Format-8 (UTF-8)

The earlier version of IIS log file was only in English. This was a major issue for multilingual Web sites. Multilingual support is enabled by supporting UCS Transformation Format (UTF) 8 characters codes. Computer applications do not understand human-readable characters. They only understand binary code. There are conversion tables available to convert a key value to a human readable character (those tables are referred as *Local Character Sets* or *Unicode formats*). The tables were language specific. Therefore, we could not read an English log file entry in Japanese. UTF-8 format rectifies these problems. We can instruct HTTP.sys to log details in specific language format. FTP site login does not support UTF-8 login. Therefore, we can maintain multiple log files in multiple languages. UTF-8 support is available for URLs and filenames in IIS 6.0. Active Server Pages (ASP) will also have the UTF-8 support. The Unicode code is converted into UTF-8 in this instance.

XML Metabase

The information store that contains IIS configuration settings is referred as the *metabase*. The metabase is a hierarchical database in which all the information needed to configure IIS is stored.

The metabase data was in binary format in earlier IIS versions. It was difficult to edit the entries, or even to read them, since the information was in binary. The IIS 6.0 metabase, on the other hand, is in *XML format*. These Extensible Markup Language files are plain text. You can use a general text editor to change the XML entries, and these changes can even be performed when ISS 6.0 is running. Editing the XML metabase while IIS is running is referred to as "*edit while running.*" You do not need to restart IIS to reflect the changes. (Unless you make overwrite the schema file with a new version.)

This design change has also significantly increased the performance of IIS 6.0. It has reduced the start-up and shutdown time of ISS considerably. (All the IIS settings were in the inetinfo.exe and system registry. This will result in multiple reads from the registry and accessing system resources as start-up time. We also need to clear all memory references at the shutdown time. We do not need to do these functions in IIS 6.0 due to the XML metabase.)

The metabase consists of the following two XML files:

- **Metabase.xml** An XML document that contains ISS configuration values for the server (for example, Web site details, virtual directory details).

- **MBSchema.xml** An XML document in which the metabase XML schema is stored, which acts as a *validation tool* to enter correct metabase values in metabase.xml.

The metabase files are located in the **Systemroot\System32\Inetsrv** directory. You need administrator permission to view the contents of the metabase entries. You cannot edit the metabase.xml file. You will not be able to edit the MBSchema.xml file directly. The schema changes are enabled by using Active Directory Service Interface (ADSI). Editing a metabase.xml file is a tedious task. A simple approach is to use the IIS Manager interface to make the changes. However, this could save some effort for the expert users. It is possible to have simultaneous changes to the metabase.xml. (The schema is changed by ADSI while the administrator is making some changes to the metabase.xml file). We can prevent this by using access control lists (ACLs) on the metabase files. This will prevent the XML file changes when the schema changes are made. The metabase history feature stores a history of the metabase.XML file changes. This is valuable for IIS to execute new metabase changes.

Thus far, you have learned about the installation process and the new features in IIS 6.0. In the following sections, we will practice using the interface to perform common IIS management tasks. You will learn how to create, manage, stop, start, and delete IIS components. (Web, FTP, NNTP, and SMTP servers).

Managing IIS 6.0

The primary tool for managing IIS 6.0 is an MMC called **IIS Manager**. Most of the management of IIS functions can be done using the IIS Manager.

Performing Common Management Tasks

First of all, let's get familiar with the IIS Manager Console. How can we start the IIS Manager? We can load the IIS Manager in the following ways.

1. Go to **Start | Administrative Tools | Internet Information Services (IIS) Manager**.

2. Go to **My Computer | Manage.** Select and expand **IIS Manager** node.

IIS manager is the primary interface to handle all Internet-related functions. We can set up Web sites,

Site Setup

We can set up Web and FTP sites using IIS Manager. We can also configure SMTP and NNTP virtual servers using IIS Manager. The WWW, FTP, NNTP, and SMTP servers can be installed manually or using scripts (unattended setup). Please follow these steps to install the components manually:

1. Navigate to **Start | Control Panel | Add Remove Programs**.

2. Click the **Add Remove Windows** Component button.

3. Select the **Application Server** option from the Windows Component window, and then click **Details**.

4. Select **IIS** and click **Details** in the **Application Server** window.

5. Select the options you want to install (Web, NNTP, FTP, and SMTP).

6. Click **OK** and the installation process will begin.

7. You will be presented with a confirmation screen at the end of the installation process.

Let's look closely on how to create and maintain Web, FTP, NNTP, and SMTP sites. All these subjects will be discussed as a subsection from now on.

Setting up a Web Site

All Web sites can be created and managed in IIS Manager. This is a wizard-driven example. Therefore, it is a simple task to create a Web site from scratch. Let's learn the process to create a Web site using IIS Manager.

1. Start **IIS Manager** (refer to the previous section on Site Setup).

2. Navigate to **Web Sites** node and right-click it.

3. Select **New** then **Web Site**. You should get a screen similar to Figure 26.3. (You can also create a Web site from XML file settings. This option is commonly used to create Web sites from a backup configuration. In most case you will be using the wizard to create a new Web site.)

Figure 26.3 Creating a New Web Site in IIS Manager

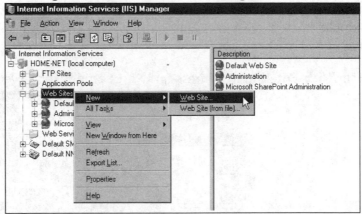

4. You will be greeted with the **Welcome to the Web Site Creation Wizard**. Click **Next** on this screen.

5. In the **Web Site Description** window enter the Web site name. We will create a Web site called "TestWebSite." Then click **Next**. Your screen should be similar to Figure 26.4

Figure 26.4 Entering the Web Site Name

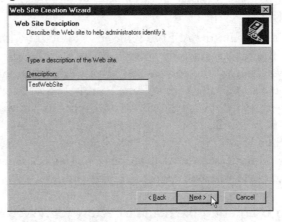

6. The next screen will be the **IP Address and Port Settings** window. Let's assume my Web site domain name is www.mytestwebsite.com and it runs on port 80. Put these details under the **Host Header** (please refer to *Hosting Multiple Web Sites* in the next section for further details) and **TCP Post this Web site should use** text boxes. Let's assume that we don't assign a specific IP address for this Web site. Therefore, leave the **Enter the IP address to use for this web site** combo box with **(All Unassigned)** property. (This is the default value.) We will not be able to refer to the Web site by its IP address if we do not assign an IP address. This could be handy for intranet development. We rely on Host Headers to find the site by selecting (All Unassigned) option. We also don't need to assign

port 80 as the default port. If any port is assigned other than port 80, then we need to change the URL to reflect that. (For example, if we run www.mytestwebsite.com on port 100, we will use www.mytestwebsitecom:100 as the URL.) After all the values are entered, please click **Next**. The screen should be similar to Figure 26.5.

Figure 26.5 Entering IP Address and Port Settings for a Web Site

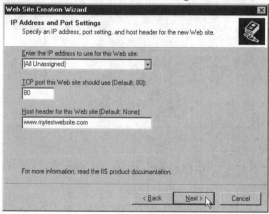

7. The next window is the **Web Site Home Directory** window (Figure 26.6). The *home directory* is where the physical files of a Web site reside. All the content and executable files are stored here.

8. Enter the path to find the ASP.NET files that associate with the Web site. In my example, the files are found at c:\inetpub\wwwroot\testWebSite directory. Therefore, when a user enters www.mytestwebsite.com, it will point to this directory. Microsoft strongly recommends that the home directory volume is an NTFS drive. Please click the **Browse** button and navigate to that folder. The **Allow anonymous access to this web site** flag is checked by default. Allowing anonymous access will enable the users to navigate the site without authenticating themselves. This is not recommended for sites with sensitive business information. Please refer to the *Configuring Authentication Settings* section for further details. Click **Next** to navigate to the next window.

Figure 26.6 Entering the Home Directory for a Web Site

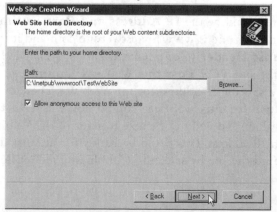

9. The next window is the **Web Site Access Permissions** screen. This is a very important screen. We can configure the access to our Web site using this screen. The **Read** and **Run scripts** options are ticked by default. The **Execute** option refers to granting execute permission for Dynamic Link Libraries (such as ISAPI DLLs or CGI applications) in IIS space. Most of the business logic and interfaces to 3rd-party business models will be stored as ISAPI DLLs or CGI Applications. Therefore we may need to enable **Execute** access to communicate with these entities. The **Write** option will enable the user of the Web site to upload/write data into the Web site's source directories (in this case, c:\inetpub\www-root\testWebSite directory). Finally, the **Browse** option will enable *directory browsing* on the Web site. This option will produce a complete directory information list (files and their attributes – size, last modified time stamp, etc.) when a user navigates to the directory. Therefore, we can get a complete file list using a Web browser interface. This is not widely recommended. (Since it exposes all the files and interfaces to Web site users. It will be a large security breach if Anonymous access is also enabled.) I have selected the default options and the screen should be similar to Figure 26.7. Finally, click **Next** to finish the creation of the Web site. You will get a window confirming your creation of the Web site.

Figure 26.7 Entering Access Permissions for a Web Site

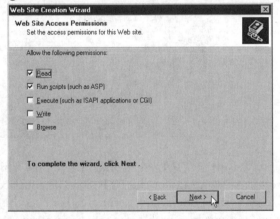

Setting up an FTP Server

The FTP site setup is similar to Web site setup. Most of the setup has the same information as the Web site setup. FTP site will enable the user to share data with others. The users can upload data or download data from our FTP site. Let's learn how to create an FTP site using IIS Manager.

1. Open IIS Manager.

2. Click the **FTP sites**, right-click and select **New**.

3. Select **FTP Site** from the context menu. (You can also read the FTP site settings from an XML configuration file.)

4. Click **Next** from the **Welcome to the FTP site Creation Wizard**.

5. Enter the FTP site name in the **FTP Site Description** window. We will name our FTP site "TestFTPSite" and click **Next**.

6. Let's enter the IP address and the port number for the Web site in the **IP Address and Port Settings** window. The default port number for an FTP site is 21. You can use a different port number than 21. (Most corporate firewalls will open port 80 for Web and 21 for FTP access. If you change the FTP port to another number, we need to reconfigure the firewall to let the traffic into the enterprise. The next step is to select the correct IP address from the combo box. We will use the default **(All Unassigned)** for our demonstration. You can also assign a dedicated IP address for the FTP site. The user will use this IP address to access the FTP site. (We are using the IP address of the IIS machine if we leave the (All Unassigned) option selected.) The screen should be similar to Figure 26.8. Click **Next** to navigate to the next window.

Figure 26.8 Entering IP Address and Port Numbers for an FTP Site

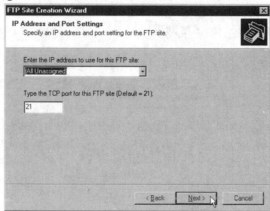

7. The next window is the **FTP User Isolation** window. This window will enable you to configure the security settings for the FTP site. The user access for FTP server can be managed in several ways. The default setting is that every user has access to other user directories. This will not be a problem in many cases since a company FTP site will distribute generic information regardless of the user (e.g., enable Beta product download to the test users). The user will have access to *all files* if the user is authenticated. In some cases this model may not work. We may need to give different users to access different information. We need to *isolate* users to different directories in this case. FTP user isolation prevents users from accessing the FTP home directory of another user on this FTP site. We can select the **Isolate users** to accommodate this scenario. This option uses NTFS directory authentication to perform this task. We can also go a step further by asking Active Directory to authenticate the user and assign an FTP home directory for the user. This can be configured using the **Isolate the users using Active Directory** option. We can also use iisftp.vbs script to perform these functions at a command line with the **/isolation** switch. This will be discussed later in the chapter. We will stick with the default and click the **Next** button. (Figure 26.9 shows the isolation options.)

Figure 26.9 FTP Site User Isolation Options

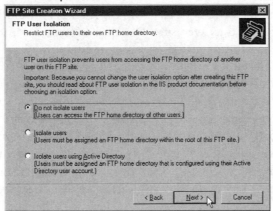

8. The next window will enable you to enter a physical directory path where the FTP site refers. We will put C:\Inetpub\ftproot\TestFTPSite as the physical directory for our FTP site. This directory will be exposed to the public access. Therefore, make sure the data in this directory is not sensitive to the organization. Click **Next.**

9. The Next window is **FTP Site Access Permission** window. The default is just read access to users. You can also enable the **Write** access if the users need to upload files to the server. This option can be helpful in some cases (for example, your sales team needs to upload sales data to the FTP server for the weekly accounting purposes). This option will enable users to upload malicious content to the server. Therefore, it is not recommend to enable **write** access unless necessary. The screen should be similar to Figure 26.10. Click **Next** and the FTP site creation process will be completed.

Figure 26.10 FTP Site Access Permissions Window

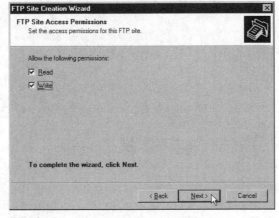

Setting up an SMTP Server

We can also set up a virtual SMTP server using IIS Manager. SMTP servers help IIS to deliver simple e-mail functionality to its Web sites. E-mail delivery is a common task for Web sites. We use e-mails to transmit business information or for administration purposes (e.g., e-mail error message to the system administrators) from our IIS components. Therefore, Microsoft included the SMTP server to be installed with IIS 6.0. SMTP server fully supports Simple Mail Transfer Protocol and is compatible with SMTP clients. SMTP servers use Transport Layer Security (TLS) encryption to protect the e-mail information. The SMTP server will communicate with the Domain Name System (DNS) to validate the recipient's e-mail address. The sent e-mails are transferred to the **drop** directory. The SMTP server will transmit all the messages in the **drop** directory. Therefore, other non-IIS 6.0 applications can also send e-mail by putting the application messages in the **drop** directory. The delivered e-mail will be picked up from a **pickup** directory. Let's learn the process to set up an SMTP server.

1. Start IIS Manager.

2. Navigate to the correct computer and select **Default SMTP Server**.

3. Right-click and select **New.** Then select **Virtual Server**.

4. Enter the SMTP site name in the **New SMTP Virtual Server Wizard.** We will use "TestSMTPServer" for our demonstration. Click **Next.** You should have a screen similar to Figure 26.11.

Figure 26.11 Entering the Name of the SMTP Virtual Server

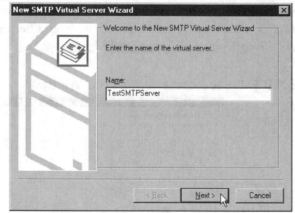

5. Select the correct IP address settings from the **Select IP Address** window. We will select 127.0.0.1. Click **Next.**

6. Select a home directory for the virtual server by using the **Browse** button of the **Select a Home Directory** screen. We will refer to C:\Inetpub\mailroot\Mailbox for our home directory. Non-IIS 6.0 applications can also use the SMTP server to send e-mail. Therefore, it is a good practice to have general access to the home directory. (It shouldn't have any restricted NTFS permissions on it. It shouldn't be an OS drive to make generic mail access from other applications.) Click **Next.**

7. Enter the domain name of the SMTP server at the **Default Domain** window and click **Finish.** You will get a message to confirm the creation of the server.

Setting up an NNTP Server

The Network News Transfer Protocol (NNTP) server helps the IIS 6.0 server to facilitate discussion group functionalities. The IIS setup creates an NNTP server by default. Let's try to create a new NNTP server.

1. Load IIS Manager.

2. Navigate to the correct computer and select **Default NNTP Server**.

3. Right-click and select **New.** Then select **Virtual Server**.

4. Enter the NNTP site name in the **New NNTP Virtual Server Wizard.** We will use "TestNNTPServer" for our demonstration. Click **Next.** The screen should be very similar to the initial SMTP screen.

5. Select the correct IP address settings from the **Select IP Address** window. We will select 127.0.0.1. You also need to provide a different port number for each NNTP server. The common port number associated with NNTP servers is 119. You can also use another port number. We will use 1001 for this demonstration. You can also have multiple NNTP servers. The best practice is to use different IP addresses for each NNTP site. If a lot of IP addresses are not available, then we can use multiple port numbers on a single IP address. Click **Next.** The screen should be similar to Figure 26.12.

Figure 26.12 Entering IP Address and Port Numbers for NNTP Server

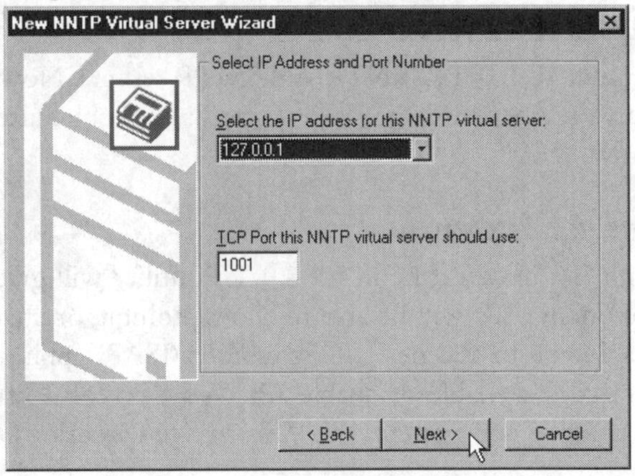

6. The Next screen will be to select a home directory for the NNTP virtual server. We will select C:\Inetpub\nntpfile\root as our home directory. Click **Next.**

7. The next window is **Select Storage Medium**. This option will enable us to choose between **File System** and **Remote Share**. This is where the news messages are stored. The **File System** option will enable the user to store the news content on the local

machine. The **Remote Share** option will enable it to be stored remotely. We need to know the machine name and user details (i.e., user name and password details) in order to store news content remotely. We will select the default **File System** option. The screen should be similar to Figure 26.13. Click **Next**.

Figure 26.13 Selecting a File System for NNTP Server

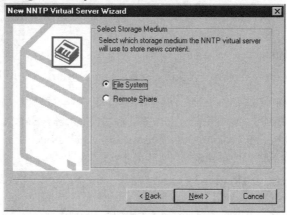

8. The next screen will enable you to define the physical directory in which the messages are going to be stored. Click the **Browse** button and navigate to the directory. We will use C:\Inetpub\nntpfile\drop as our file system location. Click **Finish** to create the NNTP virtual server. You will get a message to confirm the creation of the server.

Common Administrative Tasks

We have learned to install Web, FTP, NNTP, and SMTP servers. Now we are in a stage to practice our knowledge and dive further into the IIS 6.0 world. Let's concentrate on learning some common administrative tasks now.

Enabling Web Service Extensions

Web Service Extensions is a new feature in IIS 6.0. This utility will give a Control Panel-like function-ality on your IIS components. We will be able to allow, prohibit, or change the properties using this tool. This will also enable you to add new IIS extensions (ISAPI applications and 3rd-party IIS tools) to the IIS 6.0 server. You can also enable or disable **All Web Service Extensions** by using this manage-ment console. Here is a list of components the Web service extensions can enable or disable.

- ASP.NET executions
- ASP executions
- CGI and ISAPI Applications
- Front Page Server Extensions 2000 and 2002
- WebDAV support for IIS directories

We can get to the Web service extensions by using **Start | Administrative Tools | IIS Manager** and clicking on **Web Server Extensions** node on a selected server name. Figure 26.14 is similar to a default view of the Web service extensions window.

Figure 26.14 Web Service Extensions View

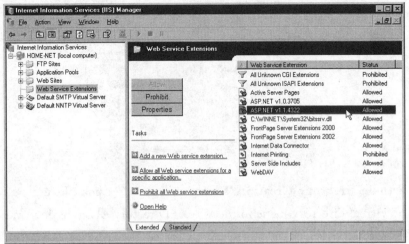

Creating and Working with Virtual Directories

Creating virtual directories is a simple task in IIS 6.0. A virtual directory is a *reference* to an existing directory by a Web or FTP site. We can get access to the subdirectories from a root Web or FTP directory. Sometimes we need to go beyond the root directory access information to process a Web request. We use virtual directories to remedy these scenarios. (For example, we can store all the images file in a large shopping catalogue in one directory. Then we can point multiple Web servers to access this images directory as a virtual directory. It will be low maintenance to modify one images directory.) The Web or FTP site will be able to refer to this directory as it exists within its directory structure (even if it physically exists out of its directory structure). One of the limitations will be the Web site deployment to a new server. Because the virtual directory is not a physical subdirectory (under the home FTP or Web directory) we simply cannot copy and paste the files to the new server. We also need to configure the virtual directories manually. Here is the process to create a virtual directory for a Web site. (The FTP server virtual directory creation process is very similar to this.)

1. Open IIS Manager.
2. Select the server and right-click on the Web site. This will be the **Default Web Site** for our demonstration purposes.
3. Select **New | Virtual Directory**. The screen should be similar to Figure 26.15

Figure 26.15 Creating a Virtual Directory for a Web Site

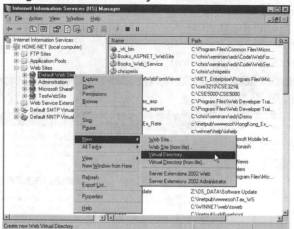

4. The **Virtual Directory Creation Wizard** will appear. Click Next.

5. Type the virtual directory name in the Virtual Directory Alias window and click Next. We will enter "TestVirtualDir" for our demonstration.

6. In the Web Site Content Directory choose the physical directory the virtual directory is point to. We will choose C:\test to point our TestVirtualDir. Therefore form the IIS point of view, every time we say TestVirtualDir it is pointing to C:\test. Click **Next**

7. Select the access permissions from the Virtual Directory Access Permissions window. The default is Read and Run Scripts. The options are very similar to Web site creation options. (Please refer to the Web Site Creation section.) Click **Next** to finish the creation process. You will be greeted with a confirmation screen. A virtual directory accessed in the same way as a subdirectory under the root directory. The external user will not know that he or she is communicating to a virtual directory (as apposed to a subdirectory under the root Web directory).

Hosting Multiple Web Sites

Hosting multiple Web sites can be done in three ways. The most common is to assign an IP address to every new Web site. This used to be the most common practice. The obvious limitation is the number of IP addresses available for the organization. This will not be a major issue for internal access within the enterprise. (Behind a corporate firewall. The enterprise will have its own private addressing range. We can use the private IP address for these Web sites.) This practice is also an expensive one to manage. The following is the IIS 6.0 process to assign an IP address for a particular site:

1. Open **IIS Manager**.

2. Select the server and right-click on the Web site. This will be the Default Web Site for our demonstration purposes.

3. Click **Properties** and select the **Web Site** tab. Your screen should be similar to Figure 26.16.

Figure 26.16 Assigning an IP Address for a Web Site

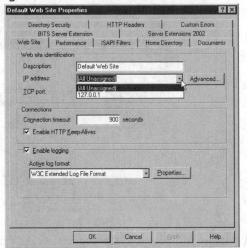

4. Click the IP address combo box and select or type the IP address your Web site should refer to. Click the **OK** button at the bottom. We will select **(All Unassigned)** for this example.

    The second option is to use the same IP address and use a different port number. A different port number will be assigned to each Web site. (For example, Web site A will run on port 1001 and Web site B will run on port 1002). This will require you to change the URL of the Web site. (For example, Web site A could be accessed as www.siteA.com:1001 and site B can be accessed as www.siteB.com:1002). This would be a great mechanism to handle internal or intranet access behind a corporate firewall.

    The last option is to assign unique host headers on a single IP address. The host headers are unique DNS names that identify different Web sites. IIS will channel all the requests for a single IP address and filter them using the *header information*. The filter process will forward them to the correct Web site according to the header name. This is a good mechanism to implement small to medium Web sites on a single machine. We need dedicated IP addresses for large Web sites. (For example, 150 Web sites running on a single IP address using host headers will affect performance and it is not scalable.) Here is the process to create a header for a site. Follow the steps from 1 to 4 from the last example. Then click the **Advance** button. You will get the following window (Figure 26.17).

Figure 26.17 Entering Header Information for a Web Site

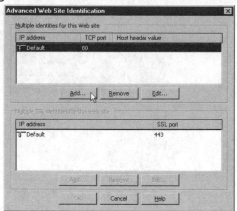

5. Click the **Add** button and you will see Figure 26.18. Choose the IP Address of the Web site and enter the port number. Then enter the header information (DNS entry) in the **Host Header value** text box and click **OK**. (We have entered a new header called www.myDefaultSite.com for our **Default Web Site**).

Figure 26.18 Entering a New Header for Default Web Site

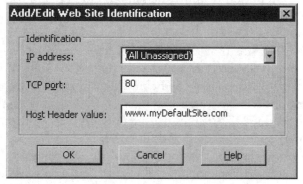

If you refer to the *Site Setup – Setting up a Web Site* section, you'll see that we already have a sample Web site called TestWebSite. It has the header www.mytestwebsite.com. Now, if we investigate closely, we have two Web sites (the **Default web site** and **TestWebSite**) running on *port 80 of the same IP address*.

Please note that the mixed case in the host header file will not matter from IIS 6.0 point of view. It is not case sensitive. The host header implementation will be an issue for SSL implementations. SSL certificates are issued for a Web site and they are tied to an IP address or machine name. The issue is all the Web sites use one IP address. Therefore, SSL-supported sites should have their dedicated IP address for the Web site.

Assigning Resources to Applications

Resources can be assigned to applications in different ways. The most common way is to use a **Properties** tab to control caching, performance, and process options. You can also use the bandwidth throttling option to restrict resources for a given Web site. (This option can be found under the **Performance** section in the **Properties** tab.) Bandwidth throttling will limit the network bandwidth resources for a Web site. The maximum bandwidth value is 1024 KB per second. This is also the default value. You can enable bandwidth throttling by ticking the **Limit the network bandwidth to this Web site** check box and specifying maximum kilobytes per second value. You can also limit the number of connections to the Web site by using this **Performance** tab. Tick the **Unlimited** or **Connection limit to** option buttons and specify a connection value.

Working with ASP.NET

ASP.NET is the advanced version of Active Server Pages. IIS 6.0 will enable you to run both ASP and ASP.NET applications. The ASP.NET scripts are built on .NET model and the ASP scripts follow the old windows Component Object Model (COM). The ASP.NET model is scalable and performs better than the ASP model. We can use ASP scripting inside ASP.NET scripts. ASP.NET applications can be built on any .NET compatible language (C#, VB.NET, Jscript.NET, etc.). We can enable ASP.NET support from the Web service extension interface. Here are the steps:

1. Navigate to **Start | Administrative Tools | IIS Manager**.

2. Click **Web Server Extensions** node on a selected server name. Figure 26.14 is similar to a default view of the Web service extensions window.

3. Select the **ASP.NET** option from the Web Service Extension window. You can click the **Allow** or **Prohibit** button to enable or disable ASP.NET access.

Backing up and Restoring the Metabase

Metabase has the IIS configuration setting as XML entries. The metabase has two components. Those are the metabase.xml and the metabase schema file. It is a good practice to back up the metabase regularly. The metabase back will back up both the metabase.xml and metabase schema files (a .md*VersionNumber* file for the metabase and .sc*VersionNumber* file for the schema file). The metabase can be safely restored (from a backup) if we lose all the IIS settings. This utility will back up only IIS entries. It does not back up the Web site content. Therefore, you need to configure the Web site manually after a restore. Here are the steps to create and restore backups:

1. Open IIS Manager.

2. Select the server and right-click and select **All Task | Backup / Restore Configuration**.

3. You will get the Configuration Backup/ Restore window (see Figure 26.19).

4. Select the **Create Backup** button to create a backup (It will take the next version number by default) or select a backup and click the Restore button to restore the IIS settings.

Figure 26.19 Backup and Restore Metabase

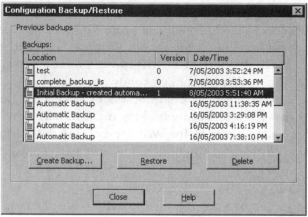

Enabling Health Detection

Health detection enables IIS to monitor its worker process functionality. We can enable pinging and configure rapid application fail over (discussed in *503 errors* under *Troubleshooting* later in the chapter). You can also set the start up and shut down time for a worker process using the option.

Enable Health Detection

You can enable health detection by following this process. This process only works if you're running in worker process isolation mode.

1. Start **IIS Manager**.

2. Select **Application Pools**.

3. Navigate to the correct Web site

4. Right-click on the site and click **Properties**.

5. Select the **Health** tab and enter your settings. You can configure the *ping* interval using the *Enable Pinging* group box. This interval describes the timeframe to contact a worker process to make sure it is functioning accordingly. The default setting is 240 seconds. *Enable Rapid fail-over* group box functionality is explained in the *503 error* section. You can also configure the worker process startup time (if the worker process restarts) and shutdown time (if the worker process gets into a deadlock position) using this screen.

Managing IIS Security

We are going to investigate the security concepts in ISS 6.0 in this section. The core concepts haven't changed much since IIS 5.0. Windows 2003 default installation does extend more security features than the previous Windows server versions. Internet access, ASP scripts, WebDAV, and FrontPage Extensions are all disabled by default. This adds another level of security to the server. The default Internet Explorer access is restricted to **High Security Zone** and no Web sites are permitted till they are added to the **Trusted Zone** links. Let's learn how to configure the security settings for a Web site in IIS 6.0.

Configuring Authentication Settings

The authentications setting are configured at the Web site level. There are several ways to protect your Web site from intruders. The security settings for a Web site can be viewed by right-clicking on a Web site in **IIS Manager** and selecting **Properties**. The settings can be found in the **Directory Security** tab. Figure 26.20 displays the configurable options of security settings.

Figure 26.20 Directory Security Tab for a Web Site

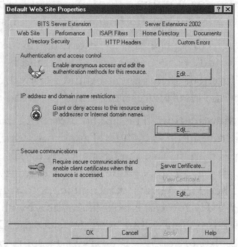

The first option is to restrict users by forcing them to authenticate to the IIS server. This can be achieved by clicking the **Edit** button of the **Authenticate and Access Control** group box. Figure 26.21 describes the options available for authenticating in IIS 6.0.

Figure 26.21 Authentication Options Available in IIS 6.0

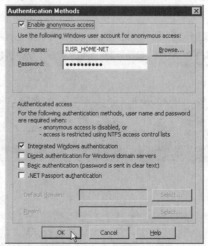

- **Enable anonymous access** This will enable the users to use the site without explicitly logging on. The IIS will impersonate the IUSR_*MachineName* account to execute scripts in this instance. A safer option is to disable the anonymous access and force the user to authenticate using one of the following methods.

- **Integrated Windows authentication** This was formally known as Windows NT Challenge / Response or NTLM. It is a secure form of authentication that hashes the user name and the password before any network transmission. It uses Kerberos version 5 for authentication if the client browser supports Kerberos. Otherwise, it will use NTLM authentication to protect user name and password data.

- **Digest authentication for Windows domain servers** This option will use Digest Authentication. Please refer to *New IIS Features* section to learn about Digest security.

- **Basic authentication** This option uses clear text username and password for authentication. This is not secure and not recommended. This could be useful in a less secure environment (e.g., a development environment behind a firewall). You can alternatively use SSL encryption to encrypt the clear text username and password details.

- **.NET Passport Authentication** This option uses .NET passports to authenticate Web users. This is a new feature in IIS 6.0. .NET Passport is a single sign-on mechanism. The incoming HTTP requests must have the passport credentials (user name and password) inside the query string or as a cookie value. (We can comprise the cookie and be exposed to malicious attacks. Therefore, Microsoft recommends to run **.NET Passport Authentication** over SSL.) You can enable this option by clicking the **.NET Passport Authentication** check box. You will be asked to select the **Domain** the IIS server belongs to and the **Realm** to configure the .NET passport credentials. These details need to be available to the client for future requests to the Web server.

The second option is to restrict users on an IP address level. We can list all the permitted IP addresses using this method. The users are denied access if they are not accessing from this permitted list. This could be achieved by clicking the **Edit** button under **IP Address and Domain name restrictions** group box on the Web site's Properties window (Figure 26.20). You will be presented with Figure 26.22.

Figure 26.22 Assigning IP Address Restrictions on a Web Site

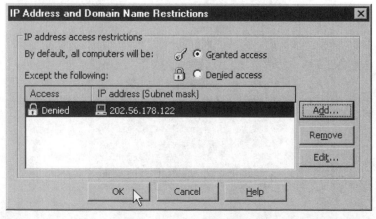

In this demonstration, we enable all computers to have access to our Web site by default. We can also restrict access to users by including their IP address in a list. You do this by clicking the **Add** button and entering the IP address. The above example will let any user access the Web site **unless** their IP address is 202.56.178.122.

The third option is to enable SSL and attach security certificates to the Web site. You do this by using the buttons on the **Secure Communications** group box (Figure 26.20). The **Server Certificate** button will initiate a wizard to configure a certificate for the Web site. The **Edit** button will enable you to view any existing certificate entries. The Certificate will have information on the version, serial number, signature algorithm (e.g., sha1RSA), Issuer, Valid From, Valid To, Subject, and Public key information. The certificate has keys that are used to authenticate the server and the client for SSL encryption. The Web server will create a **Session** or **Encryption** key according to the security certificate. This key is used to encrypt all the communication with the server and the client. The strength of the encryption is measured by the length of the encryption key (this is in bits). The encryption strength can be either 40 bits or 128 bits. The choice of the strength of the encryption depends on the sensitivity of the data. (High importance will require 128 bits – as apposed to 40).

Troubleshooting IIS 6.0

Let's concentrate our attention on some of the troubleshooting associated with IIS 6.0. We can divide this troubleshooting section into three subsections: content errors, connection errors, and miscellaneous errors. First we look at content errors.

Troubleshooting Content Errors

Content errors are caused by ASP or ASP.NET application code. We need the application code or scripts to perform business intelligence task to derive data. These errors are associated with these scripts. We will try to get familiar with these errors. Her are some of the common ones.

Static Files Return 404 Errors

This is the most common IIS error. This could be due to two main reasons. The user may type in an incorrect URL. Or the file extension is invalid. IIS is configured to only accept requests from files that have a valid extension. (For example, IIS will understand the "aspx" extension, but it will not understand ".abc" file extension.)

IIS checks for the file extension as soon as it gets a request. All the valid file extensions are available as Multipurpose Internet Mail Extensions (MIME) formats in IIS. MIME types will instruct the Web server how to process the incoming requests. (For example, if you get ".aspx" file, the Web server knows to instruct ASP.NET to process the request.) The MIME type does not have any effect on the returned data to the client. (The returned data will be in HTML for most HTTP requests.) IIS will start to process the file if the incoming file extension is present in the MIME list for IIS 6.0.

Dynamic Content Returns a 404 Error

IIS 6.0 default installation does not activate ASP.NET and CGI applications. These have to be manually enabled using Web Service Extensions module (discussed above). If the ASP.NET or CGI applications are not enabled, you will get a 404 error on dynamic content.

Sessions Lost Due to Worker Process Recycling

Sessions were very popular in ASP scripts. (A "Session" could be described as a data storage mechanism for a single user on a Web site. We use to manipulate HTTP cookies to store information about the user activities. This information is referred as Session data.) These ASP sessions were alive till we restarted the IIS server. IIS 6.0 works on a **worker process model**. Therefore, when the worker process stops, we lose all the session information. The default installation will configure IIS to recycle worker process every 120 minutes. (Session data can grow to a large number in a high-scale Web farm. This could have an adverse affect on the performance and the memory management of the Web servers. Therefore, IIS 6.0 will *empty* the session information by recycling the worker process every 120 minutes by default.) We can either disable worker process recycling or extend the time span to get over this problem. Here are the steps.

Configure Worker Process Recycling

1. Open **IIS Manager**.
2. Select **Application Pools** and right-click the correct application pool for your Web site.
3. Select Properties.
4. Select **Recycling** tab.
5. To disable worker process recycling, **untick** the **Recycle worker process (in minutes)** check box. Alternatively you can tick the box and enter a figure to extend the time.
6. Click **OK**.

ASP.NET Pages are Returned as Static Files

ASP.NET files should be processed at the server and the HTML is returned to the browser. (In some cases this could be DHTML, depending on the complexity of the browser.) If the IIS server does not recognize an ASP.NET file (.aspx file extension), the server will return the static text as the reply. This can happen if you reinstall IIS without reregistering ASP.NET.

Troubleshooting Connection Errors

Let's concentrate on the Connection errors now. Mainly connection issues with IIS and ASP.NET cause these errors.

503 Errors

This error is generally caused by HTTP.sys overload. It could be due to two reasons. Either the request queue length has exceeded the number of available application pool resources, or the problem is **rapid-fail protection** initiated by IIS.

Every application pool has a configurable queue length. If the request pool queue exceeds this amount, the HTTP.sys will not be able to process the requests. This will result in a **503 error** been thrown at the client.

Extend The Queue Length of An Application Pool

We can investigate the process to increase the queue length of the application process. The default value for the queue length is 2000 requests. We can extend the value by following these steps:

1. Open **IIS Manager**.

2. Select **Application Pools** and right-click the correct application pool for your Web site.

3. Select **Properties**.

4. Select **Performance** tab.

5. In the **Request Queue Limit** group box, select the **Limit the kernel request queue** tick box and put a value in the text box.

6. Click **OK**.

IIS initiates **rapid-fail protection** when too many application pool errors are generated for a specified time frame. The default is five errors occurring in five minutes. This scenario will trigger the IIS to restart and issue a **503 error** to the client.

Extend The Error Count and Timeframe

Use the following steps to increase the error count and expand the timeframe. Usually this is resulting from a memory leak in the application code. Here is the process to configure rapid-fail protection:

1. Open **IIS Manager**.

2. Select **Application Pools** and right-click the correct application pool for your Web site.

3. Select **Properties**.

4. Select the **Health** tab.

5. In the **Enable rapid-fail protection** group box, enter the value for **Failures** and **Time Period (in minutes)** spaces.

6. Click **OK**.

Clients Cannot Connect to Server

Windows 2003 server comes with an inbuilt software firewall. **Internet Connection Firewall** is disabled by default. If you enable the firewall, you need to provide the correct settings to let your clients into the system. Please refer to the **Internet Connection Firewall** section for configuration details.

401 Error—Sub Authentication Error

Anonymous accesses to Web sites are managed by the **sub-authentication component (iissuba.dll).** This DLL is not enabled by default in IIS 6.0. The reason is to avoid potential security risks due to anonymous access. We can enable the sub-authentication component by registering iissuba.dll and setting the **AnonymousPasswordSync** attribute in the Metabase to **true**. The IIS administrator will get a warning when anonymous access is enabled.

Client Requests Timing Out

There was less emphasis on time out connections in IIS 5.0 and below. IIS 6.0 has made some considerable ground on this issue. IIS 6.0 has locked down and reduced the size of many client request properties. This has resulted in better efficiency and performance. Here are the new features in IIS 6.0 to deal with time outs:

- **Limits on response buffering** We can buffer all the process output at the server end and send the whole output to the client as a single entity (as apposed to processing some data and sending the information and starting to process the next bit of the initial request). This is referred to as **Response buffering**. Limits on response buffering is 4.0 M. A timeout will result if the buffer exceeds the limit. This feature can be modified by using the **ASPBufferingLimit** metabase property.

- **Limits on posts** The maximum ASP post size is 204,800 bytes. (**Post** refers to a HTTP POST response to the Web server. This is usually done as an HTML form submission. Sometimes these HTML form variables can be very lengthy. The maximum size allowed as HTTP POST request is referred to as **Post limit/size**.) Each individual field can have up to 100 kilobits of data. If these fields are exceeded, a time out error is thrown. This property can also be modified from the **AspMaxRequestEntityAllowed** property of the metabase.

- **Header size limitation** HTTP.sys only accepts a request that has less than 16K as the request header. HTTP.sys believes that anything larger is malicious and terminates the connection. You can change this value by modifying the **MaxRequestBytes** registry key.

Troubleshooting Other Errors

We will investigate some miscellaneous troubleshooting errors in this section. These errors do not clearly fall into content or connection categories.

File Not Found Errors for UNIX and Linux Files

IIS 6.0 can access and share information with UNIX and Linux systems. IIS 6.0, UNIX, and Linux all support mixed-case filenames. Unfortunately, IIS **static file cache** stores filenames as upper case. Therefore, the first file access will be trouble-free. The subsequent access to the same file will result in a "**File Not Found**" error because IIS 6.0 will try to extract it from the static file cache. The remedy is to disable static file cache if you deal with UNIX or Linux systems.

ISAPI Filters Are Not Automatically Visible as Properties of the Web Site

IIS 5.0 used to display all the ISAPI filters that are associated with a particular site. IIS 6.0 does not load an ISAPI DLL till it is actually invoked from a client request. Therefore, until the ISAPI DLL is loaded, it will not show up in the **ISAPI tab** of the **Properties** window. Please run IIS 6.0 in isolation mode if you want to get a complete list of ISAPI DLLs available for a site. (Refer to the **New Reliability Features** section to learn how to run IIS 6.0 in isolation mode).

The Scripts and Msadc Virtual Directories Are Not Found in IIS 6.0

IIS 5.0 had executable permission on the **Scripts** and **Msadc** directories. This was one of the common security breaches of IIS 5.0. A malicious user can start to execute code in these virtual directories and take control of the IIS server. Therefore, IIS 6.0 is configured not to have these two directories to beef up security.

Using New IIS Command-Line Utilities

IIS Manager is the GUI interface for all IIS management functions. You can also perform these management functions by using command-line tools. All these command line tools are VBScript functions with "***.vbs:** file extensions. You can get the complete help file information by applying the **/?** Switch on each utility. Let's go through them one by one.

iisweb.vbs

The insweb.vbs utility is used to create and manage Web sites in IIS 6.0. This utility is stored at **System Root\system 32** directory. Iisweb.vbs comes with six main switches. The first argument for iisweb.vbs is one of these main switches. The rest of the arguments are further information to perform the task. The common syntax is:

```
Iiswab [switch] [parameters to switch]
```

iisvdir.vbs

The **iisvdir.vbs** command enables us to create virtual directories for a specific Web site. We can use create, delete, and query switches on this script. It is important to clarify that this command does not generate any new code or physical directories. This command will basically instruct the IIS configuration to point at **existing directories** and refer to it as a local directory of the Web site.

iisftp.vbs

Iisftp.vbs is the command-line tools to administer FTP sites on your IIS server. The functionality is very similar to iisweb.vbs. The only major difference is the association with Active Directories under iisftp.vbs. The parameters to switches change from switch to switch.

The use of the **iisftp /create** is very similar to **iisweb /create.** The input parameters and the command shell output are very similar.

iisftpdr.vbs

The **iisftpdr.vbs** command is very similar to iisvdir.vbs. We create virtual directories for FTP sites (not Web sites) using this command. You can use create, delete, and query switches on this script.

iisback.vbs

Use the **iisback.vbs** utility to create backups and restore IIS configurations. We can back up both the metabase and metabase XML schema data using this tool. The backup creates two files. The ".**md***VersionNumber*" file to back up the metabase and the ".**sc***VersionNumber*" file to back up the metabase schema.

iiscnfg.vbs

The **iiscnfg.vbs** script will enable you to manipulate the configuration settings for IIS 6.0. The main task is to import and export settings of the IIS metabase. You can also select a node of the IIS 6.0 and import and export settings to it. The available switches are import, export, copy, and save.

Chapter 27

Managing and Troubleshooting Terminal Services

In this chapter:

☑ **Understanding Windows Terminal Services**

☑ **Using Terminal Services Components for Remote Administration**

☑ **Installing and Configuring the Terminal Server Role**

☑ **Using Terminal Services Client Tools**

☑ **Using Terminal Services Administrative Tools**

☑ **Troubleshooting Terminal Services**

Introduction

Windows Server 2003, like Windows 2000, includes the Terminal Services component that enables you to connect from remote computers using a Terminal Services client (such as the Remote Desktop Connection [RDC] utility built into Windows XP and Windows 2003). A Windows 2003 terminal server can function in one of several ways. Using a client such as the RDC utility, administrators can perform management tasks on the server from any location on the network. When the terminal server role is installed, it turns the server into an application server, which enables multiple users to connect to the terminal server from "thin clients" or other computers running the client software. These clients can then run applications on a Windows 2003 desktop even if they are using older, less powerful operating systems or client hardware.

In this chapter, we will provide an overview of the benefits of using Windows Server 2003 Terminal Services and how to select the Terminal Services functionality that best fits your needs. We will discuss installation and configuration of the terminal server role, the Terminal Services client software, and licensing issues. You'll learn how to use the Terminal Services administrative tools, including the Terminal Services Manager and Terminal Services Configuration console tools. In addition, we'll discuss the Remote Desktop MMC snap-in, using group policies to control Terminal Services users and clients, Terminal Services extensions to the properties of user accounts and the Terminal Services command-line tools. Finally, we look at how to troubleshoot problems with Terminal Services.

Understanding Windows Terminal Services

The Microsoft Terminal Services feature has evolved and undergone major changes since Microsoft first licensed the technology from Citrix. In the beginning, using Terminal Services required purchasing a separate operating system (Windows NT 4.0 Terminal Server Edition). In Windows 2000, it was included with the Server products, but it was a component that required separate installation. In Windows 2003, the core service is installed with the operating system. This is to enable administration of the server from remote clients right out of the box, with very little additional configuration being necessary, and serves the same purpose as Terminal Services running in remote administration mode in Windows 2000.

Despite its many enhancements and new features in the area of remote administration, Terminal Services still maintains its traditional capability of serving as an application server to which multiple remote clients can connect and run sessions simultaneously. In Windows 2000, this was called *Application Server* mode; now it is referred to as the *Terminal Server* role. When the Terminal Server role is installed, users can connect and use applications that are installed on the server as if they were sitting at its keyboard. By default, when they connect, they will see a Windows 2003 desktop from the server displayed on their local systems and be able to interact with it. Most importantly, all of their session settings and application information will be kept separate from other users. This application-sharing and multi-user capability exists only when the Terminal Server role is installed; it does not exist with the *Terminal Services Remote Administration* feature that is available right out of the box.

Terminal Services Components

The Terminal Services service in Windows 2003 supports a number of components. These include the following:

- Remote Desktop for Administration (formerly called Remote Administration mode in Windows 2000)

- Remote Assistance (RA – a feature introduced in Windows XP)

- The terminal server role (formerly called Application Server mode in Windows 2000)

Remote Desktop for Administration

Remote Desktop for Administration is the key component of Terminal Services that enables remote server administration. It is installed by default, but is disabled; it must be manually enabled and configured by an administrator before you can connect to it. This component enables a maximum of two concurrent connections for the purposes of remotely administering the server. By default, when a Terminal Services client connects to this component, a new session is created and a copy of the Windows 2003 desktop is displayed in a window on the client machine.

It's important to note that this copy of the desktop is not the actual server desktop that the user would see if he or she were sitting down at the server's keyboard. That session is called the console. This is an important distinction, because often the operating system or an installed application will send a popup message to the server console. An administrator connecting to the server using Terminal Services will not see the console by default, and thus will not see the popup messages. You also will not see any applications that might be running on the console session – unless you use the *Remote Desktop Protocol* (RDP) 5.1 or later client to run a remote console session.

In Windows 2000, there was no way to view the console session remotely. However, one of the new Terminal Services client utilities (discussed in more detail later in the chapter) includes this capability.

Remote Assistance

Remote Assistance (RA) depends on and uses the Terminal Services service. However, the way you connect to it is substantially different from the methods used to establish a session with Remote Desktop for Administration or a client session connecting to the multi-user terminal server. RA enables a user at one computer (whom we'll call the Novice) to ask for help from a user at another computer (whom we'll call the Expert or the assistant), on the LAN or across the Internet. This request can be made through Windows Messenger, e-mail, or through a transferred file. The Expert can also offer remote assistance without receiving an explicit request from the Novice (if Group Policy settings are configured to enable offering of remote assistance and the Expert user is listed as an assistant in the Offer Remote Assistance policy, or is a local administrator), but the Novice must grant permission; the Expert can never take over the Novice's computer without the Novice's agreement. This differs from Remote Desktop, in that administrators and users on the Remote Desktop Users list can start a remote session without getting permission from the person who is using the computer locally.

When an Expert receives a request from a Novice, he or she can initiate a connection to the Novice's computer. When connected, the Expert is able to view the actual desktop and applications that are being used by the Novice on his or her computer. In addition, a special application is launched on the Novice's computer that enables him or her to chat with the Expert and control the session, either via text messages or audio (as long as both computers are equipped with full-duplex sound cards, speakers, and microphones). If the Novice desires, the Expert can be allowed to control the Novice's desktop and applications, including taking control of the Novice's cursor. In addition, files can be transferred easily between the two through the RA interface.

RA requires that both computers be running Windows XP or Server 2003. Because security is always a concern in the business environment, RA invitations can require that the assistant provide a password, to prevent an imposter from connecting to the computer while pretending to be the assistant. You can also specify the amount of time for which an RA invitation will remain valid. Users also have the option to turn off the RA feature entirely.

The Terminal Server Role

The original purpose of the Terminal Services was to enable Windows servers to be used in a thin client environment without expensive third-party software such as Citrix MetaFrame. The development of Microsoft's Terminal Services involved the creation of several components that worked together, including a a core architectural component known as *Multi-Win* and a special presentation layer protocol, the Remote Desktop Protocol (RDP) .

The Multi-Win Component

The Multi-Win component sits at a very low level in the operating system and enables more than one user to be logged in locally. The Multi-Win technology was originally created by Citrix for WinFrame and licensed to Microsoft for Windows NT 4.0 Terminal Server Edition. It is a core component of Terminal Services and is used in Remote Desktop for Administration (RDA), Remote Assistance (RA), and the Terminal Server role. Prior to its development, only the user that actually logged on at a server's keyboard (the local console session) was considered a local user. The creation of Multi-Win enabled remote users to log on and use the server as if they were local users. The Multi-Win component not only allows for multiple local users, but it also keeps each of their system and application settings separate, even when many are logged on at the same time.

This new capability enables remote users to actually launch and use applications on the remote system. A Terminal Services session is altogether different. When you establish a terminal server session, by default you see a copy of the desktop from the server to which you have connected. When using Remote Desktop for Administration or the Terminal Server role, by default each terminal user works in his or her own virtual Windows 2003 computer that has been created for that user by the Terminal Services service on the Windows 2003 server. When you double-click an icon within this session and launch an application, it launches in your session on the server. It uses the server's processor, the server's memory, and accesses the server's hard disk. Only images of the screen transfer to the local computer; the application files never leave the server.

The Remote Desktop Protocol (RDP)

The second important Terminal Services component, the Remote Desktop Protocol (RDP), handles the transfer of the screen information from the server to your client. It also ensures that your cursor movements and keystrokes make it from the client back to your session on the server. RDP was based on a set of International Telecommunications Union (ITU) T.120 protocol family. Windows 2000 Terminal Services included RDP v5.0, which increased performance. Windows XP and Server 2003 use RDP 5.1. RDP communicates on port 3389; it uses encryption to protect the information that is sent between the terminal server and the client computer.

Comparing Remote Desktop for Administration and the Terminal Server Role

The primary difference between Remote Desktop for Administration and the Terminal Server role is the number of simultaneous connections that are allowed and the extent to which settings from multiple users are accommodated and kept separate. As mentioned, RDA enables only two simultaneous remote connections, which do not require separate licensing. With the Terminal Server role installed, you are allowed a number of connections equal to the number of terminal server licenses you have purchased.

Unlike RDA, with the terminal server role installed, applications are installed in special way that enables Terminal Services to make sure all settings are always kept and tracked separately. However, keeping up with all this information requires system resources. A tremendous amount of resources are used up by the Terminal Server role to keep track of multiple user sessions and maintain all of their settings separately. Because of the overhead associated with the Terminal Server role, it is recommended that you do not install it on a domain controller or other resource-intensive application server, such as an SQL server or e-mail server. Unlike with Remote Desktop for Administration and RA, an administrator must explicitly install the terminal server role.

In the following sections, we will examine in detail how to configure and use the Windows Server 2003 Terminal Services in each of these ways.

Using Terminal Services Components for Remote Administration

As mentioned, no installation is necessary for the Remote Desktop for Administration component of Terminal Services. It is installed with the operating system by default. However, for security purposes it is not enabled by default. After it is enabled, members of the administrators group can connect and use it by default. Non-administrators must be specifically granted access. Let's take a look at how to enable and configure this critical component.

Configuring RDA

To configure Remote Desktop for Administration, select **Start | Control Panel | System** and click the **Remote** tab. To enable the feature, simply check the box next to **Allow users to connect remotely to this computer** located in the **Remote Desktop** section of the tab.

Enabling RDA Access

When RDA is enabled, any user accounts that are members of the *Administrators* built-in group on the server will be allowed to establish a remote session. However, other accounts must be explicitly approved for access. There are two different ways this can be accomplished. The first is to simply add any accounts that require access to the **Remote Desktop Users** group on the server.

The second, simpler way to access the **Remote Desktop Users** group and grant access is to use an option provided in the **Remote** tab in the **System** properties located in **Control Panel**. To use this method, perform the following steps:

1. In the Remote Desktop section of the **Remote** tab, click the **Select Remote Users…** button.

2. In the **Remote Desktop Users** dialog box that appears, click the **Add** button.

3. Type (or search for and select) the account name of the user requiring access. (

4. Click the **OK** button.

Remote Desktop Security Issues

When enabled, Remote Desktop for Administration opens port 3389 and listens for connection requests. This port is a significant target and is often sought during port scans. Most open ports link to applications that must be attacked in complex ways to permit administrator level access to a computer. This service is designed to actually provides administrator level access, which makes it a prime target for attackers. There are several best practices that you should follow to maximize the security of this component.

It goes without saying that users that do not require RDA should not be granted access. In addition, it is important to enforce strong security precautions on all accounts that are enabled to connect using Remote Desktop for Administration. Strong passwords and the use of account lock out are essential to make it difficult for an attacker to successfully use a brute force attack to gain system access. Administrators should be required to log on using a standard user account and perform administrative duties in the session using the **Run as...** feature.

All users should be required to use the most recent client available for their platform. This will ensure that the latest security features are available to them. It should be standard policy to check frequently for software updates to both client and server components, because these may contain critical security fixes. In addition, users should be discouraged from storing their log-on credentials in the properties of the client. This enables anyone with physical access to the user's machine to establish a session. It also stores sensitive information such as the user's username and domain in a clear text file with an RDP extension in the user's My Documents folder.

Finally, denial of service is a significant possibility when using Remote Desktop for Administration because it enables only two sessions to exist on the server. Both active and disconnected sessions count. The solution to this may appear to be seting the timeout settings so that sessions are reset shortly after they enter the disconnected state. However, this can cause serious problems.

An administrator may establish a session, begin an installation process and then disconnect to enable the installation to finish unmonitored. The previous settings would terminate the session, including the installation routine it was running, with potentially disastrous effects for the server. Special circumstances like these must be taken into account when configuring your policies. Because session timeout settings can be set at the user property level, Microsoft recommends the use of a special shared administrative account for circumstances like this. The strategy applies a timeout for disconnected sessions that are started by every user account except the shared account, which has no timeout settings applied. In this way, there should always be one connection available to a server, even though the second allowed connection is being consumed by a session involving the shared administrative account.

Using Remote Assistance

As with Remote Desktop for Administration, the Remote Assistance (RA) components of Windows 2003 install with the operating system and must be enabled and configured before they become functional.

Two major services comprise the default installation: the *Terminal Services* service and the *Remote Desktop Help Session Manager service*. In addition to installing these two components, Microsoft also creates a special user account for connections involving RA, called *HelpAssistant_XXXXXX*. On your system, the X's will be replaced with a unique alphanumeric code and the account name will appear as something similar to this: HelpAssistant_e4bb43. This account will be disabled until you enable RA. As we've mentioned, although RA is based on and uses Terminal Services, it works very differently from Remote Desktop for Administration or the terminal server role.

Configuring Remote Assistance for Use

RA is relatively easy to configure; you use the same tab that is used to configure Remote Desktop for Administration. To enable RA, go to **Control Panel** and select the **Remote** tab in the **System** properties. Select the check box next to **Turn on Remote Assistance and allow invitations to be sent from this computer**, located in the **Remote Assistance** section of the tab.

Invitations have an expiration time of one hour by default, but the Novice (referring to our earlier example) can alter the expiration time of the invitations sent, from 0 minutes to 99 days. The acceptance and opening of a session in response to an invitation does not cause it to expire; it is good until it reaches the specified expiration time. To modify the default expiration time, perform the following steps:

1. Click **Start | Control Panel | System**.

2. Click the **Remote** tab.

3. Click the **Advanced...** button.

4. Choose the desired number (0 to 99) and interval (minutes, hours, or days) under the **Invitations** section in the **Remote Assistance Settings** dialog box.

In addition to modifying the expiration time, the **Remote Assistance Settings** dialog box can be used to enable (or not enable) the Expert to control the Novice's desktop and applications during an RA session. When the **Allow this computer to be controlled remotely** box is checked, the Expert will be allowed to send mouse and keyboard input to the Novice's system and interact directly with his or her desktop and applications. When it is unchecked, the Expert will be able to see the Novice's desktop and any actions the Novice performs, but cannot control the cursor or send keyboard commands.

Asking for Assistance

A Novice can use a variety of methods to request help by sending an invitation using RA:

- The request can be sent using Windows Messenger.

- The request can be sent via e-mail.

■ The request can be saved to a file.

To create an invitation, open **Help and Support** from the Windows **Start** menu. On the right side of the **Help and Support Center** utility, click **Remote Assistance** under the Support heading. In the next screen, click the **Invite someone to help you** link. You will then be able to select the method that you want to use in asking for assistance, as shown in Figure 27.1. A request using Windows Messenger requires that Windows Messenger be installed and configured. A request using email requirest an email client be installed and configured, though most users already have an email client installed.

Figure 27.1 The "Pick how you want to contact your assistant" Screen in Remote Assistance

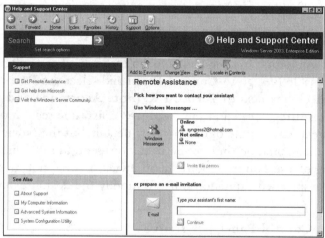

Managing Open Invitations

Sometimes you might want to know the names of users with whom you have active RA invitations open. You might want to cancel an invitation because you've solved the problem or because you want someone else to help you. Help and Support Center provides a number of options for managing open invitations.

To manage your active invitations, follow these steps:

1 Open the **Help and Support** utility from the Windows **Start** menu.

2 On the right side of the Help and Support Center screen, click **Remote Assistance** under the Support heading.

3 On the following screen, click the **View Invitation Status (X)** link. The **(X)** will be replaced on your screen by the number of invitations you have outstanding.

4 The next screen will show you a list of the invitations that are outstanding. The list consists of three columns: **Sent To**, **Expiration Time**, and **Status**. The Sent To column contains the name of the person to whom you sent the Windows Message or e-mail. If you saved the request to a file, this column will display the word "Saved." The **Expiration Time** column will show the date and time that the invitation will expire. The **Status** column

will show whether the invitation's status is Open or Expired. Now you can view or modify any of these invitations.

Each invitation will have a radio button next to it, as shown in Figure 27.2. You can click a radio button to select one of the invitations, and then choose an action to perform using the buttons under the list box.

Figure 27.2 The "View or change your invitation settings" Screen in Remote Assistance

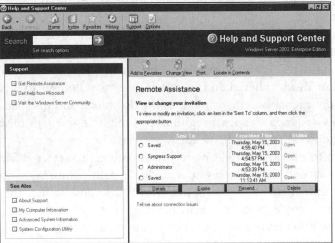

Remote Assistance Security Issues

RA is a valuable tool, but it also contains serious security risks that must be planned for and managed. RA makes it easy for any user to ask virtually anyone using a Windows XP or Server 2003 computer to connect to his or her desktop. This person can be inside or a friend that is outside of your company. Although an outside person may be qualified to assist the user, in doing so they will likely receive full control of a client in your network.

This, of course, is unacceptable, because they could place malicious software on the system while in control of it, view sensitive company information that normally isn't allowed outside of the organization, etc. The best way to prevent this is to use your company's firewalls to prevent connection to RA from outside the company's network. RA uses the same port that all Terminal Services components do: 3389. Simply blocking this port on your external firewalls prevents this type of unauthorized access and protects from malicious external port scanning.

Several other key security concerns should be addressed in your company's remote assistance policies. E-mail and file-based invitations enable you to specify passwords. An invitation without password protection can be used by anyone that receives it by accident or intercepts it illegitimately. Because of this, always mandate the use of these passwords.

Your company may also want to protect traffic that contains RA requests. E-mail is normally sent in unencrypted form on the network. This means that the URL that is sent in the e-mail invitation is available for easy interception while it is in transit on the network. Likewise, a simple XML format is used for the invitation file. A simple patter match could be used when monitoring the network to detect and automatically save this information to an unauthorized system while it is being sent across the network. If the e-mail or file invitations do not have passwords, they can be used immediately when they are captured in this way. Even if a password is specified, there is no limit to the number of times requests like these can be used for connection. A brute force attack could be used to attempt to break the password and successfully establish a session. For this reason, it is important that your remote assistance policy also specify a short expiration time for the invitation. Once expired, no connections are possible with it. A shorter time reduces the chances of success using a brute force attack. And, if no password is specified, at least the open window for misuse of the invitation is shorter.

You should also educate your users on when it is appropriate to accept RA requests. As mentioned previously, a request saved to a file is stored in a standard XML file. These can easily be modified to perform malicious actions when run by a user on a local system. The e-mail request contains a URL to click and can also be altered. In this case it may take the user to a page that performs malicious actions on their local system, or requires the download and installation of an unauthorized ActiveX control that is designed to appear legitimate to the user. Even an unsolicited request received through Windows messaging has security worries.

The best option is to maintain a tight policy that asks users to reject RA invitations in all but a few instances. What is acceptable will relate specifically to your company. Some organizations allow acceptance only from immediate co-workers and known help desk staff. Others are more liberal and allow invitations to be accepted from any verifiable employee within the company. The most important rule is to not allow connections from outside of the organization.

Installing and Configuring the Terminal Server Role

Unlike the remote administration components in Windows 2003, the terminal server role requires separate installation by an administrator. In addition, it requires the terminal server licensing component to be added to a Windows 2003 server on the network. If the license server component is not added, or if it is added but valid client licenses are not installed on it, no remote connections to the terminal server will be allowed 120 days after the first client connects.

Install the Terminal Server Role

The terminal server role can be installed from the **Manage Your Server** utility, which is opened from the Windows **Start | Administrative Tools** menu. Open the utility and follow these steps:

1. Click the **Add or remove a role** link. This will display the **Configure Your Server Wizard** with its first page displayed.

2. Read the recommendations and click the **Next** button.

3. A **Configure Your Server Wizard** dialog box will pop up, informing you that the underlying network settings are being detected. When detection is complete, you will see the **Configuration Options** screen in the wizard.

4. Select the radio button next to **Custom configuration** and click the **Next** button.

5. On the **Server Role** screen, click **Terminal server** to highlight the role in the list (it should say **No** under the **Configured** column if the terminal server role has not already been installed). Click the **Next** button.

6. The **Summary of Selections** screen should read **Install Terminal Server**. Ensure that it does, and then click **Next**.

7. At this point, another **Configure Your Server** pop-up dialog box will appear to inform you that the server will reboot automatically as part of the installation process. Click the **OK** button in this dialog box.

8. The wizard will switch to the **Applying Selections** screen, launch the **Windows Component Wizard**, finish the installation based on your selections, and reboot.

9. When the reboot has completed, log on as an administrator. When your logon is completed, the **Configure Your Server Wizard** will appear to let you know that your server is now a terminal server. Click the **Finish** button.

10. The **Manage Your Server** utility will reappear in the background. A help window also opens when you log on with the terminal server help topic displayed.

Install Terminal Server Licensing

After you have installed the Terminal Server role on one of your servers, it's time to install terminal server licensing. If you fail to do so, all terminal server connections will be rejected 120 days after the first client logs on. Microsoft recommends that you install terminal server licensing on a server that does not host the terminal server role. So, it will take at least two Windows 2003 servers to properly implement a terminal server environment.

The terminal server licensing component is not available from the **Configure Your Server Wizard** and must be added using **Add or Remove Programs** from **Control Panel** in the Windows **Start** menu. To install it, follow these steps:

1. In the **Add or Remove Programs** utility, click the **Add/Remove Windows Components** button on the left side of the screen. A **Windows Setup** pop-up dialog box will briefly appear, followed by the **Windows Components Wizard**.

2. In the **Components:** list, scroll down to select the check box next to **Terminal Server Licensing** and click the **Next** button.

3. On the **Terminal Server Licensing Setup** page of the wizard, select the way you will use this license server on your network.

4. You can also specify where you would like to place the license database. The default location, **C:\WINDOWS\System32\LServer** is displayed in the **Install license server database at this location:** text box. When you have made your selections, click the **Next** button.

5. The wizard will switch to the **Configuring Components** screen and will begin the installation. Unlike the terminal server role installation, the license component requires the Windows 2003 installation CD. If it is not in the CD-ROM drive, you will be prompted for it.

6. The final screen in the wizard is entitled **Completing the Windows Component Wizard**. Review the information it contains and click the **Finish** button.

7. When the wizard disappears, if you do not wish to add additional components, close the **Add or Remove Programs** utility.

It is important to note that you can also install the Terminal Server role and most other Windows components from the **Add or Remove Programs** utility in **Control Panel**.

After you have installed the licensing component, you must complete the licensing process by adding client licenses. Refer to Microsoft's Web site for additional details on how to complete this process. While it is also covered in Windows 2003's help materials, this can be a complex process and it is best to ensure that you have the latest information and fixes from Microsoft.

Using Terminal Services Client Tools

There are three primary tools you can use to connect from a client system to Terminal Services. These tools include:

- The Remote Desktop Connection (RDC) utility
- The Remote Desktops MMC snap-in
- The Remote Desktop Web Connection utility

Each is designed to fill a very specific role, and it is important for you to be familiar with the capabilities and uses of each. In the following sections, we examine how to install and use these utilities.

Installing and Using the Remote Desktop Connection (RDC) Utility

The *Remote Desktop Connection* (RDC) utility (formerly the *Terminal Services Client Connection Manager*) is the standard client for connecting to Terminal Services, via RDA on a server or Terminal Services on a terminal server. It can be used for remote administration or full terminal server client use. It enables a user to connect to a single server running Terminal Services using the RDP protocol over TCP/IP. The utility is installed with the operating system in Windows XP and Server 2003. It is accessed via the **Start | Programs | Accessories | Communications** menu in those operating systems. The RDC utility can also be installed and used on a number of older Windows operating systems, including Windows 2000, NT, ME, 98, and 95.

The older Terminal Services Client Connection Manager can still be used to connect to a terminal server from a Windows 3.11 computer with the 32-bit TCP/IP stack installed. There is also a 16-bit version of the Windows 2000 TS client for Windows for Workgroups 3.11 and a Macintosh client. If you need to connect MS-DOS, Linux, or other client operating systems, you will need third-party RDP or ICA client software. The Remote Desktop Connection utility is backward compatible and capable of communicating with Terminal Services in Windows XP, Windows 2000, and Windows NT 4.0, Terminal Server Edition.

Installing the Remote Desktop Connection Utility

If you want to use the Remote Desktop Connection utility on systems older than Windows XP, you'll need to install it first. This means you'll need the installation files. You can get them from the Microsoft Web site, or if you have installed Windows Server 2003, you can share the client setup folder located at %SystemRoot%\system32\clients\tsclient. After you share this folder, computers on the network can connect to the share and run the Setup.exe utility in the Win32 folder. If you want to deploy the client using Group Policy, Microsoft also includes an MSI installation file, Msrdpcli.msi, in this directory.

Perform the following steps to install the RDC client:

1. When you double-click the **Setup.exe** file, the installation wizard will launch. Read the initial welcome screen, and then click the **Next** button.

2. Review the license agreement, and then click the radio button next to **I accept the terms of the license agreement**, followed by the **Next** button.

3. On the Customer Information screen, enter your name for licensing purposes in the **User Name:** text box, and your company for licensing purposes in the **Organization:** text box.

4. In the **Install this application for:** section, select the radio button next to **Anyone who uses this computer (all users)** if you want the utility to be available on the Windows Start menu for every user that logs on to the system. Select the radio button next to **Only for me (-)** if you want the utility to appear only in your Windows Start menu. When you've finished making your selection, click the **Next** button.

5. On the next screen, click the **Install** button to proceed with the installation or the **Back** button to review your choices. The application will remove any previously installed similar applications, and then complete its own installation.

6. Click the **Finish** button to close the wizard.

Launching and Using the Remote Desktop Connection Utility

After the application is installed, open the Windows **Start** menu and click **Remote Desktop Connection** in the **Programs | Accessories | Communications** menu. This will open the utility, with most of its configuration options hidden. To proceed with the connection at this point, simply type the name or IP address of the terminal server, Windows Server 2003 computer, or Windows XP Professional computer to which you want to connect in the **Computer:** drop-down box, or select it from the drop-down list if you have previously established a session to it. By default, the name or IP address of the last computer to which you connected will be displayed. Finally, click on the **Connect** button.

A Remote Desktop window will open. If the user name and password with which you are logged on to your current system are valid for connection to Terminal Services on the server, you will be automatically logged on and a session will appear. If not, you will be prompted to enter a valid user name and password. When you are connected, the remote desktop will appear in a window on your system by default. You can move your cursor over it, click, and use any item in the remote desktop just as you would if you were using your local system. You can also copy and paste between the remote and local computers, using the standard methods of doing this.

Connecting is a simple process; however, terminating your session requires a bit more explanation. There are two methods that you can use to end your session:

- Logging off
- Disconnecting

To log off, simply click the Windows **Start** menu on the remote desktop, and then click the **Log Off** button. When you do this, it will completely log you out of the remote system in much the same way as if you logged out on your local system. Registry entries are properly written, programs are elegantly closed, etc. The session is completely removed from the Terminal Services computer, freeing up any system resources that were being used by your session. Make sure that you select **Log Off,** rather than **Shut Down**. If you select **Shut Down**, and you are logged onto the remote session with rights that enable your account to shut down the server, it will power down or reboot the server. This will affect everyone who is currently using the server.

The second method of terminating your session is to use the process known as disconnection. When you disconnect from Terminal Services, your session remains on the server and is not removed. It continues to consume resources, although the video stream coming to your local computer and input stream going from your local computer to the Terminal Services system are terminated. When you launch the RDC utility again and connect to the same computer running Terminal Services, your session will still be there, exactly as you left it, and you can take up where you left off. This can be helpful in cases where you are running an application that requires lengthy processing. You do not have to remain connected for the application to run and you can check back in later and obtain the result.

In general, it is best to properly log off and free up the resources being used by a session you no longer need. As we'll see a bit later, an administrator can cause a disconnected session to be reset if you don't return to it for a specified period of time. If you've left unsaved documents or other files open in your session, resetting will cause you to lose all work. Thus, it is usually safest to save your work and disconnect. You can disconnect from your session by clicking the close button (the X) in the top right corner of the Remote Desktop window.

You can also log off or disconnect using the Windows Security dialog box. This can be accessed by opening the Windows **Start** menu and selecting **Windows Security**, or by using the **CTRL + ALT + END** key combination from within the session (this has the same effect as CTRL + ALT + DEL on the local machine). Once in the dialog, you can log off by clicking the **Log Off...** button, or by selecting **Log Off** from the drop-down box that appears if you click the **Shut Down...** button. This same drop-down box also contains the option to **Disconnect**.

Configuring the Remote Desktop Connection Utility

In the previous section, we simply launched the Remote Desktop Connection utility and established a connection. When you initially launch the utility, most of its configuration information is hidden. To display it before you use it to establish a connection, click the **Options** button. This will reveal a series of tabs and many additional settings that have be configured. Let's take a look at each in the following sections.

The General Tab

The General tab contains the **Computer:** drop-down box, which contains names and IP addresses of computers to which you have previously connected, along with an option to browse the network for computers not listed. It also contains **User name:**, **Password:**, and **Domain:** text boxes. Remember, by default the credentials with which you are logged on locally are used to establish your remote session. If you always want to ensure that a specific set of credentials is used to log on to Terminal Services, you can type the account information into these text boxes.

You might be using an earlier Windows operating system that does not require you to log on. These boxes can be used in this instance if you want to avoid being prompted for a user name and password when you connect with the utility.

This tab also enables you to save your connection settings. You might have several different systems to which you connect using Terminal Services. If so, it is helpful to not have to configure the utility each time you open it. When you click the **Save As...** button, a **Save As** dialog box opens, asking you where you'd like to save the file that contains your configuration information. You can save the file with an RDP extension and can double-click it later to establish a terminal session. You can also use the **Open...** button on this tab to specify that the settings from a previously saved RDP file be loaded into the utility.

The Display Tab

The display tab controls how the remote desktop appears on your client computer. The top portion of the screen contains a slider that controls the size of the remote desktop that will be displayed on your screen. The slider has four possible positions: 640x480, 800x600, 1024x768, and Full Screen. The default is 800x600.

The next portion of this tab controls the color depth (in bits) of the remote desktop when it is displayed on your local computer. The drop-down list box contains the following options: 256 colors, High Color (15 bit), High Color (16 bit), and True Color (24 bit). Higher color depths require more resources. Note that the settings on the server itself may override your selection.

Finally, the bottom of the tab contains a check box entitled **Display the connection bar when in full screen mode**. When selected, this setting places a small bar, shown in Figure 27.3, at the top of a full screen remote desktop, which makes it easier to size, minimize or maximize (to full screen), or close the Remote Desktop window.

Figure 27.3 The Full Screen Connection Bar

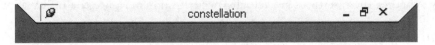

The Local Resources Tab

The Local Resources tab enables you to control whether or not client resources are accessible in your remote session. Remember that when you are working in a session, you are actually working on the remote computer. This means that when you open Windows Explorer, the disk drives you see are the ones that are physically located on the Terminal Services computer, not the ones installed on your local computer. Selections on the Local Resources tab can be used to make your local drives, client-attached printers, and similar client-side resources available for use within your remote desktop session.

The first setting on the tab deals with whether audio will be used in the session. The default setting, **Bring to this Computer**, enables you to transfer any sounds played in the session from the Terminal Services computer to the client. Audio transfer can be bandwidth intensive in a thin client environment, so Microsoft also gives you the opportunity to not transfer this audio. The **Leave at Remote Computer** setting plays the audio in the session on the Terminal Services computer but does not transfer the audio to the client. The **Do not play** setting prevents audio in the session altogether.

The next setting on the Local Resources tab relates to whether keyboard shortcut combinations are used by the local operating system or the Remote Desktop window. There are three possible settings for keyboard shortcut combinations:

- **In full screen mode only**. In this mode (which is the default), when you use a shortcut combination, the system applies it to the local operating system, unless there is a full screen Remote Desktop window open.

- **On the local computer**. This setting applies all shortcut combinations to the local operating system.

- **On the remote computer**. This setting applies all shortcut combinations to the Remote Desktop window.

It is important to note that you cannot redirect the **CTRL + ALT + DEL** keyboard combination. This combination works only on the local operating system. An equivalent that can be used in the Remote Desktop window (mentioned earlier in the chapter) is **CTRL + ALT + END**.

The final section of the tab contains a series of check boxes that can be selected to determine which devices from the client system are automatically made available to the user within the remote desktop session. By default, the following are selected: Disk drives, Printers, and Smart cards (if installed). An additional one, Serial ports, is not selected by default. When Disk drives, Serial ports, or Smart cards are selected, you may see a Remote Desktop Connection Security Warning box pop up when you begin the connection process. This happens because opening up devices that enable input or may relate to the underlying security of your local machine can be risky. You should consider carefully whether these settings are actually needed, and configure the utility appropriately.

The Programs Tab

By default, when you connect to a Terminal Services session, you will receive a Windows 2003 desktop. The selections on this tab enable you to receive only a specified application instead. If Terminal Services is being used to provide only a single application for each user, this setting can increase security by ensuring that users do not receive a full desktop upon connection. This will prevent them from performing tasks on the server other than running the specified application. If the check box next to **Start the following program on connection** is selected, only that application will be available in the session.

Selecting the box enables the **Program path and file name:** text box. If the path to the application is already contained in one of the Windows path variables on the Terminal Services computer, you can just type the name of the application's executable file in this box. If not, you must include the full path and file name of the executable. The check box also enables the **Start in the following folder:** text box. If the application requires the specification of a working directory, enter it here. This is often the same directory in which the application itself is installed.

After the connection is made with a specified program starting, the traditional methods of ending your session (discussed earlier) will not always be possible. Most programs have an Exit command on a menu, embedded in a button or contained in a link. When you have specified an initial program, the Exit command is the equivalent of logging out. To disconnect, simply close the Remote Desktop Connection utility.

The Experience Tab

The Experience tab enables you to customize several performance features that control the overall feel of your session. All of these settings except **Bitmap Caching** can generate substantial amounts of additional bandwidth and should be used sparingly in low bandwidth environments. The check boxes on this page include the following:

- **Desktop background** Enables the background image of the desktop (wallpaper) in the remote session to be transferred to and displayed on the client.

- **Show contents of window while dragging** Rapidly refreshes a window so that its contents are visible as the user moves it around the screen in his or her Remote Desktop window.

- **Menu and window animation** Enables some sophisticated effects, such as the Windows Start menu fading in and out, to be displayed in the Remote Desktop window on the client computer.

- **Themes** Enables any themes used in the remote session to be enabled and transferred to the Remote Desktop window on the client.

- **Bitmap Caching** Enables bitmaps to be stored locally on the client system and called up from cache, rather than being transmitted multiple times across the network. Examples of bitmaps include desktop icons and icons on application toolbars. This setting improves performance, but not all thin client systems have a hard drive or other storage mechanism in which to store the bitmaps.

At the top of this tabbed page, there is a dropdown box that contains several predefined combinations of these settings that Microsoft has optimized for different levels of available bandwidth. Table 27.1 shows which bandwidth level corresponds to which settings:

Table 27.1 Preconfigured Bandwidth Settings

Connection Speed Selection	Desktop Background	Show Contents of Window while Dragging	Menu and Window Animation	Themes	Bitmap Caching
Modem (28.8 Kbps)					X
Modem (56 Kbps) – default				X	X
Broadband (128 Kbps – 1.5 Mbps)		X	X	X	X
LAN (10 Mbps or higher)	X	X	X	X	X
Custom				X	X

The Experience tab also contains a check box entitled **Reconnect if connection is dropped,** which is selected by default. The versions of Terminal Services included with Windows Server 2003 and Windows XP SP1 or later include the Automatic Reconnection feature. If dropped packets, network service interruptions, or other network errors cause your Terminal Services connection to disconnect, this feature will automatically attempt to reconnect to your session without requiring you to reenter your log-on credentials. By default, there will be a maximum of twenty reconnection attempts, which occur at five-second intervals. Generally, a notification message will pop up, informing you that the connection has been lost and counting down the remaining connection attempts.

Installing and Using the Remote Desktops MMC Snap-In

The *Remote Desktops* (RD) MMC snap-in is another utility that can be used to establish Terminal Services connections to Windows 2003 servers and terminal servers. The RD MMC snap-in can safely be considered the primary Terminal Services client connection tool for administrators. It contains two outstanding features that are not found in the Remote Desktop Connection (RDC) utility:

- **The RD MMC can be used to connect to multiple Windows 2003 servers using Terminal Services.** An administrator can configure and save the MMC with connection information for multiple servers. These connections can be used to establish and switch between sessions. With the RD MMC, you can quickly click between multiple, running terminal sessions, as shown in Figure 27.4.

Figure 27.4 The Remote Desktops MMC Snap-In

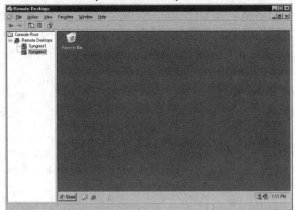

- **The Remote Desktops MMC enables a remote connection to the console session.** Inability to connect to the console session has prevented many administrators from being able to use Terminal Services in the past for remote administration. There was simply no way for the Administrator to connect to the existing console session and see pop up messages. RD MMC allows the Administrator to see and respond to these console session messages.

Install the Remote Desktops MMC Snap-In

To prepare the Remote Desktops MMC snap-in for use, you begin by opening a blank MMC console. Click **Start | Run** and type **MMC** in the **Open:** dialog box.

In the MMC window that appears, click **File | Add/Remove Snap-in…**. In the Add/Remove Snap-in dialog box, click the **Add…** button. Select **Remote Desktops** from the **Available Standalone Snap-ins:** list in the Add Standalone Snap-in dialog box and click the **Add** button followed by the **Close** button. In the Add/Remove Snap-in dialog box, click the **OK** button. Remote Desktops should now be visible in the tree view on the left side of the window under Console Root. By default, no connections are configured, so if you click the Remote Desktops node at this point, nothing will appear to happen.

Configure a New Connection in the RD MMC

1. From the Windows **Start** menu, click **Run**, and type **MMC** in the **Open:** dialog box.

2. In the MMC window that appears, click **File | Add/Remove Snap-in…**.

3. In the Add/Remove Snap-in dialog box, click the **Add…** button.

4. Select **Remote Desktops** from the **Available Standalone Snap-ins:** list in the Add Standalone Snap-in dialog box and click the **Add** button; then click the **Close** button.

5. In the Add/Remove Snap-in dialog box, click the **OK** button.

6. Right-click the **Remote Desktops** node in the tree view in the left console pane.

7. Select **Add new connection...**from the context menu.

8. In the **Server name or IP address:** text box, enter the fully qualified domain name (FQDN), NetBIOS name, or IP address of the server to which you wish to connect.

9. Next type an identifying name for the connection in the **Connection Name:** text box, or accept the default.

10. Leave the **Connect to console** check box selected if you want to connect to the server's console. Deselect the check box if you want Terminal Services to create a new session for you to use.

11. To store your user credentials in the connection, enter your log-on name in the **User name:** text box, enter your password in the **Password:** text box, and enter the name of the domain in the **Domain:** text box.

12. Select the **Save Password** check box if you want the entered password saved.

13. Click the **OK** button to save the connection.

Configure a Connection's Properties

You can configure several properties for saved connections. Right-click the node in the left pane of the MMC that represents the connection you want to modify, and select **Properties** from the context menu. The Properties window will appear, with the General tab displayed. This tab is essentially the same as the Add New Connection window and contains the same fields for configuration. You can change any of the settings you made when you created the connection.

Click the **Screen Options** tab to bring it to the foreground. This tab enables you to choose the size of the remote desktop window that will appear in the snap-in. The desktop will appear in the currently blank space on the right side of the MMC window. You can select the size of desktop that appears there. The default is for the desktop to fill all the available space in the right pane of the MMC window. This default setting is called **Expand to fill MMC Result Pane** in Properties window. You can change this by selecting the radio button next to one of the other choices on the tab. The second choice is entitled **Choose desktop size:**. When selected, it enables a drop-down box containing two standard resolutions: 640x480 and 800x600. The final option on the tab is **Enter custom desktop size:**. When selected, it enables two text boxes: **Width:** and **Height:**. If the other available options do not provide you with the desired desktop size, you can manually enter the size you want into these text boxes.

Click the **Other** tab at the top of the Window to view the final set of options. You will see some settings that are familiar from your experience with the RDC utility: the capability to start a program and/or redirect local drives.

By default, you will receive a Windows 2003 desktop when you connect to a terminal session. The first selection on this tab enables you to receive only a specified application instead. If the check box next to **Start the following program on connection:** is selected, only that application will be available in the session. Selecting the box enables the **Program path and file name:** text box. If the path to the application is already contained in one of the Windows path variables, you can type the filename of the application's executable file in this box. If not, you must include the full path and filename of the executable. The check box also enables the **Working directory:** text box. If the application requires the specification of a working directory, enter it here. This is often the same directory into which the application itself is installed.

At the bottom of this tab is another check box, entitled **Redirect local drives when logged on to the remote computer**. If this check box is selected, the drives on the client will be visible from within the session. This provides you with access to those local drives from Windows Explorer, as well as Open and Save As dialog boxes within applications. If it is not necessary to allow clients access to their local drives, you should leave this option disabled for security purposes. Note that there is no option to redirect local printers, serial ports, and smart cards as with the RDC utility.

Connecting and Disconnecting

When you have your connection added and configured, connecting is a snap. To connect, simply right-click the node that represents your saved connection in the tree view in the left MMC pane and select **Connect** from the context menu. If you did not save your log-on information in the properties of the connection, the information you provided was incorrect, or you want to log on with a different account, you will be required to enter a user name and password when the session appears in the right pane of the snap-in.

Disconnecting is just as simple. Right-click the node that represents your saved connection in the tree view in the left MMC pane, and then select **Disconnect** from the context menu. You can also use some of the other methods for logging off and disconnecting that we mentioned earlier in the chapter.

Installing and Using the Remote Desktop Web Connection Utility

The Remote Desktop Web Connection utility is designed to access a Terminal Services session through Microsoft Internet Explorer (MSIE) over TCP/IP. It consists of an ActiveX component that is downloaded to the client browser and sample Web pages that the client uses IE to connect to. It replaces Windows 2000's Terminal Services Advanced Client (TSAC).

This utility depends on Internet Information Services 6 (IIS6), which is not installed by default. Thus, to use the Remote Desktop Web Connection utility, you must begin by installing IIS6. This is accomplished via **Start | Programs | Administrative Tools | Add or remove a role.**

Install the Remote Desktop Web Connection Utility

The Remote Desktop Web Connection utility does not install automatically with IIS6. It is not available for installation from the **Configure Your Server Wizard**, but must be added using **Add or Remove Programs** from **Control Panel** in the Windows **Start** menu. To install it, follow these steps:

1. In the **Add or Remove Programs** utility, click the **Add/Remove Windows Components** button on the left side of the screen. A **Windows Setup** pop-up dialog box will briefly appear, followed by the **Windows Components Wizard**.

2. In the **Components:** list, scroll down to select the check box next to **Application Server** and click the **Details...** button.

3. In the **Application Server** dialog box that appears, select **Internet Information Services (IIS)** and click the **Details...** button.

4. In the **Internet Information Services (IIS)** dialog box, select **World Wide Web Service** and click on the **Details...** button.

5. In the **World Wide Web service** dialog box, select the check box next to **Remote Desktop Web Connection**, as shown in Figure 27.5, and click the **OK** button. Also click the **OK** buttons on the **Internet Information Services (IIS)** and **Application Server** dialog boxes.

Figure 27.5 Installing the Remote Desktop Web Connection Utility

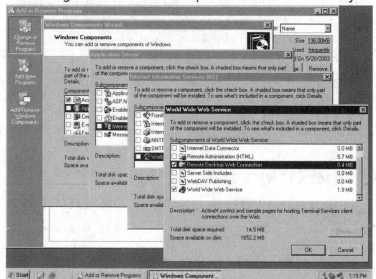

6. This will return you to the main screen of the **Windows Components Wizard**, where you should click the **Next** button. You should still have the Windows 2003 CD-ROM in the drive if you are installing from the CD. If you are installing from a network share, you will need to enter its path or browse to it again.

7. The wizard will switch to the **Configuring Components** screen and begin the installation. The final screen in the wizard is entitled **Completing the Windows Component Wizard**. Review the information it contains and click the **Finish** button to close the wizard.

8. A small Windows Setup pop-up box may appear briefly. When the wizard disappears, if you do not wish to add more components, close the **Add or Remove Programs** utility.

Using the Remote Desktop Web Connection Utility from a Client

To use the Remote Desktop Web Connection utility, open a version of Internet Explorer 5 or later on a client computer on the network, and connect to the following URL: http://*SERVER NAME OR IP address*/tsweb. When you do so, the default.htm Web page for the utility will appear. It will automatically detect whether you have the Remote Desktop ActiveX Control installed. If you do not, a **Security Warning** dialog box will appear, asking if you'd like to install it. Click the **Yes** button, as shown in Figure 27.6, to proceed with the installation. The control will then download and install on your system, and the default Web page will appear when installation is complete.

Figure 27.6 Installing the Remote Desktop ActiveX Control

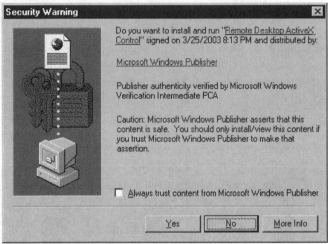

The default Web page contains two options. The **Server:** text box is used to enter the name or IP address of the server to which you want to connect. The **Size:** drop-down box contains a number of different screen resolutions that can be specified for the connection. The default is Full Screen, but other available options include: 640x480, 800x600, 1024x768, 1280x1224, and 1600x1200. There is also a check box entitled **Send logon information for this connection**. When selected, it adds two text boxes to the screen:

- **User name:** can be used to specify the account with which you want to connect
- **Domain:** can be used to specify the domain in which the account is located.

If you do not select this check box, you will be prompted for log-on information when you attempt to connect. After you have made your selections, click the **Connect** button, shown in Figure 27.7.

Figure 27.7 The Remote Desktop Web Connection Log-On Page

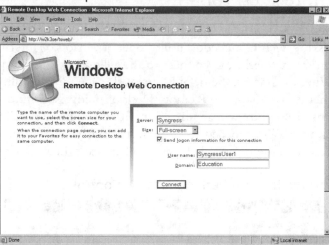

If you select any size setting less than Full Screen, the session will appear in the Web page itself, as shown in Figure 27.8.

Figure 27.8 Viewing a Session that is Embedded in a Browser Window

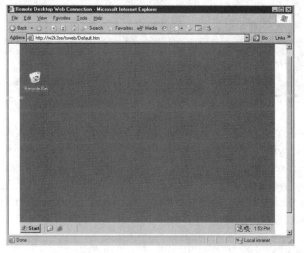

When you scroll through the Web page, the Terminal Services session will move with it. When you log off using the method described earlier in the chapter, the desktop disappears and the Web page displays the connection information and text boxes again. If you select Full Screen, a separate connection window is launched. The Web page changes to display a large blank box with text at the bottom of the page that indicates you are connected. The Remote Desktop can be minimized, sized, disconnected from, and logged off, in all the ways mentioned earlier in the chapter.

Regardless of how you connect, a full session is established, which enables you to interact with a complete Windows 2003 desktop and all applications, as with the other clients. An important advantage of the Web client is that it does not require any client software to be installed. The ActiveX control that downloads to the browser upon connection to the default Web page is the only client software needed. In other words, if you are away from the computer you normally use for administration, this client can be used to administer one of your servers in an emergency from anywhere in the world. All that is needed on the client system is IE 5 or later.

Using Terminal Services Administrative Tools

Microsoft provides several utilities to administer different aspects of Terminal Services. The two primary tools are as follows:

- Terminal Services Manager, which is used to administer sessions
- Terminal Services Configuration, which is use to create and manage the properties of listener connections

In addition to these tools, Microsoft also provides extensions to the properties of user accounts, which enable them to receive individual Terminal Services settings. Virtually all of the settings available at the user properties level, as well as in the properties of a connection in the Terminal Services Configuration utility, can also be configured within Group Policy. Finally, there are a number of command-line utilities that can be used for administrative scripting of Terminal Services. In the following sections, we take a detailed look at these tools.

Use Terminal Services Manager to Connect to Servers

Terminal Services Manager is opened from the **Start | Programs | Administrative Tools** menu. The left pane contains a tree view that shows servers and sessions. The primary top-level nodes in the tool are as follows:

- This Computer
- Favorite Servers
- All Listed Servers

If the tool is used on a Terminal Services computer, or from within a session, **This Computer** appears in the tree to represent the local computer. You can right-click the name of any Terminal Services computer in the tree and select **Add to Favorites** from the menu that appears. Doing so will add the server under the **Favorite Servers** node in the tree. Finally, **All Listed Servers** shows aggregate information from all the Terminal Services computers to which the utility is connected.

The **Action** menu can be used to connect to additional Terminal Services computers by selecting the **Connect to Computer** option (You can also do this by right-clicking **All Listed Servers** and selecting **Connect to Computer...** in the context menu). New Terminal Services systems that are added will appear in the tree view on the left side of the screen.

You can disconnect from any server listed in the tree view by right-clicking its name and selecting **Disconnect**. When you are connected to a server, the utility tracks statistics, such as which users are connected, the number of disconnected sessions per server, and much more. This all consumes bandwidth, so if you have added a number of servers to the utility, it may be best not to leave them all connected to prevent excessive use of network resources by the utility. Microsoft recommends that you connect to only one terminal server at a time with the TS Manager. By default, the servers to which you connect are not remembered if you close and reopen the TS Manager. To have them remembered, click **Options** in the **Tools** menu and select the check box next to **Remember server connections**.

Manage Users with the Terminal Services Manager Tool

When you select any of the server nodes or the **All Listed Servers** node in the tree view in the left pane of TS Manager, a series of tabs appears in the **Results** pane on the right side of the screen, labeled as follows:

- Users
- Sessions
- Processes

The **Users** tab can be used to view information about and manage the users who are consuming terminal server resources. It shows both currently connected users and users who have disconnected sessions still running on the server. The Users tab is shown in Figure 27.9.

Figure 27.9 The Users Tab in Terminal Services Manager

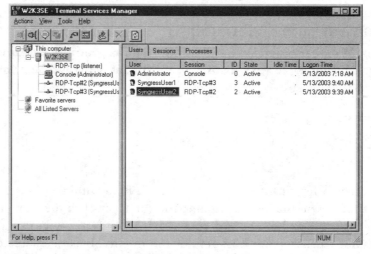

Manage Sessions with the Terminal Services Manager Tool

When you select any of the server nodes or the **All Listed Servers** node in the tree view in the left pane of the TS Manager, a series of tabs appear in the results pane on the right side of the screen. The Sessions Tab is used to view information about, and manage, the sessions that are consuming terminal server resources. The tab shows currently connected sessions, disconnected sessions, listener sessions, and the console session.

Right-clicking on a session brings up a number of different options, which are the same as those discussed in regard to the Users tab, except that there is no **Log off** option, as shown in Figure 27.10. The Sessions tab is shown in Figure 27.11.

Figure 27.10 Sending a Message to a User in a Session

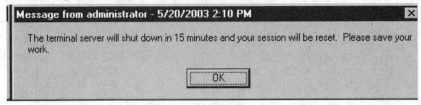

Figure 27.11 The Sessions Tab in Terminal Services Manager

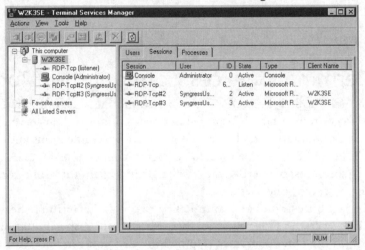

Manage Processes with the Terminal Services Manager Tool

The Processes tab is the third and final tab that is available when you select any of the server nodes or the All Listed Servers node in the tree view in the left pane of the TS Manager. The Processes tab can be used to terminate individual processes that are running on the server, including those running inside sessions. To terminate a process, simply right-click it and select **End Process** from the context menu. Then click the **OK** button in the Terminal Services Manager pop-up box that asks you to verify the termination. The process will be terminated and removed from the list. Figure 27.12 shows the Processes tab.

Figure 27.12 The Processes Tab in Terminal Services Manager

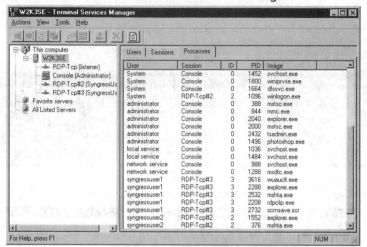

Using the Terminal Services Configuration Tool

A listener connection (also called the RDP-Tcp connection) must be configured and exist on the server for clients to successfully establish Terminal Services sessions to that server. Administrators use the Terminal Services Configuration tool to create new listener connections and configure the ones that currently exist. This tool can also be used to configure connections for ICA (Citrix) clients using IPX, SPX, Asynchronous, or NetBIOS as well as TCP. Finally, the Configuration tool is also used to configure some server policy settings.

Microsoft recommends that you use Group Policy to configure Terminal Services connection settings, if possible. However, the Configuration tool enables you to specify settings separately for multiple connections on the same computer – something that you can't do with Group Policy. You can also use the Configuration tool for terminal servers that run pre-Windows Server 2003 operating systems.

Understanding Listener Connections

Listener connections can be configured for RDP only over TCP/IP, and only one listener can be configured for each network interface card (NIC) in the Terminal Services computer. By default, the RDP-Tcp listener is created that is bound to all of the NICs in the server. If the server has more than one NIC, an administrator can configure the default listener connection to only be associated with one NIC, and create new listener connections for each of the other NICs in the Terminal Services computer. You must be a member of the Administrators group, or be delegated the authority, in order to create new listener connections.

Creating new listener connections might be desirable if each NIC is attached to a separate segment, and only certain users should be enabled to access the Terminal Services computer from each segment. Permissions can be granted within the listener connection that specify who can and cannot connect. By default, all users are configured to connect using terminal servers. If you disable this in a user's properties, he or she will not be able to access any Terminal Services. If you want to enable a user to connect, but only from one segment that is attached to the terminal server, you can use the permissions associated with a listener connection to accomplish this.

In truth, it's pretty unusual for people to create their own listener connections, so the following section focuses on how to configure existing ones. All of the settings that relate to configuring listener connections also relate to settings you provide when you create one. You should also note that the term "listener connection" is an older term that is not used in Windows 2003. The Windows 2003 documentation refers to it as an RDP-TCP connection. We're using it here because there is no distinction made in the Windows Server 2003 Help files between a connection as configured in the Terminal Services Configuration tool, and a connection made from a client to Terminal Services running on a server. While we'll be using the term "listener connection" to help you keep them straight, the exam may not be so kind.

Modifying the Properties of an Existing Connection

To modify an existing listener connection, open the **Terminal Services Configuration** tool from the **Administrative Tools** folder in the **Windows Start | Programs** menu, and follow these steps:

1. In the tree view on the left pane of the Configuration tool, click the **Connections** node.

2. Existing listener connections should appear in the **Results** pane on the right side of the screen.

3. The default listener connection that is created during installation is entitled RDP-Tcp. Right-click this (or any other listener connection you may have) and click **Properties**. This will open a multi-tabbed dialog box with which you can configure the settings for this connection. We will discuss each tab in detail in the following sections.

The most important thing to remember is that *every property you set affects all users who connect through the listener connection.* Many of the property settings for a listener connection can also be set at the client and user account property levels. By default, the listener connections are almost always set to default to the client– or user-level setting. This is to give you greater granularity of control. If you change these settings to be applied at the listener connection level, the client and user account-level settings will be ignored.

Now let's look at each of the tabs in the RDP-Tcp Properties dialog box. Keep in mind that you must be an administrator, or be delegated the proper authority, to change the settings we discuss in the following sections.

The General tab

This tab identifies the connection type (RDP-Tcp) and RDP version number. There is a Comment text box in which you can store information for administrative purposes.

More importantly, this tab enables you to specify the level of encryption that will be required for connection to Terminal Services. The default encryption setting is Client Compatible. This setting attempts to use the maximum level of encryption allowed on the client. If you have multiple clients that use different encryption levels, this is the preferred setting. The other possible settings are:

- Low (56 bit)
- High (128 bit)
- FIPS Compliant.

All encryption levels use RC4 encryption. If you select High, any client that does not support 128-bit encryption will be unable to connect. The same will be true if you select Low and the client cannot support 56-bit encryption.

FIPS stands for Federal Information Processing Standard and should be used where required for work with the government. If the **System cryptography: Use FIPS compliant algorithms for encryption, hashing and signing** Group Policy has been enabled, you will not be able to change the encryption level using the Configuration tool. Remember that Group Policy settings take precedence over settings made with the Configuration tool.

The bottom of the tab contains a check box entitled **Use standard Windows authentication**. It is not checked by default and under normal circumstances, selection of this check box is not required. However, if you have installed a third-party authentication provider, but you want to use Windows authentication for Terminal Services connections instead of the third-party provider, check this box.

The General tab is shown in Figure 27.13.

Figure 27.13 The General Tab in the RDP-Tcp Connection's Properties

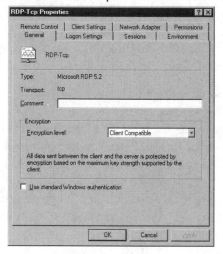

The Logon Settings tab

All Terminal Services clients are capable of providing log-on information to the Terminal Services computer. Typically, this includes a user name, password, and domain. The default setting on this tab, **Use client-provided logon information**, ensures that the credentials passed from the client are accepted at the server. If no credentials are passed, or incorrect credentials are passed, the user will be prompted for valid log-on information.

The other major option on this page is entitled **Always use the following logon information:**. When selected, it enables the **User name:**, **Domain:**, **Password:**, and **Confirm password:** text boxes. Information entered in these fields will be used for logon. This will enable users to log on to the server automatically, without providing credentials.

It is important to remember that settings done at the listener connection level affect everyone who connects using the NIC or NICs to which it is bound. As a result, if this option is enabled, *everyone attempting to establish a session through this listener connection will be logged on with the same credentials.* This will make it virtually impossible to audit "who did what" later. If the credentials typed into these text boxes are incorrect, the users will still be prompted for valid log-on information. It is usually best for automatic log-on credentials to be set at the client level.

The last setting on this page is entitled **Always prompt for password**. If it is selected, the password in the **Password:** and **Confirm password:** fields will be ignored and the user will be prompted to supply a valid password. The Logon Settings tab is displayed in Figure 27.14.

Figure 27.14 The Logon Settings Tab in the RDP-Tcp Connection's Properties

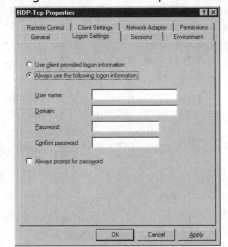

The Sessions tab

The Sessions tab enables you to control how long a user may remain actively connected to a session and how long a disconnected session should be allowed to remain on the Terminal Services computer. Even though they are not active, disconnected sessions can use substantial resources on the Terminal Services computer because applications are still running on them. Depending on your environment, it may be advisable to terminate them after a specific period of time.

By default, most of the settings on this page are configured to use the user account property settings and several settings are grayed out. This can be overridden by selecting the check box next to **Override user settings**. When user settings are overridden, several settings are no longer grayed out; these include:

- **End a disconnected session:** Used to specify the amount of time a disconnected session can remain running on the Terminal Services computer.

- **Active session limit:** Used to specify the amount of time an actively used session can remain connected and in use.

- **Idle session limit:** Used to specify the amount of time an idle session can remain connected to the Terminal Services computer.

Each of these settings has a drop-down box that follows it. The drop-down box contains a range from Never (the default) to 2 days. If you select Never, sessions will be allowed to continue indefinitely. If the setting you prefer is not listed in the box, you can type it in and it will be added. For instance, if you type in **5 days,** a new entry (5 days) will appear in the box and be selected. Just be certain to follow the correct format when typing it in, as shown in the other entries (<number> <minutes/hours/days>).

The next configuration item on the screen is **When a session limit is reached or connection is broken:**. This setting contains two possible options and relates to the **Active session limit:** and **Idle session limit:** settings. When one of these limits is reached, you can choose to have the user disconnected from the session, but leave the session running until the **End disconnected session:** limit is reached by choosing the radio button next to the **Disconnect user from session** option. Or, you can chose to simply have the session terminated by selecting the radio button next to **End session**. If you do this, applications that are running will be shut down and data may be lost.

The final setting on this tab is **Allow reconnection:**. You can use it to specify whether a user can reconnect to a session only from the original client that was used to establish it (**From previous client**) or from any client (**From any client**). This setting can be used only with ICA (Citrix) clients. If you do not have ICA clients, this option will be grayed out.

Remember that all of these time limits apply to all users who log on to the terminal server using this connection. Also remember that all of these settings can also be made using Group Policy (Microsoft's recommended method).

The Sessions tab is shown in Figure 27.15.

Figure 27.15 The Sessions Tab in the RDP-Tcp Connection's Properties

The Environment Tab

This tab can be used to specify that upon connection, the user should see only a running application, instead of receiving the default desktop. It can also be used to provide a custom shell or run a batch script, which in turn calls the desktop. By default, the setting is configured to be inherited from the client or user account properties. If you override the client and user settings at the listener connection level, two previously grayed out text boxes become activated:

- **Program path and file name:** is used to enter the full path to the program, including the name of the executable file.

- The **Start in:** text box is where you can enter a working directory for the application if it requires one. This is often the same folder that contains the executable.

The Environment Tab is shown in Figure 27.16.

Figure 27.16 The Environment Tab in the RDP-Tcp Connection's Properties

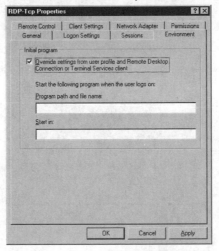

The Remote Control Tab

As mentioned in the Terminal Services Manager section of the chapter, remote control is a feature that enables an administrator to connect to, view, and interact with a user's session. It is ideal for remote troubleshooting or educating a user on the proper way to do something without leaving your desk.

The default setting on this tab is **Use remote control with user default settings**, which accepts the remote control configuration settings stored in the properties of a user's account. The second option on this tab, **Do not allow remote control,** blocks any use of remote control and should be used in secure environments where this might be necessary. Finally, you can select the third option to both enable remote control and customize its settings at the listener connection level, instead of at the user property level. This setting is entitled **Use remote control with the following settings:** and when chosen it activates a number of options. As with all listener-level configurations, these settings will apply to all users who connect to the terminal server using this connection.

You can choose to enable remote control of a session with or without the user's permission by selecting or deselecting the check box next to **Require user's permission**. If this box is checked, a message will be displayed on the client, requesting permission to view or control the session.

You can specify the level of control you have over the sessions by selecting the radio button next to the appropriate option. The first option, **View the session,** enables you to see the user's desktop but does not enable you to provide any input to it. The second option, **Interact with the session,** enables you to view the desktop and provide cursor and keyboard input.

Any changes you make to the Remote Control settings won't apply to sessions that are already connected when you make the changes.

The Remote Control tab is shown in Figure 27.17.

Figure 27.17 The Remote Control Tab in the RDP-Tcp Connection's Properties

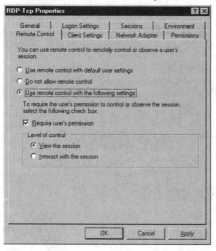

The Client Settings Tab

Remember that when you connect to a Terminal Services session, you are really working on the server. The desktop that is displayed on your local system reflects what is happening on the server. When you open Windows Explorer, the local drives displayed are actually the server's disk drives. The **Client Settings** tab contains a number of settings that can be used to make your local client resources (disk drives, printers, bar code scanner, etc.) also available from within your session.

As with many of the settings on these tabs, some of the configuration items default to settings at the user account property level. To override these settings at the listener connection level (that is, for all users using this connection), clear the check box next to **Use connection settings from user settings**. The settings include the following:

- **Connect client drives at logon** Makes your mapped local client's drives accessible from within Windows Explorer, Save As, and Open windows in the session. Note that this option is available for clients running any edition of Windows Server 2003; it is not supported for other clients.

- **Connect client printers at logon** Makes the mapped printers installed in your local client's Printers folder accessible within the session.

- **Default to main client printer** Makes the default printer in the session the same as the default printer that is specified on the client computer. If you don't select this option, the default printer for the session will be the server's default printer.

It is important to realize that these settings can cause substantial additional bandwidth to be used. When you access client drives from within your session, the data must transfer from the client system to the Terminal Services computer. Likewise, when you print to a client-attached printer from within a session, the print job must transfer from the Terminal Services computer to your local client. In most cases, these transfers occur outside the RDP protocol and can consume substantial additional bandwidth.

The next section on this tab contains the **Limit Maximum Color Depth** drop-down box. This can be used to specify the maximum color bit depth settings that will be available for connecting clients and overrides the settings in the client software. Even if a client asks to use a higher setting in a session, and is capable of doing so, it will not be allowed. The higher the bit depth settings, the more bandwidth consumed. The available settings are: 8, 15, 16, and 24 bit.

The final section on the tab is entitled **Disable the following:**, and contains settings that enable you to prevent certain types of communication from occurring between the client and server or being made available within the session. The options include the following:

- **Drive mapping** Blocks connection to and use of client drives from within a session. You might be asking yourself how this differs from the previous similar setting. If **Connect client drives at logon** is not selected, the drives will not be added to the session upon connection, but this does not prevent them from being manually added later. Disabling them here prevents this. Drive mapping is enabled by default.

- **Windows printer mapping** Blocks connection to and use of client printers from within Windows. If you want to block all use of client printers, you should also be sure to disable **LPT port mapping** and **COM port mapping**. The **Windows printer mapping** setting will not prevent someone from connecting to the client printer manually at the command prompt using LPT port mapping or COM port mapping. Printer mapping is enabled by default.

- **LPT port mapping** Blocks connection to and use of devices connected to the LPT ports on the local client computer and makes these ports unavailable in the port list of the Add Printer Wizard. LPT port mapping is enabled by default.

- **COM port mapping** Blocks connection to and use of devices (including printers) connected to the COM ports on the local client computer and makes COM ports unavailable in the port list of the Add Printer Wizard. COM port mapping is enabled by default.

- **Clipboard mapping** Prevents clipboard synchronization between the remote session and the local client operating system. Although clipboard mapping can be very convenient, it can be very bandwidth intensive and may be too resource intensive for a thin client environment. When enabled, it essentially results in a shared clipboard between the session running on the Terminal Services system and the local operating system, which can be used for copying and pasting data between applications on the local machine and applications on the terminal server. When data is copied to one of the clipboards, it is transferred across the network to the other machine (note that you do not have full clipboard functionality between the local computer and terminal server; you can only copy and paste data, not files and folders).

■ **Audio mapping** Prevents the transmission of audio information from the Terminal Services computer to the local client's audio subsystem. Audio mapping is disabled (the box is checked) by default.

The Network Adapter Tab

As mentioned previously, only one listener connection can be associated with each NIC in the Terminal Services computer. However, by default one listener connection is associated with all NICs in the system. On this tab, you can specify with which NIC the listener connection is associated.

The top of the tab has a **Network Adapter:** drop-down box, which contains an entry for each NIC as well as an entry for **All network adapters configured for this protocol**. Remember that by default, there is only one set of protocols enabled, RDP over TCP/IP. The lower portion of the tab enables you to specify the maximum number of sessions that can connect to this listener connection at any given time. If you have not installed the terminal server role, the maximum number in this box is 2 (which is the limit for Remote Desktop for Administration). If the terminal server role is installed, you can select **Unlimited connections** or set a number in the **Maximum connections** box to prevent overloading the terminal server.

The Permissions Tab

As we mentioned earlier, you can set access permissions on each listener connection. This is accomplished using settings contained in the **Permissions** tab. The tab contains a standard Windows access control list, but the permissions available differ from those found elsewhere and are shown in Table 27.2.

It's important to note that by clicking the **Advanced** button, you can set specialized permissions and enable auditing for Terminal Services connections.

Table 27.2 Standard Permissions

Standard Permission	What the Permission Allows
Full Control	Lets you query to find out information about a session. Lets you change connection parameters. Lets you terminate a session using Reset. Lets you take control of another user's session. Lets you log on to a session that is running on the server. Lets you log off another user from an existing session. Lets you send a message to another user within an existing session. Lets you connect to an existing session. Lets you disconnect another user's session. Lets you use virtual channels to provide access to client devices from a program on the server.
Service	Lets the service query to find out information about a session. Lets the service send a message to another session.
User Access	Lets you log on to a session that is running on the server. Lets you query to find out information about a session. Lets you send messages to another user within an existing session. Lets you connect to an existing session.
Guest Access	Lets you log on to a session that is running on the server.

Terminal Services Configuration Server Settings

The **Server Settings** node in Terminal Services Configuration controls a number of server-wide settings that affect all sessions running on the server. In an Active Directory environment, these settings can also be configured using Group Policy. If configured in both Group Policy and within Terminal Services Configuration, the Group Policy settings will take precedence.

To configure these settings, click the Server Settings node in the tree view in the left pane of the Terminal Services Configuration tool. The configuration options, described below, will appear in the Results pane on the right side of the screen. To configure one of the options, right-click it and select Properties from the context menu. If the option is a simple Yes/No setting, the context menu will contain whichever selection is the opposite of the current configuration setting and can be changed from this menu.

- **Delete temporary folders on exit** Deletes a session's temporary folder when the user logs off. This setting is configured to **Yes** by default.

- **Use temporary folders per session** Creates a separate temporary folder for each new user session created on the server. This typically does not need to remain on the server after the session has been terminated. This setting is configured to **Yes** by default.

- **Licensing** Allows for the administrator to configure the server as a terminal server or Remote Desktop for Administration computer. This setting is configured to Remote Desktop for Administration if the terminal server role has not been installed. If it has, this setting reflects the licensing choice made when you installed the terminal server role (per Device or per User) and can be changed here.

- **Active Desktop** Enables the use of Active Desktop technologies in Terminal Services sessions. These desktops can use considerably more bandwidth than traditional desktops. This setting is configured to be enabled by default.

- **Permission Compatibility** Full security is the only choice available for Remote Desktop for Administration. A second mode, Relaxed Security, is added when the terminal server role is installed on the server, which loosens security to accommodate older Windows computers and legacy applications. This is configured as Full Security by default.

- **Restrict each user to one session** Can be used to ensure that users do not establish more than one session to a Terminal Services system. Savvy users may be able to work around this setting by specifying a different program to start upon connection for each different session.

User Account Extensions

Windows 2003 user accounts contain four property tabs that are designed for the control of the Terminal Services session at the user level. The tabs are entitled Terminal Services Profile, Sessions, Environment, and Remote Control. The same tabs exist in domain and local user accounts. The same tabs are present whether the Terminal Services computer is configured for Remote Desktop for Administration or the terminal server role. You can use these dialog boxes to control Terminal Services settings on a per-user basis. The settings you make here will apply only to that user account.

To access these tabs, right-click the user account you wish to configure in either the **Active Directory Users and Computers**, **Computer Management**, or **Local Users and Groups** MMC snap-in. From the context menu, select **Properties** and click the appropriate tab.

The Terminal Services Profile Tab

The bottom of the **Terminal Services Profile** tab contains perhaps the most important check box contained on any of the Terminal Services property tabs, **Allow logon to terminal server**. This check box is selected by default on all user accounts and enables any user to log on and use either Remote Desktop for Administration (if his or her account is added to the Remote Desktop Users list) or the terminal server. If you want to prevent a single user from accessing Terminal Services, simply clear this check box in the user's account properties.

The top section of this tab enables you to specify a separate profile and home directory for use when the user is logged on to a Terminal Services session. By default, these are blank. That means that the effective settings come from the Profile tab in the user's properties. The Profile tab was originally intended to be used to specify the profile and home directory locations when the user is logged on locally. Many companies leave the Terminal Services Profile tab blank, allowing the settings on the user's Profile tab to be the effective settings whether the user is logged on locally or with Terminal Services. Because the user's profile contains that user's desktop settings, sometimes a user can get confused when logging on to a session and finding a different desktop than when logged on locally. Likewise, if the user saves files to the home directory all day long and then is connected to a different home directory when using Terminal Services, this can be confusing.

Figure 27.18 shows the Terminal Services Profile tab on a user's account properties.

Figure 27.18 The Terminal Services Profile Tab in a User's Properties

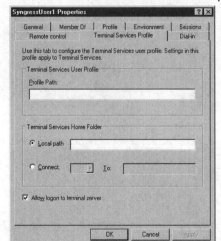

The Sessions Tab

The **Sessions** tab in the user's properties contains many of the same settings that we saw while we were examining the Terminal Services Configuration tool. At that level, they applied to all users connecting over a specified connection to the server. Here they apply to only one user. Thus, if the **Override user settings** check box is selected on any of the settings at the connection level, those that are set here at the user level are ignored. Likewise, if the defaults are left in place at the connection level, the configurations in the user's properties are the effective settings.

The settings on this tab include the following:

- **End a disconnected session** (select a duration from Never to 2 days)
- **Active session limit** (select a duration from Never to 2 days)
- **Idle session limit** (select a duration from Never to 2 days)

- **When a session limit is reached or broken**:

  - Disconnect from session

  - End session

- **Allow reconnection**:

  - From any client

  - From originating client only

Again, the settings on this tab affect only the user whose properties are being modified. However, they perform the exact same actions as described in the Terminal Services Configuration section. This tab is displayed in Figure 27.19.

Figure 27.19 The Sessions Tab in a User's Properties

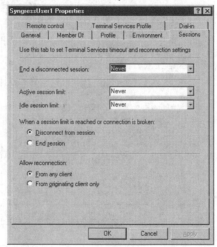

The Environment Tab

As with the **Sessions** tab, the settings on the **Environment** tab in the user's properties are identical to several settings we've already seen in the Terminal Services Configuration tool. As with the **Sessions** tab, when overridden at the connection level or by Group Policy, the settings on this tab are ignored. However, by default they are the effective settings. The top section of the tab contains the **Start the following program at logon** check box, which is not selected by default. When selected, the **Program file name:** and **Start in:** text boxes are enabled. The **Program file name:** text box corresponds to the **Program path and file name:** text box on the **Environment** tab in the Terminal Services Configuration tool. Likewise, the **Start in:** text box is identical to the box of the same name on that tab in Terminal Services Configuration. Refer to the Terminal Services Configuration section of this chapter for more information about how to use these.

The lower section of the **Environment** tab in the user's properties also contains settings identical to several we've already discussed in the section on the Client Settings tab in the Terminal Services Configuration tool. These include the following:

- Connect client drives at logon

- Connect client printers at logon

- Default to main client printer

Again, by default the user's settings are effective unless overridden with the Terminal Services Configuration tool or by Group Policy. The **Environment** tab is shown in Figure 27.20.

Figure 27.20 The Environment Tab

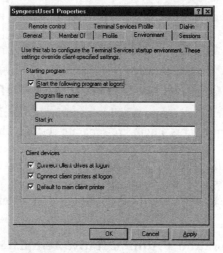

The Remote Control Tab

As with the previous two tabs, the settings on the **Remote Control** tab also mirror those in the Terminal Services Configuration tool and were described in that section of this chapter. As with the other settings, the default is for the settings at the user property level to be effective. As we saw earlier, these settings can be overridden at the connection level using Terminal Services Configuration if desired, or by Group Policy. The following settings are available at the user property level:

- **Enable remote control**

- **Require user's permission**

- **Level of control:**

  - View the user's session

  - Interact with the session

For more detailed information on each of these settings, refer to the Terminal Services Configuration section of the chapter. The **Remote Control** tab is shown in Figure 27.21.

Figure 27.21 The Remote Control Tab in a User's Properties

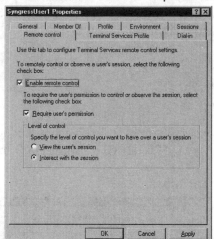

Using Group Policies to Control Terminal Services Users

There are over 900 group policy settings in Windows 2003, of which approximately 50 relate specifically to Terminal Services components. There are separate settings that can be applied at the computer and user levels, as well as separate settings for Terminal Services and RA. Virtually all of the actions performed by these settings have already been described, because similar settings exist on many of the tabs and property sheets we've already discussed.

Terminal services settings can be found in the following locations within the **Group Policy Object Editor**:

- **Computer Configuration | Administrative Templates | Windows Components | Terminal Services**

- **Computer Configuration | Administrative Templates | System | Remote Assistance**

- **User Configuration | Administrative Templates | Windows Components | Terminal Services**

    Some of the key Group Policy settings that have not already been covered elsewhere in this chapter include the following:

- **Deny log off of an administrator logged in to the console session**, which can be used to prevent the automatic logoff of the administrator currently using the Terminal Services computer's console session by another administrator attempting to connect to it. Remember that by default, only one administrator can be logged on and viewing the console session at a time. When an administrator attempts to connect, by default any currently connected administrator is logged off and all unsaved work is lost. It is also important to note that the console session is the only one that cannot be used with Remote Control, in either View Only or Interaction mode.

- **Remove Windows Security item from Start menu**, which can be used to control how a user may terminate his or her session. The Windows Security dialog is the dialog box that comes up on a local system when you use the key combination **CTRL + ALT + DEL**. Because this key combination is never redirected to a remote session, Microsoft puts a link to it on the Start menu in a session. The Windows Security dialog box contains buttons for locking the remote desktop, logging off, shutting down (if you have the appropriate permissions and this is not grayed out, it will shut down the Terminal Services computer not the local computer), changing your password, and accessing Task Manager on the Terminal Services computer. It may be appropriate in your environment to remove this link for security or log-off control purposes. However, even if this link is not present, the key combination **CTRL + ALT + END** can be used to bring up the Windows Security dialog box within the terminal session.

- **Remove Disconnect option from Shut Down dialog**, which enables you to remove the disconnect option from the Shut Down Windows dialog box. This dialog box appears when you select Shut Down from the Windows Start menu or Windows Security dialog box. It is important to note that removing this option from the Shut Down dialog does not prevent someone from disconnecting. The user can still click the **X** button in the top righthand corner of the Remote Desktop window to disconnect.

There are many more Group Policy templates that can be used to control Terminal Services. For some settings, Group Policy is the only way to configure a particular setting. For example, you can specify whether to allow time zone redirection, prevent license upgrade, or enable users to offer remote assistance.

Using the Terminal Services Command-Line Tools

In addition to the graphical tools and clients described earlier, Windows 2003 also provides a number of command-line utilities for both administrators and end users to manage connections. The primary benefit of these command-line tools is that they can be used in scripts to automate Terminal Services tasks. The basic set of commands, as listed in the Windows Server 2003 Help files, is described in Table 27.3.

Table 27.3 Terminal Services Command-Line Tools

Command	Description
change logon	Temporarily disables logons to a terminal server
change port	Used to change COM port mappings for MS-DOS program compatibility
change user	Changes the .ini file mapping for the current user
Cprofile	Removes user-specific file associations from a user profile
Flattemp	Enables or disables flat temporary directories
Logoff	Logs off a user from a session and deletes the session from the server
Msg	Sends a message to a user or group of users

Continued

Table 27.3 Terminal Services Command-Line Tools

Command	Description
Mstsc	Displays the Remote Desktop Connection to establish a connection with a terminal server
query process	Displays information about processes running on a terminal server
query session	Displays information about sessions on a terminal server
query termserver	Displays a list of all terminal servers on the network
query user	Displays information about user sessions on a terminal server
Register	Registers applications to execute in a global context on the system
reset session	Resets a session to known initial values
Shadow	Monitors another user's session
Tscon	Connects to another existing terminal server session
Tsdiscon	Disconnects a client from a terminal server session
Tskill	Ends a process
Tsprof	Copies user configuration and changes profile path
Tsshutdn	Shuts down a terminal server

Use Terminal Services Manager to Reset a Session

1. Open Terminal Services Manager from **Administrative Tools** in the Windows **Start | Programs** menu.

2. If necessary, expand the **This Computer** node.

3. If necessary, expand the node that corresponds to the name of your Windows 2003 server.

4. Right-click the session you wish to terminate.

5. In the context menu that appears, select **Reset**.

6. Close Terminal Services Manager.

Troubleshooting Terminal Services

Troubleshooting Terminal Services components is never an easy task. The complexity of Terminal Services often makes for strange occurrences, which are difficult to track down so this section contains a number of troubleshooting tips you can use to find and solve Terminal Server problems.

The most important keys to understanding how to troubleshoot Terminal Services come from all the background knowledge presented in this chapter. Knowing how it all works is essential to troubleshooting problems quickly and effectively.

Not Automatically Logged On

A common problem occurs when you want to be able to automatically log on to the server, but you're still prompted for your user credentials when you connect to the terminal server. There are a number of possible causes and solutions.

If you are using a Windows NT 4.0 Terminal Services client, be aware that these clients are not always able to detect and pass on the underlying system logon credentials to the Windows Server 2003 terminal server even if your system logon credentials are the same as those for the terminal server. In the NT 4.0 Client Connection Manager, configure **Automatic logon** on the **General** tab in the **Properties** box for the connection. Enter the appropriate logon credentials in the **User name, Password** and **Domain** text boxes.

If you are using a Windows 2000 TS client or the RDC client, it is possible that you entered the incorrect credentials on the **General** tab. If you mistyped the user name or password, the terminal server will not be able to verify your credentials and will prompt you for the correct ones. The solution is to edit the **User name**, **Password**, and/or **Domain** text box(es) on the **General** tab of the client utility.

Another possibility is that your client settings are configured correctly, but Group Policy is configured to require users to enter at least part of the credentials (the password). Group Policy settings override client settings. The only way to correct this is to remove the Group Policy setting that is enforcing this restriction.

"This Initial Program Cannot Be Started"

Occasionally a client may receive a message stating, "This initial program cannot be started." At the client level, a user can specify that program be launched when they connect to a server instead of receiving a desktop. Likewise, an administrator can specify this at the connection level for all users that connect to a specific listener connection. Finally, this can also be set in Group Policy.

The error may be caused by something as simple as an input error. You should first check to ensure that the path and executable names specified are correct. If you have entered them incorrectly, they will be pointing to a file that does not exist. This will make it impossible for Windows Server 2003 to launch the application.

Another possibility is that the correct permissions are not set on the executable file. If Windows cannot access the file, it will not be able to launch the program for you. You should verify that the appropriate read and execute permissions are applied to both the file and the working directory (if specified). If neither of these two possible solutions resolves the issue, the application may have become corrupt. Try to launch the application from the server console. If it will not open, you may need to uninstall and reinstall the application.

Clipboard Problems

Ordinarily, when you copy text to the clipboard in a session, it is synchronized with the local clipboard on the client. Because the text is available on each clipboard, it should be available to paste into local applications as well as applications running remotely in a session. You should note that it works the same way when you copy text to the clipboard locally. It is synchronized with the clipboard running in your Terminal Services session and can be used in either local or remote applications.

Microsoft states that there are instances in which text that is copied to the clipboard in a remote session is unable to be pasted into an application on the local client. Currently, there is no fix available for this problem. First, try to reinstall the client application you are using. If it is still malfunctioning, try to uninstall the client application and reinstall it.

License Problems

For remote administration, licenses come built in to the Windows Server 2003. The terminal server role, however, requires the installation and proper configuration of the terminal server licensing component. Because of this, license problems typically relate only to the terminal server role. If you receive messages similar to those below, you have license component problems.

- The remote session was disconnected because there are no terminal server client access licenses available for this computer. Please contact the server administrator.

- The remote session was disconnected because there are no Terminal Server License Servers available to provide a license. Please contact the server administrator.

Error messages such as these can indicate several different types of issues. First, verify that the license server is online and able to communicate on the network. It's also important to verify name resolution during this step. Next, ensure that the license server component has been activated properly. Check event logs on the license server and look for more subtle problems than simple connectivity checks will not spot.

Verify that the license server has a sufficient number of valid client licenses for your network, and that the licenses are valid. The terminal server draws licenses from the license server so you should also ensure that these two servers can communicate with each other. Finally, don't forget to check the clients. It is possible that the clients never received a valid license. By default, clients often receive temporary licenses that expire after 90 days and prevent further connections. If they did receive full licenses, the licenses may have become corrupt and need to be replaced or overwritten.

Index

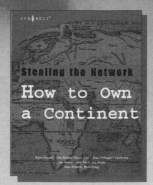